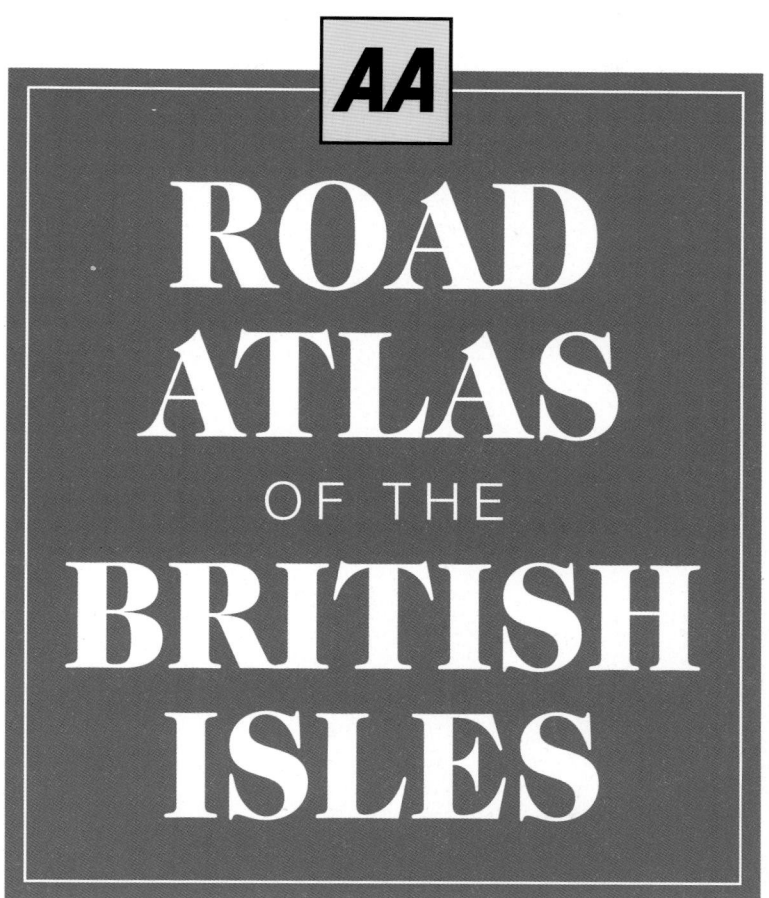

ROAD ATLAS OF THE BRITISH ISLES

1: 200,000

Approximately 3 miles to 1 inch

6th edition September 1995
5th edition September 1994
4th edition September 1993
Reprinted October 1993
3rd edition September 1992
Reprinted October 1992
2nd edition September 1991
Reprinted October 1991
1st edition September 1990

Published by AA Publishing (a trading name of Automobile Association Developments Limited, whose registered office is Norfolk House, Priestley Road, Basingstoke, Hampshire RG24 9NY. Registered number 1878835).

Mapping produced by the Cartographic Department of The Automobile Association. This atlas has been compiled and produced from the Automaps database utilising electronic and computer technology.

ISBN 0 7495 1245 8

A CIP catalogue record for this book is available from the British Library.

Printed by L.E.G.O. SpA, Vicenza, Italy.

The contents of this atlas are believed to be correct at the time of printing. Nevertheless, the publishers cannot be held responsible for any errors or omissions, or for changes in the details given. They would welcome information to help keep this atlas up to date; please write to the Cartographic Editor, Publishing Division, The Automobile Association, Norfolk House, Priestley Road, Basingstoke, Hampshire RG24 9NY.

Information on National Parks provided by the Countryside Commission for England and the Countryside Council for Wales.
Information on National Scenic Areas in Scotland provided by the Scottish Natural Heritage.
Information on Forest Parks provided by the Forestry Commission.
The RSPB sites shown are a selection chosen by the Royal Society for the Protection of Birds.
National Trust properties shown are those open to the public as indicated in the handbooks of the National Trusts of England, Wales and Northern Ireland, and Scotland.

contents

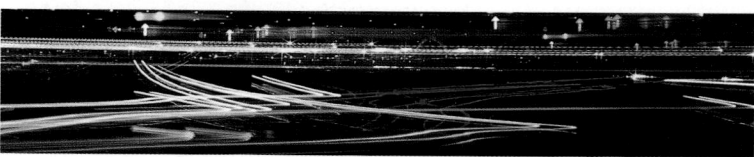

THE TOURIST'S BRITISH ISLES
· SYMBOLS ·

Rochester Castle, in Kent, is a fine example of Norman military architecture.

WHETHER you are looking to spend an afternoon with the family or want to plan a holiday, knowing exactly where to go and what you can see when you get there can often be a problem. The following pages have been designed to give you an idea of what is on offer wherever you happen to be visiting.

Your needs could be as simple as locating a suitable place to enjoy a picnic, where to launch your boat for a day's sailing or where you can find further information about the area.

Whatever your requirement, some 50 symbols, highlighting over 8,000 features of interest, give you a chance to choose what interests you.

Pages 6 to 48 give a taste of what can be seen and where to find it.

Each place located on the atlas by the use of red symbols, has been chosen because it is open and has reasonable access for the public. Although some places may not be open to the public, they have been included simply because they are an interesting feature or landmark, waterfall, windmill etc.

The AA is constantly checking and updating these entries in its atlases and other publications to ensure accurate, up-to-date information is given. All the attractions featured in *Days Out in Britain*, published annually by the AA, are highlighted in this atlas by the red symbols. The atlas, however, includes even more places and the information on locations such as country parks, nature reserves, nature trails, RSPB sites and Forest Parks, is supplied by the numerous authorities and national bodies such as the Countryside Commission, the Forestry Commission and many others.

There is a wide range of interests to choose from.

For cultural tastes, museums, art galleries, historic houses, castles, abbeys and cathedrals are featured. A stately home like Stourhead, in Wiltshire, may be more famous for its garden than its house and will therefore be depicted by the red garden symbol. Others, like Chatsworth in Derbyshire, which are better known for the architectural splendour of the house, even though they are also renowned for their garden features, will be indicated by the red house symbol. Larger, specific garden features, classified as arboreta, are depicted accordingly. Major sporting venues such as athletics stadiums, county cricket grounds and horse racing courses are located by appropriate symbols. It is not possible to indicate league football grounds because of their large numbers and the limitations of the map scale. However, some are shown on the town plans at the back of the atlas where appropriate.

For those who like to participate rather than spectate, outdoor and leisure-type facilities, such as ski slopes, golf courses and coastal launching sites for boats are located.

If you have a particular interest in Ancient Britain, you can choose from the various hill-forts, Roman antiquities and prehistoric monuments which are found throughout the country. Even battle

The places behind Portsmouth's tourist symbols. Left *Tourist Information at The Hard.* Below left *Industrial Interest with restored steam pumping engines at Eastney.* Below right *The Cathedral.* Right *HMS Warrior, just one of the city's many Museums.*

sites, where the course of history has often been changed, are shown. Some of these have interpretative centres which help you to relive and understand the events that occurred there.

Animal lovers can visit the major wildlife collections (both mammals and birds), zoos, and aquariums, or see nature in the wild at one of the numerous nature reserves, Forest Parks and RSPB sites. Another option is to follow one of the nature trails through the countryside. The more adventurous can attempt part or all of one of the national trails which traverse some of Britain's most spectacular scenic areas.

Industrial interest covers a wide spectrum from heritage centres and museums to mills, mines and slate caverns. Old railways, many of which served these industries in the past, now delight the public with a taste of the golden days of steam.

Family days out are catered for by the theme parks. The AA has selected eight of these for inclusion on the basis that they provide multi-purpose entertainment and leisure facilities

and have numerous fairground attractions that are unnervingly described as 'white knuckle' rides. Along with the country parks, they make ideal places to spend the whole day rather than just a quick visit.

Picnic sites are selected and inspected by the AA on a regular basis and are easily accessible, being sited on or by A and B roads. Viewpoints are shown if they offer vistas of at least 180 degrees, and many have panoramic 360 degree views.

Other places of interest which are worth visiting but do not fall easily into the categories symbolised are indicated by a small red star alongside their name. There is a great variety of these – waterfalls, water mills, visitor centres and market crosses, among others.

New additions for the 1990s include the National Parks of England and Wales and the National Scenic Areas of Scotland, along with 930 miles of Heritage Coasts along the shores of England and Wales.

When the red symbols are boxed, this indicates the attractions are in

urban areas. Some of these places may seem bare compared to the surrounding countryside. However, it may be that one symbol for a museum covers several museums in the town, but it is not practical to include them all because of space limitations.

Ireland is included in this special tourist section, and places of interest are located in the atlas, but the scale of mapping does not allow a large selection. Nevertheless, all the most important of Ireland's many tourist attractions are clearly marked.

Wherever possible, the red pictorial symbols used in the atlas are based on the Department of Transport's brown tourist signposts, so that the maps correspond with the road signs. In addition to all this information in the special tourist spreads, a month by month calendar on pages 46 and 47 tells you which customs and events occur throughout the year. This can assist you in deciding when to go. Page 48 describes the services offered by Britain's Tourist Information Centres to help you get the most out of your visits

Abbey, cathedral
or priory

Ruined abbey,
cathedral or
priory

Top *Tintern Abbey: majestic roofless ruin beside the River Wye in Gwent.* Above *St David's Cathedral, Dyfed, where the bones of St David lie.*

Abbeys
Cathedrals
Priories

Augustinian, Benedictine, Cistercian and Dominican – the monastic orders which preserved ideals and scholarship after the fall of Rome have left a rich heritage in stone across Britain. Each imposing ruin or active place of worship tells its own story. All evoke a sense of wonder at the faith and industry of the medieval builders and monks. Which of any of them is the loveliest, however, will for ever be a matter of personal preference.

Burnt down in 1174, four years after Becket's murder, the choir of **Canterbury Cathedral** was rebuilt in a manner worthy of the martyr and appears today much as it was in the early 16th century. The 'Altar of the Sword's Point' and a modern cruciform sculpture, dedicated in 1986, mark the site of Becket's martyrdom. The long vistas back to the nave, at a lower level than the choir aisles, show the evolution of Gothic style over three centuries.

The west front of **York**, the largest Gothic church north of the Alps, presents an almost 13th-century 'French' outline, with its glorious façades. The Minster contains the largest single collection of medieval stained glass in England – the West Window painted in 1339 by Master Robert and the East Window, the work of John Thornton of Coventry, between 1405 and 1408. The Pilgrim Window dates from about 1312 and the Bellfounders' Window was given by Richard Tunnoc, buried in the Minster in 1330.

A fire, started by lightning on 9 July 1984, destroyed much of the south transept. Craftsmen, incorporating 20th-century improvements for future safety, restored the medieval beauty of the transept, reopened by the Queen in October 1988.

Embodiment of the spirit of the nation, **Westminster**, the Norman abbey of Edward the Confessor, took on its Gothic appearance after its rebuilding by Henry III. Fortunately, when the 600-year-old Benedictine community was disbanded, the buildings were spared. The Lady Chapel houses the Confessor's shrine, ringed by the tombs of five kings and three queens. In the centre is the Coronation Chair and below the oaken seat the Stone of Scone.

In the Sanctuary beyond the choir every monarch since the Conqueror has been crowned, with the exception of Edward V and Edward VIII. Early Parliaments met in the Chapter House, and the Henry VII Chapel has a superb fan-vaulted roof – the most glorious, some would say, in the country. Near the West Door lies the 'Unknown Warrior', brought back from France after World War I to sleep among the nation's great.

On its rocky promontory dominating the city and a loop in the River Wear, the Norman architecture of **Durham Cathedral** gives an impression, inside as well as out, of overwhelming power. Huge, deeply grooved columns alternating with massive piers support gallery, clerestory and beautiful vault. The Early English Chapel of the Nine Altars is a 13th-century addition, its tall lancet windows paralleled only in the now ruined Fountains Abbey. In the Treasury are evocative relics of the 7th-century St Cuthbert, including his tiny portable altar, his delicate gold pectoral cross and the remains of his original carved oak coffin.

One of the most delicate of England's cathedrals must be **Salisbury**, built in the 40 years following 1220 of local silver-grey limestone with pointed arches and soaring windows. The spire, at 404 feet (123m), is the tallest in the country. It is such inspired work that it blends perfectly with the rest, though crossing piers of clustered black marble had to be reinforced in the 15th century to support the added 6,500 tons of the spire.

Wells is the first cathedral church in the Early English style. Its west front is still, despite Puritan vandalism, one of England's richest displays of 13th-century sculpture. Inside, the most striking feature is the inverted arches, built from 1338 to 1348 to combat subsidence of the tower.

The Norman crypt and transepts of **Winchester Cathedral** survive, the rest being 13th and 14th century. At 556 feet (169m) it is the longest Gothic church in Europe. Saved from demolition in 1652 by a petition of the citizens, it was again saved at the beginning of this century by a diver, William Walker. Working alone, from 1906 to 1912, in pitch dark waters of the marshy foundations, he replaced the rotting 13th-century beech tree raft (on which the cathedral had originally been built) with cement.

Near York are three jewels – Beverley, Selby and Ripon. **Beverley Minster** houses the Percy Tomb, the most splendid of British Decorated funerary monuments. It shares, with St Mary's Church nearby, wonderful misericords and the largest collection of carvings of medieval musical instruments anywhere in the world.

Benedictine **Selby Abbey**, founded in 1069, predates Durham. The west front ranges in style from strength and simplicity to later elegance. The easternmost arches of the nave have distorted spectacularly, due to a high water table. High up above the south side of the choir is a 14th-century window with the arms of the Washington family – the 'Stars and Stripes' motif of the American flag.

Ripon Cathedral is built over the tiny 11 by 8 ft (3.4 x 2.4m) Saxon crypt of St Wilfrid's Church, one of the few Saxon structures left in England. The cathedral has a beautiful Early English west front. One woodcarver, working from 1939 to 1945, replaced all the 'idolatrous images' on the choir screen, destroyed by Puritans in 1643.

There are modern cathedrals, too. The new **Coventry Cathedral** appears to grow out of the old St Michael's and the overwhelming

impression is of height, light and colour. South-facing angled windows enable sunlight to flood the nave with colour. Dominating the whole cathedral is the huge tapestry designed by Graham Sutherland, *Christ in Glory*.

Liverpool's **Anglican Cathedral** is, in the words of Sir John Betjeman, 'vastness, strength and height no words can describe'. Sir Giles Gilbert Scott designed Britain's largest cathedral in medieval style but on a scale which no medieval builder would have attempted. His memorial is set in the floor of the central space under the tower. He, a Catholic, is buried just outside the West Door.

The **Metropolitan Cathedral of Christ the King** in Liverpool, often irreverently called 'Paddy's Wigwam', stands above the huge crypt of the cathedral which Sir Edwin Lutyens started before the war. Inside the 194ft (59m) circular nave, completed by Sir Frederick Gibberd, every member of the 2,300 congregation has an uninterrupted view of the white marble high altar.

A cathedral conveys 'city status' on a town, however small. Pass through the gatehouse at **St David's**, Dyfed, and the lichen-encrusted purple stone of Wales's greatest church is dramatically revealed. It was restored in Decorated Gothic style after an earthquake in 1248 and the whole building slopes upwards some 14 feet (4m) from west to east – an unnerving first glimpse for the visitor entering at the western end

of the nave. The relics of St David rest in an oak and iron reliquary, hidden at the Reformation and discovered during restoration work in 1866.

St Asaph Cathedral, in Clwyd, is on the site of a monastic community founded in AD570. It houses the tomb of Bishop William Morgan, translator of the Bible into Welsh, and the 16th-century Bible itself, which was used at the Investiture of the Prince of Wales in 1969.

Henry VIII's Dissolution left a legacy of ruined religious centres across the country, many of which still survive today in all their shattered glory.

Perhaps one of the most magnificent monastic ruins is **Rievaulx Abbey**, two miles north-west of Helmsley. It was founded in 1131 and is the first Cistercian house in the north of England. The name, pronounced 'Reevo', comes from Rye Vallis or valley of the River Rye, above which it stands, surrounded by wooded hills. Its chief glory is its choir built *c*. 1225. The scale of the buildings gives an idea of the activities and work of the 600 and more monks and lay brothers who lived here in the 13th century.

The Cistercian community of **Fountains Abbey**, near Ripon, became the centre of an enormous enterprise, with fish-farms, forestry,

iron-workings and, above all, sheep, which funded its building. It was one of the first foundations to be sold by Henry VIII in 1540. In 1768 the Aislabie family bought it as a picturesque addition to their Studley Royal estate.

The condition of the Benedictine **Whitby Abbey** cannot wholly be blamed on King Henry. The gaunt ruins of the clifftop site, chosen by St Hilda in AD657, became the setting for Bram Stoker's *Dracula* and suffered further indignity when they were bombarded by German warships during World War I.

The 7th-century buildings at **Much Wenlock** were destroyed by the Danes and later refounded by Leofric, husband of Lady Godiva. Today's ruins are the remains of the church built in the 1220s by Prior Humbert, whose lodging is one of the finest examples of English domestic architecture from around the 1500s.

Abbey, cathedral
or priory

Ruined abbey,
cathedral or
priory

Right The ancient kings of Northumbria lie buried near Tynemouth Priory. Below Cistercian Fountains Abbey, now part of the Studley Royal estate.

Castle

Castles

Maiden Castle to Balmoral, Mousa Broch to Dover – Britain is rich in castles dating from Bronze to Victorian ages. The very name 'castle', conjuring up visions of power, of menace and later of opulence, has often been affected by builders of lesser dwellings.

Castles begin with the hillforts of the Bronze Age and stone brochs of pre-Christian Scotland, primarily refuges for men and cattle in time of local warfare. The ruins of Norman timber-built motte and bailey castles – a stone keep on a mound, surrounded by a defensive wall – later converted by the Plantagenets to stone fortresses, still dominate many towns, river crossings and strategic points across the country.

These were not solely refuges, but administrative headquarters, stores and living quarters. Even in times of peace they would have been bustling centres of activity; in time of war, life must have been pretty chaotic, with garrisons, stores, cattle and weaponry increased and as many of the local population as

Below Orford Castle, in Suffolk, has a remarkable 18-sided polygonal keep. *Inset* The Welsh border castle of Goodrich, in the Wye Valley.

could be squeezed in taking refuge in the bailey. Castles were not designed for passive defence but for vigorous action. They were not safe refuges in which to avoid conflict, but ingeniously contrived to make the enemy fight at a disadvantage – they were meant to be costly to capture – both in time and in lives. Henry II (1154-1189), after the mayhem of Stephen's reign 'took every castle of England into his hands', destroyed about 500 unlicensed castles and founded a line of castle-building kings – Richard, John, Henry III, Edward I and III.

Visiting some of these castles, it needs only a little imagination to bring to life the history of their times. The castles of Edward I (1272-1307) around the coast of North Wales are symbols of the organising ability and engineering skills as well as reminders of the vast expense of castle building in the Middle Ages.

Norman and Plantagenet castles vary to suit the site on which they are built but the first criterion was always that of aggressive defence. Where possible a ditch or moat – dry or flooded – was dug to prevent besiegers tunnelling under the walls. Towers without sharp

corners were less likely to be undermined, and so became the fashion.

From about 1268, the date of **Caerphilly Castle** in Mid Glamorgan, the defenders of the outer curtain wall and its towers would be supported by covering fire from higher inner walls. A formidable array of outworks defends gateways and sluices, further protected by drawbridge and portcullis. Barbicans and towers ensured that attackers were subjected to murderous flanking crossfire before they got anywhere near anything so flammable as a wooden gate.

Caerphilly, at 30 acres the largest castle in Wales, surpassed only by **Dover** and **Windsor**, is sufficiently well preserved to give a vivid idea of the way these defensive ideas worked together. It has wide water defences, in imitation of those which Henry III had built at **Kenilworth** and which Simon de Montfort held so successfully against him. Edward I, on his return from the Crusades, liked what he saw at Caerphilly and began to turn the **Tower of London** into a concentric castle. He also introduced at **Caernarfon** and **Conwy** an idea from his campaigns in Gascony –

Castle

the 'bastide' – an extension of the bailey to enclose a small town in which traders, labourers and craftsmen could live under the protection of the castle.

Edward I's castle building in North Wales is well documented and throws fascinating light on the feudal power and organisation at the King's command. Ditch diggers were recruited from the Fens and marched across by mounted serjeants – to discourage deserters – to dig the canal around **Rhuddlan Castle.**

At **Conwy**, Edward's young Spanish queen, Eleanor, homesick for the courts and fountains of her native Castile, had a small garden and fishpond built in the castle's east barbican. In the hot summer of 1283 a labourer hauled water from the well, to 'water the Queen's new grass'. Here at Conwy it is believed that Eleanor introduced one of our favourite summer flowers – the sweet pea.

At **Caernarfon Castle** where his son, later Edward II, was born on 25 April 1284, Edward sought to bring Arthurian and Welsh legends to life and make the seat of his government in Wales a new imperial Constantinople. Octagonal towers are set in a single curtain wall, banded with red sandstone in imitation of those of the 5th-century Turkish capital. Defended passages within the thickness of the masonry and ingenious triple arrow slits allowed three bowmen a wide angle of fire through only one external opening.

The more settled times of the Tudor dynasty after the Wars of the Roses reduced the military significance of the castle. Gunpowder played no little part in this. Castles continued to be built, but design changed. Henry VIII began a series of symmetrically planned coastal 'artillery forts' from the Thames to Dorset in 1538. **Deal, Walmer** and **Sandgate** are three, but these were garrisoned rather than lived in – the garrisons complaining that 'they stank of gunpowder and dogs'. Comfort and elegance dictated the style of Elizabethan and Jacobean buildings, though many were still castellated and defensible.

The Civil War saw many castles used again as strongpoints. They stood up so well, even to improved 17th-century firepower, that the victorious Parliamentarians decreed that those which had been so vigorously defended should be 'slighted' – demolished so as to make them useless for military purposes. Some of these 'ruins Cromwell knocked about a bit', if not too badly damaged, became the

Above *Caernarfon Castle, Gwynedd, built by Edward I to subdue the Welsh.* Right *St Andrews' 13th-century castle overlooks the North Sea.*

local prison and the Norman word for the keep – *donjon* – became the English dungeon.

In Scotland, Northumberland, Cumbria and the troubled lands of the Borders, there are over 1,100 'castles' of one sort or another, excluding the baronial houses of the last 200 years. Most are tower houses or 'peles', built in stone, for timber was always short in the region, and usually several storeys high. **Craigievar**, west of Aberdeen, is the masterpiece of this uniquely Scottish style. Seven storeys high with, even today, few windows in its pink granite walls, it must have been a formidable sight for any would-be attacker.

Many peles have been absorbed into later houses. **Traquair House** west of Galashiels, now more 'château' than castle, claims to be the oldest continuously inhabited house in Scotland. Buried within the north-east corner is a pele tower dating back to the reign of Alexander I (1107-24).

Stirling Castle, which looked down on Edward II's ignominious defeat at Bannockburn in 1314, was still an earthen and timber construction. The 'Gateway to the Highlands' was transformed under the Stuarts, first into a stone fortress, then into a splendid Renaissance royal palace.

Castles lived on in the romantic imaginations of later centuries. Sir Charles Cavendish, son of Bess of Hardwick, built his mansion at **Bolsover**, Derbyshire, in the 1620s with the turrets, crenellations and medieval fancies so popular with the Elizabethans. As tastes began to rebel against Classical symmetry and long for 'the good old days', mock medieval 'castles' were built

and some genuine 14th-century castles, such as **Croft**, in Shropshire, were 'gothicised'.

William Burges built two for the Marquess of Bute, at **Cardiff** and **Castell Coch**, reconstructing the motte and bailey castle the Normans had built at Cardiff within a Roman fort into an extravaganza rivalling the creations of Ludwig of Bavaria – with a medieval tower suite complete with smoking room, Gothic chapel and banqueting hall. At Castell Coch, to the north of Cardiff, Burges transformed the ruins of a keep destroyed in the 15th century into a mock 13th-century retreat. Its conical roofs recall the illustrations in the Duc de Berry's 'Book of Hours' but the thick walls have arrow slits and 'murder holes' and a portcullis and drawbridge which function.

The last such conceit built in Britain was designed by Edwin Lutyens, who in 1901 had made a comfortable home for the publisher of *Country Life* magazine within the ramparts of **Lindisfarne**, off the Northumbrian coast. For 20 years, from 1910, **Castle Drogo**, Lutyen's composite Norman and Tudor 'castle' arose overlooking the River Teigne in Devon, home to the founder of the Home & Colonial Stores and is – to date, at any rate – Britain's 'last castle'.

Historic house

National Trust properties

Historic Houses

The Greek historian, Thucydides said 'Men, not walls, make a city'. The same holds true for a house and the human stories of the builders, owners or residents add interest to it, however humble, however grand. Membership of the National Trust and English Heritage – an outlay quickly recouped if you are going to visit even half a dozen properties in a season – will give you a wonderful selection from which to choose, rich in architecture and in treasures, but above all in personalities.

The name 'Mote' at **Ightham Mote** in Kent recalls the 'moot', the council which met here, in the Great Hall, dating from 1340. Three centuries of continuous ownership by the Selby family have left their mark, from Jacobean fireplaces through 17th-century wallpaper to Victorian bedrooms. All told there are 600 years of England's history to be discerned at Ightham.

Ightham Mote, Kent, is one of the best examples of a medieval manor house.

Built in 1340 by a Lord Mayor of London, the Great Hall at **Penshurst Place** in Kent is the finest to have survived. Birthplace of the Elizabethan courtier, soldier and poet, Sir Philip Sidney, the house remains in the same family today. Later ranges of building have left it light and airy. The Long Gallery marries house to garden and medieval to Renaissance, a fitting memorial to the man who personified all that was best in the Elizabethan age.

The Elizabethan house Bess of Hardwick built with Sir William Cavendish at **Chatsworth** in Derbyshire has been absorbed into the present house. Chatsworth is the home of the Cavendish family, the Dukes of Devonshire, the first of whom, in the early 1700s, transformed the house into a baroque palace, a second Versailles. Treasures are everywhere – in the Painted Hall, the State Rooms, Sculpture Gallery – works by famous artists, painters and sculptors abound. The Library has over 17,000 volumes, among them those of Henry Cavendish, the 18th-century discoverer of hydrogen. Capability Brown laid out much of the garden, but retained Grillet's 1696 Cascade, the sound of the water varying as it falls over steps of different height. Joseph Paxton, too, worked here, and his Great Conservatory was the forerunner of the Crystal Palace.

Montacute in Somerset is one of the least altered of late Elizabethan houses. Begun in the year of the Armada, it expresses the rise to power of an astute lawyer, Edward Phelips. He led the prosecution of Guy Fawkes and became Speaker of the House of Commons. The house, with its mullioned front and statues standing in their lofty niches, is the masterpiece of a local genius, William Arnold. No one, though, who has seen the charming Elizabethan pavilions can ever doubt the delicacy and humour of this Elizabethan mason who has so completely captured his master's wish to display his continuing good fortune.

After a spell in the Tower and a stiff fine, Sir John Thynne retired to his Wiltshire estate at **Longleat**, following his support of the disgraced Lord Protector to Edward VI. He began Longleat in about 1546, and today it is still home to the Thynne family, now the Marquesses of Bath. The Great Hall, with its 16th-century fireplace and hunting scenes, is the least altered part of the house. Sir John broke from the tradition of the Elizabethan 'E-shaped' house and built around two inner courts. The top floor of the house was the library and home of Thomas Ken, Bishop of Bath and Wells, who was given refuge

here when he fell foul of both James II and William and Mary. Lord Bath, an innovator like his ancestor, opened his house to the public in 1949 and in 1966 introduced the 600-acre safari park, a 'drive-through' reserve of giraffes, rhinoceroses, elephants, tigers – and the well-known 'lions of Longleat'.

Bess of Hardwick married four times, each time increasing her fortune. She married Sir William Cavendish when she was 27 and their second son inherited Chatsworth. She left her fourth husband, the Earl of Shrewsbury, for his alleged infatuation with his prisoner, Mary, Queen of Scots. Then, aged 70, she began to build **Hardwick Hall**. The accounts of the building reflect the imperiousness of the owner who, living a hundred yards away in her old hall, strode across to inspect and criticise every day. Her descendants preferred Chatsworth and Hardwick remained, frozen in time, one of the purest examples of 16th-century design and decor in the country, a memorial to the indomitable woman whose portrait stares down from the tapestried wall of the Long Gallery.

Robert Cecil, first Earl of Salisbury, builder of **Hatfield House**, Hertfordshire, was adviser to both Elizabeth I and James I. James suggested that Robert Cecil exchange the house his father, Lord Burghley, had built at Theobalds, for the palace at Hatfield – a 'suggestion' he could scarcely refuse. Between 1607 and 1611, Cecil built himself a vast new house nearby.

Great Halls and Long Galleries were by then going out of fashion, but Hatfield would have lost much had Cecil not been traditionalist enough to include them. His own quarters and the guest wing, however, have smaller rooms. Here conversation and gracious living could flourish. The style of the great house was changing. It was a later Cecil, Marquess of Salisbury, three times Prime Minister to Queen Victoria and amateur scientist, who installed electricity in 1881 and it is reported that 'the naked wires on the Gallery ceiling tended to burst into flame, being extinguished by members of the family who threw cushions a them before returning to their conversation'.

By the time **Petworth** was built, 70 years or so after Hatfield, Long Galleries and Great Halls had gone completely from the English building scene. The house passed by marriage from the Percys to the 'Proud Duke' of Somerset, who began building – using his wife's fortune – in 1688. The name and skill of Grinling Gibbons will always be associated with Petworth. His mastery of limewood carving is complete. The house also

Historic house

National Trust
properties
Scotland

boasts excellent tracery work by Jonathan Ritson, and the Marble Hall has wonderful carving by John Selden, the Duke's estate carpenter.

Just to the south of Wrexham lies **Erddig**. It was completed by a local mason in 1689 and owned by the Yorke family since 1733, who collected much and threw little away! Subsidence from coal mining almost destroyed the house and restoration began in 1973. The interest of the house is not in its architecture or its treasures, but in the relationship that a local family maintained with their servants. Portraits of master and servant hang in drawing room and servants' hall, many with little poems and descriptions. There are frequent group photographs of the whole staff, enabling us to follow some servants right through their careers. Erddig is one of the few houses to show the public the maids' bedrooms as well as the public rooms. Here, 200 years of the running of a self contained estate come vividly to life.

Soldier turned dramatist on his return to England in 1692, John Vanbrugh came to the notice of Charles Howard, 3rd Earl of Carlisle, perhaps through his popular and bawdy plays. Howard chose this enthusiastic amateur to build him a home fitted to the position of an Earl, and so Castle Howard came about. Vanbrugh was widely helped by one of Sir Christopher Wren's assistants, Nicholas Hawksmoor, who turned Vanbrugh's ideas into working drawings. Castle Howard impresses

but does not overawe, as does their later work at Blenheim. At the heart of the house is the Great Hall, rising 70 feet (21m) through two storeys into the painted dome. It is the most light-hearted but impressive concept of English architecture. Treasures and portraits abound, including one of a stricken Henry VIII, painted by Holbein just after the execution of Catherine Howard, and a portrait of her uncle, Thomas Howard, who escaped the block because the king died on the day of his execution.

The story of **Blenheim Palace** is full of powerful men and women. It was built for John Churchill, Duke of Marlborough. Queen Anne instigated the idea of the palace as a reward for Churchill's victory over the French and Bavarians at the battle of Blenheim. She later quarrelled with Sarah, Duchess of Marlborough, as did Vanbrugh, the architect. Sarah wanted a comfortable country house and Vanbrugh wanted something even greater than Castle Howard. Sir Winston Churchill, born here, became Prime Minister at a time when a man of Marlborough's character was again needed.

William Adam began to build **Mellerstain** in the Scottish borders for George Baillie in 1725 and his son, Robert, finished it in 1770. It is the interiors, by Robert, that are the main attraction, for William was never able to finish the exterior as planned and it lacks a noble central block. The colours Adam used in his decorations make the rooms particularly attractive.

Above *Vanbrugh's spectacular Castle Howard, in North Yorkshire.*
Right *The beautiful Georgian mansion of Mellerstain, in the Borders.*

The National Trust
Many of the historic houses mentioned on these two pages are in the care of the National Trust of England, Wales and Northern Ireland and the National Trust for Scotland. Apart from maintaining many of Britain's finest buildings the Trust also owns gardens such as the renowned Hidcote Manor Garden near Chipping Campden, ruins such as **Fountains Abbey** in North Yorkshire, tracts of especially scenic shoreline, such as 110 miles of spectacular Cornish coast, follies, windmills, locks and even pubs, of which *The Fleece Inn* at Bretforton, on the edge of the Cotswolds, is a particularly attractive example. The letters 'NT' designate where the Trust owns property or land.

Museum or art gallery

Concorde 01 is on show at the Imperial War Museum, Duxford, Cambridgeshire.

Museums
Art Galleries

Among the prized possessions of the British Museum in its early days were a landscape painted on a spider's web, a two-headed chicken, Chinese shoes, figures of King William III and Queen Mary carved out of walnut shells and various unpleasant-looking things preserved in spirits and hidden in the basement in case they might frighten pregnant women. A far cry from the British Museum of today with its Elgin Marbles, Assyrian winged bulls and the Sutton Hoo treasure included in its fabulous array of objects from every corner of the globe.

The ancestors of today's museums and art galleries were the collections of classical sculptures and antiquities formed during the Renaissance period by rulers, wealthy churchmen and merchant princes like the Medicis of Florence. They were inspired by the devouring interest which had sprung up in ancient Greece and Rome. With interest also rapidly developing in science, others assembled natural history collections and 'cabinets of curiosities', which contained animal bones, weapons, coins, shells, oddly shaped plants or stones – anything that took the collector's fancy.

In England the two John Tradescants, father and son, who were keen naturalists, plant-hunters and gardeners to Charles I in the 17th century, formed a substantial collection, or 'museum' as it was called: one of its star pieces was a stuffed dodo. The collection passed to Elias Ashmole, the antiquary, herald and pioneer Freemason, who added to it and passed it on in turn to Oxford University. Twelve wagon loads of objects were conveyed to Oxford, to form the nucleus of the **Ashmolean Museum**, opened to the public in 1683 and the oldest museum in Britain.

The Ashmolean today glories in its Egyptian mummy cases and medieval jewellery, its Old Master paintings and British art, but it still honours Ashmole's memory and items from the original Tradescant collection can be seen, with other curiosities such as Guy Fawkes's lantern.

The **British Museum** opened its doors in London to 'studious and curious persons' in 1759, the word 'museum' now meaning the building in which a collection was kept rather than the collection itself. It was established by Parliament and funded by a state lottery to house the collections of Robert Harley, Earl of Oxford, and the books and manuscripts assembled by Sir Robert Cotton – which included the Lindisfarne Gospels and two copies of Magna Carta. Also included was the astonishing collection of no less than 79,575 objects put together by Sir Hans Sloane. A successful London doctor, Sloane's fanatical zeal as a collector extended to classical antiquities, coins, jewels, fossils, plants, butterflies, zoological specimens and oddities of every kind. Those who came to feast their eyes on these items consisted, as the Trustees reported in 1784, 'chiefly of Mechanics and persons of the lower Classes'.

Zeal to improve and educate 'persons of the lower classes' gained strength in the 19th century, especially in the heavily populated towns created by the industrial revolution, and prompted the establishment of numerous museums and art galleries. The splendid **City Art Gallery** in Manchester, for example was opened in 1834 and is today noted for its superb Victorian and Pre-Raphaelite paintings. The **Birmingham Museum and Art Gallery** was founded in 1867 and the building it now occupies was opened in 1885. Approximately a hundred museums opened in Britain in the 1870s and '80s.

The Victorian boom in museums and art galleries was also stimulated by an ambition to promote scientific and technological advance and to improve standards of design. This was why the **Victoria & Albert Museum** in London was founded by the Prince Consort in 1852, originally as a 'museum of manufactures', in the wake of the Great Exhibition of the previous year.

National and civic pride were also a factor. The **National Gallery** in

London is now the country's premier collection of Western painting down to 1900 (developments since then are the preserve of the **Tate Gallery**). It was founded in 1824 to emulate the national art galleries already established in Vienna, Paris, Berlin and other European capitals. The government bought 38 paintings to start it off from the collection of a banker, Sir John Julius Angerstein: they included the Rubens *Rape of the Sabine Women*, two Rembrandts and Raphael's *Portrait of Julius II*.

Major museums and galleries generally have two functions and there is often a tension between them. The obvious function is to instruct and entertain the public. The other, carried on out of the public eye, is the advancement of scholarship. An example of this dual role is the **National Museum of Wales** in Cardiff, opened in 1927 (in a building which has leaked ever since). It was founded to inform both the Welsh and the rest of the world about Wales, which it does. However, its own staff and visiting academics also work behind the scenes on collections far too voluminous for public display – 230,000 pressed plant specimens, more than 300,000 fossils, serried multitudes of dead beetles.

The museum is also a good example of the fact that the functions of an institution of this kind today go far beyond the display of objects in showcases. Activities include lectures, the loan of items to schools, and guided family walks with experts from the staff discoursing learnedly along the way.

Museums like this take a wide range of subjects for their province. Others concentrate on specialised areas. There is a museum of Scottish tartans at **Comrie**, for example, of stained glass at **Ely**, of horse racing at **Newmarket**. Military museums concentrate on regiments: the **Durham Light Infantry** in Durham, the **Staffordshire Regiment** in Lichfield, the **Royal Green Jackets** at Winchester. Some museums concentrate on World War II, such as the **German Occupation Museum** in Guernsey. Portsmouth has an unrivalled battery of naval attractions, with the excellent **Royal Naval Museum**, Nelson's flagship **HMS *Victory***, the Tudor warship *Mary Rose* and the **Submarine Museum** in Gosport among others.

There are museums which concentrate on a single famous person: **John Bunyan** in Bedford, **Jane Austen** at Chawton, **Captain Cook** in Middlesbrough, **Barbara Hepworth** at St Ives. There are also galleries which preserve a collection formed by a single person or family – the enchanting **Lady Lever Art Gallery** at Port Sunlight, for instance, or the gorgeous **Bowes Museum** at Barnard Castle. Some of the most rewarding preserve a collection accumulated by a business firm: **Colman's Mustard** in Norwich, the **Harvey's Wine Museum** in Bristol, the **Pilkington Glass Museum** in St Helen's, the **Bass Museum of Brewing** at Burton upon Trent, treasures of **Minton** at Stoke-on-Trent, **Wedgwood** at Barlaston, **Royal Crown Derby** in Derby.

There are agricultural museums, costume museums, museums which collect whole buildings, like the **Weald and Downland Museum** in Sussex. So does the sparkling **Welsh Folk Museum** in St Fagans, founded in 1947 and an example of the growing post-war interest in the lives of ordinary people in the past.

The **North of England Open Air Museum** at Beamish in County Durham, which is showered with awards like confetti, re-creates the way of life of working-class people in the North around the turn of the century.

Since the 1950s there has been a second museum boom, on a far greater scale than the first. There were perhaps 700 museums all told in Britain when World War II ended. There are now more than 2,000. A substantial number of these, about a third, are independent institutions, not set up by the government or the local authorities, but by private operators. To survive, they depend on their ability to attract and please paying customers and among them are some of the best museums in the country. The **National Motor Museum** at Beaulieu in Hampshire has more than 250 historic vehicles on show and visitors are carried in moving 'pods' past displays which show how motoring developed in Britain from the late 19th century on and how it may develop in the future. In Shropshire there is the marvellous **Ironbridge Gorge** complex of museums, bringing one of the key sites of the industrial revolution to life. In the old canal docks at Gloucester is the immensely enjoyable and nostalgic **Robert Opie Collection** of packets, wrappers, tins and advertising material, a museum of all our domestic yesterdays.

The best independents have contributed to the general enlivening of museums over the last 20 years. The old, musty institution of yore, full of mournful stuffed birds, prehistoric flint implements and dauntingly uninformative captions, is now a collector's item, if you can find one.

Some of the newest museums and galleries have been encouraged or funded by local authorities bent on developing tourist attractions to bring visitors and money into an area. In Bradford, for example, the **National Museum of Photography, Film and Television** opened in 1983, with the biggest cinema screen in Britain. It has galleries with 'interactive displays', where you can see yourself reading the news on TV!

There are teapots to admire in **Norwich**, trams to ride at **Crich** in Derbyshire, pork pies in **Melton Mowbray** and buns in **Abingdon**, voices in Lincolnshire dialect to listen to on the telephone in **Lincoln**, while the **Town Docks Museum** in Hull echoes to the voices of whales moaning in the deep. Certainly no one could sensibly complain of a lack of variety and interest in Britain's museums and galleries today.

Museum or art gallery

Below *The ship's wheel of HMS Warrior on show at Portsmouth.* Bottom *One of the locomotives at the National Railway Museum, in York.*

13

Industrial interest

Tourist railway or steam centre

Industrial Interest Tourist Railways and Steam Centres

Agriculture, industry and transport are the three principal activities through which successive generations have altered the appearance and character of Britain's landscape. Far back in the Stone Age there were axe factories in the Lake District and men wielding deer antlers as picks were digging shafts 40ft (12m) deep to mine for flint in Norfolk and Sussex. Since then the face of the land has been scarred wherever opportunity offered, by quarrying for building stone and mining for coal, iron ore, copper, lead and tin.

The great majority of Britain's sites of industrial interest today are legacies from the industrial revolution. They date roughly from the 1750s on, when water power and subsequently steam power were harnessed to the mass production of goods in mills and factories. The products were efficiently transported to customers along

Below Handsome 18th-century Quarry Bank Mill, at Styal in Cheshire. Bottom The splendid iron bridge in Ironbridge in Shropshire.

improved roads, later by canals and in the 19th century by railways.

Interest in preserving what was left of the old industrial heritage gathered strength after World War II. The term 'industrial archaeology' was coined in about 1950 and since then some exceptionally impressive sites have been rescued from dereliction or threatened destruction.

Perhaps the single most important one is the **Ironbridge Gorge** in Shropshire, where the River Severn cuts its way through steep, wooded hills. Here in the mining village of Coalbrookdale, the Darby dynasty of ironmasters succeeded in 1709 in smelting iron with coke – a fundamental advance in technology which led to the mass production of iron. It was in Coalbrookdale that the great Iron Bridge across the Severn was cast, the first important iron bridge in the world. The bridge is still there and the complex of museums and sites in the area today includes blast furnaces and engines, and a charmingly restored 1890s industrial community at Blists Hill, with a working foundry, a candle mill, other installations and railway exhibits.

The Darby family and other ironmasters pressed on to exploit the use of steam. One of the pioneers was John Wilkinson, known as 'Iron-Mad Wilkinson' because of his passionate advocacy of iron for every conceivable use. He wore an iron hat, was buried in an iron coffin when he died in 1808, and an iron obelist was raised to his memory. It was Wilkinson who patented the method of boring cylinders which made James Watt's steam engine a practical proposition. His ironworks at **Bersham**, near Wrexham in North Wales, is today the centrepiece of an industrial heritage centre. This itself is on an eight-mile trail which traces the industrial history of this area from Roman times to the present day.

Another pioneer was Richard Arkwright, the Lancashire barber turned textile magnate, who built a water-powered cotton mill in the 1770s at **Cromford** in Derbyshire, with model housing for his factory hands. The site is being restored by the Arkwright Society. In Cheshire the National Trust owns **Quarry Bank Mill** at Styal, where another factory town was created round the cotton mill by the Greg family from the 1780s on. The machinery is running again, cotton goods woven in the mill are on sale and visitors can see the huge 85ft (26m) water-wheel, the village and the house where the pauper children lived.

The vast, dinosaur-like wheels and engines of the early industrial

age always attract and awe visitors. Lead mining was long an important industry on the northern moors and an enormous wheel is the most striking feature of the **Killhope Lead Mine** in Weardale, County Durham. In Cornwall giant engines were needed to pump water out of the shafts of tin mines driven 2,000ft (610m) deep and sometimes far out under the sea. The ruined engine houses and chimney stacks of abandoned tin mines are a dramatic and melancholy feature of the Cornish landscape. The National Trust preserves two of the engines at **East Pool Mine**, near Camborne. North of St Austell, in the strange white moonscape of china clay heaps, the 19th-century **Wheal Martyn** pit is a museum of the industry.

The titanic 1876 steam engine which pumped Brighton's water up from 160ft (49m) below ground has been restored, with many other engines, at the **British Engineerium** in Hove. Machinery clatters and rattles energetically away at the **Stott Park Bobbin Mill** in Cumbria, now in the care of English Heritage. This bobbin factory built in the 1830s is virtually unchanged. Wheels turn and fan-belts flap alarmingly at **Camden Works** in Bath, in the former brass foundry of J B Bowler. Here the most elementary safety precautions were ignored. The firm also made dubious aerated soft drinks. Nothing was ever thrown away at Bowler's and the whole ramshackle place is a delight.

Scotland is not as rich in industrial sites as it might be, but drinks of quite a different kind can be sampled in a clutch of whisky distilleries in the Dufftown area. There is a 70-mile, eight-distillery Whisky Trail for enthusiasts, who are urged to let someone else do the driving.

Coal mining and ironworking were carried on for centuries on a small scale in the Forest of Dean. One of the eerier experiences in Britain is to make your way down into the echoing tunnels and caverns of the **Clearwell Caves Iron Mine**, which had its heyday between 1850 and 1900.

In Wales, among the mountains of Snowdonia, there are dramatic sites where the hillsides are torn and broken by quarrying for slate, the principal industry of the area for 200 years until quite recently. At the **Llechwedd Slate Caverns** near Blaenau Ffestiniog, visitors are taken deep underground into the tunnels and caverns, and there are demonstrations of the skilled art of slate-splitting. Close by is the **Gloddfa Ganol Slate Mine**, once the biggest in the world. At Llanberis there is a museum of the

industry in the workshops of the now-closed **Dinorwic Quarry**.

The country's most dramatic and convincing coal mining museum is in South Wales. This is **Big Pit**, near Blaenafon in Gwent, in a colliery which closed in 1980. You go down almost 300ft (90m) in the cage, wearing your miner's helmet with lamp – which you need – and an ex-miner guides the party through the tunnels.

The application of steam power to transport created the great age of railways in Britain in the 19th and 20th centuries. The landscape was changed for every by the Herculean works involved; the construction of embankments, cuttings and tunnels, the throwing of noble bridges and soaring viaducts across rivers and valleys. The sight of a powerful steam locomotive hammering along the rails at full tilt under a plume of smoke, the screaming of its whistle echoing across country, became part of the right order of things. When steam gave way to diesel and electric power, and much-loved branch lines were closed down in the 1950s and '60s, preservation societies were formed to keep steam lines running or restore them to operation.

Many of the preserved lines go through particularly attractive stretches of country. The **Severn Valley Railway** runs more trains than any other, for 16 miles close to the River Severn between Bridgnorth, Bewdley and Kidderminster. Among its steam warhorses are some fine old Great Western locomotives.

The **Bluebell Railway** in Sussex has five miles of track between Sheffield Park and Horsted Keynes, through woods shining with bluebells in the spring. The **North Yorkshire Moors Railway** steams the 18 miles from Pickering to Grosmont through superlative scenery in the North York Moors National Park and runs a Pullman service regularly. There are gaslit stations on the **Keighley and Worth Valley Railway**, whose headquarters are at Haworth in the Brontë Country. The **Lakeside & Haverthwaite Railway** puffs amicably through the Cumbrian woods to connect with the steamers on Lake Windermere.

In 19th-century England and Scotland the standard gauge of 4ft 8$\frac{1}{2}$in held sway, but elsewhere, especially in mountainous areas, a narrow gauge might be better suited

to the terrain – the **Isle of Man Railway's** 15-mile line from Douglas to Port Erin, has a 3ft gauge. Wales has a special reputation for its 'great little trains', on which the traveller can enjoy the steam, the shining paintwork and polished brass, and extremely spectacular scenery.

The **Vale of Rheidol Railway**, for instance, which opened in 1902, clanks its way along the mountainsides and round sharp bends from Aberystwyth to the famous beauty spot of the Devil's Bridge. The **Ffestiniog Railway**, originally built to haul slate, clambers up into Snowdonia from the harbour of Porthmadog past lakes and waterfalls and into the mountains. Some of its genial, round-faced engines have been making the trip for a hundred years. The **Talyllyn Railway**, which has been running since 1865, travels seven miles inland from Tywyn on Cardigan Bay, with splendid mountain prospects. This was the first railway in Britain to be saved by volunteers from destruction. It set an example many were glad to follow.

A vintage steam engine on the Brecon Mountain Railway near Merthyr Tydfil.

Industrial interest

Tourist railway or steam centre

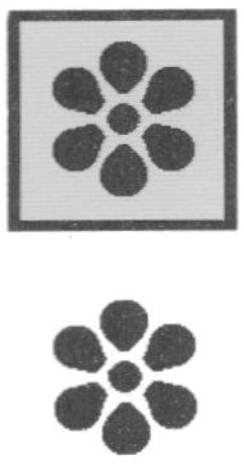

Garden

Arboretum

Gardens
Arboreta

'An Englishman's home is his castle' and round his castle he creates a garden. Despite – or perhaps because of – the vagaries of our climate, the closeness of the Gulf Stream and the collections brought back from all over the world particularly in the 18th and 19th centuries, Britain has a wonderful heritage of gardens and arboreta.

The **Royal Horticultural Society**, inaugurated in 1804, has gardens at **Wisley**, near Woking, **Rosemoor**, in Devon, as well as close affiliations with the College of Horticulture, at **Pershore** and Liverpool University Botanic Garden, at **Ness**, on the Wirral. The RHS has, since 1889, published '*The Garden*', describing what can be seen, when and where. At all these places, keen gardeners can readily obtain advice and information.

The **Royal Botanic Garden** at Kew was established in 1759, in the reign of George II. Joining the traditional Victorian Palm and Temperate Houses, is Kew's latest feature, the Princess of Wales Conservatory, a

The gardens at Bodnant, Gwynedd, are among the most beautiful in Britain.

complex of 10 independently controlled climatic environments, growing a range of plants from desert to tropical forest species.

Since 1965 the National Trust property at **Wakehurst Place**, near Ardingly, has been 'Kew in the country' and it is here that a national seed bank is maintained.

As we become increasingly aware of the fragile nature of our planet's eco-system, plant collections and gene banks are more and more a vital part of horticulture. The National Council for the Conservation of Plants and Gardens has, since 1982, co-ordinated collections such as the magnolias at **Savill Garden**, near Windsor, violas at **Leicester University,** clematis at **Tenbury**, peonies at **Hidcote** and rhododendrons at **Leonardslee**, **Nymans** and at **Exbury**. **Abbotsbury,** in Devon, looks after eucalyptus and in scores of smaller gardens, amateurs as well as professionals nurture border plants, primroses, celandines, buddleias and asters. For bigger specimens, arboreta play their part. Seventeen miles of pathways lead through the 500 acres of the Forestry Commission's **Westonbirt Arboretum** in Gloucestershire, where plantings have been

continuous for 150 years. Oak, chestnut, pine and beech shelter more exotic specimens, such as acers and willows, azaleas and rhododendrons.

The **Granada Arboretum**, in Manchester, and the National Trust's **Winkworth Arboretum**, in Surrey, maintain sorbus and malus. Winter-flowering plants such as daphnes, honeysuckle, camellias and viburnum can be seen at the **Hillier Arboretum**, near Romsey, and plants which flourish on chalky soils are the specialty of **Hidcote Manor Garden**, north of Chipping Campden.

Many of the gardens lovingly tended in the past have now been restored. At **New Place,** in Surrey, the Edwardian garden of Gertrude Jekyll was recovered from beneath couch grass and poppies. At East Grinstead, the mullioned windows of 16th-century **Gravetye Manor** now reflect the glory of a Victorian garden created by William Robinson. At **Erddig**, near Wrexham, another 18th-century design has been re-created in the grounds of the National Trust house and **Culpeper Flower Garden** now flourishes at **Leeds Castle**, in Kent, 17th-century home of the Culpeper family. The 18th-century garden at

Painshill Park in Surrey was laid out in the 1740s by Charles Hamilton. Sadly decayed, the combination of classical architecture, lake and landscaping is being restored and it may once again rival the garden of Hamilton's friend, Henry Hoare at Stourhead.

Gardens stretch the length and breadth of the British isles. **Inverewe**, in Wester Ross, despite its northern latitude, enjoys frost-free conditions, due to the warm North Atlantic Drift, and **Tresco Abbey Gardens** in the Scilly Isles, created and maintained since 1834 by successive generations of the same family, relishes mild, moist weather. In the 1790s garden of 13th-century **Drum Castle**, near Aberdeen, a collection illustrating the development of roses from the 17th-century has recently been created by the National Trust for Scotland.

The **University Botanic Gardens** at St Andrews, training ground for future professionals, also provide a well laid out and informative garden for the visitor. Its high point is the peat, water and rock complex simulating the natural progression from mountain crag to scree to meadow and bog. The **Royal Botanic Garden**, in Edinburgh, second oldest in the country after Oxford, also has a superb rock garden and, like the new conservatory at Kew, grows the astonishing *Victoria Amazonica* water lily, its huge leaves capable of supporting a small child, but which grow from seed annually.

Across on the west coast are the gardens of **Brodick Castle**, on the Isle of Arran. Sir John Ramsden, then owner of **Muncaster Castle**, in Cumbria, after a visit to Brodick sent his hostess some rhododendrons for her garden – in all 80 tons! In 1953 an expedition to Burma brought back hundreds more plants and yet more varieties, most of which flourish in the mild climate.

At **Belsay**, north of Newcastle, English Heritage has restored the gardens, partly in the quarry used by Charles Monck, a keen member of the Horticultural Society. At **Thorp Perrow**, near Ripon, there is a cherry avenue which is a riot of blossom in May. Several 'autumn bays' provide colour from September to November and there is a rowan avenue, with spring blossom and autumn berries.

John Aislabie, Chancellor of the Exchequer at the time of the South Sea Bubble, retired to his estate at **Studley Royal**, in Yorkshire, albeit under something of a cloud. The garden he designed is a work of true inspiration, anticipating

Stourhead by 40 years. It now incorporates the ready-made 'folly', so essential to Romantic landscaping, acquired when his son purchased the nearby Fountains Abbey.

Harlow Carr Botanical Garden, near Harrogate, has been since 1948 the headquarters of the Northern Horticultural Society, working closely with the RHS and offering a similar range of walks, workshops and demonstrations as Wisley. **Newby Hall,** near Ripon, has something to delight the eye all year round, but is best known for its display of roses in early summer and its herbaceous border plants.

At **Eaton Hall**, Eccleston, near Chester, there is an unheated glasshouse 360 feet (110m) long, with camellias which are usually at their best in April. **Bodnant**, near Llandudno, always associated with the Aberconway family, has rhododendrons, azaleas, magnolias and camellias. Here, too, there is a wonderful laburnum walk where, on a sunny day in May, you can walk through a tunnel of glorious yellow blossom. Near Welshpool is **Powis Castle**, once the home of Clive of India. Its terraces are one of the few remaining medieval-style gardens in the country.

Doddington Hall, south-west of Lincoln, was built by the Elizabethan architect, Smythson, who designed Longleat and Hardwick Hall. The garden, even as late as 1919, had cattle grazing on the lawns, but now the walled west garden is full of the old-fashioned roses for which Doddington is famous, as well as a profusion of irises.

Near Colchester, **Beth Chatto's Garden** covering 12 acres, has developed into a centre where gardeners can pick up hints on what grows best in hard-baked sandy soil, sour silt or waterlogged clay. At **Sissinghurst**, in Kent, the garden of this Tudor house is a monument to Vita Sackville-West who, in the 1930s, created walks where each of the gardens opening off had its own colour scheme.

In **Sheffield Park**, near East Grinstead, famous for its autumn colours, you can wander away from the lakeside rhododendrons and discover the wonderful collection of conifers. One group of maritime pines is reputed to have been planted by Sir Joseph Banks, a founder of the RHS. David Douglas, after whom the Douglas fir is named, brought Monterey pines here from California and there is a dwarf Siberian pine planted in the 1920s, which has just about reached five feet (one and a half metres) and can thus be highly recommended for the small garden!

The National Trust property at **Kingston Lacy** in Dorset, has a delightful fernery planted with snowdrops for an early effect and the Cedar Walk has carefully recorded plantings by the Duke of Wellington, King Edward VII, the Kaiser and King George V, who planted an oak here to commemorate his Coronation. At **Stourhead**, north of Shaftesbury, lake, bridge, temples and grottoes combine to achieve one of the finest 'landscaped' gardens in the world, the creation of Henry Hoare in the 1740s, a generation before Capability Brown began diverting rivers and moving mountains around many of the great houses of his day.

Penjerrick, in Cornwall, was begun in the 1830s and many exotic plants here were grown from seed brought into nearby Falmouth by clipper captains, but rhododendrons remain one of its glories.

Wherever you go, at no matter what season of the year, there are gardens to be enjoyed all over Britain. Provided you do not pick a Bank Holiday weekend, in most cases you will find someone ready to pass on the secret of their success to you.

Hillier Arboretum in Hampshire.

Garden

Arboretum

Country park

The forested slopes at Afan Argoed resemble those in Switzerland.

Country Parks

In the 1960s and '70s, increasing affluence, more leisure time, more cars and faster roads combined to bring the open countryside within the reach of far more people. The number of townspeople and suburbanites driving out for a day in the country was growing rapidly and there was a need to accommodate the demand without spoiling the countryside which everyone was eager to enjoy.

In 1966 a government white paper on 'Leisure in the Countryside' suggested the establishment of country parks and the idea was taken up in the Countryside Acts which followed. The two Countryside Commissions, one for England and Wales, the other for Scotland, were given the responsibility for stimulating the creation of country parks, providing advice and grants of taxpayers' money to projects they approved.

Most of the country parks have been set up by local authorities. One of their fundamental functions is to make available country places where visitors know they have a right to be. Opinion polls and studies have shown time and time again that people are held back from enjoying the countryside by an uneasy feeling that they may be trespassing or at least not wanted. A country park is a place where you are welcome. It is also a place where there will be toilets and somewhere to park the car.

There are now more than 200 country parks in Britain, varying considerably in size and character. The larger ones have visitor centres where you will find information about the landscape, the wildlife and often the area's history; wardens or rangers who keep an eye on things and provide help and information when needed; way-marked paths; amusements for children, and refreshments.

Country parks are usually open every day during daylight hours, and in the great majority of them admission is free, though boating, bowls or other special facilities may have to be paid for. Activities vary from one park to another – from riding, fishing, hang-gliding and grass-skiing to orienteering, golfing, boating and sailing.

Some of the earliest country parks were areas which were already heavily visited and where better facilities were needed. An example is **Box Hill**, near Dorking in Surrey, named after the rare wild box trees on the chalk hill. For centuries past people have loved to walk there and admire the views of the Weald. Much of the area is owned by the National Trust and there is a car park, information room and shop.

Another case in point is **Butser Hill**, a much-visited beauty spot on the A3 south of Petersfield where

Hampshire County Council created the **Queen Elizabeth Country Park,** opened by the Queen in 1976. The park covers 1,400 acres of downs, Forestry Commission beechwoods and stands of yew at the western edge of the South Downs Way footpath. There are splendid views from the top of Butser Hill, a nature reserve and waymarked trails, with downland plants and flowers to see, woodpeckers, butterflies and deer. The Ancient Farm Research Project here farms the way Iron Age man did 2,000 years ago and the park has an information centre with an audio-visual programme, a café and a picnic area.

Another heavily visited area is the **Brimham Rocks Country Park** on the moors near Pateley Bridge in North Yorkshire. The rocks, weathered into strange shapes over the centuries, drew sightseers in such numbers that the area was in danger of being badly damaged. It is owned by the National Trust and the threat to the rocks has been brought under control.

Since country parks were intended primarily for town dwellers, they tend to be more numerous close to heavily populated urban areas. They are not thick on the ground in Norfolk and Suffolk, for example, but there is quite a concentration of them in Essex, nearer London. One of these is the attractive **Hatfield Forest Country Park**, near Bishop's Stortford, an area of ancient hunting forest which was only just rescued from the developer's grasp in the 1920s and which is famous for its hornbeams and its nightingales.

Similarly, there are fewer country parks in North and Central Wales than in the former mining and industrial areas of South Wales. One of the biggest and best is **Margam Country Park**, near Port Talbot. Its 850 acres include what were once the stately grounds of the Mansel family's fine house. There are landscaped gardens, a deer park, a handsome orangery which is used for concerts, a theatre, a large maze and boating on the lake, which is also occupied by swans, coots and moorhens. A herd of Glamorgan cattle and an Iron Age hillfort with commanding views over the Bristol Channel add to its enormous appeal. There is an adventure playground, a heronry in the nature reserve and there are skylarks and buzzards. Just outside the park is the ruined church of 12th-century Margam Abbey.

Many other parks have solved the problem of what to do with fine country estates the owners can no longer keep up. **Mount Edgcumbe Country Park**, which looks out over Plymouth Sound, preserves the formal gardens with their statues and fountains laid out for the Edgcumbe family in the 18th century. Stretching for miles along the coast, it boasts follies, woods, a deer park and a fabulous collection of camellias.

Many country parks, by contrast, have contributed to the reclamation of derelict industrial wasteland. East of Sheffield, on the border of Yorkshire and Derbyshire, the **Rother Valley Country Park** has arisen phoenix-like from an area of opencast coal mining, with 350,000 freshly planted trees and no less than three lakes for fishing and watersports. There are footpaths and visitors can hire cycles to ride along the network of bicycle tracks.

The **Strathclyde Country Park** in the south-eastern outskirts of Glasgow was formally opened in 1978. Millions of pounds were spent to take a derelict, stagnant wasteland of exhausted colliery workings and desolate spoil heaps and turn it back into pleasant countryside. The River Clyde was diverted to create a 200-acre loch, trees and shrubs and long stretches of grass were planted, paths were laid out by the loch and picnic areas and car parks provided.

Now the trees have matured. The loch, almost two miles long, is a watersports centre for sailing, canoeing and waterskiing. There is a golf course and sports pitches, an interpretation centre and a nature reserve which attracts wintering whooper swans and other waterfowl. Also inside the park are the remains of a Roman fort and a peculiar 19th-century mausoleum, which was constructed for the Dukes of Hamilton but turned out to have such a noisy echo in the chapel inside that it was impossible to use it.

Country park landscapes vary from the heath and scrub of **Cannock Chase** in Staffordshire to the giant trees in **Sherwood Forest**, the ducal landscape by Capability Brown not far away in **Clumber Park** in Nottinghamshire and on to the deer and rugged rocks of **Bradgate Park** in Leicestershire, with the ruins of the house in which the tragic Lady Jane Grey grew up. On top of **Ham Hill** in Somerset, the grassed-over stone quarries make a wonderful arena for hide-and-seek. On **Berry Head**, south of Torbay in South Devon, towering cliffs command bracing views of the English Channel and the nests of kittiwakes and guillemots. The need to protect the wild orchids and other rare plants here was one reason why the local council bought the land in 1968. Further on along the Channel coast, at the **Lepe Country Park** in Hampshire, you can look across the Solent to the Isle of Wight and idly watch the ships and the black-headed gulls go by.

One question which remains is: are the visitors at country parks enjoying real countryside or a mock-up? Nowadays the Countryside Commission believes that the parks should be treated less as ends in themselves and more as gateways to the true countryside beyond.

Brimham Rocks, in North Yorkshire, where the rocks form weird shapes.

Theme park

The 'Thunder River' rapid-water ride, for all the family, at Thorpe Park.

Theme Parks

The British theme park has its spiritual ancestor across the Atlantic. Disneyland, which opened in Anaheim in the southern suburbs of Los Angeles in 1955, combined four basic characteristics. First there was a central theme – the world of Disney cartoons and films. Second, there were illusions, using the latest technology, and visitors experienced a simulated river trip in the African jungle, or thought they were going deep underwater in a submarine, when in fact they were only a few inches beneath the surface. Next, there were 'white knuckle' rides – an exciting roller-coaster, a terrifying helter-skelter and other thrilling fairground rides, again using the latest technology. And last, Disneyland catered for the motor car, the family with children and modern mass tourism, with a parking lot of gargantuan proportions and an ample supply of toilets and places to eat.

The lessons of Disneyland were absorbed and put to use at **Alton Towers**, the 500-acre 'leisure park' in Staffordshire which is now attracting two and a half million visitors a year. Alton Towers employs a staff of 1,400 people during the summer and has six different restaurants, of varying types and price levels, with innumerable kiosks scattered about the grounds selling ice-creams and soft drinks. There is no single central theme, but six 'themed areas', which include Fantasy World, Aqualand and Kiddies Kingdom. Among the 'white knuckle' rides are the gravity-defying Corkscrew Roller-coaster, which lives up to its name, as well as the New Black Hole, the Alton Beast, and the water-based Log Flume

and Grand Canyon Rapids Ride.

There are gentler rides for those of nervous disposition or with small children, with a beautiful carousel, and a mass of indoor attractions and Disney-style parades with bands, floats and performers in life-size animal costumes.

In addition to all this is a wonderful Victorian Gothic ruin and some of the most spectacular gardens in the country, inherited from the Earls of Shrewsbury, whose country seat Alton Towers used to be. The 15th and 16th Earls constructed an enormous pseudo-medieval fantasy palace here, replete with towers and spires, turrets and battlements. A W Pugin himself, the high priest of Victorian Gothic, was called in to preside over the interior decor. Outside, meanwhile, a fortune was spent to lay out a magnificent park and gardens. Lakes and pools were dug out, fed by water brought from a spring two miles off. Terraces, miles of walks, giant stairways and grand glasshouses were built at colossal expense by an army of workmen.

The future Queen Victoria visited Alton in 1832, at the age of 13, and was entertained to luncheon on gold plates. The Chinese-style Pagoda Fountain was built, and shoots a jet of water 70ft (21m) high. A Swiss cottage was erected on the hillside to provide a fine prospect over the grounds while a blind Welsh harper was stationed there to play soothing music. Today it is a restaurant.

In later years it proved impossible to keep the house up and the mansion fell into the condition of picturesque ruin in which visitors see it now. The gardens were properly maintained, however, and are a delight to walk in today.

More 'white knuckle' rides can be found by the adventurous at the **Chessington World of Adventures**, in Surrey. 'This Ride Is Not For The

Faint-Hearted' one sign warns. There is a blood chilling roller-coaster called the Vampire, which zooms along at tree-top height and dives underground. It is set in a 'Transylvania' village which also has a bubble works fantasy ride for children through a simulated fizzy pop factory, and a restaurant wittily named the Black Forest Chateau.

The theme areas at Chessington feature encounters with horrible science fiction monsters, and Calamity Canyon, where there's a Wild West trading post, a shooting gallery and a roller-coaster called the Runaway Mine Train. In the Mystic East area visitors see the Palace of the Nine Dragons, the Giant Buddha and the Cambodian temple of Angkor Wat, and go on a 'dragon river' water ride through a bamboo jungle, where the boat is attacked by a crocodile. In addition, Chessington has a zoo, a circus, a miniature railway, plenty of eating places and live entertainment with bands, dancers, clowns, street performers and 'madcap' characters in costume.

Halfway between Derby and Nottingham may seem an odd place to meet cowboys and shoot-outs, but the Wild West is one of the main themes at the **American Adventure**, near Ilkeston in Derbyshire. Pistol-packing posses career through town, bullets fly and saloon girls squeal as badmen get their come-uppances. There is live entertainment in Lazy Lil's Saloon and jazz on a Mississippi riverboat.

The numerous rides include a double-drop log flume in Thunder Canyon and a charge through the raging torrents of the Great Niagara Rapids. Or you can take a triple-looping roller-coaster called the Missile and blast off to the stars from Space Port USA. There are special attractions to keep small children happy in Pioneer Playland, including a cartoon cinema.

At the **Pleasurewood Hills American Theme Park**, near Lowestoft in Suffolk, southern fried chicken is on the menu, and attractions range from the evil Rattlesnake roller-coaster and the New Tempest, which hangs you upside down 100ft (30m) in the air, to a waterborne voyage to Aladdin's Cave, a land of dinosaurs, fairground big wheels, a spooky haunted castle and shows by performing sea lions and parrots.

In Yorkshire, near Ripon, the **Lightwater Valley Theme Park**, in the 1970s a peaceful pig farm, prides itself on the sheer appalling terror of its 'white knuckle' rides. It opened the longest roller-coaster ride in the world in 1990, at a cost of over £5 million, running close to

1¹/₂ miles (2.4km) with a drop of 158ft (48m) and a top speed of about 60mph. This joined a nightmare ride called The Rat, which runs entirely underground in pitch darkness, 'through smelly sewers alive with the shrieks and shrills of rats' – rated tops for sheer horror by the *Daily Mirror*.

There are calmer pleasures at Lightwater Valley, too – a nine-hole golf course, three boating lakes, an old-fashioned fairground, a miniature railway and a shopping centre. There is skateboarding, a go-kart track, an adventure playground for smaller children and a theatre with live entertainment.

At Charnock Richard in Lancashire, there awaits 'an enchanted day out for the whole family' in 'the magical kingdom' of **Camelot.** The theme here is the world of King Arthur and his heroic knights of the Round Table. Knights in full armour thunder into combat on their chargers in the jousting arena. Jesters and grotesque animal figures wander about. A chilling roller-coaster hurtles into the Tower of Terror, where something unspeakable called the Beast lurks in its dark lair. Guinevere's swan ride negotiates Merlin's magic mountain, the Grail trail crosses a swinging rope bridge and Sir Bedevere's Bridge leads to the enchantments of the Wild Wood.

You can eat at the Round Table Burger Bar, naturally, but altogether Camelot has 28 outlets selling food and drink. It reckons to cook 2¹/₂ miles of sausages every season, as well as 250,000 pounds of dragon burgers and 315,000 pounds of chips.

The 'family leisure park' at **Thorpe Park**, near Chertsey in Surrey, is close to both the M3 and the M25. It opened in 1979 on the site of old gravel workings, which gave it plenty of lakes and pools. Water skiing, windsurfing and other watersports rank high among its pleasures, water barges carry visitors from one area of the park to another and there are river-boat restaurants.

The original theme was Britain's maritime history, but now, with the need to attract repeat visitors, the emphasis has changed. 'White knuckle' rides are not particularly important here and the park concentrates more on entertainments and amusements which families with children aged about four to 14 can all enjoy together. There is live entertainment at two theatres, lots of street entertainment, musicians, clowns and giant sub-Disney animal grotesques, and a large amusement centre with

video games and one-armed bandits. The log flume ride in the Canadian Rockies theme area has a drop of 50ft and there is a fast Space Station Zero ride, but more typical is the complete working farm, which operates as it did in the 1930s. A simulated medieval town square has a double-decker carousel and other attractions include a nature trail, miniature railway, roller skating rink, crazy golf and a cartoon cinema.

All theme parks are geared to a safe, enjoyable family day out, and you pay once, on entry, and get the rides and other attractions thrown in. Alton Towers is the kingpin in terms of visitor figures, but the numbers rung up at the other parks – over a million and a quarter at Chessington – suggest that this type of transatlantic family attraction is in Britain to stay.

The 'Runaway Mine Train' at Chessington World of Adventures.

Theme Park

Zoo

Wildlife collection – mammals

Wildlife collection – birds

Aquarium

Zoos
Wildlife Collections
Aquariums

The oldest picture of an elephant in England is in Exeter Cathedral, a 13th-century wood carving under one of the choir seats. It is quite likely to be a portrait of a real African elephant, the one which was presented to Henry III by the King of France in 1253. Its arrival in England created a sensation and people flocked to see the great beast as it tramped from the port of Sandwich to London.

Zoos
The century before, Henry I had established a menagerie at Woodstock in Oxfordshire. It was later moved to the Tower of London and survived there until well into the 19th century. The public was let in to see the animals, which in 1609 consisted of 11 lions, two leopards, a jackal, two mountain cats, three eagles and two owls.

Kings and noblemen continued to keep private menageries, but the 19th century saw the creation of public zoological gardens – zoos for short – as part of the same educational and improving impulse responsible for the establishment of so many museums. The first in the field was the **Regent's Park Zoo** in London, laid out by Decimus Burton and opened in 1828 by the recently founded Zoological Society of London. The animals from the Tower were moved here.

Municipal zoos now opened, combining serious study of animals with public instruction and entertainment. In Dublin, for example, the Royal Zoological Society of Ireland opened a zoo in **Phoenix Park** in 1830. It gained a substantial reputation for breeding lions, as **Glasgow Zoo** breeds porcupines and Edinburgh Zoo is famous for its penguins.

Wildlife Collections
After World War II, a tide of disapproval set in against the old-fashioned 19th-century zoo, which seemed little better than a prison with its cramped cages and unnatural conditions, and against the whole attitude to animals which this type of zoo was felt to represent. The consequence was the modernisation of many zoos and the coming of the safari park and a new style of wildlife collection.
The development of the open-range zoo, where animals roam in large enclosures instead of being penned in cages, had begun in 1931, when the Zoological Society of London opened a country branch at **Whipsnade Park** in Bedfordshire, near Dunstable. Whipsnade covers

The famous lions of Longleat.

more than 500 acres, most of the animals live in herds in sizeable paddocks and well over 90 per cent of them were born in the zoo. In the last 30 years many other zoos have moved closer to the open-range system.

Britain's first safari park opened in 1966 at **Longleat** in Wiltshire, the palatial Elizabethan seat of the Marquess of Bath. The prime movers in the enterprise were the Marquess himself and Jimmy Chipperfield, of the well-known circus family, an experienced supplier of wild animals to zoos. The idea was for visitors to drive through the spacious enclosures where the animals roamed: in other words, for a change, the animals would be free and the public confined. The project proved extremely popular.

Lions were the first and have always been the foremost attraction at Longleat, but many other animals can be seen there today – including the country's only white Bengal tiger, as well as white rhinos, camels, giraffes and gorillas. The monkeys enjoy riding on visitors' cars and there are boat trips to see hippos and sea lions. In some areas visitors can leave their cars and stroll about or even have a picnic among the animals. Like other safari parks, Longleat depends on and provides for the motor car and there is plenty of parking with no problem about finding a restaurant or a toilet.

The Duke of Bedford was not far behind in opening a safari park of his own at his stately Bedfordshire mansion of **Woburn**. Jimmy Chipperfield was again involved. But Woburn already had a distinguished history of keeping and breeding wild animals. Père David's deer are named after a French missionary, who saw the only remaining herd of them in the imperial park outside Peking where they were kept in the 19th century. A few animals were grudgingly shipped out to European zoos and

Flamingoes at Slimbridge Wildfowl Trust

when the Chinese herd was wiped out, the 16 Père David's deer in Europe were the only ones left. The 11th Duke of Bedford rounded all 16 up in 1894 and settled them in his park at Woburn, where they prospered and multiplied. All the Père David's deer in the world are descended from them, and in 1985 some were sent back to China, to the same park outside Peking.

Woburn also played a part in saving the European bison from extinction. The Père David's deer are still there, and so are the bison, and the **Woburn Wild Animal Kingdom** today is Britain's largest drive-through collection of wild creatures. A ride in aerial cars gives a bird's eye view of the park and there are performing sea lions, and even performing macaws.

A wildlife collection of an entirely different flavour can be enjoyed at **Chillingham**, in Northumberland, where visitors can cautiously inspect the 50-strong herd of wild white cattle. With their wicked, curving horns, they are the nearest thing to prehistoric cattle still in existence. They have been kept in the park at Chillingham for centuries and have never been crossbred.

John Aspinall has set up two Kent

Zoo

Wildlife collection – mammals

Wildlife collection – birds

Aquarium

zoo parks: **Howletts**, near Canterbury, famous for breeding gorillas and African elephants, and its sister at **Port Lympne**, near Hythe. Here magnificent Siberian tigers, black rhino and the country's only breeding colony of majestic Barbary lions loll about in aristocratic splendour.

Breeding animals, and especially breeding species which in the wild are threatened with extinction, has become an important function of zoos, safari parks and wildlife collections, and a key justification of their existence. **Chester Zoo**, for example, which ranks second only to London in its tally of visitors and has a wide range of animals in attractive grounds, has successfully bred orang-utans, Madagascan tree boas and rare fruit bats, among other species. **Bristol Zoo**, where the creatures on view range from tigers to tarantulas and penguins to piranhas, counts gorillas and orang-utans, Persian leopards, colobus monkeys and long-tailed macaques among its breeding successes. **Twycross Zoo**, near Atherstone in Warwickshire, a small zoo with a remarkable collection of apes and monkeys, has a notable breeding record and **Marwell**, near Winchester, breeds rare Sumatran tigers and the endangered oryx.

In 1947 there were only 50 breeding pairs of the Hawaiian geese (called nene) left in the world, all of them in Hawaii. The species was saved by successful breeding at the Wildfowl & Wetlands Trust reserve at **Slimbridge** in Gloucestershire, founded by the late Sir Peter Scott. Some of the birds from here were later sent back to Hawaii in the hope of re-establishing them in their native land.

The splendid Slimbridge reserve is on the bank of the River Severn. Other Wildfowl Trust reserves include those at **Arundel** in Sussex, **Washington** in Tyne and Wear, and **Caerlaverock**, near Dumfries in Scotland. At **Stagsden** in Bedfordshire is one of the first specialist bird collections in Britain. The Bird Gardens concentrate on cranes, but there are 150 species or more on view in all. **Birdworld**, near Farnham in Surrey, has a collection ranging from tiny hummingbirds to outsize ostriches, and is successfully breeding Humboldt penguins.

Aquariums
The first public aquarium in Britain opened in London in 1853. It was not until a hundred years later that the first massive sea aquariums, or oceanariums, opened in the United States, with huge tanks containing

The 'Penguin Parade' – the star attraction at Edinburgh Zoo.

hundreds of fish of different species swimming together. The example has been followed in Britain, for example at the **Sea Life Centre** in Weymouth, which opened in 1983 with the biggest display tank in Europe. Visitors can see dolphins and porpoises, British sharks, octopus and squid and evil-looking conger eels, and fish in drifting droves. There is a special flatfish tank and a tank with a simulated sunken wreck and the marine life that would gather around it. There are also 'touch pools' and plenty of fun for children.

Of the same genre, but on a much more modest scale, is **Anglesey Sea Zoo**, near Brynsiencyn, close to the shore of the Menai Strait, with its tanks of fish, lobsters and crabs from the local waters and 'touch tanks' for the children.

There is plenty of enjoyment and discovery at other sea life centres in seaside towns, like Brighton, Blackpool and Southsea and at Barcaldine in Scotland where young seals can be viewed prior to their release back into the wild. While wildlife is increasingly threatened in the wild, it flourishes in British zoos, safari parks and aquariums.

Nature reserve

RSPB site

Nature Reserves
Nature Trails
RSPB Sites

Brownsea Island is a much-treasured Dorset beauty spot, a 500-acre island in Poole Harbour, accessible only by boat. It has an honoured place in the history of the Boy Scouts, as it was here in 1907 that General Baden-Powell held his first scout camp. A succession of wealthy and sometimes eccentric owners preserved the island from contamination by development until, with the death of the last of them in 1961, it passed to the National Trust. It was then a wildly overgrown paradise for red squirrels, the late owner's peacocks, Sika deer, herons and seabirds. The National Trust has protected it ever since and thousands of visitors go there every year to enjoy the beaches, walk the heathland and woodland glades and admire stunning views of the Dorset coast.

A substantial area of the island is sealed off against casual visitors dropping in, though parties are guided round at regular intervals. This is a nature reserve, managed by the Dorset Trust for Nature Conservation, with a heronry, two lakes and a marsh fringed with reeds, where wildfowl congregate in

A view from a hide overlooking Welney Wildfowl Refuge, in Norfolk.

safety – terns and oystercatchers, godwits and sandpipers, dunlins and redshanks.

Nature Reserves
Unlike a National Park or a country park, a nature reserve is not protected for the sake of human visitors, but for the sake of the wild creatures, birds, insects and rare plants, and the habitats and conditions they need to survive and flourish. Many nature reserves are open to the general public; at others a permit may be needed or access may be limited, but some are closed altogether.

As long ago as 1912 the need to set aside areas in which threatened species could survive was recognised with the founding of the Society for the Promotion of Nature Reserves by the pioneering naturalist Charles Rothschild. When he died the movement lost impetus. After World War II, however, the pressure of expanding population and expanding leisure time bore so heavily on the country's wildlife that something plainly needed to be done. In 1949 the government set up the Nature Conservancy Council (NCC) as its wildlife protection arm, and one of the new body's responsibilities was 'to establish, manage and maintain nature reserves'.

At the same time vigorous county and local wildlife protection trusts were forming and establishing nature reserves of their own. Charles Rothschild's society re-emerged into the limelight as the national organisation and mouthpiece of these groups, as the Royal Society for Nature Conservation.

Today Britain has more than 2,000 nature reserves, occupying more than half a million acres of land between them. Some are managed by the NCC, but a far larger number are run by the county or local trusts for nature conservation, naturalists' trusts or wildlife trusts. Others are owned and managed by the Forestry Commission, others again by local authorities and conservation bodies.

From a visitor's point of view, nature reserves supply a way of seeing and coming close to the full range of Britain's wildlife and plant life without any danger of trespassing or going where one is not wanted. They can be found on the coast and inland, on high ground and on low, in a great variety of countryside.

At **Caerlaverock**, for instance, on the Solway Firth coast of Scotland, the NCC established a reserve in 1957 on the low-lying saltmarshes among muddy flats and creeks. Multitudes of birds feed and roost there: golden plovers in legions,

greylag geese, pintail and all manner of ducks and waders. Thousands of barnacle geese fly in from the Arctic every winter, and there are birds of prey, as well as saltmarsh plants in abundance. This is also one of the breeding grounds of the rare and noisy natterjack toad. Visitor access is limited, partly because the flats and creeks are dangerous when the tide sweeps in suddenly. There is also a Wildfowl Trust refuge close by and the romantic pink ruin of Caerlaverock Castle to visit.

By contrast, not so many miles away inland, east of Newton Stewart, the NCC runs the **Cairnsmore of Fleet** nature reserve, largely a trackless waste of peat and heather moorland, bog and mountainside. It is important as the home of the red deer, wild goats and ravens. Access is again restricted.

Similarly, there is a cluster of contrasting nature reserves in the Gower Peninsula of South Wales, which is famed for packing a remarkable variety of scenery into a small area, and for the accompanying wealth of wildlife. At **Cwmllwyd Wood**, west of Swansea, for instance, West Glamorgan County Council has a reserve of oak woods, grassland and marsh, with hides from which to watch snipe and woodcock. At **Oxwich** on the south coast there is an NCC reserve of quite different character in an area of sand dunes, wooded headlands and marshes, explored by nature trails. Keep an eye out for adders on the slopes.

RSPB Sites

Some of the most rewarding nature reserves in the country belong to the Royal Society for the Protection of Birds (RSPB). Founded in 1889, the RSPB is devoted to the conservation of wild birds. It has built up a portfolio of well over a hundred reserves in which the habitats of breeding and wintering birds and birds of passage are preserved.

Some of the RSPB reserves are as far flung as the **Orkneys** and **Shetlands**, but most of them are more accessible. There is one at **Dungeness** on the Kent coast, where the nuclear power station broods over a desolate landscape of shingle beach, ponds and abandoned gravel workings, and tangled gorse and brambles. But there is plenty of life here – marsh frogs, plants like viper's bugloss, and waterfowl in huge numbers, with many migrating birds making a landfall at this point.

Up in Lancashire, at **Leighton Moss** near Silverdale, the RSPB preserves an area of swamp,

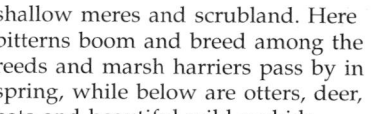

The 300ft (91m) high cliffs of Marwick Head's RSPB reserve, Orkney.

shallow meres and scrubland. Here bitterns boom and breed among the reeds and marsh harriers pass by in spring, while below are otters, deer, bats and beautiful wild orchids.

The Forest of Dean is one of the few remaining ancient royal forests left in England. Although commercial forestry plantations have replaced much of the original oak woods, there are still a few areas where magnificent oaks over 150 years old can be found. One of these is at the RSPB **Nagshead Reserve** which covers some of the best remaining oak woodland and has a rich bird community. Summer visitors include wood warblers, redstarts and pied flycatchers as well as the whole range of woodland species including all three species of woodpecker, sparrowhawks, treecreepers and nuthatches.

At **Nene Washes** in Cambridgeshire the RSPB reserve, saved from drainage and ploughing, is an example of a landscape now nearly lost. Once, hay meadows like these – rich in flowers in spring and full of birds in winter – were common; now there are only scattered remnants left. It is ironic that the washes are entirely man-made, created in the 18th century as part of flood control and drainage schemes. Breeding birds here include redshanks, snipe, sedge warblers, yellow wagtails and shovelers. Winter brings Bewick's swans, wigeon, teal and pintails in large numbers.

On the north-west tip of Holy Island, is the RSPB reserve of **South Stack Cliffs**. This reserve consists of two separate areas: the dramatic sea cliffs and heathland of Holyhead Mountain make up the northern part, while the maritime heathland of Penrhosfeilw Common is the

southern section. The most numerous seabirds are guillemots but there are razorbills, puffins and kittiwakes. The reserve is one of the foremost migration watchpoints in North Wales, both for landbirds and seabirds. On most summer days, especially with a westerly wind, Manx shearwaters and gannets may be seen flying past, while in spring and autumn large movements of passerines can be recorded in suitable weather conditions. Hundreds of wheatears and swallows may pass through daily, with smaller numbers of willow and grasshopper warblers, whinchats and ring ouzels. In early winter thousands of starlings, chaffinches and other species pass westward to the warmer climate of Ireland.

One of the RSPB's most celebrated reserves is **Bempton Cliffs** near Goole. These spectacular 445ft chalk cliffs hold the largest breeding colony of seabirds in England. Puffins and guillemots nest here but the most famous of Bempton's seabirds is the gannet, whose colony is the only mainland one in Britain. Seawatching can be exceptionally good, especially in the autumn, when the terns and skuas are moving south. The narrow band between the cliffs and the cliff-top fields is an excellent place for wild flowers.

Though the primary purpose of a reserve is protection, the RSPB welcomes visitors – the general public as well as its own members – in order to encourage public sympathy and support for conservation. Trails and hides are provided to help visitors see as much as possible, while interfering as little as possible with the birds.

National trail

National Trails

Enthusiasm for long distance walking has grown apace in Britain since World War II, as part of a general quickening of appetite for exploring and enjoying the countryside at first hand, away from main roads and crowded tourist spots. The first national long distance walking route, the Pennine Way, was declared open in 1965. Since then many more paths have been established. Ten of them are now classified by the Countryside Commission as 'national trails'. These are continuous routes over substantial distances, which can take a week or more to traverse though, of course, many people enjoy walking for only a few hours or a day or two on part of one of the routes.

The ten national trails in England and Wales are: the Cleveland Way; the North Downs Way; the Offa's Dyke Path; the Peddars Way and Norfolk Coast Path; the Pembrokeshire Coast Path; the Pennine Way; the Ridgeway Path; the South Downs Way; the South

Below *Offa's Dyke Path traces the 8th-century English – Welsh boundary.* Bottom *The 50 miles of the Peddar's Way, in Norfolk, follow a Roman road.*

West Coast path; and the Wolds Way. Placed end to end, these 10 routes together cover approximately 1,750 miles. Three of them are in the South of England, one is in East Anglia, two are in Wales and the Marches, and three in the North. There are also three more long distance walking routes in Scotland.

The founding father of this whole network was the late Tom Stephenson of the Ramblers' Association, who in 1935 put forward the idea of a continuous public footpath running the whole length of the Pennine Chain to the Cheviots and the Scots Border. It took 30 years during which much opposition had to be overcome, but he lived to see his brainchild brought safely to birth as the Pennine Way.

The **Pennine Way** runs 250 miles up the backbone of England from the High Peak in Derbyshire to the Scottish border. It starts in the Peak District National Park and crosses two other National Parks – the Yorkshire Dales and Northumberland – as well as an Area of Outstanding Natural Beauty in the North Pennines.

You can walk it either way, naturally, but travelling from south to north keeps the weather at the walker's back and the route is usually described in this direction. It starts at Edale in the delectable valley of the River Noe, close to Castleton and its deep, eerie limestone caverns. The Way goes up across the Kinder Scout plateau (there are alternative routes here and elsewhere along the trail) to the aptly named wasteland of Bleaklow. It then passes by Blackstone Edge, with its exceptionally well preserved stretch of Roman road, and across the Calder Valley close to Hebden Bridge, where the rows of millhands' houses cling to the steep hillsides, to the beauty spot of Hardcastle Crags. North from here are the wild moors of the Brontë Country, near Haworth, and the bleak scenery and atmosphere of *Wuthering Heights* at the ruined farmhouse at Withins.

The Way crosses the Craven district to reach the tremendous limestone scenery of the Yorkshire Dales National Park: 'a strange landscape,' as the great fell-walker Wainwright has written, 'almost lunar, in places awesome, in places beautiful, and everywhere fascinating.' From Malham, the beetling gorge of Gordale Scar is a mile or so off the path, which scrambles up the sheer curving cliff of Malham Cove, close to 250ft (76m) high, to the cracked and fissured limestone 'pavement' on top. Malham Tarn is the lake where Charles Kingsley was inspired to

create *The Water Babies*. Further on is the isolated hump of Pen-y-ghent, 2,273ft (693m).

On to Ribblesdale and to Wensleydale, at Hawes, and close to Hardraw Force, where the water tumbles over a 100ft (30m) rock. Further on is Middleton in Teesdale and the Way follows the swirling, rock-strewn Tees to three spectacular waterfalls in succession: Low Force, High Force and Cauldron Snout, where the river boils and rages down the rock ledges for 200ft (61m). At the stupendous horseshoe of High Cup Nick an immense abyss opens, whose sides are sheer for almost 1,000ft (305m).

Northwards again, up the valley of the South Tyne to Hadrian's Wall, getting on for 1,900 years old now, but still swooping athletically over the crags. The Way follows it for nine miles, passing Housesteads, where there are the remains of a substantial Roman fort, with legionary latrines and a museum. Then the route lies on north over heathery moors to Bellingham, across Redesdale and through the forest to the high Cheviots, the lonely open spaces of the Northumberland National Park, and the Border at last, coming to a final grateful halt at Kirk Yetholm.

The **Wolds Way** in the old East Riding of Yorkshire is about as unlike the Pennine Way as two walking routes in the same country could conceivably be. In length, by comparison, the Wolds Way is a mere pygmy of 79 miles all told. It is easy going where the Pennine Way is hard. And instead of daring the wild and lonely places, and scenes of spectacular grandeur, the Wolds Way walker is in placid, pretty country and never far from a small town or a village, a bed, a drink, a meal, a drink.

Open since 1982, the Wolds Way begins at Hessle on the north bank of the Humber and runs under the northern end of the mighty Humber Suspension Bridge. Then the route heads north to the Yorkshire Wolds, rounded chalk hills with attractive valleys. The path lies through farming country and woods, over gentle slopes, along farm tracks and roads. A point of special interest is the deserted village of Wharram Percy, north of Thixendale. It was abandoned in Tudor times and only the ruined church is still standing.

From the northern scarp of the Wolds there are fine views across the Vale of Pickering to the North York Moors, and later to the North Sea as the footpath comes to the Victorian seaside resort of Filey. It passes close to Filey Brigg, a mile-long finger of rock protruding into the sea, going on along the cliffs to

join the Cleveland Way.

The **Cleveland Way** was the second long distance footpath to be opened, in 1969. It steers its course northwards along the Yorkshire coast by Scarborough and Whitby to Saltburn. There it turns inland and changes course to the south-west, to spend the rest of its energies in the Cleveland Hills and the North York Moors National Park before coming to an end at Helmsley, not far from the haunting ruins of Rievaulx Abbey.

The **Pembrokeshire Coast Path**, 180 miles round Wales's south-western corner, and the **South West Coast Path** both take the walker through heroic coastal scenery of massive sea-beaten cliffs, coves and sandy beaches, lighthouses, vast seaward panoramas and superlative sunsets. The South West Coast Path follows the entire coastline from Minehead on the Bristol Channel in Somerset, along the North Devon shore, all round Cornwall by Land's End and the Lizard, back along the South Devon coast and the Dorset shoreline to finish on the edge of Poole Harbour.

The longest of the Scottish long distance paths is the **Southern Upland Way**, 212 miles clear across the country between Cockburnspath, east of Dunbar on the North Sea shore, and Portpatrick, looking out over the Irish Sea from the Rhinns of Galloway. This is a demanding route over a great variety of Border landscape, and positively dripping in history – passing through the Lammermuirs and the Scott Country, by the austere Jacobite mansion of Traquair, past St Mary's Loch and across the wild country of the Galloway Forest Park.

The 95 miles of the **West Highland Way**, opened in 1980, also make a romantic pilgrimage. The route is by Loch Lomond, across bleak Rannoch Moor and past the grim mountain gates of Glen Coe to Kinlochleven and Fort William, in the shadow of Ben Nevis.

The English and Welsh paths, too, have historic roots. **Offa's Dyke Path**, which is quite heavily trampled in some sections but satisfactorily lonely in others, runs the whole length of the Welsh Marches for 168 miles. From Chepstow on the River Severn it goes up the entrancing Wye Valley and long the edge of the Brecon Beacons National Park, then makes its way through the solitary, eerie Shropshire Hills and over the Clwydian Range to reach the coast of North Wales at Prestatyn. For about one-third of a distance it follows the line of the formidable bank and ditch constructed by Offa, 8th-century King of Mercia, to mark and defend his frontier with the Welsh.

The **North Downs Way**, similarly, 140 miles from Farnham to Dover and Folkestone, in part runs along the traditional medieval pilgrims' route to Canterbury, to the shrine of St Thomas à Becket. The **South Downs Way** runs 106 miles on prehistoric tracks from towering Beachy Head across Sussex and Hampshire to Winchester, commanding on the way wonderful views over the English Channel and across the Sussex Weald. The **Peddars Way**, again, follows an ancient track from the Suffolk border across Norfolk to the coast, and the **Ridgeway Path** across Wiltshire is an immensely ancient route, passing close to the important prehistoric monuments of Avebury, Wayland's Smithy and the White Horse of Uffington. On these timeworn, well-trodden ways, today's walkers tread in the footsteps of travellers of long ago.

National trail

A view from Benbrack Hill, along the Southern Upland Way in Galloway.

Cave

Prehistoric monument

Hillfort

Roman antiquity

Stonehenge is one of the most famous prehistoric monuments in Europe.

Caves
Prehistoric Monuments
Hillforts
Roman Antiquities

As the last great Ice Age held Britain in its grip, early man and the animals he hunted with increasingly sophisticated stone weapons followed shifts of climate. Small family groups took refuge from the sleet-lashed tundra in many natural limestone caverns.

Caves

Creswell Crags, in Derbyshire, one of the most important Palaeolithic sites in Britain, has a visitor centre which illustrates the life they must have led, both in the main cave and in nearby **Pin Hole** and **Robin Hood's Cave**. At **Cheddar Gorge**, Gough's Cave and Cox's Cave have displays in a nearby museum. Other caves worth visiting are the remains of mine workings for lead and later for semi-precious fluorspar near Castleton, Derbyshire – the **Treak Cliff** and **Speedwell Caverns**, near Buxton, as well as the **Blue John Cavern** itself.

Prehistoric Monuments

Long after the retreating glaciers and rising sea levels had submerged the mud flats to the east of Britain, agriculturalists arrived from Europe.

By about 5000BC, they had given the British upland landscape a basic appearance which was to remain largely unchanged until the introduction of intensive farming methods in the 20th century. But in that landscape began to appear burial mounds and much larger monuments.

Most famous must be **Stonehenge**, but from **Callanish**, on the Isle of Lewis, through **Arbor Low** and the **Nine Ladies**, near Matlock, to the **Rollright Stones**, north of Oxford, similar circles have filled later generations with awe. Possibly built, like **Castlerigg** in Cumbria and the **Ring of Brodgar** on Orkney, in connection with solar or lunar observation and associated rituals, the 'alignments' so often attributed to these circles, and to groups such as the **Devil's Arrows**, near Boroughbridge, should be treated with caution. Stonehenge pre-dates the Druid cult by 3,000 years and yet, in the Romantic age and the 19th century was thought to have been a Druid temple. In today's 'computer climate' it has become, for some, an astronomical calculator.

Orientation to the rising and setting sun does appear to have influenced the builders of most of the megalithic burial mounds in Britain. One of these, at **Newgrange**, north of Dublin, a splendid example of Neolithic

carving in its own right, is so aligned that the midwinter sunrise casts a beam directly into the tomb chamber. Newgrange predates Stonehenge by a thousand years and the positions of earth and sun, of sunrise – midwinter or midsummer – have changed, but the east–west alignments remain an intriguing facet of the study of all these monuments.

The village of **Avebury**, in Wiltshire, is set within another huge stone circle and earthwork rampart. A museum here displays finds and explains the way in which rampart and circle were constructed. **Stonehenge** has seen many phases in its construction, from its origins in 3000BC to its present form, which dates from around 1800BC. The sheer manpower involved is amazing. Four million cubic feet of chalk were dug out at Avebury, using antler picks. This and the hauling on raft and sledge of the Stonehenge bluestones from the Preseli Mountains in Wales and the transport of the 80 huge sarsens from the Marlborough Downs, tells us something of the beliefs and about the organisational ability of the builders of both monuments. Illiterate agriculturalists they may have been – certainly they were ignorant of the use of iron – and yet their kings and priests were able to organise and plan huge civil engineering projects.

Associated with Stonehenge is the huge circular timber building – **Woodhenge**. It is not difficult to imagine a conical thatched roof supported by timber uprights, their positions now marked by concrete posts. When was it built? Around 2750BC – that at least is known. Why was it built? Who used it? There is no scatter of the usual debris associated with hut circles and their domestic middens, so Woodhenge and the nearby **Durrington Walls** site would seem to have a public and ceremonial function. Perhaps the forest of tree trunk pillars recalled forest groves which had long had religious significance. At Woodhenge a three-year-old child, its skull split, was buried, perhaps as a dedication, at the centre of the complex. When the timbers at last decayed, a memorial stone was placed at the centre of the circle.

Silbury Hill, near Avebury, has so far yielded up few of its secrets. Why this 130ft (40m) mound, covering over five acres at its base, was raised is still a mystery. Trenches have been dug, seeking a burial somewhere within, but all these excavations have found is that it was very carefully built. Inside the turf mound is a stepped cone of compacted chalk rubble, each layer being finished with smooth chalk blocks. The steps were later filled with earth except for the topmost one, still visible as a terrace. The fact that the whole of the Stonehenge circle would fit comfortably within this topmost terrace gives an idea of the scale of the mound.

Carbon-14 dating has placed its construction at around 2600BC – and the trenches have told us that it was started in July or August, for right at the core have been found winged ants – but maybe there is a more important burial still to be discovered. Nearby is **West Kennet Long Barrow** and its sarsen façade – burial chamber perhaps, of the chieftains who commanded the building of Avebury.

Hillforts

The 'Beaker Folk', so called from the distinctive pottery vessels found in their graves, arrived in Britain around 2700BC. They brought with them the Aryan roots of our language and their knowledge of metal working was gradually learnt by the established communities into which they merged. By 1800BC the British climate was deteriorating and tribes vied for workable land. Local chiefs gained power and protected their arable land and pasture from the safety of upland hillforts, which gradually became tribal 'capitals'

rather than merely bolt holes in case of war.

Thousands of these hillforts dot the landscape, and many were inhabited well into the Roman age. **Ingleborough**, just north of the National Park Centre at Clapham, North Yorkshire, is the highest in Britain. Life must have been very hard on this high windswept plateau. Earlier settlers in the area possibly make themselves a warmer home in the cave systems nearby, at **Ingleborough Show Cave** and **Gaping Gill**. One of the largest and most important hill-forts in Britain is **Maiden Castle**. Built initially around 300BC, it finally fell to Vespasian's troops in AD43. Boards around the two-mile perimeter provide much information and the museum in nearby Dorchester displays finds from the site.

Often associated with these hill-forts are the figures carved into the chalk hillsides – horses and giant figures – but only a handful can be said with certainty to be 'pre-historic'. **Uffington White Horse**, between Swindon and Wantage, certainly is. Overlooking the Ridgeway Path, an ancient trade route across the north Berkshire Downs, its disintegrated simplicity resembles the horses – tribal totems, perhaps – which feature on Celtic coinage. The **Cerne Abbas Giant,** north of Dorchester, is probably not more than 1,500 years old, but its club-wielding phallic figure possibly represents Hercules, part of a god-cult which flourished around AD100. The iron Age enclosure above him was used for May Day and fertility ceremonies long after the foundation of the nearby Benedictine priory in the 10th century. **Wilmington Long Man**, near Alfriston, inland from Beachy Head, could well be Romano-British, too.

From 700BC onwards, Celtic settlers brought their language, their chariots and a love of finery, gold and ornaments. Iron swords gave them an ascendancy in battle over the native Britons, who were pushed westwards. Celtic immigrant groups shared a common dialect but their lack of any concept of 'nationhood' left their society an easy prey to the civilising might of Rome.

Roman Antiquities

The lure of corn, gold, iron, slaves and hunting dogs was enough to make the Romans decide that an invasion of Britannia in the summer of AD43 was worthwhile. By AD70 50 or more towns were linked by a network of roads. *Lex Romana* tamed the unruly land and Latin became yet another rootstock from

which English would eventually spring. Evidence of Roman military occupation is everywhere – from **Hadrian's Wall** and the lighthouse in **Dover Castle**, to the legionary fortress at **Caerleon** in Gwent.

Many of the civilising influences of Rome can still be seen today – an aqueduct which supplied fresh water 12 miles along the Frome Valley to Dorchester, sewers in Lincoln, Colchester and York, and bath houses. The finest of these, at **Bath**, is rivalled by the complex of baths and exercise halls at Viroconium, near **Wroxeter**. Theatres such as those of Verulamium and Caerleon, and the busy shopping centres which developed around the forum or the town gates, attracted people to the towns. Mosaic floors like those at **Aldborough**, in Yorkshire, reflect a very comfortable style of life. This wealth is mirrored, too, by the remains of many Roman villas such as those at Lullingstone, near **Eynsford** in Kent, **Fishbourne** in Sussex and **Chedworth** in Gloucestershire.

Below Westbury White Horse, on Bratton Down, Wiltshire. Bottom Housesteads Fort along Hadrian's Wall, in Northumbria.

Cave

Prehistoric monument

Hillfort

Roman antiquity

Battle site with year

THE BATTLE OF FLODDEN FIELD

9th September 1513

Above *The site of the Battle of Flodden. Inset A display board at Flodden chronicles the battle which was fought here.* Top right *According to tradition, men watched London's Great Fire from Outwood Mill, Surrey.* Bottom *Porthcurno's Minack open-air theatre.*

Windmill

Other place of interest

Battlefields
Windmills
Other Places of Interest

Normans and Plantagenets, wars in Scotland and Wales, the Wars of the Roses, the Civil War and the Jacobite risings, have all left the map of Britain dotted with 'crossed swords' symbols. In the 250 years that separate us from Culloden, in 1746, the last battle on British soil, farming, roads and railways, canals and houses have changed the fields on which the history of the nation was written.

Battlefields

We do not commemorate our battles as lavishly as the Visitor Centres at places such as Waterloo or Gettysburg, but there are still fields where there is something to be seen today. Facilities are available, mainly in the tourist season, for organised groups to be taken round and it is worth telephoning to see whether you can join one.

The Battle of **Hastings**, on 14 October 1066, certainly changed things in England. Stories of the battle are well enough known – Harold's forced march of 250 miles from battle against the Norwegian king at Stamford Bridge, near York, to meet the Norman invaders; the Norman minstrel Taillefer charging

the shield-wall; the hail of arrows harassing the axemen; the final stand of the house-carles around the royal standard of Wessex. All are vividly recalled in an audio-visual presentation in the Tourist Office on the green just opposite the gateway of the Abbey which William founded, its altar traditionally on the spot where Harold fell. Now an English Heritage property, the pathways around and overlooking main sectors of the battlefield are well signposted, with information boards at regular intervals.

In the **Bannockburn** Heritage Centre the full story of the battle of 24 June 1314, is graphically told in an audio-visual entitled *The Forging of a Nation*. On the field itself is preserved the Borestone, where Robert the Bruce raised his banner before this decisive culmination of the Wars of Independence.

From the top of the Durham Cathedral tower the battlefield of **Neville's Cross** can be seen as it was by the monks who gave 'moral support' by singing hymns there in 1346. A leaflet explaining the battle is available from the Tourist Office and a half mile walk from the city brings the visitor to the battlefield itself.

An exhibition is mounted on **Bosworth** battlefield, near Sutton

Cheney, with an audio-visual presentation including scenes from Laurence Olivier's *Richard III*. There is a battlefield trail, with another information centre halfway round at Shenton Station. Here, Richard of Gloucester, uncle of the Princes in the Tower, met his end, having found no one to answer his cry 'My kingdom for a horse!'

At a call from France for help from the 'auld alliance', James IV of Scotland marched into England. On Pipers' Hill, at **Flodden Edge**, is a monument 'To the Brave of both Nations', with the battlefield spread out below. A booklet and map from nearby Coldstream enable you to follow the course of the battle. King Henry VIII had left the old Earl of Surrey, a veteran of Bosworth, to defend the north. Surrey had borrowed the banner of St Cuthbert, obviously a powerful morale raiser, from Durham Cathedral. But it was artillery fire that stung the Scots into premature offensive action, allowing English archers to reach the crest of Pipers' Hill and pour a murderous arrow storm into the massed pikemen below. Flodden was the last major battle won largely by the longbow.

The Castle Inn, in **Edgehill,** was built on the spot where King Charles raised his Standard. There

is a memorial on the field below and a map and guidebook will enable you to follow the course of the fighting. Neither side seemed willing to strike the first blow until a Parliamentary gunner spotted the King on the hill, fired – and missed. Prince Rupert charged – found an ally in the inaptly named Sir Faithful Fortescue, one of the Parliamentary cavalry commanders – and they all dashed the two miles or so to Kineton, where they rested their horses and indulged in a little light looting. Roundhead foot soldiers were about to finish off the exhausted Royalists when they were attacked owing to the opportune return of Prince Rupert and the cavalry. Captain John Smith, of the King's Lifeguard, met a party of Roundheads escorting a Royalist prisoner and the Royal Standard which they had just captured. The prisoner recognised Smith and called to him. Smith charged, killed one Roundhead, wounded another and the other four fled. He was knighted on the spot by the King for recovering the Standard, which had not been in Parliamentary hands above fifteen minutes.

In the village of **Naseby** is a museum with dioramas and a ten minute commentary of different stages of the battle of 14 July 1645.

Should the museum be closed, then try the village shop or the church for the descriptive leaflet and map, which will make the whole encounter more easy to follow.

A drive up the Naseby-Sibbertoft road takes you to a monument marking the position from which Cromwell led his cavalry to win the day and from where there is a good view over the whole battlefield.

Information about the battle of **Worcester**, 3 September 1651, is available from both the Tourist Office and the Civil War Centre at the Commandery. Worcester was the scene of the first and last battles of the war. During the summer, frequent 're-enactments' are staged by several groups, particularly in September.

Sedgemoor, the last battle fought on English soil, on 6 July 1685, followed the landing by the Duke of Monmouth, illegitimate son of Charles II, to claim the throne of James II. A stone monument marks the site of the battle, and information can be obtained from the Admiral Blake Museum in Bridgwater.

The Battle of **Culloden**, on the moors outside Inverness, ended the Jacobite Rising in 1746. Bonnie Prince Charlie, with the help of Flora Macdonald, escaped 'over the sea to Skye' and the Stuart cause was swept away. The whole story is graphically told in the visitor centre on the battlefield, which has been restored to its 18th-century appearance, but now dotted with emotive memorial cairns and the Graves of the Clans, on which no heather ever grows.

Since Culloden, we may be thankful that no armies have fought on British soil – only *above* it, in 1940. Aerial bombardment brought the realities of war much closer to the public than did any of the very localised combats of the previous 700 years.

Windmills

Few things add as much atmosphere to the countryside as a windmill. They have drained marshlands and ground corn since medieval times. One tradition suggests that they were introduced by crusaders returning home from the wars. Whether or not this is true, we know for a fact that they were first built here some eight centuries ago. None of the original structures remain, but some have survived a few hundreds years. Still in working order is **Berney Arms Mill**, in Norfolk, from the top of which there is a splendid view and the working wind pump at **Wicken Fen**, a remnant of the wetlands drained by Dutch engineers, which

became England's first nature reserve, in 1899. **Bourn Mill**, near Cambridge, is a 17th-century 'post mill', the oldest surviving mill in the country. Unlike the conical tower windmills with a rotating cap, here the sails and machinery all turn together, revolving round a central post. A tide mill has stood on the river bank at **Woodbridge** in Suffolk since the 12th century and the present one was working until 1956, when the shaft of the waterwheel broke. Careful restoration has successfully restored it to working condition.

Other Places of Interest

There is a wide range of other places of interest which are well worth visiting. From waterfalls, wells, bridges and towers to dovecotes, follies, monuments and parks, Britain has something to offer every visitor.

Not far from Land's End, on the cliffs near Porthcurno, is the **Minack Theatre**, carved out of the living rock in the 1930s, with the sea as a backdrop for the stage. North of Tavistock is **Lydford Gorge**, a deep wooded gorge with the lovely White Lady Waterfall at the end of a mile or so walk.

Further along the coast, north-west of Weymouth, the extraordinary Chesil Beach, a 12-mile long pebble bank, shelters the **Abbotsbury Swannery**, where swans were bred for the table by the monks as long ago as the 14th century. Today it is a breeding haven for hundreds of wild mute swans. At St Fagans, to the west of Cardiff, is the **Welsh Folk Museum,** a collection of rural buildings from the 17th century onwards from all over Wales, carefully re-erected in the grounds of St Fagans Castle, an elegant Elizabethan mansion.

Waterfalls abound, but one not to be missed is **Hardraw Force**, north of Hawes, North Yorkshire, a spectacular 90ft (27m) drop into a glen which has been used for brass band contests – a great local tradition – on account of its splendid acoustics. Further north, near Moffat on the A708, is one of Scotland's highest falls, the **Grey Mare's Tail**, where Loch Skeen plunges 200ft (61m) to meet Moffat Water.

Shire horses, Clydesdales and Suffolk Punches have ploughed England's fields – and delivered England's beer – for centuries. In the **National Shire Horse Centre**, at Plymouth, there is stabling dating back to 1772 and three parades a day are staged in summer. Courage Breweries have a **Shire Horse Centre** near Maidenhead, as do Whitbread at their **Hop Farm**, on the B2015, east of Tonbridge.

Battle site with year

Windmill

Other place of interest

Viewpoint

Picnic site

Agricultural showground

Viewpoints
Picnic Sites
Agricultural Showgrounds

The **Clee Hills** of Shropshire, in the Welsh Marches, are in a remote and exceptionally attractive area of the country – an official Area of Outstanding Natural Beauty, in fact. They are 'young' hills, geologically, jagged and more impressive than their official height statistics would suggest, and in the past were heavily quarried for coal, building stone, iron and copper. A wealth of folklore still attaches to them, with sinister tales of witches and evil forces. They are also the site of a spectacular viewpoint.

Viewpoints

The viewpoint is on the A4117, six miles east of Ludlow. In the immediate foreground to the north is the bulk of Titterstone Clee, 1,750ft (533m) with its aerials and radar dishes, and one of the biggest Iron Age hillforts in Britain on its summit. Beyond the hill is the long,

Below *The picnic site at David Marshall Lodge, Aberfoyle.*
Bottom *View of South Stack lighthouse from the viewpoint on Anglesey.*

wooded ridge of Wenlock Edge and to the west beyond Ludlow rise the mountains of Wales.

Viewpoints, as marked in AA Road Atlases, are all easily accessible by car and have a plaque to identify landmarks and places of interest in the area. Each viewpoint has a prospect of at least 180 degrees and some command wider vistas still. The **Cockleroy** viewpoint, two miles south of Linlithgow in the Lothian region of Scotland, has marvellous views over the full 360 degrees. To the east the eye ranges over Edinburgh to the Firth of Forth, to the south-east lie the Pentland Hills, in the west is Glasgow and in the north the outlying bastions of the Highlands.

The viewpoint is in the Beecraigs Country Park, among the Bathgate Hills, with trails through the woodland, a reservoir with hides for watching the numerous waterfowl and a deer farm with a viewing platform. At Linlithgow are the romantic ruins of the palace of the Stuart kings, where Mary, Queen of Scots was born, and the church where she was christened. Not far away is Torphichen Preceptory, once the Scottish base of the crusading order of the Knights of St John of Jerusalem. A little to the south there are superlative views again, from Cairnpaple Hill, where prehistoric men buried their dead over a period of 2,500 years and more.

On the other side of Glasgow, the **Lyle Hill** viewpoint is just outside the former shipbuilding town of Greenock, the birthplace of James Watt, and during World War II the principal Free French naval base. The viewpoint is near the war memorial to those sailors, an anchor surmounted by a Cross of Lorraine. Down below is the Firth of Clyde and its swarming ferries. To the north and north-west lie Holy Loch and the woods and mountains of the Argyll Forest Park on the Cowal Peninsula, with the serrated crests of The Cobbler in the distance. West and south-west are the Isle of Bute, separated from the mainland by the narrow Kyles of Bute, the Isle of Arran rising to Goat Fell and, beyond Arran, the Kintyre Peninsula.

Far away at the other end of the country, in Cornwall, the majestic harbour of Carrick Roads was an important United States Navy base during the war. The viewpoint is on **Pendennis Point**, outside Falmouth, commanding a sweeping prospect of the harbour and out to the English Channel and the Lizard Peninsula. Close at hand is the round keep of Pendennis Castle,

one of the artillery strongpoints built along the coast in Henry VIII's time against attack by the French. Across the water is its other half, St Mawes Castle. These twin fortresses have done their job, and no enemy force has ever attempted to penetrate Carrick Roads.

Another viewpoint with naval connections lies eastward along the coast, on **Portsdown Hill** in Hampshire, a mile north of Cosham. Immediately to the south sprawls Portsmouth, with its historic harbour and the Royal Navy dockyard where Nelson's HMS *Victory* rests in honourable retirement. Birds wheel above the Farlington Marshes at the northern end of Langstone Harbour and the eagle eye pierces 10 miles across the Solent to the Isle of Wight. For visitors who would like something to eat as well as watch, there is a picnic site here.

So there is at the viewpoint at **David Marshall Lodge**, the Forestry Commission visitor centre in the scenic Trossachs area, in the Central region of Scotland, a mile north of Aberfoyle on A821. There are spectacular views here of Ben Lomond, the Highland mountains and the valleys of the Forth.

The haunting beauty of the Trossachs – 'So wondrous wild, the whole might seem the scenery of a fairy dream' – with its lochs, peaks and 'wildering forest' – was praised by Sir Walter Scott in 1810 in his immensely popular poem *The Lady of the Lake*. To add to its romantic attractions, much of the area was Rob Roy country.

Strictly speaking, the Trossachs ('the cross places' in Gaelic) means the narrow belt of land between Loch Katrine and Loch Achray, but the name is more often used broadly for the whole area between Loch Lomond and Callander. Much of it is now in the Forestry Commission's enormous Queen Elizabeth Forest Park. After Scott, tourists began to flock to the area in such numbers that the local landowner, the Duke of Montrose, built the road north from Aberfoyle which is now the A821, or Duke's Road. There are parking places and a picnic site along it, and more along the Forestry Commission's one-way Achray Forest Drive, which leaves the Duke's Road to make its way seven miles through the woods, by Loch Drunkie and Loch Achray. There are more scenic viewpoints here and a waymarked forest walk.

Picnic Sites

One of the Countryside Commission's achievements has been to stimulate local authorities to

provide places where motorists could pull off the road to enjoy a picnic. Opinion surveys and studies repeatedly made it clear that many people were deterred from enjoying the countryside by an uneasy fear of trespassing or going where they were not wanted; an official picnic spot is somewhere where you know you are entitled to be. Although most sites have been organised by county councils, many have been provided by the Forestry Commission, others by the National Trust and by private landowners.

Many sites provide a view of attractive scenery or are close to an outstanding attraction. There is one near the ruins of **Mount Grace Priory**, for instance, the medieval Carthusian monastery near Osmotherley in North Yorkshire (where each of the tiny hermit-like cells had running water, incidentally) and there is one close to the **Hardraw Force** waterfall, off the Pennine Way. In Wales there are several with views of **Llyn Clywedog**, near Llanidloes in Powys, a three-mile long reservoir. An old iron mine can also be visited here, and not far away is another picnic site beside the infant River Severn, as it starts its long journey to the sea from the high moors of Plynlimon. There are more looking over **Lake Vyrnwy** in Powys, a beautiful 1880s reservoir with wooded shores and a striking Victorian Gothic tower. In England too, reservoirs make pleasing picnic spots, as at **Rutland Water** in Leicestershire, or **Grafham Water** in Cambridgeshire.

Agricultural Showgrounds

The 'traditional' English landscape of green fields, hedgerows and narrow lanes was created by the agricultural revolution of the 18th century, which introduced improved farming methods. County agricultural societies were formed to spread knowledge of the new ways and raise standards. They organised annual county shows at which farmers and breeders showed off their achievements and competed against each other. For 200 years and more these agricultural shows have been part of the accustomed round of country life, with their marquees and bands, their displays of the latest farm machinery and equipment, and their classes for heavy horses, cattle and sheep. One of the oldest is the **Royal Bath and West Show**, which can trace its history back to 1777 and draws 100,000 people every year to its permanent showground near Shepton Mallet in Somerset. Before the War, the county shows normally moved around from one

Viewpoint

Picnic site

Agricultural showground

country estate or farmer's fields to another, year by year. After 1945 the cost of staging a show escalated alarmingly. Some shows folded up, some amalgamated and others established permanent showgrounds. The leader in the field was the Yorkshire Agricultural Society, which planted its **Great Yorkshire Show** on a permanent site at Harrogate. The **Royal Highland Show** chose a location at Ingliston, a few miles west of Edinburgh, for its shows.

Other leading shows which have equipped themselves with fixed locations include the **Three Counties** at Great Malvern (the three counties being Herefordshire, Worcestershire and Gloucestershire), the **South of England** at Ardingly in Sussex, the **Royal Cornwall** at Wadebridge, the

A plaque marking the viewpoint on Sugar Loaf Mountain in Wales.

East of England near Peterborough and the **Royal Welsh** at Builth Wells. The Royal Agricultural Society of England, founded in 1838, held its first show at Oxford the following year. The 'Royal' moved about the country every year until 1963, when it settled at Stoneleigh in Warwickshire, in a permanent home where the **National Agriculture Centre** evolved in the 1970s. The agricultural shows have had heavy weather to come through in recent years, but they have survived, and altogether are estimated to attract about three million visitors a year to share country triumphs and pleasures.

33

Horse racing

Show jumping and equestrian circuit

Horse Racing
Show Jumping and
Equestrian Circuits
Athletics Stadiums
Motor Racing Circuits

Becher's Brook . . . Valentine's . . . the Canal Turn . . . the Chair. The familiar litany of names conjures up **Aintree** on Grand National Day – the jostle at the start, the crash and crackle of horse meeting thorn-and-fir fence, horses and jockeys falling, the clamour of the crowd. The early history of the great race is obscure, but it is usually traced back to the Grand Liverpool Steeplechase of 1839. That race was won by a horse appropriately named Lottery and that was the year the gallant Captain Becher, a well-known gentleman rider of the day, fell into the brook that bears his name. His horse, named Conrad, fell in as well.

Horse Racing
A steeplechase as the name implies, did not originally take place on a course at all. A by-product of hunting, it was a wild pell-mell gallop across country over hedges and ditches, towards a distant steeple or other agreed marker. Not

World famous Derby Day, at Epsom Race Course in Surrey.

until the 19th century did organised racing over artificial jumps on a set course begin. Racing started at Aintree in 1829, on the course owned by the Earls of Sefton for another 120 years. The course, in a dreary northern suburb of Liverpool, has the most formidable fences in the sport and in 1928 a horse named Tipperary Tim won the Grand National simply by being the only finisher of 42 starters. Far and away the most famous horse associated with Aintree and the National, however, is Red Rum, the only three-time winner (in 1973, 1974 and 1977).

The most prestigious steeplechase course in England is at **Cheltenham**, in a delightful country situation outside the town, at Prestbury Park, under the looming Cotswold bulwark of Cleeve Hill. It is a testing track on heavy clay. The major event of the year is the Cheltenham Gold Cup in March, first held in 1924. The great horse Golden Miller won it five years in succession from 1932 to 1936 (and in 1934 won the Grand National as well). The Champion Hurdle at Cheltenham is the premier hurdle event in the country.

The capital of the flat racing industry is across the other side of the country at **Newmarket**. The

town developed as a racing and breeding centre for 'the sport of kings' under royal patronage. Charles II rode his own horses in races there: hence the name Rowley Mile for one of Newmarket's two courses, from the king's nickname, Old Rowley. In the mid-18th century the aristocratic Jockey Club was founded at Newmarket. It owns the two courses and Newmarket Heath, the open country around the town on which strings of staggeringly valuable racehorses can be seen exercising. It occupies a suitably august red brick building in the centre of the town, and nearby is the highly enjoyable National Horseracing Museum, which opened in 1983.

Two of the five 'classic' races are held at Newmarket: the Two Thousand Guineas, and the One Thousand Guineas for fillies only, inaugurated in 1809 and 1814 respectively. Both are run on the Rowley Mile course, which has a long flat straight, followed by a dip and rise to the finish. Long races cannot easily be seen from the grandstands because the course was laid out long before the days of packed modern race crowds.

The most famous race in the world is run early in June every year at **Epsom.** It is named after the

12th Earl of Derby, though it might easily have been called the Bunbury. Lord Derby and Sir Charles Bunbury tossed a coin in 1780 to decide the name of a new race for three-year-old colts and fillies. As if in compensation, Bunbury's horse Diomed won the first Derby, and Lord Derby had to wait until 1787 to win with Sir Peter Teazle.

The other classic race at Epsom, the Oaks, restricted to fillies, was first run in 1779 and was named after a house which Lord Derby had taken nearby.

W P Frith's well-known painting *Derby Day* gives a vivid impression of the occasion in Victorian times, when it was virtually a public holiday. Huge numbers of people swarmed to enjoy a day out and all the fun of the fair on Epsom Downs. The Derby course is more or less level for the first three-quarters of a mile and then drops to a sharp turn at Tattenham Corner before the run-in.

The last of the classics, in September, is the oldest; the St Leger, which goes all the way back to 1776 and is named after a prominent Yorkshire sportsman of the time. It is run at **Doncaster,** on the Town Moor, the common land outside the town which, as at Epsom, was the natural place for the races.

One of the oldest courses in the country, and one of the oddest, is the Roodee at **Chester,** where there was apparently organised racing in Henry VIII's time. The course has the River Dee on one side with the old city wall on the other and is circular, with almost no straight. At **York,** there was racing on the Knavesmire, common land outside the city, early in the 18th century. Here in August is contested the Gimcrack Stakes, named in honour of a famous grey. The sport's most attractive setting is claimed by **Goodwood,** near Chichester in Sussex, where the course was laid out by the 3rd Duke of Richmond with the first meeting staged in 1801.

The smartest social occasion of the racing year is the **Royal Ascot** meeting in June, attended by the Queen, with a royal procession up the straight in carriages and much media fuss about fashionable hats. Races were first held at Ascot, in Berkshire, in 1711. The King George VI and Queen Elizabeth Diamond Stakes, run in July with the richest prize money in the sport, was inaugurated in 1951 to mark the Festival of Britain.

Showjumping and Equestrian Circuits

The first show jumping contest on record was held in London in 1869. From 1912 the sport was regularly included in the Olympic Games, but it is only since 1945 that it has attracted strong public and media interest. The popular Horse of the Year show, at **Wembley Arena** in London, dates from 1949. The same year saw the first horse trials at **Badminton,** in Avon, on a testing course laid out in the grounds of his palatial mansion by the Duke of Beaufort. Himself a redoubtable huntsman, the duke was determined to do something about the indifferent showing of the British equestrian team in the 1948 Olympics. The three day event at Badminton in the spring now draws spectators in thousands. In 1984 Lucinda Green won Badminton for a record sixth time, on six different horses. Another stately home course is the one at **Burghley House,** near Stamford, in the grounds of the palace of the Cecils, right-hand men to Elizabeth I and James I. The Marquess of Exeter, a former Olympic athlete, offered a home for a three day event here, first held in 1961. The Burghley Horse Trials in September are now firmly established as a prestigious occasion in the show jumping calendar.

The sport's equivalent of Aintree and Epsom combined is the course at **Hickstead** in Sussex, opened in 1960 at his home by a leading rider, Douglas Bunn, to provide a permanent arena with formidable obstacles. The first British Show Jumping Derby was held there in 1961.

Athletics Stadiums

Athletics is less well equipped with tracks and grounds than other major sports. The principal arena for international athletics is at the **Crystal Palace** in South London, where a 12,000-seater stadium was opened in 1964. Ten years later, an all-weather track was installed in the town stadium at **Gateshead,** and home-town athlete Brendan Foster set a new 3,000m world record to celebrate. The cross-country course at Gateshead is also well known.

Athletics stadium

Motor Racing Circuits

The magic name from the early history of motor racing in England is **Brooklands**, the track near Weybridge in Surrey which, sadly, closed in 1939. Every great figure of the early days raced there and John Cobb set a lap record of 143mph in a Napier-Railton in 1935. Another leading venue was **Donington Park**, near Derby, where Grand Prix events were held in the 1930s. During the war the site was taken over by the Army. Years later the circuit was reopened for racing, in the 1970s. The Motor Museum there has a notable collection of Grand Prix racing cars.

Since 1945 the two major British circuits have been Silverstone and Brands Hatch. **Silverstone**, in Northamptonshire near Towcester, opened in 1948 on a former airfield, hence the name Hangar Straight for part of the course. The British Grand Prix is staged there, but for many years it alternated with Brands Hatch, near Farningham in Kent. It opened for Formula Three racing in 1949 and in 1960 opened the Grand Prix course.

Motor racing circuit

A rider in the TT races, held every June on the Isle of Man.

Golf course

County cricket ground

National rugby ground

A scene at Lord's, the home of Middlesex County Cricket Club.

Golf Courses
County Cricket Grounds
National Rugby Grounds
Ski Slopes
Coastal Launching Sites

Of all the world's great golf courses, the most august is the venerable and venerated Old Course at **St Andrews** in Scotland, where the Victorian clubhouse of the Royal and Ancient Golf Club is the temple and citadel of the game. A links, or seaside course – as all the country's top courses are – the Old Course is four miles in length and so many golfers are keen to play it that it normally opens at six o'clock in the morning. The notorious par 4 17th, or Roadhole, is said to have driven more great golfers to rage and bitter despair than any other golf hole in the world.

Golf Courses

Golf was played at St Andrews on the springy turf beside the North Sea as long ago as the 15th century, it seems, and when 22 noblemen and gentlemen founded the Society of St Andrews Golfers in 1754, they described the game as an 'ancient and healthful exercise'. The club was dubbed 'royal' in 1834 by King William IV and became the governing body of the game.

Another illustrious club is the Honourable Company of Edinburgh Golfers, which was founded in 1744 (as the Gentlemen Golfers of Leigh), ten years before the Royal and Ancient. It drew up the first set of

rules, which the R and A adopted. The club now has its headquarters at **Muirfield**, a famous championship course on the outskirts of the village of Gullane, east of Edinburgh. It is close to the shore of the Firth of Forth, whose invigorating breezes are claimed to account for the great age which the Edinburgh Golfers commonly attain. The course is known for its meticulously constructed bunkers. Jack Nicklaus won his first British Open at Muirfield in 1966 and Nick Faldo won there in 1987.

There is a clutch of notable courses across on the Ayrshire shore, on hillocky ground on the sandy turf and coarse grass beside the sea. The **Prestwick** club organised the first British Open championship in 1860 and it was played there many times, but after 1925 the course was no longer big enough for the crowds which the event was beginning to attract. Few of them are these days.

Royal Troon, just to the north, has holes with names – they start with Seal and to on to Postage Stamp and Rabbit. In the 1973 Open two holes-in-one were scored at Postage Stamp. One was by the veteran American Gene Sarazen and the other by the amateur David Russell, who happened to be respectively the oldest and the youngest players in the field.

There is another group of redoubtable courses in England along the Lancashire coast. **Royal Lytham and St Anne's**, near Blackpool, was in open countryside when the club was founded in 1886, but is now an oasis in a desert of housing estates. Here, the first Ladies Open was played in 1893 and Tony Jacklin had his Open triumph in 1969. Near Southport is another crack course, **Royal Birkdale,** and further south on the tip of the Wirral Peninsula, is **Hoylake,** where the first British Amateur championship was contested in 1885. The demanding course is no longer considered adequate to cope with Open crowds. The Open is still played over the **Royal St George's** course at Sandwich on the Kent coast, one of the toughest in Britain, and the scene of a famous fictitious match in Ian Fleming's *Goldfinger*.

Other courses are celebrated not for the championships fought out over them, but for their associations with heroic figures of the past. The legendary James Braid, five times Open champion, was professional at **Walton Heath** in Surrey for 45 years until he died in 1950 at the age of 80. On his birthday he invariably went out and played the course in as many strokes as his age or less.

His contemporary, the incomparable John Henry Taylor, learned his golf at the **Royal North Devon's** links at Westward Ho!, on the bumpy sandy ground of the Burrows, frequented by horses, cows and sheep as well as golfers.

Speaking of animals on a course, in 1934 the professional at the **St Margaret's at Cliffe** club in Kent killed a cow with his tee shot to the 18th. And in 1975 at **Scunthorpe**, Humberside, a drive at the 14th hole, named the Mallard, hit and killed a mallard duck in flight.

Cricket Grounds
Cricket, like golf, emerged from the mists of obscurity into the light of history in the 18th century. The most famous ground in the country, and the world, is **Lord's** in the St John's Wood district of London. It takes its name from its original proprietor, a Yorkshireman named Thomas Lord, who came to London in 1787, was instrumental in the founding of the MCC (Marylebone Cricket Club) and opened the St John's Wood ground in 1812. Lord's is also the home of the Middlesex County Cricket Club. The original pavilion, a one-room hut, and the tavern provided by Thomas Lord have been replaced over the years by a Victorian pavilion and modern stands. The grand entrance gates to the ground were specially designed in 1923 as a memorial to W G Grace, the greatest cricketer of his age, and Lord's now has a good museum of cricket.

The other famous London ground is the **Oval,** in Kennington, south of the river. Originally a market garden, and long famed for a fine view of the local gasometers, the ground has been the headquarters of the Surrey county club since its formation in a nearby pub in 1845. Like Lord's, the Oval is a regular Test match arena. The highest innings ever recorded in Test cricket was notched up there in 1938, when England scored 903 for 7 declared, with Len Hutton making 364.

One of cricket's most attractive settings is the county ground at **Worcester,** where the cathedral rises nobly in the background across the Severn. The drawback is that when the river floods, as in 1990, the pitch is covered with tons of thick black mud. Another attractive county cricket arena is the St Lawrence ground at **Canterbury** in Kent. The Canterbury Week cricket festival has been held since 1847.

The ground at **Old Trafford** in the southern suburbs of Manchester has seen many a Test match and many a tussle between the red rose of Lancashire and the white rose of Yorkshire. The principal Yorkshire

ground is at **Headingley,** a couple of miles from the centre of Leeds. Two other grounds regularly used for Test cricket are **Trent Bridge** in Nottingham, where cricket has been played since 1838, and **Edgbaston,** the Warwickshire county ground in Birmingham.

Rugby Grounds
Rugby's equivalent of Lord's is the 'cabbage patch' at **Twickenham,** a market garden bought by the Rugby Union in 1907. The choice was fiercely criticised for being too far from Piccadilly Circus, but the motor car changed all that and the ground has been developed into a spanking modern arena. For Welsh rugby men, however, the holy of holies of their national game is **Cardiff Arms Park**, beside the River Taff close to the heart of the city, where the stands echo on great occasions to the impassioned sound of Welsh singing. The Cardiff Football Club began to practise on a piece of meadow here beside the river in 1876. Today it is a thoroughly up-to-date arena with

base for the nearby Cairngorms ski area, with its chairlifts and ski tows.

There are cross-country ski trails of varying degrees of difficulty in this area, too. The other main Scottish ski areas are **Glenshee**, south of Braemar on the A93, Britain's highest main road, the **Lecht** area on the A939 near Tomintoul and the **Glencoe** area above the A82, where the road crosses Rannoch Moor.

Coastal Launching Sites
Sailing has also become more popular. Most of its enthusiasts are weekend sailors, who do not go far from shore, and there are boat launching sites at harbours and marinas all round the coast, from **St Ives** harbour in Cornwall to **Thurso Bay** on the north coast of Scotland. They vary from the broad, sheltered expanses of **Carrick Roads** or **Plymouth Sound** to the flat shingle shore at **Deal** in Kent, close to the historic anchorage of The Downs, or the exposed Suffolk coastline at **Walberswick** or **Southwold.**

Natural ski slope

Artificial ski slope

Coastal launching site

Above *The clubhouse at St Andrew's.* Right *Skiing in the Cairngorms, one of Scotland's busiest resorts.*

two stadiums. The two other home international grounds are Murrayfield in Edinburgh and Lansdowne Road in Dublin.

Ski Slopes
Increasing affluence since 1945 has brought skiing within the reach of far more people than before, and although all the major ski slopes are abroad, a skiing industry has developed in Scotland. The Highland village of **Aviemore**, a quiet haven for anglers and mountaineers, was transformed into a thriving winter sports resort in the 1960s. There are ski schools and dry-ski slopes, and Aviemore is the

Above *Looking across Embleton Bay, a view for Dunstanburgh Castle.*
Left *Spectacular rock formation at Elegug stacks, Pembrokeshire.*

Heritage Coasts

For centuries the white cliffs of Dover have stood as symbols of English nationhood, independence and pride, confronting foes across the Channel with unyielding defiance. It was the sight of the white cliffs which told generations of weary English travellers that they were nearing home. Today, to keep the white cliffs unspoiled, they have to be protected as two four-mile stretches of Heritage Coast, either side of Dover.

Heritage Coasts

Before World War II, concern was growing about the substantial areas of coastline which had been ruined by commercial development and the threat that what was left would go the same way, disappearing under an ever-rising tide of cliff-top bungalows and caravan sites. The

Coastal Preservation Committee mounted a campaign in the 1930s. During the War, the distinguished geographer J A Steers surveyed the coast for the government, and his work would later be the basis on which Heritage Coasts were chosen.

In 1965 the National Trust, thoroughly alarmed, launched Enterprise Neptune, a campaign to raise money to buy threatened coastline. This campaign continues and the Trust now owns and protects more than one mile in every six along the shoreline of England, Wales and Northern Ireland, including the **Giant's Causeway** on the scenic North Antrim seacoast of Northern Ireland and more than a quarter of the entire coast of **Cornwall.**

In 1970 the Countryside Commission recommended to the government that scenically outstanding stretches of undeveloped coast should be designated as Heritage Coasts and protected against undesirable development. This was duly set in train and by the end of the 1980s there were some 850 miles of Heritage Coast in total, amounting to a little over 30 per cent of the coastline of England and Wales. In Scotland more than 20 stretches of coastline of scenic, ecological or environmental importance have been designated by the Scottish

Development Department as Preferred Conservation Zones.

The Heritage Coasts reflect much of the wide variety of scenery and wildlife of the shores of England and Wales. Atop the sheer chalk cliffs of **Dover**, **Beachy Head** and the **Seven Sisters** orchids grow, and they make good places to watch jackdaws and swallows as well as seabirds. Right across on the other side of the country, the granite **Isles of Scilly** lie 28 miles out to sea off Land's End. In legend the islands are all that is left above the surface of the lost land of Lyonesse, which sank beneath the waves when King Arthur's reign came to an end.

The local environmental trust manages 40 miles of Heritage Coast in the Scillies, where the long Atlantic rollers cream on sandy beaches and rocky coves. The mild climate fosters a wealth of wildlife – snails and worms, sea urchins and anemones in the sand or in rock pools, seaweed trailing and undulating in the waves. Here Manx shearwaters, stormy petrels and puffins breed and there are multitudes of terns and gulls. Marram and sand sedge grow in the dunes, with the dwarf pansy – found only here and in the Channel Islands.

The **Suffolk** Heritage Coast is altogether different. This is an understated shore of low cliffs under enormous skies, and shingle beaches where the sea's melancholy retreating roar rattles the pebbles. The sea has swallowed up stretches of this coast, but

contrariwise has constructed the shingle bulk of Orford Ness and the long shingle spit that runs six miles down the North Weir Point. Martello towers stud the shoreline. The country's principal breeding colony of avocets has been established by the RSPB in the reserve at Havergate Island. Further north is the Sizewell nuclear power station and beyond is the RSPB reserve at Minsmere. Here among the marshes and shallow 'scrapes', or lagoons, are more avocets, as well as bitterns, marsh harriers, nightingales and nightjars, all told the largest number of breeding bird species on any British reserve.

Bird sanctuaries are again a feature of the **North Norfolk** Heritage Coast between Holme-next-the-Sea and Weybourne. This is a hauntingly desolate coast and another shifting shoreline, which has left places 'next the sea' – like Holme, Cley and Wells – marooned some distance inland. Along the shore an almost unbroken succession of nature reserves protects the saltmarshes, sand dunes and shingle spits, where mats of sea lavender edge the muddy inlets. Hundreds of species of moths gladden the hearts of entomologists here, and there are birds in millions. Rarities sometimes seen include hoopoes and ospreys. The nature reserve on Scolt Head Island is famous for its nesting terns and there are more at Blakeney Point.

Though it faces the same North Sea, the **North Yorkshire and Cleveland** Heritage Coast is a different matter altogether. Lying north of Scarborough and on either side of Whitby, this is the seaward edge of the North York Moors National Park, a line of high cliffs and bays, dramatic headlands and narrow, wooded ravines. Fishing villages huddle in deep clefts, and this is where the great explorer Captain Cook first learned his seamanship. Geologically it is an area of unusual interest and pieces of jet picked up along the shore are the foundation of the trade in Whitby jet ornaments. At Robin Hood's Bay the village houses crowd above each other on a 1-in-3 gradient.

Further up the same coast is the **North Northumberland** area, where there is a different landscape again, with miles of delectable sandy beaches, many of them owned by the National Trust. There are no titanic cliffs here, but low, rocky headlands thrust into the sea. On one of them sprawls ruined Dunstanburgh Castle, lazily menacing like a lion lying in the sun. Bamburgh Castle looks out seawards to the Farne Islands bird sanctuaries and there are memories here of gallant Grace Darling, the lighthouse keeper's daughter who in 1838 rowed out in a storm to rescue shipwrecked sailors. The tides race in across the gleaming mudflats to cut Lindisfarne off from the mainland.

The only Heritage Coast in Cumbria and Lancashire is the short section round **St Bees Head.** The sheer red sandstone cliffs here command views of the Isle of Man on a clear day and the seabirds wheel and cry – fulmars, herring gulls, black-headed gulls and kittiwakes. Thrift, harebell and wild thyme grow by the cliff path.

The Great Orme is another dramatic headland with stark cliffs looming above Llandudno on the North Wales coast. Further south, miles more of formidable cliff scenery have been designated as Heritage Coasts: around the **Lleyn Peninsula**, along the **Pembrokeshire** shore and in **Devon, Cornwall** and **Dorset**.

Heritage Coasts have a great variety of owners, not all of whom are equally conscientious in their stewardship: from the National Trust, the RSPB and other conservation bodies to county councils, local authorities, farmers, private estates and individuals. The Countryside Commission itself gives advice and financial help, but does not own any of the land.

Where a piece of Heritage Coast is owned by an organisation like the National Trust or the RSPB, the public can feel entirely certain there will be proper protection. Matters are not as straightforward along the other Heritage Coasts. Here, each area has a Heritage Coast plan, drawn up by the local authority on Countryside Commission guidelines. The aim is to involve all local interests in a common approach to the management of the area, to conserve it and to encourage locals and visitors to take tender care of it.

Pollution Free Beaches

Quite apart from the physical constitution of the coastline, there is concern about polluted beaches. In 1988 one-third of the bathing beaches in England, Wales and Northern Ireland failed to meet EEC standards of cleanliness: sewage levels in the water were too high. This was at least an improvement on 1986, when half the beaches had failed the test. The great majority of bathing beaches in Cornwall, Devon, Dorset, East Anglia, Wales and Northern Ireland were passed as clean. Along the Kent, Sussex and Hampshire shore, in southern Northumberland and especially in the North-West, the situation was not so good.

Large amounts of money are being spent on the problem. The Marine Conservation society publishes *The Good Beach Guide*, which gives lists and details of the country's cleanest beaches. These include most of those which have won a Blue Flag award from the Tidy Britain Group. The Blue Flag winners were mostly town beaches; those which are cleaned every day during the season and where water cleanliness is high. More beaches in Britain are clean than are not, but there is still work to be done.

Alum Bay, Isle of Wight, whose colourful sands are sold as souvenirs.

National Parks

National Park

Wordsworth, in his *Guide to the Lakes* wrote: 'the Lakes are a sort of national property, in which every man has a right and interest who has an eye to perceive and a heart to enjoy'. In the 19th century 'being outdoors' was seen as being good for body and soul.

Earlier this century, on many wild moors shooting took precedence over amenities for walkers. In the Peak District, an area much appreciated by those wishing to escape for a while from nearby large industrial communities, a mass trespass took place on Kinder Scout in 1932 and five men were arrested and imprisoned.

The Standing Committee on National Parks (SCNP) met for the first time on 26 May 1936, the start of an organised effort to protect and to make available to all the wild landscapes of Britain. The Council for National Parks now oversees the 11 National Parks in Britain, which have been set up since the National Parks and Access to the Countryside Act became law in 1949.

Reservoirs, power lines, roads, quarrying, forestry, TV transmitter

A spectacular view towards Derwent Dale, in the Peak District.

masts, power boats, caravan sites, even the tourists themselves by eroding footpaths are all potential threats to the preservation of the National Parks. But, provided informed and responsible public opinion and a spirit of co-operation prevail, all these amenities will be available to future generations.

It is fitting that, after the Kinder Scout protest, the **Peak District** should have been established as the first National Park. The Pennine Way was opened on the anniversary of the protest in 1965 and follows the backbone of England from Edale in Derbyshire, across Hadrian's Wall, to Kirk Yetholm, in the Cheviots. Seventeen million people live within a couple of hours' drive of the park and many come to enjoy walking the deep dales of the White Peak or the dramatic moors and peat bogs of the Dark Peak. Fishing, cycling and rock climbing on the gritstone edges have been joined as leisure activities by gliding and hang-gliding. An Iron Age fort on Man Tor overlooks Roman lead workings and the mine near Castleton, where deposits of decorative fluorspar – blue john – have been worked since Roman times. Heather covers one third of the Park and provides food for the red grouse.

Largest of the National Parks, the **Lake District** combines mountain and lake, woodland and farmland. Moving ice shaped these troughs and corries and glacial rubble dammed the valleys, but the underlying rock dictated whether the hills were softly rounded, like Skiddaw, or wildly rugged, like Scafell and Helvellyn. Broad-leaved woodland like the Borrowdale and Witherslack woods, of great interest to conservationists, cover about five per cent of the Park.

The Snowdon massif is the heartland of the **Snowdonia National Park** and Cader Idris is one of the most popular areas. Half a million people reach Snowdon Summit each year and only a quarter of them admit to using the railway! Many fewer visit the Aran Mountains in the south, or the rugged Rhynogydd. Harlech Castle lies on part of the park's 20 or so miles of sweeping sandy coastline, backed by beautiful mountain scenery. For the 'railway buff' there are six narrow-gauge railways to enjoy and to the 5,000 acres of ancient broad-leaved woodland have been added another 5,000, which with commercial forestry, now cover over 10 per cent of the Park.

Two plateaux make up **Dartmoor,** the largest and wildest stretch of open country in southern Britain, rising to over 2,000ft (610m). Covered with

blanket bog and heather moorland, they are divided by the River Dart. Granite tors protrude near the edges, where other rivers have eroded deep valleys. Over a third of the Park is farmland and the high northern moors have been a military training area since the 1870s. The Dartmoor pony – descendant of ponies turned out to graze in the Middle Ages – grazes much of the lower lying heather moorland. There are hundreds of ancient sites – chambered tombs, hillforts and stone circles – in the Park and medieval crosses and waymarks can still be useful to today's traveller.

The **Pembrokeshire Coast National Park**, the smallest of the Parks, hugs the coast and is only three miles wide along most of its length. Steep cliffs display spectacularly folded and twisted rock formations, while sheltered bays invite bathing, and scuba diving. Offshore, islands such as Skomer and Skokholm support huge colonies of seabirds, among them the world's largest concentration of Manx shearwaters and puffins. Inland from the Milford Haven oil terminal, with its facilities for 300,000-ton tankers, is the Daugleddau, a drowned river valley with dense woodlands and in the north, the windswept moorlands of the Preseli Hills, source of the 'bluestones' of Stonehenge.

Though Middlesbrough and York are not far away, the **North York Moors** is a relatively quiet Park. The moors rise sharply from Pickering in the south, Teesside in the north and the Vale of York in the west. The eastern boundary is the sea, with Staithes, home of Captain Cook, and Whitby (outside the Park boundaries), famous for its clifftop Abbey and its jet – a fossilised black amber – so popular with the Victorians. Rievaulx and Rosedale Abbeys are within the Park, as is Mount Grace Priory, the best preserved Carthusian priory in Britain. Evidence of man's occupation of the high moors ranges from the burial mounds of the neolithic farmers who first cleared the land to the giant golf ball-like radar domes of the Fylingdales early warning system.

Nearly half of the **Yorkshire Dales** is farmland, but there is little woodland. Over four centuries the monasteries' sheep walks developed into the start of a road system across the fells, the best known today being the green lane between Kilnsey and Malham. Miles of dry stone walling are a man-made feature of the landscape, as is the Settle–Carlisle railway with its spectacular Ribblehead Viaduct. Public transport facilities being poor,

the Dalesrail scheme makes recreational use of this line for walkers, who form the second largest group of visitors, after the touring motorist. As well as a part of the Pennine Way, there are popular areas for walkers and day trippers around Malham Cove and Tarn, with its fascinating limestone pavement 'grikes' – sheltered habitats for lime- and shade-loving plants. Aysgarth Falls, in Wensleydale, attract over half a million visitors a year. There is a 'Bunk House Barns' project, offering basic shelter for walkers in field barns which used to over-winter the dairy cattle.

R D Blackmore's *Lorna Doone* has made **Exmoor** known to many, as has Williamson's *Tarka the Otter*. The heartland, rising to 1,500ft (460m), from Chapman Barrows to Dunkery Beacon is still the windswept haunt of falcon and hawk. The 'hog's back' cliffs along the coast are broken by deep valleys with waterfalls which make protected breeding sites for seabirds. Exmoor is known for its Bronze and Iron Age sites, and a recent aerial survey has added over 2,000 fresh areas to be investigated. The medieval Tarr Steps bridge in the Barle Valley is a popular tourist attraction. With the Quantocks, Exmoor is the last secure habitat in the south of England for the red deer. The number of Exmoor ponies, adapted to rough grazing and wild winters, is declining, but a small herd has been established to maintain the breed.

Cheviot sheep graze the open moorland which makes up most of the **Northumberland National Park.** Remote from all settlements and mostly above 1,000ft (300m), it is often a harsh environment and must have seemed the end of the world to Roman legionaries from sunny Spain and Italy who manned Hadrian's Wall, part of which runs along the southern edge of the Park. Housesteads fort and Vindolanda have interesting visitor centres and museums. Otterburn and other battles over the 300 years up to the Union of Crowns in 1603 have given rise to many a Border ballad.

The **Brecon Beacons,** four high red sandstone mountain blocks, divide the ancient rocks of mid-Wales from the coalfields and industrialisation further south. From the Black Mountains, near Hay-on-Wye, through the Brecon Beacons and Fforest Fawr, the Park stretches to Black Mountain in the west. Along its southern edge a limestone belt provides a dramatic change in scenery with hundreds of sink-holes and cave systems. The most spectacular are the Dan-yr-Ogof Caves, on the A4067, at the head of the Tawe valley. The ruins of Carreg Cennen Castle, a 13th-century stronghold on sheer limestone cliffs, lie just off the A40, near Llandeilo.

The **Broads Authority** was rejected together with the Sussex Downs from the twelve candidates in 1949, but was established as a National Park on 1 April 1989. We owe Britain's most famous stretch of inland waterways to the peat-digging activities of our ancestors in the 9th century, which caused flooding in the 14th, and its survival as a recreational area to the strenuous efforts of the Broads Authority, in the 1980s, to halt the environmental degradation. Algae flourished on increased nutrients from effluents and fertilisers, the water 'died', reed cover was lost and the banks became eroded. Much has been done, but care is still needed.

The **New Forest** is the latest area to be granted the status of a National Park, although, as it is administered by the Forestry Commission, the status is not 'real'.

National Park

Hound Tor, an example of Dartmoor's striking landscape.
Inset *The deep waters of Llyn Cau, from Cader Idris, Gwynedd.*

National Scenic Areas (Scotland)

Where England and Wales have National Parks, Scotland has National Scenic Areas. There are 40 of them, designated in 1978 by the Countryside Commission for Scotland, established to conserve Scotland's natural beauty and improve public access to and enjoyment of it. Though the Commission's stated policy is not 'to see land in Scotland managed as though it were a museum', the National Scenic Areas are protected from development which would harm their scenic qualities. Between them they cover close to one eighth of the total area of Scotland.

Inevitably, the great majority of these National Scenic Areas lie in the Highlands and Islands, along or north of the Highland Line, the geological fault which separates Highland from Lowland Scotland. It runs diagonally from south-west to north-east clear across the country from the Isle of Arran to Stonehaven on the east coast. North and west of this line Scotland's wilder, more solitary, most spectacular and least spoiled landscapes are to be found. The land to the south and east is far more given to farming and industry, and some of it is heavily populated.

A few of the areas lie south of the Highland Line, however. In the Borders, for instance, the **Eildon and Leaderfoot** area includes the uncannily beautiful Eildon Hills. The Leader Water runs south to join the River Tweed below the three volcanic Eildon peaks, the highest rising to 1,385ft (422m). These

Looking out to Scarista Bay, from Borve on the west coast of Harris.

shapely hills are steeped in legend and romance. King Arthur and his gallant knights of the Round Table are said to lie sleeping beneath them, under an enchantment, awaiting the time of their recall to life. It was here that Thomas the Rhymer, the 13th-century poet and prophet, encountered the Queen of Fairyland. Dressed all in green, and very fair, she took him away to her magic realm for seven years and gave him the power to see into the future. Here, below the hills, lies ruined Melrose Abbey, where the heart of Robert the Bruce was buried, and close by is Abbotsford, the house Sir Walter Scott built for himself in the countryside he loved.

Scott's immensely popular poems and novels whetted the appetite of prospective tourists for his native land. The process was helped along by Queen Victoria and Prince Albert, who made themselves a Highland retreat at Balmoral in the 1840s. They loved to go stalking deer in the mountains, picnicking at the remote shielings, or shepherds' huts, and fishing for trout in a lumbering rowing boat on Loch Muick.

The region today is the **Deeside and Lochnagar** National Scenic Area, which is the only one in the Grampian Region. The high granite ridge of Lochnagar, a favourite with climbers, rises to 3,786ft (1,154m) to the south of Braemar, in an area of mountain and forest where the River Dee flows past Balmoral Castle on its way to the North Sea at Aberdeen. Lord Byron wrote rhapsodically of 'the crags that are wild and majestic, the steep frowning slopes of dark Lochnagar'. Ever since Queen Victoria's time,

the Highland Gathering at Braemar has been regularly attended by the royal family and marks the annual apogee of the Highland Games season.

From Deeside westwards, the pass called the Lairg Ghru runs through another National Scenic Area, negotiating the heart of the **Cairngorm Mountains** on its way to Speyside. This is the largest tract of land above 3,000ft (915m) in Britain. Rearing up between Braemar and the valley of the Spey, the lofty granite summits of Ben Macdhui, Braeriach, Cairn Toul and Cairn Gorm itself all clear 4,000ft (1,220m) and are outstripped in height only by Ben Nevis.

The lures of hill walking, rock climbing and wintersports draw visitors here. The Forestry Commission manages an extensive Forest Park and near Loch an Eilein are Scots pines at least 250 years old. A hundred square miles of nature reserve lie to the south of Glen More and includes both Braeriach and Cairn Toul. Arctic and alpine plant rarities grow here, with all sorts of mosses and ferns. Reindeer were reintroduced a few years ago and red deer and wildcat roam the mountainsides. Golden eagles soar above the corries and in the woods capercaillies make popping noises like corks.

Scottish scenery is renowned not only for its breathtaking grandeur, its harmony of sky and mountain and water, but for the romantic and often violent history which seems to cling still to every peak and corrie, every pass and glen. The **Ben Nevis** and **Glen Coe** areas contain both the highest mountain in Britain at 4,408ft (1,344m) and one of the most notorious localities in all Scotland's bloody and tragic past. Ben Nevis, which is more of a hump than a peak, can be climbed fairly easily in good weather, though it will take a good many hours up and down, and there are colossal views from the top on a clear day. In Fort William, down below the mountain, the West Highland Museum illuminates the natural and the human history of the district.

To the south are the peaks which tower above Glen Coe, on an overcast day one of the bleakest and most melancholy places in the British Isles. The celebrated and treacherous massacre of the local Macdonalds by a party of Campbell soldiery occurred on a bitter February night in 1692. The site of the Macdonald settlement and much of the surrounding country is now owned by the National Trust for Scotland, which has a visitor centre in the glen. There is also a folk museum in Glencoe village. Further

south still, and part of the National Scenic Area, is the brooding wasteland of Rannoch Moor, with its peaty bogs and lochans, vividly described in an episode of Robert Louis Stevenson's *Kidnapped.*

Famed again in song and story are the **Cuillin Hills** of the Isle of Skye, which reach up in savage splendour above dramatic Loch Coruisk. These are black, jagged, precipitous, sinister mountains, the highest peak being Sgurr Alasdair at 3,309ft (1,009m). The Cuillins are an irresistible magnet to rock climbers, but they have an old reputation for treachery – compasses go oddly astray, mists descend suddenly, climbers are lost and cut off. Among marginally safer attractions on Skye are Talisker malt whisky and the MacLeods' ancestral castle at Dunvegan with its singularly daunting dungeon.

There is wonderful mountain and loch scenery again to the north, where six massive ranges rear their peaks to the sky in the National Scenic Area of **Wester Ross.** The sun glitters on Loch Maree and its islands, and the warmth of the North Atlantic Drift fosters a subtropical paradise in the luxuriant gardens at Inverewe, at the head of Loch Ewe. The gardens were created from the 1860s on by Osgood Mackenzie on what was initially barren peat wasteland.

The island of Foula is included in the Shetlands National Scenic Area, and so is Fair Isle, familiar from weather forecasts. In the Orkneys the island of **Hoy** is protected, with its dramatic isolated 450ft (137m) stack, the Old Man of Hoy. Man-made Orkney attractions include the Stone Age village of Skara Brae and the enormous Stone Age tomb of Maes Howe, as well as the cathedral of St Magnus in Kirkwall.

Though most of the National Scenic Areas protect mountain scenery, one of them is centred on the old town of **Dunkeld** in the Tayside Region, where the River Tay sweeps past the ruined cathedral among its lawns and sheltering trees. There are memorials in the church to a renowned Scottish regiment, the Black Watch, and to the Scottish Horse, a regiment raised by the Duke of Atholl to fight in the Boer War. An attractive walk through the woods by the River Braan leads to a waterfall and an 18th-century folly. Not far away in the opposite direction is the Loch of the Lowes nature reserve, run by the Scottish Wildlife Trust, where visitors who are lucky may see ospreys. *Macbeth's* Birnam Wood is not far away either.

Lying across the Highland Line are the 'bonnie banks' of **Loch Lomond,** 24 miles long and the largest stretch of inland water in Britain. This is another National Scenic Area. The narrow northern end of the loch protrudes into the Highlands between Ben Vorlich and Ben Lomond, both over 3,000ft (915m). The southern end, with its numerous islands, lies in more

Top *The rocks and tumbling waters of the River Dee, in Royal Deeside.*
Above *Beinn Alligin's peak, with Upper Loch Torridon in the foreground.*

placid country. The burial place of the outlawed Clan MacGregor is on the island of Inchaillach, which is part of the nature reserve at the lower end of the loch.

To the south-west there is a return to mountain landscape in the National Scenic Area of **North Arran,** among the jagged heights of this island in the Firth of Clyde. The highest is Goat Fell at 2,866ft (874m), which can be climbed from the town of Brodick and offers wonderful views, stretching on a clear day to England, Ireland and the Isle of Man. It is to be hoped that the National Scenic Areas will continue to reward Scots and their visitors for many generations to come.

Forest Park

Forest Drive

Forest Parks
Forest Drives

Long ago, before man began to make his mark, most of the land surface of Britain was thickly covered with trees. Far back in the New Stone Age, 6,000 years ago or more, farmers began to fell and burn the woodlands to make clearings for crops and pasture stock. By the Middle Ages more than 80 per cent of the original woodland cover had been cleared. Little is left today of the tangled Wealden forest through which the defeated English were chased by William the Conqueror's Normans after Hastings, or of the oaks and glades of Sherwood Forest where Robin Hood and his outlaws hunted.

In this century huge new man-made forests have been created by the Forestry Commission, set up in 1919 to repair the ravages of World War I, when no timber was imported. The Commission's principal purpose has always been a commercial one, to grow saleable timber. It planted pine, larch and spruce – fast-growing softwood trees that thrive in poor soil and are ready for harvesting in 25 or 30 years – and it has been fiercely criticised for its regimented ranks of

This vast, wooded region of Argyll became Scotland's first Forest Park.

conifers marching monotonously over hill and dale. Increasingly, however, the Commission has recognised the importance of its role as a provider of recreation and its responsibility to the environment.

Forest Parks

In Scotland, where it is the largest landowner, the Commission began to create Forest Parks in scenically attractive areas. The first of them, set under way as far back as 1935, was the **Argyll Forest Park,** extending over 100 square miles of the Cowal Peninsula in the Strathclyde region. Lying between Loch Fyne and Loch Long, it is mountain country, long dominated by the Campbell clan, who feuded with the local Lamonts. The ruined Campbell hold of Carrick Castle glowers out over Loch Goil and the churchyard of Kilmun on Holy Loch was the traditional burying place of the Campbell chiefs.

Visitors can enjoy driving the forest roads, walking on miles of tracks, pony trekking, fishing, sailing and waterskiing. Deer, wildcats, otters, golden eagles and ravens live here. Near the head of Loch Long are fine peaks, including The Cobbler at 2,891ft (881m) and the pass called 'Rest and be Thankful' on the A83, named from the inscription on a stone seat that used to be there. Close to the

southern end of Loch Eck, Benmore House, weirdly and wonderfully Scots Baronial, was given to the Forestry Commission in 1928. The Younger Botanic Garden here is open to the public and is celebrated for its marvellous azaleas and rhododendrons. A brook runs through Puck's Glen, a narrow cleft among the rocks with rare mosses and ferns.

Further south and more than twice as big in area is the **Galloway Forest Park,** designated in 1943, a wild area of wooded mountains, moorland, lochs and streams lying to the north of Newton Stewart. There are ten peaks above 2,000ft (610m), the highest being Merrick, 2,766ft (843m) near the centre of the park. There is climbing, walking, fishing and swimming to enjoy, and a tremendous richness of wildlife – deer, wild goats, pine martens, wildcats, red squirrels, golden eagles and hen harriers.

There are miles of trails for walkers, but motor roads are few and far between in this part of the world. North of Newton Stewart, Loch Trool, bowered among wooded slopes, has a good forest trail. The main road in the park is the Queen's Drive, or more prosaically the A712, from New Galloway to Newton Stewart. Bruce's Stone marks the place where Robert the Bruce scored an early

victory over the English and the man-made Clatteringshaws Loch is part of a hydro-electric scheme. The Galloway Deer Museum is informative not only about the deer but the park and its wildlife in general. The Raiders' Road Forest Drive turns off to the south and follows an old cattle thieves' route through the woods for 10 miles beside the Black Water of Dee, with bathing places and picnic spots.

The **Glen More Forest Park** is in the National Scenic Area of the Cairngorms. The **Queen Elizabeth Forest Park,** designated in 1953, links two National Scenic Areas, Loch Lomond and the Trossachs. In the Tayside Region there is pony trekking, mountain biking and fishing in the **Tummel Forest Park,** with numerous walks of varying length and degrees of difficulty. Forestry Commission walks are graded as 'Easy', 'Strenuous' or 'Difficult'. There are camp sites, picnic sites and plenty of car parks, with deer, red squirrels and capercaillies to watch. The forest here has mostly been planted since World War II, but a specially enticing attraction is a guided walk through the magically named Black Wood of Rannoch. On the south shore of Loch Rannoch, this is one of the rare remaining fragments of the great Caledonian pine forest, which once stretched for hundreds of miles. The visitor centre for the Forest Park is above Loch Tummel at the Queen's View, where you can stand in the footsteps of Queen Victoria, who admired the prospect in 1866. She also admired the Pass of Killiecrankie, not far away, a wooded gorge and battlefield where the National Trust for Scotland has a visitor centre.

The Forest Park idea spread from Scotland south into England. The **Border Forest Park,** designated in 1955, straddles the high sparse moors on both sides of the Anglo-Scots border, where so many raiding and rustling parties rode about their nefarious business in past centuries. Ruins of pele towers and castles testify to a violent history of feuding and marauding. At the heart of the park lies Kielder Water, a spectacular man-made reservoir seven miles long in the valley of the North Tyne, holding 40 million gallons of water. Ferry boats ply across it in the summer, and it is reached by the 12-mile Kielder Forest Drive from the A68. The drive runs past viewpoints and picnic spots to the Forestry Commission's visitor centre at Kielder Castle. In the remoter areas, you may catch sight of red deer, wild goats, blue hares and red squirrels.

On a much smaller scale is the **Grizedale Forest Park,** occupying a slice of Lake District scenery between Coniston Water and Esthwaite Water, south-west of Hawkshead. There are walks and guided tours, orienteering courses, cycle trails, a disabled trail, and a theatre. A trail bears witness to past industries: bloomeries where iron ore was smelted, charcoal pits, potash pits for soap-making, kilns, a tannery and a blast furnace.

The **North Riding Forest Park** lies north-east of Pickering in the rolling landscape of the North York Moors. Centred on the Dalby Valley, in the Middle Ages it was part of the much larger royal hunting forest of Pickering. A nine-mile forest drive takes the motorist gently through the woodland today, with an ample supply of parking pull-offs and places for a picnic. Leaflets detail forest walks for those who want to stretch their legs. Part of the drive follows the Staindale Beck, which was dammed to create an attractive lake, and there is a walk from here to the strange rock formations called the Bridestones, in a nature reserve run by the National Trust and the Yorkshire Wildlife Trust.

Forest Drives

Where there is no Forest Park, there is still occasionally a forest drive: as in the **Hamsterley Forest,** the largest area of woodland in County Durham. It covers 5,000 acres west of Bishop Auckland, off the A68. The Forestry Commission bought the estate from the last Surtees owner, a descendant of the famous Victorian sporting novelist R S Surtees. The drive runs for four miles along the Bedburn Beck and the Spurlswood Beck, through

Right Helpful information at the Visitor Centre in the Borders Forest Park. Below Kielder Forest Drive, between Kielder Castle and Redesdale.

woodland which sports much pine and fir, spruce and larch. There are no less than 60 varieties of tree here all told, with oak and ash, beech and thorn among them. Red squirrels and roe deer, bats and lizards frequent these woods and there are large numbers of woodpeckers and fungi. There are waymarked walks, though more adventurous visitors can explore wherever they like.

In South Wales, meanwhile, it takes a tough cyclist to manage the splendid **Cwmcarn Forest Drive.** The seven-mile drive starts at an excellent new visitor centre south of Abercarn, near Newport. Higher up are picnic places and barbecue spots with commanding views across country and to the Bristol Channel. Walks lead off at intervals, including one which climbs to the summit. The trees are mostly spruce, larch and pine, but oaks, beeches and rowans temper the conifers.

The drive runs through part of the Forestry Commission's Ebbw Forest, a distant man-made descendant of the ancient forest of Machen, which was eaten away over the centuries by sheep and charcoal burners and finally fell victim to the devouring demand for timber in the South Wales coal mines. So here man has put back something of what he has destroyed.

Forest Park

Forest Drive

45

THE TOURIST'S BRITISH ISLES
·CALENDAR·

SPRING

MARCH

Whuppity Scoorie
Lanark, Strathclyde
(March 1)

Ideal Home Exhibition
Earls Court, London
(early March to early April)

Belfast Musical Festival
Belfast
(March – 3rd week)

Oxford v Cambridge Boat Race
Putney to Mortlake,
London
(late March or early April)

APRIL

Midgley Pace Egg Play
Calder Valley, West
Yorkshire
(Good Friday)

Nutters Dance
Bacup, Lancashire
(Easter Saturday)

Easter Parade
Battersea Park, London
(Easter Monday)

Harness Horse Parade
Regent's Park, London
(Easter Monday)

Hare Pie Scramble and Bottle Kicking
Hallaton, Leicestershire
(Easter Monday)

Hocktide Festival
Hungerford, Berkshire
(Easter Tuesday)

Northumbria Gathering
Morpeth, Northumbria
(week after Easter)

The Grand National
Aintree, Merseyside
(April – 2nd Saturday)

Shakespeare's Birthday Celebrations
Stratford-upon-Avon,
Warwickshire
(April 21)

Spring Flower Show
Harrogate, North Yorkshire
(late April)

Badminton Three Day Event
Badminton, Avon
(late April or early May)

MAY

May Morning Ceremony
Oxford
(May 1)

Royal May Day Celebrations
Knutsford, Cheshire
(May – 1st Saturday)

Flower Parade
Spalding, Lincolnshire
(early May)

Furry Dance
Helston, Cornwall
(May 8)

Garland Day
Abbotsbury, Dorset
(May 13)

Goat Fell Race
Isle of Arran, Strathclyde
(May – 2nd or 3rd
Saturday)

Bath International Festival of the Arts
Bath, Avon
(late May to early June)

Chelsea Flower Show
Royal Hospital, Chelsea,
London
(late May to early June)

TT Motorcycle Races
Isle of Man
(late May to early June)

Arbor Tree Day
Aston on Clun, Shropshire
(late May)

Garland Day
Castleton, Derbyshire
(May 29)

Dickens Festival
Rochester, Kent
(late May or early June)

Royal Bath and West Show
Shepton Mallet, Somerset
(late May or early June)

Woolsack Races
Tetbury, Gloucestershire
(Spring Bank Holiday)

SUMMER

JUNE

The Derby
Epsom, Surrey
(June – 1st Wednesday)

Scuttlebrook Wake
Chipping Campden,
Gloucestershire
(Saturday following Spring
Bank Holiday)

Appleby Horse Fair
Appleby, Cumbria
(June – 2nd Tuesday and
Wednesday)

Trooping the Colour
Horse Guards Parade,
London
(June – 2nd Saturday)

Royal Cornwall Show
Wadebridge, Cornwall
(June – 2nd week)

Aldeburgh Festival of Music and the Arts
Aldeburgh, Suffolk
(June – 2nd to 4th
weeks)

Selkirk Common Riding
Selkirk, Borders
(mid-June)

Three Counties Agricultural Show
Great Malvern, Hereford &
Worcester
(mid-June)

Stour Music Festival
Boughton Aluph, Kent
(June – 2nd half)

Royal Highland Show
Ingliston, Lothian
(June – 3rd week)

Royal Ascot Race Meeting
Ascot, Berkshire
(late June)

Wimbledon Lawn Tennis Championships
Wimbledon, London
(late June to early July)

JULY

Tynwald Day
Isle of Man
(July 5)

Henley Royal Regatta
Henley on Thames,
Oxfordshire
(July – 1st week)

Cheltenham International Festival of Music
Cheltenham,
Gloucestershire
(July – 1st and 3rd weeks)

British Rose Festival
Gardens of the Rose,
Chiswell Green,
Hertfordshire
(July – 1st or 2nd week)

Royal International Agricultural Show
Stoneleigh, Warwickshire
(early July)

Great Yorkshire Agricultural Show
Harrogate, North Yorkshire
(July – 2nd week)

International Musical Eisteddfod
Llangollen, Clwyd
(early July)

Sham Fight
Scarva, Co Down
(July 13)

Royal Welsh Show
Builth Wells, Powys
(July – 3rd week)

Black Cherry Fair
Chertsey, Surrey
(July – 3rd Saturday)

Royal Tournament
Earls Court, London
(mid-July)

Buxton International Arts Festival
Buxton, Derbyshire
(mid-July to early August)

Tweedmouth Salmon Feast
Tweedmouth,
Northumberland
(Sunday after July 18)

Tolpuddle Martyrs Procession
Tolpuddle, Dorset
(July – 3rd Sunday)

Durham Miners Gala
Durham
(July – Saturday of 2nd
week)

Croagh Patrick Pilgrimage
Near Westport, Co Mayo
(July-last Sunday)

AUGUST

Royal National Eisteddfod
Varying locations in Wales
(August – 1st week)

The Burry Man Festival
Queensferry, Lothian
(August – 2nd Friday)

Cowes Week
Cowes, Isle of Wight
(August – 2nd week)

Puck Fair
Killorglin, Co Kerry
(August 10–12)

Marymass Festival
Irvine, Strathclyde
(August – 2nd or 3rd
weeks)

**Edinburgh International
Festival**
Edinburgh
(August – last three weeks)

Priddy Sheep Fair
Priddy, Somerset
(mid-August)

Grasmere Sports
Grasmere, Cumbria
(Thursday nearest
August 20)

Burning of Bartle
West Witton, North
Yorkshire
(Saturday nearest
August 24)

Oul' Lammas Fair
Ballycastle, Co Antrim
(August – last Tuesday)

Plague Sunday Service
Eyam, Derbyshire
(August – last Sunday)

Navy Days
Plymouth and Portsmouth
(August Bank Holiday)

AUTUMN

SEPTEMBER

Ben Nevis Hill Race
Fort William, Highland
(September – 1st Saturday)

Braemar Gathering
Braemar, Grampian
(September – 1st Saturday)

Hop Hoodening
Canterbury, Kent
(early September)

St Giles's Fair
Oxford
(September – 1st full week)

Horn Dance
Abbots Bromley,
Staffordshire
(Monday after 1st Sunday
following September 4)

Burghley Horse Trials
Burghley House, Stamford
(early September)

Blackpool Illuminations
Blackpool, Lancashire
(early September to early
November)

International Air Show
Farnborough, Hampshire
(September – 1st week)

**Clarinbridge Oyster
Festival**
Clarinbridge, Co Galway
(early or mid-September)

**World Carriage Driving
Championships**
Windsor, Berkshire
(September – 3rd week)

Victorian Festival
Llandrindod Wells, Powys
(September – 3rd week)

**Great Autumn Flower
Show**
Harrogate, North Yorkshire
(mid-September)

Dr Johnson's Birthday
Lichfield, Staffordshire
(on or near September 18)

Egremont Crab Fair
Egremont, Cumbria
(Saturday nearest
September 18)

Barnstaple Old Fair
Barnstaple, Devon
(September – 3rd week)

**Painswick Church
Clipping**
Painswick, Gloucestershire
(September – 3rd week)

Dublin Theatre Festival
Dublin
(late September to early
October)

OCTOBER

Nottingham Goose Fair
Nottingham
(early October)

Tavistock Goose Fair
Tavistock, Devon
(October 10)

Pack Monday Fair
Sherborne, Dorset
(1st Monday after
October 10)

Border Shepherds Show
Alwinton, Northumberland
(October – 2nd week)

Horse of the Year Show
Wembley Arena, London
(mid-October)

Stratford Mop Fair
Stratford-upon-Avon,
Warwickshire
(mid-October)

Wexford Opera Festival
Wexford, Co Wexford
(late October to
mid-November)

NOVEMBER

**London to Brighton
Veteran Car Run**
Hyde Park Corner, London
(November – 1st Sunday)

Guy Fawkes Night
Lewes, East Sussex, and
elsewhere
(November 5)

Tar-Barrel Rolling
Ottery St Mary, Devon
(November 5)

Lord Mayor's Show
Guildhall to the Strand,
London
(November – 2nd Saturday)

Belfast Festival at Queen's
Belfast
(mid to late November)

**Contemporary Music
Festival**
Huddersfield, West
Yorkshire
(late November)

WINTER

DECEMBER

Royal Smithfield Show
London
(early December)

**Festival of Carols and
Lessons**
King's College Chapel,
Cambridge
(December 24)

Ba' Games
Kirkwall, Orkney Islands
(December 25 and
January 1)

Greatham Sword Dance
Greatham, Cleveland
(December 26)

**Allendale Tar-Barrel
Ceremony**
Allendale, Northumberland
(December 31)

Fireball Ceremony
Stonehaven, Grampian
(December 31)

Flambeaux Procession
Comrie, Tayside
(December 31)

JANUARY

Haxey Hood Game
Haxey, Humberside
(January 5 or 6)

Straw Bear Festival
Whittlesey, Cambridgeshire
(Friday and Saturday
before Plough Monday)

Plough Stots Service
Goathland, North
Yorkshire
(Monday after January 6)

Burning the Clavie
Burghead, Grampian
(January 11)

Wassailing the Apple Tree
Carhampton, Somerset
(January 17)

Up Helly Aa
Lerwick, Shetland Islands
(January – last Tuesday)

FEBRUARY

Jorvik Viking Festival
York, North Yorkshire
(February – whole month)

Pancake Day Race
Olney, Buckinghamshire
(Shrove Tuesday)

Shrovetide Football
Ashbourne, Derbyshire
(Shrove Tuesday)

Shrovetide Skipping
Scarborough, North
Yorkshire
(Shrove Tuesday)

*Left Traditional maypole
dancing at Chipping Campden
in Gloucestershire.
Inset A familiar sight in The
Mall, the Household Cavalry.
Above Wimbledon draws the
crowds each summer.
Below May Day celebrations
in Oxford, which were started
in the mid-17th century.*

*Tourist
Information
Centre*

*Tourist
Information
Centre
(Summer only)*

Tourist Information Centres

With over 800 offices nationwide, Britain's Tourist Information Centres offer a free service, welcoming calls both in person and by phone.

Whatever your query – whether you are looking for something new to do on a Sunday, somewhere to take the family for the day or simply a good place to eat, your local Tourist Information Centre is only too willing to help.

The staff at each centre have details on just about everything within a 50-mile radius and this is backed up by a comprehensive range of brochures, pamphlets and guides both free and for sale.

They can help with excursions and outings, giving you details and route directions to a variety of places, from castles and craft centres to model villages and museums, tell you which bus to catch, the best place for a picnic, or a walk or a scenic drive. They can even advise on which restaurant is likely to provide a high-chair for the baby or which stately home involves a lot of walking about. They also have details of local events: concerts, carnivals, festivals and fêtes and

*Inside the London Tourist Board
Information Centre at Victoria.*

what is on in town in the evenings.

Another invaluable service is to offer on-the-spot help with finding places to stay. Most centres have up-to-date lists of all kinds of holiday accommodation in the area such as hotels, holiday homes and campsites. They can make local reservations for you, if available, or reservations at any other town which has a centre offering this facility, for the same or the following day. A fee or deposit may be payable for these services.

Most of the centres keep regular office hours from 9 to 5, Monday to Friday, but many are also open at weekends or for longer periods, especially in the summer. Some, however, are open from Easter to September only, but you can always refer your enquiries to the nearest all-year-round centre.

Britain's Tourist Information Centres are at your service and are always happy to help, no matter what the query.

The following signs indicate where you will find a Tourist Information Centre in a town.

 – directional sign for road traffic

 – sign for pedestrians

 – this sign means a Tourist Information Centre is just a few yards away

ROAD ATLAS
OF THE
BRITISH ISLES

Map pages

Clear, easy-to-read mapping helps you to plan more detailed journeys, and provides a wealth of information for the motorist.

All motorways, primary, A and B roads, and unclassified roads are shown. The atlas also identifies interchanges, roundabouts and those roads outside urban areas which are under construction.

Additional features include rivers, lakes and reservoirs, railway lines, interesting places to visit, picnic sites and Tourist Information Centres. To assist you in estimating journey length, distances are shown in miles between blue marker symbols.

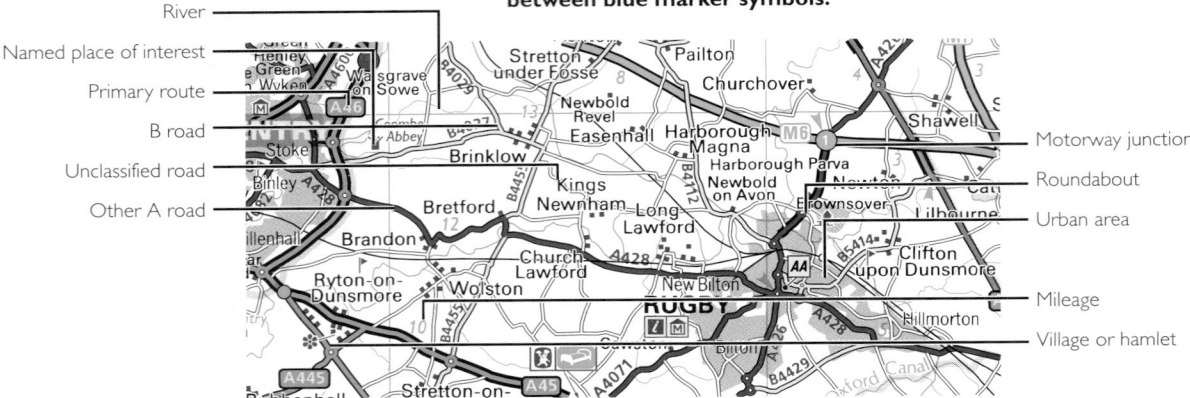

Ferry and rail routes

Useful ferry and rail information.

To assist in planning journeys overseas mapping of coastal regions provides basic off-shore information including ferry routes. Throughout the atlas, railway lines with stations and level crossings are shown to assist with general navigation or rail travel requirements.

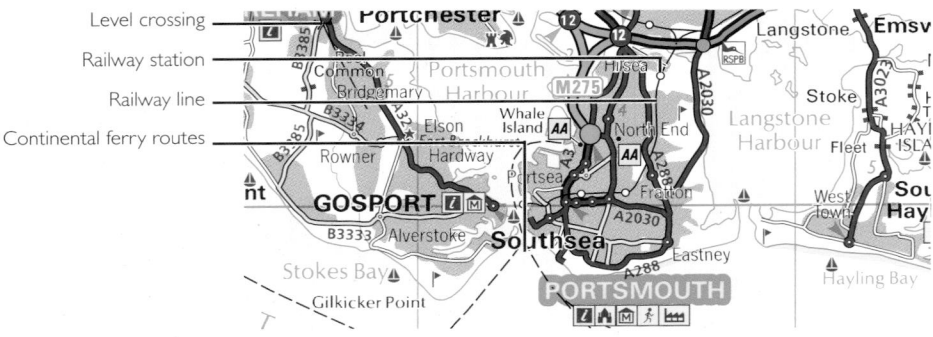

Tourism and leisure

Places of interest to note in the area you are visiting.

Red pictorial symbols and red type highlight numerous places of interest, catering for every taste. Red symbols within yellow boxes show tourist attractions in a town. Use them to plan days out or places to visit on holiday. To avoid disappointment remember to check opening times before you visit.

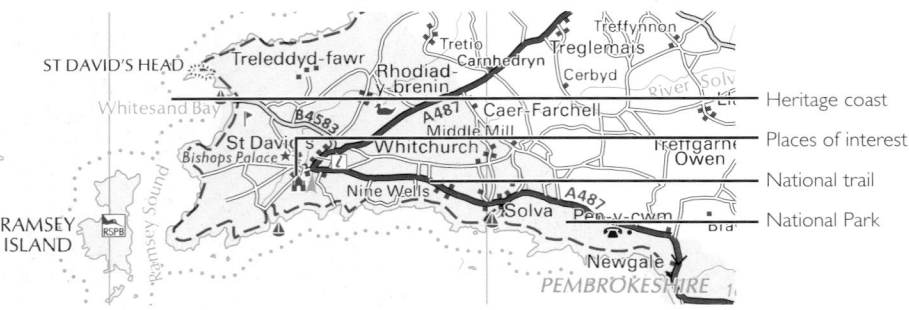

using this atlas

Motorways – restricted junctions

Motorway junctions, displayed as diagrams,

highlight individual restrictions.

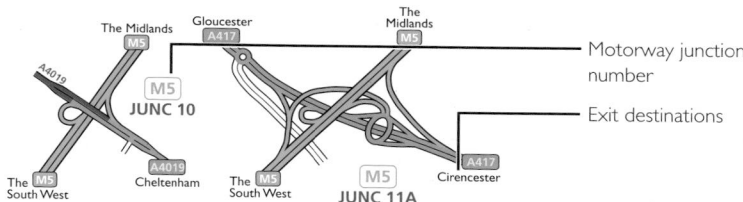

— Motorway junction number

— Exit destinations

Town plans

Up-to-date, fully indexed town plans show AA

recommended roads and other practical

information, such as one-way streets, car parks

and restricted roads,

making navigation much easier.

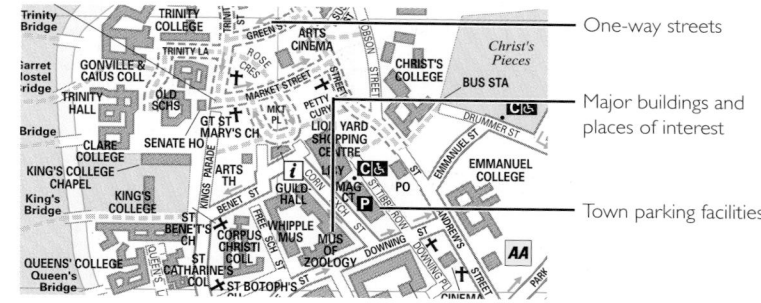

— One-way streets

— Major buildings and places of interest

— Town parking facilities

London

Easy-to-read, fully indexed street maps of inner

London provide a simple guide to finding your

way around the city.

Underground railway stations —
Major places of tourist interest —
Garage parking —
One-way systems —

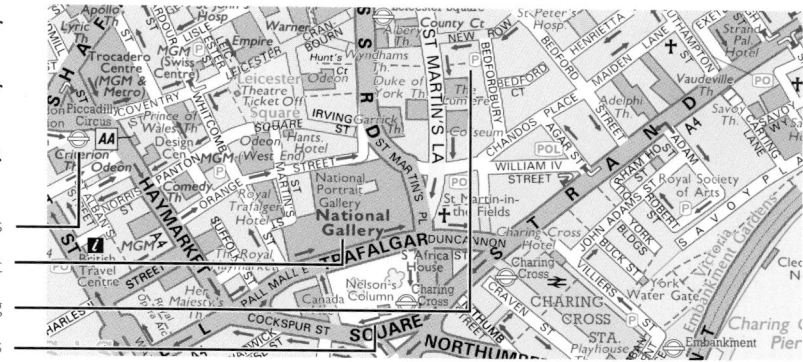

Ports and airports

Car parking —
Airport terminal —
Public transport stops —

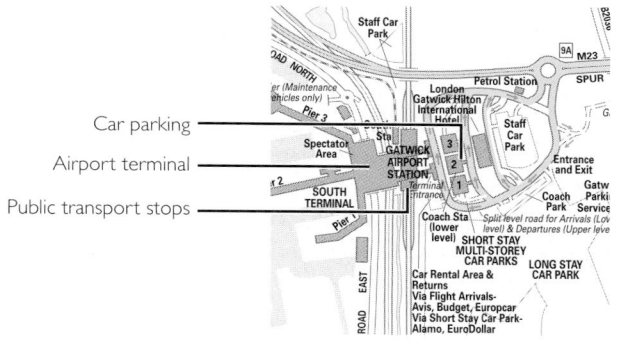

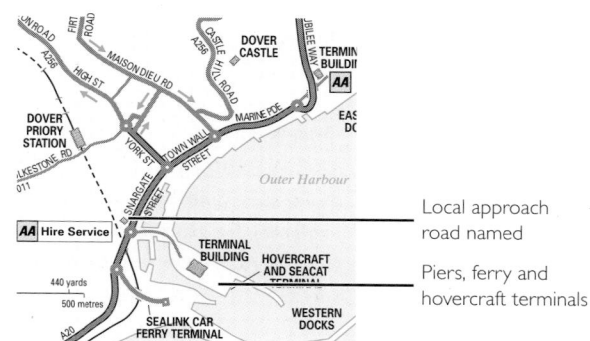

— Local approach road named

— Piers, ferry and hovercraft terminals

Delays and hold-ups

Despite ever-increasing levels of traffic, motorways are still the quickest means of getting from A to B. Nevertheless, a hold-up on a motorway can easily delay your journey for several hours. There are a number of ways of gleaning information about the stretches of motorway to avoid: by phone, radio and newspaper.

AA Roadwatch

This service provides up-to-the-minute information on traffic conditions, roadworks and the weather for the whole country. See page XII for numbers to call.

Radio

Frequent radio bulletins are issued by both the BBC and independent local radio stations about road and weather conditions, and likely hold-ups. By tuning into the local radio stations you can avoid delays and prepare to make changes to your route. However, local radio does not yet cover the entire country.

Call AA Roadwatch or listen to local radio to avoid delays on your journey.

Daily checks

Before you start every journey you should always ensure that:
- You check the dashboard warning lights before and after starting the engine
- There are no unusual noises once the engine is running
- All the lights are both clean and working
- The windscreen and all other windows are clean
- You have sufficient fuel for your journey

Weekly checks

Before you set out on a journey you should also ensure that:
- The engine oil level is correct, looking for obvious signs of leakage
- The coolant level is correct, checking the anti-freeze before the onset of winter
- The battery connections and terminals are clean and free from corrosion
- The brake (and clutch, if hydraulic) fluid is correct
- The tyres, including the spare, are properly inflated and not damaged
- The tyres are changed if the tread falls below 2mm
- The fan-belt is not worn or damaged, and that the tension is correct
- The windscreen wipers are clean and that the screen wash reservoir is full

Carry out regular checks to make sure that you and your car arrive safely.

Fit to drive

Many accidents are caused by one or more of the drivers involved being unfit to drive when the accident occurred. The most obvious reason for such accidents is alcohol; even the smallest quantity can affect driving. The only safe advice is: if you drive, don't drink – if you drink, don't drive. However, alcohol is just one of a number of factors that can make someone unfit to drive.

Tiredness

Some people become tired sooner than others, but the following are guidelines which you should aim to keep: for every three hours on the road, take 20 minutes rest; if possible, share the driving; limit yourself to a maximum of eight hours behind the wheel in any one day; and try to avoid driving at times when you would normally be asleep or resting. You should also avoid driving after hard exercise, a large meal and, of course, after consuming alcohol. Other factors which can contribute to tiredness are temperature inside the car and medication; a stuffy atmosphere – and some drugs – can induce drowsiness. If you are on medication, check with your doctor whether you should be driving at all. One final point: not driving during peak hours keeps delays to a minimum, reduces frustration and minimises journey time.

Driving abroad

Always ensure you know the specific legal requirements and road signs before you set out – and make sure your car conforms to such requirements. If you take an overnight ferry crossing you will probably be tired the next morning; do not set yourself too long a drive after arriving on the Continent. When you begin driving again after taking a break be especially careful to keep on the correct side of the road.

Are you fit to drive? Food, tiredness, drink and medicine all affect your driving.

journey planning

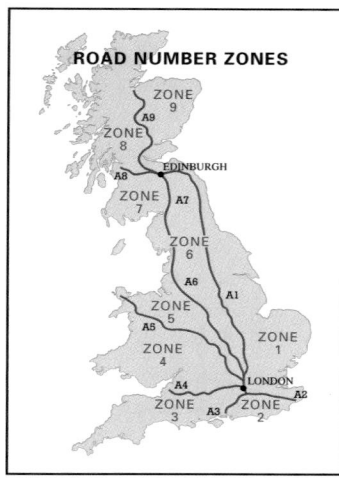

ROAD NUMBER ZONES

How to get there

Special route planning maps on pages XII–XVII enable you to devise a basic route before referring to the main pages of the atlas for greater detail.

Road classification

London is the hub for the spokes of roads numbered A1 to A6, Edinburgh the hub for A7, A8 and A9. Beginning with the A1, running north from London, the roads radiate clockwise from the capital: A2 runs roughly east, the A3 west, and so forth. The system has made the numbering of other roads very simple. Generally, the lower the subsequent number, the closer the road's starting point to London (or Edinburgh).

using the national grid

One of the unique

features of AA

mapping is the use of

the National Grid

System.

The National Grid

The National Grid covers Britain with an imaginary network of squares, using blue vertical lines called eastings and horizontal lines called northings. On the atlas pages these lines are numbered along the bottom and on the left-hand side.

The index

Each entry in the index is followed by a page number, two letters denoting an area on the map and a 4-figure grid reference. You will not need to use the two letters for simple navigation, but they come in useful if you want to use your map in relation to the rest of the country and other map series.

Quick reference

For quick reference, the four figures of the grid reference in the index are arranged so that the 1st and 3rd are in a bolder type than the 2nd and 4th. The 1st figure shows the number along the bottom of the grid, and the 3rd figure, the number up the left-hand side. These will indicate the square in which you will find the place name.

Pinpoint accuracy

However, to pinpoint a place more accurately you will also need to use the 2nd and 4th numbers. The second will tell you how many imaginary tenths along the bottom line to go from the first number, and the 4th will tell you how many tenths to go up from the third number. Where these two lines intersect, you will find your place name. For example: Skegness 77TF**5**6**6**3. Skegness is located on page 77 within grid square 56 in National Grid square TF. Its exact location is **5**6**6**3.

Skegness **77**TF**5663**

Skegness is located on page **77**

within grid square **56**

in National Grid square **TF**

Its exact location is **5663**

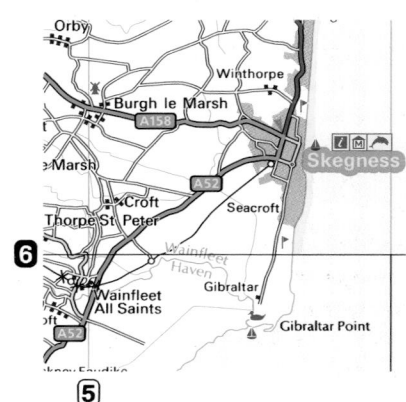

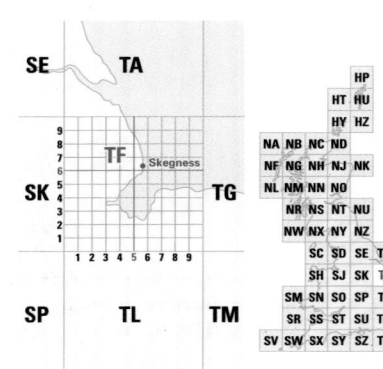

Classes of signs

A consistent and comprehensive set of road signs provides information and warning to the motorist.

These are based on an internationally agreed system, with variations specific to Britain. Signs which give orders and prohibitions are usually circular, and if the background is blue, their instructions are compulsory. Triangular signs carry warning messages and rectangular signs give information.

There are three shapes of road signs: triangles, circles and rectangles. Red triangles warn. Red circles prohibit

Blue circles give positive instruction. Blue rectangles give general information. Green rectangles are used for direction signs on primary routes.

Junctions and roundabouts

Warning signs lead up to a junction or roundabout and provide information about the nature of the junction.

Warning signs will probably be followed by a give way or stop sign. The road markings at a stop sign consist of solid white lines identifying the farthest point to which you may drive. It is obligatory to stop and look to see that it is possible to enter the major road in safety. The give way sign has different road markings – a pair of white dashed lines – and drivers are required to delay joining the main road until it is safe to do so. If the main road is clear, there is no obligation to stop completely.

Countdown markers approaching a major junction

Crossroads

Side road

T-junction

Staggered junction

Stop sign

Give way

No vehicles

Distance to STOP sign

Distance to GIVE WAY sign

Roundabout

Mini-roundabout, give way to vehicles from the right

Advance warning of no through road

No through road

The road ahead

Advance warning of how the road ahead is laid out helps a driver plan his/her approach.

The information given is generally precise about which side of the road is affected or which direction the road will take. The triangular signs give warnings, the circular signs must be obeyed.

Bend to left

Double bend, first to left

Bend to right

Double bend, first to right

Road hump or series of road humps ahead

Worded warning sign

Dual carriageway ends

Axle weight limit (in tonnes)

Steep incline

No vehicles over height shown

Dual carriageway ahead

No goods vehicles over maximum gross weight shown (in tonnes)

Steep decline

Sharp deviation

Traffic merging with equal priority from left

Road narrows on left

Traffic merging with equal priority from right

Road narrows on right

Road narrows on both sides

road signs

Hazards ahead

The signs warning of hazards ahead should never be ignored, and provide valuable information about what is round the next corner or just ahead.

Pedestrian crossing ahead	Hospital ahead with accident and emergency facilities	Slippery road	Cattle grid	Road works ahead	Children	Wild animals	Wild horses	Cattle	Other danger

Uneven road	Traffic signals ahead	Children going to or from school	Stop at sign	School crossing patrol ahead	School crossing patrol; vehicles must stop

Hump-backed bridge	Opening or swing bridge	Risk of falling rocks	Quayside or river bank	Overhead electric cable

Traffic behaviour

Information about the way traffic should be organised is given in a series of specific signs.

These signs govern the speed and general approach at any situation. They are signs which must be obeyed.

No stopping (clearway)	National speed limits apply	No U-turns	Give priority to vehicles from opposite direction	No overtaking	Motor vehicles prohibited except for access	No entry for vehicles	Two-way traffic	No right turn	No left turn

Turn left ahead		Turn left	Pass either side to reach same destination	Ahead only	Keep left

Level crossings

There are several different types of level crossing. Many have barriers which may cross half or all of the road.

Level crossings may be worked automatically by the approach of the train or they may be operated by an attendant. When flashing lights and bell signals are in operation you should not pass. If you are already crossing when the amber lights flash and the bells start, keep crossing.

				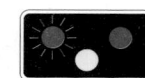
Level crossing without gate or barrier	Level crossing with gate or barrier	Level crossing without gate or barrier	Countdown markers	Alternate flashing lights means YOU MUST STOP

M1 London–Leeds

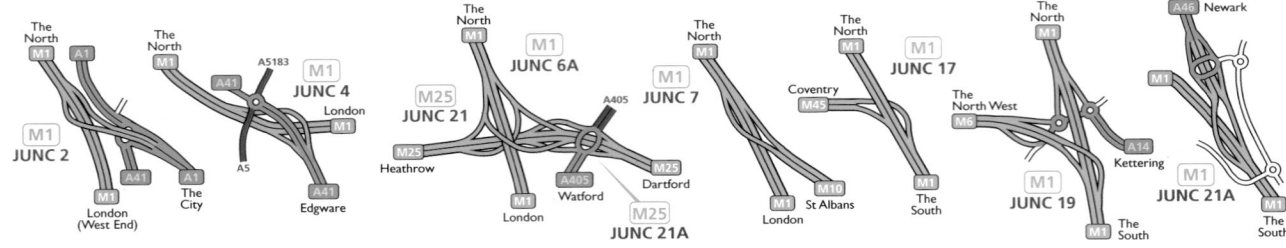

M1 London–Leeds   M2 Rochester–Faversham   M3 Sunbury–Southampton

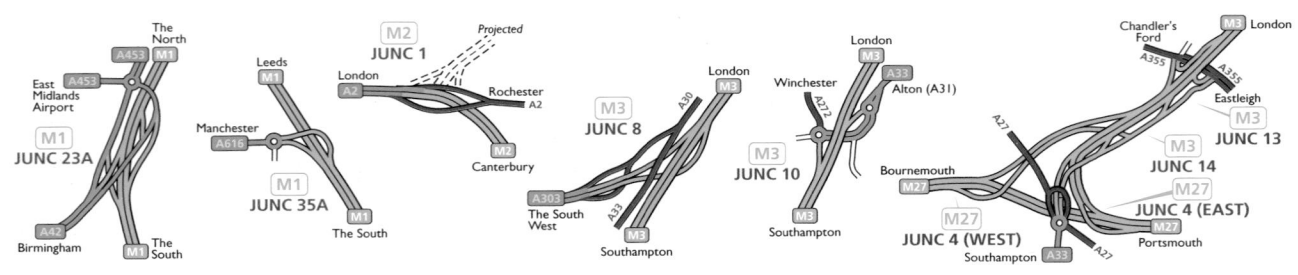

M4 London–South Wales   M5 Birmingham–Exeter

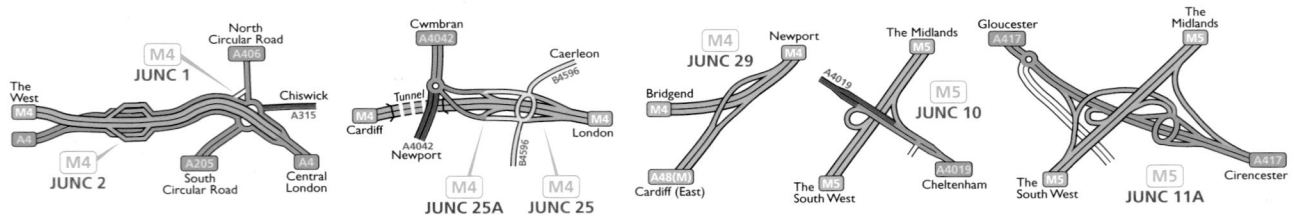

M5 Birmingham–Exeter   M6 Rugby–Carlisle

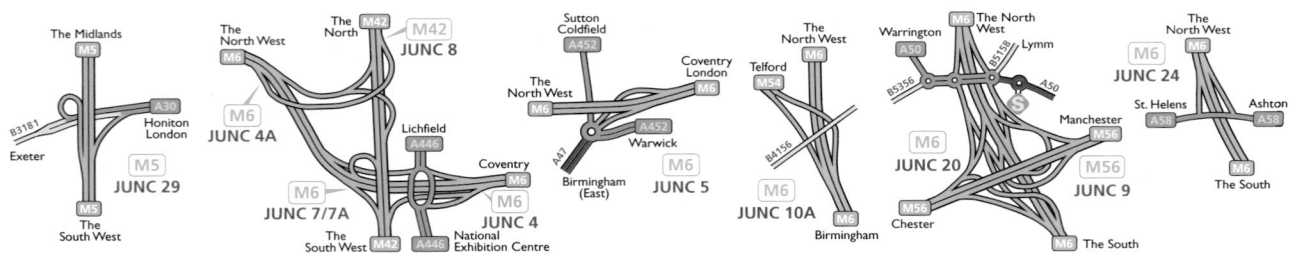

M6 Rugby–Carlisle   M8 Edinburgh–Bishopton

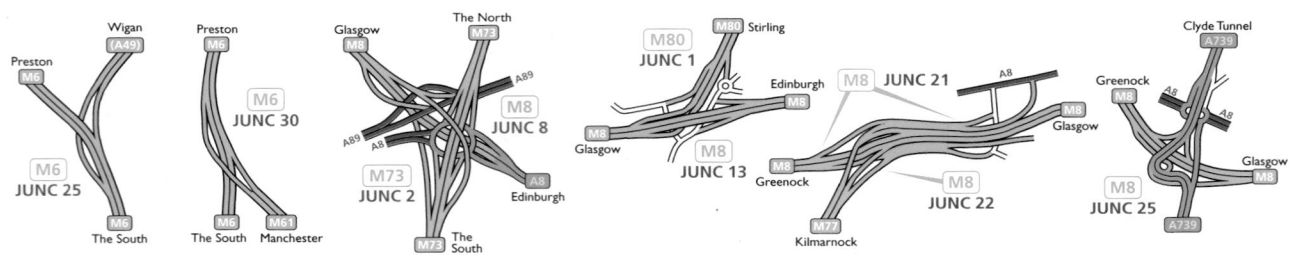

motorways –restricted junctions

Diagrams of selected motorway junctions which have entry and exit restrictions

M8 Edinburgh–Bishopton   M9 Edinburgh–Dunblane   M11 London–Cambridge

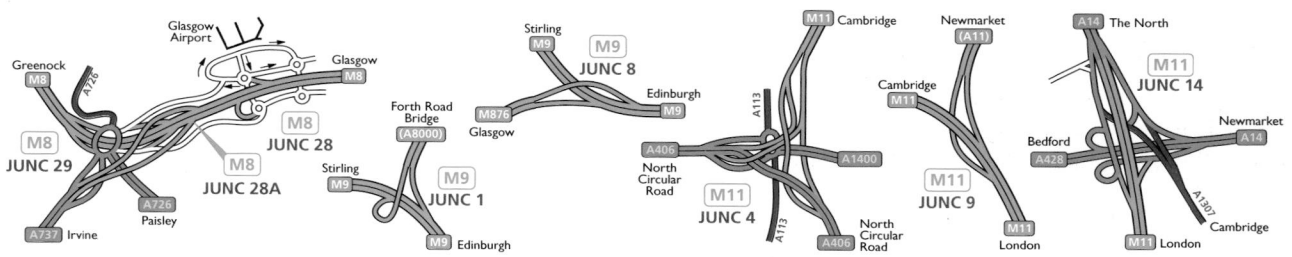

M20 Swanley–Folkestone   M25 London Orbital   M27 Cadnam–Portsmouth   M40 London–Birmingham

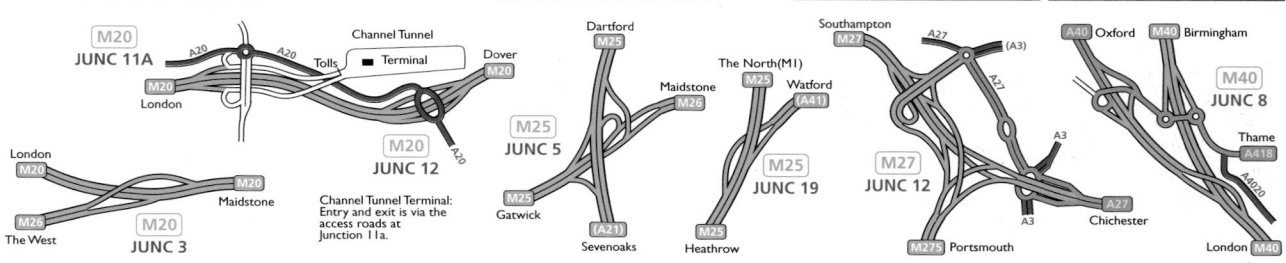

M42 Bromsgrove–Measham   M56 North Cheshire Motorway   M62 Liverpool–Humberside

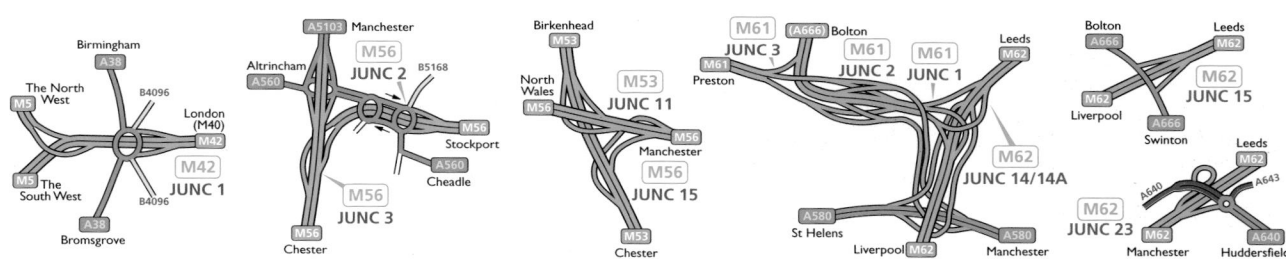

M63 Greater Manchester   M73 East of Glasgow   M74 Glasgow–Gretna

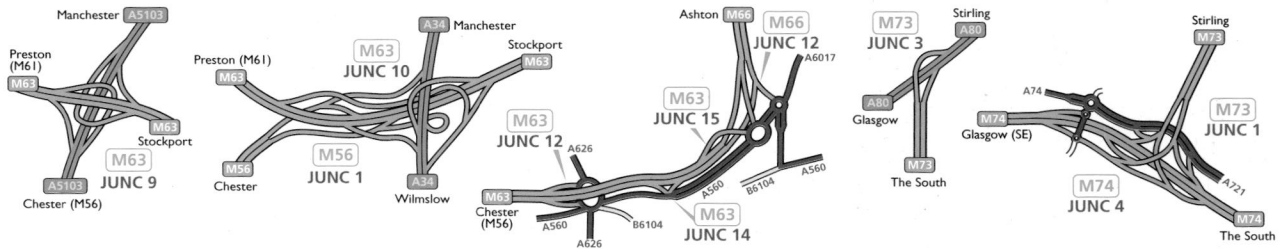

M74, A74(M) Glasgow–Gretna   M80 Glasgow–Stirling   M90 Forth Road Bridge–Perth   A1(M) Scotch Corner–Tyneside

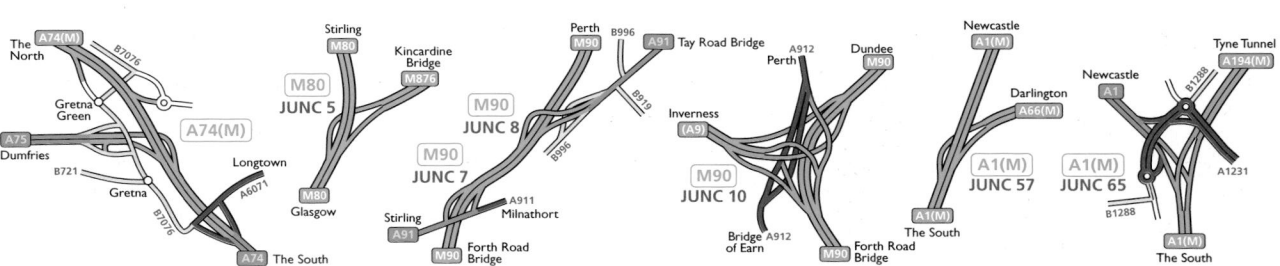

route planner

Planning your route

The route-planning maps on the following pages show principal routes throughout the country and pinpoint the major towns and cities. Detailed routes can be worked out from the maps in the main atlas section of this book. You may find it useful to make a note of road numbers and route directions. You are advised to avoid driving through towns and built-up areas whenever possible, even if such routes appear to be more direct on the map. Delays caused by traffic lights, one-way systems and other road-users will almost certainly be encountered in such areas.

The length of the journey is a fundamental consideration when planning a route. The mileage chart on the inside back cover gives the distances between main towns and can be used to make a rough calculation of the total journey length. The time needed for the journey can then be estimated.

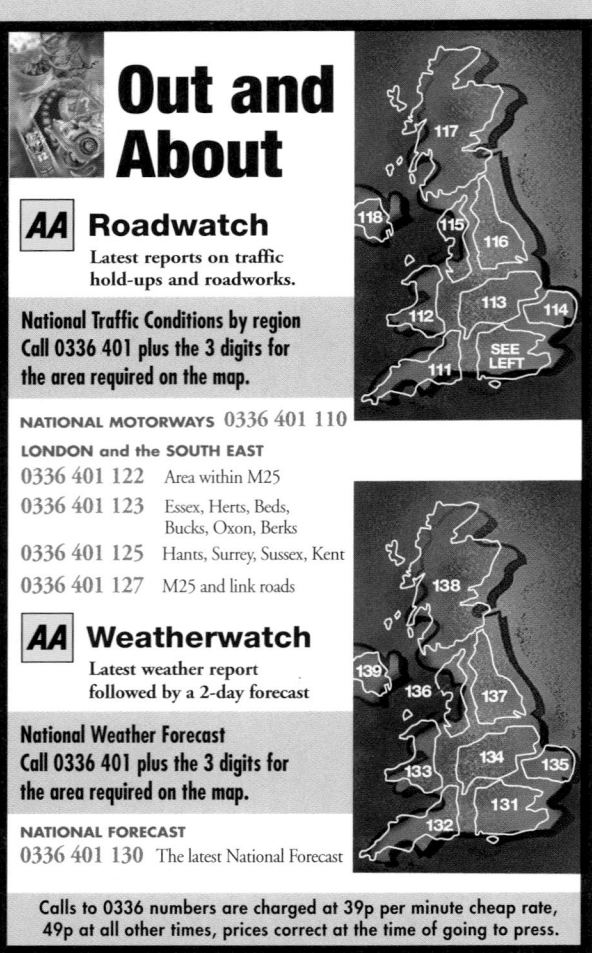

Out and About

AA Roadwatch
Latest reports on traffic hold-ups and roadworks.

National Traffic Conditions by region
Call 0336 401 plus the 3 digits for the area required on the map.

NATIONAL MOTORWAYS 0336 401 110

LONDON and the SOUTH EAST

0336 401 122   Area within M25

0336 401 123   Essex, Herts, Beds, Bucks, Oxon, Berks

0336 401 125   Hants, Surrey, Sussex, Kent

0336 401 127   M25 and link roads

AA Weatherwatch
Latest weather report followed by a 2-day forecast

National Weather Forecast
Call 0336 401 plus the 3 digits for the area required on the map.

NATIONAL FORECAST
0336 401 130   The latest National Forecast

Calls to 0336 numbers are charged at 39p per minute cheap rate, 49p at all other times, prices correct at the time of going to press.

Motorway	
Primary route dual carriageway	
Primary route single carriageway	
Other A roads	

| 0 | 10 | 20 | 30 miles |
| 0 | 10 | 20 | 30 | 40 | 50 km |

SCALE approx 1:1,400,000

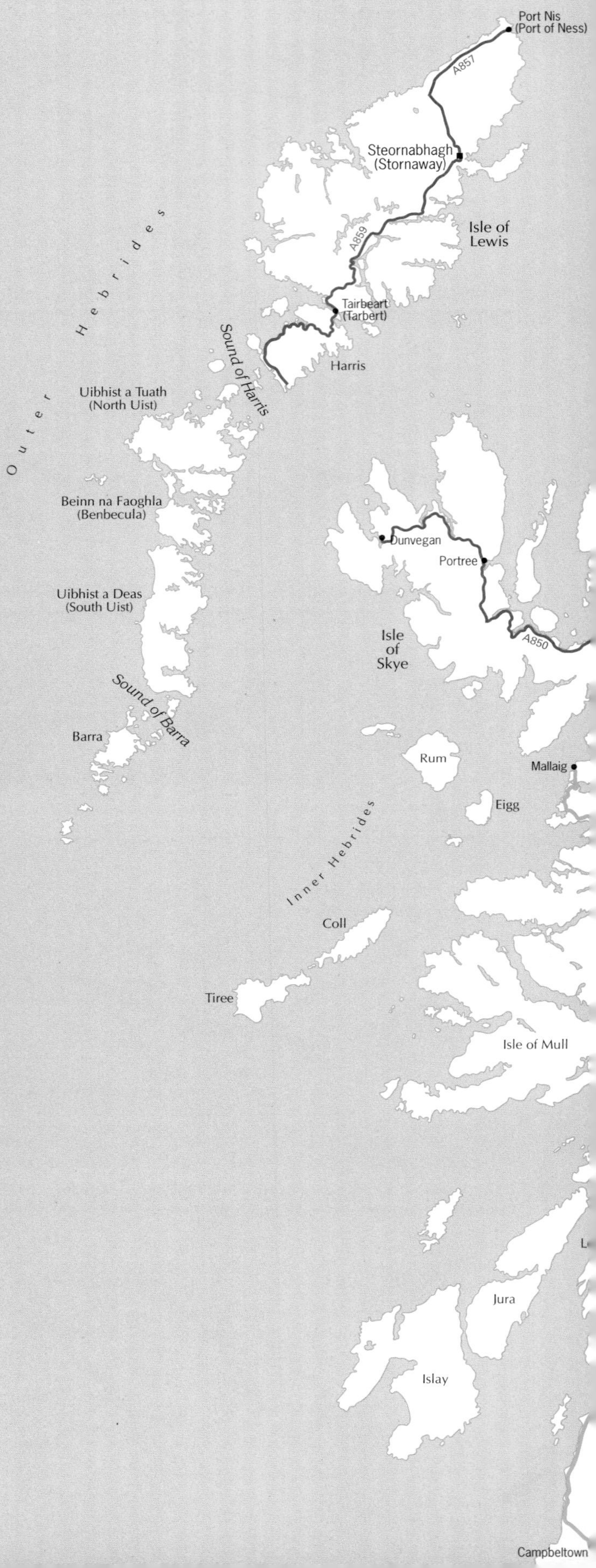

Port Nis (Port of Ness)

A857

Steornabhagh (Stornaway)

Isle of Lewis

A859

Tairbeart (Tarbert)

Harris

Sound of Harris

Outer Hebrides

Uibhist a Tuath (North Uist)

Beinn na Faoghla (Benbecula)

Uibhist a Deas (South Uist)

Sound of Barra

Barra

Dunvegan

Portree

Isle of Skye

A850

Inner Hebrides

Rum

Mallaig

Eigg

Coll

Tiree

Isle of Mull

Jura

Islay

Campbeltown

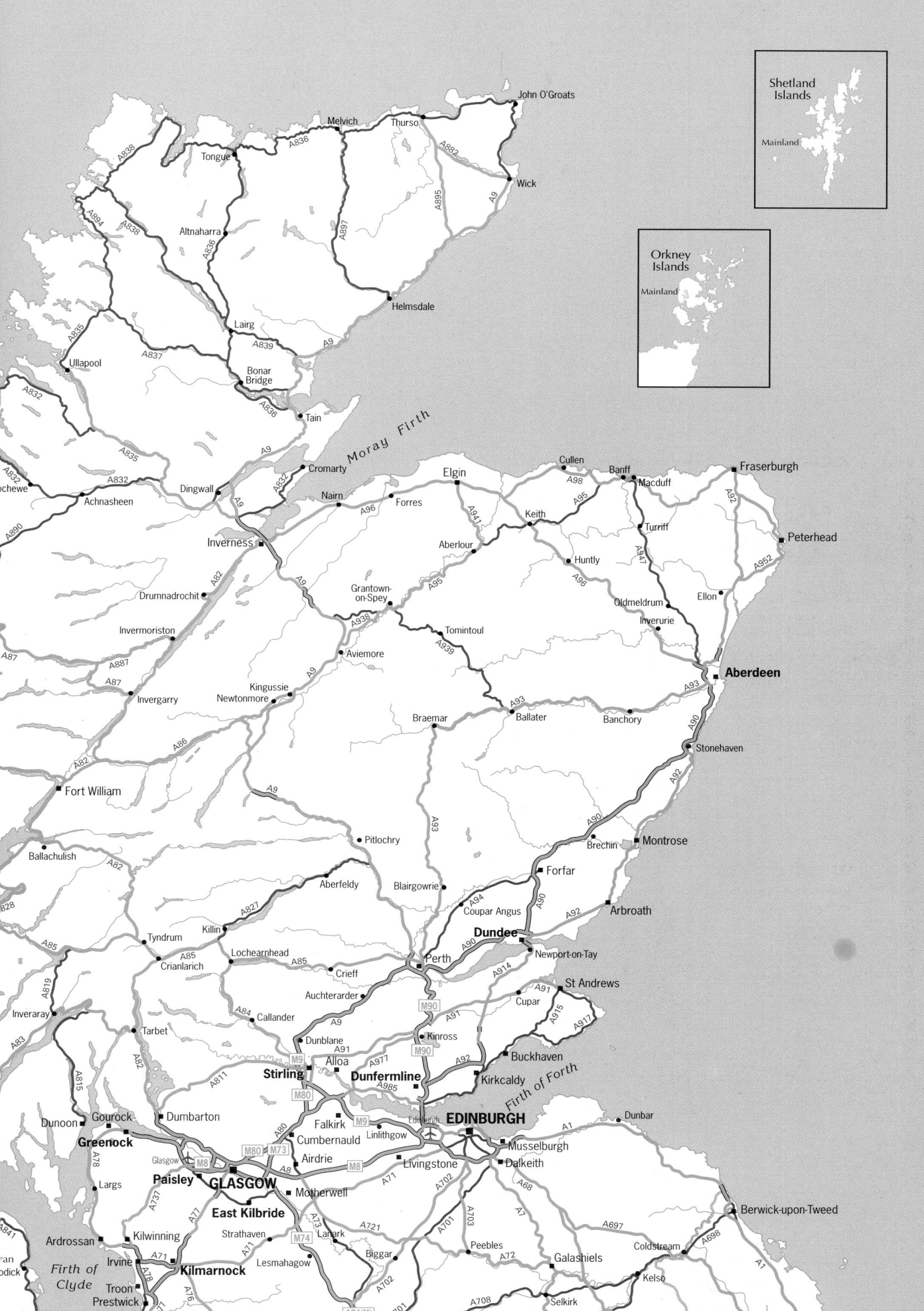

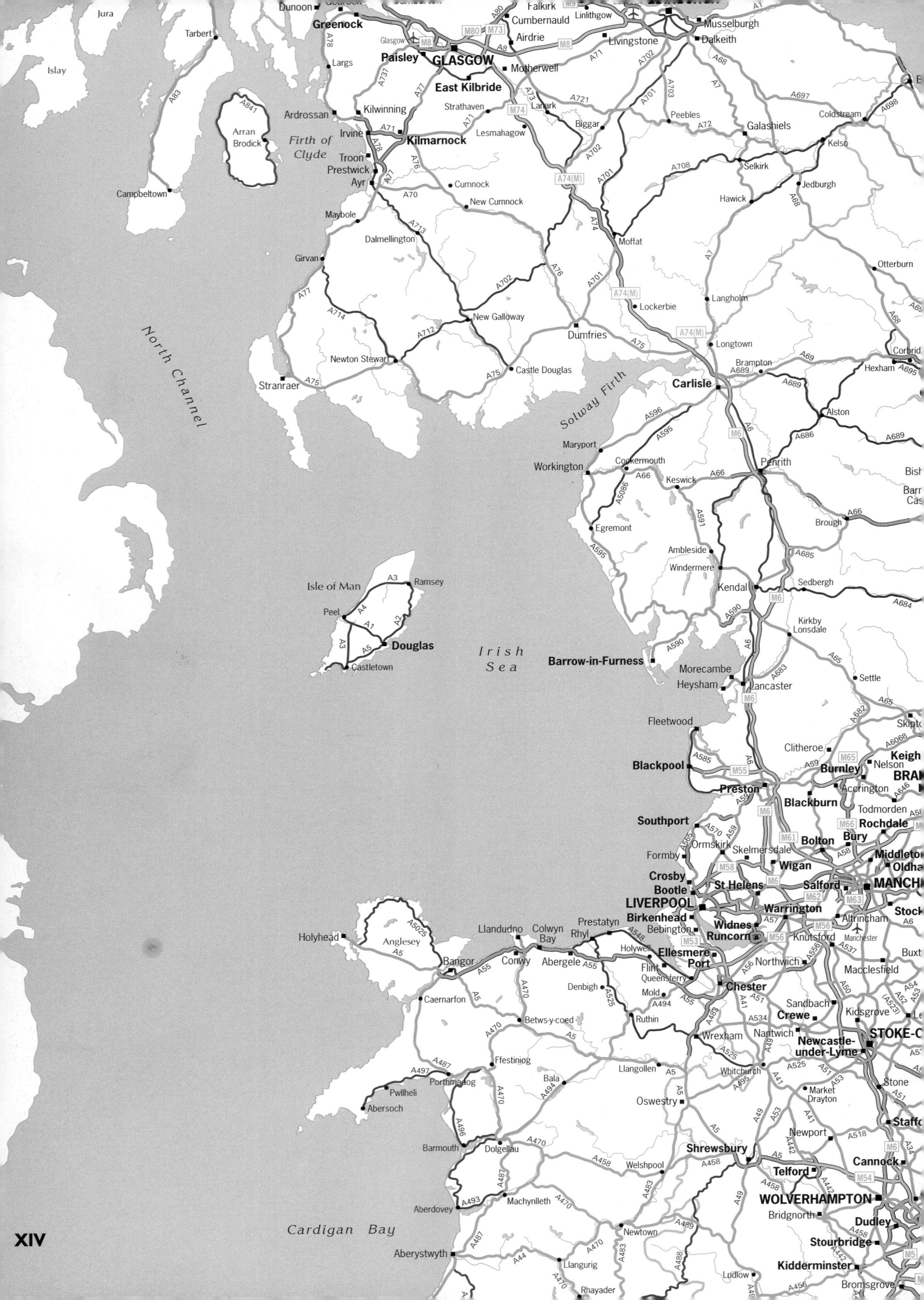

N O R T H

S E A

...eed

...hlington

Whitley Bay
Tynemouth
South Shields
NEWCASTLE UPON TYNE
Jarrow
ey
Sunderland

A19

A1(M)

Spennymoor
Hartlepool
A19
A89
A689
Stockton-on-Tees
Middlesbrough
Darlington
A66
A171
cotch
orner
Whitby
A172

A19
A168
A684 Northallerton
A171
A169
Scalby
Scarborough
Thirsk
A170
A170
A185
Filey
A168
A64
Malton
A166
Bridlington
A61
A19
A166
Driffield
gate
A59
A163
A1079
York
Wetherby
A64
A163
A614
Market Weighton
Beverley
A165
LEEDS
A61
A58
A19
A1
A63
Selby
A63
Hessle
HULL
A645
A63
M62
Goole
Barton-upon-Humber
M62
ry
Wakefield
Pontefract
M18
A15
Immingham
A160
Grimsby
M1
A61
A628
Thorne
Scunthorpe
M180
A18
Cleethorpes
Barnsley
M180
A16
A635
Brigg
A46
Doncaster
A159
A15
Rotherham
Bawtry
Gainsborough
A631
A16
A1031
FFIELD
A1(M)
A631
Market Rasen
Louth
Mablethorpe
nfield
A57
Worksop
A156
A46
M1
Staveley
A619
A1
A158
A16
A52
A619
A614
A57
A158
Chesterfield
Lincoln
Horncastle
A15
A158
Skegness
Mansfield
A617
Alfreton
A6
A38
Newark-on-Trent
A6097
A17
A46
A52
NOTTINGHAM
A1
Sleaford
A17
Boston
The Wash
ourne
Ilkeston
Sheringham
Cromer
A149
RBY
Grantham
A52
Hunstanton
A148
Long Eaton
A52
North Walsham
A6
A453
A606
A607
A15
Spalding
A17
King's Lynn
A148
Fakenham
A140
A149
rton upon Trent
Loughborough
A46
A50
M1
Melton Mowbray
Bourne
A151
A1065
East Dereham
A1067
by-de-Zouch
A1
A16
Wisbech
A10
Swaffham
A47
Norwich
Caister-on-Sea
A42
A50
Oakham
A606
Stamford
A47
A1122
A47
A47
A143
Great Yarmouth
LEICESTER
Wigston
A47
Peterborough
March
Downham Market
A11
A146
Lowestoft
Hinckley
Market Harborough
A6003
A605
A1141
A134
Attleborough
A143
eaton
M1
A5
A6116
Corby
A1
Chatteris
A1065
Bungay
Beccles
XV
HAM
M69
A427
Kettering
A14
A605
Ely
A11
A1066
Diss
A143
Southwold
COVENTRY
M6
A43
A45
Huntingdon
A10
A142
A14
eamington Spa
M45
A14
Bury St Edmunds

map pages

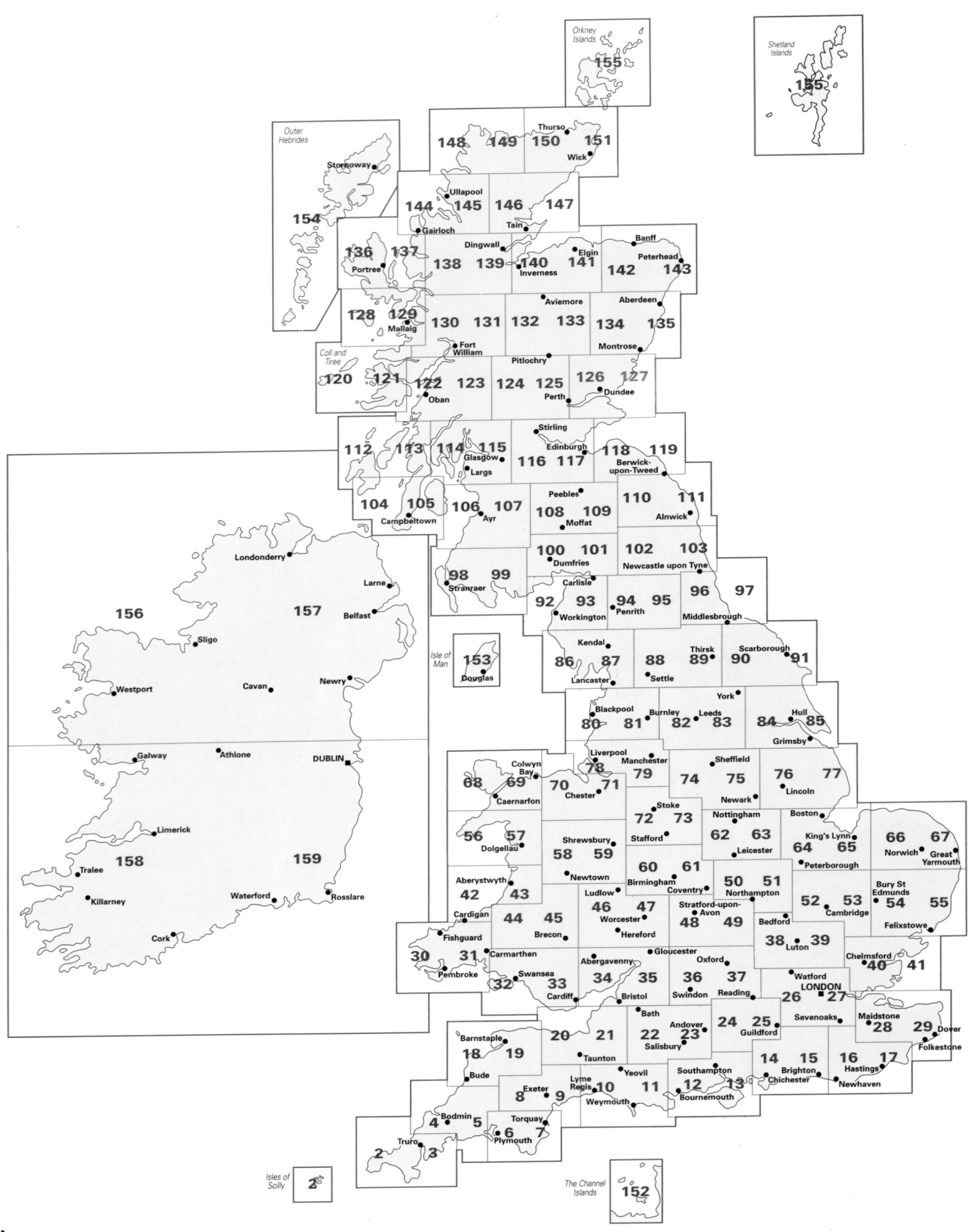

map symbols

motoring information

M4	Motorway with number
11	Motorway junction with and without number
3	Motorway junction with limited access
S Fleet	Motorway service area
	Motorway and junction under construction
A3	Primary route single/dual carriageway
S Oxford	Primary route service area
BATH	Primary route destination
A1123	Other A road single/dual carriageway
B2070	B road single/dual carriageway
	Unclassified road single/dual carriageway
	Roundabout
	Interchange
	Narrow primary, other A or B road with passing places (Scotland)
	Road under construction
	Road tunnel
	Steep gradient (arrows point downhill)
Toll	Road toll
5	Distance in miles between symbols

— V —	Vehicle ferry – Great Britain
BERGEN V	Vehicle ferry – Continental
— H —	Hovercraft ferry
✈	Airport
H	Heliport
	Railway line/in tunnel
	Railway station and level crossing
	Tourist railway
AA	AA Shop
☎	AA telephone
☎	BT telephone in isolated places
	Urban area/village
628 ▲	Spot height in metres
	River, canal, lake
	Sandy beach
	County/regional boundary
	National boundary
85	Page overlap and number

tourist information

i	Tourist Information Centre
i	Tourist Information Centre (seasonal)
	Abbey, cathedral or priory
	Ruined abbey, cathedral or priory
	Castle
	Historic house
M	Museum or art gallery
	Industrial interest
❉	Garden
	Arboretum
	Country park
	Agricultural showground
	Theme park
	Zoo
	Wildlife collection – mammals
	Wildlife collection – birds
	Aquarium
	Nature reserve
RSPB	RSPB site
....	Forest drive
– – – –	National trail
☀	Viewpoint
	Picnic site
	Hill-fort

	Roman antiquity
	Prehistoric monument
✕ 1066	Battle site with year
	Steam centre (railway)
	Cave
	Windmill
	Golf course
	County cricket ground
	Rugby Union national ground
	International athletics ground
	Horse racing
	Show jumping/ equestrian circuit
	Motor racing circuit
	Coastal launching site
	Ski slope – natural
	Ski slope – artificial
NT	National Trust property
NTS	National Trust property Scotland
★	Other places of interest
☐	Boxed symbols indicate attractions within urban areas
	National Park (England & Wales)
	National Scenic Area (Scotland)
	Forest Park
	Heritage Coast

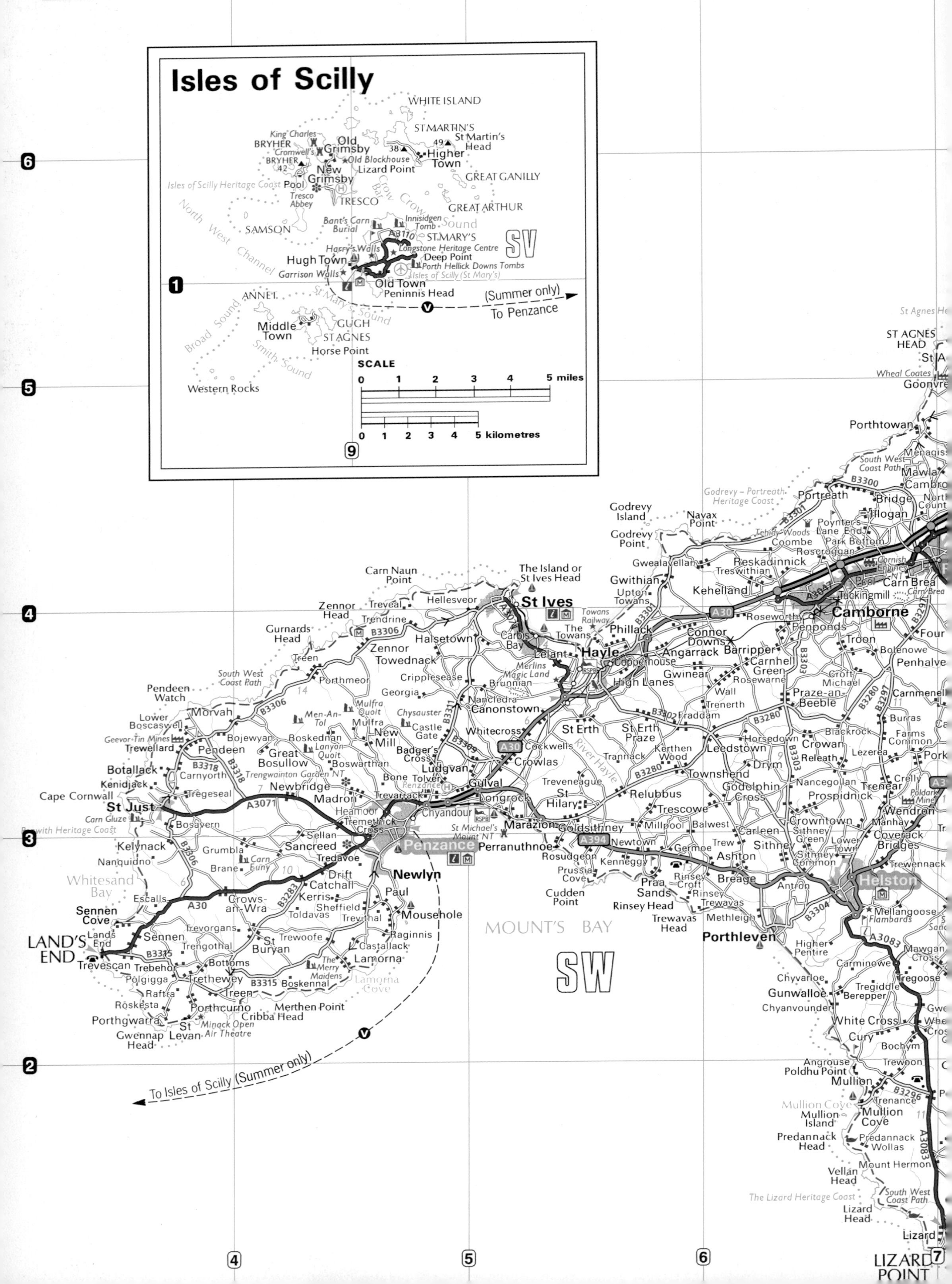

2

Isles of Scilly

WHITE ISLAND

ST MARTIN'S
St Martin's Head

King Charles
BRYHER
Cromwell's
Old Grimsby
38
49
Higher Town
BRYHER
Old Blockhouse
42
New Grimsby
Lizard Point
GREAT GANILLY

Isles of Scilly Heritage Coast
Pool
Tresco Abbey
TRESCO
Crow Crow Sound
GREAT ARTHUR

North West Channel

SAMSON

Bant's Carn Burial
Innisidgen Tomb
B3110
ST. MARY'S
SV

Harry's Walls
Longstone Heritage Centre
Deep Point
Hugh Town
Porth Hellick Downs Tombs
Garrison Walls
Old Town
Isles of Scilly (St Mary's)

ANNET
Peninnis Head
(Summer only)
To Penzance

St Mary's Sound

Middle Town
GUGH
ST AGNES
Horse Point

Broad Sound
Smith Sound

Western Rocks

SCALE

0   1   2   3   4   5 miles

0 1 2 3 4 5 kilometres

9

St Agnes He
ST AGNES HEAD
St A

Wheal Coates
Goonvre

Porthtowan

South West Coast Path
Menagis
Mawla
Cambo
Nort
Coun

Godrevy – Portreath Heritage Coast
B3300
Portreath
Bridge
Illogan

Godrevy Island
Navax Point
B3301
Poynter's
Lane End
Tehidy Woods
Coombe
Roscroggan
Cornish Engines
Pool
Carn Brea
Carn Brea

Godrevy Point
Gwealavellan
Reskadinnick
Tuckingmill
Carn Brea

The Island or St Ives Head
Upton Towans
Gwithian

Carn Naun Point

Kehelland
A30
Roseworthy
Camborne

Zennor Head
Treveal
Hellesveor
St Ives
The Towans
Towans Railway
Phillack
Connor Downs
Penponds

Trendrine
Carbis Bay
Hayle
Angarrack
Barripper
Troon
Four

Gurnards Head
B3306
Halsetown
Leliant
Copperhouse
Carnhell Green
Bolenowe
Penhalve

Zennor Head
Zennor
Towednack
Merlins Magic Land
Brunman
High Lanes
Gwinear
Rosewarne
Croft Michael
Carnmenel

South West Coast Path
Porthmeor
Cripplesease
Nancledra
Canonstown
Wall
Trenerth
Praze-an-Beeble
Burras

14
Georgia
B3302
Fraddam
B3280
Carnmenel

Pendeen Watch
Mulfra Quoit
Chysauster
Whitecross
St Erth
Kerthen Wood
Horsedown
Crowan
Blackrock
Farms Common

Lower Boscaswell
Men-An-Tol
Mulfra
New Mill
Castle Gate
B3311
St Erth Praze
Trannack
Drym
Releath
Lezerea
Pork

Morvah
B3306
Boskednan
Badger's Cross
A30
Cockwells
Crowlas
Leedstown
Townshend
B3280
Crelly
Trenear

Geevor Tin Mines
Bojewyan
Lanyon Quoit
Boswarthan
Bone Tolver
Ludgvan
River Hayle
Trescowe
Nancegollan Cross
Prospidnick
Wendron
Manhay

Trewellard
Pendeen
Great Bosullow
Trengwainton Garden NT
Madron
Gulval
Treveneague
Relubbus
Godolphin Cross
Carleen
Poldark Mine

Botallack
Carnyorth
B3318
7
Newbridge
Trevarrack
Longrock
St Hilary
Millpool
Balwest
Crowntown
Sithney
Green
Trenear

Kenidjack
Tregeseal
Heamoor
Tremethick Cross
Chyandour
Marazion
Goldsithney
Germoe
Lower Sithney Common
Trewennack

Cape Cornwall
A3071
St Michael's Mount NT
Penzance
Perranuthnoe
A394
Newtown
Trew
Ashton
Helston

St Just
Carn Gluze
Bosavern
Sancreed
Rosudgeon
Kenneggy
Breage
Antron
B3304

Tinners Heritage Coast
Kelynack
Grumbla
Tredavoe
Newlyn
Prussia Cove
Praa Sands
Rinsey
Trewavas
Methleigh
Mellangoose
Flambards

Nanquidno
Brane
Carn Euny
Drift
Catchall
Paul
Cudden Point
Rinsey Head
Trewavas Head
Porthleven
A3083

Whitesand Bay
Escalls
A30
Crows-an-Wra
Kerris
Mousehole
MOUNT'S BAY
Higher Pentire
Mawgan Cross

Sennen Cove
Sellan
Sheffield
Trevithal
SW
Carminowe
Tregoose

LAND'S END
Land's End
Sennen
Trevorgans
Toldavas
Raginnis
Chyvarloe
Tregiddle
Berepper
Gwe

Trevescan
Trebeho
Trengothal
St Buryan
Castallack
Lamorna
Gunwalloe
White Cross
Whe
Cros

Polgigga
Trethewey
Bottoms
Trewoofe
The Merry Maidens
Lamorna Cove
Chyanvounder
Cury

Raftra
Treen
Boskennal
B3315
Bochym

Roskesta
Porthcurno
Merthen Point
Minack Open Air Theatre
Cribba Head
Trewoon

Porthgwarra
St Levan
Angrouse
Poldhu Point
Mullion

Gwennap Head
Predannack Wollas
B3296
Mullion Island
Mullion Cove

To Isles of Scilly (Summer only)

Mullion Cove
Predannack Head
Mount Hermon

Vellan Head
The Lizard Heritage Coast
South West Coast Path
Lizard Head
Lizard

LIZARD POINT
7

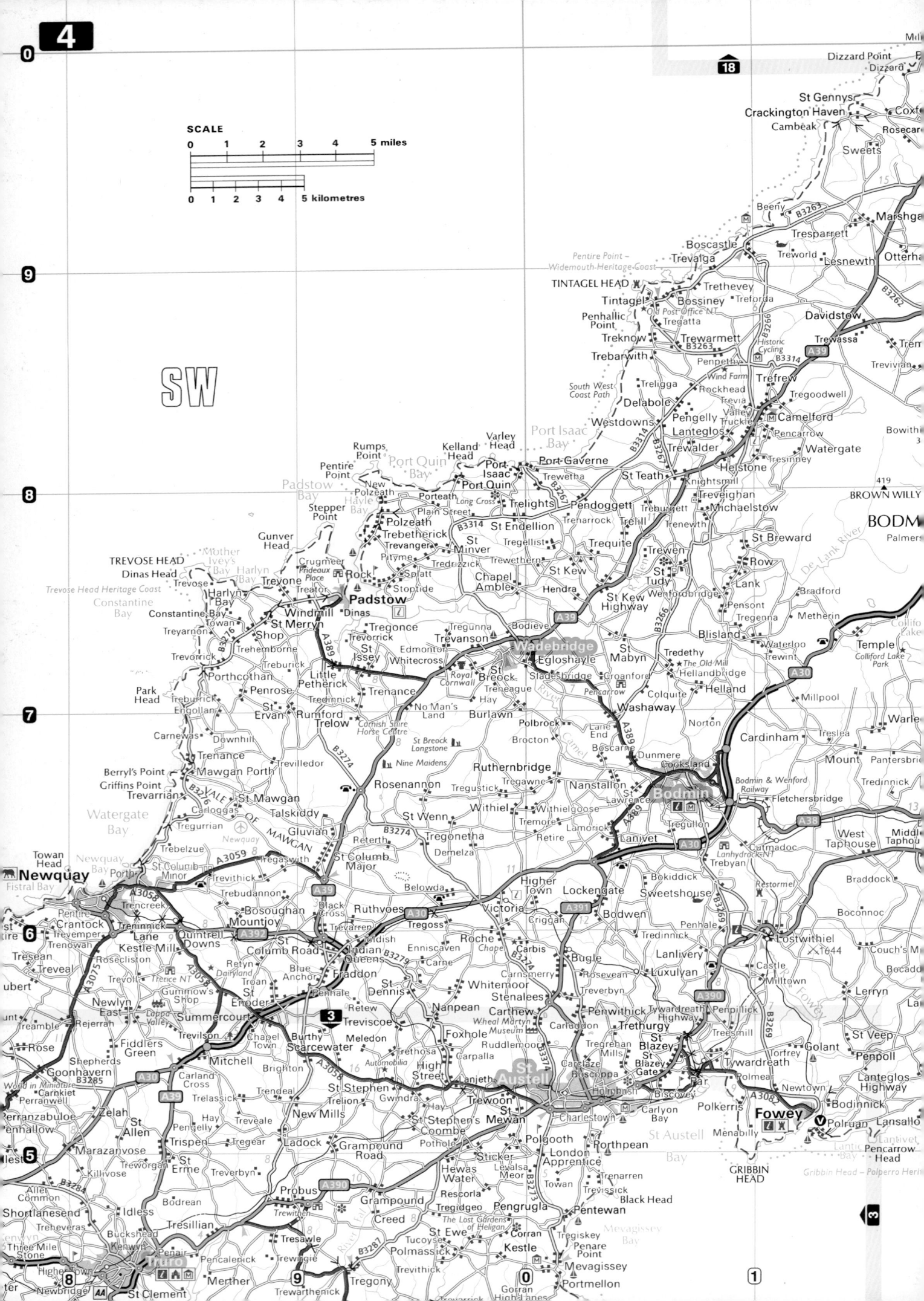

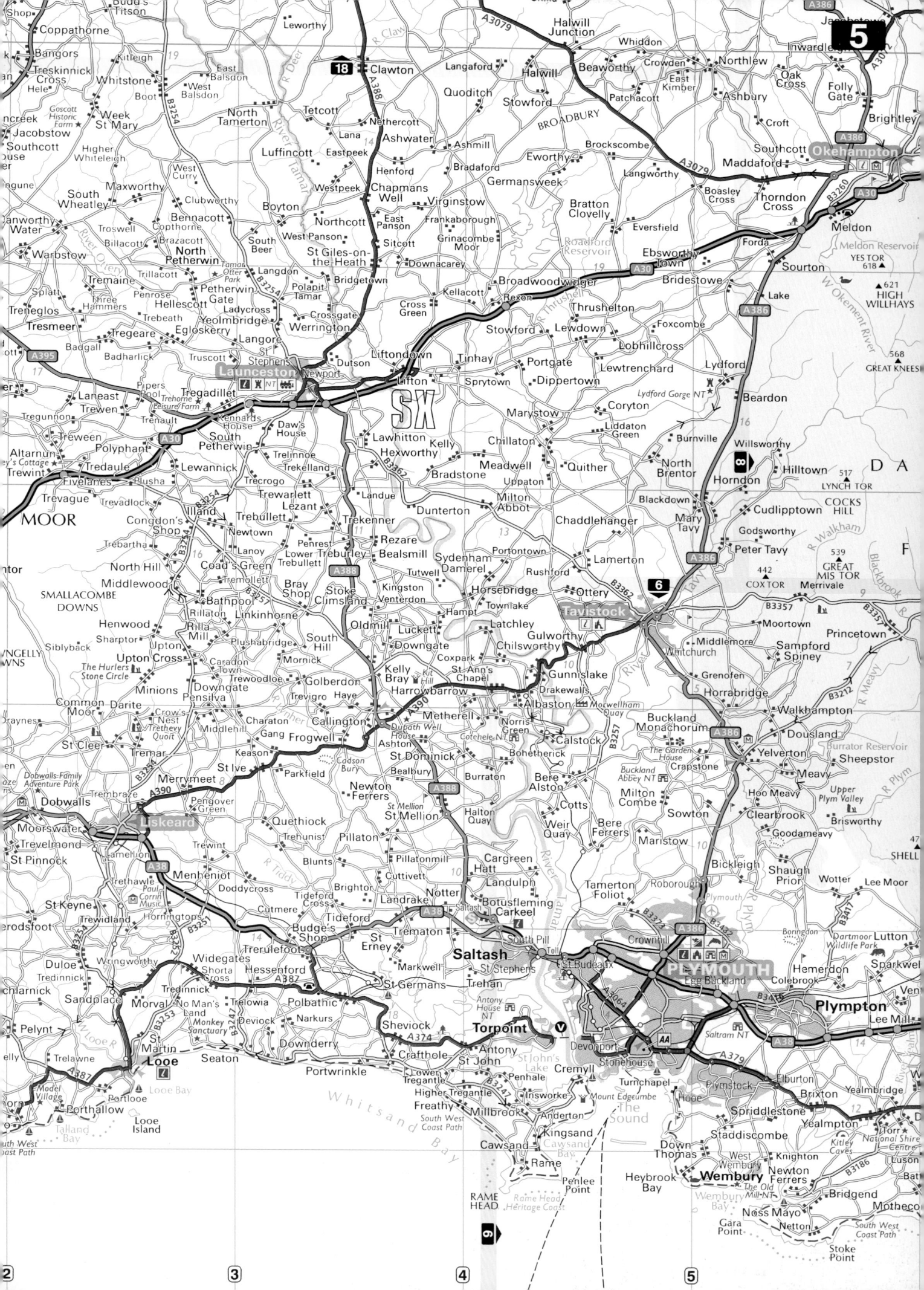

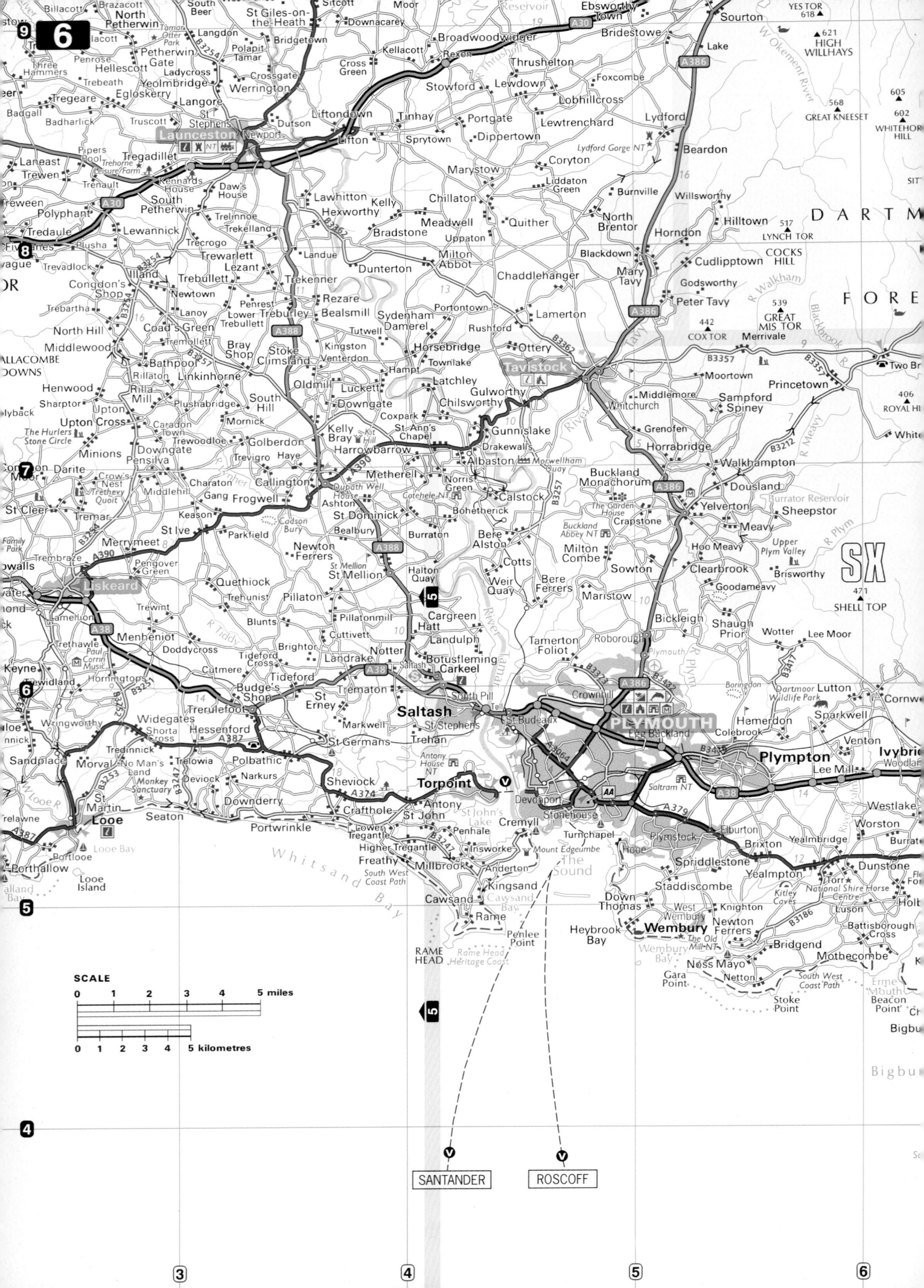

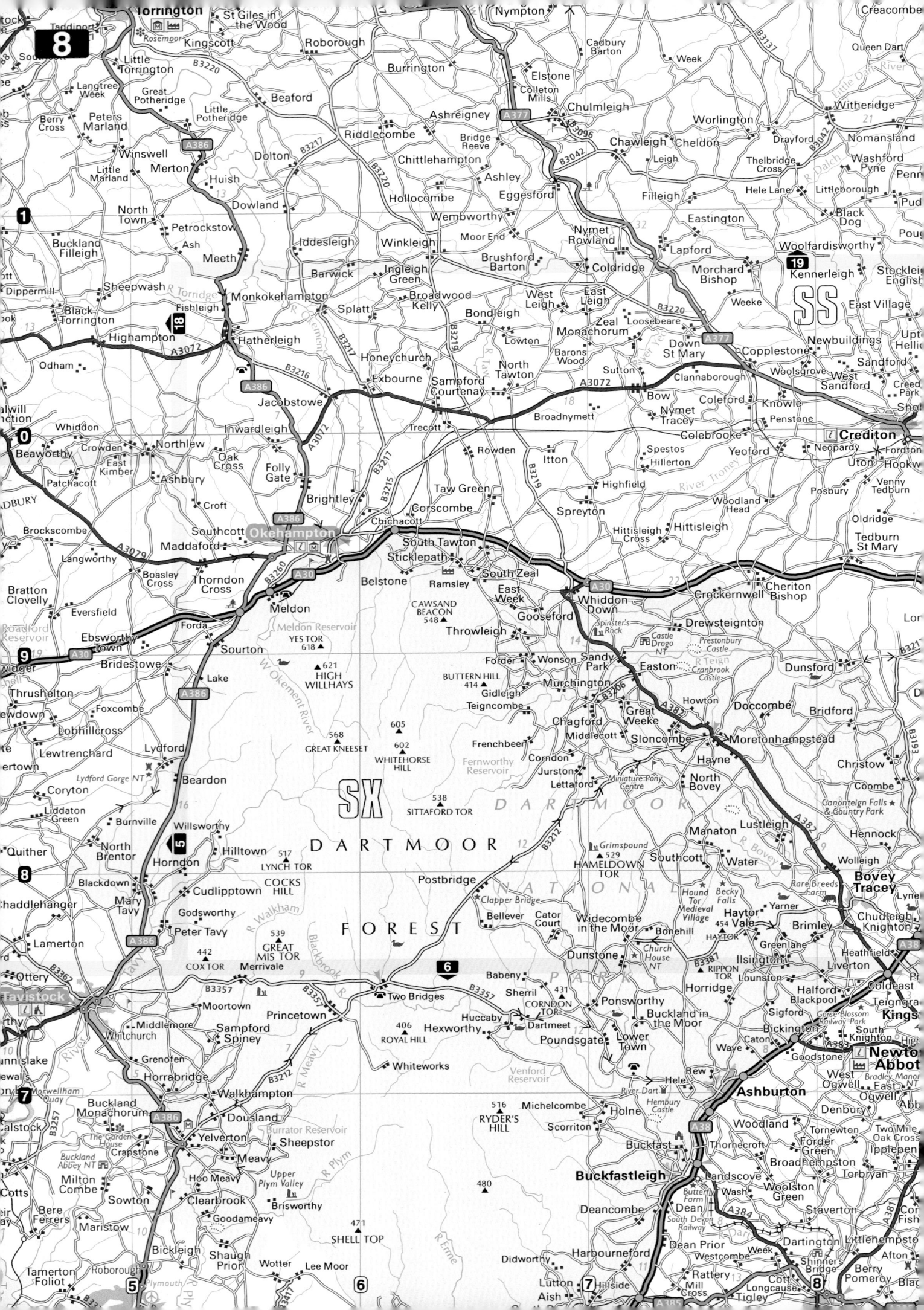

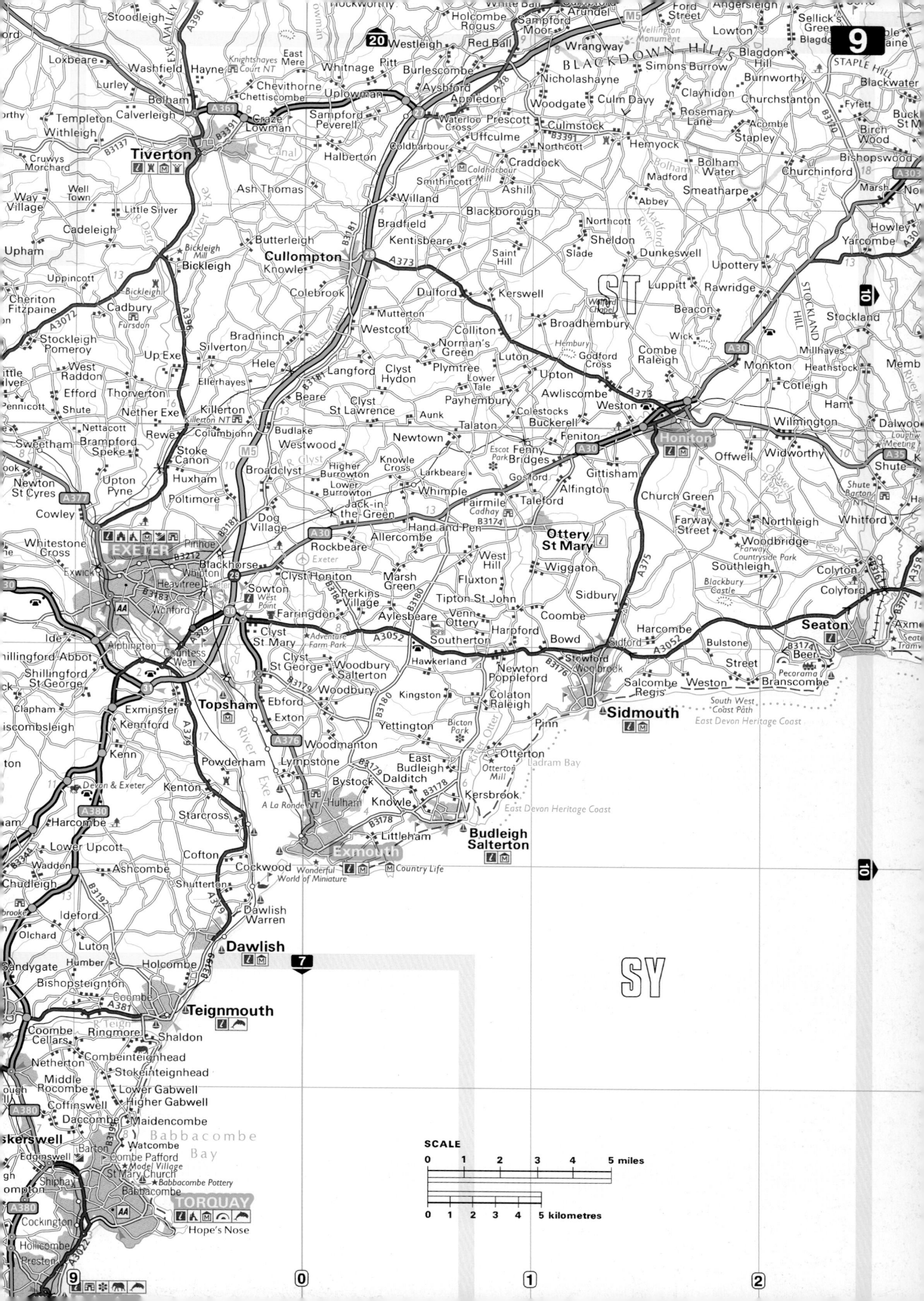

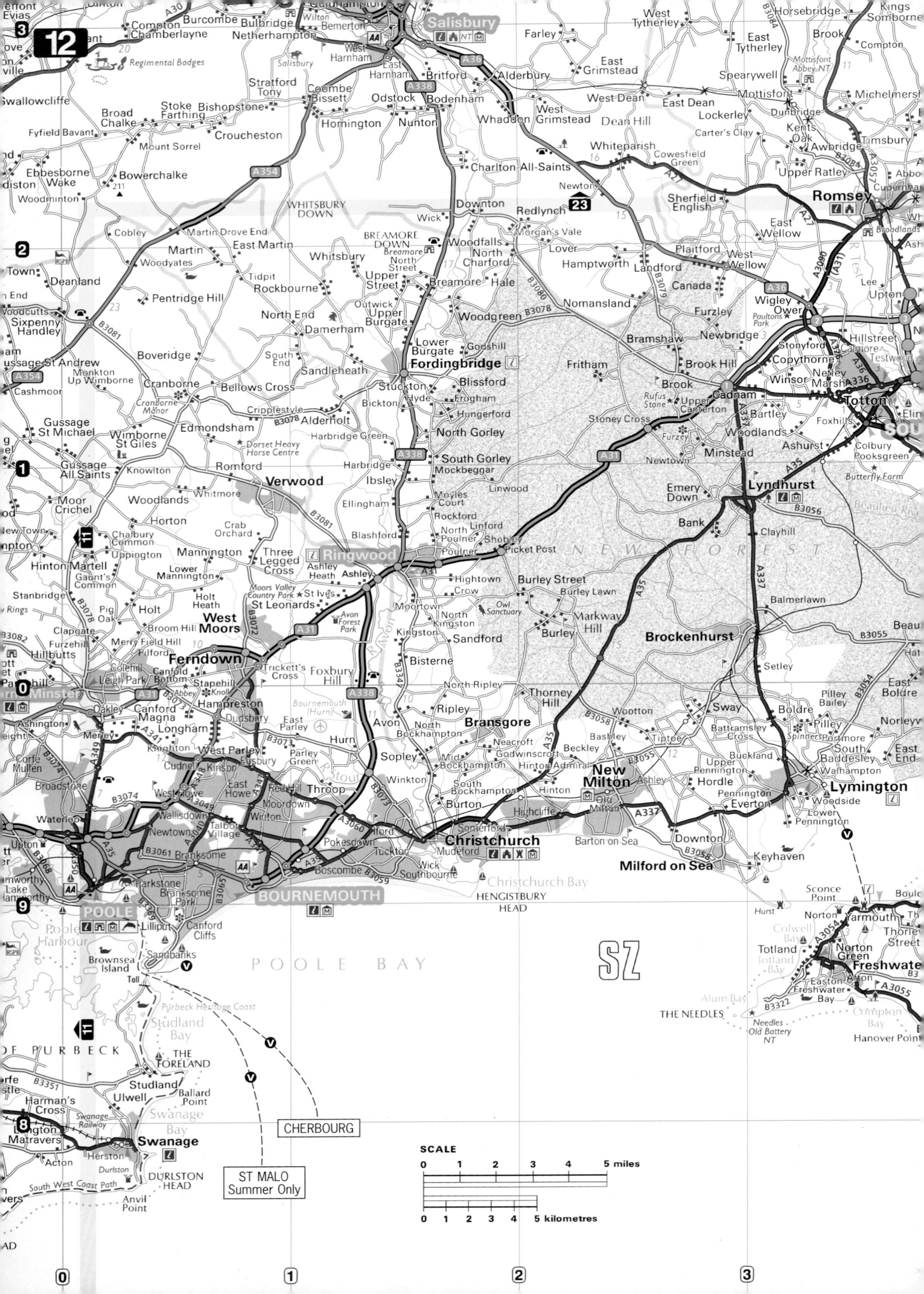

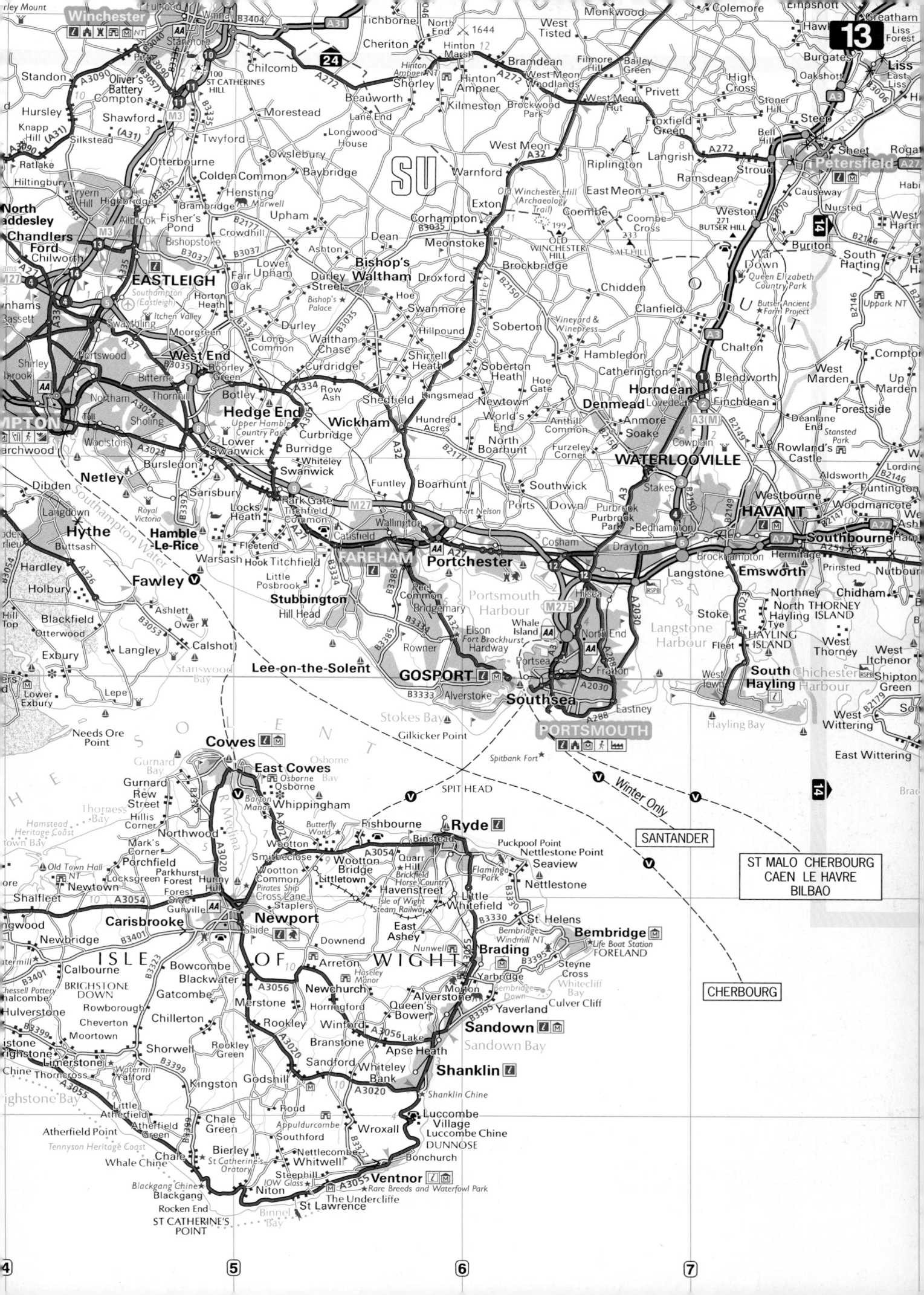

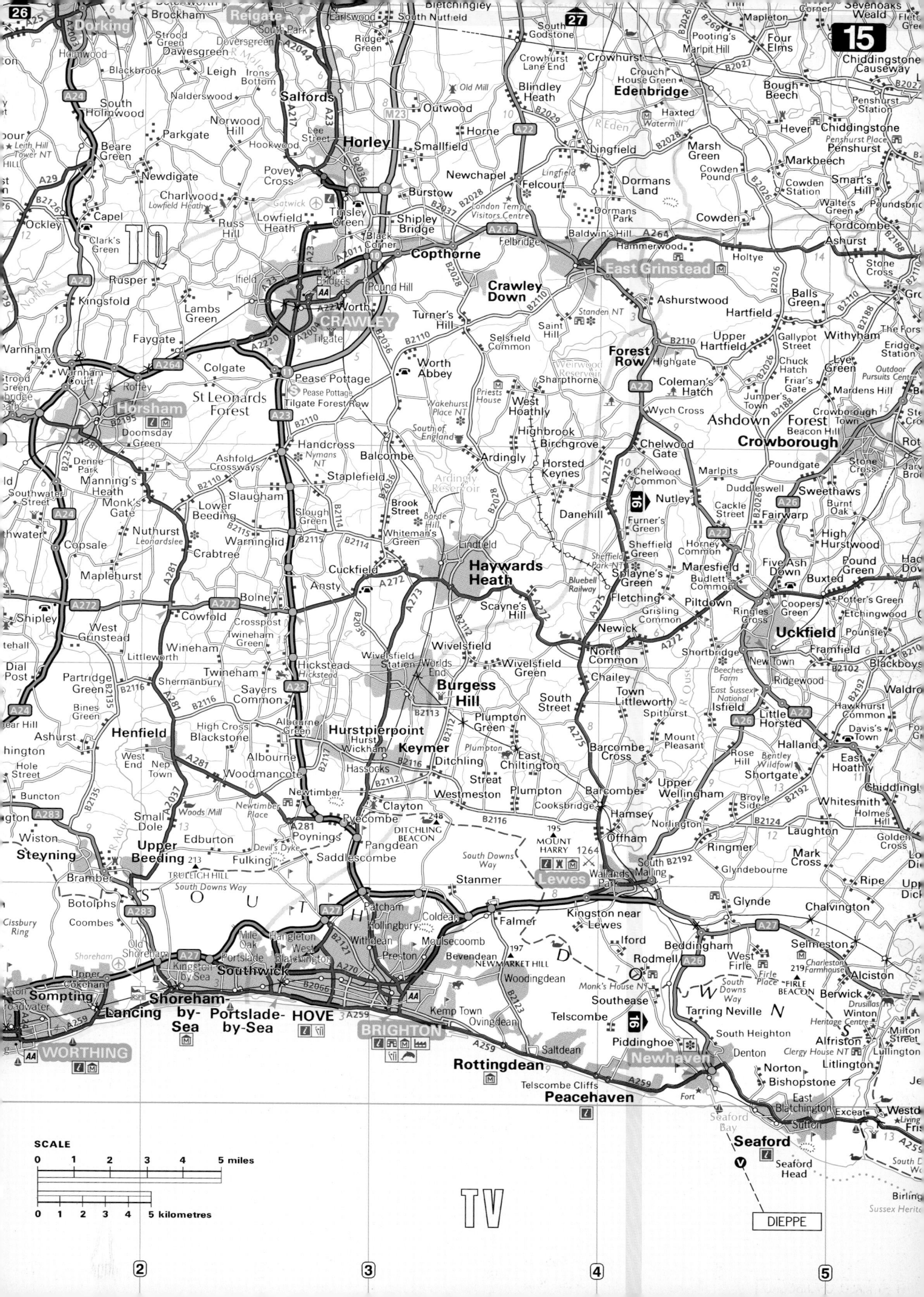

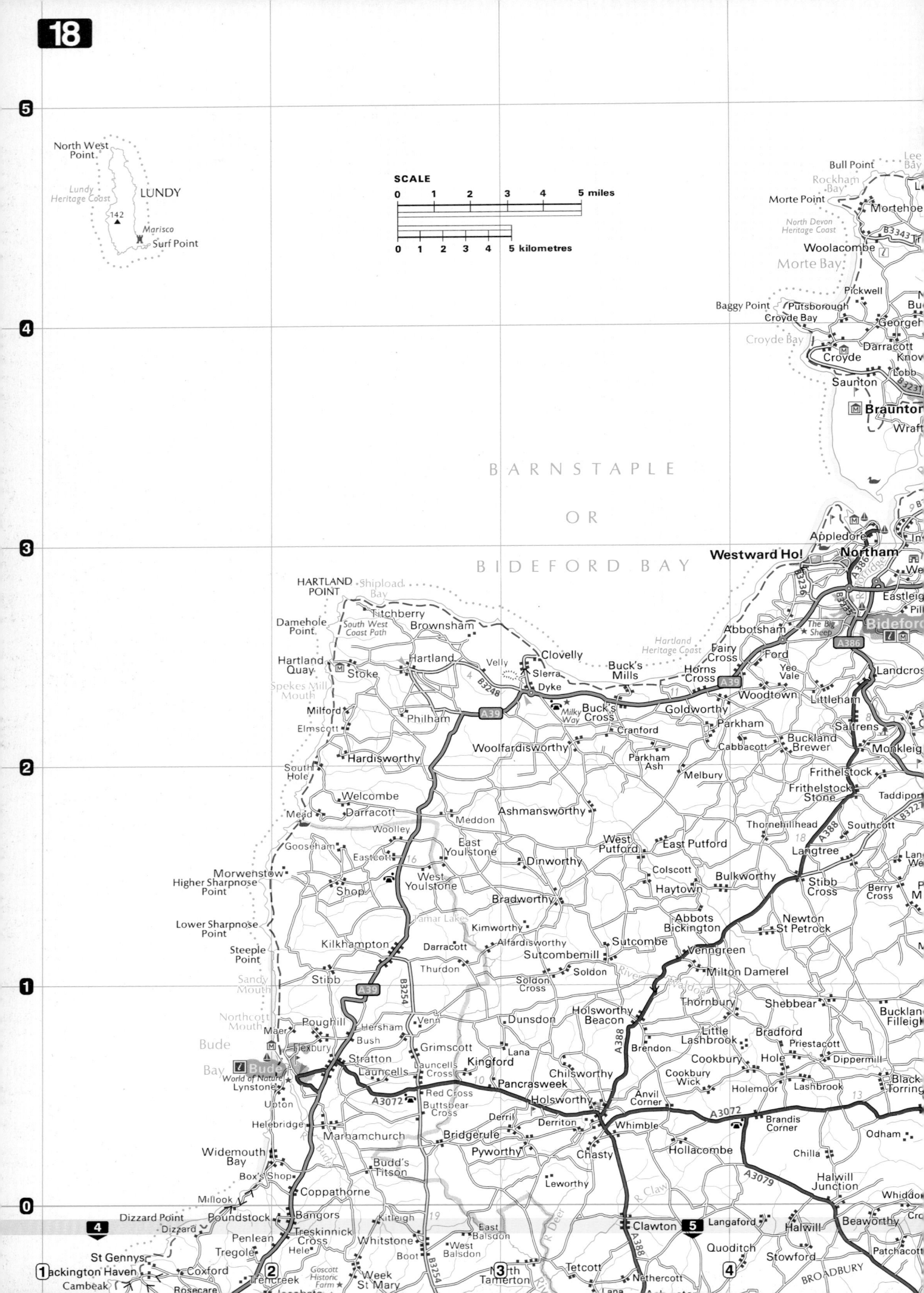

SS

EXMOOR FOREST

EXMOOR

NATIONAL PARK

Foreland Point
Lynmouth Bay
Countisbury Cove
Woody Bay
Lynton
Brass Rubbing Centre
Countisbury
Exmoor Heritage Coast
Hurtstone Point
Porlock Bay
Bossington
Lynch

Combe Martin Bay
Water Mouth
Combe Martin
Watermouth
Hele Bay
Elwill Bay
Martinhoe
Trentishoe
Hunter's Inn
Woody Bay
Lynbridge
Dean
Toll
West Lyn
Wilsham
Barbrook
Brendon
Rockford
Watersmeet House NT
Tippacott
Malmsmead
Oare
Culbone
Porlock Weir
West Porlock
Porlock
Lyn

Hele
Haggington Hill
Hele Mill
Combe Martin
Kemacott
Heale
Killington
West Ilkerton
East Ilkerton
Cheriton
Lucott
Horner
Luccomb

Chambercombe Manor
Sterridge
Berrynarbor
Ruggaton
Bodstone Barton Farm Park
Dean
Parracombe
Woolhanger
Furzehill
HOAROAK HILL 474
DRY HILL 444
DUNKERY HILL
519

Two Pots
Mullacott Cross
A3123
Berry Down Cross
Patchole
Kentisbury
Kentisbury Ford
Churchtown
River Exe
410
Edgcott
Exford
Luckwell Bridge
Gre Nurc

West Down
Bittadon
Churchill
East Down
Arlington Beccott
Stowford
Wistlandpound Reservoir
Swincombe
Challacombe
B3358
Simonsbath
B3223
Newland
Blackland
WINSFORD HILL

Halsinger
Higher Muddiford
Milltown
Muddiford
Upcott
Arlington
Arlington Court NT
Exmoor Bird Gardens
Knightacott
Barton Town
Leworthy
SPAN HEAD 493
Whitefield
Withypool
Winsford
Wee

Marwood
Pippacott
Guineaford
Kingsheanton
Prixford
Shirwell
Shirwell Cross
Loxhore
Loxhore Cott
Lower Loxhore
Bratton Fleming
Benton
Fullaford
Lydcott
Kinsford Water
WORTH HILL
Knaplock
Liscombe
Tarr

Heanton Punchardon
Ashford
Bradiford
Pilton
Burridge
Northleigh
Goodleigh
Willesleigh
Gunn
Stoke Rivers
Brayford
High Bray
Bentwichen
North Radworthy
Tarr Steps
Hawkridge
H Co

Barnstaple
Derby
Newport
Bickington
Lake
Landkey Town
Bishop's Tawton
Bradninch
Accott
Whitsford
Charles
Stoodleigh
North Heasley
Heasley Mill
South Radworthy
Twitchen
Northmoor
Dulverton

St John's Chapel
Horsacott
Tawstock
Landkey
Swimbridge Newland
West Buckland
Yarnacott
Elwell
East Buckland
Bremridge
North Molton
Upcott
Molland
Slade
West Anstey
East Anstey
Battleto

Hannaford
Kerscott
Swimbridge
Castle Hill
South Molton
Aller
Bish Mill
Newtown
Radley
Bishop's Nympton
Ash Mill
Knowstone
Oldways End
Sowerhill
Nightcott
Ex

Harracott
Herner
Cobbaton
East Stowford
Filleigh
Quince Honey Farm
B3227
Crooked Oak
Yeo Mill
East Knowstone
Roachill
Oakfordbrid

Newton Tracey
Hiscott
Ensis
Week
Chapelton
A377
Chittlehampton
Clapworthy
George Nympton
Alswear
Mariansleigh
Yard
Rose Ash
Knowstone
Oakford
Westcott

Delley
Yarnscombe
Atherington
Umberleigh
Warkleigh
Satterleigh
Romansleigh
Meshaw
A361
Creacombe
Rackenford
Loxbeare

Huntshaw Cross
Langridge Ford
B3227
High Bickington
Chittlehamholt
King's Nympton
Cadbury Barton
Week
Queen Dart
Witheridge
Edgeworthy
Templeto
Withleigh

Great Torrington
High Bullen
Dodscott
St Giles in the Wood
Kingscott
Roborough
Burrington
Elstone
Colleton Mills
Chulmleigh
Worlington
Cheldon
Drayford
Nomansland
Pennymoor
Way Village
Well Town
Cruwys Morchard
Cadelei

Rosemoor
Beaford
Riddlecombe
Ashreigney
Chittlehampton
Bridge Reeve
A377
B3096
Chawleigh
Leigh
Thelbridge Cross
Washford Pyne
Littleborough
Puddington
Poughill
Upham

A386
Little Potheridge
Dolton
Hollocombe
Ashley
Eggesford
B3042
Filleigh
Eastington
Hele Lane
Black Dog

Merton
Huish
Dowland
Wembworthy
Nymet Rowland
Lapford
Woolfardisworthy
Kennerleigh
Stockleigh English
East Village
Cheriton Fitzpaine
Uppincott

Petrockstow
Ash
Meeth
Iddesleigh
Winkleigh
Moor End
Brushford Barton
Coldridge
Morchard Bishop
Weeke
Stockleigh Pomeroy
West Raddon
Efford

Fishleigh
Monkokehampton
Barwick
Ingleigh Green
Broadwood Kelly
West Leigh
East Leigh
Zeal Monachorum
Looseleare
Down St Mary
Newbuildings
Sandford
Lower Creedy
Chilton
Little Silver

Hatherleigh
Splatt
Bondleigh
Lowton
Barons Wood
Sutton
Clannaborough
Bow Nymet Tracy
Coleford
Knowle
Penstone
Woolsgrove
West Sandford
Creedy Park
Shobrooke
Pennicott
Shute

Jacobstowe
Honeychurch
North Tawton
A3072
Coldridge
Golebrooke
Crediton
Uton
Hookway
Wyke
Smallbrook
Bran

Inwardleigh
Northlew
Oak Cross
Ashbury
Croft
Folly Gate
Exbourne
Sampford Courtenay
Trecott
Rowden
Itton
Taw Green
Highfield
Hillerton
Spestos
Yeoford
Neopardy
Fordton
Venny Tedburn
Sweetham
Netta
Newton St Cyres

Brightley
Corscombe
Spreyton
Woodland Head

SX
A386
A3072

River Taw
River Bray
River Mole
River Yeo
River Troney
R Torridge
R Okement
R Dalch
Little Dart River

MARGATE
Foreness Point
B2051
Cliftonville Kingsate
Westgate on Sea
Westbrook Northdown
NORTH FORELAND
Minnis Bay
Birchington
Dent-de-Lion
Garling
Reading Street
St Peter's
Westwood
Broadstairs
Dumpton
Hereson
Ramsgate
OOSTENDE
DUNKERQUE

Herne Bay
Bishopstone
Reculver
Potten Street
Brooks End
Hampton
Beltinge
Hillborough
A28
ISLE OF THANET
Salmestone Grange
Haine
Manston
Whitstable
Tankerton
Swalecliffe
B2205
Greenhill
Eddington
Broomfield
Highstead
St Nicholas at Wade
Acol
A299
A28
Whitstable Bay
Chestfield
Bullockstone
Herne
Boyden Gate
Sarre
Gore Street
Monkton
A253
Manston
St Lawrence
Seasalter
South Street
Herne Common
Brambles
Maypole
Hoath
Chislet
A28
Hoo
Durlock
Cliffsend
Way
Viking Ship 'Hugin'
Pegwell
Yorkletts
Highstreet
Dargate
Honey Hill
Tyler Hill
Upstreet
West Stourmouth
Plucks Gutter
Minster
St Augustine's Cross
Pegwell Bay
Hernhill
Denstroude
Broad Oak
Westbee
Hersden
East Stourmouth
Westmarsh
Paramour Street
Richborough
Blean
Staplestreet
Calcott
Sturry
Grove
Preston Street
Goldstone
Cop Street
Cooper St
Great Stonar
Sandwich Bay
Dunkirk
Upper Harbledown
Hales Place
Fordwich
Stodmarsh
Preston
Hoaden
Weddington
Royal St George's
Hickmans Green
uth Street
A2050
Wickhambreaux
Littlebourne
Seaton
Ickham
Hoaden
Guilton
Ash
A257
versland
Harbledown
AA
Canterbury
Thanington
Howletts
Bekesbourne Hill
Shatterling
Wingham
Durlock
Marshborough
Stone Cross
Woodnesborough
Sandwich
Chartham Hatch
Bramling
Staple
Barnsole
Worth
ives
Chartham
A2
Bekesbourne
Goodnestone
Eastry
Statenborough
Ham
Hacklinge
Shalmsford Street
Bridge
Patrixbourne
Adisham
TR
Ratling
Chillenden
Heronden
Fingelsham
Marley
A258
Mountain Street
A28
Garlinge Green
Nackington Street End
Bishopsbourne
North Downs Way
B2046
Nonington
Knowlton
Bettshanger
Sholden
The Downs
Petham
Lower Hardres
Pett Bottom
Easole Street
Northbourne
Upper Deal
Deal
A28
Sole Street
Anvil Green
Kingston
Out Elmstead
Aylesham
Holt St
Elvington
Great Mongham
Little Mongham
Walmer
Crundale
Whiteacre
Waltham
Marley
Barham
Womenswold
Frogham
Lower Eythorne
Sutton
Ripple
Ringwould
Pet Street
Hassell Street
North Leigh
Derringstone
Woolage Village
A2
Eythorne
Ashley
East Studdal
Sutton Downs
Martin
Kingsdown
Bodsham Green
Hastingleigh
Elmsted Court
Stelling Minnis
Breach
Woolage Green
Barfrestone
Shepherdswell
Coldred
West Langdon
St Margarets Bay
West Brabourne
Whatsole Street
Maxted St
Bladbean
Denton
Rural Heritage Centre
Geddinge
Wootton
Whitfield
East Langdon
A256
A258
Six Mile Cottages
Wheelbarrow Town
North Elham
Selsted
Lydden
Temple Ewell
Guston
West Cliffe
St Margaret's at Cliffe
Brabourne
Lymbridge Green
Exted
Swingfield Street
Ewell Minnis
Kearsney
River
A2
South Foreland Heritage Coast
SOUTH FORELAND
Brabourne Lees
Stowting Common
Stowting
Rhodes Minnis
Elham
Swingfield Minnis
Alkham
Chilton
Wolverton
Buckland
A256
South Foreland Lighthouse NT
Smeeth
Monks Horton
Ottinge
Ridge Row
Densole
Upper Standen
South Alkham
St Radigund's
Maxton
DOVER
CALAIS
M20
Moorstock
Postling
Lyminge
Newbarn
Paddlesworth
Hawkinge
Drellingore
West Hougham
Farthingloe
A20
B2011
Stonestreet Green
Sellindge
Stanford
Newington
Peene
Lower Standen
Capel le Ferne
Satmar
H
Aldington
Westenhanger
Folkestone
Pedlinge
Newingreen
Lympne
Cheriton
Morehall
A2011
Dover-Folkestone Heritage Coast
CALAIS
Channel Tunnel Terminal
Eurotunnel Exhibition Centre
Brockhill
Horn St
11A
FOLKESTONE
East Wear Bay
Court-at-Street
Port Lympne Sanctuary
Botolph's Bridge
Lympne
B61
Saltwood
Seabrook
Sandgate
AA
A2067
West Hythe
Donkey Street
Hythe
BOULOGNE
Burmarsh
A259
Romney, Hythe & Dymchurch Railway
Dymchurch
Martello Tower
St Mary's Bay
B2071
Littlestone-on-Sea
Greatstone-on-Sea
ney

SCALE
0 1 2 3 4 5 miles
0 1 2 3 4 5 kilometres

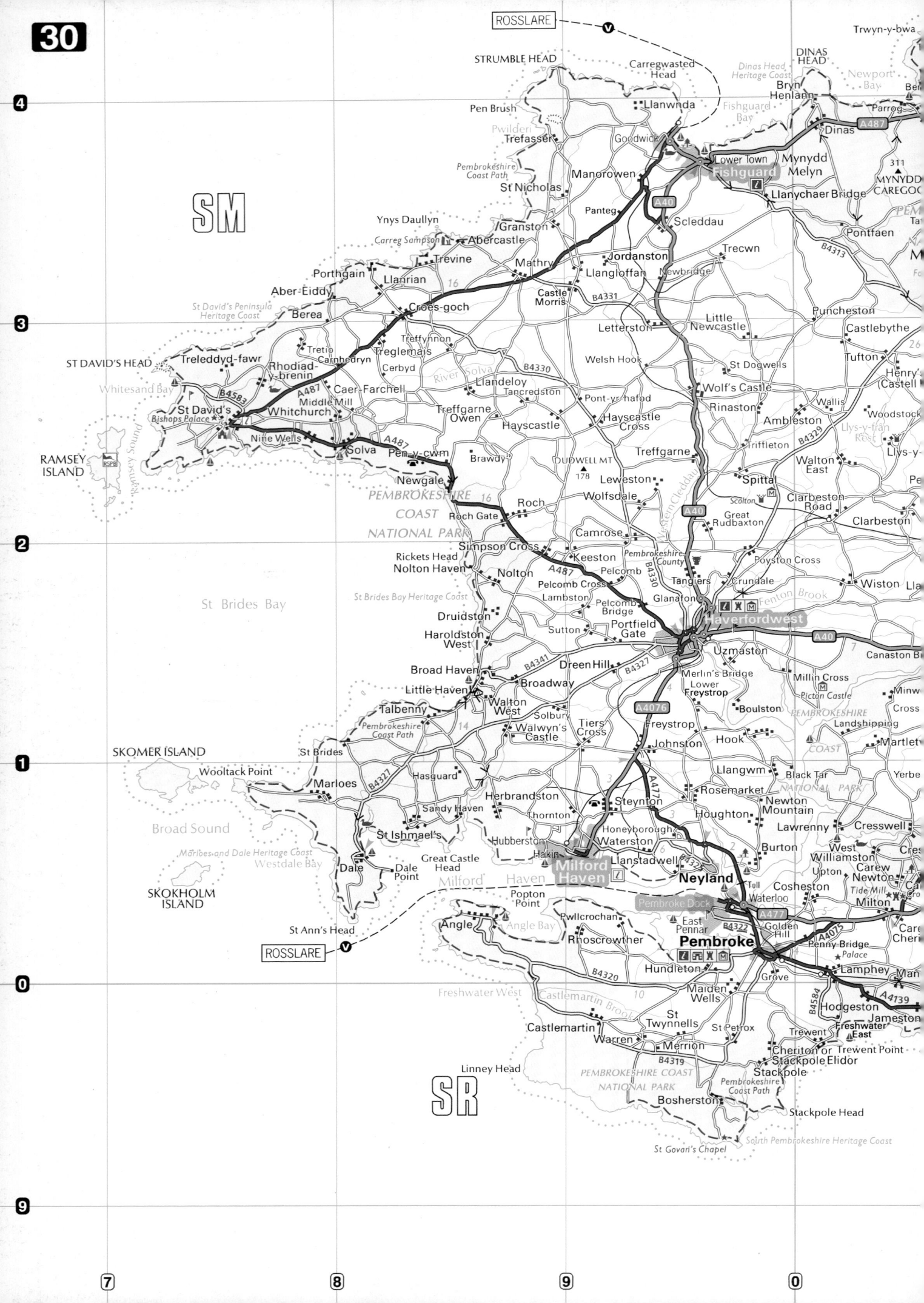

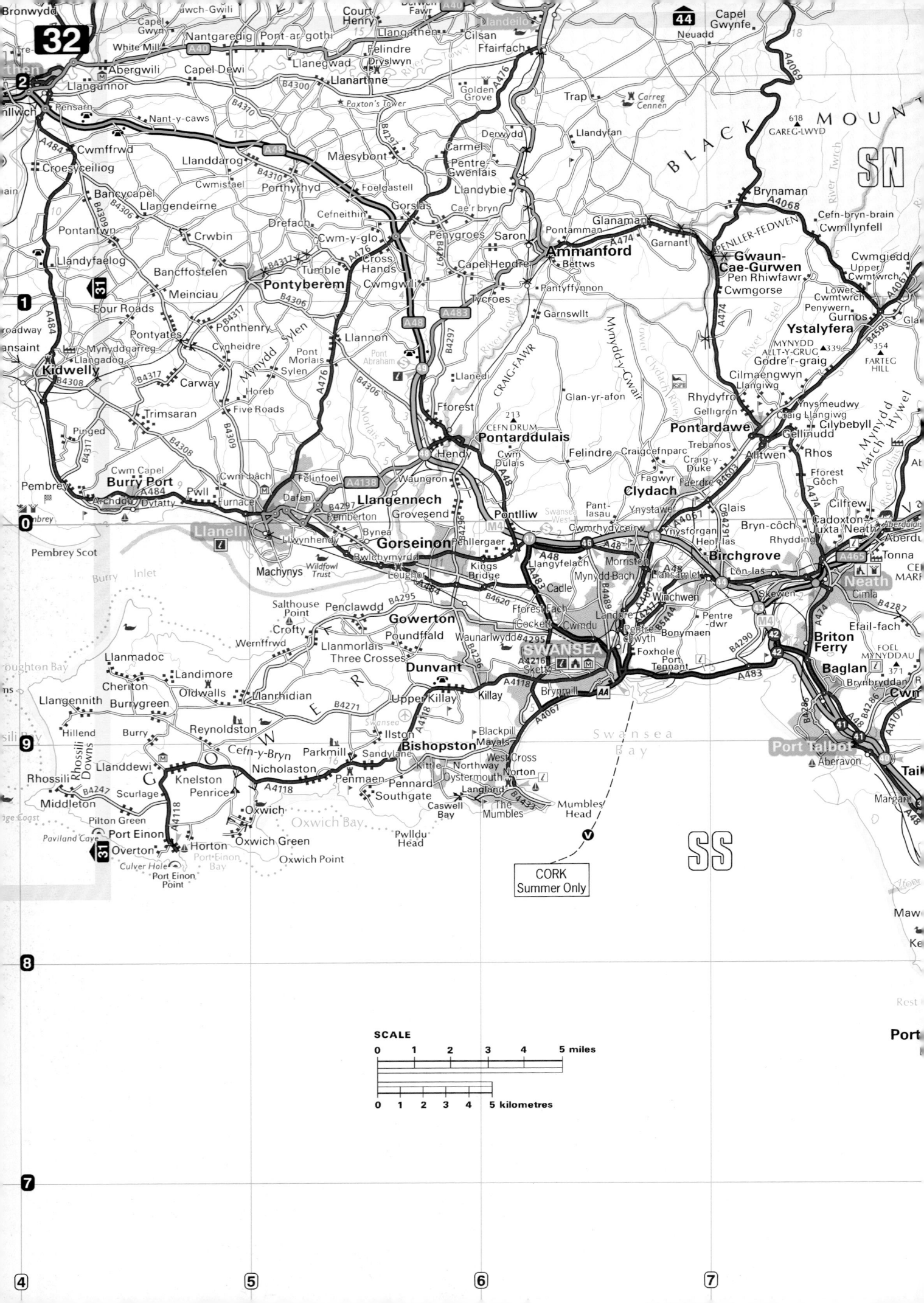

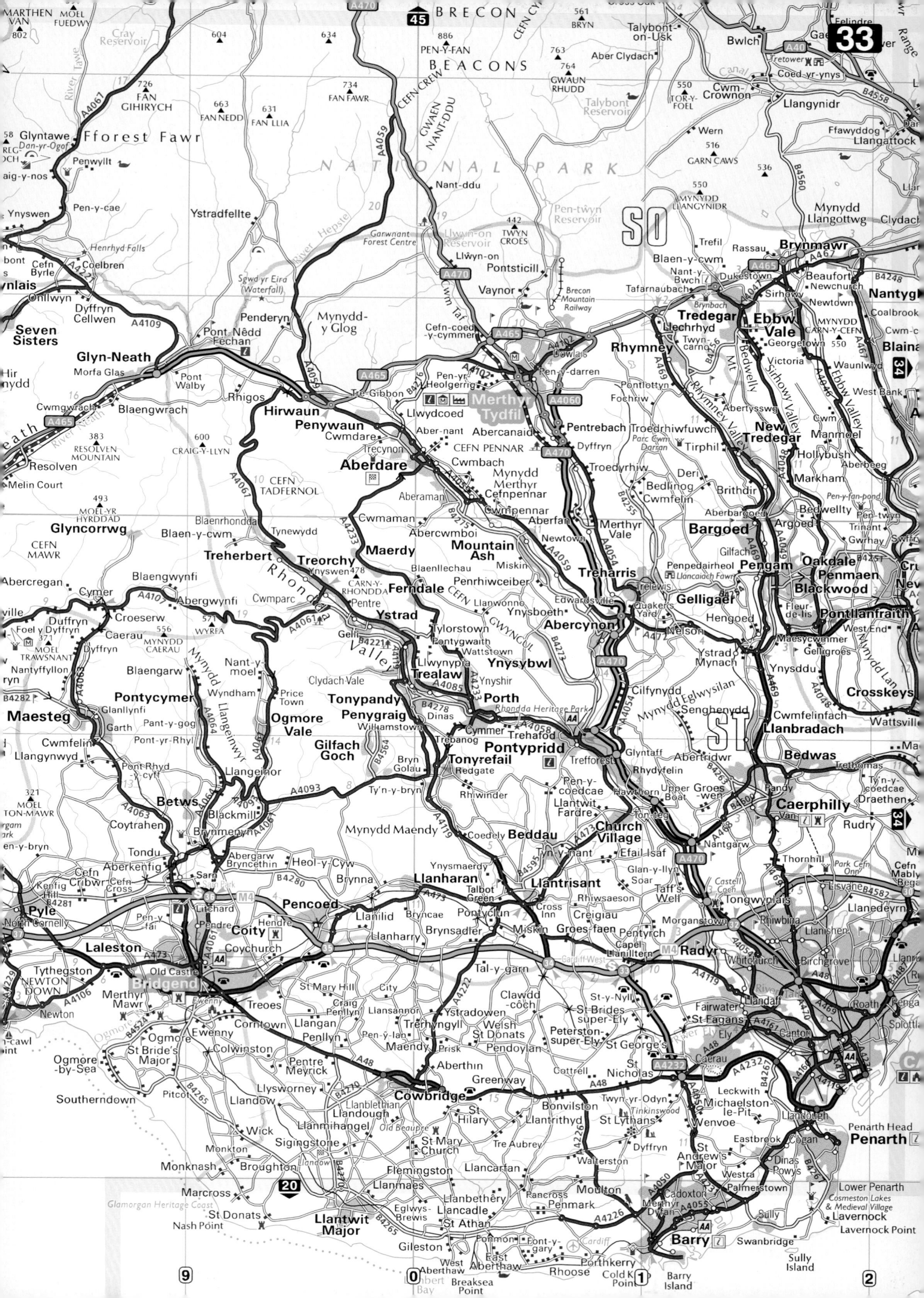

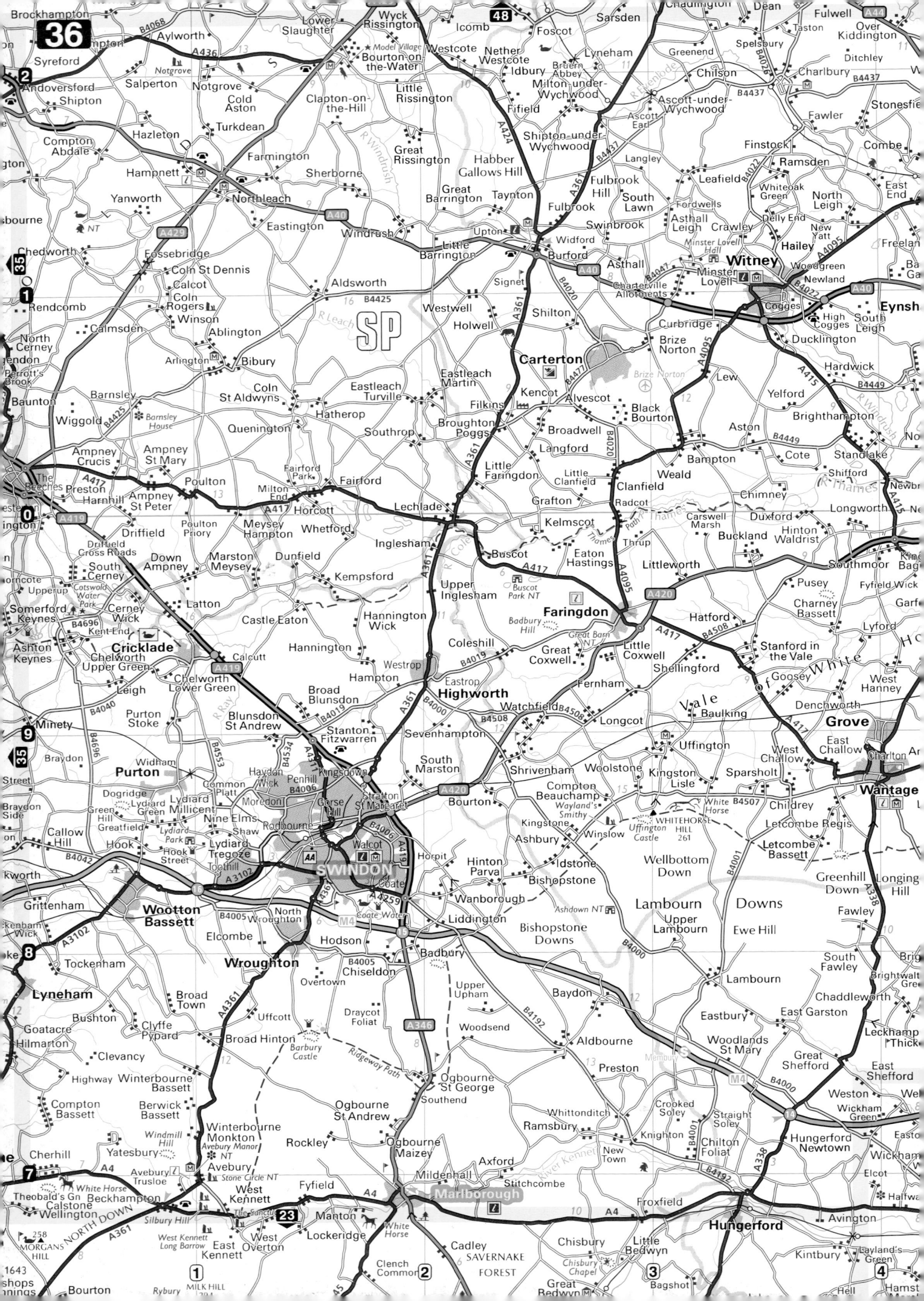

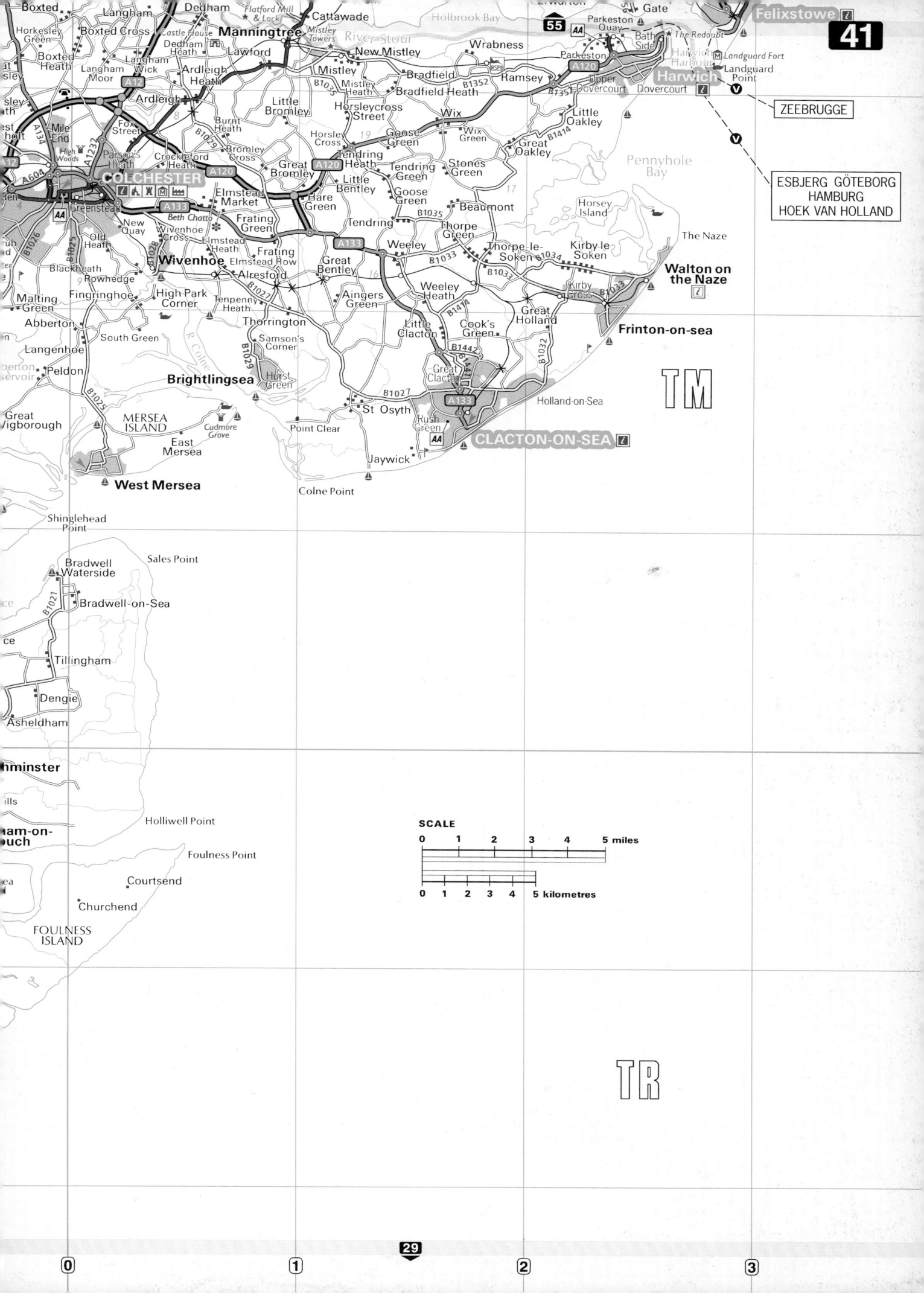

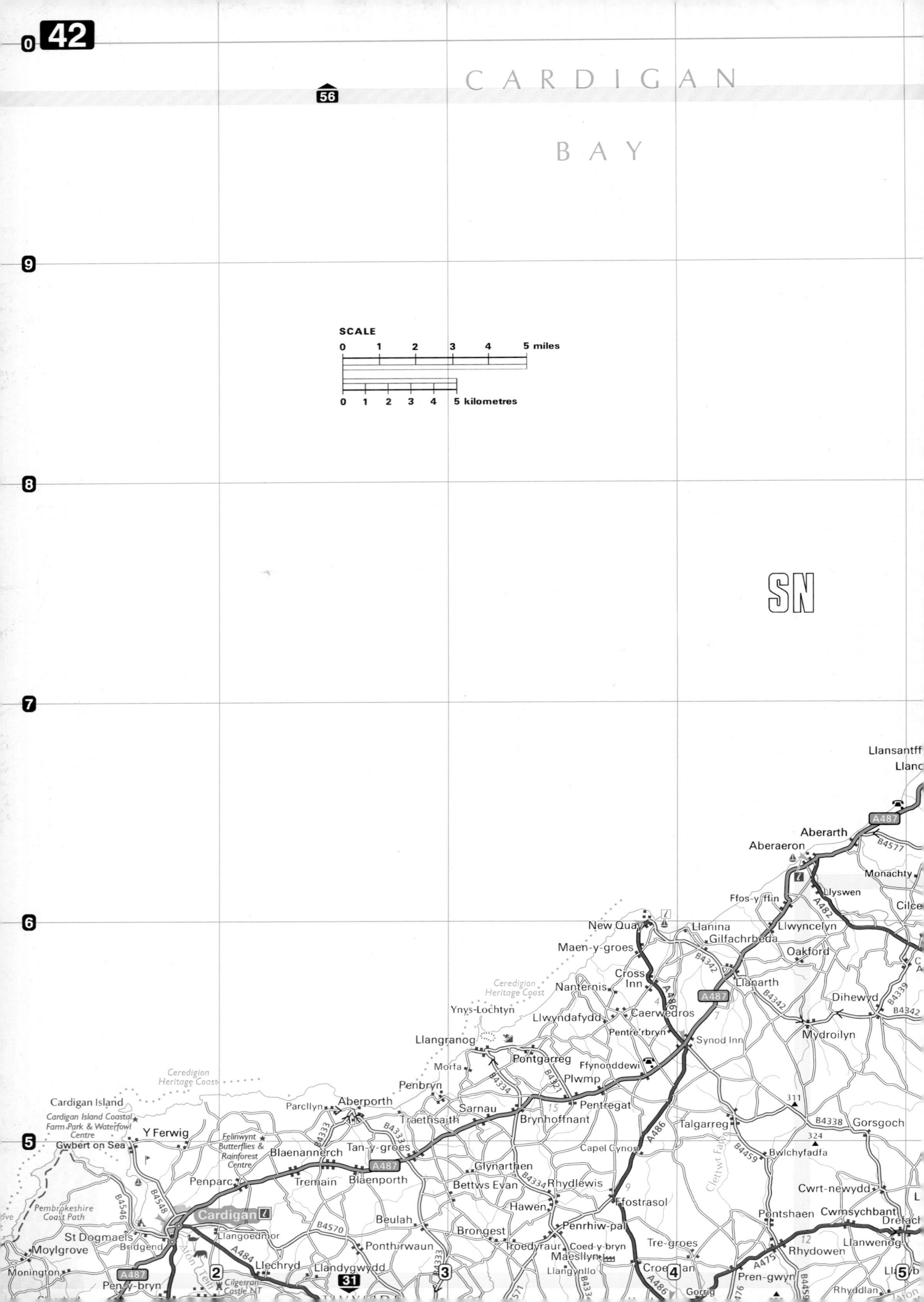

C A R D I G A N

B A Y

56

SCALE

0   1   2   3   4   5 miles

0   1   2   3   4   5 kilometres

SN

Llansantff
Lland

Aberarth
A487
Aberaeron   B4577
Monachty
Ffos-y-ffin   Llyswen   A482   Cilce
New Quay   Llanina   Llwyncelyn
Maen-y-groes   Gilfachrheda   Oakford
Cross   B4342
Ceredigion   Nanternis   Inn   A487   Llanarth   C A
Heritage Coast   A486   B4342   Dihewyd   B4342
Ynys-Lochtyn   Caerwedros   7
Llwyndafydd   Mydroilyn
Llangranog   Pentre'rbryn   Synod Inn
Pontgarreg   Ffynonddewi
Morfa   Plwmp   311
Penbryn   B4334   B4321   B4338   Gorsgoch
Cardigan Island   Parcllyn   Aberporth   Sarnau   Pentregat   324
Cardigan Island Coastal   Traethsaith   Brynhoffnant   Talgarreg   Bwlchyfadfa
Farm Park & Waterfowl   A486
Centre   Y Ferwig
Gwbert on Sea   Felinwynt   Tan-y-groes   Capel Cynon   B4459
Butterflies &   A487   Glynarthen   Cwrt-newydd
Rainforest   Blaenannerch   Bettws Evan   Rhydlewis   9
Penparc   Centre   Blaenporth   B4334   Pontshaen   Cwmsychbant
Tremain   Hawen   Ffostrasol   Drefac
Cardigan   Beulah   Penrhiw-pal   Tre-groes   Llanweno
St Dogmaels   Brongest   Troedyraur   Coed-y-bryn   12
Moylgrove   Llangoedmor   B4570   Ponthirwaun   Croe   Rhydowen   Ll
Bridgend   Llechryd   Llangynllo   Pren-gwyn   Rhydlan
Monington   A487   A484   Llandygwydd   Gorrig
Pen-y-bryn   Cilgerran   31   3
Castle NT

Ceredigion
Heritage Coast

Pembrokeshire
Coast Path

5

2   4   5

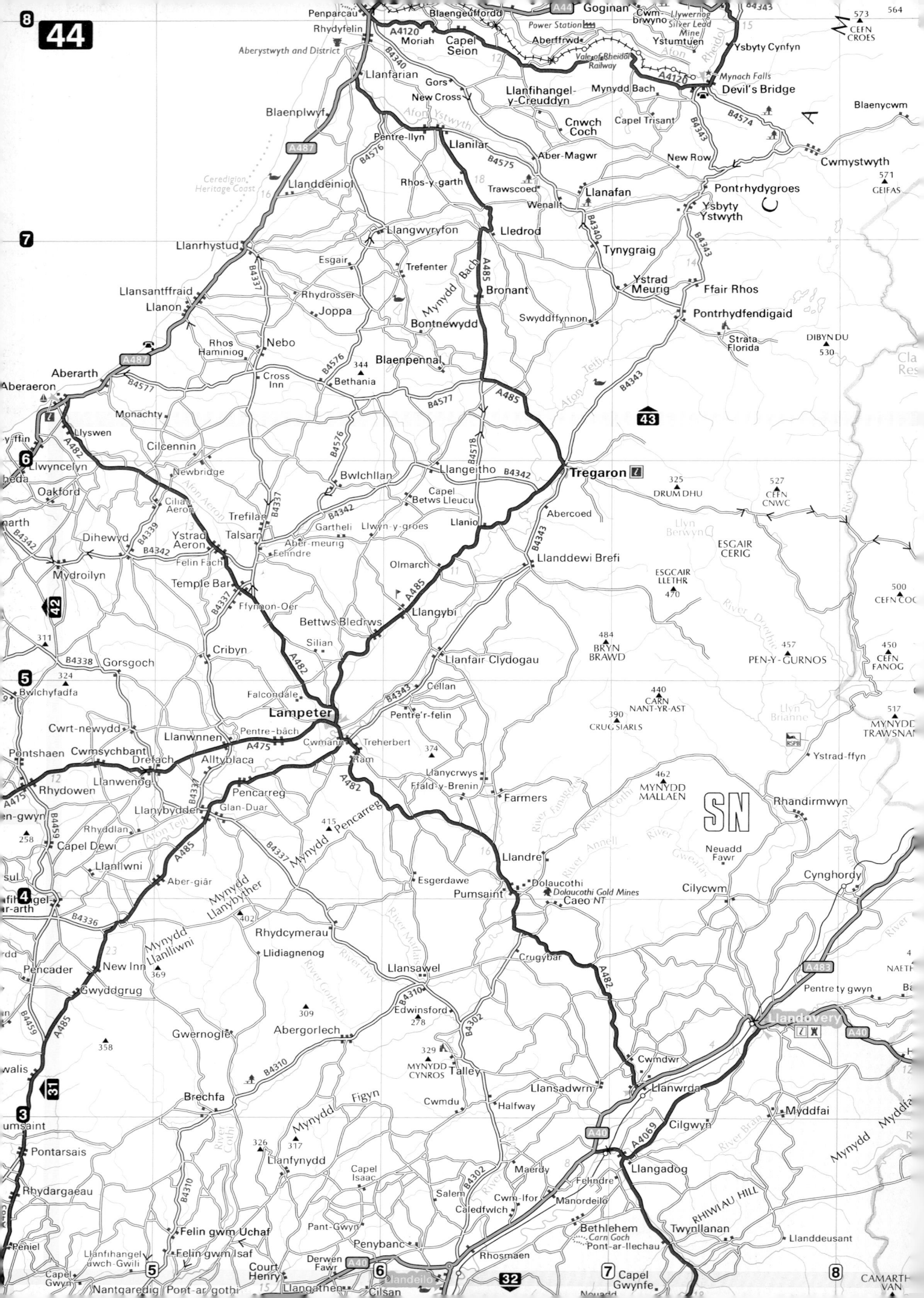

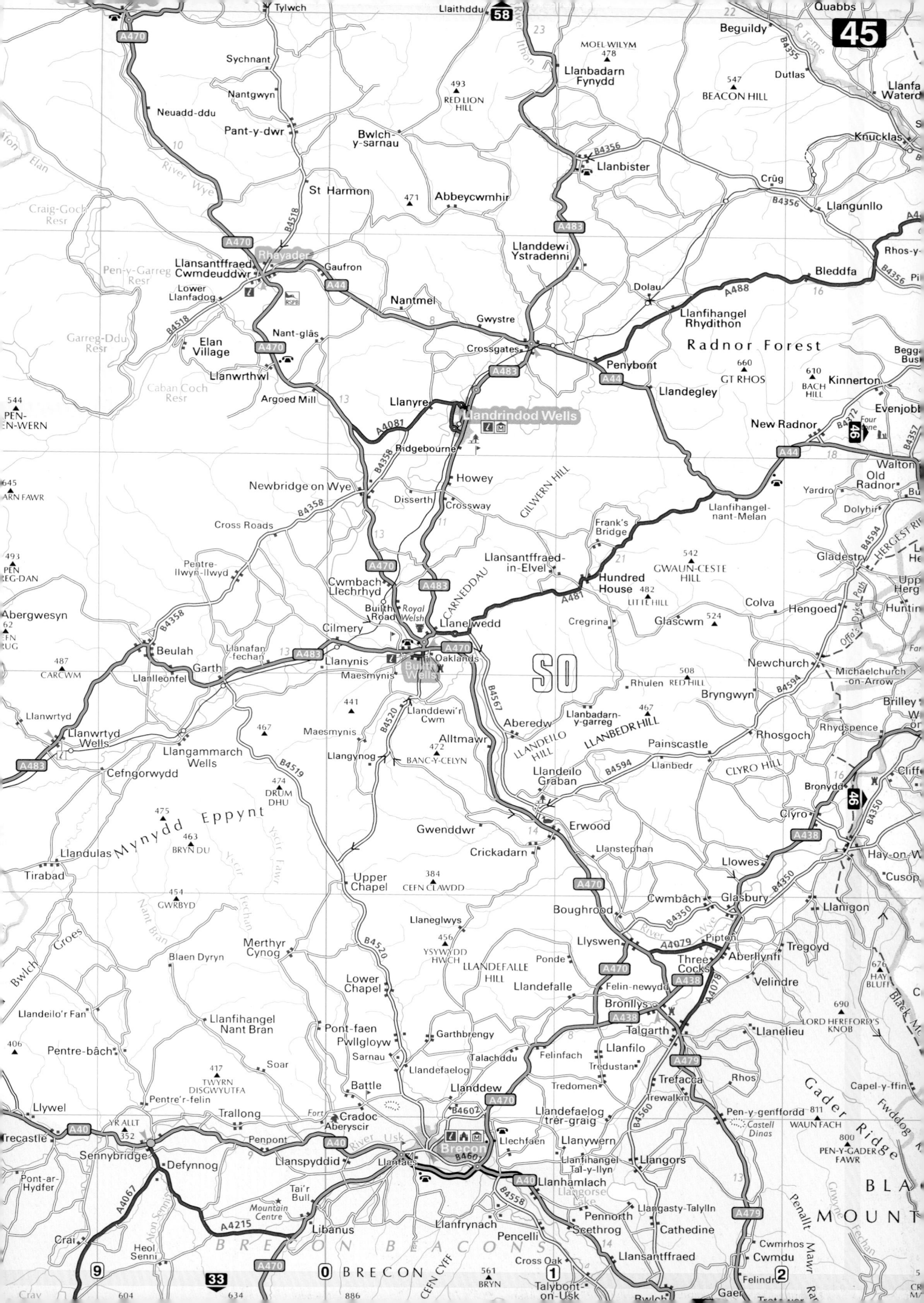

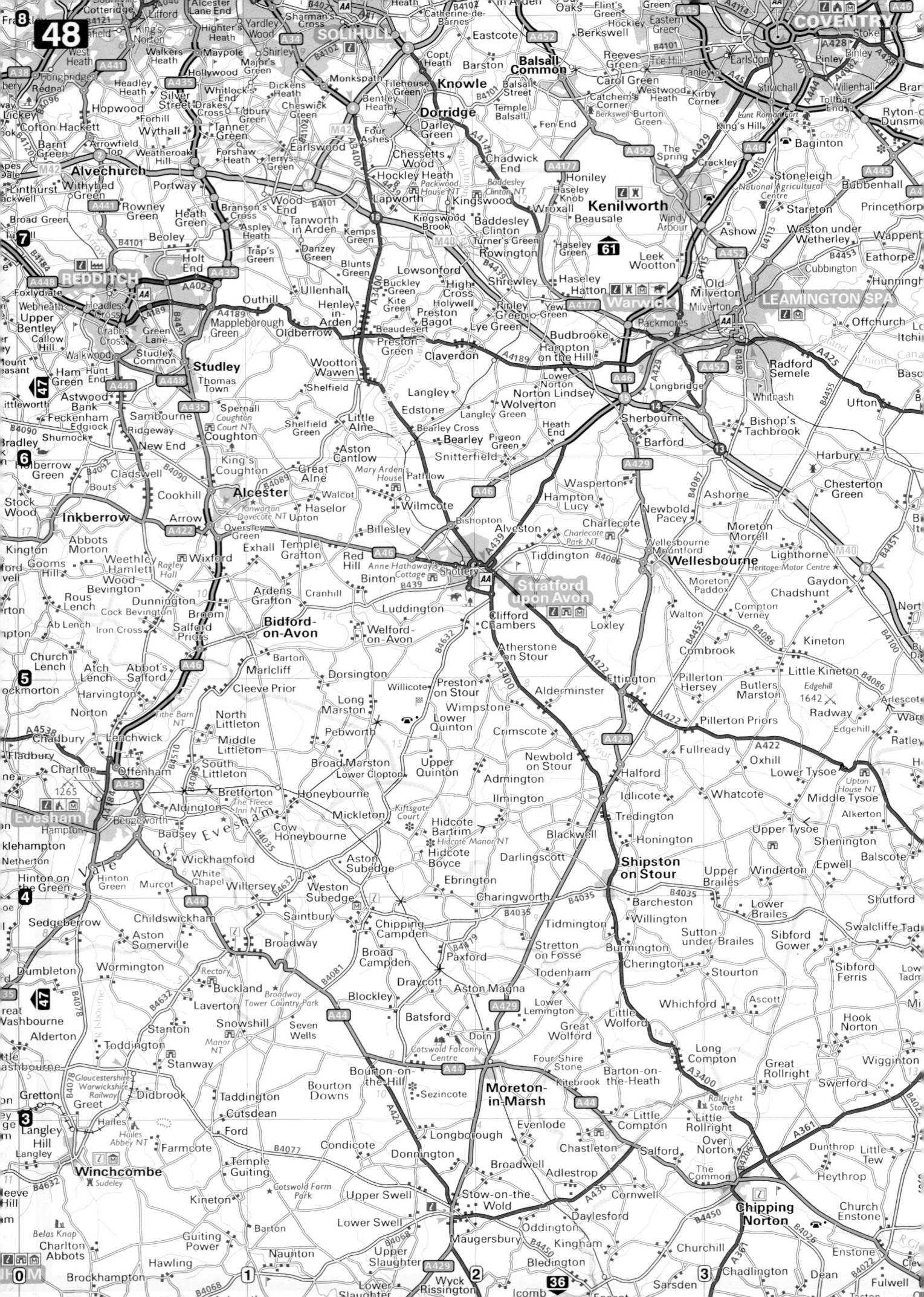

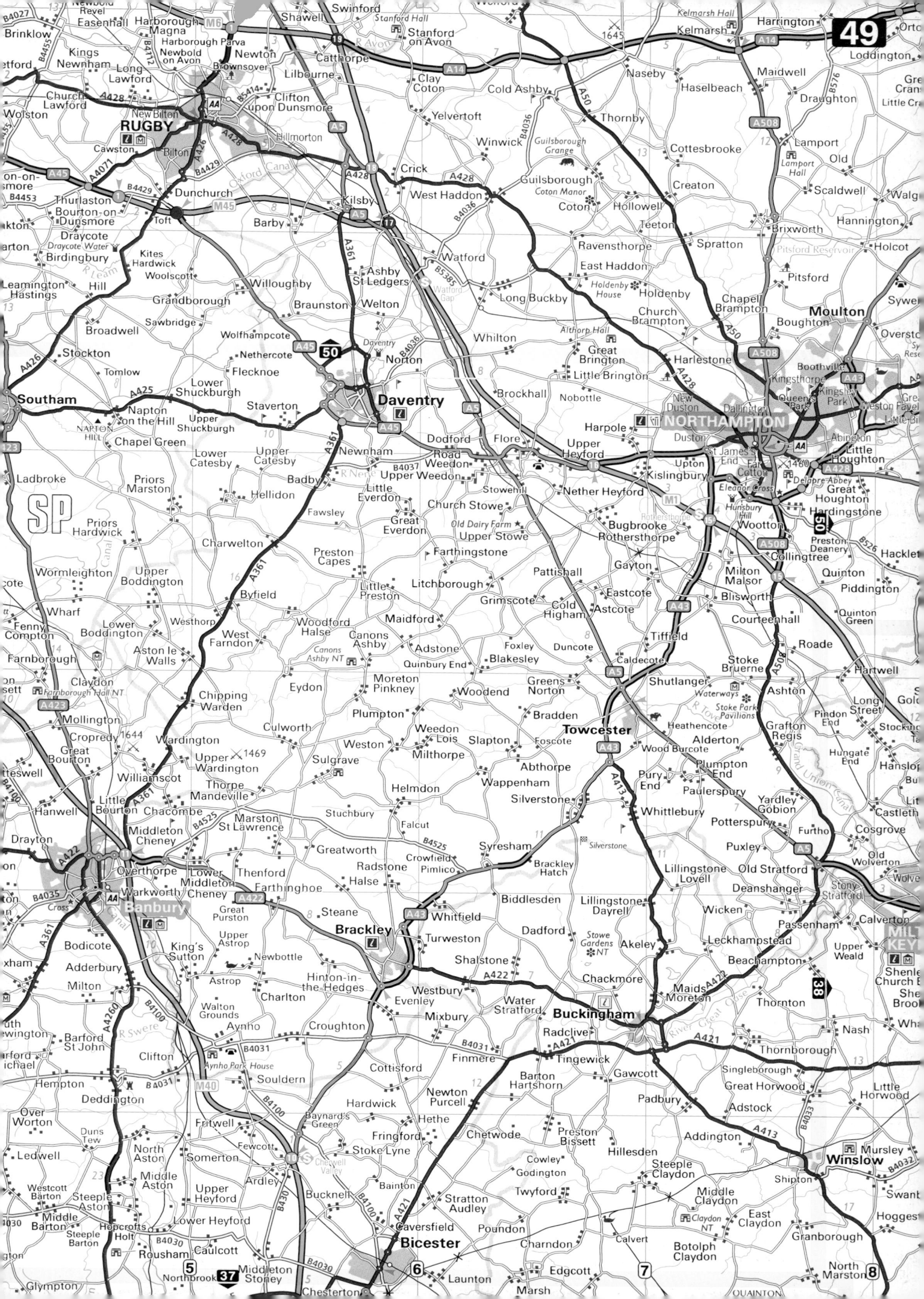

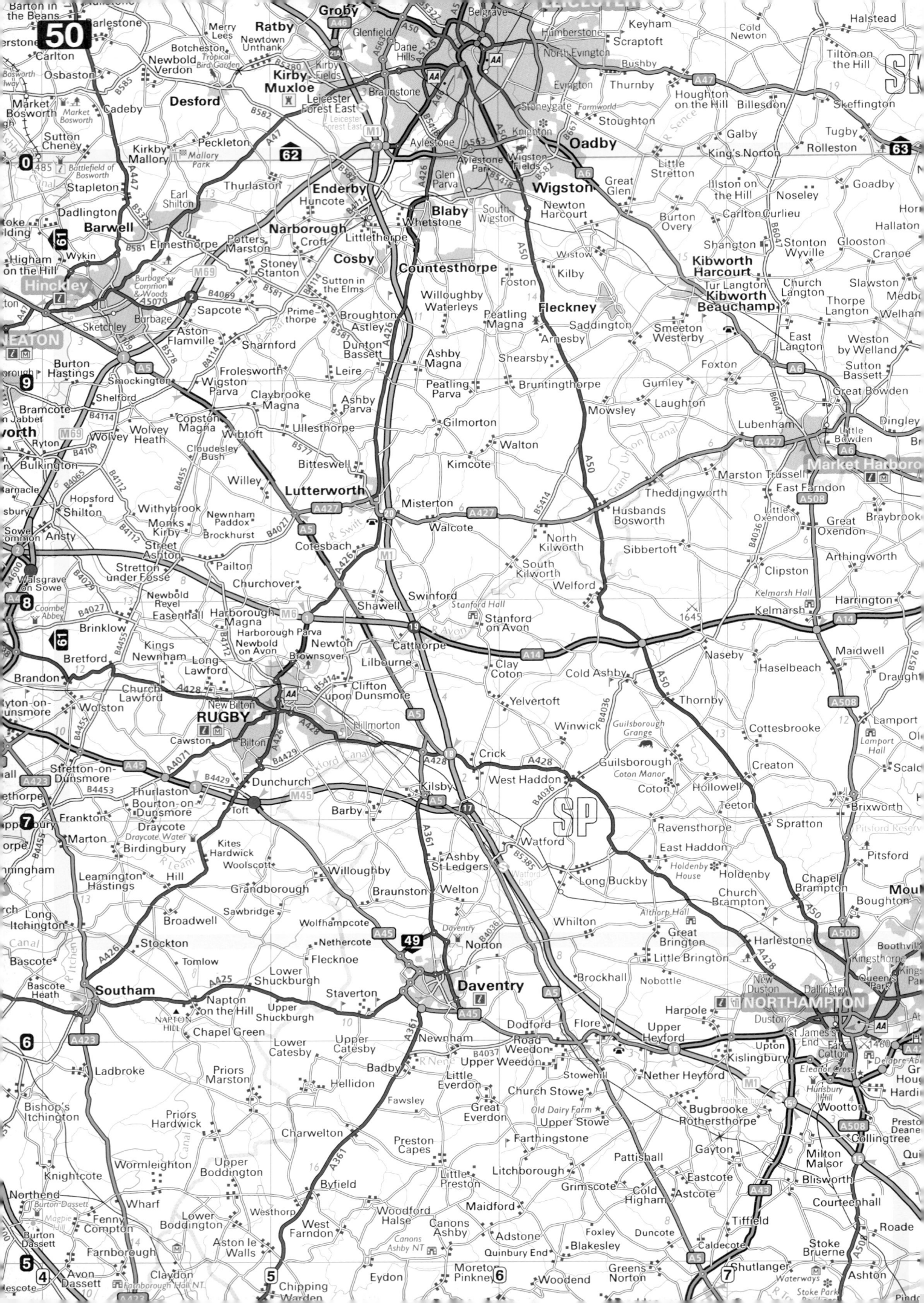

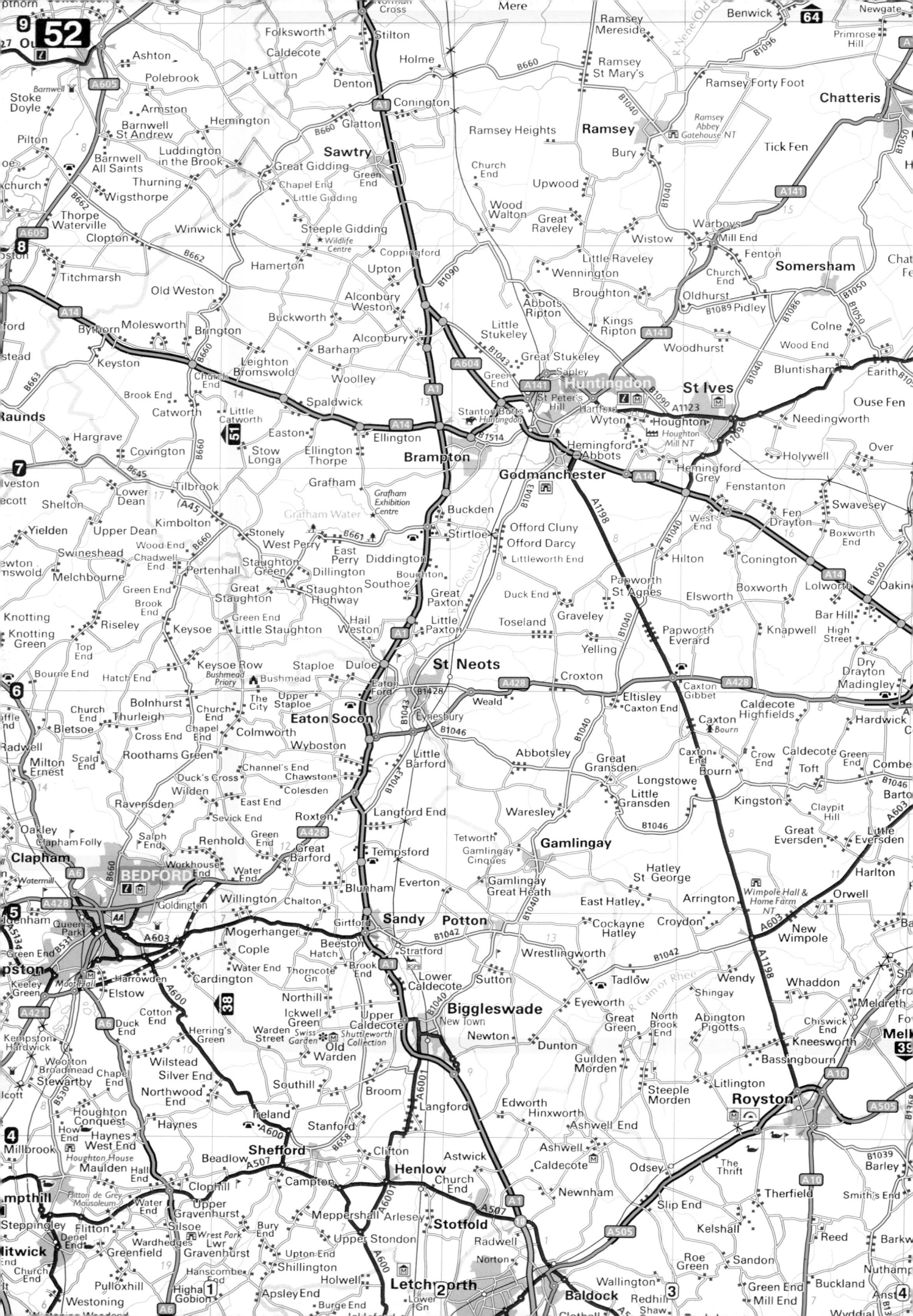

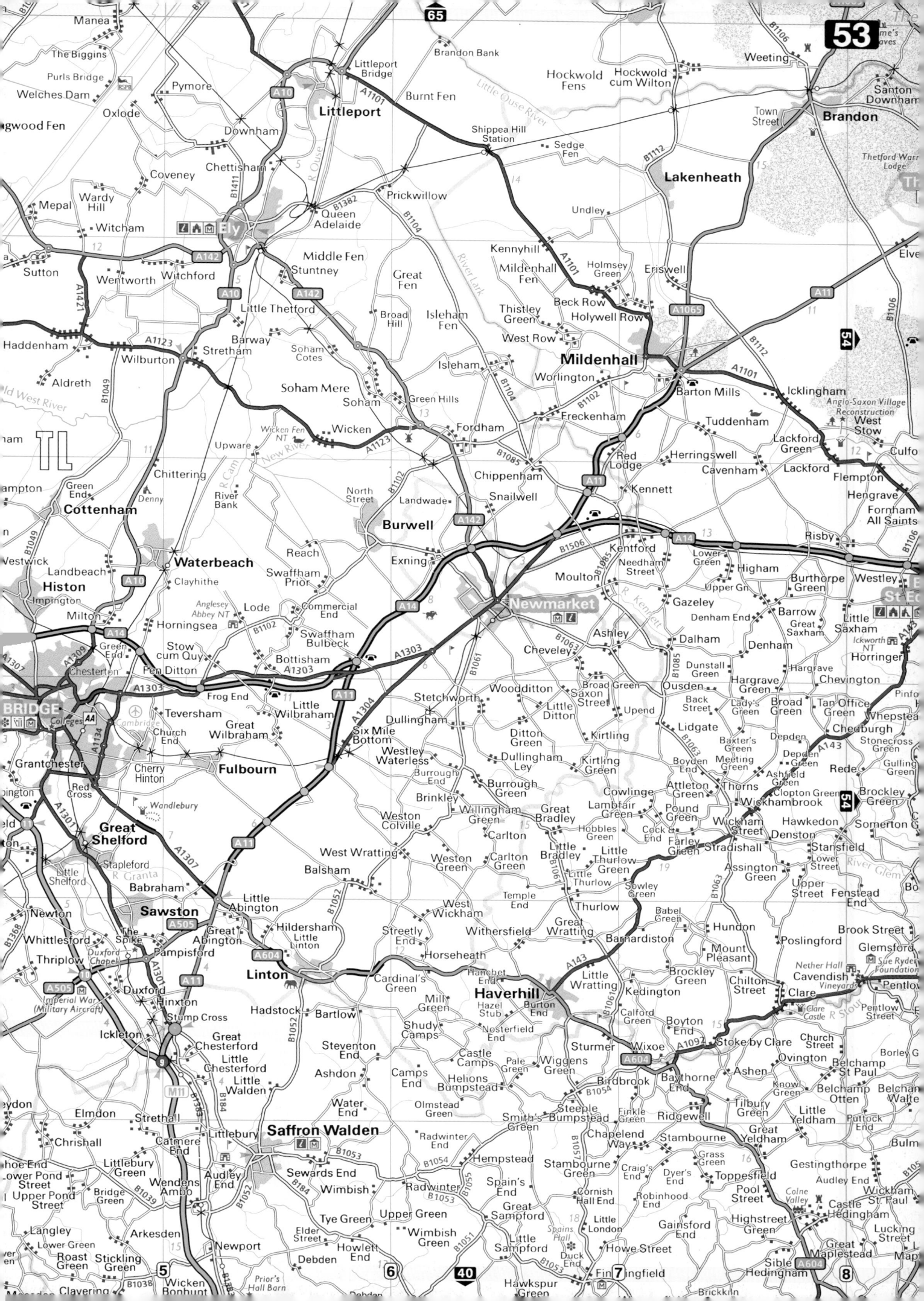

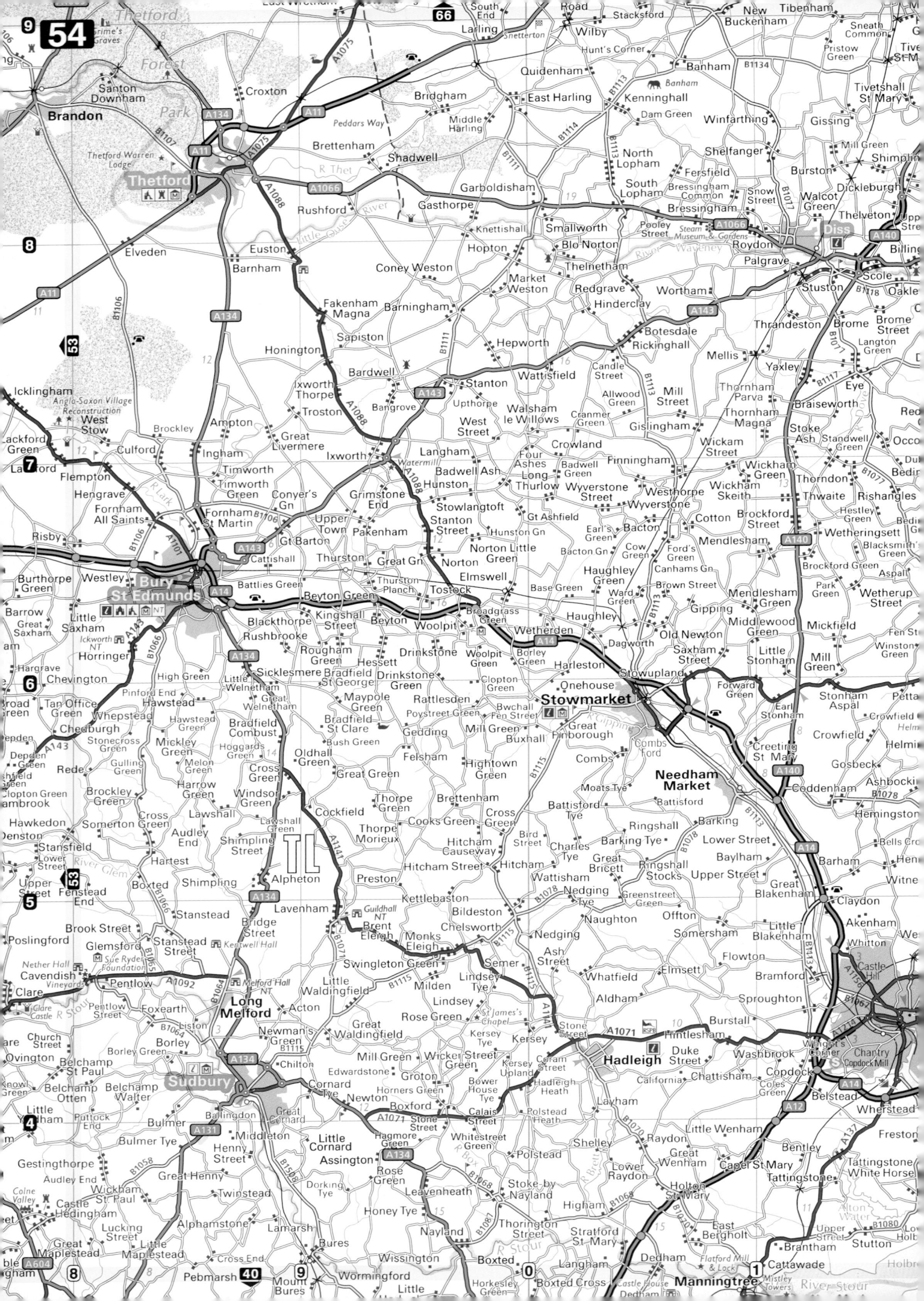

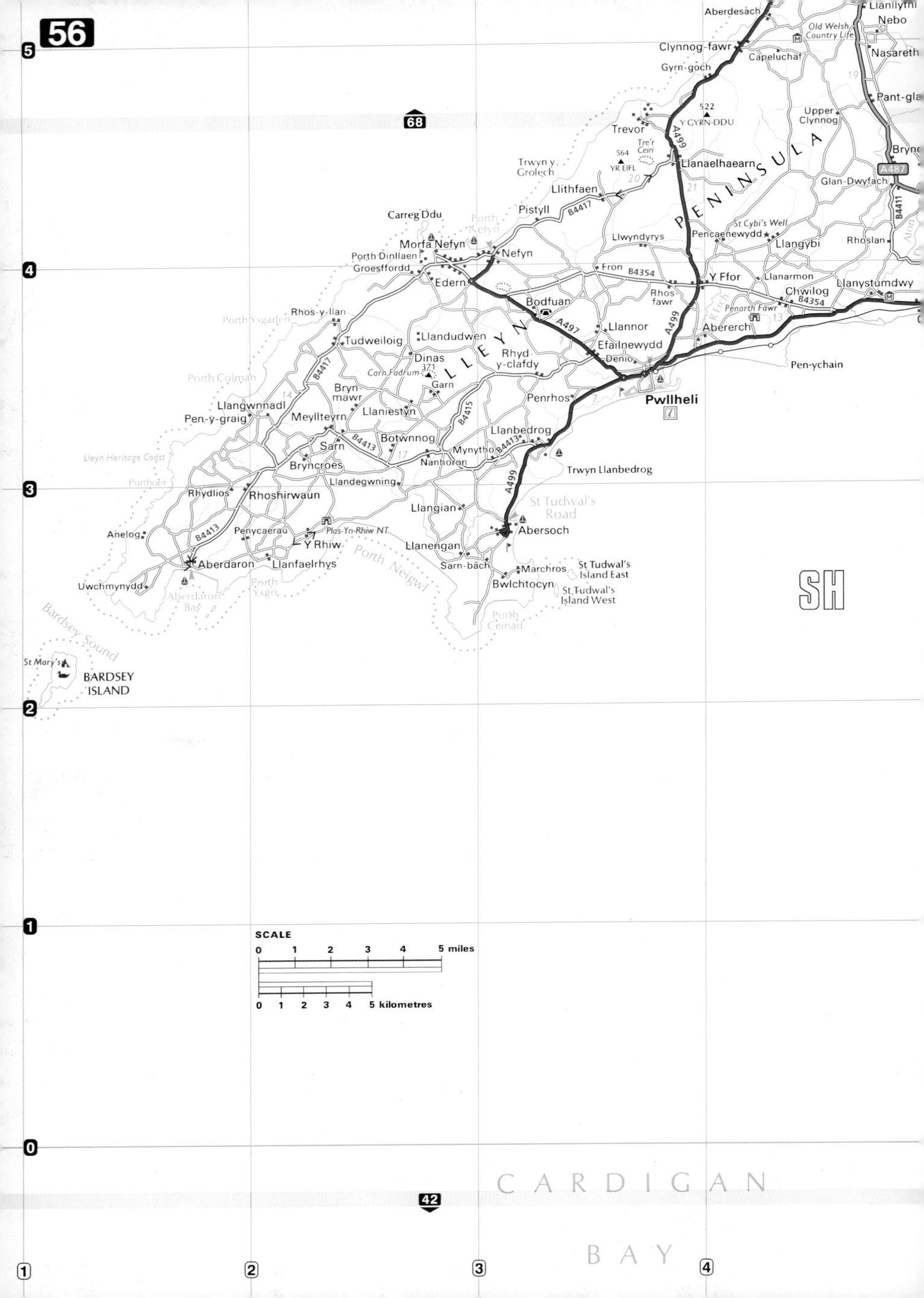

68

Aberdesach
Llanllyfni
Nebo
Clynnog-fawr
Gyrn-goch
Capeluchaf
Nasareth
Old Welsh
Country Life
Pant-gla
522
Y GYRN-DDU
Upper
Clynnog
Trevor
Tre'r
Ceiri
564
YR EIFL
Llanaelhaearn
Bryn
A487
Trwyn y
Grolech
Llithfaen
Llwyndyrys
St Cybi's Well
Pistyll
Pencaenewydd
Glan-Dwyfach
B4411
Carreg Ddu
B4417
Porth
Nefyn
Rhoslan
Morfa Nefyn
Nefyn
Fron
B4354
Llangybi
Porth Dinllaen
Llanarmon
Groesffordd
Edern
Y Ffor
Chwilog
Llanystumdwy
Bodfuan
Rhos
fawr
Penarth Fawr
B4354
Rhos-y-llan
A497
Abererch
Tudweiloig
Llandudwen
Llannor
Abererch
Dinas
Rhyd
y-clafdy
Efailnewydd
Pen-ychain
371
Garn
Denio
Carn Fadrum
Bryn-
mawr
Penrhos
Pwllheli
Llaniestyn
B4415
Llangwnnadl
Pen-y-graig
Meyllteyrn
B4413
Botwnnog
Llanbedrog
Sarn
Mynytho
B4413
Bryncroes
Nanhoron
Trwyn Llanbedrog
Llandegwning
St Tudwal's
Road
Rhydlios
Llangian
Rhoshirwaun
Abersoch
Anelog
B4413
Penycaerau
Plas-Yn-Rhiw NT
Llanengan
St Tudwal's
Island East
Y Rhiw
Aberdaron
Llanfaelrhys
Sarn-bach
Marchros
St Tudwal's
Island West
Porth Neigwl
Uwchmynydd
Bwlchtocyn
Porth
Ysgo
SH
Aberdaron
Bay
Porth
Ceiriad

Bardsey Sound
St Mary's
BARDSEY
ISLAND

LLEYN

PENINSULA

Porth Ysgaden

Porth Colman

Porthor

Lleyn Heritage Coast

SCALE
0   1   2   3   4   5 miles
0 1 2 3 4 5 kilometres

42

C A R D I G A N

B A Y

1   2   3   4

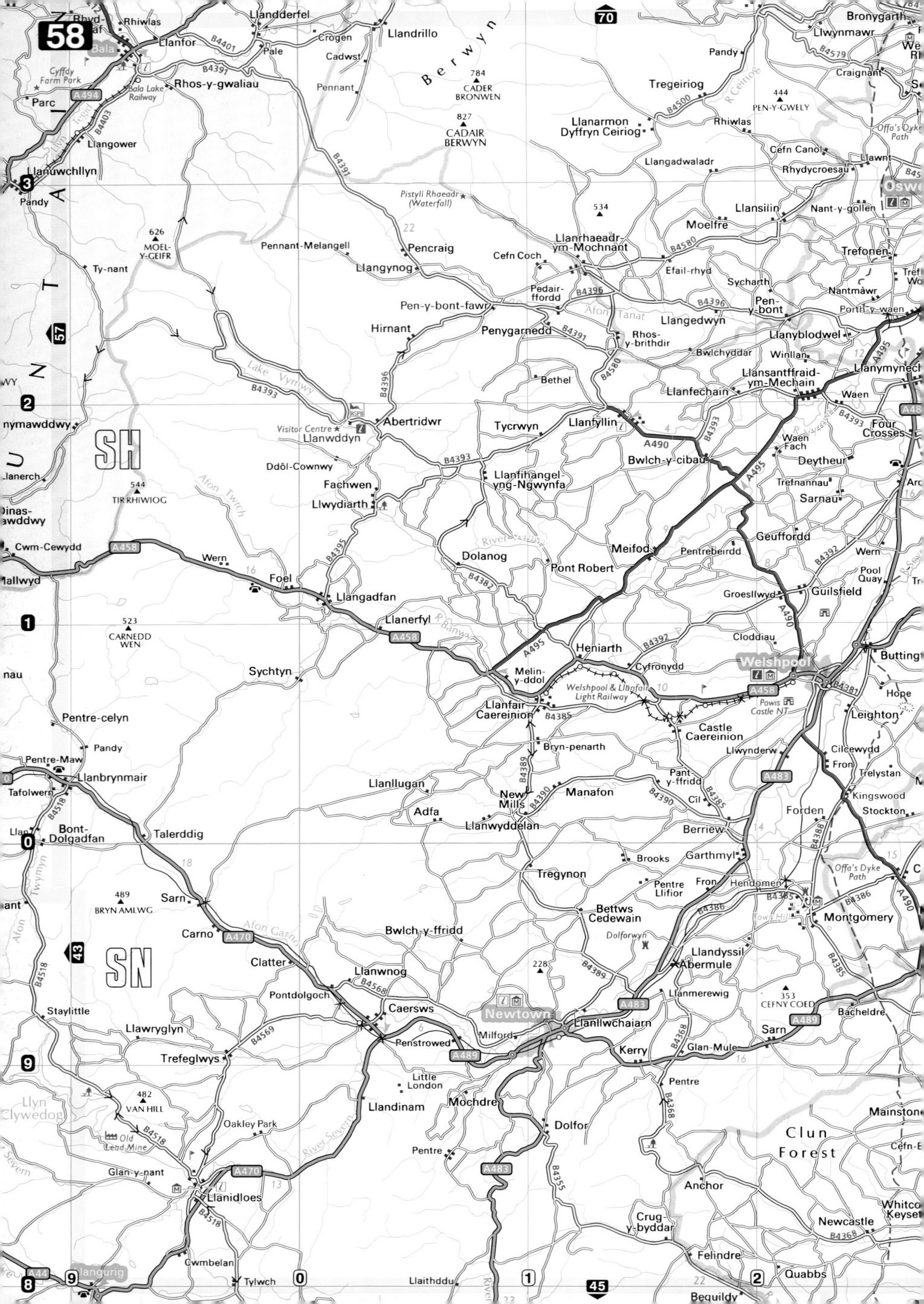

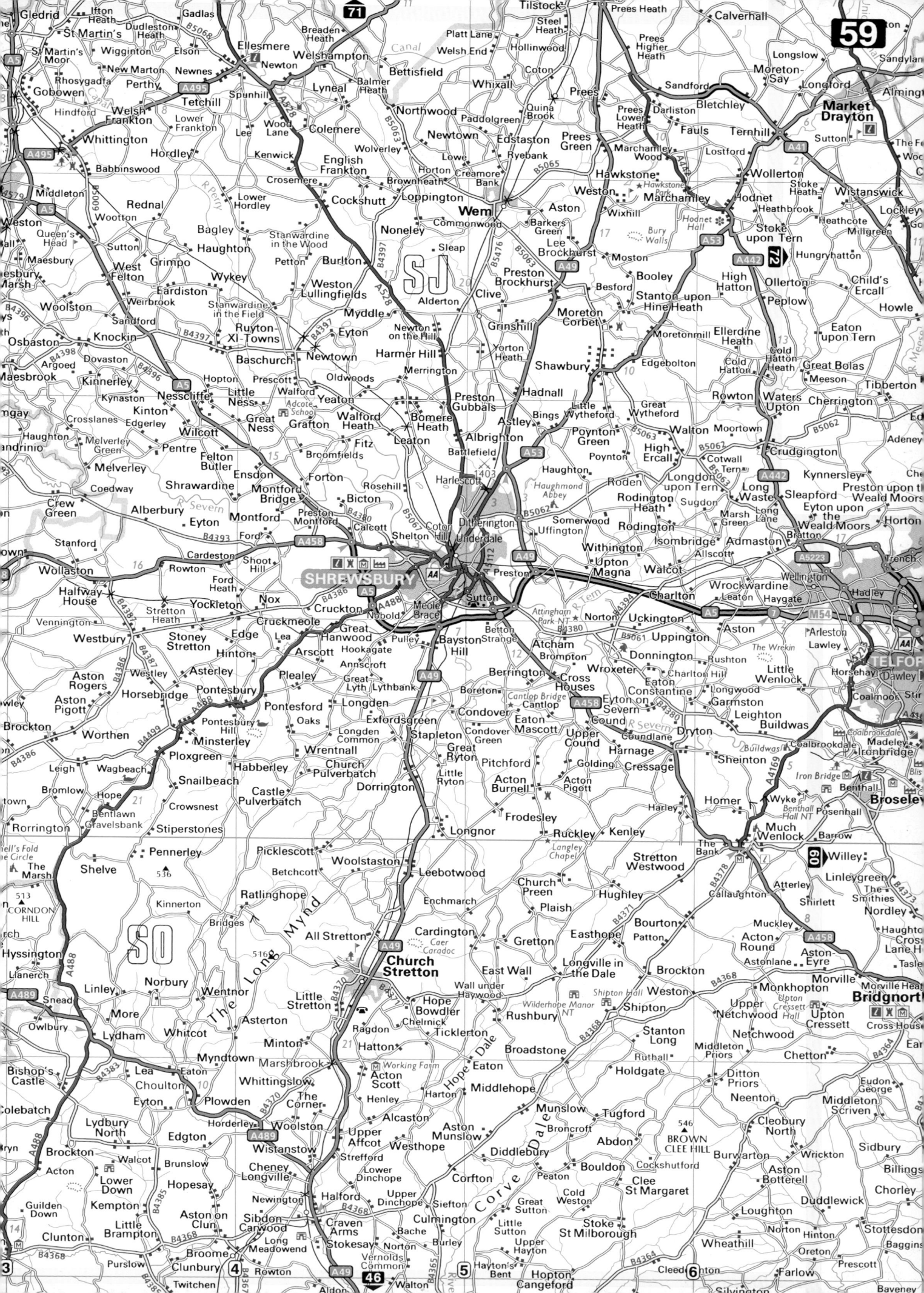

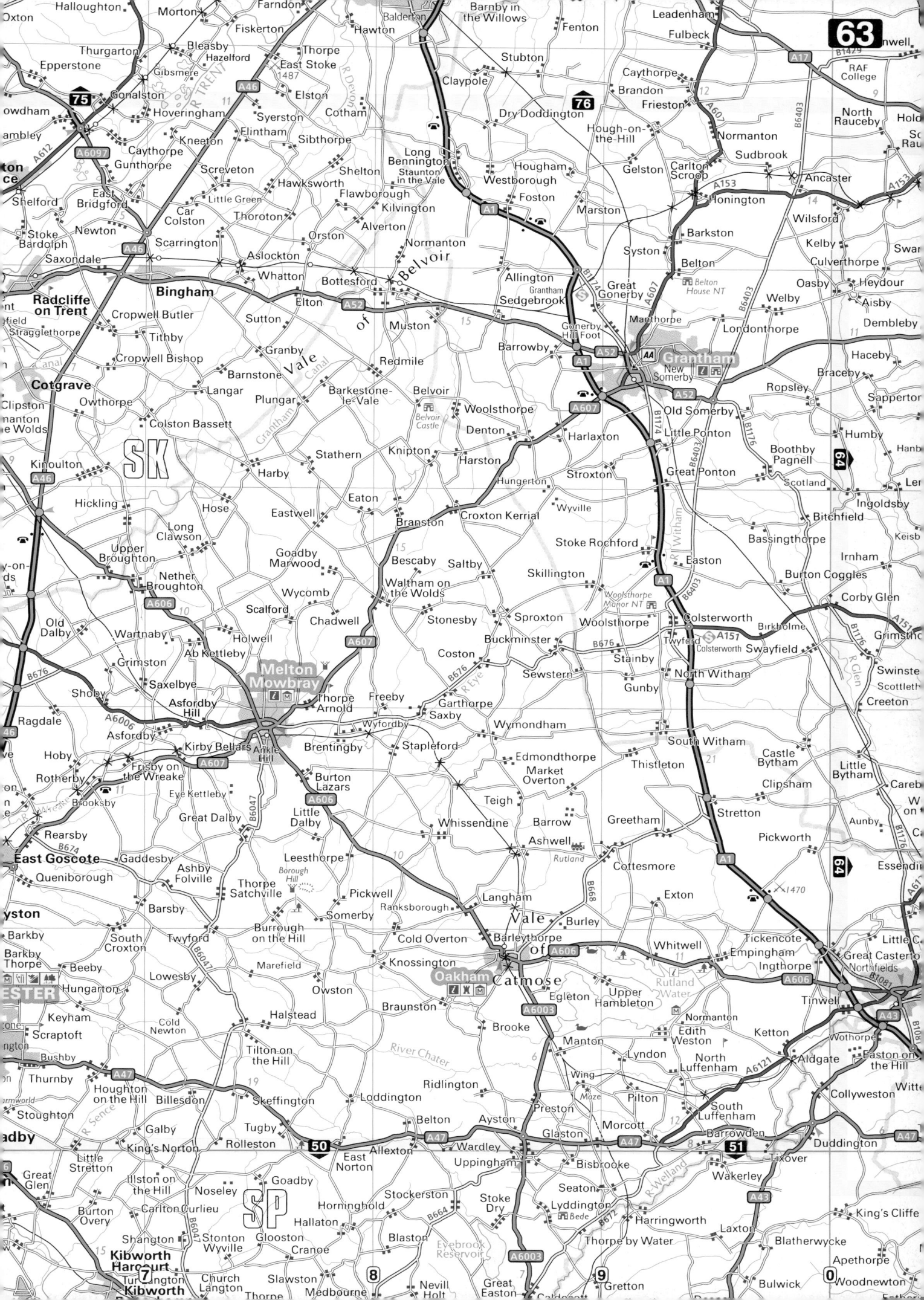

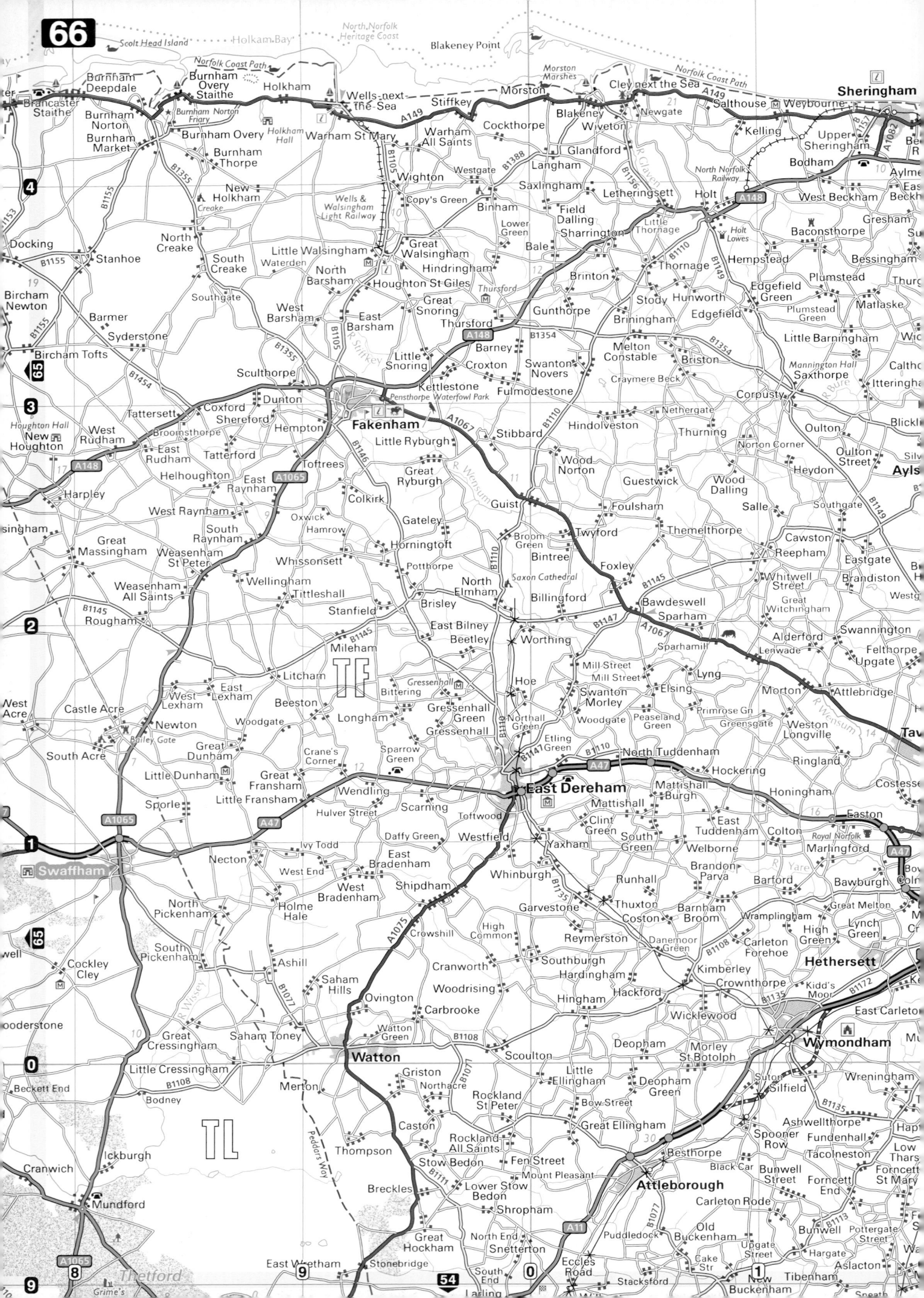

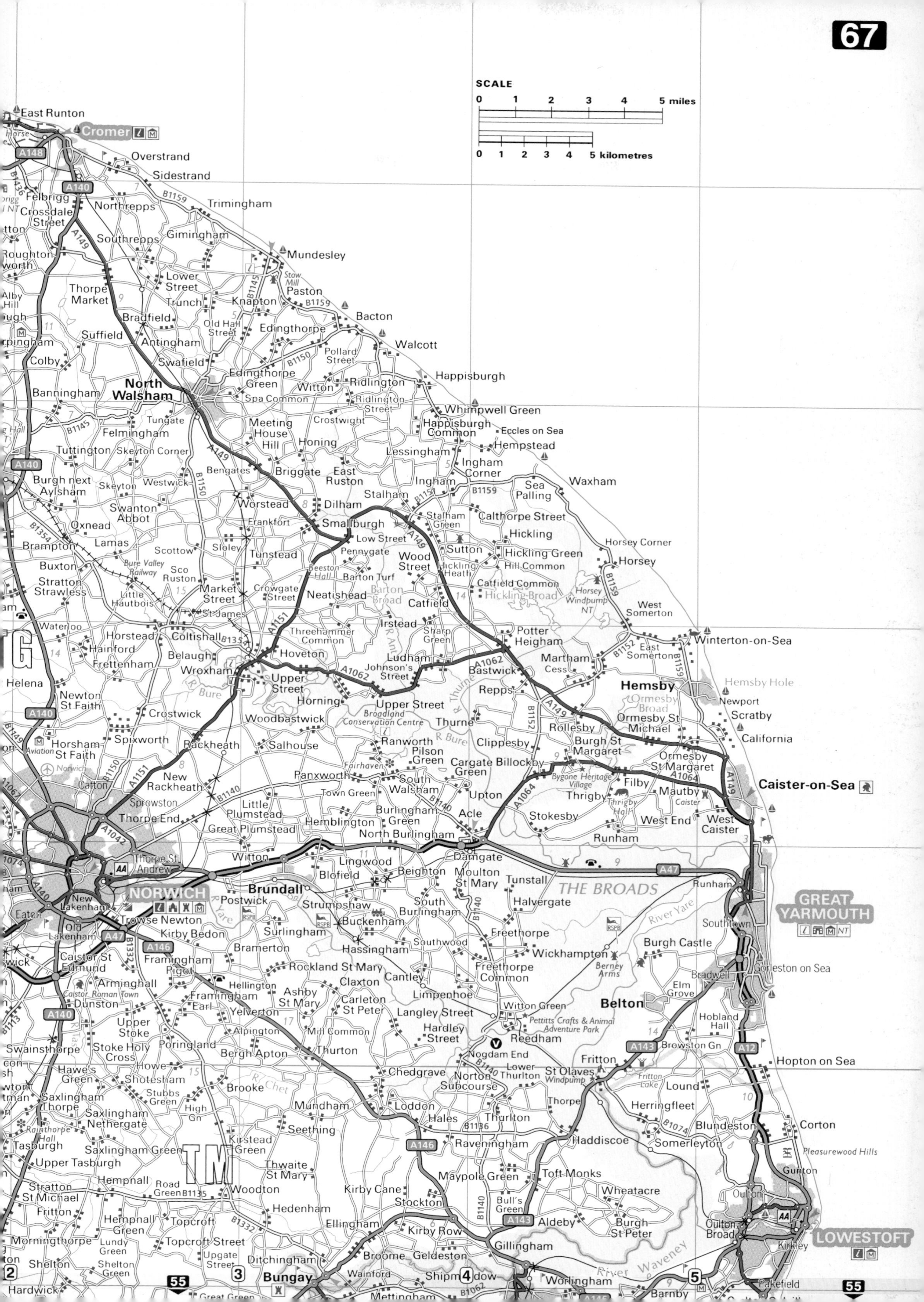

SCALE
0 1 2 3 4 5 miles
0 1 2 3 4 5 kilometres
East Runton
Cromer
A148
Overstrand
Sidestrand
A140
Felbrigg
B1159
Trimingham
Northrepps
Crossdale Street
Southrepps
Gimingham
Roughton
A149
Mundesley
Lower Street
Stow Mill
Thorpe Market
Trunch
Paston
B1145
Knapton
B1159
Bradfield
Old Hall Street
Bacton
Suffield
Edingthorpe
Antingham
Walcott
Pollard Street
Colby
Swafield
B1150
Edingthorpe Green
Happisburgh
Ridlington
North Walsham
Witton
Banningham
Spa Common
Ridlington Street
Whimpwell Green
Tungate
Meeting House Hill
Crostwight
Happisburgh Common
Eccles on Sea
Felmingham
B1145
Honing
Hempstead
Tuttington
Skeyton Corner
Lessingham
Ingham Corner
A140
A149
Bengates
Briggate
East Ruston
Burgh next Aylsham
Skeyton
Westwick
B1150
Ingham
Sea Palling
Waxham
Stalham
B1159
Swanton Abbot
Worstead
Dilham
B1151
Oxnead
Frankfort
Smallburgh
Stalham Green
Calthorpe Street
B1354
Low Street
A149
Hickling
Brampton
Lamas
Sloley
Pennygate
Sutton
Horsey Corner
Scottow
Tunstead
Wood Street
Hickling Green
Buxton
Bure Valley Railway
Sco Ruston
Beeston Hall
Hickling Heath
Hill Common
Horsey
Stratton Strawless
Barton Turf
Barton Broad
Catfield Common
B1159
Little Hautbois
Market Street
Crowgate Street
Neatishead
Catfield
Hickling Broad
Horsey Windpump NT
West Somerton
St James
Waterloo
Irstead
A1151
Threehammer Common
Sharp Green
Potter Heigham
Horstead
Coltishall
B1354
Winterton-on-Sea
Hainford
R Ant
East Somerton
Belaugh
Hoveton
Martham
B1152
Frettenham
Ludham
Cess
A1062
Johnson's Street
B1159
Wroxham
Bastwick
Helena
Upper Street
Hemsby
Hemsby Hole
A1062
Ormesby Broad
Bure
Repps
Newport
Newton St Faith
Horning
R Thurne
Upper Street
B1152
A149
Ormesby St Michael
Scratby
A140
Crostwick
Broadland Conservation Centre
Thurne
Rollesby
California
Woodbastwick
Horsham St Faith
Spixworth
Ranworth
R Bure
Clippesby
Burgh St Margaret
Aviation
Rackheath
Salhouse
Pilson Green
Ormesby St Margaret
Norwich
B1150
Fairhaven
Cargate Green
Billockby
A1064
Bygone Heritage Village
Filby
Catton
A1151
New Rackheath
Panxworth
South Walsham
Mautby
A149
Caister-on-Sea
Town Green
Thrigby
Caister
Sprowston
Little Plumstead
B1140
Upton
A1064
Thrigby Hall
Burlingham Green
Acle
Stokesby
West End
West Caister
Thorpe End
Plumstead
Hemblington
Great Plumstead
A1042
North Burlingham
Runham
Damgate
Witton
Lingwood
Thorpe St Andrew
Blofield
Beighton
Moulton St Mary
A47
Tunstall
Runham
NORWICH
Brundall
THE BROADS
GREAT YARMOUTH
Postwick
Halvergate
New Lakenham
Strumpshaw
South Burlingham
Eaton
R Yare
River Yare
Southtown
Trowse Newton
Old Lakenham
Buckenham
B1140
Freethorpe
Kirby Bedon
Surlingham
A47
B1332
A146
Bramerton
Hassingham
Southwood
Wickhampton
Burgh Castle
Caistor St Edmund
Framingham Pigot
Rockland St Mary
Freethorpe Common
Berney Arms
Gorleston on Sea
Bradwell
Arminghall
Hellington
Cantley
Claxton
Elm Grove
Caistor Roman Town
Framingham Earl
Ashby St Mary
Limpenhoe
Dunston
Carleton St Peter
Belton
A140
Yelverton
Witton Green
Langley Street
Hobland Hall
Upper Stoke
Alpington
Pettitts Crafts & Animal Adventure Park
Mill Common
Hardley Street
Reedham
Swainsthorpe
Poringland
A143
Browston Gn
A12
Stoke Holy Cross
Bergh Apton
Thurton
Nogdam End
Howe
Fritton
Hopton on Sea
Hawe's Green
Lower Thurlton
Shotesham
Chedgrave
St Olaves
B1140
Norton Subcourse
St Olaves Windpump
Fritton Lake
Lound
Stubbs Green
Brooke
R Chet
Saxlingham Thorpe
High Gn
Mundham
Loddon
Thorpe
Herringfleet
Saxlingham Nethergate
Hales
Thurlton
Rainthorpe Hall
B1136
B1074
Blundeston
Corton
Seething
Tasburgh
Kirstead Green
Haddiscoe
Somerleyton
Saxlingham Green
TM
A146
Raveningham
Pleasurewood Hills
Upper Tasburgh
Thwaite St Mary
Toft Monks
Gunton
Maypole Green
Hempnall
Road Green
B1135
Woodton
Kirby Cane
Wheatacre
Oulton
Stratton St Michael
B1140
Bull's Green
Fritton
Hedenham
Stockton
Hempnall Green
Topcroft
B1332
A143
Aldeby
Burgh St Peter
Oulton Broad
Ellingham
Kirby Row
Morningthorpe
Lundy Green
Topcroft Street
Gillingham
Kirkley
LOWESTOFT
Upgate Street
Ditchingham
Shelton
Shelton Green
Broome
Geldeston
River Waveney
Wainford
Bungay
Shipmeadow
Worlingham
B1062
Hardwick
Great Green
Mettingham
Barnby
Pakefield
A146
2
3
4
5
55
55

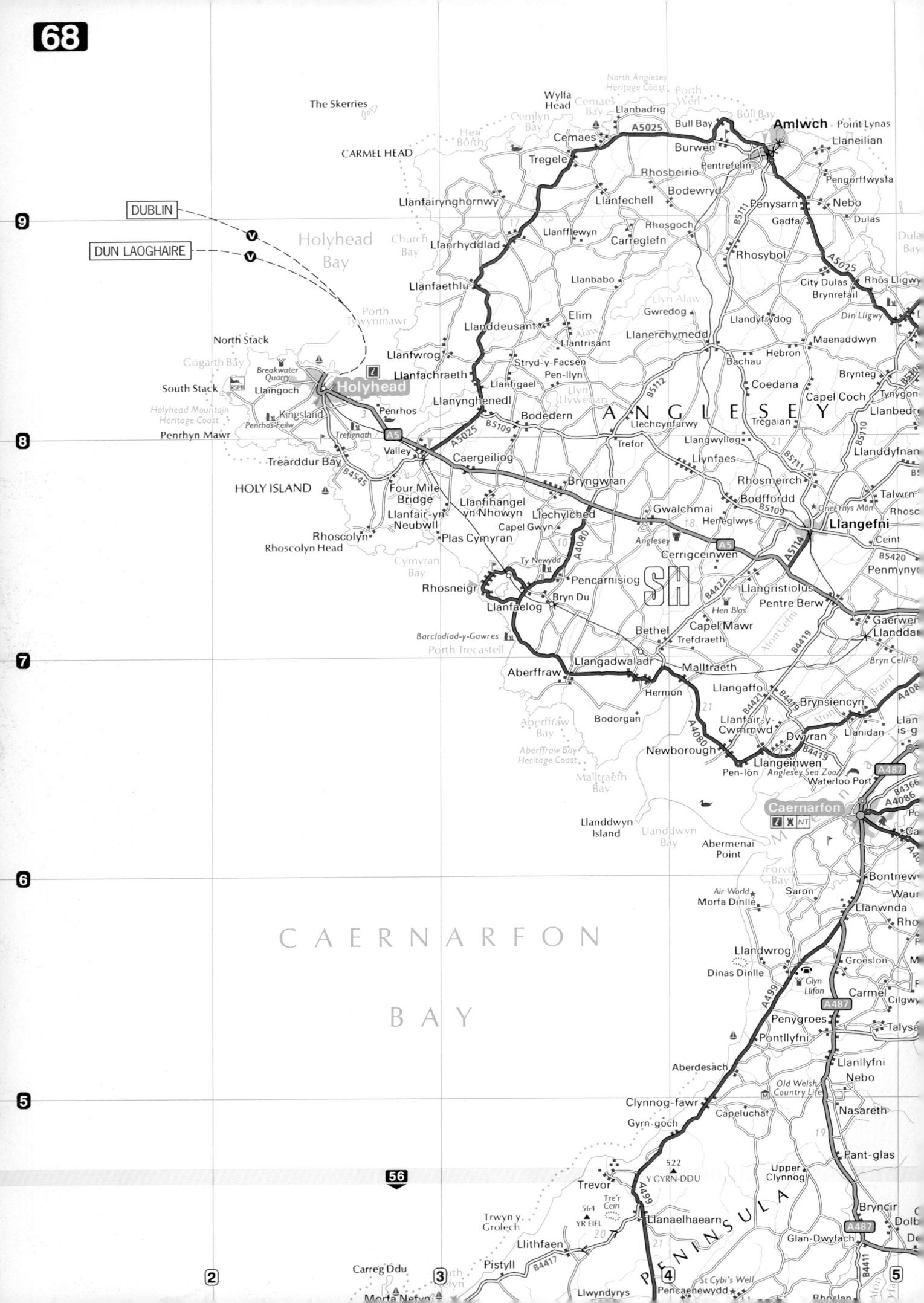

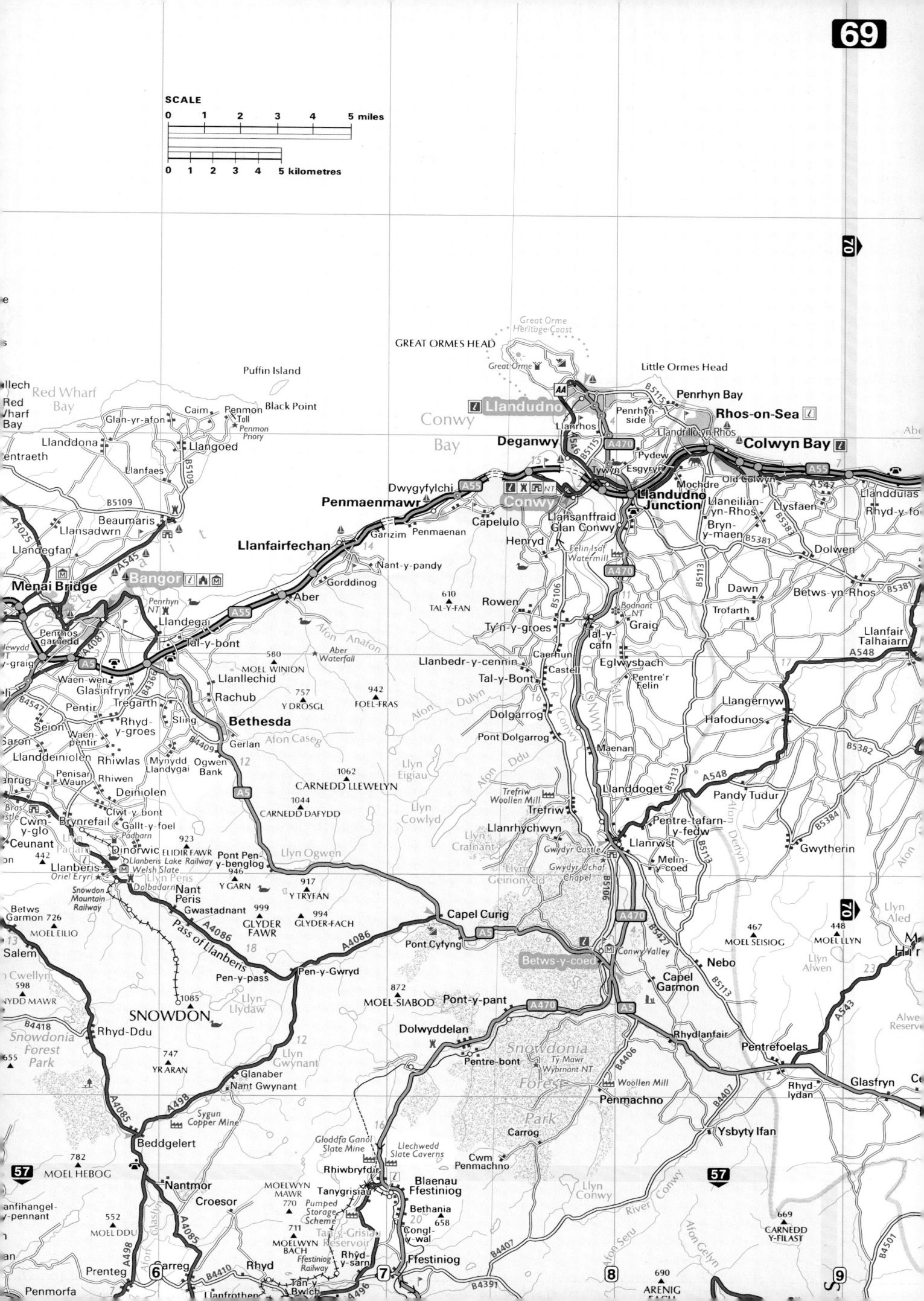

SCALE

0 1 2 3 4 5 miles

0 1 2 3 4 5 kilometres

70

Great Orme
Heritage Coast

GREAT ORMES HEAD

Great Orme

Little Ormes Head

Puffin Island

Penrhyn Bay

Black Point

Llandudno

Penrhyn-
side

Rhos-on-Sea

Conwy
Bay

Llanrhos

Deganwy

Llandrillo-yn-Rhos

Colwyn Bay

Pydew

Red Wharf
Bay

Red
Wharf
Bay

Glan-yr-afon

Caim

Penmon
Toll

Penmon
Priory

Mochdre

Old Colwyn

A55 7

Llanddulas

entraeth

Llanddona

Llangoed

B5109

15

Tywyn

Esgyryn

Conwy

**Llandudno
Junction**

Llaneilian-
yn-Rhos

Llysfaen

Rhyd-y-fo

Llanfaes

Dwygyfylchi

A55

Bryn-
y-maen

Penmaenmawr

Capelulo

Llansanffraid
Glan Conwy

B5381

Dolwen

Beaumaris

B5109

Garizim

Penmaenan

Henryd

Felin Isaf
Waterfall

Llanfairfechan

B5106

A470

Dawn

Betws-yn-Rhos

B5381

Llansadwrn

A545

Bangor

Nant-y-pandy

Rowen

Bodnant
NT

Graig

Trofarth

Hafodunos

Llanfair
Talhaiarn

A548

Menai
Bridge

Aber

610
TAL-Y-FAN

Ty'n-y-groes

Tal-y-
cafn

Langernyw

Llandegfan

Penrhyn
NT

Llandegai

Tal-y-bont

Caerhun

Eglwysbach

Pentre'r
Felin

17

Llanddeiniolen

A5

Waen-wen

Glasinfryn

Pentir

MOEL WINION

Llanbedr-y-cennin

Castell

Tal-y-Bont

Dolgarrog

A548

Pandy Tudur

B5382

Seion

Rhyd-
y-groes

Tregarth

Sling

Llanllechid

Rachub

757
Y DROSGL

942
FOEL-FRAS

Pont Dolgarrog

Llanddoget

B5113

Pentre-tafarn-
y-fedw

Gwytherin

B5384

Bethesda

Gerlan

Afon Caseg

12

Maenan

Rhiwlas

Mynydd
Llandygai

Ogwen
Bank

Trefriw
Woollen Mill

Llanrwst

Penisar
Waun

Deiniolen

1062

CARNEDD LLEWELYN

Llyn
Eigiau

Trefriw

Melin-
coed

Rhiwen

1044
CARNEDD DAFYDD

Llanrhychwyn

Gwydyr Castle

Brynrefail

Clwt-y-bont

Gallt-y-foel

923

Pont Pen-
y-benglog

Llyn
Cowlyd

Gwydyr Uchaf
Chapel

Cwm-
y-glo

Dinorwic

ELIDIR FAWR

946

Y GARN

B5106

442

Dolbadarn

Llanberis
Lake Railway

Welsh Slate

Llyn
Crafnant

Oriel Eryri

Llyn Peris

Dolbadarn

Nant
Peris

917
Y TRYFAN

Geirionydd

Snowdon
Mountain Railway

Gwastadnant

999

994

Capel Curig

Conwy
Valley

Betws
Garmon 726

MOEL EILIO

GLYDER
FAWR

GLYDER-FACH

A5

467
MOEL SEISIOG

448
MOEL LLYN

70

Llyn
Aled

Salem

Pont Cyfyng

6

Betws-y-coed

A470

B5427

Pen-y-pass

Llyn
Llydaw

872
MOEL-SIABOD

Pont-y-pant

Nebo

Llyn
Alwen

23

Pen-y-Gwryd

M

Hir

598
NYDD MAWR

Capel
Garmon

B5113

SNOWDON

Rhyd-Ddu

12

Snowdonia
Forest
Park

747
YR ARAN

Llyn
Gwynant

Dolwyddelan

A470

Rhydlanfair

A5

Pentrefoelas

A543

Glanaber

Nant Gwynant

Pentre-bont

Ty Mawr
Wybrnant-NT

Snowdonia

A4406

Woollen Mill

12

Rhyd-
lydan

Glasfryn

Ce

A4085

Sygun
Copper Mine

Forest

Penmachno

B4407

Rhyd

Beddgelert

782

Park

A4407

Ysbyty Ifan

57

MOEL HEBOG

Nantmor

Croesor

Gloddfa Ganol
Slate Mine

Llechwedd
Slate Caverns

Carrog

Cwm
Penmachno

Llyn
Conwy

57

nfihangel-
pennant

552

MOELWYN
MAWR

770

Rhiwbryfdir

Blaenau
Ffestiniog

MOEL DDU

A498

A4085

Tanygrisiau

Bethania

Pumped
Storage
Scheme

Congl-
y-wal

669
CARNEDD
Y-FILAST

711
MOELWYN
BACH

Tan-y-Grisiau
Reservoir

20

658

Prenteg

Carreg

B4410

Rhyd
y-sarn

Ffestiniog
Railway

Ffestiniog

690
ARENIG
FACH

B4501

Penmorfa

Rhyd

Tan-y-
Bwlch

6

7

B4391

B4407

Afon Serw

Afon Gelyn

8

9

86

To Douglas (Summer Only)

5

Fleetwood
Rossall Point
Cleveleys

Knott End-on-Sea
Pilling Lane
Pilling
Preesall
Fisher's Row
Small Wood Hey
Stake Pool
COCKERHAM MOSS

Overton
Sunderland
River Lune
Glasson
Conder Green
Galgate
Ellel
Smith Green
Hampson Green
Bay Horse
Dolphin Lee
Street

Cockersand
Winmarleigh
Cabus
Scorton
R Grizedale

Cockerham
Potters Brook
Forton
Hollins Lane

4

A585
Stalmine
Burn Naze
Trunnah
Stanah
Staynall
Hambleton
Thornton
Little Thornton
Norcross
Little Bispham
Norbreck
Churchtown
Bispham
Carleton
Warbreck
North Shore
BLACKPOOL
Hoohill
Norcross
Normoss
Newton
Staining
Great Marton
Model Village

Stalmine Moss Side
Moor End
Hale Nook
Sower Carr
Hambleton Moss Side
Whin Lane End
Little Singleton
Singleton
Hardhorn
Greenhalgh
Weeton
Mythop

Moss Edge
Out Rawcliffe
Ratten Row
Larbreck
Great Eccleston
Copp
Lane Heads
Inskip Moss Side
Elswick
Thistleton
Esprick
Wharles
Medlar
Corner Row
Moor Side

Eagland Hill
Nateby
Churchtown
St Michael's on Wyre
R Brock
Bilsborrow
Inskip
Roseacre
Lewth
Catforth
Swillbrook
Treales

Garstang
Bonds
Bowgreave
Catterall
Brock
Cuddy Hill
Newsham
Moor Side
Woodplumpton

A6
M6

M55
Great Plumpton
A583
Wesham
Kirkham
Dowbridge
Scales
Lea Town
Cottam
Lower Bartle
Higher Bartle
Cadley

3

South Shore
A5230
Common Edge
Peel
Blackpool
B5261
B5233
Hey Houses
Royal Lytham
St Anne's
Ansdell
St Anne's
Fairhaven
Lytham St Anne's

Little Plumpton
Westby
Lower Ballam
Higher Ballam
Moss Side
Wrea Green
Bryning
Kellamergh
Ribby
B5259
Newton
Hall Cross
Clifton
A584
A583
Saltcotes
Freckleton
Warton
Lytham
River Ribble

Higher Penwortham
Bottom of Hutton
Hutton
Longton
New Longton
A59
Walmer Bridge
Midge Hall
Leyland
Faringt
White Stake
Penw
A582

SCALE
0 1 2 3 4 5 miles
0 1 2 3 4 5 kilometres

Hesketh Bank
Hundred End
Becconsall
Banks
Tarleton
B5248
Much Hoole
Much Hoole Town
Cocker Bar
Bretherton
B5253

2

Marshside
SOUTHPORT
Churchtown
Blowick
Birkdale
The Royal Birkdale
Ainsdale-on-Sea
Ainsdale

Crossens
A565
Mere Brow
Sollom
A581
Croston
Eccleston
Leisure Lakes
Holmeswood
B5246
Rufford
Rufford Old Hall NT
Sollom
R Douglas

Newtown
Shaw Green
B5253
Eccleston Green
Heskin Green

Brown Edge
B5243
Snape Green
Bescar
Martin Mere
Scarisbrick
Pinfold
New Lane
Tarlscough
Burscough Bridge
Hoscar
Parbold

Shirdley Hill
Hurlston Green
Heaton's Bridge
Mawdesley
Wrightington Bar
Bispham Green
Grimshaw Green
Mossy Lea
Robin Hood

1

78
A565
Woodvale
Formby
Formby Point
Raven Meols
Little Altcar
North End
Hightown
Great Altcar
B5195
Ince Blundell
Homer Green
Lunt

Barton
Haskayne
Halsall
Bangor's Green
Primrose Hill
Downholland Cross
Aughton
Holt Green
Bowker's Green

A570
Burscough
Ring o' Bells
Newburgh
Ormskirk
AA
Westhead
Scarth Hill
Town Green
Blaguegate
Stanley Gate
A506
Royal Oak
Lydiate
Moss Side
Melling Mount

A59
Stormy Corner
Skelmersdale
Digmoor
Bickerstaffe
Barrow Nook

Appley Bridge
Holland Lees
Dalton
Roby Mill
Elmers Green
Up Holland
Crawford
M58
Orrell
Longshaw
Common
Rainford
King's Moss
B5205
Cha

0

2
Blundellsands
Little Crosby
Thornton
3
Sefton
Sefton Town
Maghull
Waddicar
Netherton
Kennessee Green
Melling
A59
4
Melling Mount
KIRKBY
5
Crank

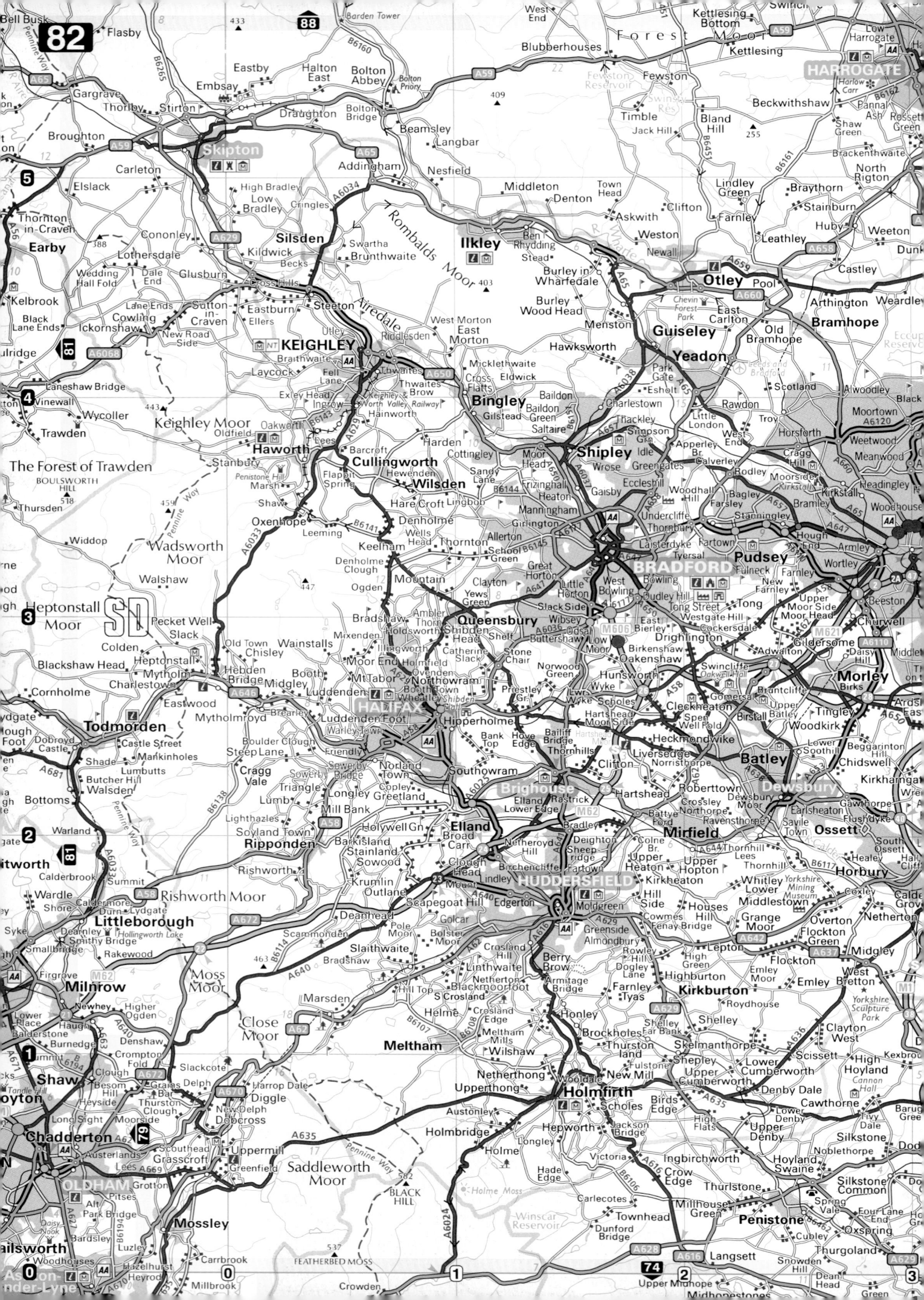

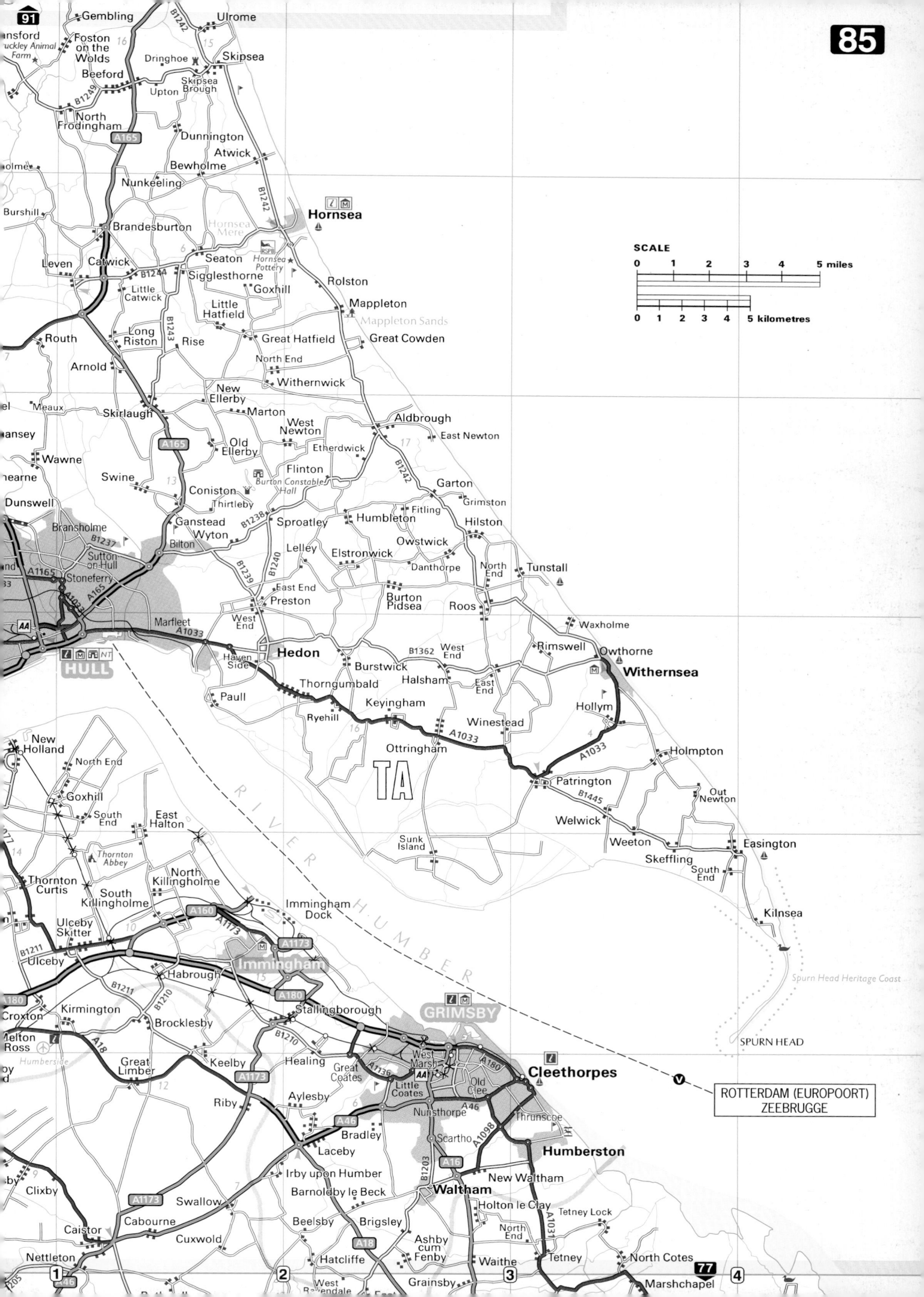

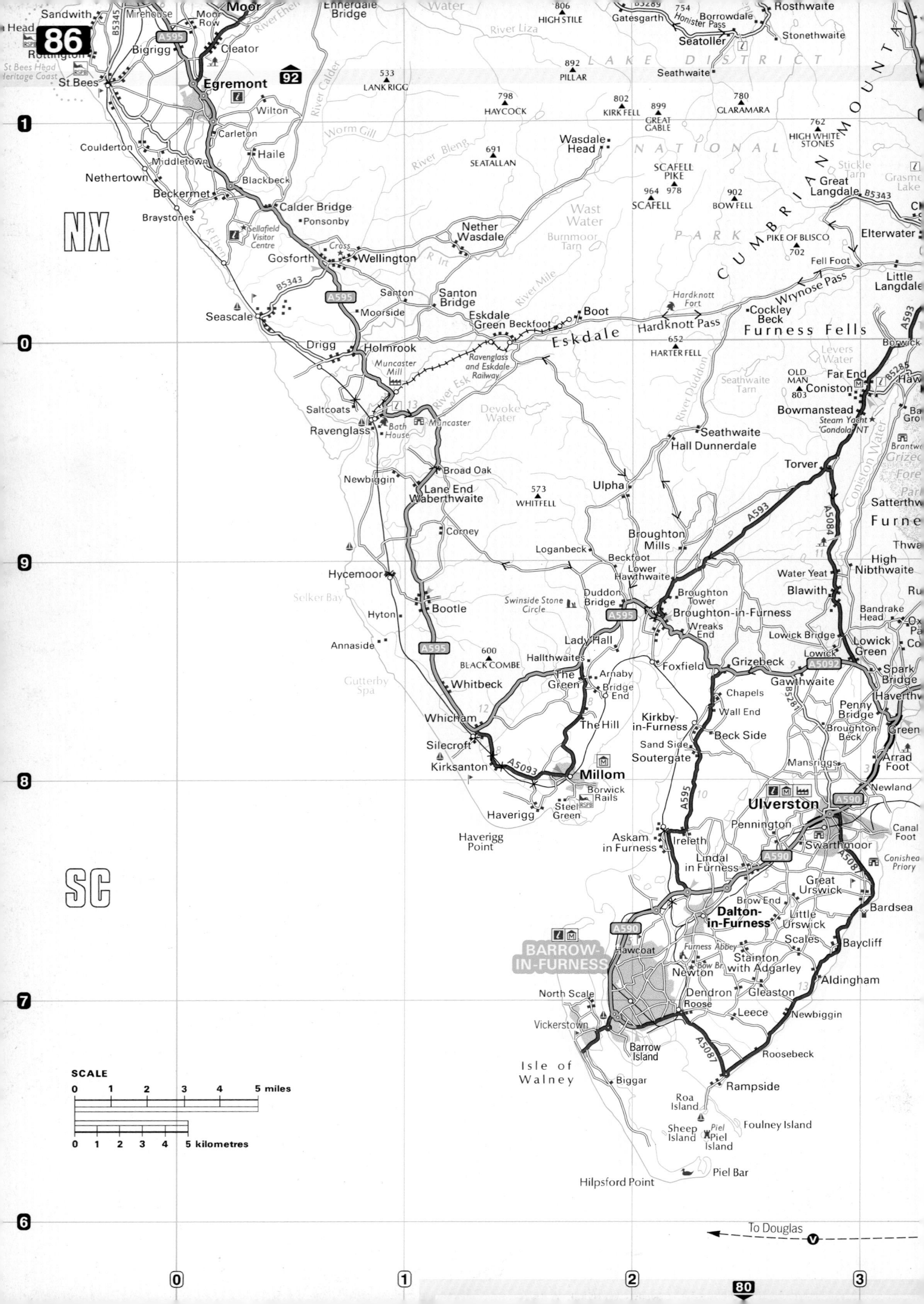

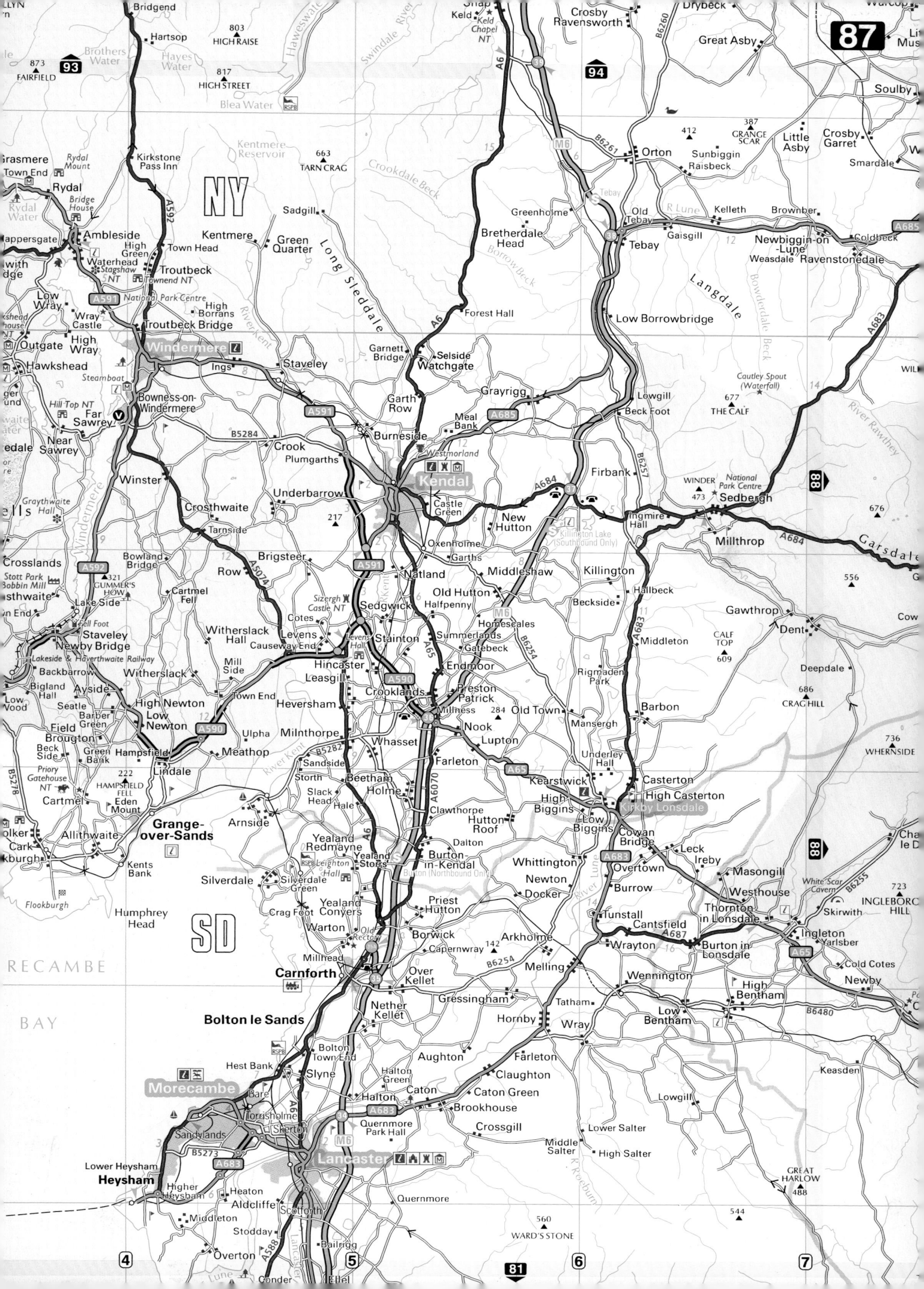

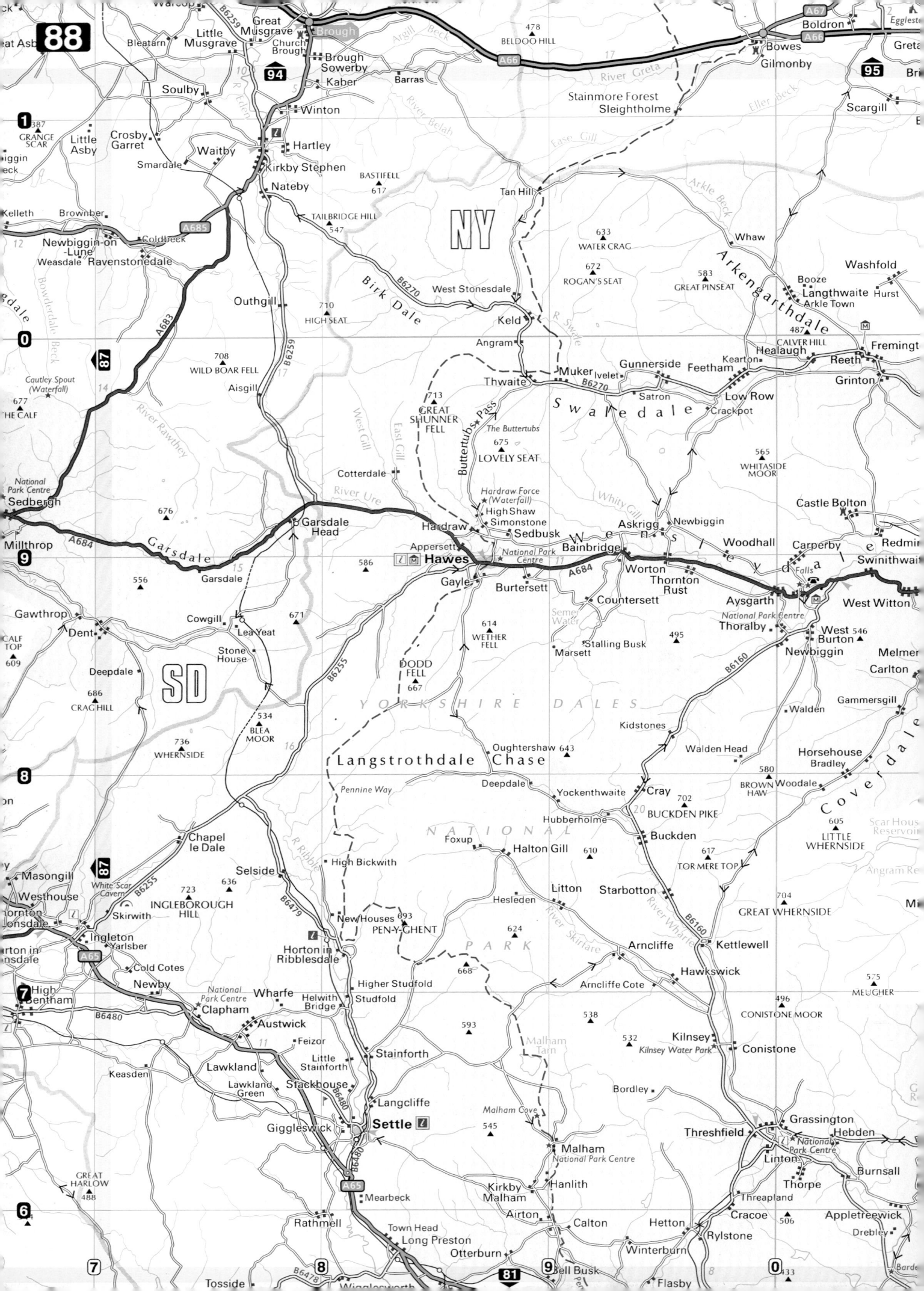

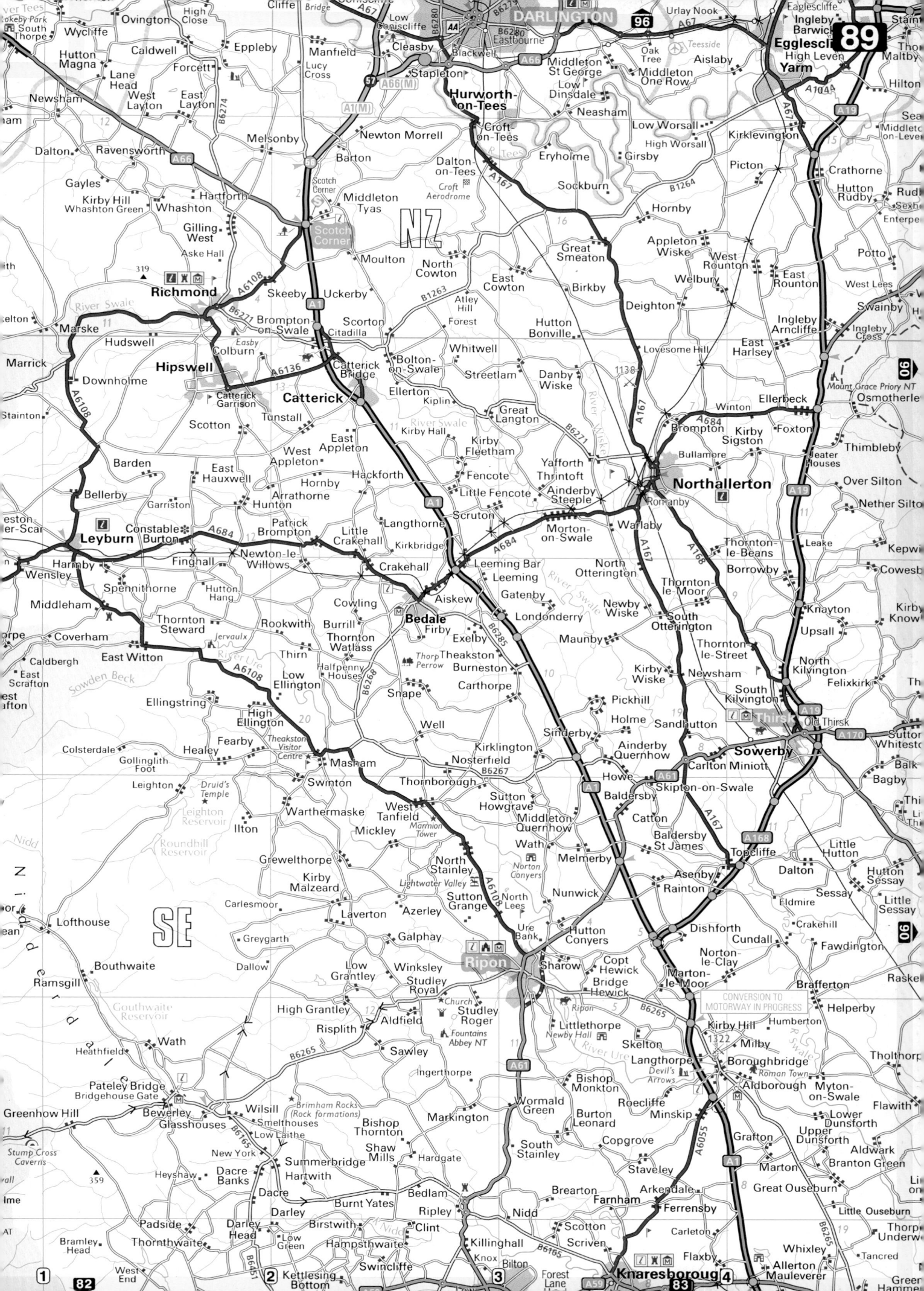

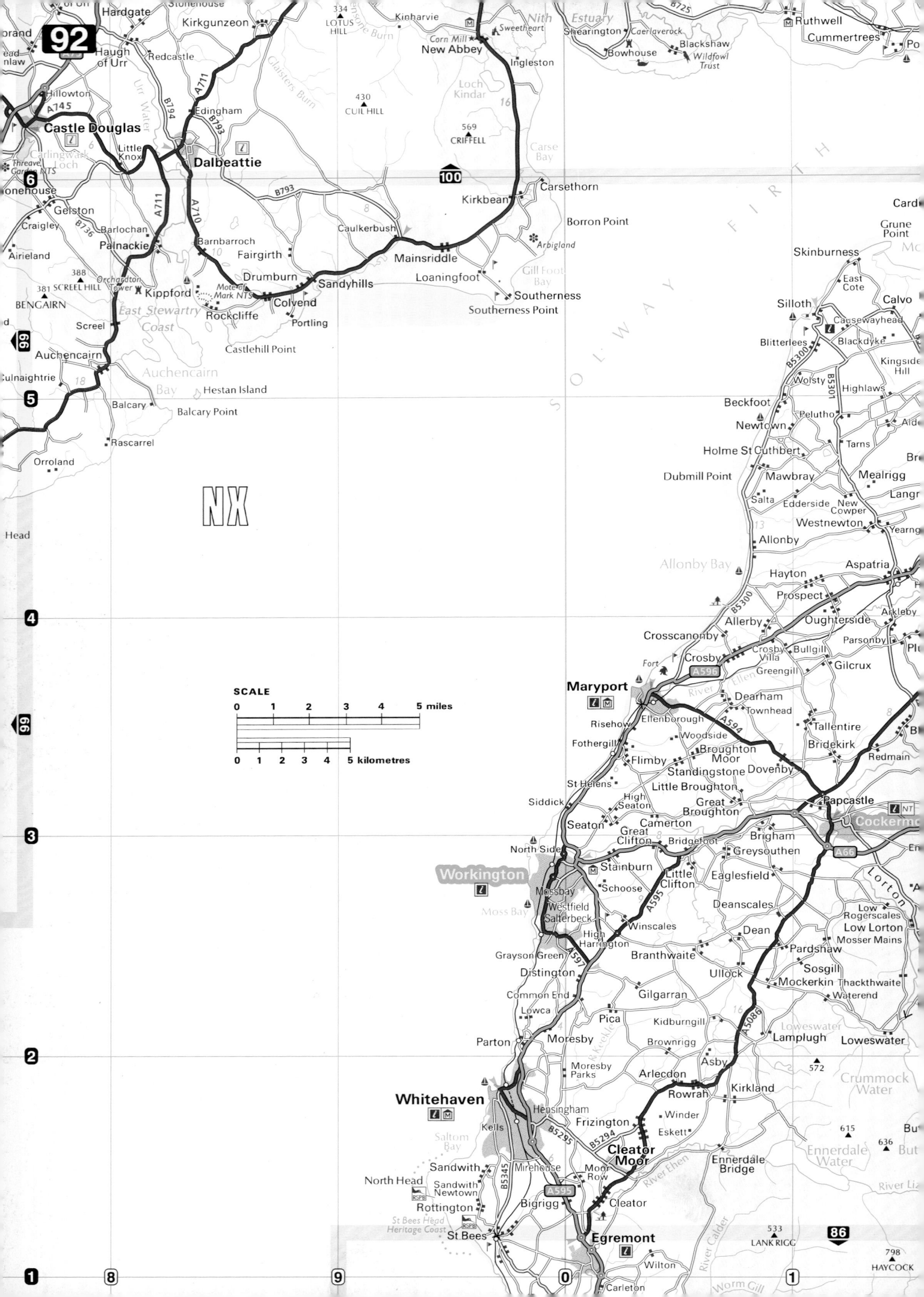

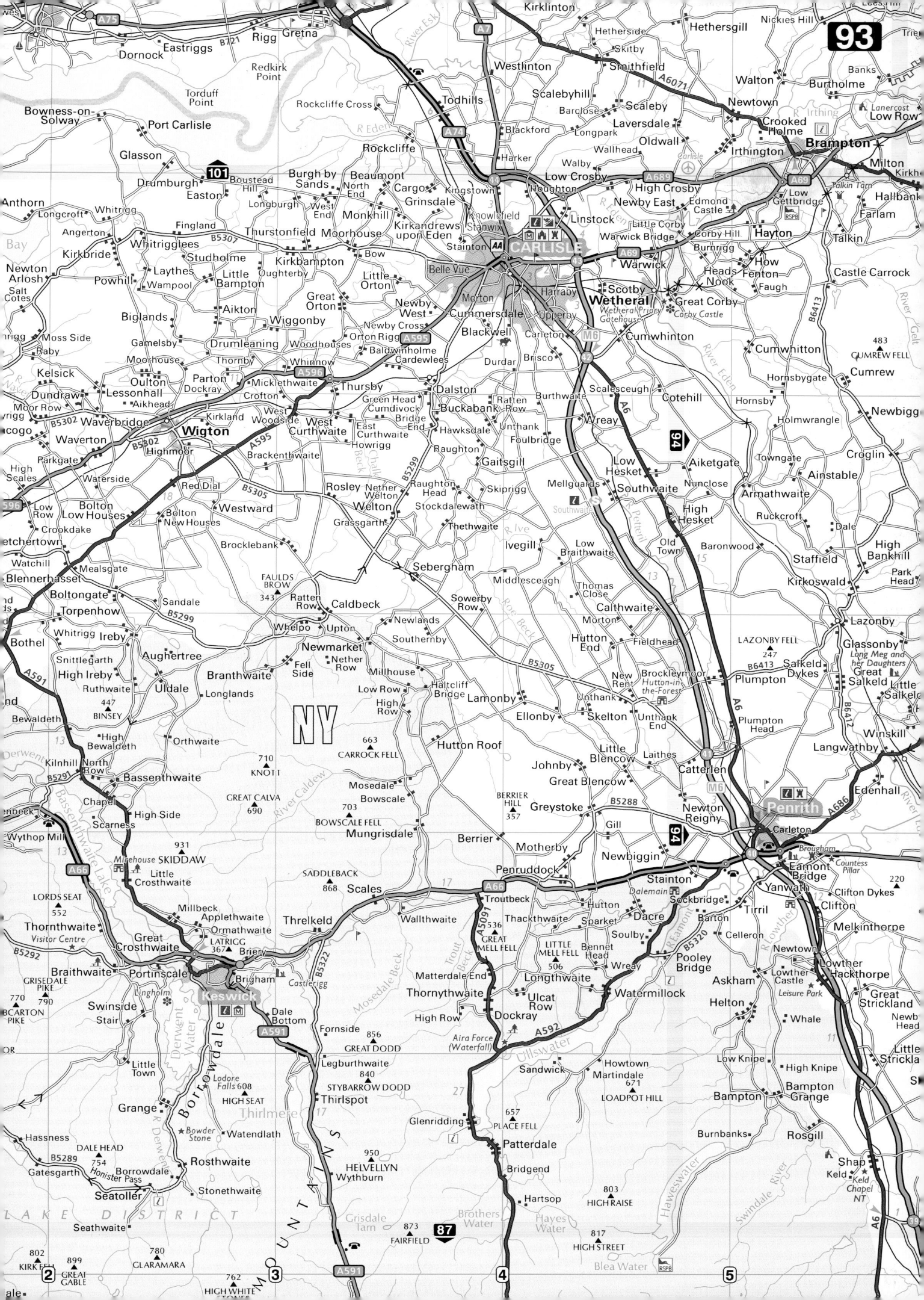

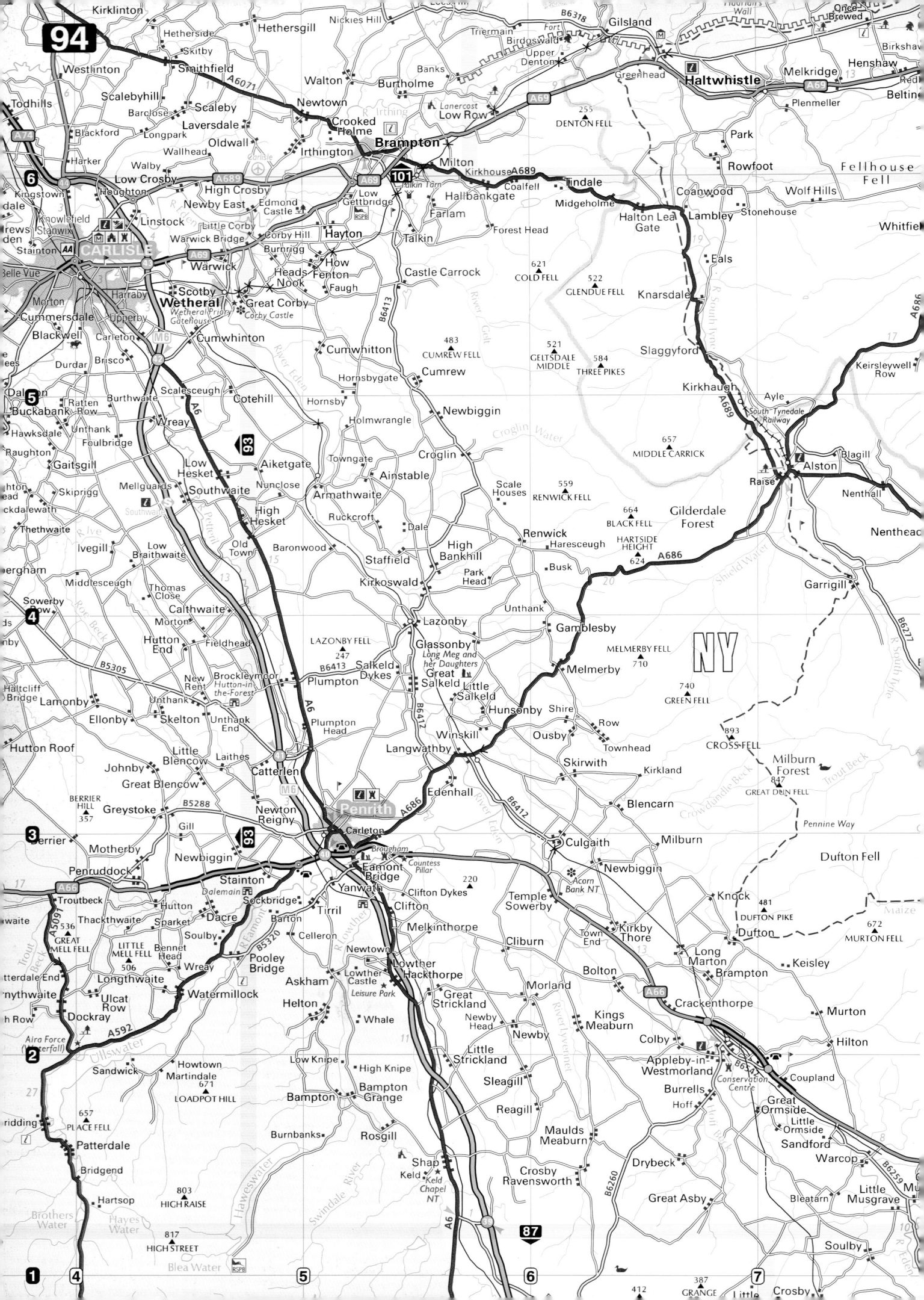

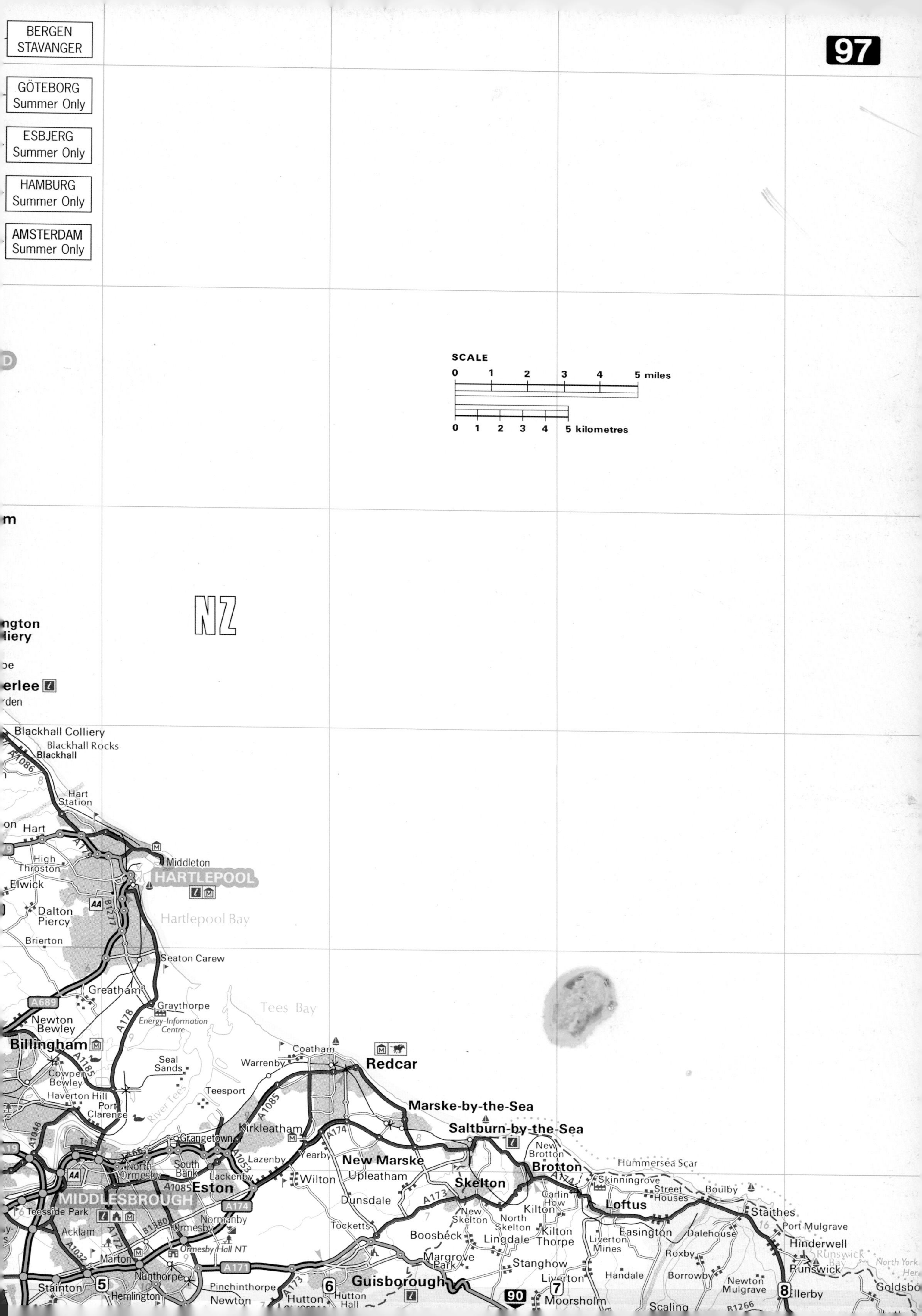

BERGEN
STAVANGER

GÖTEBORG
Summer Only

ESBJERG
Summer Only

HAMBURG
Summer Only

AMSTERDAM
Summer Only

SCALE

0   1   2   3   4   5 miles

0   1   2   3   4   5 kilometres

NZ

ngton
liery

be

erlee 🛈

rden

Blackhall Colliery
Blackhall Rocks
Blackhall

Hart
Station

on Hart

High
Throston

Middleton

HARTLEPOOL

🛈

Elwick

AA

Dalton
Piercy

Hartlepool Bay

Brierton

Seaton Carew

Greatham

A689

Graythorpe

Newton
Bewley

Energy Information
Centre

Billingham

Tees Bay

Seal
Sands

Coatham

Cowpen
Bewley

Warrenby

Redcar

Haverton Hill

Teesport

A1085

Port
Clarence

Marske-by-the-Sea

Teesside Park

Kirkleatham

Saltburn-by-the-Sea

Grangetown

A174

New
Brotton

Lazenby

Yearby

New Marske

Hummersea Scar

South
Bank

Lackenby

Wilton

Upleatham

Brotton

A174

Skinningrove

MIDDLESBROUGH

AA

North
Ormesby

Eston

A1085

Dunsdale

Skelton

Carlin
How

Street
Houses

Boulby

A174

Teesside Park

Ormesby

Normanby

Tocketts

New
Skelton

North
Skelton

Kilton

Loftus

Staithes

Acklam

Ormesby Hall NT

Boosbeck

Lingdale

Kilton
Thorpe

Liverton
Mines

Easington

Dalehouse

Port Mulgrave

Marton

Margrove
Park

Stanghow

Roxby

Hinderwell

Stainton

Liverton

Handale

Borrowby

Newton
Mulgrave

Runswick

Hemlington

Nunthorpe

Newton

Hutton
Hall

Guisborough

Moorsholm

Scaling

Ellerby

Goldsbo

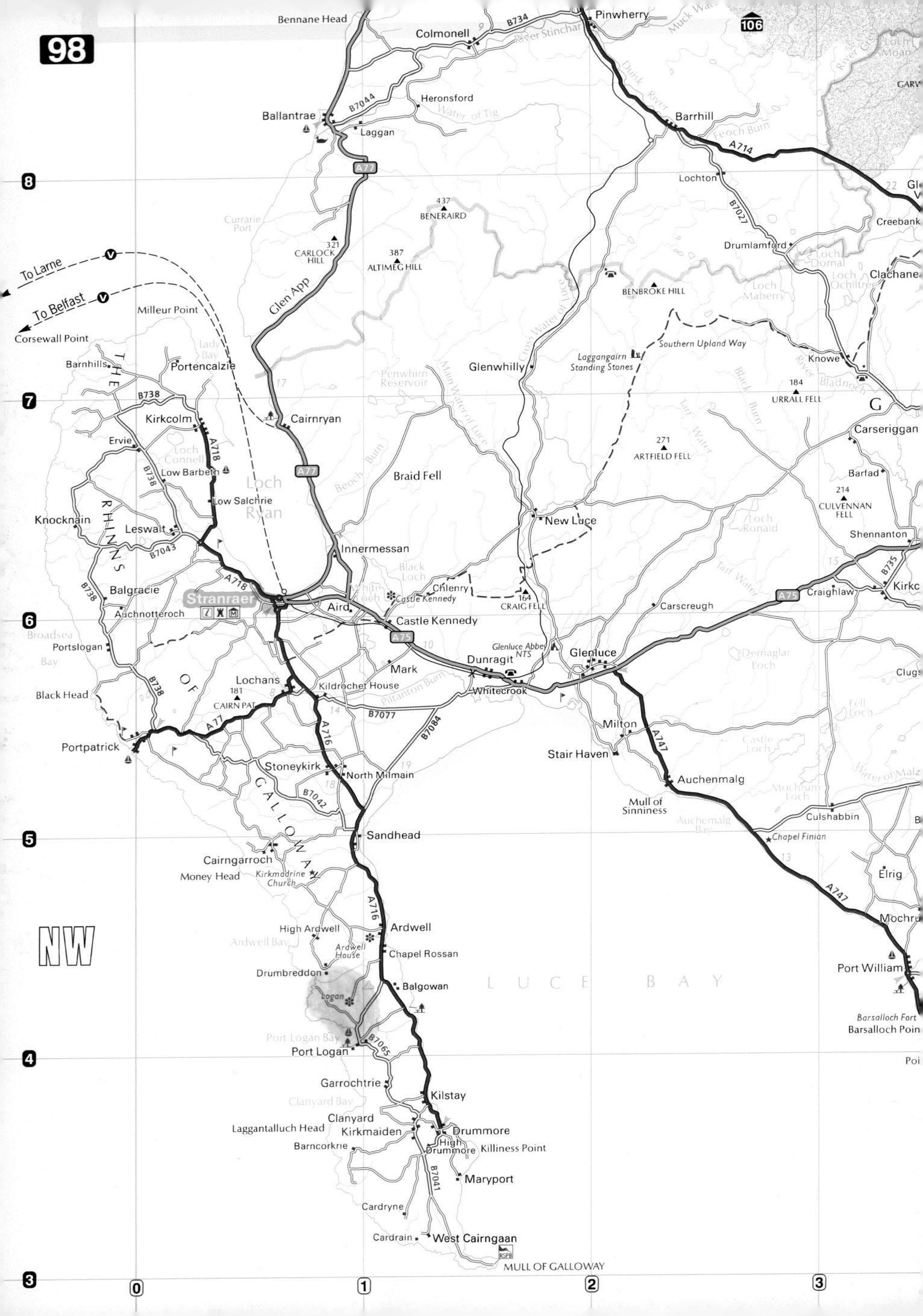

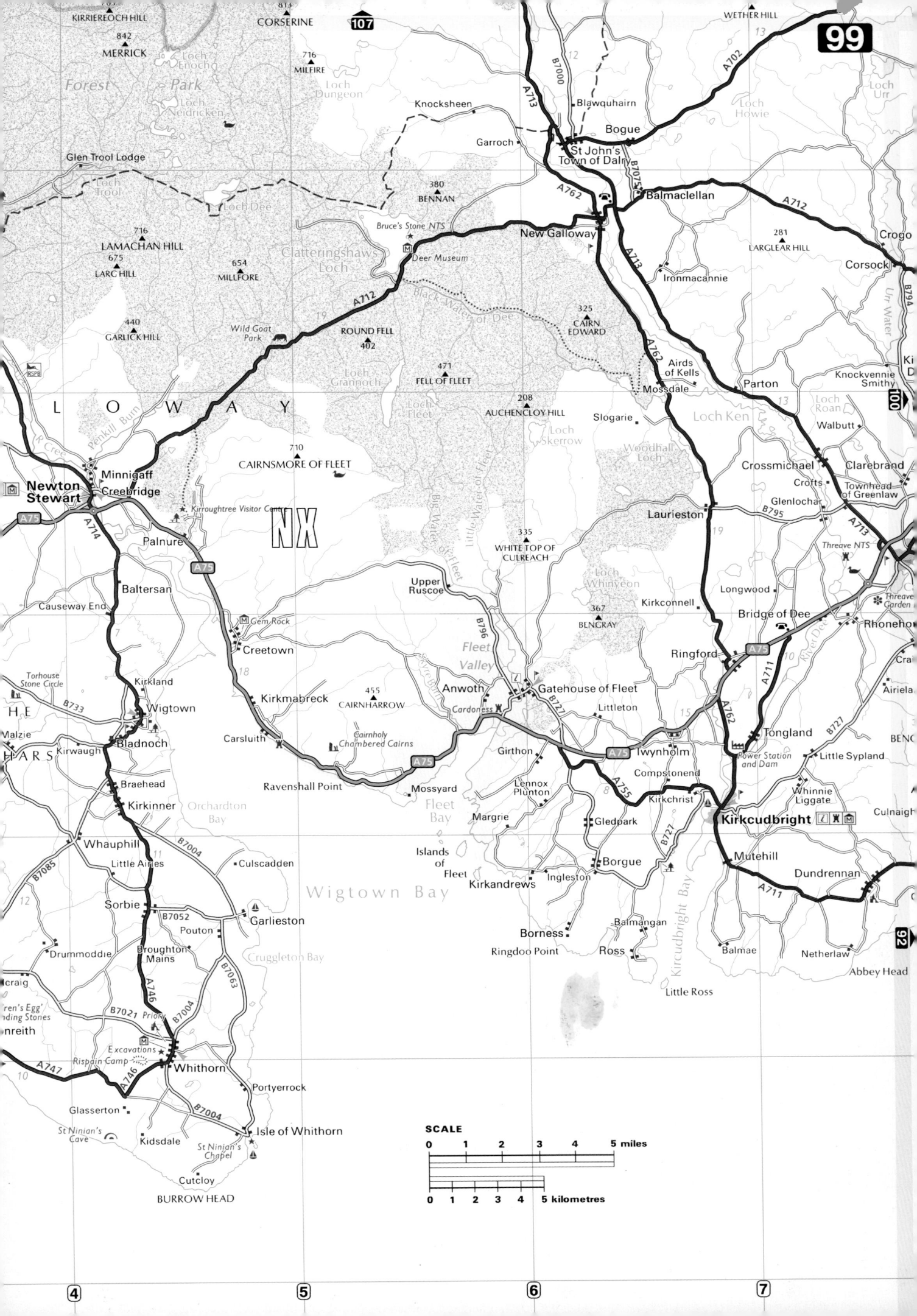

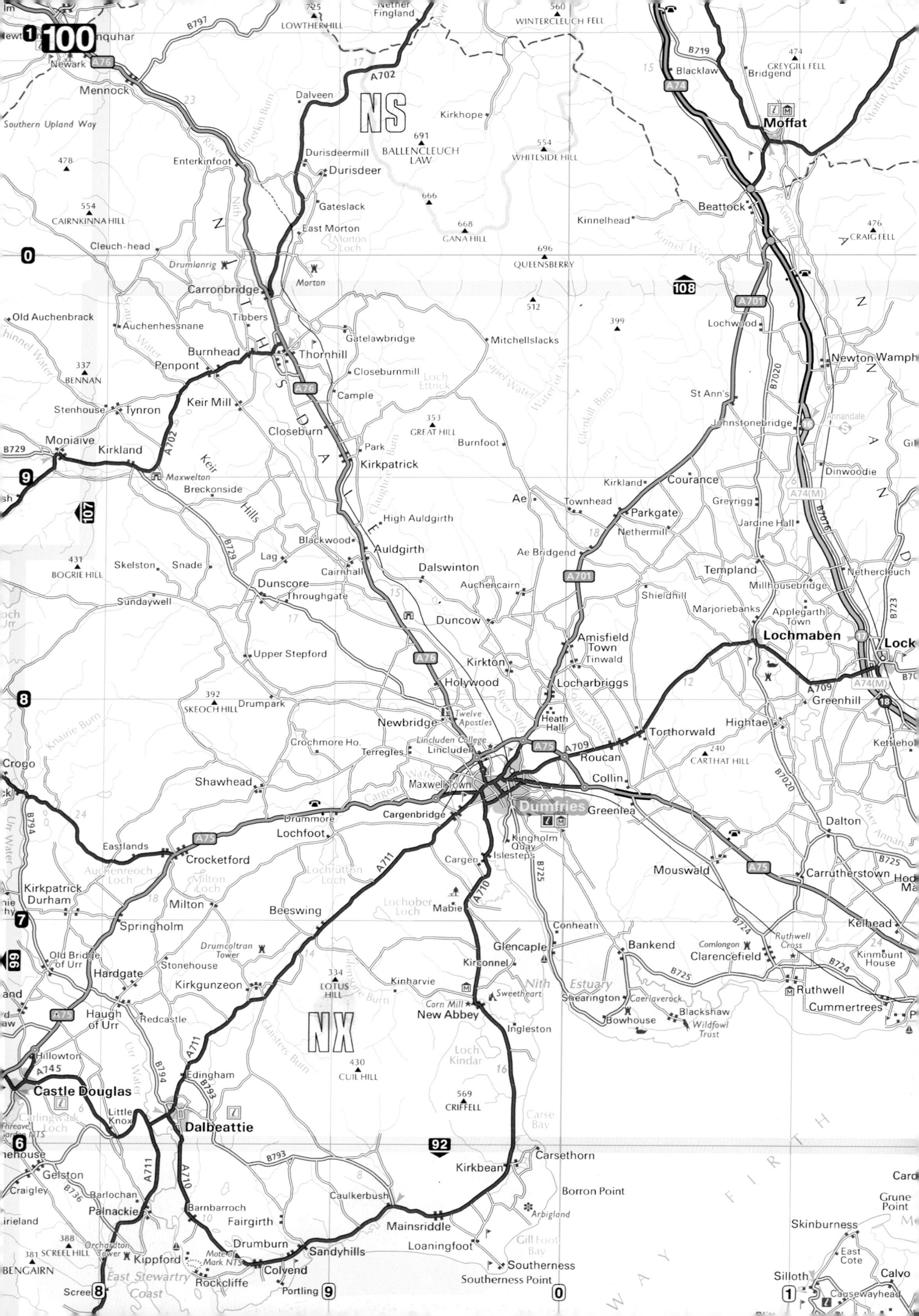

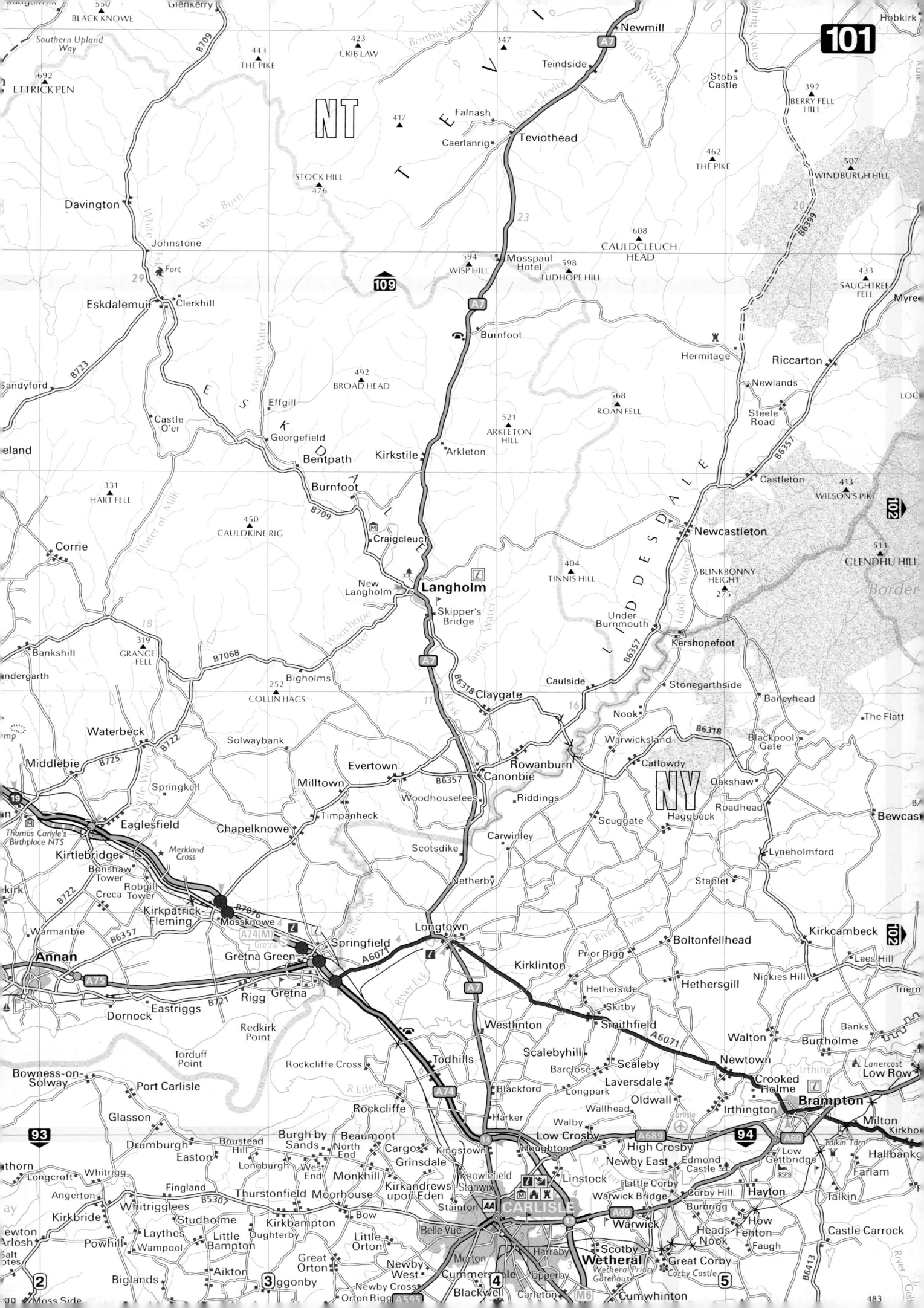

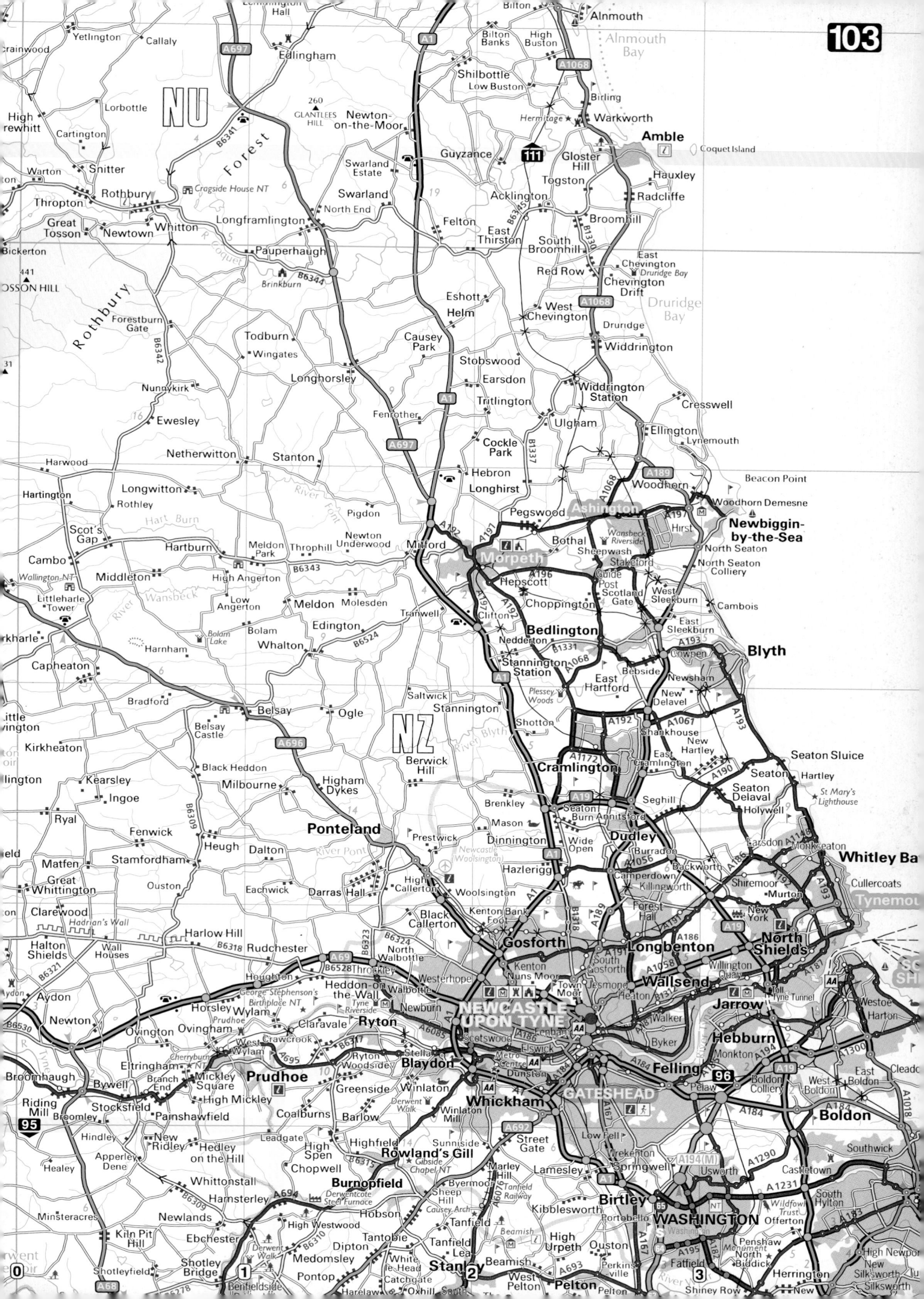

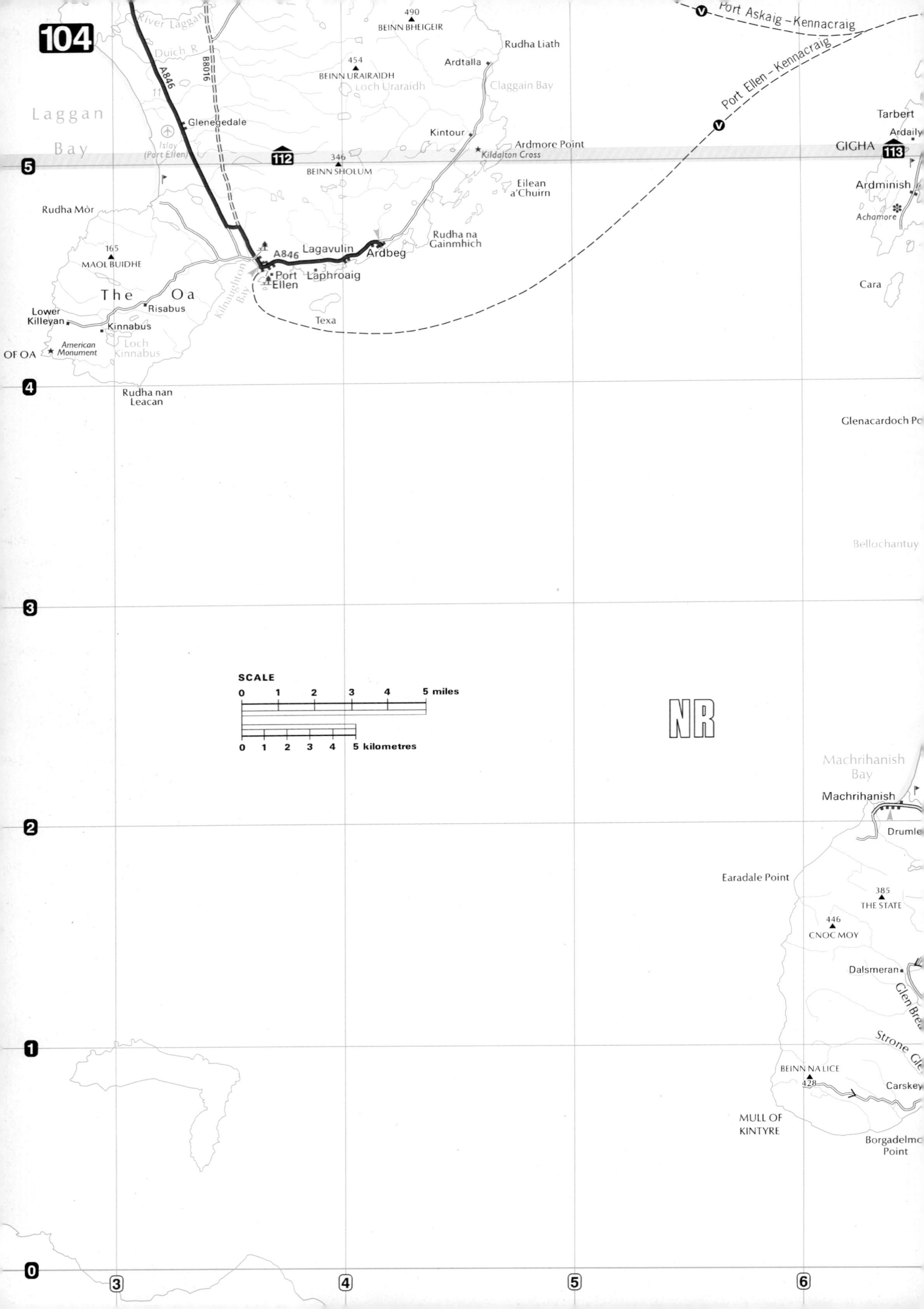

River Laggan
Duich R.
490
BEINN BHEIGEIR
Rudha Liath
Ardtalla
454
BEINN URAIRAIDH
Loch Uraraidh
Claggain Bay
A846
B8016
Glenegedale
Laggan
Bay
Islay
(Port Ellen)
112
Kintour
346
BEINN SHOLUM
Ardmore Point
Kildalton Cross
Eilean
a'Chuirn
Rudha Mòr
165
MAOL BUIDHE
Rudha na
Gainmhich
A846
Lagavulin
Ardbeg
The   Oa
Kilnaughton Bay
Port
Ellen
Laphroaig
Cara
Lower
Killeyan
Risabus
Kinnabus
Texa
American
Monument
Loch
Kinnabus
OF OA
Rudha nan
Leacan

Port Askaig – Kennacraig
Port Ellen – Kennacraig
Tarbert
Ardaily
GIGHA
113
Ardminish
Achamore

Glenacardoch Po

Bellochantuy

SCALE

| 0 | 1 | 2 | 3 | 4 | 5 miles |

| 0 | 1 | 2 | 3 | 4 | 5 kilometres |

NR

Machrihanish
Bay
Machrihanish
Drumle
Earadale Point
385
THE STATE
446
CNOC MOY
Dalsmeran
Glen Bree
Strone Gle
BEINN NA LICE
428
Carskey
MULL OF
KINTYRE
Borgadelmo
Point

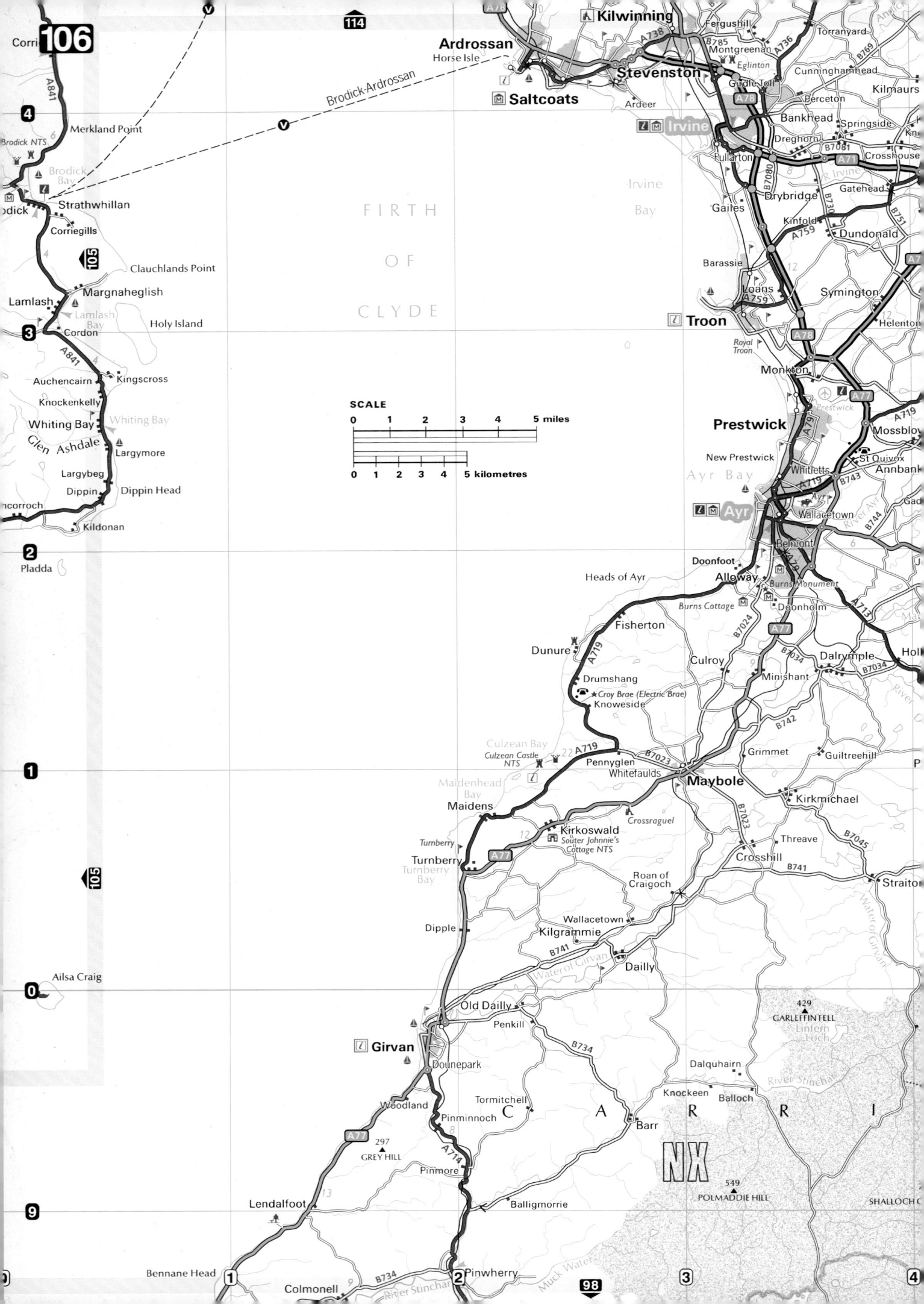

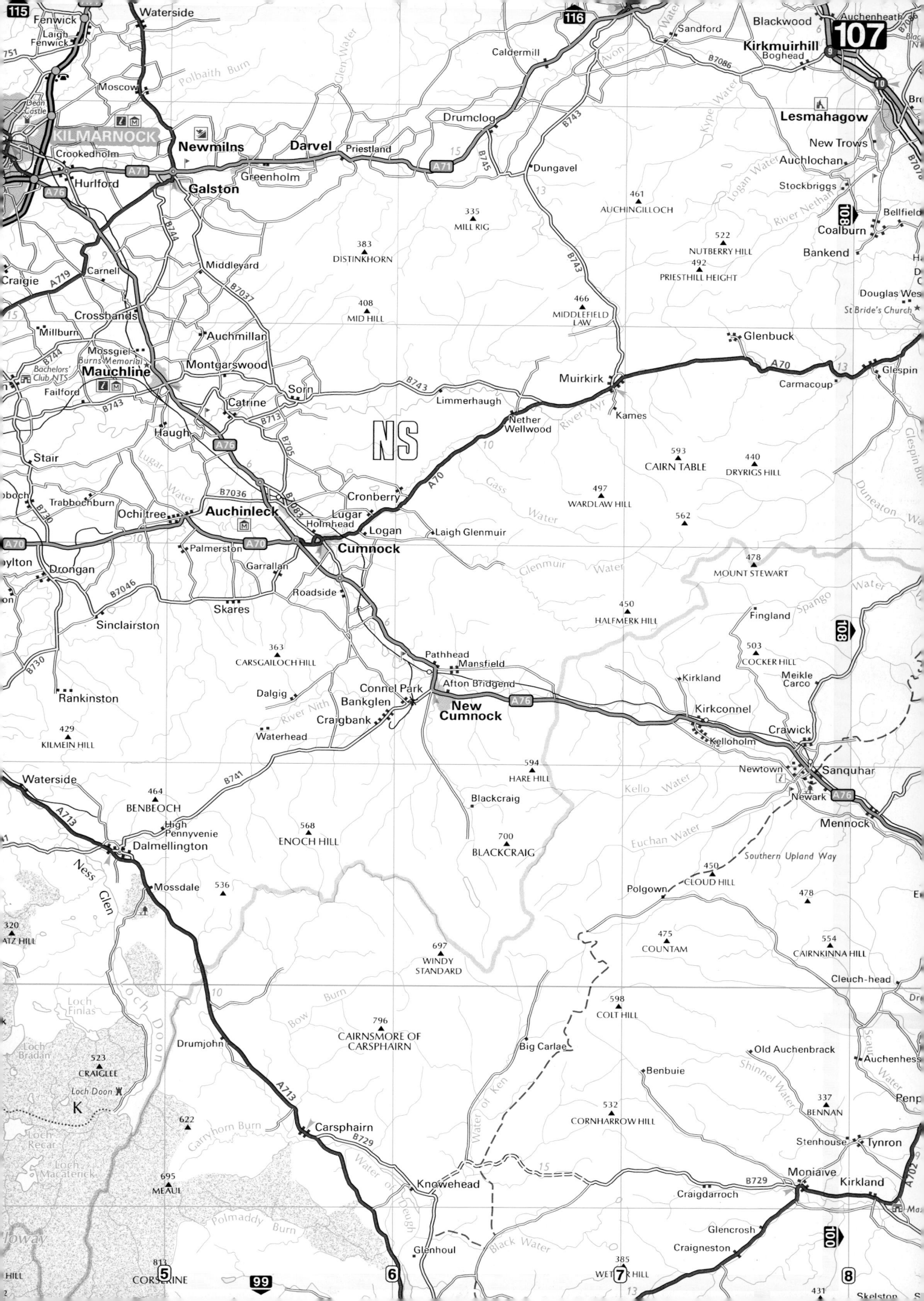

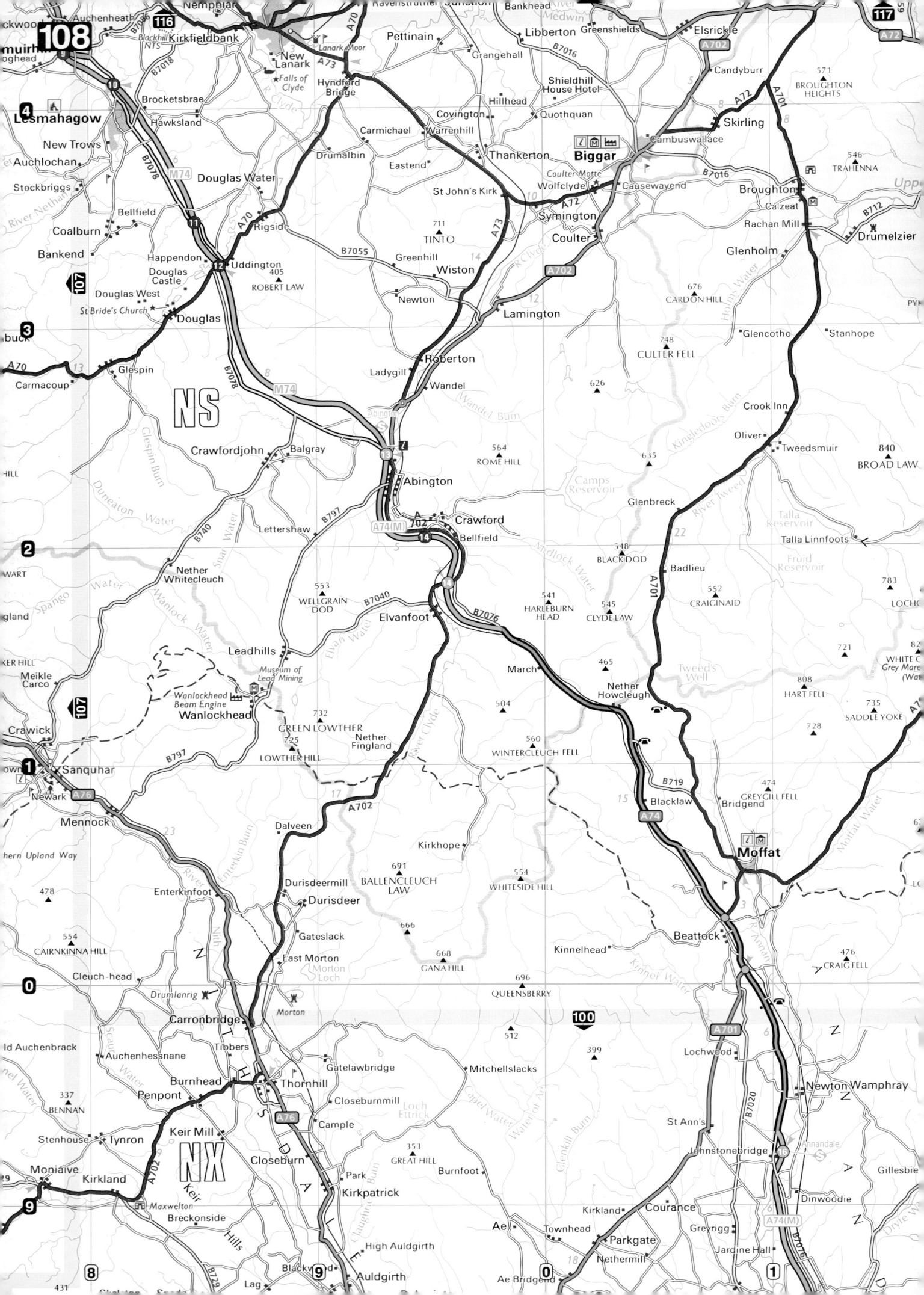

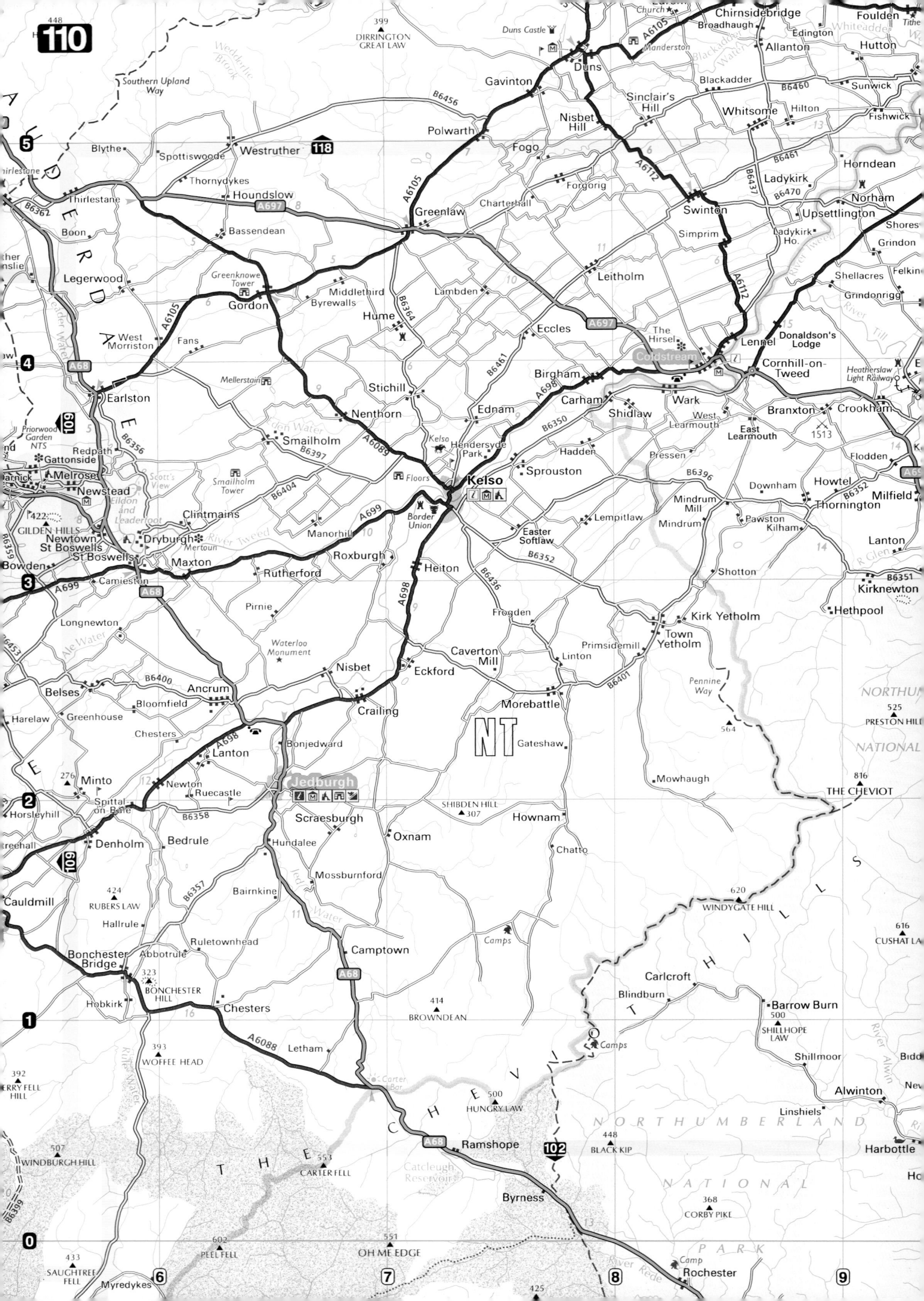

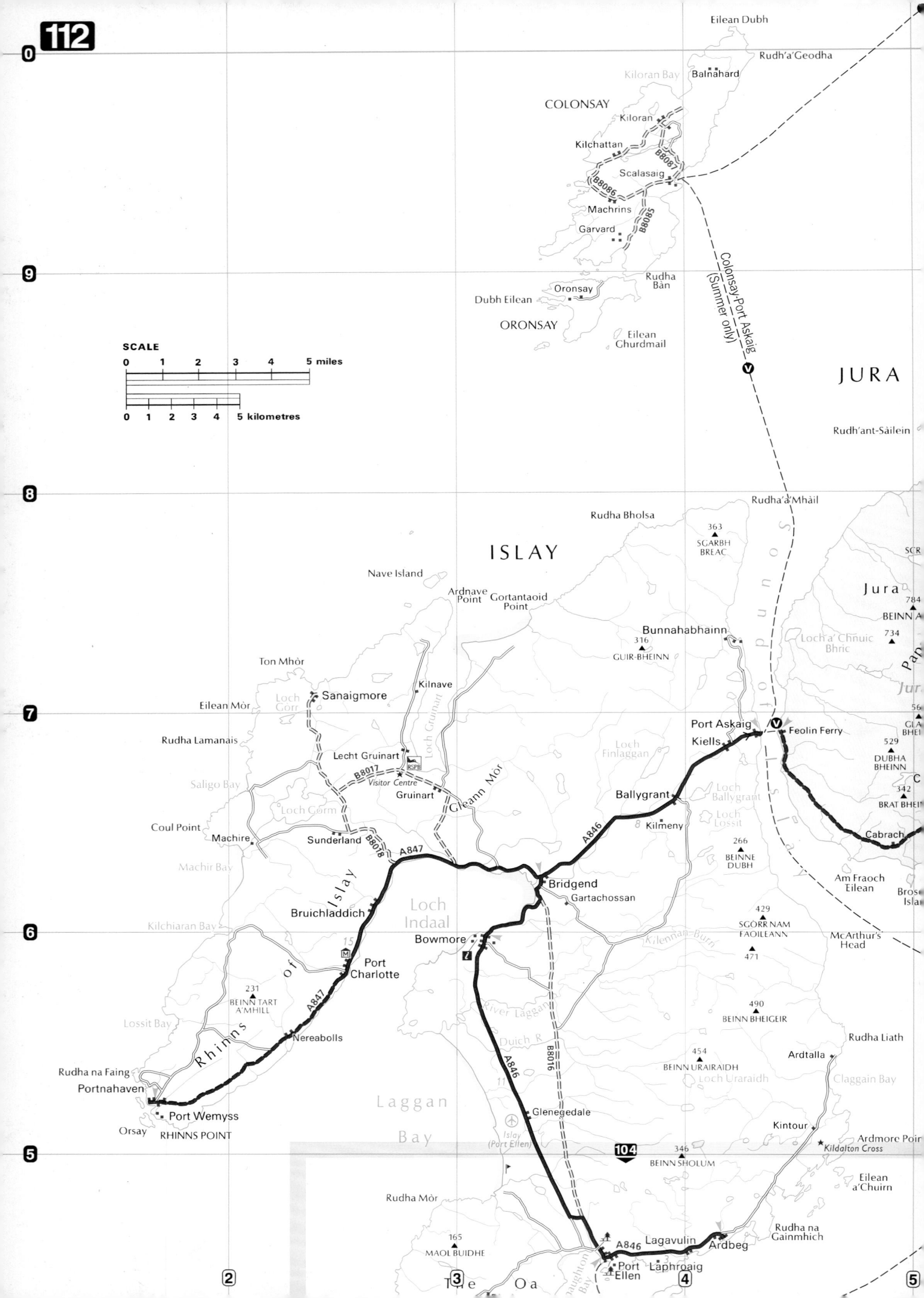

SCALE

0   1   2   3   4   5 miles

0   1   2   3   4   5 kilometres

COLONSAY

Eilean Dubh

Rudh'a'Geodha

Kiloran Bay   Balnahard

Kiloran

Kilchattan   B8081

Scalasaig

B8086

Machrins   B8085

Garvard

Rudha Bàn

Oronsay

Dubh Eilean

ORONSAY

Eilean Ghurdmail

Colonsay-Port Askaig
(Summer only)

JURA

Rudh'ant-Sàilein

Rudha'a'Mhàil

Rudha Bholsa

363 ▲ SGARBH BREAC

ISLAY

Nave Island

Ardnave Point   Gortantaoid Point

Bunnahabhainn

316 ▲ GUIR-BHEINN

Jura

784 ▲ BEINN A

734 ▲ Loch a' Chnuic Bhric

SCR

Ton Mhòr

Eilean Mòr

Loch Gorr

Sanaigmore   Kilnave

Rudha Lamanais

Loch Gruinart

Lecht Gruinart   RSPB

B8017   Visitor Centre   Gruinart

Port Askaig   V   Feolin Ferry

Kiells

56

Saligo Bay

Loch Gorm

Gleann Mòr

Loch Finlaggan

Ballygrant

529 GLA BHEI

DUBHA BHEINN

342 BRAT BHEI

C

Coul Point   Machire

Sunderland   B8018   A847

A846   8   Kilmeny

Loch Ballygrant

Loch Lossit

Cabrach

Machir Bay

Kilchiaran Bay

Bruichladdich

Loch Indaal

Bridgend
Gartachossan

266 ▲ BEINNE DUBH

Am Fraoch Eilean

Bros Isla

429 ▲ SGORR NAM FAOILEANN

McArthur's Head

231 ▲ BEINN TART A'MHILL

15   M   Port Charlotte

A847

Bowmore   i

471 ▲

Rhinns of Islay

Lossit Bay

Nereabolls

River Laggan

Duich R.

A846   B8016

490 ▲ BEINN BHEIGEIR

Rudha na Faing

Portnahaven

Port Wemyss

Orsay   RHINNS POINT

Laggan Bay

Glenegedale

Islay (Port Ellen)

454 ▲ BEINN URAIRAIDH   Loch Urairaidh

Ardtalla

Rudha Liath

Claggain Bay

Rudha Mòr

165 ▲ MAOL BUIDHE

The Oa

104

346 ▲ BEINN SHOLUM

Kintour

Ardmore Poir

Kildalton Cross

Eilean a'Chuirn

A846   Lagavulin

Port Ellen   Laphroaig   Ardbeg

Rudha na Gainmhich

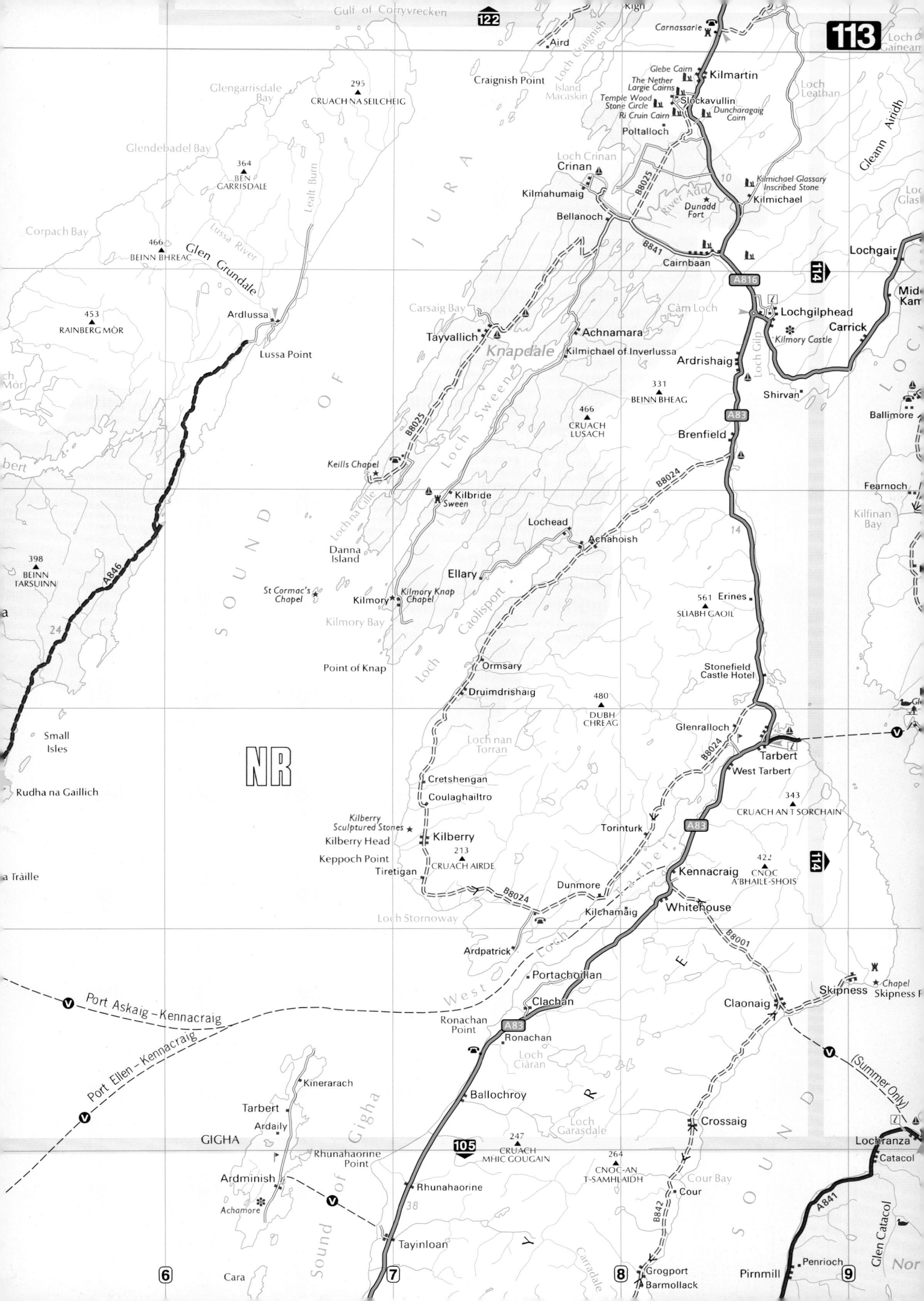

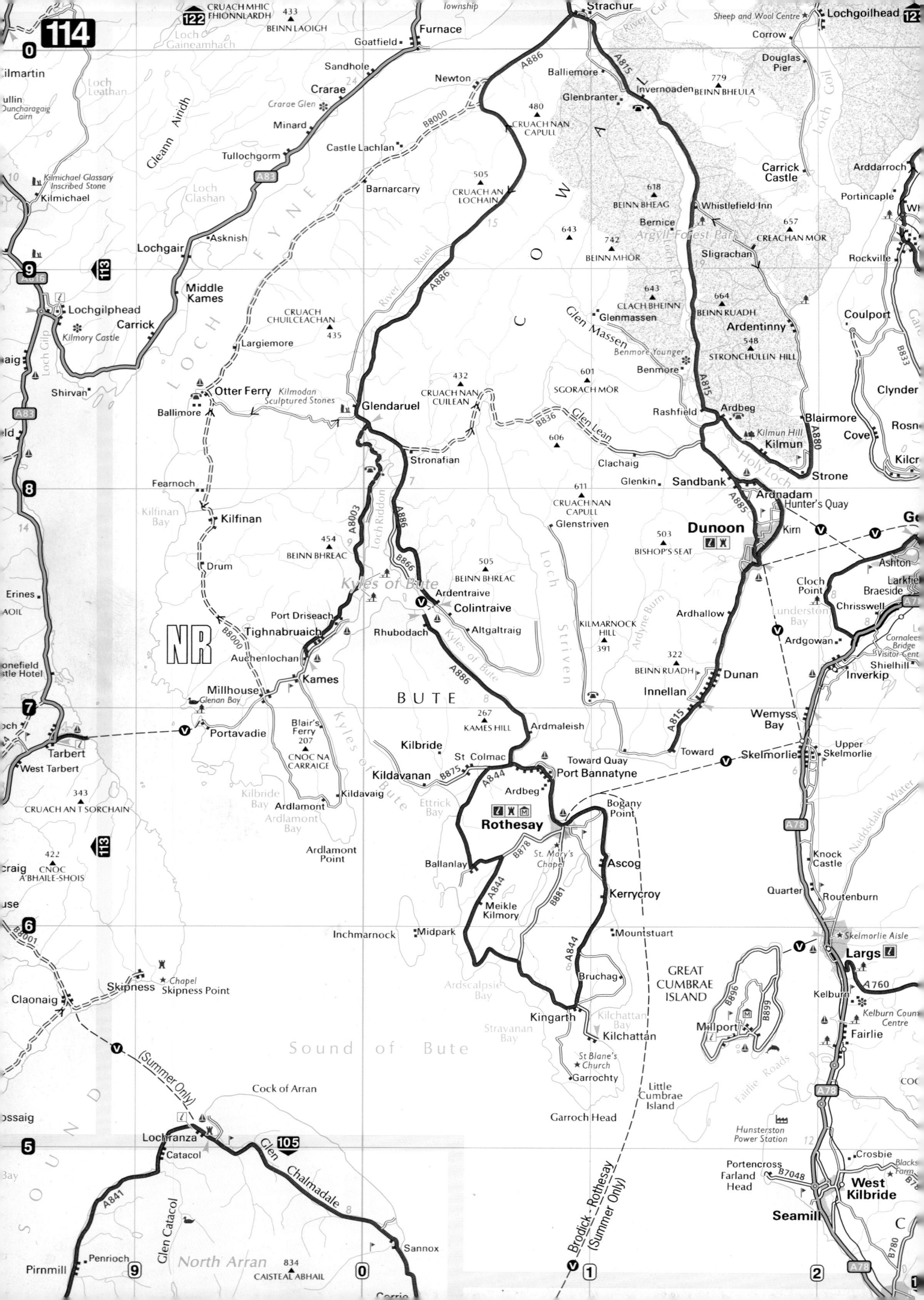

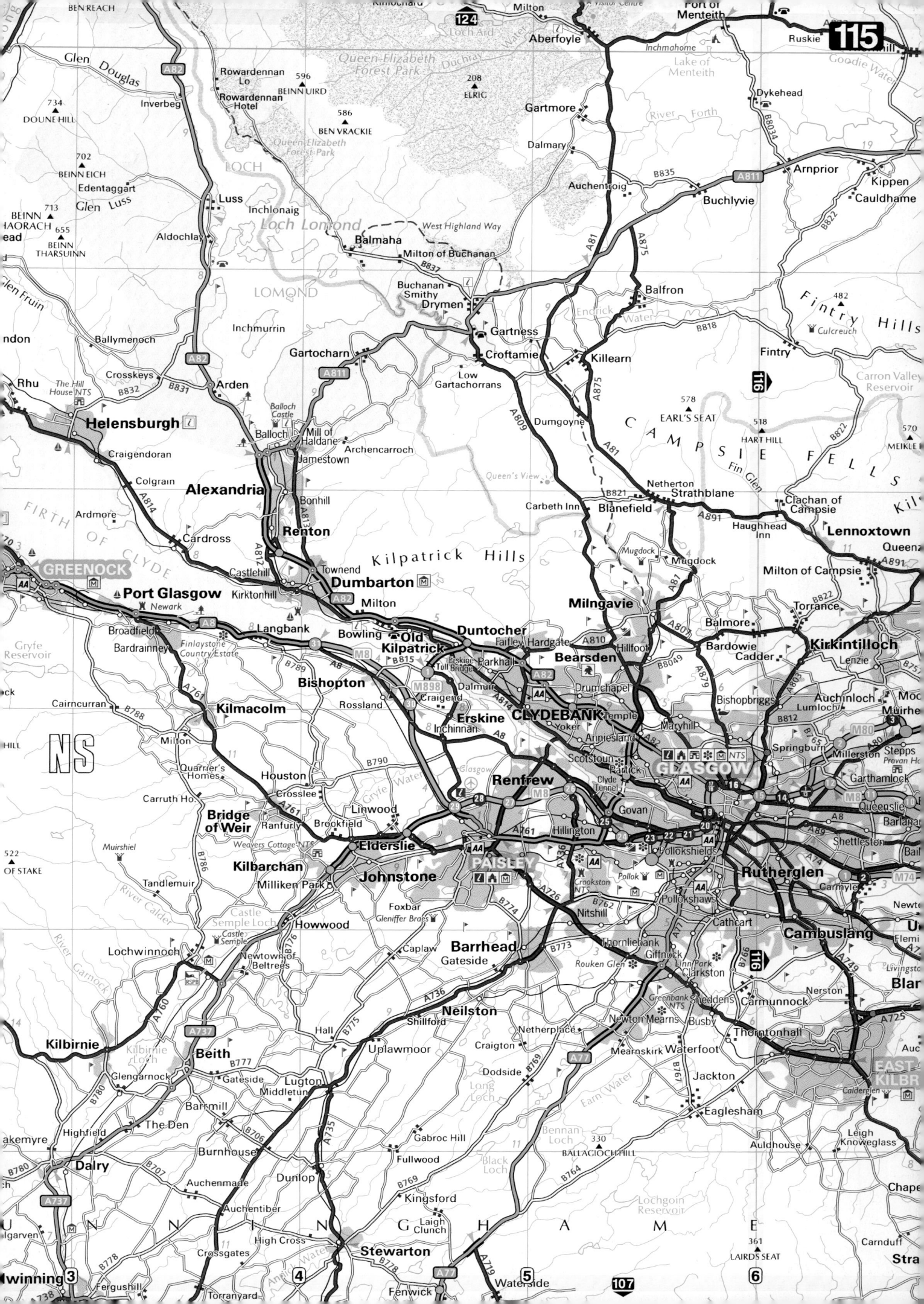

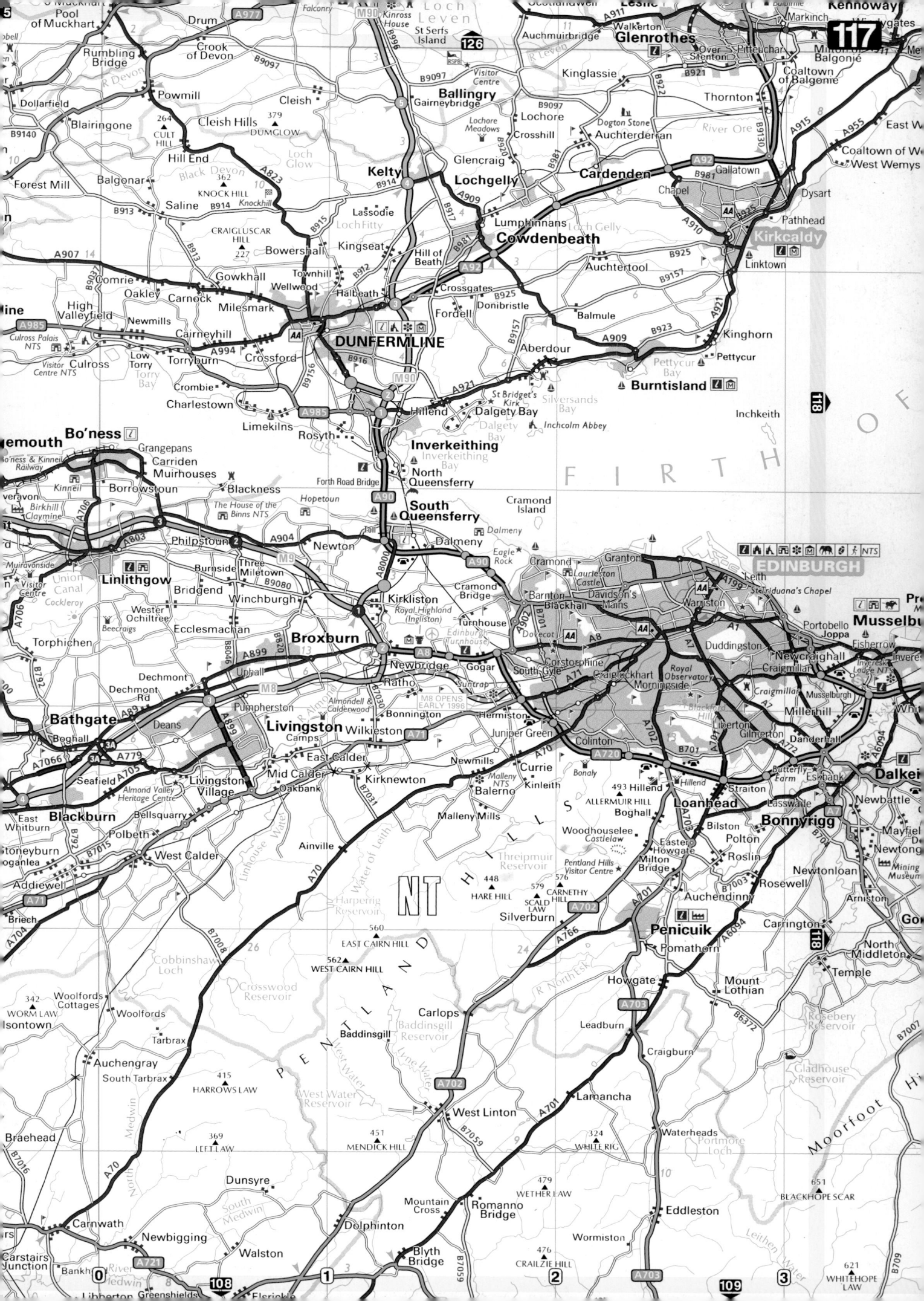

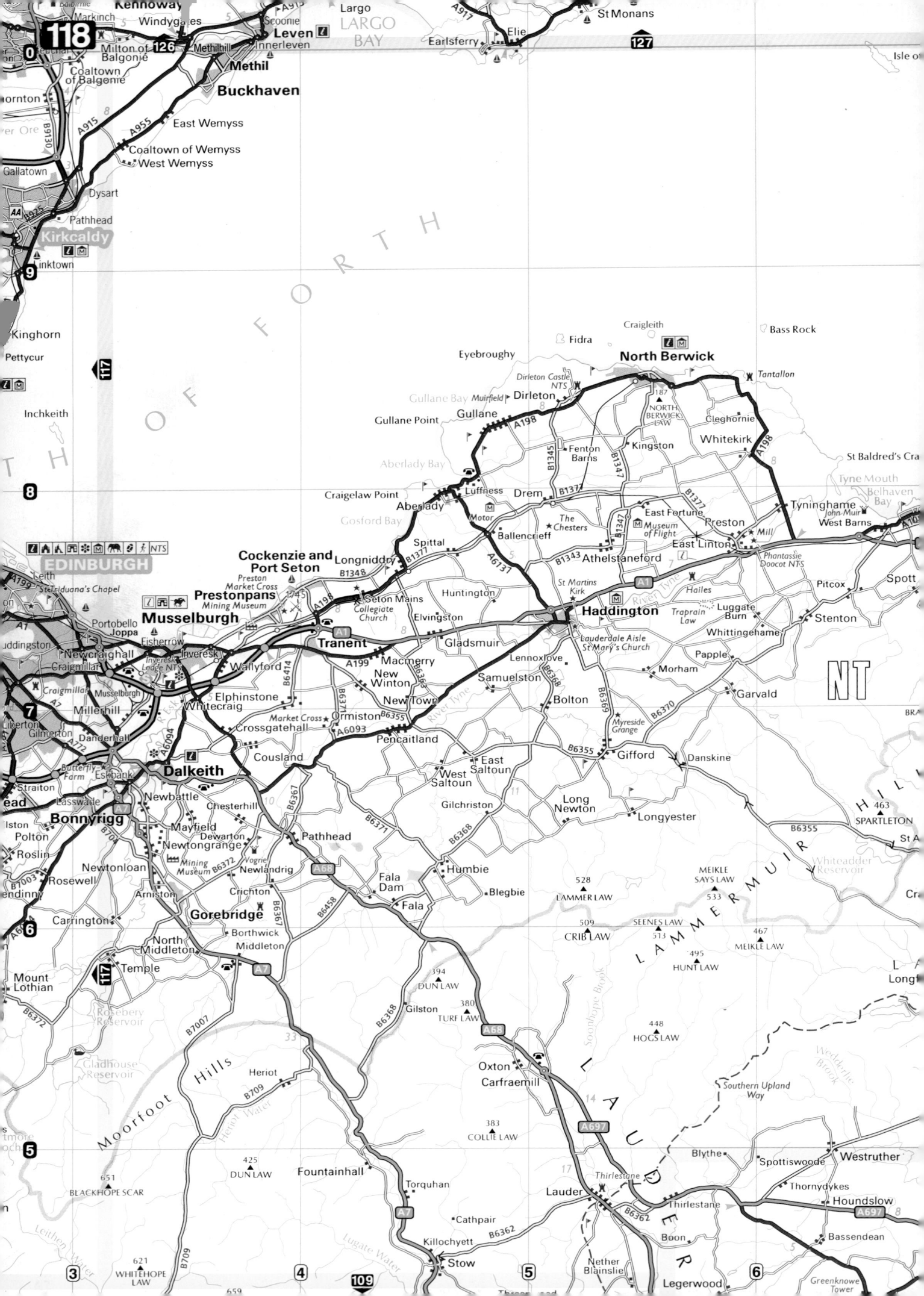

SCALE

0 1 2 3 4 5 miles

0 1 2 3 4 5 kilometres

NU

...ar

...oxburn

Barns Ness

...650

East Barns

Chapel Point

Skateraw

Torness Power Station

Thorntonloch

Innerwick

Crowhill

319

COCKLAW HILL

Dunglass

Collegiate Church

Reed Point

Cove

Pease Bay

Siccar Point

Fast Castle Head

Oldhamstocks

Cockburnspath

ST ABB'S HEAD

A1

Ecclaw

Southern Upland Way

A1107

196

BROWN RIG

St Abbs

391

HEART LAW

Grantshouse

Coldingham

Coldingham Bay

Butterdean

Eye Water

21

Houndwood

22

Eyemouth

Quixwood

Heugh Head

Cairncross

A6112

Abbey St Bathans

262

HORSELEY HILL

B6438

Reston

A1

Ellemford

14

Edin's Hall Broch

Ayton

Burnmouth

...itchester

325

COCKBURN LAW

Marygold

Auchencrow

B6437

E R M I R

B6355

Lintlaw

B6355

Lamberton

Marshall Meadows Bay

...99

Primrosehill

Preston

Chirnside

North Northumberland Heritage Coast

...NGTON

...AT LAW

B6365

Cumledge

Edrom

Church

15

Chirnsidebridge

Foulden

Tithe Barn

1333

A6105

A1

Duns Castle

Broadhaugh

Edington

Whiteadder

Water

A6105

Duns

Manderston

Allanton

Hutton

Paxton

Barracks

Town Ramparts

Berwick-upon-Tweed

Gavinton

Blackadder

Water

Blackadder

B6460

Sunwick

B6461

Tweedmouth

Polwarth

Nisbet Hill

Sinclair's Hill

Whitsome

Hilton

Fishwick

Loanend

East Ord

Spittal

B6456

13

A698

Huds Head

110

Fogo

6

7

A6105

Charterhall

A6112

Forgorig

Swinton

B6461

Horndean

Ladykirk

Murton

Thornton

Unthank

Scremerston

111

Greenlaw

11

Simprim

Ladykirk Ho.

B6437

B6470

Norham

Upsettlington

Shoreswood

Grindon

West Allerdean

B6354

B6525

Cheswick

A1

7

8

9

0

Ancroft

Göswick

Haggerston

Felkington

128

Eilean Mòr

Rudha Mòr

Rudha Sgor-inn

Bousd

Sorisdale

Cliad Bay

Gallanach

B8072

Arnabost

Grishipoll

Clabhach

Loch Cliad

B8071

COLL

Hogh Bay

Ballyhaugh

Arinagour

Totronald

Acha

B8070

Arileod

Uig

Friesland Bay

Eilean Ornsay

V

Feall Bay

Loch Breachacha

Calgary Point

Crossapol Bay

Rudha Pàsachd

V

Gunna

V

5

Caoles

Rudha Dubh

Rudha Port Bhiosd

Clachan

Mor

Balephetrish Bay

B8069

Ruaig

Loch Bhasapoll

Haugh Bay

Ballevullin

Cornaigmore

B8068

Kenovay

Gott Bay

Tiree-Oban

V

Kilkenneth

B8068

Tiree

Scarinish

Moss

Middleton

Heylipoll

B8065

Crossapoll

Barrapoll

Hynish Bay

TIREE

TRESHNISH
ISLES

Lunga

Loch a' Phuill

Balemartine

B8067

Mannel

nn Thorbhais

4

Balephuil Bay

Hynish

Bac Mòr or
Dutchman's Cap

Bac Beag

NL

3

IONA

Abbey

Baile Mór

Maclean's Cross

Nunnery

Fion

2

Soa Island

Erraid

Torran Rocks

6

0   **1**   **2**   **3**

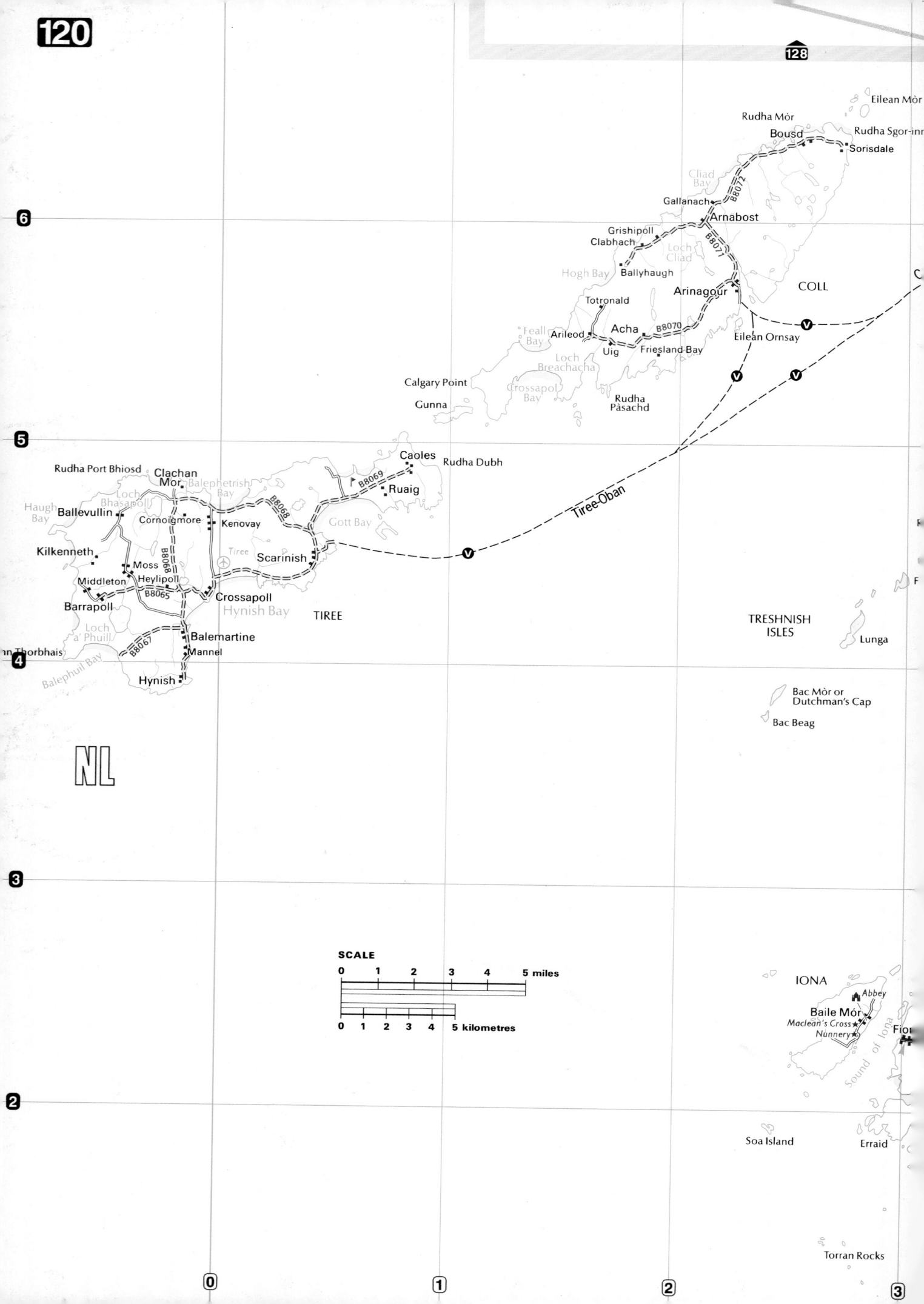

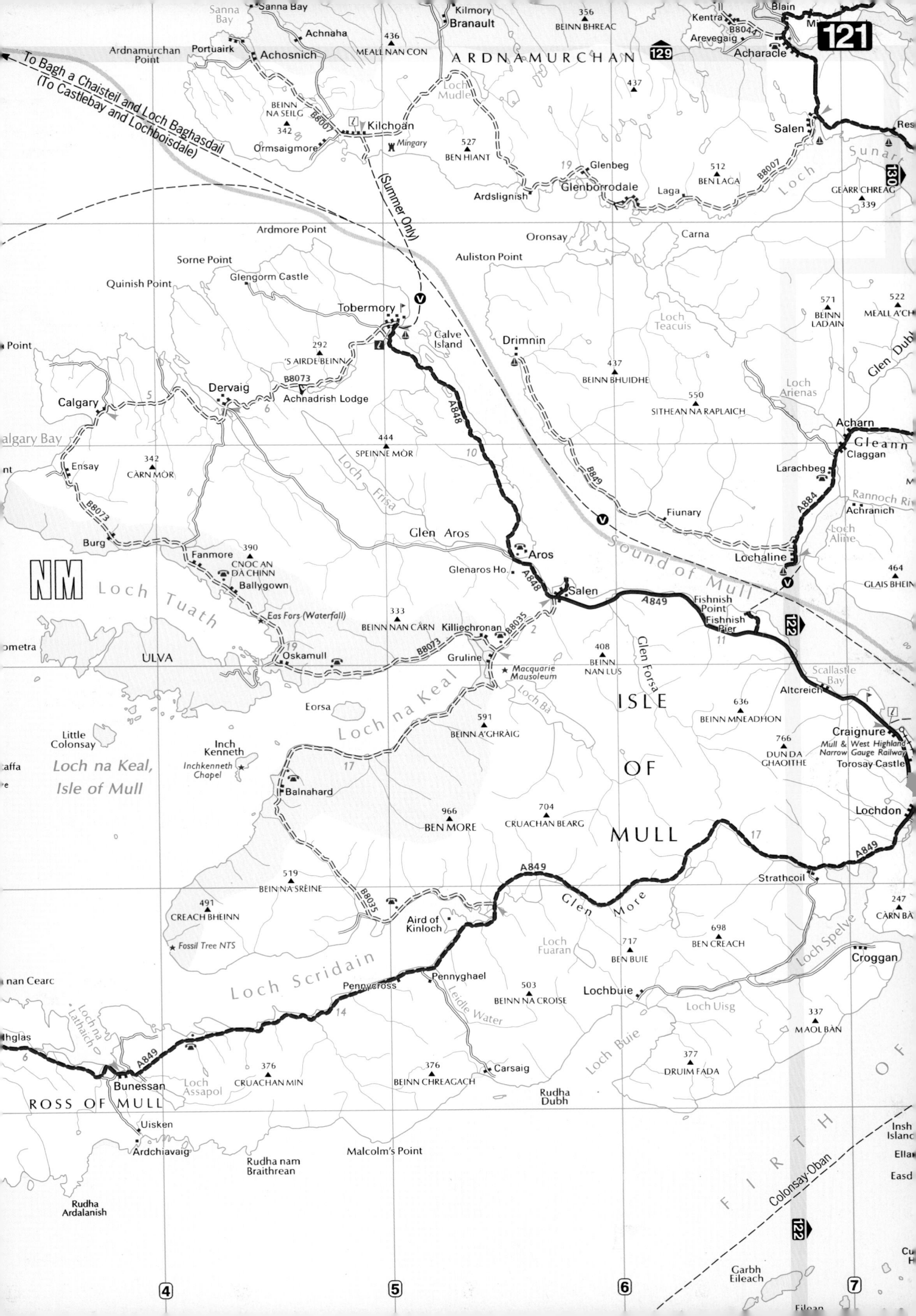

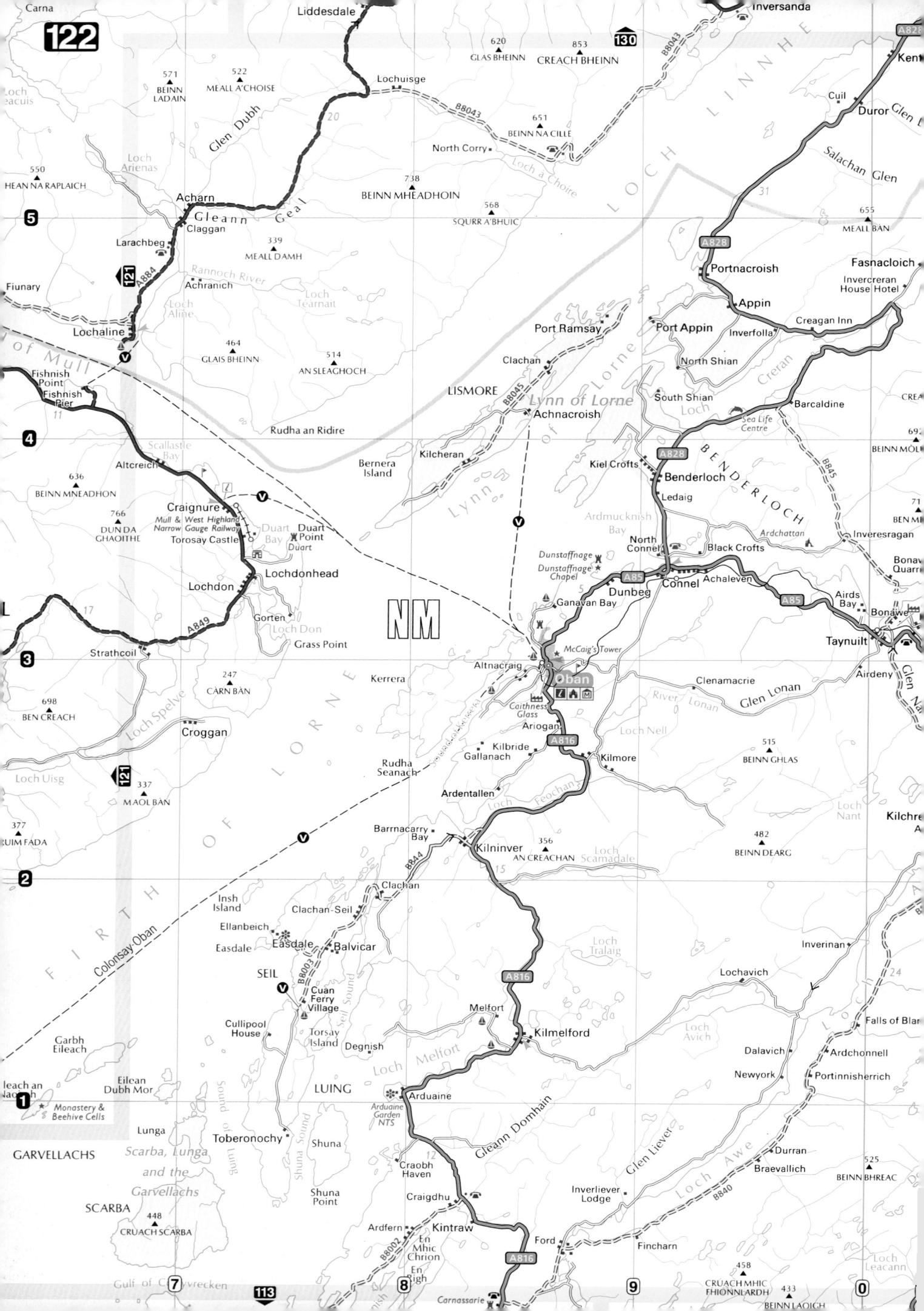

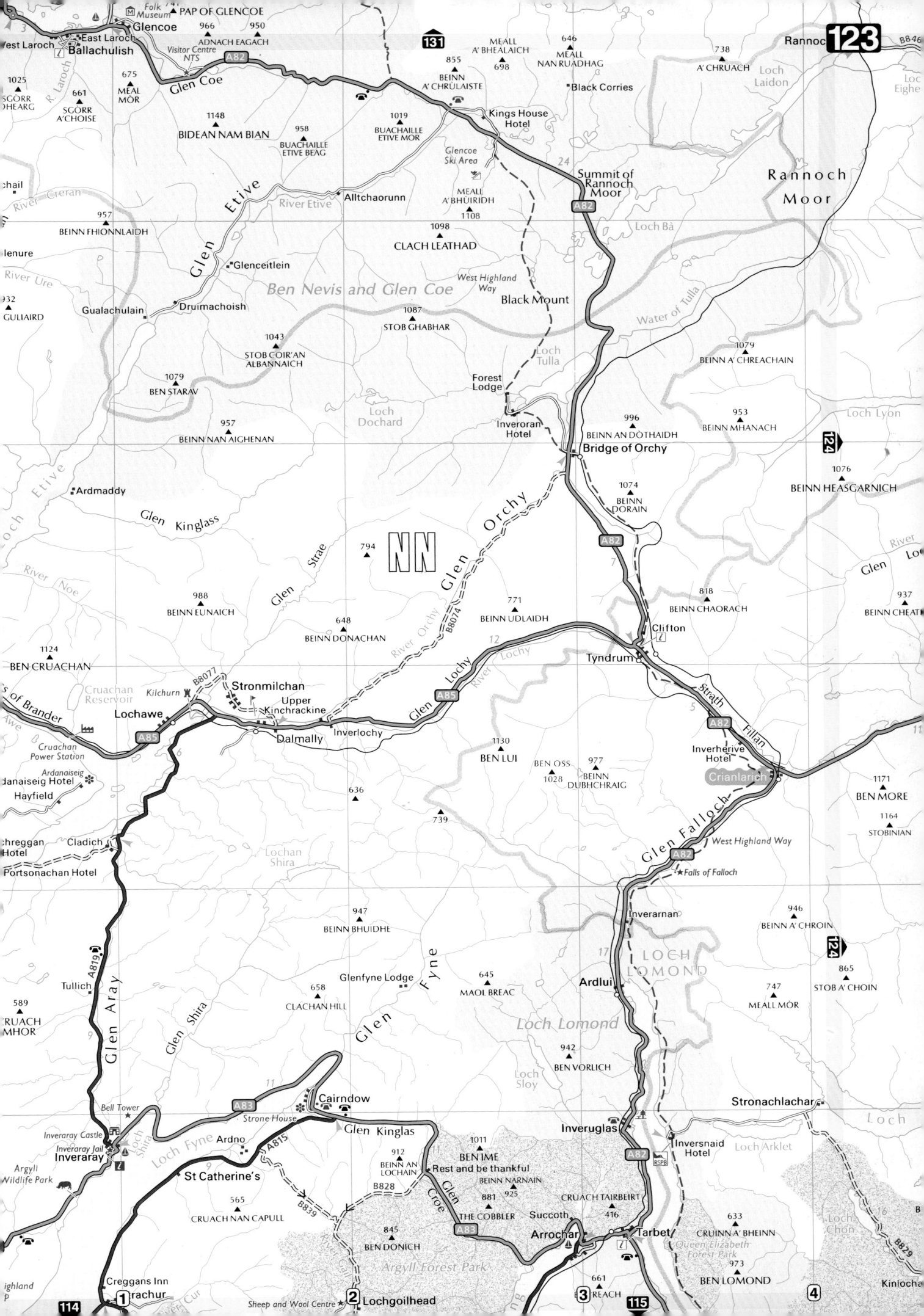

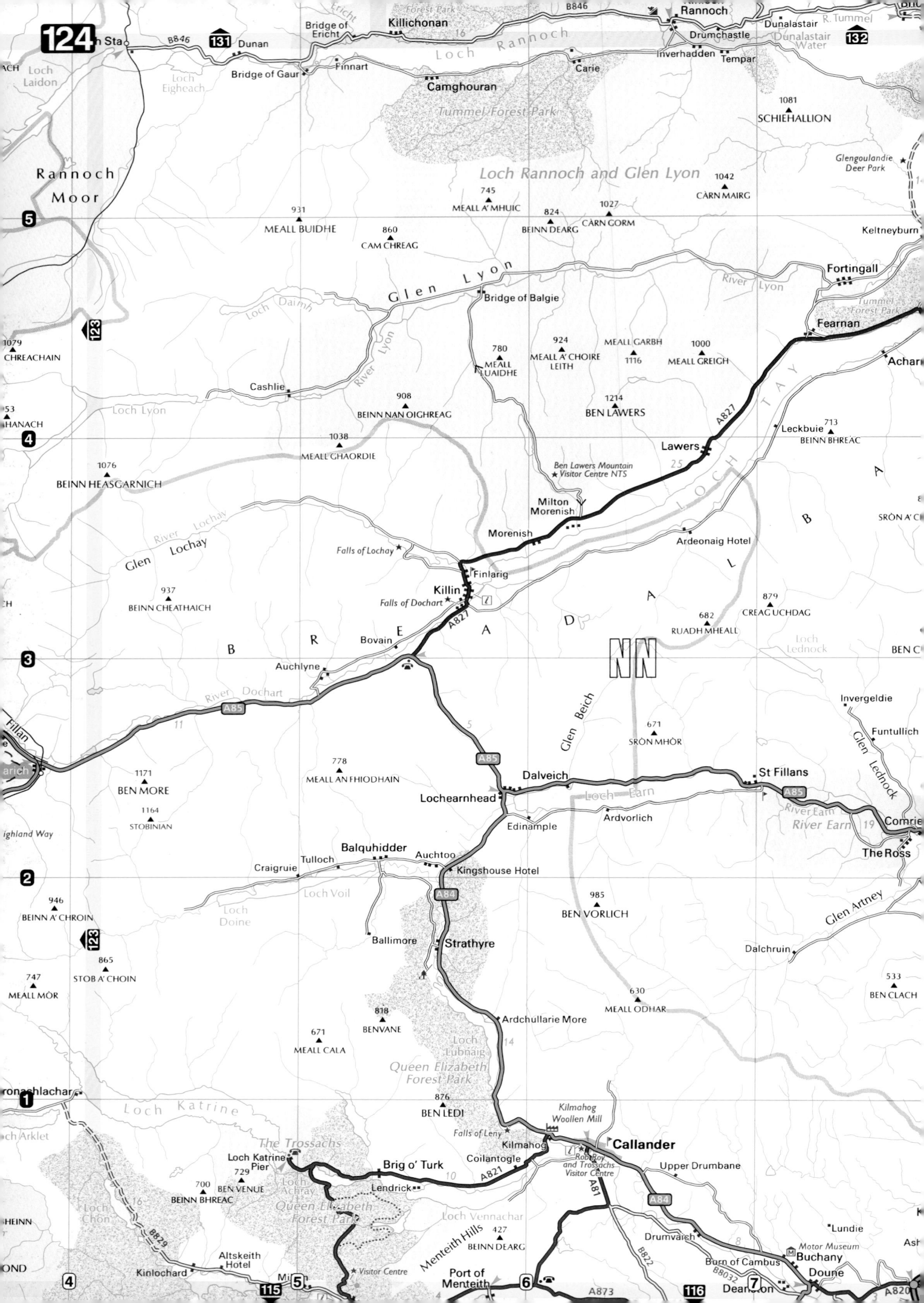

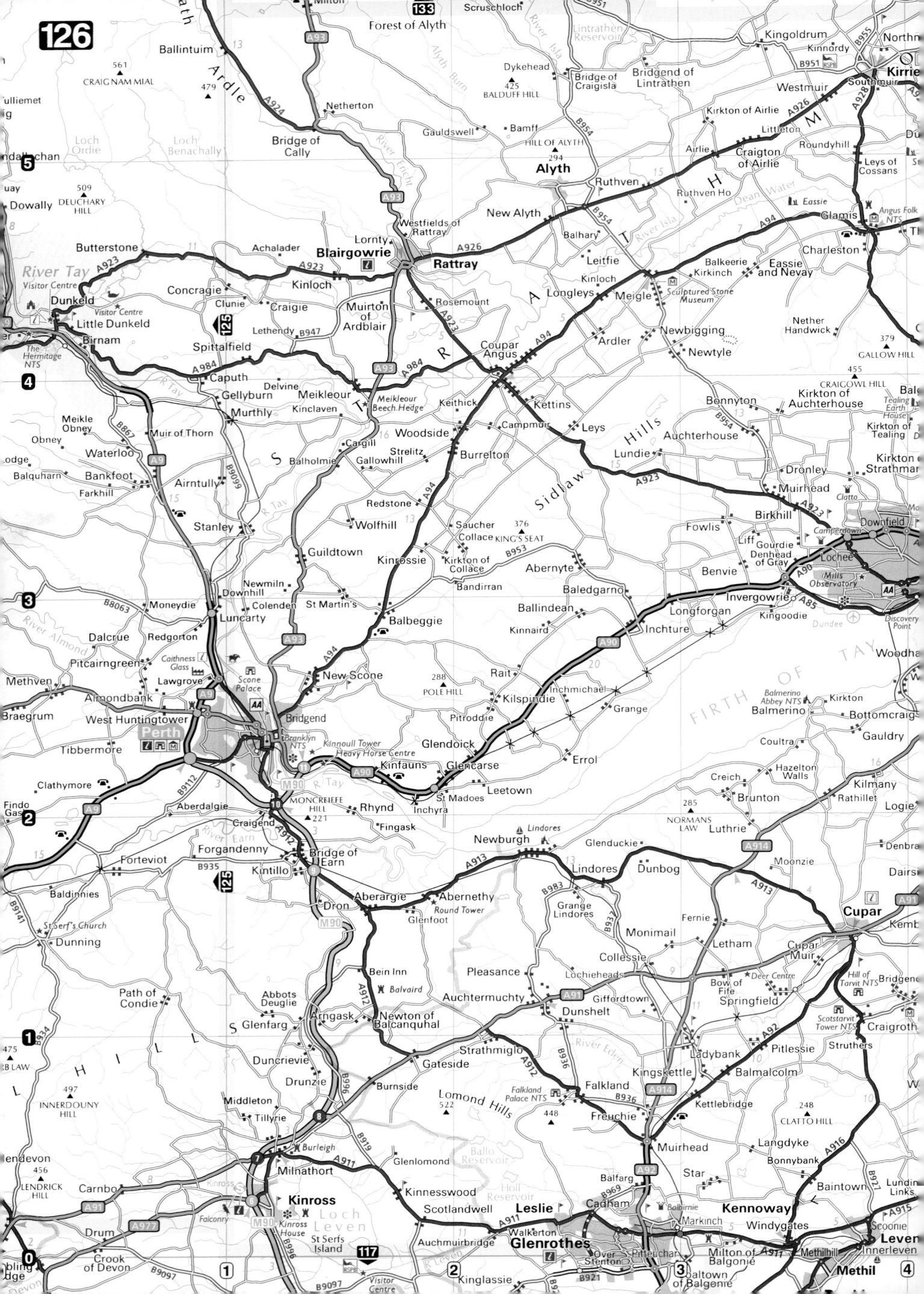

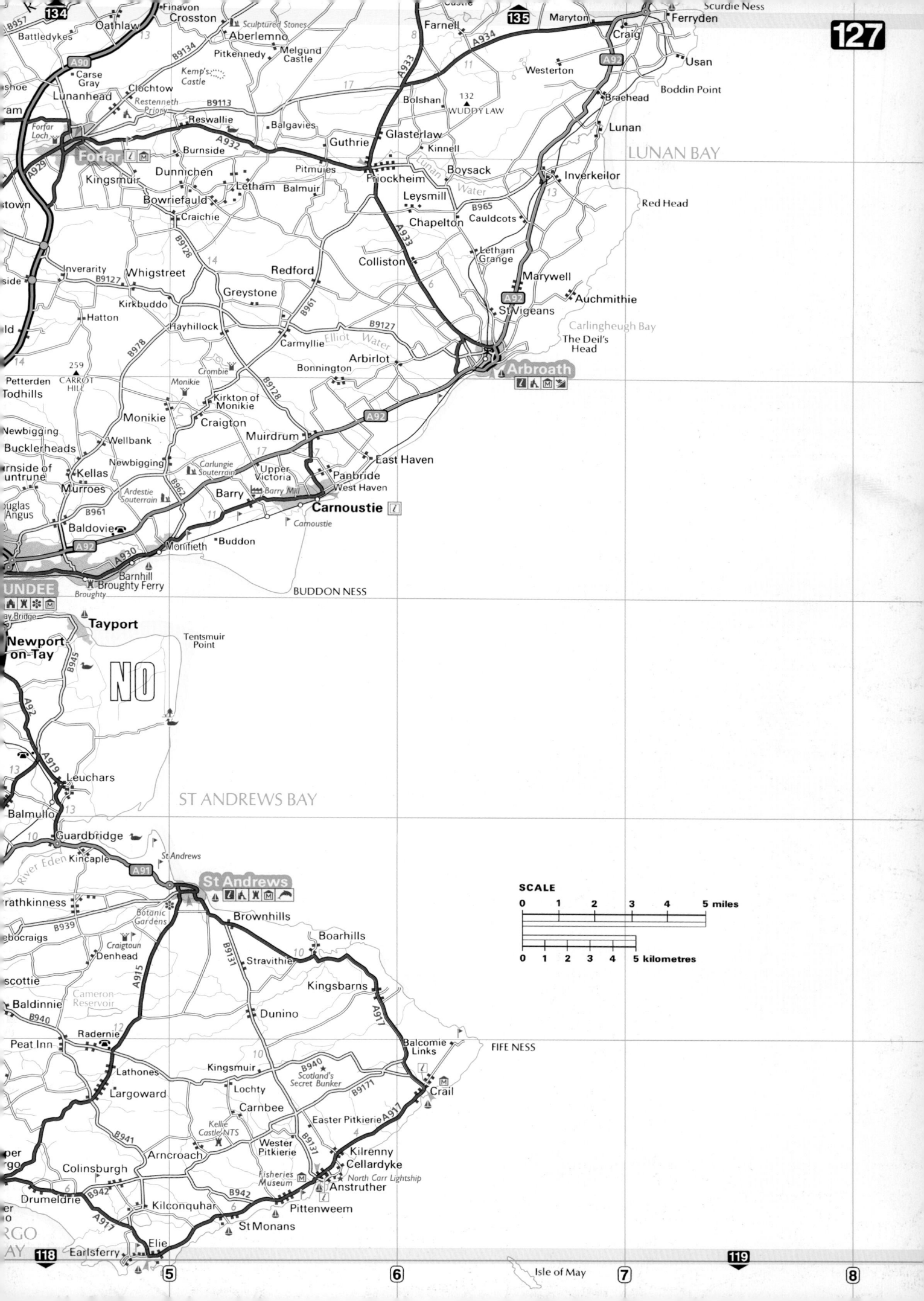

Battledykes
Oathlaw
B957
Finavon
Crosston
Sculptured Stones
Aberlemno
Pitkennedy
Melgund Castle
Kemp's Castle
A90
Carse Gray
shoe
Lunanhead
Clochtow
am
Restenneth Priory
Reswallie
B9113
Forfar Loch
Forfar
Kingsmuir
Dunnichen
Burnside
Bowriefauld
Letham
Craichie
Balmuir
town
A929
A932
Pitmuies
Inverarity
B9127
Whigstreet
Redford
side
B961
Kirkbuddo
Greystone
ld
Hatton
Hayhillock
B9127
Carmyllie
Petterden
259
Todhills
CARROT HILL
Crombie
Monikie
14
B978
Bonnington
Arbirlot
Newbigging
Bucklerheads
Monikie
Kirkton of Monikie
Wellbank
Craigton
Muirdrum
Newbigging
rnside of
Kellas
untrune
B962
Carlungie Souterrain
Upper Victoria
Barry Mill
Murroes
B961
Ardestie Souterrain
Barry
Carnoustie
uglas
Angus
Baldovie
11
Carnoustie
A92
Monifieth
Buddon
Barnhill
A930
Broughty Ferry
UNDEE
Broughty
Tayport
Newport-on-Tay
Tentsmuir Point
NO
B945
A92
A919
Leuchars
13
Balmullo
13
10
Guardbridge
St Andrews
River Eden
Kincaple
A91
rathkinness
St Andrews
Brownhills
Botanic Gardens
Boarhills
B939
ebocraigs
Craigtoun
Stravithie
scottie
Denhead
A915
Kingsbarns
Baldinnie
Cameron Reservoir
Dunino
B940
B9131
Peat Inn
Radernie
12
Kingsmuir
Lathones
10
Lochty
Largoward
Carnbee
B941
Kellie Castle NTS
Colinsburgh
Arncroach
Wester Pitkierie
B942
Drumeldrie
B942
Kilconquhar
Pittenweem
RGO
A917
St Monans
Earlsferry
Elie
AY

Finavon
Castle
Farnell
Maryton
Scurdie Ness
135
A934
Craig
Ferryden
A933
Westerton
Usan
A92
11
Boddin Point
132
Braehead
Bolshan
WUDDY LAW
Lunan
Guthrie
Glasterlaw
Kinnell
LUNAN BAY
Friockheim
Boysack
Inverkeilor
Leysmill
13
Red Head
A933
Chapelton
Cauldcots
B965
Colliston
Letham Grange
Marywell
6
A92
St Vigeans
Auchmithie
Carlingheugh Bay
The Deil's Head
Arbroath

East Haven
Panbride
West Haven

BUDDON NESS

ST ANDREWS BAY

A917
Balcomie Links
FIFE NESS
Scotland's Secret Bunker
Crail
B940
B9171
Easter Pitkierie
A917
Kilrenny
Cellardyke
Fisheries Museum
North Carr Lightship
Anstruther

SCALE

0   1   2   3   4   5 miles

0   1   2   3   4   5 kilometres

Isle of May

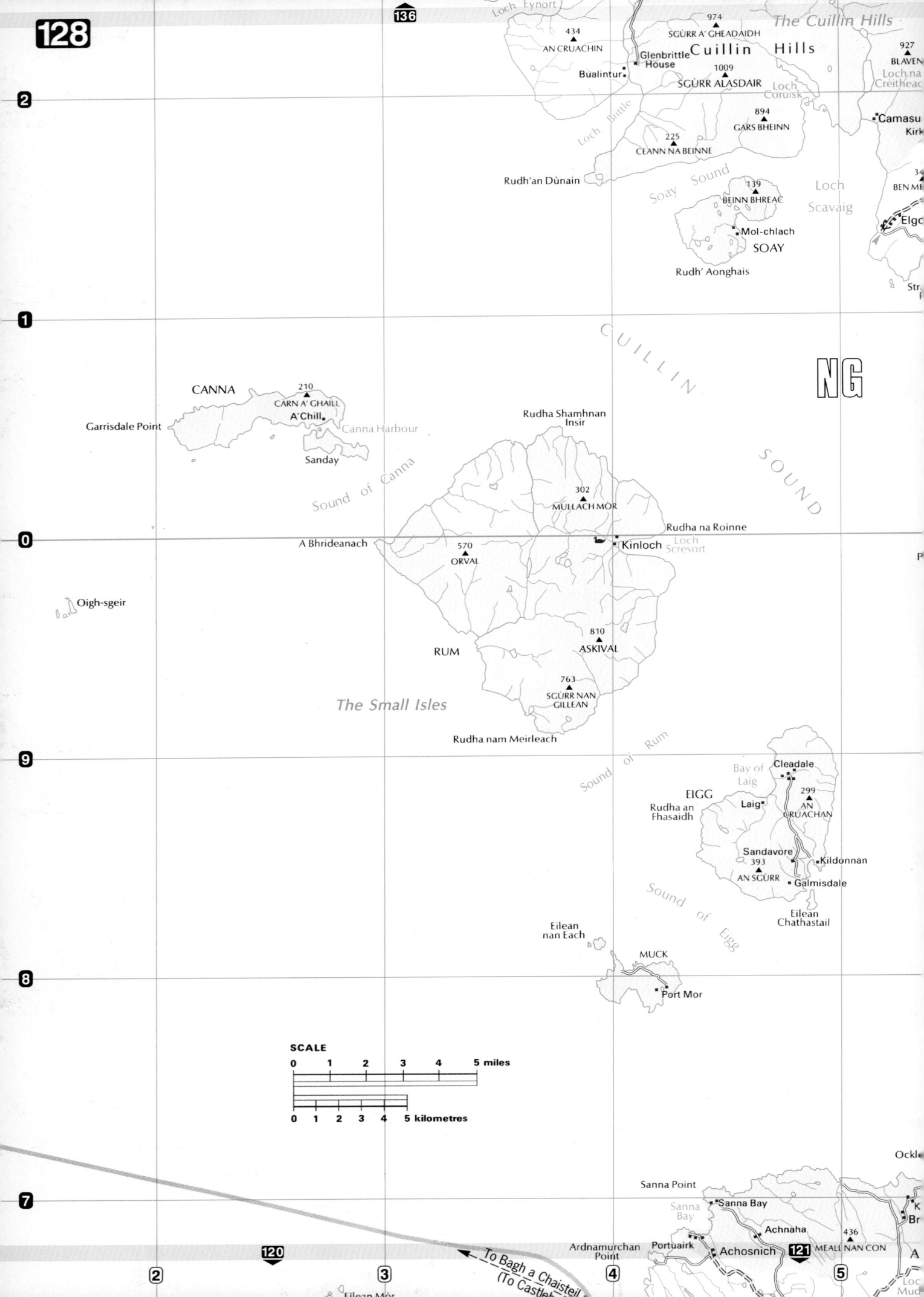

136

Loch Eynort

The Cuillin Hills

974
SGÙRR A' GHEADAIDH ▲

434
AN CRUACHIN ▲

Cuillin Hills

927
BLAVEN ▪

Glenbrittle
House ▪

Bualintur ▪

1009
SGÙRR ALASDAIR ▲

Loch
Coruisk

Loch na
Crèitheac

894
GARS BHEINN ▲

▪ Camasu
Kirk

225
CEANN NA BEINNE ▲

Rudh'an Dùnain ▪

Soay Sound

34
BEN ME ▪

139
BEINN BHREAC ▲

Loch
Scavaig

Elgo ▪

Mol-chlach ▪

SOAY

Str

Rudh' Aonghais ▪

Loch
Scavaig

NG

CANNA

210
CÀRN A' GHAILL ▲

A'Chill ▪

Garrisdale Point ▪

Canna Harbour

Rudha Shamhnan
Insir

CUILLIN SOUND

Sanday

Sound of Canna

Oigh-sgeir

302
MULLACH MÒR ▲

Rudha na Roinne

A Bhrideanach ▪

570
ORVAL ▲

Kinloch ▪

Loch
Scresort

P

810
ASKIVAL ▲

RUM

763
SGÙRR NAN
GILLEAN ▲

The Small Isles

Rudha nam Meirleach

Sound of Rum

Bay of
Laig

Cleadale ▪

EIGG

299
AN
CRUACHAN ▲

Rudha an
Fhasaidh

Laig ▪

Sandavore ▪

393
AN SGÙRR ▲

Kildonnan ▪

Sound of Eigg

Galmisdale ▪

Eilean
Chathastail

Eilean
nan Each

MUCK

Port Mor ▪

SCALE

0 1 2 3 4 5 miles

0 1 2 3 4 5 kilometres

Ockl

Sanna Point

Sanna
Bay

Sanna Bay ▪

K
Br ▪

Achnaha ▪

436
MEALL NAN CON ▲

Ardnamurchan
Point

Portuairk ▪

Achosnich ▪

To Bagh a Chaisteil
(To Castle

A

Loch
Mud

2   3   4   5

Eilean Mor

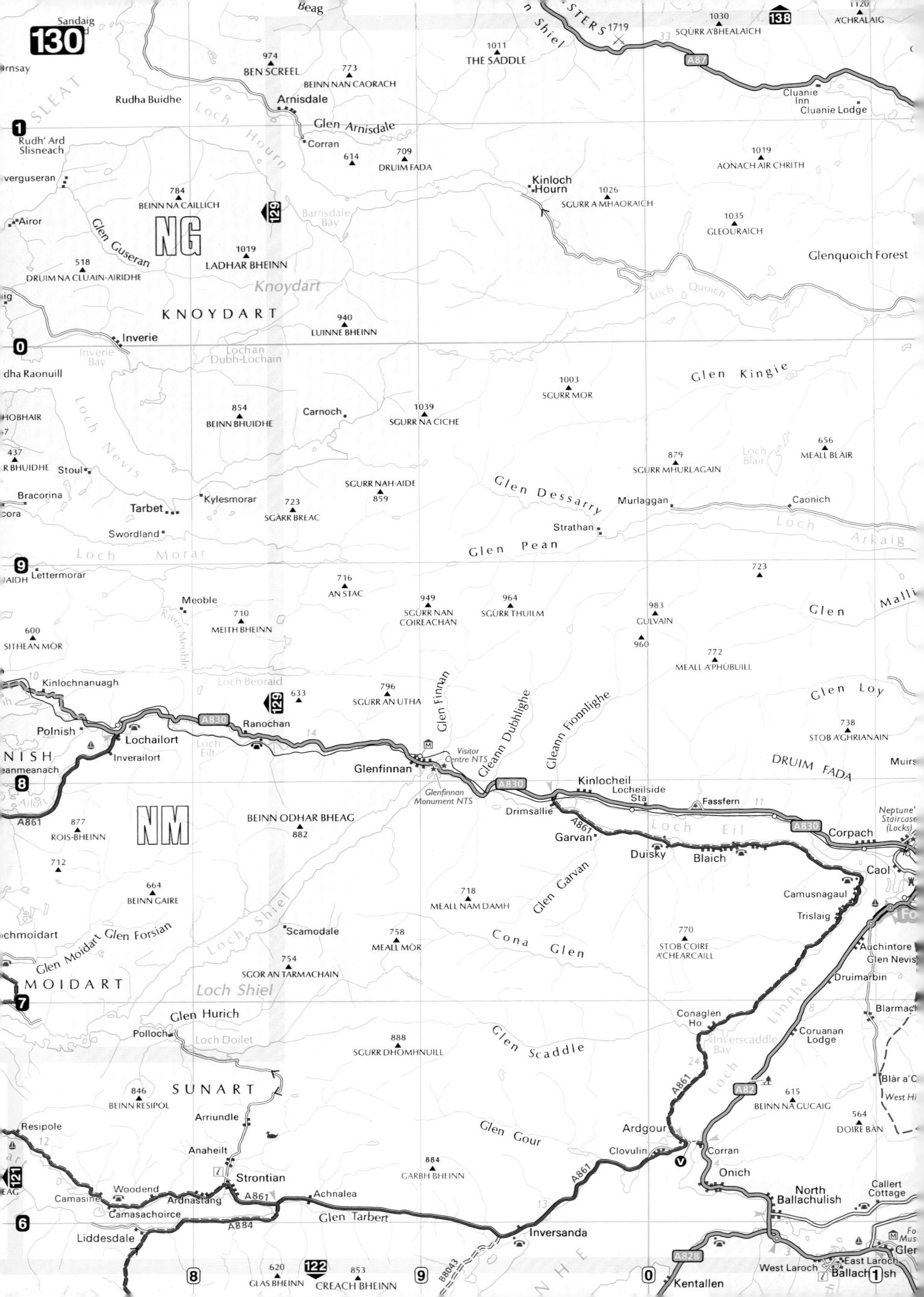

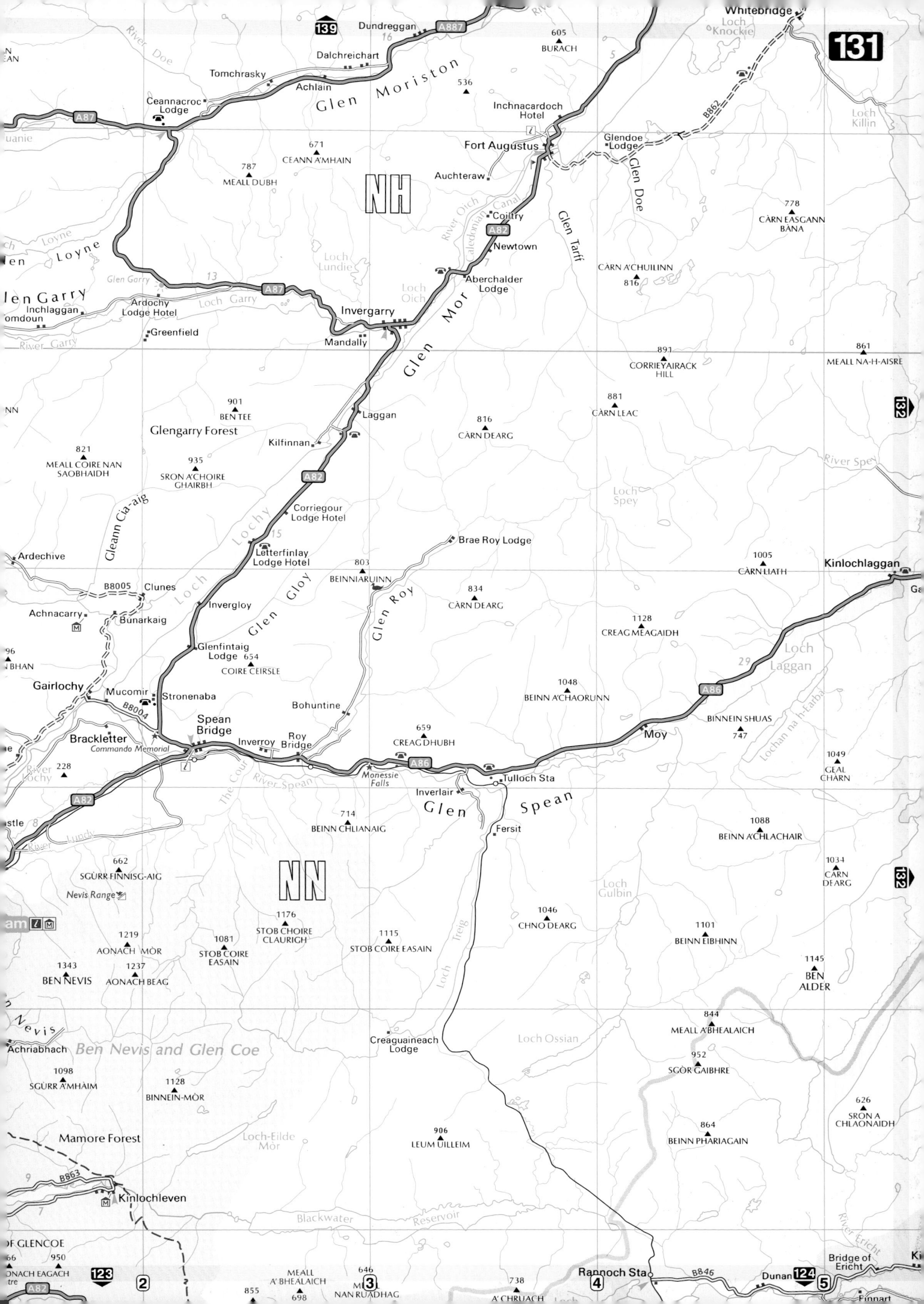

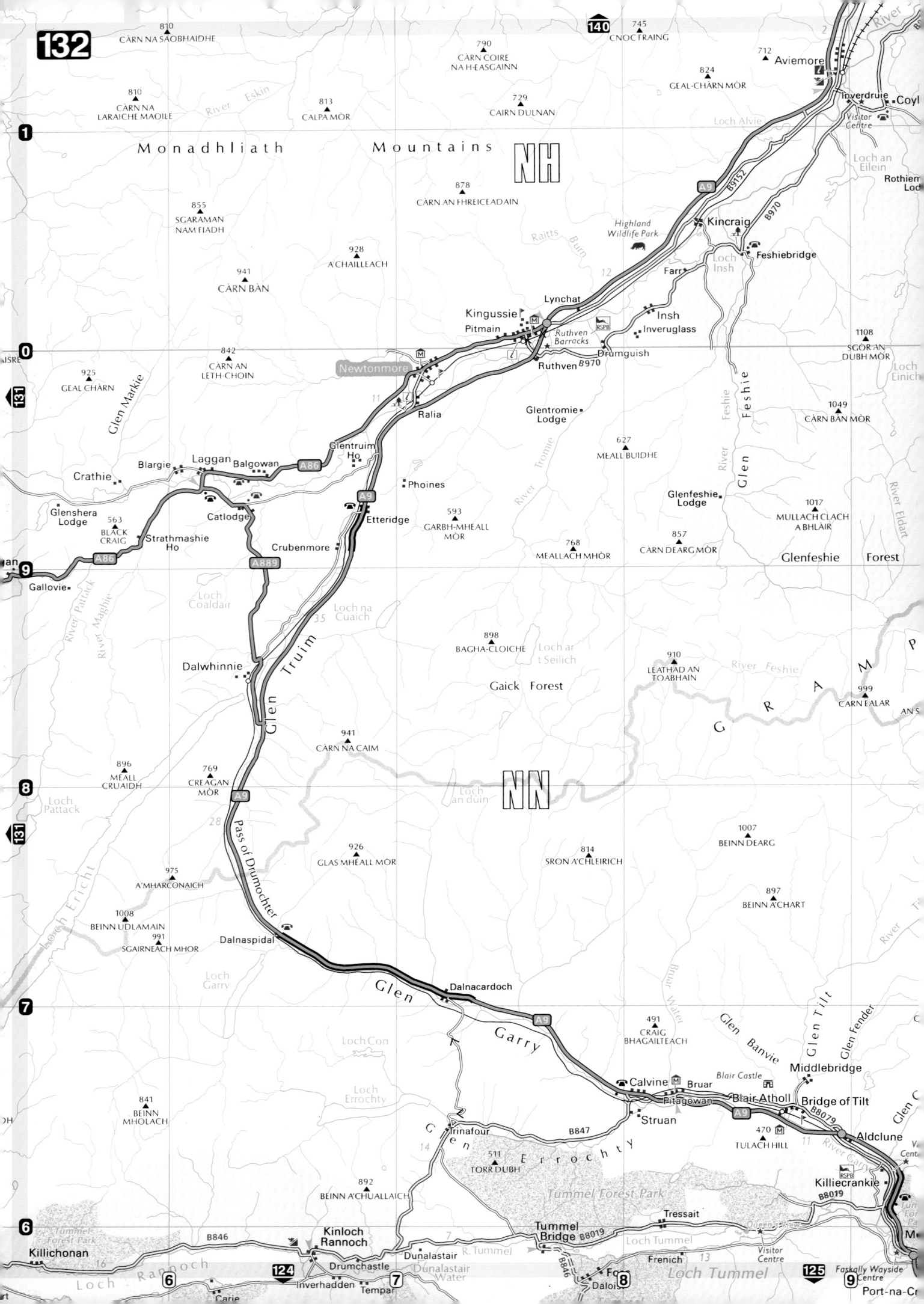

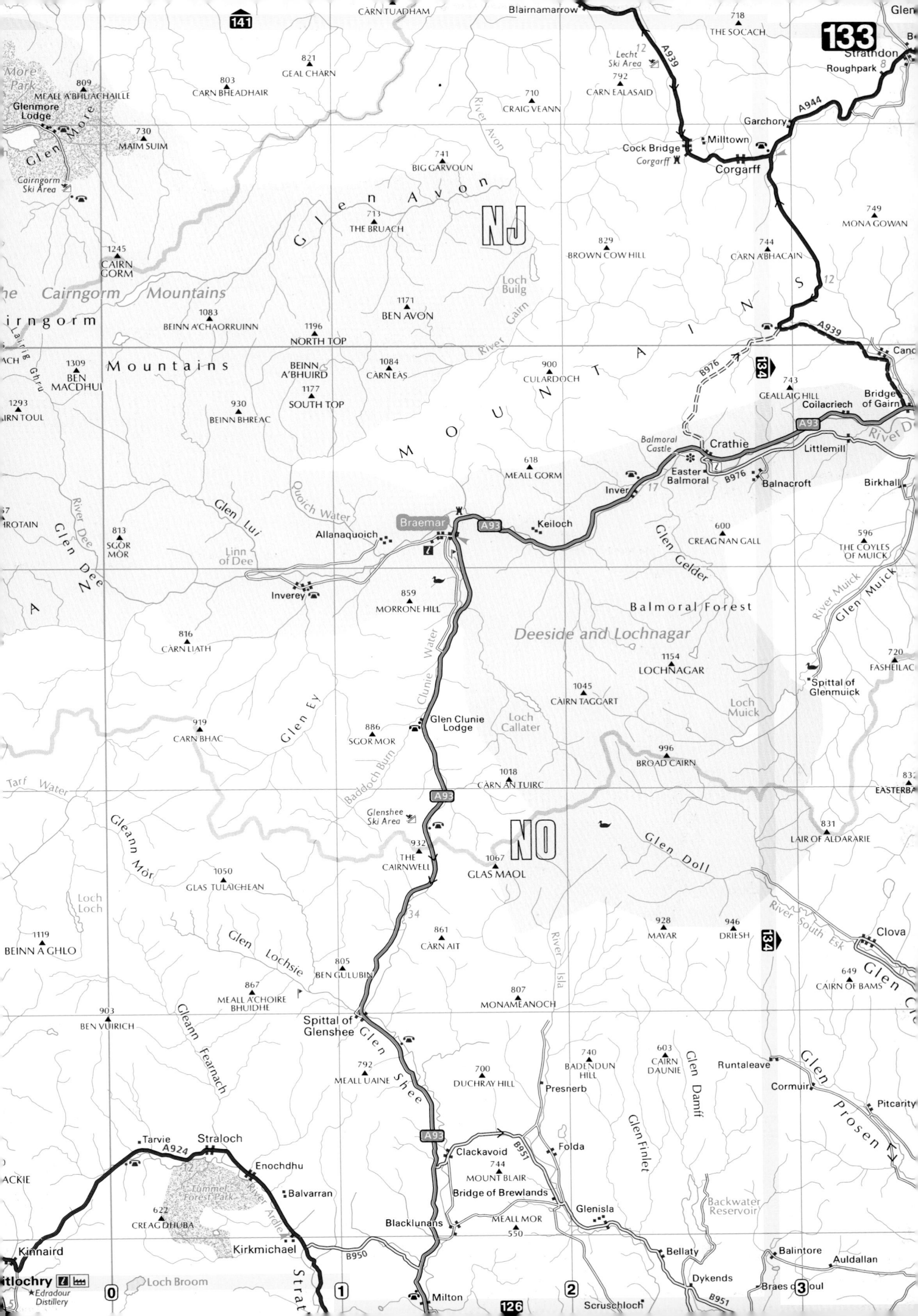

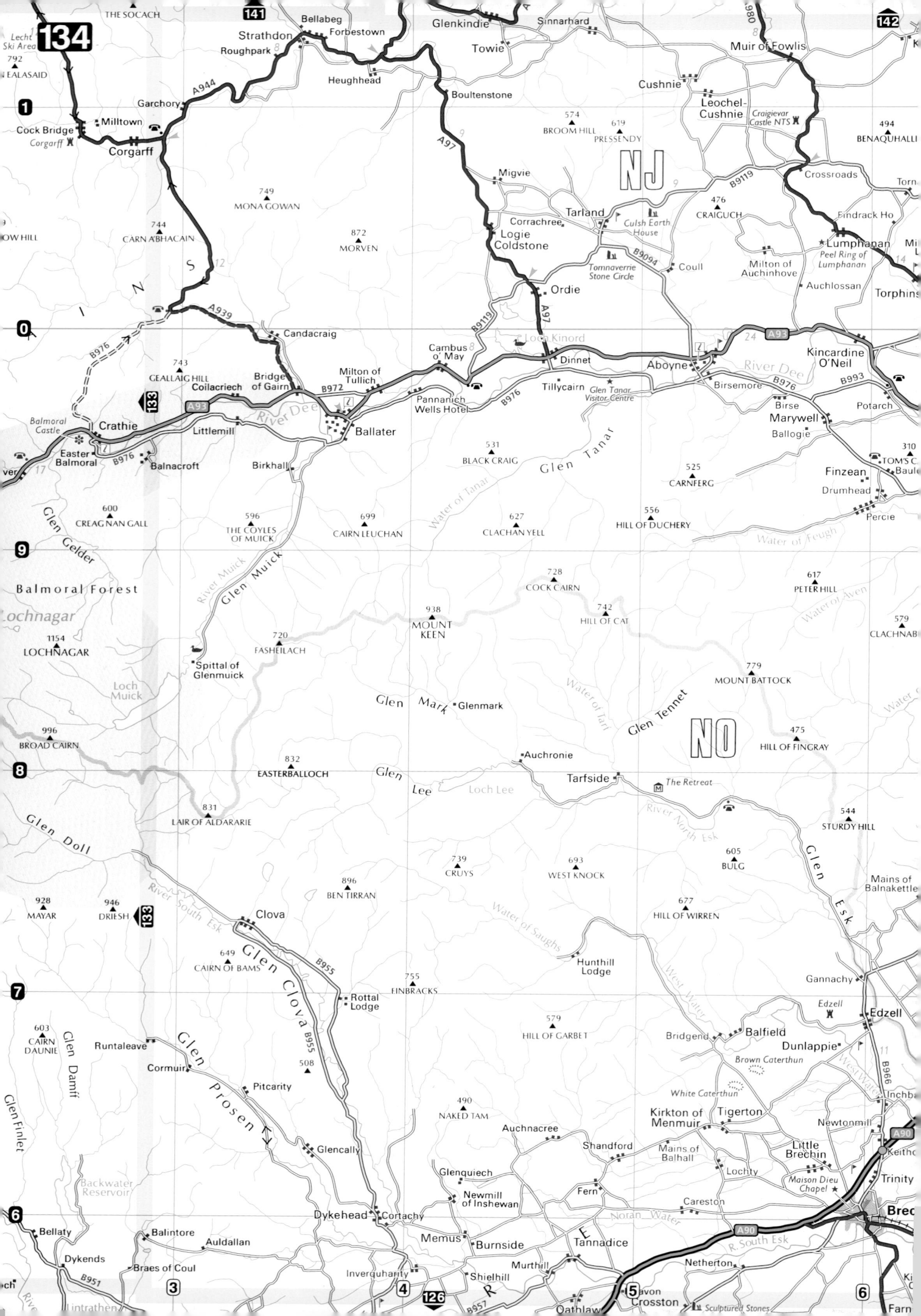

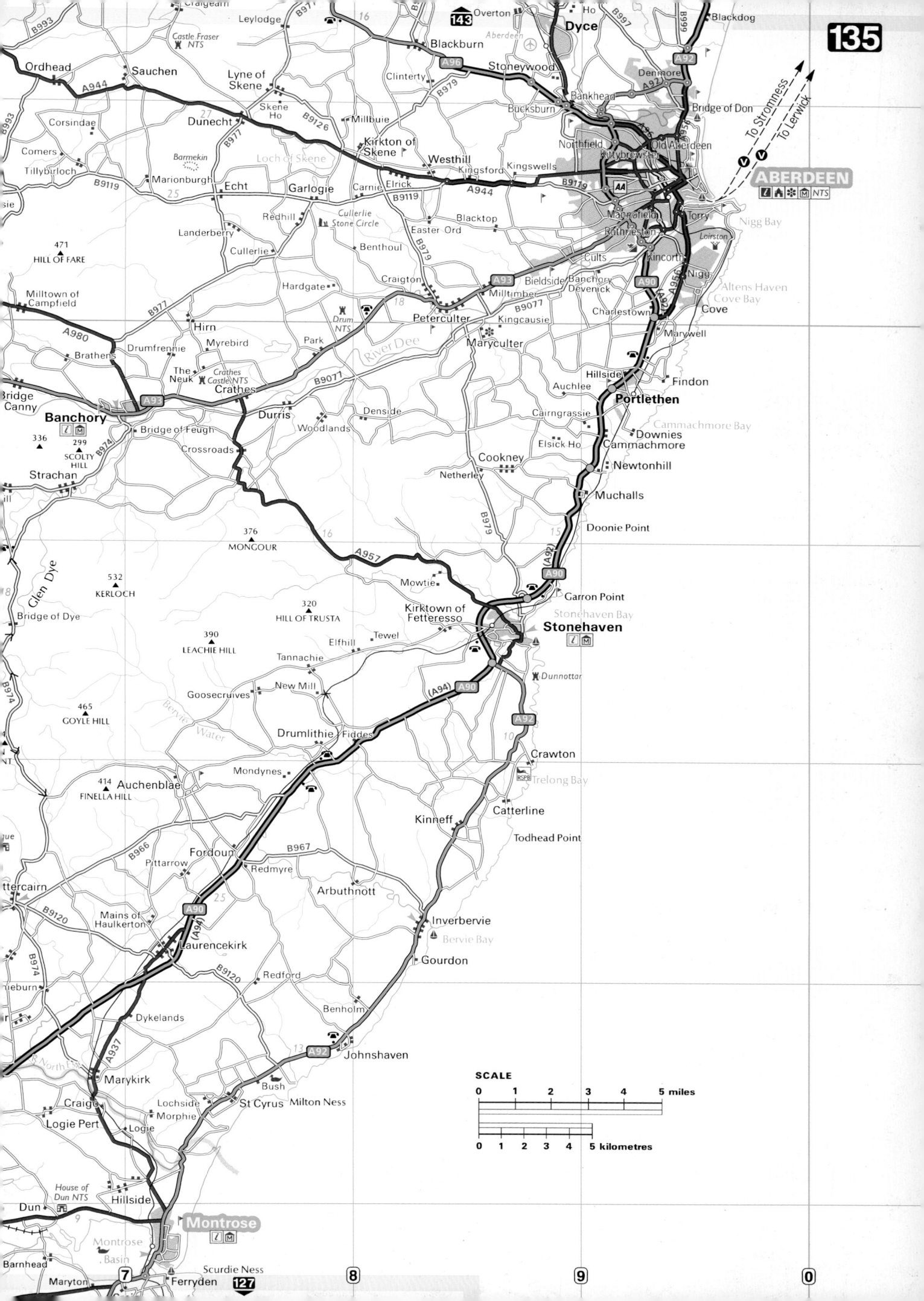

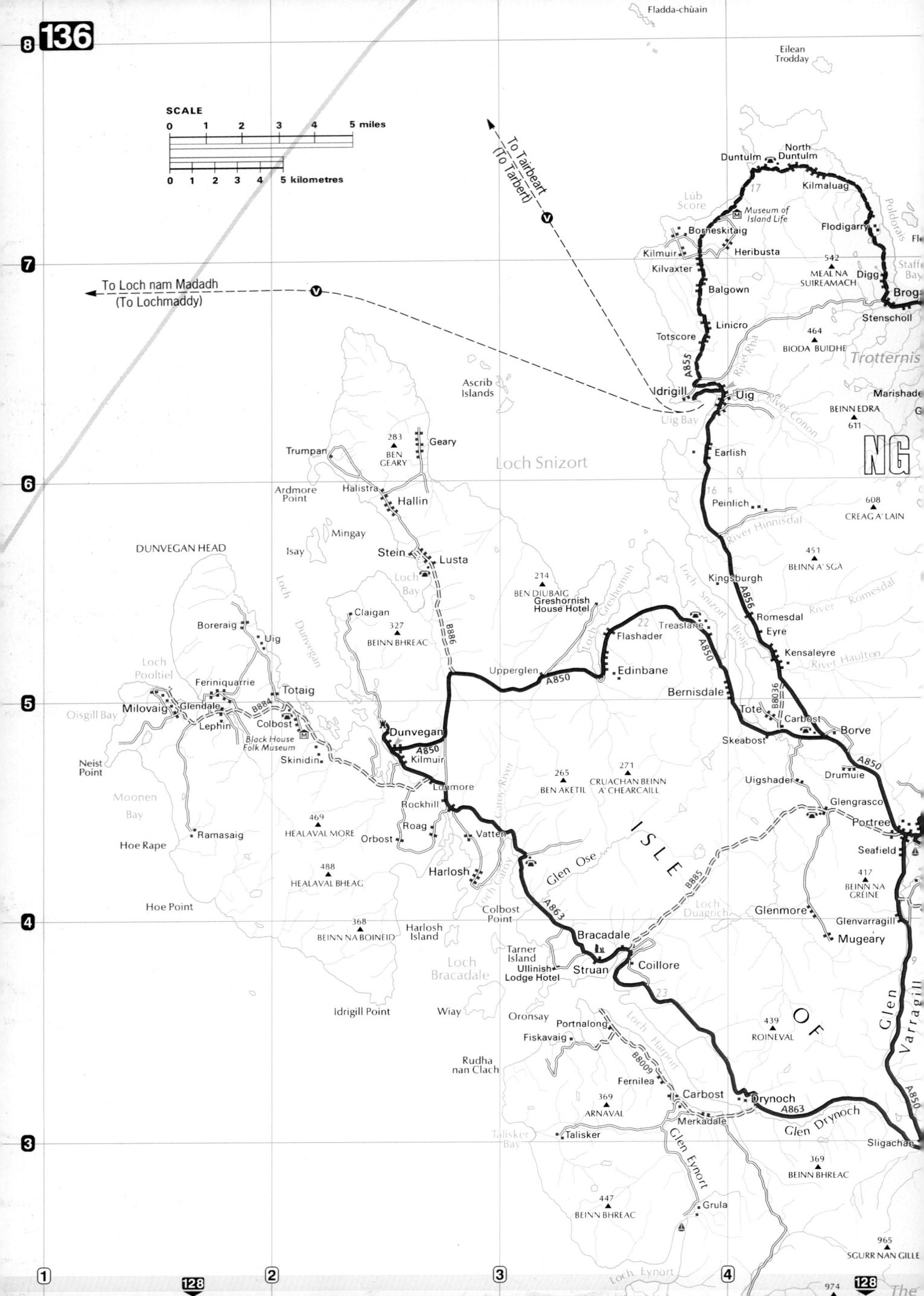

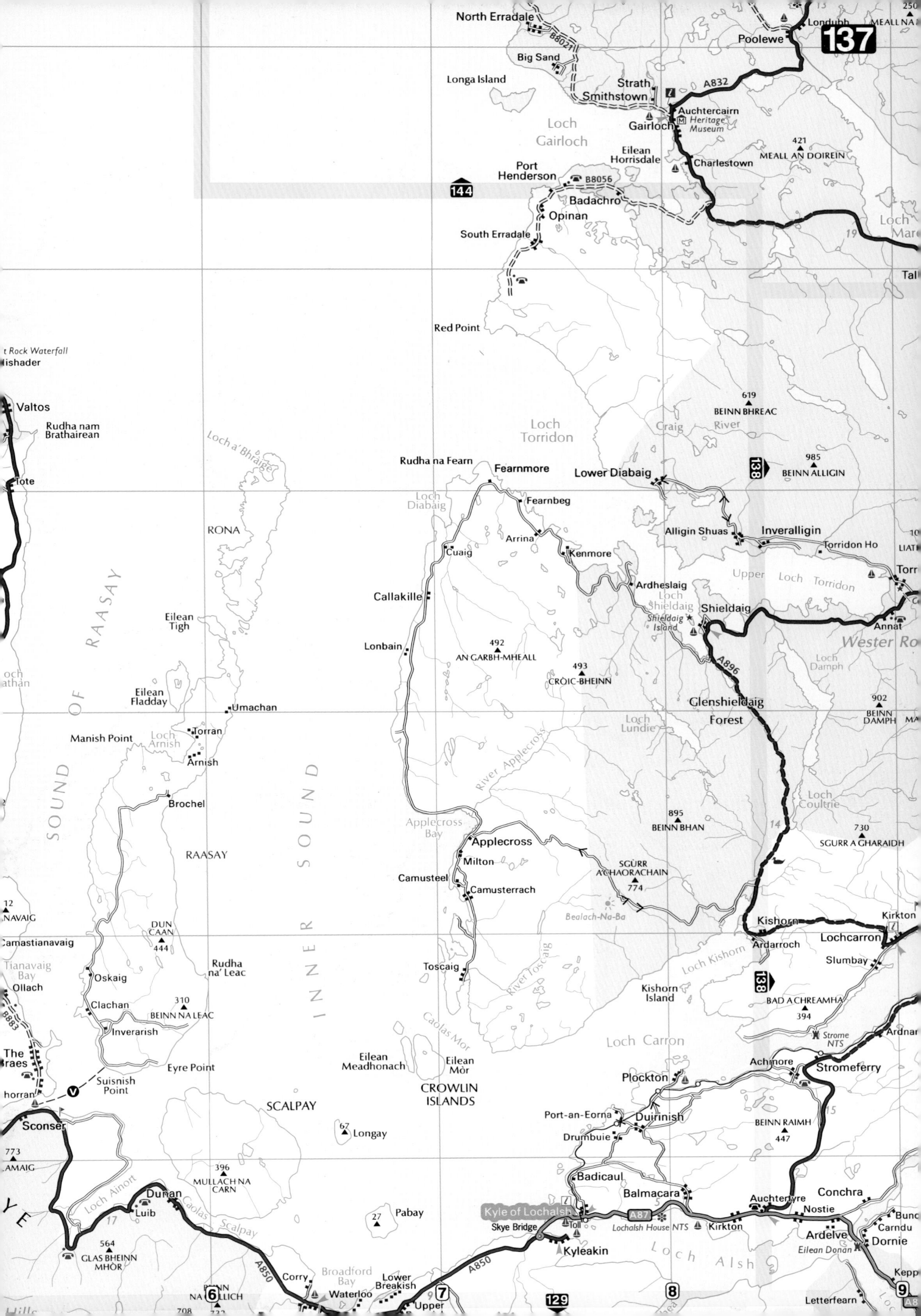

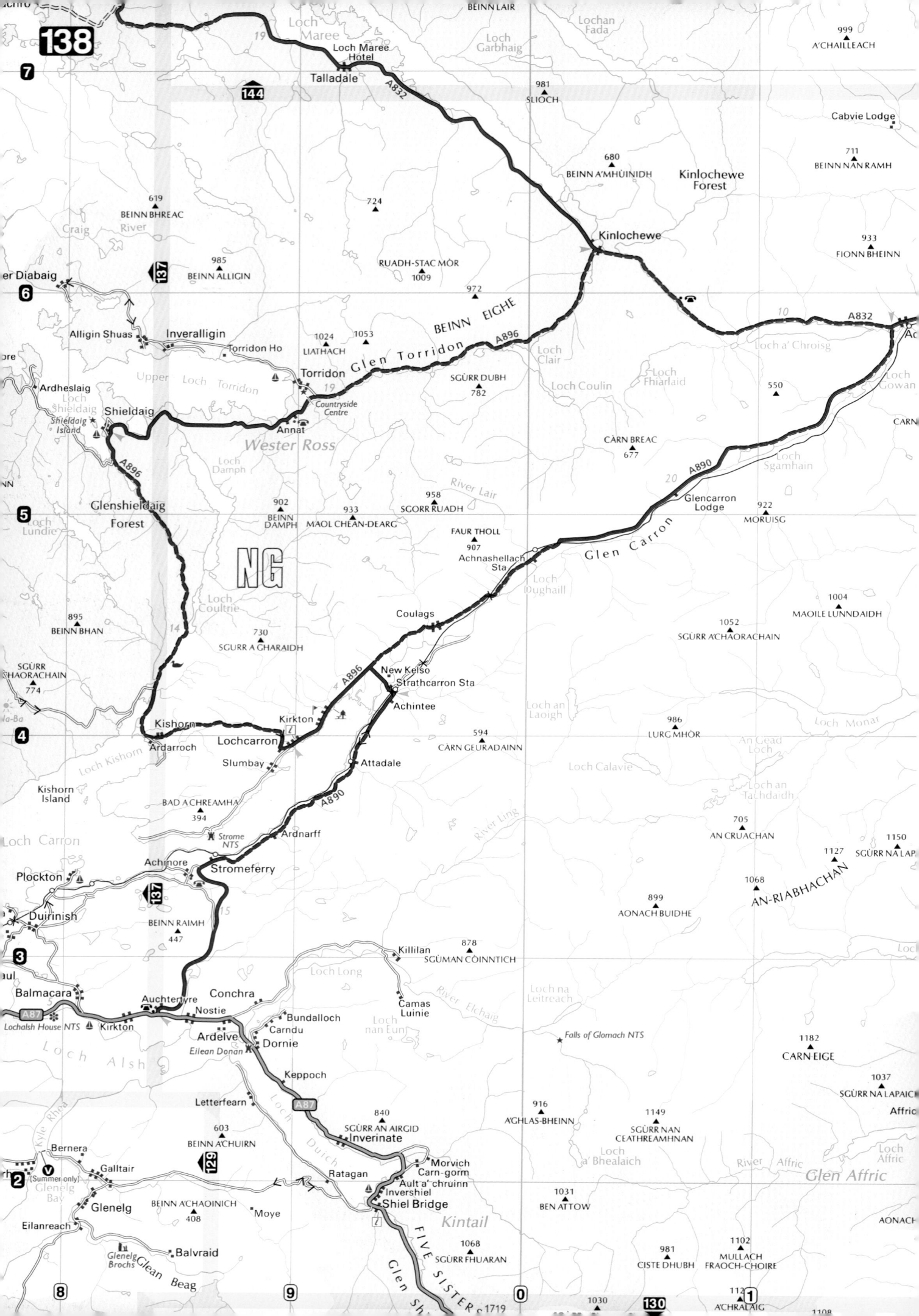

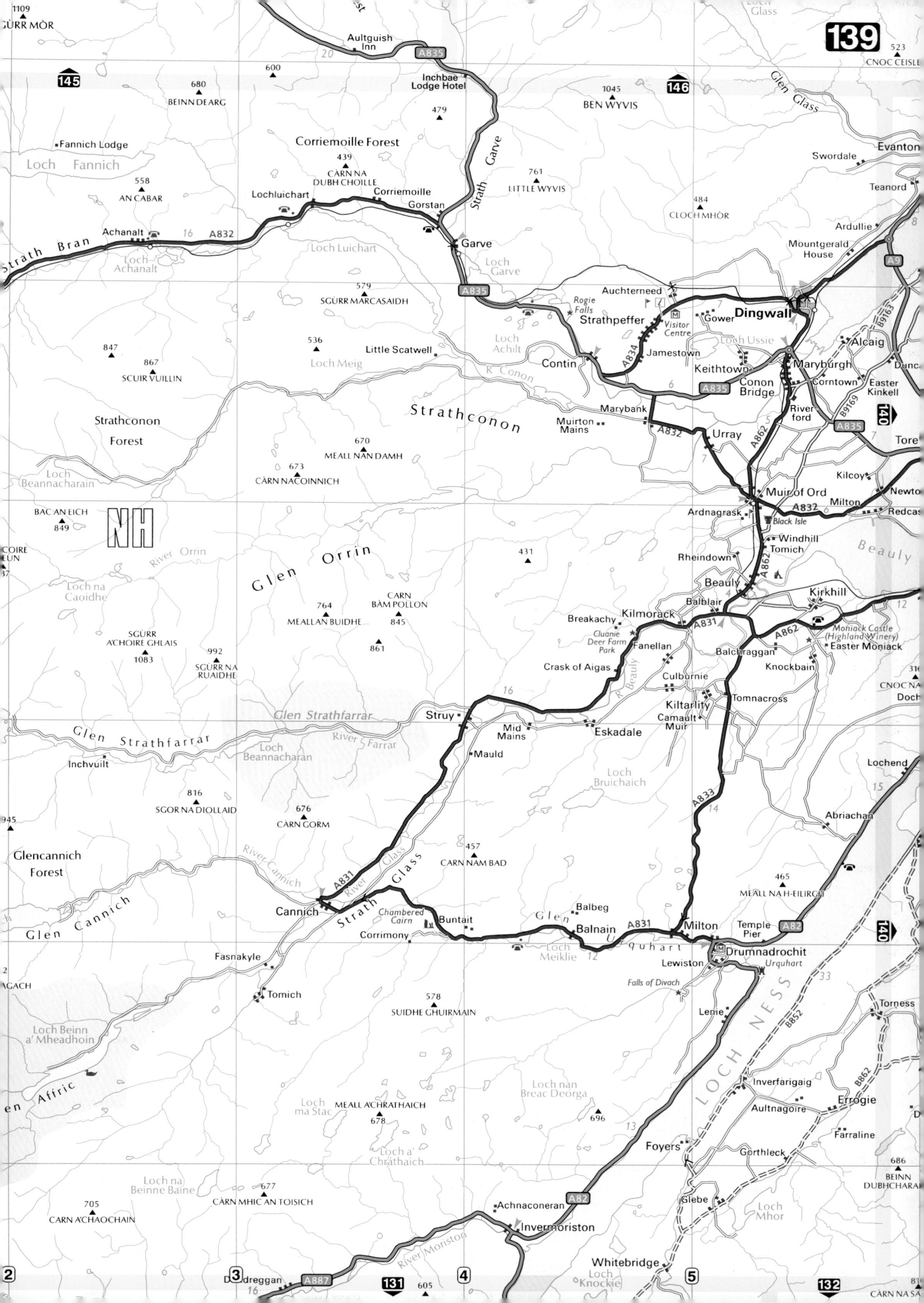

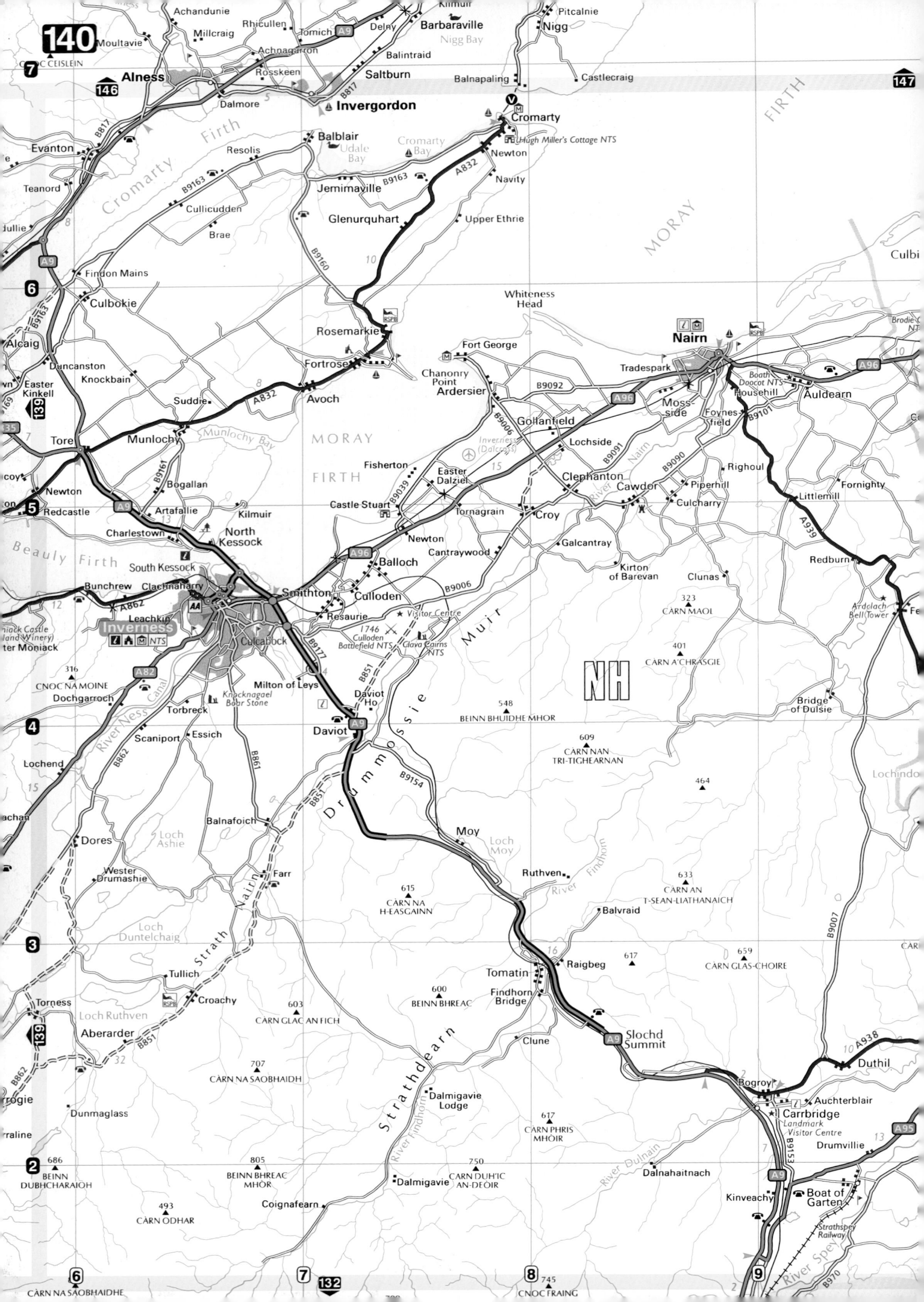

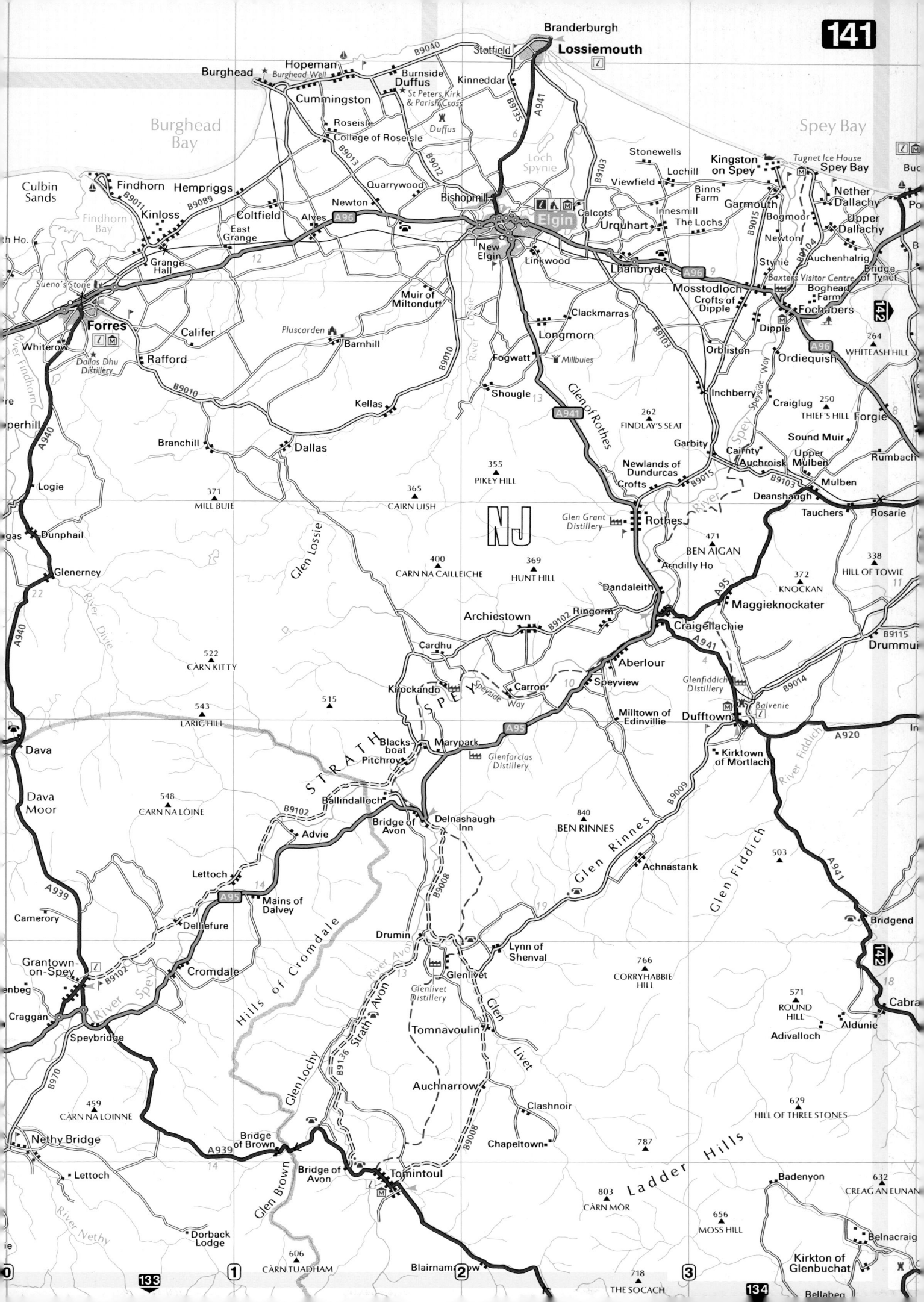

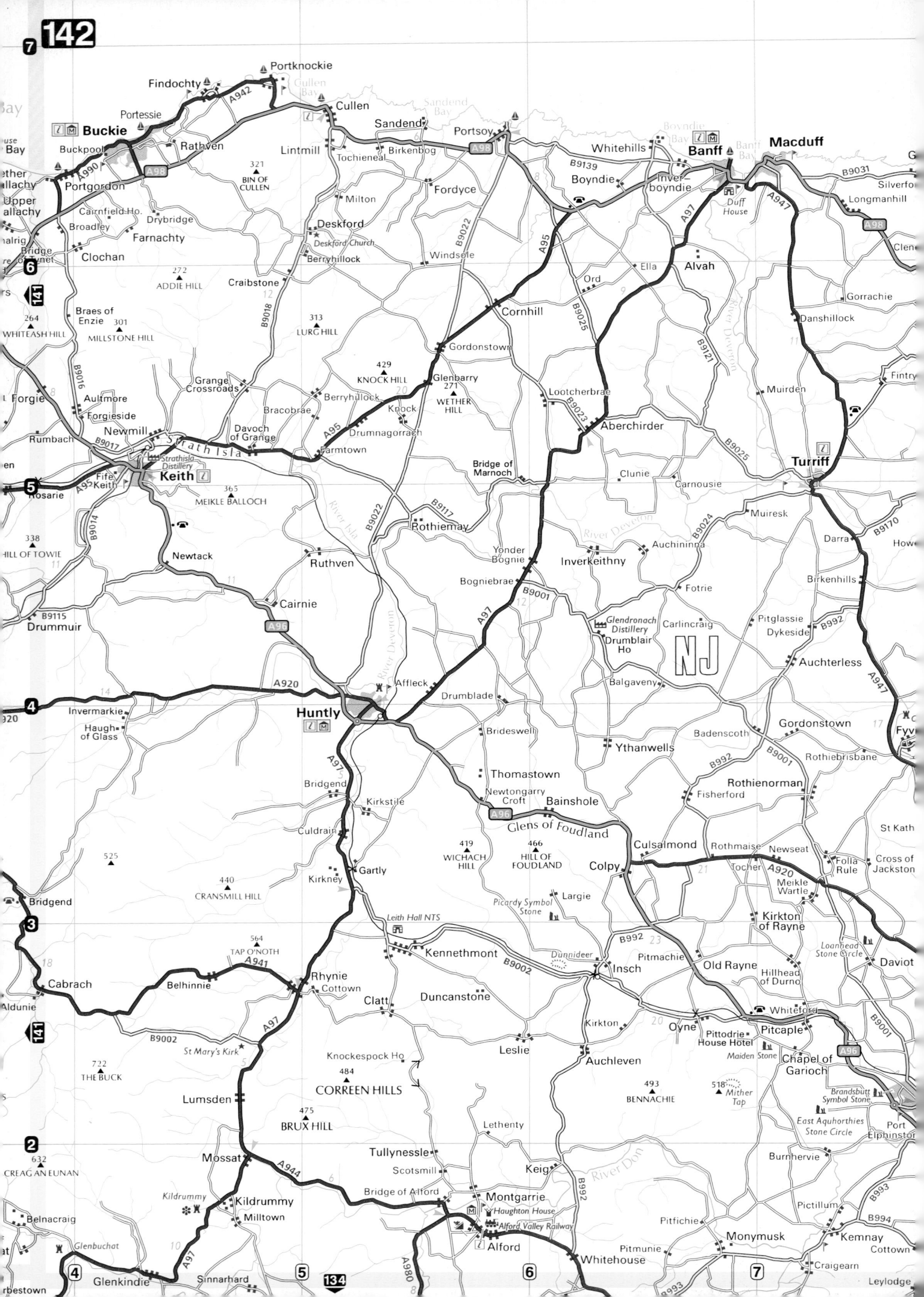

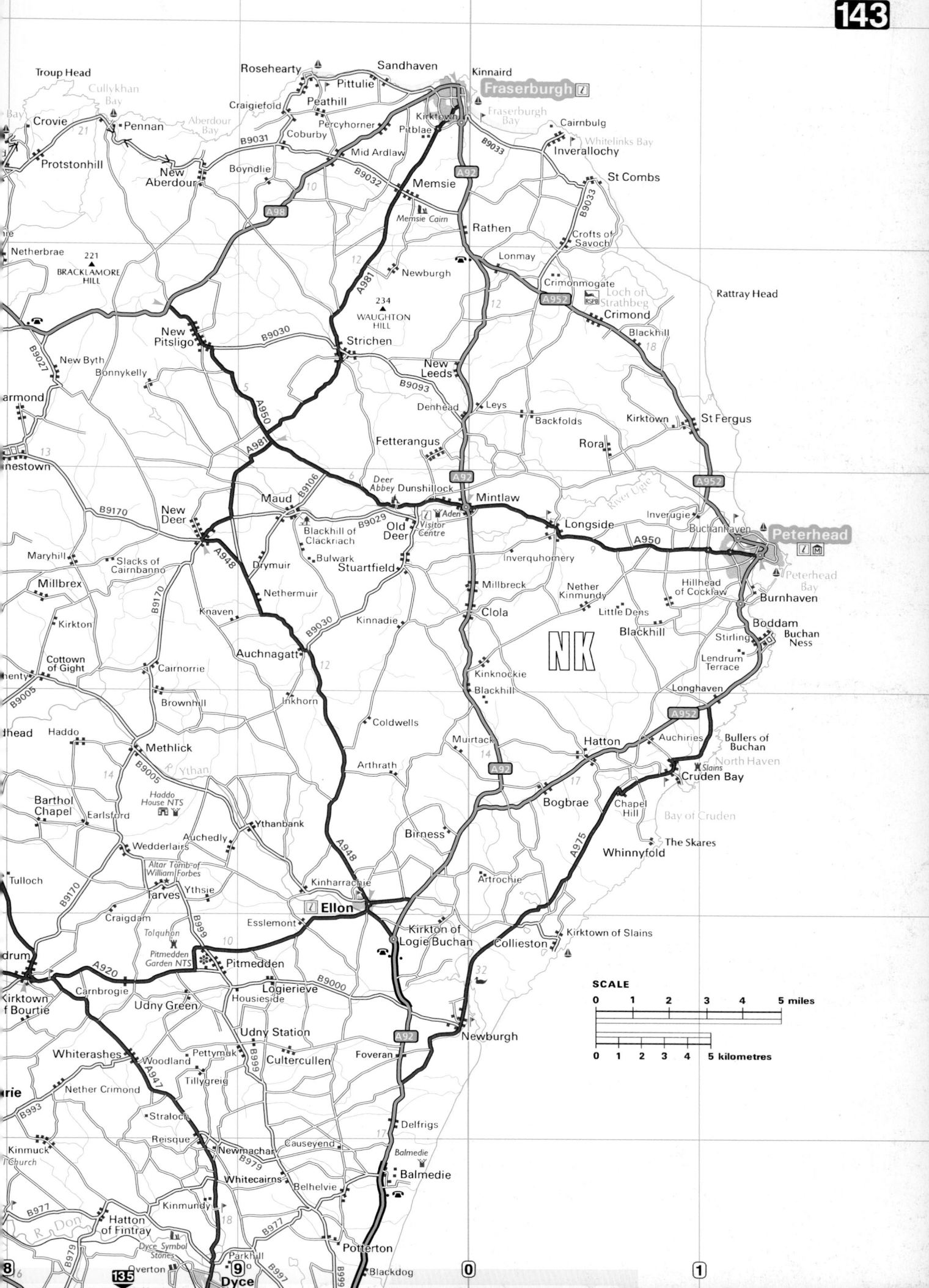

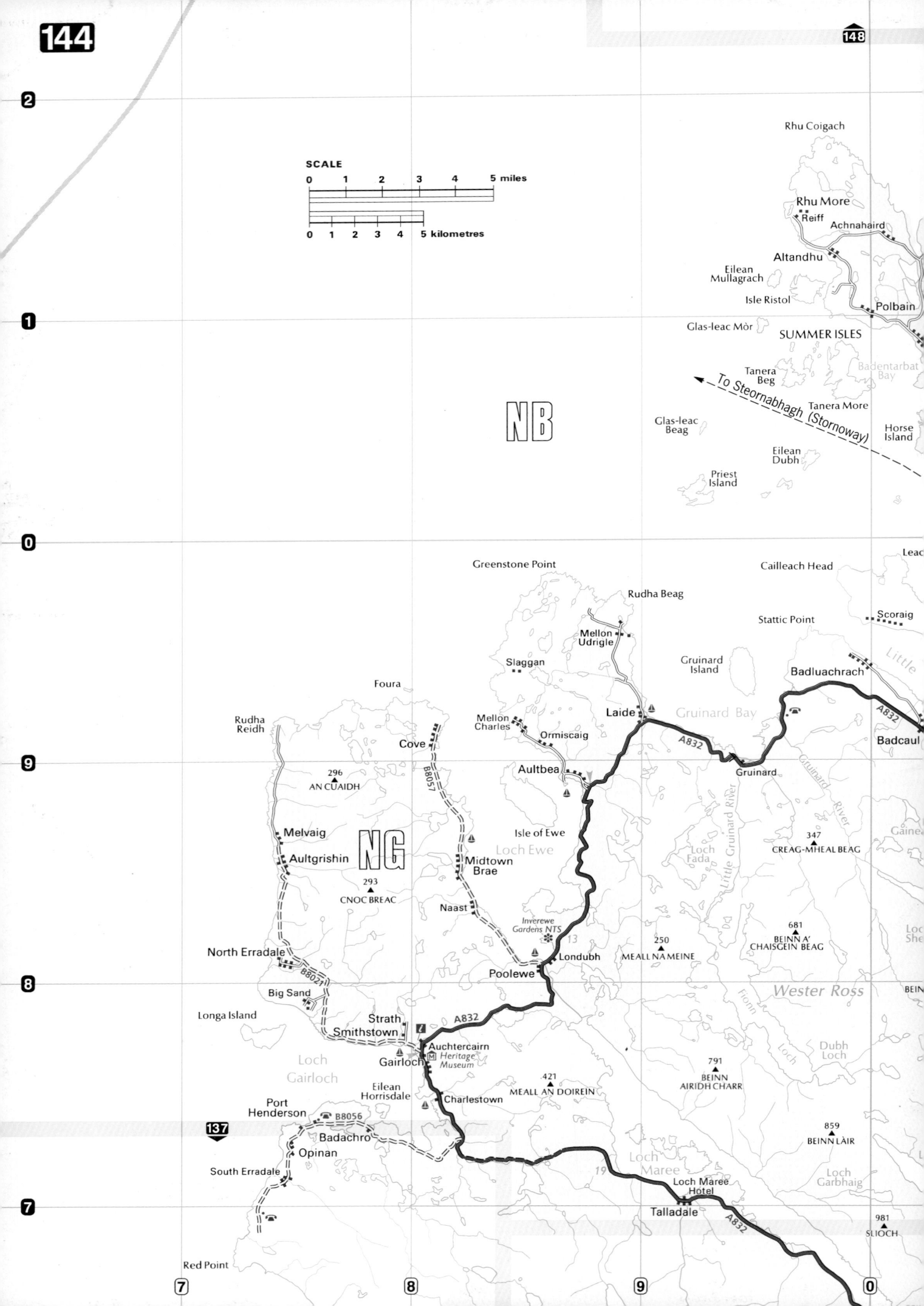

2

1

0

9

8

7

SCALE

0 1 2 3 4 5 miles

0 1 2 3 4 5 kilometres

NB

NG

137

Rhu Coigach

Rhu More
Reiff
Achnahaird

Eilean
Mullagrach
Altandhu

Isle Ristol
Polbain

Glas-leac Mòr
SUMMER ISLES

Badentarbat
Bay

Tanera
Beg

To Steornabhagh (Stornoway)
Tanera More

Glas-leac
Beag
Horse
Island

Eilean
Dubh

Priest
Island

Greenstone Point

Cailleach Head

Leac

Rudha Beag

Mellon
Udrigle

Scoraig

Stattic Point

Slaggan

Gruinard Island

Badluachrach

Little

Foura

Mellon
Charles
Ormiscaig

Laide

Gruinard Bay

A832

Rudha
Reidh

A832

Badcaul

Cove

Aultbea

Gruinard

B8057

Gruinard River

296
AN CUAIDH

Isle of Ewe
Loch Ewe

Loch
Fada

Little Gruinard River

347
CREAG-MHEAL BEAG

Gaine

Melvaig
Aultgrishin

293
CNOC BREAC

Midtown
Brae

250
MEALL NA MEINE

681
BEINN A'
CHAISGEIN BEAG

Loch
She

Naast

Inverewe
Gardens NTS

13

North Erradale

B8021

Big Sand

Poolewe

Londubh

Wester Ross

BEIN

Fronn

Longa Island

Strath
Smithstown

A832

Loch
Gairloch

Auchtercairn
Heritage
Museum
Gairloch

Charlestown

.421
MEALL AN DOIREIN

791
BEINN
AIRIDH CHARR

Dubh
Loch

Eilean
Horrisdale

Port
Henderson

B8056

Badachro

Opinan

South Erradale

859
BEINN LÀIR

Loch
Maree

19

Loch
Garbhaig

Loch Maree
Hotel

Talladale

A832

981
SLIOCH

Red Point

7

8

9

0

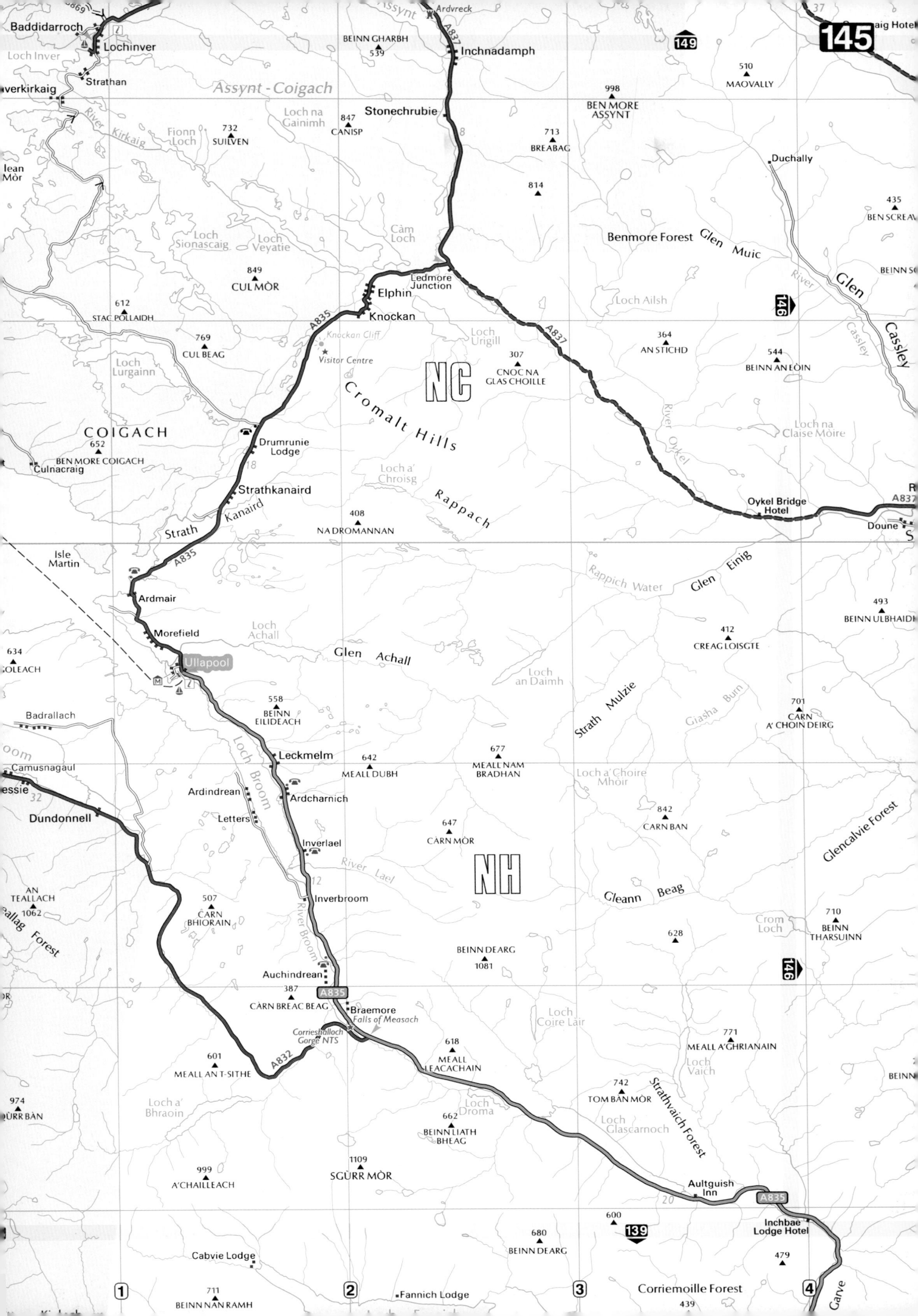

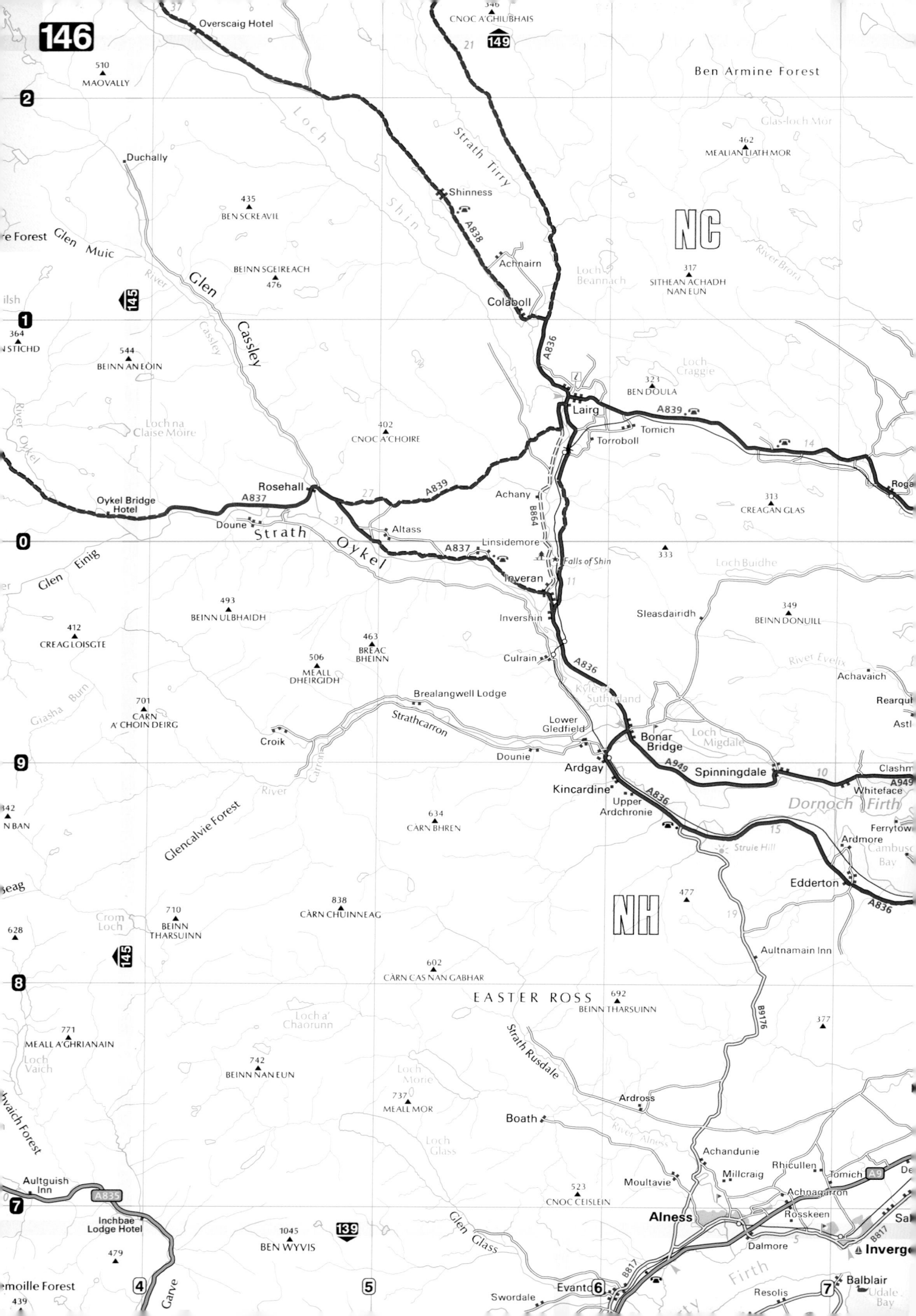

BREUN-CHOILLE

CREAG NAM FIADH

& Stone Circle

CREAG SCALABSDALE

150

151

Langwell Ho.

147

Strath of Kildonan

Kildonan Lodge

Kildonan 416

BEINN DUBHAIN

CNOC NA MAOILE

401

A9

Ord of Caithness

Torrish

River Helmsdale

A897

404

CNOC NA H-INNSE MOIRE

337

CNOC NAN CRUBAG MOR

421

BEINN DHORAIN

624

Timespan

West Helmsdale

Navidale House Hotel

East Helmsdale

Helmsdale

ND

BEINN NA MEILICH

591

Gartymore

Portgower

Glen Loth

Lothmore

Balnacoil Lodge

COL-BHEINN

539

Lothbeg

HD

Strath Brora

River Brora

A9

21

reavoch Lodge

Loch Brora

BEN HORN

520

Dalchalm

CAGAR FEOSAIG

378

Brora

446

BEINN LUNDIE

Backies

Doll

Golspie Burn

Rhives

Cairn Liath

Dunrobin Castle

Golspie

A9

Loch Fleet

Skelbo

Skelbo Street

Fourpenny

SCALE

0   1   2   3   4   5 miles

0 1 2 3 4   5 kilometres

chin

Embo

B9168

Embo Street

Pitgrudy

A949

Camore

Dornoch

3

hill

Tarbat Ness

Innis Mhor

Brucefield

Wilkhaven

NJ

Dornoch Firth

Portmahomack

Rockfield

Inver

Arboll

B9165

Toulvaddie

ie

m

ain

A9

B9165

Rhynie

Loch Eye

Fearn

Newfield

11

B9165

Hill of Fearn

Balmuchy

Hilton of Cadboll Chapel

Tullich

Hilton of Cadboll

B9166

B9175

Balintore

Milton

Ankerville

Shandwick

Shandwick Bay

Kilmuir

Pitcalnie

baraville

Nigg

Nigg Bay

Balnapaling

140

Castlecraig

Burghead

Hopeman

Burghead Well

141

Cummingston

FIRTH

Cromarty

Roseisle

Burghead Bay

College of

8

h Miller's Cottage NTS

9

0

1

Newton

B832

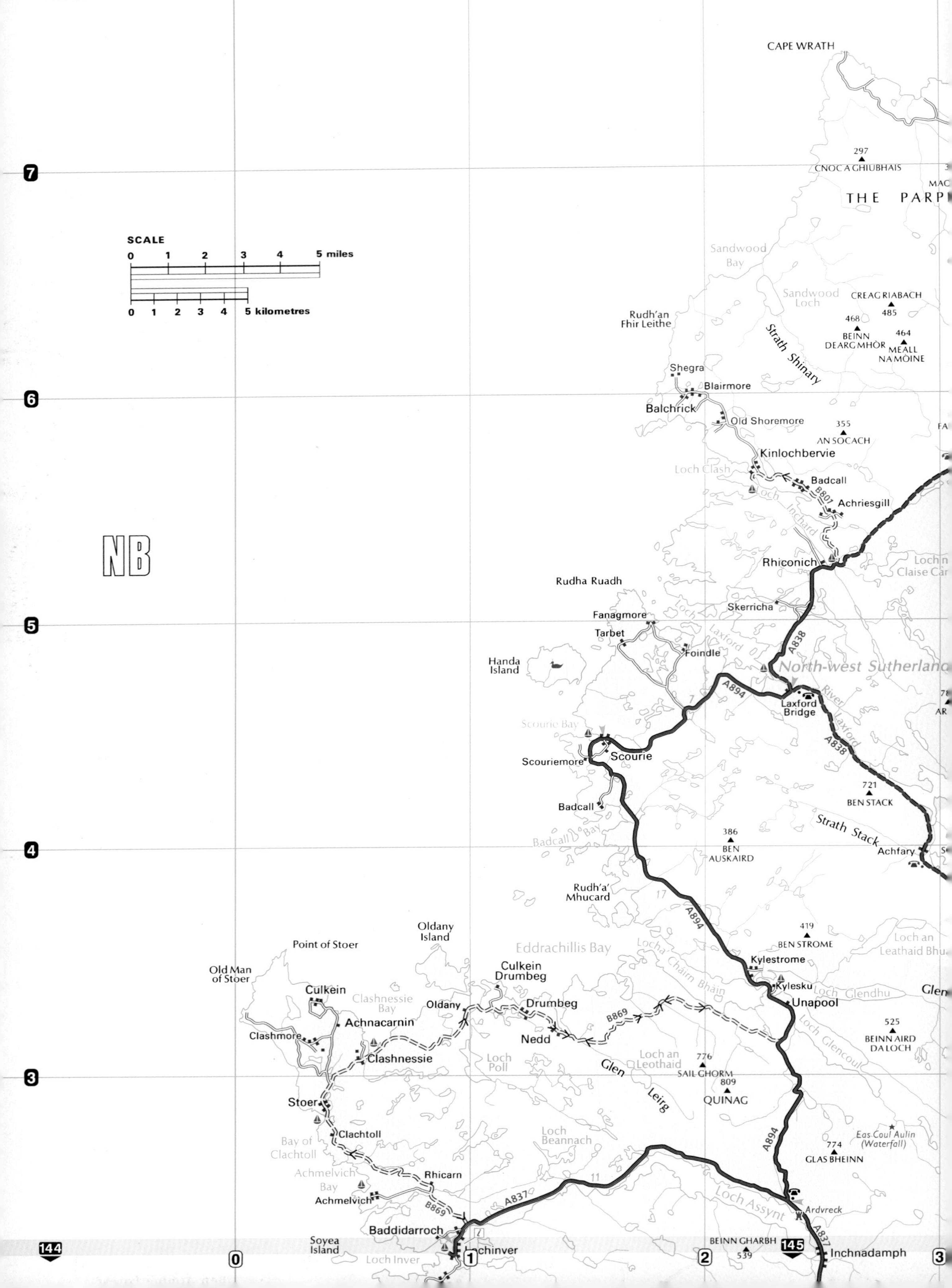

CAPE WRATH

THE PARP

MAC

297
▲
CNOC A GHIUBHAIS

SCALE

0   1   2   3   4   5 miles

0   1   2   3   4   5 kilometres

Sandwood
Bay

Sandwood
Loch

CREAG RIABACH
▲
485

468
▲

464
▲

BEINN
DEARG MHÒR

MEALL
NA MÒINE

Strath Shinary

Rudh'an
Fhir Leithe

Shegra

Blairmore

Balchrick

Old Shoremore

355
▲

AN SOCACH

Kinlochbervie

Loch Clash

Badcall

B807

Achriesgill

FA

NB

Rhiconich

Loch 'n
Claise Car

Rudha Ruadh

Fanagmore

Tarbet

Foindle

Skerricha

A838

North-west Sutherland

Handa
Island

River Laxford

78

AR

A894

Laxford
Bridge

A838

Scourie Bay

Scourie

Scouriemore

Badcall

721
▲
BEN STACK

Strath Stack

Badcall Bay

386
▲
BEN
AUSKAIRD

Achfary

S

Rudh'a'
Mhucard

17

A894

419
▲
BEN STROME

Loch an
Leathaid Bhu

Point of Stoer

Oldany
Island

Eddrachillis Bay

Loch a Chàrn Bhain

Kylestrome

Old Man
of Stoer

Culkein
Drumbeg

Kylesku

Loch Glendhu

Glen

Old Man
of Stoer

Culkein

Clashnessie
Bay

Oldany

Drumbeg

B869

Unapool

Loch Glencoul

525
▲
BEINN AIRD
DA LOCH

Achnacarnin

Nedd

Clashmore

Clashnessie

Loch
Poll

Glen
Leirg

Loch an
Leothaid

776
▲
SAIL GHORM

809
▲
QUINAG

Stoer

Clachtoll

Bay of
Clachtoll

Loch
Beannach

Eas Coul Aulin
(Waterfall)

774
▲
GLAS BHEINN

Achmelvich
Bay

Rhicarn

A837

11

A894

Achmelvich

B869

Loch Assynt

Ardvreck

Soyea
Island

Baddidarroch

Lochinver

BEINN GHARBH
539

A837

Inchnadamph

Loch Inver

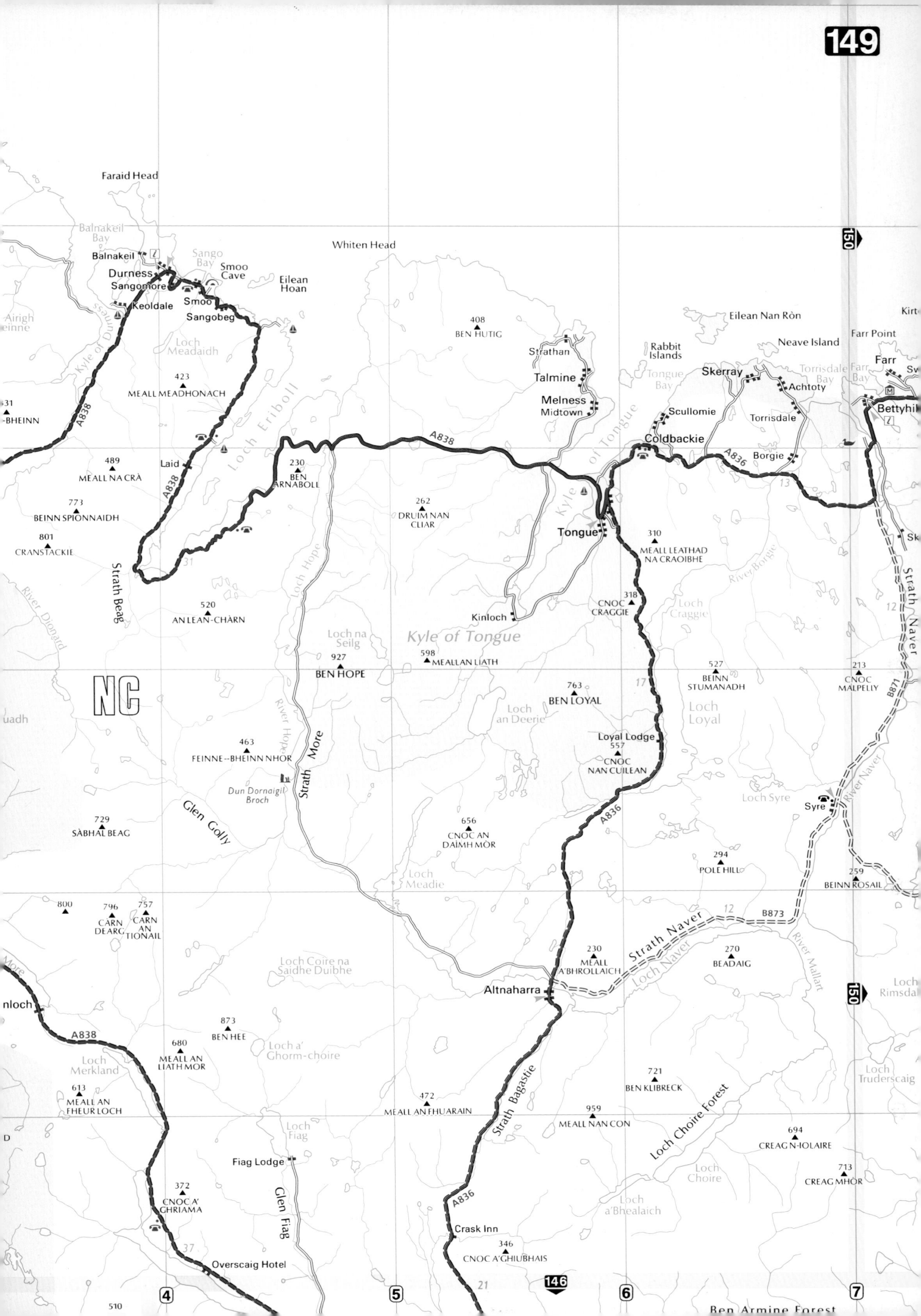

Faraid Head

Balnakeil Bay

Whiten Head

Eilean Nan Ròn

Farr Point

150

Balnakeil
Durness
Sango Bay
Smoo Cave
Eilean Hoan

Strathan
Rabbit Islands
Neave Island
Farr
Sv
Kirt

Airigh einne
31 -BHEINN

Sangomore
Keoldale
Smoo
Sangobeg

Loch Meadaidh

408 ▲ BEN HUTIG

Talmine

Skerray
Achtoty
Bettyhi

423 ▲ MEALL MEADHONACH

Melness
Midtown

Scullomie

Torrisdale Bay
Farr

A838
Loch Eriboll
A838

Torrisdale

Bettyhi

489 ▲ MEALL NA CRÀ

Laid

230 ▲ BEN ARNABOLL

Coldbackie

A836
Borgie
13

773 ▲ BEINN SPIONNAIDH

262 ▲ DRUIM NAN CLIAR

Kyle of Tongue

River Borgie

Strath Naver

801 ▲ CRANSTACKIE

Tongue

310 ▲ MEALL LEATHAD NA CRAOIBHE

Sk

River Dionard

Strath Beag

520 ▲ AN LEAN-CHÀRN

Loch na Seilg

Kinloch

318 ▲ CNOC CRAGGIE

Loch Craggie

12

NC

598 ▲ MEALLAN LIATH

Kyle of Tongue

17

527 ▲ BEINN STUMANADH

213 ▲ CNOC MALPELLY

B871

927 ▲ BEN HOPE

763 ▲ BEN LOYAL

Loch an Deerie

Loch Loyal

uadh

463 ▲ FEINNE--BHEINN NHOR

Strath More

River Hope

Loyal Lodge
557 ▲ CNOC NAN CUILEAN

Glen Golly

Dun Dornaigil Broch

Loch Syre

Syre

River Naver

729 ▲ SÀBHAL BEAG

656 ▲ CNOC AN DAIMH MÒR

A836

294 ▲ POLE HILL

259 ▲ BEINN ROSAIL

800 ▲
796 ▲ CARN DEARG
757 ▲ CARN AN TIONAIL

Loch Meadie

Strath Naver
12
B873

Loch Coire na Saidhe Duibhe

230 ▲ MEALL A'BHROLLAICH

Loch Naver

270 ▲ BEADAIG

River Mallart

150

Loch Rimsdal

nloch

A838

Altnaharra

873 ▲ BEN HEE

Loch a' Ghorm-choire

Strath Bagastie

721 ▲ BEN KLIBRECK

Loch Choire Forest

Loch Truderscaig

Loch Merkland

680 ▲ MEALL AN LIATH MOR

613 ▲ MEALL AN FHEUR LOCH

472 ▲ MEALL AN FHUARAIN

959 ▲ MEALL NAN CON

694 ▲ CREAG N-IOLAIRE

D

Loch Fiag

Loch a'Bhealaich

Loch Choire

713 ▲ CREAG MHOR

Fiag Lodge

372 ▲ CNOC A' GHRIAMA

Glen Fiag

A836

Crask Inn

346 ▲ CNOC A'GHIUBHAIS

Overscaig Hotel

37

21

510

4   **5**   **146**   **6**   **7**

Ben Armine Forest

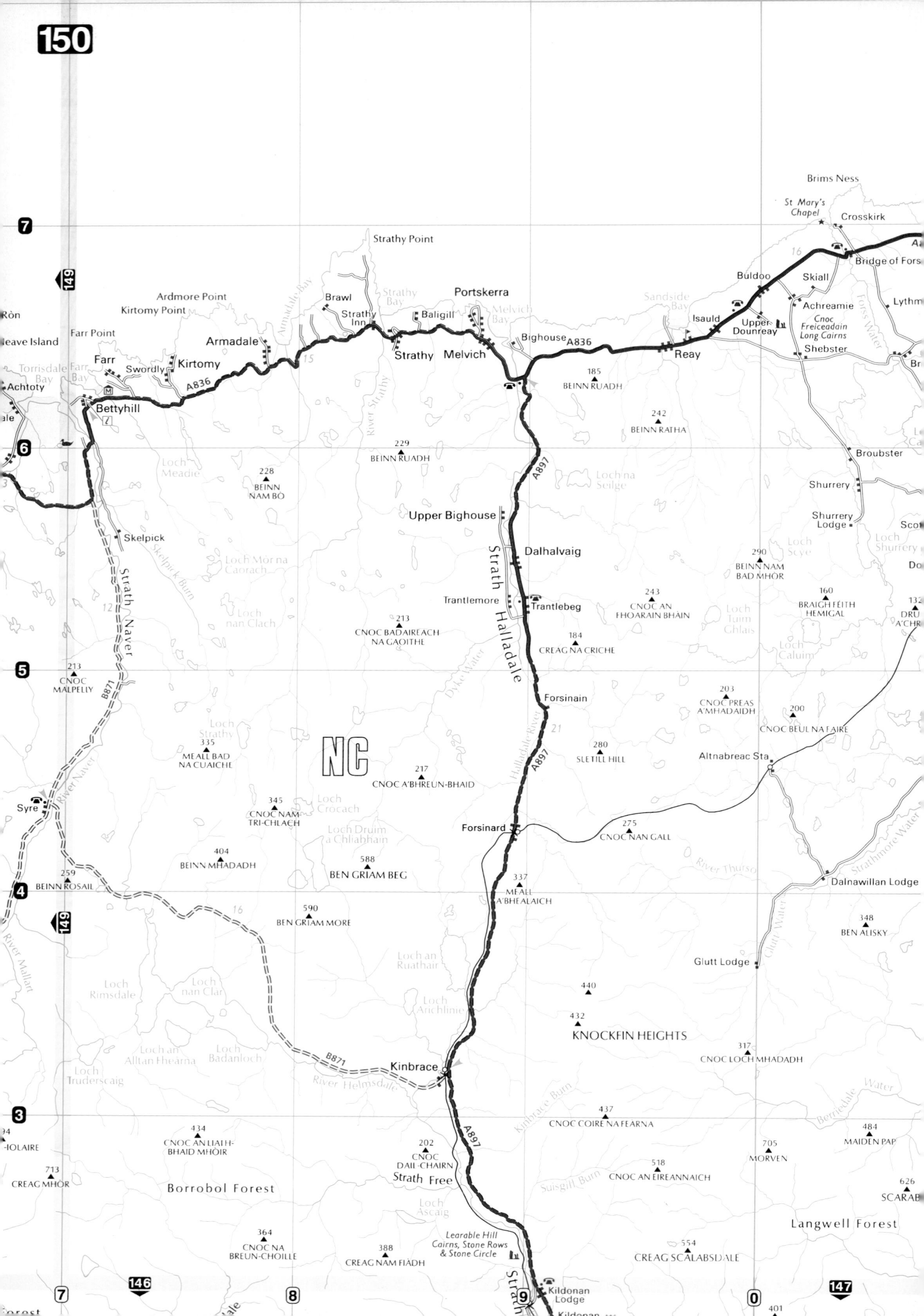

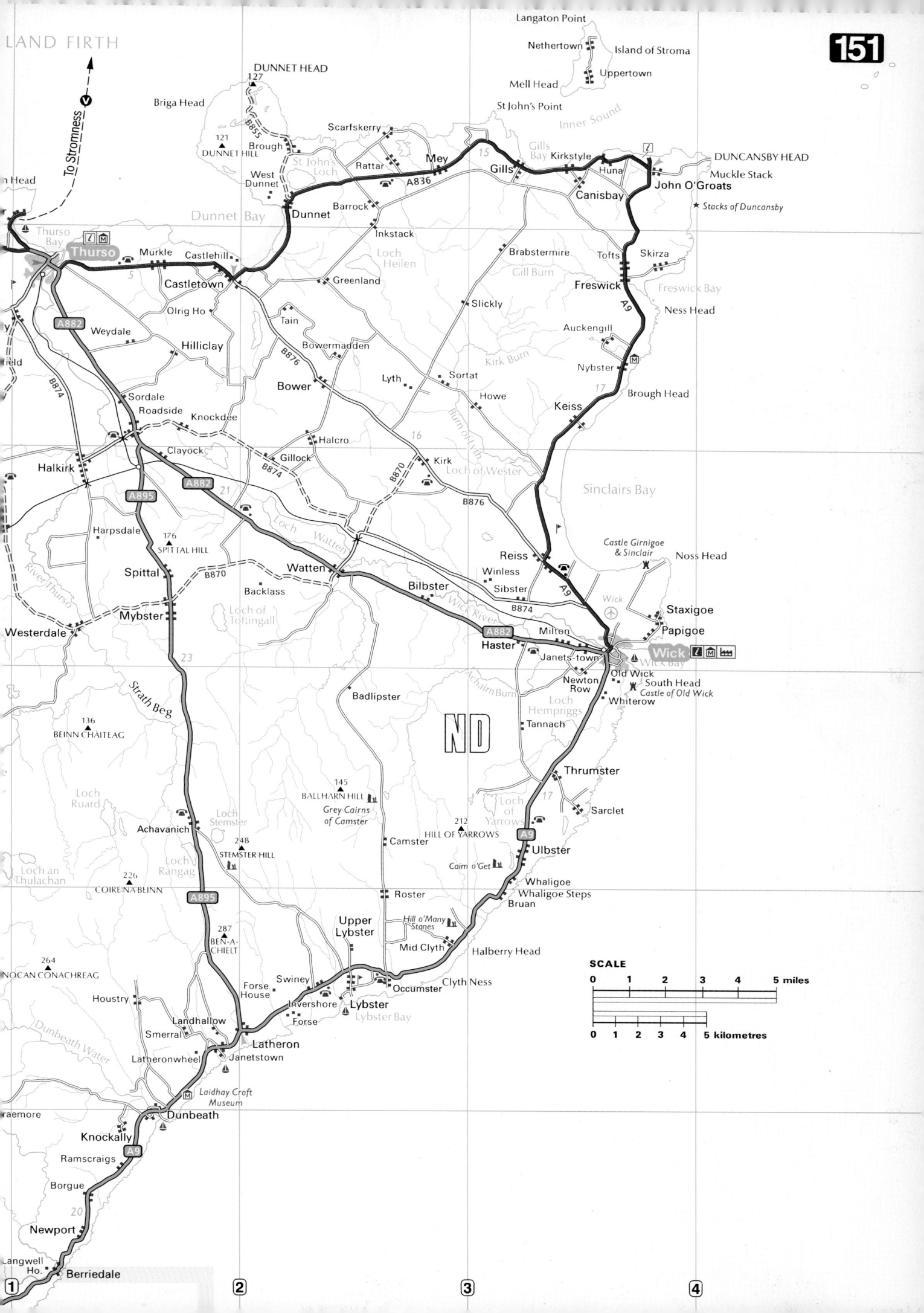

The Channel Islands

ALDERNEY — St Anne

GUERNSEY — St Peter Port — HERM — SARK

JERSEY — St Helier

FRANCE

Guernsey

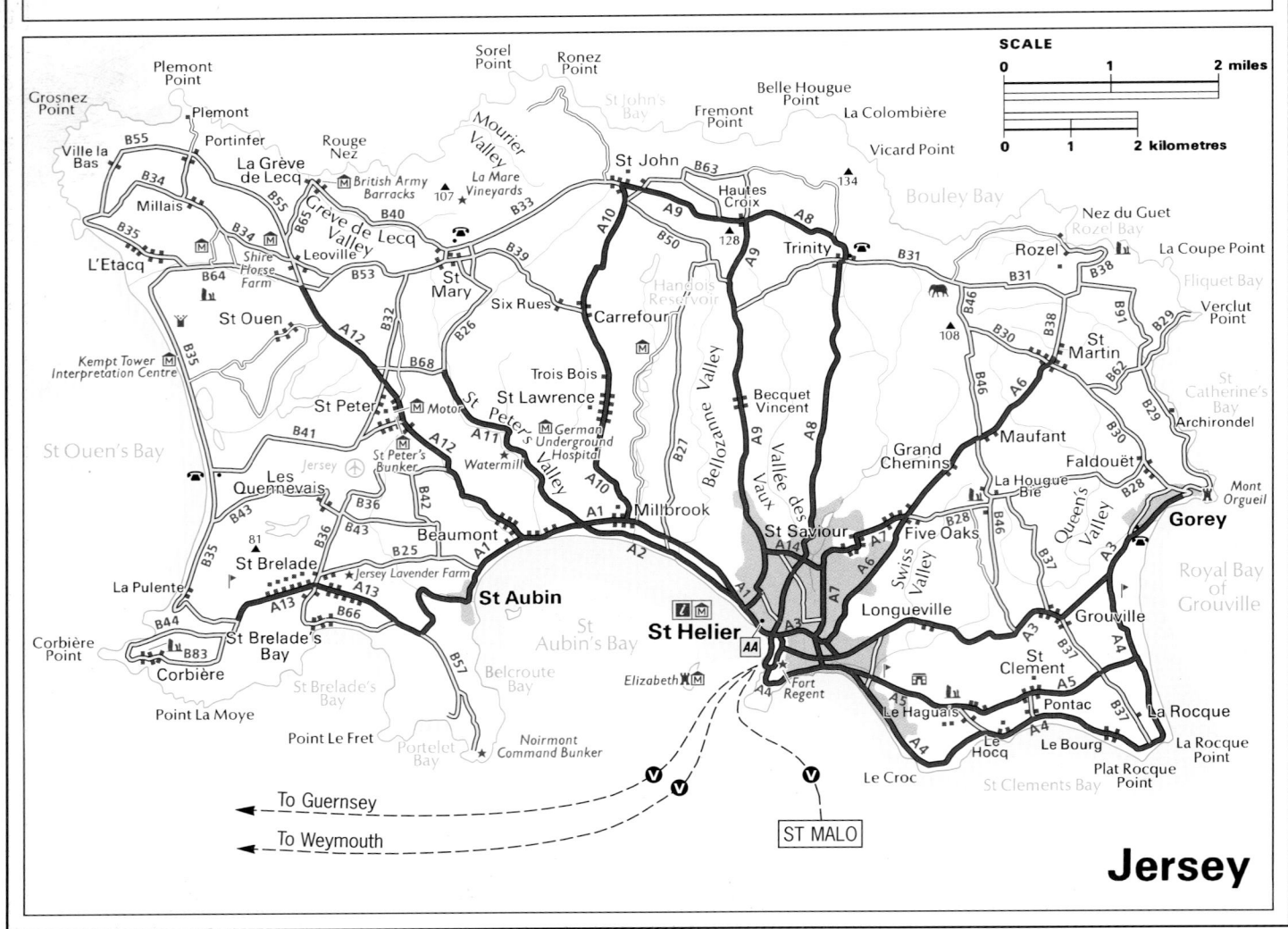

Jersey

Isle of Man

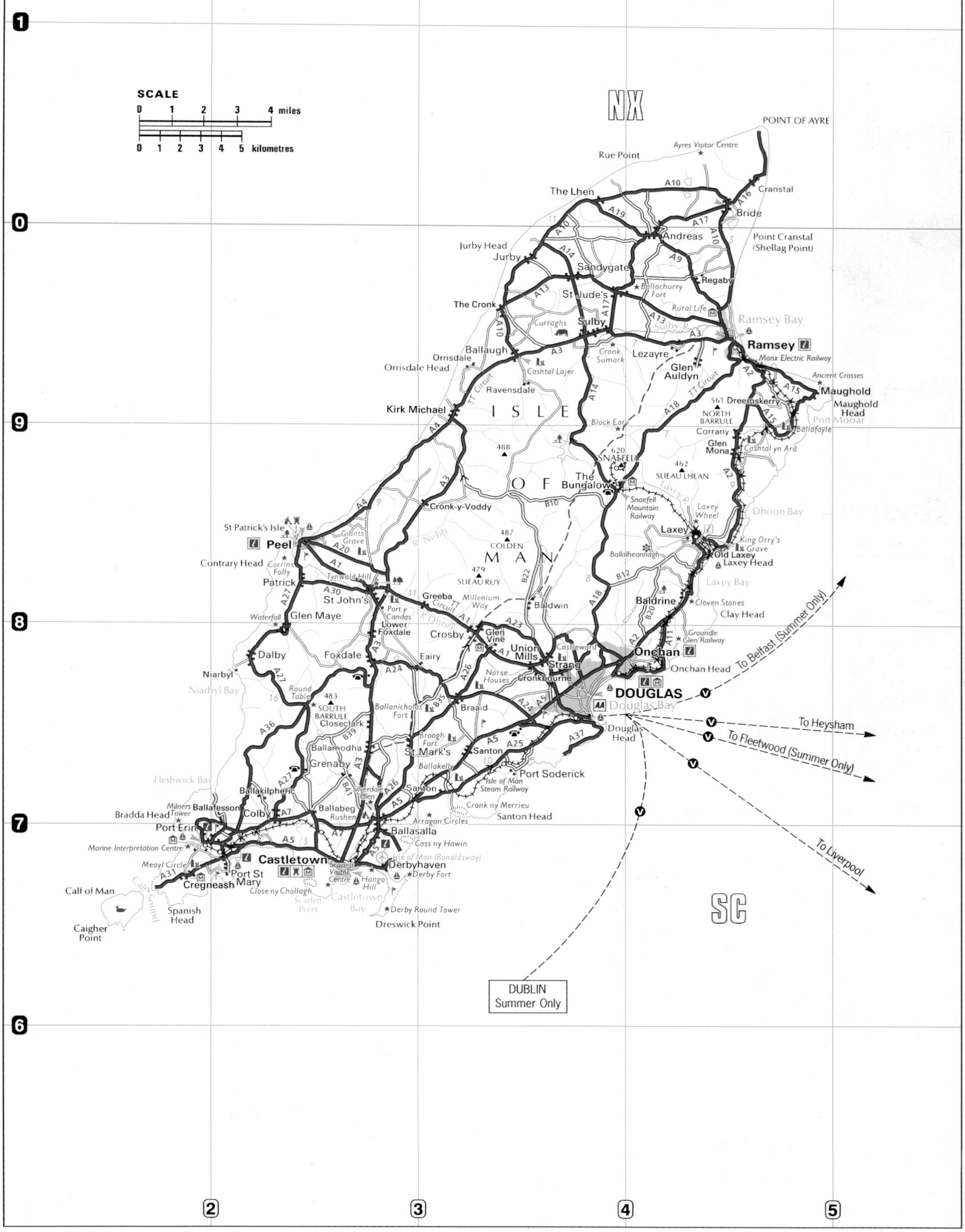

SCALE

0 1 2 3 4 miles

0 1 2 3 4 5 kilometres

NX

POINT OF AYRE

Ayres Visitor Centre

Rue Point

The Lhen

A10

A16 Cranstal

Bride

A17

A19

Andreas

A10

Point Cranstal (Shellag Point)

Jurby Head

Jurby

A14

A10

A9

Sandygate

A13

St Jude's

Ballachurry Fort

Regaby

The Cronk

A17

Sulby

Rural Life

A3

A73

Curraghs

Ramsey Bay

Manx Electric Railway

Ballaugh

A3

Cronk Sumark

Lezayre

Ramsey

Orrsdale

A10

Ravensdale

Cashtal Lajer

A14

Glen Auldyn

A2

Ancient Crosses

Orrisdale Head

ISLE

A18

TT Circuit

A75

Maughold

Kirk Michael

561 Dreemskerry

Maughold Head

A14

TT Circuit

NORTH BARRULE

Corrany

A15

Port Mooar

488

Block Eary

620 SNAEFELL

O F

Glen Mona

Cashtal yn Ard

Ballafayle

A4

Cronk-y-Voddy

462 SLIEAU LHEAN

A2

A18

St Patrick's Isle

Giants Grave

B10

Snaefell Mountain Railway

Dhoon Bay

Peel

A20

487 COLDEN

Laxey Wheel

Laxey

King Orry's Grave

Contrary Head

Corrins Folly

A1

M A N

B22

Ballalheannagh

Old Laxey

Patrick

A27

Tynwald Hill

479 SLIEAU RUY

Laxey Head

A30

St John's

11

Greeba

TT Circuit

Millenium Way

Baldwin

B12

Laxey Bay

Waterfall

Glen Maye

A1

Port y Candas

Lower Foxdale

A3

Crosby

Glen Vine

A18

Baldrine

Cloven Stones

Dalby

Foxdale

Eairy

A26

Union Mills

Castleward

B20

Clay Head

Niarbyl

A27

A24

Norse Houses

Strang

Onchan

Groundle Glen Railway

Niarbyl Bay

Round Table

483 SOUTH BARRULE

Ballanicholas Fort

Closeclark

B35

Braaid

Cronkbourne

A2

A11

Onchan Head

To Belfast (Summer Only)

16

A36

B39

Brough Fort

A5

St Mark's

A25

DOUGLAS

Ballamodha

Santon

Douglas Bay

Fleshwick Bay

Grenaby

A26

Ballakelly

Isle of Man Steam Railway

Port Soderick

A37

Douglas Head

To Heysham

Bradda Head

Milners Tower

Ballakilpheric

A3

Silverdale Glen

Santon

Cronk ny Merrieu

Santon Head

To Fleetwood (Summer Only)

Port Erin

Colby

A7

Ballabeg

Ballasalla

Arragon Circles

To Liverpool

Marine Interpretation Centre

A5

Rushen

A1

Cass ny Hawin

Meayll Circle

Port St Mary

A31

Castletown

Isle of Man (Ronaldsway)

SC

Cregneash

Scarlett Visitor Centre

Derbyhaven

Derby Fort

Calf of Man

Close ny Chollagh

Hango Hill

Castletown

Scarlett Point

Derby Round Tower

Caigher Point

Spanish Head

Scarlett Bay

Dreswick Point

DUBLIN
Summer Only

The Western Isles

SCALE

0 — 5 — 10 miles

0 — 5 — 10 kilometres

THE WESTERN ISLES

The Western Isles, na h-Eileanan Siar, stretch for 130 miles along the edge of the Atlantic, fringed on the west by mile after mile of clean, sandy beaches. The islands have a distinctive culture and Gaelic is the first language of the majority of islanders. Roadside placename signs are in Gaelic. Although one island, Lewis (north) and Harris (south) are very different. Lewis is low-lying and covered with bleak peat moors, whereas Harris is rocky and mountainous, with fertile green 'machair' land to the west.

North Uist, Benbecula and South Uist offer beaches and low-lying 'machair' to the west and mountains and moorland to the east, while Barra has a rocky, broken east coast and fine-sand bays on the west, rising to a summit at Heaval.

Ferry Services

Lewis is linked by ferry to the mainland at Ullapool, with daily sailings (except Sunday). Harris is linked to Skye at Uig, and North Uist at Loch nam Madadh in a triangular service. North Uist is served from Uig and Tairbeart (Harris), also in a triangular service. South Uist is served from Oban (mainland), as is Barra, with the ferry arriving at Bagh a Chaisteil.

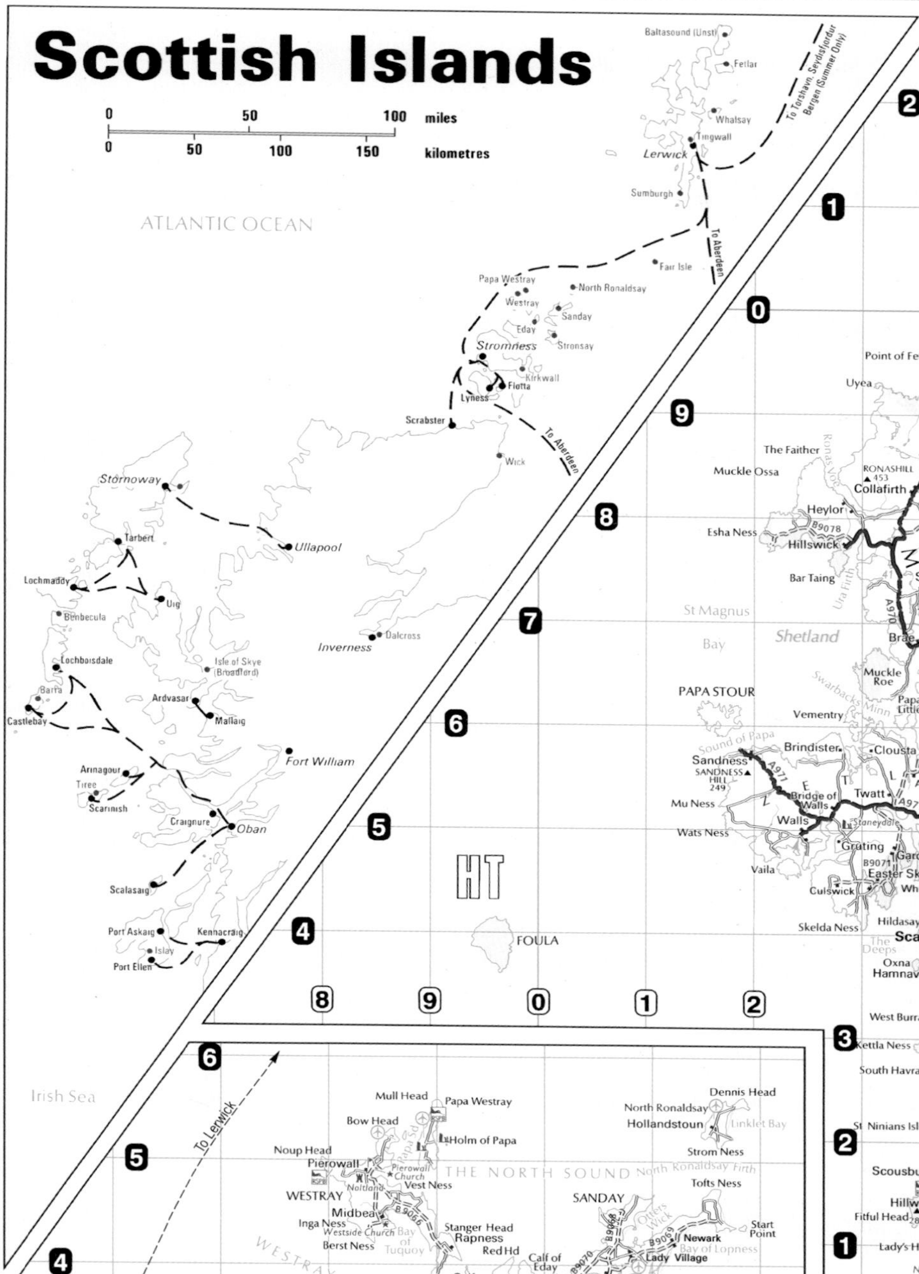

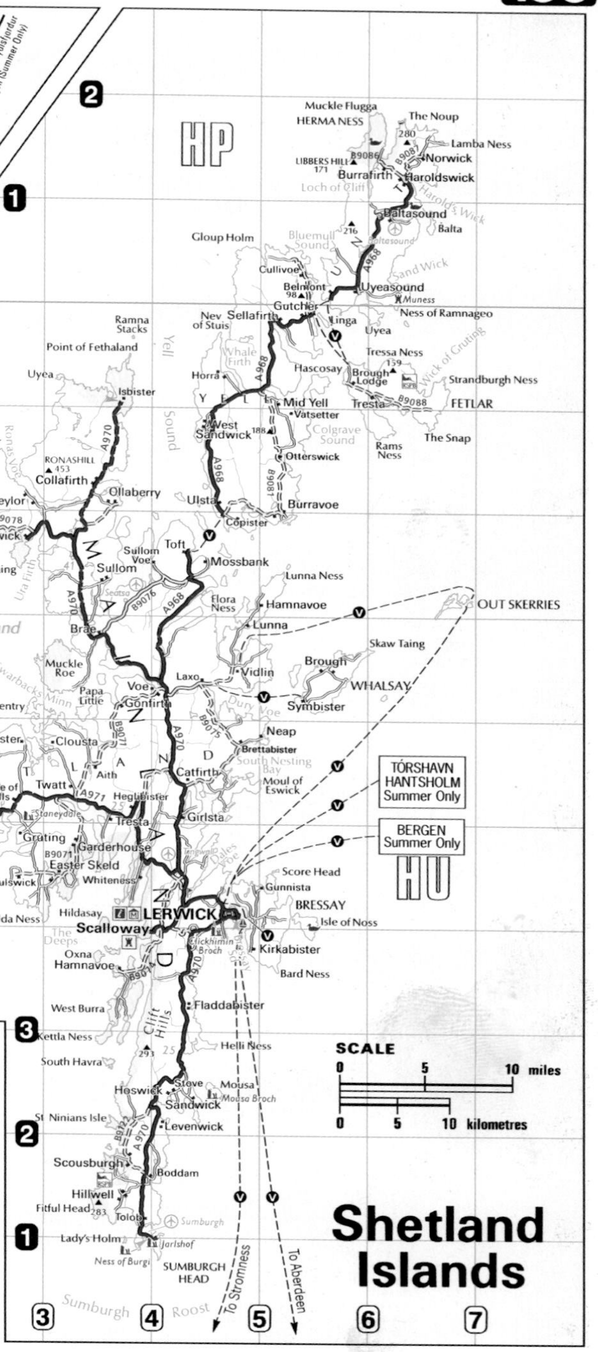

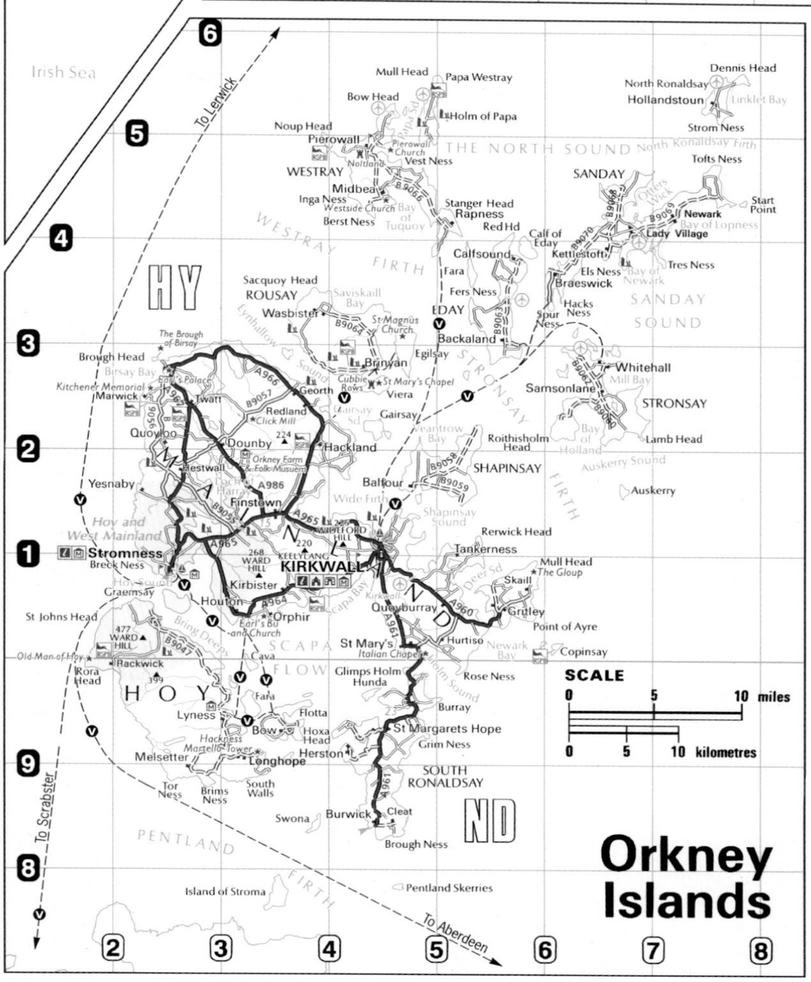

Scottish Islands

ATLANTIC OCEAN

HP

HT

HU

Shetland Islands

Orkney Islands

THE SHETLAND ISLES
The most northerly of all Britain's islands, this group numbers 100, though only 15 are inhabited. Most people live on the largest island, Mainland, on which Lerwick is the only town of importance. The scenery is magnificent, with unspoiled views, and the islands' northerly position means summer days have little or no darkness.

Ferry Services
The main service from the mainland is from Aberdeen to the island port of Lerwick. A service from Stromness (Orkney) to Lerwick is also available. During the summer months there are also services linking Shetland with Faroe, Norway and Denmark. Shetland Islands Council operates an inter-island service.

THE ORKNEY ISLANDS
Lying 20 miles north of the Scottish mainland, Orkney comprises 70 islands, of which 18 are inhabited, Mainland being the largest. Apart from Hoy, Orkney is generally green and flat, with few trees. The islands abound with prehistoric antiquities and rare bird life. The climate is one of even temperatures and 'twilight' summer nights but with violent winds at times.

Ferry Services
The main service is from Scrabster on the Caithness coast to the island port of Stromness. A service from Aberdeen to Stromness provides a link to Shetland at Lerwick. Inter-island services are also operated (advance reservations necessary).

Ireland

Abbeydorney G2
Abbeyfeale G2
Abbeyleix G4
Adamstown G4
Adare H2
Adrigole H2
Ahascragh F3
Ahoghill D5
Allihies H1
Anascaul H1
Annalong E5
Annestown H4
Antrim D5
Ardagh G2
Ardara D3
Ardcath F5
Ardee E4
Ardfert G2
Ardfinnan G3
Ardglass E5
Ardgroom H1
Arklow G5
Arless G4
Armagh D4
Armoy C5
Arthurstown H4
Arvagh E4
Ashbourne F5
Ashford F5
Askeaton G2
Athboy E4
Athea G2
Athenry F3
Athleague F3
Athlone F3
Athy F4
Augher D4
Aughnacloy D4
Aughrim G5
Avoca G5

Bailieborough E4
Balbriggan F5
Balla E2
Ballacolla G4
Ballaghaderreen E3
Ballina E2
Ballina E2
Ballinafad E3
Ballinagh E4
Ballinakill G4
Ballinalee E3
Ballinamallard D4
Ballinamore F3
Ballinamore E3
Ballinascarty H2
Ballindine E2
Ballineen H2
Ballingarry G3
Ballingarry G2
Ballingeary H2
(Béal Átha an Ghaorthaidh)
Ballinhassig H2
Ballinlough E3
Ballinrobe E2
Ballinspittle H2
Ballintober E3
Ballintra D3
Ballivor F4
Ballon G4
Ballybaun F3
Ballybay E4
Ballybofey D3
Ballybunion G2
Ballycanew G5
Ballycarry D5
Ballycastle D2
Ballycastle C5
Ballyclare D5
Ballyconneely F1
Ballycotton H3
Ballycumber F3
Ballydehob J2
Ballydesmond H2
Ballyduff H3
Ballyduff G2
Ballyfarnan E3
Ballygalley D5
Ballygar F3
Ballygawley D4
Ballygowan D5
Ballyhaise E4
Ballyhale G4
Ballyhaunis E3
Ballyhean E2
Ballyheige G2
Ballyjamesduff E4
Ballykeeran F3
Ballylanders G3
Ballylongford G2
Ballylooby G3
Ballylynan G4
Ballymahon F3
Ballymakeery H2
Ballymaloe H3
Ballymena D5
Ballymoe E3

Ballymoney C4
Ballymore F3
Ballymore Eustace F4
Ballymote E3
Ballynahinch D5
Ballynure D5
Ballyragget G4
Ballyronan D4
Ballyroan F4
Ballysadare E3
Ballyshannon D3
Ballyvaughan F2
Ballywalter D5
Balrothery F5
Baltimore J2
Baltinglass G4
Banagher F3
Banbridge D5
Bandon H2
Bangor D5
Bangor Erris E2
Bansha G3
Banteer H2
Bantry H2
Barryporeen G3
Beaufort H2
Belcoo D3
Belfast D5
Belgooly H2
Bellaghy D4
Belleek D3
Belmullet D2
(Béal an Mhuirhead)
Belturbet E4
Benburb D4
Bennettsbridge G4
Beragh D4
Birr F3
Blacklion D3
Blackwater G5
Blarney H3
Blessington F4
Boherbue H3
Borris G4
Borris-in-Ossory F3
Borrisokane F3
Borrisoleigh G3
Boyle E3
Bracknagh F4
Bray F5
Bridgetown H4
Brittas F4
Broadford G3
Broadford G2
Broughshane D5
Bruff G3
Bruree G3
Bunclody G4
Buncrana C4
Bundoran D3
Bunmahon H4
Bunnahowen D2
Bunnyconnellan E2
Bushmills C4
Butler's Bridge E4
Buttevant H2

Cadamstown F3
Caherconlish G3
Caherdaniel H1
Cahersiveen H1
Cahir G3
Caledon D4
Callan G4
Caltra F3
Camolin G4
Camp G1
Cappagh White G3
Cappamore G3
Cappoquin H3
Carlanstown E4
Calingford E5
Carlow G4
Carndonagh C4
Carnew G4
Carnlough C5
Carracastle E3
Carrick D3
(An Charraig)
Carrickfergus D5
Carrickmacross E4
Carrickmore D4
Carrick-on-Shannon E3
Carrick-on-Suir G4
Carrigahorig F3
Carrigaline H3
Carriganimmy H2
Carrigans C4
Carrigtohill H3
Carrowkeel C4
Carryduff D5
Cashel G3
Castlebar E2
Castlebellingham E5
Castleblayney E4
Castlebridge G4
Castlecomer G4

Castle Cove H1
Castlederg D4
Castledermot G4
Castleisland G2
Castlemaine H2
Castlemartyr H3
Castleplunkett E3
Castlepollard E4
Castlerea E3
Castlerock C4
Castleshane E4
Castletown F4
Castletownbere H1
Castletownroche H3
Castletownshend J2
Castlewellan E5
Causeway G2
Cavan E4
Celbridge F4
Charlestown E3
Clady D4
Clane F4
Clara F3
Clarecastle G2
Claremorris E2
Clarinbridge F2
Clashmore H3
Claudy C4
Clifden F1
Cliffony D3
Clogh G4
Cloghan F3
Clogheen H3
Clogher D4
Clohamon G4
Clonakilty H2
Clonard F4
Clonaslee F4
Clonbulloge F4
Clonbur (An Fhairche) E2
Clondalkin F5
Clones E4
Clonmany C4
Clonmel G3
Clonmellon E4
Clonmore G4
Clonony F3
Clonoulty G3
Clonroche G4
Clontibret E4
Cloonbannin H2
Cloondara E3
Cloonkeen H2
Cloonlara G3
Clough D5
Cloughjordan F3
Cloyne H3
Coagh D4
Coalisland D4
Cobh H3
Coleraine C4
Collinstown E4
Collon E4
Collooney E3
Comber D5
Conna H3
Cookstown D4
Coole E4
Cooraclare G2
Cootehill E4
Cork H3
Cornamona E2
Corofin F2
Courtmacsherry H2
Courtown Harbour G5
Craigavon D5
Craughwell F3
Creggs F3
Cresslough C3
Croagh G2
Crolly (Croithlí) C3
Crookedwood E4
Crookhaven J1
Crookstown H2
Croom G2
Crossakeel E4
Cross Barry H2
Crosshaven H3
Crossmaglen E4
Crossmolina E2
Crumlin D5
Crusheen F2
Culdaff C4
Culleybackey D5
Curracloe G4
Curraghboy F3
Curry E3
Cushendall C5

Daingean F4
Delvin E4
Derrygonnelly D3
Derrylin E4
Dervock C5
Dingle (An Daingean) H1
Doagh D5
Donaghadee D5
Donaghmore G3

Donegal D3
Doneraile H3
Doonbeg G2
Douglas H3
Downpatrick D5
Dowra D3
Draperstown D4
Drimoleague H2
Dripsey H2
Drogheda E5
Droichead Nua F4
(Newbridge)
Dromahair D3
Dromcolliher G2
Dromore D5
Dromore H3
Dromore West D3
Drum E4
Drumconrath E4
Drumkeeran E3
Drumlish E3
Drumod E3
Drumquin D4
Drumshanbo E3
Drumsna E3
Duagh G2
Dublin F5
Duleek E5
Dunboyne F4
Duncormick H4
Dundalk E5
Dunderrow H3
Dunfanaghy C3
Dungannon D4
Dungarvan H3
Dungarvan G4
Dungiven C4
Dungloe C3
Dungourney H3
Dunkineely D3
Dún Laoghaire F5
Dunlavin F4
Dunleer E5
Dunloy C5
Dunmanway H2
Dunmore E3
Dunmore East H4
Dunmurry D5
Dunshaughlin F4
Durrow G4
Durrus H2

Easky D2
Edenderry F4
Edgeworthstown E4
Eglinton C4
Elphin E3
Emyvale D4
Enfield F4
Ennis F2
Enniscorthy G4
Enniscrone D2
Enniskean H2
Enniskillen D4
Ennistymon F2
Eyrecourt F3

Farnaght E3
Farranfore H2
Feakle F3
Fenagh E3
Fermoy H3
Ferns G4
Fethard H3
Fethard G4
Finnea E4
Fintona D4
Fivemiletown D4
Fontstown F4
Foulkesmills H4
Foxford E2
Foynes G2
Freemount H2
Frenchpark E3
Freshford G4
Fuerty F3

Galbally G3
Galway F2
Garrison D3
Garristown F5
Garvagh C4
Geashill F4
Gilford D5
Glandore J2
Glanworth H3
Glaslough D4

Glassan F3
Glenamaddy E3
Glenarm C5
Glenavy D5
Glenbeigh H1
Glencolumbkille D3
(Gleann Cholm Cille)
Glendalough G4
Glenealy G5
Glenfarne D3
Glengarriff H2
Glenmore H4
Glenties D3
Glenville H3
Glin G2
Glinsk F2
(Glinsce)
Golden G3
Goleen J2
Goresbridge G4
Gorey G5
Gort F2
Gortin D4
Gowran G4
Graiguenamanagh G4
Grallagh E3
Granard E4
Grange E3
Greencastle E5
Greyabbey D5
Greystones F5
Gulladuff D4

Hacketstown G4
Headford F2
Herbertstown G3
Hillsborough D5
Hilltown E5
Hospital G3
Holycross G3
Holywood D5
Howth F5

Inch H1
Inchigeelagh H2
Inishannon H2
Irvinestown D4

Johnstown G3

Kanturk H2
Keadue E3
Keady E4
Keel E1
Keenagh E3
Kells D5
Kells E4
Kenmare H2
Kesh D3
Kilbeggan F3
Kilberry E4
Kilbrittain H2
Kilcar D3
(Cill Charthaigh)
Kilcock F4
Kilcolgan F2
Kilconnell F3
Kilconnell F3
Kilcoole F5
Kilcormac F3
Kilcullen F4
Kilcurry E5
Kildare F4
Kildavin G4
Kildorrery H2
Kildress D4
Kilfenora F2
Kilfinnane G3
Kilgarvan H2
Kilkee G2
Kilkeel E5
Kilkelly E3
Kilkenny G4
Kilkieran F2
(Cill Ciaráin)
Kilkinlea G2
Kill H4
Killadysert G2
Killala D2
Killaloe G3
Killarney H2
Killashandra E4
Killashee E3
Killeagh H3
Killeigh F4
Killenaule G3
Killimer G2
Killimor F3

Killiney F5
Killinick H4
Killorglin H1
Killough E5
Killucan F4
Killybegs D3
Killyleagh D5
Kilmacanoge F5
Kilmacrenan C3
Kilmacthomas H4
Kilmaganny G4
Kilmaine F2
Kilmallock G3
Kilmanagh G4
Kilmanahan G3
Kilmeaden H4
Kilmeage F4
Kilmeedy G2
Kilmore Quay H4
Kilnaleck E4
Kilrea C4
Kilrush G2
Kilsheelan G3
Kiltealy G4
Kiltegan G4
Kiltimagh E2
Kiltoom F3
Kingscourt E4
Kinlough D3
Kinnegad F4
Kinnitty F3
Kinsale H3
Kinvarra F2
Kircubbin D5
Knock E2
Knockcroghery F3
Kocklofty G3
Knockmahon H4
Knocktopher G4

Lahinch F2
Lanesborough E3
Laragh F5
Larne D5
Lauragh H1
Laurencetown F3
Leap J2
Leenane F2
Leighlinbridge G4
Leitrim E3
Leixlip F4
Lemybrien H3
Letterfrack E2
Letterkenny C4
Lifford D4
Limavady C4
Limerick G3
Lisbellaw D4
Lisburn D5
Liscarroll G2
Lisdoonvarna F2
Lismore H3
Lisnaskea D4
Lisryan E4
Listowel G2
Loghill G2
Londonderry C4
Longford E3
Loughbrickland D5
Loughgall D4
Loughglinn E3
Loughrea F3
Louisburgh E2
Lucan F4
Lurgan D5
Lusk F5

Macroom H2
Maghera E5
Maghera D4
Magherafelt D4
Maguiresbridge D4
Malahide F5
Malin C4
Malin More D3
Mallow H2
Manorhamilton D3
Markethill D4
Maynooth F4
Mazetown D5
Middletown D4
Midleton H3
Milford C4
Milltown H2
Milltown H2
Milltown Malbay G2
Mitchelstown H3

Moate F3
Mohill E3
Molls Gap H2
Monaghan E4
Monasterevin F4
Moneygall G3
Moneymore D4
Monivea F3
Mooncoin H4
Moorfields D5
Mount Bellew F3
Mount Charles D3
Mountmellick F4
Mountrath F4
Mountshannon F3
Mourne Abbey H3
Moville C4
Moy D4
Moylett E4
Moynalty E4
Moyvore F3
Muckross H2
Muff C4
Muine Bheag G4
Mullabohy E4
Mullagh F4
Mullinavat G4
Mullingar F4
Myshall G4

Naas F4
Nad H2
Naul F5
Navan E4
Neale E2
Nenagh G3
Newbliss E4
Newcastle E5
Newcastle West G2
Newinn G3
Newmarket H2
Newmarket-on-Fergus G2
Newport F2
Newport E2
New Ross G4
Newry E5
Newtown G4
Newtownabbey D5
Newtownards D5
Newtownmountkennedy F5
Newtownstewart D4
Newtown Butler E4
Newtown Forbes E3
Nobber E4

Oilgate G4
Oldcastle E4
Omagh D4
Omeath E5
Oola G3
Oranmore F2
Oughterard F2
Ovens H3

Pallas Grean G3
Parknasilla H1
Partry E2
Passage East H4
Passage West H3
Patrickswell G2
Paulstown G4
Pettigo D3
Plumbridge D4
Pomeroy D4
Portadown D5
Portaferry D5
Portarlington F4
Portavogie D5
Portglenone D5
Portlaoise F4
Portmarnock F5
Portrane F5
Portroe G3
Portrush C4
Portstewart C4
Portumna F3
Poyntzpass D5

Raharney F4
Randalstown D5
Rasharkin C5
Rathangan F4
Rathcoole F4
Rathcormack H3
Rathdowney G3
Rathdrum G5
Rathfriland E5

Rathkeale G2
Rath Luric G2
(Charleville)
Rathmelton C4
Rathmolyon F4
Rathmore H2
Rathmullan C4
Rathnew F5
Rathowen E4
Rathvilly G4
Ratoath F4
Ray C4
Ring H3
(An Rinn)
Ringaskiddy H3
Riverstown F3
Rockcorry E4
Roosky E3
Rosapenna C3
Rosbercon G4
Roscommon E3
Roscrea F3
Ross Carbery J2
Rosscor D3
Rosses Point D3
Rosslare Harbour H4
Roslea E4
Rostrevor E5
Roundstone F2
Roundwood F5
Rush F5

St Johnstown C4
Saintfield D5
Sallins F4
Scarriff F3
Scartaglen H2
Scarva D5
Schull J2
Scramoge E3
Scribbagh D3
Seskinore D4
Shanagolden G2
Shannonbridge F3
Shercock E4
Shillelagh G4
Shinrone F3
Shrule F2
Silvermines G3
Sion Mills D4
Sixmilebridge G2
Skerries F5
Skibbereen J2
Slane E4
Sligo D3
Smithborough E4
Sneem H1
Spiddal F2
(An Spidéal)
Stewartstown D4
Stonyford G4
Strabane D4
Stradbally F4
Stradone E4
Strangford D5
Stranorlar D3
Stratford F4
Strokestown E3
Summerhill F4
Swanlinbar E3
Swatragh D4
Swinford E2
Swords F5

Taghmon G4
Tagoat G4
Tahilla H1
Tallaght F5
Tallow H3
Tallowbridge H3
Tandragee D5
Tang F3
Tarbert G2
Templemore G3
Templepatrick D5
Templetouhy G3
Termonfeckin F5
Thomas Street F3
Thomastown G4
Thurles G3
Timahoe F4
Timoleague H2
Tinahely G4
Tipperary G3
Tobercurry E3
Togher F5
Toomyvara G3
Toormore J2
Tralee G2
Tramore H4
Trim F4
Tuam F2
Tuamgraney G3
Tulla G2
Tullamore F4
Tullow G4
Tulsk E3
Turlough E2
Tyholland D4
Tyrrellspass F4

Urlingford G3

Virginia E4

Waddington H4
Warrenpoint E5
Waterford H4
Watergrasshill H3
Waterville H1
Westport E2
Wexford G4
Whitegate H3
Whitehead D5
Wicklow G5
Woodenbridge G5
Woodford F3

Youghal H3

Aran Island

Gweebarra
Rossan Point
Malin More
Glencolumbkille (Gleann Cholm Cille)
Glencolumbkille Folk Museum M
Carrick (An Charraig)
Killybe
Kilcar (Cill Charthaigh)
SLIEVE LEAGUE 601
St John's Point
Donegal Bay
Inishmurray
Grange
Lissadell
BENB
525
Rosses Point
Sligo Bay
Strandhill
Sli
Ballysadare
R292
R291
Colooney

Erris Head
Broad Haven
Downpatrick Head
Ballycastle
Easky
Dromore West
R314
R315
R297
Killala
Enniscrone
N59
Belmullet (Béal an Mhuirhead)
Bunnahowen
R313
Bangor Erris
Inishkea
Duvillaun Móre
Blacksod Bay
Crossmolina
Ballina
Bunnyconnellan
OX MTS
Tobercurry
R294
722
806 NEPHIN
SLIEVE MORE 671
Keel
Foxford
Curry
Ballina
Achill Head
Achill Island
Lough Feeagh
R317
Swinford
Charlestown
Carracastle
Ballaghaderree
Newport
Turlough
Knock Regional Airport
Clare Island
Clew Bay
Castlebar
Kiltimagh
Kilkelly
R325
Westport
Ballyhean
Balla
Knock
Loughglin
Louisburgh
CROAGH PATRICK 765
Castlerea

C

D

E

1

2

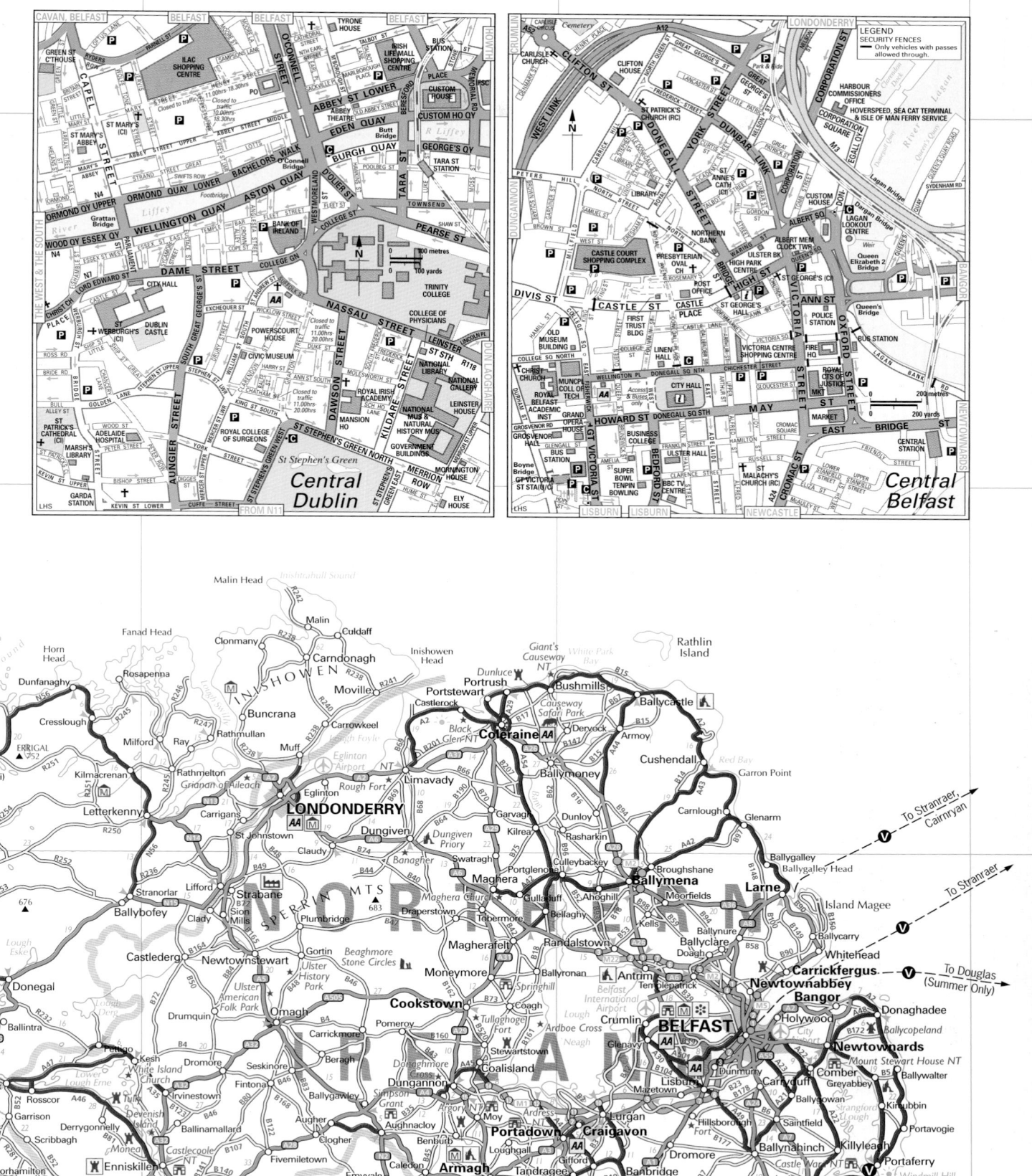

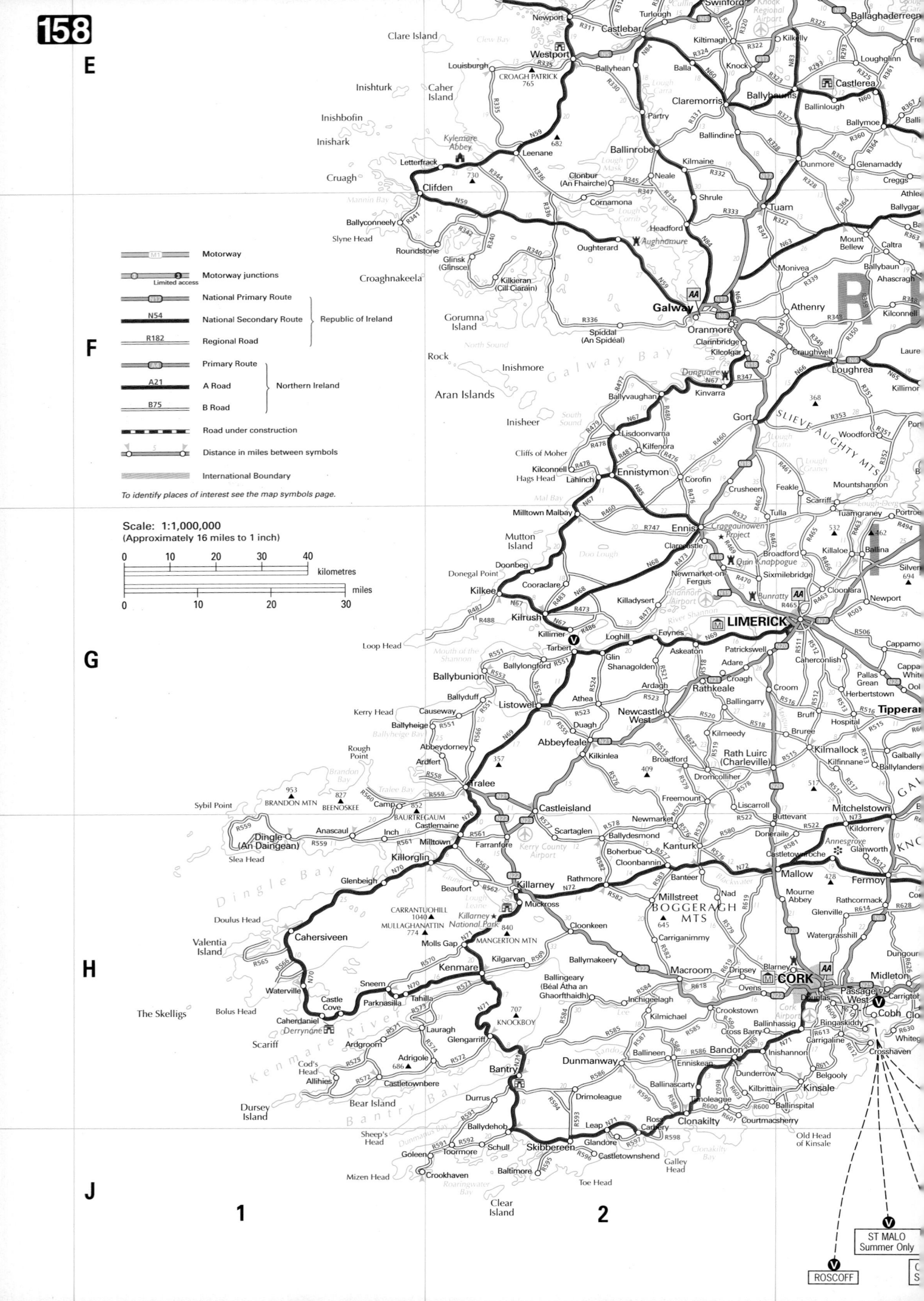

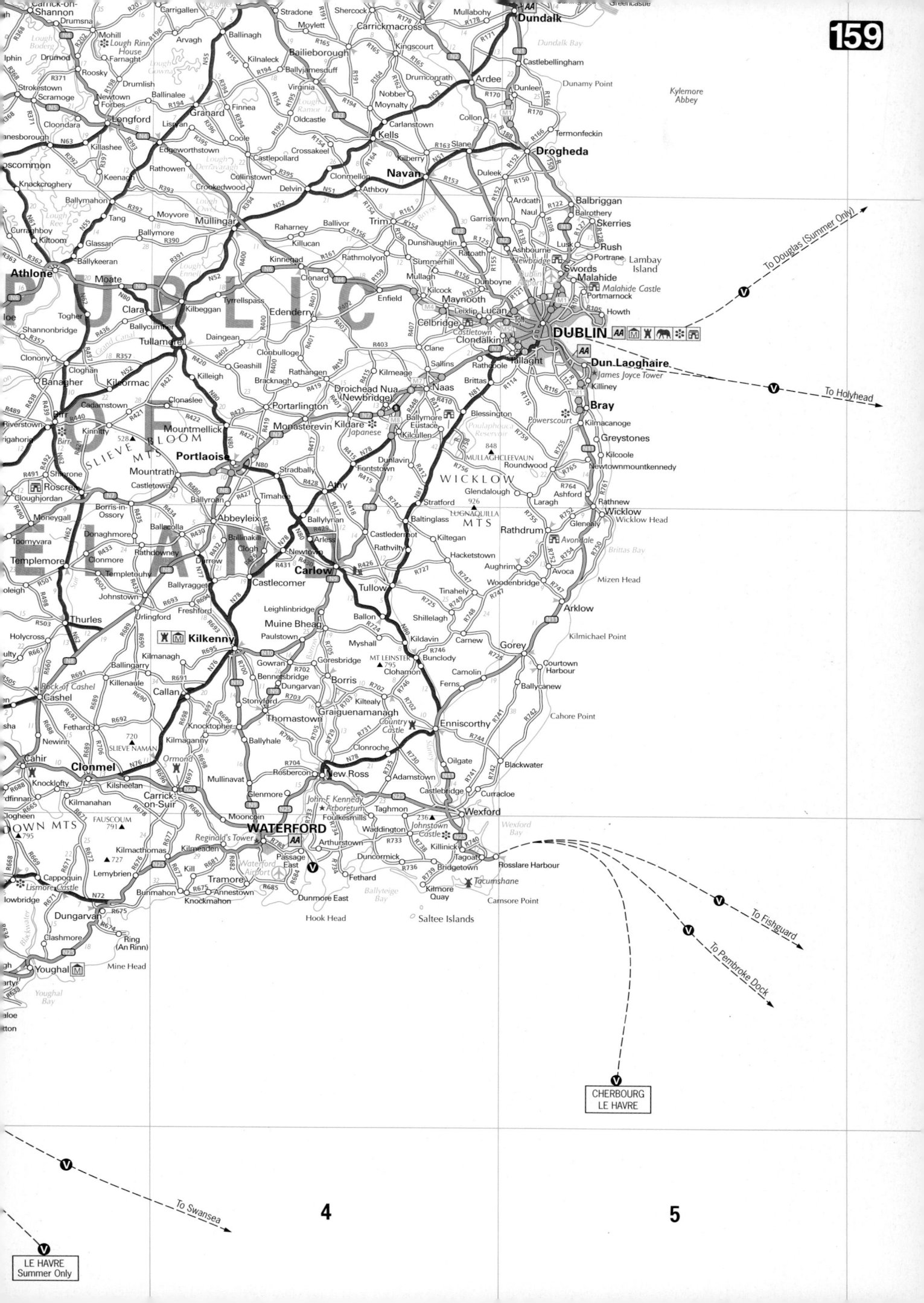

ports and airports

The following pages detail the major airports and seaports which help to provide a comprehensive domestic and international communications network. The maps indicate the approach roads into each complex with information on parking. Telephone numbers are provided to obtain details on cost and other travel information.

Gatwick and Heathrow are two of the busiest airports in the world and many of the smaller airports listed below are constantly improving and expanding available services and destinations. The name of the airline concerned, or the flight number, must be known before aircraft arrivals and departures can be checked. Generally, no contact may be made with the passengers after they have cleared Customs on departure or before they have done so on arrival.

Always use the designated car parks. Your vehicle is liable to be removed if left unattended - even for very short periods - on any roads near the airport terminals. Facilities for the disabled traveller are provided at the listed air and seaports and in some cases parking concessions are available for Orange Badge holders. If special assistance is required the relevant airline or shipping company should be contacted.

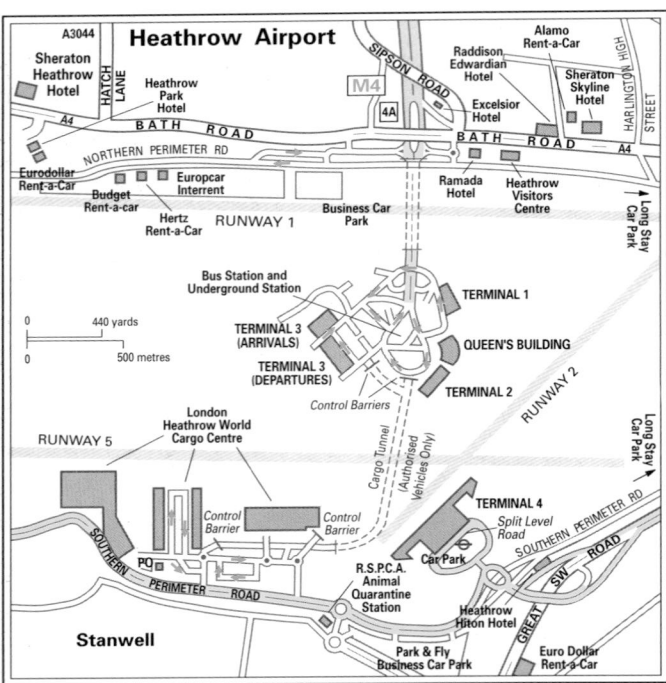

Heathrow Airport - 16 miles west of London

Telephone: 0181 759 4321
Parking: Short-stay, Long-stay and business parking available. For charge details tel: 0181 745 7160
Public Transport: Coach, Bus and London Underground
There are several 4-star and 3-star hotels within easy reach of the airport and car hire facilities are available

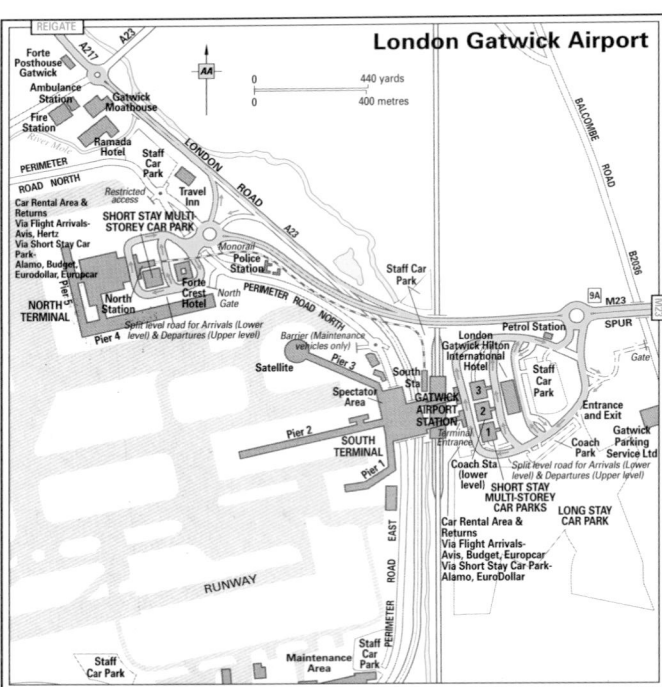

Gatwick Airport - 28 miles south of London

Telephone: 01293 535353
Parking: Short and Long-stay parking available at both the North and South terminal. For charge details tel: 01293 502390 (short-stay) and either 0800 128128 or 01293 569222 (long stay)
Public Transport: Coach, Bus and Rail. There are several 4-star and 3-star hotels within easy reach of the airport and car hire facilities are available

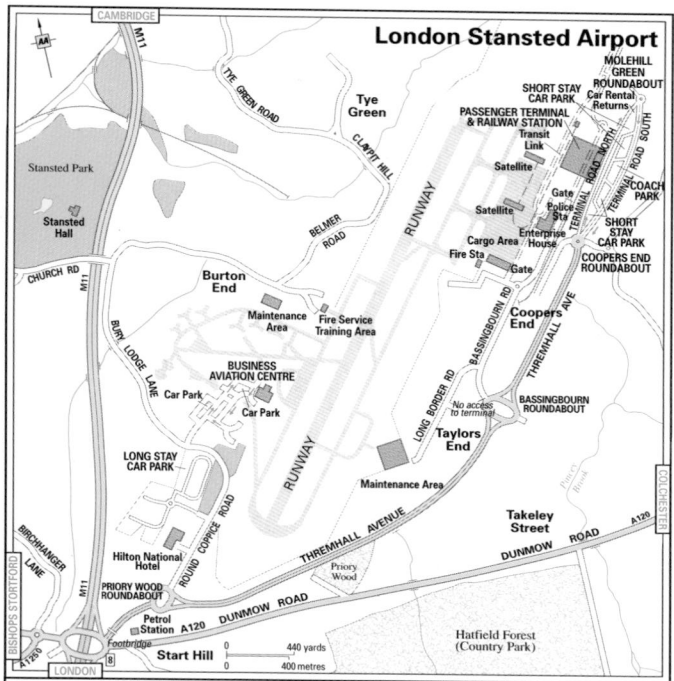

London Stansted Airport - 38 miles north-east of London

Telephone: 01279 680500
Parking: Short and Long-stay open air parking available. For charge details tel: 01279 662373
Public Transport: Coach, Bus and a direct Rail link to London on the 'Stansted Express'
There are several 4-star and 3-star hotels within easy reach of the airport and car hire facilities are available

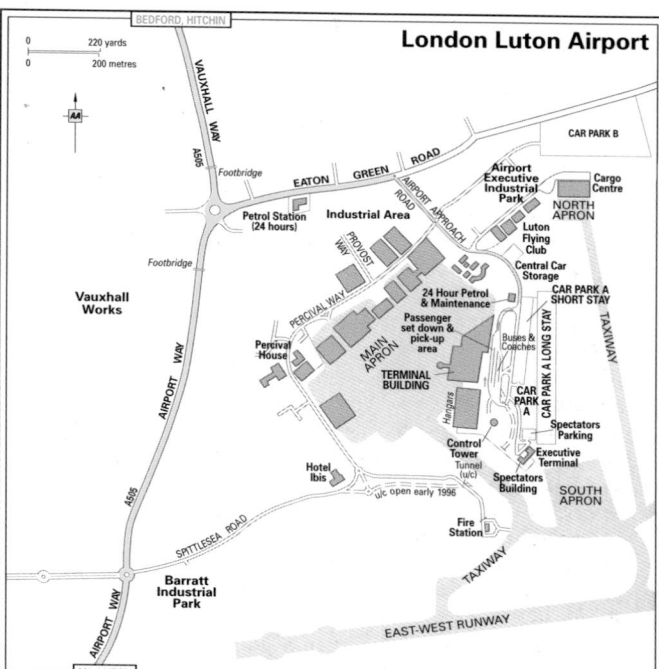

London Luton Airport - 35 miles north of London

Telephone: 01582 405100
Parking: Short and Long-stay open air parking available
Public Transport: Coach, Bus and Rail
There is one 2-star hotel at the airport and several 3-star hotels within easy reach of the airport. Car hire facilities are available

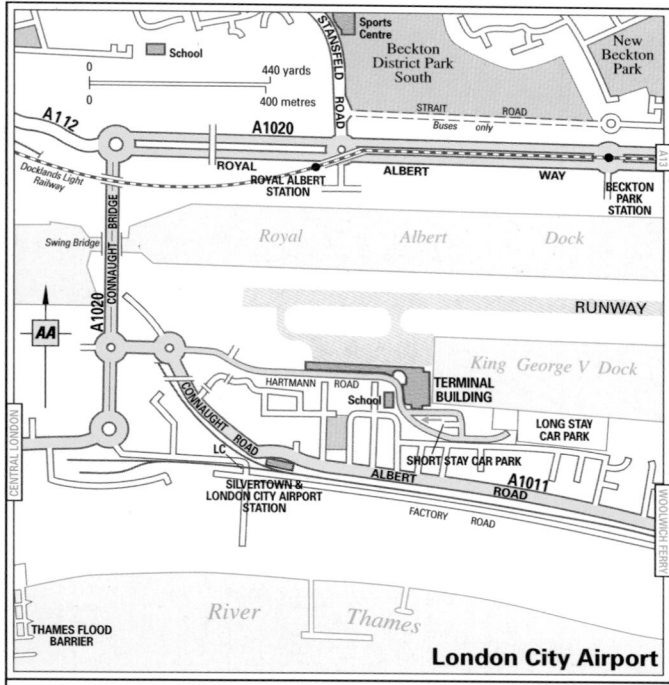

London City Airport - 6 miles east of London

Telephone: 0171 474 5555
Parking: Short and Long-stay parking available
Public Transport: 'Shuttlebus' service into London. Easy access to Rail network and London Underground
There is a 4-star and 2-star hotel within easy reach of the airport and car hire facilities are available

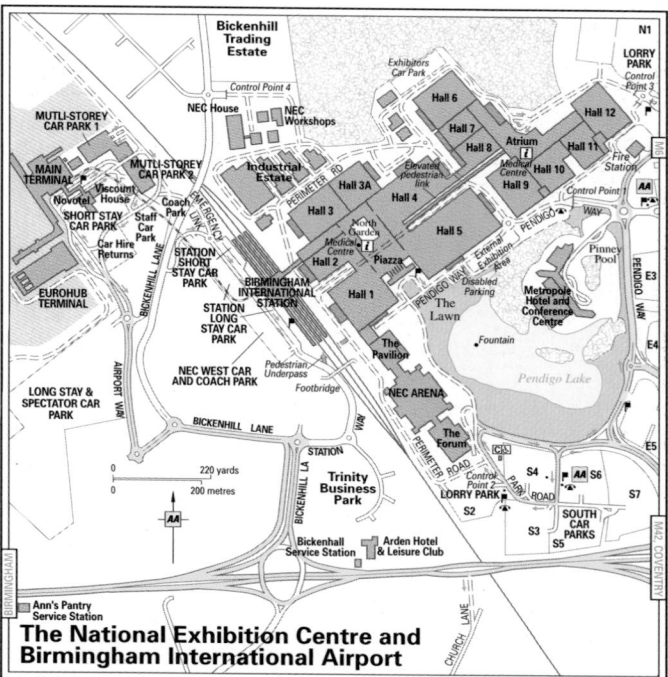

The National Exhibition Centre and Birmingham International Airport

Birmingham International Airport - 8 miles east of of Birmingham

Telephone: 0121 767 5511 (Main Terminal), 0121 767 7502 (Eurohub Terminal)
Parking: Short and Long-stay parking available
For charge details tel: 0121 767 7861
Public Transport: Bus Service. Maglev transit system offers a 90 second shuttle service to Birmingham International Railway Station
There are several 3-star hotels within easy reach of the airport and car hire facilities are available

East Midlands International Airport
15 miles southwest of Nottingham. Next to the M1 at junctions 23A and 24

Telephone: 01332 852852
Parking: Short and Long-stay parking available
Public Transport: Bus and coach services to major towns and cities in the East Midlands
There are several 3-star hotels in easy reach of the airport and car hire facilities are available

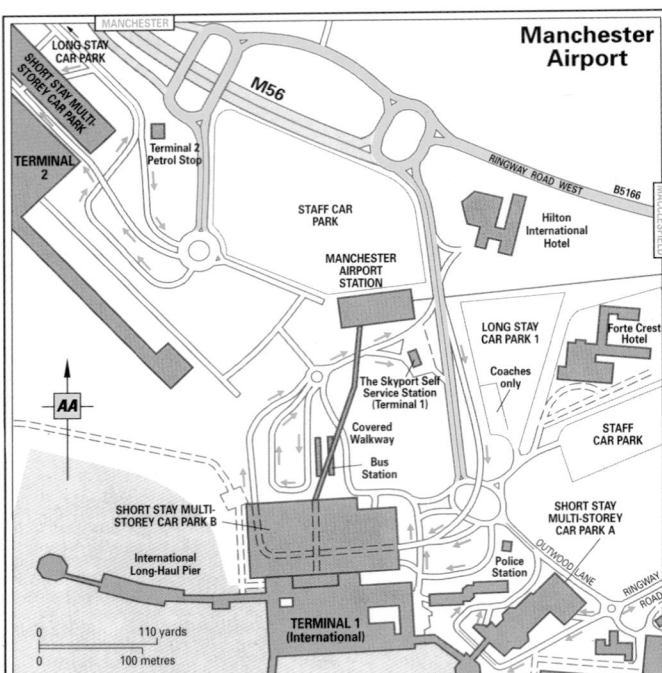

Manchester Airport - 10 miles south of Manchester

Telephone: 0161 489 3000
Parking: Short and Long-stay parking available.
Public Transport: Bus, Coach and Rail. Manchester airport railway station connects with the Rail network
There are several 4-star and 3-star hotels within easy reach of the airport and car hire facilities are available

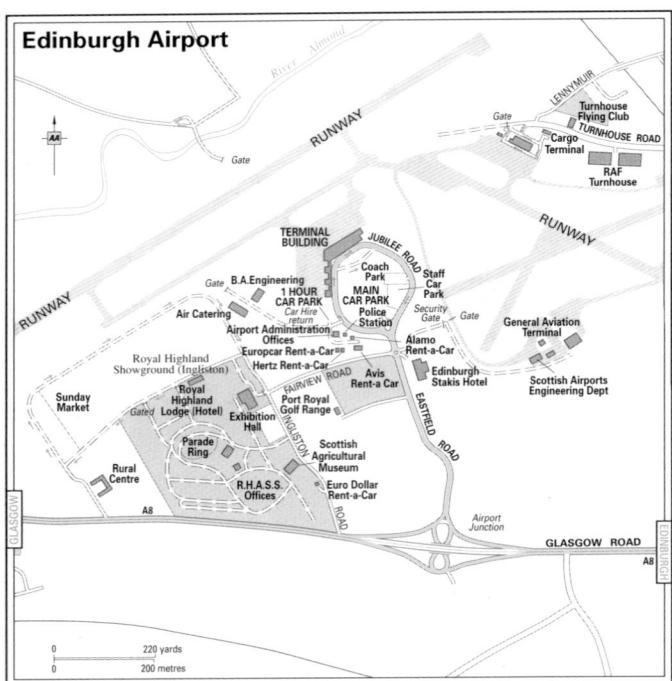

Edinburgh Airport - 7 miles west of Edinburgh

Telephone: 0131 333 1000
Parking: Open air parking is available. For charge details tel: 0131 344 3197
Public Transport: Regular coach services operate between central Edinburgh and Glasgow
There is one 4-star are several 3-star hotels within easy reach of the airport and car hire facilities are available

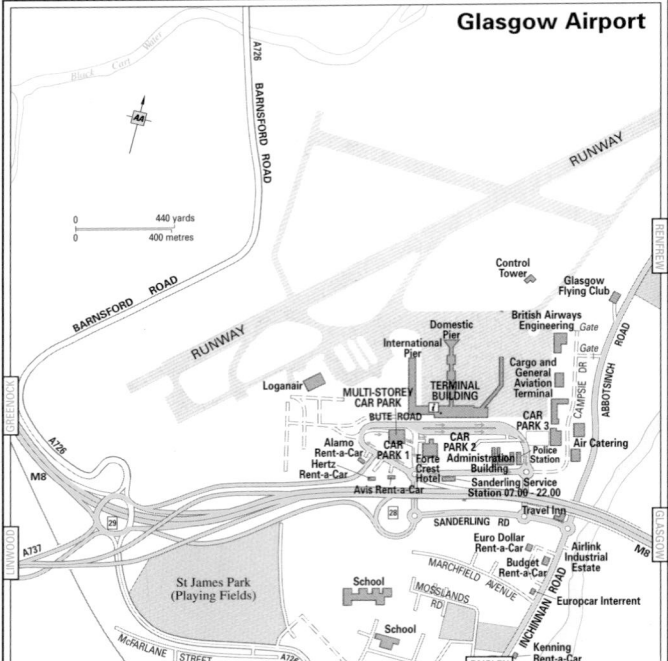

Glasgow Airport - 8 miles west of Glasgow

Telephone: 0141 887 1111
Parking: Short and Long-stay parking is available, mostly open air. For charge details tel: 0141 889 2751
Public Transport: Regular coach services operate between central Glasgow and Edinburgh
There are several 3-star hotels within easy reach of the airport and car hire facilities are available

Dover

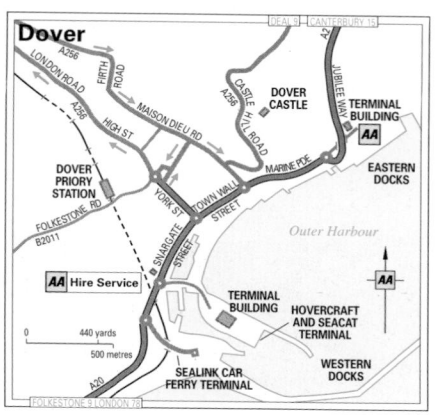

Pay and display parking available at the Dover Eastern and Western Docks and Hoverport Terminal. Other long-stay parking facilities are available with collection and delivery service, for charge details tel: 01304 203777, 208041 or 201227

Felixstowe

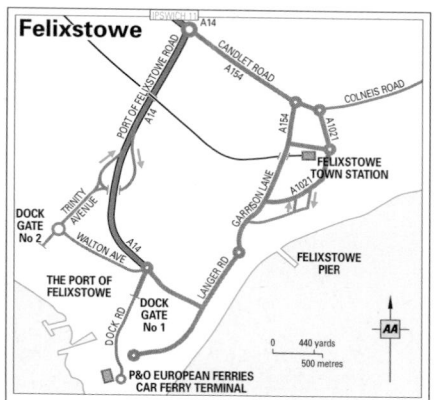

Open-air parking available at the terminal, for charge details tel: 01394 604040

Harwich International Port

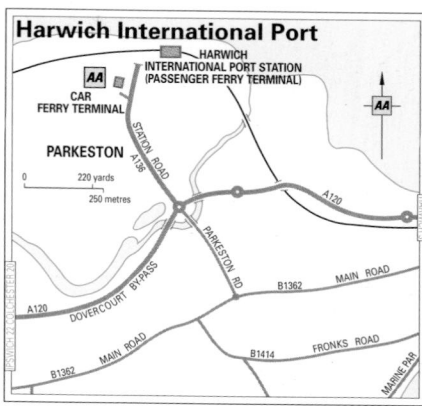

Open-air parking available at the terminal, for charge details tel: 01255 242000. Further parking 5 miles from Harwich International Port with collection and delivery service, for charge details tel: 01255 870217

Holyhead

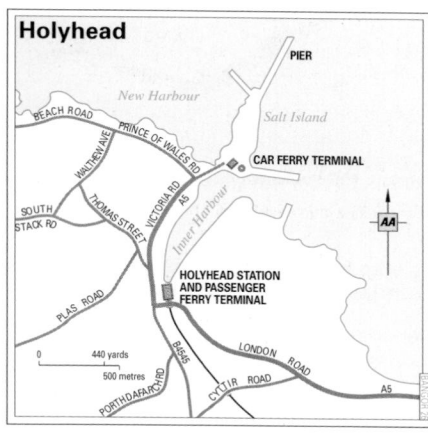

Open-air pay and display parking available close to the Passenger Terminal, for charge details tel: 01407 762304

Hull

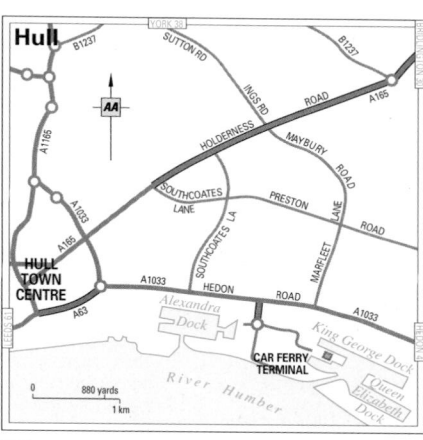

Free open-air parking at King George Dock (left at owners risk), tel: 01482 795141. Undercover parking available, for charge details tel: 01482 781021

Plymouth

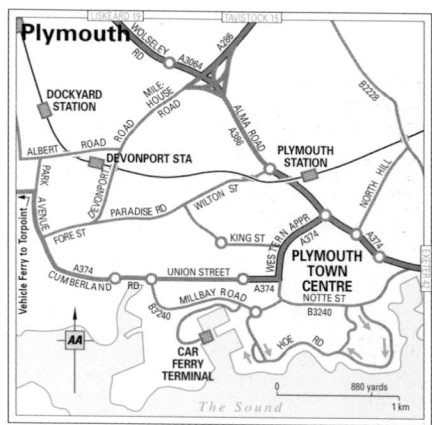

Free open-air parking available outside the terminal building, tel: 01752 221321

Poole

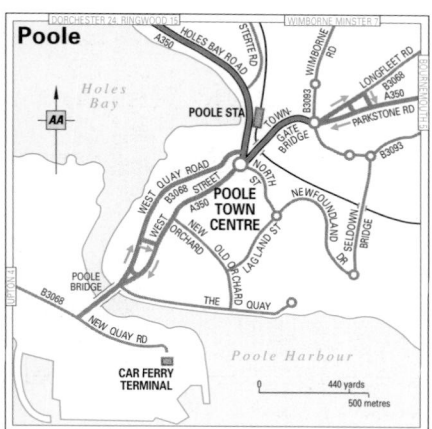

Free open-air parking available adjacent to ferry terminal, tel: 01202 685311

Portsmouth

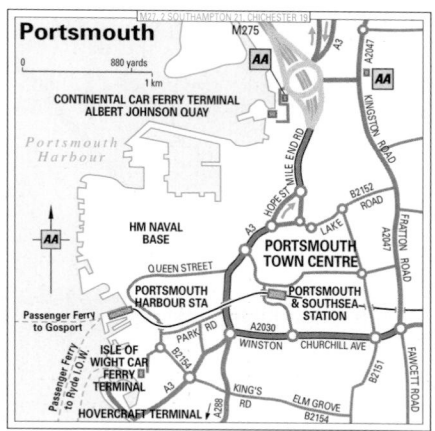

Lock-up parking spaces available at Albert Johnson Quay, for charge details tel: 01705 751261.
Pay and display parking available opposite the Hovercraft Terminal. Mutli-storey parking is also available close to the Isle of Wight Passenger Ferry Terminal, for charge details tel: 01705 823153 or 812071

Southampton

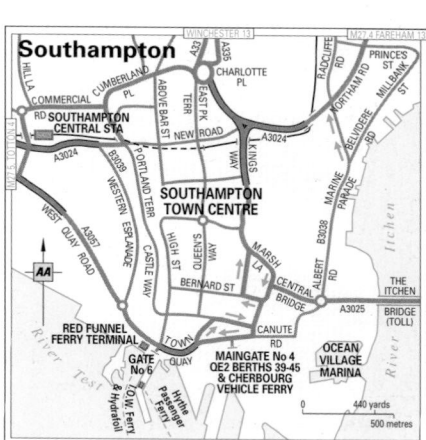

Covered or fenced compound parking within the Western Docks with a collection and delivery service, for charge details tel: 01703 228001/2/3

the Channel Tunnel

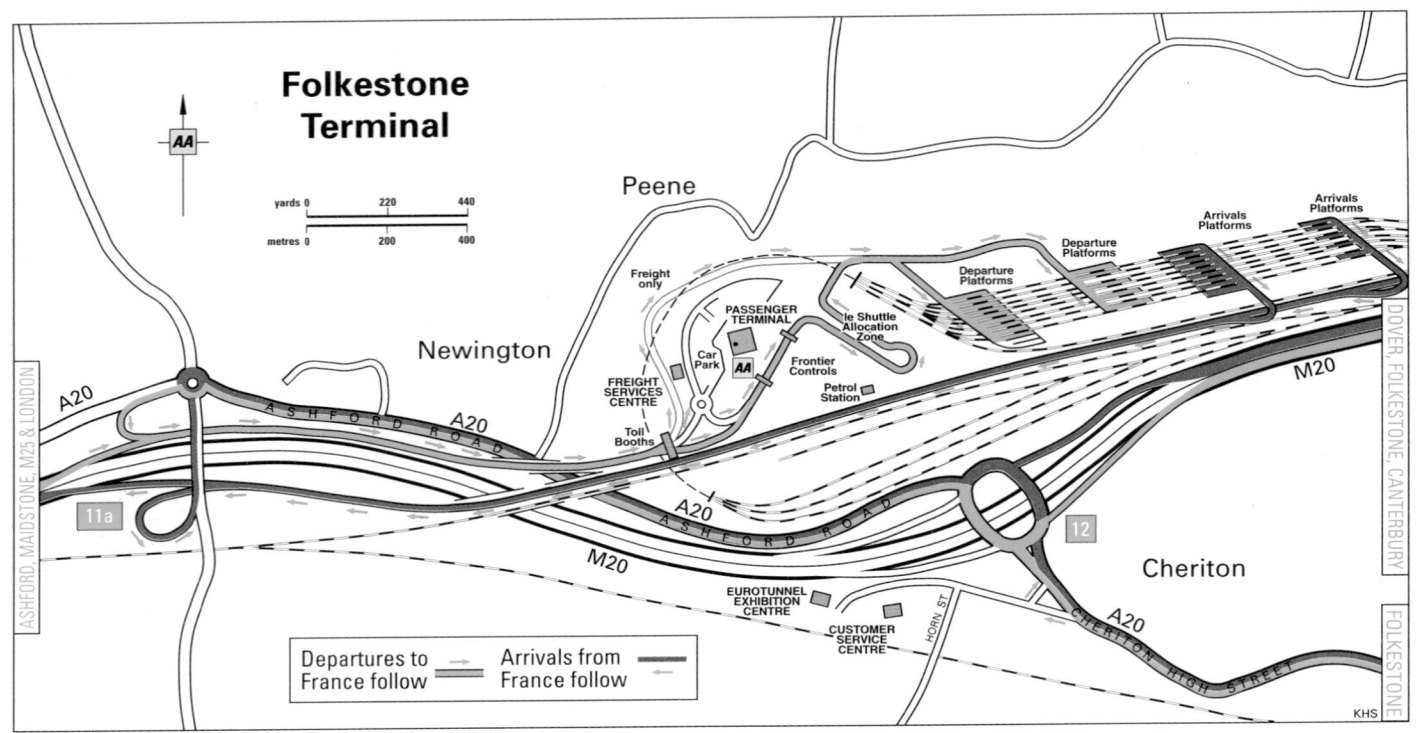

Folkestone Terminal

Departures to France follow →   Arrivals from France follow ←

SERVICES TO THE CONTINENT

The Le Shuttle service for cars, motorcycles and HGV vehicles runs between terminals at Folkestone and Calais. Coaches, caravans and trailers will not be carried until late 1995. Considerable improvements to the road network on both sides of the channel allows easy access to both terminals. It takes just over one hour to travel from the M20 motorway via the tunnel to the A16 autoroute.

Travellers are not required to make advance reservations as there are so many trains a day - just turn up and go. Call Le Shuttle Customer Services Department tel: 0990 353535 for further information.

Trains run at 15 minute intervals at peak times with the journey in the tunnel from platform to platform taking just 35 minutes.

You pass through British and French frontier controls on departure saving time on the other side of the channel. Each terminal has tax and duty free shops, bureau de change, restaurants and a variety of shops. In Calais the Cité de l'Europe contains further shops, restaurants, hotels and a hypermarket.

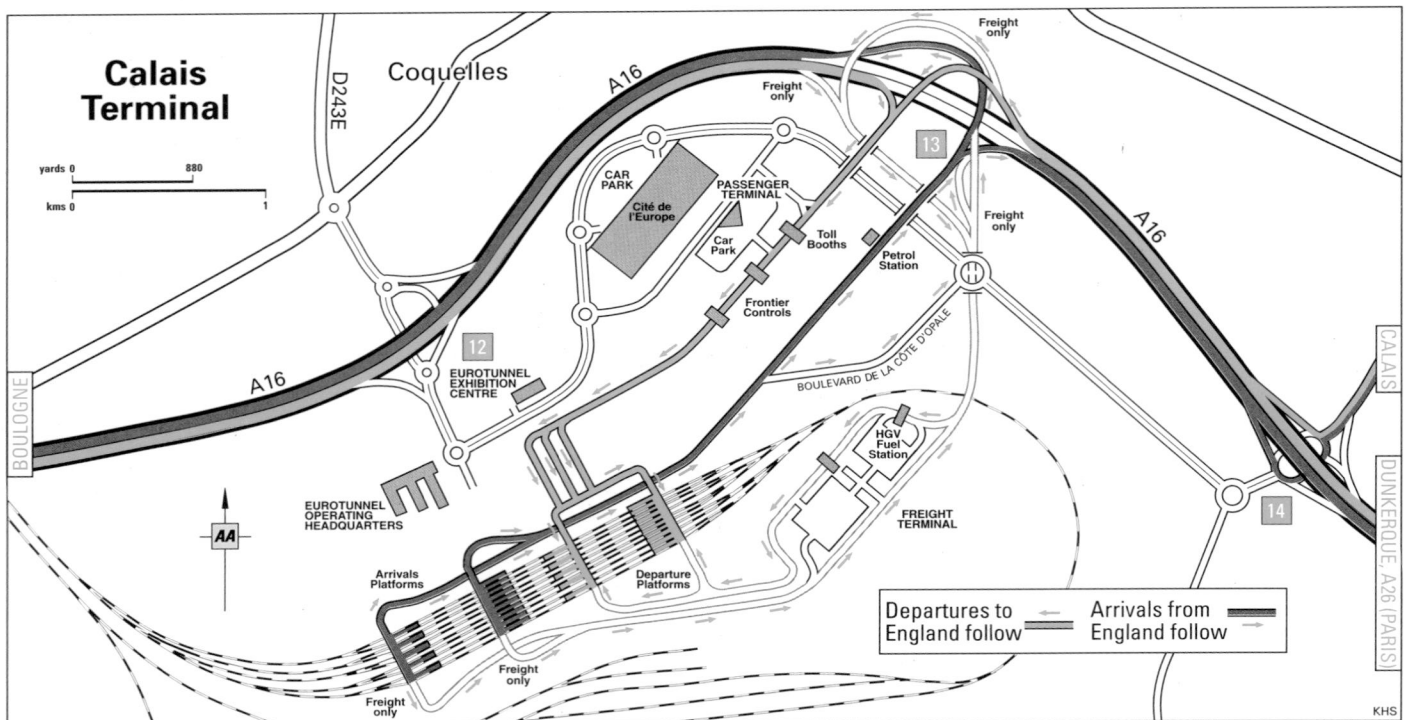

Calais Terminal

Departures to England follow →   Arrivals from England follow ←

ferry routes

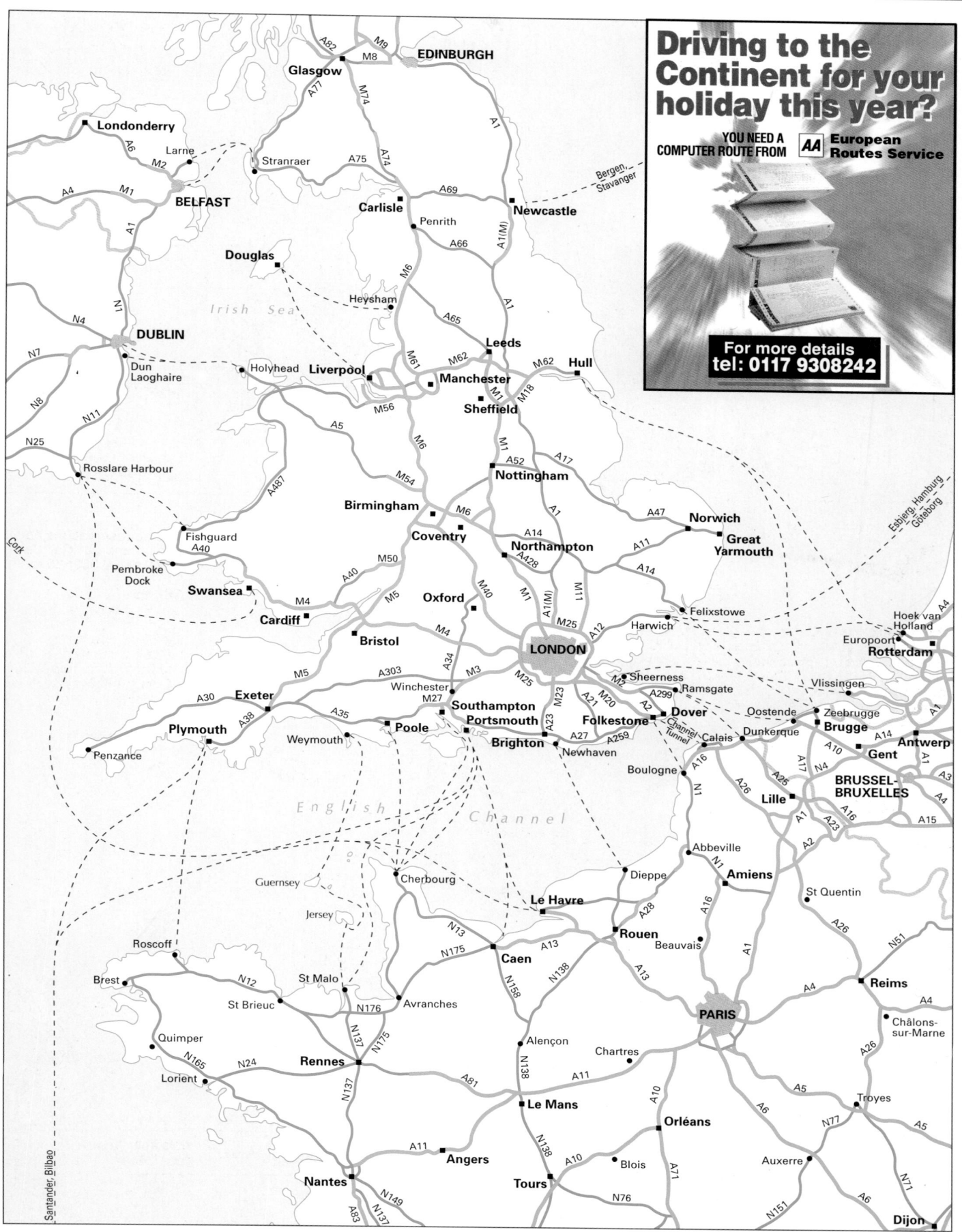

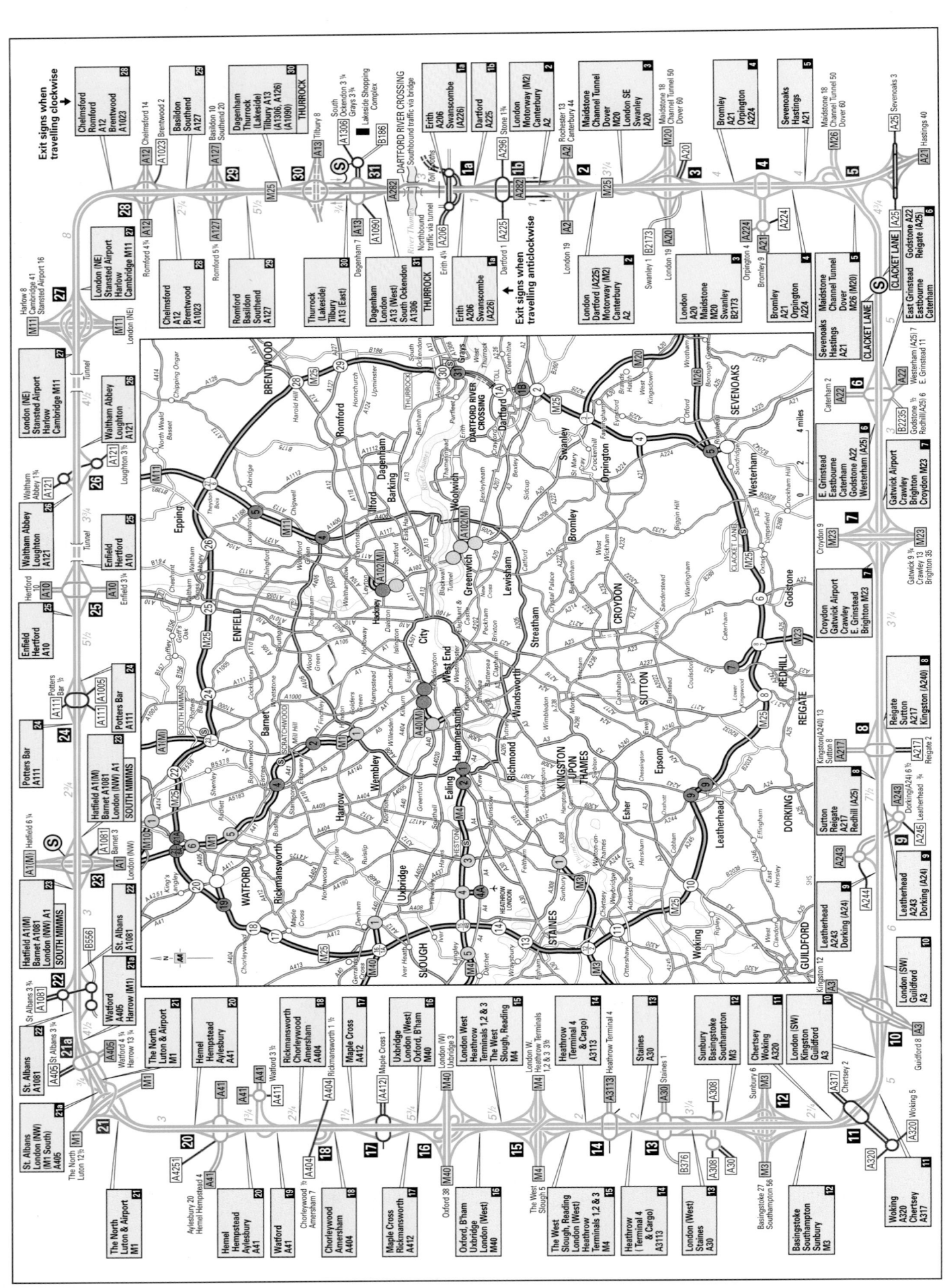

town plans

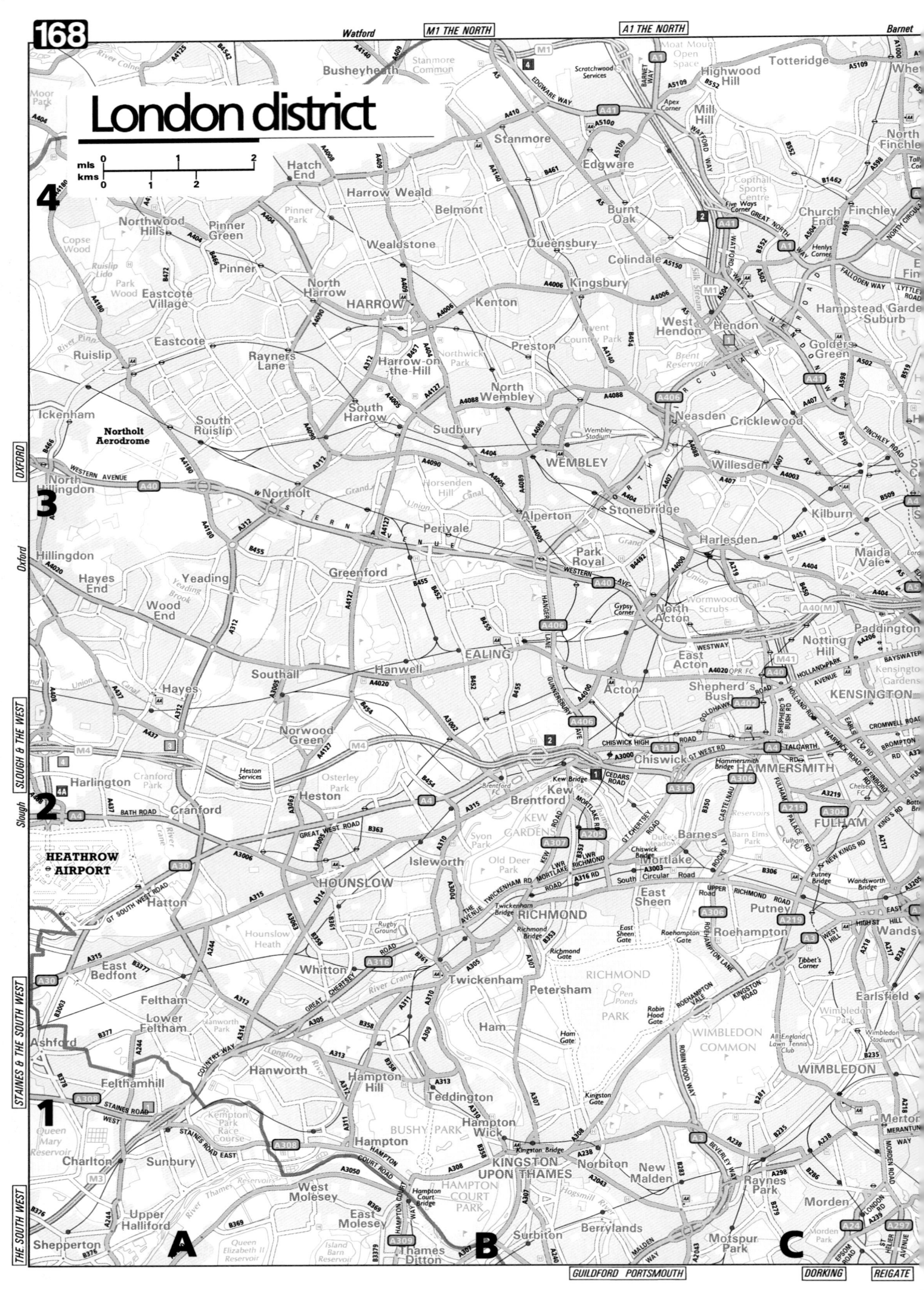

London district

London

Inset locator map (page references)
171 172 173
178 179
174 175 176 177 180

ST PANCRAS
BLOOMSBURY
FINSBURY
PADDINGTON
MARYLEBONE
SOHO
HOLBORN
CITY
WHITECHAPEL
STEPNEY
MAYFAIR
STRAND
KNIGHTSBRIDGE
SOUTH KENSINGTON
WESTMINSTER
LAMBETH
SOUTHWARK
BERMONDSEY
ROTHERHITHE
ISLE OF DOGS
MILLWALL
GREENWICH
NEWINGTON
VAUXHALL
CHELSEA
Hyde Park
Green Park
St James Park
Regent's Park
Southwark Park

Scale: 1:10,000
approx 6 inches to 1 mile

0 220 440 660 yards
0 250 500 750 m

Legend

	Motorway
	Primary route single/dual
	Other A road single/dual
	B road single/dual
	Unclassified road single/dual
	Unclassified road wide/narrow
	Road under construction
	Road tunnel wide/narrow
	Restricted road (access only/private)*
	Footpath
	Track
	Pedestrian street
	Railway line/in tunnel
←	One-way street
↰	Compulsory turn
↰	Banned turn
↰	Banned turn (restricted periods only)
•	Mini-roundabout
=	Barrier
⇌	British Rail station
⊖	London Regional Transport station
•	Docklands Light Railway station
Ⓟ	Parking
PO	Post office
POL	Police station
	Steps
✝	Church
AA	AA Shop
ℹ	Tourist Information Centre
ℹ	Tourist Information Centre (summer only)

Royal Parks (Opening and closing times for traffic)

Green Park — Constitution Hill is always open except Sundays when it is closed 08.00–dusk

Hyde Park — 05.00–midnight

Regents Park — 05.00–dusk

St James Park — The Mall is always open except on Sundays when it is closed 08.00–dusk

New traffic regulations in the City of London include security checkpoints and restrict the number of entry and exit points. Changes may occur.

* Note: Oxford Street is closed to through traffic (except buses & taxis) 07.00–19.00 hrs Monday–Saturday

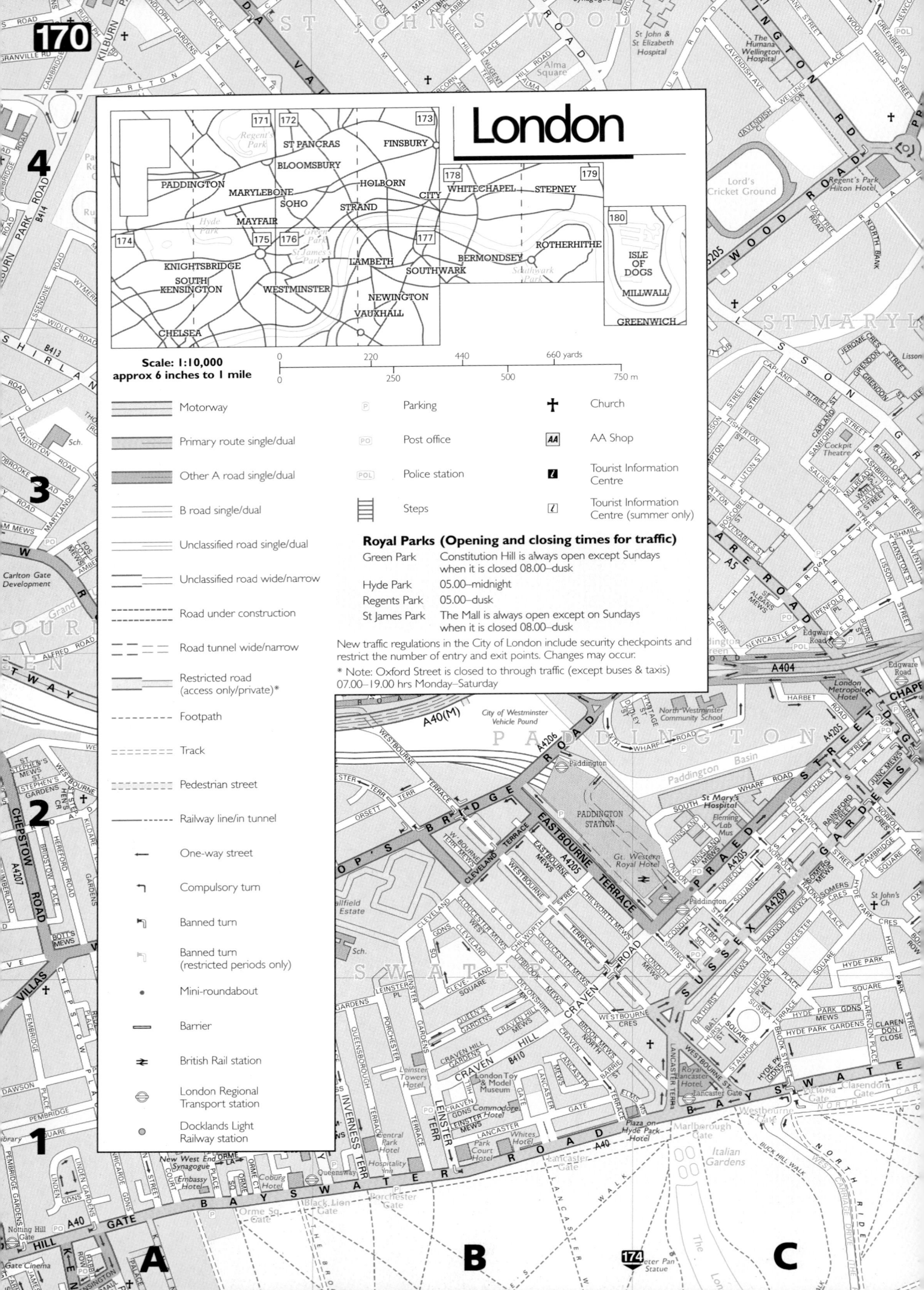

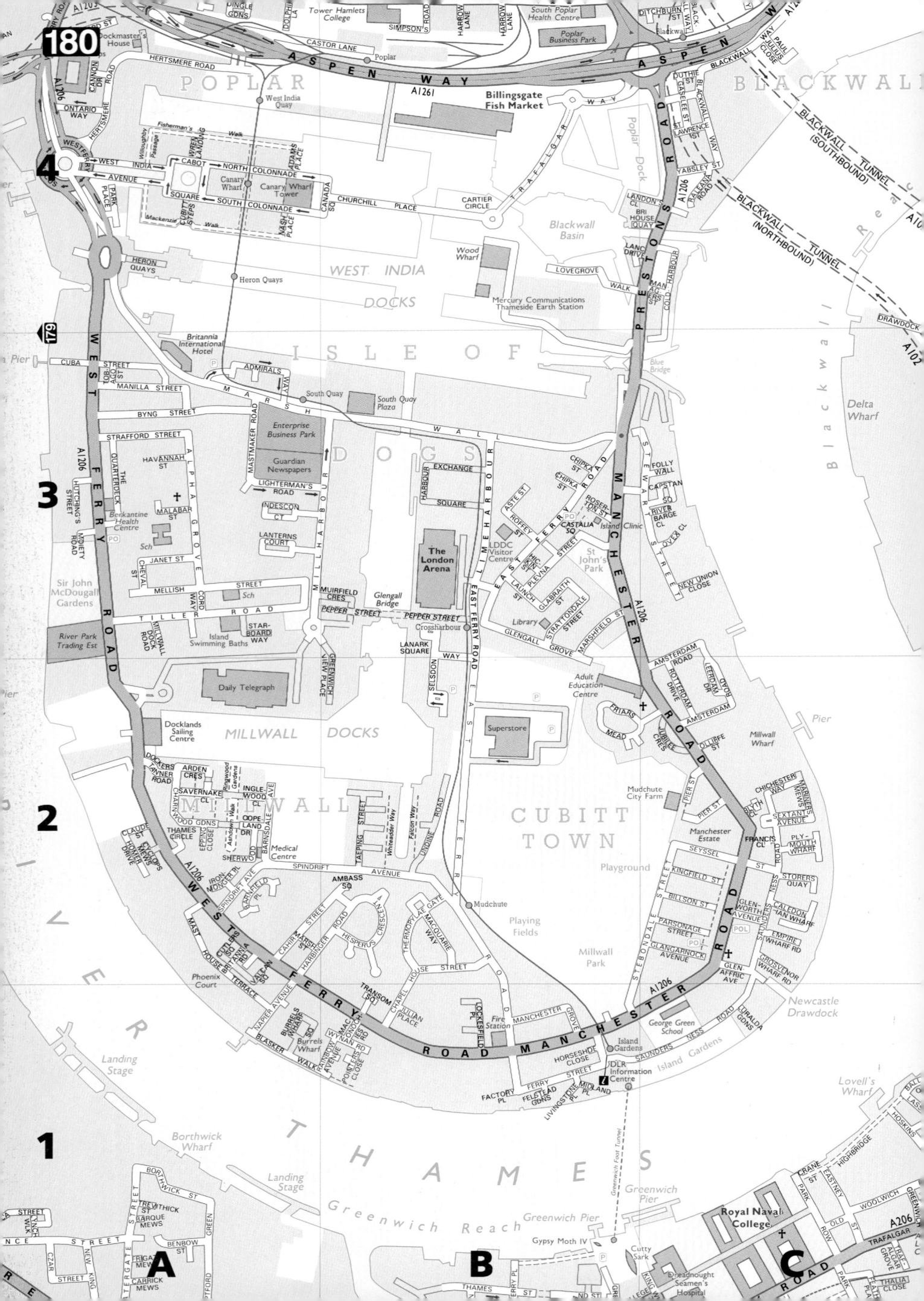

4

3

2

1

179

POPLAR

BLACKWALL

ISLE OF DOGS

MILLWALL DOCKS

CUBITT TOWN

RIVER THAMES

Greenwich Reach

A **B** **C**

London street index

In the index the street names are listed in alphabetical order and written in full, but may be abbreviated on the map. Postal codes are listed where information is available. Each entry is followed by its map page number in bold type, and an arbitrary letter and grid reference number . For example for Exhibition Road SW7 **174** C3, turn to page '**174**'. The letter 'C' refers to the grid square located at the bottom of the page. The figure '3' refers to the grid square located at the lefthand side of the page. Exhibition Road is found within the intersecting square. SW7 refers to the postcode. A proportion of street names and their references are also followed by the name of another street in italics. These entries do not appear on the map due to insufficient space but can be located adjacent to the name of the road in italics.

A

Abbey Orchard Street SW1 ... **176** B3
Abbey Street SE1 **178** A1
Abbots Lane SE1 **178** A2
Abchurch Lane EC4 **173** F1
Aberdour Street SE1 **177** F2
Abingdon Road W8 **174** A3
Abingdon Street SW1 **176** B3
Abingdon Villas W8 **174** A3
Achilles Way W1 **175** E4
Ackroyd Drive E3 **179** F4
Acorn Walk SE16 **179** F2
Acton Street WC1 **172** C4
Adam And Eve Court W1 **171** E1
Oxford Street
Adam And Eve Mews W8 **174** A3
Adam Street WC2 **172** B1
Adam's Row W1 **171** E1
Adams Place E14 **180** A4
Addington Street SE1 **176** C3
Addle Hill EC4 **173** E1
Addle Street EC2 **173** E2
Adelaide Street WC2 **172** B1
William IV Street
Adelina Grove E1 **178** D4
Adeline Place WC1 **172** B2
Adelphi Terrace WC2 **172** B1
Adams Street
Adler Street E1 **178** B4
Admiral Place SE16 **179** E2
Admirals Way E14 **180** A3
Adpar Street W2 **170** C3
Adrian Mews SW10 **174** A1
Agar Street WC2 **172** B1
Agatha Close E1 **178** C2
Agdon Street EC1 **173** D3
Agnes Street E14 **179** F4
Ainstey Street SE16 **179** D1
Brunel Road
Air Street W1 **172** A1
Alaska Street SE1 **176** C4
Albany Mews SE5 **177** E1
Albany Road SE5 **177** E1
Albany Street NW1 **171** F4
Albatross Way SE16 **179** D1
Albemarle Street W1 **171** F1
Albemarle Way EC1 **172** C3
Clerkenwell Road
Albert Court SW7 **174** C3
Albert Embankment SE1 **176** B1
Albert Gardens E1 **179** D3
Albert Hall Mansions SW7 **174** C3
Albert Mews W8 **174** B3
Albert Place W8 **174** B3
Alberta Street SE17 **177** D1
Albion Close W2 **171** D1
Albion Mews W2 **171** D1
Albion Place EC1 **173** D3
Albion Street SE16 **179** D1
Albion Street W2 **171** D1
Albion Way EC1 **173** E2
Aldburgh Mews W1 **171** E2
Marylebone Lane
Aldenham Street NW1 **172** A4
Aldermanbury EC2 **173** E2
Aldermanbury Square EC2 **173** E2
Aldermanbury
Alderney Street SW1 **175** F2
Aldersgate Street EC1 **173** E3
Aldford Street W1 **171** E1
Aldgate EC3 **178** A3
Aldgate High Street EC3 **178** A3
Aldwych WC2 **172** C1
Alexander Place SW7 **174** C2
Alexander Square SW3 **174** C2
Alford Place N1 **173** E4
Alfred Mews W1 **172** A3
Alfred Place WC1 **172** A3
Alice Street SE1 **177** F3
Alie Street E1 **178** B3
All Hallows Lane EC4 **173** F1
All Soul's Place W1 **171** F2
Langham Street
Allen Street W8 **174** A3
Allington Street SW1 **175** F3
Allsop Place NW1 **171** D3
Alpha Grove E14 **180** A3
Alpha Place SW3 **175** D1
Alsace Road SE17 **177** F1
Alscot Road SE1 **178** B1
Alvey Street SE17 **177** F2
Ambassador Square E14 **180** B2
Ambergate Street SE17 **177** D1
Ambrosden Avenue SW1 **176** A3
Amelia Street SE17 **177** E2
Amen Corner EC4 **173** D2
Amen Court EC4 **173** D2
America Square EC3 **178** A3
America Street SE1 **177** E4
Amoy Place E14 **179** F3
Ampton Place WC1 **172** C4
Ampton Street WC1 **172** C4
Amsterdam Road E14 **180** C2
Amwell Street EC1 **172** C4
Anderson Street SW3 **175** D2
Andrew Borde Street WC2 ... **172** B2
Charing Cross Road
Angel Court EC2 **173** F2
Angel Passage EC4 **173** F1
Angel Place SE1 **177** E4
Angel Street EC1 **173** E2
Ann Moss Way SE16 **179** D1
Ansdell Street W8 **174** A3
Antill Terrace E1 **179** D4
Apothecary Street EC4 **173** D2
New Bridge Street
Apple Tree Yard SW1 **172** A1
Appold Street EC2 **173** F3
Aquinas Street SE1 **177** D4
Arbour Square E1 **179** D4
Archangel Street SE16 **179** E1
Archer Street W1 **172** A1
Arden Crescent E14 **180** A2
Argent Street SE1 **177** E4
Loman Street
Argyle Square WC1 **172** B4
Argyle Street WC1 **172** B4
Argyle Walk WC1 **172** B4
Argyll Road W8 **174** A3
Argyll Street W1 **171** F2
Arlington Street SW1 **175** F4
Arlington Way EC1 **173** D4
Arne Street WC2 **172** B2
Arneway Street SW1 **176** A2
Arnside Street SE17 **177** E1
Arthur Street EC4 **173** F1
Artichoke Hill E1 **178** C3
Artillery Lane E1 **178** A4
Artillery Passage E1 **178** A4
Artillery Lane
Artillery Row SW1 **176** A3
Artizan Street E1 **178** A4
Harrow Place
Arundel Street WC2 **172** C1
Ashbridge Street NW8 **170** C3
Ashburn Gardens SW7 **174** B2
Ashburn Mews SW7 **174** B2
Ashburn Place SW7 **174** B2
Ashby Street EC1 **173** D4
Ashdown Walk E14 **180** A2
Asher Drive E1 **178** B3
Ashfield Street E1 **178** C4
Ashland Place W1 **170** E3
Ashley Place SW1 **175** F3
Ashmill Street NW1 **170** C3
Aske Street N1 **173** F4
Aspen Way E14 **180** B4
Assam Street E1 **178** B4
Assembly Passage E1 **179** D4
Aste Street E14 **180** B3
Astell Street SW3 **175** D2
Aston Street E14 **179** E4
Astwood Mews SW7 **174** B2
Atherstone Mews SW7 **174** B2
Atterbury Street SW1 **176** B2
Attneave Street WC1 **172** C4
Auckland Street SE11 **176** C1
Augustus Street NW1 **171** F4
Aulton Place SE11 **177** D1
Austin Friars EC2 **173** F2
Austin Friars Square EC2 **173** F2
Austin Friars
Austral Street SE11 **177** D2
Ave Maria Lane EC4 **173** E2
Aveline Street SE11 **176** C1
Avery Row W1 **171** F1
Avis Square E1 **179** E4
Avon Place SE1 **177** E3
Avonmouth Street SE1 **177** E3
Aybrook Street W1 **171** E2
Aylesbury Road SE17 **177** F1
Aylesbury Street EC1 **173** D3
Aylesford Street SW1 **176** A1
Aylward Street E1 **179** D4
Ayres Street SE1 **177** E4

B

Babmaes Street SW1 **176** A4
Jermyn Street
Bacchus Walk N1 **173** F4
Bache's Street N1 **173** F4
Back Church Lane E1 **178** B4
Back Hill EC1 **173** D3
Bacon Grove SE1 **178** A1
Bainbridge Street WC1 **172** B2
Baker Street W1 & NW1 **171** D3
Baker's Mews W1 **171** E2
Baker's Row EC1 **173** F3
Baker's Yard EC1 **173** D3
Baker's Row
Bakers Hall Court EC3 **178** A3
Harp Lane
Balcombe Street NW1 **171** D3
Balderton Street W1 **171** E1
Baldwin Street EC1 **173** F4
Baldwin's Gardens EC1 **172** C3
Balfe Street N1 **172** B4
Balfour Mews W1 **171** E1
Balfour Place W1 **171** E1
Balfour Street SE17 **177** F2
Ballast Quay SE10 **180** C1
Balneil Gate SW1 **176** A1
Baltic Street EC1 **173** E3
Balvaird Place SW1 **176** B2
Bancroft Road E1 **176** C1
Bank End SE1 **177** E4
Bankside Jetty SE1 **173** E1
Banner Street EC1 **173** E3
Banyard Road SE16 **178** C1
Barbon Close WC1 **172** C3
Barge House Street SE1 **173** D1
Barkston Gardens SW5 **174** A2
Barleycorn Way E14 **179** F3
Barlow Place W1 **171** F1
Barlow Street SE17 **177** F2
Barnaby Place SW7 **174** C2
Barnardo Street E1 **179** D3
Barnby Street NW1 **172** A4
Barnes Street E14 **179** E4
Barnfield Place E14 **180** A2
Barnham Street SE1 **178** A2
Barnsdale Avenue E14 **180** A2
Baron's Place SE1 **177** D3
Barque Mews SE8 **180** A1
Barrett Street W1 **171** E2
Barrie Street W2 **170** B1
Barrow Hill Road NW8 **170** C4
St Johns Wood High Street
Barter Street WC1 **172** B2
Barth Lane EC2 **173** F2
Bartholomew Close EC1 **173** E2
Bartholomew Square EC1 **173** E3
Bartholomew Street SE1 **177** F2
Barton Street SW1 **176** B3
Basil Street SW3 **175** D3
Basinghall Avenue EC2 **173** E2
Basinghall Street EC2 **173** E2
Bastwick Street EC1 **173** E3
Bate Street E14 **179** F3
Bateman Street W1 **172** A2
Bath Court EC1 **172** C3
Warner Street
Bath Place N1 **173** F4
Bath Street EC1 **173** E4
Bath Terrace SE1 **177** E3
Bathurst Mews W2 **170** C1
Bathurst Street W2 **170** C1
Battle Bridge Lane SE1 **177** F4
Batty Street E1 **178** B4
Bayley Street WC1 **172** A2
Baylis Road SE1 **176** C3
Bayswater Road W2 **170** A1
Baythorne Street E3 **179** F4
Beaconsfield Road SE17 **177** F1
Beak Street W1 **172** A1
Bear Gardens SE1 **173** E1
Bear Lane SE1 **177** D4
Bear Street WC2 **172** B1
Cranbourn Street
Beatrice Place W8 **174** A2
Beauchamp Place SW3 **175** D3
Beauchamp Street EC1 **173** D3
Brooke Street
Beaufort Gardens SW3 **175** D3
Beaufort Street SW3 **174** B1
Beaumont Mews W1 **171** E2
Beaumont Place W1 **172** A3
Beaumont Street W1 **171** E3
Beccles Street E14 **179** F3
Beckway Street SE17 **177** F2
Bedale Street SE1 **177** E3
Borough High Street
Bedford Avenue WC1 **172** B2
Bedford Court WC2 **172** B1
Bedford Gardens W8 **174** A4
Bedford Place WC1 **172** B3
Bedford Row WC1 **172** C3
Bedford Square WC1 **172** B2
Bedford Street WC2 **172** B1
Bedford Way WC1 **172** B3
Bedfordbury WC2 **172** B1
Bedser Close SE11 **176** C1
Beech Street EC2 **173** E3
Beeston Place SW1 **175** F3
Bekesbourne Street E14 **171** E2
Marylebone Lane
Belgrave Mews North SW1 **175** E3
Belgrave Mews South SW1 **175** E3
Belgrave Mews West SW1 **175** E3
Belgrave Place SW1 **175** E3
Belgrave Road SW1 **175** F2
Belgrave Square SW1 **175** E3
Belgrave Street E1 **179** E3
Belgrove Street WC1 **172** B4
Bell Lane E1 **178** A4
Bell Street NW1 **170** C3
Bell Yard WC2 **172** C2
Belvedere Buildings SE1 **177** E3
Belvedere Road SE1 **176** C4
Ben Jonson Road E1 **179** E4
Ben Smith Way SE16 **178** C1
Benbow Street SE8 **180** A1
Bendall Mews W1 **171** D3
Bennet's Hill EC4 **173** E1
Castle Baynard Street
Benson Quay E1 **179** D3

Langton Close

Onslow Mews

Langton Close WC1 172 C3
Lansdowne Row W1 171 F1
Lansdowne Terrace WC1 172 B3
Lant Street SE1 177 E3
Lanterns Court E14 180 A3
Larcom Street SE17 177 E2
Lassell Street SE10 180 C1
Launcelot Street SE1 176 C3
Lower Marsh
Launceston Place W8 174 B3
Launch Street E14 180 B3
Laurence Pountney Lane EC4 173 F1
Lavender Close SW3 174 C1
Lavender Road SE16 179 E2
Laverton Place SW5 174 A2
Lavington Street SE1 177 E4
Law Street SE1 177 F3
Lawn Lane SW8 176 B1
Lawrence Lane EC2 173 E2
Trump Street
Lawrence Street SW3 174 C1
Laxton Place NW1 171 F3
Laystall Street EC1 172 C3
Layton's Buildings SE1 177 E4
Borough High Street
Leadenhall Place EC3 173 F1
Leadenhall Street EC3 173 F2
Leake Street SE1 176 C3
Leather Lane EC1 173 D3
Leathermarket Street SE1 177 F3
Lecky Street SW7 174 C1
Leedam Drive E14 180 C2
Lees Place W1 171 E1
Leicester Court WC2 172 B1
Cranbourn Street
Leicester Place WC2 172 A1
Lisle Street
Leicester Square WC2 172 B1
Leicester Street WC2 172 B1
Leigh Hunt Street SE1 177 E3
Leigh Street WC1 172 B4
Leinster Gardens W2 170 B1
Leinster Mews W2 170 B1
Leinster Place W2 170 B1
Leinster Terrace W2 170 B1
Leman Street E1 178 B3
Lennox Gardens SW1 175 D2
Lennox Gardens Mews SW1 175 D2
Leonard Street EC2 173 F3
Leopold Street E3 179 F4
Leroy Street SE1 177 F2
Lever Street EC1 173 E4
Leverett Street SW3 175 D2
Mossop Street
Lewisham Street SW1 176 B3
Lexham Gardens W8 174 A2
Lexham Mews W8 174 A2
Lexington Street W1 172 A1
Leyden Street E1 178 A4
Leydon Close SE16 179 E2
Library Place E1 178 C3
Library Street SE1 177 D3
Lightermans Road E14 180 A3
Lilestone Street NW8 170 C3
Lillie Yard SW6 174 A1
Lime Close E1 178 B2
Lime Street EC3 173 F1
Lime Street Passage EC3 173 F1
Lime Street
Limeburner Lane EC4 173 D2
Limeharbour E14 180 B3
Limehouse Causeway E14 179 F3
Limehouse Link Tunnel E14 179 E3
Limerston Street SW10 174 B1
Lincoln Street SW3 175 D2
Lincoln's Inn Fields WC2 172 C2
Linden Gardens W2 170 A1
Lindley Street E1 178 C4
Lindsay Square SW1 176 B2
Lindsey Street EC1 173 E3
Linhope Street NW1 170 D3
Linsey Street SE16 178 B1
Lion Street E1 172 C2
Lipton Road E1 179 D3
Lisle Street W1 172 A1
Lisson Grove NW1 & NW8 170 C3
Lisson Street NW1 170 C3
Litchfield Street WC2 172 B1
Little Albany Street NW1 171 F4
Little Argyll Street W1 176 A2
Regent Street
Little Britain EC1 173 E2
Little Chester Street SW1 175 E3
Little College Street SW1 176 B3
Little Dorrit Close SE1 177 E4
Little Edward Street NW1 171 F4
Little George Street SW1 176 B3
Great George Street
Little Marlborough Street
W1 171 F1
Kingly Street
Little New Street EC4 173 D2
New Street Square
Little Newport Street WC2 172 B1
Little Portland Street W1 171 F2
Little Russell Street WC1 172 B2
Little Sanctuary SW1 176 B3
Broad Sanctuary
Little Smith Street SW1 176 B3
Little Somerset Street E1 176 A3
Little St James's Street SW1 176 A4
Little Titchfield Street W1 171 F2
Little Trinity Lane EC4 173 E1
Liverpool Grove SE17 177 E1
Liverpool Street EC2 173 F2
Livingstone Place E14 180 B1
Livonia Street W2 172 A2
Lizard Street EC1 173 E4
Llewellyn Street SE16 178 B1
Lloyd Baker Street WC1 172 C4
Lloyd Square WC1 172 C4
Lloyd Street WC1 172 C4
Lloyd's Avenue EC3 178 A3
Lloyd's Row EC1 173 D4
Lockesfield Place E14 180 B1
Locksley Street E14 179 F4
Lockwood Square SE16 178 C1
Lodge Road NW8 170 C4
Loftie Street SE16 178 B1
Lolesworth Close E1 178 B4
Lollard Street SE11 176 C2
Loman Street SE1 177 E4
Lomas Street E1 178 C4
Lombard Lane EC4 173 A2
Temple Lane
London Bridge EC4 & SE1 173 F1
London Bridge Street SE1 177 F4
London Road SE1 177 D3
London Street EC3 178 A3
London Street W2 170 C2
London Wall EC2 173 E2
Long Acre WC2 172 B1
Long Lane EC1 173 E2
Long Lane SE1 177 F3
Long Walk SE1 178 A1
Long Yard WC1 172 C3
Longford Street NW1 171 F3
Longmoore Street SW1 175 F2
Longville Road SE11 177 D2
Lord North Street SW1 176 B3
Lordship Place SW3 174 C1
Lawrence Street
Lorenzo Street WC1 172 C4
Lorrimore Road SE7 177 E1
Lorrimore Square SE17 177 E1
Lothbury EC2 173 F2
Loughborough Street SE11 176 C1
Lovat Lane EC3 173 F1
Love Lane EC2 173 E2
Lovegrove Walk E14 180 B4
Lovell Place SE16 179 E1
Lovers' Walk W1 175 E4
Lowell Street E14 179 E4
Lower Belgrave Street SW1 175 E3
Lower Grosvenor Place SW1 175 F3
Lower James Street W1 172 A1
Lower John Street W1 172 A1
Lower Marsh SE1 176 C3
Lower Road SE8 & SE16 179 D1
Lower Sloane Street SW1 175 E1
Lower Thames Street EC3 173 F1
Lowndes Place SW1 175 E3
Lowndes Square SW1 175 D3
Lowndes Street SW1 175 E3
Lowood Street E1 178 C3
Bewley Street
Loxham Street WC1 172 B3
Cromer Street
Lucan Place SW3 174 C2
Lucerne Mews W8 174 A4
Lucey Road SE16 178 B1
Ludgate Broadway EC4 173 D2
Pilgrim Street
Ludgate Circus EC4 173 D2
Ludgate Square EC4 173 D2
Luke Street EC2 173 F3
Lukin Street E1 179 D3
Lumley Street W1 171 E1
Brown Hart Garden
Lupus Street SW1 175 F1
Luralda Gardens E14 180 C1
Luton Street NW8 170 C3
Luxborough Street W1 171 E3
Lyall Street SW1 175 E3
Lygon Place SW1 175 F3
Lynch Walk SE8 180 A1
Lytham Street SE17 177 F1

M

Mabledon Place WC1 172 B4
Macclesfield Road EC1 173 E4
Mackenzie Walk E14 180 A4
Macklin Street WC2 172 B2
Mackworth Street NW1 171 F4
Macleod Street SE17 177 E1
Maconochies Road E14 180 B1
Macquarie Way E14 180 B2
Maddox Street W1 171 F1
Magdalen Street SE1 178 A2
Magee Street SE11 177 D1
Maguire Street SE1 178 B2
Mahognay Close SE16 179 E2
Maiden Lane WC2 172 B1
Maiden Lane SE1 177 E4
Makins Street SW3 178 D2
Malabar Street E14 180 A3
Malet Street WC1 172 A3
Mallord Street SW3 174 C1
Mallory Street NW8 170 C3
Mallow Street EC1 173 F3
Malta Street EC1 173 D3
Maltby Street SE1 178 A1
Maltravers Street WC2 172 C1
Managers Street E14 180 C4
Manchester Grove E14 180 B2
Manchester Road E14 180 B3
Manchester Square W1 171 E2
Manchester Street W1 171 E2
Manciple Street SE1 177 F3
Mandarin Street E14 179 F3
Mandeville Place W1 171 E2
Manette Street W1 172 B2
Manilla Street E14 180 A3
Manningford Close EC1 173 D4
Manningtree Street E1 178 B4
Commercial Road
Manor Place SE17 177 E1
Manresa Road SW3 174 C1
Mansell Street E1 178 B3
Mansfield Mews W1 171 F2
Mansfield Street
Mansfield Street W1 171 F2
Mansion House Place EC4 173 A1
St Swithun's Lane
Manson Mews SW7 174 B2
Manson Place SW7 174 C2
Maple Leaf Square SE16 179 E2
Maple Street W1 171 F3
Maples Place E1 178 C4
Marble Arch W1 171 D1
Marchmont Street WC1 172 B3
Margaret Court W1 171 F2
Margaret Street
Margaret Street W1 171 F2
Margaretta Terrace SW3 174 C1
Margery Street WC1 172 C4
Marigold Street SE16 178 C1
Mariners Mews E14 180 C2
Marjorie Mews E1 179 D4
Mark Lane EC3 178 A3
Market Court W1 171 E1
Oxford Street
Market Mews W1 175 E4
Market Place W1 171 F2
Markham Square SW3 175 D2
Markham Street SW3 175 D2
Marlborough Close SE17 177 E2
Marlborough Road SW1 176 A4
Marlborough Street SW3 174 C2
Marloes Road W8 174 A3
Marlow Way SE16 179 D2
Marne Street W10 178 B1
Maroon Street E14 179 E4
Marsh Street E14 180 A2
Marsh Wall E14 180 A3
Marshall Street W1 172 A1
Marshall's Place SE16 178 B1
Marshalsea Road SE1 177 E4
Marsham Street SW1 176 B3
Marshfield Street E14 180 B3
Marsland Close SE17 177 E1
Martha Street E1 178 C3
Martin Lane EC4 173 F1
Martin's Street WC2 172 B1
Martlett Court WC2 172 B2
Marylebone High Street W1 171 E3
Marylebone Lane W1 171 E2
Marylebone Mews W1 171 E2
Marylebone Road NW1 171 D3
Marylebone Street W1 171 E2
Marylee Way SE11 176 C2
Mason Street SE17 177 F2
Mason's Arms Mews W1 171 F1
Maddox Street
Mason's Place EC1 173 E4
Mason's Yard SW1 171 E2
Duke Street St James's
Massinger Street SE17 177 F2
Mast House Terrace E14 180 A2
Master's Street E1 179 E4
Mastmaker Road E14 180 A2
Matlock Street E14 179 E4
Matthew Parker Street SW1 176 B3
Maunsel Street SW1 176 A2
May's Court WC2 172 B1
St Martin's Lane
Mayfair Place W1 175 F4
Mayflower Street SE16 179 D1
Maynards Quay E1 178 C3
McAuley Close SE1 176 C3
McCleod's Mews SW7 174 B2
Mead Row SE1 177 D3
Meadcroft Road SE11 177 D1
Meadow Row SE1 177 E2
Meard Street W1 172 A2
Mecklenburgh Place WC1 172 C3
Mecklenburgh Square WC1 172 C3
Mecklenburgh Street WC1 172 C3
Mecklenburgh Square
Medway Street SW1 176 A2
Melbury Terrace NW1 171 D3
Melcombe Place NW1 171 D3
Melcombe Street NW1 171 D3
Melior Place SE1 177 F4
Snowsfields
Mellish Street E14 180 A3
Melon Place W8 174 A4
Kensington Church Street
Melton Street NW1 172 A4
Memel Court EC1 173 E3
Baltic Street
Mepham Street SE1 176 C4
Mercer Street WC2 172 B1
Meredith Street EC1 173 D4
Merlin Street WC1 173 D4
Mermaid Court SE1 177 F4
Mermaid Row SE1 177 F3
Merrick Square SE1 177 E3
Merrington Road SW6 174 A1
Merrow Street SE17 177 E1
Methley Street SE11 177 D1
Mews Street E1 178 B2
Meymott Street SE1 177 D4
Micawber Street N1 173 E4
Middle Street EC1 173 E2
Middle Temple Lane EC4 172 C2
Middle Yard SE1 177 F4
Middlesex Street E1 178 A4
Middleton Drive SE16 179 E2
Midford Place W1 172 A3
Tottenham Court Road
Midhope Street WC1 172 B4
Midland Place E14 180 B1
Midland Road NW1 172 B4
Midship Close SE16 179 E2
Milborne Grove SW10 174 B1
Milcote Street SE1 177 D3
Mile End Road E1 178 C4
Miles Street SW8 176 B1
Milford Lane WC2 172 C1
Milk Street EC2 173 E2
Milk Yard E1 179 D3
Mill Place E14 179 F3
Mill Street SE1 178 B1
Mill Street W1 171 F1
Millbank SW1 176 B2
Millharbour E14 180 A3
Milligan Street E14 179 F3
Millman Street WC1 172 C3
Millstream Road SE1 178 A1
Millwall Dock Road E14 180 A3
Milner Street SW3 175 D2
Milton Court EC2 173 F3
Milton Street EC2 173 F3
Milverton Street SE11 177 D1
Milward Street E1 178 C4
Mincing Lane EC3 178 A3
Minera Mews SW1 175 E2
Minories EC3 178 A3
Mint Street SE1 177 E3
Miranda Close E1 178 C4
Mitchell Street EC1 173 E3
Mitre Road SE1 177 D3
Mitre Square EC3 178 A3
Mitre Street
Mitre Street EC3 178 A3
Moiety Road E14 180 A3
Molyneux Street W1 171 D2
Monck Street SW1 176 B3
Moncorvo Close SW7 174 C3
Monkton Street SE11 177 D2
Monkwell Square EC2 173 E2
Monmouth Street WC2 172 B1
Montagu Mansions W1 171 D3
Montagu Mews North W1 171 D2
Montagu Mews South W1 171 D2
Montagu Mews West W1 171 D2
Montagu Place W1 171 D2
Montagu Row W1 171 D2
Montagu Square W1 171 D2
Montagu Street W1 171 D2
Montague Close SE1 177 F4
Montague Place WC1 172 D3
Montague Street EC1 173 E2
Montague Street WC1 172 B3
Montford Place SE11 176 C1
Montpelier Mews SW7 175 D3
Montpelier Place SW7 175 D3
Montpelier Square SW7 175 D3
Montpelier Street SW7 175 D3
Montpelier Walk SW7 175 D3
Montreal Place WC2 172 C1
Montrose Court SW7 174 C3
Montrose Place SW1 175 E3
Monument Street EC3 173 F1
Monza Street E1 179 D3
Moodkee Street SE16 179 D1
Moor Lane EC2 173 F2
Moor Place EC2 173 F2
Moorfields
Moore Street SW3 172 A1
Old Compton Street
Moorfields EC2 173 F2
Moorgate EC2 173 F2
Mora Street EC1 173 E4
Morecambe Close E1 179 D4
Morecambe Street SE17 177 E2
Moreland Street EC1 173 E4
Moreton Place SW1 176 A2
Moreton Street SW1 176 A2
Moreton Terrace SW1 176 A1
Morley Street SE1 177 D3
Morocco Street SE1 177 F3
Morpeth Terrace SW1 175 F2
Morris Street E1 178 C3
Mortimer Market WC1 172 A3
Capper Street
Mortimer Street W1 171 F2
Morwell Street WC1 172 A2
Moss Close E1 178 B4
Mossop Street SW3 175 D2
Motcomb Street SW1 175 E3
Mount Pleasant WC1 172 C3
Mount Row W1 171 E1
Mount Street E1 178 C4
Mount Street W1 171 E1
Mount Terrace E1 178 C4
Moxon Street W1 171 E2
Mozart Terrace SW1 175 E2
Muirfield Crescent E14 180 B3
Mulberry Street E1 178 B4
Mulberry Walk SW3 174 C1
Mulready Street NW8 170 C3
Mulvaney Way SE1 177 F3
Mumford Court EC2 173 E2
Milk Street
Mundy Street N1 173 F4
Munster Square NW1 171 F4
Munton Road SE17 177 E2
Murphy Street SE1 176 C3
Murray Grove N1 173 E4
Musbury Street E1 179 D4
Muscovy Street EC3 178 A3
Museum Street WC1 172 B2
Myddelton Passage EC1 173 D4
Myddelton Square EC1 173 D4
Myddelton Street EC1 173 D4
Mylne Street EC1 173 D4
Myrdle Street E1 178 C4
Myrtle Walk N1 173 F4

N

Napier Avenue E14 180 A2
Narrow Street E14 179 E3
Nash Place E14 180 A4
Nash Street NW1 171 F4
Nassau Street W1 171 F2
Nathaniel Close E1 178 B4
Thrawl Street
Neal Street WC2 172 B2
Neathouse Place SW1 175 F2
Wilton Road
Nebraska Street SE1 177 E3
Neckinger SE1 178 B1
Neckinger Street SE1 178 B1
Nelson Passage EC1 173 E4
Mora Street
Nelson Place N1 173 E4
Nelson Square SE1 177 D4
Nelson Street E1 178 C4
Nelson Terrace N1 173 D4
Nelson Walk SE16 179 E2
Neptune Street SE16 179 D1
Nesham Street E1 178 B3
Neston Street SE16 179 D2
Netherton Grove SW10 174 B1
Netley Street NW1 171 F4
Nevern Place SW5 174 A2
Nevern Square SW5 174 A2
Neville Street SW7 174 C2
Neville Terrace SW7 174 C1
New Bond Street W1 171 F1
New Bridge Street EC4 173 D2
New Broad Street EC2 173 F2
New Burlington Mews W1 178 A3
Hart Street
New Burlington Place W1 171 F1
New Burlington Street W1 171 F1
New Cavendish Street W1 171 E2
New Change EC4 173 E2
New Compton Street WC2 172 B2
New Crane Place E1 179 D2
New Fetter Lane EC4 173 D2
New Globe Walk SE1 177 E4
New Goulston Street E1 178 A4
New Kent Road SE1 177 E2
New King Street SE8 180 A1
New North Place EC2 173 F3
New North Road N1 173 F4
New North Street WC1 172 C3
New Oxford Street WC1 172 B2
New Quebec Street W1 171 D2
New Ride SW7 174 C3
New Road E1 178 C4
New Row WC2 172 B1
New Spring Gardens Walk
SE11 176 B1
Goding Street
New Square WC2 172 C2
New Street EC2 178 A4
New Street Square EC4 173 D2
New Turnstile WC1 172 B2
High Holborn
New Union Close E14 180 C3
New Union Street EC2 173 F2
Newark Street E1 178 C4
Newburgh Street W1 172 F1
Foubert's Place
Newburn Street SE11 176 C1
Newbury Street EC1 173 E2
Newcastle Place W2 170 C3
Newcomen Street SE1 177 F4
Newell Street E14 179 F3
Newgate Street EC1 173 D2
Newington Butts SE1 & SE11 177 D2
Newington Causeway SE1 177 E3
Newlands Quay E1 179 D3
Newman Street W1 172 A2
Newman's Row WC2 172 C2
Lincoln's Inn Fields
Newnham Terrace SE1 176 C3
Newnhams Row SE1 178 A1
Newport Place WC2 172 B1
Newport Street SE11 176 C2
Newton Street WC2 172 B2
Nicholas Lane EC4 173 F1
Nicholson Street SE1 177 D4
Nightingale Place SW10 174 B1
Nile Street N1 173 E4
Nine Elms Lane SW8 176 A1
Noble Street EC2 173 E2
Noel Street W1 172 A2
Norbiton Road E14 179 F4
Norfolk Crescent W2 170 C2
Norfolk Place W2 170 C2
Norfolk Square W2 170 C2
Norman Street EC1 173 E4
Norris Street SW1 172 A1
North Audley Street W1 171 E1
North Bank NW8 170 C4
North Colonnade E14 180 A4
North Crescent WC1 172 A3
North Flockton Street SE16 178 B1
Chambers Street
North Gower Street NW1 172 A4
North Mews WC1 172 C3
North Ride W2 170 C1
North Row W1 171 E1
North Tenter Street E1 178 B3
North Terrace SW3 174 C2
North Wharf Road W2 170 B2
Northampton Road EC1 173 D3
Northampton Row EC1 173 D3
Exmouth Market
Northampton Square EC1 173 D4
Northburgh Street EC1 173 D3
Northchurch SE17 177 F2
Northdown Street N1 172 C4
Northington Street WC1 172 C3
Northumberland Alley EC3 178 A3
Northumberland Avenue
WC2 176 B4
Northumberland Street
WC2 176 B4
Northy Street E14 179 E3
Norway Gate SE16 179 E1
Norway Place E14 179 F3
Norwich Street EC4 173 D2
Notting Hill Gate W11 170 A1
Nottingham Place W1 171 E3
Nottingham Street W1 171 E3

O

O'leary Square E1 179 D4
O'meara Street SE1 177 E4
Oak Lane E14 179 F3
Oak Tree Road NW8 170 C4
Oakden Street SE11 177 D2
Oakfield Street SW10 174 B1
Oakley Crescent EC1 173 E4
Oakley Gardens SW3 175 D1
Oakley Street SW3 174 C1
Oat Lane EC2 173 E2
Observatory Gardens W8 174 A4
Occupation Road SE17 177 E1
Ocean Street E1 179 E4
Octagon Arcade EC2 173 F2
Odessa Street SE16 179 F1
Ogle Street W1 171 F2
Old Bailey EC4 173 D2
Old Bond Street W1 171 F1
Old Broad Street EC2 173 F2
Old Brompton Road
SW5 & SW7 174 A1
Old Burlington Street W1 171 F1
Old Castle Street E1 178 B4
Old Cavendish Street W1 171 F2
Old Church Road E1 179 D4
Old Church Street SW3 174 C1
Old Compton Street W1 172 A1
Old Court Place W8 174 A3
Old Fleet Lane EC4 173 D2
Old Gloucester Street WC1 172 B3
Old Jamaica Road SE16 178 B1
Old Jewry EC2 173 F2
Old Marylebone Road NW1 171 D2
Old Mitre Court EC4 173 D2
Fleet Street
Old Montagu Street E1 178 B4
Old North Street WC1 172 C3
Theobalds Road
Old Palace Yard SW1 176 B3
Old Paradise Street SE11 176 C2
Old Park Lane W1 175 E4
Old Pye Street SW1 176 A3
Old Quebec Street W1 171 D2
Old Queen Street SW1 176 A3
Old Square WC2 172 C2
Old Street EC1 173 E3
Old Woolwich Road SE10 180 C1
Oldbury Place W1 171 E3
Olivers Yard EC1 173 F3
Olliffe Street E14 180 C2
Olney Road SE7 177 E1
Olympia Mews W2 170 B1
Onega Gate SE16 179 E1
Ongar Road SW6 174 A1
Onslow Gardens SW7 174 B2
Onslow Mews SW7 174 C2

London district index

District names are listed in alphabetical order and are referenced to the London district map, pages 168-169. Each entry is followed by its map page number, in bold type plus a grid reference,

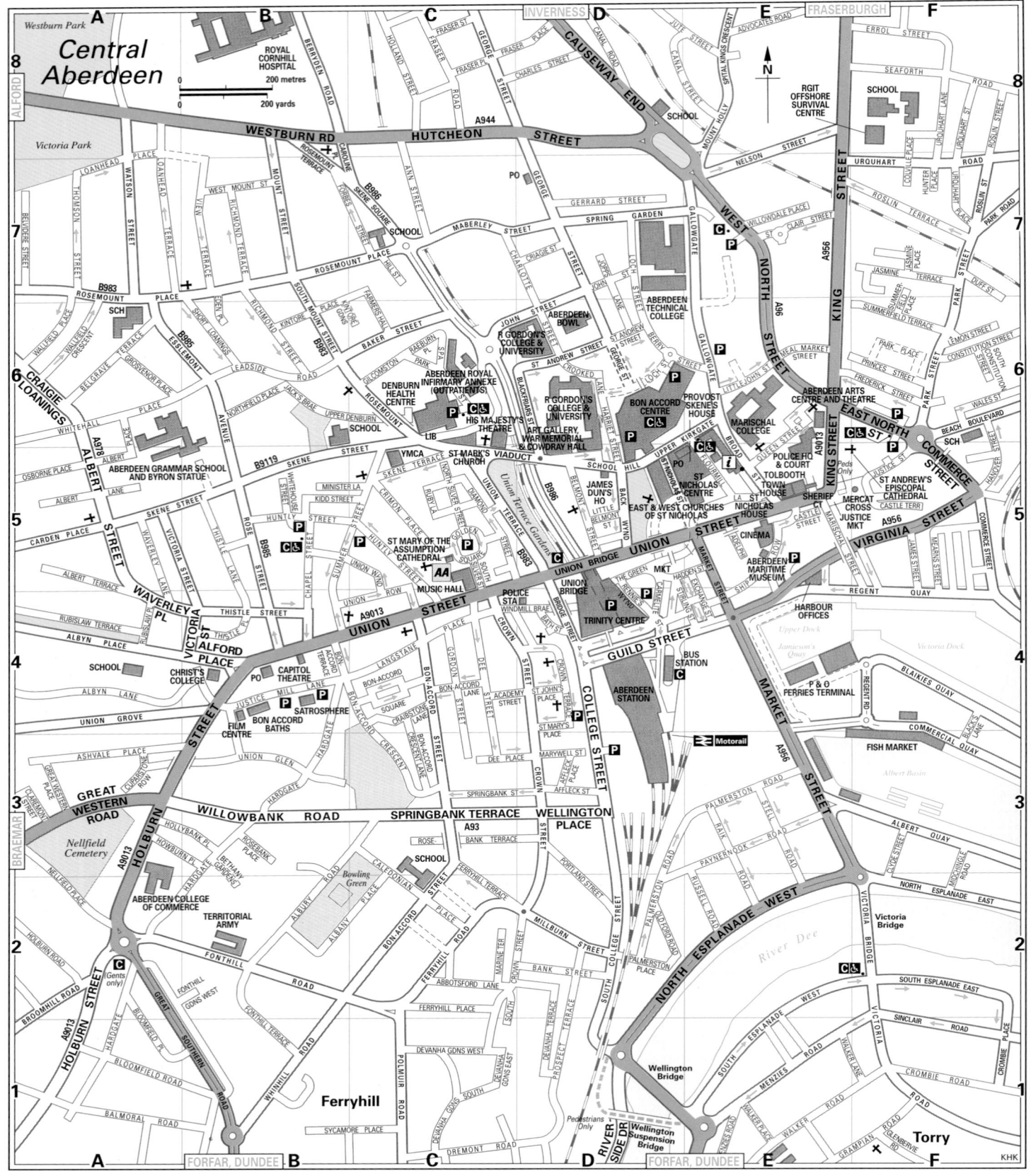

Aberdeen

Aberdeen is known as the 'Granite City', a reputation earned for the extensive use of the material and the attractiveness of its colours – white, blue, pink and grey – rather than for any suggestion of grimness. Although mostly 19th-century in character, the city is very much older. St Machar's Cathedral in Old Aberdeen was founded as far back as AD580, although rebuilt several times – principally after a devastating fire was started on the orders of Edward III of England in 1336. Old Aberdeen, close to the River Don, is traditionally the ecclesiastical and educational hub of the city, with King's College (Aberdeen University) founded in 1494. New Aberdeen, almost as old with Marischal College (also Aberdeen University) dating from 1593, is the commercial centre and has the magnificent near-mile-long Union Street at its heart. Among its many interesting features are the impressive Art Gallery, Provost Ross'. House (NTS) (Aberdeen's third oldest building, dating from 1593, and containing the Maritime Museum), 16th-century Provost Skene's House and local history museum, the 17th-century Tolbooth Tower, and Union Bridge, one of the widest single-span arches in Britain. Aberdeen is also a major fishing port and ferry terminal for the Orkneys, Shetlands and Scandinavia, and since the North Sea oil boom it has become Britain's most important administrative and off-shore oil-rig supply and maintenance centre.

190

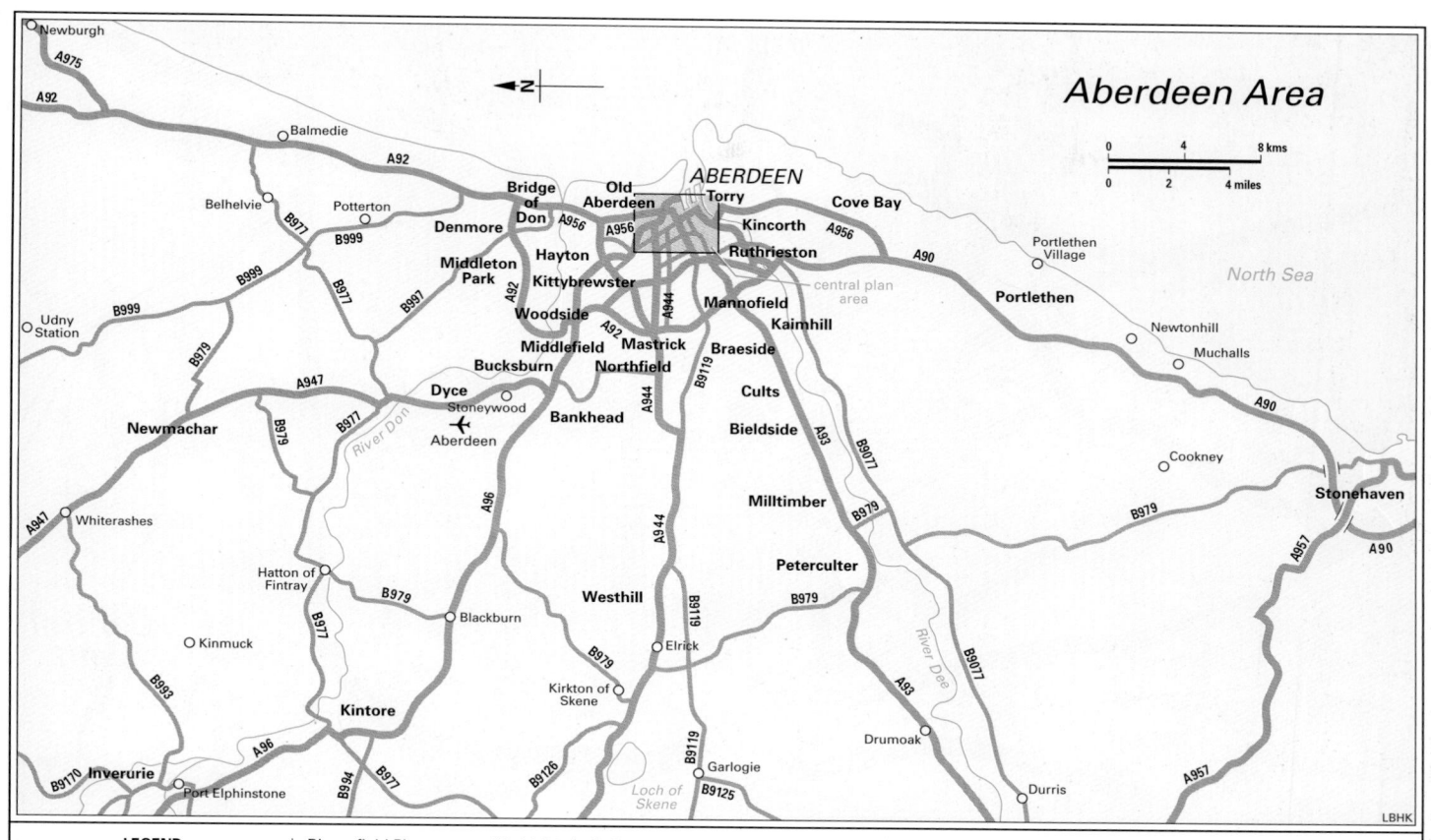

Aberdeen Area

North Sea

LBHK

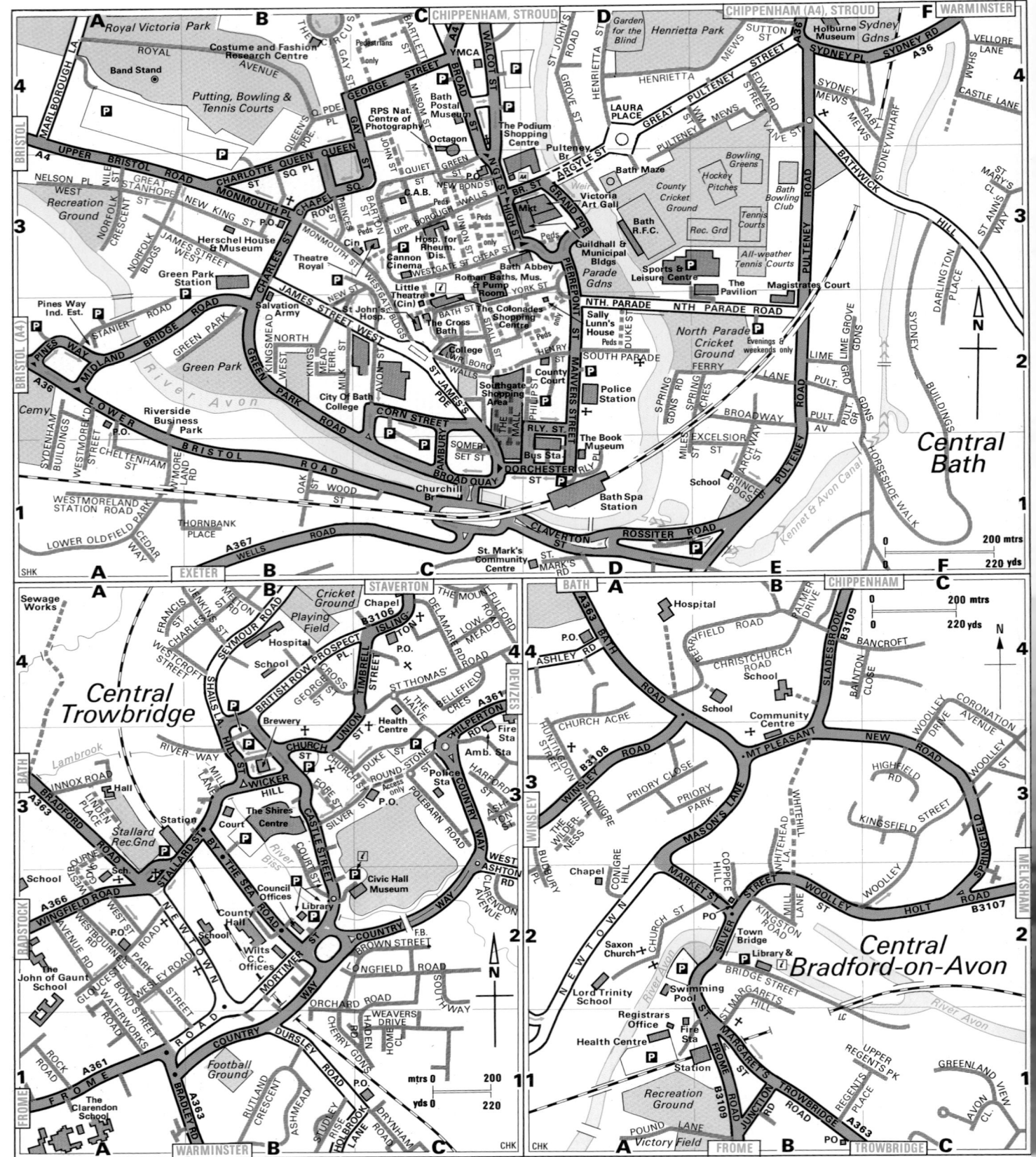

Bath

This unique city combines Britain's most impressive collection of Roman relics with a magnificent Georgian townscape. Its attraction to the Romans and fashionable 18th-century society alike was its mineral springs, which are still seen by thousands of tourists who visit the Roman Baths every year. They are the centre-piece of a Roman Museum, where exhibits give a vivid impression of life 2,000 years ago. The adjacent Pump Room to which the waters were piped for drinking was a focal-point of local social life in 18th- and 19th-century Bath.

The Georgian age of elegance also saw the building of Bath's perfectly proportioned streets, terraces and crescents. The finest examples are Queen Square, the Circus, and Royal Crescent, all built of golden local sandstone. Overlooking the city centre is the great tower of Bath Abbey – sometimes called the 'Lantern of the West' because of its large and numerous windows.

Bath has much to delight the museum-lover. The Holburne Museum houses collections of silver, porcelain, paintings, furniture and glass of all periods, and the Assembly Rooms, very much a part of the social scene in Georgian Bath, are now the home of the Museum of Costume. Also to be seen are museums covering industrial heritage, bookbinding and collecting, English Naive Art, photography, postal services, and the architecture and construction of the city. The Sally Lunn's Refreshment House and Museum is the oldest house in Bath; built in the Tudor period, its origins go back to Roman times.

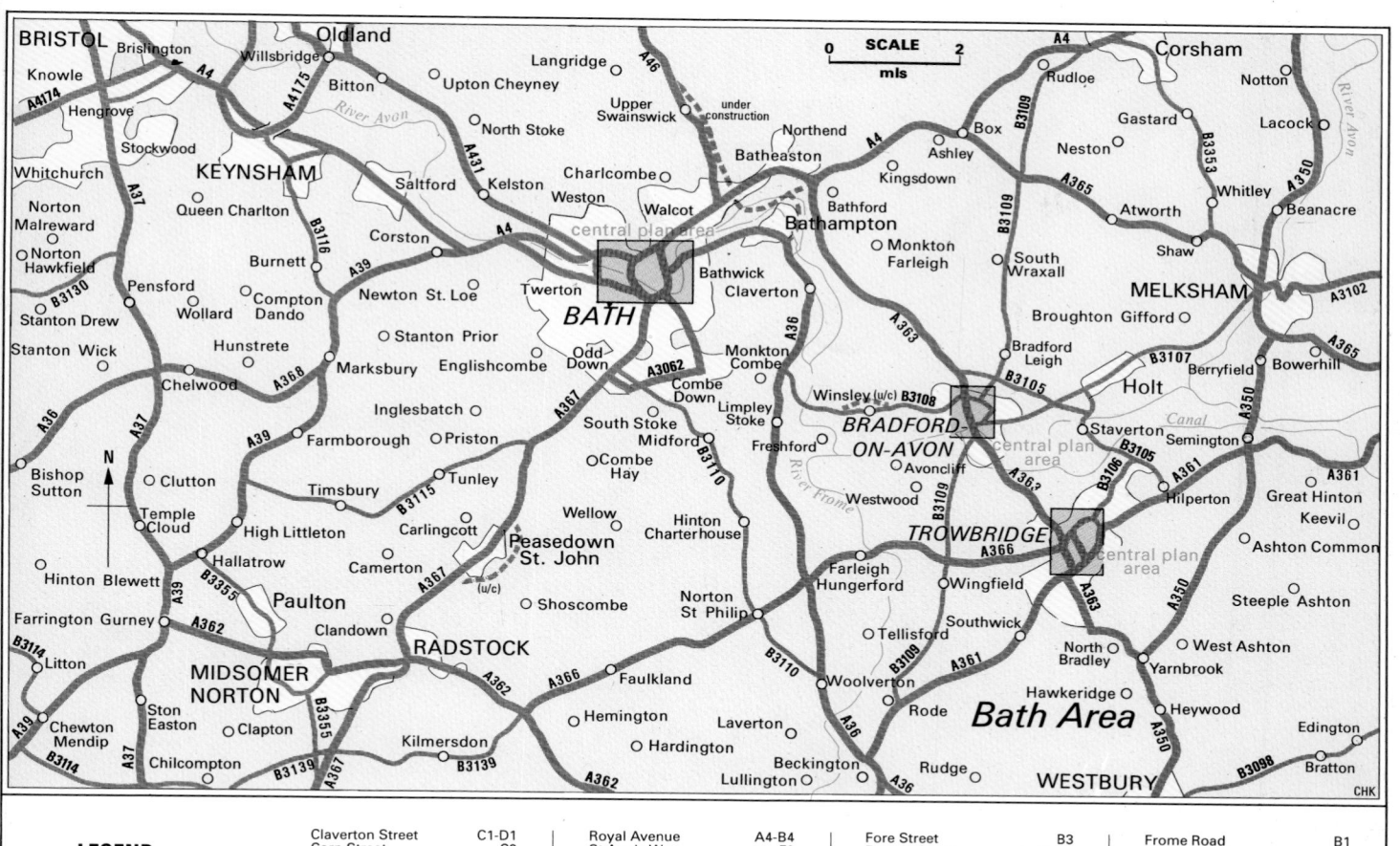

LEGEND

Town Plan

AA Recommended roads	
Other roads	
Restricted roads	
Buildings of interest	Museum
Churches	✝
Car parks	Ⓟ
Parks and open spaces	
One way streets	←

Area Plan

A roads	
B roads	
Locations	Oldland ○
Urban area	

Street Index with Grid Reference

Central Bath

Ambury	C1-C2
Archway Street	E1-E2
Argyle Street	D3-D4
Avon Street	C2
Bartlett Street	C4
Barton Street	C3
Bath Street	C2
Bathwick Hill	E4-E3-F3-F2
Bridge Street	C3-D3
Broadway	E2
Broad Street	C4
Broad Quay	C1
Cedar Way	A1
Chapel Row	B3
Charles Street	B2-B3
Charlotte Street	B3
Cheap Street	C3
Cheltenham Street	A1
Claverton Street	C1-D1
Corn Street	C2
Darlington Place	F2-F3
Dorchester Street	C1-D1
Duke Street	D2
Edward Street	E4
Excelsior Street	E1
Ferry Lane	D2-E2
Gay Street	B4-C4-C3
George Street	B4-C4
Grand Parade	D3
Great Pulteney Street	D4-E4
Great Stanhope Street	A3
Green Park	A2-B2
Green Park Road	B2-C2-C1
Green Street	C3
Grove Street	D4-D3
Henrietta Mews	D4-E4
Henrietta Street	D4
Henry Street	C2-D2
High Street	C3
Horseshoe Walk	F1
James Street West	A3-B3-B2-C2
John Street	C4-C3
Kingsmead North	B2
Kingsmead Terrace	B2
Kingsmead West	B2
Laura Place	D3-D4
Lime Grove	E2
Lime Grove Gardens	E2
Lower Bristol Road	A2-A1-B1-C1
Lower Borough Walls	C2
Lower Oldfield Park	A1
Manvers Street	D2-D1
Marlborough Lane	A4
Midland Bridge Road	A2-B2
Miles Street	D1-D2
Milk Street	B2
Mill Street	D1-D2
Milsom Street	C4-C3
Monmouth Place	B3
Monmouth Street	B3-C3
Nelson Place West	A3
New Street	B2-B3-C3
New Bond Street	C3
New King Street	A3-B3
Nile Street	A3
Norfolk Buildings	A3
Norfolk Crescent	A3
Northgate Street	C3
North Parade	D2
North Parade Road	D2-E2
Oak Street	B1
Philip Street	D2
Pierrepont Street	D3-D2
Pines Way	A2
Princes Buildings	E1
Princes Street	B3
Pulteney Avenue	E2-F2-F1
Pulteney Gardens	E2-F2-F1
Pulteney Grove	E2
Pulteney Mews	D3-D4-E4
Pulteney Road	E1-E2-E3-E4
Queen Square	B3-B4-C3-C4
Queen Square Place	B3
Queen's Parade	B4
Queen's Parade Place	B4
Quiet Street	C3
Raby Mews	E4-F4
Railway Street	D2
Rossiter Road	D1-E1
Royal Avenue	A4-B4
St Ann's Way	F3
St James's Parade	C2
St John's Road	D4
St Mark's Road	D1
St Mary's Close	F3
Sham Castle Lane	F4
Somerset Street	C1
South Parade	D2
Spring Crescent	E2
Spring Gardens Road	D2
Stall Street	C2
Stanier Road	A2
Sutton Street	E4
Sydenham Buildings	A1-A2
Sydney Buildings	F3-F2-F1
Sydney Mews	E4-F4
Sydney Place	E4-F4
Sydney Road	F4
Sydney Wharf	F3-F4
The Circus	B4
The Mall	C1-C2
Thornbank Place	B1
Union Street	C3
Upper Borough Walls	C3
Upper Bristol Road	A4-A3-B3
Vane Street	E4
Vellore Lane	F4
Walcot Street	C4
Wells Road	B1-C1
Westgate Buildings	C3-C2
Westgate Street	C3
Westmoreland Station Road	A1
Westmoreland Road	A1
Westmoreland Street	A1-A2
Wood Street	B1-C1
York Street	C2-D2-D3

Trowbridge

Ashmead	B1
Ashton Street	C3
Avenue Road	A2
Bellefield Crescent	C4
Bond Street	A2-A1
Bradford Road	A3-A2
Bradley Road	A1-B1
British Row	B4
Brown Street	B2-C2
Bythesea Road	B3-B2
Castle Street	B3-B2
Charles Street	A4-B4
Cherry Gardens	B1-C1
Church Street	B3-C3
Clarendon Avenue	C2
Country Way	A1-B1-B2-C2-C3
Court Road	B3-B2
Cross Street	B4
Delamare Road	C4
Drynham Road	C1
Duke Street	C3
Dursley Road	B1-C1
Fore Street	B3
Francis Street	A4-B4
Frome Road	A1-B1
Fulford Road	C4
George Street	B4
Gloucester Road	A2
Haden Road	C1
Harford Street	C3
Hill Street	B3
Hilperton Road	C3-C4
Holbrook Lane	B1-C1
Home Close	C1
Innox Road	A3
Islington	C4
Jenkins Street	B4
Linden Place	A3
Longfield Road	B2-C2
Lowmead	C4
Melton Road	B4
Mill Lane	B3
Mortimer Street	B4
Newtown	A2-B2
Orchard Road	B2-C2
Park Street	A2-A1-B1
Polebarn Road	C3
Prospect Place	B4-C4
River Way	A3-B3
Rock Road	A1
Roundstone Street	C3
Rutland Crescent	B1
St Thomas' Road	C4
Seymour Road	B4
Shails Lane	B4
Silver Street	B3-C3
Southway	C4
Stallard Street	A2-A3-B3
Studley Rise	B1
The Halve	C4-C3
The Mount	C4
Timbrell Street	C4
Union Street	B3-B4-C3-C4
Waterworks Road	A2-A1
Weavers Drive	C1
Wesley Road	A2-B2
West Street	B4
West Ashton Road	C3-C2
Westbourne Gardens	A2-A3
Westbourne Road	A2
Westcroft Street	A4-B4
Wicker Hill	B3
Wingfield Road	A2

Frome Road	B1
Greenland View	C1
Highfield Road	C3
Holt Road	C2
Huntingdon Street	A3
Junction Road	B1
Kingsfield	C3
Kingston Road	B2
Market Street	A2-B2
Masons Lane	A3-B3
Mill Lane	B2
Mount Pleasant	B3
Newtown	A1-A2
New Road	B3-C3
Palmer Drive	B4
Pound Lane	A1-B1
Priory Close	A3-B3
Priory Park	A3-B3
Regents Place	B1-C1
St Margaret's Hill	B1-B2
St Margaret's Street	B2-B1
Silver Street	B2
Sladesbrook	B4
Springfield	C2-C3
The Wilderness	A3
Trowbridge Road	B1
Upper Regents Park	B1-C1
Whitehill	B2-B3
Whitehead Lane	B2-B3
Winsley Road	A3-A4
Woolley Drive	C3-C4
Woolley Street	B2-C2-C3

Bradford-upon-Avon

Ashley Road	A4
Avon Close	C1
Bainton Close	B4-C4
Bancroft	B4-C4
Bath Road	A4-B4-B3
Berryfield Road	A4-B4
Bridge Street	B2
Christchurch Road	B4
Church Acre	A4
Church Street	A2-B2
Conigre Hill	A3-A2
Coppice Hill	B2
Coronation Avenue	C4-C3

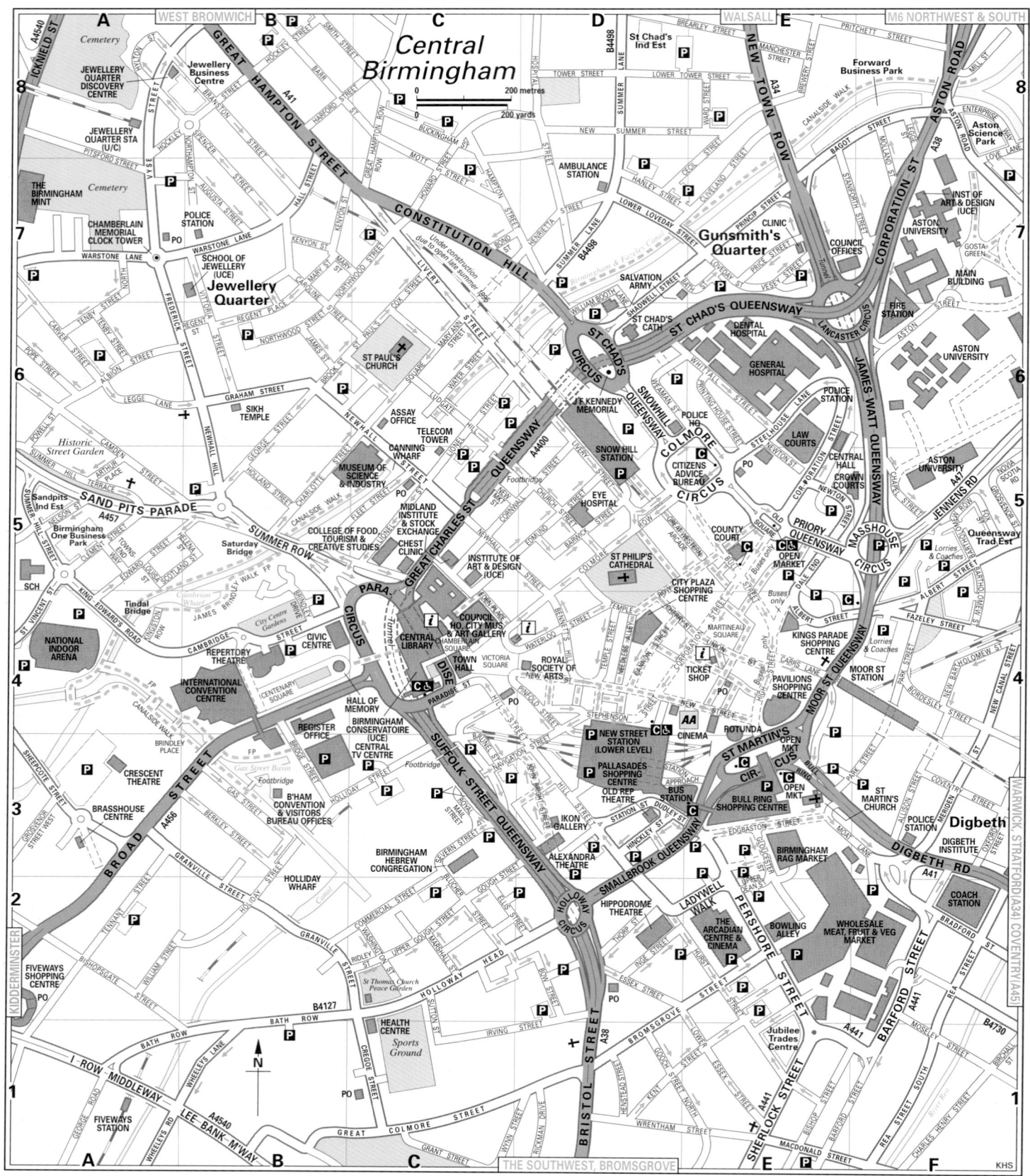

Birmingham

When the Romans were in Britain, Birmingham was little more than a staging post on Icknield Street. Throughout medieval times it was a minor agricultural centre in the middle of a heavily forested region. Timbered houses clustered together round a green that was eventually to be called the Bull Ring. But by the 16th century, although still a tiny village by today's standards, it had begun to gain a reputation as a manufacturing centre. Tens of thousands of sword blades were made here during the Civil War.

Throughout the 18th century more and more land was built on. In 1770 the Birmingham Canal was completed, expanding the possibilities of trade and dramatically increasing the town's development. All of that pales into near insignificance compared with what happened during the 19th century. Birmingham was not represented in Parliament until 1832 and had no town council until 1838. Yet by 1889 it had already

been made a city, and after only another 20 years it had become the second largest city in England. Many of Birmingham's most imposing public buildings date from the 19th century, when the city was growing rapidly. The International Convention Centre and the National Indoor Arena are two of the most recent developments. Surprisingly, the city has more miles of waterway than Venice.

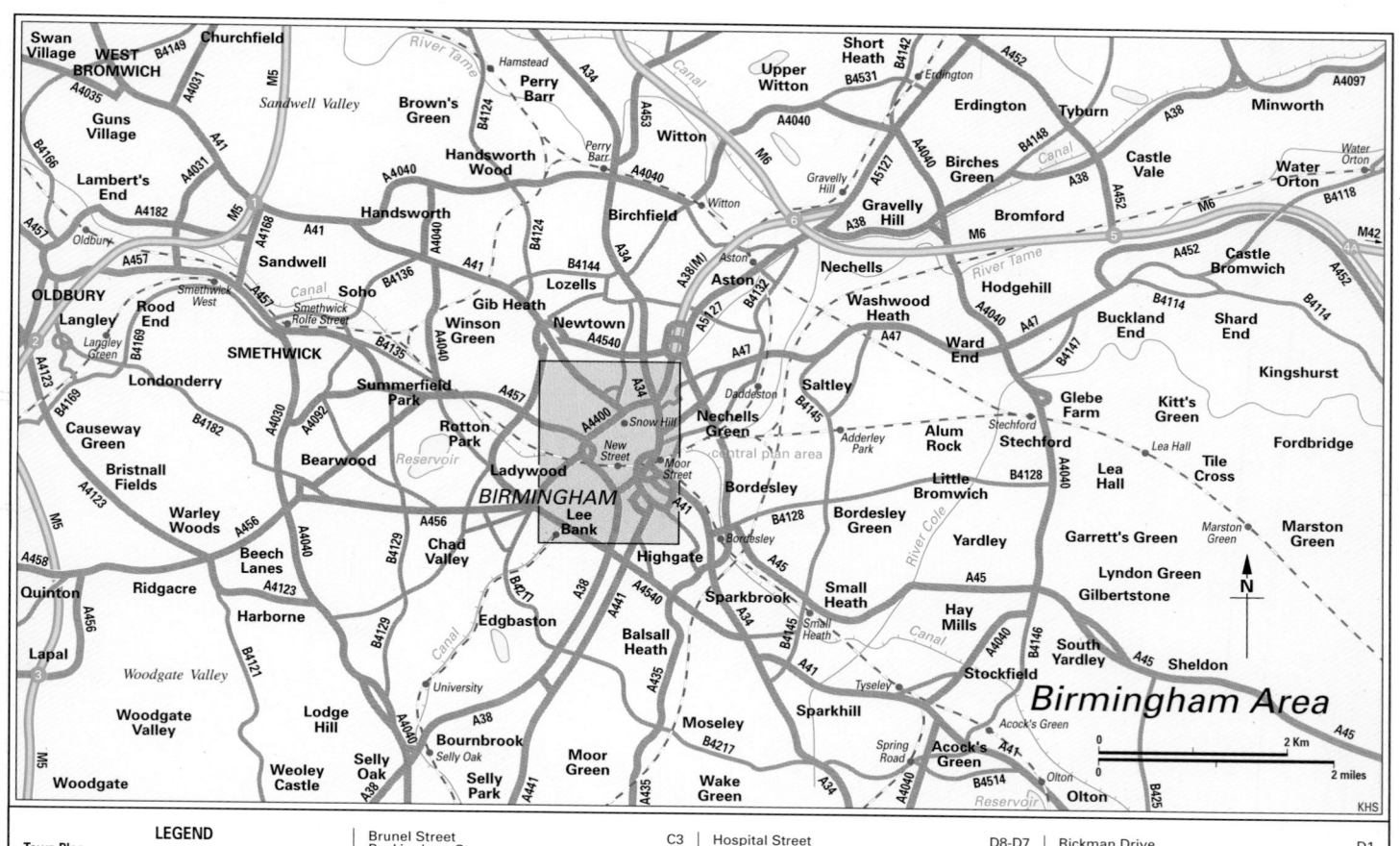

Birmingham Area

0   2 Km
0   2 miles

KHS

LEGEND

Town Plan

AA Recommended routes	
Restricted roads	
Other roads	
Buildings of interest	COLLEGE
AA Shop/Insurance	AA
Churches	+
Parks and open spaces	
Car parks	P
Toilets	C
One way streets	←

Area Plan

A roads	
B roads	

Street Index with Grid Reference

Birmingham

Albert St	E4-F4-F5
Albion Street	A6
Allison Street	F3-F4
Arthur Place	A5
Aston Road	F8-F7
Aston Street	F6-F7
Augusta Street	B7
Bagot Street	E7-E8-F8
Barford Street	F2-F1-E1
Barr Street	B8-C8
Bartholomew Row	F5
Bartholomew Street	F4-F5
Barwick Street	D5
Bath Row	A1-B1-B2-C2
Bath Street	D7-E7
Bennett's Hill	D4
Berkley Street	B3
Birchall Street	F1
Bishop Street	E1
Bishopsgate Street	A2-A1-B1
Blucher Street	C3-C2
Bond Street	C7
Bordesley Street	F4
Bow Street	D2
Bradford Street	F2
Branston Street	A8-B8-B7
Brearley Street	D8-E8
Brewery Street	E8
Bridge Street	B3-B4
Brindley Drive	B4-B5
Brindley Place	A4
Bristol Street	D1-D2
Broad Street	A2-A3-B3-B4-C4
Bromsgrove Street	D1-D2-E2
Brook Street	B6

Brunel Street	C3
Buckingham Street	C8
Bull Ring	E3-F3
Bull Street	E5-E4
Cambridge Street	A4-B4
Camden Street	A6-A5
Canalside Walk	B3-A4-A5-B5-C5
Cannon Street	D4
Caroline Street	B7-B6-C6
Carrs Lane	E4
Carver Street	A7-A6
Cecil Street	D7-E7-E8
Chamberlain Square	C4
Chapel Street	F5
Charles Henry Street	F1
Charlotte Street	B5-C6
Cherry Street	D4-E4
Church Street	D5
Clement Street	A5
Cliveland Street	D7-E7-E8
Coleshill Street	F5-F6
Colmore Circus	D5-D6-E6-E5
Colmore Row	C4-D4-D5
Commercial Street	B2-C2-C3
Constitution Hill	C7-D7-D6
Cornwall Street	C5-D5-D6
Corporation Street	D4-E4-E5-E6-E7-F7
Coventry Street	F3
Cox Street	C6-C7
Cregoe Street	C1
Dale End	E4-E5
Digbeth Road	F3
Dudley Street	D3
Eden Place	C5-C4
Edgbaston Street	E3
Edmund Street	C5-D5
Edward Street	A4-A5
Ellis Street	C2-D2
Enterprise Way	F8
Essex Street	D2
Fazeley Street	F4
Fleet Street	B5-C5
Fox Street	F5
Frederick Street	A7-A6-B6
Gas Street	B3
George Road	A1
George Street	B6-B5
Gloucester Street	E3
Gooch Street North	D1-E1
Gosta Green	F7
Gough Street	C2-C3-D3
Graham Street	B6
Grant Street	C1
Granville Street	A3-B3-B2-C2
Great Charles Street	C5
Great Colmore Street	B1-C1-C2
Great Hampton Row	C7-C8
Great Hampton Street	B8-B7
Great Western Arcade	D5-E5
Grosvenor Street	F5
Grosvenor Street West	A3
Hall Street	B7-B8
Hampton Street	D7-C7-C8
Hanley Street	D7
Harford Street	B8-C8
Helena Street	A5-B5
Henrietta Street	C7-D7
Henstead Street	D1
High Street	E4
Hill Street	C4-D3
Hinckley Street	D3
Hockley Street	A8-B8
Holland Street	B5
Holliday Street	A2-B2-B3-C3
Holloway Circus	D2
Holloway Head	C2-D2

Hospital Street	D8-D7
Howard Street	C7-C8-D8
Hurst Street	D2-E2-E1
Hylton Street	A8
Icknield Street	A8
Inge Street	D2
Irving Street	C1-D1-D2
Islington Row Middleway	A1
James Brindley Walk	A4-B4-B5
James Street	B6
James Watt Queensway	F5-F6-E6
Jennens Road	F5-F6
John Bright Street	D3
Kent Street	D1-E1
Kenyon Street	B7
King Edwards Road	A5-A4
Kingston Row	A4
Ladywell Walk	D2-E2-E3
Lancaster Circus	E7-E6-F6-F7
Lee Bank Middleway	B1
Legge Lane	A6-B6
Lionel Street	C5-C6-D6
Livery Street	C7-C6-D6-D5
Louisa Street	A5
Love Lane	F7-F8
Loveday Street	E7
Lower Essex Street	D2-E2-E1
Lower Loveday Street	D7-E7
Lower Tower Street	D8-E8
Ludgate Hill	C6-C5
Macdonald Street	E1-F1
Manchester Street	E8
Marshall Street	C2
Mary Ann Street	C6
Mary Street	B7-C7
Masshouse Circus	E5-F5
Meriden Street	F3
Mill Street	F8
Moat Lane	E3-F3
Molland Street	F8-F7
Moor Street Queensway	E4-F4
Moseley Street	F2-F1
Mott Street	C8-C7
Navigation Street	C3-D3-D4
Needless Alley	D4
Nelson Street	A5
New Bartholomew Street	F4
New Canal Street	F4
New Street	C4-D4-E4
New Summer Street	D8-E8
New Town Row	E8-E7
Newhall Hill	B6-B5
Newhall Street	B6-C6-C5-D5
Newton Street	E5-E6
Northampton Street	A8-B8-B7
Northwood Street	B6-B7-C7
Novia Scotia Road	F5
Old Square	E5
Oxford Street	F3
Paradise Circus	B4-C4-C5-B5
Paradise Street	C4
Park Street	E3-F3-F4
Pershore Street	E2
Pinfold Street	C4-D4
Pitsford Street	A7-A8
Pope Street	A7
Powell Street	A6
Price Street	E7
Princip Street	E7
Printing House Street	E6
Priory Queensway	E5
Pritchett Street	E8-F8
Queensway	C5-D6
Rea Street	F1-F2
Rea Street South	F1
Regent Place	B7-B6

Rickman Drive	D1
Ridley Street	C2
Royal Mail Street	C3
St Chad's Circus	D6
St Chad's Queensway	D6-E6-E7
St Martin's Circus	E4-E5
St Paul's	B6-C6
St Vincent Street	A4-A5
Sand Pits Parade	A5-B5
Severn Street	C3
Shadwell Street	D6-D7-E7
Sheepcote Street	A4-A3
Sherlock Street	E1
Smallbrook Queensway	D2-D3-E3
Smith Street	B8-C8
Snowhill Queensway	D6
Spencer Street	B8-B7
Square	C6-B6
Staniforth Street	E8-E7-F7
Station Street	D3
Steelhouse Lane	E5-E6
Stephenson Street	D4
Suffolk Street Queensway	C4-C3-D3-D2
Summer Hill Street	A5
Summer Hill Terrace	A5
Summer Lane	D7-D8
Summer Row	B5
Sutton Street	C2-C1
Temple Row	D5-D4-E5
Temple Street	D4
Tenby Street	A7
Tenby Street North	A6-A7
Tennant Street	A1-A2-A3
Thorp Street	D2
Tower Street	D8
Townsend Way	A5
Union Street	E4
Upper Dean Street	E2-E3
Upper Gough Street	C2
Vesey Street	E7
Vittoria Street	B7-B6
Vyse Street	A7-A8-B8
Ward Street	E8
Warstone Lane	A7-B7
Washington Street	C2
Water Street	C6
Waterloo Street	C4-D4
Weaman Street	E6-D6
Wheeleys Lane	A1-B1
Wheeleys Road	A1
Whittall Street	D6-E6
William Booth Lane	D6-D7
William Street	A2-B2
Wrentham Street	D1-E1
Wynn Street	C1-D1
AA shop	D4
134 New Street	
Birmingham B2 4NP	

Maps: © The Automobile Association 1995
Revision: © The Automobile Association 1995

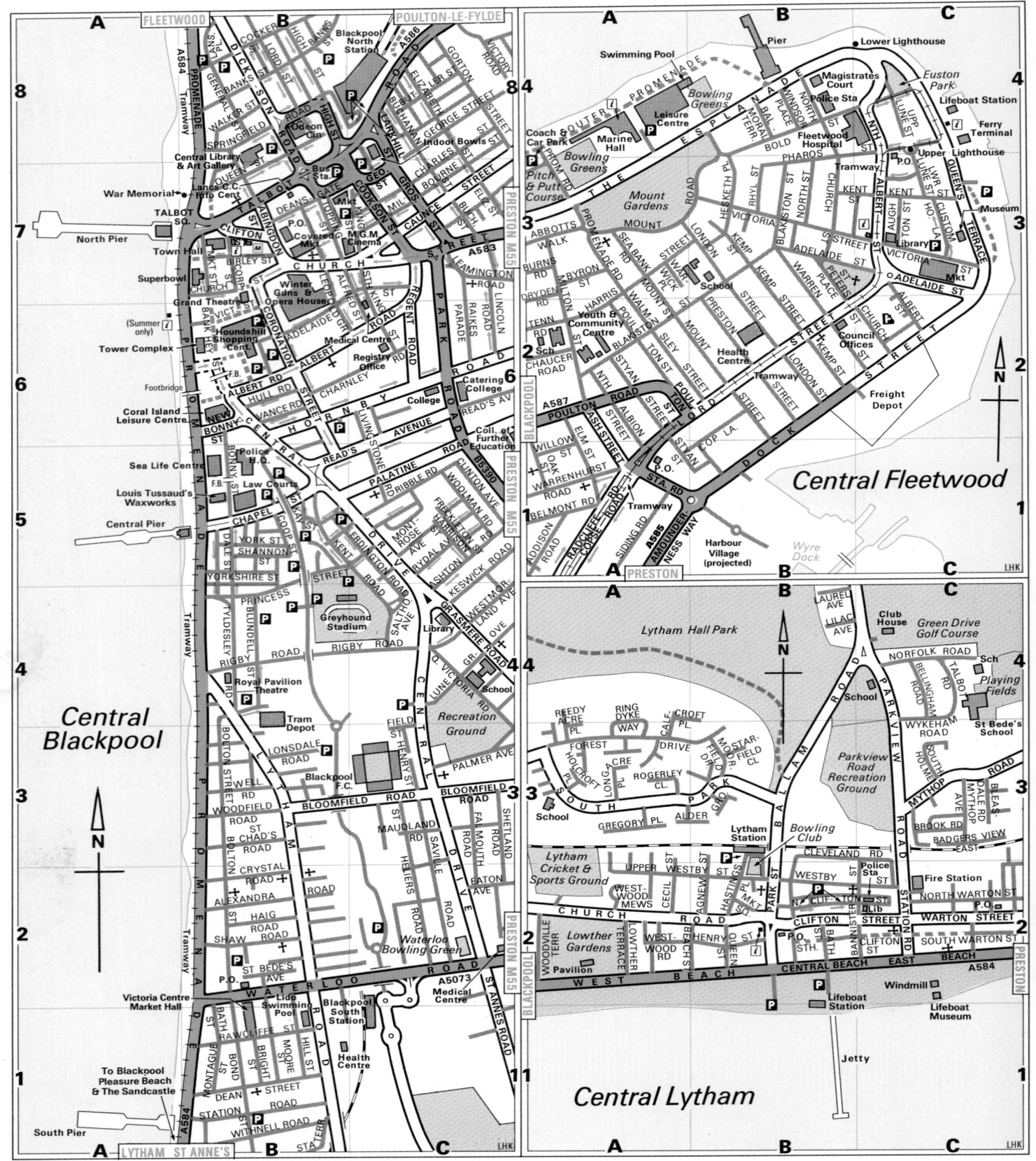

Central Fleetwood

Central Blackpool

Central Lytham

Blackpool

No seaside resort is regarded with greater affection than Blackpool. It is still the place where millions of North Country folk spend their holidays; its famous illuminations draw visitors from all over the world. It provides every conceivable kind of traditional holiday entertainment, and in greater abundance than any other seaside resort in Britain. The famous tower – built in the 1890s as a replica of the Eiffel Tower – the three piers, seven miles of promenade, five miles of illuminations, countless guesthouses, huge numbers of pubs, shops, restaurants and cafés all play host to eight million visitors a year.

At the base of the tower is a huge entertainment complex that includes a ballroom and an aquarium. Other 19th-century landmarks are North Pier and Central Pier, the great Winter Gardens and Opera House, and the famous trams that still run along the promenade – the last traditional urban tramway system still operating in Britain. The most glittering part of modern Blackpool is the famous Golden Mile, packed with amusements, novelty shops and snack stalls. Every autumn it becomes part of the country's most extravagant light show – the Illuminations – when the promenade is ablaze with neon representations of anything and everything from moon rockets to the Muppets. Autumn is also the time when Blackpool is a traditional venue for political party conferences.

196

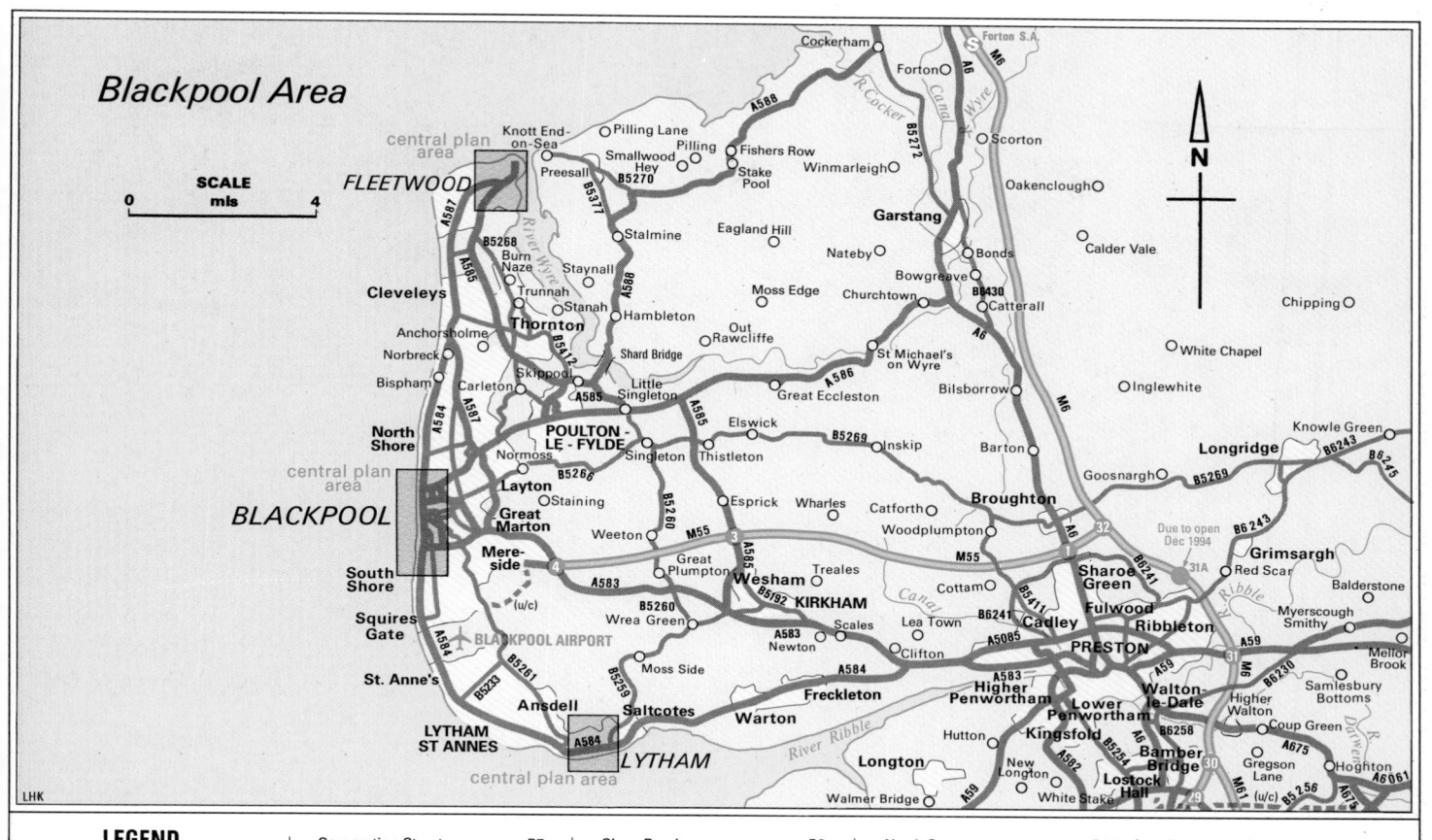

Blackpool Area

FLEETWOOD

BLACKPOOL

LYTHAM ST ANNES

LYTHAM

SCALE
mls
0   4

N

LEGEND

Town Plan

AA Recommended roads
Restricted roads
Other roads
Buildings of interest   Hall
Car parks   P
Parks and open spaces

Area Plan

A roads
B roads
Locations   Trunnah O
Urban area

Street Index with Grid Reference

Blackpool

Abingdon Street	B7
Adelaide Street	B6-B7-C7
Albert Road	B6-C6
Alexandra Road	B2
Alfred Street	B7-C7-C6
Ashton Road	C4-C5
Bank Hey Road	B6-B7
Banks Street	B8
Bath Street	B1
Birley Street	B7
Bloomfield Road	B3-C3
Blundell Street	B4
Bolton Street	B4-B3-B2
Bond Street	B1-B2
Bonny Street	B5-B6
Bright Street	B1
Buchanan Street	C8-C7
Butler Street	C8
Caunce Street	C7-C8
Central Drive	B6-B5-C5-C4-C3-C2
Chapel Street	B5
Charles Street	C7-C8
Charnley Road	B6-C6
Church Street	B7-C7
Clifton Street	B7
Clinton Avenue	C5
Cocker Street	B8
Cookson Street	B7-C7
Coop Street	B5
Coronation Street	B7-B6-B5

Corporation Street	B7
Crystal Road	B2
Dale Street	B5-B4
Deansgate	B7
Dean Street	B1
Dickson Road	B8-B7
Eaton Avenue	C2
Erdington Road	B5-C5-C4
Elizabeth Street	C8-C7
Falmouth Road	C3-C2
Field Street	C3
Freckleton Street	C5
General Street	B8
George Street	C7-C8
Gorton Street	C4
Grasmere Road	C7
Grosvenor Street	C7
Haig Road	B2
Harrison Street	C5
Henry Street	C3
High Street	B8
Hill Street	B1-B2
Hornby Road	B6-C6
Hull Road	B6
Kay Street	B5
Kent Road	B5-C5-C4
Keswick Road	C4-C5
King Street	C7
Lansdowne Place	B8
Larkhill Street	C8
Leamington Road	C7
Leopold Grove	B7-B6-C6
Lincoln Road	C7-C6
Livingstone Road	C6-C5
Lonsdale Road	B3
Lord Street	B8
Lune Grove	C4
Lytham Road	B4-B3-B2-B1
Market Street	B7
Maudland Road	C3
Milbourne Street	C7-C8
Montague Street	B1
Montrose Avenue	C5
Moore Street	B1
New Bonny Street	B6
Palatine Road	B5-C5-C6
Palmer Avenue	C7
Park Road	C7-C6-C5
Princess Street	B4-B5-C5
Promenade	B8-B7-B6-B5-B4-B3-B2-B1
Queen Street	B7-B8
Queen Victoria Road	C4-C3
Raikes Parade	C6-C7
Rawcliffe Street	B1
Read's Avenue	B5-C5-C6
Regent Road	C7-C6
Ribble Road	C5
Rigby Road	B4-C4
Rydal Avenue	C5
St Annes Road	C2-C1
St Bede's Avenue	B2
St Chad's Road	B3
St Heliers Road	C3-C2
Salthouse Avenue	C4
Saville Road	C3-C2-C3
Shannon Street	B5

Shaw Road	B2
Shetland Road	C3-C2
South King Street	C7-C6
Springfield Road	B8
Station Road	B1
Station Terrace	B1
Talbot Road	B7-B8-C8
Topping Street	B7
Tyldesley Road	B4
Vance Road	B6
Victoria Street	B6
Victory Road	C8
Walker Street	B8
Waterloo Road	B2-C2
Wellington Road	B3
Westmorland Avenue	C4
Withnell Road	B1
Woodfield Road	B3
Woolman Road	C5
York Street	B5
Yorkshire Street	B5

AA Shop
13 Clifton Street
Blackpool
Lancashire
FY1 1JD
     B7

Fleetwood

Abbotts Walk	A3
Adelaide Street	B3-C3
Addison Road	A1
Albert Street	C3-C2
Amounderness Way	A1
Ash Street	A2-A1
Aughton Street	C3
Balmoral Terrace	B4
Belmont Road	A1
Blakiston Street	A2-B2-B3
Bold Street	B4-C4
Burns Road	A3
Byron Street	A3
Chaucer Road	A2
Church Street	C2
Cop Lane	A1-B1-B2
Copse Road	A1
Custom House Lane	C3
Dock Street	B1-B2-C2
Dryden Road	A3-A2
Elm Street	A2-A1
Harris Street	A2-A3-B3
Hesketh Place	B3-B2
Kemp Street	B3-B2
Kent Street	B3-C3
London Street	A3-B3-B2
Lord Street	A1-A2-B2-C2-C3
Lower Lune Street	C3
Milton Street	A3-A2
Mount Road	A3
Mount Street	A3-A2-B2
North Albert Street	C4-C3
North Albion Street	A2-A1
North Church Street	B4-B3

North Street	B3
Oak Street	A1
Outer Promenade	A4-B4
Pharos Street	B3-C3-C4
Poulton Road	A2
Poulton Street	A2
Preston Street	B2
Promenade Road	A4-A3
Queen's Terrace	C3-C4
Radcliffe Road	A1
Rhyl Street	B3
St Peters Place	B3-B2
Sea Bank Road	A3
Siding Road	A1
Station Road	A1
Styan Street	A2-A1-B1
Tennyson Road	A2
The Esplanade	A3-A4-B4-C4
Upper Lune Street	C4
Victoria Street	C3-C3
Walmsley Street	A3-A2-B2
Warrenhurst Road	A1
Warren Street	B3-B2-C2
Warwick Place	A3
Willow Street	A1
Windsor Place	B4

Lytham

Agnew Street	B2-B3
Alder Grove	A3-B3
Badgers View East	C3
Ballam Road	B3-B4-C4
Bannister Street	B2-C2
Bath Street	B2
Beach Street	A2-B2
Bellingham Road	C4
Bleasdale Road	C3
Brook Road	C3
Calfcroft Place	A3-A4-B4
Cecil Street	A2-A3
Central Beach	B2-C2
Church Road	A2-B2
Cleveland Road	B3-C3
Clifton Street	B2-C2
East Beach	C2
Forest Drive	A3-B3
Gregory Place	A3
Hastings Place	B2-B3
Henry Street	B2
Holcroft Place	A3
Laurel Avenue	B4
Lilac Avenue	B4
Longacre Place	A3
Lowther Terrace	A2
Market Square	B2
Moorfield Drive	B3
Mythop Avenue	C3
Mythop Road	C3
Norfolk Road	C4
North Clifton Street	C2
North Warton Street	C2
Park Street	B2
Parkview Road	C4-C3-C2
Queen Street	B2

Reedy Acre Place	A4-A3
Ring Dyke Way	A4-A3
Rogerley Close	A3
South Clifton Street	B2-C2
South-Holme	C3
South Park	A3-B3
South Warton Street	C2
Starfield Close	B3
Station Road	C2
Talbot Road	C4
Upper Westby Street	A2-B2
Warton Street	C2
West Beach	A2-B2
Westby Street	B2-C2
Westwood Mews	A2
Westwood Road	A2
Woodville Terrace	A2
Wykeham Road	C3

LHK

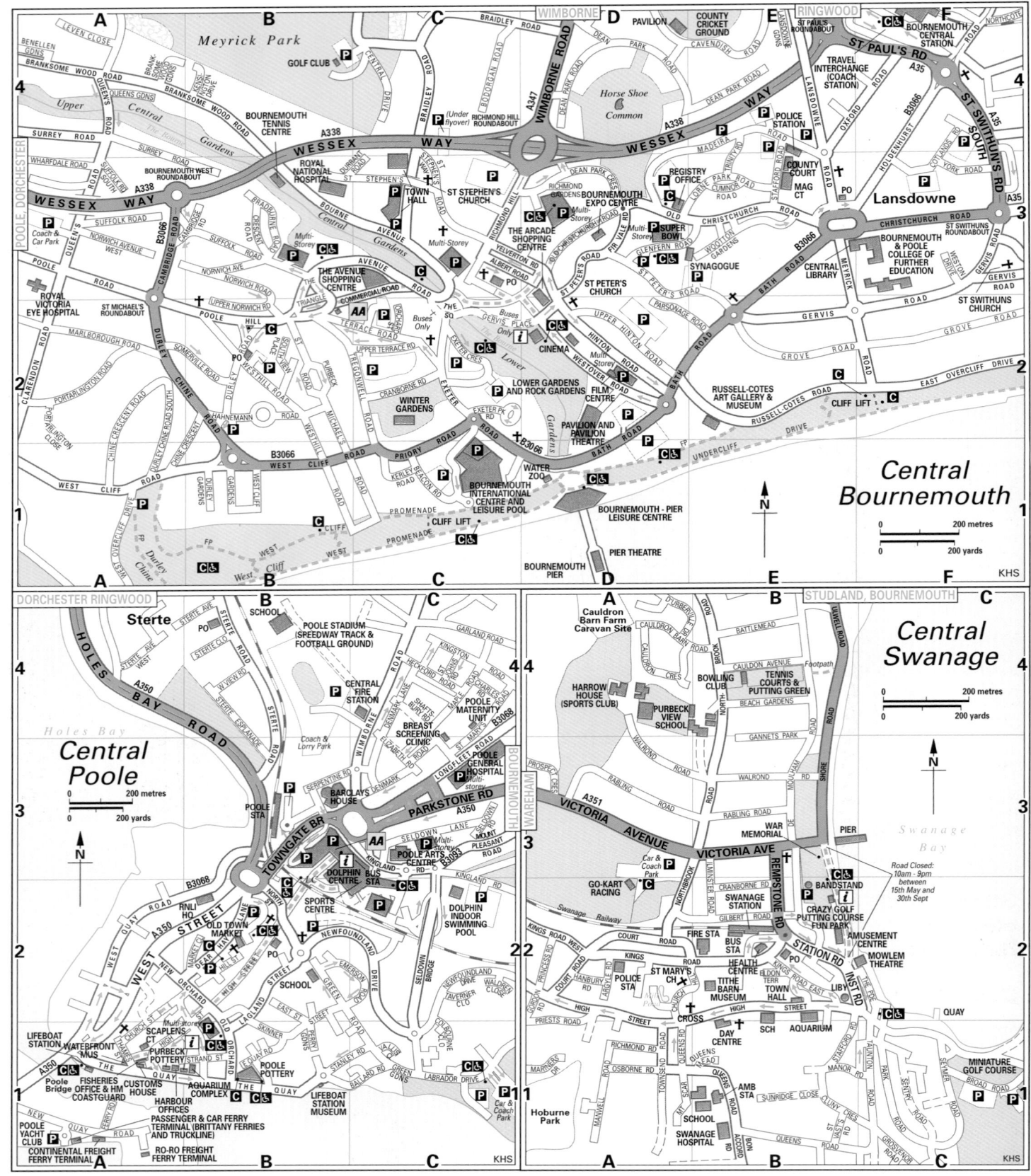

Bournemouth

Until the beginning of the 19th century the landscape was open heath. Bournemouth's rise began in Victorian times when the idea of seaside holidays was very new. Within the next 50 years it had become a major resort. Holidaymakers today enjoy miles of sandy beaches, a mild climate and a beautiful setting, along with a tremendous variety of amenities including some of the best shopping in the south. Entertainments range from variety shows and cinemas to opera and the world famous Bournemouth Symphony Orchestra. Major features of interest are the Bournemouth Expo Centre, containing the Dinosaur Safari and, at nearby Canford Cliffs, the magnificent Compton Acres Gardens overlooking Poole Harbour.

Poole is famous for its large natural harbour and the old town around the Quay with its unique historical interest. The waterfront Maritime Museum illustrates the town's associations with the sea since prehistoric times and the famous Poole Pottery offers guided tours of its workshops. Among other places to be visited are Scaplen's Court and the RNLI Headquarters Museum.

Swanage, one of Dorset's most popular holiday resorts, still retains much of its Victorian character. Dramatic coastal scenery with clifftop walks and many places of interest are within easy reach. A major attraction is the Swanage Railway, which operates steam-hauled trains to Harman's Cross and, in the near future, to Corfe Castle.

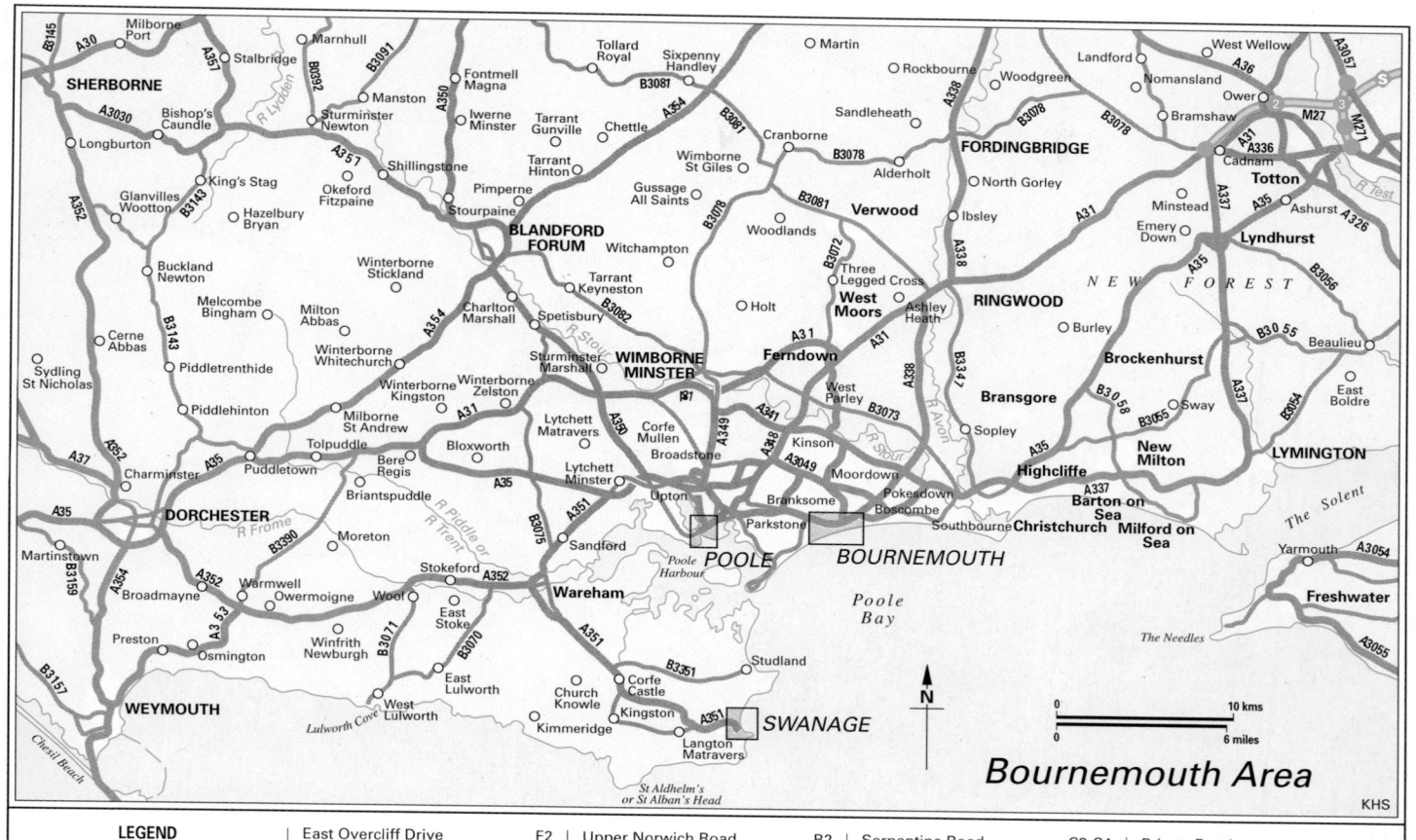

Bournemouth Area

KHS

LEGEND

Town Plan

AA Recommended routes	
Restricted roads	
Other roads	
Buildings of interest	COLLEGE
AA Shop/Insurance	AA
Churches	+
Parks and open spaces	
Car parks	P
Toilets	C C
One way streets	←

Area Plan

A roads	
B roads	
Locations	Yalding ○
Urban area	

Street Index with Grid Reference

Bournemouth

Albert Road	C3-D3
Avenue Road	B3-C3-C2
Bath Road	D1-D2-E2-E3
Beacon Road	C1
Benellen Gardens	A4
Bodorgan Road	C4
Bourne Avenue	B2-C2
Bradburne Road	B3
Braidley Road	C3-C4-D4
Branksome Wood Gardens	A4-B4
Branksome Wood Road	A4-B4
Cambridge Road	A3
Cavendish Road	D4-E4
Central Drive	B4-C4
Chine Crescent	A1-B1-B2
Chine Crescent Road	A1-A2
Christchurch Road	F3
Clarendon Road	A2-A3
Commercial Road	B2-C2-C3
Cotlands Road	F3-F4
Cranborne Road	C2
Crescent Road	B3
Cumnor Road	E3
Dean Park Crescent	C3-D3
Dean Park Road	D4-E4
Durley Chine Road	A2-B2-B1
Durley Chine Road South	A1-A2
Durley Gardens	B1
Durley Road	B2
East Overcliff Drive	F2
Exeter Crescent	C2
Exeter Park Road	C2
Exeter Road	C2-C1
Fir Vale Road	D3
Frances Road	F4
Gervis Place	C2-D2
Gervis Road	E2-F2-F3
Glenfern Road	D3-E3
Grove Road	E2-F2
Hahnemann Road	B2
Hinton Road	D2
Holdenhurst Road	E3-F3-F4
Kensington Drive	B4
Kerley Road	C1
Knyveton Road	F4
Lansdowne Gardens	E4
Lansdowne Road	E4-E3
Leven Avenue	A4
Leven Close	A4
Lorne Park Road	D3-E3
Madeira Road	D3-D4-E4-E3
Manor Road	F3
Marlborough Road	A2
Meyrick Road	E3-E2-F2
Northcote	F4
Norwich Avenue	A3-B3
Norwich Avenue West	A3
Norwich Road	B3
Old Christchurch Road	C3-C2-D3-E3
Orchard Street	C3-C2
Oxford Road	E4-F4
Parsonage Road	D2-E2
Poole Hill	A2-B2
Poole Road	A3
Portarlington Close	A2-A1
Portarlington Road	A2
Priory Road	C1-C2
Purbeck Road	B2
Queens Gardens	A4
Queens Road	A3-A4
Richmond Gardens	D3
Richmond Hill	C3-D3
Russell-Cotes Road	D2-E2
St Michael's Road	B2-B1-C1
St Paul's Road	E4-F4
St Peter's Road	E2-E3-D2-D3
St Stephen's Road	B2-C2
St Stephen's Way	C4-C3
St Swithun's Road South	F4-F3
Somerville Road	A2-B2
South View Place	B2
Southcote Road	F4
Stafford Road	E3-E4
Suffolk Road	A3-B3
Suffolk Road South	A3
Surrey Road	A4-A3-B3
Terrace Road	B2-C2
The Square	C2
The Triangle	B2
Tregonwell Road	B2-C2-C1
Trinity Road	E3-E4
Undercliff Drive	D1-E1-E2-F2
Upper Hinton Road	D2
Upper Norwich Road	B2
Upper Terrace Road	B2-C2
Wessex Way	A3-B3-B4-C4-D3-D4-E4
West Cliff Gardens	B1
West Cliff Road	A1-B1-C1
West Overcliff Drive	A1
Westhill Road	B2-B1
Weston Drive	F3
Westover Road	D2
Wharfdale Road	A3-A4
Wimborne Road	D4
Wootton Gardens	E3
Yelverton Road	C3-D3
York Road	F3

AA shop	C2
96 Commercial Road	
Bournemouth	
Dorset BH2 5LR	

Serpentine Road	C3-C4
Shaftsbury Road	B1-B2
Skinner Street	B1-C1
Stanley Road	A4-B4
Sterte Avenue	A4
Sterte Avenue West	B4
Sterte Close	B3
Sterte Esplande	B4-B3
Sterte Road	B4-B3
Strand Street	A1-B1
Taverner Close	C2
Thames Street	A1
The Quay	A1-B1
Towngate Bridge	B3
Vallis Close	C1
Waldren Close	C2
West Quay Road	A1-A2-B2-B3
West Street	A1-A2-B2
West View Road	B4
Wimborne Road	C4-C3

AA shop	B3
10 Falkland Square	
Poole	
Dorset BH15 1ER	

Poole

Ballard Road	B1-C1
Charles Road	C4
Church Street	A1-A2
Colbourne Close	C2-C1
Dear Hay Lane	A2-B2
Denmark Lane	C3-C4
Denmark Road	C3
East Quay Road	B1
East Street	B2-B1
Elizabeth Road	C3-C4
Emerson Road	B2-C2
Ferry Road	A1
Garland Road	C4
Green Road	B2-C1
Hackford Road	C4
High Street	A1-B1-B2-B3
Hill Street	B2
Holes Bay Road	B3-B4-A4
Jolliffe Road	C4
Kingland Road	B2-B3-C2
Kingston Road	C4
Labrador Drive	B1
Lagland Street	B1-B2
Longfleet Road	C3-C4
Maple Road	C3-C4
Market Close	B2
Marnhull Road	C4
Mount Pleasant Road	C3
New Orchard	A2-B2
New Quay Road	A1
Newfoundland Drive	B2-C2-C1
North Street	B2-B1
Old Orchard	B2-B1
Parkstone Road	C3
Perry Gardens	B1
St Johns Road	C4
St Mary's Road	C3-C4
Seldown Bridge	C1-C2
Seldown Lane	C3
Seldown Road	C3

Swanage

Argyle Road	A2
Battlemead	B4
Beach Gardens	B4
Bon Accord Road	B1
Broad Road	C1
Cauldon Avenue	B4
Cauldron Barn Road	A4-B4
Cauldron Crescent	A4
Church Hill	A2-B2
Cluny Crescent	B1-C1
Court Road	A2-B2
Cranborne Road	B2
De Moulham Road	B3-B4
D'Uberville Drive	A4-B4
Eldon Terrace	B2
Gannets Park	B3-B4
Gilbert Road	A2-B2
Gordon Road	A2
Grosvenor Road	C1
Hanbury Road	A2
High Street	A2-B3
Ilminster Road	B2-B3
Institute Road	B2-C2
Kings Road	A2-B2
Kings Road East	B2
Kings Road West	A2
Manor Road	B1-C1
Manwell Road	A1
Mariners Drive	A1
Mount Scar	A1
Northbrook Road	A2-A3-B3-B4
Osborne Road	A1
Park Road	C1
Princess Road	A2
Prospect Crescent	A3

Priests Road	C1
Queens Mead	B1
Queens Road	A1-B1-C1
Rabling Road	A3-B3
Rempstone Road	B2-B3
Richmond Road	A1
St Vast's Road	B1
Sentry Road	C1
Seymer Road	C1
Shore Road	B3-B4
Stafford Road	B1-B2
Station Road	B2
Sunridge Close	B1
Taunton Road	C1
The Parade	C2
Townsend Road	A1
Ulwell Road	B4
Victoria Avenue	A3-B3
Walrond Road	A3-B3

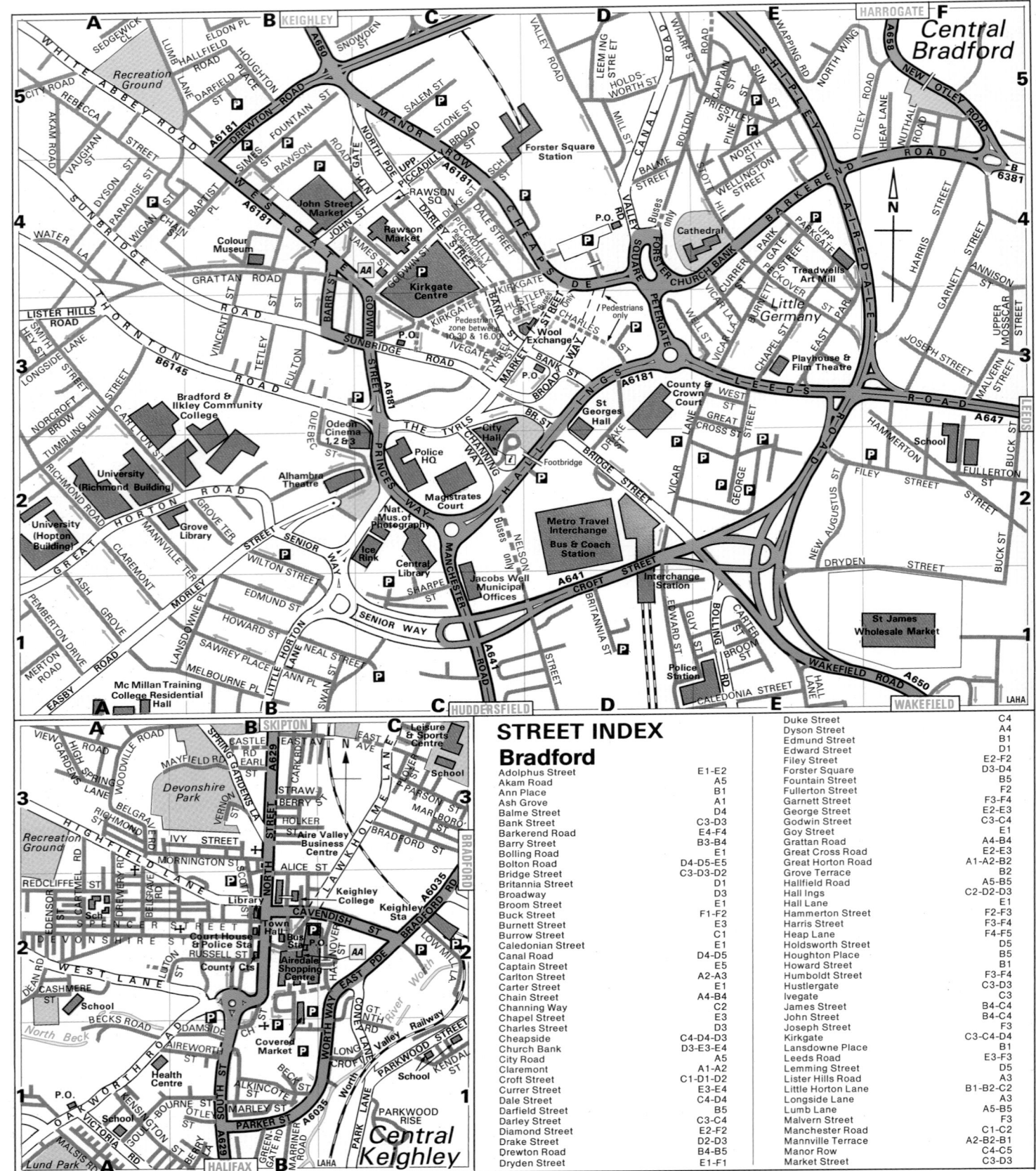

STREET INDEX
Bradford

Street	Grid
Adolphus Street	E1-E2
Akam Road	A5
Ann Place	B1
Ash Grove	A1
Balme Street	D4
Bank Street	C3-D3
Barkerend Road	E4-F4
Barry Street	B3-B4
Bolling Road	E1
Bolton Road	D4-D5-E5
Bridge Street	C3-D3-D2
Britannia Street	D1
Broadway	D3
Broom Street	E1
Buck Street	F1-F2
Burnett Street	E3
Burrow Street	C1
Caledonian Street	E1
Canal Road	E5
Captain Street	A2-A3
Carlton Street	A2-A3
Carter Street	E1
Chain Street	A4-B4
Channing Way	C2
Chapel Street	E3
Charles Street	D3
Cheapside	C4-D4-D3
Church Bank	D3-E3-E4
City Road	A5
Claremont	A1-A2
Croft Street	C1-D1-D2
Currer Street	E3-E4
Dale Street	C4-D4
Darfield Street	B5
Darley Street	C3-C4
Diamond Street	E2-F2
Drake Street	D2-D3
Drewton Road	B4-B5
Dryden Street	E1-F1
Duke Street	C4
Dyson Street	A4
Edmund Street	B1
Edward Street	D1
Filey Street	E2-F2
Forster Square	D3-D4
Fountain Street	B5
Fullerton Street	F2
Garnett Street	F3-F4
George Street	E2-E3
Godwin Street	C3-C4
Goy Street	E1
Grattan Road	A4-B4
Great Cross Road	E2-E3
Great Horton Road	A1-A2-B2
Grove Terrace	B2
Hallfield Road	A5-B5
Hall Ings	C2-D2-D3
Hall Lane	E1
Hammerton Street	F2-F3
Harris Street	F3-F4
Heap Lane	F4-F5
Holdsworth Street	D5
Houghton Place	B5
Howard Street	B1
Humboldt Street	F3-F4
Hustlergate	C3-D3
Ivegate	C3
James Street	B4-C4
John Street	B4-C4
Joseph Street	F3
Kirkgate	C3-C4-D4
Lansdowne Place	B1
Leeds Road	E3-F3
Lemming Street	D5
Lister Hills Road	A3
Little Horton Lane	B1-B2-C2
Longside Lane	A3
Lumb Lane	A5-B5
Malvern Street	F3
Manchester Road	C1-C2
Mannville Terrace	A2-B2-B1
Manor Row	C4-C5
Market Street	C3-D3

Bradford

The centre of Yorkshire's wool trade from the 19th century onwards, Bradford, like many small market towns that exploded into industrial cities almost overnight, is a mixture of grand civic buildings, factories and mills, crowded housing estates and sprawling suburbs. Impressive among the former are the Wool Exchange, with its ornate tower, and the massive city hall, topped by a 200ft-high tower. The late 15th- and 16th-century cathedral is built in the Perpendicular style with some fine carvings – notably the 20 angels supporting the nave roof.

Another notable feature of Bradford is the old German Quarter, with many commercial buildings now listed; the composer Frederick Delius was born here in 1862. Changing population patterns in recent years have brought a considerable Asian influence to the city's cuisine, clothing and culture, which has become an attraction in its own right.

Bradford's museums include the Colour Museum, giving a fascinating insight into the world of colour, the National Museum of Photography, Film and Television, which includes the famous IMAX cinema (with Britain's largest cinema screen), and the Industrial Museum, which illustrates the development of the woollen and worsted industry.

Keighley The Brontë sisters used to walk from Haworth to this pleasant 19th-century town for their shopping sprees. The Keighley and Worth Valley Railway, famous for its award-winning restored stations and the film *The Railway Children,* is a great attraction, hauling passengers up the valley to Haworth and Oxenhope.

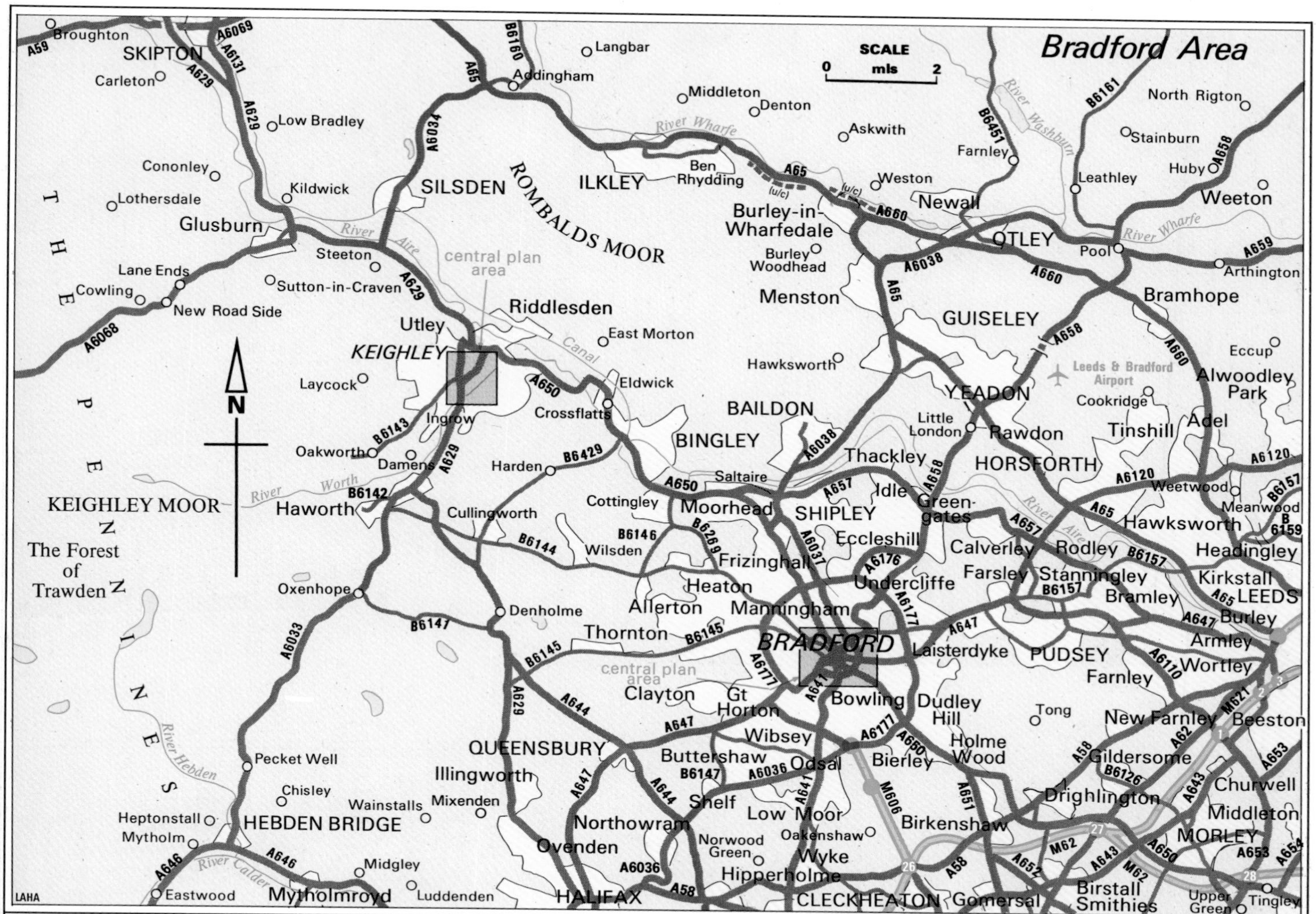

SCALE
0   mls   2

Melbourne Place	A1-B1	Thornton Road	A4-A3-B3-C3
Merton Road	A1	Tumbling Hill Street	A2-A3
Mill Street	D4-D5	Tyrrel Street	C3
Morley Street	A1-B1-B2-C2	Upper Parkgate	E4
Neal Street	B1-C1	Upper Piccadilly	C4
Nelson Street	C2-C1-D1	Valley Road	D4-D5
New Augustus Street	E2	Vaughan Street	A4
Northgate	C4-C5	Vicar Lane	D2-E2-E3
North Parade	C4-C5	Wakefield Road	E2-E1-F1
North Street	E4	Wapping Road	E5
North Wing	E4-E5	Water Lane	A4
Nuthall Road	F5	Wellington Street	E4
Otley New Road	F4-F5	Well Street	D3-E3
Otley Road	E4-F4-F5	Westgate	B4-C4-C3
Paradise Street	A4	West Street	E3
Park Gate	E4	White Abbey Road	A5-B5-B4
Peckover Street	E4-E3-F3	Wigan Street	A4-B4
Peel Street	E2-E3	Wilton Street	B1-B2
Pemberton Drive	A1	AA Shop, 101 Godwin Street	
Petergate	D3	Bradford, West Yorkshire BD1 3PP	C4
Piccadilly	C3-C4		
Pine Street	E5		
Portland Street	C1-D1	**Keighley**	
Priestly Street	E5		
Princes View	C1	Aireworth Street	A1-B1
Princes Way	C2	Alice Street	B3-C3
Quebec Street	B3-B2-C2	Alkincote Street	B1
Rawson Road	B4-C4	Beck Street	B1
Rawson Square	C4	Becks Road	A2
Rebecca Street	A5	Belgrave Road	A2-A3
Richmond Road	A2	Berry Lane	B1
Salem Street	C5	Bingley Road	C3
Sawrey Place	B1	Bradford Road	C2-C3
School Street	C4-D4-D5	Bradford Street	C3
Senior Way	B2-C1	Cark Road	B3
Sharpe Street	C1	Cartmel Road	A2-A3
Simes Street	B4	Cashmere Street	A2
Smith Street	A3	Castle Road	B3
Southgate	B3	Cavendish Street	B2-C2
Stone Street	C5	Church Street	B1-B2
Stott Hill	D4-E4	Cliffe Street	A3-B3
Sunbridge Road	A4-A3-B3-C3	Coney Lane	C1-C2
Swan Street	B1-C1	Croft Street	A1
The Tyrls	C2-C3	Damside	B1

Dean Road	A2	Strawberry Street	B3
Devonshire Street	A2-B2	Vernon Street	B3
Drewery Road	A2-A3	View Road	A3
Earl Street	B3	Victoria Road	A1
East Avenue	B3, C3	Water Lane	B1
East Parade	C2	West Lane	A2-B2
Edenser Street	A2	Woodville Road	A3-B3
Goulbourne Street	A1-B1	Worth Way	C1-C2
Greengate Road	B1		
Hanover Street	C2		
High Street	B2		
Highfield Lane	A3-A2-B2		
Holker Street	B3		
Ivy Street	A3-B3		
Kendal Street	C1		
Kensington Street	A1-B1		
Lawkholme Lane	B2-C2-C3	Maps © The AA 1981; Revision © The AA 1995	
Long Croft	B1-C1		
Lord Street	B2		
Low Mill Lane	C2		
Luton Street	A2-B2		
Malsis Road	A1		
Market Street	B1-B2		
Marlborough Street	C3		
Marley Street	B1		
Marriner Road	B1		
Mayfield Road	A3-B3		
Mornington Street	A3-B3		
North Street	B2-B3		
Oakworth Road	A1-B1-B2		
Otley Street	B1		
Park Lane	C1		
Park Wood Street	C1-C2		
Parker Street	B1		
Parson Street	C3		
Plover Street	C3		
Richmond Street	A3		
Russell Street	B2		
Scott Street	B2-B3		
South Street	B1		
Spencer Street	A2-B2		
Spring Gardens Lane	B3		
Springfield Gardens	A3		
Starkie Street	B1		

LEGEND

Town Plan

AA Recommended Route
Other roads
Restricted roads
Buildings of interest   Market
Car parks   P
Parks and open spaces
One Way Streets

Area Plan

A roads
B roads
Urban area
Locations   Richmond ○

BRADFORD
St George's, built with the profits of the wool trade, is one of Bradford's imposing Victorian buildings. It is once again being used for the purpose for which it was intended – a concert hall – and has exceptionally good acoustics.

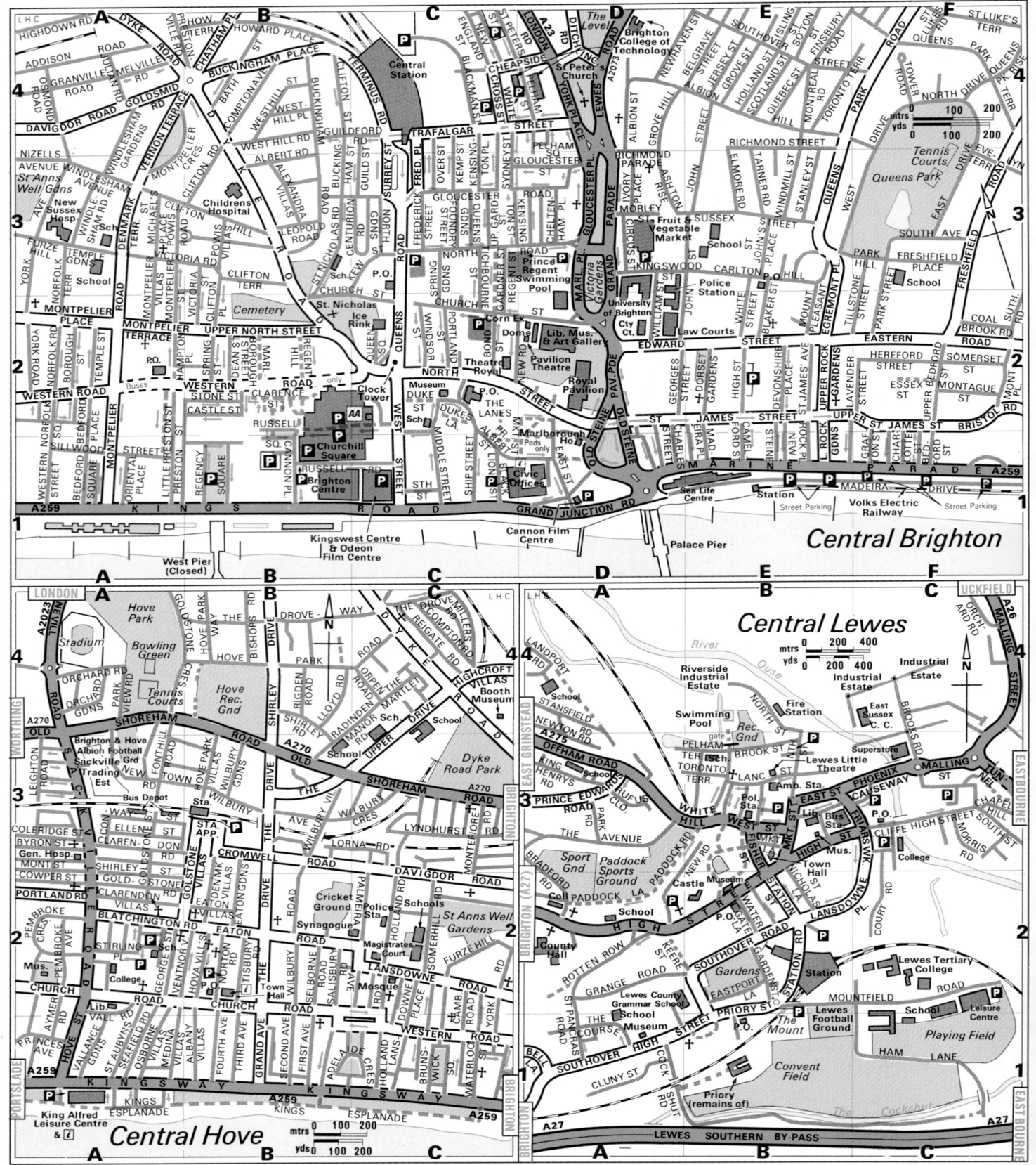

Central Brighton

Central Hove

Central Lewes

Brighton

Its habitation by the Prince of Wales during the late 18th century transformed Brighton from a fishing village into a highly fashionable Regency town. Today it is one of Britain's best-known and oldest resorts, with facilities for a multitude of interests. There are two universities, a racecourse, the largest marina in Britain, the 5,000-seat multipurpose Brighton Centre, the Sea Centre, two piers (one closed and awaiting restoration), Britain's first public electric railway

(1883), one of the largest shopping centres in the South of England, the exotic and magnificent Royal Pavilion, the Lanes (the narrow shop-lined streets of the old fishermen's quarter) and the annual veteran-car run from London.

Hove Almost inseparable from Brighton in terms of architecture, shopping and leisure facilities, Hove's main features of interest are the British Engineerium at the restored Victorian pumping station and the King Alfred Leisure Centre on the seafront.

Haywards Heath is a pleasant commuter town incorporating the attractive village of Lindfield. To the north-west is the 40-acre Borde Hill Garden.

Lewes This very old and historic market and commercial centre has a Norman castle and the 16th-century Anne of Cleves House (now a museum), and is well known for its 5th November firework celebrations. The outcome of the Battle of Lewes in 1264 between the Earl of Leicester and Henry III laid the foundations of Parliamentary democracy.

LEGEND

AA Recommended roads	Buildings of interest
Other roads	Churches
Restricted roads	Car Parks
One Way Streets	Parks and open spaces

Maps © The AA 1981
Revision © The AA 1994

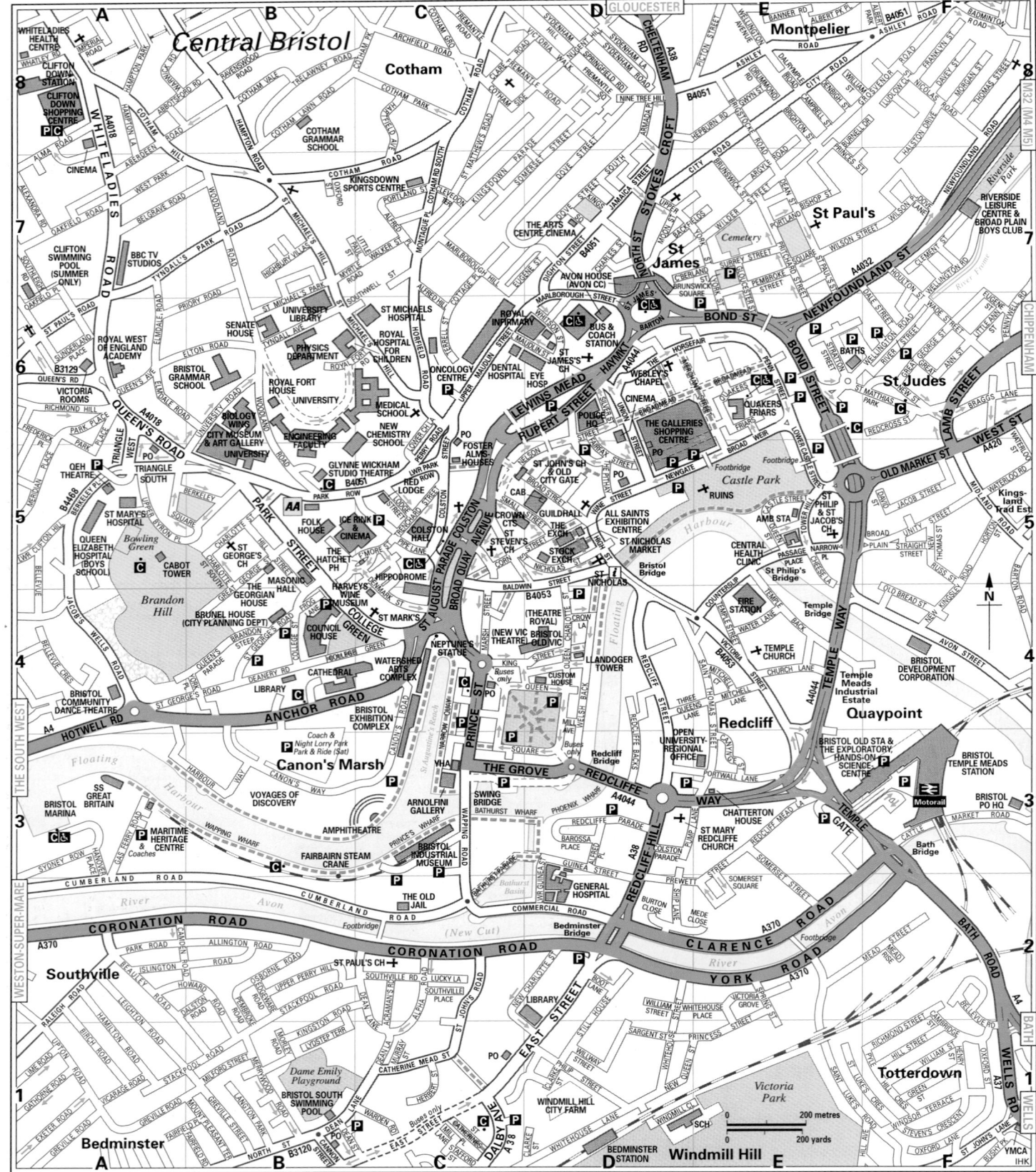

Bristol

One of Britain's most historic seaports, Bristol retains many of its visible links with the past, despite terrible damage inflicted during the bombing raids of World War II. Most imposing is the cathedral, founded as an abbey church in 1140. But perhaps even more famous than the cathedral is the Church of St Mary Redcliffe. Ranking among the finest churches in the country, it owes much of its splendour to 14th- and 15th-century merchants who bestowed huge sums of money on it. The merchant families brought wealth to the whole of Bristol, and their trading links with the world are continued in today's modern aerospace and technological industries.

Much of the best of Bristol can be seen in the area of the Floating Harbour. Several of the old warehouses have been converted into museums, galleries and exhibition centres. Scattered among them are genuinely picturesque old pubs, the best known being the Llandoger Trow, a timbered 17th-century house, the finest of its kind in Bristol. Further up the same street – King Street – is the Theatre Royal, built in 1766 and the oldest theatre in the country.

In Corn Street, the heart of the business area, is a magnificent 18th-century corn exchange. In front of it are the four pillars known as the 'nails', on which merchants used to make cash transactions, hence to 'pay on the nail'.

Forever linked with Bristol is the great engineer Isambard Kingdom Brunel. He designed the Clifton Suspension Bridge, built the Great Western Railway's line from London to Bristol's Old Station and constructed the SS *Great Britain*, the world's first screw-propelled, ocean-going iron ship – restored in the Bristol yard where she was built in 1843.

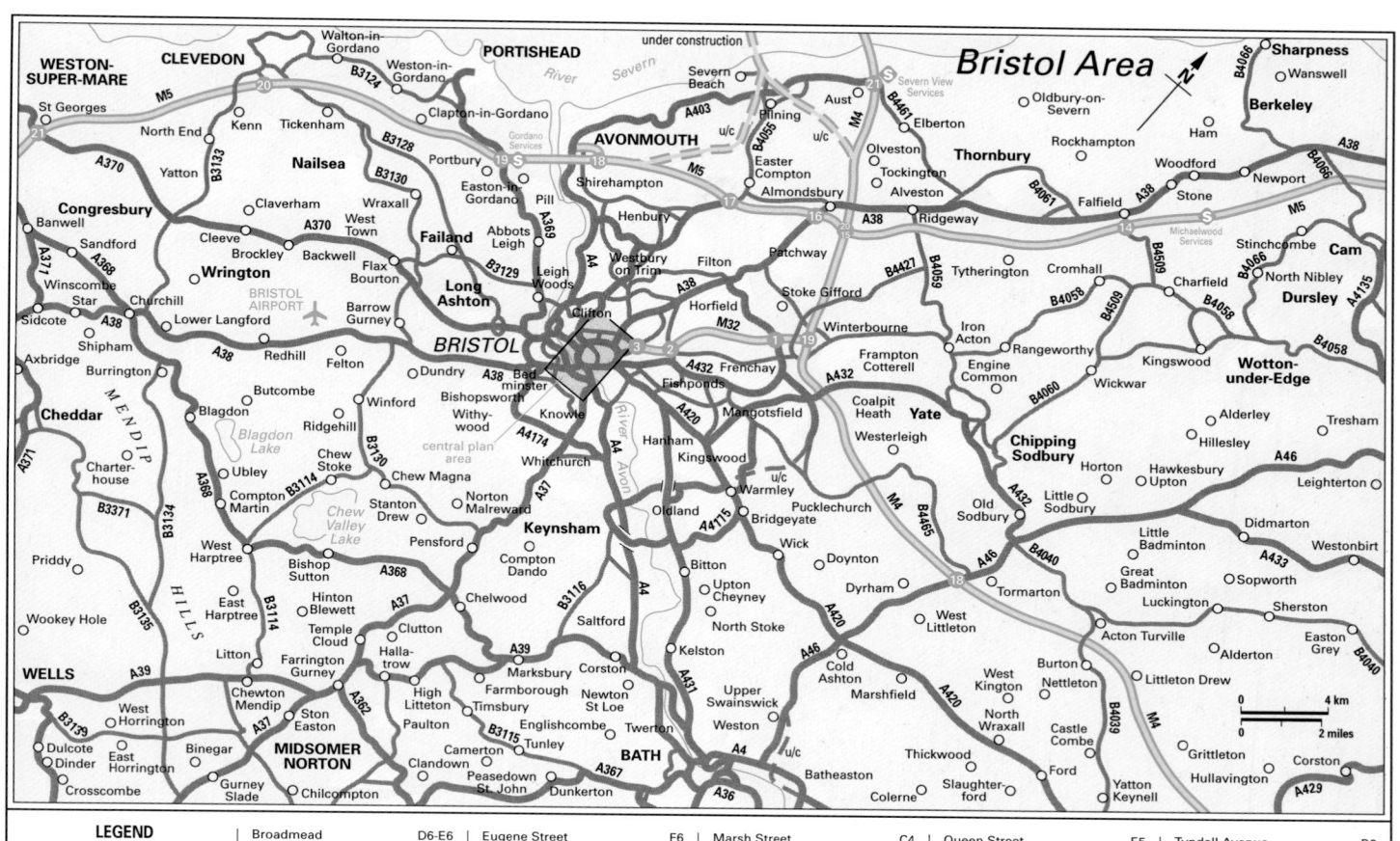

Bristol Area

LEGEND

Town Plan

AA Recommended routes	▬▬
Restricted roads	- - - -
Other roads	▬▬
Buildings of interest	COLLEGE ▢
AA shop	AA
Churches	†
Parks and open spaces	▢
Car parks	P
Toilets	C&, C
One way streets	←

Area Plan

A roads	▬▬
B roads	▬▬
Locations	Yalding ○
Urban area	▢

Street Index with Grid Reference

Bristol

Abbotsford Road	A8-B8
Aberdeen Road	A7-A8-B8
Acraman's Road	C2
Albert Park	F8
Albert Park Place	E8
Alexandra Road	A7
Alfred Hill	C7-C6
Alfred Place	D3
Allington Road	B2
Alma Road	A7-A8
Alpha Road	C1-C2
Anchor Road	A4-B4-C4
Archfield Road	C8
Argyle Road	E7-E8
Ashley Road	E8-F8
Avon Street	E4-F4
Backfields	D7-E7
Badminton Road	F8
Baldwin Street	C5-D5
Banner Road	E8
Barossa Place	D3
Barton Road	F4-F5
Bath Road	F2
Bathurst Parade	C2-C3
Beauley Road	A2-B1
Belgrave Road	A7-B7
Bellevue	A4-A5
Bellevue Crescent	A4
Bellevue Road	F2
Berkeley Place	A5
Berkeley Square	A5-B5
Birch Road	A1-A2
Bishop Street	E7
Bond Street	D6-E6
Boot Lane	D2
Bragg's Lane	F6
Brandon Steep	B4
Brighton Street	E7
Brigstocke Road	E7-E8

Broadmead	D6-E6
Broad Plain	F5
Broad Quay	C4-C5
Broad Street	C5-D5
Broad Weir	E5-E6
Brunswick Street	E7
Burnell Drive	E8-F8
Burton Close	D2
Bushy Park	F1
Cambridge Street	F1
Camden Road	A2
Campbell Street	E8
Cannon Street	B1
Canon's Road	C3-C4
Canon's Way	B3
Canynge Street	E3
Castle Street	E5
Catherine Mead Street	C1
Cattle Market Road	F3
Charles Street	D7
Charlotte Street	B5
Charlotte Street South	B5
Cheese Lane	E5
Cheltenham Road	D8
Church Lane	E4
City Road	D7-E7-E8-F8
Clare Road	C8-D8
Clarence Road	D2-E2-F3
Clarke Street	D1
Clement Street	F7
Clevedon Terrace	C7
College Green	B4-C4-B4-B5
College Street	B4
Colston Avenue	C5
Colston Parade	D3
Colston Street	C5-C6
Commercial Road	C2-D2
Corn Street	C5-D5
Coronation Road	A2-B2-C2-D2
Cotham Grove	C8
Cotham Hill	A8-B7
Cotham Lawn Road	B8
Cotham Park	C8
Cotham Road	B7-C7-C8
Cotham Road South	C7-C8
Cotham Side	C8-D8
Cotham Vale	B8
Cottage Place	C7
Countership	E4-E5
Crow Lane	D4
Cumberland Road	A2-B2-C2
Cumberland Street	D7-E7
Dalby Avenue	C1
Dale Street	F6
Dalston Road	B2
Dalrymple Road	E8
Davey Street	F8
David Street	F5
Deanery Road	B4
Dean Lane	B1-C1-C2
Dean Street	B1
Dean Street	E7
Denbigh Street	B2
Denmark Street	C5-C4
Dighton Street	C6
Dove Lane	F7
Dove Street	D7-D7-D8
Dove Street South	D7-D8
Drummond Road	F8
East Street	C1-D1-D2
Edgeware Road	B2
Elmdale Road	A7-A6-B6
Elton Road	A6-B6
Eugene Street	C7-D7

Eugene Street	F6
Exeter Road	A1
Fairfax Street	D5
Fairfield Place	A1-B1
Fairfield Road	A1
Franklyn Street	F8
Frederick Place	A6
Fremantle Road	C8-D8
Fremantle Square	D8
Frog Lane	B4
Frogmore Street	C5
Gas Ferry Road	A3
Gathorpe Road	A1
Gloucester Street	E7-E6
Great Ann Street	F6
Great George Street	B4-B5
Green Street	F1
Greville Road	A1
Greville Street	B1
Grosvenor Road	E8-F8
Guinea Street	D2-D3
Gwyn Street	E8
Halston Drive	F7-F8
Hamilton Road	A1-A2
Hampton Lane	A8
Hampton Park	A8
Hampton Road	B8
Hanover Place	A3
Harbour Way	A3-B3
Hatfield Avenue	C8
Haymarket	D6
Henry Street	F1
Hepburn Road	D8-E8
Herbert Street	C1
Highbury Villas	B7
High Street	D5
Hiill Avenue	F1
Hill Street	B5
Hill Street	F1
Horfield Road	C6-C7
Horton Road	A8
Hotwell Road	A3-A4
Houlton Street	F6-F7
Howard Road	A2-B2
Imperial Road	A2-B2
Islington Road	B1
Jacob Street	F5
Jacob's Wells Road	A4-A5
Jamaica Street	D7
Jubilee Street	F5
Kingsdown Parade	C7-C8-C8
Kings Square	D7
King Street	C4-D4
Kingston Road	B1-B2
Lamb Street	F5-F6
Langton Park	B1
Leighton Road	A1-A2
Lewins Mead	C6-D6
Lime Road	A1
Little Ann Street	F6
Little George Street	F6
Little Paul Street	B7-C7
Lodge Street	C5
Lower Castle Street	E5-E6
Lower Church Lane	C5
Lower Clifton Hill	A5
Lower Guinea Street	D2-D3
Lower Maudlin Street	D6
Lower Park Row	C5
Lucky Lane	C2
Ludlow Close	B2
Lydstep Terrace	B1-B2
Marlborough Hill	C7
Marlborough Street	D6-D7

Marsh Street	C4
Mead Rise	F2
Mead Street	E2-F2
Mede Close	E2
Merchant Street	D6-E6-E5
Meridian Place	A5-A6
Merrywood Road	B1
Midland Road	F5
Milford Street	B1
Mill Avenue	D4
Mill Lane	C1
Mitchell Court	E4
Mitchell Lane	E4
Montague Place	C7
Moon Street	D7
Morgan Street	F8
Morley Road	B1
Mount Pleasant Terrace	B1
Murray Street	C1
Myrtle Road	B7-C7
Narrow Place	E5
Narrow Quay	C3-C4
Nelson Street	C5-D5-D6
New Charlotte Street	C2-D2
Newfoundland Road	F7-F8
Newfoundland Street	E6-E7-F7
Newfoundland Way	F8
Newgate	D5-E5
New Kingsley Road	F4-F5
New Queen Street	D1
New Street	F6
New Thomas Street	F5
Nine Tree Hill	D8
North Street	B1
North Street	D7
Nugent Hill	D8
Oakfield Place	A6-A7
Oakfield Road	A7
Old Bread Street	F4
Old Market Street	E6
Osborne Road	B2
Oxford Lane	F1
Oxford Street	E7
Oxford Street	B7
Park Place	A6
Park Road	A2
Park Row	B5-C5
Park Street	B5
Passage Place	E5
Pembroke Road	B2
Pembroke Street	E7
Penn Street	E6
Pennywell Road	F7
Perry Road	C5-C6
Philip Street	D1
Picton Street	E8
Pipe Lane	C5
Portland Square	E7
Portland Street	C7
Portwall Lane	D3-E3
Prewett Street	D2-E3
Prince Street	C3-C4
Princess Street	D1-E1-E2
Princes Street	E7
Priory Road	A6-B7
Pritchard Street	E7-E6
Pump Lane	D3-E3
Pyle Hill Crescent	F1
Quakers Friars	E6
Queen Charlotte Street	D4
Queen's Avenue	A6
Queen's Parade	B4
Queen's Road	A6-B6-B5
Queen Square	C3-C4-D4-D3

Queen Street	E5
Raleigh Road	A1-A2
Ravenswood Road	B8
Redcliff Backs	D4-D3
Redcliffe Parade	D3
Redcliffe Way	D3-E3
Redcliff Hill	D2-D3
Redcliff Mead Lane	E3
Redcliff Street	D3-D4
Redcross Street	F6
Richmond Hill	A6
Richmond Street	E1-F1
River Street	F6
Royal Fort Road	B6-C6
Rupert Street	C6-D6
Russ Street	F5
St Augustine's Parade	C4-C5
St Catherines Place	C1
St George's Road	A4-B4
St James' Barton	D6
St John's Lane	F1
St John's Road	C1-C2
St Luke's Crescent	E1-F1
St Luke's Road	E2-E1-F1
St Matthew's Road	C7-C8
St Matthias Park	E6-F6
St Michael's Hill	B7-B6-C6
St Michael's Park	B6-B7
St Nicholas Road	F8
St Nicholas Street	C5-D5
St Paul's Road	A6-A7
St Paul's Street	E7
St Thomas Street	D4-E4-E3
Sargent Street	D1
Ship Lane	D2
Silver Street	D6
Small Street	C5-D5
Somerset Square	E2
Somerset Street	E2-E3
Somerset Street	C7-D7-D8
Southleigh Road	A7
Southville Place	C2
Southville Road	C2
Southwell Street	B6-C7
Springfield Road	D8
Spring Street	E2
Stackpool Road	A1-A2-B2
Stafford Street	C1
Steven's Crescent	F1
Stillhouse Lane	D1-D2
Stokes Croft	D7-D8
Straight Street	F5
Stratton Street	E6
Sunderland Place	A6
Surrey Street	E7
Sydenham Hill	D8
Sydenham Lane	D8
Sydenham Road	D8
Sydney Row	A3
Temple Back	E4-E5
Temple Gate	E3
Temple Street	E4
Temple Way	E3-E4-E5
Terrell Street	C6-C7
The Grove	C3-D3
The Horsefair	D6-E6
The Pithay	D5
Thomas Street	F8
Three Queens Lane	D4-E4
Tower Hill	E5
Trelawney Road	B8-C8
Trenchard Street	C5
Triangle South	A5
Triangle West	A6

Tyndall Avenue	B6
Tyndall's Park Road	A7-B7
Union Street	D5-D6
Unity Street	F5
University Road	B6
Upper Byron Place	A5
Upper Maudlin Street	C6
Upper Perry Hill	B2
Upper York Street	D7-E7
Upton Road	A1-A2
Vicarage Road	A1
Victoria Grove	E2
Victoria Road	E4
Victoria Walk	D8
Wade Street	F6
Walker Street	C7
Wapping Road	C3
Warden Road	C1
Warwick Road	A8
Water Lane	E4
Waterloo Road	F5
Waterloo Street	F5-F6
Wellington Avenue	E8
Wellington Road	E6-F6-F7
Wells Road	F1
Welsh Back	D3-D4-D5
West Park	A7
West Street	F5-F6
Whatley Road	A8
Whitehouse Lane	C1-D1
Whitehouse Place	D2-E2
Whitehouse Street	D1-D2
Whiteladies Road	A6-A7-A8
Whitson Street	D6
Wilder Street	D7-E7
William Street	D2
William Street	E8-F8
William Street	F1
Willway Street	D1
Wilson Place	F7
Wilson Street	E7-F7
Windmill Close	D1
Windsor Terrace	F1
Wine Street	D5
Woodland Road	B5-B6-B7
York Place	B4
York Road	D2-E2-F2
York Street	E6-E7

AA shop
Fanum House
26-32 Park Row
Bristol
BS1 5LY   B5

Maps: © The AA 1994
Revision: © The AA 1994

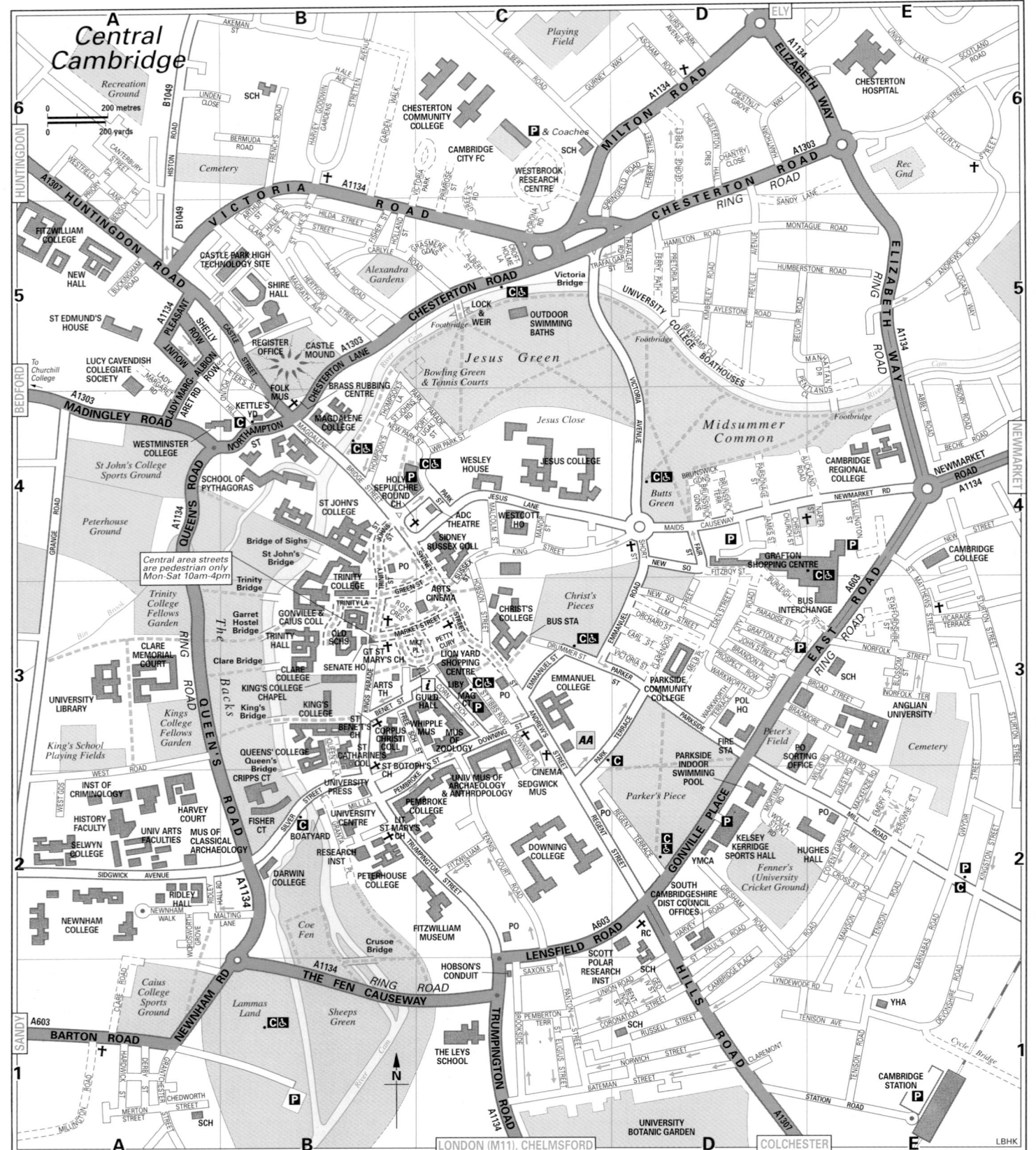

Central Cambridge

London (M11), Chelmsford · Colchester · Ely · Newmarket

Central area streets are pedestrian only Mon-Sat 10am-4pm

Cambridge

Few views in England, perhaps even in Europe, are as memorable as that from the Cambridge Backs towards the colleges. Dominating the scene in every sense is King's College Chapel. One of the finest Gothic buildings in Europe, it was built in three stages from 1446 to 1515.

No one would dispute that the chapel is Cambridge's masterpiece, but there are dozens of buildings here that would be the finest in any other town or city. Most are colleges, or are attached to colleges, and it is the university that permeates every aspect of Cambridge's landscape and life. In all the city has 33 university colleges and nearly all have buildings and features of great architectural interest. Guided tours of the colleges are available throughout the year.

Cambridge can provide a complete history of English architecture. The oldest surviving building is the tower of St Bene't's Church, dating back to before the Norman Conquest, and its most famous church is the Church of the Holy Sepulchre, one of only four round churches of its kind.

Of the many notable museums in Cambridge, the Fitzwilliam Museum is the most prestigious. It contains some of the best collections of ceramics, paintings, coins, medals and Egyptian, Greek and Roman antiquities outside London.

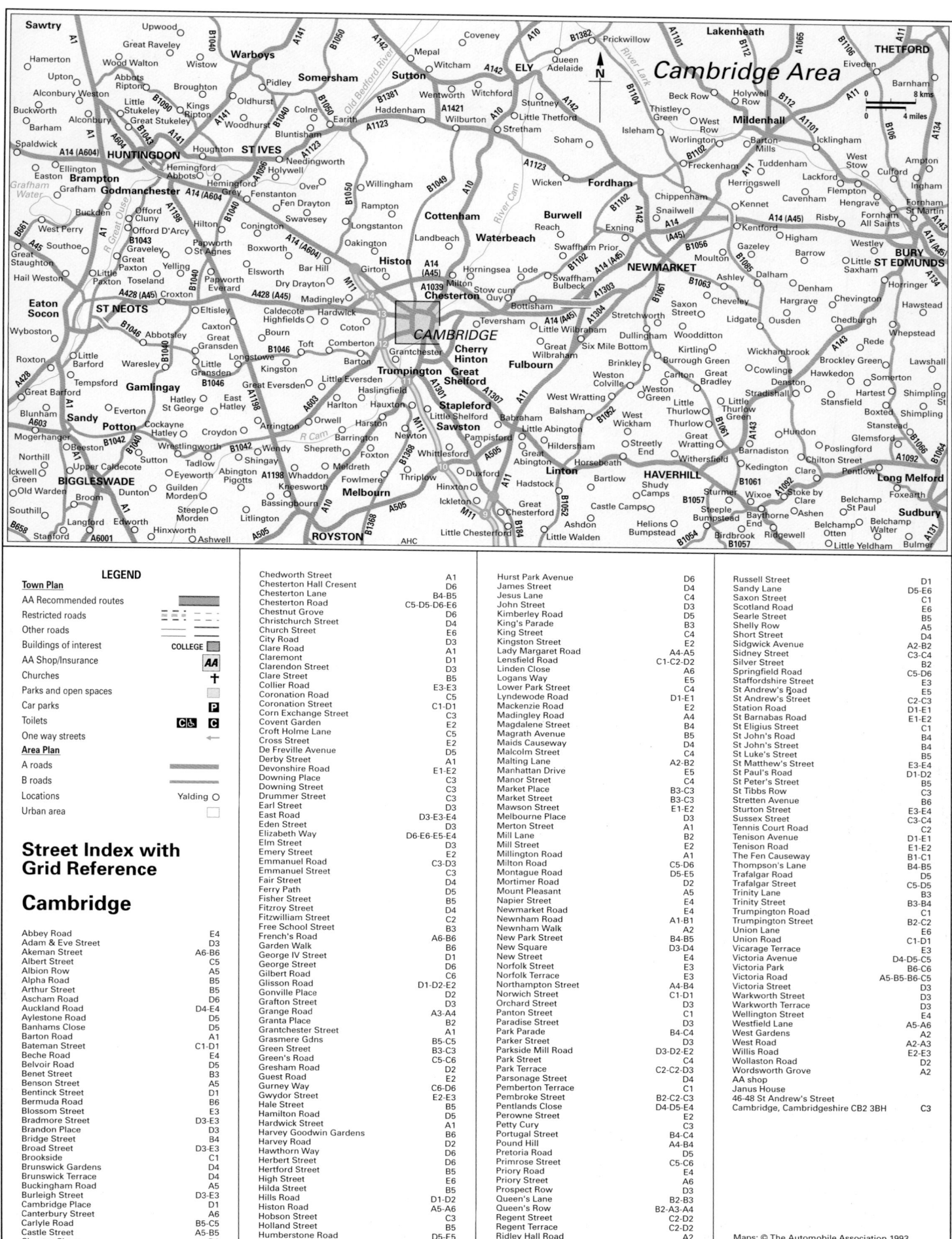

LEGEND

Town Plan

AA Recommended routes	
Restricted roads	
Other roads	
Buildings of interest	COLLEGE
AA Shop/Insurance	AA
Churches	+
Parks and open spaces	
Car parks	P
Toilets	C& C
One way streets	←

Area Plan

A roads	
B roads	
Locations	Yalding O
Urban area	

Street Index with Grid Reference

Cambridge

Abbey Road	E4
Adam & Eve Street	D3
Akeman Street	A6-B6
Albert Street	C5
Albion Row	A5
Alpha Road	B5
Arthur Street	B5
Ascham Road	D6
Auckland Road	D4-E4
Aylestone Road	D5
Banhams Close	D5
Barton Road	A1
Bateman Street	C1-D1
Beche Road	E4
Belvoir Road	D5
Benet Street	B3
Benson Street	A5
Bentinck Street	D1
Bermuda Road	B6
Blossom Street	D3-E3
Bradmore Street	D3-E3
Brandon Place	D3
Bridge Street	B4
Broad Street	D3-E3
Brookside	C1
Brunswick Gardens	D4
Brunswick Terrace	D4
Buckingham Road	A5
Burleigh Street	D3-E3
Cambridge Place	D1
Canterbury Street	A6
Carlyle Road	B5-C5
Castle Street	A5-B5
Chantry Close	D6

Chedworth Street	A1
Chesterton Hall Cresent	D6
Chesterton Lane	B4-B5
Chesterton Road	C5-D5-D6-E6
Chestnut Grove	D6
Christchurch Street	D4
Church Street	E6
City Road	D3
Clare Road	A1
Claremont	D1
Clarendon Street	D3
Clare Street	B5
Collier Road	E3-E3
Coronation Road	C5
Coronation Street	C1-D1
Corn Exchange Street	C3
Covent Garden	E2
Croft Holme Lane	C5
Cross Street	E2
De Freville Avenue	D5
Derby Street	A1
Devonshire Road	E1-E2
Downing Place	C3
Downing Street	C3
Drummer Street	D3
Earl Street	D3
East Road	D3-E3-E4
Eden Street	D3
Elizabeth Way	D6-E6-E5-E4
Elm Street	D3
Emery Street	E2
Emmanuel Road	C3-D3
Emmanuel Street	D3
Fair Street	D4
Ferry Path	D5
Fisher Street	B5
Fitzroy Street	D4
Fitzwilliam Street	C2
Free School Lane	B3
French's Road	A6-B6
Garden Walk	B6
George IV Street	D1
George Street	D6
Gilbert Road	C6
Glisson Road	D1-D2-E2
Gonville Place	D2
Grafton Street	D3
Grange Road	A3-A4
Granta Place	B2
Grantchester Street	A1
Grasmere Gdns	B5-C5
Green Street	B3-C3
Green's Road	C5-C6
Gresham Road	D2
Guest Road	E2
Gurney Way	C6-D6
Gwydir Street	E2-E3
Hale Street	B5
Hamilton Road	D5
Hardwick Street	A1
Harvey Goodwin Gardens	B6
Harvey Road	D2
Hawthorn Way	D6
Herbert Street	D6
Hertford Street	B5
High Street	E6
Hilda Street	B5
Hills Road	D1-D2
Histon Road	A5-A6
Hobson Street	C3
Holland Street	B5
Humberstone Road	D5-E5
Huntington Road	A5-A6

Hurst Park Avenue	D6
James Street	D4
Jesus Lane	C4
John Street	D3
Kimberley Road	D5
King's Parade	B3
King Street	C4
Kingston Street	E2
Lady Margaret Road	A4-A5
Lensfield Road	C1-C2-D2
Linden Close	A6
Logans Way	E5
Lower Park Street	C4
Lyndewode Road	D1-E1
Mackenzie Road	E2
Madingley Road	A4
Magdalene Street	B4
Magrath Avenue	B5
Maids Causeway	D4
Malcolm Street	C4
Malting Lane	A2-B2
Manhattan Drive	E5
Manor Street	C4
Market Place	B3-C3
Market Street	B3-C3
Mawson Street	E1-E2
Melbourne Place	D3
Merton Street	A1
Mill Lane	B2
Mill Street	E2
Millington Road	A1
Milton Road	C5-D6
Montague Road	D5-E5
Mortimer Road	D2
Mount Pleasant	A5
Napier Street	E4
Newmarket Road	E4
Newnham Road	A1-B1
Newnham Walk	A2
New Park Street	B4-B5
New Square	D3-D4
New Street	E4
Norfolk Street	E3
Norfolk Terrace	E3
Northampton Street	A4-B4
Norwich Street	C1-D1
Orchard Street	D3
Panton Street	C1
Paradise Street	D3
Park Parade	B4-C4
Parker Street	D3
Parkside Mill Road	D3-D2-E2
Park Street	C4
Park Terrace	C2-C2-D3
Parsonage Street	D4
Pemberton Terrace	C1
Pembroke Street	B2-C2-C3
Pentlands Close	D4-D5-E4
Perowne Street	E2
Petty Cury	C3
Portugal Street	B4-C4
Pound Hill	A4-B4
Pretoria Road	D5
Primrose Street	C5-C6
Priory Road	E4
Priory Street	A6
Prospect Row	D3
Queen's Lane	B2-B3
Queen's Row	B2-A3-A4
Regent Street	C2-D2
Regent Terrace	C2-D2
Ridley Hall Road	A2
Rose Cresent	B3

Russell Street	D1
Sandy Lane	D5-E6
Saxon Street	C1
Scotland Road	E6
Searle Street	B5
Shelly Row	A5
Short Street	D4
Sidgwick Avenue	A2-B2
Sidney Street	C3-C4
Silver Street	B2
Springfield Road	C5-D6
Staffordshire Street	E3
St Andrew's Road	E5
St Andrew's Street	C2-C3
Station Road	D1-E1
St Barnabas Road	E1-E2
St Eligius Street	C1
St John's Road	B4
St John's Street	B4
St Luke's Street	B5
St Matthew's Street	E3-E4
St Paul's Road	D1-D2
St Peter's Street	B5
St Tibbs Row	C3
Stretten Avenue	B6
Sturton Street	E3-E4
Sussex Street	C3-C4
Tennis Court Road	C2
Tenison Avenue	D1-E1
Tenison Road	E1-E2
The Fen Causeway	B1-C1
Thompson's Road	B4-B5
Trafalgar Road	D5
Trafalgar Street	C5-D5
Trinity Lane	B3
Trinity Street	B3-B4
Trumpington Road	C1
Trumpington Street	B2-C2
Union Lane	E6
Union Road	C1-D1
Vicarage Terrace	E3
Victoria Avenue	D4-D5-C5
Victoria Park	B6-C6
Victoria Road	A5-B5-B6-C5
Victoria Street	D3
Warkworth Street	D3
Warkworth Terrace	D3
Wellington Street	E4
Westfield Lane	A5-A6
West Gardens	A2
West Road	A2-A3
Willis Road	E2-E3
Wollaston Road	D2
Wordsworth Grove	A2
AA shop	
Janus House	
46-48 St Andrew's Street	
Cambridge, Cambridgeshire CB2 3BH	C3

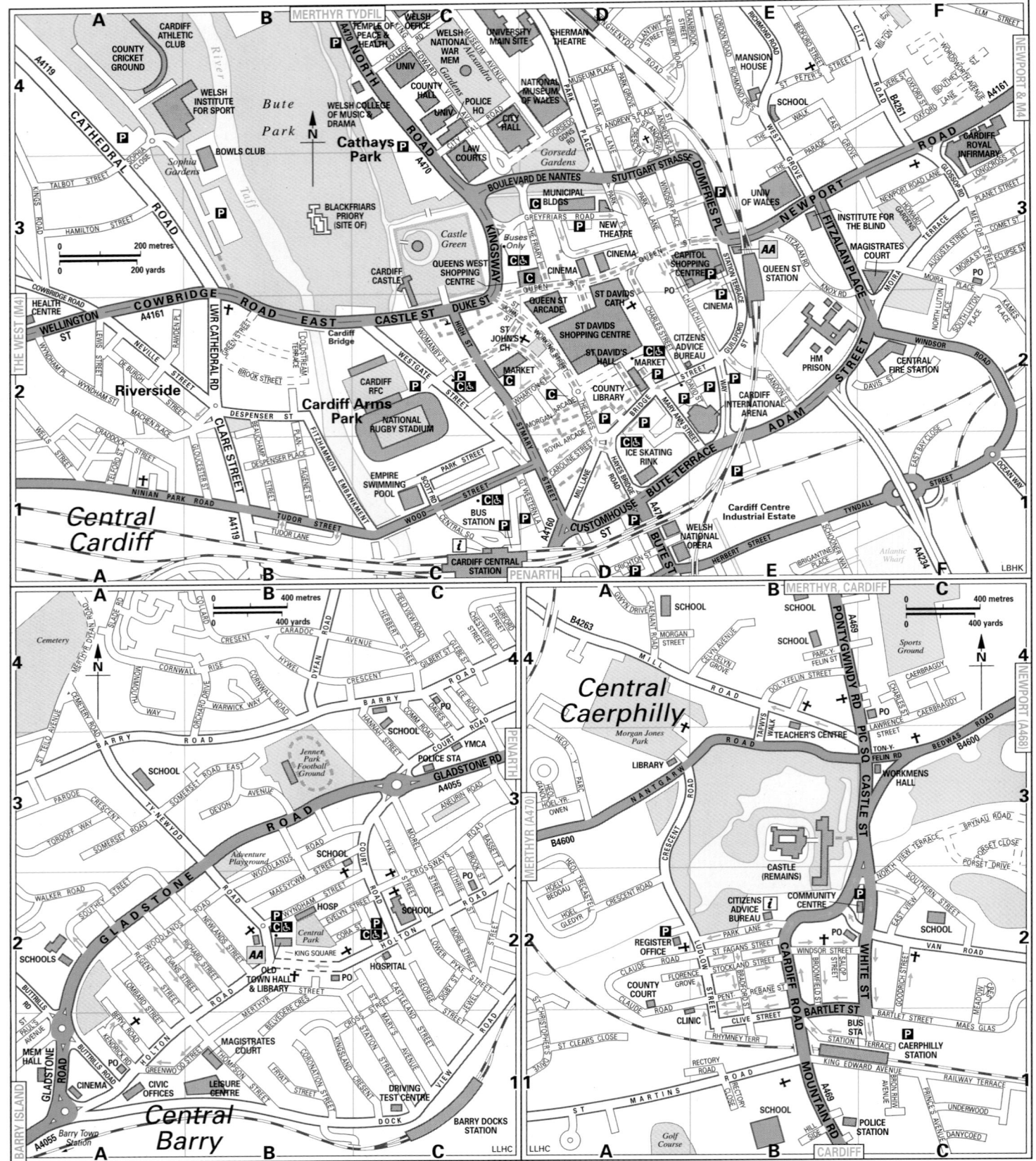

Cardiff

Once strategically important to both the Romans and the Normans, Cardiff declined to the level of a market town until transformed by the Industrial Revolution. Through the coal-mining and iron-smelting industries of the valleys it became a major export centre, and by the end of the 19th century was the world's largest coal-exporting port. Today it is a modern commercial, administrative and tourist centre, with new shopping precincts and a fine concert hall. Close to the famous castle, which encompasses features from the Roman period to the 19th century, is the Civic Centre – a fine range of early 20th-century buildings among which is the National Museum of Wales. In the docklands, an area of considerable redevelopment, is the Welsh Industrial and Maritime Museum, and at Llandaf the 13th-century cathedral contains the magnificent *Christ in Majesty* by Epstein. Cardiff is also the home of Welsh rugby, with the National Stadium at Cardiff Arms Park staging both county and international matches.

Barry Like Cardiff, Barry grew as a result of the demands for coal and iron, but now its dock complex is involved in the petro-chemical and oil industries. Nearby Barry Island, for decades a popular seaside resort for day-trippers, has a sandy beach, entertainment arcades and fun-fairs.

Caerphilly is famous for two things – its castle and its cheese. The cheese is no longer made here commercially but the massive 13th-century castle – slighted by Cromwell – still looms above its moat. With the exception of Windsor, no other castle in Britain is larger.

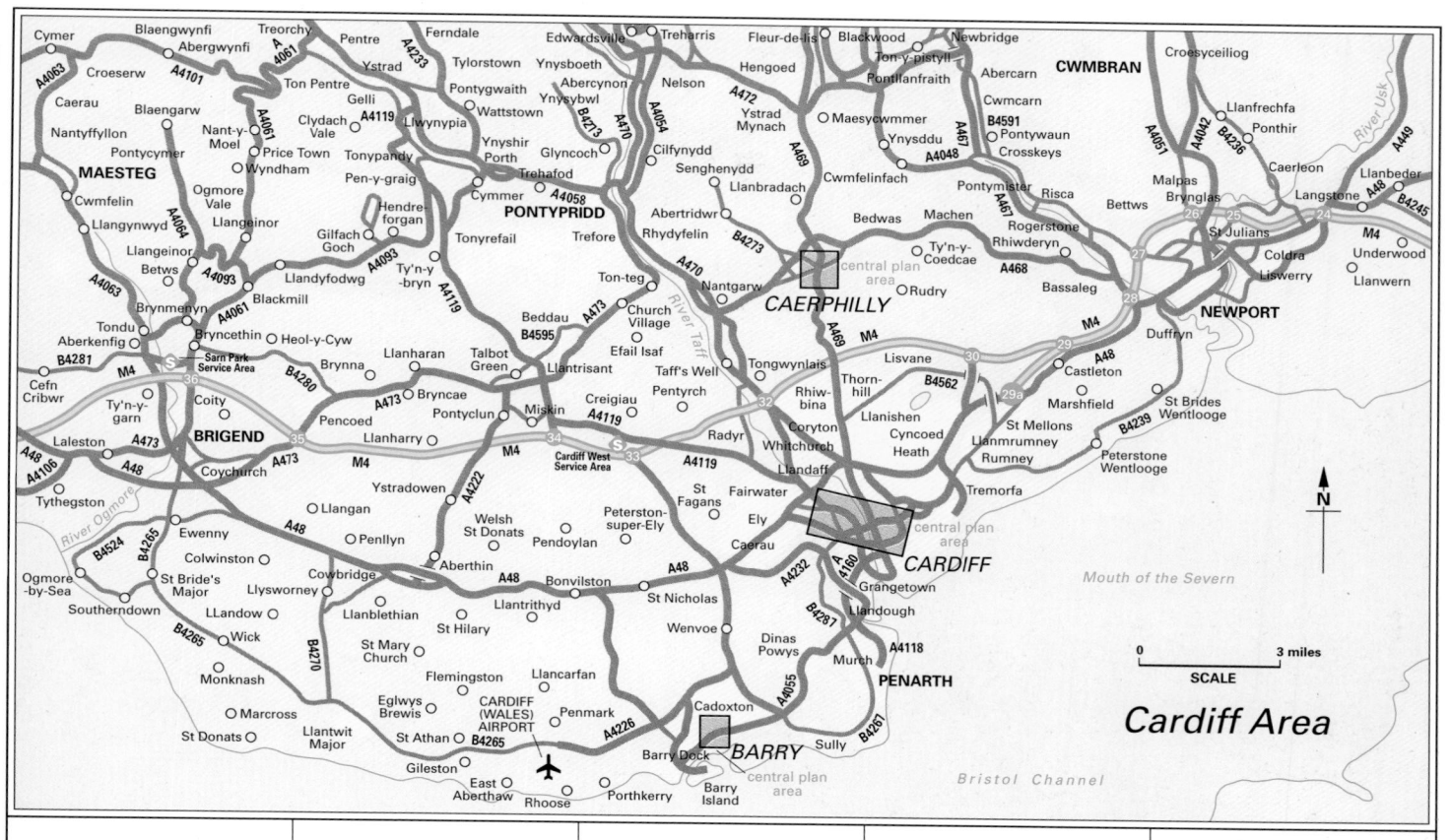

LEGEND

Town Plan

AA Recommended routes	
Restricted roads	
Other roads	
Buildings of interest	COLLEGE
AA Shop/Insurance	AA
Churches	†
Parks and open spaces	
Car parks	P
Toilets	C C
One way streets	←

Area Plan

A roads	
B roads	
Locations	Gileston ○
Urban area	

Street Index with Grid Reference

Cardiff

Adam Street	E1-E2-F2
Augusta Street	F3
Bedford Street	E4
Beauchamp Street	B1-B2
Boulevard de Nantes	C3-D3
Bridge Street	D1-D2-E2
Brigantine Place	E1
Brook Street	B2
Bute Street	D1
Bute Terrace	D1-E1
Caroline Street	D1
Castle Street	C2
Cathedral Street	A4-A3-B3
Central Square	C1
Charles Street	D2-E2
Churchill Way	E2-E3
City Hall Road	C3-C4
City Road	E4-F4
Clare Street	B1-B2
Coldstream Terrace	B2
College Road	C4
Comet Street	F3
Cowbridge Road	A2-A3
Cowbridge Road East	A2-B2-C2
Craddock Street	A1-A2
Cranbrook Street	E4
Crichton Street	D1
Customhouse Street	D1
David Street	D2-E2
Davis Street	F2
De Burgh Street	A2-B1
Despenser Place	B1
Despenser Street	B2
Duke Street	C2
Dumfries Place	E3
East Bay Close	F1-F2
East Grove	E3-F3-E4
Eclipse Street	F3
Elm Street	F4
Fitzalan Place	F2-F3-E3
Fitzalan Road	E3
Fitzhamon Embankment	B1-C1-B2
Glossop Road	F3
Gloucester Street	B1
Gordon Road	E4
Gorsedd Gardens Road	D4
Great Western Lane	D1-C1
Green Street	B2
Greyfriars Road	D3
Guildford Street	E2
Hamilton Street	A3
Hayes Bridge Road	D1
Herbert Street	E1
High Street	C2
Howard Gardens	F3
Kames Place	F2
King Edwards VII Avenue	C3-C4
King's Road	A2-A3
Kingsway	C3
Knox Road	E2-E3
Lewis Street	A2
Llanwit Street	D4
Longcross Street	F3-F4
Lower Cathedral Road	B1
Machen Place	A1-A2
Mary Ann Street	D1-D2-E1-E2
Meteor Street	F3
Mill Lane	D1
Milton Street	F4
Morgan Arcade	D2
Moira Place	F3
Moira Street	F3
Moira Terrace	F2-F3
Museum Avenue	C4-D4
Museum Place	D4
Neville Street	A2-B2
Newport Road	E3-F3-F4
Newport Road Lane	F3
Ninian Park Road	A1-B1
North Luton Place	F2-F3
North Road	B4-C4-C3
Ocean Way	F1
Oxford Lane	F4
Oxford Street	F4
Park Grove	D4
Park Lane	D4-D3
Park Place	D4-D3
Park Street	C1
Planet Street	F3
Plantagenet Street	B1-B2
Queen Street	C2-C3-D3-E3
Rawden Place	A2
Richmond Crescent	E4
Richmond Road	E4
Royal Arcade	D1-D2
St Andrew's Crescent	D3-D4
St Andrew's Lane	D4
St Andrew's Place	D4
St John Street	C2
St Mary's Street	D1-C1
St Peter's Street	E4-F4
Salisbury Road	D4
Sandon Street	E2
Schooner Way	E1
Scott Road	C1
Senghenydd Road	D4
Sophia Close	A3-A4
Southey Street	F4
South Luton Place	F2
Station Terrace	E2-E3
Stuttgart Strasse	D3-E3
The Friary	D3
The Hayes	D2
The Parade	E3-E4-F4
The Walk	E4
Talbot Street	A3
Telford Street	A1
Tressilian Way	D1
Tudor Lane	B1
Tudor Street	B1-C1
Tyndall Street	E1-F1
Vere Street	F4
Wellington Street	A2
Wells Street	A1-A2
Westgate Street	C1-C2
West Grove	E4-E3
Wharton Street	C2-D2
Windsor Place	D3
Windsor Road	F2
Womanby Street	C2
Wood Street	C1-D1
Wordsworth Avenue	F4
Working Street	D2
Wyndham Place	A2
Wyndham Street	A2

Barry

Aneurin Road	C3
Barry Road	A3-B3-B4-C4
Bassett Street	C2-C3
Belvedere Crescent	B1-B2
Beryl Road	A1-A2
Brook Street	C2-C3
Buttrills Road	A1-A2
Caradoc Avenue	B4-C4
Castleland Street	C1-C2
Cemetery Road	A3-A4
Chesterfield Street	C4
Collard Crescent	B4
Commerical Road	C3-C4
Cora Street	B2-C2
Cornwall Rise	A4-B4
Cornwall Road	B4
Coronation Street	B1
Cross Street	B1-C1-C2
Crossways Road	C2-C3
Court Road	C2-C3-C4
Davies Street	C3-C4
Devon Avenue	B3
Digby Street	C2
Dock View Road	B1-C1-C2
Dyfan Road	B4
Evans Street	A2-B2
Evelyn Street	B2-C2
Fairford Street	C4
Field View Road	C4
Fryatt Street	B1
George Street	C1-C2
Gilbert Street	C4
Gladstone Road	A1-A2-B2-B3-C3
Glebe Street	C4
Greenwood Street	A1-B1
Guthrie Street	C3-C2
Hannah Street	C4-C3
Herbert Street	C4

Caerphilly

Holton Road	A1-B1-B2-C2
Hywell Crescent	B4-C4
Jewel Street	C1-C2
Kendrick Road	A1
Kingsland Crescent	B1-C1
Kings Square	B2
Lee Road	C4
Lombard Street	A1-A2
Lower Pyke Street	C2
Maesycwm Street	B2-B3-C3
Merthyr Dyfan Road	A4
Merthyr Street	B1-B2
Monmouth Way	A4
Morel Street	C2-C3
Newlands Street	B2
Orchard Drive	B3-B4
Pardoe Crescent	A3
Pyke Street	C2-C3
Regent Street	A2-B2
Richard Street	A2-B2
St Mary's Avenue	C1-C2
St Pauls Avenue	A1
St Teilo Avenue	A3-A4
Slade Road	A4
Somerset Road	A3
Somerset Road East	A3-B3
Southey Street	A2-A3
Station Street	C1
Thompson Street	B1
Tordoff Way	A4
Ty-Newydd Road	A3-B3-B2
Walker Road	A2
Warwick Way	B4
Woodlands Road	A2-B2-B3-C3
Wyndham Street	B2-C2

Bartlet Street	B2-B1-C1
Bedwas Road	C3-C4
Bradford Street	B1-B2
Broomfield Street	B2
Bronrhiw Avenue	C1
Brynau Road	C3
Caenant Road	A4
Caer Bragdy	C4
Cardiff Road	B1-B2
Castle Street	C3
Celyn Avenue	B4
Celyn Grove	B4
Charles Street	C4
Claude Road	A1-A2-B2
Clive Street	B1-B2
Crescent Road	A2-A3-B3
Danycoed	C1
Dol-y-Felen Street	B4
East View	C2
Florence Grove	A2-B2
Goodrich Street	C1-C2
Gwyn Drive	A4
Heol Ganol	A3
Heol Gledyr	C2
Heol-y-Beddau	A2
Heol-yr-Owen	A3
Heol-y-Parc	A3-A4
Heol-Trecastell	A2-A3
King Edward Avenue	B1-C1
Lawrence Street	C3-C4
Ludlow Street	A2-B2-B1
Maes Glas	C1
Meadow Crescent	C1-C2

Mill Road	A1-A2
Morgan Street	A1
Mountain Road	B2
Nantgarw Road	A1-B1
North View Terrace	B2
Parc-y-Felin Street	C2-C3
Park Lane	B1-C1
Pentrebane Street	B2
Piccadilly Square	B3-B4
Pontgwindy Road	C3
Porset Close	C1
Porset Drive	C2
Prince's Avenue	C2
Railway Terrace	C2
Rectory Road	A4-B4-B3
Rectory Close	A4-B4
Rhymney Terrace	B1
St Christopher's Drive	A3-B3
St Clears Close	C2-C3
St Fagans Street	B4
St Martins Road	B2
Salop Street	B2
Southern Street	C3
Station Terrace	B4-C4
Stockland Street	C3
Tafwy Walk	C2-C3
Ton-y-Felin Road	C1
Underwood	C1
Van Road	A1-B1
White Street	B1
Windsor Street	B1

AA shop	E3

Fanum House
140 Queen Street
Cardiff
South Glamorgan CF1 1QS

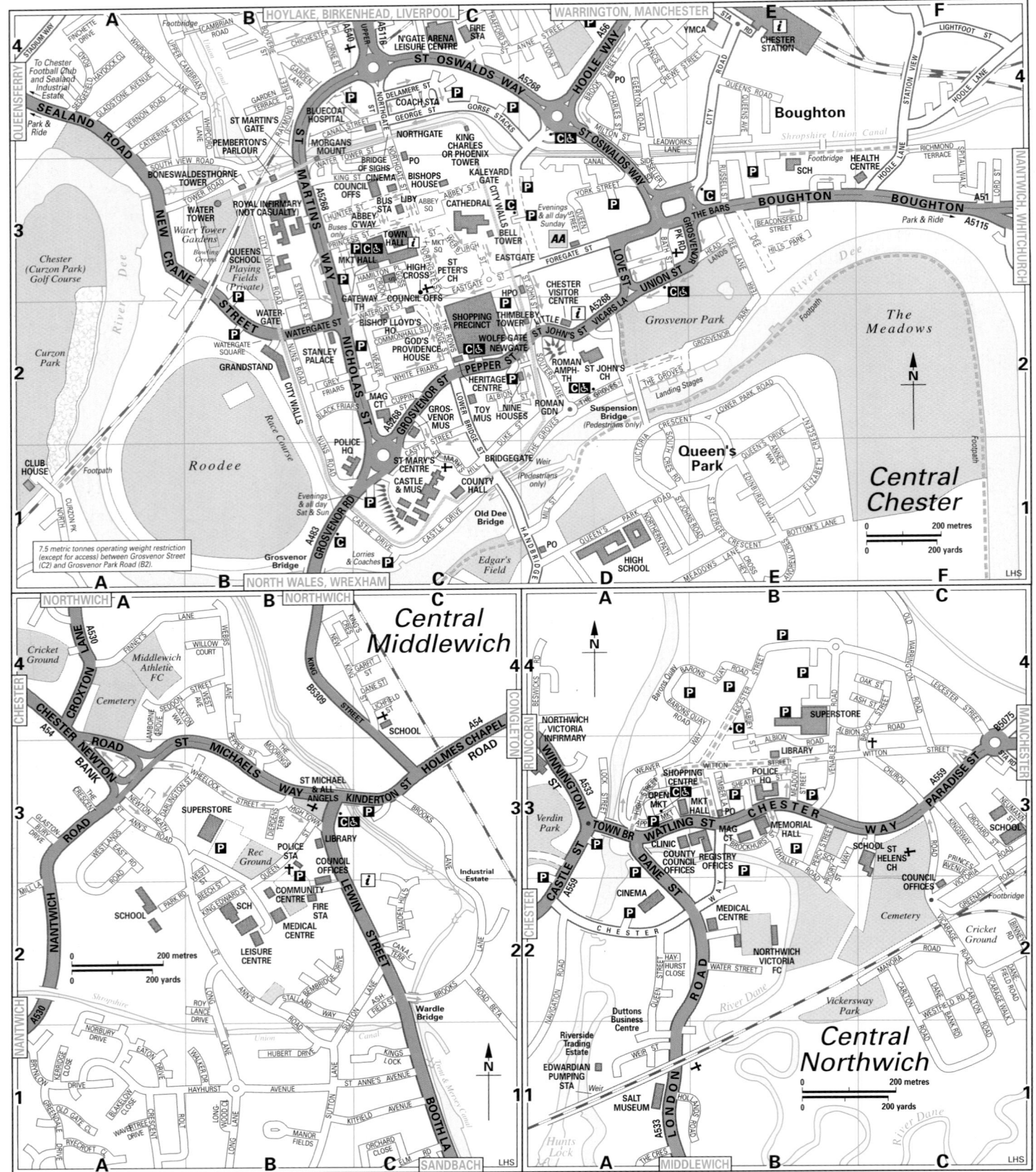

Chester

Chester is the only English city to have preserved the complete circuit of its Roman and medieval walls. On the west side the top of the wall is now at pavement level, but on the other three sides the walk along the ramparts is remarkable. Two of the old watchtowers contain small museums: the Water Tower, built to protect the old river port, displays relics of medieval Chester; King Charles'

Tower, from which Charles I watched the defeat of the Royalist army at the Battle of Rowton Moor in 1645, portrays Chester's role in the Civil War.

Looking down from the top of the Eastgate, crowned with the ornate and gaily coloured Jubilee Clock of 1897, the view of the main street (the old Roman *Via Principalis*) reveals a dazzling display of the black-and-white timbered buildings for which Chester is famous. One of these, Providence House, bears the inscription 'Gods's

Providence is Mine Inheritance', carved in thanks for sparing the survivors of the plague of 1647 that ravaged the city.

On either side of Eastgate, Watergate and Bridge Street are the Rows, a feature unique to Chester and dating back at least to the 13th century. These covered galleries of shops, raised up at first-floor level, protect pedestrians from weather and traffic. Chester's magnificent cathedral is renowned for its beautifully carved choir stalls.

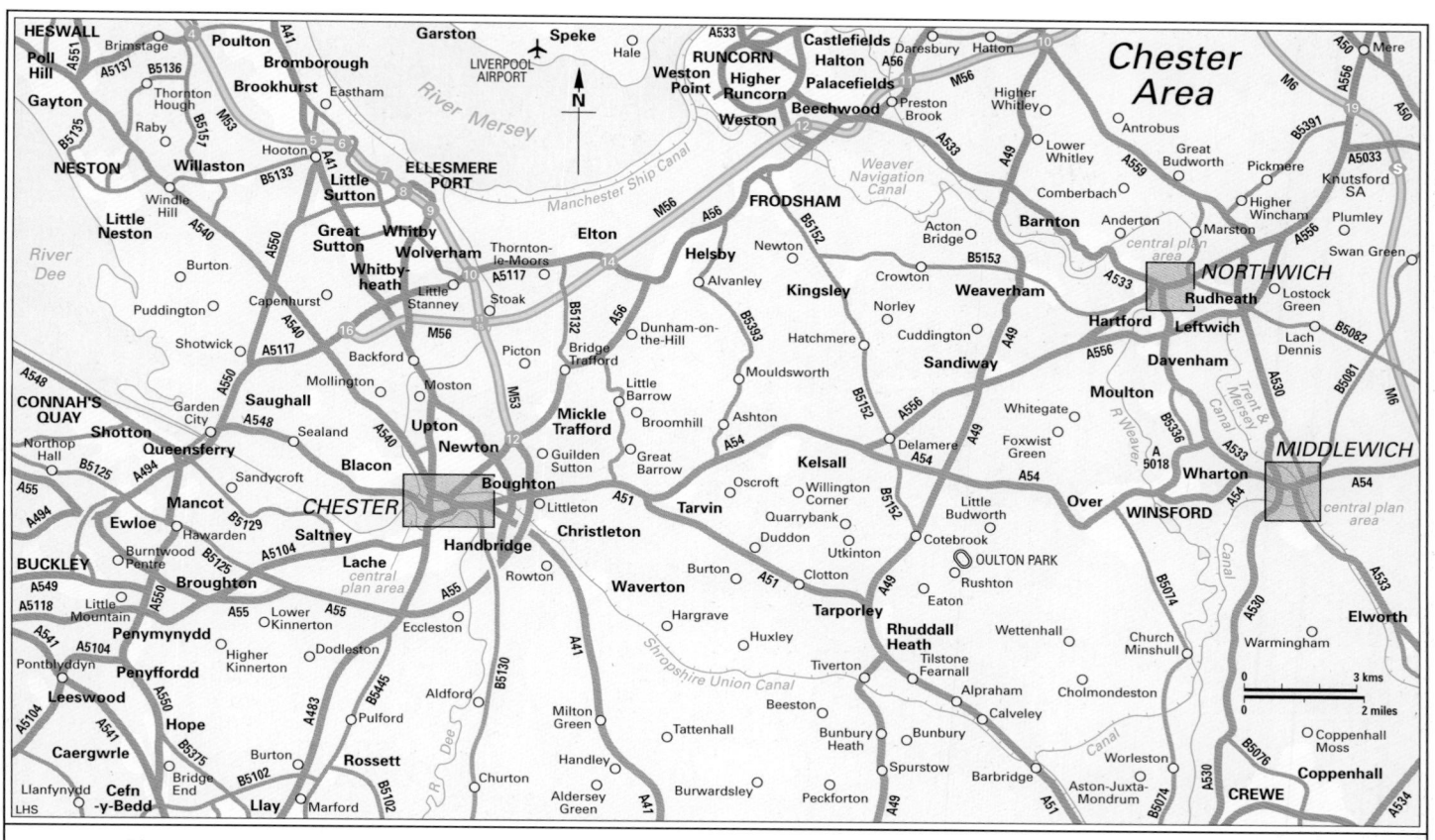

LEGEND

Town Plan

AA Recommended routes	
Restricted roads	
Other roads	
Buildings of interest	COLLEGE
AA Shop/Insurance	AA
Churches	†
Parks and open spaces	
Car parks	P
Toilets	C& C
One way streets	←

Area Plan

A roads	
B roads	
Locations	Yalding ○
Urban area	

Street Index with Grid Reference

Chester

Abbey Square	C3
Abbey Street	C3
Albion Street	C2-D2
Andrew Crescent	E1
Anne's Way	E1
Bath Street	D3
Beaconsfield Street	E3
Black Friars	B2-C2
Bottom's Lane	E1
Boughton	E3-F3
Bouverie Street	B4
Bridge Street	C2
Brook Street	D4
Cambrian Road	A4-B4
Canal Street	B4-C4
Castle Drive	C1
Castle Street	C1-C2
Catherine Street	A4-B4
Charles Street	D4
Chicester Street	B4-C4
City Road	E3-E4
City Walls Road	B3-B2
Commonhall Street	C2
Crewe Street	D4-E4
Crook Street	C3
Cross Heys	E1
Cuppin Street	C2
Curzon Park North	A1
Dee Hills Park	E3
Dee Lane	E3
Delamere Street	C4
Duke Street	C1-D1-D2
Eastgate Street	C2-C3
Edinburgh Way	E1
Egerton Road	D4
Elizabeth Crescent	E1-E2
Finchette Drive	A4
Foregate Street	D3
Forest Street	D3
Francis Street	D3
Frodsham Street	C3-D3
Garden Lane	B4-C4
Garden Terrace	B4
George Street	C4
Gladstone Avenue	A4
Gorse Stacks	C4-D4
Goss Street	C3
Grey Friars	C2
Grosvenor Park Road	D3-E3
Grosvenor Park Terrace	E2-E3
Grosvenor Road	B1-C1
Grosvenor Street	C1-C2
Hamilton Place	C3
Handbridge	C1-D1
Haydock Close	A4
Headlands	E3
Hoole Lane	F3-F4
Hoole Way	D4
Hunter Street	B3-C3
King Street	B3-C3
Leadworks Lane	D4-E4
Lightfoot Street	F4
Lord Street	F3
Lorne Street	B4
Lower Bridge Street	C2-C1
Lower Park Road	E2
Love Street	D3
Lyon Street	D4
Meadows Lane	E1
Mill Street	D1
Milton Street	D4
New Crane Street	A3-B3-B2
Nicholas Street	B2-C2-C1
Northern Path	D1
Nuns Road	B2-B1-C1
Pepper Street	C2-D2
Princess Street	B3-C3
Prince's Avenue	E4
Queen's Avenue	E4
Queen's Drive	E1-E2
Queen's Park Road	D1
Queen's Road	E4
Queen Street	D3
Raymond Street	B3-B4
Richmond Terrace	F4
Russell Street	E3
St Anne Street	C4-D4
St Georges Crescent	E4
St Johns Road	E1
St Johns Street	D2
St John Street	D3-D2
St Martins Way	C4-B4-B3-B2
St Mary's Hill	C1
St Oswalds Way	C4-D4-D3
St Werburgh Street	C3
Sealand Road	A3-A4
Sedgefield Road	A4
Seller Street	D3
Souters Lane	D2
South Crescent Road	D2-D1
South View Road	A3-B3
Spital Walk	F4-F3
Stadium Way	A4
Stanley Street	B3-B2
Station Road	E4
Station View	F4
The Bars	E3
The Groves	C1-D1-D2
The Rows	C2
Tower Road	A3-B3
Trafford Street	C4
Union Street	D2-D3
Upper Cambrian Road	A4-B4
Upper Northgate Street	C4
Vernon Road	C1
Vicars Lane	D2
Victoria Crescent	D1-D2-E2-E1
Walls Avenue	B3
Watergate Street	B2-C2
Water Tower Street	B3-C3-C4
Weaver Street	C2
White Friars	C2
Whipcord Lane	A4-B4
York Street	D3

AA shop
63-65 Foregate Street
Chester CH1 1YZ — D3

Middlewich

Ashfield Street	C2
Beech Street	B2-B3
Bembridge Drive	B2
Beta Road	C2-C1
Blakelow Close	A1
Booth Lane	C1
Brooks Lane	C3-C2
Brynlow Drive	A1
Canal Terrace	C2
Chester Road	A4-A3
Croxton Lane	A4
Darlington Street	A3-B3
Dane Street	C4
Dierdens Terrace	B3
East Road	A3
Eaton Drive	A1
Elm Road	C1
Finney's Lane	A4-B4
Garfit Street	B4-C4
Greendale Drive	A1
Glastonbury Drive	A3
Hayhurst Avenue	A1-B1
High Town	B3
Holmes Chapel Road	C3-C4
Hubert Drive	B1
Kerridge Street	A1
Kinderton Street	B3-C3
King Edward Street	B2
King's Crescent	B4-C4
King's Lock	B1-C1
King Street	B4-C4-C3
Kitfield Avenue	B1-C1
Lamborne Grove	A4
Laxton Way	A4
Lewin Street	B3-B2-C2-C1
Lichfield Street	C4
Long Lane	B1
Longwood Close	B2
Maidon Hills	C2
Manor Fields	B1
Mill Lane	A2
Nantwich Road	A1-A2-A3
New King Street	B4-C4
Newton Bank	A4-A3
Newton Heath	A3
Norbury Drive	A1-A2
Old Gate Close	A1
Orchard Close	C1
Park Road	A2-B2
Pepper Street	B4-B3
Queen Street	B2-B3
Road Beta	C1-C2
Rolt Crescent	A1-B1
Roy Lance Drive	B2
Ryecroft Close	A1
St Anne's Avenue	B1-C1
St Ann's Road	A3-B3-B2-B1
St Ann's Walk	B2-B3
St Michaels Way	A3-B3
Seddon Street	B4
Stallard Way	B2
Sutton Lane	B1-B2-C2
The Crescent	A3
The Moorings	B3
Walker Drive	B1
Wavertree Drive	A1
Webbs Lane	B4
West Avenue	B4
Westlands Road	A3-A2
West Street	B3
Wheelock Street	A3-B3
Willow Court	B4

Northwich

Albion Road	B3-B4-C4
Apple Market	A3
Ash Street	B4-C4
Barons Quay Road	A4-B4
Beswicks Road	A4
Binney Road	C2
Brockhurst Street	B3
Brook Street	B3-C3-C4
Carlton Road	C2-C1
Castle Street	A2-A3
Chester Way	A2-B2-B3-C3
Church Road	C3
Danebank Road	C2-C1
Danefield Road	C2
Dane Street	A3-A2
Greenall Road	C2-C3
Hayhurst Close	A2
High Street	A3
Hollands Road	A1-B1
Kingsway	A3
Leicester Street	B3-B4
Lock Street	A3
London Road	A1-A2-B2
Manora Road	C2
Meadow Street	B3
Navigation Road	A1-A2
Neumann Street	C3
Oak Street	B4-C4
Old Warrington Road	C4-C3
Orchard Street	C3
Paradise Street	B3
Percy Street	C3
Princes Avenue	C3
Priory Street	B2-B3
Queen Street	A2
School Way	B3
Sheath Street	B3
Station Road	C3
The Crescent	A1
Tabley Street	B4-B3
Timber Lane	B3
Town Bridge	A3
Venables Road	B3-B4
Vicarage Road	C2
Vicarage Walk	C2
Victoria Road	C2-C3
Water Street	B2
Watling Street	A3-B3
Weaver Way	A3-B3-B4
Weir Street	A1
Westfield Road	C2
Whalley Road	B3-B2
Winnington Street	A3
Witton Street	B3-C3

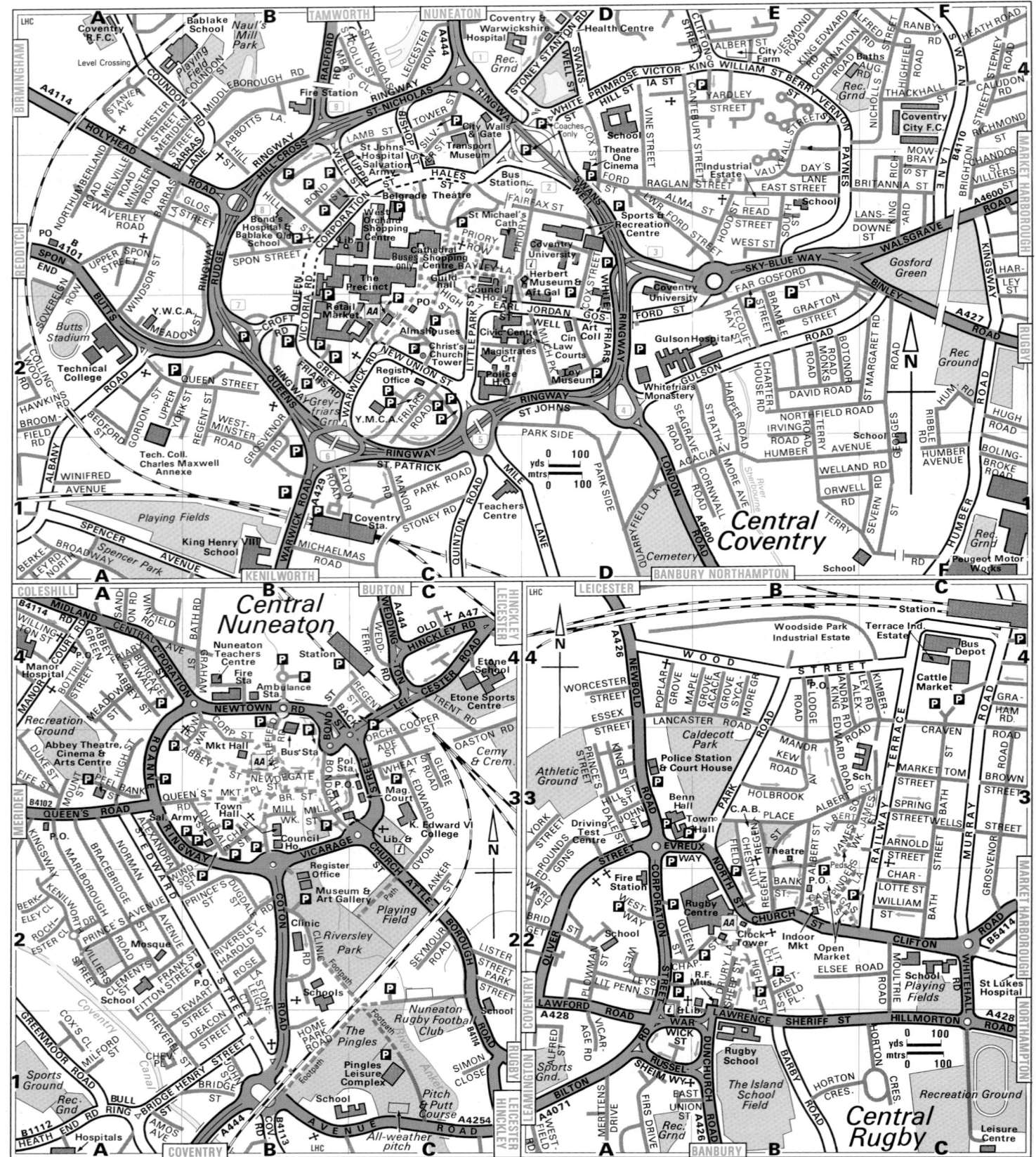

Coventry

Few British towns were as battered by the Blitz as Coventry. A raid in November 1940 flattened most of the city and left the lovely cathedral church a gaunt shell with only the tower and spire still standing. Rebuilding started almost immediately. Symbolising the creation of the new from the ashes of the old is Sir Basil Spence's cathedral, completed in 1962 beside the bombed ruins. A few medieval buildings have survived intact in the city. St Mary's Guildhall is a finely restored 14th-century building with an attractive minstrels' gallery. Whitefriars Monastery now serves as a local museum. The Herbert Art Gallery and Museum has several collections.

Coventry is an important manufacturing centre – most notably for cars – and is blessed with two universities; one in the city centre, and the other, the University of Warwickshire, with its fine campus, some three miles to the south-west.

Nuneaton is an industrial town to the north of Coventry with two distinguished old churches – St Nicholas' and St Mary's. Like Coventry it was badly damaged in the war and its centre has been rebuilt.

Rugby, known world-wide for the sport invented at its famous public school in 1823, was a market town until transformed by the railways into a major junction and industrial centre, currently producing turbines and heavy electrical equipment. The Rugby Football Museum is located in a shop which has manufactured rugby balls ever since the game was introduced.

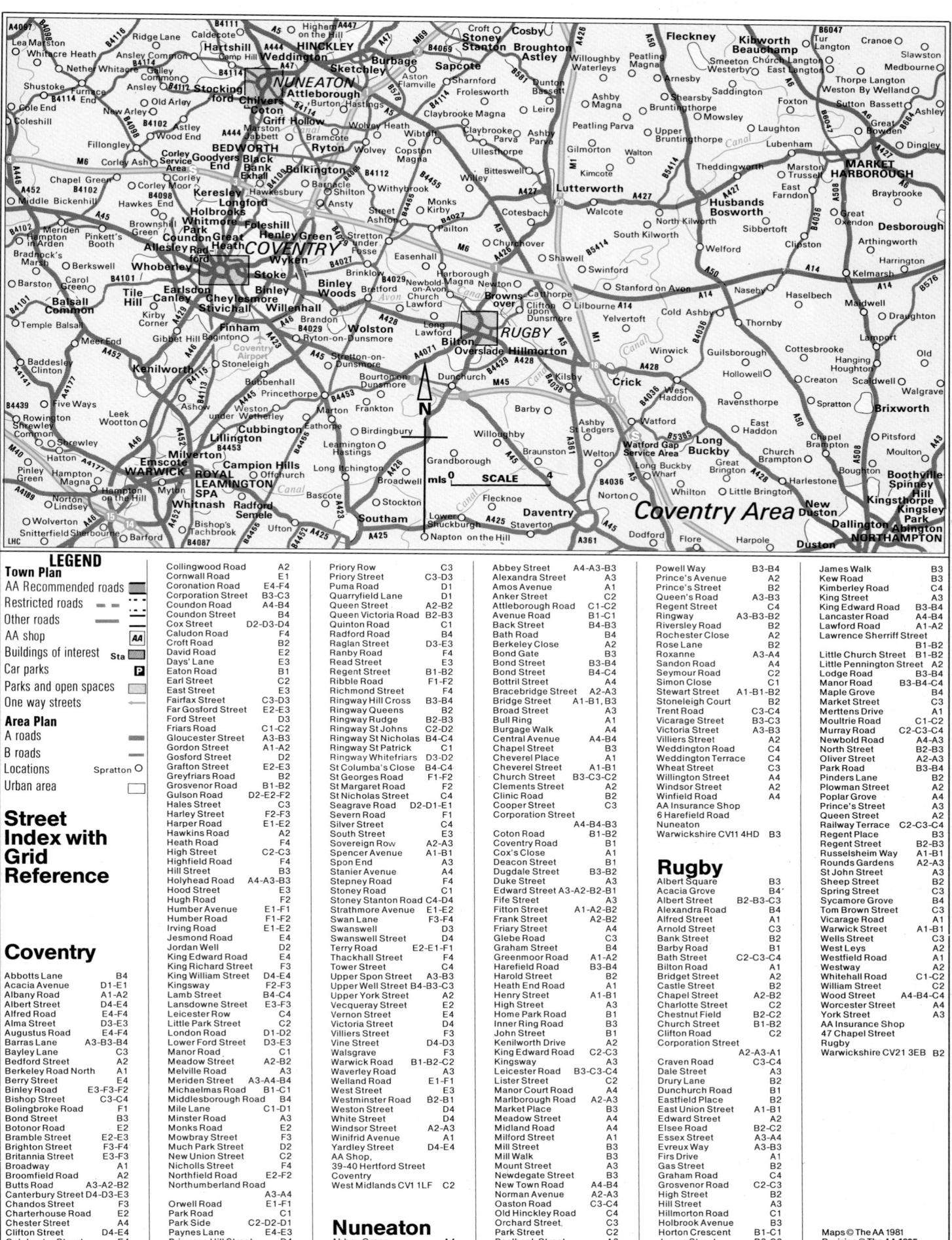

LEGEND

Town Plan

AA Recommended roads
Restricted roads
Other roads
AA shop — AA
Buildings of interest — Sta
Car parks — P
Parks and open spaces
One way streets

Area Plan

A roads
B roads
Locations — Spratton ○
Urban area

Street Index with Grid Reference

Coventry

Abbotts Lane	B4
Acacia Avenue	D1-E1
Albany Road	A1-A2
Albert Street	D4-E4
Alfred Road	E4-F4
Alma Street	D3-E3
Augustus Road	E4-F4
Barras Lane	A3-B3-B4
Bayley Lane	C3
Bedford Street	A2
Berkeley Road North	A1
Berry Street	E4
Binley Road	E3-F3-F2
Bishop Street	C3-C4
Bolingbroke Road	F1
Bond Street	B3
Botoner Road	E2
Bramble Street	E2-E3
Brighton Street	F3-F4
Britannia Street	E3-F3
Broadway	A1
Broomfield Road	A2
Butts Road	A3-A2-B2
Canterbury Street	D4-D3-E3
Chandos Street	F3
Charterhouse Road	E2
Chester Street	A2
Clifton Street	D4-E4
Colchester Street	E4

Collingwood Road	A2
Cornwall Road	E1
Coronation Road	E4-F4
Corporation Street	B3-C3
Coundon Road	A4-B4
Coundon Street	B4
Cox Street	D2-D3-D4
Caludon Road	F4
Croft Road	B2
David Road	E2
Days' Lane	E3
Eaton Road	B1
Earl Street	C2
East Street	E3
Fairfax Street	C3-D3
Far Gosford Street	E2-E3
Ford Street	D3
Friars Road	C1-C2
Gloucester Street	A3-B3
Gordon Street	A1-A2
Gosford Street	D2
Grafton Street	E2-E3
Greyfriars Road	B2
Grosvenor Road	B1-B2
Gulson Road	D2-E2-F2
Hales Street	C3
Harley Street	F2-F3
Harper Road	E1-E2
Hawkins Road	A2
Heath Road	F4
High Street	C2-C3
Highfield Road	F4
Hill Street	B3
Holyhead Road	A4-A3-B3
Hood Street	E3
Hugh Road	F2
Humber Avenue	E1-F1
Humber Road	F1-F2
Irving Road	E1-E2
Jesmond Road	E4
Jordan Well	D2
King Edward Road	E4
King Richard Street	F3
King William Street	D4-E4
Kingsway	F2-F3
Lamb Street	B4-C4
Lansdowne Street	E3-F3
Leicester Row	C4
Little Park Street	C2
London Road	D1-D2
Lower Ford Street	D3-E3
Manor Road	C1
Meadow Street	A2-B2
Melville Road	A3
Meriden Street	A3-A4-B4
Michaelmas Road	B1-C1
Mile Lane	C1-D1
Minster Road	A3
Monks Road	E2
Mowbray Street	F3
Much Park Street	D2
New Union Street	C2
Nicholls Street	E4
Northfield Road	E2-F2
Northumberland Road	A3-A4
Orwell Road	E1-F1
Park Road	C1
Park Side	C2-D2-D1
Paynes Lane	E4-E3
Primrose Hill Street	D4

Priory Row	C3
Priory Street	C3-D3
Puma Road	D1
Quarryfield Lane	D1
Queen Street	A2-B2
Queen Victoria Road	B2-B3
Quinton Road	C1
Radford Road	B4
Raglan Street	D3-E3
Ranby Road	F4
Read Street	E3
Regent Street	B1-B2
Ribble Road	F1-F2
Richmond Street	F4
Ringway Hill Cross	B3-B4
Ringway Queens	B2
Ringway Rudge	B2-B3
Ringway St Johns	C2-D2
Ringway St Nicholas	B4-C4
Ringway St Patrick	C1
Ringway Whitefriars	D3-D2
St Columba's Close	B4-C4
St Georges Road	F1-F2
St Margaret Road	F2
St Nicholas Street	C4
Seagrave Road	D2-D1-E1
Severn Road	F1
Silver Street	C4
South Street	E3
Sovereign Row	A2-A3
Spencer Avenue	A1-B1
Spon End	A3
Stanier Avenue	A4
Stepney Road	F4
Stoney Road	C1
Stoney Stanton Road	C4-D4
Strathmore Avenue	E1-E2
Swan Lane	F3-F4
Swanswell	D3
Swanswell Street	D4
Terry Road	E2-E1-F1
Thackhall Street	F4
Tower Street	C4
Upper Spon Street	A3-B3
Upper Well Street	B4-B3-C3
Upper York Street	A2
Vecqueray Street	E2
Vernon Street	E4
Victoria Street	D4
Villiers Street	F3
Vine Street	D4-D3
Walsgrave	F3
Warwick Road	B1-B2-C2
Waverley Road	A3
Welland Road	E1-F1
West Street	E3
Westminster Road	B2-B1
Weston Street	D4
White Street	D4
Windsor Street	A2-A3
Winifrid Avenue	A1
Yardley Street	D4-E4
AA Shop,	
39-40 Hertford Street	
Coventry	
West Midlands CV1 1LF	C2

Nuneaton

Abbey Green	A4
Abbey Street	A4-A3-B3
Alexandra Street	A3
Amos Avenue	A1
Anker Street	C2
Attleborough Road	C1-C2
Avenue Road	B1-C1
Back Street	B4-B3
Bath Road	B4
Berkeley Close	A2
Bond Gate	B3
Bond Street	B3-B4
Bond Street	B4-C4
Bottril Street	A4
Bracebridge Street	A2-A3
Bridge Street	A1-B1, B3
Broad Street	B3
Bull Ring	A1
Burgage Walk	A4
Central Avenue	A4-B4
Chapel Street	B3
Cheveral Place	A1
Cheverel Street	A1-B1
Church Street	B3-C3-C2
Clements Street	A2
Clinic Road	B2
Cooper Street	C3
Corporation Street	A4-B4-B3
Coton Road	B1-B2
Coventry Road	B1
Cox's Close	A1
Deacon Street	B1
Dugdale Street	B3-B2
Duke Street	B2
Edward Street	A3-A2-B2-B1
Fife Street	A3
Fitton Street	A1-A2-B2
Frank Street	A2-B2
Friary Street	A4
Glebe Road	C3
Graham Street	A4
Greenmoor Road	A1-A2
Harefield Road	B3-B4
Harold Street	B2
Heath End Road	A1
Henry Street	A1-B1
High Street	A3
Home Park Road	B1
Inner Ring Road	B3
John Street	B1
Kenilworth Drive	A2
King Edward Road	C2-C3
Kingsway	A3
Leicester Road	B3-C3-C4
Lister Street	C2
Manor Court Road	A4
Marlborough Road	A2-A3
Market Place	B3
Meadow Street	A3
Midland Road	A4
Milford Street	B3
Mill Street	B3
Mill Walk	B3
Mount Street	A3
Newdegate Street	B3
New Town Road	A4-B4
Norman Avenue	A2-A3
Oaston Road	C3-C4
Old Hinckley Road	C4
Orchard Street	C3
Park Street	C2
Peelbank Street	A3

Powell Way	B3-B4
Prince's Avenue	A2
Prince's Street	B2
Queen's Road	A3-B3
Regent Street	C4
Ringway	A3-B3-B2
Riversley Road	B2
Rochester Close	A2
Rose Lane	B2
Roxanne	A3-A4
Sandon Road	A4
Seymour Road	C2
Simon Close	C1
Stewart Street	A1-B1-B2
Stoneleigh Court	B2
Trent Road	C3-C4
Vicarage Street	B3-C3
Victoria Street	A3-B3
Villiers Street	A2
Weddington Road	C4
Weddington Terrace	C4
Wheat Street	C3
Willington Street	A4
Windsor Street	A2
Winfield Road	A4
AA Insurance Shop	
6 Harefield Road	
Nuneaton	
Warwickshire CV11 4HD	B3

Rugby

Albert Square	B3
Acacia Grove	B4
Albert Street	B2-B3-C3
Alexandra Road	B4
Alfred Street	A1
Arnold Street	C3
Bank Street	B2
Barby Road	B3
Bath Street	C2-C3-C4
Bilton Road	A1
Bridget Street	A2
Castle Street	B2
Chapel Street	A2-B2
Charlotte Street	C2
Chestnut Field	B2-C2
Church Street	B1-B2
Clifton Road	C2
Corporation Street	A2-A3-A1
Craven Road	C3-C4
Dale Street	A3
Drury Lane	B2
Dunchurch Road	B1
Eastfield Place	B2
East Union Street	A1-B1
Edward Street	A2
Elsee Road	B2-C2
Essex Street	A3-A4
Evreux Way	A3-B3
Firs Drive	A1
Gas Street	B2
Graham Road	C4
Grosvenor Road	C2-C3
High Street	A3
Hill Street	A3
Hillmorton Road	C1
Holbrook Avenue	B3
Horton Crescent	B1-C1
James Street	B3-C3

James Walk	B3
Kew Road	B3
Kimberley Road	C4
King Street	B3
King Edward Road	B3-B4
Lancaster Road	A4-B4
Lawford Road	A1-A2
Lawrence Sherriff Street	B1-B2
Little Church Street	B1-B2
Little Pennington Street	A2
Lodge Road	A2
Manor Road	B3-B4-C4
Maple Grove	B4
Market Street	C3
Merttens Drive	A1
Moultrie Road	C1-C2
Murray Road	C2-C3-C4
Newbold Road	A4-A3
North Street	B2-B3
Oliver Street	A2-A3
Park Road	B3-B4
Pinders Lane	B2
Plowman Street	A2
Poplar Grove	A4
Prince's Street	A3
Queen Street	A2
Railway Terrace	C2-C3-C4
Regent Place	B3
Regent Street	B2-B3
Russelsheim Way	A1-B1
Rounds Gardens	A2-A3
St John Street	B2
Sheep Street	B2
Spring Street	C3
Sycamore Grove	B4
Tom Brown Street	C3
Vicarage Road	A1
Warwick Street	A1-B1
Wells Street	C3
West Leys	A2
Westfield Road	A1
Westway	A2
Whitehall Road	C1-C2
William Street	C2
Wood Street	A4-B4-C4
Worcester Street	A4
York Street	A3
AA Insurance Shop	
47 Chapel Street	
Rugby	
Warwickshire CV21 3EB	B2

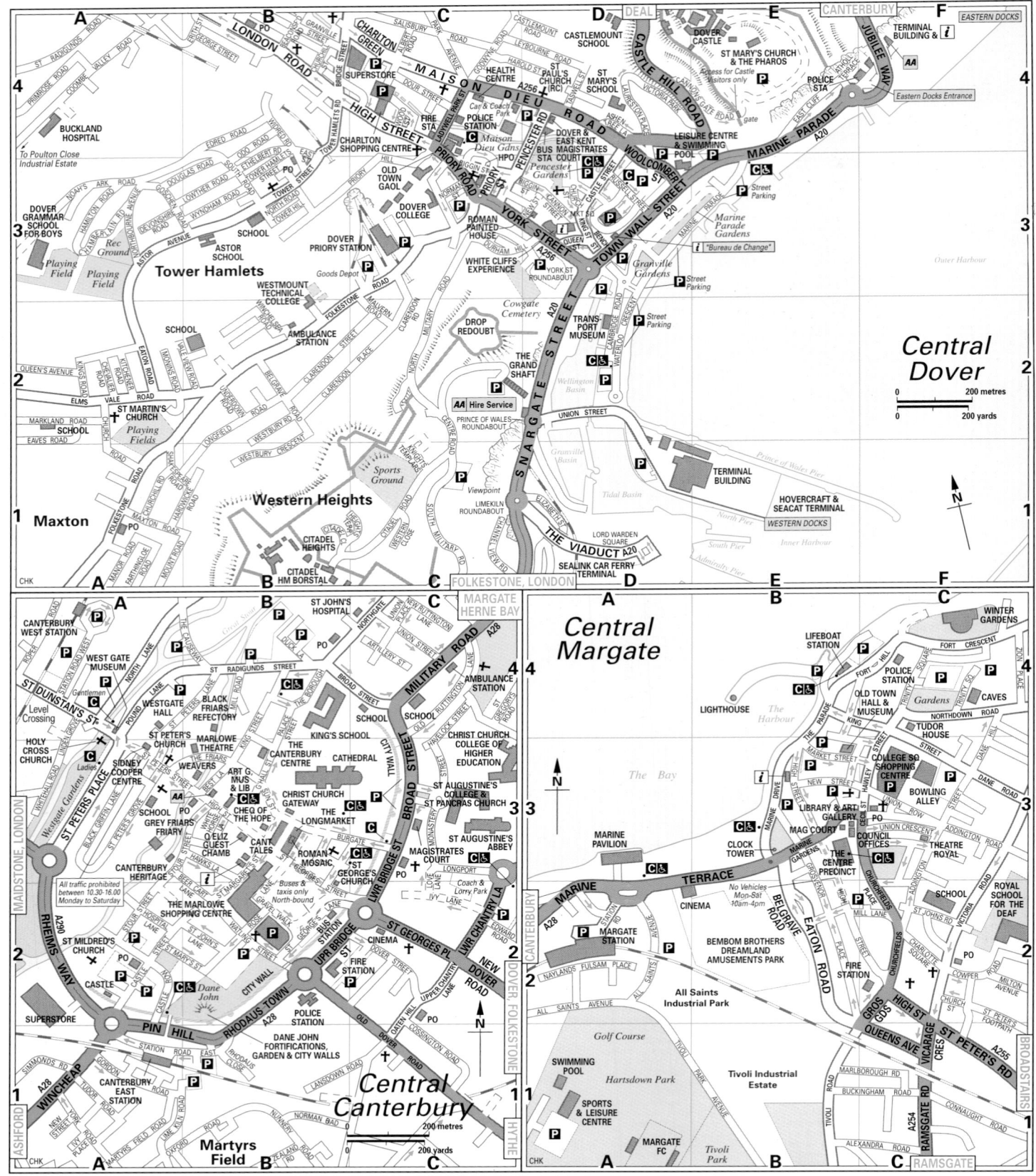

Dover

One of the busiest passenger ports in England, travellers tend to rush through Dover and by so doing miss an exciting town with much of interest. The huge fortifications of the castle have guarded the town since the 12th century, but within its walls are even older structures – a Saxon church and a Roman lighthouse called the Pharos. In the town itself the walls of a 13th-century building, called the Maison Dieu, encircle the Town Hall. The Roman Painted House in New Street consists of the substantial remains of a Roman town house and include the best-preserved Roman wall paintings north of the Alps.

Canterbury is one of Britain's most historic cities. It is the seat of the Church of England, and has been a religious centre since St Augustine began his mission here in the 6th century. The cathedral is a priceless work of art containing many other works of art, including superb displays of medieval carving and stained glass. Partly built on Roman foundations, the ancient city walls still circle parts of Canterbury and a wealth of grand public buildings and charming private houses of many periods line the maze of lanes in the shadow of the cathedral.

Margate was the first seaside resort to introduce bathing machines over 200 years ago, and **Ramsgate**, a commercial port since 1749, once owned the largest fishing fleet on the south coast. Both have safe sandy beaches and good entertainment facilities for holidaymakers.

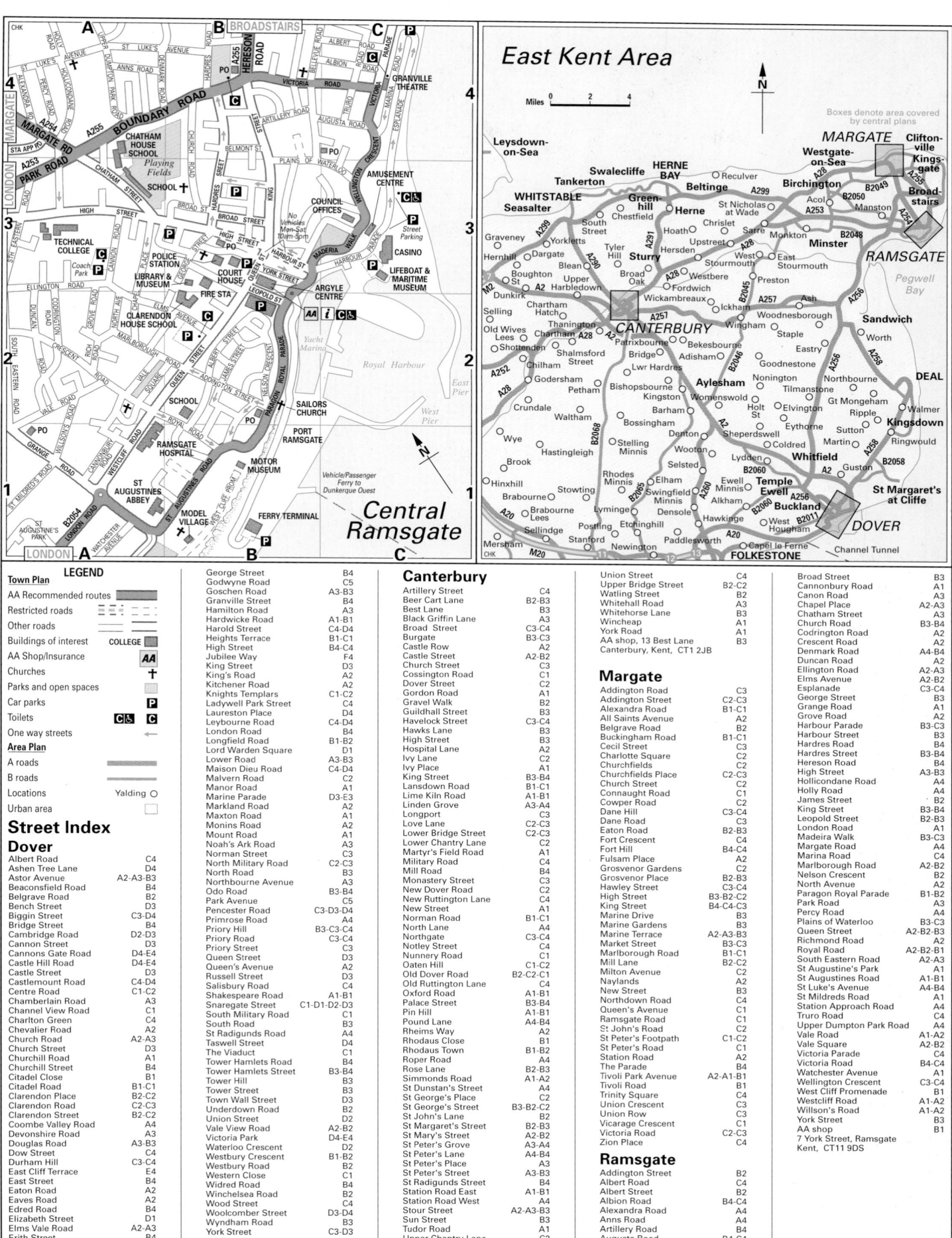

Central Ramsgate

East Kent Area

Miles 0 2 4

N

Boxes denote area covered by central plans

Maps: © The AA 1994
Revision: © The AA 1995

LEGEND

Town Plan

AA Recommended routes
Restricted roads
Other roads
Buildings of interest — COLLEGE
AA Shop/Insurance — *AA*
Churches — †
Parks and open spaces
Car parks — P
Toilets — ♿ ⚹
One way streets

Area Plan

A roads
B roads
Locations — Yalding ○
Urban area

Street Index

Dover

Albert Road	C4
Ashen Tree Lane	D4
Astor Avenue	A2-A3-B3
Beaconsfield Road	B2
Belgrave Road	B2
Bench Street	D3
Biggin Street	C3-D4
Bridge Street	B4
Cambridge Road	D2-D3
Cannon Street	D3
Cannons Gate Road	D4-E4
Castle Hill Road	D4-E4
Castle Street	D3
Castlemount Road	C4-D4
Centre Road	C1-C2
Chamberlain Road	A3
Channel View Road	C1
Charlton Green	C4
Chevalier Road	A2
Church Road	A2-A3
Church Street	D3
Churchill Road	A1
Churchill Street	B4
Citadel Close	C1
Citadel Road	B1-C1
Clarendon Place	B2-C2
Clarendon Road	C2-C3
Clarendon Street	B2-C2
Coombe Valley Road	A4
Devonshire Road	A3
Douglas Road	A3-B3
Dow Street	C4
Durham Hill	C3-C4
East Cliff Terrace	E4
East Street	B4
Eaton Road	A2
Eaves Road	A2
Edred Road	B4
Elizabeth Street	D1
Elms Vale Road	A2-A3
Erith Street	B4
Ethelbert Road	B3-B4
Farthingloe Road	A1
Folkestone Road	A1-A2-B2-C3

George Street	B4
Godwyne Road	C5
Goschen Road	A3-B3
Granville Street	B4
Hamilton Road	A3
Hardwicke Road	A1-B1
Harold Street	C4-D4
Heights Terrace	B1-C1
High Street	B4-C4
Jubilee Way	F4
King Street	D3
King's Road	A2
Kitchener Road	A2
Knights Templars	C1-C2
Ladywell Park Street	C4
Laureston Place	D4
Leybourne Road	C4-D4
London Road	B4
Longfield Road	B1-B2
Lord Warden Square	D1
Lower Road	A3-B3
Maison Dieu Road	C4-D4
Malvern Road	C2
Manor Road	A1
Marine Parade	D3-E3
Markland Road	A2
Maxton Road	A1
Monins Road	A2
Mount Road	A1
Noah's Ark Road	A3
Norman Street	C3
North Military Road	C2-C3
North Road	B3
Northbourne Avenue	A3
Odo Road	B3-B4
Park Avenue	C5
Pencester Road	C3-D3-D4
Primrose Road	A4
Priory Hill	B3-C3-C4
Priory Road	C3-C4
Priory Street	C3
Queen Street	D3
Queen's Avenue	A2
Russell Street	D3
Salisbury Road	C4
Shakespeare Road	A1-B1
Snaregate Street	C1-D1-D2-D3
South Military Road	C1
South Road	B3
St Radigunds Road	A4
Taswell Street	D4
The Viaduct	C1
Tower Hamlets Road	B4
Tower Hamlets Street	B3-B4
Tower Hill	B3
Tower Street	B3
Town Wall Street	D3
Underdown Road	B2
Union Street	D2
Vale View Road	A2-B2
Victoria Park	D4-E4
Waterloo Crescent	D2
Westbury Crescent	B1-B2
Westbury Road	B2
Western Close	C1
Widred Road	B4
Winchelsea Road	B2
Wood Street	B4
Woolcomber Street	D3-D4
Wyndham Road	B3
York Street	C3-D3

AA Port shop
Eastern Dock Terminal
Dover, Kent, CT16 1JA

Canterbury

Artillery Street	C4
Beer Cart Lane	B2-B3
Best Lane	B3
Black Griffin Lane	A3
Broad Street	C3-C4
Burgate	B3-C3
Castle Row	A2
Castle Street	A2-B2
Church Street	C3
Cossington Road	C1
Dover Street	C2
Gordon Road	A1
Gravel Walk	B2
Guildhall Street	B3
Havelock Street	C3-C4
Hawks Lane	B3
High Street	B3
Hospital Lane	A2
Ivy Lane	C2
Ivy Place	A1
King Street	B3-B4
Lansdown Road	B1-C1
Lime Kiln Road	A1-B1
Linden Grove	A3-A4
Longport	C3
Love Lane	C2-C3
Lower Bridge Street	C2-C3
Lower Chantry Lane	C2
Martyr's Field Road	A1
Military Road	C4
Mill Road	B4
Monastery Street	C3
New Dover Road	C2
New Ruttington Lane	C4
New Street	A1
Norman Road	B1-C1
North Lane	A4
Northgate	C3-C4
Notley Street	C4
Nunnery Road	C1
Oaten Hill	C1-C2
Old Dover Road	B2-C2-C1
Old Ruttington Lane	C4
Oxford Road	A1-B1
Palace Street	B3-B4
Pin Hill	A1-B1
Pound Lane	A4-B4
Rheims Way	A2
Rhodaus Close	B1
Rhodaus Town	B1-B2
Roper Road	A4
Rose Lane	B2-B3
Simmonds Road	A1-A2
St Dunstan's Street	A4
St George's Place	C2
St George's Street	B3-B2-C2
St John's Lane	B2
St Margaret's Street	B2-B3
St Mary's Street	A2-B2
St Peter's Grove	A3-A4
St Peter's Lane	A4-B4
St Peter's Place	A3
St Peter's Street	A3-B3
St Radigunds Street	B4
Station Road East	A1-B1
Station Road West	A1
Stour Street	A2-A3-B3
Sun Street	B3
Tudor Road	A1
Upper Chantry Lane	C2
The Borough	B4
The Causeway	B4
The Friars	A3-B3
Union Street	C4
Upper Bridge Street	B2-C2
Watling Street	B2
Whitehall Road	A3
Whitehorse Lane	A3
Wincheap	A1
York Road	A1

AA shop, 13 Best Lane
Canterbury, Kent, CT1 2JB

Margate

Addington Road	C3
Addington Street	C2-C3
Alexandra Road	B1-C1
All Saints Avenue	A2
Belgrave Road	B2
Buckingham Road	B1-C1
Cecil Street	C2
Charlotte Square	C2
Churchfields	C2
Churchfields Place	C2-C3
Church Street	C2
Connaught Road	C1
Cowper Road	C2
Dane Hill	C3-C4
Dane Road	B2-B3
Eaton Road	C4
Fort Crescent	C4
Fort Hill	B4-C4
Fulsam Place	A2
Grosvenor Gardens	C2
Grosvenor Place	B2-B3
Hawley Street	C3-C4
High Street	B3-B2-C2
King Street	B4-C4-C3
Marine Drive	B3
Marine Gardens	C3
Marine Terrace	A2-A3-B3
Market Street	B3-C3
Marlborough Road	B1-C1
Mill Lane	B2-C2
Milton Avenue	A2
Naylands	A2
New Street	B3
Northdown Road	C4
Queen's Avenue	C1
Ramsgate Road	C1
St John's Road	C2
St Peter's Footpath	C1-C2
St Peter's Road	C1
Station Road	A2
The Parade	B4
Tivoli Park Avenue	A2-A1-B1
Tivoli Road	B1
Trinity Square	C4
Union Crescent	C3
Union Row	C3
Vicarage Crescent	C1
Victoria Road	C2-C3
Zion Place	C4

Ramsgate

Addington Street	B2
Albert Road	C4
Albert Street	B2
Albion Road	B4-C4
Alexandra Road	A4
Anns Road	A4
Artillery Road	B4
Augusta Road	B4-C4
Bellevue Road	B4
Belmont Street	B4
Boundary Road	A4-B4
Broad Street	B3
Cannonbury Road	A1
Canon Road	A3
Chapel Place	A2-A3
Chatham Street	A3
Church Road	B3-B4
Codrington Road	A2
Crescent Road	A2
Denmark Road	A4-B4
Duncan Road	A2
Ellington Road	A2-A3
Elms Avenue	A2-B2
Esplanade	C3-C4
George Street	B3
Grange Road	A1
Grove Road	A2
Harbour Parade	B3-C3
Harbour Street	B3
Hardres Road	B4
Hardres Street	B3-B4
Hereson Road	B4
High Street	A3-B3
Hollicondane Road	A4
Holly Road	A4
James Street	B2
King Street	B3-B4
Leopold Street	B2-B3
London Road	A1
Madeira Walk	B3-C3
Margate Road	A4
Marina Road	C4
Marlborough Road	A2-B2
Nelson Crescent	B2
North Avenue	A2
Paragon Royal Parade	B1-B2
Park Road	A3
Percy Road	A4
Plains of Waterloo	B3-C3
Queen Street	A2-B2-B3
Richmond Road	A2
Royal Road	A2-B2-B1
South Eastern Road	A2-A3
St Augustine's Park	A1
St Augustines Road	A1-B1
St Luke's Avenue	A4-B4
St Mildreds Road	A1
Station Approach Road	A4
Truro Road	C4
Upper Dumpton Park Road	A4
Vale Road	A1-A2
Vale Square	A2-B2
Victoria Parade	C4
Victoria Road	B4-C4
Watchester Avenue	A1
Wellington Crescent	C3-C4
West Cliff Promenade	B1
Westcliff Road	A1-A2
Willson's Road	A1-A2
York Street	B3

AA shop
7 York Street, Ramsgate
Kent, CT11 9DS

215

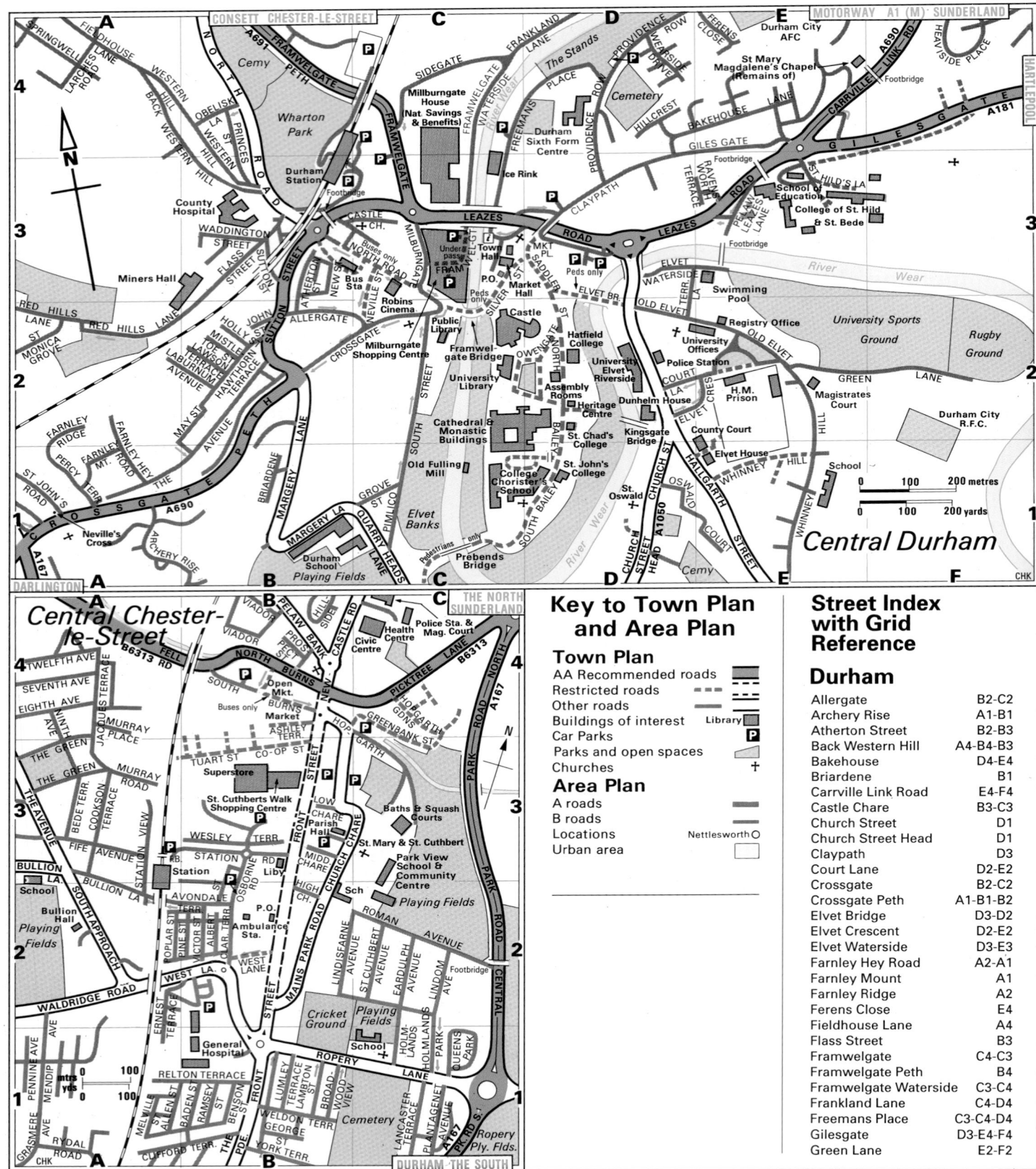

Central Durham

Key to Town Plan and Area Plan

Town Plan

AA Recommended roads	
Restricted roads	
Other roads	
Buildings of interest	Library
Car Parks	P
Parks and open spaces	
Churches	+

Area Plan

A roads	
B roads	
Locations	Nettlesworth ○
Urban area	

Central Chester-le-Street

Street Index with Grid Reference

Durham

Durham

The castle and the cathedral stand side by side high above the city like sentinels, dramatically symbolising the military and religious power Durham wielded in the past. Its origins date from about 995, when the remains of St Cuthbert arrived from Lindisfarne and his shrine became a popular centre of pilgrimage. Soon after that early fortifications were built, later replaced by a stone castle which became the residence of the Prince-Bishop of Durham – powerful feudal rulers appointed by the king. Today the city's university, the oldest in England after Oxford and Cambridge, occupies the castle and most of the buildings around the peaceful, secluded Palace Green. The splendid Norman cathedral, sited on the other side of the green, is considered to be one of the finest in Eurpoe. Its combination of strength and size, tempered with grace and beauty, is awe-inspiring.

Under the shadow of these giants the old city streets, known as vennels, ramble down the bluff past the 17th-century Bishop Cosin's House and the old grammar school, to the thickly wooded banks of the Wear. Here three historic bridges link the city's heart with the pleasant Georgian suburbs on the other side of the river.

Although Durham is not an industrial city, it has become the venue for the North-East Miners' annual Gala Day in July.

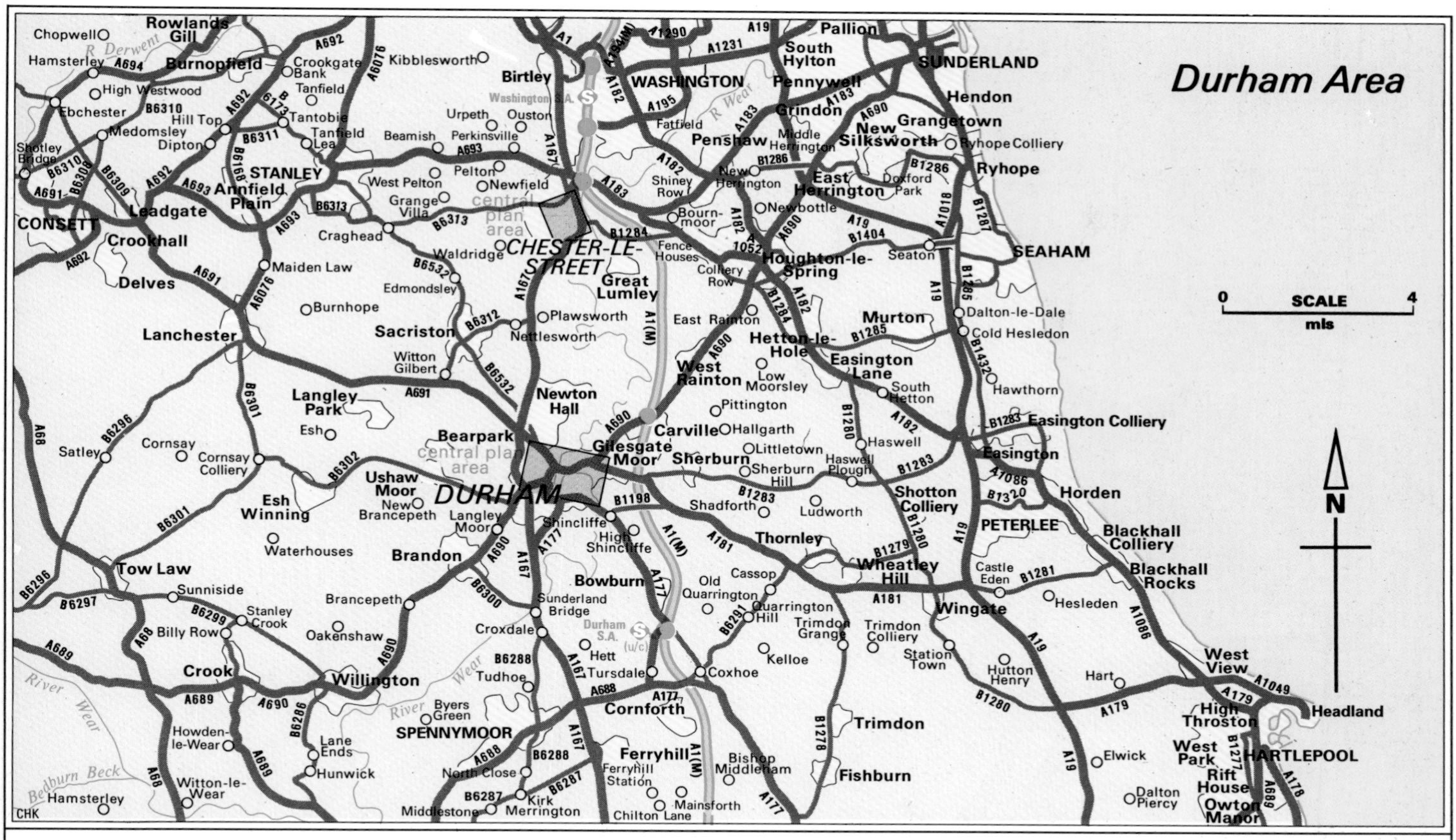

Durham Area

Grove Street	C1
Hallgarth Street	D1-E1
Hawthorn Terrace	B2
Heaviside Place	F4
Hillcrest	D4
Holly Street	B2
John Street	B2
Laburnum Street	A2-B2
Larches Road	A4
Lawson Terrace	B2
Leazes Road	C3-D3-E3
Margery Lane	B1-B2
Market Place	C3-D3
May Street	A2-B2
Milburngate	C3
Mistletoe Street	B2
New Elvet	D3-D2
New Street	B3
Neville Street	C2-C3
North Bailey	D1-D2
North Road	B4-B3-C3-C2
Obelisk Lane	B4
Old Elvet	D2-E2
Owengate	C2-D2
Oswald Court	D1-E1
Pelaw Leazes Lane	E3
Percy Terrace	A1
Pimlico	C1
Princes Street	B4-B3
Providence Row	D3-D4
Quarry Heads Lane	C1
Ravensworth Terrace	E3
Red Hills Lane	A2-B2
St Hild's Lane	E3
St John's Road	A1
St Monica Grove	A2

Saddler Street	D3-D2
Sidegate	C4
Silver Street	C2-C3
South Bailey	C1-D1
South Street	C1-C2
Springwell	A4
Sutton Street	B2-B3
Territorial Lane	D2-D3
The Avenue	A1-B1-B2
Waddington Street	B3
Wearside Drive	D4
Western Hill	A4-B4-B3
Whinney Hill	E1-E2

Chester-le-Street

Albert Street	B2-B3
Allen Street	A1
Ashley Terrace	B4
Avondale Terrace	A2-B2
Baden Street	B1
Bede Street	A3
Benson Street	B1
Broadwood View	B1
Bullion Lane	A3-A2
Church Chare	B2-B3-C3
Clarence Terrace	B2
Clifford Terrace	A1-B1
Cookson Terrace	A3
Co-operative Street	B3
Eardulph Street	C2
Eigth Avenue	A4
Ernest Terrace	A1-A2
Fell Road	A4-B4
Fife Avenue	A3
Front Street	B1-B2-B3-B4

George Street	B1
Grasmere Avenue	A1
Greenbank Street	C4-C3
High Chare	B2
Hillside	B4
Holmlands	C1-C2
Holmlands Park	C1-C2
Hopgarth	B4-C4-C3
Hopgarth Gardens	C4
Jacques Terrace	A3-A4
Lambton Street	B1
Lancaster Terrace	C1
Lindisfarne Avenue	B2
Lindom Avenue	C2
Low Chare	B3
Lumley Terrace	B1
Mains Park Road	B2
Melville Street	A1
Mendip Avenue	A1-A2
Middle Chare	B3
Murray Place	A4
Murray Road	A3
Newcastle Road	B4-C4
Ninth Avenue	A4-A3
North Burns	B4
Osborne Road	B2-B3
Park Road Central	C3-C2-C1
Park Road North	C3-C4
Park Road South	C1
Pelaw Bank	B4
Penine Avenue	A1
Picktree Lane	B4-C4
Pine Street	B2
Plantaganet Avenue	C1
Poplar Street	A2
Prospect Street	B4

Queens Park	C1
Ramsey Street	B1
Relton Terrace	A1-B1
Roman Avenue	C2
Ropery Lane	B1-C1
Rydal Road	A1
St Cuthbert Avenue	C2
Seventh Avenue	A4
South Approach	A3-A2
South Burns	B4
Station Road	B3
Station View	A2-A3
The Avenue	A3
The Green	A3-A4
The Parade	B1
Tuart Street	B3
Twelth Avenue	A4
Viador	B4
Victor Street	B2
Waldridge Road	A2
Weldon Terrace	B1
Wesley Terrace	B3
West Lane	A2-B2
York Terrace	B1

DURHAM
High above the wooded banks of the River Wear, Durham's castle and cathedral crown the steep hill on which the city is built. They share the site with several of the university's attractive old buildings.

217

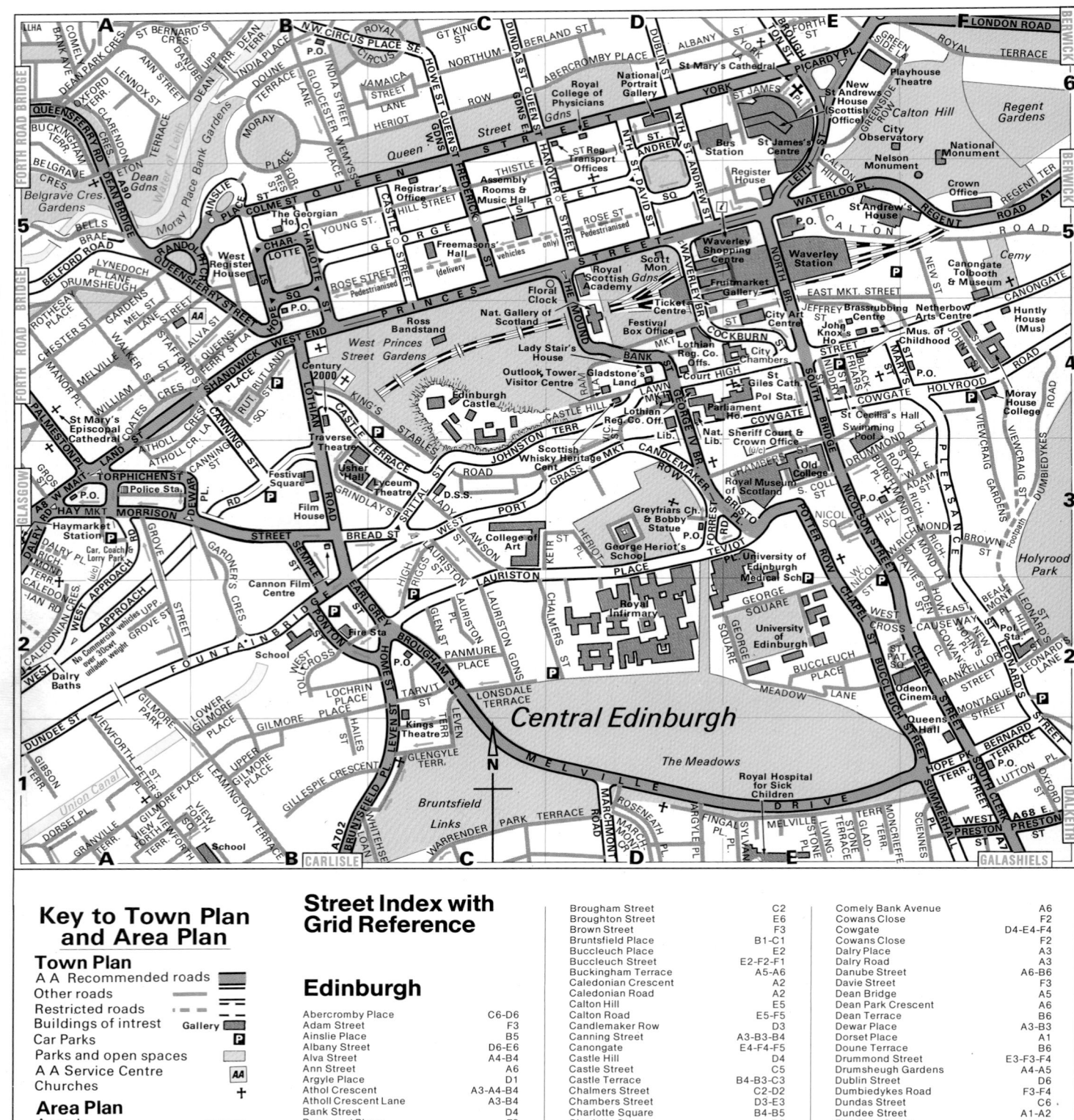

Key to Town Plan and Area Plan

Town Plan

A A Recommended roads	
Other roads	
Restricted roads	
Buildings of intrest	Gallery
Car Parks	P
Parks and open spaces	
A A Service Centre	AA
Churches	+

Area Plan

A roads	
B roads	
Locations	Newcraighall O
Urban area	

Street Index with Grid Reference

Edinburgh

Edinburgh

Dubbed the 'Athens of the North', Scotland's ancient capital is one of the most splendid cities in the whole of Europe. Its buildings, history and cultural life give it an international importance which is celebrated every year in the world-famous festival. The whole city is overshadowed by the craggy castle which seems to grow out of the rock itself. There has been a fortress here since the 7th century and most of the great figures of Scottish history have been associated with it. The old town grew up around the base of Castle Rock, within the boundaries of the defensive King's Wall; unable to spread outwards, the town grew upwards in a maze of tenements. However, during the 18th century new prosperity from the shipping trade resulted in the building of the New Town, and the regular, spacious layout of the Georgian development makes a striking contrast with the hotch-potch of streets of the old quarter. Princes Street is the main east–west thoroughfare, with shops on one side and Princes Street Gardens, with their famous floral clock, on the south side.

As befits such a splendid capital city there are numerous museums and art galleries packed with priceless treasures. Among these are the famous picture gallery in 16th-century Holyrood Palace (the present Royal Palace) and the fascinating and unusual Museum of Childhood.

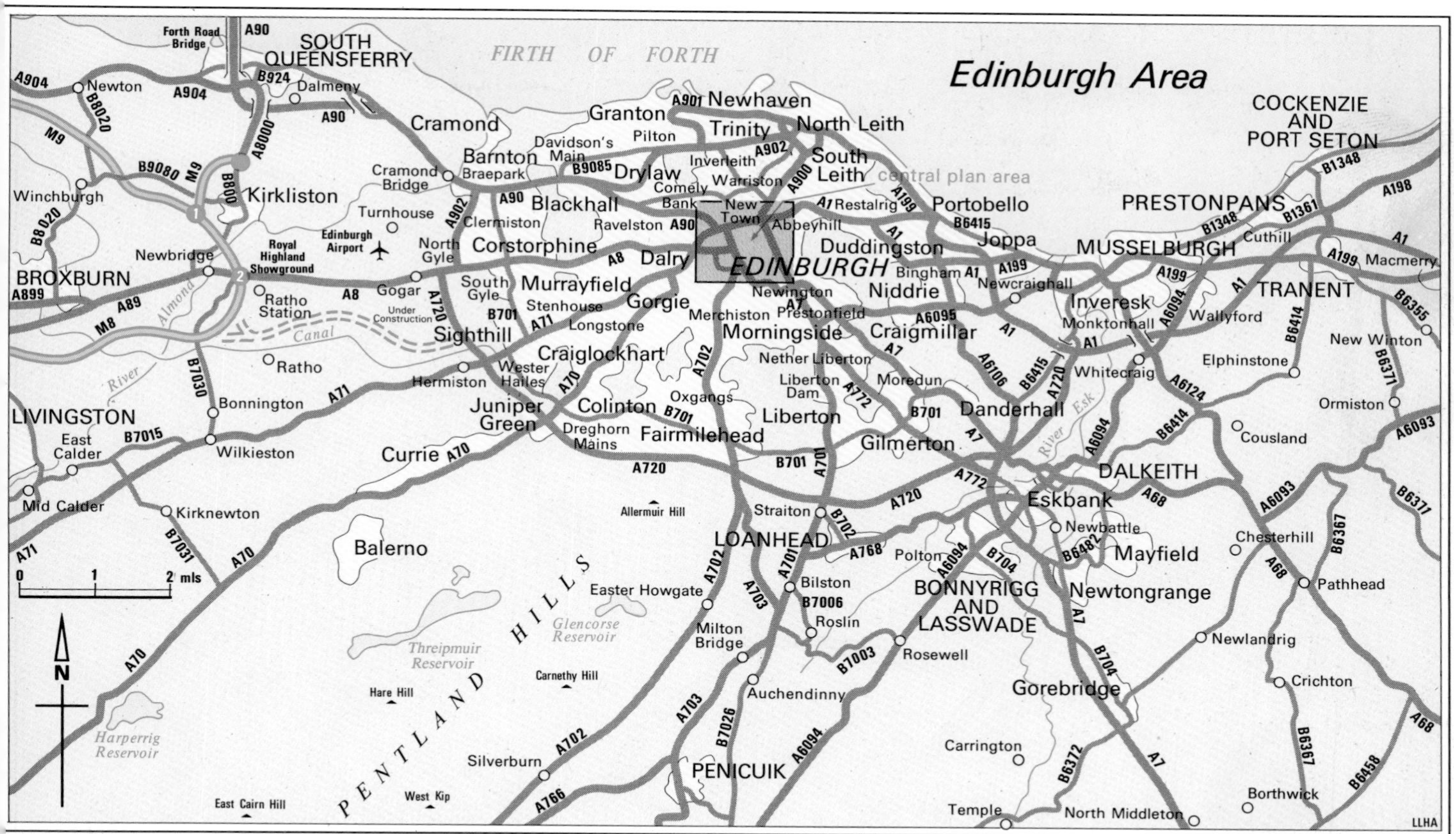

Edinburgh Area

COCKENZIE AND PORT SETON

PRESTONPANS

MUSSELBURGH

TRANENT

DALKEITH

EDINBURGH

LLHA

Maps: © The Automobile Association 1981
Revision: © The Automobile Association 1995

EDINBURGH
Holyrood Palace orginated as a guest house for the Abbey of Holyrood in the 16th century, but most of the present building was built for Charles II. Mary Queen of Scots was one of its most famous inhabitants.

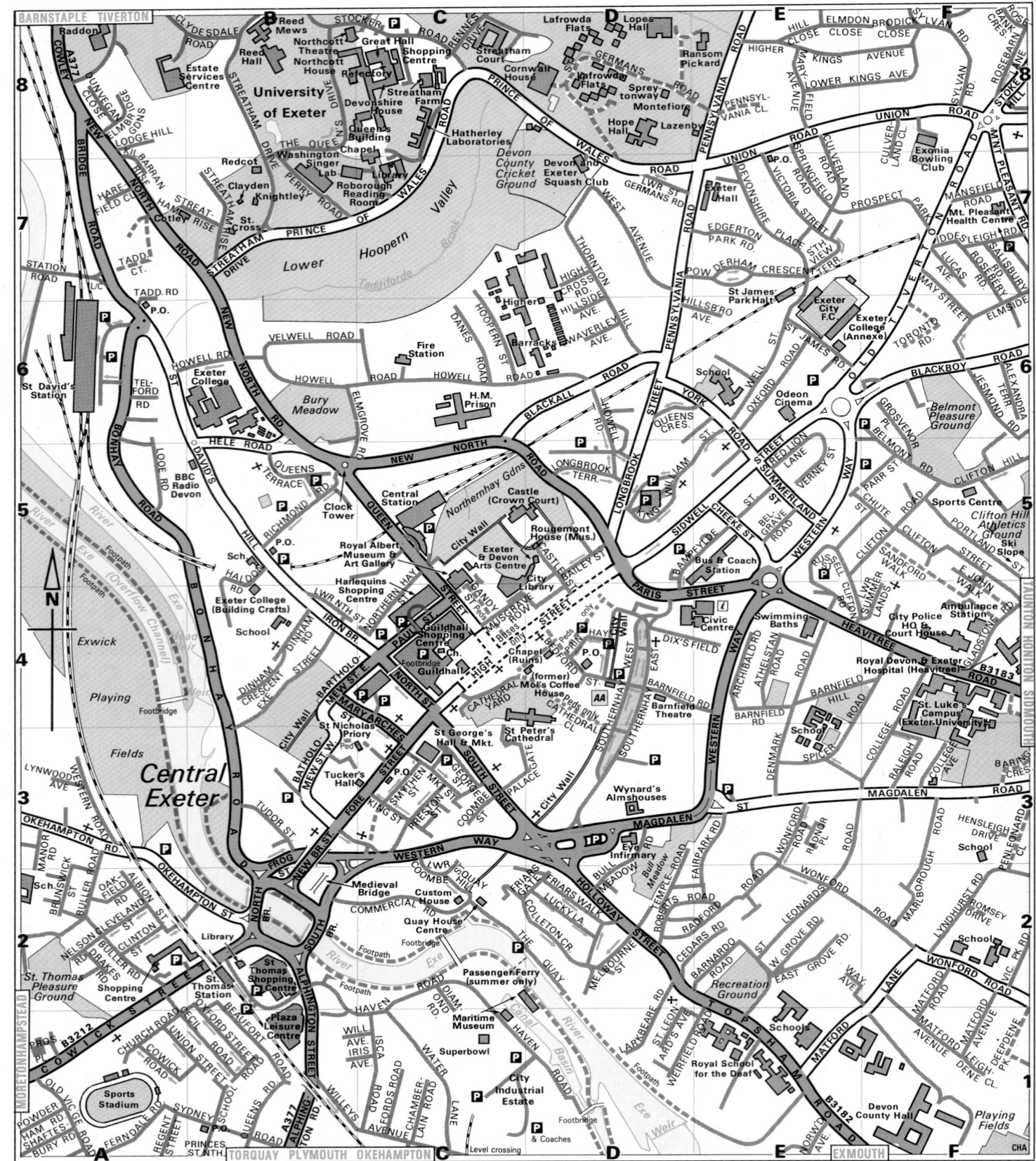

Exeter

The cathedral is Exeter's greatest treasure. Founded in 1050, but rebuilt by the Normans during the 12th century and again at the end of the 13th century, it has many beautiful and outstanding features – especially the exquisite rib-vaulting of the nave. Perhaps most remarkable is the fact that it remained intact while much around it was flattened during the bombing raids of World War II.

There are still plenty of reminders of Old Exeter: Roman and medieval walls encircle parts of the city; 14th-century underground passages can be explored; the Guildhall is 15th-century; and Sir Francis Drake is said to have met his explorer companions at Mol's Coffee House. Of the city's ancient churches the most interesting are St Mary Steps, St Mary Arches and St Martin's. The extensive Maritime Museum has over 100 boats from all over the world. Other museums include the Rougemont House, the Devonshire Regiment and the Royal Albert Museum and Art Gallery.

Exmouth has a near-perfect position at the mouth of the Exe estuary. On one side it has expanses of sandy beach, on another a wide estuary alive with wildfowl and small boats, and inland is beautiful Devon countryside.

Honiton is famous for traditional hand-made lace and pottery, which can still be bought in the busy town.

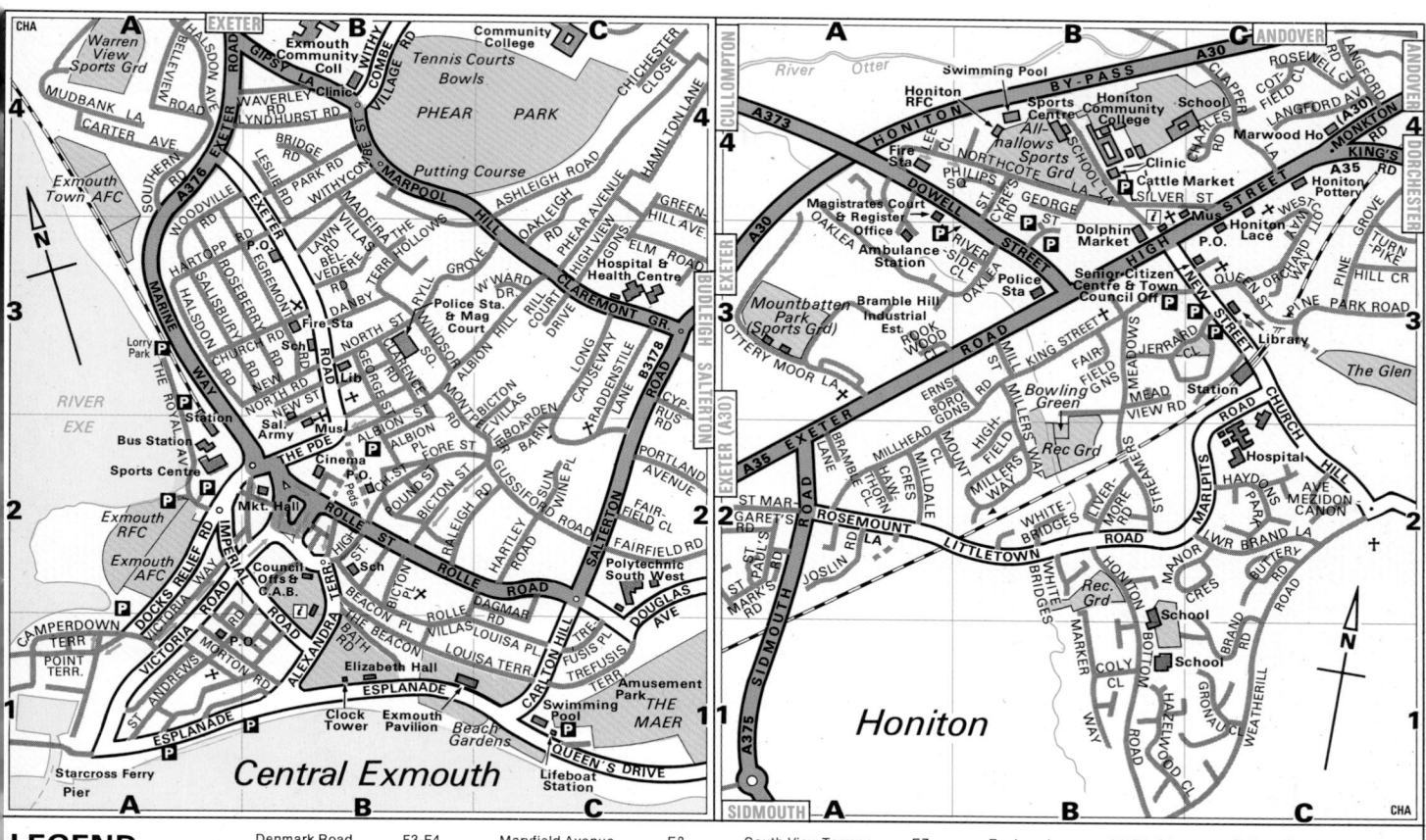

LEGEND

- AA Recommended roads
- Other roads
- Restricted roads
- Buildings of interest
- Churches †
- Car parks ℗
- Parks, open spaces
- One way streets
- AA shop 🅰🅰

Exeter

Albion Street	A2
Alexandra Terrace	F6
Alphington Road	B1
Alphington Street	B1-B2
Archibald Road	E4
Athelstan Road	E4
Bailey Street	D5
Bampfylde Street	D4-D5-E5
Baring Crescent	F3
Barnado Road	E2
Barnfield Hill	E4-F4
Barnfield Road	D4-E4
Bartholomew St. East	B4-C4
Bartholomew St. West	B3
Bedford Street	D4
Belgrave Road	F5
Belmont Road	F6-F5
Blackall Road	C6-D6
Blackboy Road	F6
Bonhay Road	A5-B4-B3
Brodick Close	F8
Brunswick Street	B4
Buller Road	A2-A3
Bull Meadow Road	D2
Castle Street	D5
Cathedral Close	D4
Cathedral Yard	D4
Cecil Road	A1-B1
Cedars Road	E2
Chamberlain Road	C1
Cheeke Street	E5
Church Road	A1-A2-B2
Chute Street	E5-F5
Clevedon Street	A2
Clifton Hill	E5
Clifton Road	E5-F5
Clifton Street	F4-F5
Clinton Street	A2
Clydesdale Road	A8-B8
College Avenue	F3
College Road	F3-F4
Colleton Crescent	C2-D2
Commercial Road	B2-C2
Coombe Street	C3
Cowick Road	A1
Cowick Street	A1-A2-B2
Cowley Bridge Road	A6-A7-A8
Culverland Close	F7-F8
Culverland Road	E7-E8
Danes Road	C6
Deepdene Park	F1
Denmark Road	F3-F4
Devonshire Place	E7
Diamond Road	C2-C1
Dineham Crescent	B4
Dinham Road	B4
Dix's Field	D4
Drakes Road	A2
East John Walk	F4-F5
Dunvegan Close	A8
East Grove Road	E2
Edgerton Park Road	E7
Elmbridge Gardens	E1
Elmdon Close	E8-F8
Elmgrove Road	B6-C6-B5
Elmside	F6
Exe Street	B4
Fairpark Road	E2-E3
Ferndale Road	A1
Fords Road	C1
Fore Street	B3-C3
Friars Gate	C2-D2
Friars Walk	D2
Frog Street	B3
Gandy Street	C4
George Street	C3
Gladstone Road	F4
Grosvenor Place	F6
Haldon Road	B4-B5
Harefield Close	A2
Haven Road	C1-C2-D1
Heavitree Road	E4-F4
Hele Road	B6-B5
Hensleigh Drive	F3
Highcross Road	D7
Higher Kings Avenue	E8-F8
High Street	C4-D4-D5
Hill Close	E8
Hillsborough Avenue	D6-E6
Hillside Avenue	D6
Holloway Street	D2
Hoopern Street	C6-C7
Howell Road	A6-D6
Iddesleigh Road	F7
Iris Avenue	B1-C1
Iron Bridge	B4-C4
Isca Road	C1
Jesmond Road	F6-F5-F6
Kilbarran Rise	A7-A8
King Street	C3
King William Street	D5-E6
Larkbeare Road	D1-D2
Leighdene Close	F1
Lodge Hill	A8
Longbrook Street	D5-D6
Longbrook Terrace	D5
Looe Road	A5-A6
Lower Coombe Street	C2
Lower Kings Avenue	E8-F8
Lower North Street	B4
Lower St Germans Road	D7
Lower Summerlands	F4
Lucas Avenue	F2
Lucky Lane	D2
Lyndhurst Road	F2
Lynwood Avenue	A3
Magdalen Road	E3-F3
Magdalen Street	D3-E3
Manor Road	A3
Mansfield Road	F7
Market Street	C3
Marlborough Road	F2-F3
Mary Arches Street	B4-C3

Maryfield Avenue	E8
Matford Avenue	F2-F1-F2
Matford Lane	E1-F1-F2
Matford Road	F1
May Street	F7-F6
Melbourne Street	D2
Mount Pleasant Road	F8-F7
Musgrave Row	C4-C5
Nelson Road	A2
New Bridge Street	B2-B3
New North Road	A7-D5
North Bridge	B2
Northernhay Street	C4-C5
North Street	C3
Norwood Avenue	E1
Oakfield Road	A2
Oakhampton Street	A2-B2
Okehampton Road	A3-B2
Old Tiverton Road	E6-F7
Old Vicarage Road	A1
Oxford Road	E6
Oxford Street	B1-B2
Palace Gate	C3-D3
Paris Street	D5-D4-E4
Parr Street	F5
Paul Street	C4
Penleonard Close	F3
Pennsylvania Close	E8
Pennsylvania Road	D6-E8
Perry Road	B7
Portland Street	F5
Powderham Crescent	D7-E7
Powderham Road	A1
Preston Street	C3
Prince of Wales Rd.	B7-C8-D7
Princes Way	D4
Princes Street North	B1
Prospect Park	E7-F7
Prospect Place	A1
Quay Hill	C2
Queens Crescent	D6
Queens Road	B1
Queen Street	B5-C5-C4
Queens Terrace	B5
Radford Road	D2-E2
Radnor Place	E3
Raleigh Road	F3
Red Lion Lane	E5
Regent Street	A1
Rennes Drive	C8
Richmond Road	B5
Roberts Road	D2-E2
Romsey Drive	F2
Rosebank Crescent	F8
Rosebarn Lane	F8
Rosebery Road	F6-F7
Russell Street	E5
St David's Hill	B4
St Germans Road	D8-E8
St James Road	D4
St Leonards Avenue	D1-E1
St Leonards Road	E2-E3
Salisbury Road	F7-F6
Sandford Walk	F5
School Road	A1
Shaftesbury Road	A1
Sidwell Street	D5-E5-E6
Smythen Street	C3
South Bridge	B1
Southernhay East	D3-D4
Southernhay West	D3-D4
South Street	D3

South View Terrace	E7
Spicer Road	E3-E4-F4
Springfield Road	E8-E7
Station Road	A7
Stocker Road	B8-C8
Stoke Hill	F8
Streatham Drive	B7-B8
Streatham Rise	A7-B7
Summerland Street	E5
Sydney Road	A1-B1
Sylvan Road	F8
Taddiforde Court	A1
Taddiforde Road	A6-A7
Telford Road	A6
Temple Road	D2-D3
The Quay	C2-D2
The Queen's Drive	B8
Thornton Hill	D7-D6
Topsham Road	E2-E1-F1
Toronto Road	F6
Tudor Street	B3
Union Road	E7-E8-F8
Union Street	A1-B1
Velwell Road	B6-C6
Verney Street	E5
Victoria Park Road	F2
Victoria Street	E7
Water Lane	C1
Waverley Avenue	C6
Way Avenue	C2
Weirfield Road	D1-E1
Well Street	E6
West Avenue	D7
Western Road	A3
Western Way	E3-E5, C3
West Grove Road	E2
Willeys Avenue	B1-C1
Williams Avenue	B1-C1
Wonford Road	E3-E2-F2
York Road	D6-E6-E5

Exmouth

Albion Hill	B3-C3
Albion Place	B3
Albion Street	B2-B3
Alexandra Terrace	B1-B2
Ashleigh Road	C4
Bath Road	B1-B2
Beacon Place	B2
Belle View Road	A4
Belvedere Road	B3
Bicton Place	B2
Bicton Street	B2-C2
Bicton Villas	C3
Boarden Barn	C2
Bridge Road	B4
Camperdown Terrace	A1
Carter Avenue	A4
Carlton Hill	C1-C2
Chichester Close	C4
Church Road	A3-B3
Church Street	B2
Claremont Grove	C3
Clarence Road	B3
Cyprus Road	C3
Dagmar Road	B2
Danby Terrace	B3
Docks Relief Road	B1
Douglas Avenue	C1-C2
Egremont Road	B3
Elm Road	C3

Esplanade	A1-B1-C1
Exeter Road	B3-A4
Fairfield Close	C2
Fairfield Road	C2
Fore Street	B2-C2
Gipsy Lane	A4-B4
George Street	B3
Green Hill Avenue	C3-C4
Gussiford Road	C2
Halsdon Avenue	A4
Hamilton Lane	C4
Hartley Road	C2
Hartopp Road	A3-B3
Halsdon Road	A3
High Street	B2
High View Gardens	C3
Imperial Road	A2-B1
Lawn Road	B3
Leslie Road	B4
Long Causeway	C3
Louisa Place	B1-C1
Louisa Terrace	B1-C1
Lyndhurst Road	A4-B4
Madeira Villas	B3-B4
Marine Way	A3
Marpool Hill	B4-C3
Montpellier Road	B3-B2-C2
Morton Road	A1-B1
Mudbank Lane	A4
New North Road	B3
New Street	B3
North Street	B3
Oakleigh Road	C3-C4
Park Road	B4
Phear Avenue	C3-C4
Point Terrace	A1
Portland Avenue	C2
Pound Street	B2
Queens Drive	C1
Raddenstile Lane	C2
Raleigh Road	B2-C2
Rill Court Drive	C2
Rolle Road	B2-C2
Rolle Street	B2
Rolle Villas	B1-B2
Ryll Grove	B3-C3
St Andrews Road	A1-B1-B2
Salisbury Road	A3-B3
Salterton Road	C2-C3
Southern Road	A4
Sunwine Place	B2
The Beacon	B1-B2
The Hollows	B2
The Parade	B2
The Royal Avenue	A2
Trefusis Place	C1
Trefusis Terrace	C1
Victoria Road	A1-A2-B2
Victoria Way	A2
Waverley Road	B4
Westward Drive	C3
Windsor Square	B2
Withycombe Road	B3-B4
Withycombe Village Road	B4
Woodville Road	A3-A4-B2

Honiton

Avenue Mezidon-Canon	C2
Bramble Lane	A2
Brand Road	C1

Buttery Road	C2
Charles Road	C4
Church Hill	C2-C3
Clapper Lane	C4
Coly Close	B1
Cotfield Close	C2
Dowell Street	A4-B3
Ernsborough Gardens	A3
Exeter Road	A2-B3
Fairfield Gardens	B3
George Street	B4
Gronau Close	C1
Hawthorn Close	A2
Haydons Park	C2
Hazelwood Close	B1
Highfield	B2
High Street	B3-C4
Hill Crescent	C3
Honiton Bottom Road	B1-B2
Honiton By-Pass	A4-B4
Jerrard Close	B3-C3
Jerrard Crescent	C3
Joslin Road	A2
King's Road	C4
Kings Road	B3
Langford Avenue	C4
Langford Road	C4
Lee Close	A4
Littledown Road	A2
Livermore Road	B2
Lower Brand Lane	C2
Manor Crescent	B2-C2
Marker Way	B1
Marlpits Road	C2
Mead View Road	B3
Milldale Crescent	A2
Millers Way	B2-B3
Millhead Road	A2-B3
Mill Street	B3
Monkton Road	C4
Mount Close	A2
New Street	C3
Northcote Lane	B4
Oaklea	A3
Orchard Way	C3
Ottery Moor Lane	A3
Philips Square	B4
Pine Grove	C3-C4
Pine Park Road	C3
Queen Street	C3
Riverside Close	B3
Rookwood Close	A3
Rosemount Lane	A2
Rosewell Close	C4
St Cyre's Road	B4
St Margaret's Road	A2
St Mark's Road	A2
St Paul's Road	A2
School Lane	B4
Sidmouth Road	A1-A2
Silver Street	B4-C4
Streamers Meadows	B2-B3
Turnpike	C3
Westcott Way	A2
Whitebridges	B2

AA SHOP – Bedford Street
Exeter EX1 1LD D4

Maps © The AA 1981
Revision © The AA 1993

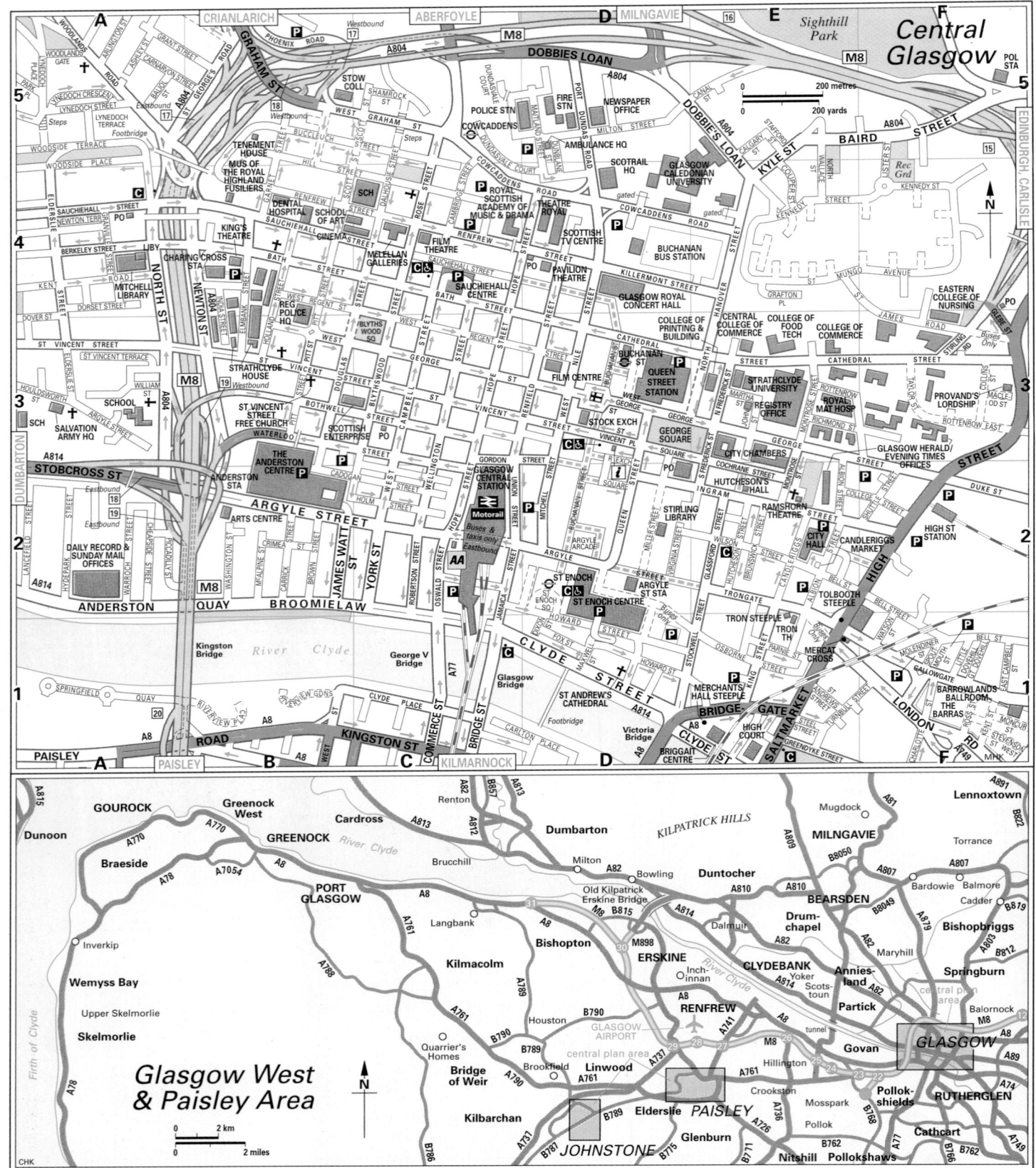

Glasgow

Although much of Glasgow is distinctly Victorian its roots are very much older. The cathedral was founded in the 6th century and has features from many succeeding centuries, notably an exceptional 13th-century crypt. Provand's Lordship, built in 1471 and now a museum, is the city's oldest house while Provan Hall also dates from the 15th century. Glasgow is one of the art capitals of the world, with many fine paintings and treasures in the city's Art Gallery and Museum, the Hunterian Art Gallery and Museum, Pollok House and the internationally famous Burrell Collection. Other major attractions are the People's Palace Museum of city life on Glasgow Green, the Museum of Transport and a new international concert hall. Although an industrial city, Glasgow also has many large and attractive parks.

Paisley is famous for the fabric pattern to which it gives its name. The pattern was derived from fabrics brought from India in the early 19th century, and its manufacture, along with the production of thread, is still important. The town museum, which has many fine examples of Paisley work, also runs the Coats Observatory – one of the best-equipped in Britain. Paisley Abbey is a fine 14th- and 15th-century building with a rare crown spire.

Johnstone grew rapidly as a planned industrial town in the 19th century, but suffered later from the decline in the textile trade. Today, engineering is the main industry.

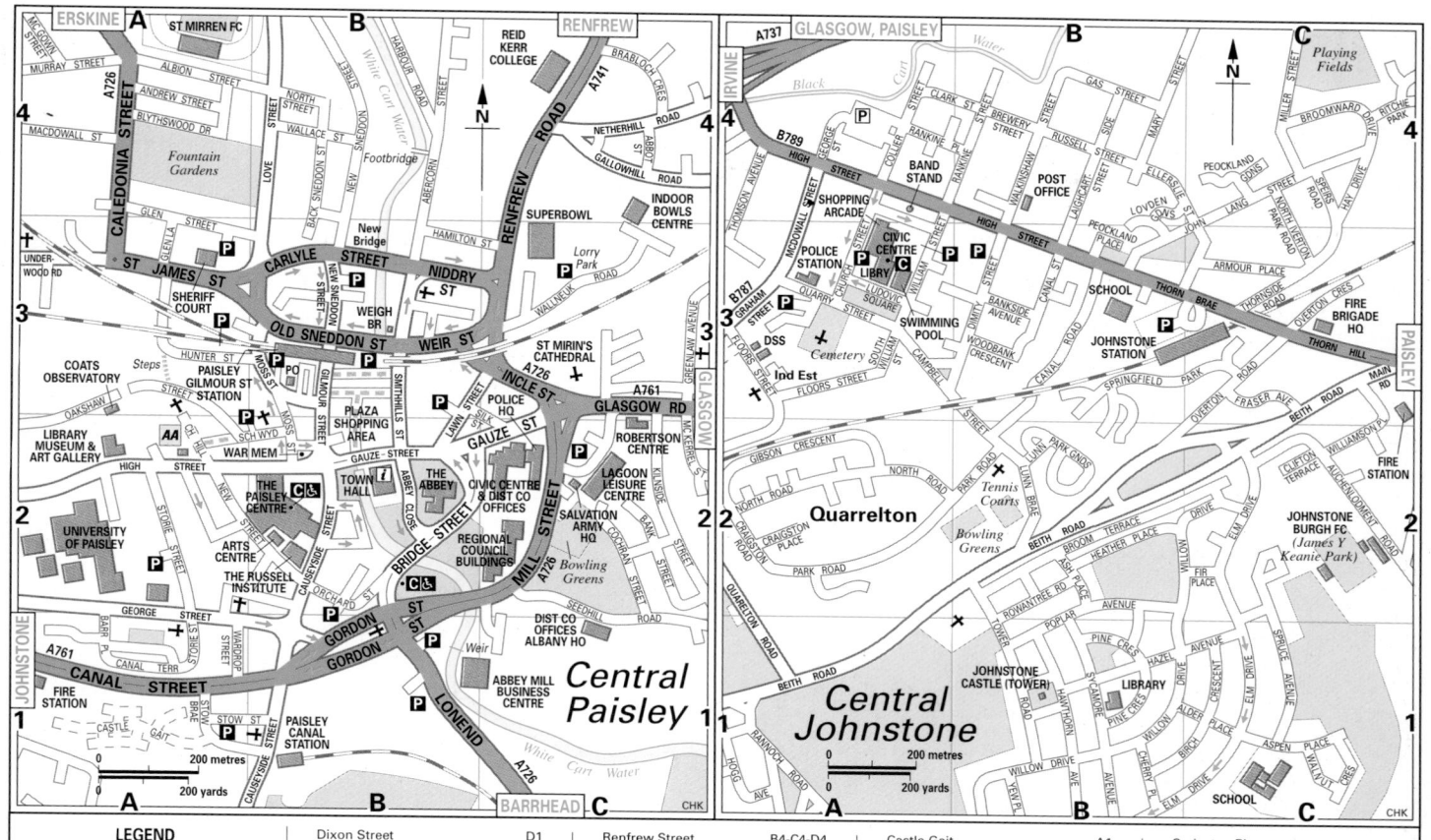

LEGEND

Town Plan

AA Recommended routes

Restricted roads

Other roads

Buildings of interest COLLEGE

AA Shop/Insurance AA

Churches †

Parks and open spaces

Car parks P

Toilets C& C

One way streets

Underground stations

Area Plan

A roads

B roads

Locations Yalding ○

Urban area

Street Index with Grid Reference

Glasgow

Albion Street	E1-E2
Anderston Quay	A2-B2
Argyle Arcade	D2
Argyle Street	A3-B2-C2-D2
Arlington Street	A5
Ashley Street	A5
Baird Street	E5-F5
Baliol Street	A5
Bath Street	B4-C4-C3-D3
Bell Street	E2-E1-F1-F3
Berkeley Street	A4
Blythswood Square	C3
Blythswood Street	C3-C4
Bothwell Street	B3-C3
Bridgegate	D1-E1
Bridge Street	C1
Broomielaw	B2-C1
Brown Street	B2
Brunswick Street	E2
Buccleuch Street	B5-C5
Buchanan Street	D2-D3-D4
Cadogan Street	B2-C2
Calgary Street	E5
Canal Street	E5
Candleriggs	E2
Cambridge Street	C4
Carlton Place	C1-D1
Carnarvon Street	A5-B5
Carrick Street	B2
Cathedral Street	D3-E3-F3
Charlotte Street	F1
Cheapside Street	A2
Clyde Place	B1-C1
Clyde Street	C1-D1-E1
Cochrane Street	E2
College Street	E2-F2
Collins Street	F3
Commerce Street	C1
Couper Street	E4
Cowcaddens Road	C5-C4-D4-E4
Crimea Street	B2
Dalhousie Street	C4-C5

Dixon Street	D1
Dobbies Loan	C5-D5-E5-E4
Dorset Street	A4
Douglas Street	B3-C4
Dover Street	A3-A4
Duke Street	F2
Dunblane Street	D4-D5
Dundasvale Court	C5
East Campbell Street	F1
Elderslie Street	A4-A3
Elmbank Street	B3-B4
Fox Street	D1
Gallowgate	E1-F1
Garnet Street	B4-B5
George V Bridge	C1
George Square	D3-E3
George Street	E3-F2
Glasgow Bridge	C1
Glassford Street	E2
Glebe Street	F5
Gordon Street	C3-D3
Grafton Place	E4
Grant Street	A5-B5
Granville Street	A4
Great Dovehill	F1
Greendyke Street	E1
High Street	F2-F3
Hill Street	B5-B4-C4
Houldsworth Street	A3
Holland Street	B3-B4
Holm Street	C2
Hope Street	C2-C3-C4-D4
Howard Street	D1
Hutcheson Street	E2
Hydepark Street	A2
India Street	B3-B4
Ingram Street	D2-E2-F2
Jamaica Street	C1-C2
James Watt Street	B2
John Street	E3
Kennedy Street	E4-F4
Kent Road	A4
Kent Street	F1
Killermont Street	D4-E4
King Street	E1
Kingston Bridge	B1
Kingston Street	B1-C1
Kyle Street	E4-E5
Lancefield Street	A2
Little Dovehill	F1
Lister Street	F4-F5
London Road	E1-F1
Lynedoch Crescent	A5
Lynedoch Place	A5
Lynedoch Street	A5
Lynedoch Terrace	A5
McAlpine Street	B2
Macleod Street	F3
Maitland Street	D5-D4
Maxwell Street	D1
Miller Street	D2
Milton Street	D5
Mitchell Street	D2-D3
Molendinar Street	F1
Moncur Street	F1
Montrose Street	E2-E3
Newton Terrace	A4
North Street	A4-A3
North Frederick Street	E3
North Hanover Street	E3-E4
North Wallace Street	E4
Osborne Street	E1
Oswald Street	C2
Paisley Road	A1-B1
Park Place	A5
Parnie Street	E1
Phoenix Road	B5
Piccadilly Street	A2
Pitt Street	B3-B4
Port Dundas Road	D5-D4
Queen Street	D2
Renfield Street	C3-D3-D4

Renfrew Street	B4-C4-D4
Richmond Street	E3
Riverview Gardens	B1
Riverview Place	B1
Robertson Street	C2
Rose Street	C4-C5
Ross Street	F1
Rottenrow	E3
Rottenrow East	F3
Royal Exchange Square	D3-D2
St Andrew's Street	E1
St Enoch Square	D1-D2
St George's Road	A5-B5
St James Road	E4-F3
St Mungo Avenue	E4-F4
St Vincent Place	D3
St Vincent Street	A3-B3-C3-D3
St Vincent Terrace	A3
Saltmarket	E1
Sauchiehall Street	A4-B4-C4-D4
Scott Street	B4-C5
Shamrock Street	B5
Shuttle Street	F2
South Frederick Street	E2-E3
Spoutmouth Street	F1
Springfield Quay	A1
Stafford Street	E5-E4
Steel Street	E1
Stevenson Street West	F1
Stirling Road	F3
Stobcross Street	A3-A2
Stockwell Street	D1-E1-E2
Taylor Street	F3
Trongate	E2
Turnbull Street	E1-F1
Union Street	C2
Virginia Street	D2
Warroch Street	A2
Washington Street	B2
Waterloo Street	B3-C3
Watson Street	F1
Wellington Street	C2-C3
West Street	B1
West Campbell Street	C2-C3-C4
West George Street	B3-C3-D3
West Graham Street	B5-C5
West Nile Street	D3-D4
West Regent Street	B4-C3-D3
William Street	A3
Wilson Street	E2
Woodlands Gate	A5
Woodlands Road	A5
Woodside Place	A5
Woodside Terrace	A5
York Street	C2

AA shop
269 Argyle Street
Glasgow
Strathclyde
G2 8DW C2

Paisley

Abbey Close	B2
Abbot Street	C4
Abercorn Street	B3-B4
Albion Street	A4-B4
Andrew Street	A4
Back Sneddon Street	B3-B4
Bank Street	C2
Barr Place	A1
Blythswood Drive	A4
Brabloch Crescent	C4
Bridge Street	B2
Caledonia Street	A3-A4
Canal Street	A1-B1
Canal Terrace	A1
Carlyle Street	B3

Castle Gait	A1
Causeyside Street	A1-B1-B2
Church Hill	A2
Cochran Street	C2
Cotton Street	B2
Gallowhill Road	C4
Gauze Street	B2-C2-C3
George Street	A2-A1-B1
Gilmour Street	B2-B3
Glasgow Road	C3
Glen Lane	C3
Glen Street	A4-A3-B3
Gordon Street	B1-B2
Greenlaw Avenue	C3
Hamilton Street	B3-C3
Harbour Road	B4
High Street	A2-B2
Hunter Street	A3-B3
Incle Street	C3
Kilnside Road	C3
Lawn Street	B2-B3-C3
Lonend	B1-C1
Love Street	B3-B4
Macdowall Street	A4
McGown Street	A4
McKerrel Street	C2
Mill Street	C2
Moss Street	B3-B2
Murray Street	A4
Netherhill Road	C4
New Sneddon Street	B3-B4
New Street	A2-B2
Niddry Street	B3-C3
North Street	B4
Oakshaw Street	A2-A3-A2
Old Sneddon Street	B3
Orchard Street	B2
Renfrew Road	C3-C4
St James Street	A3
School Wynd	A2-B2
Seedhill Road	C2-C1
Silk Street	B3-C3-C2
Smithhills Street	B3-B2
Storie Street	A2-A1
Stow Brae	A1
Stow Street	A1-B1
Underwood Road	B4
Wallace Street	B4
Wallneuk Road	C3
Wardrop Street	B2
Weir Street	B3-C3

AA shop
36 High Street
Paisley
Renfrewshire
PA1 2DQ A2

Johnstone

Alder Place	B1-C1
Armour Place	C3
Ash Place	B2
Aspen Place	C1
Auchenlodment Road	C2
Bankside Avenue	B3
Beith Road	A1-A2-B2-C2-C3
Birch Crescent	B1-C1
Brewery Street	B2
Broom Terrace	B2-C2
Broomward Drive	B1
Campbell Street	A3-B3-B2
Canal Road	B2-B3
Canal Street	B3
Cherry Place	B1
Church Street	A3-A4
Clark Street	A4-B4
Clifton Terrace	C2
Collier Street	A4

Craigston Place	A2
Craigston Road	A2
Dimity Street	A3-B3
Ellerslie Street	B4-C4-C3
Elm Drive	B1-C1-C2
Fir Place	C2
Floors Street	A3
Fraser Avenue	C3
Gas Street	B4
George Street	A4
Gibson Crescent	A2
Graham Street	A3
Hawthorn Avenue	B1
Hay Drive	C4
Hazel Avenue	B1-C1
Heather Place	B2
High Street	A4-B4-B3
Hogg Avenue	A1
John Lang Street	B3-C3-C4
Kings Road	A3
Laighcartside Street	B3-B4
Linn Park Gardens	B4
Lovden Gardens	B4-B3
Ludovic Square	B2
Lunn Brae	A2
McDowall Street	A3-A4
Main Road	A3-A4
Mary Street	B4-C4
Miller Street	C4
North Iverton Park Road	C4-C3
North Road	A2
Overton Crescent	C3
Overton Road	B2-C3
Park Road	A2-B2
Peockland Gardens	C4
Peockland Place	B3
Pine Crescent	B1
Poplar Avenue	B1-B2
Quarrelton Road	A2-A1
Quarry Street	A3
Rankine Place	A4-B4
Rankine Street	A4-B4
Rannoch Road	A1
Ritchie Park	C4
Rowantree Road	B1-B2
Russell Street	B4
South William Street	A3
Speirs Road	B2
Springfield Park	B3-C3-B2
Spruce Avenue	C2-C1
Sycamore Avenue	B1
Thomson Avenue	A3-A4
Thorn Brae	B3-C3
Thorn Hill	C3
Thornside Road	B2-B1
Tower Road	B2-B1
Walkinshaw Street	B3-B4
Walnut Crescent	C1
Williamson Place	C2
William Street	A3
Willow Drive	B1-B2-C2
Woodbank Crescent	B3
Yew Place	B1

Maps: © The Automobile Association 1994
Revision: © The Automobile Association 1994

223

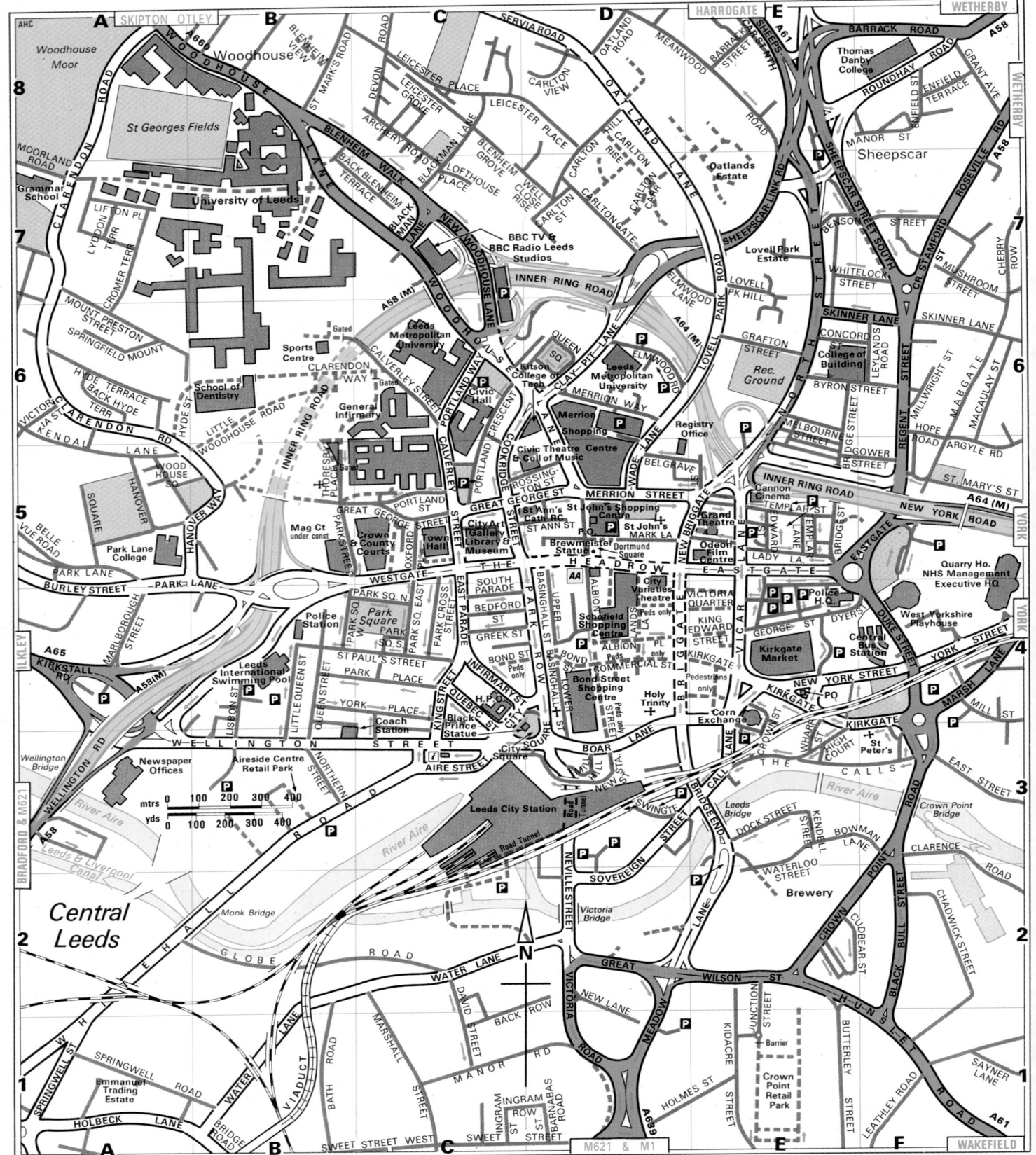

Leeds

The magnificent colonnaded Town Hall, with a 225ft-high clock-tower, is an obvious symbol of the city's pride. For centuries a major centre of the wool trade, Leeds has evolved into a city renowned for its engineering, textiles and ready-made clothes industries. Nevertheless, it also has many features to interest the tourist. The Art Gallery and Museum has sculptures by Henry Moore (a former student at the Leeds School of Art) and near by on the Headrow, the city's foremost shopping street, is the City Varieties Theatre, perhaps best known for the 'Good Old Days' TV programme. Off the Headrow are numerous attractive shopping arcades and, not far away, Kirkgate Market is the largest covered market in the North of England. The museum at Armley Mills (once the world's largest woollen mill) recalls the woollen industry, while Tetley's Brewery Wharf on the River Aire illustrates the history of the British pub. Thwaite Mills at Stourton is an industrial water-mill and the preserved Middleton Railway at Hunslet is the world's oldest non-passenger railway, authorised in 1758. At Kirkstall are the substantial remains of the 12th-century abbey and the Abbey House folk museum, while east of the city are the Tudor and Jacobean mansion of Temple Newsam House, set in a 1,200-acre park.

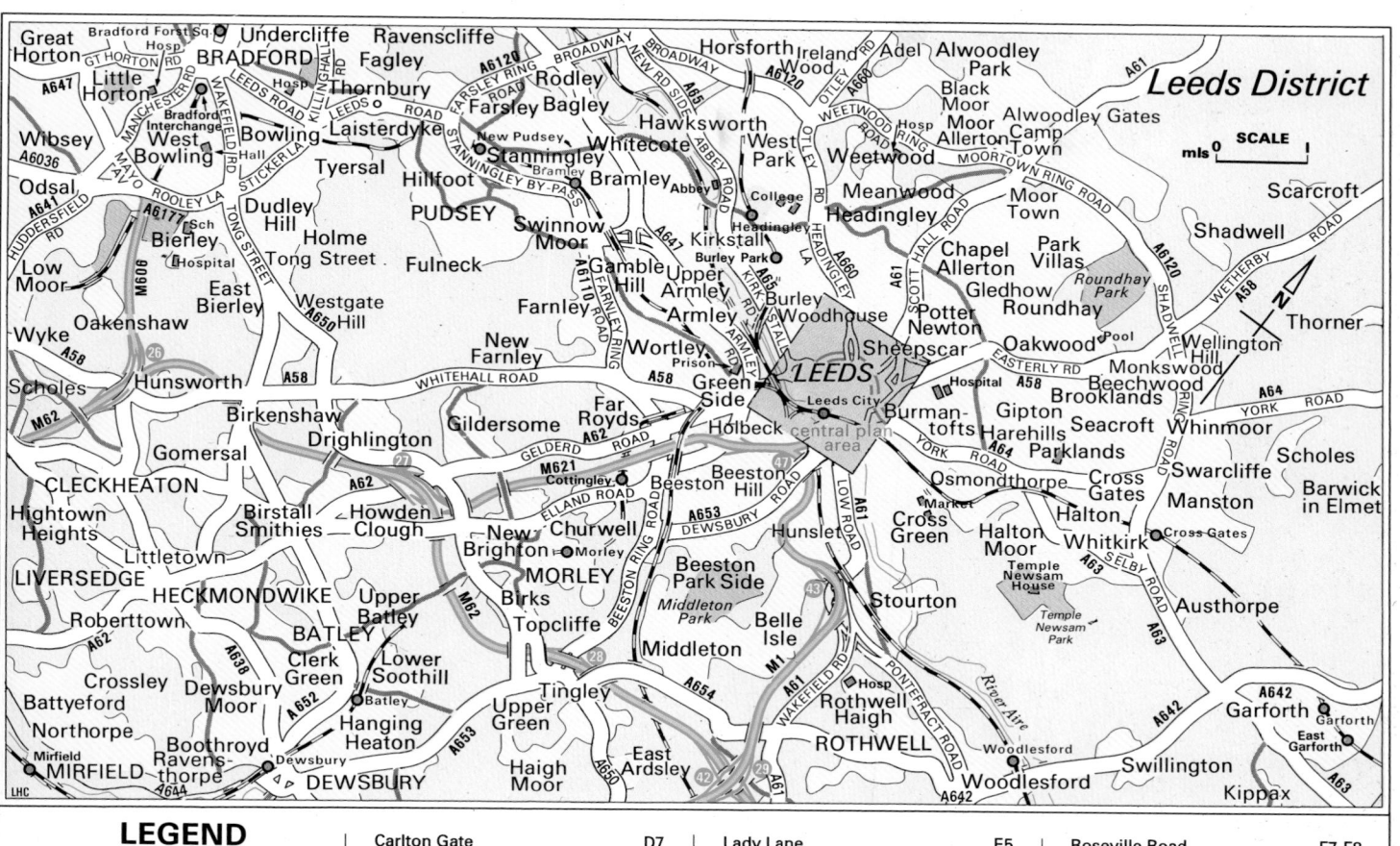

Leeds District

SCALE mls 0

LEGEND

Town Plan

AA Recommended roads	
Other roads	
Restricted roads	
Buildings of interest	Museum
AA Shop/Insurance	AA
Parks and open spaces	
Car parks	P
Churches	†
One-way streets	→

District Plan

A roads	
B roads	
Railway station	Kirkgate
Urban area	
Buildings of interest	Hospital

Street Index with Grid Reference

Leeds

Aire Street	C3
Albion Place	D4
Albion Street	D3-D4-D5
Archery Road	C7-C8
Argyle Road	F5
Back Hyde Terrace	A6
Back Row	C1-C2-D2
Barrack Road	E8-F8
Barrack Street	E8
Bath Road	B1-B2
Bedford Street	C4
Belgrave Street	D5-E5
Belle Vue Road	A5
Benson Street	E7-F7
Back Blenheim Terrace	C7
Black Bull Street	F1-F2-F3
Blackman Lane	C7-C8
Blenheim Grove	C8-C7-D7
Blenheim View	B8
Blenheim Walk	B8-C8-C7
Boar Lane	D3-D4
Bond Street	C4-D4
Bowman Lane	E3-F3
Bridge End	D3-E3
Bridge Road	B1
Bridge Street	E5-E6
Briggate	D3-D4-D5
Burley Street	A4-A5
Butterley Street	E1-E2
Byron Street	E6-F6
Call Lane	E3
Calverley Street	C5-C6
Carlton Carr	D7

Carlton Gate	D7
Carlton Hill	D7-D8
Carlton Rise	D7-D8
Carlton Street	D7
Carlton View	D8
Chadwick Street	F2
Cherry Row	F7
City Square	C3-C4-D4-D3
Clarence Road	F3-F2
Clarendon Road	A8-A7-A6-A5-B5
Clarendon Way	B6-C6
Clay Pit Lane	D6
Commercial Street	D4
Concord Street	E6-F6
Cookridge Street	C5-C6-D6
Cromer Terrace	A7
Cross Stamford Street	F7
Crown Street	E3-E4
Crown Point Road	E2-F2-F3
Cudbear Street	E2
David Street	C1-C2
Devon Road	C8
Dock Street	E3
Duke Street	F4
Dyer Street	E4-F4
East Parade	C4-C5
East Street	F3
Eastgate	E5-F5
Edward Street	E5
Elmwood Lane	D7-E7
Elmwood Road	D6
Enfield Street	F8
Enfield Terrace	F8
George Street	E4
Globe Road	A2-B2-C2
Gower Street	E5-F5
Grafton Street	E6
Grant Avenue	F8
Great George Street	B5-C5-D5
Great Wilson Street	D2-E2
Greek Street	C4
Hanover Square	A5
Hanover Way	A5-B5
High Court	E3
Holbeck Lane	A1-B1
Holmes Street	D1-E1
Hope Road	F5-F6
Hunslet Road	E2-F2-F1
Hyde Street	A6
Hyde Terrace	A6
Infirmary Street	C4-D4
Ingram Row	C1-D1
Ingram Street	C1
Inner Ring Road	B5-C6-D7-E6-E5
Junction Street	E1-E2
Kendal Lane	A5-A6
Kendell Street	E3
Kidacre Street	E1-E2
King Street	C3-C4
King Edward Street	D4-E4
Kirkgate	E4-E3-F3-F4
Kirkstall Road	A4

Lady Lane	E5
Lands Lane	D4-D5
Leathley Road	F1
Leicester Place	C8-D8
Leicester Grove	C8
Leylands Road	F6
Lifton Place	A7
Lisbon Street	B3-B4
Little Queen Street	B3-B4
Little Woodhouse Street	B6
Lofthouse Place	C7
Lovell Park Hill	E7
Lovell Park Road	D6-E6-E7
Lower Basinghall Street	D3-D4
Lyddon Terrace	A7
Mabgate	F6
Macaulay Street	F6
Manor Road	C1-D1
Manor Street	F8
Mark Lane	D5
Marlborough Street	A4
Marsh Lane	F4
Marshall Street	C1-C2
Meadow Lane	D1-D2-E2-E3
Meanwood Road	D8-E8
Melbourne Street	E6
Merrion Street	D5-E5
Merrion Way	D6
Mill Hill	D3
Mill Street	F4
Millwright Street	F6
Moorland Road	A7-A8
Mount Preston Street	A6-A7
Mushroom Street	F6-F7
Neville Street	D2-D3
New Briggate	D5-E5
New Lane	D2-D1
New Station Street	D3
New Woodhouse Lane	C6-C7
New York Road	F5
New York Street	E4-F4
North Street	E5-E6-E7
Northern Street	B3
Oatland Lane	D8-D7-E7
Oatland Road	D8
Oxford Place	C5
Park Cross Street	C4-C5
Park Lane	A5-B5-B4
Park Place	B4-C4
Park Row	C5-D5-D4
Park Square East	C4
Park Square North	B4-C4
Park Square South	C4
Park Square West	B4
Park Street	B5-C5
Portland Crescent	C5-C6
Portland Street	B5-C5
Portland Way	C6
Quebec Street	C3-C4
Queen Square	C6-D6
Queen Street	B3-B4
Regent Street	F5-F6

Roseville Road	F7-F8
Rossington Street	C5-D5
Roundhay Road	E8-F8
St Ann Street	C5-D5
St Barnabas Road	D1
St Mark's Road	B8
St Mary's Street	F5
St Paul's Street	B4-C4
Servia Road	C8-D8
Sayner Lane	F1
Sheepscar Link Road	E7-E8
Sheepscar Street North	E8
Sheepscar Street South	E8-E7-F7
Skinner Lane	E6-F6
South Parade	C4
Sovereign Street	D2-D3-E3
Springfield Mount	A6
Springwell Road	A1-B1
Springwell Street	A1
Sweet Street	C1-D1
Sweet Street West	B1-C1
Swinegate	D3
The Calls	E3-F3
The Headrow	C5-D5
Templar Lane	E5
Templar Street	E5
Thoresby Place	B5-B6
Upper Basinghall Street	D4-D5
Vicar Lane	E4-E5
Victoria Quarter	E4
Victoria Road	D1-D2
Victoria Street	A6
Wade Lane	D5-D6
Water Lane	B1-B2-C2-D2
Waterloo Street	E2-E3
Well Close Rise	D7
Wellington Road	A3
Wellington Street	A3-B3-C3
Westgate	B4-B5-C4
Wharf Street	E3-E4
Whitehall Road	A1-A2-B2-B3-C3
Whitelock Street	E7-F7
Woodhouse Lane	B8-C7-C6-D5-D4
York Place	B4-C4
York Street	F4

AA Shop,	D5
95, The Headrow,	
Leeds, West Yorkshire	
LS1 6LU	

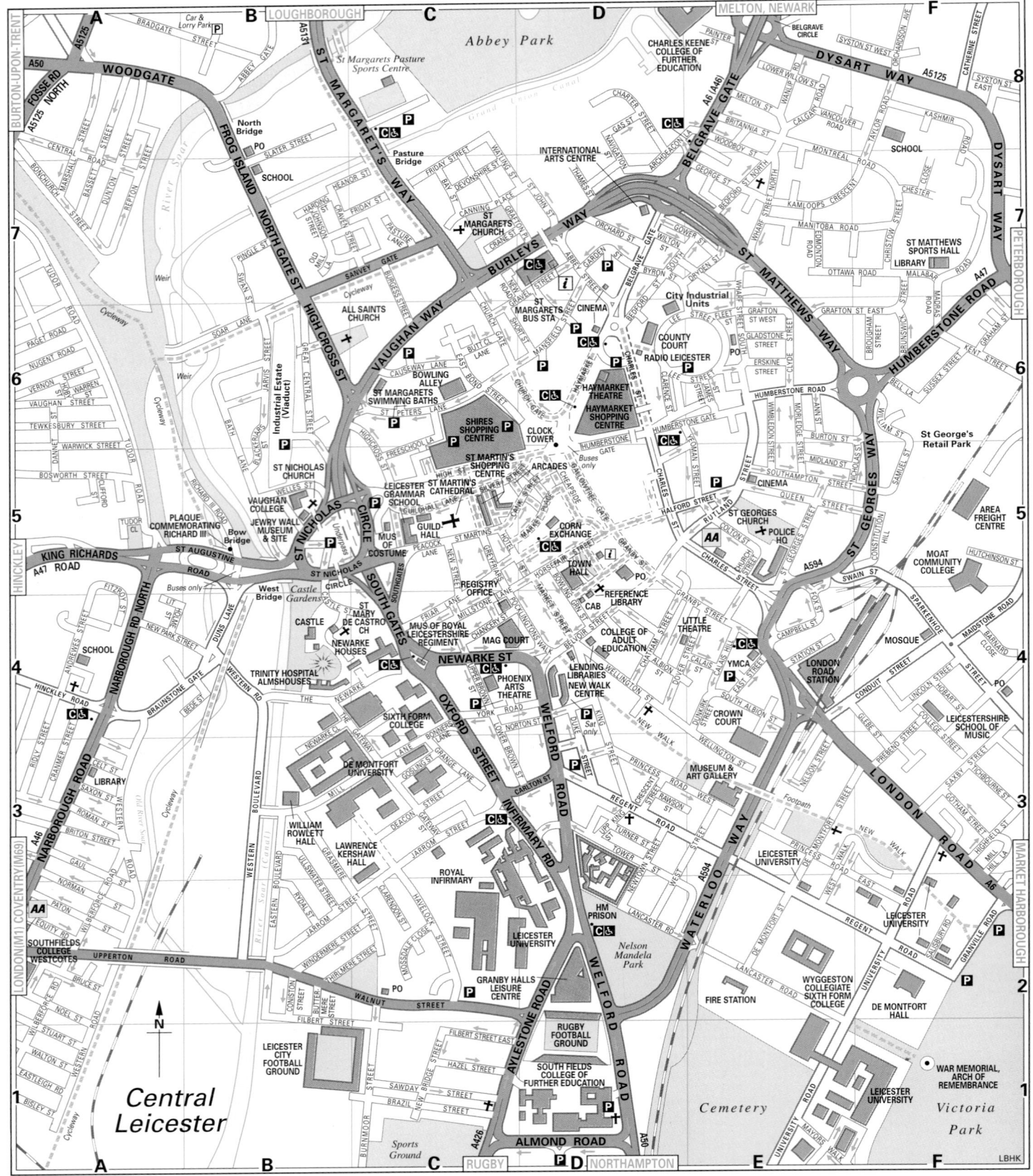

Leicester

Founded as a regional capital in Roman times and later occupied in turn by Danes, Saxons and Normans, Leicester retains many buildings from an eventful and distinguished past. Frequently visited by Richard III, it was from here that he set out, only to be killed, for the Battle of Bosworth. Today Leicester is a thriving contrast between modern shopping, leisure, academic develop-

ments and heritage. The oldest feature is the Jewry Wall, a 30ft-high section of Roman masonry, with other remains and an archaeological museum near by. Of the Norman castle little remains except the motte and great hall. The cathedral is 13th- to 15th- century, and there are several churches even older St Nicholas being of Saxon origin. The Guildhall is a magnificent timbered building dating back in part to 1340, and Newarke Houses, two adjoining 16th-century houses, contain the

museum of the city's and county's social history to the present day. Adjacent is the Museum of the Royal Leicestershire Regiment. Also of interest are the Wygston's House Museum of Costume, the 18th-century Belgrave Hall, the Leicestershire Museum of Technology and the city's Museum and Art Gallery. Situated in the northern suburbs is the Leicester north terminus of the preserved Great Central Railway to Loughborough.

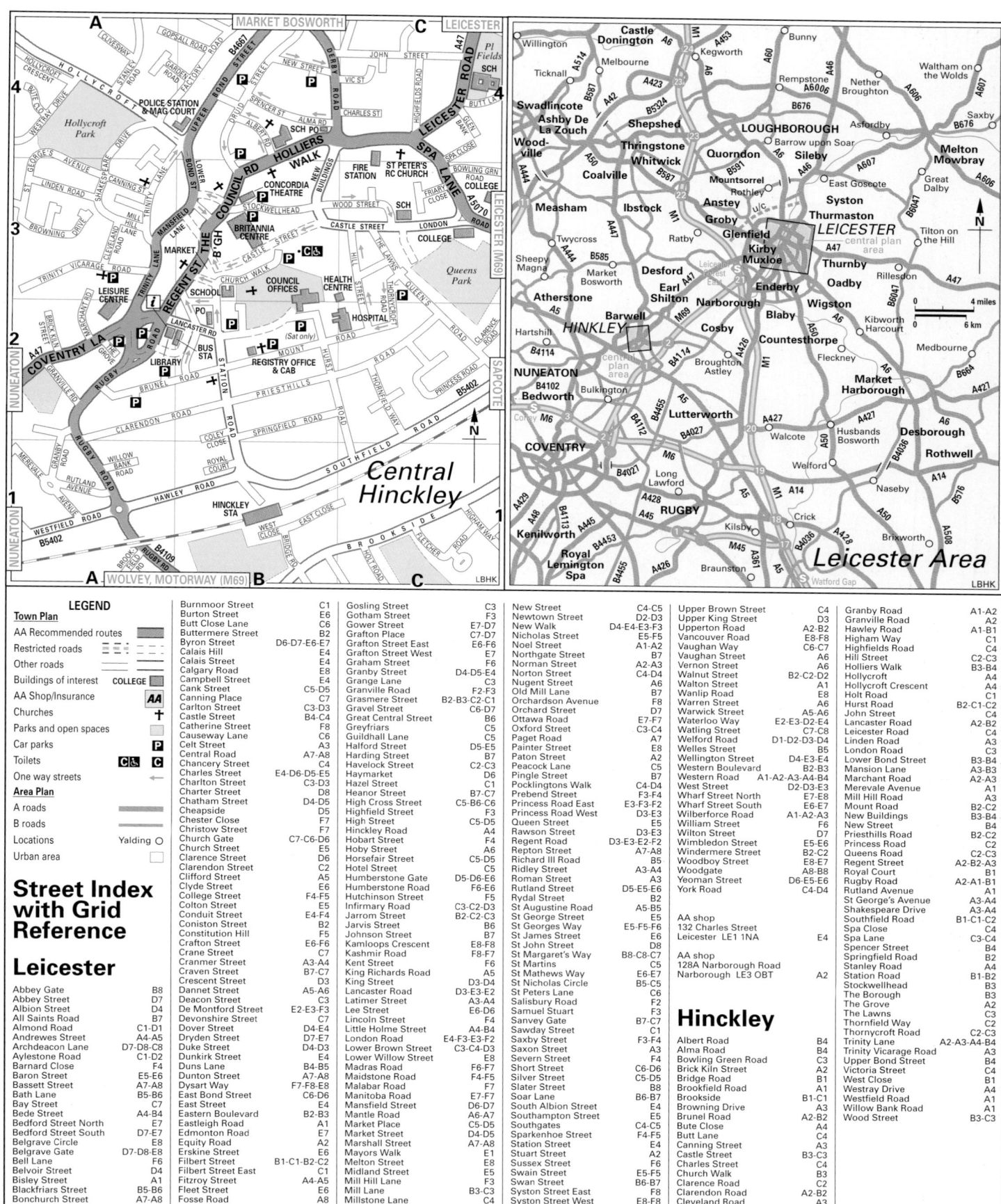

LEGEND

Town Plan

AA Recommended routes	
Restricted roads	
Other roads	
Buildings of interest	COLLEGE
AA Shop/Insurance	AA
Churches	†
Parks and open spaces	
Car parks	P
Toilets	C&C
One way streets	←

Area Plan

A roads	
B roads	
Locations	Yalding O
Urban area	

Street Index with Grid Reference

Leicester

Abbey Gate	B8
Abbey Street	D7
Albion Street	D4
All Saints Road	B7
Almond Road	C1-D1
Andrewes Street	A4-A5
Archdeacon Lane	D7-D8-C8
Aylestone Road	C1-D2
Barnard Close	F4
Baron Street	E5-E6
Bassett Street	A7-A8
Bath Lane	B5-B6
Bay Street	C7
Bede Street	A4-B4
Bedford Street North	A4-B4
Bedford Street South	D7-E7
Belgrave Circle	E8
Belgrave Gate	D7-D8-E8
Bell Lane	F6
Belvoir Street	D4
Bisley Street	A1
Blackfriars Street	B5-B6
Bonchurch Street	A7-A8
Bonners Lane	C4
Bosworth Street	A5
Bowling Green Street	D5-D4
Bradgate Street	A8-B8
Braunstone Gate	A4-B4
Brazil Street	C1
Britannia Street	E8
Briton Street	A3
Brougham Street	F6
Bruce Street	A2
Brunswick Street	F6-F7
Burgess Street	C6-C7
Burleys Way	C7-D7
Burnmoor Street	C1
Burton Street	E6
Butt Close Lane	C6
Buttermere Street	B2
Byron Street	D6-D7-E6-E7
Calais Hill	E4
Calais Street	E4
Calgary Road	E8
Campbell Street	E4
Cank Street	C5-D5
Canning Place	C7
Carlton Street	C3-D3
Castle Street	B4-C4
Catherine Street	F8
Causeway Lane	C6
Celt Street	A3
Central Road	A7-A8
Chancery Street	C4
Charles Street	E4-D6-D5-E5
Charlton Street	C3-D3
Charter Street	D8
Chatham Street	D4-D5
Cheapside	D5
Chester Close	F7
Christow Street	D3
Church Gate	C7-C6-D6
Church Street	D6
Clarence Street	D6
Clarendon Street	C2
Clifford Street	A5
Clyde Street	E6
College Street	F4-F5
Colton Street	E5
Conduit Street	E4-F4
Coniston Street	B2
Constitution Hill	F5
Crafton Street	E6-F6
Crane Street	C7
Cranmer Street	A3-A4
Craven Street	B7-C7
Crescent Street	D3
Dannet Street	A5-A6
Deacon Street	C5
De Montfort Street	E2-E3-F3
Devonshire Street	C7
Dover Street	D4-E4
Dryden Street	D7-E7
Duke Street	D4-D3
Dunkirk Street	E4
Duns Lane	B4-B5
Dunton Street	A7-A8
Dysart Way	F7-F8-E8
East Bond Street	C6-D6
East Street	E4
Eastern Boulevard	B2-B3
Eastleigh Road	A1
Edmonton Road	E7
Equity Road	A2
Erskine Street	E6
Filbert Street	B1-C1-B2-C2
Filbert Street East	C1
Fitzroy Street	A4-A5
Fleet Street	E6
Fosse Road	A8
Fox Street	E4
Freeschool Lane	C5-C6
Friar Lane	C5-C4
Friday Street	B7-C7-C8
Frog Island	B7-B8
Gallowtree Gate	D5
Garden Street	D7
Gas Street	D8
Gateway Street	B4-C4-C3
Gaul Street	A3-A2
George Street	E7
Gladstone Street	E6
Glebe Street	F3-F4
Gosling Street	C3
Gotham Street	F3
Gower Street	E7-D7
Grafton Place	C7-D7
Grafton Street East	E6-F6
Grafton Street West	E7
Graham Street	F6
Granby Street	D4-D5-E4
Grange Lane	C3
Granville Road	F2-F3
Grasmere Street	B2-B3-C2-C1
Gravel Street	C6-D7
Great Central Street	B6
Greyfriars	C5
Guildhall Lane	C5
Halford Street	D5-E5
Harding Street	B7
Havelock Street	C2-C3
Haymarket	D6
Hazel Street	C1
Heanor Street	B7-C7
High Cross Street	C5-B6-C6
Highfield Street	F3
High Street	C5-D5
Hinckley Road	A4
Hobart Street	F4
Hoby Street	A6
Horsefair Street	C5-D5
Hotel Street	C5
Humberstone Gate	D5-D6-E6
Humberstone Road	F6-E6
Hutchinson Street	F5
Infirmary Road	C3-C2-D3
Jarrom Street	B2-C2-C3
Jarvis Street	B7
Johnson Street	A7
Kamloops Crescent	E8-F8
Kashmir Road	F8-F7
Kent Street	F6
King Richards Road	A5
King Street	D3-D4
Lancaster Road	D3-E3-E2
Latimer Street	A3-A4
Lee Street	E6-D6
Lincoln Street	F4
Little Holme Street	A4-B4
London Road	E4-F3-E3-F2
Lower Brown Street	C3-C4-D3
Lower Willow Street	E8
Madras Road	F6-F7
Maidstone Road	F4-F5
Malabar Road	F7
Manitoba Road	E7-F7
Mansfield Street	D6-D7
Mantle Road	A6-A7
Market Place	C5-D5
Market Street	D4-D5
Marshall Street	A7-A8
Mayors Walk	E1
Melton Street	E8
Midland Street	E5
Mill Hill Lane	F3
Mill Lane	B3-C3
Millstone Lane	C4
Morledge Street	E5-E6
Montreal Road	E7-E8-F7
Mossdale Close	C2
Narborough Road	A2-A3-A4
Narborough Road North	A3-A4-A5
Navigation Street	D7-D8
Nelson Street	E3
Newarke Close	B3-B4
Newarke Street	C4-D4
Newbridge Street	C1
New Park Street	A4-B4
New Road	C7-D7
New Street	C4-C5
Newtown Street	D2-D3
New Walk	D4-E4-E3-F3
Nicholas Street	E5-F5
Noel Street	A1-A2
Northgate Street	B7
Norman Street	A2-A3
Norton Street	C4-D4
Nugent Street	A6
Old Mill Lane	B7
Orchardson Avenue	F8
Orchard Street	D7
Ottawa Road	E7-F7
Oxford Street	C3-C4
Paget Road	A7
Painter Street	E8
Paton Street	A2
Peacock Lane	C5
Pingle Street	B6
Pocklingtons Walk	C4-D4
Prebend Street	F3-F4
Princess Road East	E3-F3-F2
Princess Road West	D3-E3
Queen Street	E3
Rawson Street	D4-D5
Regent Road	D3-E3-E2-F2
Repton Street	A7-A8
Richard III Road	B5
Ridley Street	A3-A4
Roman Street	A3
Rutland Street	D5-E5-E6
Rydal Street	B2
St Augustine Road	A5-B5
St George Street	E5
St Georges Way	E5-F5-F6
St James Street	E6
St John Street	D8
St Margaret's Way	B8-C8-C7
St Martins	C5
St Mathews Way	E6-E7
St Nicholas Circle	B5-C5
St Peters Lane	C6
Salisbury Road	F2
Samuel Stuart	F3
Sanvey Gate	B7-C7
Sawday Street	C3
Saxby Street	F3-F4
Saxon Street	A3
Severn Street	F4
Short Street	C6-D6
Silver Street	C5-D5
Slater Street	B7
Soar Lane	B6-B7
South Albion Street	E4
Southampton Street	E5
Southgates	C4-C5
Sparkenhoe Street	F4-F5
Station Street	E4
Stuart Street	A2
Sussex Street	F6
Swain Street	E5-F5
Swan Street	B6-B7
Syston Street East	F8
Syston Street West	E8-F8
The Newarke	B4-C4
Taylor Road	F7-F8
Tewkesbury Street	A6
The Gateway	B4-C3
Thames Street	D7
Thirlemere Street	B2-C3
Tichbourne Street	F3
Tower Street	D2-D3
Tudor Close	A5
Tudor Road	A5-A6-A7
Turner Street	D3
Ullswater Street	B3-B2
University Road	E1-E2-F2-F3
Upper Brown Street	C4
Upper King Street	D3
Upperton Road	A2-B2
Vancouver Road	E8-F8
Vaughan Way	C6-C7
Vaughan Street	A6
Vernon Street	A6
Walnut Street	B2-C2-D2
Walton Street	A1
Wanlip Road	E8
Warren Street	A6
Warwick Street	A6-A5
Waterloo Way	E2-E3-D2-E4
Watling Street	C7-C8
Welford Road	D1-D2-D3-D4
Welles Street	B5
Wellington Street	D4-E3-E4
Western Boulevard	B2-B3
Western Road	A1-A2-A3-A4-B4
Wharf Street North	E7-E8
Wharf Street South	E6-E7
Wilberforce Road	A1-A2-A3
William Street	F6
Wilton Street	D7
Wimbledon Street	E5-E6
Windermere Street	B2-C2
Woodboy Street	E8-E7
Woodgate	A8-B8
Yeoman Street	D6-E5-E6
York Road	C4-D4

AA shop
132 Charles Street
Leicester LE1 1NA — E4

AA shop
128A Narborough Road
Narborough LE3 0BT — A2

Hinckley

Albert Road	B4
Alma Road	B4
Bowling Green Road	C3
Brick Kiln Street	A2
Bridge Road	B1
Brookfield Road	A1
Brookside	B1-C1
Browning Drive	A3
Brunel Road	A2-B2
Bute Close	A4
Butt Lane	C4
Canning Street	A2
Castle Street	B3-C3
Charles Street	C4
Church Walk	B3
Clarence Road	C2
Clarendon Road	A2-B2
Cleveland Road	A3
Clivesway	A4
Coley Close	B2
Council Road	B3
Coventry Lane	A2
Derby Road	B4
Druid Street	B3-B4
East Close	B1-C1
Factory Road	A4-B4
Fletcher Road	A4
Friary Close	C2
Garden Road	A4-B4
Glen Bank	C4
Gopsall Road	B4
Granby Road	A1-A2
Granville Road	A2
Hawley Road	A1-B1
Higham Way	C1
Highfields Road	C4
Hill Street	C2-C3
Holliers Walk	B3-B4
Hollycroft	A4
Hollycroft Crescent	A4
Holt Road	C1
Hurst Road	B2-C1-C2
John Street	B1
Lancaster Road	A2-B2
Leicester Road	C4
Linden Road	A3
London Road	C3
Lower Bond Street	B3-B4
Mansion Lane	A3-B3
Marchant Road	A2-A3
Merevale Avenue	A1
Mill Hill Road	A3
Mount Road	B2-C2
New Buildings	B3-B4
New Street	B4
Priesthills Road	B2-C2
Princess Road	C2
Queens Road	C2
Regent Street	A2-B2-A3
Royal Court	B1
Rugby Road	A2-A1-B1
Rutland Avenue	A1
St George's Avenue	A3-A4
Shakespeare Drive	A3
Southfield Road	B1-C1-C2
Spa Close	C3
Spa Lane	C3-C4
Spencer Street	B2
Springfield Road	B2
Stanley Road	A4
Station Road	B1-B2
Stockwellhead	B3
The Borough	B3
The Grove	A2
The Lawns	C3
Thornfield Way	C2
Thornycroft Road	C2-C3
Trinity Lane	A2-A3-A4-B4
Trinity Vicarage Road	A3
Upper Bond Street	B4
Victoria Street	C4
West Close	B1
Westray Drive	A4
Westfield Road	A1
Willow Bank Road	A1
Wood Street	B3-C3

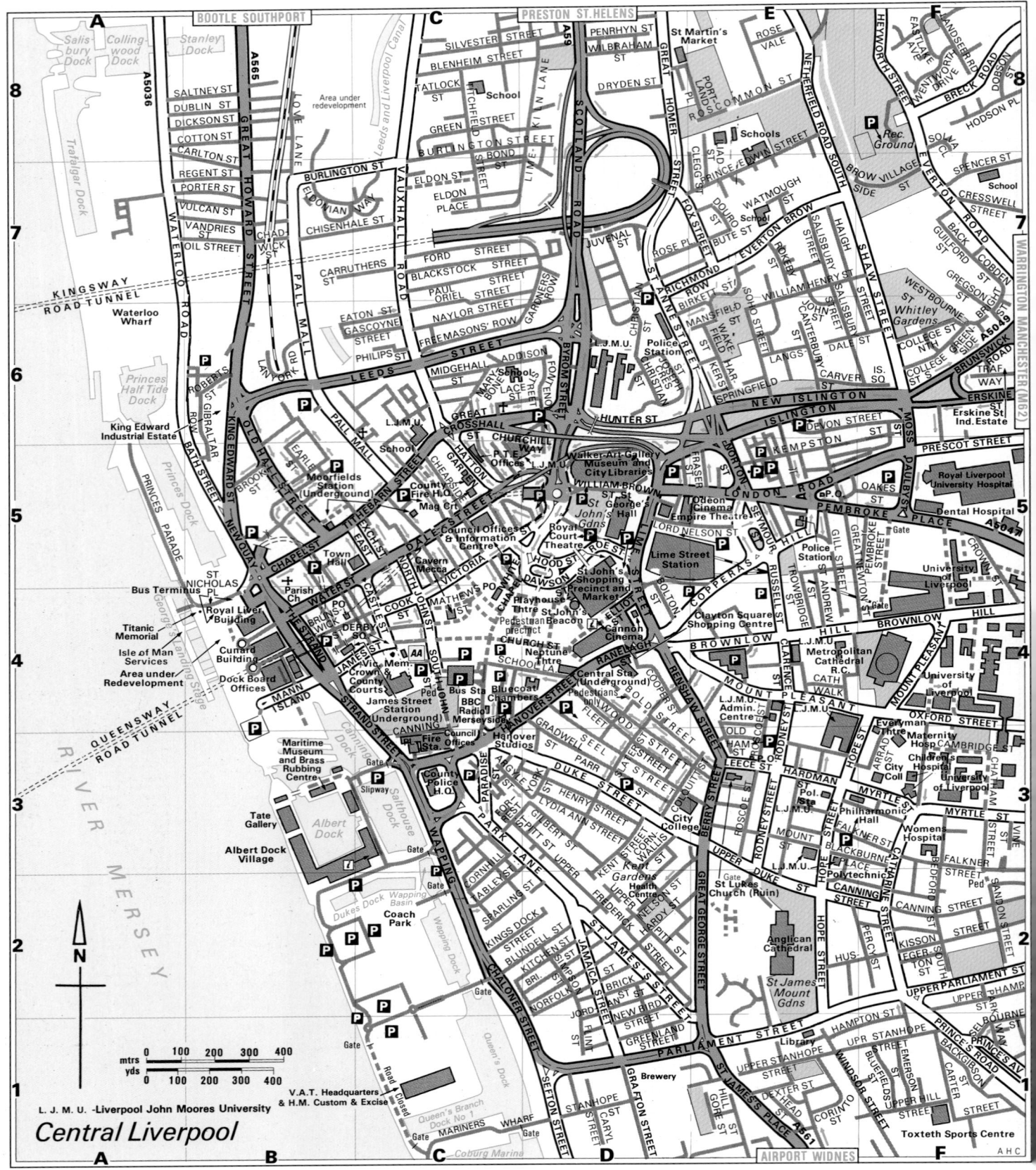

Liverpool

Although its dock area has been much reduced, Liverpool is still a thriving successful port. Formerly the centrepiece of the docks area are three monumental buildings: the Dock Board Offices, built in 1907 with a huge copper-covered dome; the Cunard Building, dating from 1912 and decorated with an abundance of ornamental carving; and the Liver Building, with two 'liver birds' crowning its twin cupolas. The entire waterfront south of the Liver Building has been transformed into one of the north-west's biggest tourist attractions. New offices and marinas have replaced most of the old warehouses, but one outstanding group, the Albert Dock Village, has survived and contains Britains largest collection of Grade I listed buildings. Among the buildings of the 1845 dock are the Tate Gallery and the Maritime Museum and Brassrubbing Centre.

Other museums and galleries include the Walker Art Gallery, with excellent collections of European painting and sculpture, Liverpool City Libraries, one of the oldest and largest public libraries in Britain, and Bluecoat Chambers, a Queen Anne building now used as a gallery and concert hall. Liverpool has two outstanding cathedrals: the Roman Catholic, completed in 1967 in an uncompromising controversial style; and the Anglican, constructed in the great tradition of Gothic architecture, but begun in 1904 and only recently completed. Also of interest are the 450ft-high St John's Beacon, with a viewing gallery, St George's Hall, possibly Europe's finest Greco-Roman-style building, the Cavern Mecca Shopping Centre, famed for its Beatles' connections and Cavern Club reconstruction, and a new Battle of the Atlantic exhibition.

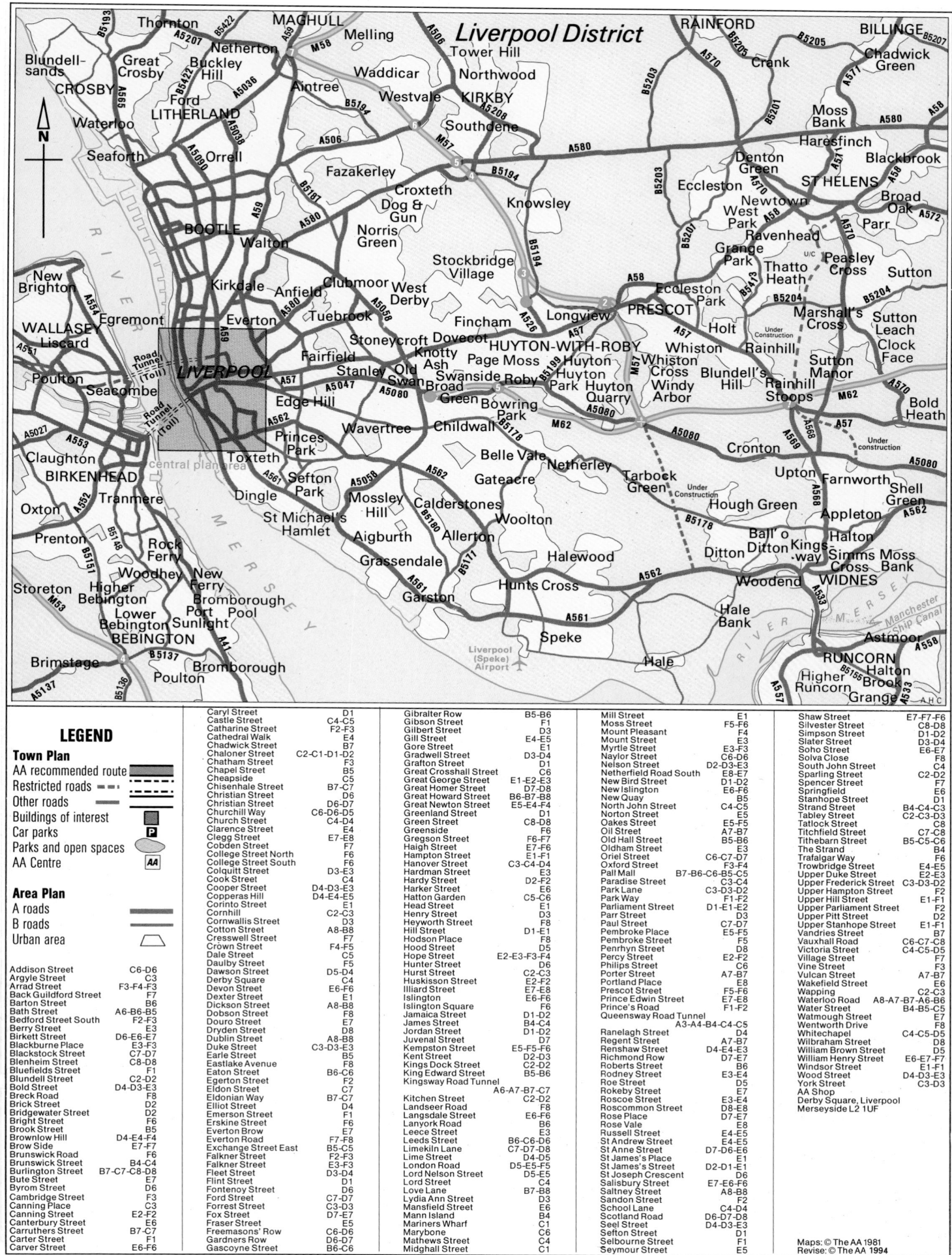

Liverpool District

LEGEND

Town Plan

AA recommended route
Restricted roads
Other roads
Buildings of interest
Car parks
Parks and open spaces
AA Centre

Area Plan

A roads
B roads
Urban area

Street	Grid
Addison Street	C6-D6
Argyle Street	C3
Arrad Street	F3-F4-F3
Back Guildford Street	F7
Barton Street	B6
Bath Street	A6-B6-B5
Bedford Street South	F2-F3
Berry Street	E3
Birkett Street	D6-E6-E7
Blackburne Place	E3-F3
Blackstock Street	C7-D7
Blenheim Street	C8-D8
Bluefields Street	F1
Blundell Street	D2-D2
Bold Street	D4-D3-E3
Breck Road	F8
Brick Street	D2
Bridgewater Street	D2
Bright Street	E4
Brook Street	B5
Brownlow Hill	D4-E4-F4
Brow Side	E7-F7
Brunswick Road	F6
Brunswick Street	B4-C4
Burlington Street	B7-C7-C8-D8
Bute Street	E7
Byrom Street	D6
Cambridge Street	F3
Canning Place	C3
Canning Street	E2-F2
Canterbury Street	E6
Carruthers Street	B7-C7
Carter Street	F1
Carver Street	E6-F6
Caryl Street	D1
Castle Street	C4-C5
Catharine Street	F2-F3
Cathedral Walk	E4
Chadwick Street	B7
Chaloner Street	C2-C1-D1-D2
Chatham Street	F3
Chapel Street	B5
Cheapside	C5
Chisenhale Street	D6
Christian Street	D6-D7
Christian Street	D6
Churchill Way	C6-D6-D5
Church Street	C4-D4
Clarence Street	E4
Clegg Street	E7-E8
Cobden Street	E7
College Street North	F6
College Street South	F6
Colquitt Street	D3-E3
Cook Street	C4
Cooper Street	D4-D3-E3
Copperas Hill	D4-E4-E5
Corinto Street	E1
Cornhill	C2-C3
Cornwallis Street	D3
Cotton Street	A8-B8
Cresswell Street	F7
Crown Street	F4-F5
Dale Street	C5
Daulby Street	F5
Dawson Street	D5-D4
Derby Square	C4
Devon Street	E6-F6
Dexter Street	E1
Dickson Street	A8-B8
Dobson Street	F8
Douro Street	E7
Dryden Street	D8
Dublin Street	A8-B8
Duke Street	C3-D3-E3
Earle Street	B5
Eastlake Avenue	F8
Eaton Street	B6-C6
Egerton Street	F2
Eldon Street	C7
Eldonian Way	B7-C7
Elliot Street	D4
Emerson Street	F1
Erskine Street	F6
Everton Brow	E7
Everton Road	F7-F8
Exchange Street East	B5-C5
Falkner Street	F2-F3
Falkner Street	E3-F3
Fleet Street	D3-D4
Flint Street	D1
Fontenoy Street	D6
Ford Street	C7-D7
Forrest Street	C3-D3
Fox Street	D7-E7
Fraser Street	E5
Freemasons' Row	C6-D6
Gardners Row	D6-D7
Gascoyne Street	B6-C6
Gibralter Row	B5-B6
Gibson Street	F1
Gilbert Street	D3
Gill Street	E4-E5
Gore Street	E1
Gradwell Street	D3-D4
Grafton Street	D1
Great Crosshall Street	C6
Great George Street	E1-E2-E3
Great Homer Street	D7-D8
Great Howard Street	B6-B7-B8
Great Newton Street	E5-E4-F4
Greenland Street	D1
Green Street	C8-D8
Greenside	F6
Gregson Street	F6-F7
Haigh Street	E7-F6
Hampton Street	E1-F1
Hanover Street	C3-C4-D4
Hardman Street	E3
Hardy Street	D2-F2
Harker Street	E6
Hatton Garden	C5-C6
Head Street	E1
Henry Street	D3
Heyworth Street	F7-F6
Hill Street	D1-E1
Hodson Place	F8
Hood Street	D5
Hope Street	E2-E3-F3-F4
Hunter Street	D6
Hurst Street	C2-C3
Huskisson Street	E2-F2
Illiard Street	E7-E8
Islington	E6-F6
Islington Square	F6
Jamaica Street	D1-D2
James Street	B4-C4
Jordan Street	D1-D2
Juvenal Street	D7
Kempston Street	E5-F5-F6
Kent Street	D2-D3
Kings Dock Street	D2
King Edward Street	B5-B6
Kingsway Road Tunnel	A6-A7-B7-C7
Kitchen Street	C2-D2
Landseer Road	F8
Langsdale Street	E6-F6
Lanyork Road	B6
Leece Street	E3
Leeds Street	B6-C6-D6
Limekiln Lane	C7-D7-D8
Lime Street	D5-E5-F5
London Road	D5-E5-F5
Lord Nelson Street	D5-E5
Lord Street	C4
Love Lane	B7-B8
Lydia Ann Street	D3
Mansfield Street	E6
Mann Island	B4
Mariners Wharf	C1
Marybone	C6
Mathews Street	C4
Midghall Street	C1
Mill Street	E1
Moss Street	F5-F6
Mount Pleasant	F4
Mount Street	E3
Myrtle Street	E3-F3
Naylor Street	C6-D6
Nelson Street	D2-D3-E3
Netherfield Road South	E8-E7
New Bird Street	D1-D2
New Islington	E6-F6
New Quay	B5
North John Street	C4-C5
Norton Street	E5
Oakes Street	E5-F5
Oil Street	A7-B7
Old Hall Street	B5-B6
Oldham Street	E1
Oriel Street	C6-C7-D7
Oxford Street	E3-F3
Pall Mall	B7-B6-C6-B5-C5
Paradise Street	C3-C4
Park Lane	C3-D3-D2
Park Way	F1-F2
Parliament Street	D1-E1-E2
Parr Street	D3
Paul Street	C7-D7
Pembroke Place	E5-F5
Pembroke Street	F5
Penrhyn Street	D8
Percy Street	E2-F2
Philips Street	C6
Porter Street	A7-B7
Portland Place	E8
Prescot Street	F5-F6
Prince Edwin Street	E7-E8
Prince's Road	F1-F2
Queensway Road Tunnel	A3-A4-B4-C4-C5
Ranelagh Street	D4
Regent Street	A7-B7
Renshaw Street	D4-E4-E3
Richmond Row	D7-E7
Roberts Street	B6
Rodney Street	E3-E4
Roe Street	D5
Rokeby Street	E7
Roscoe Street	E3-E4
Roscommon Street	D8-E8
Rose Place	D7-E7
Rose Vale	E8
Russell Street	E4-E5
St Andrew Street	E4-E5
St Anne Street	D7-D6-E6
St James's Place	E1
St James's Street	D2-D1-E1
St Joseph Crescent	D6
Salisbury Street	E7-E6-F6
Saltney Street	A8-B8
Sandon Street	F2
School Lane	C4-D4
Scotland Road	D6-D7-D8
Seel Street	D3-D4-E3
Sefton Street	D1
Selbourne Street	F1
Seymour Street	E5
Shaw Street	E7-F7-F6
Silvester Street	C8-D8
Simpson Street	D1-D2
Slater Street	D3-D4
Soho Street	E6-E7
Solva Close	F8
South John Street	C4
Sparling Street	C2-D2
Spencer Street	F7
Springfield	E6
Stanhope Street	D1
Strand Street	B4-C4-C3
Tabley Street	C2-C3-D3
Tatlock Street	C8
Titchfield Street	C7-C8
Tithebarn Street	B5-C5-C6
The Strand	B4
Trafalgar Way	F6
Trowbridge Street	E4-E5
Upper Duke Street	E2-E3
Upper Frederick Street	C3-D3-D2
Upper Hampton Street	F2
Upper Hill Street	E1-F1
Upper Parliament Street	F2
Upper Pitt Street	D2
Upper Stanhope Street	E1-F1
Vandries Street	B7
Vauxhall Road	C6-C7-C8
Victoria Street	C4-C5-D5
Village Street	F7
Vine Street	F3
Vulcan Street	A7-B7
Wakefield Street	E6
Wapping	C2-C3
Waterloo Road	A8-A7-B7-A6-B6
Water Street	B4-B5-C5
Watmough Street	E7
Wentworth Drive	F8
Whitechapel	C4-C5-D5
Wilbraham Street	D8
William Brown Street	D5
William Henry Street	E6-E7-F7
Windsor Street	E1-F1
Wood Street	D4-D3-E3
York Street	C3-D3

AA Shop
Derby Square, Liverpool
Merseyside L2 1UF

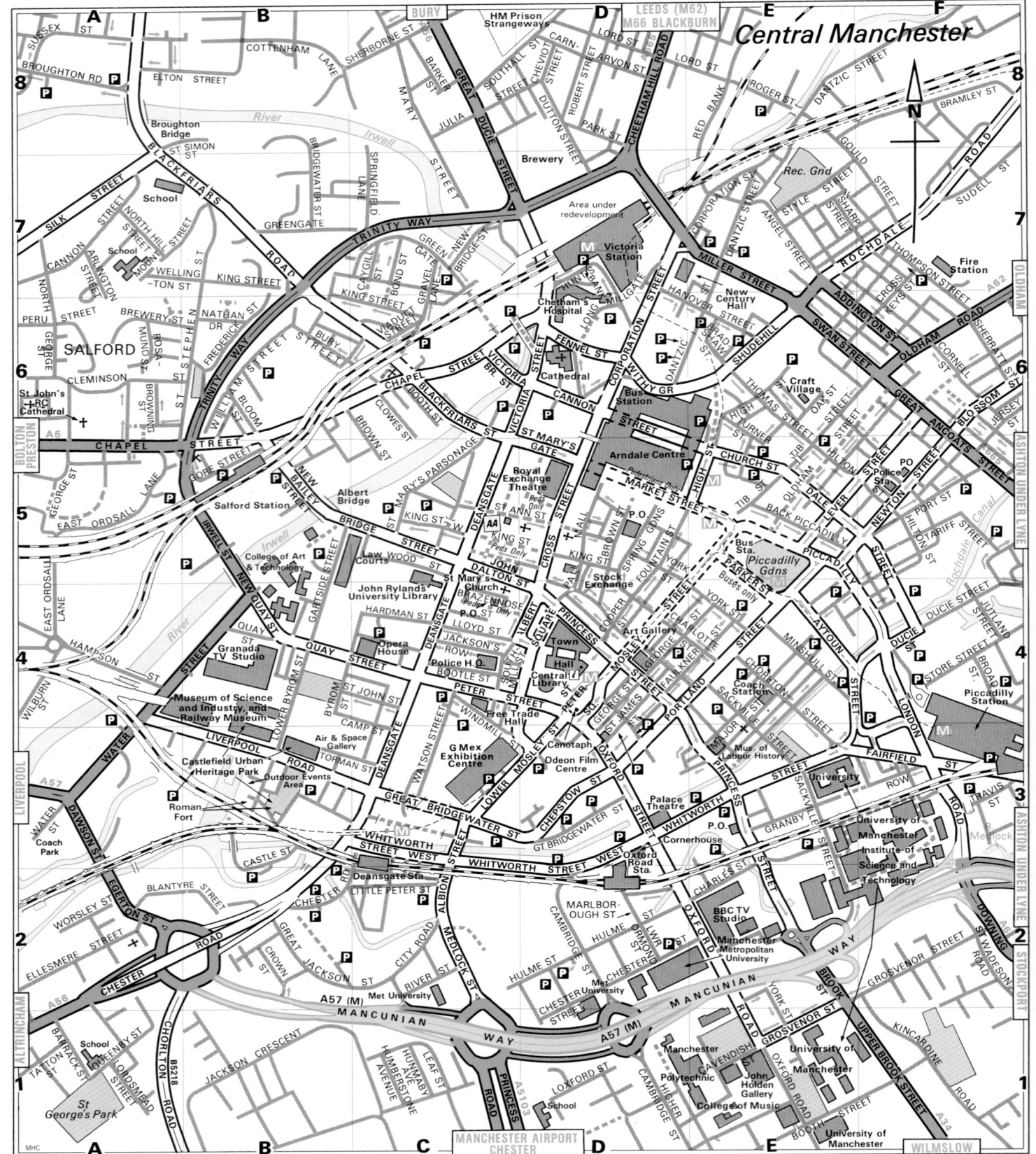

Manchester

Manchester is the regional centre for North-west England, with a population of over half a million. Commerce and industry are vital aspects of the city's character, but it is also an important cultural centre – the Hallé Orchestra has its home at the Free Trade Hall (a venue for many concerts besides classical music), there are several theatres, the John Rylands Library, which houses one of the most important collections of books in the world, and a number of

museums and galleries, including the Whitworth Gallery with its lovely watercolours.

Like many great cities it suffered badly during World War II, but some older buildings remain including the massive Gothic-style town hall of 1877.

Manchester Cathedral dates mainly from the 15th century and is noted for its fine tower and outstanding carved woodwork. Near by is Chetham's Hospital, also 15th-century. Much new development has taken place, and more is planned. The massive Arndale shopping centre caters for the vast population, and there are

huge international-standard hotels. The Museum of Science and Industry in the Castlefield Urban Heritage Park contains exhibits from the Industrial Revolution to the Space Age and includes the world's first passenger railway station. Near by are the Granada Television Studios where visitors can walk through the various film sets, including the famous 'Coronation Street', and the impressive G-Mex exhibition centre. Manchester is also the first city in Britain to reinstate an on-street tramway route as part of its new Light Rapid Transit system.

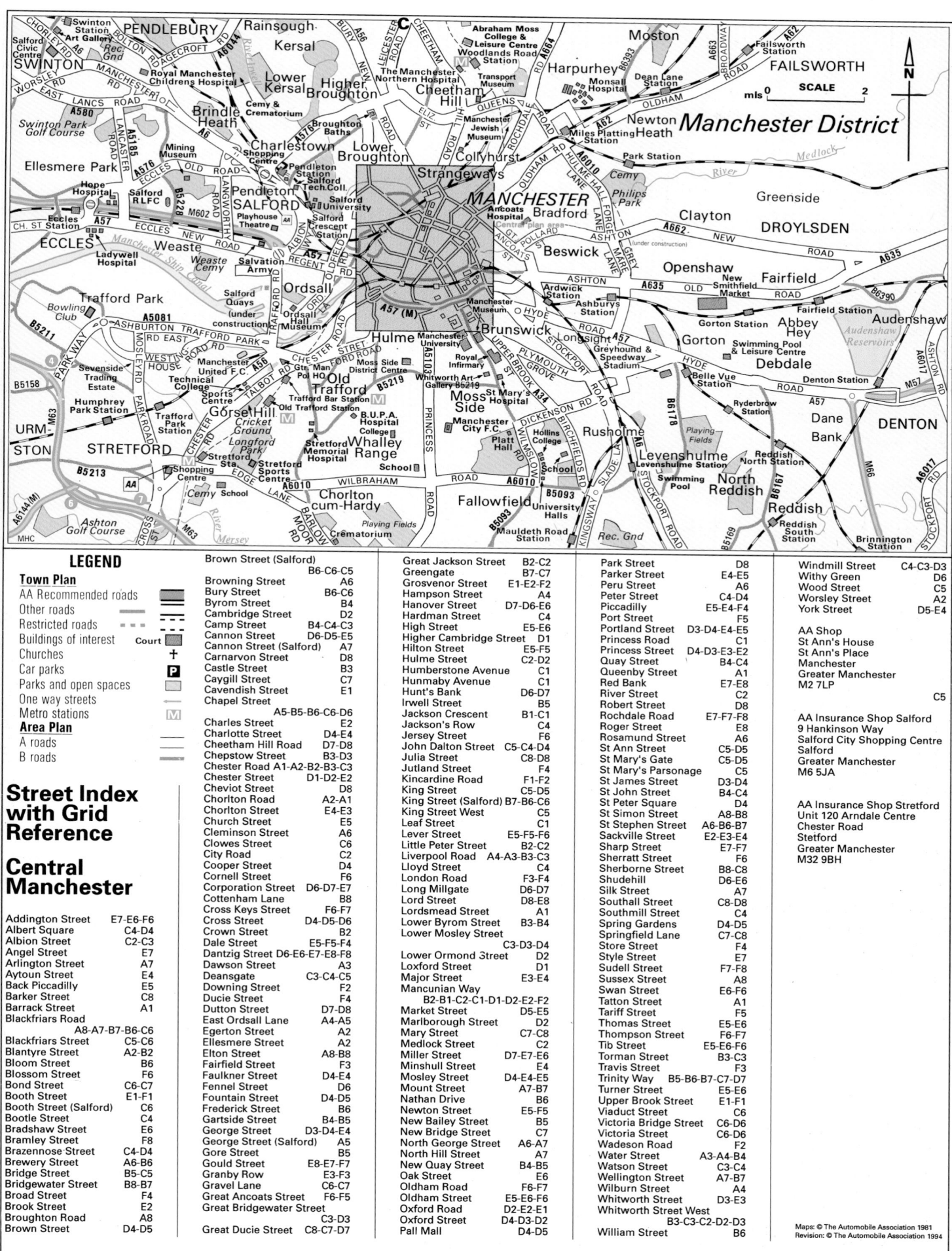

LEGEND

Town Plan

AA Recommended roads
Other roads
Restricted roads
Buildings of interest   Court
Churches   †
Car parks   P
Parks and open spaces
One way streets
Metro stations   M

Area Plan

A roads
B roads

Street Index with Grid Reference

Central Manchester

Addington Street	E7-E6-F6
Albert Square	C4-D4
Albion Street	C2-C3
Angel Street	E7
Arlington Street	A7
Aytoun Street	E4
Back Piccadilly	E5
Barker Street	C8
Barrack Street	A1
Blackfriars Road	A8-A7-B7-B6-C6
Blackfriars Street	C5-C6
Blantyre Street	A2-B2
Bloom Street	B6
Blossom Street	F6
Bond Street	C6-C7
Booth Street	E1-F1
Booth Street (Salford)	C6
Bootle Street	C4
Bradshaw Street	E6
Bramley Street	F8
Brazennose Street	C4-D4
Brewery Street	A6-B6
Bridge Street	B5-C5
Bridgewater Street	B8-B7
Broad Street	F4
Brook Street	E2
Broughton Road	A8
Brown Street	D4-D5

Brown Street (Salford)	B6-C6-C5
Browning Street	A6
Bury Street	B6-C6
Byrom Street	B4
Cambridge Street	D2
Camp Street	B4-C4-C3
Cannon Street	D6-D5-E5
Cannon Street (Salford)	A7
Carnarvon Street	D8
Castle Street	B3
Caygill Street	C7
Cavendish Street	E1
Chapel Street	A5-B5-B6-C6-D6
Charles Street	E2
Charlotte Street	D4-E4
Cheetham Hill Road	D7-D8
Chepstow Street	B3-D3
Chester Road	A1-A2-B2-B3-C3
Chester Street	D1-D2-E2
Cheviot Street	D8
Chorlton Road	A2-A1
Chorlton Street	E4-E3
Church Street	E5
Cleminson Street	A6
Clowes Street	C6
City Road	C2
Cooper Street	D4
Cornell Street	F6
Corporation Street	D6-D7-E7
Cottenham Lane	B8
Cross Keys Street	F6-F7
Cross Street	D4-D5-D6
Crown Street	B2
Dale Street	E5-F5-F4
Dantzig Street	D6-E6-E7-E8-F8
Dawson Street	A3
Deansgate	C3-C4-C5
Downing Street	F2
Ducie Street	F4
Dutton Street	D7-D8
East Ordsall Lane	A4-A5
Egerton Street	A2
Ellesmere Street	A2
Elton Street	A8-B8
Fairfield Street	F3
Faulkner Street	D4-E4
Fennel Street	D6
Fountain Street	D4-D5
Frederick Street	B6
Gartside Street	B4-B5
George Street	D3-D4-E4
George Street (Salford)	A5
Gore Street	B5
Gould Street	E8-E7-F7
Granby Row	E3-F3
Gravel Lane	C6-C7
Great Ancoats Street	F6-F5
Great Bridgewater Street	C3-D3
Great Ducie Street	C8-C7-D7

Great Jackson Street	B2-C2
Greengate	B7-C7
Grosvenor Street	E1-E2-F2
Hampson Street	A4
Hanover Street	D7-D6-E6
Hardman Street	C4
High Street	E5-E6
Higher Cambridge Street	D1
Hilton Street	E5-F5
Hulme Street	C2-D2
Humberstone Avenue	C1
Hunmaby Avenue	C1
Hunt's Bank	D6-D7
Irwell Street	B5
Jackson Crescent	B1-C1
Jackson's Row	C4
Jersey Street	F6
John Dalton Street	C5-C4-D4
Julia Street	C8-D8
Jutland Street	F4
Kincardine Road	F1-F2
King Street	C5-D5
King Street (Salford)	B7-B6-C6
King Street West	C5
Leaf Street	C1
Lever Street	E5-F5-F6
Little Peter Street	B2-C2
Liverpool Road	A4-A3-B3-C3
Lloyd Street	C4
London Road	F3-F4
Long Millgate	D6-D7
Lord Street	D8-E8
Lordsmead Street	A1
Lower Byrom Street	B3-B4
Lower Mosley Street	C3-D3-D4
Lower Ormond Street	D2
Loxford Street	D1
Major Street	E3-E4
Mancunian Way	B2-B1-C2-C1-D1-D2-E2-F2
Market Street	D5-E5
Marlborough Street	D2
Mary Street	C7-C8
Medlock Street	C2
Miller Street	D7-E7-E6
Minshull Street	E4
Mosley Street	D4-E4-E5
Mount Street	A7-B7
Nathan Drive	B6
Newton Street	E5-F5
New Bailey Street	B5
New Bridge Street	C7
North George Street	A6-A7
North Hill Street	A7
New Quay Street	B4-B5
Oak Street	E6
Oldham Road	F6-F7
Oldham Street	E5-E6-F6
Oxford Road	D2-E2-E1
Oxford Street	D4-D3-D2
Pall Mall	D4-D5

Park Street	D8
Parker Street	E4-E5
Peru Street	A6
Peter Street	C4
Piccadilly	E5-E4-F4
Port Street	F5
Portland Street	D3-D4-E4-E5
Princess Road	C1
Princess Street	D4-D3-E3-E2
Quay Street	B4-C4
Queenby Street	A1
Red Bank	E7-E8
River Street	C2
Robert Street	D8
Rochdale Road	E7-F7-F8
Roger Street	E8
Rosamund Street	A6
St Ann Street	C5-D5
St Mary's Gate	C5-D5
St Mary's Parsonage	C5
St James Street	D3-D4
St John Street	B4-C4
St Peter Square	D4
St Simon Street	A8-B8
St Stephen Street	A6-B6-B7
Sackville Street	E2-E3-E4
Sharp Street	E7-F7
Sherratt Street	F6
Sherborne Street	B8-C8
Shudehill	D6-E6
Silk Street	A7
Southall Street	C8-D8
Southmill Street	C4
Spring Gardens	D4-D5
Springfield Lane	C7-C8
Store Street	F4
Style Street	E7
Sudell Street	F7-F8
Sussex Street	A8
Swan Street	E6-F6
Tatton Street	A1
Tariff Street	F5
Thomas Street	E5-E6
Thompson Street	F6-F7-F7
Tib Street	E5-E6-F6
Torman Street	B3-C3
Travis Street	F3
Trinity Way	B5-B6-B7-C7-D7
Turner Street	E5-E6
Upper Brook Street	E1-F1
Viaduct Street	C6
Victoria Bridge Street	C6-D6
Victoria Street	C6-D6
Wadeson Road	F2
Water Street	A3-A4-B4
Watson Street	C3-C4
Wellington Street	A7-B7
Wilburn Street	A4
Whitworth Street	D3-E3
Whitworth Street West	B3-C3-C2-D2-D3
William Street	B6

Windmill Street	C4-C3-D3
Withy Green	D6
Wood Street	C5
Worsley Street	A2
York Street	D5-E4

AA Shop
St Ann's House
St Ann's Place
Manchester
Greater Manchester
M2 7LP
   C5

AA Insurance Shop Salford
9 Hankinson Way
Salford City Shopping Centre
Salford
Greater Manchester
M6 5JA

AA Insurance Shop Stretford
Unit 120 Arndale Centre
Chester Road
Stetford
Greater Manchester
M32 9BH

Maps: © The Automobile Association 1981
Revision: © The Automobile Association 1994

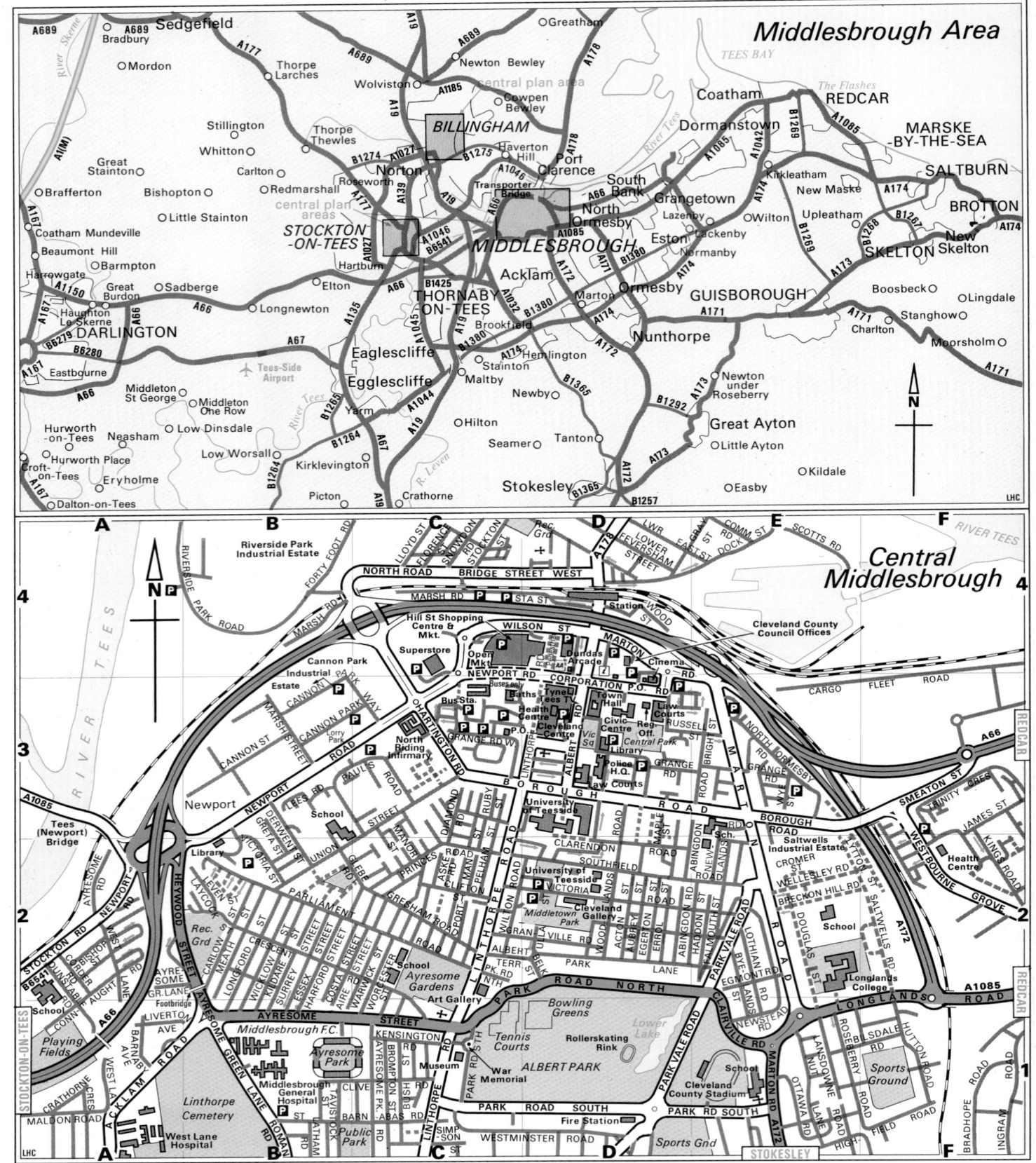

Middlesbrough

Middlesbrough was a small village on the River Tees when the Stockton & Darlington Railway purchased land there in the 1830s and transformed it into a busy coal exporting town. Within ten years it had become, and remains, a major centre of iron and steel-making. Now all the heavy industry has moved away, with steel-making transferred to a modern plant near Redcar, and the town has developed a new role as the commercial and administrative centre for Teesside.

Middlesbrough's most notable structure is the Transporter Bridge, built across the Tees in 1911. It is one of only two bridges of its type left in Britain. The town centre is modern with spacious shopping areas and new public buildings. The Dorman Museum covers the region's history and there are two major art galleries.

Stockton has a place in transport history; it was here, on 27 September 1825, that the world's first steam railway passenger service began. The town, also situated on the River Tees, became an engineering and shipbuilding centre, and is still an important industrial site today. It has a town hall of 1763 standing in the middle of one of the widest main streets in England.

Billingham Although a very old settlement, it has a modern centre with fine sports and leisure facilities at the Forum and Forum Theatre. There is also an international folklore festival held every August. Dominating the town are the petro-chemical industries.

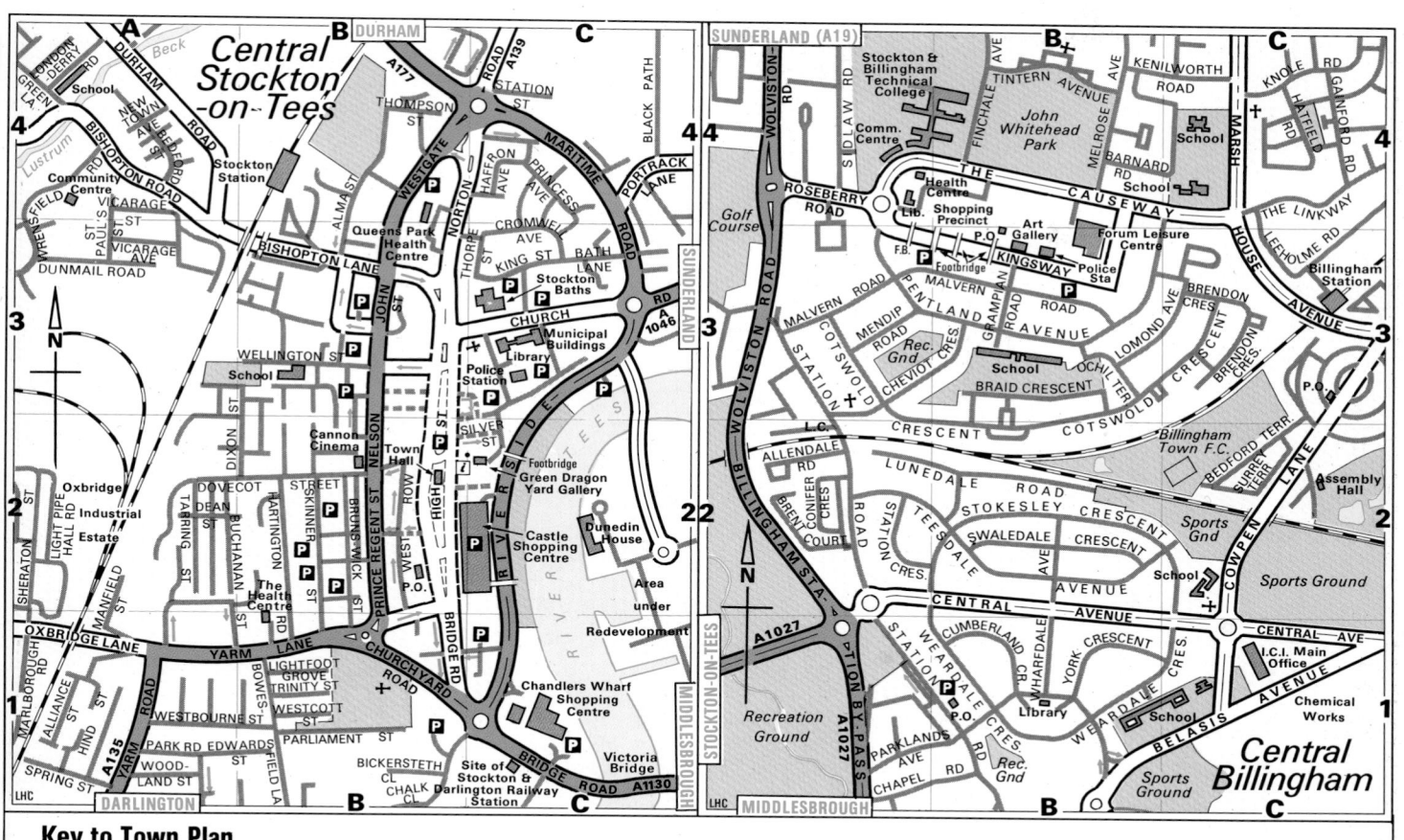

Key to Town Plan and Area Plan

Town Plan

- AA Recommended roads
- Other roads
- Restricted roads
- Buildings of interest
- Car parks **P**
- Parks and open spaces
- Churches +

Area Plan

- A roads
- B roads
- Locations Aycliffe ○
- Urban area

Street Index with Grid Reference

Middlesbrough

Stockton-on-Tees

Billingham

233

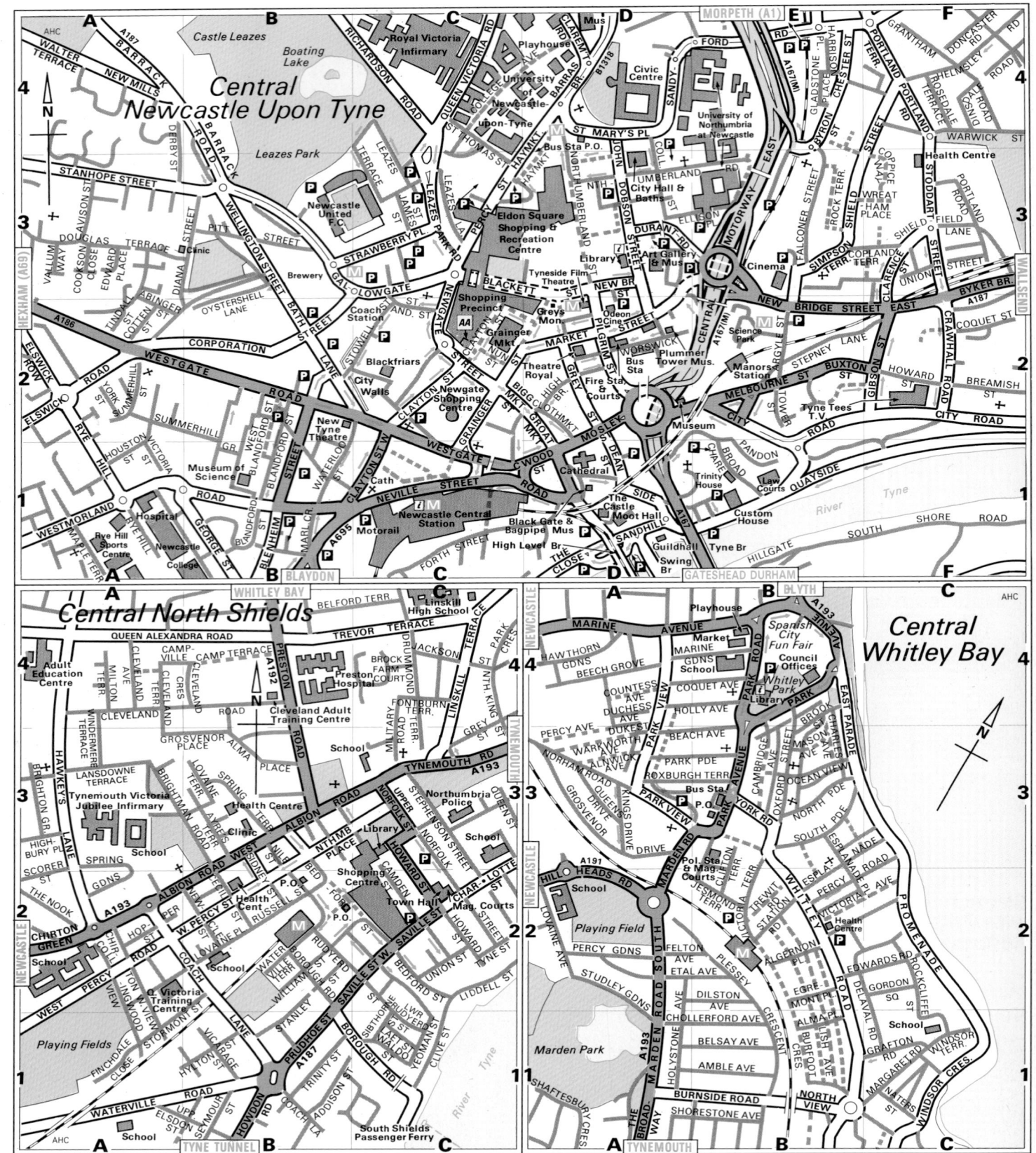

Newcastle

A city full of impressive features, Newcastle boasts no less than six road and rail bridges across the River Tyne. One of them, the High-level Bridge built by Robert Stephenson in 1845-49, is unusual in being a two-level bridge carrying both road and rail decks. At its north end is the 13th-century castle with a massive 82ft-high keep, while near by is the old cathedral with a graceful crown spire rising to 194ft.

Mostly rebuilt between 1835 and 1840, the city centre has many fine buildings and streets, among them the Central Station of 1849 and the magnificent curving Grey Street which leads up to the 135ft-high Grey Monument. Adjacent to the monument are the contrasting buildings of the Grainger Market (1835) and the vast Eldon Square shopping, sports and leisure centre.

Newcastle has two universities and a host of museums: the Museum of Science and Engineer-ing; the Hancock Museum (one of the finest natural history museums in the country); the Laing Art Gallery & Museum; the John George Joicey Museum; and the Bagpipe Museum. In addition there are three further museums within the University of Newcastle.

The city also has a pioneering light railway metro system and one of the largest public open spaces anywhere – Town Moor on the north side of the city centre covering nearly a thousand acres.

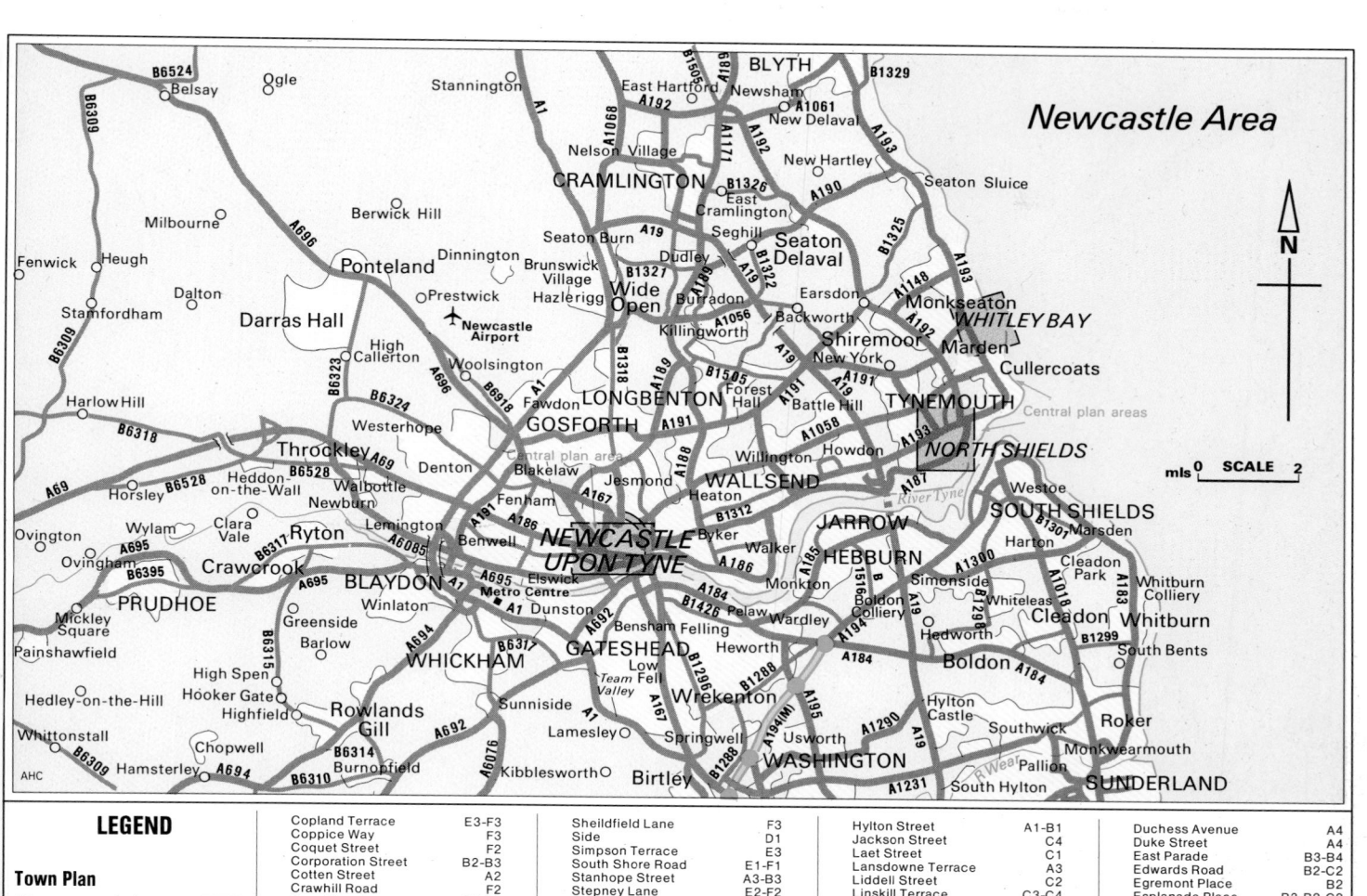

LEGEND

Town Plan

AA recommended route
Restricted roads
Other roads
Buildings of interest — Library 🅿
Car parks — 🅿
Parks and open spaces
Metro stations — Ⓜ
One way streets
Churches — ✝

Area Plan

A roads
B roads
Locations — Dudley ○
Urban area — ▭

Street Index with Grid Reference

Newcastle

Abinger Street	A2
Argyle Street	E2
Avison Street	A3
Barrack Road	A4-B4-B3
Barras Bridge	D4
Bath Lane	B2-C2
Bigg Market Street	C2-D2
Blackett Street	C3-D3-D2
Blandford Street	B1
Blenheim Street	B1-B2
Breamish Street	F2
Broad Chare	E1
Buxton Street	E2
Byker Bridge	F2-F3
Byran Street	E3-E4
Central Motorway	E1-D1-D2-E2-E3-E4
Chester Street	F2-F3
City Road	E1-E2-F2
Clarance Street	F2-F3
Claremont Road	D4
Clayton Street	C2
Clayton Street West	B1-C1-C2
Clothmarket	D2
College Avenue	C4-D4
College Street	D3-D4
Collingwood Street	C1-D1
Cookson Close	A3

Copland Terrace	E3-F3
Coppice Way	F3
Coquet Street	F2
Corporation Street	B2-B3
Cotten Street	A2
Crawhill Road	F2
Dean Street	D1-D2
Derby Street	A3-A4
Diana Street	A2-A3-B3
Dinsdale Place	F4
Doncaster Road	F4
Douglas Terrace	A3-B3
Durant Road	D3
Edward Street	A3
Ellison Place	D3-E3
Elswick Road	A2
Elswick Row	A2
Falconer Street	E3
Forth Street	C1-D1
Gallowgate	B3-C3
George Street	A1-B1
Gibson Street	F2
Gladstone Place	E4
Grainger Street	C1-C2-D2
Grantham Road	F4
Grey Street	D2
Great Market	D1-D2
Harrison Place	E4
Haymarket	D3-D4
Helmsley Road	F4
High Bridge	D2
Hillgate	E1
Houston Street	A1
Howard Street	F2
John Dobson Street	D3-D4
Leazes Lane	C3
Leazes Park Road	C3-C4
Leazes Terrace	C3-C4
Maple Terrace	A1
Market Street	D2
Marlborough Crescent	B1
Melbourne Street	E2-F2
Moseley Street	D1-D2
Neville Street	C1
New Bridge Road	F2-F3
New Bridge Street	D3-E3-E2-F2
New Bridge Street East	E2-F2
Newgate Street	C2-C3
New Mills	A4
Northumberland Street	D4-D3-E4
Nun Street	C2
Oakes Place	A2-B2-B3
Oystershell Lane	B2-B3
Pandon	E1
Percy Street	C3-D3-D4
Pilgrim Street	D2
Pitt Street	B3
Portland Road	F3-F4
Portland Terrace	F4
Quayside	D1-E1-F1-F2
Queen Victoria Road	C4
Rock Terrace	E3
Rosedale Terrace	F4
Rye Hill	A1-A2
St Andrews Street	C2
St James Street	C3
St Mary's Place	D4
St Nicholas Square	D1-D2
St Thomas Street	C3-C4
Sandyford Road	D4-E4
Sandhill	D1
Shield Street	E3-F3-F4

Sheildfield Lane	F3
Side	D1
Simpson Terrace	E3
South Shore Road	E1-F1
Stanhope Street	A3-B3
Stepney Lane	E2-F2
Stoddart Street	F3
Stowell Street	B2-C2
Strawberry Place	B3-C3
Summerhill Grove	A2-B2-B1
Summerhill Street	A2
The Close	D1
Tindall Street	A2
Tower Street	E2
Union Street	F3
Vallum Way	A3
Victoria Square	E4
Victoria Street	A1
Walter Terrace	A4
Warwick Street	F4
Waterloo Street	B1-B2-C2
Wellington Street	B3
Westgate Road	A2-B2-C2-C1-D1
Westmorland Road	A1-B1
West Blandford Street	B1-B2
Worswick Street	D2
Wreatham Place	E3-F3
York Street	A2
AA Shop	
33-35 Whitecrossway	
Newgate Mall, Eldon Centre	
Newcastle, Tyne & Wear NE1 7YN	
	C2

North Shields

Addison Street	B1
Albion Road	B3-C3
Albion Road West	A2-B2-B3
Alma Place	B3
Ayre's Terrace	B3
Bedford Street	B3-B2-C2
Belford Terrace	B4-C4
Borough Road	B2-B1-C1
Brightman Road	A3-B3
Brighton Grove	A3
Brock Farm Court	C4
Camden Street	C2-C3
Camp Terrace	B4
Campville	A4-B4
Cecil Street	B2
Charlotte Street	C2-C3
Chirton Green	A2
Chirton West View	A1-A2
Cleveland Avenue	A4
Cleveland Crescent	A4
Cleveland Road	A4-B4
Cleveland Terrace	A3-A4
Clive Street	C1-C2
Coach Lane	A2-B2-B1
Collingwood View	A1-A2
Drummond Terrace	C3-C4
Finchdale Close	A1
Fontbarn Terrace	C4
Grey Street	C3-C4
Grosvenor Place	A3-B3
Hawkey's Lane	A2-A3-A4
Highbury Place	A2
Hopper Street	A2
Howard Street	C2-C3
Howdon Road	B1

Hylton Street	A1-B1
Jackson Street	C4
Laet Street	C1
Lansdowne Terrace	A3
Liddell Street	C2
Linskill Terrace	C3-C4
Lovaine Place	B2
Lovaine Terrace	B3
Lower Rudyerd Street	C1
Military Road	C3-C4
Milton Terrace	A4
Nile Street	B3
Norfolk Street	C2-C3
North King Street	C3-C4
Northumberland Place	B3-C3
Park Crescent	C4
Preston Road	B3-B4
Prudhoe Street	B1-B2
Queen Alexandra Road	A4-B4
Queen Street	C3
Rudyerd Street	B2-C2-C1
Russell Street	B2
Sackville Street West	B2-C2
Saville Street	C2
Scorer Street	A2-A3
Seymour Street	B1
Sibthorpe Street	C1-C2
Sidney Street	B2-B3
Spring Gardens	A2-A3
Spring Terrace	B3
Stanley Street	B1-B2
Stephenson Street	C2-C3
Stormont Street	A1-A2-B2
The Nook	A2
Trevor Terrace	B4-C4
Trinity Street	B1
Tyne Street	C2
Tynemouth Road	B3-B4
Union Street	C2
Upper Elsdon Street	A1-B1
Upper Norfolk Street	C3
Vicarage Street	B1
Waldo Street	C1
Waterville Road	A1-B1
Waterville Terrace	B2
West Percy Road	A1-A2
West Percy Street	A2-B2-B3
William Street	B2-C2
Windermere Terrace	A3-A4
Yeoman Street	C1-C2

Whitley Bay

Algernon Place	B2
Alma Street	B1
Alnwick Avenue	A3
Amble Avenue	A1-B1
Beach Avenue	A3-B3-B4
Beech Grove	A4
Belsay Avenue	A1-B1
Brook Street	B3-B4
Burfoot Crescent	B1
Burnside Road	A1-B1
Cambridge Avenue	B3-B4
Charles Avenue	B3-B4
Chollerford Avenue	A1-B1
Clifton Terrace	B2-B3
Coquet Avenue	A4-B4
Countess Avenue	A4
Delaval Road	B2-C2-C1
Dilston Avenue	A2-B2

Duchess Avenue	A4
Duke Street	A4
East Parade	B3-B4
Edwards Road	B2-C2
Egremont Place	B2
Esplanade Place	B3-B2-C2
Etal Avenue	A2-B2
Felton Avenue	A2-B2
Gordon Square	C2
Grafton Road	C1
Grosvenor Drive	A3
Hawthorne Gardens	A4
Hill Heads Road	A2-A3-A2
Holly Avenue	A4-B4
Holystone Avenue	A1-A2
Jesmond Terrace	A2-B2
Kings Drive	A3
Lish Avenue	B1
Lovaine Avenue	A2
Marden Road	A2-A3-B3
Marden Road South	A1-A2
Margaret Road	C1
Marine Avenue	A4-B4
Marine Gardens	A4-B4
Mason Avenue	B3
Naters Street	C1
Norham Road	A3
North Parade	B3
North View	B1
Ocean View	B3
Oxford Street	B3-B4
Park Avenue	B3-B4
Park Parade	A3-B3
Park Road	B4
Park View	A3-A4
Percy Avenue	A3-A4
Percy Gardens	A2
Percy Road	B2-C2-C3
Plessey Crescent	A2-B2-B1
Promenade	C1-C2-C3
Queens Drive	A3
Rockcliffe Street	C1-C2
Roxburgh Terrace	A3-B3
Shaftesbury Crescent	A1
Shorestone Avenue	A1-B1
South Parade	B3
Station Road	B2
Studley Gardens	A1-A2
The Broadway	A1
Trewit Road	B2
Victoria Avenue	B2-C2
Victoria Terrace	B2-B3
Warkworth Avenue	A3
Whitley Road	B1-B2-B3
Windsor Crescent	C1
Windsor Terrace	C1
York Road	B3

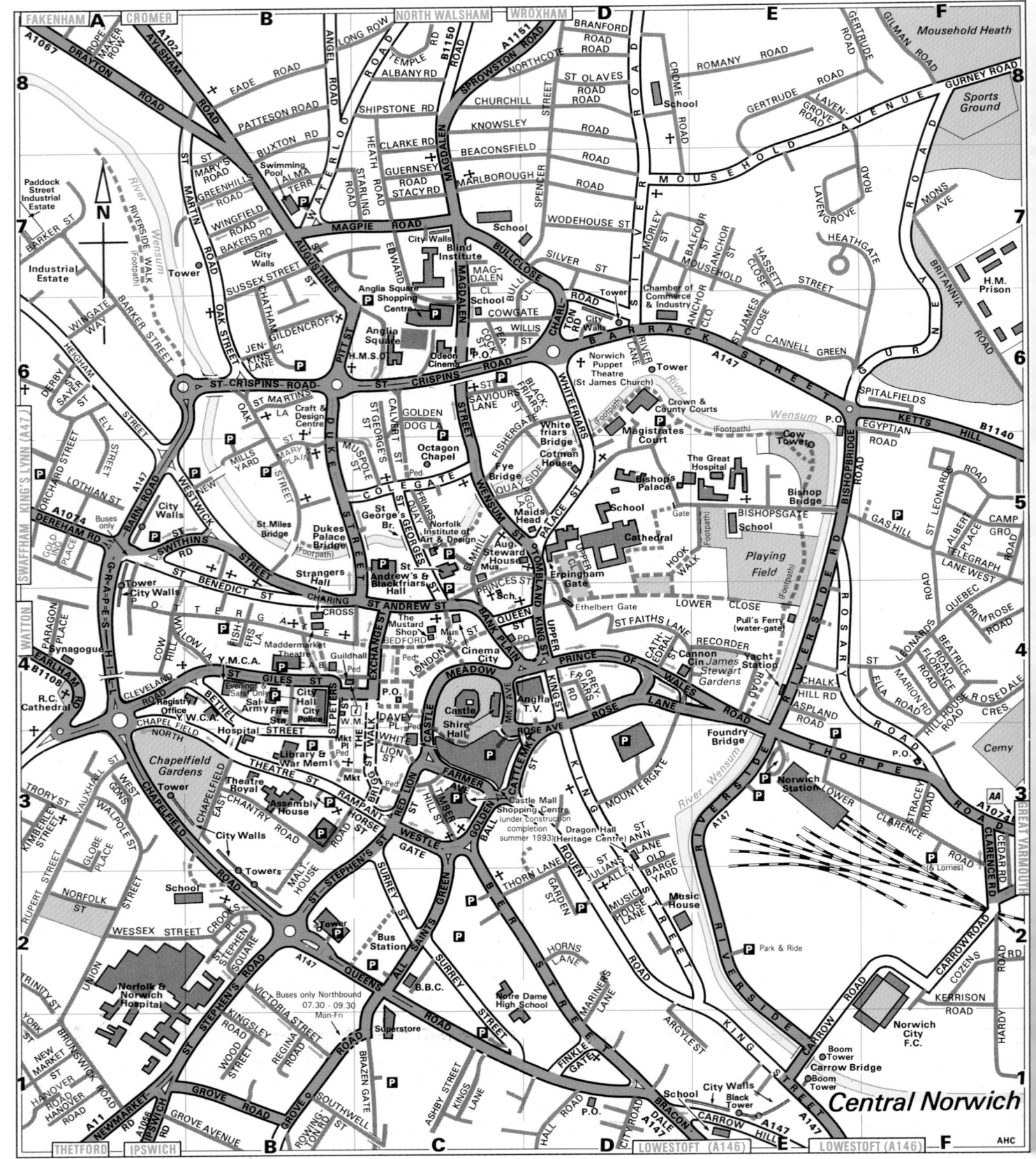

Norwich

This beautiful medieval walled city on the River Wensum has been a regional capital for centuries, and was once second only in importance to London. It is still a major commercial and administrative centre and fortunately has not been spoiled by insensitive redevelopment. Norwich still has the greatest number of surviving medieval churches (31) of any city in Europe and retains many quiet narrow streets and ways, such as Elm Hill, lined with fine old buildings.

Dominating the city centre from its substantial mound is the stone keep of the Norman castle, now in use as the Castle Museum and housing collections on local history and the Norwich school of painters. To the north-east is the magnificent Norman cathedral, a huge landmark with a graceful tower and spire soaring to 315ft and second only in height to Salisbury. Among the cathedral's many features are the largest cloisters in Britain, 800 carved roof bosses, the finely carved choir stalls and the oldest bishops' throne (possibly Saxon) in England.

Other major places of interest are the Guildhall and

the late 14th-century Bridewell Museum, the Royal Norfolk Regimental Museum in the Shirehall, the St Peter Hungate Church Museum containing the Brassrubbing Centre, and Strangers' Hall, a notable 15th-century building now housing a folk museum. At the University of East Anglia, the Sainsbury Centre for Visual Arts displays 19th- and 20th-century European art and worldwide ethnographical art. Pull's Ferry (the cathedral water gate), pleasant riverside walks, extensive markets, theatres, medieval halls, Georgian buildings and two cathedral gateways are yet more reasons for visiting this fine city.

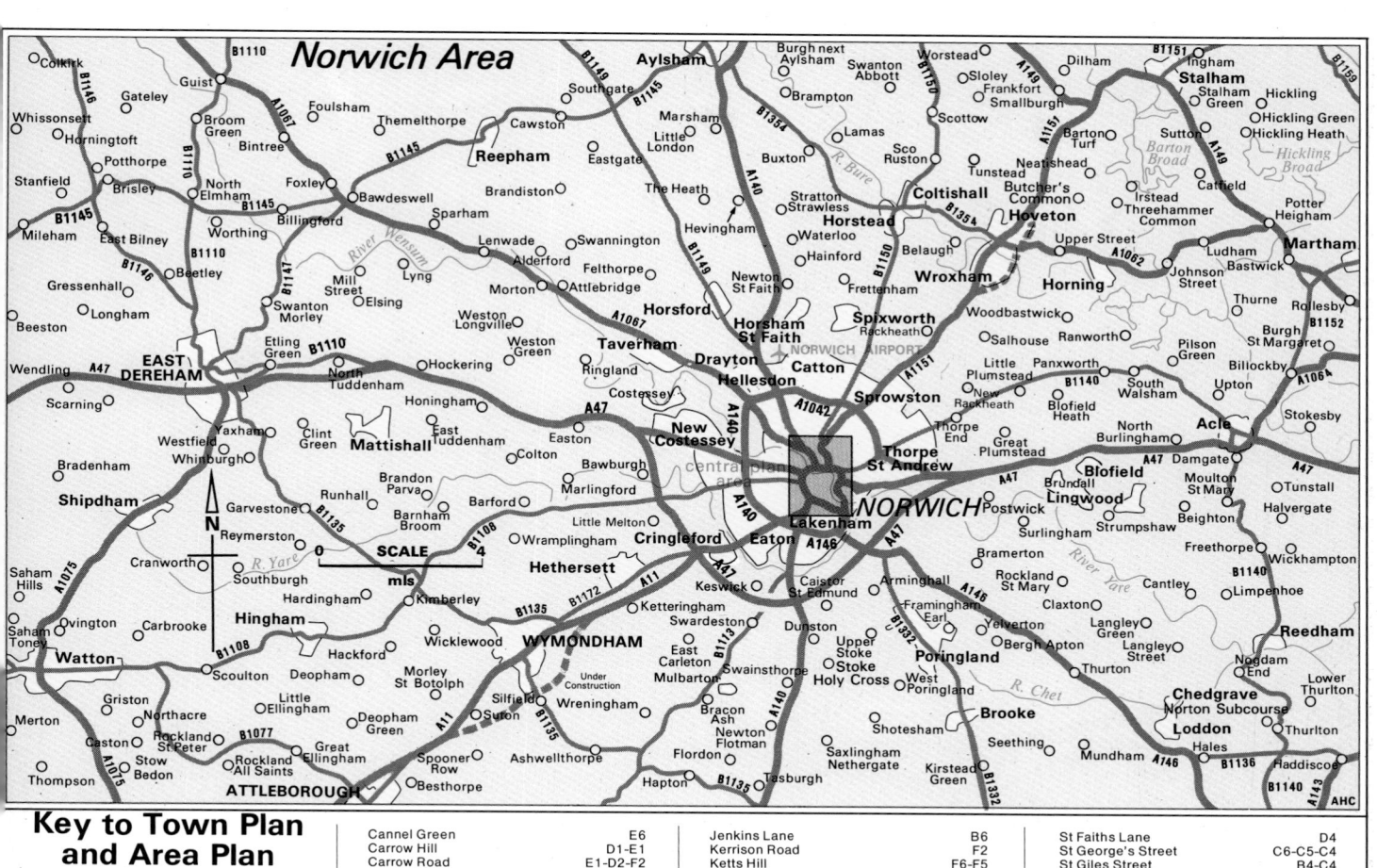

Norwich Area

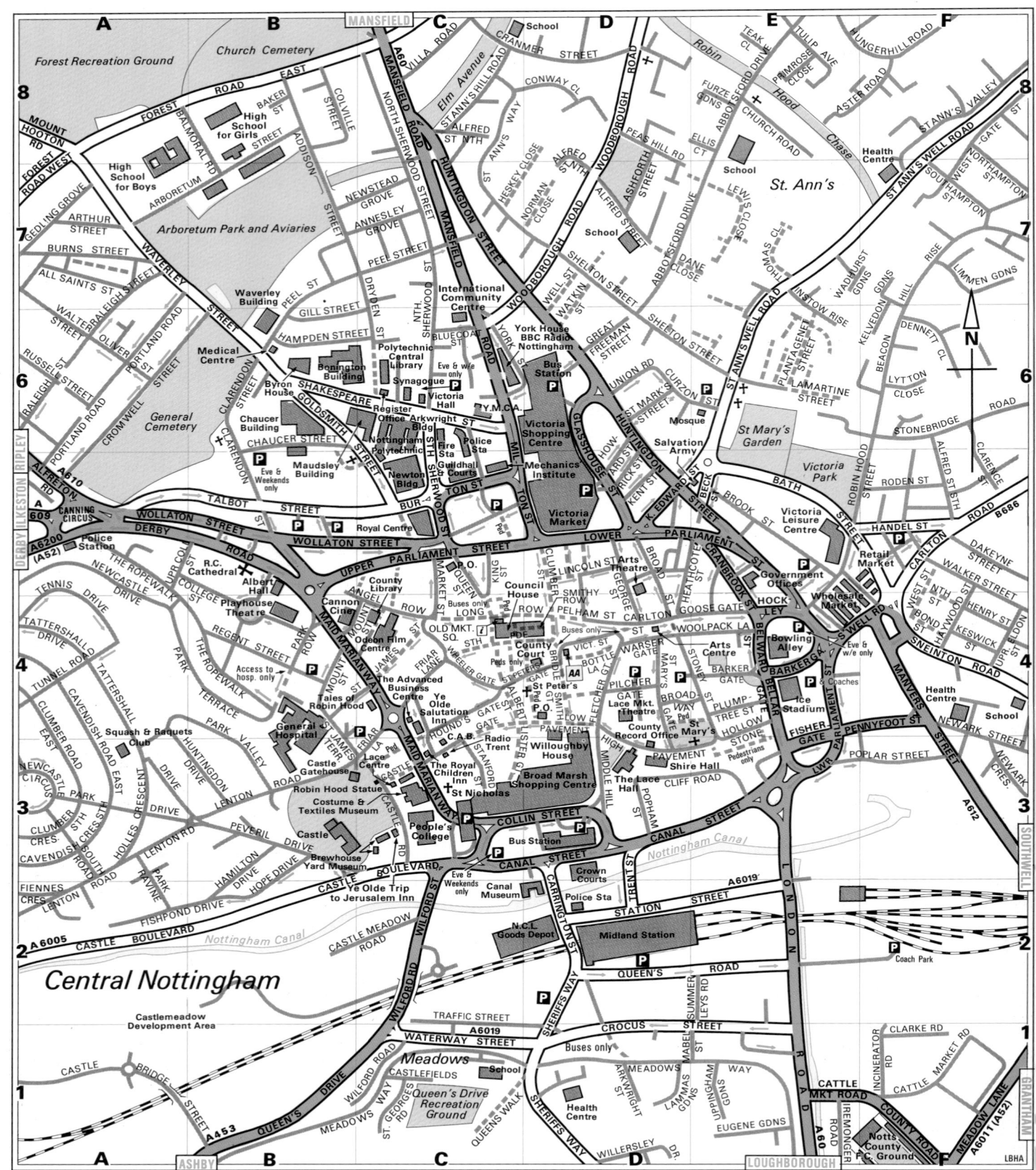

Nottingham

Hosiery and lace were the foundations upon which Nottingham's prosperity were built. The stockings came first – a knitting machine for these had been invented by a Nottinghamshire man as early as 1589 – but a machine called a 'tickler', which enabled simple patterns to be created in the stocking fabric, prompted the development of machine-made lace. The earliest fabric was produced in 1768, and an example from that period is kept in the city's Museum of Costume and Textiles in Castlegate. In fact, the entire history of lacemaking is beautifully explained in this converted row of Georgian terraces. The Industrial Museum at Wollaton Park has many other machines and exhibits tracing the development of the knitting industry, as well as displays on the other industries which have brought wealth to the city – tobacco, pharmaceuticals, engineering and printing.

Also at Wollaton Park is the Natural History Museum, while nearer the city centre are the Canal Museum and the Brewhouse Yard Museum, a marvellous collection of items from daily life in the city up to the present day. No visit to Nottingham is complete without mention of Robin Hood, the partly mythical figure whose statue stands in the castle grounds. Although the castle itself has Norman foundations, the present structure is largely Victorian and currently houses a museum.

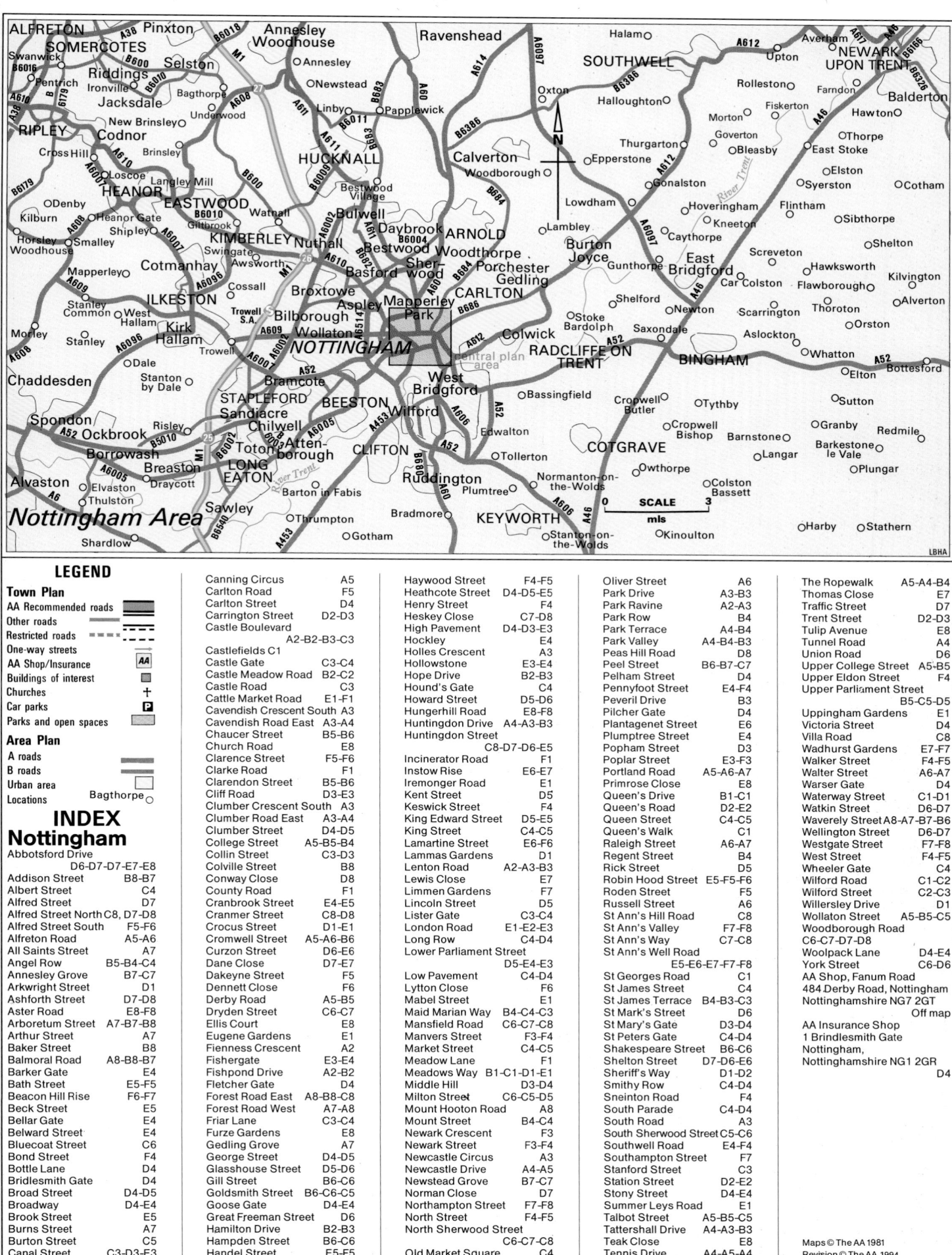

Nottingham Area

LEGEND

Town Plan
- AA Recommended roads
- Other roads
- Restricted roads
- One-way streets
- AA Shop/Insurance
- Buildings of interest
- Churches
- Car parks
- Parks and open spaces

Area Plan
- A roads
- B roads
- Urban area
- Locations — Bagthorpe

INDEX
Nottingham

Abbotsford Drive D6-D7-D7-E7-E8
Addison Street B8-B7
Albert Street C4
Alfred Street D7
Alfred Street North C8, D7-D8
Alfred Street South F5-F6
Alfreton Road A5-A6
All Saints Street A7
Angel Row B5-B4-C4
Annesley Grove B7-C7
Arkwright Street D1
Ashforth Street D7-D8
Aster Road E8-F8
Arboretum Street A7-B7-B8
Arthur Street A7
Baker Street B8
Balmoral Road A8-B8-B7
Barker Gate E4
Bath Street E5-F5
Beacon Hill Rise F6-F7
Beck Street E5
Bellar Gate E4
Belward Street E4
Bluecoat Street C6
Bond Street F4
Bottle Lane D4
Bridlesmith Gate D4
Broad Street D4-D5
Broadway D4-E4
Brook Street E5
Burns Street A7
Burton Street C5
Canal Street C3-D3-E3

Canning Circus A5
Carlton Road F5
Carlton Street D4
Carrington Street D2-D3
Castle Boulevard A2-B2-B3-C3
Castlefields C1
Castle Gate C3-C4
Castle Meadow Road B2-C2
Castle Road C3
Cattle Market Road E1-F1
Cavendish Crescent South A3
Cavendish Road East A3-A4
Chaucer Street B5-B6
Church Road E8
Clarence Street F5-F6
Clarke Road F1
Cliff Road D3-E3
Clumber Crescent South A3
Clumber Road East A3-A4
Clumber Street D4-D5
College Street A5-B5-B4
Collin Street C3-D3
Colville Street B8
Conway Close D8
County Road F1
Cranbrook Street E4-E5
Cranmer Street C8-D8
Crocus Street D1-E1
Cromwell Street A5-A6-B6
Curzon Street D6-E6
Dane Close D7-E7
Dakeyne Street F5
Dennett Close F6
Derby Road A5-B5
Dryden Street C6-C7
Ellis Court E8
Eugene Gardens E1
Fienness Crescent A2
Fishergate E3-E4
Fishpond Drive A2-B2
Fletcher Gate D4
Forest Road East A8-B8-C8
Forest Road West A7-A8
Friar Lane C3-C4
Furze Gardens E8
Gedling Grove A7
George Street D4-D5
Glasshouse Street D5-D6
Gill Street B6-C6
Goldsmith Street B6-C6-C5
Goose Gate D4-E4
Great Freeman Street D6
Hamilton Drive B2-B3
Hampden Street B6-C6
Handel Street E5-F5

Haywood Street F4-F5
Heathcote Street D4-D5-E5
Henry Street F4
Heskey Close C7-D8
High Pavement D4-D3-E3
Hockley E4
Holles Crescent A3
Hollowstone E3-E4
Hope Drive B2-B3
Hound's Gate C4
Howard Street D5-D6
Hungerhill Road E8-F8
Huntingdon Drive A4-A3-B3
Huntingdon Street C8-D7-D6-E5
Incinerator Road F1
Instow Rise E6-E7
Iremonger Road E1
Kent Street D5
Keswick Street F4
King Edward Street D5-E5
King Street C4-C5
Lamartine Street E6-F6
Lammas Gardens D1
Lenton Road A2-A3-B3
Lewis Close E7
Limmen Gardens F7
Lincoln Street D5
Lister Gate C3-C4
London Road E1-E2-E3
Long Row C4-D4
Lower Parliament Street D5-E4-E3
Low Pavement C4-D4
Lytton Close F6
Mabel Street E1
Maid Marian Way B4-C4-C3
Mansfield Road C6-C7-C8
Manvers Street F3-F4
Market Street C4-C5
Meadow Lane F1
Meadows Way B1-C1-D1-E1
Middle Hill D3-D4
Milton Street C6-C5-D5
Mount Hooton Road A8
Mount Street B4-C4
Newark Crescent F3
Newark Street F3-F4
Newcastle Circus A3
Newcastle Drive A4-A5
Newstead Grove B7-C7
Norman Close D7
Northampton Street F7-F8
North Street F4-F5
North Sherwood Street C6-C7-C8
Old Market Square C4

Oliver Street A6
Park Drive A3-B3
Park Ravine A2-A3
Park Row B4
Park Terrace A4-B4
Park Valley A4-B4-B3
Peas Hill Road D8
Peel Street B6-B7-C7
Pelham Street D4
Pennyfoot Street E4-F4
Peveril Drive B3
Pilcher Gate D4
Plantagenet Street E6
Plumptree Street E4
Popham Street D3
Poplar Street E3-F3
Portland Road A5-A6-A7
Primrose Close E8
Queen's Drive B1-C1
Queen's Road D2-E2
Queen Street C4-C5
Queen's Walk C1
Raleigh Street A6-A7
Regent Street B4
Rick Street D5
Robin Hood Street E5-F5-F6
Roden Street F5
Russell Street A6
St Ann's Hill Road C5
St Ann's Valley F7-F8
St Ann's Way C7-C8
St Ann's Well Road E5-E6-E7-F7-F8
St Georges Road C1
St James Street C4
St James Terrace B4-B3-C3
St Mark's Street D6
St Mary's Gate D3-D4
St Peters Gate C4-D4
Shakespeare Street B6-C6
Shelton Street D7-D6-E6
Sheriff's Way D1-D2
Smithy Row C4-D4
Sneinton Road F4
South Parade C4-D4
South Road A3
South Sherwood Street C5-C6
Southwell Road E4-F4
Southampton Street F7
Stanford Street C3
Station Street D2-E2
Stony Street D4-E4
Summer Leys Road E1
Talbot Street A5-B5-C5
Tattershall Drive A4-A3-B3
Teak Close E8
Tennis Drive A4-A5-A4

The Ropewalk A5-A4-B4
Thomas Close E7
Traffic Street D7
Trent Street D2-D3
Tulip Avenue E8
Tunnel Road A4
Union Road D6
Upper College Street A5-B5
Upper Eldon Street F4
Upper Parliament Street B5-C5-D5
Uppingham Gardens E1
Victoria Street D4
Villa Road C8
Wadhurst Gardens E7-F7
Walker Street F4-F5
Walter Street A6-A7
Warser Gate D4
Waterway Street C1-D1
Watkin Street D6-D7
Waverely Street A8-A7-B7-B6
Wellington Street D6-D7
Westgate Street F7-F8
West Street F4-F5
Wheeler Gate C4
Wilford Road C1-C2
Wilford Street C2-C3
Willersley Drive D1
Wollaton Street A5-B5-C5
Woodborough Road C6-C7-D7-D8
Woolpack Lane D4-E4
York Street C6-D6

AA Shop, Fanum Road
484 Derby Road, Nottingham
Nottinghamshire NG7 2GT
Off map

AA Insurance Shop
1 Brindlesmith Gate
Nottingham,
Nottinghamshire NG1 2GR
D4

Maps © The AA 1981
Revision © The AA 1994

239

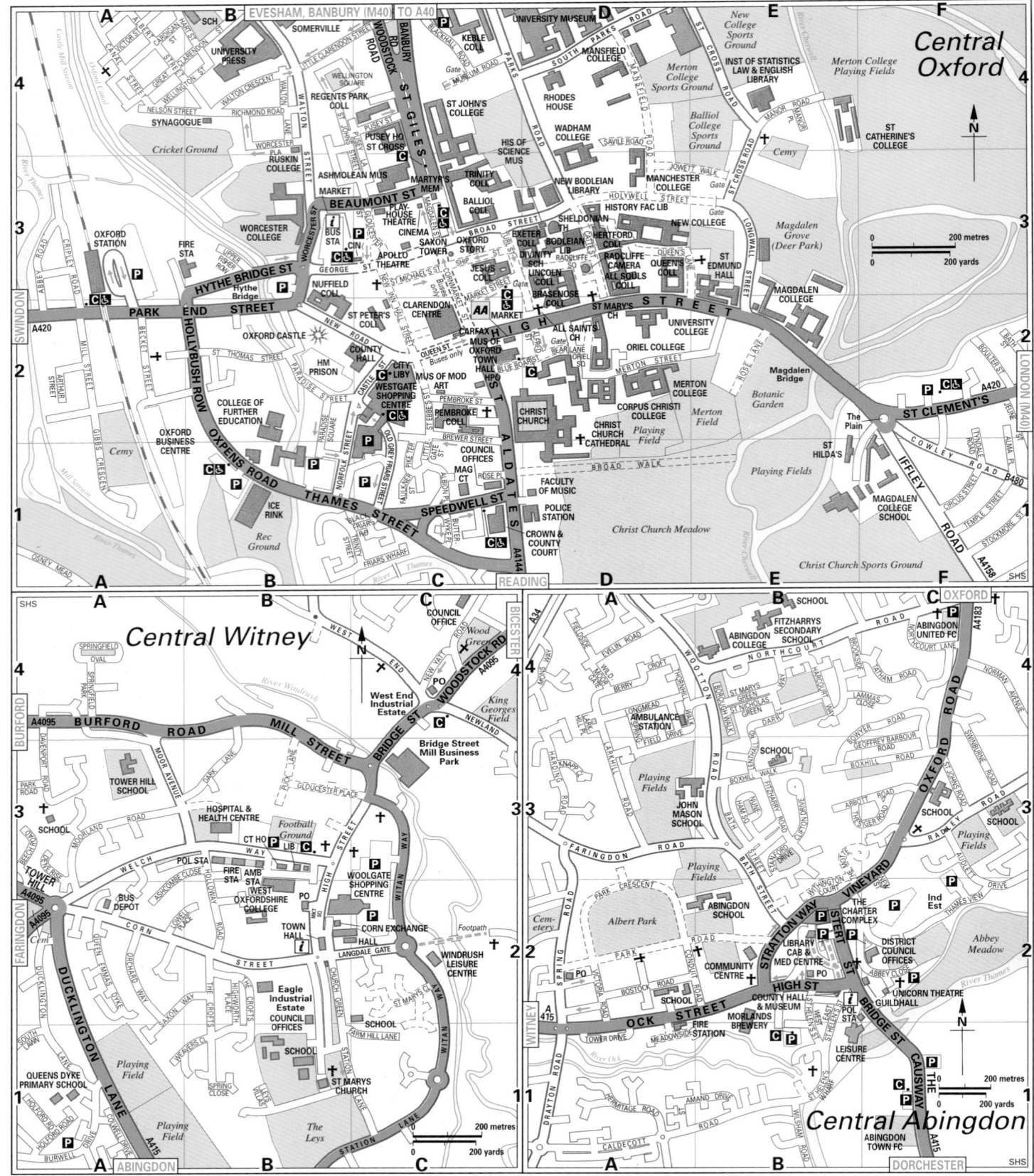

Oxford

From Carfax, at the centre of the city, round to Magdalen Bridge stretches High Street, one of England's best and most interesting thoroughfares. Shops rub shoulders with churches and colleges, alleyways lead to ancient inns and to a large covered market, and little streets lead to views of some of the finest architecture to be seen anywhere. Catte Street, beside St Mary's Church (whose lovely in England. Footpaths lead through panoramic view of Oxford), opens out into Radcliffe Square, dominated by the Radcliffe Camera, a great round structure built in 1749. Close by is the Bodleian Library, one of the finest collections of books and manuscripts in the world. All around are ancient college buildings. Close to Magdalen Bridge is Magdalen College, founded in 1448 and certainly not to be missed. Across the High Street are the Botanical Gardens, founded in 1621, and the oldest such foundation in England. Footpaths lead through Christ Church Meadow to Christ Church College and the cathedral. Tom Tower is the college's most notable feature: the cathedral is actually its chapel. Among much else not to be missed in Oxford is the Ashmolean Museum, whose vast collections of precious and beautiful objects from all over the world repay many hours of study; perhaps the loveliest treasure is the 9th-century Alfred Jewel.

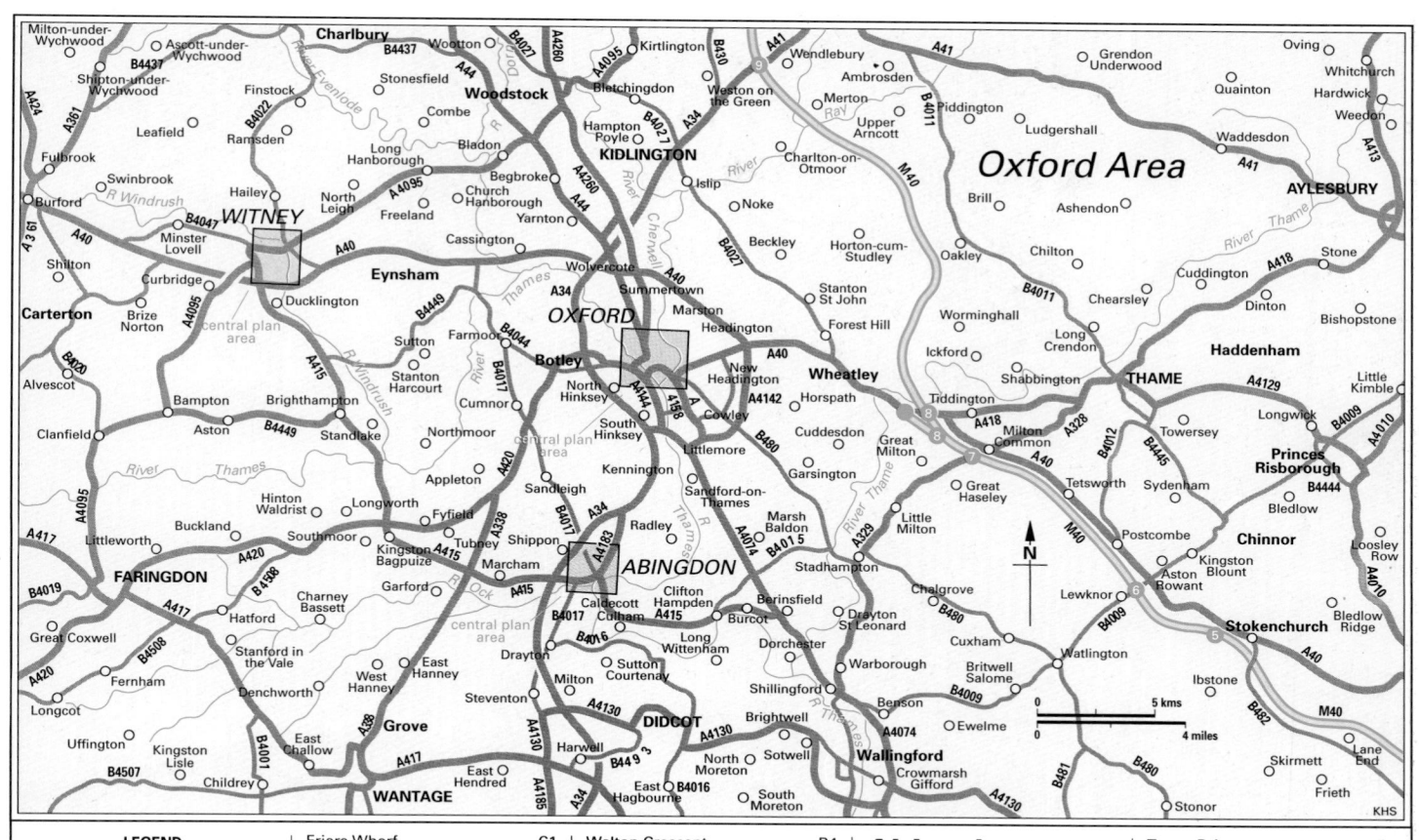

KHS

LEGEND

Town Plan

AA Recommended routes	
Restricted roads	
Other roads	
Buildings of interest	COLLEGE
AA Shop/Insurance	AA
Churches	†
Parks and open spaces	
Car parks	P
Toilets	C C
One way streets	←

Area Plan

A roads	
B roads	
Locations	Yalding ○
Urban area	

Street Index with Grid Reference

Oxford

Abbey Road	A2-A3
Adelaide Street	B5
Albert Street	A4-B4
Albion Place	C1
Alfred Street	D2
Alma Place	F1-F2
Arthur Street	A2
Banbury Road	C4
Bath Street	F2
Bear Lane	D2
Beaumont Street	B3-C3
Becket Street	A2
Blackfriars Road	B1-C1
Blackhall Road	C4
Blue Boar Street	C2-D2
Boulter Street	F2
Brewer Street	C2
Broad Street	C3-D3
Broad Walk	C1-D1-E1
Butter Wyke Place	C1
Canal Street	A4
Cardigan Street	A4
Castle Street	B2-C2
Catte Street	D3
Circus Street	F1
Cornmarket Street	C2-C3
Cowley Road	F1-F2
Cripley Road	A2-A3
Faulkner Street	C1

Friars Wharf	C1
George Street	B3-C3
Gibbs Crescent	A1-B1
Gloucester Street	C3
Great Clarendon Street	A4-B4
Hart Street	A4-B4
High Street	C2-D2-E2-F2
Hollybush Row	A2-B2
Holywell Street	D3-E3
Hythe Bridge Street	B2-B3
Iffley Road	F1-F2
Jowett Walk	D3-E3
Little Clarendon Street	B4-C4
Littlegate Street	C1-C2
Longwall Street	E2-E3
Magdalen Street	C3
Manor Place	E4
Manor Road	E4
Mansfield Road	D3-D4
Market Street	C2-C3
Merton Street	D2-E2
Mill Street	A2
Museum Road	C4
Nelson Street	A4-B4
New Inn Hall Street	C2-C3
New Road	B2-C2
Norfolk Street	B1-B2
Old Grey Friars Street	C1-C2
Oriel Square	D2
Osney Mead	A1
Oxpens Road	B1-B2
Paradise Square	B1-B2
Paradise Street	B2
Park End Street	A2-B2
Parks Road	C4-D4-D3
Pembroke Street	C2
Pike Terrace	C1-C2
Pusey Lane	B3-C3
Pusey Street	C4
Queen Street	C2
Queens Lane	D3
Radcliffe Square	D3
Richmond Road	B4
Rose Lane	E2
Rose Place	C1
St Aldates	C1-C2
St Clements	F2
St Cross Road	E3-E4-D4
St Ebbe's Street	C1-C2
St Giles	C3
St John's Street	B4-B3-C3
St Michael's Street	C2-C3
St Thomas Street	B2
Savile Road	D4
Ship Street	C3
South Parks Road	D4
Speedwell Street	C1
Stockmore Street	F1
Temple Street	F1
Thames Street	B1-C1
Trinity Street	B1-C1
Turl Street	C3
Tyndale Road	F1-F2
Upper Fisher Row	B3
Victor Street	A4

Walton Crescent	B4
Walton Lane	B4
Walton Street	B4-B3
Wellington Square	B4
Wellington Street	A4-B4
Woodstock Road	C4
Worcester Place	B4
Worcester Street	B2-B3

AA shop,
133-134 High Street   C2
Oxford OX1 4DN

Witney

Ashcombe Close	A2-A3-B3
Beech Road	A3
Bridge Street	C3-C4
Burford Road	A4-B4
Burwell Drive	A1
Church Green	B1-B2
Colwell Drive	A1
Corn Street	A2-B2
Dark Lane	B3-B4
Davenport Road	A3-A4
Dene Rise	A3
Ducklington Lane	A1-A2
Farm Hill Lane	B1-C1
Gloucester Place	B3-C3
High Street	B2-B3-C3
Highworth Place	B1-B2
Holford Road	A1
Holloway Road	B2-B3
Langdale Gate	B2-C2
Leys Villas	B1
Lowell Place	A2-B2
Market Square	B2
Mill Street	B4-B3-C3
Moor Avenue	A4-A3-B3
Moorland Road	A2-A3
Newland	C3-C4
New Yatt Road	C4
Orchard Way	A2
Park Road	A3
Puck Lane	B3-C4
Queen Emmas Dyke	A2
St Marys Close	A2-B2
Saxon Way	A1-A2-B2
South Lawn	A1
Spring Close	B1
Springfield Oval	A4
Springfield Park	A4
Station Lane	B1-C1
The Crofts	B1-B2
Tower Hill	A2
Weavers Close	A1-B1
Welch Way	A2-A3-B3
West End	B4-C4
Witan Way	C1-C2-C3
Woodstock Road	C4

Abingdon

Abbey Close	B2-C2
Abbott Road	B3-C3
Audlett Drive	C2-C3
Bath Street	B2-B3
Berry Croft	A4
Borough Walk	B4
Bostock Road	A2
Bowyer Road	B3-B4-C4
Boxhill Road	B3-C3
Boxhill Walk	B3
Bridge Street	B2-C2-C1
Brookside	B4
Caldecott Road	A1-B1
Clifton Drive	B3
Conduit Road	A2-B2
Darrel Way	B4
Drayton Road	A1
East St Helens Street	B1-B2
Evelin Road	A4
Faringdon Road	A3-B3
Fieldside	A4
Fitzharrys Road	B3
Geoffrey Barbour Road	B3-C3-C4
Harcourt Way	B4
Harding Road	A3-A4
Hermitage Road	A1
High Street	B2
Knapp Close	A3
Lammas Close	B4-C4
Larkhill Place	A4
Larkhill Road	A3-A4
Lenthall Road	B3-B4
Longmead	A4
Meadowside	A1-B1
Mons Way	A4
New Street	C2-C3
Norman Avenue	C4
Northcourt Lane	C4
Northcourt Road	B4-C4
Nuneham Square	B3
Ock Street	A1-A2-B2
Oxford Road	C3-C4
Park Crescent	A2-A3
Park Road	A2-B2
Radley Road	C3
St Amand Drive	A1-B1
St Helens Wharf	B1
St Johns Road	C3
St Marys Green	B4
St Nicholas Green	B4
Springfield Drive	A4-A3
Spring Road	A1-A2-A3
Stanford Drive	B3
Stert Street	B2
Stratton Way	B2
Swinburne Road	C3-C4
Tatham Road	C4
Thames View	C2
The Causeway	C1
The Motte	B2-B3
Thesiger Road	B3-C3
Thornhill Walk	A4

Tower Drive	A1
Victoria Road	A2
Vineyard	B2-C2-C3
West St Helens Street	B1-B2
Wildmoor Gate	A4
Wilsham Road	B1
Withington Court	B2-B3
Wootton Road	A4-B4-B3

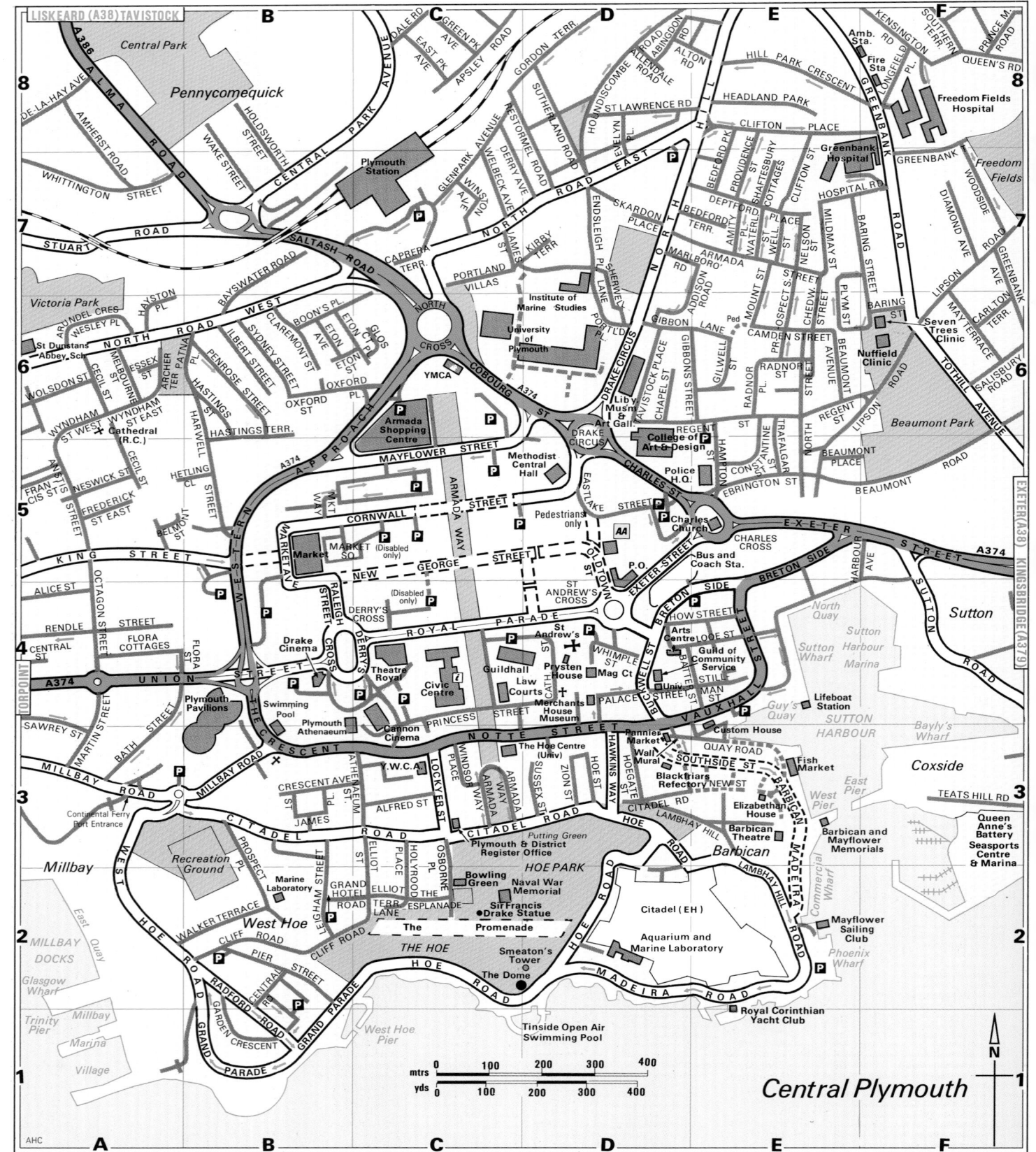

Plymouth

Ship's, sailors and the sea permeate every aspect of Plymouth's life and history. Its superb natural harbour – Plymouth Sound – has ensured its importance as a port, yachting centre and naval base (at Devonport) for centuries. Sir Francis Drake is undoubtedly the city's most famous sailor. His statue stands on the Hoe – where he really did play bowls before tackling the Spanish Armada. Also on the Hoe are Smeaton's Tower, once the upper part of the third Eddystone Lighthouse, and the impressive Royal Navy War Memorial. Just east of the Hoe is the Royal Citadel, an imposing fortress built in 1666 by order of Charles II. Sutton Harbour is perhaps the most atmospheric part of Plymouth, where fishing boats bob up and down in a harbour whose quays are lined with attractive old houses, inns and warehouses. One of the memorials, on Mayflower Quay, just outside the harbour commemorates the sailing of the *Mayflower* from here in 1620.

Plymouth's modern shopping centre was built after the old centre was badly damaged in World War II. Near by is the 200ft-high tower of the impressive Civic Centre. Some old buildings escaped destruction, such as the Elizabethan House, the Merchant's House (now a museum) and the 500-year-old Prysten House, next to which is 15th-century St Andrew's Church with stained glass by John Piper. Also of interest are the City Art Gallery and Museum, the Plymouth Dome visitor centre and the Plymouth Pavilions, a conference centre with ice-rink, leisure pool and shops.

242

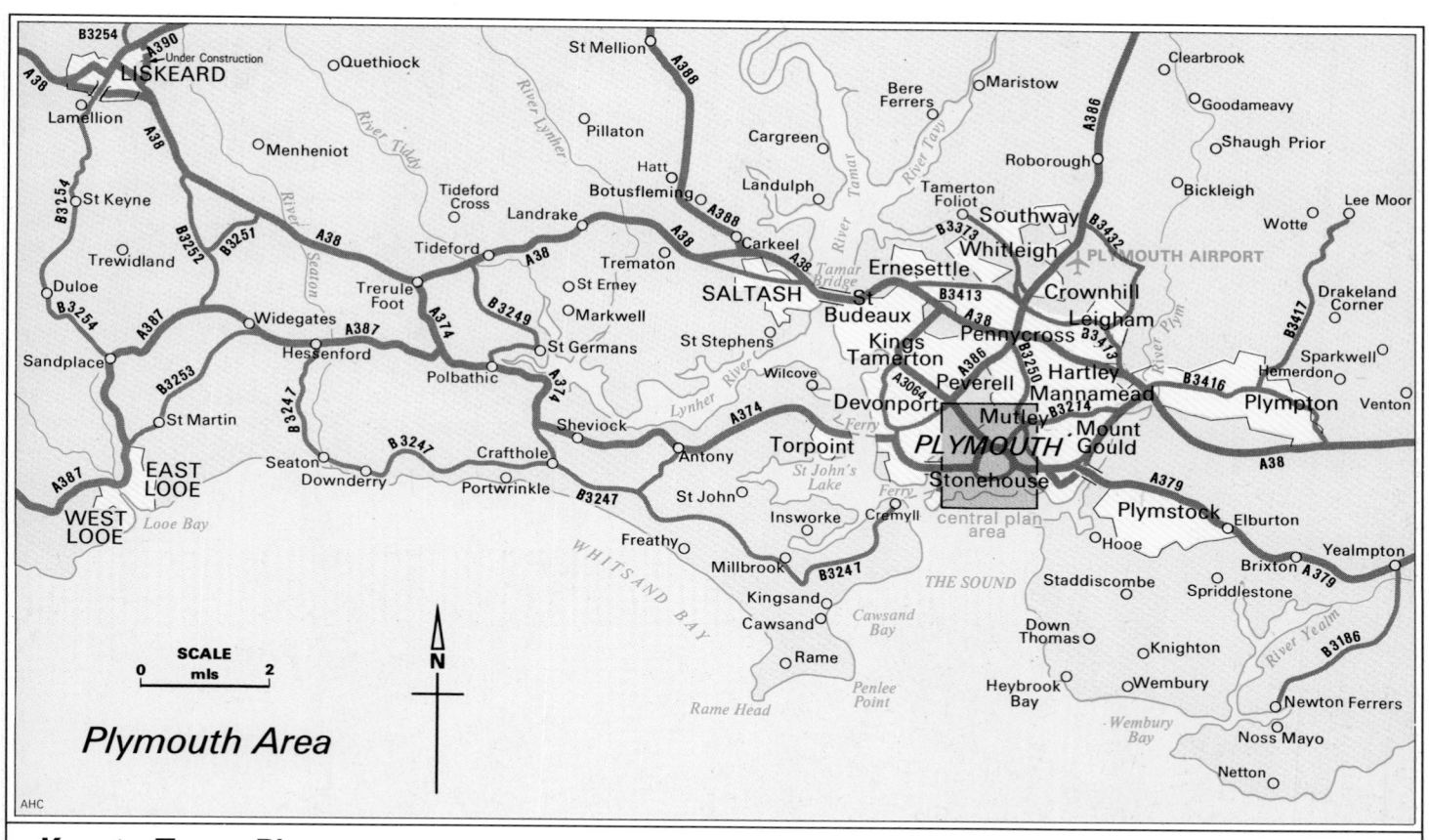

Plymouth Area

SCALE
0 mls 2

N

AHC

Key to Town Plan and Area Plan

Town Plan

AA Recommended roads
Other roads
Restricted roads
Buildings of interest
Car Parks
Parks and open spaces
AA Shop

P

AA

Area Plan

A roads
B roads
Locations   Sandplace O
Urban area

Street Index with Grid Reference

Plymouth

AA Shop
10 Old Town Street
Plymouth
Devon PL11DE
                         D5

AA Port Shop
Millbay Docks, Plymouth
Devon PL1 3DS
                         A2

Maps:
© The Automobile Association 1981
Revision:
© The Automobile Association 1993

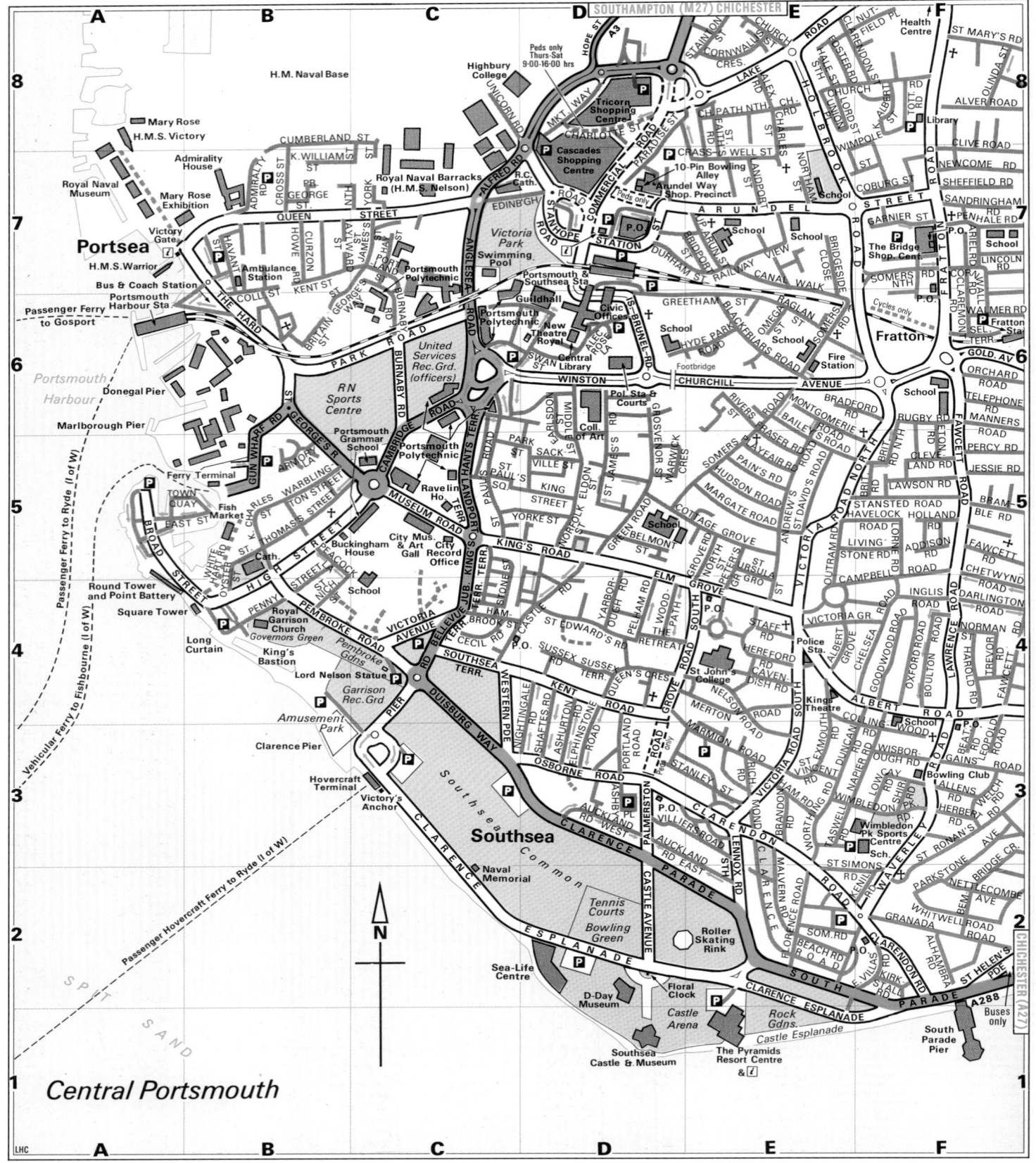

Portsmouth

A busy ferry port and one of Britain's two major naval bases, Portsmouth is world famous as the home of Nelson's flagship *Victory*, Henry VIII's *Mary Rose*, spectacularly raised from the seabed in 1982, and HMS *Warrior*, the world's first iron-hulled warship. All are located at the 300-acre dockyard, which also contains the Royal Naval and Mary Rose museums (the latter housing thousands of artefacts recovered from the ship), and many listed Georgian buildings. The city has been a naval port since the 13th century and has a cathedral dating from the 12th century. Notable fortifications are the 15th-century Round Tower, an excellent viewpoint at the harbour entrance, and Fort Nelson, one of a ring of Napoleonic defences, several of which are open to the public. The great novelist Charles Dickens was born in Portsmouth in 1805 and his birthplace is now a museum. The city was heavily bombed during World War II and the centre has been extensively rebuilt, but the old town by the harbourmouth escaped severe damage and now forms an attractive and fashionable area.

Southsea developed in the 19th century as an elegant seaside resort with fine houses and terraces, an esplanade and an extensive sea-front common where the Sea-Life Centre, Southsea Castle and Museum, the D-Day Museum (containing the 272ft-long Overlord Embroidery) and Pyramids Leisure Centre are situated. The Royal Marines Museum and the offshore Spit Bank Fort are also worth a visit.

244

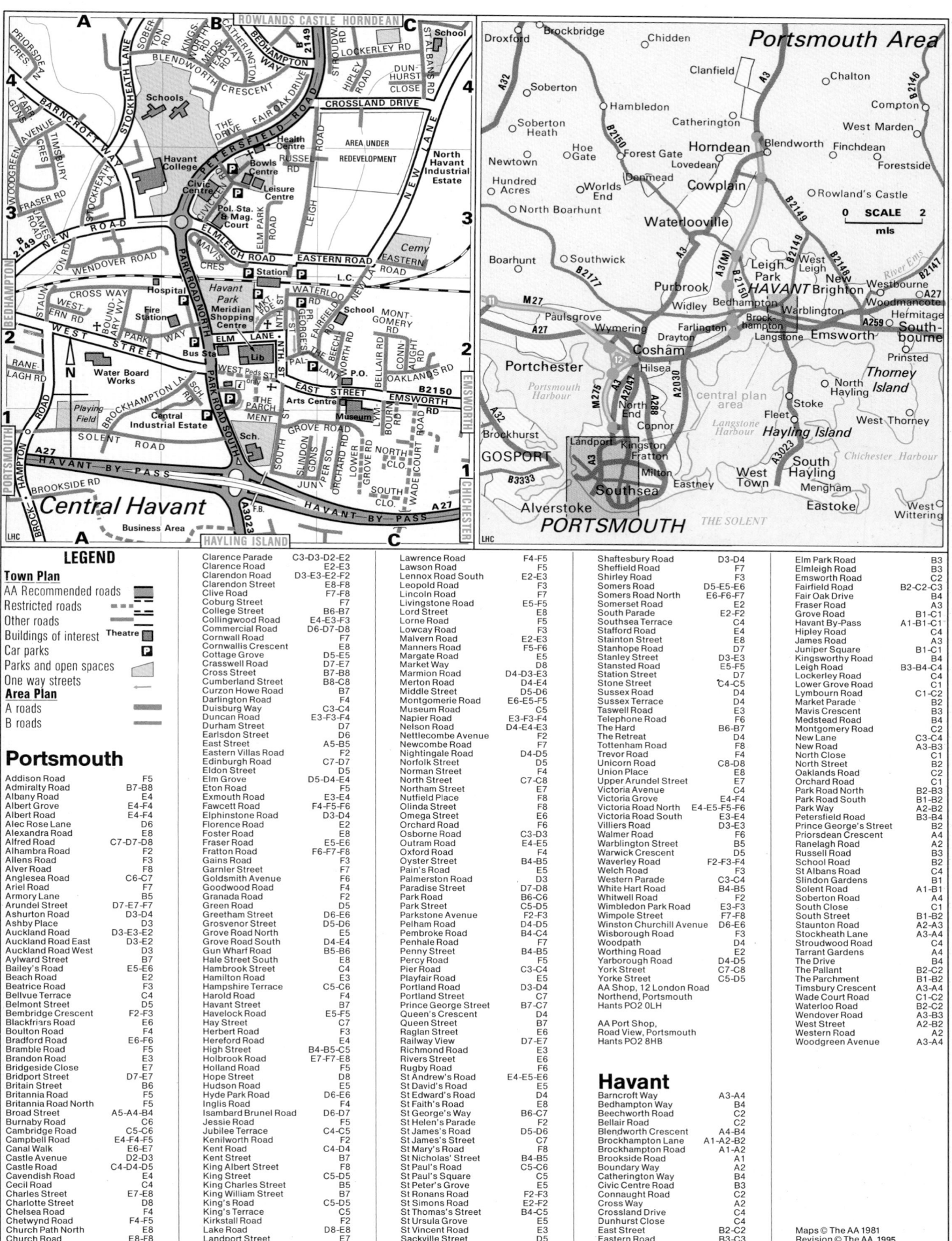

LEGEND

Town Plan
- AA Recommended roads
- Restricted roads
- Other roads
- Buildings of interest — Theatre
- Car parks — P
- Parks and open spaces
- One way streets

Area Plan
- A roads
- B roads

Portsmouth

Addison Road	F5	Lawrence Road	F4-F5
Admiralty Road	B7-B8	Lawson Road	F5
Albany Road	E4	Lennox Road South	E2-E3
Albert Grove	E4-F4	Leopold Road	F3
Albert Road	E4-F4	Lincoln Road	E8
Alec Rose Lane	D6	Livingstone Road	E5-F5
Alexandra Road	E8	Lord Street	E8
Alfred Road	C7-D7-D8	Lorne Road	F5
Alhambra Road	F2	Lowcay Road	F3
Allens Road	F3	Malvern Road	E2-E3
Alver Road	F7	Manners Road	F5-F6
Ariel Road	F8	Margate Road	E5
Anglesea Road	C6-C7	Market Way	D8
Armory Lane	B5	Marmion Road	D4-D3-E3
Arundel Street	D7-E7-F7	Merton Road	D4-E4
Ashurton Road	D3-D4	Middle Street	D5-D6
Ashby Place	D3	Montgomerie Road	E6-E5-F5
Auckland Road	D3-E3-E2	Museum Road	C5
Auckland Road East	D3-E2	Napier Road	E3-F3-F4
Auckland Road West	D3	Nelson Road	D4-E4-E3
Aylward Street	B7	Nettlecombe Avenue	F2
Bailey's Road	E5-E6	Newcombe Road	F7
Beach Road	E2	Nightingale Road	D4-D5
Beatrice Road	F3	Norfolk Street	D5
Bellvue Terrace	C4	Norman Street	F4
Belmont Street	D5	North Street	C7-C8
Bembridge Crescent	F2-F3	Northam Street	E7
Blackfriars Road	E6	Nutfield Place	F8
Boulton Road	F4	Olinda Street	F8
Bradford Road	E6-F6	Omega Street	E6
Bramble Road	F5	Orchard Road	F6
Brandon Road	E3	Osborne Road	C3-D3
Bridgeside Close	E7	Outram Road	E4-E5
Bridport Street	D7-E7	Oxford Road	F4
Britain Street	B6	Oyster Street	B4-B5
Britannia Road	F5	Pain's Road	E5
Britannia Road North	F5	Palmerston Road	D3
Broad Street	A5-A4-B4	Paradise Street	D7-D8
Burnaby Road	C6	Park Road	B6-C6
Cambridge Road	C5-C6	Park Street	C5-D5
Campbell Road	E4-F4-F5	Parkstone Avenue	F2-F3
Canal Walk	E6-E7	Pelham Road	D4-D5
Castle Avenue	D2-D3	Pembroke Road	B4-C4
Castle Road	C4-D4-D5	Penhale Road	F7
Cavendish Road	E4	Penny Street	B4-B5
Cecil Road	C4	Percy Road	F5
Charles Street	E7-E8	Pier Road	C3-C4
Charlotte Street	D8	Playfair Road	E5
Chelsea Road	F4	Portland Road	D3-D4
Chetwynd Road	F4-F5	Portland Street	C7
Church Path North	E8	Prince George Street	B7-C7
Church Road	E8-F8	Queen's Crescent	D4
Clarence Esplanade	C3-E1	Queen Street	B7
Clarence Parade	C3-D3-D2-E2	Raglan Street	E6
Clarence Road	E2-E3	Railway View	D7-E7
Clarendon Road	D3-E3-E2-F2	Richmond Road	E3
Clarendon Street	E8-F8	Rivers Street	E6
Clive Road	F7-F8	Rugby Road	F6
Coburg Street	F7	St Andrew's Road	E4-E5-E6
College Street	B6-B7	St David's Road	E5
Collingwood Road	E4-E3-F3	St Edward's Road	D4
Commercial Road	D6-D7-D8	St Faith's Road	E8
Cornwall Road	F7	St George's Way	B6-C7
Cornwallis Crescent	E8	St Helen's Parade	F2
Cottage Grove	D5-E5	St James's Road	D5-D6
Crasswell Road	D7-E7	St James's Street	C7
Cross Street	B7-B8	St Mary's Road	F8
Cumberland Street	B8-C8	St Nicholas' Street	B4-B5
Curzon Howe Road	B7	St Paul's Road	C5-C6
Darlington Road	F4	St Paul's Square	C5
Duisburg Way	C3-C4	St Peter's Grove	C5
Duncan Road	E3-F3-F4	St Ronans Road	F2-F3
Durham Street	D7	St Simons Road	E2-F2
Earlsdon Street	D6	St Thomas's Street	B4-C5
East Street	A5-B5	St Ursula Grove	E5
Eastern Villas Road	F2	St Vincent Road	E3
Edinburgh Road	C7-D7	Sackville Street	D5
Eldon Street	D5	Sandringham Road	F7
Elm Grove	D5-D4-E4	Shaftesbury Road	D3-D4
Eton Road	F5	Sheffield Road	F7
Exmouth Road	E3-E4	Shirley Road	F3
Fawcett Road	F4-F5-F6	Somers Road	D5-E5-E6
Elphinstone Road	D3-D4	Somers Road North	E6-F6-F7
Florence Road	E2	Somerset Road	E2
Foster Road	E8	South Parade	E2-F2
Fraser Road	E5-E6	Southsea Terrace	C4
Fratton Road	F6-F7-F8	Stafford Road	E4
Gains Road	F3	Stainton Street	E8
Garnier Street	F7	Stanhope Road	D7
Goldsmith Avenue	F6	Stanley Street	D3-E3
Goodwood Road	F4	Stansted Road	E5-F5
Granada Road	F2	Station Street	D7
Green Road	D5	Stone Street	C4-C5
Greetham Street	D6-E6	Sussex Road	D4
Grosvenor Street	D5-D6	Sussex Terrace	E3
Grove Road North	E5	Taswell Road	E3
Grove Road South	D4-E4	Telephone Road	F6
Gun Wharf Road	B5-B6	The Hard	B6-B7
Hale Street South	E8	The Retreat	D4
Hambrook Street	C4	Tottenham Road	F8
Hamilton Road	E5	Trevor Road	F4
Hampshire Terrace	C5-C6	Unicorn Road	C8-D8
Harold Road	F4	Union Place	E8
Havant Street	B7	Upper Arundel Street	E7
Havelock Road	E5-F5	Victoria Avenue	C4
Hay Street	C7	Victoria Grove	E4-F4
Herbert Road	E6	Victoria Road North	E4-E5-F5-F6
Hereford Road	E4	Victoria Road South	E3-E4
High Street	B4-B5-C5	Villiers Road	D3-E3
Holbrook Road	E7-F7-F8	Walmer Road	F5
Holland Road	F6	Warblington Street	B5
Hope Street	D8	Warwick Crescent	D5
Hudson Road	E5	Waverley Road	F2-F3-F4
Hyde Park Road	D6-E6	Welch Road	F3
Inglis Road	F4	Western Parade	C3-C4
Isambard Brunel Road	D6-D7	White Hart Road	B4-B5
Jessie Road	F5	Whitwell Road	F2
Jubilee Terrace	C4-C5	Wimbledon Park Road	E3-F3
Kenilworth Road	F2	Wimpole Street	F7-F8
Kent Road	C4-C5	Winston Churchill Avenue	D6-E6
Kent Street	B7	Wisborough Road	F3
King Albert Street	F7	Woodpath	D4
King Street	C5-D5	Worthing Road	E2
King Charles Street	B5	Yarborough Road	D4-D5
King William Street	B7	York Street	C7-C8
King's Road	C5-D5	Yorke Street	C5-D5
King's Terrace	C5		
Kirkstall Road	F5	AA Shop, 12 London Road	
Lake Road	D8-E8	Northend, Portsmouth	
Landport Street	E7	Hants PO2 0LH	
Landport Terrace	C5		
		AA Port Shop,	
		Road View, Portsmouth	
		Hants PO2 8HB	

Havant

Barncroft Way	A3-A4
Bedhampton Way	B4
Beechworth Road	C2
Bellair Road	C2
Blendworth Crescent	A4-B4
Brockhampton Lane	A1-A2-B2
Brockhampton Road	A1-A2
Brookside Road	A1
Boundary Way	A2
Catherington Way	B4
Civic Centre Road	B3
Connaught Road	C2
Cross Way	A2
Crossland Drive	C4
Dunhurst Close	C4
East Street	B2-C2
Eastern Road	B3-C3
Elm Lane	B2

Elm Park Road	B3
Elmleigh Road	B3
Emsworth Road	C2
Fairfield Road	B2-C2-C3
Fair Oak Drive	B4
Fraser Road	A3
Grove Road	B1-C1
Havant By-Pass	A1-B1-C1
Hipley Road	C4
James Road	A3
Juniper Square	B1-C1
Kingsworthy Road	B4
Leigh Road	B3-B4-C4
Lockerley Road	C4
Lower Grove Road	C1
Lymbourn Road	C1-C2
Market Parade	B2
Mavis Crescent	B3
Medstead Road	B4
Montgomery Road	C4
New Lane	C3-C4
New Road	A3-B3
North Close	C1
North Street	B2
Oaklands Road	C2
Orchard Road	C2
Park Road North	B2-B3
Park Road South	B1-B2
Park Way	A2-B2
Petersfield Road	B3-B4
Prince George's Street	B2
Priorsdean Crescent	A4
Ranelagh Road	A2
Russell Road	B3
School Road	B2
St Albans Road	C4
Slindon Gardens	B1
Solent Road	A1-B1
Soberton Road	A4
South Close	C1
South Street	B1-B2
Staunton Road	A2-A3
Stockheath Lane	A3-A4
Stroudwood Road	C4
Tarrant Gardens	A4
The Drive	B4
The Pallant	B2-C2
The Parchment	B1-B2
Timsbury Crescent	A3-A4
Wade Court Road	C1-C2
Waterloo Road	B2-C2
Wendover Road	A3-B3
West Street	A2-B2
Western Road	A2
Woodgreen Avenue	A3-A4

Maps © The AA 1981
Revision © The AA 1995

245

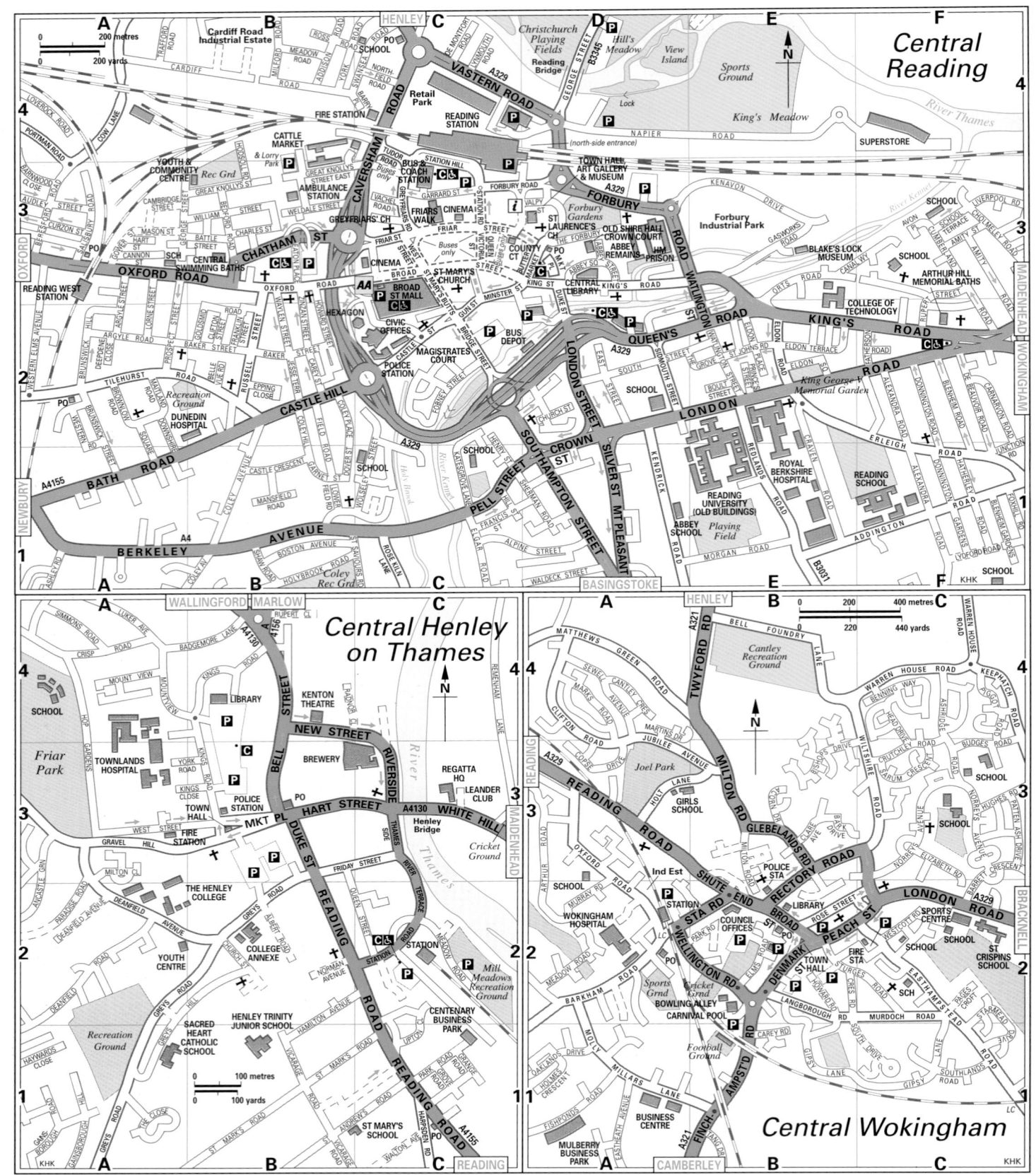

Reading

A major commercial and administrative centre with ultra-modern office blocks contrasting with Victorian buildings, a university, the county hall, large shopping centres and the well-known Hexagon Theatre, Reading is very much a town of the present. It does, however, have a long history, with the abbey founded by Henry I in 1121 becoming one of the most important in England. It suffered badly in the Dissolution and only a few ruins are left. The town's once important cloth trade was finally destroyed by the Civil War, and it was not until the opening of the Kennet and Avon Canal, followed by the coaching routes and finally the coming of the Great Western Railway, that prosperity returned. Reading's industrial past is displayed in the Blake's Lock Museum, while the local history, including exhibits from the Roman town at nearby Silchester, can be seen in the Old Town Hall. Farm and domestic equipment is on show at the Museum of English Rural Life in Whiteknights Park.

Henley-on-Thames, famous for its annual rowing regatta, is a lovely old town, well-provided with old coaching inns, Georgian façades and numerous listed buildings.

Wokingham has been a market town for centuries and over the years has been known for its silk industry and its bell-foundry. Half-timbered gabled houses can be seen in the town centre, although modern development surrounds it.

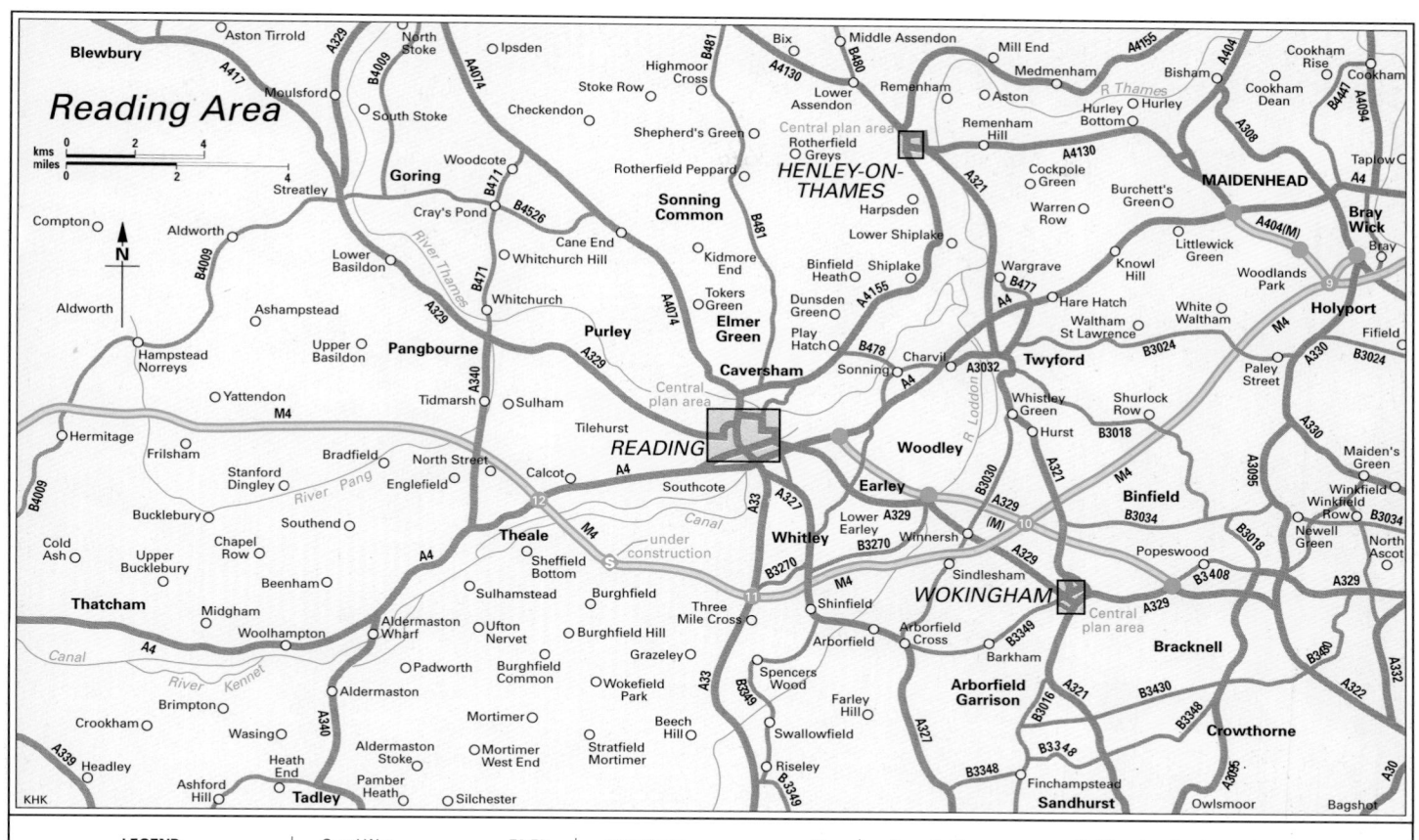

Reading Area

kms 0 2 4
miles 0 2 4

(Map of Reading Area showing locations including Blewbury, Aston Tirrold, North Stoke, Ipsden, Bix, Middle Assendon, Mill End, Bisham, Cookham Rise, Cookham, Moulsford, Stoke Row, Highmoor Cross, Lower Assendon, Remenham, Aston, Medmenham, Hurley Bottom, Hurley, Cookham Dean, South Stoke, Checkendon, Shepherd's Green, Remenham Hill, Cockpole Green, Burchett's Green, MAIDENHEAD, Taplow, Goring, Woodcote, Rotherfield Peppard, HENLEY-ON-THAMES, Rotherfield Greys, Warren Row, BRAY WICK, Bray, Cray's Pond, Sonning Common, Harpsden, Lower Shiplake, Knowl Hill, Littlewick Green, Woodlands Park, Holyport, Streatley, Compton, Aldworth, Lower Basildon, Whitchurch Hill, Cane End, Kidmore End, Binfield Heath, Shiplake, Wargrave, Hare Hatch, White Waltham, Fifield, Ashampstead, Whitchurch, Purley, Tokers Green, Dunsden Green, Waltham St Lawrence, Aldworth, Hampstead Norreys, Upper Basildon, Pangbourne, Elmer Green, Play Hatch, Charvil, Twyford, Paley Street, Maiden's Green, Hermitage, Yattendon, Tidmarsh, Sulham, Caversham, Sonning, Whistley Green, Shurlock Row, Frilsham, Tilehurst, READING, Woodley, Hurst, Winkfield, Winkfield Row, North Ascot, Stanford Dingley, Bradfield, North Street, Calcot, Southcote, Earley, Sindlesham, Popeswood, Newell Green, Cold Ash, Upper Bucklebury, Chapel Row, Southend, Englefield, Theale, Sheffield Bottom, Whitley, Lower Earley, Winnersh, Bracknell, Thatcham, Midgham, Woolhampton, Aldermaston Wharf, Ufton Nervet, Burghfield, Three Mile Cross, Shinfield, WOKINGHAM, Arborfield Cross, Barkham, Arborfield Garrison, Brimpton, Padworth, Burghfield Common, Grazeley, Wokefield Park, Spencers Wood, Arborfield, Farley Hill, Crowthorne, Crookham, Wasing, Aldermaston, Mortimer, Beech Hill, Swallowfield, Headley, Heath End, Aldermaston Stoke, Mortimer West End, Stratfield Mortimer, Riseley, Finchampstead, Ashford Hill, Pamber Heath, Silchester, Sandhurst, Owlsmoor, Bagshot, Tadley, KHK)

LEGEND

Town Plan

AA Recommended routes	
Restricted roads	
Other roads	
Buildings of interest	COLLEGE
AA Shop/Insurance	AA
Churches	†
Parks and open spaces	
Car parks	P
Toilets	C C
One way streets	←

Area Plan

A roads	
B roads	
Locations	Yalding
Urban area	

Street Index with Grid Reference

Reading

Abbey Square	D3	Canal Way	E2-F2	King Street	D3	
Abbey Street	D3	Cannon Street	A3	Liverpool Road	F3	
Addington Road	E1-F1	Cardiff Road	A4	London Road	D2-E2-F2	
Addison Road	B4	Carey Street	B2	London Street	D2	
Alexandra Road	F1-F2	Carnavon Road	F2	Lorne Street	A2-A3	
Alpine Street	C1-D1	Castle Crescent	B1	Loverock Road	A4	
Amity Road	F3-F2	Castle Hill	B2	Lower Field Road	B1	
Amity Street	F3	Castle Street	C2	Lydford Road	F1	
Ashley Road	A1	Caversham Road	C3-C4	Lynmouth Road	C4	
Avon Place	F3	Charles Street	B3	Maitland Road	A2	
Argyle Road	A2	Chatham Street	B3	Mansfield Road	B1	
Argyle Street	A2-A3	Cholmeley Road	F3	Market Place	D3	
Audley Street	A3	Church Street	D2	Mason Street	A3	
Baker Street	A2	Clifton Street	B2	Meadow Road	B4	
Barnwood Close	A3	Coley Avenue	B1-B2	Milford Road	B4	
Barry Place	C4	Coley Hill	B2	Minster Street	C3	
Bath Road	A1-B2	Coley Place	B2	Morgan Road	E1	
Battle Street	B3	Cow Lane	A4	Mount Pleasant	D1	
Bedford Road	B3	Craven Road	E1-E2	Napier Road	D4-E4	
Bellevue Road	B2	Crown Street	D1-D2	Northfield Road	C4	
Beresford Road	A3	Cumberland Road	F3-F2	Orts Road	E2-F2	
Berkeley Avenue	A1-B1-C1	Curzon Street	A3	Oxford Road	A3-B2	
Blenheim Gardens	F1	De Beauvoir Road	F2	Pell Street	C1-D1	
Blenheim Road	F2	De Montfort Road	C4	Portman Road	A3-A4	
Boston Avenue	B1	Deepdene Close	A2	Princess Street	E2	
Boult Street	E2	Donnington Gardens	F1	Prospect Street	A2-A3	
Bridge Street	C2	Donnington Road	F1-F2	Queen's Road	D2-E2	
Broad Street	C3	Dover Street	B1	Queen Victoria Street	C3	
Brownlow Road	A2	Downshire Square	B1-B2	Redlands Road	E1-E2	
Brunswick Hill	A2	Duke Street	D2-D3	Ross Road	B4-C4	
Brunswick Street	A1-A2	East Street	D3	Rupert Street	F2-F3	
Buttermarket	D3	Eaton Place	B3	Russell Street	B2	
Cambridge Street	A3	Eldon Place	E2	St Johns Road	E2	
		Eldon Road	E2	St Mary Butts	C2-C3	
		Eldon Terrace	E2	St Saviours Road	C1	
		Eldon Square	E2	Salisbury Road	A3	
		Elgar Road	C1	School Terrace	F3	
		Elm Park Road	A2-A3	Sidmouth Street	D2	
		Epping Close	B2	Silver Street	D1	
		Erleigh Road	E2-F1	Shaw Road	B1	
		Fatherson Place	F2	Sherman Road	D1	
		Field Road	B2-B1	Southampton Street	D2-D1	
		Fobney Street	C2	South Street	D2-E2	
		Forbury Gardens	C3-D3	Station Hill	C3	
		Forbury Road	D3-E3-E2	Station Road	C3	
		Foxhill Road	F1	Swansea Road	C4	
		Francis Street	C1	The Forbury	D3	
		Franklin Street	B2	The Grove	E2	
		Friar Street	C3-D3	Trafford Road	B4	
		Garnet Street	B1	Tudor Road	C4	
		Garrard Street	C3	Vachel Road	C3	
		Gasworks Road	E3	Valpy Street	D3	
		George Street	A3-B3	Vastern Road	C4-D4	
		George Street	D4	Waldeck Street	D1	
		Goldsmid Road	B2	Watlington Street	E2	
		Gower Street	A2	Waylen Street	B2	
		Great Knollys Street	B3	Weldale Street	B2	
		Great Knollys Street East	B3	Western Elms Avenue	A2-A3	
		Greyfriars Road	C2	Western Road	A2	
		Gun Street	C2-C3	West Street	C3	
		Hart Street	A3	William Street	B3	
		Hatherley Road	F1	Wolseley Street	C1-C2	
		Henry Street	C1-C2	York Road	B4-C4	
		Hill Street	C1	Zinzan Street	B2	
		Hodsoll Road	B4-B3			
		Holybrook Road	B1	**AA shop**		
		Howard Street	B3-B2	45 Oxford Road, Reading		
		Jesse Terrace	B2	Berkshire RG1 7QL	C2	
		Junction Road	F1			
		Katesgrove Lane	C1-C2	### Henley		
		Kenavon Drive	D3-E3			
		Kendrick Road	D1-D2	Albert Road	B2	
		King's Road	D3-E3			

Wokingham (area index column 4)

Ancastle Green	A2-A3	Easthampstead Road	B2-C2-C1			
Badgemore Lane	A4-B4	Eastheath Avenue	A1			
Bell Street	B3-B4	Elizabeth Road	C3-C2			
Church Street	B2	Elms Road	B2			
Crisp Road	A4	Finchampstead Road	A1-B1-B2			
Deanfield Avenue	A3-A2-B2	Fishponds Road	A1			
Deanfield Road	A2	Gipsy Lane	B2-B1-C1-C2			
Duke Street	B3	Glebelands Road	B3			
Friday Street	B3-C3	Headington Drive	C4-C3			
Gainsborough Hill	A1	Holmes Crescent	A1			
Gainsborough Road	A1	Holt Lane	A3-B3			
Grange Road	C1	Howard Road	B2			
Gravel Hill	A3-B3	Hughes Road	C3			
Greys Hill	A1-A2-B2	Jubilee Avenue	A4-A3-B3			
Greys Road	A1-A2-B2-B3	Keephatch Road	C4-C3			
Grove Road	C1	Langborough Road	B2			
Hamilton Avenue	B1-B2-C2	London Road	C2			
Harpsden Road	C1	Marks Road	A4			
Hart Street	B3-C3	Martins Drive	A4			
Hayswards Close	A1	Matthewsgreen Road	A4-B4			
Hop Gardens	A4-A3	Meadow Road	A2			
King's Close	A3-B3	Milton Road	B4-B3-B2			
King's Road	B3-B4	Molly Millars Lane	A2-A1-B1			
Luker Avenue	A4	Murdoch Road	B2-C2			
Market Place	B3	Murray Road	A2			
Meadow Road	C2	Norreys Avenue	C3			
Milton Close	A3	Oaklands Drive	A3			
Mount View	A4-B4	Oxford Road	A3-A2			
New Street	B4-C4-C3	Pages Croft	C2			
Norman Avenue	B2	Park Road	A2-B2			
Queen Street	B3-B2-B1	Patten Ash Drive	C3			
Paradise Road	A2-A3	Peach Street	B2-C2			
Park Road	C2	Piggot Road	C4-C3			
Radnor Close	B4-C4	Reading Road	A3-B3			
Reading Road	B3-B2-C2-C1	Rectory Road	B2-B3			
Remenham Lane	C4-C3	Rose Street	B2			
Riverside	C2	Sarum Crescent	C3			
River Terrace	C3-C2	Sewell Avenue	A4			
Rupert Close	B2	Shute End	B2			
St Andrew's Road	B1-C1	South Drive	B1-C1			
St Mark's Road	B1-C1	Southlands Road	C1			
Simmons Road	A4	Starmead Drive	C2-C1			
Station Road	C2	Station Road	A2-B2			
Thames Side	C3	Sturges Road	B2-C2			
The Close	A1	Tangley Drive	B1			
Upton Close	C1-C2	Twyford Road	B4			
Vicarage Road	B1	Warren House Road	B4-C4			
Walton Avenue	C1	Wellington Road	A2-B2			
West Street	A3-B3	Westcott Road	C2			
White Hill	C3	Wiltshire Road	B4-B3-C3			
York Road	A3-B3					

Wokingham

Acorn Drive	B3			
Arthur Road	A2-A3			
Ashridge Road	C4-C3			
Barkham Road	A1-A2			
Barkhart Drive	B3			
Barrett Crescent	C2-C3			
Bell Foundry Lane	B4			
Benning Way	C4			
Bishops Drive	B3			
Broad Street	B2			
Budges Road	C3			
Cantley Crescent	A4			
Carey Road	B1			
Clare Avenue	B2			
Clifton Road	A4-A3			
Copse Drive	A3			
Crutchley Road	C3			
Denmark Street	B2			

Maps: © The Automobile Association 1994
Revision: © The Automobile Association 1994

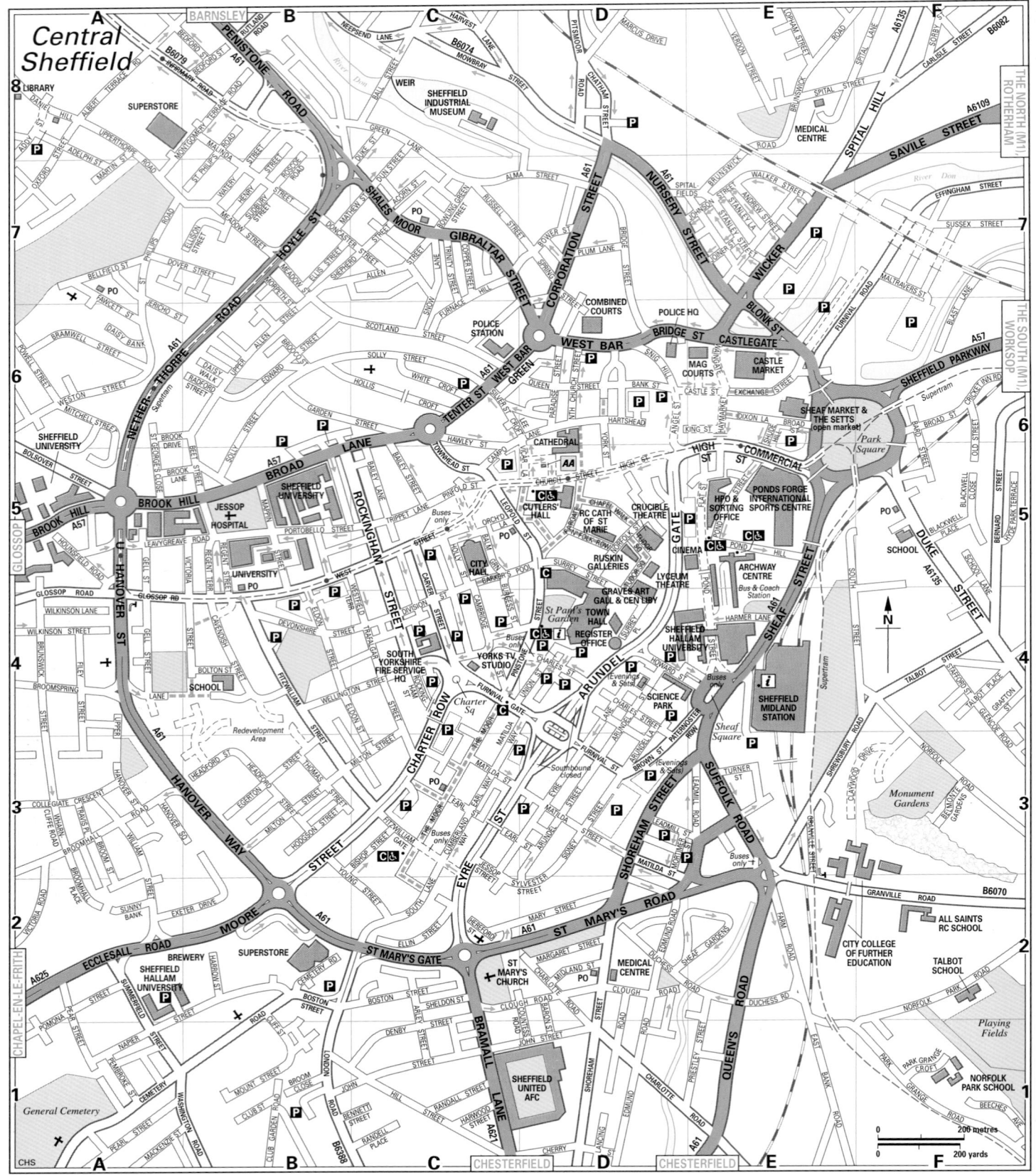

Sheffield

Cutlery – which has made Sheffield famous throughout the world – has been manufactured here since the time of Chaucer. Steel production, a vital component of the industry, was greatly improved when the crucible process was invented here in 1740 and this has created a major industry in high quality specialised steels and heavy engineering. Cutlers' Hall, the headquarters of the Honourable Company of Cutlers, has a vast display of silverware craftmanship covering every year since 1773, and the City Museum contains the world's largest collection of cutlery, dating back through time to the Paleolithic age. Abbeydale Industrial Hamlet and the Shepherd Wheel illustrate early steel and cutlery manufacture, and the city's industrial history is demonstrated in the Industrial Museum at Kelham Island.

Set on five rivers among the foothills east of the Peak District, Sheffield has many interesting and historic buildings, such as the Town Hall with a 193ft-high clock-tower, two cathedrals, two universities and a very fine and extensive shopping centre. The modern Crucible Theatre is famous as the venue of the world snooker championships. Recent developments around the city have been the Ponds Forge International Sports Centre, the Meadowhall Shopping Centre and the Don Valley Stadium used for the World Student Games in 1991. Sheffield is also the second city in Britain to construct a new supertram light railway system.

248

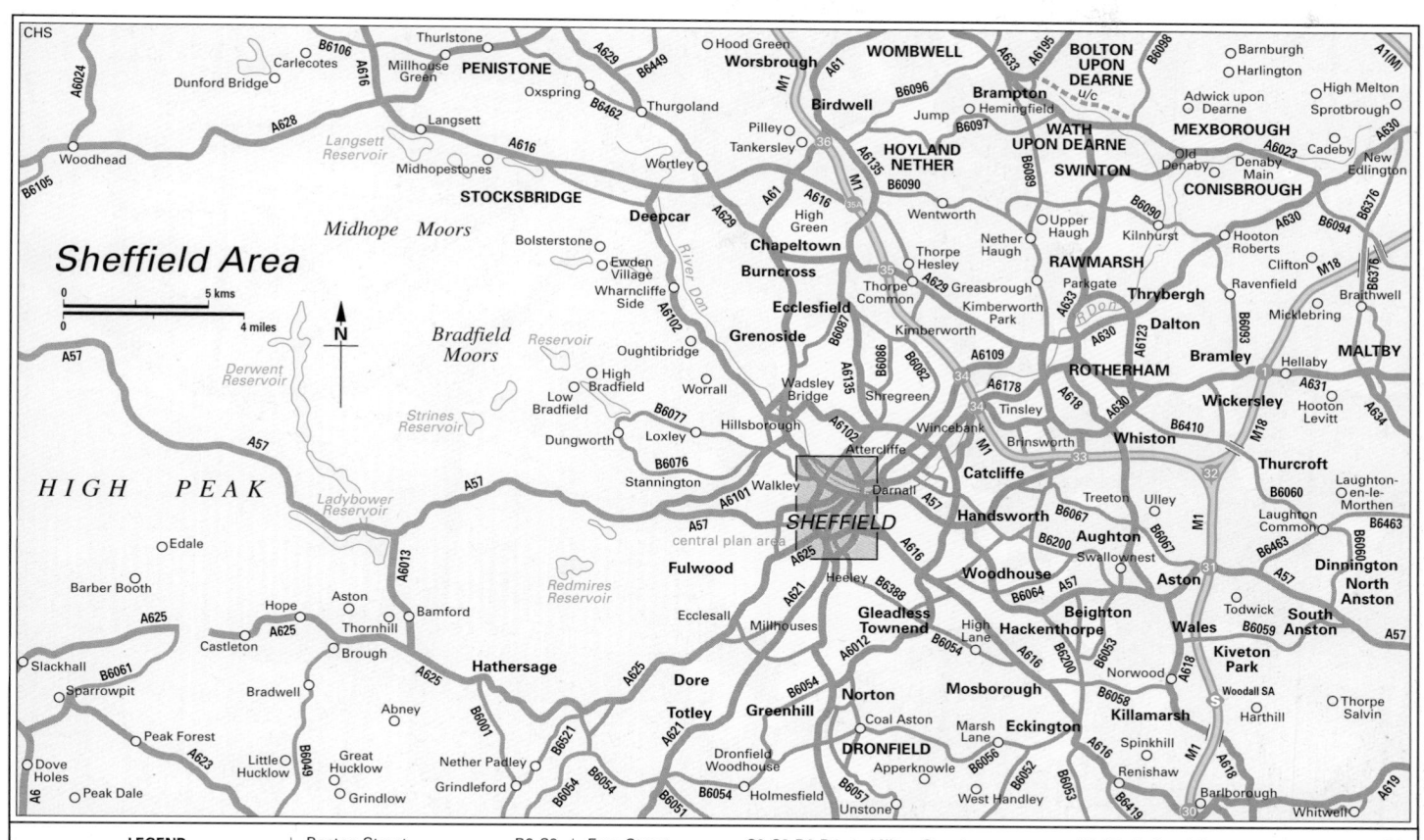

Sheffield Area

CHS

0 — 5 kms
0 — 4 miles

N

Maps: © The Automobile Association 1994
Revision: © The Automobile Association 1995

LEGEND

Town Plan

AA Recommended routes	
Restricted roads	
Other roads	
Buildings of interest	COLLEGE
AA Shop/Insurance	AA
Churches	†
Parks and open spaces	
Car parks	P
Toilets	C & C
One way streets	←

Area Plan

A roads	
B roads	
Locations	Yalding ⊙
Urban area	

Street Index with Grid Reference

Sheffield

Street	Grid
Acorn Street	C7
Adelphi Street	A7 -A8
Addy Street	A8
Albert Terrace Road	A8
Allen Street	C7
Alma Street	C7-D7
Andrew Street	E7
Angel Street	D5-D6
Arley Street	C1-C2
Arundel Gate	D4-D5
Arundel Street	D3-D4
Bailey Lane	C5
Bailey Street	C5
Ball Street	C8
Balm Green	C5
Bank Street	D6
Bard Street	F5-F6
Barker's Pool	C4-C5-D5
Baron Street	D1-D2
Bedford Street	B8
Beeches Avenue	F1
Beet Street	B5-B6
Belmonte Gardens	F3
Bennet Street	B1-C1
Bernard Street	F4-F5-F6
Bishop Street	B2-C2
Blackwell Close	F5
Blackwell Place	F5
Blast Lane	F6-F7
Blonk Street	E6
Bolton Street	B4
Bolsover Street	A5
Boston Street	B2-C2
Bower Street	C7-D7
Bowling Green Street	C7
Bramall Lane	C1-C2
Bramwell Street	A6
Bridge Street	D7-D6-E6
Broad Lane	B5-C5-C6
Broad Street	F6
Brocco Street	B6
Brook Drive	A6-B6
Brook Hill	A5-B5
Brook Lane	A5-B5
Broom Close	C1-B1
Broom Street	A3-A2
Broomhall Place	A2-A3
Broomhall Road	A3
Broomspring Lane	A4-B4
Brown Street	D3
Brunswick Street	A3-A4
Brunswick Road	E7-E8
Burgess Street	C4-C5
Cambridge Street	C4
Campo Lane	C5-D5-D6
Carlisle Street	F8
Carver Street	C4-C5
Castle Street	D6-E6
Castlegate	E6
Cavendish Street	B4
Cemetery Road	A1-B1-B2
Chapel Walk	D5
Charles Street	D5
Charlotte Road	D2-D1-E1
Charter Row	C3-C4
Chatham Street	D7-D8
Cherry Street	D1
Church Street	C5-D5
Claywood Drive	E3-F3
Cliff Street	B1
Clough Road	C2-D2
Club Garden Road	B1
Club Street	B1
Collegiate Crescent	A3
Commercial Street	E5
Copper Street	C7
Corporation Street	D6-D7
Countess Road	D1-D2
Cricket Inn Road	F6
Cumberland Way	C3
Daisy Bank	A6
Daisy Walk	B6
Daniel Hill	A8
Denby Street	C1
Devonshire Street	B4-C4
Division Street	C4
Doncaster Street	B7-C7
Dover Street	D2-E2
Duchess Road	C6-C6
Duke Street	C8
Duke Street	F4-F5
Earl Street	C3-D3
Earl Way	C3
East Bank Road	E1-E2
Ecclesall Road	A2-B2
Edmund Road	D1-D2
Edward Street	B6
Effingham Street	F7
Egerton Street	B3
Eldon Street	B4-C4
Ellin Street	C2
Ellis Street	B7
Ellison Street	B7
Eyre Street	C2-C3-D3-D4
Exchange Street	E6
Exeter Drive	A2-B2
Eyre Lane	C3-D3
Fargate	D5
Farm Road	E2
Fawcett Street	A6-A7
Filey Street	A3-A4
Fitzwilliam Gate	C3
Fitzwilliam Street	B4-B3-C3
Flat Street	E5
Furnace Hill	C6-C7
Furnival Gate	C4-D4
Furnival Road	E6-F6-F7
Furnival Street	D3
Garden Street	B6-C6
Gell Street	A4-A5
Gibraltar Street	D7-C7-D6
Glencoe Road	F3-F4
Glossop Road	A4-B4
Grafton Street	F4
Granville Road	E2-F2
Granville Street	E3-E4
Green Lane	B8-C8-C7
Hanover Square	A3
Hanover Way	A3-B3-B2
Harmer Lane	E5
Harrow Street	B2
Hartshead	D6
Harvest Lane	C8
Harwood Street	C1
Hawley Street	C6-C5
Haymarket	E6
Headford Street	B3
Henry Street	B7
Hereford Street	C2
High Street	D5-E5
Hill Street	B1-C1
Hodgson Street	B3
Hollis Croft	B6-C6
Holly Street	C4-C5
Hounsfield Road	A5
Howard Street	D4-E4
Hoyle Street	B7
Hyde Park Terrace	F5
Infirmary Road	A8-B8
Jericho Street	A6-A7
Jessop Street	C2-C3
John Street	B1-C1-D1
Johnson Street	D7-E7
Joiner Street	E7
King Street	D5-E5
Lancing Road	D1
Leadmill Street	D3
Leadmill Road	D3
Leavygreave Road	A5-B5
Lee Croft	C6
Leopold Street	C5-C6
London Road	B1-B2-C2
Lopham Street	E8
Mackenie Street	A1
Maltravers Street	F6-F7
Mappin Street	B5
Marcus Drive	D8
Margaret Street	D2
Martin Street	A7-A8
Mary Street	C2-D2
Mathew Street	B7-C7
Matilda Street	C3-D3-D2
Matilda Way	C3-C4
Meadow Street	B6-B7
Milton Street	B3-C3
Mitchell Street	A5-A6
Montgomery Terrace Road	A7-B8-A8
Moore Street	B2-B3-C3
Morpeth Street	B6-B7
Mount Street	B1
Mowbray Street	C8-D8
Napier Street	A2-A1-B2
Neepsend Lane	B8-C8
Netherthorpe Road	A5-A6-B6-B7
Norfolk Park Road	E1-E2-F2
Norfolk Road	F3-F4
Norfolk Row	D5
Norfolk Street	D5
North Church Street	D6
Nursery Street	D7-E7-E6
Old Street	F6-F5
Orchard Lane	C5
Oxford Street	A7-A8
Paradise Street	D6
Park Grange Croft	F1
Park Grange Road	E1-F1
Park Square	E5-E6-F6-F5
Paternoster Row	D3-D4-E4
Pear Street	A1-A2
Pearl Street	A1
Pembroke Street	A1
Penistone Road	B7-B8
Pinfold Street	C5
Pinstone Street	C4-D4-D5
Pitsmoor Road	D8
Plum Lane	D7
Pomona Street	A1-A2
Pond Hill	E5
Pond Street	E5
Portobello Street	B5-C5
Powell Street	A7
Priestley Street	D1-E1-E2
Queen Street	C6-D6
Queen's Road	E1-E2
Radford Street	B6
Randall Street	C1
Randall Place	C1
Regent Street	B4-B5
Regent Terrace	A4-B5
Rockingham Street	B5-C5-C4
Roscoe Road	B7
Russell Street	C7
Rutland Road	B8
St Georges Close	A5-A6
St Mary's Gate	C2
St Mary's Road	C2-D2-E2
St Philip's Road	A6-A7-B7-B8
Savile Street	E7-F7-F8
School Lane	F5
Scotland Street	B6-C6
Shales Moor	B7-C7
Sheaf Gardens	D2-E2
Sheaf Street	E4-E5
Sheffield Parkway	F6
Shepherd Street	B6-B7-C7
Shoreham Street	D1-D2-D3-E3
Shrewsbury Road	E3-E4-F3-F4
Shude Hill	E5-E6
Sidney Street	D3
Silver Street	C6
Snig Hill	D6
Snow Lane	C6-C7
Solly Street	B5-B6-C6
Sorby Street	F8
South Lane	C2
South Street	E4-E5
Spitalfields	D7-E7
Spital Hill	E7-E8-E8
Spital Lane	F8
Spital Street	E8-F8
Spring Street	D6-E7
Stafford Street	F4
Stanley Lane	E7
Stanley Street	E7
Sudbury Street	F7
Suffolk Road	E3
Summerfield Street	A2-A1
Sunny Bank	A2
Surrey Place	D4
Surrey Street	D5
Sussex Street	F7
Sylvester Street	C2-D2
Talbot Place	F4
Talbot Street	F4
Tenter Street	C6
The Moor	C3-C4
Thomas Street	B3
Townhead Street	C5
Trippet Lane	C5
Trafalgar Street	C3-C4
Travis Place	A3
Trinity Street	C7
Tudor Square	D4-D5
Turner Street	E3
Union Street	C4-D4
Upper Allen Street	B6
Upper Hanover Street	A3-A4-A5
Upperthorpe Road	A7-A8
Verdon Street	E8
Vicar Lane	C5-D5
Victoria Road	A2-A3
Victoria Street	B4-B5
Waingate	E6
Walker Street	E8
Washington Road	A1-B1
Watery Street	B7-B8
Wellington Street	B4-C4
West Bar	D6
West Bar Green	C6-D6
West Street	B4-B5-C5
Westfield Terrace	B4-C5
Weston Street	A5-A6
Wharncliffe Road	A3
White Croft	C6
Wicker	E6-E7
Wilkinson Lane	A4
Wilkinson Street	A4
William Street	A2-A3
York Street	D5-D6
Young Street	B3-C2
AA shop, 5 St James Row, Sheffield, South Yorks S1 1AY	D5

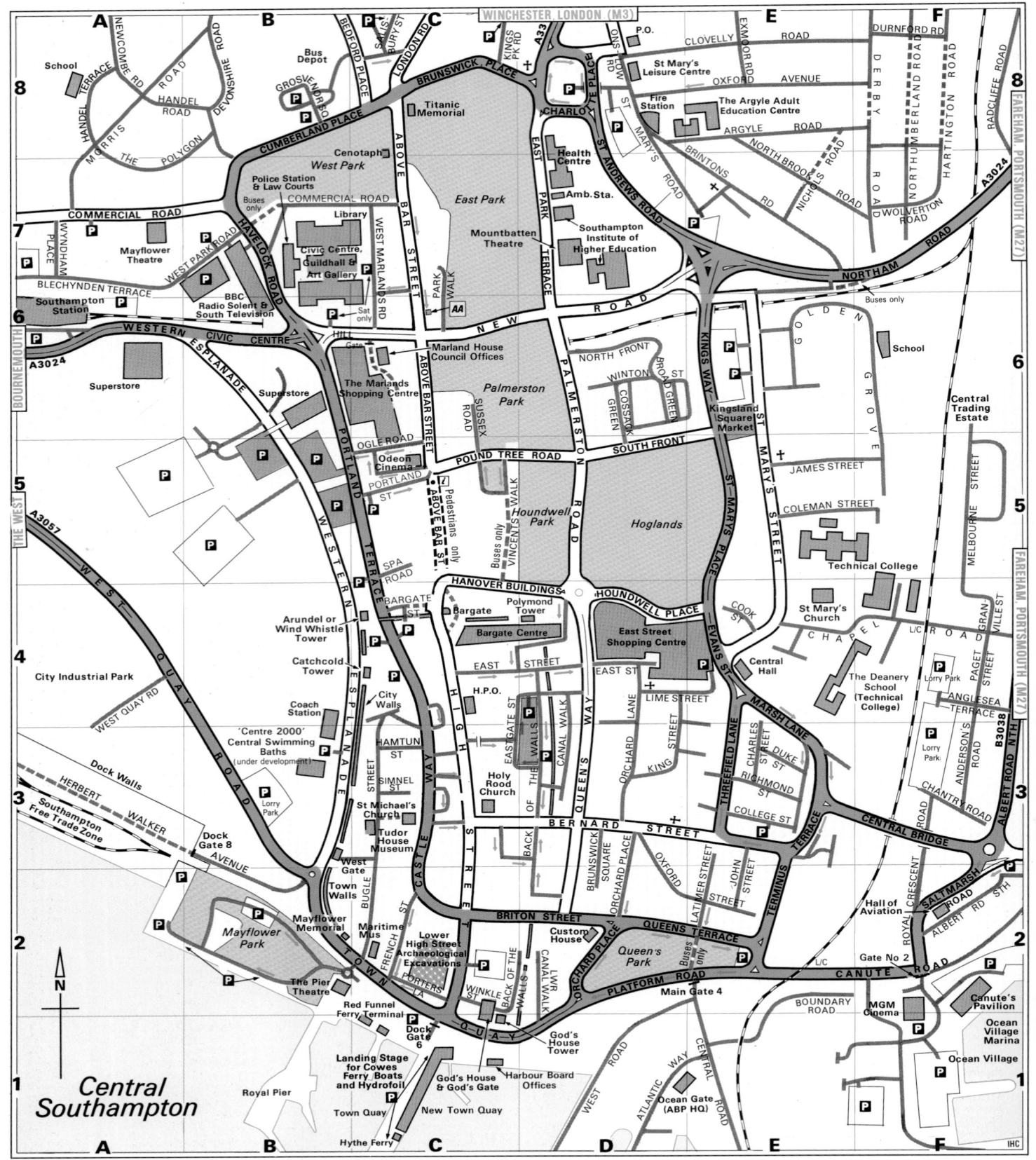

Southampton

Britain's premier passenger port in the days of the great ocean liners, Southampton is now a major container terminal and is still visited regularly by cruise ships. The unique double tide of the Solent waters, protected by the Isle of Wight, has meant that Southampton has always been a superb and important port. Although it was devastated by wartime bombing, many ancient features still survive. Outstanding are the medieval town walls, particularly impressive along the Western Esplanade. The main landward entrance to the walled town was the Bargate, a superb gateway with a guildhall (now a museum) on its upper floor. Founded in 1070, St Michael's Church is the oldest in the city and contains a rare Tournai marble font. Opposite is the Tudor House Museum, dating from the end of the 15th century, with a reconstructed Tudor garden. There are old houses along Bugle Street, with the town walls and 13th-century West Gate near by (through which Henry V passed in 1415 while embarking for Agin-

court). Housed in a 14th-century warehouse is the Maritime Museum. By the Town Quay is God's House Tower, now containing the city's archaeological museum. In part of the redeveloped Eastern Docks are the popular Ocean Village Marina and Canute's Pavilion. The Hall of Aviation, built round an enormous four-engined Sandringham Flying Boat includes a Spitfire created at nearby Woolston. The impressive Civic Centre has the largest art gallery in the South of England.

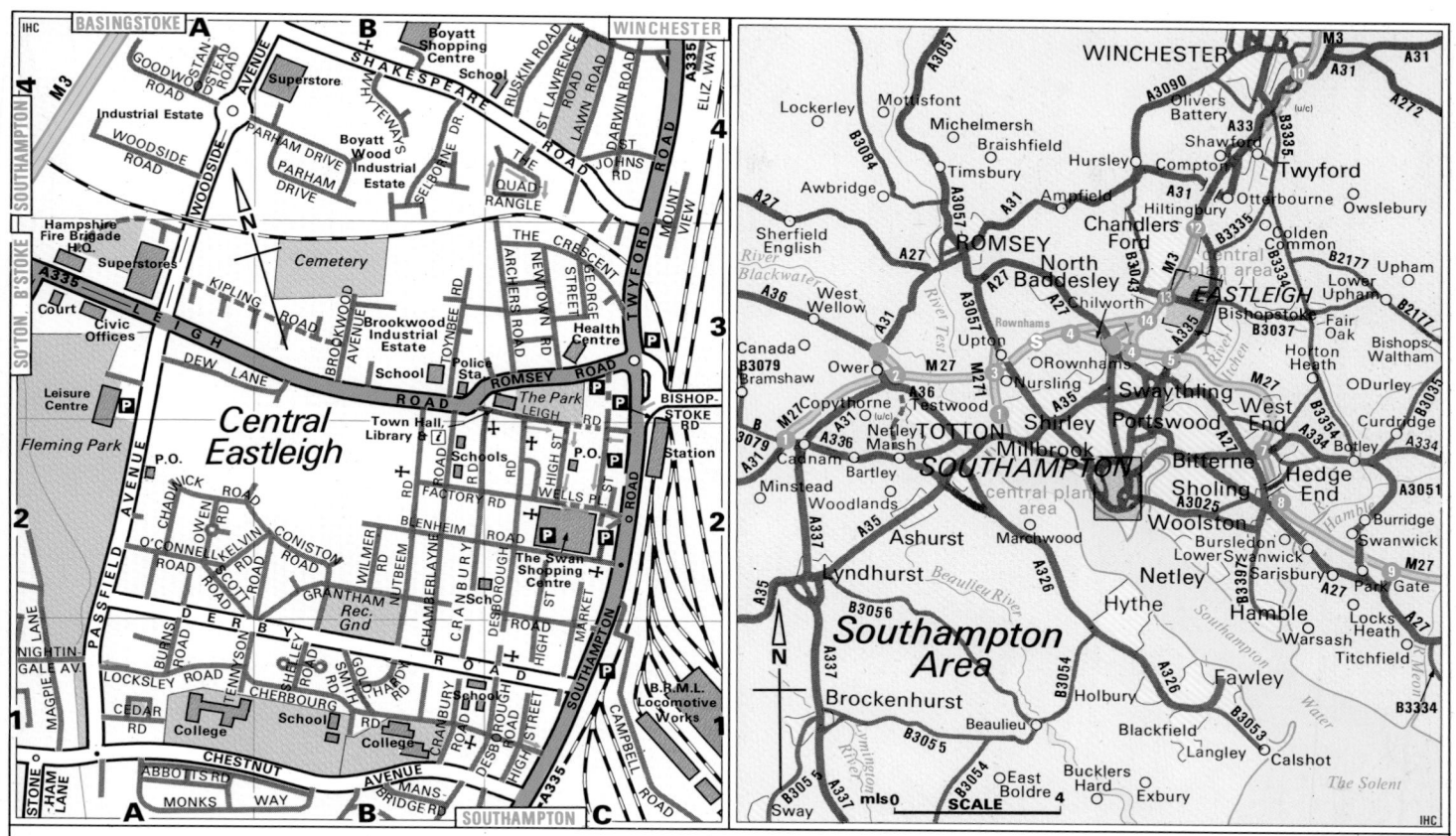

Key to Town Plan and Area Plan

Town Plan

A.A. Recommended roads
Other roads
Restricted roads
Buildings of interest — Cinema
A A Service Centre — AA
Car Parks — P
Parks and open spaces
One way streets

Area Plan

A roads
B roads
Locations — Ower O
Urban Area

Street Index with Grid Reference

Southampton

Above Bar Street	C8-C7-C6-C5
Albert Road North	F3-F4
Albert Road South	F2
Anderson's Road	F3-F4
Anglesea Terrace	F4
Argyle Road	D8-E8-F8
Atlantic Way	D1-E1
Back of the Walls	C2-D2-D3-D4
Bargate Street	C4
Bedford Place	B8-C8
Bernard Street	C3-D3-E3
Blechynden Terrace	A7
Boundary Road	E2
Brintons Road	D8-E7
Briton Street	C2-D2
Broad Green	D6
Brunswick Place	C8-D8
Brunswick Square	D2-D3
Bugle Street	C2-C3
Canal Walk	D3-D4
Canute Road	E2-F2
Castle Way	C2-C3-C4
Central Bridge	E3-F3
Central Road	E1-E2
Chantry Road	F3
Chapel Road	E4-F4
Charles Street	E3
Charlotte Place	D8
Civic Centre Hill	B6-C6
Clovelly Road	D8-E8-F8
Coleman Street	E5-F5
College Street	E3
Commercial Road	A7-B7-C7
Cook Street	E4
Cossack Green	D6-D5
Cumberland Place	B7-B8-C8
Derby Road	F8-F7
Devonshire Road	B8
Duke Street	E3
Durnford Road	F8
East Street	C4-D4
East Park Terrace	D6-D7-D8
Eastgate Street	D3-C3-C4-D4
Evans Street	E4
Exmoor Road	E8
French Street	C2
Golden Grove	E6-F6-F5
Granville Street	F4
Grosvenor Square	B8
Hamtun Street	C3
Handel Road	A8-B8
Handel Terrace	A8
Hanover Buildings	C5-C4-D4
Hartington Road	F7-F8
Havelock Road	B7-B6
Herbert Walker Avenue	A3-B3-B2
High Street	C4-C3-C2
Houndwell Place	D4-E4
James Street	E5-F5
John Street	E2-E3
Kings Way	E6-E7
King Street	D3-D4
Kings Park Road	C8
Latimer Street	E2-E3
Lime Street	D4-E4
London Road	C8
Lower Canal Walk	D2-D1
Marsh Lane	E4-E3
Melbourne Street	F4-F5-F6
Morris Road	A7-A8-B8
New Road	C6-D6-D7
Newcombe Road	A8
Nichols Road	E7-E8
Northbrook Road	E8-E7-F7
North Front	D6
Northam Road	E7-F7
Northumberland Road	F7-F8
Ogle Road	C5
Onslow Road	D8
Orchard Lane	D3-D4
Orchard Place	D2-D3
Oxford Avenue	D8-E8-F8
Oxford Street	D3-D2-E2
Paget Street	F4
Palmerston Road	D6-D5
Park Walk	C6-C7

Platform Road	D2-E2
Porters Lane	C2
Portland Street	C5
Portland Terrace	B6-B5-C5-C4
Pound Tree Road	C5-D5
Queens Terrace	D2-E2
Queen's Way	D2-D3-D4
Radcliffe Road	F7-F8
Richmond Street	E3
Royal Crescent Road	F2-F3
St Andrews Road	D8-D7
St Mary's Place	E5-E4
St Mary's Road	D8-D7-E7
St Mary's Street	E6-E5-E4
Salisbury Street	C8
Saltmarsh Road	F2-F3
Simnel Street	C3
South Front	D5-E5-E6
Spa Road	C5
Sussex Road	C6-C5
The Polygon	A8-A7-B7-B8
Terminus Terrace	E2-E3
Threefield Lane	E3-E4
Town Quay	B2-C2-C1-D1
Vincents Walk	C5
West Marlands Road	C6-C7
West Road	D1-D2-E2
West Park Road	A7-B7
West Quay Road	A5-A4-B4-B3-B2
Western Esplanade	A6-B6-B5-B4-C4-B3
Winkle Street	C2
Winton Street	D6-E6
Wolverton Road	F7
Wyndham Place	A7

AA Shop
126 Above Bar Street
Southampton
Hampshire SO9 1GY   C6

Eastleigh

Abbotts Road	A1
Archers Road	C3
Blenheim Road	B2-C2
Bishopstoke Road	C3
Brookwood Avenue	B3
Burns Road	A1
Campbell Road	C1
Cedar Road	A1
Chadwick Road	A2-B2
Chamberlayne Road	B1-B2-B3
Cherbourg Road	A1-B1-C1
Chestnut Avenue	A1-B1-C1
Coniston Road	B2
Cranbury Road	B1-C1-C2-C3
Darwin Road	C4
Derby Road	A2-A1-B1-C1

Desborough Road	B1-C1-C2
Dew Lane	A3-B3
Elizabeth Way	C4
Factory Road	B2-C2
George Street	C3
Goldsmith Road	B1
Goodwood Road	A4
Grantham Road	B2-C2-C1
Hardy Road	B1
High Street	C1-C2
Kelvin Road	A2-B2
Kipling Road	A3-B3
Lawn Road	C4
Leigh Road	A3-B3-C3-C2
Locksley Road	A1
Magpie Lane	A1-A2
Mansbridge Road	B1
Market Street	C1-C2-C3
Monks Way	A1-B1
Mount View	C3-C4
Newtown Road	C3
Nightingale Avenue	A1
Nutbeem Road	B1-B2-B3
O'Connell Road	A2
Owen Road	A2
Parham Drive	A4-B4
Passfield Avenue	A1-A2-A3
Romsey Road	B3-C3
Ruskin Road	C4
St John's Road	C4
St Lawrence Road	C4
Scott Road	A2
Selborne Drive	B4
Shakespeare Drive	B4-C4
Shelley Road	B1
Southampton Road	C1-C2
Stanstead Road	A4
Stoneham Lane	A1
The Crescent	C3
The Quadrangle	C4
Tennyson Road	A1-B2
Toynbee Road	B3
Twyford Road	C3-C4
Wells Place	C2
Whyteways	B4
Wilmer Road	B2
Woodside Avenue	A3-A4-B4
Woodside Road	A4

Maps: © The Automobile Association 1981
Revision: © The Automobile Association 1994

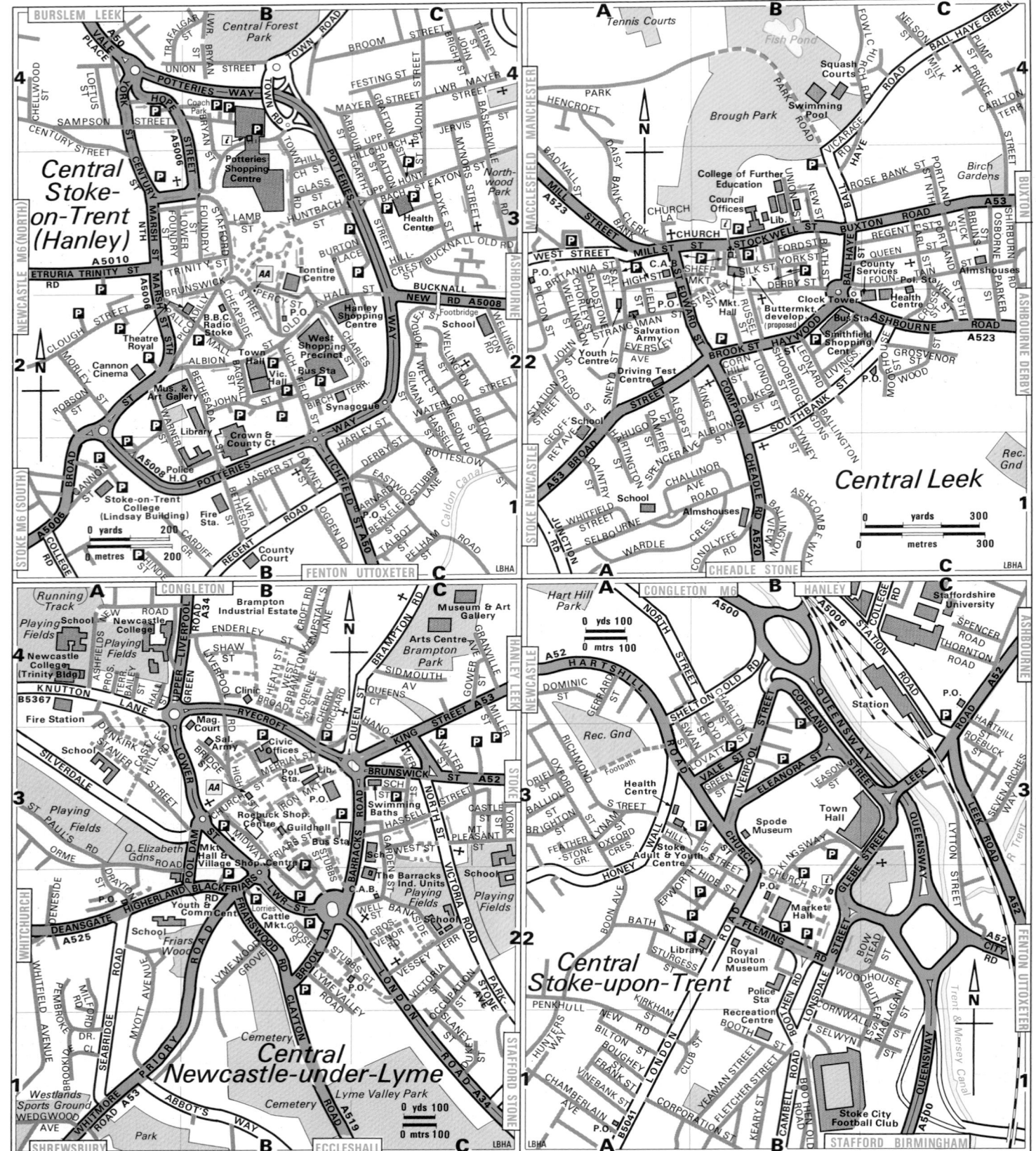

Stoke-on-Trent

Wedgwood, Spode and Royal Doulton are among the names that spring to mind when the city of Stoke-on-Trent is mentioned. Renowned for many years as the capital of the pottery industry, there are numerous museums dealing with the industry's history as well as with leading figures involved in it, and tours of pottery factories can be arranged. Of particular interest is the Gladstone Pottery Museum at Longton, which retains all the original buildings and equipment including some of the once ubiquitous bottle kilns. On the sporting front, Stoke City football team, which plays in the Endsleigh League, boasts Sir Stanley Matthews among its former players.

Hanley is the birthplace of novelist Arnold Bennett, who immortalised the Potteries in his stories about the 'Five Towns'. Reginald Mitchell, designer of the legendary Spitfire aircraft, was also born here. A great attraction of Hanley for many is the fine woodland expanse of 90-acre Central Forest Park, recently the venue of a national garden festival.

Leek was once renowned for silk and dye, but now attracts visitors to its antique shops. Among its interesting older buildings is Brindley Mill and Museum, specialising in the work of 18th-century canal builder James Brindley.

Newcastle-under-Lyme boasts a fine old Guildhall and several inns dating from the 17th and 18th centuries. Keele University, to the south-west, has contributed to the town's cultural activities in recent years.

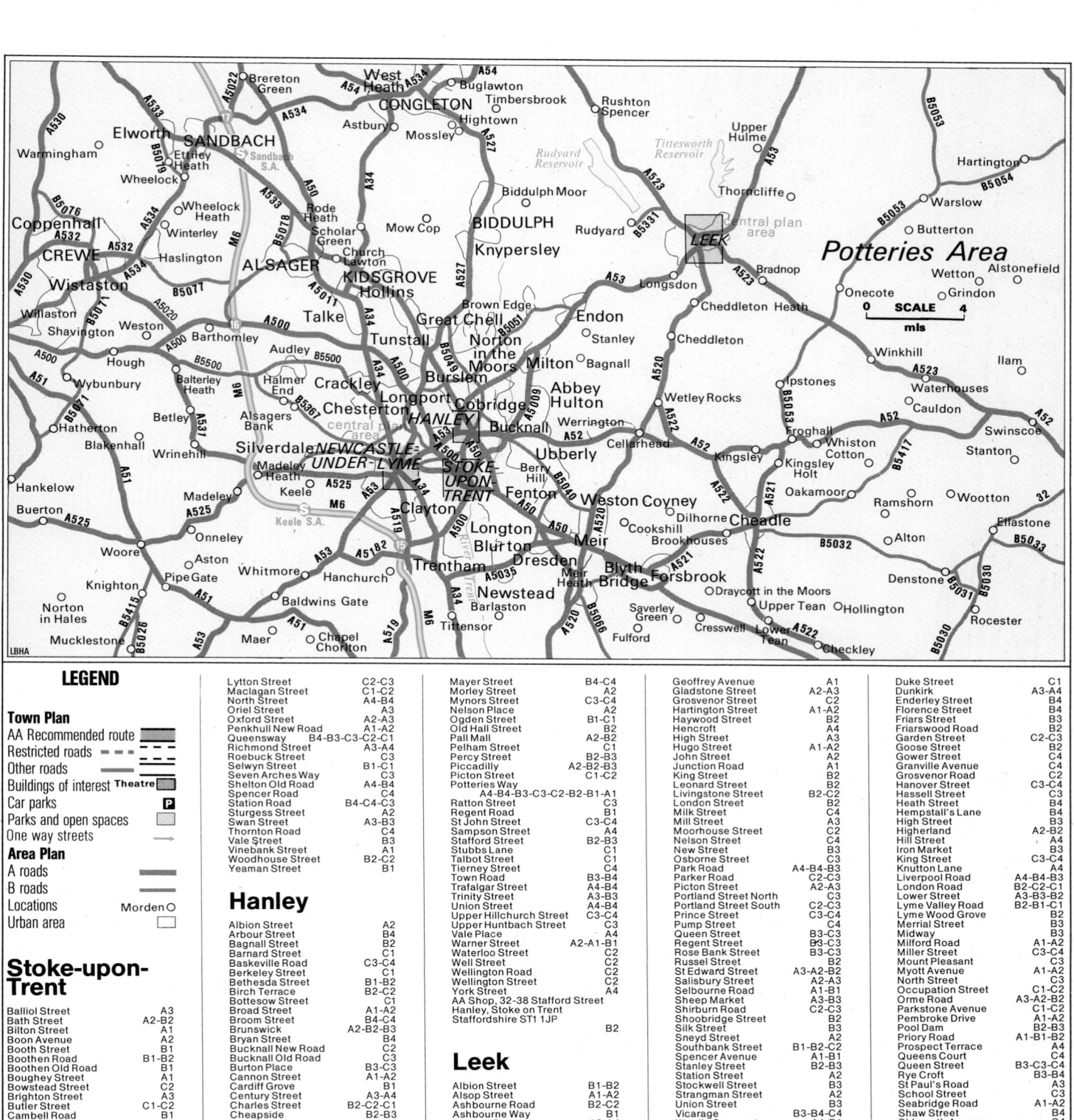

LEGEND

Town Plan

AA Recommended route
Restricted roads
Other roads
Buildings of interest — Theatre
Car parks — P
Parks and open spaces
One way streets

Area Plan

A roads
B roads
Locations — Morden ○
Urban area

Stoke-upon-Trent

Balliol Street	A3
Bath Street	A2-B2
Bilton Street	A1
Boon Avenue	A2
Booth Street	B1
Boothen Road	B1-B2
Boothen Old Road	B1
Boughey Street	A1
Bowstead Street	C2
Brighton Street	A3
Butler Street	C1-C2
Cambell Road	A1
Chamberlain Avenue	A1
Charlton Street	B4
Church Street	B3-B2-C2
City Road	C2
Club Street	A1
College Road	C4
Copeland Street	B4-B3-C3
Cornwallis Street	B2-B1-C1
Corporation Street	A1-B1
Dominic Street	A4
Eleanora Street	B3
Epworth Street	A2-A3-B3
Featherstone Grove	A3
Fleming Road	B2
Fletcher Street	B1
Floyd Street	B3-B4
Frank Street	A1
Gerrard Street	A4
Glebe Street	B2-B3-C3-C2
Harthill Road	C3-C4
Hartshill Road	A4-A3-B3
Hide Street	A2-B2
Hill Street	A3-B3-B2
Honeywall	A2-A3
Hunters Way	A1-A2
Keary Street	B1
Kingsway	B2-B3
Kirkham Street	A1-A2
Leason Road	B3
Leek Road	C3-C4
Liverpool Street	B3-B4
London Road	A1-A2-B2-B1
Lonsdale Street	B1-B2
Lovatt Street	A3-B3
Lynam Street	A3
Lytton Street	C2-C3
Maclagan Street	C1-C2
North Street	A4-B4
Oriel Street	A3
Oxford Street	A2-A3
Penkhull New Road	A1-A2
Queensway	B4-B3-C3-C2-C1
Richmond Street	A3-A4
Roebuck Street	C3
Selwyn Street	B1-C1
Seven Arches Way	C3
Shelton Old Road	A4-B4
Spencer Road	A1
Station Road	B4-C4-C3
Sturgess Street	A2
Swan Street	A3-B3
Thornton Road	C4
Vale Street	B3
Vinebank Street	A1
Woodhouse Street	B2-C2
Yeaman Street	B1

Hanley

Albion Street	A2
Arbour Street	B4
Bagnall Street	B2
Barnard Street	B2
Baskeville Road	C3-C4
Berkeley Street	C1
Bethesda Street	B1-B2
Birch Terrace	B2-C2
Bottesow Street	C1
Broad Street	A1-A2
Broom Street	B4-C4
Brunswick	A2-B2-B3
Bryan Street	B4
Bucknall New Road	C2
Bucknall Old Road	C3
Burton Place	B3-C3
Cannon Street	A1-A2
Cardiff Grove	B1
Century Street	A3-A4
Charles Street	B2-C2-C1
Cheapside	B2-B3
Chelwood Street	A4
Clough Street	A2
College Road	A1
Derby Street	B1-C1
Downey Street	B1
Dyke Street	C3
Eastwood Road	C1
Eaton Street	C3
Etruria Road	A3
Festing Street	B4-C4
Foundary Street	B3
Garth Street	C3
Gilman Street	C2
Glass Street	B3-C3
Grafton Street	C3-C4
Harley Street	B1-C1-C2
Hassell Street	C2
Hillchurch Street	B3
Hillcrest Street	C3
Hinde Street	A1
Hope Street	A4-B4-B3
Hordley Street	C2
Huntbach Street	B3-C3
Jervis Street	C4
John Street	B1
Johnbright Street	C4
Lamb Street	B2
Lichfield Street	B2-B1-C1
Loftus Street	A4
Lower Bethesda Street	B1
Lower Bryan Street	B4
Lower Foundary Street	A3
Lower Mayer Street	A4
Marsh Street North	A3
Marsh Street South	A2

Mayer Street	B4-C4
Morley Street	A2
Mynors Street	C3-C4
Nelson Place	A2
Ogden Street	B1-C1
Old Hall Street	C1
Pall Mall	A2-B2
Pelham Street	B2-B3
Percy Street	A2
Piccadilly	A2-B2-B3
Picton Street	C1-C2
Potteries Way	A4-B4-B3-C3-C2-B2-B1-A1
Ratton Street	C3
Regent Road	B1
St John Street	C3-C4
Sampson Street	A4
Stafford Street	B2-B3
Stubbs Lane	C1
Talbot Street	C1
Tierney Street	C4
Town Road	B3-B4
Trafalgar Street	B4
Trinity Street	A3-B3
Union Street	A4-B4
Upper Hillchurch Street	C3-C4
Upper Huntbach Street	C3
Vale Place	A4
Warner Street	A2-A1-B1
Waterloo Street	B1
Well Street	C2
Wellington Road	C2
Wellington Street	C2
York Street	A4

AA Shop, 32-38 Stafford Street
Hanley, Stoke on Trent
Staffordshire ST1 1JP — B2

Leek

Albion Street	B1-B2
Alsop Street	A1-A2
Ashbourne Road	B2-C2
Ashbourne Way	B1
Badnall Street	A3-A4
Ball Haye Green	A4-C4
Ball Haye Road	B3-B4-C4
Ball Haye Street	B3
Ballington Gardens	B2
Ballington View	B2
Bath Street	B3
Britannia Street	A2-A3
Broad Street	A1-A2-B2
Brook Street	B2
Brunswick Street	C3
Buxton Road	B3-C3
Carlton Terrace	C4
Challinor Avenue	A1-B1
Chorley Street	A2-A3
Church Lane	A3
Church Street	A3-B3
Clerk Bank	A3
Compton Cheadle Road	B1-B2
Condlyffe Road	B1
Corn Hill Street	B2
Cross Street	C2-C3
Cruso Street	A2
Daintry Street	A1
Daisy Bank	A3-A4
Dampier Street	A1-A2
Derby Street	B2-B3
Duke Street	B2
Earl Street	C3
Eversley Avenue	A2
Field Street	A2-A3
Ford Street	B3
Fountain Street	B3-C3
Fowlchurch Road	B4-C4
Fynney Street	B1-B2

Geoffrey Avenue	A1
Gladstone Street	A2-A3
Grosvenor Street	C2
Hartington Street	A1-A2
Haywood Street	B2
Hencroft	A4
High Street	A3
Hugo Street	A1-A2
John Street	A2
Junction Road	A1
King Street	B2
Leonard Street	B2
Livingstone Street	B2-C2
London Street	B2
Milk Street	C4
Mill Street	A3
Moorhouse Street	C2
Nelson Street	C4
New Street	B3
Osborne Street	C3
Park Road	A4-B4-B3
Parker Road	C2-C3
Picton Street	A2-A3
Portland Street North	C3
Portland Street South	C2-C3
Prince Street	C3-C4
Pump Street	C4
Queen Street	B3-C3
Regent Street	B3-C3
Rose Bank Street	B3-C3
Russel Street	B2
St Edward Street	A3-A2-B2
Salisbury Street	A2-A3
Selbourne Road	A1-B1
Sheep Market	A3-B3
Shirburn Street	C2-C3
Shoobridge Street	B3
Silk Street	B3
Sneyd Street	B3
Southbank Street	B1-B2-C2
Spencer Avenue	A1-B1
Stanley Street	B2-B3
Station Street	A2
Stockwell Street	B3
Strangman Street	A2
Union Street	B3
Vicarage	B3-B4-C4
Wardle Crescent	A1-B1
Well Street	C2-C3
Wellington Street	A2-A3
West Street	A3
Whitfield Street	A1
Wood Street	C2
York Street	B3

Newcastle-under-Lyme

Abbot's Way	A1-B1
Ashfields New Road	A4
Bailey Street	A4
Bankside	
Barracks Road	B2-C2-C3
Blackfriars Road	B2
Brampton Road	C4
Bridge Street	B3
Broad Street	B2
Brook Lane	B2
Brookside Close	A1
Brunswick Street	C3
Castle Street	C3
Castlehill Road	A3-A4
Cherry Orchard	B4
Church Street	B3
Clayton Road	B2-B1-C1
Croft Road	B4
Deansgate	A2
Deneside	A2
Drayton Street	A2

Duke Street	C1
Dunkirk	A3-A4
Enderley Street	B4
Florence Street	B4
Friars Street	B3
Friarswood Road	B2
Garden Street	C2-C3
Goose Street	B2
Gower Street	C4
Granville Avenue	C4
Grosvenor Road	C2
Hanover Street	C3-C4
Hassell Street	B3
Heath Street	B4
Hempstall's Lane	B4
High Street	B3
Higherland	A2-B2
Hill Street	A4
Iron Market	B3
King Street	C3-C4
Knutton Lane	A4
Liverpool Road	A4-B4-B3
London Road	B2-C2-C1
Lower Street	A3-B3-B2
Lyme Valley Road	B2-B1-C1
Lyme Wood Grove	
Merrial Street	B3
Midway	
Milford Road	A1-A2
Miller Street	C3-C4
Mount Pleasant	C3
Myott Avenue	A1-A2
North Street	C3
Occupation Street	C1-C2
Orme Road	A3-A2-B2
Parkstone Avenue	C1-C2
Pembroke Drive	A1-A2
Pool Dam	B2-B3
Priory Road	A1-B1-B2
Prospect Terrace	A4
Queens Court	C4
Queen Street	B3-C3-C4
Rye Croft	B3-B4
St Paul's Road	A3
School Street	C3
Seabridge Road	A1-A2
Shaw Street	B4
Sidmouth Avenue	C4
Silverdale	A3-B3
Slaney Street	C1
Stanier Street	A3-B3
Stubbs Gate	B2-C2
Upper Green	A4-B4
Victoria Road	C2-C3
Vessey Terrace	C2
Water Street	C2
Wedgewood Avenue	A1
Well Street	B2-C2
West Brampton	B4
West Street	C3
Whitfield Avenue	A1-A2
Whitmore Road	A1
York Street	B3

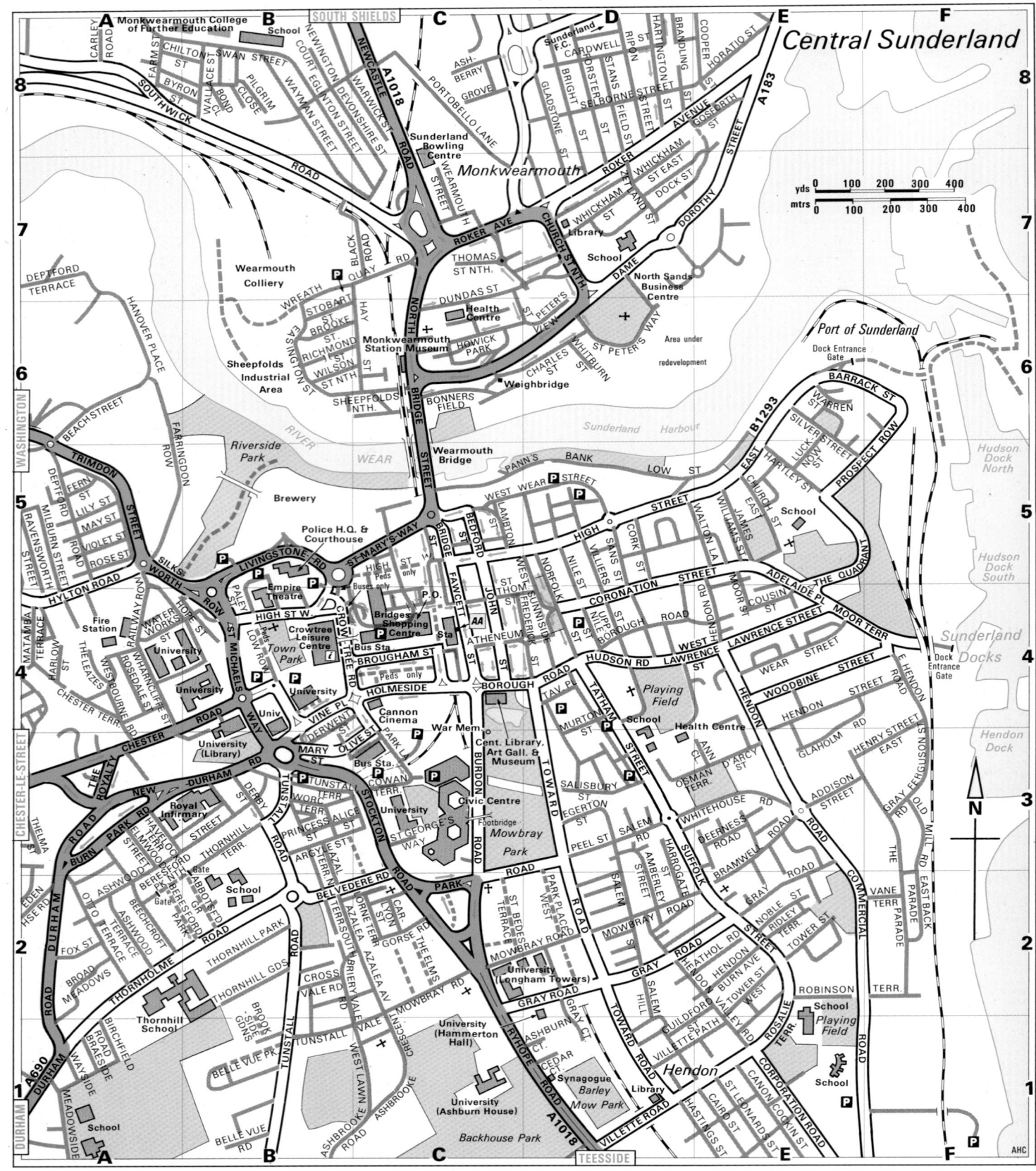

Central Sunderland

Sunderland

Britain's newest city, Sunderland was granted the honour by Her Majesty the Queen to celebrate the fortieth anniversary of her accession to the throne. It recognised the achievement of a community which overcame the loss of its traditional shipbuilding industry, replacing it with modern hi-tech business including the giant Nissan factory. Home to St Bede, the father of English history,

Sunderland was an early centre of Christianity; the church of St Peter's dates back to 674. The city has a modern covered shopping centre, an unrivalled range of leisure facilities, and fine beaches at Roker and Seaburn.

Washington, a former new town, is now part of Sunderland. Its imaginative mix of housing, factories and greenscape was designed to revive a collection of former mining villages. In Washington Village itself stands 17th-century

Washington Old Hall, the former home of George Washington's ancestors. Now in the care of the National Trust, it has been fully restored in period style. The Wildfowl Trust's 103-acre park on the north bank of the Wear enables visitors to observe in landscaped surroundings a colourful collection of the world's rarest waterfowl.

254

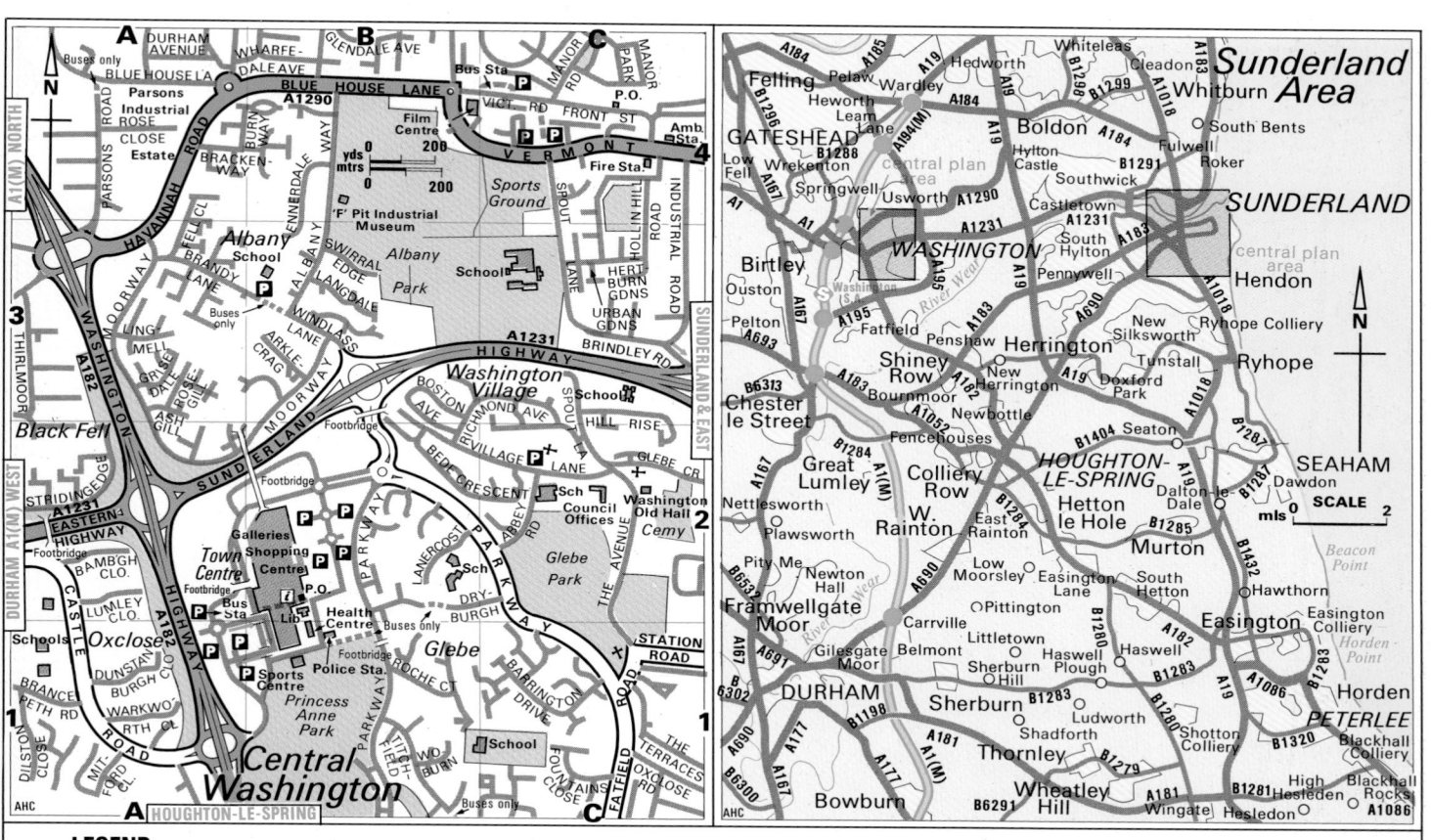

LEGEND

Town Plan

- AA recommended route
- Restricted roads
- Other roads
- Buildings of interest — Cinema
- Car parks — P
- Parks and open spaces
- One way streets
- AA shop — AA

Area Plan

- A roads
- B roads
- Locations — Lingfield ○
- Urban area

Street Index

Sunderland

Abbotsford Grove	B2	Burdon Road	C3-C4	Hope Street	A4-B4
Addison Street	E3	Burlington Road	E2-E3	Horatio Street	E8
Adelaide Place	E4-E5	Burn Park Road	A3	Howick Park	C6
Alice Street	B3	Byron Street	A8-B8	Hudson Road	D4
Amberley Street	D2-D3	Cairo Street	E1	Hylton Road	A4-A5
Ann Close	E3	Canon Cocking Street	E1	James Villiers Street	E5
Argyle Street	B3-C3	Cardwell Street	D8	J. A. Williams Street	E5
Ashberry Grove	C8	Carley Road	A8	John Street	C4-C5
Ashbrooke Crescent	C1	Carlyon Street	C2	Lambton Street	C5
Ashbrooke Road	B1-C1	Cedar Court	D1	Lawrence Street	E4
Ashburn Court	D1	Charles Street	C6-D6	Lily Street	A5
Ashwood Street	A2-A2-B3	Chester Road	A3-A4-B4	Livingstone Road	B5
Ashwood Terrace	A2	Chester Terrace	A4	Lorne Terrace	C2
Athenaeum	C4	Chilton Street	A8-B8	Low Road	B4
Athol Road	E2	Church Street East	E5	Low Street	D5-E5
Avon Street	E3-E4	Church Street North	D7	Lucknow Street	E5
Azalea Avenue	C2	Commercial Road	F1-F2	Matamba Terrace	A4
Azalea Terrace North	B3	Cooper Street	E8	Matlock Street	C5
Azalea Terrace South	B2-C2	Cork Street	D5	May Street	A5
Barrack Street	E6-F6	Coronation Street	D4-D5-D5	Meadowside	A1
Beach Street	A6	Corporation Road	E1	Milburn Street	A5
Beechcroft	A2	Cousin Street	E4	Moor Street	E4-E5
Bedford Street	C5	Cowan Terrace	C3	Moor Terrace	E4-F4
Belle Vue Park	B1	Cross Vale Road	B2	Mowbray Road	C2-D2
Belle Vue Road	B1	Crowtree Road	B4-C4	Murton Street	D3-D4
Belvedere Road	B2-C2	Dame Dorothy Street	C6-E8	Newcastle Road	C7-C8
Beresford Park	B2	D'Arcy Street	E3	New Durham Road	A3-B3
Beresford Park North	A2-B3	Deerness Road	E3	Newington Court	B8
Birchfield Road	A1	Deptford Road	A5	Nile Street	D5
Black Road	C7	Deptford Terrace	A7	Noble Street	E2
Bond Close	B8	Derby Street	B3	Norfolk Street	D4-D5
Bonners Field	C6	Devonshire Street	B8-C8	North Bridge Street	C5-C6-C7
Borough Road	C4-D4	Derwent Street	B3-B4-C4	Old Mill Road	F3
Braeside	A1	Dock Street	D7	Olive Street	B3-C3-C4
Brandling Street	D8	Dundas Street	C6-C7	Osman Terrace	D3
Bridge Street	C5	Durham Road	A1-A2-A3	Otto Terrace	A2
Briery Vale Road	B2	Easington Street	B8-C7	Paley Street	B4-B5
Bright Street	D8	East Back Parade	F2	Pann's Bank	C5-D5
Broad Meadows	A2	East Hendon Road	F4	Park Lane	C3
Brook Street	B6	Eden House Road	A2	Park Road	C2-C3-D3
Brookside Gardens	B1	Egerton Street	D3	Park Place	D2
Brougham Street	C4	Elmwood Street	A3	Park Place West	D2
		Farm Street	A8	Peel Street	D3
		Farringdon Row	A5-A6	Pilgrim Close	B8
		Fawcett Street	C4-C5	Portobello Lane	C7-C8
		Ferguson Street	F3	Princess Street	B3
		Fern Street	A5	Prospect Row	E5-F5-F6
		Forster Street	D8	Railway Row	A4-A5
		Fox Street	A2	Ravensworth Street	A5
		Frederick Street	D4	Richmond Street	B6
		Gladstone Street	D7-D8	Ridley Terrace	E2
		Glaholm Road	E3-E4	Ripon Street	D8
		Gorse Road	C2	Robinson Terrace	E2-F2
		Gosforth Street	E8	Roker Avenue	C7-D7-D8-E8
		Gray Court	D1-D2	Rosalie Terrace	E1-E2
		Gray Road	D2	Rosedale Street	A4
		Guildford Street	D1-E2	Rose Street	A5
		Hanover Place	A6	Ryhope Road	C1-C2-D1
		Harlow Street	A4	St Bedes Terrace	C2
		Harrogate Street	D2-D3	St George's Way	C3
		Hartington Street	D8	St Leonards Street	E1
		Hartley Street	E5	St Mary's Way	B5-C5
		Hastings Street	D1-E1	St Peter's View	B4
		Havelock Terrace	A3	St Peter's Way	D6
		Hay Street	C6-C7	St Michael's Way	B4
		Hendon Burn Avenue	E2	St Thomas Street	C4
		Hendon Road	E3-E4-E5	Salem Hill	D1-D2
		Hendon Street	E4-F4	Salem Road	D3
		Hendon Valley Road	D2-E1-E2	Salem Street	D2-D3
		Henry Street East	E3-F3-F4	Salisbury Street	D3
		High Street East	D5-E5-E6	Sans Street	D5
		High Street West	B4-B5-C5	Selborne Street	D8
		Holmeside	C4	Sheepfolds North	B6-C6

Silksworth Row	A5-B4	Blue House Lane	A4-B4
Silver Street	E5-E6	Boston Avenue	B2-B3
Southwick Road	A8-B8-B7-C7	Bracken Way	A4
Stansfield Street	D8	Brancepeth Road	A1
Stobart Street	B6	Brandy Lane	A3
Stockton Road	B3-C2-C3	Brindley Road	C3
Suffolk Street	D3-E2	Burn Way	B3
Swan Street	A8-B8	Castle Road	A1-A2
Tatham Street	D3-D4	Dilston Close	A1
Tavistock Place	D4	Dryburgh	B2-C2
The Elms	C2	Dunstanburgh Close	A1
The Leazes	A4	Durham Avenue	A4
Thelma Street	A3	Eastern Highway	A2
Thomas Street North	C7	Ennerdale	B4
Thornhill Gardens	B2	Fatfield Road	C1
Thornhill Park	B2	Fell Close	A3-A4
Thornhill Terrace	B3	Fountains Close	C1
Thornholme Road	A1-A2-B2	Front Street	C4
Toward Road	D1-D2-D3-D4	Glebe Crescent	C2
Tower Street	E2	Glendale Avenue	B4
Tower Street West	E2	Grisedale	A3
Trimdon Street	A5	Havannah Road	A3-A4
Tunstall Road	B1-B2-B3	Hertburn Gardens	C1
Tunstall Terrace	B3-C3	Hill Rise	C3
Tunstall Vale	B1-C1	Hollin Hill Road	C3-C4
The Parade	F2-F3	Industrial Road	C3-C4
The Royalty	A3	Lancercost	B2
The Quadrant	E5-F5	Langdale	B3
Upper Nile Street	D4	Lingmell	A3
Vane Terrace	F2	Lumley Close	A2
Villette Path	D1-E1	Manor Park	C4
Villette Road	D1	Manor Road	C4
Vine Place	B4	Mitford Close	A1
Violet Street	A5	Moorway	A3-B3
Wallace Street	B8	Oxclose Road	C4
Walton Lane	D5-E5	Parkway	B1-B2-C2-C1
Warren Street	E6	Parsons Road	A4
Warwick Street	C8	Richmond Avenue	B2-B3-C3
Waterworks Street	A5	Roche Court	B1
Wayman Street	B7-B8	Rose Close	A4
Wayside	A1	Rosegill	A3
Wearmouth Street	C7	Spout Lane	C2-C3-C4
Wear Street	E4	Station Road	C1
Westbourne Street	A4	Stridingedge	A2-C3
West Lawn	C1	Sunderland Highway	A2-C3
West Lawrence Street	D4-D5	The Avenue	C1-C2
West Sunniside	D4-D5	The Terraces	C1
West Wear Street	C5-D5	Thirlmoor	A3
Wharncliffe Street	A4	Titchfield	B1
Whickham Street	D7	Urban Gardens	C3
Whickham Street East	D7-D8	Vermont	B4-C4
Whitburn Street	D6	Victoria Road	B4-C4
White House Road	D3-E3	Village Lane	B2-C2
Wilson Street North	B6	Warkworth Close	A1
Woodbine Street	E4-F4	Washington Highway	A1-A4
Worcester Terrace	A4	Wharfedale Avenue	A4-B4
Wreath Quay Road	B6-B7-C7	Windlass Lane	B3
AA Insurance Shop		Wirral Edge	B3
6 North of England House		Woburn	B1
49 Fawcett Street, Sunderland			
Tyne & Wear SR1 1BR	C4		

Washington

Abbey Road	C2
Albany Way	B3-B4
Arklecrag	B3
Ashgill	A2
Bamborough Close	A2
Barrington Drive	C1
Bede Crescent	B3-B2-C2

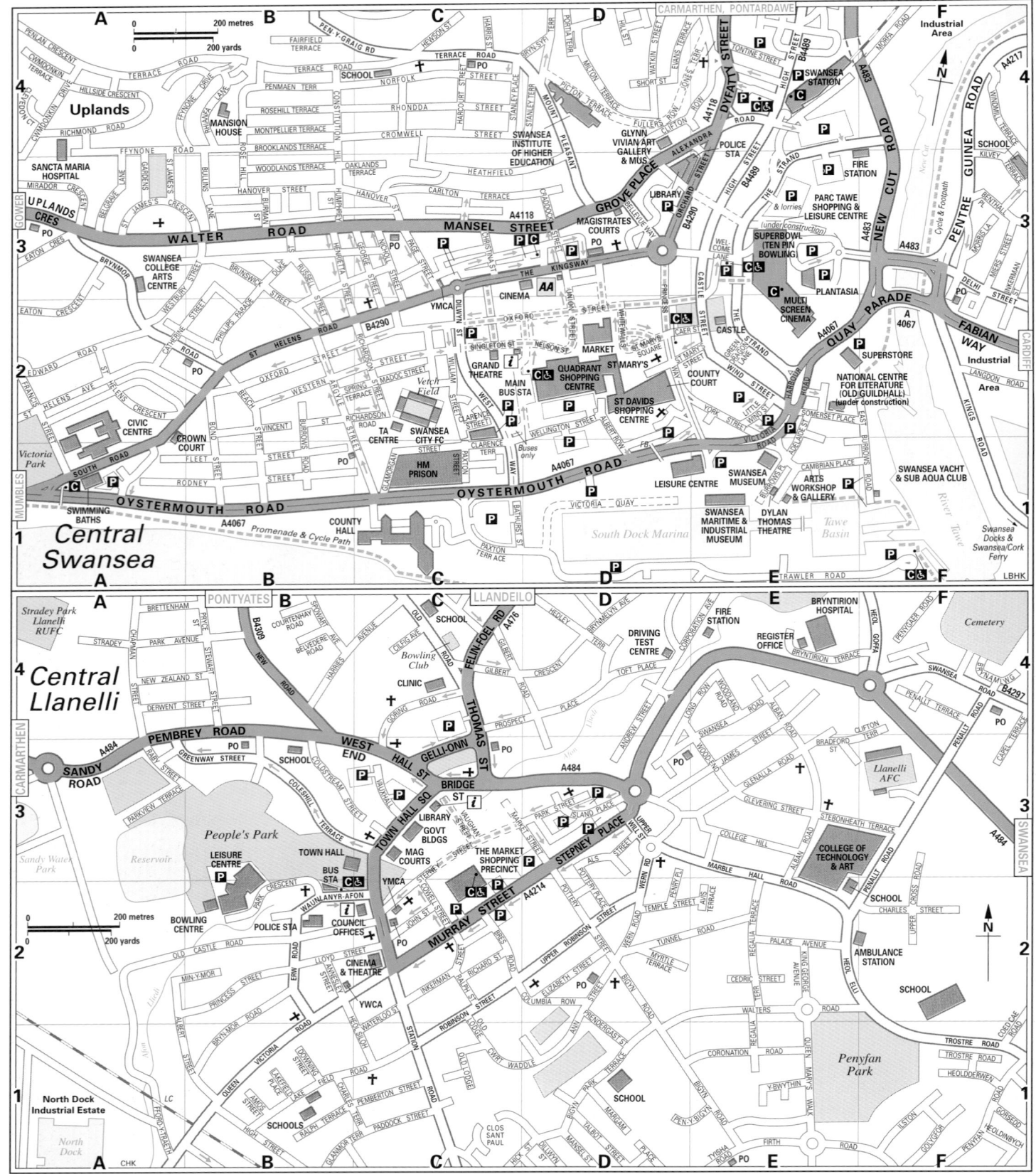

Swansea

Situated at the mouth of the River Tawe, almost at the centre of a wide bay, the city and port of Swansea developed from a 9th-century Viking settlement called Sweyn's Ea (Ea meaning island). Swansea grew rapidly during the Industrial Revolution and became infamous for the pollution caused by its numerous ironworks, non-ferrous ore smelters, factories and coal mines. Today the picture is very different. Light industry and commerce have replaced the heavy industries and slag-heaps; the city centre (much rebuilt after wartime devastation) has many fine shops, and there are hundreds of acres of parkland and open space. To the west, beyond the fine university, lies the Gower Peninsula – one of the most beautiful areas of Wales. The western docks have been transformed into the award-winning Maritime Village and marina, and at the Parc Tawe leisure centre is the unique Plantasia, a pyramidal hothouse containing over 5,000 plants from around the world. The city's history is displayed in both the Maritime and Industrial Museum and the nearby Swansea Museum, while the Glynn Vivian Art Gallery contains notable paintings and porcelain. Swansea was also the birthplace of the poet Dylan Thomas.

Llanelli is the largest town in south-east Dyfed. Originally a market centre, its rapid growth began with the 19th-century introduction of ironworks and tin manufacturing, and continued with the exploitation of its coal resources – which in turn have given way to the modern tinplate works and numerous light industries.

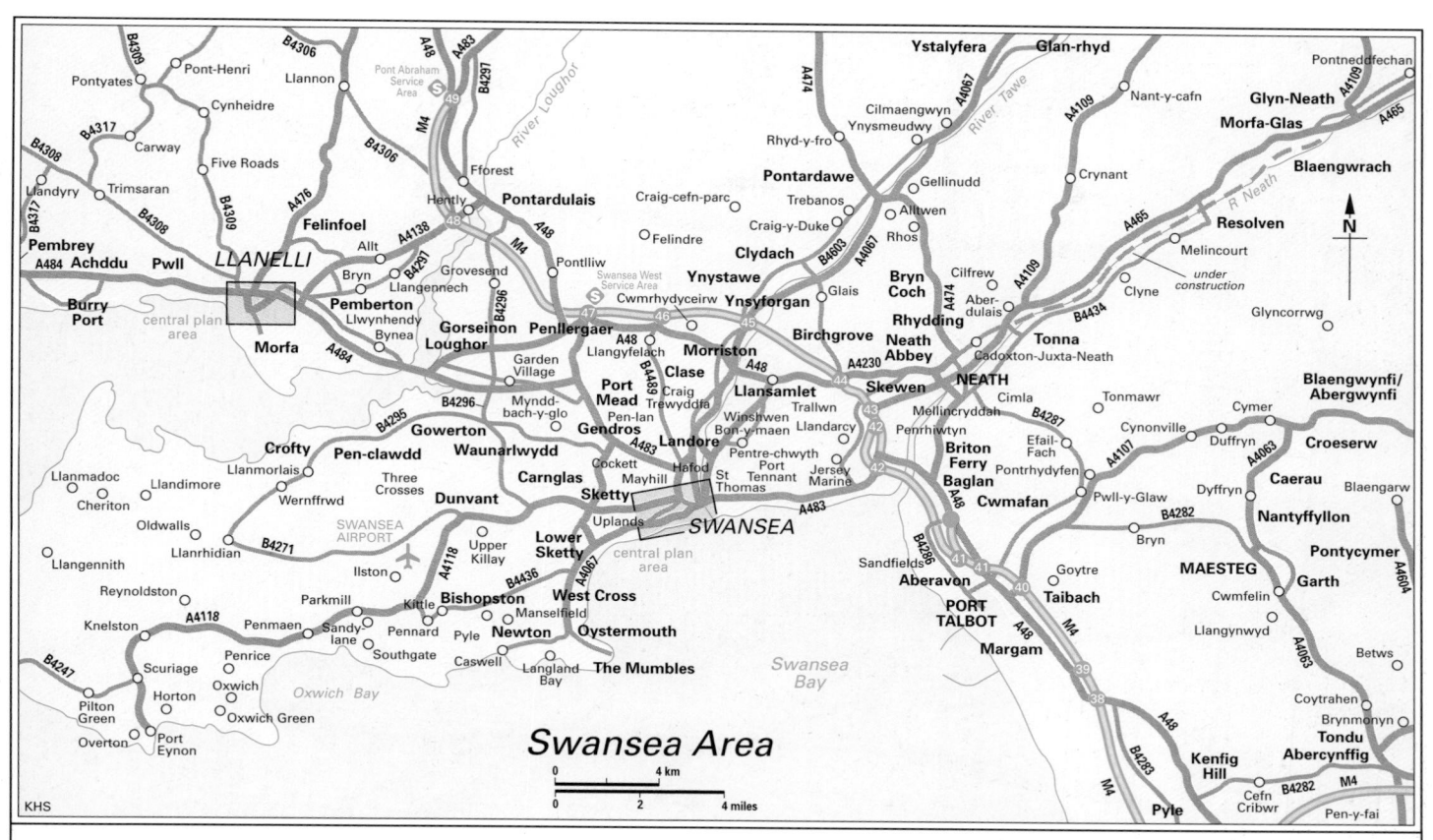

Swansea Area

0 ____ 4 km
0 __ 2 __ 4 miles

KHS

LEGEND

Town Plan

AA Recommended routes
Restricted roads
Other roads
Buildings of interest   COLLEGE
AA Shop/Insurance   AA
Churches   +
Parks and open spaces
Car parks   P
Toilets   C& C
One way streets   ←

Area Plan

A roads
B roads
Locations   Yalding O
Urban area

Street Index with Grid Reference

Swansea

Adelaide Street	E1-E2
Albert Row	D2-D1
Alexandra Road	D3-D4-E3
Argyle Street	B2-B1
Bathurst Street	C1
Beach Street	B2-B1
Belgrave Lane	A3
Bellevue Way	D3
Benthall Place	F3
Bond Street	B2-B1
Brooklands Terrace	B4
Brunswick Street	B3-B2
Bryn-y-mor Road	A3-B2
Bryn-Syfi Terrace	D4
Bullins Lane	B3
Burman Street	B3
Burrows Place	E1
Burrows Road	B2-B1
Caer Street	D2-E2
Cambrian Place	E1
Carlton Terrace	C3-D3
Castle Street	E3-E2
Catherine Street	A2-B2
Christina Street	C3
Clarence Street	C2
Clarence Terrace	C1
Clevedon Court	A4
Clifton Row	D4-E4
Constitution Hill	B4-B3
Craddock Street	D3
Cromwell Street	B4-C4
Cwmdonkin Drive	A4
Cwmdonkin Terrace	A4
Delhi Street	F3-F2
Dilwyn Street	C2
Duke Street	B3

Dyfatty Street	E4
East Burrows Road	F2-F1
Eaton Crescent	A2-A3
Evans Terrace	D4
Fabian Way	F2
Fairfield Terrace	B4
Ffynone Drive	A4-B4
Ffynone Road	A4-B4
Fleet Street	A1-B1
Francis Street	A2-A1
Fullers Row	D4
George Street	C3-C2
Glamorgan Street	C1
Green Dragon Lane	E2
Grove Place	D3
Hanover Lane	A3-B3
Hanover Street	B3-C3
Harbour Road	E2
Harcourt Street	C4
Heathfield	C3
Henrietta Street	B3-B2
Hewson Street	C4
High Street	E3-E4
Hill Street	D4
Hillside Crescent	A4
Humphrey Street	B3
Inkerman Street	F2-F3
Jones Terrace	D4-E4
Kilvey Terrace	F3
King Edward Road	A2
Kings Road	F2-F1
Langdon Road	F2
Little Wynd Street	E2
Madoc Street	C2
Mansel Street	C3-D3
Miers Street	F3
Milton Street	D4
Mirador Crescent	A3
Montpellier Terrace	B4
Morfa Road	E4-F4
Morris Lane	F3
Mount Pleasant	D4-D3
Nelson Street	D2
New Cut Road	F3-F4
Nicholl Street	C3
Norfolk Street	B4-C4
Oaklands Terrace	B3-C3
Orchard Street	D3-E3-E4
Oxford Street	B2-C2-D2
Oystermouth Road	A2-B1-C1-D1
Page Street	C3
Paxton Street	C1
Paxton Terrace	C1
Penlan Crescent	A4
Penmaen Terrace	B4
Pentre Guinea Road	F3-F4
Pen-y-Graig Road	B4-C4
Phillips Parade	B2-B3
Picton Terrace	D4
Portia Terrace	D4
Princess Way	D3-D2
Quay Parade	F2-F2
Rhianfa Lane	B4
Rhondda Street	B4-C4
Richardson Road	D3-E3-E4
Richardson Street	B2
Richmond Road	A4
Rodney Street	A1-B1

Rose Hill	B4-B3
Rosehill Terrace	B4
Russell Street	B3-B2
St Helens Avenue	A2
St Helens Crescent	A2
St Helens Road	A2-B2-C2
St James's Crescent	A3-B3
St James's Gardens	A3
St Mary's Square	D2
St Mary's Street	D2-E2
Short Street	D4
Singleton Street	C2
Somerset Place	E2
South Road	A1
Spring Terrace	B2-C2
Stanley Place	C4
Stanley Terrace	D4
Terrace Road	C4
The Kingsway	C3-D3
The Strand	E2-E3-E4-F4
Tontine Street	E4
Trawler Road	E1-F1
Union Street	D3-D2
Uplands Crescent	A3
Victoria Road	E1-E2
Victoria Quay	D1
Vincent Street	B2
Walter Road	A3-B3
Watkin Street	D4
Welcome Lane	E3
Wellington Street	D2
West Way	C2-C1
Westbury Street	A2-B3
Western Street	B2-C2
Whitewalls	D2
William Street	C2
Wind Street	E2
Windmill Terrace	F4
Woodlands Terrace	B3
York Street	E2
AA shop	C3
20 Union Street	
Swansea	
West Glamorgan	
SA1 3EH	

Llanelli

Alban Road	E3-E4
Albert Street	A2-B2-B1
Als Street	D3
Amos Street	B1
Andrew Street	D3-D4
Ann Street	D1-D2
Annesley Street	B2
Avis Terrace	E2
Belvedere Road	B4
Bigyn Park Terrace	D1
Bigyn Road	D2-D1-E1
Bradford Street	E3
Bres Road	C2
Brettenham	A4-B4
Bridge Street	C3
Bryn-mor Road	B1-B2
Brynamlwg	F4
Brynmelyn Avenue	E4
Bryntirion Terrace	E4
Capel Terrace	F3-F4

Cedric Street	E2
Chapman Street	A4
Charles Street	F2
Charles Terrace	B1-C1
Cilfig Avenue	C4
Clifton Terrace	E3-E4-F4
Clos Sant Paul	C1
Coed Cae Road	F1-F2
Coldstream Street	B3-C3
Coleshill Terrace	B3-C3
College Hill	E3
Columbia Row	D2
Coronation Road	D1-E1
Corporation Avenue	D4-E4
Courtenhay Road	B4
Cowell Street	C2
Cwrt Waddle	C1-D1
Derwent Street	A4-B4
Dillwyn Street	D1
Downing Street	B1
Elizabeth Street	D2
Erw Road	B2
Felin-Foel Road	C4
Fford-y-Traeth	A1
Firth Road	E1-E2
Gelli-Onn	C3
Gilbert Crescent	C4-D4
Gilbert Road	C4-D4
Glanmor Terrace	B1-C1
Glenalla Road	D3-E3
Glevering Street	E3
Golygfor	F1
Goring Road	C3-C4
Gorsedd	F1
Greenway Street	A3-B3
Hall Street	C3
Harries Avenue	B4-C4
Hedley Terrace	D4
Heol Dderwen	F1
Heol Dinbych	F1
Heol Elli	E2-F2
Heol Goffa	F4
Heol Siloh	B2-C2-C1
Hick Street	C1-D1
High Street	B1
Ilston	F1
Inkerman Street	C2
Island Place	C2
James Street	D3-E3-E4
John Street	C2
King George Avenue	E2
Lakefield Place	B1
Lakefield Road	B1-C1
Lliedi Crescent	D4
Lloyd Street	B2-C2
Long Row	D3-D4-E4
Mansel Street	D1
Marble Hall Road	D3-E3-E4
Margam Place	D1
Market Street	C3-D3
Min-y-mor	B2
Murray Street	C2-D2-D3
Myrtle Terrace	D2
New Road	B4
New Zealand Street	A4-B4
Old Castle Road	A2-B2
Old Lodge	C1
Old Road	C4

Paddock Street	C1
Palace Avenue	E2
Park Crescent	B2
Park Street	D3
Parkview Terrace	A3-B3
Pemberton Street	B1-C1
Pembrey Road	A3-B3-B4
Pen-y-bigy	D1-E1
Penyfan Road	F1
Penallt Road	E2-F2-F3-F4
Penallt Terrace	F4
Penry Place	D2-D3
Penygaer Road	F4
Pottery Place	D3-D2
Pottery Road	D3-D2
Prendergast Street	D2-D1
Princess Street	B2
Prospect Place	C4-D4
Pryce Street	B4
Queen Mary's Walk	E2-E1
Queen Victoria Road	
	A1-B1-B2-C2
Raby Street	A3-B3
Ralph Street	C2
Ralph Terrace	B1
Regalia Terrace	E1-E2
Richard Street	C2
Robinson Street	C1-C2
Sandy Road	A3
Spowart Avenue	B4
Station Road	C2-C1
Stebonheath Terrace	E3-F3
Stepney Place	D3
Stepney Street	C2-C3
Stewart Street	B4
Stradey Park Avenue	A4-B4
Swansea Road	D3-E4-F4
Talbot Street	D1
Temple Street	D2-E2
Thomas Street	C4-C3
Toft Place	D4
Town Hall Square	C3
Trostre Road	F1
Tunnel Road	D2-E2
Tyisha Road	E1
Upper Cross Road	F2-F3
Upper Robinson Street	D2
Upper William Street	D3
Vaughan Street	C3
Vauxhall	C3
Walters Road	D2-E2
Waterloo Street	C1-C2
Waunlanyrafon	B2
Wern Road	D2-D3
West End	B3-C3
Woodend	E3
Woodland Road	E4
Y-Bwythin	E1

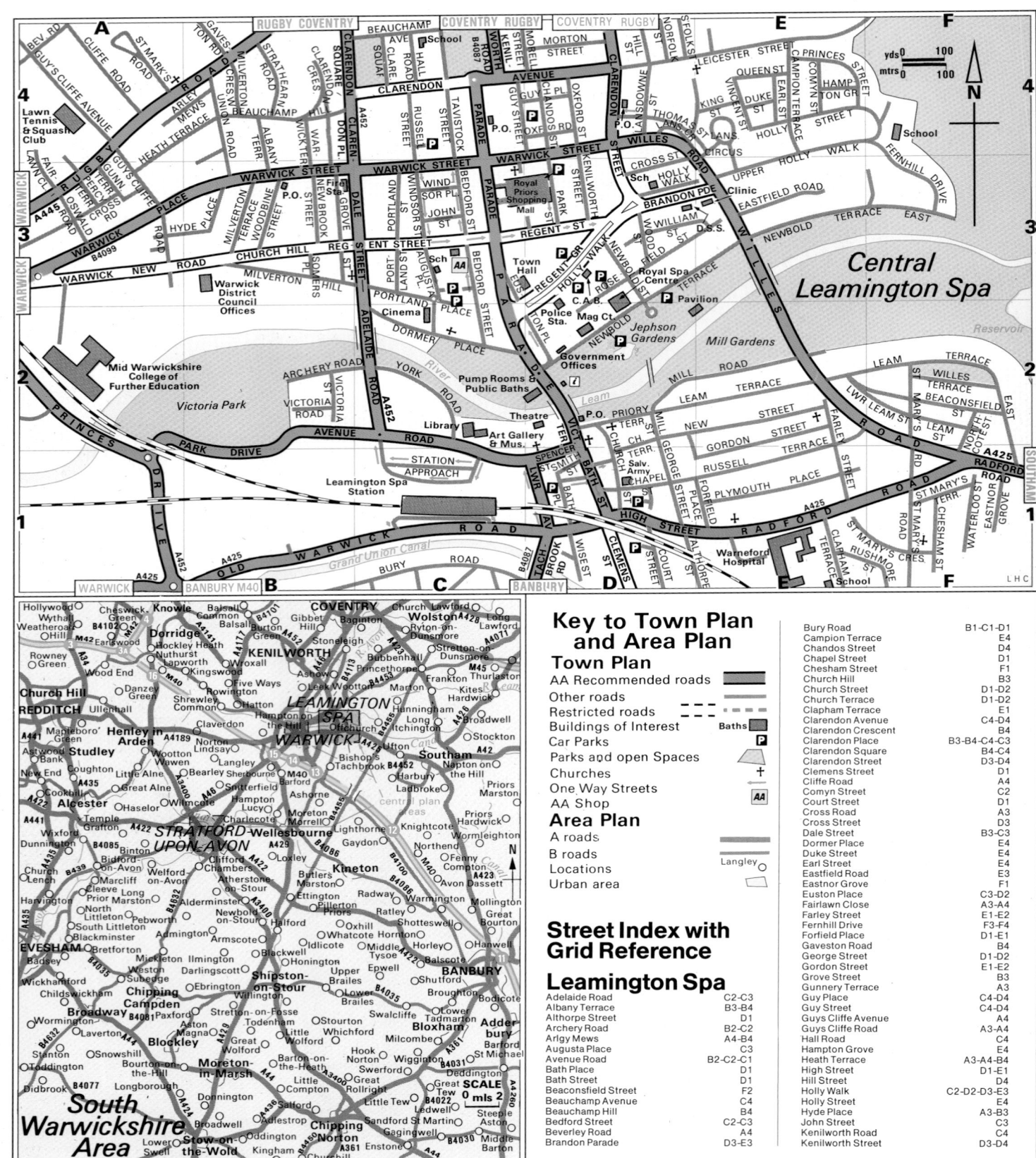

Key to Town Plan and Area Plan

Town Plan

AA Recommended roads	▬▬▬
Other roads	
Restricted roads	- - -
Buildings of Interest	Baths
Car Parks	P
Parks and open Spaces	
Churches	†
One Way Streets	→
AA Shop	AA

Area Plan

A roads	
B roads	
Locations	Langley ○
Urban area	

Street Index with Grid Reference

Leamington Spa

Adelaide Road	C2-C3
Albany Terrace	B3-B4
Althorpe Street	D1
Archery Road	B2-C2
Arlgy Mews	A4-B4
Augusta Place	C3
Avenue Road	B2-C2-C1
Bath Place	D1
Bath Street	D1
Beaconsfield Street	F2
Beauchamp Avenue	C4
Beauchamp Hill	B4
Bedford Street	C2-C3
Beverley Road	A4
Brandon Parade	D3-E3

Bury Road	B1-C1-D1
Campion Terrace	E4
Chandos Street	D4
Chapel Street	D1
Chesham Street	F1
Church Hill	B3
Church Street	D1-D2
Church Terrace	D1-D2
Clapham Terrace	E1
Clarendon Avenue	C4-D4
Clarendon Crescent	B4
Clarendon Place	B3-B4-C4-C3
Clarendon Square	B4-C4
Clarendon Street	D3-D4
Clemens Street	D1
Cliffe Road	A4
Comyn Street	C2
Court Street	D1
Cross Road	A3
Cross Street	D3
Dale Street	B3-C3
Dormer Place	E4
Duke Street	E4
Earl Street	E4
Eastfield Road	E3
Eastnor Grove	F1
Euston Place	C3-D2
Fairlawn Close	A3-A4
Farley Street	E1-E2
Fernhill Drive	F3-F4
Forfield Place	D1-E1
Gaveston Road	B4
George Street	D1-D2
Gordon Street	E1-E2
Grove Street	B3
Gunnery Terrace	A3
Guy Place	C4-D4
Guy Street	C4-D4
Guys Cliffe Avenue	A4
Guys Cliffe Road	A3-A4
Hall Road	C4
Hampton Grove	E4
Heath Terrace	A3-A4-B4
High Street	D1-E1
Hill Street	D4
Holly Walk	C2-D2-D3-E3
Holly Street	E4
Hyde Place	A3-B3
John Street	C3
Kenilworth Road	C4
Kenilworth Street	D3-D4

Warwick

The old county town of the shire, Warwick is famous for its massive historic castle standing beside the River Avon. Thomas Beauchamp and his son built the huge towers and curtain walls in the 14th century, but it was the Jacobean holders of the earldom, the Grevilles, who transformed the medieval stronghold into a nobleman's residence. In 1694 the heart of the town was almost comp-

letely destroyed by fire, and the few medieval buildings that survived lie on the outskirts of the present 18th-century centre. Of these Oken House, now a doll museum, and Lord Leycester's Hospital, almshouses dating back to the 14th century, are particularly striking. Also of interest are the county museum and the Warwickshire Yeomanry Museum.

Stratford-upon-Avon, as the birthplace of William Shakespeare, England's most famous poet and playwright, is second only to London as a tourist

attraction. This charming old market town is a living memorial to him; his plays are performed in the Royal Shakespeare Theatre which dominates the river bank, a museum specialises in scenes from his works, and his birthplace in Henley Street contains Elizabethan artefacts and a museum of costume.

Leamington Spa, an elegant Regency spa town, gained the prefix 'Royal' after a visit by Queen Victoria in 1838. It has an impressive new shopping mall and a good art gallery and museum.

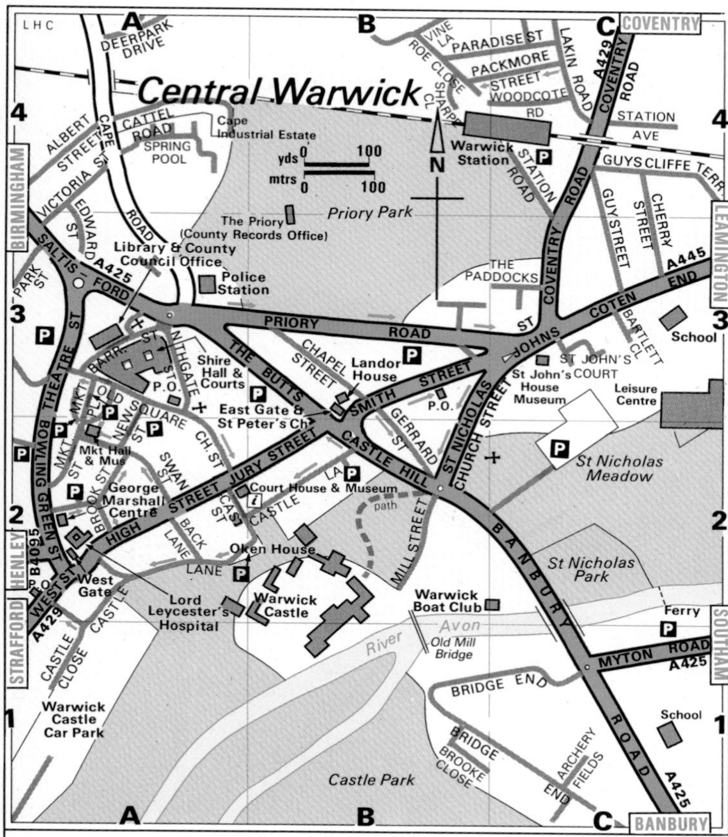

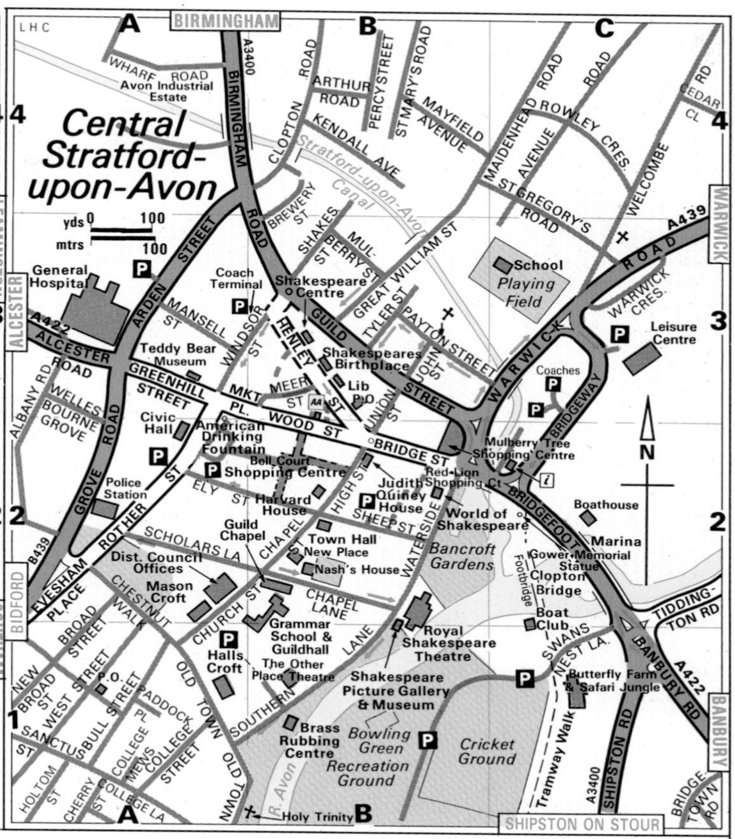

Central Warwick

(street map of Central Warwick, grid reference A–C / 1–4)

Central Stratford-upon-Avon

(street map of Central Stratford-upon-Avon, grid reference A–C / 1–4)

Warwick

Stratford-upon-Avon

WARWICK
These pretty brick and timbered cottages standing in the shadow of the great medieval towers of Warwick Castle are among the few buildings in the town that survived a devastating fire in the late 17th century.

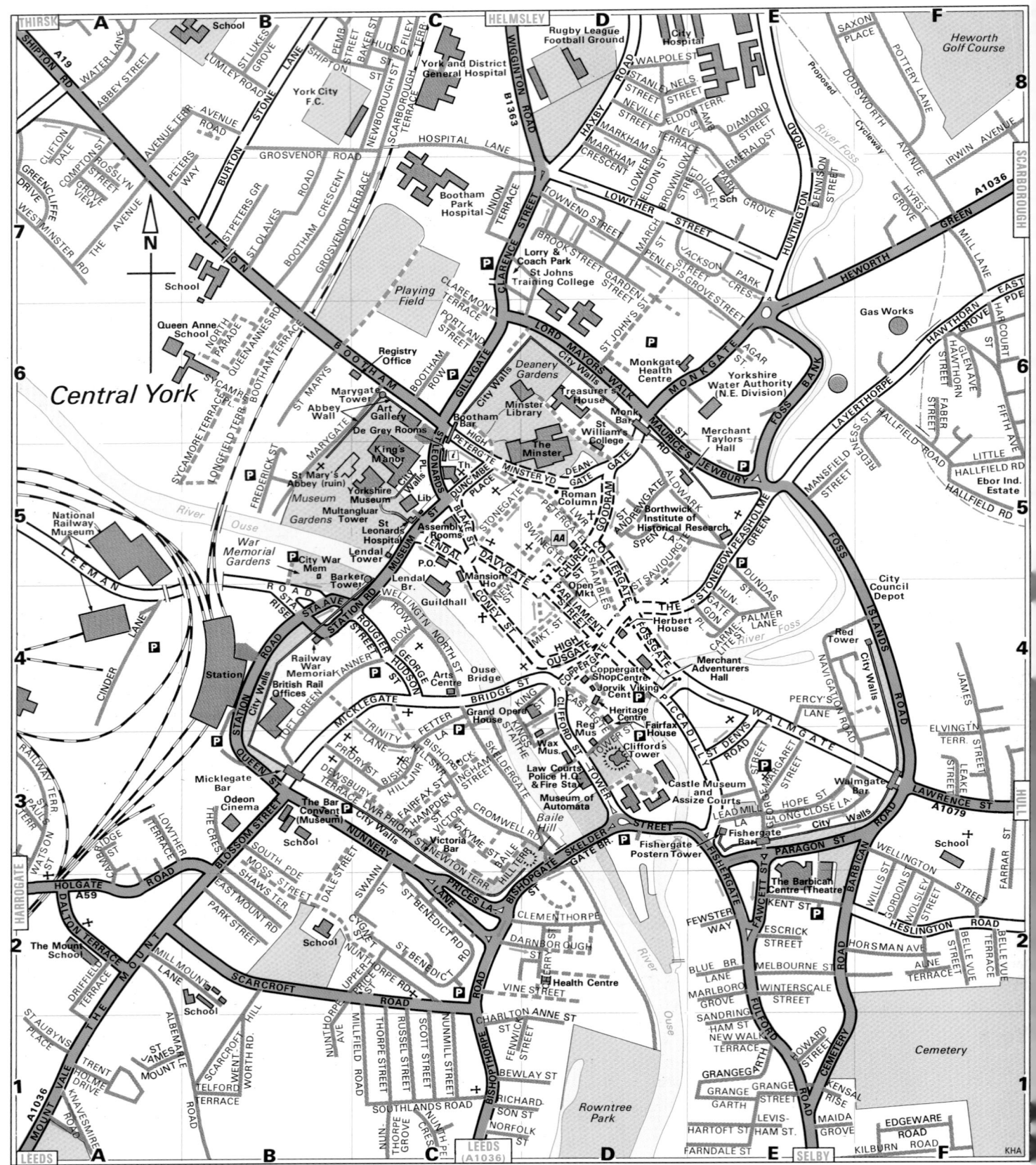

York

Unquestionably the city's outstanding glory, York Minster is considered to be one of the greatest cathedral churches in Europe. It is especially famous for its magnificent windows which contain more than half the medieval stained glass in England.

Great medieval walls enclose the historic city centre and their three-mile circuit offers impressive views of the Minster, York's numerous fine buildings, churches and the River Ouse. The ancient streets consist of a maze of alleys and lanes, some of them so narrow that the overhanging upper storeys of the houses almost touch. The most famous of these picturesque streets is The Shambles, formerly the butchers' quarter of the city, but now colonised by antique and tourist shops. York flourished throughout Tudor, Georgian and Victorian times and handsome buildings from these periods also feature throughout the city.

The Castle Museum gives a fascinating picture of York as it used to be, and the Heritage Centre interprets the social and architectural history of the city. Other places of exceptional note in this city of riches include the Merchant Adventurer's Hall; the Treasurer's House, now owned by the National Trust and filled with fine paintings and furniture; the Jorvik Viking Centre, where there is an exciting restoration of the original Viking settlement at York; and the National Railway Museum.

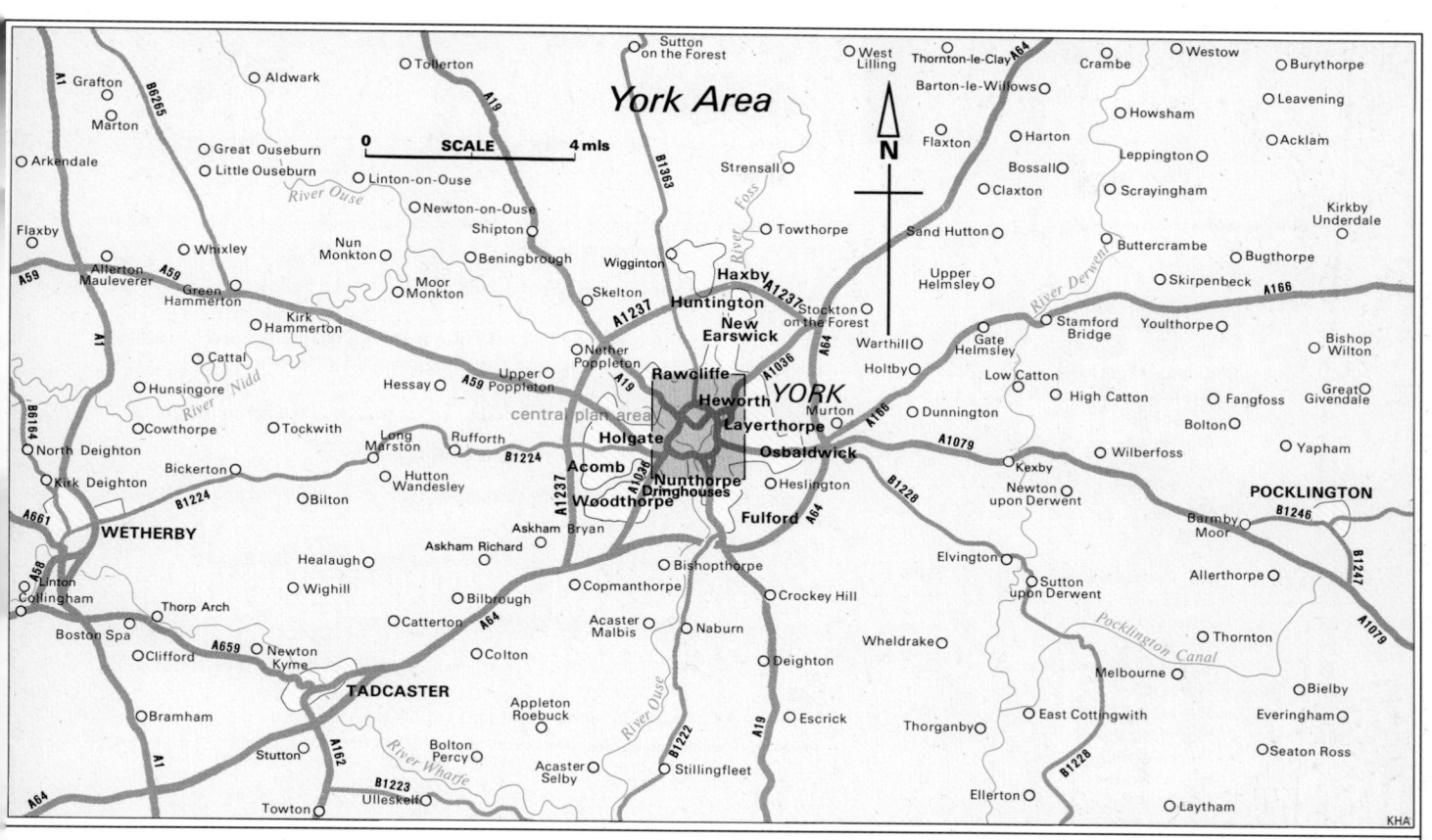

York Area

SCALE 0   4 mls

N

Maps: © The AA 1981
Revision: © The AA 1994

Key to Town Plan and Area Plan

Town Plan

AA Recommended roads
Other roads
Restricted roads
Buildings of interest   Station
Churches
Car Parks
Parks and open spaces
AA Service Centre
One Way Streets

Area Plan

A roads
B roads
Locations   Fangfoss O
Urban area

Street Index with Grid Reference

York

Abbey Street	A8
Agar Street	E6
Albemarle Road	A2-A1-B1
Aldwark	D5-E5
Alne Terrace	F2
Amber Street	E8
Anne Street	D1
Avenue Road	B8
Avenue Terrace	A7-A8-B8
Baile Hill Terrace	C2-C3-D3
Baker Street	C8
Barbican Road	E2-F2-F3-E3
Belle Vue Street	F2
Belle Vue Terrace	F2
Bewlay Street	C1-D1
Bishopgate Street	C2-D2-D3
Bishophill Junior	C3
Bishophill Senior	C3
Bishopthorpe Road	C1-C2
Blake Street	C5
Blossom Street	B2-B3
Blue Bridge Lane	C1
Bootham	B6-C6
Bootham Crescent	B7-C7-C8
Bootham Row	C6
Bootham Terrace	B6
Bridge Street	C4-D4
Brook Street	D7
Brownlow Street	D7-E7-E8
Buckingham Street	C3
Burton Stone Lane	B7-B8
Cambridge Street	A2-A3
Carmelite Street	D4-E4
Castlegate	D3-D4
Cemetery Road	E1-E2
Charlton Street	C1-D1
Cherry Street	D2
Church Street	D5
Cinder Lane	A4
Claremont Terrace	C6-C7
Clarence Street	C6-C7-D7
Clementhorpe	C2-D2
Clifford Street	D3-D4
Clifton	A8-A7-B7
Clifton Dale	A7-A8
Colliergate	D4-D5
Compton Street	A7-A8
Coppergate	D4
Cromwell Road	C3-D3
Cygnet Street	C2
Dale Street	B2-B3
Dalton Terrace	A2
Darnborough Street	C2-D2
Davygate	C5-C4-D4-D5
Deangate	D5
Dennison Street	E7
Dewsbury Terrace	B3-C3
Diamond Street	E8
Dodsworth Avenue	E8-F8-F7
Driffield Terrace	A2
Dudley Street	D7-E7
Duncombe Place	C5
Dundas Street	E4-E5
East Parade	F6-F7
East Mount Road	B2
Ebor Street	C2-D2
Edgeware Road	F1
Eldon Terrace	D8-E8
Elvington Terrace	F3
Emerald Street	E7-E8
Escrick Street	E2
Faber Street	F6
Fairfax Street	C3
Farndale Street	E1
Farrar Street	F2-F3
Fawcett Street	E2-E3
Fenwick Street	C1-D1
Fetter Lane	C3-C4
Fewster Way	E2
Fifth Avenue	F5-F6
Filey Terrace	C8
Fishergate	E2-E3
Foss Bank	E5-E6
Fossgate	D4
Foss Islands Road	E4-E5-F5-F4
Frederick Street	B5
Fulford Road	E1-E2
Garden Street	D7
George Hudson Street	C4
George Street	E3-E4
Gillygate	C6
Glen Avenue	F6
Goodramgate	D5-D6
Gordon Street	F2
Grange Garth	E1

Grange Street	E1
Greencliffe Drive	A7-A8
Grosvenor Road	B8-C8
Grosvenor Terrace	B6-B7-C7-C8
Grove View	A7
Hallfield Road	F5-F6
Hampden Street	C3
Harcourt Street	F6
Harloft Street	E1
Hawthorn Grove	F6
Hawthorne Street	F6
Haxby Road	D7-D8
Heslington Road	E2-F2
Heworth Green	E6-E7-F7
High Ousegate	D4
High Petergate	C5-C6
Holgate Road	A2-A3-B3
Hope Street	E3
Horsman Avenue	E2-F2
Hospital Lane	C8
Howard Street	E1
Hudson Street	C8
Hungate	E4
Huntington Road	E6-E7-E8
Hyrst Grove	F7
Irwin Avenue	F7-F8
Jackson Street	D7-E7
James Street	F3-F4
Jewbury	E5
Kensal Rise	F7
Kent Street	E2
Kilburn Road	E1-F1
Kings Staithe	C4-D4-D3
King Street	C4-D4
Knavesmire Road	A1
Kyme Street	C3
Lawrence Street	F3
Layerthorpe	E5-E6-F6
Lead Mill Lane	E3
Leake Street	F4
Leeman Road	A5-A4-B5-B4
Lendal Coney Street	C5-C4-D4
Levisham Street	E1
Little Hallfield Road	F5
Long Close Lane	E3-F3
Longfield Terrace	B5-B6
Lord Mayors Walk	C6-D6
Lumley Road	B8
Love Lane	A1-A2
Lower Eldon Street	D7
Lower Petergate	D5
Lower Priory Street	C3
Lowther Street	D7-E7
Lowther Terrace	A3
Maida Grove	E1
Mansfield Street	E5
March Street	D7
Margaret Street	E3
Market Street	D4
Markham Crescent	D7-D8
Markham Street	D7-D8
Marlborough Grove	E2
Marygate	B5-B6-C6
Melbourne Street	E2
Micklegate	B3-B4-C4
Millfield Road	C1-C2
Mill Lane	F7
Mill Mount Lane	A2-B2
Minster Yard	C5-D5
Monkgate	D6-E6

Moss Street	B2-B3
Mount Vale	A1
Museum Street	C5
Navigation Road	E4-E3-F3
Nelson Street	D8-E8
Neville Street	D8
Neville Terrace	D8-E8
Newborough Street	C8
New Street	C4-C5
Newton Terrace	C2-C3
New Walk Terrace	E1
Norfolk Street	C1-D1
North Parade	B6
North Street	C4
Nunmill Street	C1-C2
Nunnery Lane	B3-C3-C2
Nunthorpe Avenue	B1-B2
Nunthorpe Grove	C1
Nunthorpe Road	B2-C2
Palmer Lane	E4
Paragon Street	E3-F3
Park Crescent	E7
Park Grove	E7-E8
Park Street	B2
Parliament Street	D4-D5
Peasholme Green	E5
Pembroke Street	B8
Penley's Grove Street	D7-E7-E6
Percy's Lane	E4
Peters Way	A7-B7-B8
Piccadilly	D4-D3-E3-E4
Portland Street	C6
Pottery Lane	F8
Prices Lane	C2
Priory Street	B3-C3
Queen Annes Road	B6
Queen Street	B3
Railway Terrace	A3
Redness Street	F5-F6
Richardson Street	C1-D1
Rosslyn Street	A7
Rougier Street	C4
Russel Street	C1-C2
St Andrewgate	D5
St Aubyns Place	A1
St Benedict Road	C2
St Denys Road	E3-E4
St James Mount	A1
St Johns Street	D6-D7
St Leonards Place	D5-D6
St Lukes Grove	B8
St Marys	B6
St Maurices	D6-D5-E5
St Olaves Road	B7-B8
St Pauls Terrace	A3
St Peters Grove	B7
St Saviourgate	D4-D5-E5
Sandringham Street	E1
Saxon Place	E8-E8
Scarborough Terrace	C8
Scarcroft Hill	B1-B2
Scarcroft Road	A2-B2-C2-C1
Scott Street	C1-C2
Shambles	D4-D5
Shaws Terrace	B2-B3
Shipton Road	A8
Shipton Street	B8-C8
Skeldergate	C4-C3-D3
Skeldergate Bridge	D3
South Esplanade	D3

Southlands Road	C1
South Parade	B2-B3
Spen Lane	D5
Stanley Street	D8
Station Avenue	B4
Station Rise	B4
Station Road	B3-B4-C4-C5
Stonegate	C5-D5
Swann Street	C9
Swinegate	D5
Sycamore Place	B6
Sycamore Terrace	A5-B5-B6
Tanner Row	B4-C4
Telford Terrace	B1
The Avenue	A7
The Crescent	B3
The Mount	A1-A2-B2
The Stonebow	D4-E4-E5
Thorpe Street	C1-C2
Toft Green	B3-B4
Tower Street	D4-D3-E3
Townend Street	D7
Trent Holme Drive	A1
Trinity Lane	C3-C4
Union Terrace	C7
Upper Price Street	B2-C2
Victor Street	C3
Vine Street	C2-D2
Walmgate	D4-E4-E3-F3
Walpole Street	D8-E8
Water Lane	A8
Watson Street	A2-A3
Wellington Row	C4
Wellington Street	F2-F3
Wentworth Road	B1
Westminster Road	A7
Willis Street	F2-F3
Winterscale Street	E2
Wolsley Street	F2

AA Shop
5a and 6 Church Street
York, North Yorks YO1 2BG   D5

KHA

index

Each place name entry in this index is identified by its county or region name. These are shown in italic.

A list of the abbreviated forms used is shown on the left.

To locate a place name in the atlas turn to the map page indicated in bold type in the index and use the 4-figure grid reference.

For example, Hythe *Kent* **29** TR**1634** is found on page 29.

The two letters 'TR' refer to the National Grid.

To pinpoint our example the first bold figure '**1**' is found along the bottom edge of the page.

The following figure '6' indicates how many imaginary tenths to move east of the line '**1**'.

The next bold figure '**3**' is found along the left-hand side of the page.

The last figure '4' shows how many imaginary tenths to move north of line '**3**'.

You will locate **Hythe** where these two lines intersect.

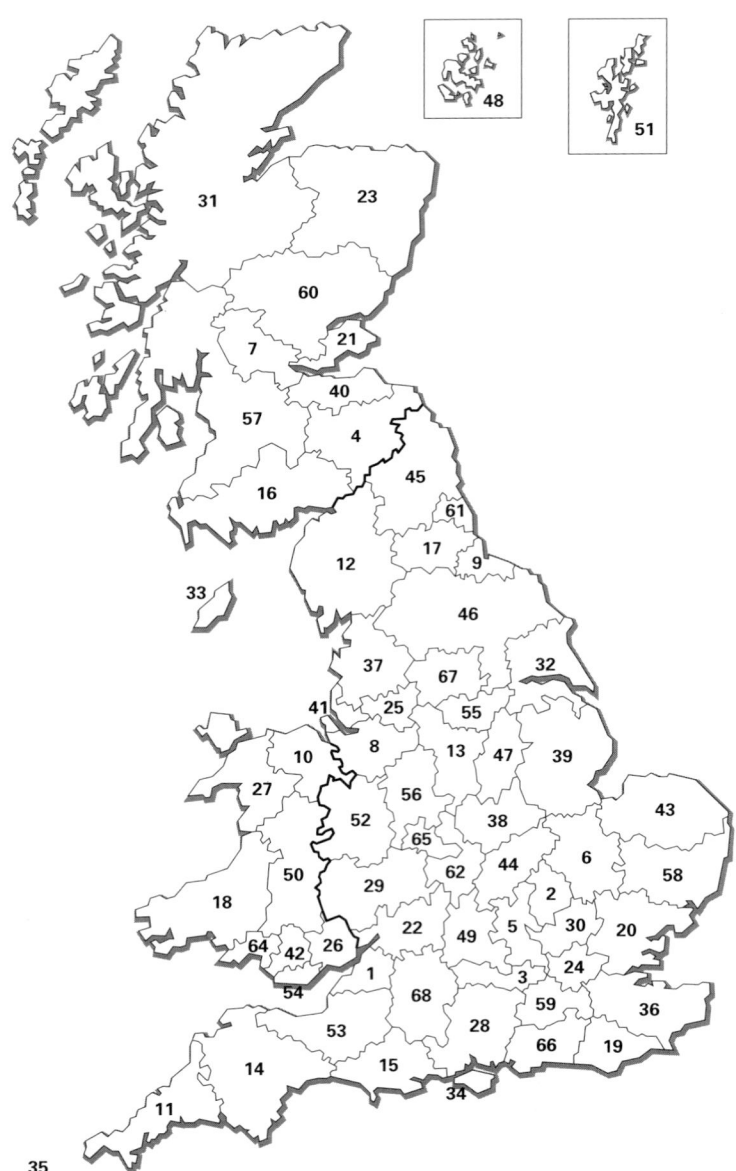

A'Chill

Amber Row

A

A'Chill *Highld*	128	NG2705
Ab Kettleby *Leics*	63	SK7223
Ab Lench *H & W*	47	SP0151
Abbas Combe *Somset*	22	ST7022
Abberley *H & W*	47	SO7567
Abberley Common *H & W*	47	SO7467
Abberton *Essex*	41	TM0019
Abberton *H & W*	47	SO9953
Abberwick *Nthumb*	111	NU1313
Abbess Roding *Essex*	40	TL5711
Abbey *Devon*	9	ST1410
Abbey Dore *H & W*	46	SO3830
Abbey Green *Staffs*	72	SJ9757
Abbey Hill *Somset*	10	ST2718
Abbey St Bathans *Border*	119	NT7661
Abbey Town *Cumb*	93	NY1750
Abbey Village *Lancs*	81	SD6422
Abbey Wood *Gt Lon*	27	TQ4779
Abbeycwmhir *Powys*	45	SO0571
Abbeydale *S York*	74	SK3281
Abbeystead *Lancs*	81	SD5654
Abbot's Chair *Derbys*	74	SK0290
Abbot's Salford *Warwks*	48	SP0650
Abbotrule *Border*	110	NT6113
Abbots Bickington *Devon*	18	SS3813
Abbots Bromley *Staffs*	73	SK0724
Abbots Deuglie *Tays*	126	NO1111
Abbots Langley *Herts*	26	TL0901
Abbots Leigh *Avon*	34	ST5474
Abbots Morton *H & W*	48	SP0255
Abbots Ripton *Cambs*	52	TL2377
Abbots Worthy *Hants*	24	SU4932
Abbotsbury *Dorset*	10	SY5785
Abbotsford *Border*	109	NT5034
Abbotsham *Devon*	18	SS4226
Abbotskerswell *Devon*	7	SX8568
Abbotsleigh *Devon*	7	SX8048
Abbotsley *Cambs*	52	TL2256
Abbotstone *Hants*	24	SU5634
Abbotswood *Hants*	23	SU3623
Abbott Street *Dorset*	11	ST9800
Abbotts Ann *Hants*	23	SU3243
Abcott *Shrops*	46	SO3978
Abdon *Shrops*	59	SO5786
Abenhall *Gloucs*	35	SO6717
Aber *Gwynd*	69	SH6572
Aber Clydach *Powys*	33	SO1021
Aber-arad *Dyfed*	31	SN3140
Aber-banc *Dyfed*	31	SN3541
Aber-giar *Dyfed*	44	SN5040
Aber-Magwr *Dyfed*	43	SN6673
Aber-meurig *Dyfed*	44	SN5656
Aber-nant *M Glam*	33	SO0103
Aberaeron *Dyfed*	42	SN4562
Aberaman *M Glam*	33	SO0100
Aberangell *Powys*	57	SH8410
Aberarder *Highld*	140	NH6225
Aberargie *Tays*	126	NO1615
Aberarth *Dyfed*	42	SN4763
Aberavon *W Glam*	32	SS7489
Aberbargoed *M Glam*	33	SO1500
Aberbeeg *Gwent*	33	SO2002
Abercairny *Tays*	125	NN9222
Abercanaid *M Glam*	33	SO0503.
Abercarn *Gwent*	33	ST2194
Abercastle *Dyfed*	30	SM8533
Abercegir *Powys*	57	SH8001
Aberchalder Lodge *Highld*	131	NH3403
Aberchirder *Gramp*	142	NJ6252
Abercoed *Dyfed*	44	SN6757
Abercraf *Powys*	33	SN8212
Abercregan *W Glam*	33	SS8496
Abercwmboi *M Glam*	33	ST0299
Abercych *Dyfed*	31	SN2441
Abercynon *M Glam*	33	ST0794
Aberdalgie *Tays*	125	NO0720
Aberdare *M Glam*	33	SO0002
Aberdaron *Gwynd*	56	SH1726
Aberdeen *Gramp*	135	NJ9306
Aberdesach *Gwynd*	68	SH4251
Aberdour *Fife*	117	NT1985
Aberdulais *W Glam*	32	SS7799
Aberdyfi *Gwynd*	43	SN6196
Aberedw *Powys*	45	SO0847
Abereiddy *Dyfed*	30	SM7931
Abererch *Gwynd*	56	SH3936
Aberfan *M Glam*	33	SO0700
Aberfeldy *Tays*	125	NN8549
Aberffraw *Gwynd*	68	SH3569
Aberffrwd *Dyfed*	43	SN6878
Aberford *W York*	83	SE4337
Aberfoyle *Cent*	115	NN5200
Abergarw *M Glam*	33	SS9184
Abergarwed *W Glam*	33	SN8102
Abergavenny *Gwent*	34	SO2914
Abergele *Clwyd*	70	SH9477
Abergorlech *Dyfed*	44	SN5833
Abergwesyn *Powys*	45	SN8552
Abergwili *Dyfed*	31	SN4320
Abergwydol *Powys*	57	SH7903
Abergwynfi *W Glam*	33	SS8995
Abergynolwyn *Gwynd*	57	SH6806
Aberhosan *Powys*	43	SN8197
Aberkenfig *M Glam*	33	SS8984
Aberlady *Loth*	118	NT4679
Aberlemno *Tays*	127	NO5255
Aberllefenni *Gwynd*	57	SH7609
Aberllynfi *Powys*	45	SO1737
Aberlour *Gramp*	141	NJ2642
Abermorddu *Clwyd*	71	SJ3056
Abermule *Powys*	58	SO1694
Abernant *Dyfed*	31	SN3323
Abernethy *Tays*	126	NO1816
Abernyte *Tays*	126	NO2531
Aberporth *Dyfed*	42	SN2651
Abersoch *Gwynd*	56	SH3127
Abersychan *Gwent*	34	SO2603
Aberthin *S Glam*	33	ST0074
Abertillery *Gwent*	33	SO2104
Abertridwr *M Glam*	33	ST1289
Abertridwr *Powys*	58	SJ0319
Abertysswg *M Glam*	33	SO1305
Aberuthven *Tays*	125	NN9615
Aberyscir *Powys*	45	SN9929
Aberystwyth *Dyfed*	43	SN5881
Abingdon *Oxon*	37	SU4997
Abinger *Surrey*	14	TQ1145
Abinger Hammer *Surrey*	14	TQ0947
Abington *Nhants*	50	SP7861
Abington *Strath*	108	NS9323
Abington Pigotts *Cambs*	39	TL3044
Ablington *Gloucs*	36	SP1007
Ablington *Wilts*	23	SU1546
Abney *Derbys*	74	SK1980
Above Church *Staffs*	73	SK0150
Aboyne *Gramp*	134	NO5298
Abram *Gt Man*	78	SD6001
Abriachan *Highld*	139	NH5535
Abridge *Essex*	27	TQ4696
Abson *Avon*	35	ST7074
Abthorpe *Nhants*	49	SP6446
Aby *Lincs*	77	TF4078
Acaster Malbis *N York*	83	SE5845
Acaster Selby *N York*	83	SE5741
Accott *Devon*	19	SS6432
Accrington *Lancs*	81	SD7628
Acha *Strath*	120	NM1854
Acha Mor *W Isls*	154	NB3029
Achahoish *Strath*	113	NR7877
Achalader *Tays*	126	NO1245
Achaleven *Strath*	122	NM9233
Achanalt *Highld*	139	NH2661
Achandunie *Highld*	146	NH6472
Achany *Highld*	146	NC5602
Acharacle *Highld*	121	NM6767
Acharn *Highld*	122	NM7050
Acharn *Tays*	124	NN7543
Achavanich *Highld*	151	ND1842
Achduart *Highld*	145	NC0403
Achfary *Highld*	148	NC2939
Achiltibuie *Highld*	144	NC0208
Achinhoan *Strath*	105	NR7516
Achintee *Highld*	138	NG9441
Achlain *Highld*	131	NH2812
Achmelvich *Highld*	148	NC0524
Achmore *Highld*	138	NG8533
Achmore *W Isls*	154	NB3029
Achnacarnin *Highld*	148	NC0432
Achnacarry *Highld*	131	NN1787
Achnacloich *Highld*	129	NG5908
Achnaconeran *Highld*	139	NH4118
Achnacroish *Strath*	122	NM8541
Achnadrish Lodge *Strath*	121	NM4652
Achnafauld *Tays*	125	NN8736
Achnagarron *Highld*	146	NH6870
Achnaha *Highld*	128	NM4668
Achnahaird *Highld*	144	NC0013
Achnairn *Highld*	146	NC5512
Achnalea *Highld*	130	NM8561
Achnamara *Strath*	113	NR7887
Achnasheen *Highld*	138	NH1658
Achnashellach Station *Highld*	138	NH0048
Achnastank *Gramp*	141	NJ2733
Achosnich *Highld*	121	NM4467
Achranich *Highld*	122	NM7047
Achreamie *Highld*	150	ND0166
Achriabhach *Highld*	131	NN1468
Achriesgill *Highld*	148	NC2554
Achtoty *Highld*	149	NC6762
Achurch *Nhants*	51	TL0283
Achvaich *Highld*	146	NH7194
Acklam *Cleve*	97	NZ4817
Acklam *N York*	90	SE7861
Ackleton *Shrops*	60	SO7698
Acklington *Nthumb*	103	NU2301
Ackton *W York*	83	SE4121
Ackworth Moor Top *W York*	83	SE4316
Acle *Norfk*	67	TG4010
Acock's Green *W Mids*	61	SP1283
Acol *Kent*	29	TR3067
Acomb *N York*	83	SE5651
Acomb *Nthumb*	102	NY9366
Acombe *Somset*	9	ST1914
Aconbury *H & W*	46	SO5133
Acre *Lancs*	81	SD7924
Acrefair *Clwyd*	70	SJ2743
Acresford *Derbys*	61	SK2913
Acton *Ches*	71	SJ6352
Acton *Dorset*	11	SY9978
Acton *Gt Lon*	26	TQ2080
Acton *H & W*	47	SO8467
Acton *Shrops*	59	SO3185
Acton *Staffs*	72	SJ8241
Acton *Suffk*	54	TL8945
Acton Beauchamp *H & W*	47	SO6850
Acton Bridge *Ches*	71	SJ6075
Acton Burnell *Shrops*	59	SJ5302
Acton Green *H & W*	47	SO6950
Acton Park *Clwyd*	71	SJ3451
Acton Pigott *Shrops*	59	SJ5402
Acton Round *Shrops*	59	SO6395
Acton Scott *Shrops*	59	SO4589
Acton Trussell *Staffs*	72	SJ9318
Acton Turville *Avon*	35	ST8080
Adbaston *Staffs*	72	SJ7627
Adber *Dorset*	21	ST5920
Adbolton *Notts*	62	SK5938
Adderbury *Oxon*	49	SP4735
Adderley *Shrops*	72	SJ6640
Adderstone *Nthumb*	111	NU1330
Addiewell *Loth*	117	NS9962
Addingham *W York*	82	SE0749
Addington *Bucks*	49	SP7428
Addington *Gt Lon*	27	TQ3664
Addington *Kent*	28	TQ6559
Addiscombe *Gt Lon*	27	TQ3366
Addlestone *Surrey*	26	TQ0564
Addlestonemoor *Surrey*	26	TQ0565
Addlethorpe *Lincs*	77	TF5468
Adeney *Shrops*	72	SJ6918
Adeyfield *Herts*	38	TL0708
Adfa *Powys*	58	SJ0601
Adforton *H & W*	46	SO4071
Adisham *Kent*	29	TR2253
Adlestrop *Gloucs*	48	SP2426
Adlingfleet *Humb*	84	SE8421
Adlington *Ches*	79	SJ9180
Adlington *Lancs*	81	SD6013
Admaston *Shrops*	59	SJ6313
Admaston *Staffs*	73	SK0423
Admington *Warwks*	48	SP2045
Adsborough *Somset*	20	ST2729
Adscombe *Somset*	20	ST1837
Adstock *Bucks*	49	SP7329
Adstone *Nhants*	49	SP5951
Adswood *Gt Man*	79	SJ8888
Adversane *W Susx*	14	TQ0723
Advie *Highld*	141	NJ1234
Adwalton *W York*	82	SE2328
Adwell *Oxon*	37	SU6999
Adwick Le Street *S York*	83	SE5308
Adwick upon Dearne *S York*	83	SE4701
Ae *D & G*	100	NX9889
Ae Bridgend *D & G*	100	NY0186
Affetside *Gt Man*	81	SD7513
Affleck *Gramp*	142	NJ5540
Affpuddle *Dorset*	11	SY8093
Affric Lodge *Highld*	138	NH1822
Afon-wen *Clwyd*	70	SJ1371
Afton *Devon*	7	SX8462
Afton *IOW*	12	SZ3486
Afton Bridgend *Strath*	107	NS6213
Agglethorpe *N York*	89	SE0885
Aigburth *Mersyd*	78	SJ3886
Aike *Humb*	84	TA0446
Aiketgate *Cumb*	94	NY4846
Aikhead *Cumb*	93	NY2349
Aikton *Cumb*	93	NY2753
Ailby *Lincs*	77	TF4376
Ailey *H & W*	46	SO3348
Ailsworth *Cambs*	64	TL1198
Ainderby Quernhow *N York*	89	SE3480
Ainderby Steeple *N York*	89	SE3392
Aingers Green *Essex*	41	TM1120
Ainsdale *Mersyd*	80	SD3112
Ainsdale-on-Sea *Mersyd*	80	SD2912
Ainstable *Cumb*	94	NY5246
Ainsworth *Gt Man*	79	SD7610
Ainthorpe *N York*	90	NZ7007
Aintree *Mersyd*	78	SJ3898
Ainville *Loth*	117	NT1063
Aird *D & G*	98	NX0960
Aird *Strath*	113	NM7600
Aird *W Isls*	154	NB5635
Aird a Mhulaidh *W Isls*	154	NB1810
Aird Asaig *W Isls*	154	NB1202
Aird of Kinloch *Strath*	121	NM5228
Aird of Sleat *Highld*	129	NG5900
Aird Uig *W Isls*	154	NB0533
Airdeny *Strath*	122	NM9929
Airdrie *Strath*	116	NS7565
Airdriehill *Strath*	116	NS7867
Airds Bay *Strath*	122	NM9932
Airds of Kells *D & G*	99	NX6770
Airidh a bhruaich *W Isls*	154	NB2417
Airieland *D & G*	99	NX7556
Airlie *Tays*	126	NO3150
Airmyn *Humb*	84	SE7224
Airntully *Tays*	125	NO0935
Airor *Highld*	129	NG7205
Airth *Cent*	116	NS9087
Airton *N York*	88	SD9059
Aisby *Lincs*	76	SK8692
Aisby *Lincs*	64	TF0138
Aisgill *Cumb*	88	SD7797
Aish *Devon*	7	SX6960
Aish *Devon*	7	SX8458
Aisholt *Somset*	20	ST1935
Aiskew *N York*	89	SE2788
Aislaby *Cleve*	89	NZ4012
Aislaby *N York*	90	NZ8608
Aislaby *N York*	90	SE7785
Aisthorpe *Lincs*	76	SK9480
Aith *Shet*	155	HU3455
Akeld *Nthumb*	111	NT9529
Akeley *Bucks*	49	SP7037
Akenham *Suffk*	54	TM1449
Albaston *Devon*	6	SX4270
Alberbury *Shrops*	59	SJ3614
Albourne *W Susx*	15	TQ2516
Albourne Green *W Susx*	15	TQ2616
Albrighton *Shrops*	59	SJ4918
Albrighton(Wolverhampton) *Shrops.*	60	SJ8004
Alburgh *Norfk*	55	TM2687
Albury *Herts*	39	TL4324
Albury *Oxon*	37	SP6505
Albury *Surrey*	14	TQ0447
Albury End *Herts*	39	TL4223
Albury Heath *Surrey*	14	TQ0646
Alby Hill *Norfk*	67	TG1934
Alcaig *Highld*	139	NH5657
Alcaston *Shrops*	59	SO4587
Alcester *Warwks*	48	SP0857
Alcester Lane End *W Mids*	61	SP0780
Alciston *E Susx*	16	TQ5005
Alcombe *Wilts*	35	ST8169
Alconbury *Cambs*	52	TL1875
Alconbury Weston *Cambs*	52	TL1777
Aldborough *N York*	89	SE4066
Aldborough *Norfk*	66	TG1834
Aldbourne *Wilts*	36	SU2676
Aldbrough *Humb*	85	TA2438
Aldbury *Herts*	38	SP9612
Aldcliffe *Lancs*	87	SD4660
Aldclune *Tays*	132	NN8964
Aldeburgh *Suffk*	55	TM4656
Aldeby *Norfk*	67	TM4493
Aldenham *Herts*	26	TQ1498
Alder Moor *Staffs*	73	SK2226
Alderbury *Wilts*	23	SU1827
Aldercar *Derbys*	62	SK4447
Alderford *Norfk*	66	TG1218
Alderholt *Dorset*	12	SU1212
Alderley *Gloucs*	35	ST7690
Alderley Edge *Ches*	79	SJ8478
Aldermans Green *W Mids*	61	SP3683
Aldermaston *Berks*	24	SU5965
Alderminster *Warwks*	48	SP2348
Aldershot *Hants*	25	SU8650
Alderton *Gloucs*	47	SP0033
Alderton *Nhants*	49	SP7446
Alderton *Shrops*	59	SJ4924
Alderton *Suffk*	55	TM3441
Alderton *Wilts*	35	ST8482
Alderwasley *Derbys*	73	SK3053
Aldfield *N York*	89	SE2669
Aldford *Ches*	71	SJ4159
Aldgate *Leics*	63	SK9804
Aldham *Essex*	40	TL9126
Aldham *Suffk*	54	TM0545
Aldingbourne *W Susx*	14	SU9205
Aldingham *Cumb*	86	SD2870
Aldington *H & W*	48	SP0644
Aldington *Kent*	29	TR0736
Aldington Corner *Kent*	29	TR0636
Aldivalloch *Gramp*	141	NJ3526
Aldochlay *Strath*	115	NS3591
Aldon *Shrops*	46	SO4379
Aldoth *Cumb*	92	NY1448
Aldreth *Cambs*	53	TL4473
Aldridge *W Mids*	61	SK0500
Aldringham *Suffk*	55	TM4461
Aldro *N York*	90	SE8162
Aldsworth *Gloucs*	36	SP1509
Aldsworth *W Susx*	14	SU7608
Aldunie *Gramp*	141	NJ3626
Aldwark *Derbys*	74	SK2257
Aldwark *N York*	89	SE4663
Aldwick *W Susx*	14	SZ9198
Aldwincle *Nhants*	51	TL0081
Aldworth *Berks*	37	SU5579
Alexandria *Strath*	115	NS3979
Aley *Somset*	20	ST1838
Alfardisworthy *Devon*	18	SS2911
Alfington *Devon*	9	SY1197
Alfold *Surrey*	14	TQ0333
Alfold Bars *W Susx*	14	TQ0333
Alfold Crossways *Surrey*	14	TQ0335
Alford *Gramp*	142	NJ5715
Alford *Lincs*	77	TF4575
Alford *Somset*	21	ST6032
Alfreton *Derbys*	74	SK4155
Alfrick *H & W*	47	SO7453
Alfrick Pound *H & W*	47	SO7452
Alfriston *E Susx*	16	TQ5103
Algarkirk *Lincs*	64	TF2935
Alhampton *Somset*	21	ST6234
Alkborough *Humb*	84	SE8821
Alkerton *Gloucs*	35	SO7705
Alkerton *Oxon*	48	SP3743
Alkham *Kent*	29	TR2542
Alkington *Shrops*	71	SJ5339
Alkmonton *Derbys*	73	SK1838
All Cannings *Wilts*	23	SU0661
All Saints South Elmham *Suffk*	55	TM3482
All Stretton *Shrops*	59	SO4595
Allaleigh *Devon*	7	SX8053
Allanaquoich *Gramp*	133	NO1291
Allanbank *Strath*	116	NS8458
Allanton *Border*	119	NT8654
Allanton *Strath*	116	NS7454
Allanton *Strath*	116	NS8457
Allaston *Gloucs*	35	SO6304
Allbrook *Hants*	13	SU4521
Allen End *Warwks*	61	SP1696
Allen's Green *Herts*	39	TL4516
Allendale *Nthumb*	95	NY8355
Allenheads *Nthumb*	95	NY8645
Allensford *Dur*	95	NZ0750
Allensmore *H & W*	46	SO4635
Allenton *Derbys*	62	SK3732
Aller *Devon*	19	SS7625
Aller *Somset*	21	ST4029
Allerby *Cumb*	92	NY0839
Allercombe *Devon*	9	SY0494
Allerford *Somset*	20	SS9046
Allerston *N York*	90	SE8782
Allerthorpe *Humb*	84	SE7847
Allerton *Mersyd*	78	SJ3987
Allerton *W York*	82	SE1234
Allerton Bywater *W York*	83	SE4227
Allerton Mauleverer *N York*	89	SE4157
Allesley *W Mids*	61	SP3080
Allestree *Derbys*	62	SK3439
Allet Common *Cnwll*	3	SW7948
Allexton *Leics*	51	SK8100
Allgreave *Ches*	72	SJ9767
Allhallows *Kent*	28	TQ8377
Allhallows-on-Sea *Kent*	40	TQ8478
Alligin Shuas *Highld*	137	NG8357
Allimore Green *Staffs*	72	SJ8519
Allington *Dorset*	10	SY4693
Allington *Kent*	28	TQ7557
Allington *Lincs*	63	SK8540
Allington *Wilts*	35	ST8975
Allington *Wilts*	23	SU0663
Allington *Wilts*	23	SU2039
Allithwaite *Cumb*	87	SD3876
Alloa *Cent*	116	NS8892
Allonby *Cumb*	92	NY0842
Allostock *Ches*	79	SJ7471
Alloway *Strath*	106	NS3318
Allowenshay *Somset*	10	ST3913
Allscott *Shrops*	59	SJ6113
Allscott *Shrops*	60	SO7396
Alltami *Clwyd*	70	SJ2665
Alltchaorunn *Highld*	123	NN1951
Alltmawr *Powys*	45	SO0746
Alltwalis *Dyfed*	31	SN4431
Alltwen *W Glam*	32	SN7303
Alltyblaca *Dyfed*	44	SN5245
Allweston *Dorset*	11	ST6614
Allwood Green *Suffk*	54	TM0472
Almeley *H & W*	46	SO3351
Almeley Wooton *H & W*	46	SO3352
Almer *Dorset*	11	SY9199
Almholme *S York*	83	SE5808
Almington *Staffs*	72	SJ7034
Almodington *W Susx*	14	SZ8297
Almondbank *Tays*	125	NO0625
Almondbury *W York*	82	SE1614
Almondsbury *Avon*	34	ST6084
Alne *N York*	90	SE4965
Alnesbourn Priory *Suffk*	55	TM1940
Alness *Highld*	146	NH6569
Alnham *Nthumb*	111	NT9810
Alnmouth *Nthumb*	111	NU2410
Alnwick *Nthumb*	111	NU1813
Alperton *Gt Lon*	26	TQ1883
Alphamstone *Essex*	54	TL8735
Alpheton *Suffk*	54	TL8750
Alphington *Devon*	9	SX9190
Alpington *Norfk*	67	TG2901
Alport *Derbys*	74	SK2264
Alpraham *Ches*	71	SJ5859
Alresford *Essex*	41	TM0621
Alrewas *Staffs*	61	SK1614
Alsager *Ches*	72	SJ7955
Alsagers Bank *Staffs*	72	SJ7948
Alsop en le Dale *Derbys*	73	SK1554
Alston *Cumb*	94	NY7146
Alston *Devon*	10	ST3002
Alston Sutton *Somset*	21	ST4151
Alstone *Gloucs*	47	SO9832
Alstone *Somset*	21	ST3146
Alstone Green *Staffs*	72	SJ8518
Alstonefield *Staffs*	73	SK1355
Alswear *Devon*	19	SS7222
Alt *Gt Man*	79	SD9403
Altandhu *Highld*	144	NB9812
Altarnun *Cnwll*	5	SX2281
Altass *Highld*	146	NC5000
Altcreich *Strath*	122	NM6938
Altgaltraig *Strath*	114	NS0473
Altham *Lancs*	81	SD7732
Althorne *Essex*	40	TQ9198
Althorpe *Humb*	84	SE8309
Altnabreac Station *Highld*	150	ND0045
Altnacraig *Strath*	122	NM8429
Altnaharra *Highld*	149	NC5635
Altofts *W York*	83	SE3823
Alton *Derbys*	74	SK3664
Alton *Hants*	24	SU7139
Alton *Staffs*	73	SK0741
Alton *Wilts*	23	SU1546
Alton Barnes *Wilts*	23	SU1062
Alton Pancras *Dorset*	11	ST7002
Alton Priors *Wilts*	23	SU1162
Altrincham *Gt Man*	79	SJ7687
Altskeith Hotel *Cent*	124	NN4602
Alva *Cent*	116	NS8897
Alvah *Gramp*	142	NJ6760
Alvanley *Ches*	71	SJ4974
Alvaston *Derbys*	62	SK3833
Alvechurch *H & W*	60	SP0272
Alvecote *Warwks*	61	SK2404
Alvediston *Wilts*	22	ST9723
Alveley *Shrops*	60	SO7584
Alverdiscott *Devon*	19	SS5225
Alverstoke *Hants*	13	SZ6098
Alverstone *IOW*	13	SZ5785
Alverthorpe *W York*	82	SE3121
Alverton *Notts*	63	SK7942
Alves *Gramp*	141	NJ1362
Alvescot *Oxon*	36	SP2704
Alveston *Avon*	35	ST6388
Alveston *Warwks*	48	SP2356
Alvingham *Lincs*	77	TF3691
Alvington *Gloucs*	34	SO6000
Alwalton *Cambs*	64	TL1396
Alwinton *Nthumb*	110	NT9106
Alwoodley *W York*	82	SE2840
Alwoodley Gates *W York*	82	SE3140
Alyth *Tays*	126	NO2448
Amber Hill *Lincs*	76	TF2346
Amber Row *Derbys*	74	SK3856

Ambergate
Aswardby

Ambergate *Derbys* 74 SK3451
Amberley *Gloucs* 35 SO8501
Amberley *W Susx* 14 TQ0213
Ambirstone *E Susx* 16 TQ5911
Amble *Nthumb* 103 NU2604
Amblecote *W Mids* 60 SO8985
Ambler Thorn *W York* 82 SE0929
Ambleside *Cumb* 87 NY3704
Ambleston *Dyfed* 30 SN0025
Ambrosden *Oxon* 37 SP6019
Amcotts *Humb* 84 SE8514
America *Cambs* 53 TL4378
Amersham *Bucks* 26 SU9597
Amersham on the Hill *Bucks* 26 SU9798
Amerton *Staffs* 73 SJ9927
Amesbury *Wilts* 23 SU1541
Amhuinnsuidhe *W Isls* 154 NB0408
Amington *Staffs* 61 SK2304
Amisfield Town *D & G* 100 NY0082
Amlwch *Gwynd* 68 SH4492
Ammanford *Dyfed* 32 SN6212
Amotherby *N York* 90 SE7473
Ampfield *Hants* 13 SU4023
Ampleforth *N York* 90 SE5878
Ampney Crucis *Gloucs* 36 SP0601
Ampney St Mary *Gloucs* 36 SP0802
Ampney St Peter *Gloucs* 36 SP0801
Amport *Hants* 23 SU3044
Ampthill *Beds* 38 TL0337
Ampton *Suffk* 54 TL8671
Amroth *Dyfed* 31 SN1608
Amwell *Herts* 39 TL1613
An T-ob *W Isls* 154 NG0286
Anaheilt *Highld* 130 NM8162
Ancaster *Lincs* 63 SK9843
Anchor *Shrops* 58 SO1785
Ancroft *Nthumb* 111 NT9945
Ancrum *Border* 110 NT6224
Ancton *W Susx* 14 SU9800
Anderby *Lincs* 77 TF5275
Andersea *Somset* 21 ST3333
Andersfield *Somset* 20 ST2434
Anderson *Dorset* 11 SY8897
Anderton *Ches* 79 SJ6475
Anderton *Cnwll* 6 SX4351
Andover *Hants* 23 SU3645
Andoversford *Gloucs* 35 SP0219
Andreas *IOM* 153 SC4199
Anelog *Gwynd* 56 SH1527
Anerley *Gt Lon* 27 TQ3369
Anfield *Mersyd* 78 SJ3692
Angarrack *Cnwll* 2 SW5838
Angarrick *Cnwll* 3 SW7937
Angelbank *Shrops* 46 SO5776
Angersleigh *Somset* 20 ST1918
Angerton *Cumb* 93 NY2257
Angle *Dyfed* 30 SM8603
Angmering *W Susx* 14 TQ0604
Angram *N York* 88 SD8899
Angram *N York* 83 SE5248
Angrouse *Cnwll* 2 SW6619
Anick *Nthumb* 102 NY9465
Ankerville *Highld* 147 NH8174
Ankle Hill *Leics* 63 SK7518
Anlaby *Humb* 84 TA0328
Anmer *Norfk* 65 TF7429
Anmore *Hants* 13 SU6611
Anna Valley *Hants* 23 SU3543
Annan *D & G* 101 NY1966
Annaside *Cumb* 86 SD0986
Annat *Highld* 138 NG8954
Annat *Strath* 122 NN0322
Annathill *Strath* 116 NS7270
Annbank *Strath* 106 NS4023
Annesley *Notts* 75 SK5053
Annesley Woodhouse *Notts* 75 SK4953
Annfield Plain *Dur* 96 NZ1651
Anniesland *Strath* 115 NS5368
Annitsford *T & W* 103 NZ2674
Annscroft *Shrops* 59 SJ4507
Ansdell *Lancs* 80 SD3428
Ansford *Somset* 21 ST6433
Ansley *Warwks* 61 SP3091
Anslow *Staffs* 73 SK2125
Anslow Gate *Staffs* 73 SK1924
Anslow Lees *Staffs* 73 SK2024
Ansteadbrook *Surrey* 14 SU9332
Anstey *Hants* 24 SU7240
Anstey *Herts* 39 TL4033
Anstey *Leics* 62 SK5508
Anstruther *Fife* 127 NO5703
Ansty *W Susx* 15 TQ2923
Ansty *Warwks* 61 SP4083
Ansty *Wilts* 22 ST9526
Ansty Cross *Dorset* 11 ST7603
Anthill Common *Hants* 13 SU6312
Anthony's *Surrey* 26 TQ0161
Anthorn *Cumb* 93 NY1958
Antingham *Norfk* 67 TG2533
Antony *Cnwll* 5 SX4054
Antrobus *Ches* 79 SJ6480
Antron *Cnwll* 2 SW6327
Anvil Corner *Devon* 18 SS3704
Anvil Green *Kent* 29 TR1049
Anwick *Lincs* 76 TF1150
Anwoth *D & G* 99 NX5856
Aperfield *Gt Lon* 27 TQ4158
Apes Dale *H & W* 60 SO9972
Apethorpe *Nhants* 51 TL0295
Apeton *Staffs* 72 SJ8518
Apley *Lincs* 76 TF1075
Apperknowle *Derbys* 74 SK3878
Apperley *Gloucs* 47 SO8628
Apperley Bridge *W York* 82 SE1937
Apperley Dene *Nthumb* 95 NZ0558
Appersett *N York* 88 SD8690
Appin *Strath* 122 NM9346
Appleby *Humb* 84 SE9514
Appleby Magna *Leics* 61 SK3109
Appleby Parva *Leics* 61 SK3008
Appleby Street *Herts* 39 TL3304
Appleby-in-Westmorland *Cumb* 94 NY6820
Applecross *Highld* 137 NG7144
Appledore *Devon* 18 SS4630
Appledore *Devon* 9 ST0614
Appledore *Kent* 17 TQ9529
Appledore Heath *Kent* 17 TQ9530
Appleford *Oxon* 37 SU5293
Applegarth Town *D & G* 100 NY1084
Applehaigh *S York* 83 SE3512
Appleshaw *Hants* 23 SU3048
Applethwaite *Cumb* 93 NY2625
Appleton *Ches* 78 SJ5186
Appleton *Ches* 79 SJ6184
Appleton *Oxon* 37 SP4401
Appleton Roebuck *N York* 83 SE5542
Appleton Thorn *Ches* 79 SJ6383
Appleton Wiske *N York* 89 NZ3804
Appleton-le-Moors *N York* 90 SE7387
Appleton-le-Street *N York* 90 SE7373
Appletreehall *Border* 109 NT5117
Appletreewick *N York* 88 SE0560
Appley *Somset* 20 ST0721
Appley Bridge *Lancs* 78 SD5209
Apse Heath *IOW* 13 SZ5683
Apsley End *Beds* 38 TL1232
Apsley Heath *Warwks* 61 SP0970
Apuldram *W Susx* 14 SU8403
Arbirlot *Tays* 127 NO6040
Arboll *Highld* 147 NH8781
Arborfield *Berks* 24 SU7567
Arborfield Cross *Berks* 24 SU7666
Arbourthorne *S York* 74 SK3785
Arbroath *Tays* 127 NO6441
Arbuthnott *Gramp* 135 NO8074
Arcadia *Kent* 28 TQ8836
Archddu *Dyfed* 32 SN4401
Archdeacon Newton *Dur* 96 NZ2517
Archencarroch *Strath* 115 NS4182
Archiestown *Gramp* 141 NJ2244
Archirondel *Jersey* 152 JS0000
Arclid Green *Ches* 72 SJ7861
Ardaily *Strath* 104 NR6450
Ardalanish *Strath* 121 NM3619
Ardanaiseig Hotel *Strath* 123 NN0824
Ardarroch *Highld* 137 NG8339
Ardarroch *Strath* 114 NS2494
Ardbeg *Strath* 104 NR4146
Ardbeg *Strath* 114 NS0766
Ardbeg *Strath* 114 NS1583
Ardcharnich *Highld* 145 NH1788
Ardchiavaig *Strath* 121 NM3818
Ardchonnel *Strath* 122 NM9812
Ardchullarie More *Cent* 124 NN5813
Arddleen *Powys* 58 SJ2616
Ardechive *Highld* 131 NN1490
Ardeer *Strath* 106 NS2740
Ardeley *Herts* 39 TL3027
Ardelve *Highld* 138 NG8627
Arden *Strath* 115 NS3684
Ardens Grafton *Warwks* 48 SP1154
Ardentallen *Strath* 122 NM8324
Ardentinny *Strath* 114 NS1887
Ardentraive *Strath* 114 NS0374
Ardeonaig Hotel *Cent* 124 NN6735
Ardersier *Highld* 140 NH7855
Ardessie *Highld* 145 NH0689
Ardfern *Strath* 122 NM8004
Ardgay *Highld* 146 NH5990
Ardgour *Highld* 130 NN0163
Ardgowan *Strath* 114 NS2073
Ardhallow *Strath* 114 NS1674
Ardhasig *W Isls* 154 NB1202
Ardheslaig *Highld* 137 NG7855
Ardindrean *Highld* 145 NH1588
Ardingly *W Susx* 15 TQ3429
Ardington *Oxon* 36 SU4388
Ardington Wick *Oxon* 36 SU4389
Ardlamont *Strath* 114 NR9865
Ardleigh *Essex* 41 TM0529
Ardleigh Heath *Essex* 41 TM0430
Ardler *Tays* 126 NO2642
Ardley *Oxon* 49 SP5427
Ardley End *Essex* 39 TL5214
Ardlui *Strath* 123 NN3115
Ardlussa *Strath* 113 NR6487
Ardmaddy *Strath* 123 NN0837
Ardmair *Highld* 145 NH1097
Ardmaleish *Strath* 114 NS0768
Ardminish *Strath* 104 NR6448
Ardmolich *Highld* 129 NM7172
Ardmore *Highld* 146 NH7086
Ardmore *Strath* 115 NS3178
Ardnadam *Strath* 114 NS1780
Ardnagrask *Highld* 139 NH5249
Ardnarff *Highld* 138 NG8935
Ardnastang *Highld* 130 NM8061
Ardno *Strath* 123 NN1508
Ardochy Lodge Hotel *Highld* 131 NH2002
Ardpatrick *Strath* 113 NR7559
Ardrishaig *Strath* 113 NR8585
Ardross *Highld* 146 NH6174
Ardrossan *Strath* 106 NS2342
Ardsley *S York* 83 SE3805
Ardsley East *W York* 82 SE3025
Ardslignish *Highld* 121 NM5661
Ardtalla *Strath* 112 NR4654
Ardtoe *Highld* 129 NM6270
Arduaine *Strath* 122 NM7910
Ardvasar *Highld* 129 NG6303
Ardvorlich *Tays* 124 NN6322
Ardvourlie *W Isls* 154 NB1810
Ardwell *D & G* 98 NX1045
Ardwick *Gt Man* 79 SJ8597
Areley Kings *H & W* 60 SO7970
Arevegaig *Highld* 129 NM6568
Arford *Hants* 14 SU8236
Argoed *Gwent* 33 ST1799
Argoed *Shrops* 59 SJ3220
Argoed Mill *Powys* 45 SN9963
Argos Hill *E Susx* 16 TQ5728
Aribruach *W Isls* 154 NB2417
Aridhglas *Strath* 120 NM3123
Arileod *Strath* 120 NM1655
Arinagour *Strath* 120 NM2257
Ariogan *Strath* 122 NM8627
Arisaig *Highld* 129 NM6586
Arisaig House *Highld* 129 NM6984
Arkendale *N York* 89 SE3861
Arkesden *Essex* 39 TL4834
Arkholme *Lancs* 87 SD5871
Arkle Town *N York* 88 NZ0001
Arkleby *Cumb* 92 NY1439
Arkleton *D & G* 101 NY3791
Arkley *Gt Lon* 26 TQ2295
Arksey *S York* 83 SE5807
Arkwright *Derbys* 74 SK4270
Arle *Gloucs* 47 SO9223
Arlecdon *Cumb* 92 NY0418
Arlescote *Warwks* 48 SP3848
Arlesey *Beds* 39 TL1936
Arleston *Shrops* 60 SJ6609
Arley *Ches* 79 SJ6680
Arley *Warwks* 61 SP2890
Arlingham *Gloucs* 35 SO7010
Arlington *Devon* 19 SS6140
Arlington *E Susx* 16 TQ5407
Arlington *Gloucs* 36 SP1006
Arlington Beccott *Devon* 19 SS6241
Armadale *Highld* 150 NC7864
Armadale *Highld* 129 NG6303
Armadale *Loth* 116 NS9368
Armaside *Cumb* 92 NY1527
Armathwaite *Cumb* 94 NY5046
Arminghall *Norfk* 67 TG2504
Armitage *Staffs* 73 SK0715
Armitage Bridge *W York* 82 SE1313
Armley *W York* 82 SE2833
Armshead *Staffs* 72 SJ9348
Armston *Nhants* 51 TL0685
Armthorpe *S York* 83 SE6204
Arnabost *Strath* 120 NM2159
Arnaby *Cumb* 86 SD1884
Arncliffe *N York* 88 SD9371
Arncliffe Cote *N York* 88 SD9470
Arncroach *Fife* 127 NO5105
Arndilly House *Gramp* 141 NJ2847
Arne *Dorset* 11 SY9788
Arnesby *Leics* 50 SP6192
Arnfield *Derbys* 79 SK0197
Arngask *Tays* 126 NO1410
Arnicle *Strath* 105 NR7138
Arnisdale *Highld* 130 NG8410
Arnish *Highld* 137 NG5948
Arniston *Loth* 118 NT3362
Arnol *W Isls* 154 NB3148
Arnold *Humb* 85 TA1241
Arnold *Notts* 62 SK5845
Arnprior *Cent* 116 NS6194
Arnside *Cumb* 87 SD4578
Aros *Strath* 121 NM5645
Arowry *Clwyd* 71 SJ4639
Arrad Foot *Cumb* 86 SD3080
Arram *Humb* 84 TA0344
Arrathorne *N York* 89 SE2093
Arreton *IOW* 13 SZ5386
Arrina *Highld* 137 NG7458
Arrington *Cambs* 52 TL3250
Arriundle *Highld* 130 NM8264
Arrochar *Strath* 123 NN2904
Arrow *Warwks* 48 SP0856
Arrowfield Top *H & W* 61 SP0374
Arscott *Shrops* 59 SJ4307
Artafallie *Highld* 140 NH6349
Arthington *W York* 82 SE2644
Arthingworth *Nhants* 50 SP7581
Arthog *Gwynd* 57 SH6414
Arthrath *Gramp* 143 NJ9636
Arthursdale *W York* 83 SE3737
Artrochie *Gramp* 143 NK0031
Arundel *W Susx* 14 TQ0106
Asby *Cumb* 92 NY0620
Ascog *Strath* 114 NS1062
Ascot *Berks* 25 SU9268
Ascott *Warwks* 48 SP3234
Ascott Earl *Oxon* 36 SP3018
Ascott-under-Wychwood *Oxon* 36 SP3018
Asenby *N York* 89 SE3975
Asfordby *Leics* 63 SK7019
Asfordby Hill *Leics* 63 SK7219
Asgarby *Lincs* 64 TF1145
Asgarby *Lincs* 77 TF3366
Ash *Devon* 19 SS5208
Ash *Devon* 7 SX8349
Ash *Dorset* 11 ST8610
Ash *Kent* 27 TQ6064
Ash *Kent* 29 TR2858
Ash *Somset* 20 ST2822
Ash *Somset* 21 ST4720
Ash *Surrey* 25 SU9051
Ash Green *Surrey* 25 SU9049
Ash Green *Warwks* 61 SP3384
Ash Magna *Shrops* 71 SJ5739
Ash Mill *Devon* 19 SS7823
Ash Parva *Shrops* 71 SJ5739
Ash Priors *Somset* 20 ST1529
Ash Street *Suffk* 54 TM0146
Ash Thomas *Devon* 9 ST0010
Ash Vale *Surrey* 25 SU8951
Ashampstead *Berks* 37 SU5676
Ashampstead Green *Berks* 37 SU5677
Ashbocking *Suffk* 54 TM1754
Ashbocking Green *Suffk* 54 TM1854
Ashbourne *Derbys* 73 SK1746
Ashbourne Green *Derbys* 73 SK1948
Ashbrittle *Somset* 20 ST0521
Ashburnham Place *E Susx* 16 TQ6814
Ashburton *Devon* 7 SX7570
Ashbury *Devon* 5 SX5098
Ashbury *Oxon* 36 SU2685
Ashby *Humb* 84 SE8908
Ashby by Partney *Lincs* 77 TF4266
Ashby cum Fenby *Humb* 77 TA2500
Ashby de la Launde *Lincs* 76 TF0555
Ashby Folville *Leics* 63 SK7012
Ashby Magna *Leics* 50 SP5690
Ashby Parva *Leics* 50 SP5288
Ashby Puerorum *Lincs* 77 TF3271
Ashby St Ledgers *Nhants* 50 SP5768
Ashby St Mary *Norfk* 67 TG3202
Ashby-de-la-Zouch *Leics* 62 SK3516
Ashchurch *Gloucs* 47 SO9233
Ashcombe *Avon* 21 ST3361
Ashcombe *Devon* 9 SX9179
Ashcott *Somset* 21 ST4336
Ashdon *Essex* 53 TL5842
Ashe *Hants* 24 SU5350
Asheldham *Essex* 41 TL9701
Ashen *Essex* 53 TL7442
Ashendon *Bucks* 37 SP7014
Asheridge *Bucks* 38 SP9304
Ashfield *Cent* 124 NN7803
Ashfield *H & W* 46 SO5923
Ashfield *Hants* 12 SU3619
Ashfield *Suffk* 55 TM2062
Ashfield Green *Suffk* 53 TL7655
Ashfield Green *Suffk* 55 TM2573
Ashfields *Shrops* 72 SJ7026
Ashfold Crossways *W Susx* 15 TQ2328
Ashford *Devon* 19 SS5335
Ashford *Devon* 7 SX6948
Ashford *Kent* 28 TR0142
Ashford *Surrey* 26 TQ0771
Ashford Bowdler *Shrops* 46 SO5170
Ashford Carbonel *Shrops* 46 SO5270
Ashford Hill *Hants* 24 SU5562
Ashford in the Water *Derbys* 74 SK1969
Ashgill *Strath* 116 NS7850
Ashill *Devon* 9 ST0811
Ashill *Norfk* 66 TF8804
Ashill *Somset* 10 ST3217
Ashingdon *Essex* 40 TQ8693
Ashington *Dorset* 11 SZ0098
Ashington *Nthumb* 103 NZ2687
Ashington *Somset* 21 ST5621
Ashington *W Susx* 15 TQ1315
Ashkirk *Border* 109 NT4722
Ashlett *Hants* 13 SU4603
Ashleworth *Gloucs* 47 SO8125
Ashleworth Quay *Gloucs* 47 SO8125
Ashley *Cambs* 53 TL6961
Ashley *Ches* 79 SJ7784
Ashley *Devon* 19 SS6511
Ashley *Dorset* 12 SU1304
Ashley *Gloucs* 35 ST9394
Ashley *Hants* 23 SU3831
Ashley *Hants* 12 SZ2595
Ashley *Kent* 29 TR3048
Ashley *Nhants* 50 SP7990
Ashley *Staffs* 72 SJ7636
Ashley *Wilts* 22 ST8268
Ashley Green *Bucks* 38 SP9705
Ashley Heath *Dorset* 12 SU1204
Ashley Moor *H & W* 46 SO4767
Ashmansworth *Hants* 24 SU4157
Ashmansworthy *Devon* 18 SS3418
Ashmead Green *Gloucs* 35 ST7699
Ashmill *Devon* 5 SX3995
Ashmore *Dorset* 11 ST9117
Ashmore Green *Berks* 24 SU5069
Ashorne *Warwks* 48 SP3057
Ashover *Derbys* 74 SK3463
Ashover Hay *Derbys* 74 SK3460
Ashow *Warwks* 61 SP3170
Ashperton *H & W* 47 SO6441
Ashprington *Devon* 7 SX8157
Ashreigney *Devon* 19 SS6313
Ashridge Park *Herts* 38 SP9912
Ashtead *Surrey* 26 TQ1857
Ashton *Cambs* 64 TF1005
Ashton *Ches* 71 SJ5069
Ashton *Cnwll* 2 SW6028
Ashton *Cnwll* 5 SX3868
Ashton *Devon* 8 SX8584
Ashton *H & W* 46 SO5164
Ashton *Hants* 13 SU5419
Ashton *Nhants* 49 SP7649
Ashton *Nhants* 51 TL0588
Ashton *Somset* 21 ST4149
Ashton *Strath* 114 NS2377
Ashton Common *Wilts* 22 ST8958
Ashton Hill *Wilts* 22 ST9057
Ashton Keynes *Wilts* 36 SU0494
Ashton under Hill *H & W* 47 SO9937
Ashton upon Mersey *Gt Man* 79 SJ7892
Ashton Watering *Avon* 21 ST5369
Ashton-in-Makerfield *Gt Man* 78 SJ5798
Ashton-under-Lyne *Gt Man* 79 SJ9399
Ashurst *Hants* 12 SU3310
Ashurst *Kent* 16 TQ5138
Ashurst *W Susx* 15 TQ1715
Ashurstwood *W Susx* 15 TQ4136
Ashwater *Devon* 5 SX3895
Ashwell *Herts* 39 TL2639
Ashwell *Leics* 63 SK8613
Ashwell *Somset* 10 ST3616
Ashwell End *Herts* 39 TL2540
Ashwellthorpe *Norfk* 66 TM1497
Ashwick *Somset* 21 ST6348
Ashwicken *Norfk* 65 TF7018
Ashwood *Staffs* 60 SO8688
Askam in Furness *Cumb* 86 SD2177
Aske Hall *N York* 89 NZ1703
Askern *S York* 83 SE5613
Askerswell *Dorset* 10 SY5292
Askett *Bucks* 38 SP8105
Askham *Cumb* 94 NY5123
Askham *Notts* 75 SK7374
Askham Bryan *N York* 83 SE5548
Askham Richard *N York* 83 SE5347
Asknish *Strath* 114 NR9391
Askrigg *N York* 88 SD9491
Askwith *N York* 82 SE1648
Aslackby *Lincs* 64 TF0830
Aslacton *Norfk* 54 TM1590
Aslockton *Notts* 63 SK7440
Asney *Somset* 21 ST4636
Aspall *Suffk* 54 TM1664
Aspatria *Cumb* 92 NY1441
Aspenden *Herts* 39 TL3528
Asperton *Lincs* 64 TF2637
Aspley *Staffs* 72 SJ8133
Aspley Guise *Beds* 38 SP9335
Aspley Heath *Beds* 38 SP9334
Aspull *Gt Man* 78 SD6108
Aspull Common *Gt Man* 79 SJ6498
Asselby *Humb* 84 SE7127
Asserby *Lincs* 77 TF4977
Asserby Turn *Lincs* 77 TF4777
Assington *Suffk* 54 TL9338
Assington Green *Suffk* 53 TL7751
Astbury *Ches* 72 SJ8461
Astcote *Nhants* 49 SP6753
Asterby *Lincs* 77 TF2679
Asterley *Shrops* 59 SJ3707
Asterton *Shrops* 59 SO3991
Asthall *Oxon* 36 SP2811
Asthall Leigh *Oxon* 36 SP3013
Astle *Highld* 146 NH7391
Astley *Gt Man* 79 SD7000
Astley *H & W* 47 SO7867
Astley *Shrops* 59 SJ5218
Astley *W York* 83 SE3828
Astley *Warwks* 61 SP3189
Astley Abbots *Shrops* 60 SO7096
Astley Bridge *Gt Man* 81 SD7111
Astley Cross *H & W* 47 SO8069
Astley Green *Gt Man* 79 SJ7099
Astley Town *H & W* 47 SO7968
Aston *Berks* 37 SU7884
Aston *Ches* 71 SJ5578
Aston *Ches* 71 SJ6146
Aston *Clwyd* 71 SJ3067
Aston *Derbys* 74 SK1783
Aston *H & W* 46 SO4662
Aston *H & W* 46 SO4671
Aston *Herts* 39 TL2722
Aston *Oxon* 36 SP3403
Aston *S York* 75 SK4685
Aston *Shrops* 59 SJ5328
Aston *Shrops* 59 SJ6109
Aston *Shrops* 60 SO8093
Aston *Staffs* 72 SJ7541
Aston *Staffs* 72 SJ8923
Aston *Staffs* 72 SJ9130
Aston *W Mids* 61 SP0888
Aston Abbotts *Bucks* 38 SP8420
Aston Botterell *Shrops* 59 SO6384
Aston Cantlow *Warwks* 48 SP1460
Aston Clinton *Bucks* 38 SP8812
Aston Crews *H & W* 47 SO6723
Aston Cross *Gloucs* 47 SO9433
Aston End *Herts* 39 TL2724
Aston Fields *H & W* 47 SO9669
Aston Flamville *Leics* 50 SP4692
Aston Heath *Ches* 71 SJ5678
Aston Ingham *H & W* 47 SO6823
Aston juxta Mondrum *Ches* 72 SJ6456
Aston le Walls *Nhants* 49 SP4950
Aston Magna *Gloucs* 48 SP1935
Aston Munslow *Shrops* 59 SO5186
Aston on Clun *Shrops* 59 SO3981
Aston Pigott *Shrops* 59 SJ3305
Aston Rogers *Shrops* 59 SJ3406
Aston Rowant *Oxon* 37 SU7299
Aston Sandford *Bucks* 37 SP7507
Aston Somerville *H & W* 48 SP0438
Aston Subedge *Gloucs* 48 SP1441
Aston Tirrold *Oxon* 37 SU5586
Aston Upthorpe *Oxon* 37 SU5586
Aston-Eyre *Shrops* 59 SO6594
Aston-upon-Trent *Derbys* 62 SK4129
Astonlane *Shrops* 59 SO6494
Astrop *Nhants* 49 SP5036
Astrope *Herts* 38 SP8914
Astwick *Beds* 39 TL2138
Astwith *Derbys* 75 SK4464
Astwood *Bucks* 38 SP9547
Astwood *H & W* 47 SO9365
Astwood Bank *H & W* 48 SP0462
Aswarby *Lincs* 64 TF0639
Aswardby *Lincs* 77 TF3770

Atch Lench
Barlby

Atch Lench *H & W*	**48**	SP0350
Atcham *Shrops*	**59**	SJ5409
Athelhampton *Dorset*	**11**	SY7694
Athelington *Suffk*	**55**	TM2171
Athelney *Somset*	**21**	ST3428
Athelstaneford *Loth*	**118**	NT5377
Atherfield Green *IOW*	**13**	SZ4679
Atherington *Devon*	**19**	SS5922
Atherington *W Susx*	**14**	TQ0000
Atherstone *Somset*	**10**	ST3816
Atherstone *Warwks*	**61**	SP3097
Atherstone on Stour *Warwks*	**48**	SP2051
Atherton *Gt Man*	**79**	SD6703
Atley Hill *N York*	**89**	NZ2802
Atlow *Derbys*	**73**	SK2248
Attadale *Highld*	**138**	NG9238
Attenborough *Notts*	**62**	SK5034
Atterby *Lincs*	**76**	SK9792
Attercliffe *S York*	**74**	SK3788
Atterley *Shrops*	**59**	SO6397
Atterton *Leics*	**61**	SP3598
Attleborough *Norfk*	**66**	TM0495
Attleborough *Warwks*	**61**	SP3790
Attlebridge *Norfk*	**66**	TG1216
Attleton Green *Suffk*	**53**	TL7454
Atwick *Humb*	**85**	TA1850
Atworth *Wilts*	**22**	ST8565
Auberrow *H & W*	**46**	SO4947
Aubourn *Lincs*	**76**	SK9262
Auchedly *Gramp*	**143**	NJ8933
Auchenblae *Gramp*	**135**	NO7279
Auchenbowie *Cent*	**116**	NS7987
Auchencairn *D & G*	**92**	NX7951
Auchencairn *D & G*	**100**	NX9884
Auchencairn *Strath*	**105**	NS0427
Auchencrow *Border*	**119**	NT8560
Auchendinny *Loth*	**117**	NT2561
Auchengray *Strath*	**117**	NS9954
Auchenhalrig *Gramp*	**141**	NJ3761
Auchenheath *Strath*	**108**	NS8043
Auchenhessnane *D & G*	**100**	NX8096
Auchenlochan *Strath*	**114**	NR9772
Auchenmade *Strath*	**115**	NS3548
Auchenmalg *D & G*	**98**	NX2352
Auchentibber *Strath*	**116**	NS6755
Auchentiber *Strath*	**115**	NS3647
Auchentroig *Cent*	**115**	NS5493
Auchindrean *Highld*	**145**	NH1980
Auchininna *Gramp*	**142**	NJ6546
Auchinleck *Strath*	**107**	NS5521
Auchinloch *Strath*	**116**	NS6570
Auchinstarry *Strath*	**116**	NS7176
Auchintore *Highld*	**130**	NN0972
Auchiries *Gramp*	**143**	NK0737
Auchlee *Gramp*	**135**	NO8996
Auchleven *Gramp*	**142**	NJ6224
Auchlochan *Strath*	**107**	NS7937
Auchlossan *Gramp*	**134**	NJ5601
Auchlyne *Cent*	**124**	NN5129
Auchmillan *Strath*	**107**	NS5129
Auchmithie *Tays*	**127**	NO6743
Auchmuirbridge *Fife*	**126**	NO2101
Auchnacree *Tays*	**134**	NO4663
Auchnagatt *Gramp*	**143**	NJ9241
Auchnarrow *Gramp*	**141**	NJ2023
Auchnotteroch *D & G*	**98**	NW9960
Auchroisk *Gramp*	**141**	NJ3351
Auchronie *Tays*	**134**	NO4480
Auchterarder *Tays*	**125**	NN9412
Auchteraw *Highld*	**131**	NH3507
Auchterblair *Highld*	**140**	NH9222
Auchtercairn *Highld*	**144**	NG8077
Auchterderran *Fife*	**117**	NT2195
Auchterhouse *Tays*	**126**	NO3337
Auchterless *Gramp*	**142**	NJ7141
Auchtermuchty *Fife*	**126**	NO2311
Auchterneed *Highld*	**139**	NH4959
Auchtertool *Fife*	**117**	NT2190
Auchtertyre *Highld*	**138**	NG8427
Auchtoo *Cent*	**124**	NN5520
Auckengill *Highld*	**151**	ND3663
Auckley *S York*	**75**	SE6400
Audenshaw *Gt Man*	**79**	SJ9197
Audlem *Ches*	**72**	SJ6543
Audley *Staffs*	**72**	SJ7950
Audley End *Essex*	**39**	TL5337
Audley End *Essex*	**54**	TL8137
Audley End *Suffk*	**54**	TL8553
Audmore *Staffs*	**72**	SJ8321
Audnam *W Mids*	**60**	SO8986
Aughertree *Cumb*	**93**	NY2538
Aughton *Humb*	**84**	SE7038
Aughton *Lancs*	**78**	SD3905
Aughton *Lancs*	**87**	SD5567
Aughton *S York*	**75**	SK4586
Aughton *Wilts*	**23**	SU2356
Aughton Park *Lancs*	**78**	SD4006
Auldallan *Tays*	**134**	NO3158
Auldearn *Highld*	**140**	NH9255
Aulden *H & W*	**46**	SO4654
Auldgirth *D & G*	**100**	NX9186
Auldhouse *Strath*	**116**	NS6250
Ault a' chruinn *Highld*	**138**	NG9420
Ault Hucknall *Derbys*	**75**	SK4665
Aultbea *Highld*	**144**	NG8789
Aultgrishin *Highld*	**144**	NG7485
Aultguish Inn *Highld*	**145**	NH3570
Aultmore *Gramp*	**142**	NJ4053
Aultnagoire *Highld*	**139**	NH5423
Aultnamain Inn *Highld*	**146**	NH6681
Aunby *Lincs*	**64**	TF0214
Aunk *Devon*	**9**	ST0400
Aunsby *Lincs*	**64**	TF0438
Aust *Avon*	**34**	ST5788
Austendike *Lincs*	**64**	TF2821
Austerfield *S York*	**75**	SK6694
Austerlands *Gt Man*	**79**	SD9505
Austhorpe *W York*	**83**	SE3733
Austonley *W York*	**82**	SE1107
Austrey *Warwks*	**61**	SK2906
Austwick *N York*	**88**	SD7668
Authorpe *Lincs*	**77**	TF3980
Authorpe Row *Lincs*	**77**	TF5373
Avebury *Wilts*	**36**	SU1069
Avebury Trusloe *Wilts*	**36**	SU0969
Aveley *Essex*	**27**	TQ5680
Avening *Gloucs*	**35**	ST8898
Averham *Notts*	**75**	SK7654
Aveton Gifford *Devon*	**7**	SX6947
Aviemore *Highld*	**132**	NH8913
Avington *Berks*	**23**	SU3767
Avoch *Highld*	**140**	NH7055
Avon *Dorset*	**12**	SZ1498
Avon Dassett *Warwks*	**49**	SP4150
Avonbridge *Cent*	**116**	NS9172
Avonmouth *Avon*	**34**	ST5178
Avonwick *Devon*	**7**	SX7158
Awbridge *Hants*	**12**	SU3224
Awkley *Avon*	**34**	ST5985
Awliscombe *Devon*	**9**	ST1301
Awre *Gloucs*	**35**	SO7008
Awsworth *Notts*	**62**	SK4844
Axborough *H & W*	**60**	SO8579
Axbridge *Somset*	**21**	ST4354
Axford *Hants*	**24**	SU6043
Axford *Wilts*	**36**	SU2370
Axminster *Devon*	**10**	SY2998
Axmouth *Devon*	**10**	SY2591
Axton *Clwyd*	**70**	SJ1080
Aycliffe *Dur*	**96**	NZ2822
Aydon *Nthumb*	**103**	NZ0065
Aylburton *Gloucs*	**34**	SO6101
Ayle *Cumb*	**94**	NY7149
Aylebridge *Cnwll*	**18**	SS2103
Aylesbeare *Devon*	**9**	SY0392
Aylesbury *Bucks*	**38**	SP8213
Aylesby *Humb*	**85**	TA2007
Aylesford *Kent*	**28**	TQ7359
Aylesham *Kent*	**29**	TR2452
Aylestone *Leics*	**50**	SK5700
Aylestone Park *Leics*	**50**	SK5800
Aylmerton *Norfk*	**66**	TG1839
Aylsham *Norfk*	**67**	TG1926
Aylton *H & W*	**47**	SO6537
Aylworth *Gloucs*	**36**	SP1021
Aymestrey *H & W*	**46**	SO4265
Aynho *Nhants*	**49**	SP5133
Ayot Green *Herts*	**39**	TL2214
Ayot St Lawrence *Herts*	**39**	TL1916
Ayot St Peter *Herts*	**39**	TL2115
Ayr *Strath*	**106**	NS3321
Aysgarth *N York*	**88**	SE0088
Ayshford *Devon*	**9**	ST0415
Ayside *Cumb*	**87**	SD3983
Ayston *Leics*	**51**	SK8600
Aythorpe Roding *Essex*	**40**	TL5815
Ayton *Border*	**119**	NT9260
Azerley *N York*	**89**	SE2574

B

Babbacombe *Devon*	**7**	SX9265
Babbington *Notts*	**62**	SK4943
Babbinswood *Shrops*	**59**	SJ3329
Babbs Green *Herts*	**39**	TL3916
Babcary *Somset*	**21**	ST5628
Babel *Dyfed*	**44**	SN8235
Babel Green *Suffk*	**53**	TL7348
Babell *Clwyd*	**70**	SJ1573
Babeny *Devon*	**7**	SX6775
Babington *Somset*	**22**	ST7051
Bablock Hythe *Oxon*	**36**	SP4304
Babraham *Cambs*	**53**	TL5150
Babworth *Notts*	**75**	SK6880
Bachau *Gwynd*	**68**	SH4383
Bache *Shrops*	**59**	SO4681
Bacheldre *Powys*	**58**	SO2492
Bachelor Bump *E Susx*	**17**	TQ8412
Back o' th' Brook *Staffs*	**73**	SK0751
Back of Keppoch *Highld*	**129**	NM6587
Back Street *Suffk*	**53**	TL7458
Backaland *Ork*	**155**	HY5630
Backbarrow *Cumb*	**87**	SD3584
Backe *Dyfed*	**31**	SN2615
Backfolds *Gramp*	**143**	NK0252
Backford *Ches*	**71**	SJ3971
Backford Cross *Ches*	**71**	SJ3873
Backies *Highld*	**147**	NC8302
Backlass *Highld*	**151**	ND2053
Backwell *Avon*	**21**	ST4968
Backworth *T & W*	**103**	NZ3072
Bacon's End *W Mids*	**61**	SP1888
Baconsthorpe *Norfk*	**66**	TG1236
Bacton *H & W*	**46**	SO3732
Bacton *Norfk*	**67**	TG3433
Bacton *Suffk*	**54**	TM0567
Bacton Green *Suffk*	**54**	TM0365
Bacup *Lancs*	**81**	SD8622
Badachro *Highld*	**137**	NG7873
Badbury *Wilts*	**36**	SU1980
Badby *Nhants*	**49**	SP5658
Badcall *Highld*	**148**	NC1541
Badcall *Highld*	**148**	NC2455
Badcaul *Highld*	**144**	NH0291
Baddeley Edge *Staffs*	**72**	SJ9150
Baddeley Green *Staffs*	**72**	SJ9151
Baddesley Clinton *Warwks*	**61**	SP2070
Baddesley Ensor *Warwks*	**61**	SP2798
Baddidarroch *Highld*	**145**	NC0822
Baddinsgill *Border*	**117**	NT1254
Badenscoth *Gramp*	**142**	NJ6938
Badenyon *Gramp*	**141**	NJ3319
Badgall *Cnwll*	**5**	SX2486
Badgeney *Cambs*	**65**	TL4397
Badger *Shrops*	**60**	SO7699
Badger's Cross *Cnwll*	**2**	SW4833
Badgers Mount *Kent*	**27**	TQ4962
Badgeworth *Gloucs*	**35**	SO9019
Badgworth *Somset*	**21**	ST3952
Badharlick *Cnwll*	**5**	SX2686
Badicaul *Highld*	**137**	NG7529
Badingham *Suffk*	**55**	TM3068
Badlesmere *Kent*	**28**	TR0153
Badlieu *Border*	**108**	NT0518
Badlipster *Highld*	**151**	ND2448
Badluachrach *Highld*	**144**	NG9994
Badninish *Highld*	**147**	NH7594
Badrallach *Highld*	**145**	NH0691
Badsey *H & W*	**48**	SP0743
Badshot Lea *Surrey*	**25**	SU8648
Badsworth *W York*	**83**	SE4614
Badwell Ash *Suffk*	**54**	TL9868
Badwell Green *Suffk*	**54**	TM0169
Bag Enderby *Lincs*	**77**	TF3571
Bagber *Dorset*	**11**	ST7513
Bagby *N York*	**89**	SE4680
Bagendon *Gloucs*	**35**	SP0106
Bagginswood *Shrops*	**60**	SO6881
Baggrow *Cumb*	**93**	NY1741
Bagh a Chaisteil *W Isls*	**154**	NL6698
Bagham *Kent*	**29**	TR0753
Bagillt *Clwyd*	**70**	SJ2175
Baginton *Warwks*	**61**	SP3474
Baglan *W Glam*	**32**	SS7492
Bagley *Shrops*	**59**	SJ4027
Bagley *Somset*	**21**	ST4645
Bagley *W York*	**82**	SE2235
Bagmore *Hants*	**24**	SU6544
Bagnall *Staffs*	**72**	SJ9250
Bagnor *Berks*	**24**	SU4569
Bagot *Shrops*	**46**	SO5873
Bagshot *Surrey*	**25**	SU9063
Bagshot *Wilts*	**23**	SU3165
Bagstone *Avon*	**35**	ST6987
Bagthorpe *Notts*	**75**	SK4651
Bagworth *Leics*	**62**	SK4408
Bagwy Llydiart *H & W*	**46**	SO4426
Baildon *W York*	**82**	SE1539
Baildon Green *W York*	**82**	SE1439
Baile a Mhanaich *W Isls*	**154**	NF7755
Baile Ailein *W Isls*	**154**	NB2920
Baile Mor *Strath*	**120**	NM2824
Bailey Green *Hants*	**13**	SU6627
Baileyhead *Cumb*	**101**	NY5179
Bailiff Bridge *W York*	**82**	SE1425
Baillieston *Strath*	**116**	NS6764
Bailrigg *Lancs*	**87**	SD4858
Bainbridge *N York*	**88**	SD9390
Bainshole *Gramp*	**142**	NJ6035
Bainton *Cambs*	**64**	TF0906
Bainton *Humb*	**84**	SE9652
Bainton *Oxon*	**49**	SP5827
Baintown *Fife*	**126**	NO3503
Bairnkine *Border*	**110**	NT6515
Baker Street *Essex*	**40**	TQ6381
Baker's End *Herts*	**39**	TL3917
Bakewell *Derbys*	**74**	SK2168
Bala *Gwynd*	**58**	SH9235
Balallan *W Isls*	**154**	NB2920
Balbeg *Highld*	**139**	NH4431
Balbeggie *Tays*	**126**	NO1629
Balblair *Highld*	**139**	NH5145
Balblair *Highld*	**140**	NH7066
Balby *S York*	**75**	SE5600
Balcary *D & G*	**92**	NX8149
Balchraggan *Highld*	**139**	NH5343
Balchrick *Highld*	**148**	NC1960
Balcombe *W Susx*	**15**	TQ3130
Balcombe Lane *W Susx*	**15**	TQ3132
Balcomie Links *Fife*	**127**	NO6209
Baldersby *N York*	**89**	SE3578
Baldersby St James *N York*	**89**	SE3676
Balderstone *Gt Man*	**79**	SD9010
Balderstone *Lancs*	**81**	SD6332
Balderton *Notts*	**75**	SK8151
Baldhu *Cnwll*	**3**	SW7743
Baldinnie *Fife*	**127**	NO4211
Baldinnies *Tays*	**125**	NO0216
Baldock *Herts*	**39**	TL2434
Baldovie *Tays*	**127**	NO4533
Baldrine *IOM*	**153**	SC4281
Baldslow *E Susx*	**17**	TQ8013
Baldwin *IOM*	**153**	SC3581
Baldwin's Gate *Staffs*	**72**	SJ7939
Baldwin's Hill *Surrey*	**15**	TQ3839
Baldwinholme *Cumb*	**93**	NY3351
Bale *Norfk*	**66**	TG0136
Baledgarno *Tays*	**126**	NO2730
Balemartine *Strath*	**120**	NL9841
Balerno *Loth*	**117**	NT1666
Balfarg *Fife*	**126**	NO2803
Balfield *Tays*	**134**	NO5468
Balfour *Ork*	**155**	HY4716
Balfron *Cent*	**115**	NS5489
Balgaveny *Gramp*	**142**	NJ6540
Balgavies *Tays*	**127**	NO5451
Balgonar *Fife*	**117**	NT0293
Balgowan *D & G*	**98**	NX1142
Balgowan *Highld*	**132**	NN6494
Balgown *Highld*	**136**	NG3868
Balgracie *D & G*	**98**	NW9860
Balgray *Strath*	**108**	NS8824
Balgray *Tays*	**126**	NO4038
Balham *Gt Lon*	**27**	TQ2873
Balhary *Tays*	**126**	NO2646
Balholmie *Tays*	**126**	NO1436
Baligill *Highld*	**150**	NC8565
Balintore *Highld*	**147**	NH8675
Balintore *Tays*	**133**	NO2859
Balintraid *Highld*	**146**	NH7370
Balivanich *W Isls*	**154**	NF7755
Balk *N York*	**89**	SE4780
Balkeerie *Tays*	**126**	NO3244
Balkholme *Humb*	**84**	SE7828
Ball *Shrops*	**59**	SJ3026
Ball Green *Staffs*	**72**	SJ8952
Ball Haye Green *Staffs*	**72**	SJ9856
Ball Hill *Hants*	**24**	SU4163
Ball's Green *Gloucs*	**35**	ST8699
Ballabeg *IOM*	**153**	SC2570
Ballachulish *Highld*	**130**	NN0858
Ballafesson *IOM*	**153**	SC2070
Ballakilpheric *IOM*	**153**	SC2271
Ballamodha *IOM*	**153**	SC2773
Ballanlay *Strath*	**114**	NS0462
Ballantrae *Strath*	**98**	NX0882
Ballards Gore *Essex*	**40**	TQ9092
Ballards Green *Warwks*	**61**	SP2791
Ballasalla *IOM*	**153**	SC2870
Ballater *Gramp*	**134**	NO3695
Ballaugh *IOM*	**153**	SC3493
Ballchraggan *Highld*	**147**	NH7675
Ballechin *Tays*	**125**	NN9353
Ballencrieff *Loth*	**118**	NT4878
Ballevullin *Strath*	**120**	NL9546
Ballidon *Derbys*	**73**	SK2054
Balliekine *Strath*	**105**	NR8739
Balliemore *Strath*	**114**	NS1099
Balligmorrie *Strath*	**106**	NX2290
Ballimore *Cent*	**124**	NN5317
Ballimore *Strath*	**114**	NR9283
Ballindalloch *Gramp*	**141**	NJ1636
Ballindean *Tays*	**126**	NO2529
Ballingdon *Essex*	**54**	TL8640
Ballinger Common *Bucks*	**38**	SP9103
Ballingham *H & W*	**46**	SO5731
Ballingry *Fife*	**117**	NT1797
Ballinluig *Tays*	**125**	NN9752
Ballinshoe *Tays*	**126**	NO4153
Ballintuim *Tays*	**126**	NO1055
Balloch *Highld*	**140**	NH7247
Balloch *Strath*	**106**	NX3295
Balloch *Strath*	**116**	NS7374
Balloch *Strath*	**115**	NS3982
Balloch *Tays*	**125**	NN8419
Ballochroy *Strath*	**113**	NR7352
Ballogie *Gramp*	**134**	NO5795
Balls Cross *W Susx*	**14**	SU9826
Balls Green *E Susx*	**16**	TQ4936
Ballygown *Strath*	**121**	NM4343
Ballygrant *Strath*	**112**	NR3966
Ballyhaugh *Strath*	**120**	NM1758
Ballymenoch *Strath*	**115**	NS3086
Ballymichael *Strath*	**105**	NR9231
Balmacara *Highld*	**137**	NG8028
Balmaclellan *D & G*	**99**	NX6579
Balmae *D & G*	**99**	NX6844
Balmaha *Cent*	**115**	NS4290
Balmalcolm *Fife*	**126**	NO3208
Balmangan *D & G*	**99**	NX6445
Balmedie *Gramp*	**143**	NJ9618
Balmer Heath *Shrops*	**59**	SJ4434
Balmerino *Fife*	**126**	NO3524
Balmerlawn *Hants*	**12**	SU3003
Balmore *Strath*	**115**	NS5973
Balmuchy *Highld*	**147**	NH8678
Balmuir *Tays*	**127**	NO5648
Balmule *Fife*	**117**	NT2088
Balmullo *Tays*	**127**	NO4220
Balnacoil Lodge *Highld*	**147**	NC8011
Balnacroft *Gramp*	**133**	NO2894
Balnafoich *Highld*	**140**	NH6835
Balnaguard *Tays*	**125**	NN9451
Balnahard *Strath*	**121**	NM4534
Balnahard *Strath*	**112**	NR4199
Balnain *Highld*	**139**	NH4430
Balnakeil *Highld*	**149**	NC3968
Balnapaling *Highld*	**147**	NH7969
Balne *N York*	**83**	SE5918
Balquharn *Tays*	**125**	NO0235
Balquhidder *Cent*	**124**	NN5320
Balsall Common *W Mids*	**61**	SP2376
Balsall Heath *W Mids*	**61**	SP0784
Balsall Street *W Mids*	**61**	SP2276
Balscote *Oxon*	**48**	SP3942
Balsham *Cambs*	**53**	TL5850
Baltasound *Shet*	**155**	HP6208
Balterley *Staffs*	**72**	SJ7650
Balterley Green *Staffs*	**72**	SJ7650
Baltersan *D & G*	**99**	NX4261
Baltonsborough *Somset*	**21**	ST5434
Balvarran *Tays*	**133**	NO0761
Balvicar *Strath*	**122**	NM7616
Balvraid *Highld*	**129**	NG8416
Balvraid *Highld*	**140**	NH8231
Balwest *Cnwll*	**2**	SW5930
Bamber Bridge *Lancs*	**81**	SD5625
Bamber's Green *Essex*	**40**	TL5722
Bamburgh *Nthumb*	**111**	NU1734
Bamff *Tays*	**126**	NO2251
Bamford *Derbys*	**74**	SK2083
Bamford *Gt Man*	**81**	SD8612
Bampton *Cumb*	**94**	NY5118
Bampton *Devon*	**20**	SS9522
Bampton *Oxon*	**36**	SP3103
Bampton Grange *Cumb*	**94**	NY5218
Banavie *Highld*	**130**	NN1177
Banbury *Oxon*	**49**	SP4540
Banc-y-ffordd *Dyfed*	**31**	SN4037
Bancffosfelem *Dyfed*	**32**	SN4811
Banchory *Gramp*	**135**	NO6995
Banchory-Devenick *Gramp*	**135**	NJ9002
Bancycapel *Dyfed*	**31**	SN4214
Bancyfelin *Dyfed*	**31**	SN3218
Bandirran *Tays*	**126**	NO2030
Bandrake Head *Cumb*	**86**	SD3187
Banff *Gramp*	**142**	NJ6863
Bangor *Gwynd*	**69**	SH5772
Bangor's Green *Lancs*	**78**	SD3709
Bangor-is-y-coed *Clwyd*	**71**	SJ3845
Bangors *Cnwll*	**18**	SX2099
Bangrove *Suffk*	**54**	TL9372
Banham *Norfk*	**54**	TM0687
Bank *Hants*	**12**	SU2807
Bank Ground *Cumb*	**86**	SD3196
Bank Newton *N York*	**81**	SD9053
Bank Street *H & W*	**47**	SO6362
Bank Top *Lancs*	**78**	SD5207
Bank Top *W York*	**82**	SE1024
Bankend *D & G*	**100**	NY0268
Bankend *Strath*	**108**	NS8033
Bankfoot *Tays*	**125**	NO0635
Bankglen *Strath*	**107**	NS5912
Bankhead *Gramp*	**135**	NJ9009
Bankhead *Strath*	**106**	NS3739
Bankhead *Strath*	**116**	NS9844
Banknock *Cent*	**116**	NS7779
Banks *Cumb*	**101**	NY5664
Banks *Lancs*	**80**	SD3920
Banks Green *H & W*	**47**	SO9967
Bankshill *D & G*	**101**	NY1982
Banningham *Norfk*	**67**	TG2129
Bannister Green *Essex*	**40**	TL6920
Bannockburn *Cent*	**116**	NS8190
Banstead *Surrey*	**27**	TQ2559
Bantham *Devon*	**7**	SX6643
Banton *Strath*	**116**	NS7480
Banwell *Avon*	**21**	ST3959
Bapchild *Kent*	**28**	TQ9263
Bapton *Wilts*	**22**	ST9938
Bar Hill *Cambs*	**52**	TL3863
Barabhas *W Isls*	**154**	NB3649
Barassie *Strath*	**106**	NS3232
Barbaraville *Highld*	**146**	NH7472
Barber Booth *Derbys*	**74**	SK1184
Barber Green *Cumb*	**87**	SD3982
Barbieston *Strath*	**107**	NS4317
Barbon *Cumb*	**87**	SD6282
Barbridge *Ches*	**71**	SJ6156
Barbrook *Devon*	**19**	SS7147
Barby *Nhants*	**50**	SP5470
Barcaldine *Strath*	**122**	NM9641
Barcheston *Warwks*	**48**	SP2639
Barclose *Cumb*	**101**	NY4462
Barcombe *E Susx*	**15**	TQ4114
Barcombe Cross *E Susx*	**15**	TQ4115
Barcroft *W York*	**82**	SE0437
Barden *N York*	**89**	SE1493
Barden Park *Kent*	**16**	TQ5746
Bardfield End Green *Essex*	**40**	TL6231
Bardfield Saling *Essex*	**40**	TL6826
Bardney *Lincs*	**76**	TF1269
Bardon *Leics*	**62**	SK4412
Bardon Mill *Nthumb*	**102**	NY7764
Bardowie *Strath*	**115**	NS5873
Bardown *E Susx*	**16**	TQ6629
Bardrainney *Strath*	**115**	NS3373
Bardsea *Cumb*	**86**	SD3074
Bardsey *W York*	**83**	SE3643
Bardsley *Gt Man*	**79**	SD9201
Bardwell *Suffk*	**54**	TL9473
Bare *Lancs*	**87**	SD4564
Bareppa *Cnwll*	**3**	SW7729
Barewood *H & W*	**46**	SO3856
Barfad *D & G*	**98**	NX3266
Barford *Norfk*	**66**	TG1107
Barford *Warwks*	**48**	SP2760
Barford St John *Oxon*	**49**	SP4433
Barford St Martin *Wilts*	**23**	SU0531
Barford St Michael *Oxon*	**49**	SP4332
Barfrestone *Kent*	**29**	TR2650
Bargate *Derbys*	**62**	SK3546
Bargeddie *Strath*	**116**	NS6964
Bargoed *M Glam*	**33**	ST1599
Bargrennan *D & G*	**98**	NX3577
Barham *Cambs*	**52**	TL1375
Barham *Kent*	**29**	TR2050
Barham *Suffk*	**54**	TM1451
Barholm *Lincs*	**64**	TF0810
Barkby *Leics*	**63**	SK6309
Barkby Thorpe *Leics*	**63**	SK6309
Barkers Green *Shrops*	**59**	SJ5228
Barkestone-le-Vale *Leics*	**63**	SK7734
Barkham *Berks*	**25**	SU7766
Barking *Gt Lon*	**27**	TQ4484
Barking *Suffk*	**54**	TM0753
Barking Tye *Suffk*	**54**	TM0652
Barkingside *Gt Lon*	**27**	TQ4489
Barkisland *W York*	**82**	SE0519
Barkla Shop *Cnwll*	**3**	SW7350
Barkston *Lincs*	**63**	SK9341
Barkston Ash *N York*	**83**	SE4936
Barkway *Herts*	**39**	TL3835
Barlanark *Strath*	**116**	NS6664
Barlaston *Staffs*	**72**	SJ8938
Barlavington *W Susx*	**14**	SU9716
Barlborough *Derbys*	**75**	SK4777
Barlby *N York*	**83**	SE6333

Berrick Prior
Blatherwycke

Berrick Prior *Oxon* 37 SU6294
Berrick Salome *Oxon* 37 SU6293
Berriedale *Highld* 147 ND1222
Berrier *Cumb* 93 NY3929
Berriew *Powys* 58 SJ1801
Berrington *H & W* 46 SO5767
Berrington *Nthumb* 111 NU0043
Berrington *Shrops* 59 SJ5206
Berrington Green *H & W* 46 SO5766
Berrow *H & W* 47 SO7934
Berrow *Somset* 20 ST2951
Berrow Green *H & W* 47 SO7458
Berry Brow *W York* 82 SE1314
Berry Cross *Devon* 18 SS4714
Berry Down Cross *Devon* 19 SS5743
Berry Hill *Dyfed* 30 SN0640
Berry Hill *Gloucs* 34 SO5712
Berry Pomeroy *Devon* 7 SX8261
Berry's Green *Gt Lon* 27 TQ4359
Berryhillock *Gramp* 142 NJ5054
Berryhillock *Gramp* 142 NJ5060
Berrynarbor *Devon* 19 SS5646
Bersham *Clwyd* 71 SJ3049
Berthengam *Clwyd* 70 SJ1179
Berwick *E Susx* 16 TQ5105
Berwick Bassett *Wilts* 36 SU0973
Berwick Hill *Nthumb* 103 NZ1775
Berwick St James *Wilts* 23 SU0739
Berwick St John *Wilts* 22 ST9422
Berwick St Leonard *Wilts* 22 ST9233
Berwick-upon-Tweed *Nthumb* 119 NT9953
Bescaby *Leics* 63 SK8126
Bescar *Cumb* 80 SD3913
Besford *H & W* 47 SO9144
Besford *Shrops* 59 SJ5525
Besom Hill *Gt Man* 79 SD9508
Bessacarr *S York* 75 SE6100
Bessels Leigh *Oxon* 37 SP4501
Besses o' th' Barn *Gt Man* 79 SD8005
Bessingby *Humb* 91 TA1566
Bessingham *Norfk* 66 TG1636
Bestbeech Hill *E Susx* 16 TQ6231
Besthorpe *Norfk* 66 TM0595
Besthorpe *Notts* 75 SK8264
Beswick *Humb* 84 TA0147
Betchcott *Shrops* 59 SO4398
Betchworth *Surrey* 26 TQ2150
Bethania *Dyfed* 43 SN5763
Bethania *Gwynd* 57 SH7044
Bethel *Gwynd* 68 SH3970
Bethel *Gwynd* 68 SH5265
Bethel *Gwynd* 70 SH9839
Bethel *Powys* 58 SJ1021
Bethersden *Kent* 28 TQ9240
Bethesda *Dyfed* 31 SN0918
Bethesda *Gwynd* 69 SH6266
Bethlehem *Dyfed* 44 SN6825
Bethnal Green *Gt Lon* 27 TQ3482
Betley *Staffs* 72 SJ7548
Betsham *Kent* 27 TQ6071
Betteshanger *Kent* 29 TR3152
Bettiscombe *Dorset* 10 ST3900
Bettisfield *Clwyd* 59 SJ4635
Betton *Shrops* 72 SJ6936
Betton Strange *Shrops* 59 SJ5009
Bettws *Gwent* 34 ST2890
Bettws Bledrws *Dyfed* 44 SN5952
Bettws Cedewain *Powys* 58 SO1296
Bettws Evan *Dyfed* 42 SN3047
Bettws-Newydd *Gwent* 34 SO3606
Bettyhill *Highld* 150 NC7061
Betws *Dyfed* 32 SN6311
Betws *M Glam* 33 SS9086
Betws Garmon *Gwynd* 69 SH5357
Betws Gwerfil Goch *Clwyd* 70 SJ0346
Betws-y-coed *Gwynd* 69 SH7956
Betws-yn-Rhos *Clwyd* 69 SH9073
Beulah *Dyfed* 42 SN2846
Beulah *Powys* 45 SN9251
Bevendean *E Susx* 15 TQ3306
Bevercotes *Notts* 75 SK6972
Beverley *Humb* 84 TA0339
Beverstone *Gloucs* 35 ST8694
Bevington *Gloucs* 35 ST6596
Bewaldeth *Cumb* 93 NY2034
Bewcastle *Cumb* 101 NY5674
Bewdley *H & W* 60 SO7875
Bewerley *N York* 89 SE1565
Bewholme *Humb* 85 TA1649
Bewlbridge *Kent* 16 TQ6834
Bexhill *E Susx* 17 TQ7407
Bexley *Gt Lon* 27 TQ4973
Bexleyheath *Gt Lon* 27 TQ4875
Bexleyhill *W Susx* 14 SU9125
Bexwell *Norfk* 65 TF6303
Beyton *Suffk* 54 TL9363
Beyton Green *Suffk* 54 TL9363
Bhaltos *W Isls* 154 NB0936
Bibstone *Avon* 35 ST6991
Bibury *Gloucs* 36 SP1106
Bicester *Oxon* 49 SP5823
Bickenhill *W Mids* 61 SP1882
Bicker *Lincs* 64 TF2237
Bicker Bar *Lincs* 64 TF2438
Bicker Gauntlet *Lincs* 64 TF2139
Bickershaw *Gt Man* 79 SD6201
Bickerstaffe *Lancs* 78 SD4404
Bickerton *Ches* 71 SJ5052
Bickerton *Devon* 7 SX8139
Bickerton *N York* 83 SE4550
Bickerton *Nthumb* 103 NT9900
Bickford *Staffs* 60 SJ8814
Bickington *Devon* 19 SS5332
Bickington *Devon* 7 SX8072
Bickleigh *Devon* 9 SS9407
Bickleigh *Devon* 6 SX5262
Bickleton *Devon* 19 SS5030
Bickley *Ches* 71 SJ5348
Bickley *Gt Lon* 27 TQ4268
Bickley *H & W* 47 SO6371
Bickley *N York* 91 SE9191
Bickley Moss *Ches* 71 SJ5448
Bicknacre *Essex* 40 TL7802
Bicknoller *Somset* 20 ST1139
Bicknor *Kent* 28 TQ8658
Bickton *Hants* 12 SU1412
Bicton *H & W* 46 SO4764
Bicton *Shrops* 59 SJ4415
Bicton *Shrops* 59 SO2983
Bidborough *Kent* 16 TQ5643
Bidden *Hants* 24 SU7049
Biddenden *Kent* 28 TQ8538
Biddenden Green *Kent* 28 TQ8842
Biddenham *Beds* 38 TL0250
Biddestone *Wilts* 35 ST8673
Biddisham *Somset* 21 ST3853
Biddlesden *Bucks* 49 SP6340
Biddlestone *Nthumb* 111 NT9508
Biddulph *Staffs* 72 SJ8858
Biddulph Moor *Staffs* 72 SJ9058
Bideford *Devon* 18 SS4526
Bidford-on-Avon *Warwks* 48 SP1052
Bidston *Mersyd* 78 SJ2890
Bielby *Humb* 84 SE7843
Bieldside *Gramp* 135 NJ8702
Bierley *IOW* 13 SZ5078
Bierton *Bucks* 38 SP8415
Big Balcraig *D & G* 99 NX3843
Big Carlae *D & G* 107 NX6597
Big Sand *Highld* 144 NG7578
Bigbury *Devon* 7 SX6646
Bigbury-on-Sea *Devon* 7 SX6544
Bigby *Lincs* 84 TA0507
Biggar *Cumb* 86 SD1966
Biggar *Strath* 108 NT0437
Biggin *Derbys* 74 SK1559
Biggin *Derbys* 73 SK2549
Biggin *N York* 83 SE5434
Biggin Hill *Gt Lon* 27 TQ4159
Biggleswade *Beds* 39 TL1944
Bigholms *D & G* 101 NY3180
Bighouse *Highld* 150 NC8964
Bighton *Hants* 24 SU6134
Bigland Hall *Cumb* 87 SD3583
Biglands *Cumb* 93 NY2553
Bignor *W Susx* 14 SU9814
Bigrigg *Cumb* 92 NY0013
Bilborough *Notts* 62 SK5241
Bilbrook *Somset* 20 ST0341
Bilbrook *Staffs* 60 SJ8703
Bilbrough *N York* 83 SE5346
Bilbster *Highld* 151 ND2853
Bildershaw *Dur* 96 NZ2024
Bildeston *Suffk* 54 TL9949
Billacott *Cnwll* 5 SX2690
Billericay *Essex* 40 TQ6794
Billesdon *Leics* 63 SK7202
Billesley *Warwks* 48 SP1456
Billingborough *Lincs* 64 TF1133
Billinge *Mersyd* 78 SD5200
Billingford *Norfk* 66 TG0120
Billingford *Norfk* 54 TM1678
Billingham *Cleve* 97 NZ4624
Billinghay *Lincs* 76 TF1554
Billingley *S York* 83 SE4304
Billingshurst *W Susx* 14 TQ0825
Billingsley *Shrops* 60 SO7085
Billington *Beds* 38 SP9422
Billington *Lancs* 81 SD7235
Billington *Staffs* 72 SJ8820
Billockby *Norfk* 67 TG4313
Billy Row *Dur* 96 NZ1637
Bilsborrow *Lancs* 80 SD5139
Bilsby *Lincs* 77 TF4776
Bilsham *W Susx* 14 SU9702
Bilsington *Kent* 17 TR0434
Bilsthorpe *Notts* 75 SK6460
Bilsthorpe Moor *Notts* 75 SK6560
Bilston *Loth* 117 NT2664
Bilston *W Mids* 60 SO9596
Bilstone *Leics* 62 SK3605
Bilting *Kent* 28 TR0549
Bilton *Humb* 85 TA1632
Bilton *N York* 83 SE4749
Bilton *N York* 89 SE3157
Bilton *Nthumb* 111 NU2210
Bilton *Warwks* 50 SP4873
Bilton Banks *Nthumb* 111 NU2010
Binbrook *Lincs* 76 TF2093
Binchester Blocks *Dur* 96 NZ2232
Bincombe *Dorset* 11 SY6884
Binegar *Somset* 21 ST6149
Bines Green *W Susx* 15 TQ1817
Binfield *Berks* 25 SU8471
Binfield Heath *Oxon* 37 SU7477
Bingfield *Nthumb* 102 NY9772
Bingham *Notts* 63 SK7039
Bingham's Melcombe *Dorset* 11 ST7702
Bingley *W York* 82 SE1039
Bings *Shrops* 59 SJ5318
Binham *Norfk* 66 TF9839
Binley *Hants* 24 SU4253
Binley *W Mids* 61 SP3778
Binnegar *Dorset* 11 SY8887
Binniehill *Cent* 116 NS8572
Binns Farm *Gramp* 141 NJ3164
Binscombe *Surrey* 25 SU9645
Binsey *Oxon* 37 SP4907
Binstead *Hants* 25 SU7740
Binstead *IOW* 13 SZ5892
Binsted *W Susx* 14 SU9806
Binton *Warwks* 48 SP1454
Bintree *Norfk* 66 TG0123
Binweston *Shrops* 59 SJ3004
Birch *Essex* 40 TL9419
Birch *Gt Man* 79 SD8507
Birch Close *Dorset* 11 ST8803
Birch Cross *Staffs* 73 SK1230
Birch Green *Essex* 40 TL9418
Birch Green *Herts* 39 TL2911
Birch Heath *Ches* 71 SJ5461
Birch Hill *Ches* 71 SJ5173
Birch Vale *Derbys* 74 SK0286
Birch Wood *Somset* 9 ST2414
Bircham Newton *Norfk* 65 TF7733
Bircham Tofts *Norfk* 65 TF7732
Birchanger *Essex* 39 TL5122
Birchburn *Strath* 105 NR9129
Birchencliffe *W York* 82 SE1218
Bircher *H & W* 46 SO4765
Birchfield *W Mids* 61 SP0790
Birchgrove *E Susx* 15 TQ4029
Birchgrove *S Glam* 33 ST1679
Birchgrove *W Glam* 32 SS7098
Birchington *Kent* 29 TR3069
Birchley Heath *Warwks* 61 SP2894
Birchmoor Green *Beds* 38 SP9534
Birchover *Derbys* 74 SK2362
Birchyfield *H & W* 47 SO6453
Bircotes *Notts* 75 SK6391
Bird End *W Mids* 60 SP0194
Bird Street *Suffk* 54 TM0052
Birdbrook *Essex* 53 TL7041
Birdforth *N York* 90 SE4875
Birdham *W Susx* 14 SU8200
Birdingbury *Warwks* 50 SP4368
Birdlip *Gloucs* 35 SO9214
Birdoswald *Cumb* 102 NY6166
Birds Edge *W York* 82 SE2007
Birds Green *Essex* 40 TL5808
Birdsall *N York* 90 SE8165
Birdsgreen *Shrops* 60 SO7785
Birdsmoorgate *Dorset* 10 ST3900
Birdwell *S York* 83 SE3401
Birdwood *Gloucs* 35 SO7418
Birgham *Border* 110 NT7939
Birichin *Highld* 147 NH7592
Birkacre *Lancs* 81 SD5714
Birkby *N York* 89 NZ3202
Birkdale *Mersyd* 80 SD3214
Birkenbog *Gramp* 142 NJ5365
Birkenhead *Mersyd* 78 SJ3288
Birkenhills *Gramp* 142 NJ7445
Birkenshaw *W York* 82 SE2028
Birkhall *Gramp* 134 NO3493
Birkhill *D & G* 109 NT2015
Birkhill *Tays* 126 NO3534
Birkholme *Lincs* 63 SK9623
Birkin *N York* 83 SE5326
Birks *W York* 82 SE2626
Birkshaw *Nthumb* 102 NY7765
Birley *H & W* 46 SO4553
Birley Carr *S York* 74 SK3392
Birling *Kent* 28 TQ6860
Birling *Nthumb* 111 NU2406
Birling Gap *E Susx* 16 TV5596
Birlingham *H & W* 47 SO9343
Birmingham *W Mids* 61 SP0786
Birnam *Tays* 125 NO0341
Birness *Gramp* 143 NJ9933
Birse *Gramp* 134 NO5697
Birsemore *Gramp* 134 NO5297
Birstall *Leics* 62 SK5909
Birstall *W York* 82 SE2225
Birstwith *N York* 89 SE2359
Birthorpe *Lincs* 64 TF1033
Birtley *H & W* 46 SO3669
Birtley *Nthumb* 102 NY8778
Birtley *T & W* 96 NZ2756
Birts Street *H & W* 47 SO7836
Bisbrooke *Leics* 51 SP8899
Biscathorpe *Lincs* 76 TF2284
Biscovey *Cnwll* 3 SX0552
Bish Mill *Devon* 19 SS7425
Bisham *Berks* 26 SU8485
Bishampton *H & W* 47 SO9951
Bishop Auckland *Dur* 96 NZ2028
Bishop Burton *Humb* 84 SE9839
Bishop Middleham *Dur* 96 NZ3231
Bishop Monkton *N York* 89 SE3266
Bishop Norton *Lincs* 76 SK9892
Bishop Sutton *Avon* 21 ST5859
Bishop Thornton *N York* 89 SE2563
Bishop Wilton *Humb* 84 SE7955
Bishop's Castle *Shrops* 59 SO3288
Bishop's Cleeve *Gloucs* 47 SO9627
Bishop's Frome *H & W* 47 SO6648
Bishop's Green *Essex* 40 TL6217
Bishop's Green *Hants* 24 SU5063
Bishop's Itchington *Warwks* 48 SP3857
Bishop's Norton *Gloucs* 47 SO8424
Bishop's Nympton *Devon* 19 SS7523
Bishop's Offley *Staffs* 72 SJ7729
Bishop's Stortford *Herts* 39 TL4821
Bishop's Sutton *Hants* 24 SU6032
Bishop's Tachbrook *Warwks* 48 SP3161
Bishop's Tawton *Devon* 19 SS5729
Bishop's Waltham *Hants* 13 SU5517
Bishop's Wood *Staffs* 60 SJ8309
Bishop`s Caundle *Dorset* 11 ST6913
Bishopbridge *Lincs* 76 TF0391
Bishopbriggs *Strath* 116 NS6070
Bishopmill *Gramp* 141 NJ2163
Bishops Cannings *Wilts* 23 SU0364
Bishops Gate *Surrey* 25 SU9871
Bishops Hull *Somset* 20 ST2024
Bishops Lydeard *Somset* 20 ST1729
Bishopsbourne *Kent* 29 TR1852
Bishopsteignton *Devon* 7 SX9073
Bishopstoke *Hants* 13 SU4619
Bishopston *W Glam* 32 SS5789
Bishopstone *Bucks* 38 SP8010
Bishopstone *E Susx* 16 TQ4701
Bishopstone *H & W* 46 SO4143
Bishopstone *Kent* 26 TQ2068
Bishopstone *Wilts* 23 SU0625
Bishopstone *Wilts* 36 SU2483
Bishopstrow *Wilts* 22 ST8943
Bishopswood *Somset* 10 ST2612
Bishopsworth *Avon* 21 ST5768
Bishopthorpe *N York* 83 SE5947
Bishopton *Dur* 96 NZ3621
Bishopton *Strath* 115 NS4371
Bishopton *Warwks* 48 SP1956
Bishton *Gwent* 34 ST3887
Bishton *Staffs* 73 SK0220
Bisley *Gloucs* 35 SO9005
Bisley *Surrey* 25 SU9559
Bisley Camp *Surrey* 25 SU9357
Bispham *Lancs* 80 SD3140
Bispham Green *Lancs* 80 SD4813
Bissoe *Cnwll* 3 SW7741
Bisterne *Hants* 12 SU1401
Bitchet Green *Kent* 27 TQ5654
Bitchfield *Lincs* 63 SK9828
Bittadon *Devon* 19 SS5441
Bittaford *Devon* 7 SX6656
Bittering *Norfk* 66 TF9417
Bitterley *Shrops* 46 SO5677
Bitterne *Hants* 13 SU4513
Bitteswell *Leics* 50 SP5385
Bitton *Avon* 35 ST6869
Bix *Oxon* 37 SU7284
Blaby *Leics* 50 SP5697
Black Bourton *Oxon* 36 SP2804
Black Callerton *T & W* 103 NZ1769
Black Car *Norfk* 66 TM0995
Black Corner *W Susx* 15 TQ2939
Black Corries *Highld* 123 NN2956
Black Crofts *Strath* 122 NM9234
Black Cross *Cnwll* 4 SW9060
Black Dog *Devon* 19 SS8009
Black Heddon *Nthumb* 103 NZ0775
Black Lane *Gt Man* 79 SD7708
Black Lane Ends *Lancs* 81 SD9243
Black Moor *W York* 82 SE2939
Black Notley *Essex* 40 TL7620
Black Street *Suffk* 55 TM5186
Black Tar *Dyfed* 30 SM9909
Black Torrington *Devon* 18 SS4605
Blackadder *Border* 119 NT8452
Blackawton *Devon* 7 SX8051
Blackbank *Warwks* 61 SP3586
Blackbeck *Cumb* 86 NY0207
Blackborough *Devon* 9 ST0909
Blackborough End *Norfk* 65 TF6615
Blackboys *E Susx* 16 TQ5220
Blackbrook *Derbys* 62 SK3347
Blackbrook *Staffs* 72 SJ7638
Blackbrook *Surrey* 15 TQ1846
Blackburn *Gramp* 135 NJ8212
Blackburn *Lancs* 81 SD6827
Blackburn *Loth* 117 NS9865
Blackcraig *Strath* 107 NS6308
Blackden Heath *Ches* 79 SJ7871
Blackdog *Gramp* 135 NJ9513
Blackdown *Devon* 5 SX5079
Blackdown *Dorset* 10 ST3903
Blackdyke *Cumb* 92 NY1452
Blackenall Heath *W Mids* 60 SK0002
Blacker *S York* 83 SE3309
Blacker Hill *S York* 83 SE3602
Blackfen *Gt Lon* 27 TQ4674
Blackfield *Hants* 13 SU4402
Blackford *Cumb* 101 NY3961
Blackford *Somset* 21 ST4147
Blackford *Somset* 21 ST6526
Blackford *Tays* 125 NN8908
Blackford Bridge *Gt Man* 79 SD8007
Blackfordby *Leics* 62 SK3217
Blackgang *IOW* 13 SZ4876
Blackhall *Dur* 97 NZ4638
Blackhall *Loth* 117 NT1975
Blackhall Colliery *Dur* 97 NZ4539
Blackhaugh *Border* 109 NT4238
Blackheath *Essex* 40 TM0021
Blackheath *Gt Lon* 27 TQ3876
Blackheath *Suffk* 55 TM4274
Blackheath *Surrey* 14 TQ0346
Blackheath *W Mids* 60 SO9786
Blackhill *Dur* 95 NZ0851
Blackhill *Gramp* 143 NK0039
Blackhill *Gramp* 143 NK0755
Blackhill *Gramp* 143 NK0843
Blackhill of Clackriach *Gramp* 143 NJ9246
Blackhorse *Devon* 9 SX9893
Blackhorse Hill *E Susx* 17 TQ7714
Blackjack *Lincs* 64 TF2639
Blackland *Somset* 19 SS8336
Blackland *Wilts* 22 SU0168
Blacklaw *D & G* 108 NT0408
Blackley *Gt Man* 79 SD8502
Blacklunans *Tays* 133 NO1460
Blackmarstone *H & W* 46 SO5038
Blackmill *M Glam* 33 SS9386
Blackmoor *Avon* 21 ST4661
Blackmoor *Hants* 14 SU7733
Blackmoorfoot *W York* 82 SE0913
Blackmore *Essex* 40 TL6001
Blackmore End *Essex* 40 TL7430
Blackmore End *Herts* 39 TL1716
Blackness *Loth* 117 NT0579
Blacknest *Berks* 25 SU9568
Blacknest *Hants* 25 SU7941
Blacko *Lancs* 81 SD8541
Blackpill *W Glam* 32 SS6190
Blackpool *Devon* 7 SX8547
Blackpool *Devon* 7 SX8174
Blackpool *Lancs* 80 SD3036
Blackpool Gate *Cumb* 101 NY5377
Blackridge *Loth* 116 NS8967
Blackrock *Cnwll* 2 SW6534
Blackrock *Gwent* 33 SO2112
Blackrock *Gwent* 34 ST5188
Blackrod *Gt Man* 78 SD6110
Blacksboat *Gramp* 141 NJ1838
Blackshaw *D & G* 100 NY0465
Blackshaw Head *W York* 82 SD9527
Blacksmith's Green *Suffk* 54 TM1465
Blacksnape *Lancs* 81 SD7121
Blackstone *W Susx* 15 TQ2316
Blackthorn *Oxon* 37 SP6219
Blackthorpe *Suffk* 54 TL9063
Blacktoft *Humb* 84 SE8324
Blacktop *Gramp* 135 NJ8604
Blackwall *Derbys* 73 SK2548
Blackwater *Cnwll* 3 SW7346
Blackwater *Hants* 25 SU8459
Blackwater *IOW* 13 SZ5086
Blackwater *Somset* 10 ST2615
Blackwaterfoot *Strath* 105 NR9028
Blackwell *Cumb* 93 NY4053
Blackwell *Derbys* 74 SK1272
Blackwell *Derbys* 75 SK4458
Blackwell *Dur* 89 NZ2713
Blackwell *H & W* 60 SO9972
Blackwell *Warwks* 48 SP2443
Blackwellsend Green *Gloucs* 47 SO7825
Blackwood *D & G* 100 NX9087
Blackwood *Gwent* 33 ST1797
Blackwood *Strath* 116 NS7844
Blackwood Hill *Staffs* 72 SJ9255
Blacon *Ches* 71 SJ3868
Bladbean *Kent* 29 TR1847
Bladnoch *D & G* 99 NX4254
Bladon *Oxon* 37 SP4514
Bladon *Somset* 21 ST4220
Blaen Dyryn *Powys* 45 SN9336
Blaen-y-Coed *Dyfed* 31 SN3427
Blaen-y-cwm *Gwent* 33 SO1311
Blaen-y-cwm *M Glam* 33 SS9298
Blaenannerch *Dyfed* 42 SN2448
Blaenau Ffestiniog *Gwynd* 57 SH7045
Blaenavon *Gwent* 34 SO2508
Blaenffos *Dyfed* 31 SN1937
Blaengarw *M Glam* 33 SS9092
Blaengeuffardd *Dyfed* 43 SN6480
Blaengwrach *W Glam* 33 SN8605
Blaengwynfi *W Glam* 33 SS8996
Blaenllechau *M Glam* 33 ST0097
Blaenpennal *Dyfed* 43 SN6264
Blaenplwyf *Dyfed* 43 SN5775
Blaenporth *Dyfed* 42 SN2648
Blaenrhondda *M Glam* 33 SS9299
Blaenwaun *Dyfed* 31 SN2327
Blaenycwm *Dyfed* 43 SN8275
Blagdon *Avon* 21 ST5059
Blagdon *Devon* 7 SX8561
Blagdon *Somset* 20 ST2118
Blagdon Hill *Somset* 9 ST2117
Blagill *Cumb* 94 NY7347
Blaguegate *Lancs* 78 SD4506
Blaich *Highld* 130 NN0376
Blain *Highld* 129 NM6769
Blaina *Gwent* 33 SO2008
Blair Atholl *Tays* 132 NN8665
Blair Drummond *Cent* 116 NS7399
Blairgowrie *Tays* 126 NO1745
Blairingone *Fife* 117 NS9896
Blairlogie *Cent* 116 NS8396
Blairmore *Highld* 148 NC1959
Blairmore *Strath* 114 NS1983
Blairnamarrow *Gramp* 141 NJ2015
Blairs Ferry *Strath* 114 NR9869
Blaisdon *Gloucs* 35 SO7017
Blake End *Essex* 40 TL7023
Blakebrook *H & W* 60 SO8276
Blakedown *H & W* 60 SO8878
Blakeley Lane *Staffs* 72 SJ9746
Blakemere *Ches* 71 SJ5571
Blakemere *H & W* 46 SO3641
Blakemore *Devon* 7 SX7660
Blakeney *Gloucs* 35 SO6707
Blakeney *Norfk* 66 TG0243
Blakenhall *Ches* 72 SJ7247
Blakenhall *W Mids* 60 SO9197
Blakeshall *H & W* 60 SO8381
Blakesley *Nhants* 49 SP6250
Blanchland *Nthumb* 95 NY9650
Bland Hill *N York* 82 SE2053
Blandford Camp *Dorset* 11 ST9107
Blandford Forum *Dorset* 11 ST8806
Blandford St Mary *Dorset* 11 ST8805
Blanefield *Cent* 115 NS5479
Blankney *Lincs* 76 TF0660
Blantyre *Strath* 116 NS6957
Blar a' Chaorainn *Highld* 130 NN1066
Blargie *Highld* 132 NN6094
Blarmachfoldach *Highld* 130 NN0969
Blashford *Hants* 12 SU1506
Blaston *Leics* 51 SP8095
Blatherwycke *Nhants* 51 SP9795

Bradninch
Bromfield

Bradninch Devon 9 SS9904
Bradnop Staffs 73 SK0155
Bradnor Green H & W 46 SO2957
Bradpole Dorset 10 SY4894
Bradshaw Gt Man 81 SD7312
Bradshaw W York 82 SE0514
Bradshaw W York 82 SE0729
Bradstone Devon 5 SX3880
Bradwall Green Ches 72 SJ7563
Bradwell Bucks 38 SP8340
Bradwell Derbys 74 SK1781
Bradwell Devon 19 SS5042
Bradwell Essex 40 TL8122
Bradwell Norfk 67 TG5003
Bradwell Waterside Essex 41 TL9907
Bradwell-on-Sea Essex 41 TM0006
Bradworthy Devon 18 SS3214
Brae Highld 140 NH6662
Brae Shet 155 HU3568
Brae Roy Lodge Highld 131 NN3391
Braeface Cent 116 NS7880
Braegrum Tays 125 NO0025
Braehead D & G 99 NX4152
Braehead Strath 117 NS9550
Braehead Tays 127 NO6952
Braelangwell Lodge Highld 146 NH5192
Braemar Gramp 133 NO1591
Braemore Highld 150 ND0829
Braemore Highld 145 NH2079
Braes of Coul Tays 133 NO2857
Braes of Enzie Gramp 142 NJ3957
Braeside Strath 114 NS2374
Braeswick Ork 155 HY6137
Braevallich Strath 122 NM9507
Brafferton Dur 96 NZ2921
Brafferton N York 89 SE4370
Brafield-on-the-Green Nhants 51 SP8258
Bragar W Isls 154 NB2947
Bragbury End Herts 39 TL2621
Braidwood Strath 116 NS8448
Brailsford Derbys 73 SK2541
Brailsford Green Derbys 73 SK2541
Brain's Green Gloucs 35 SO6609
Braintree Essex 40 TL7523
Braiseworth Suffk 54 TM1371
Braishfield Hants 23 SU3725
Braithwaite Cumb 93 NY2323
Braithwaite W York 82 SE0341
Braithwell S York 75 SK5394
Braken Hill W York 83 SE4216
Bramber W Susx 15 TQ1810
Brambridge Hants 13 SU4721
Bramcote Notts 62 SK5037
Bramcote Warwks 61 SP4088
Bramdean Hants 24 SU6128
Bramerton Norfk 67 TG2904
Bramfield Herts 39 TL2915
Bramfield Suffk 55 TM3973
Bramford Suffk 54 TM1246
Bramhall Gt Man 79 SJ8984
Bramham W York 83 SE4242
Bramhope W York 82 SE2543
Bramley Derbys 74 SK4079
Bramley Hants 24 SU6458
Bramley S York 75 SK4892
Bramley Surrey 25 TQ0044
Bramley W York 82 SE2435
Bramley Corner Hants 24 SU6359
Bramley Green Hants 24 SU6658
Bramley Head N York 89 SE1258
Bramling Kent 29 TR2256
Brampford Speke Devon 9 SX9298
Brampton Cambs 52 TL2170
Brampton Cumb 101 NY5361
Brampton Cumb 94 NY6723
Brampton Lincs 76 SK8479
Brampton Norfk 67 TG2223
Brampton S York 83 SE4101
Brampton Suffk 55 TM4381
Brampton Abbotts H & W 46 SO6026
Brampton Ash Nhants 50 SP7987
Brampton Bryan H & W 46 SO3772
Brampton-en-le-Morthen S York 75 SK4887
Bramshall Staffs 73 SK0532
Bramshaw Hants 12 SU2615
Bramshill Hants 24 SU7461
Bramshott Hants 14 SU8432
Bramwell Somset 21 ST4329
Bran End Essex 40 TL6525
Branault Highld 128 NM5269
Brancaster Norfk 65 TF7743
Brancaster Staithe Norfk 66 TF7944
Brancepeth Dur 96 NZ2237
Branch End Nthumb 103 NZ0661
Branchill Gramp 141 NJ0852
Brand End Lincs 64 TF3745
Brand Green Gloucs 47 SO7328
Branderburgh Gramp 141 NJ2371
Brandesburton Humb 85 TA1147
Brandeston Suffk 55 TM2460
Brandis Corner Devon 18 SS4104
Brandiston Norfk 66 TG1421
Brandon Dur 96 NZ2340
Brandon Lincs 76 SK9048
Brandon Nthumb 111 NU0417
Brandon Suffk 53 TL7886
Brandon Warwks 50 SP4176
Brandon Bank Cambs 53 TL6288
Brandon Creek Norfk 65 TL6091
Brandon Parva Norfk 66 TG0708
Brandsby N York 90 SE5872
Brandy Wharf Lincs 76 TF0196
Brane Cnwll 2 SW4028
Branksome Dorset 12 SZ0492
Branksome Park Dorset 12 SZ0590
Bransbury Hants 24 SU4242
Bransby Lincs 76 SK8978
Branscombe Devon 9 SY1988
Bransford H & W 47 SO7952
Bransgore Hants 12 SZ1897
Bransholme Humb 85 TA1033
Bransley Shrops 47 SO6575
Branson's Cross H & W 61 SP0970
Branston Leics 63 SK8129
Branston Lincs 76 TF0166
Branston Staffs 73 SK2221
Branston Booths Lincs 76 TF0668
Branstone IOW 13 SZ5583
Brant Broughton Lincs 76 SK9154
Brantham Suffk 54 TM1034
Branthwaite Cumb 92 NY0525
Branthwaite Cumb 93 NY2937
Brantingham Humb 84 SE9429
Branton Nthumb 111 NU0416
Branton S York 83 SE6401
Branton Green N York 89 SE4362
Branxton Nthumb 110 NT8937
Brassey Green Ches 71 SJ5260
Brassington Derbys 73 SK2254
Brasted Kent 27 TQ4755
Brasted Chart Kent 27 TQ4653
Brathens Gramp 135 NO6798
Bratoft Lincs 77 TF4764
Brattleby Lincs 76 SK9481
Bratton Shrops 59 SJ6413
Bratton Somset 20 SS9446
Bratton Wilts 22 ST9152
Bratton Clovelly Devon 5 SX4691
Bratton Fleming Devon 19 SS6437
Bratton Seymour Somset 22 ST6729
Braughing Herts 39 TL3925
Braughing Friars Herts 39 TL4124
Braunston Leics 63 SK8306
Braunston Nhants 50 SP5466
Braunstone Leics 62 SK5502
Braunton Devon 18 SS4836
Brawby N York 90 SE7378
Brawdy Dyfed 30 SM8524
Brawl Highld 150 NC8166
Braworth N York 90 NZ5007
Bray Berks 26 SU9079
Bray Shop Cnwll 5 SX3374
Bray's Hill E Susx 16 TQ6714
Braybrooke Nhants 50 SP7684
Braydon Wilts 36 SU0488
Braydon Brook Wilts 35 ST9891
Braydon Side Wilts 35 SU0185
Brayford Devon 19 SS6834
Braystones Cumb 86 NY0106
Braythorn N York 82 SE2449
Brayton N York 83 SE6030
Braywick Berks 26 SU8979
Braywoodside Berks 26 SU8775
Brazacott Cnwll 5 SX2691
Breach Kent 28 TQ8465
Breach Kent 29 TR1947
Breachwood Green Herts 39 TL1522
Breaden Heath Shrops 59 SJ4436
Breadsall Derbys 62 SK3639
Breadstone Gloucs 35 SO7000
Breadward H & W 46 SO2854
Breage Cnwll 2 SW6128
Breakachy Highld 139 NH4644
Bream Gloucs 34 SO6005
Breamore Hants 12 SU1517
Brean Somset 20 ST2956
Breanais W Isls 154 NA9925
Brearley W York 82 SE0225
Brearton N York 89 SE3261
Breascleit W Isls 154 NB2135
Breasclete W Isls 154 NB2135
Breaston Derbys 62 SK4533
Brechfa Dyfed 44 SN5230
Brechin Tays 134 NO6060
Breckles Norfk 66 TL9594
Breckonside D & G 100 NX8489
Brecon Powys 45 SO0428
Bredbury Gt Man 79 SJ9291
Brede E Susx 17 TQ8218
Bredenbury H & W 46 SO6056
Bredfield Suffk 55 TM2653
Bredgar Kent 28 TQ8860
Bredhurst Kent 28 TQ7962
Bredon H & W 47 SO9236
Bredon's Hardwick H & W 47 SO9135
Bredon's Norton H & W 47 SO9339
Bredwardine H & W 46 SO3344
Breedon on the Hill Leics 62 SK4022
Breich Loth 117 NS9560
Breightmet Gt Man 79 SD7409
Breighton Humb 84 SE7033
Breinton H & W 46 SO4739
Bremhill Wilts 35 ST9773
Bremridge Devon 19 SS6929
Brenchley Kent 28 TQ6741
Brendon Devon 18 SS3607
Brendon Devon 19 SS7748
Brendon Hill Somset 20 ST0234
Brenfield Strath 113 NR8482
Brenish W Isls 154 NA9925
Brenkley T & W 103 NZ2175
Brent Eleigh Suffk 54 TL9448
Brent Knoll Somset 21 ST3350
Brent Mill Devon 7 SX6959
Brent Pelham Herts 39 TL4330
Brentford Gt Lon 26 TQ1777
Brentingby Leics 63 SK7818
Brentwood Essex 27 TQ5993
Brenzett Kent 17 TR0027
Brenzett Green Kent 17 TR0128
Brereton Staffs 73 SK0516
Brereton Green Ches 72 SJ7764
Brereton Heath Ches 72 SJ8065
Brereton Hill Staffs 73 SK0515
Bressingham Norfk 54 TM0780
Bressingham Common Norfk 54 TM0981
Bretby Derbys 73 SK2922
Bretford Warwks 50 SP4377
Bretforton H & W 48 SP0944
Bretherdale Head Cumb 87 NY5705
Bretherton Lancs 80 SD4720
Brettabister Shet 155 HU4857
Brettenham Norfk 54 TL9383
Brettenham Suffk 54 TL9654
Bretton Clwyd 71 SJ3563
Bretton Derbys 74 SK2078
Brewer Street Surrey 27 TQ3251
Brewers End Essex 39 TL5521
Brewood Staffs 60 SJ8808
Briantspuddle Dorset 11 SY8193
Brick End Essex 40 TL5725
Brick Houses S York 74 SK3081
Brickenden Herts 39 TL3208
Bricket Wood Herts 26 TL1202
Brickkiln Green Essex 40 TL7331
Bricklehampton H & W 47 SO9742
Bride IOM 153 NX4401
Bridekirk Cumb 92 NY1133
Bridell Dyfed 31 SN1742
Bridestowe Devon 5 SX5189
Brideswell Gramp 142 NJ5738
Bridford Devon 8 SX8186
Bridge Cnwll 2 SW6744
Bridge Kent 29 TR1854
Bridge End Beds 38 TL0050
Bridge End Cumb 93 NY3748
Bridge End Cumb 86 SD1884
Bridge End Devon 7 SX6946
Bridge End Dur 95 NZ0236
Bridge End Essex 40 TL6731
Bridge End Lincs 64 TF1436
Bridge End Nthumb 102 NY8965
Bridge End Surrey 26 TQ0756
Bridge Fields Leics 62 SK4827
Bridge Green Essex 39 TL4636
Bridge Hewick N York 89 SE3370
Bridge of Alford Gramp 142 NJ5617
Bridge of Allan Cent 116 NS7997
Bridge of Avon Gramp 141 NJ1835
Bridge of Avon Gramp 141 NJ1520
Bridge of Balgie Tays 124 NN5746
Bridge of Brewlands Tays 133 NO1961
Bridge of Brown Highld 141 NJ1120
Bridge of Cally Tays 126 NO1351
Bridge of Canny Gramp 135 NO6597
Bridge of Craigisla Tays 126 NO2553
Bridge of Dee D & G 99 NX7359
Bridge of Don Gramp 135 NJ9409
Bridge of Dulsie Highld 140 NH9341
Bridge of Dye Gramp 135 NO6586
Bridge of Earn Tays 126 NO1318
Bridge of Ericht Tays 131 NN5258
Bridge of Feugh Gramp 135 NO7094
Bridge of Forss Highld 150 ND0368
Bridge of Gairn Gramp 134 NO3597
Bridge of Gaur Tays 124 NN5056
Bridge of Marnoch Gramp 142 NJ5950
Bridge of Orchy Strath 123 NN2939
Bridge of Tilt Tays 132 NN8765
Bridge of Tynet Gramp 141 NJ3861
Bridge of Walls Shet 155 HU2752
Bridge of Weir Strath 115 NS3965
Bridge of Westfield Highld 150 ND0664
Bridge Reeve Devon 19 SS6613
Bridge Sollers H & W 46 SO4142
Bridge Street Suffk 54 TL8749
Bridge Trafford Ches 71 SJ4571
Bridge Yate Avon 35 ST6872
Bridgefoot Cumb 92 NY0529
Bridgehampton Somset 21 ST5624
Bridgehill Dur 95 NZ0951
Bridgehouse Gate N York 89 SE1565
Bridgemary Hants 13 SU5803
Bridgend Border 109 NT5235
Bridgend Cumb 93 NY4014
Bridgend D & G 108 NT0708
Bridgend Devon 6 SX5548
Bridgend Dyfed 42 SN1745
Bridgend Fife 126 NO3911
Bridgend Gramp 141 NJ3731
Bridgend Gramp 142 NJ5135
Bridgend Loth 117 NT0475
Bridgend M Glam 33 SS9079
Bridgend Strath 112 NR3362
Bridgend Tays 126 NO1224
Bridgend Tays 134 NO5368
Bridgend of Lintrathen Tays 126 NO2854
Bridgerule Devon 18 SS2702
Bridges Shrops 59 SO3996
Bridgetown Devon 5 SX3389
Bridgetown Somset 20 SS9233
Bridgham Norfk 54 TL9685
Bridgnorth Shrops 60 SO7193
Bridgtown Staffs 60 SJ9808
Bridgwater Somset 20 ST2937
Bridlington Humb 91 TA1866
Bridport Dorset 10 SY4692
Bridstow H & W 46 SO5824
Brierfield Lancs 81 SD8436
Brierley Gloucs 35 SO6215
Brierley H & W 46 SO4955
Brierley W York 83 SE4010
Brierley Hill W Mids 60 SO9186
Brierton Cleve 97 NZ4730
Briery Cumb 93 NY2824
Brig o'Turk Cent 124 NN5306
Brigg Humb 84 TA0007
Briggate Norfk 67 TG3127
Briggswath N York 90 NZ8608
Brigham Cumb 92 NY0830
Brigham Cumb 93 NY2823
Brigham Humb 85 TA0753
Brighouse W York 82 SE1422
Brighstone IOW 13 SZ4282
Brightgate Derbys 74 SK2659
Brighthampton Oxon 36 SP3803
Brightholmlee Derbys 74 SK2895
Brightley Devon 8 SX6097
Brightling E Susx 16 TQ6820
Brightlingsea Essex 41 TM0817
Brighton Cnwll 3 SW9054
Brighton E Susx 15 TQ3104
Brighton le Sands Mersyd 78 SJ3098
Brightons Cent 116 NS9277
Brightor Cnwll 5 SX3561
Brightwalton Berks 36 SU4279
Brightwalton Green Berks 36 SU4278
Brightwalton Holt Berks 36 SU4377
Brightwell Oxon 37 SU5790
Brightwell Suffk 55 TM2543
Brightwell Baldwin Oxon 37 SU6595
Brightwell Upperton Oxon 37 SU6594
Brignall Dur 95 NZ0712
Brigsley Humb 85 TA2501
Brigsteer Cumb 87 SD4889
Brigstock Nhants 51 SP9485
Brill Bucks 37 SP6513
Brill Cnwll 3 SW7229
Brilley H & W 46 SO2648
Brimfield H & W 46 SO5267
Brimfield Cross H & W 46 SO5368
Brimington Derbys 74 SK4073
Brimley Devon 8 SX8077
Brimpsfield Gloucs 35 SO9312
Brimpton Berks 24 SU5564
Brimscombe Gloucs 35 SO8702
Brimstage Mersyd 78 SJ3082
Brincliffe S York 74 SK3284
Brind Humb 84 SE7430
Brindham Somset 21 ST5139
Brindister Shet 155 HU2857
Brindle Lancs 81 SD5924
Brineton Staffs 60 SJ8013
Bringhurst Leics 51 SP8492
Brington Cambs 51 TL0875
Brininghaм Norfk 66 TG0434
Brinkely Notts 75 SK7153
Brinkhill Lincs 77 TF3773
Brinkley Cambs 53 TL6354
Brinklow Warwks 50 SP4379
Brinkworth Wilts 35 SU0184
Brinscall Lancs 81 SD6221
Brinscombe Somset 21 ST4251
Brinsea Avon 21 ST4461
Brinsley Notts 75 SK4548
Brinsop H & W 46 SO4444
Brinsworth S York 74 SK4289
Brinton Norfk 66 TG0335
Brinyan Ork 155 HY4327
Brisco Cumb 93 NY4252
Brisley Norfk 66 TF9421
Brislington Avon 35 ST6270
Brissenden Green Kent 28 TQ9439
Bristol Avon 34 ST5972
Briston Norfk 66 TG0632
Brisworthy Devon 6 SX5665
Britannia Lancs 81 SD8821
Britford Wilts 23 SU1627
Brithdir Gwynd 57 SH7618
Brithdir M Glam 33 SO1401
British Gwent 34 SO2503
British Legion Village Kent 28 TQ7257
Briton Ferry W Glam 32 SS7394
Britwell Salome Oxon 37 SU6792
Brixham Devon 7 SX9255
Brixton Devon 6 SX5552
Brixton Gt Lon 27 TQ3175
Brixton Deverill Wilts 22 ST8638
Brixworth Nhants 50 SP7470
Brize Norton Oxon 36 SP2907
Broad Alley H & W 47 SO8867
Broad Blunsdon Wilts 36 SU1491
Broad Campden Gloucs 48 SP1537
Broad Carr W York 82 SE0919
Broad Chalke Wilts 23 SU0325
Broad Clough Lancs 81 SD8623
Broad Ford Kent 28 TQ7139
Broad Green Cambs 53 TL6859
Broad Green Cambs 53 TL6860
Broad Green Essex 40 TL8823
Broad Green H & W 47 SO7756
Broad Green H & W 60 SO9970
Broad Green Suffk 53 TL7859
Broad Haven Dyfed 30 SM8613
Broad Hill Cambs 53 TL5976
Broad Hinton Wilts 36 SU1075
Broad Laying Hants 24 SU4362
Broad Marston H & W 48 SP1446
Broad Meadow Staffs 72 SJ8348
Broad Oak Cumb 86 SD1194
Broad Oak E Susx 17 TQ8219
Broad Oak H & W 34 SO4821
Broad Oak Hants 24 SU7551
Broad Oak Kent 29 TR1761
Broad Oak Mersyd 78 SJ5395
Broad Road Suffk 55 TM2676
Broad Street E Susx 17 TQ8616
Broad Street Essex 39 TL5516
Broad Street Kent 28 TQ7672
Broad Street Kent 28 TR1139
Broad Street Wilts 23 SU1059
Broad Street Green Essex 40 TL8509
Broad Town Wilts 36 SU0977
Broad's Green Essex 40 TL6912
Broadbottom Gt Man 79 SJ9993
Broadbridge W Susx 14 SU8105
Broadbridge Heath W Susx 15 TQ1431
Broadclyst Devon 9 SX9897
Broadfield Dyfed 31 SN1303
Broadfield Strath 115 NS3373
Broadford Highld 129 NG6423
Broadford Bridge W Susx 14 TQ0921
Broadgairhill Border 109 NT2010
Broadgate Lincs 64 TF3610
Broadgrass Green Suffk 54 TL9663
Broadhaugh Border 119 NT8655
Broadheath Gt Man 79 SJ7689
Broadheath H & W 47 SO6665
Broadhembury Devon 9 ST1004
Broadhempston Devon 7 SX8066
Broadholme Notts 76 SK8874
Broadland Row E Susx 17 TQ8319
Broadlay Dyfed 31 SN3709
Broadley Gramp 142 NJ3961
Broadley Gt Man 81 SD8816
Broadley Common Essex 39 TL4207
Broadmayne Dorset 11 SY7286
Broadmere Hants 24 SU6247
Broadmoor Dyfed 31 SN0906
Broadmoor Gloucs 35 SO6415
Broadnymett Devon 8 SS7001
Broadoak Clwyd 71 SJ3658
Broadoak Dorset 10 SY4396
Broadoak E Susx 16 TQ6022
Broadoak Gloucs 35 SO6912
Broadstairs Kent 29 TR3967
Broadstone Dorset 11 SZ0095
Broadstone Gwent 34 SO5102
Broadstone Shrops 59 SO5489
Broadwas H & W 47 SO7555
Broadwater Herts 39 TL2422
Broadwater W Susx 15 TQ1404
Broadwaters H & W 60 SO8477
Broadway Dyfed 31 SN2910
Broadway Dyfed 31 SN3808
Broadway Dyfed 30 SM8713
Broadway H & W 48 SP0937
Broadway Somset 10 ST3215
Broadway Suffk 55 TM3979
Broadwell Gloucs 34 SO5811
Broadwell Gloucs 48 SP2027
Broadwell Oxon 36 SP2504
Broadwell Warwks 50 SP4565
Broadwey Dorset 11 SY6683
Broadwindsor Dorset 10 ST4302
Broadwood Kelly Devon 8 SS6106
Broadwoodwidger Devon 5 SX4189
Brobury H & W 46 SO3444
Brochel Highld 137 NG5846
Brock Lancs 80 SD5140
Brock's Green Hants 24 SU5061
Brockamin H & W 47 SO7753
Brockbridge Hants 13 SU6118
Brockdish Norfk 55 TM2179
Brockencote H & W 60 SO8873
Brockenhurst Hants 12 SU3002
Brocketsbrae Strath 108 NS8239
Brockford Green Suffk 54 TM1265
Brockford Street Suffk 54 TM1167
Brockhall Nhants 49 SP6362
Brockham Surrey 15 TQ1949
Brockhampton Gloucs 47 SO9326
Brockhampton Gloucs 36 SP0322
Brockhampton H & W 46 SO5931
Brockhampton Green Dorset 11 ST7106
Brockholes W York 82 SE1510
Brockhurst Derbys 74 SK3364
Brockhurst Warwks 50 SP4683
Brocklebank Cumb 93 NY3042
Brocklesby Lincs 85 TA1311
Brockley Avon 21 ST4666
Brockley Suffk 54 TL8371
Brockley Green Suffk 53 TL7247
Brockley Green Suffk 54 TL8254
Brockleymoor Cumb 94 NY4937
Brockmoor W Mids 60 SO9088
Brockscombe Devon 5 SX4695
Brockton Shrops 59 SJ3104
Brockton Shrops 60 SJ7103
Brockton Shrops 59 SO3285
Brockton Shrops 59 SO5794
Brockton Staffs 72 SJ8131
Brockweir Gwent 34 SO5401
Brockwood Park Hants 13 SU6226
Brockworth Gloucs 35 SO8916
Brocton Cnwll 4 SX0168
Brocton Staffs 72 SJ9619
Brodick Strath 105 NS0135
Brodie Gramp 140 NH9757
Brodsworth S York 83 SE5007
Brogaig Highld 136 NG4767
Brogborough Beds 38 SP9638
Broken Cross Ches 79 SJ6873
Broken Cross Ches 79 SJ8973
Brokenborough Wilts 35 ST9189
Brokerswood Wilts 22 ST8352
Bromborough Mersyd 78 SJ3582
Brome Suffk 54 TM1376
Brome Street Suffk 54 TM1576
Bromeswell Suffk 55 TM3050
Bromfield Cumb 93 NY1746
Bromfield Shrops 46 SO4876

Bromham

Burton

Bromham Beds 38 TL0051
Bromham Wilts 22 ST9665
Bromley Gt Lon 27 TQ4069
Bromley S York 74 SK3298
Bromley Shrops 60 SO7395
Bromley W Mids 60 SO9088
Bromley Common Gt Lon 27 TQ4266
Bromley Cross Essex 41 TM0627
Bromlow Shrops 59 SJ3201
Brompton Kent 28 TQ7668
Brompton N York 89 SE3796
Brompton N York 91 SE9482
Brompton Shrops 59 SJ5408
Brompton Ralph Somset 20 ST0832
Brompton Regis Somset 20 SS9531
Brompton-on-Swale N York 89 SE2199
Bromsash H & W 47 SO6524
Bromsberrow Gloucs 47 SO7433
Bromsberrow Heath Gloucs 47 SO7333
Bromsgrove H & W 60 SO9670
Bromstead Heath Staffs 72 SJ7917
Bromyard H & W 47 SO6554
Bromyard Downs H & W 47 SO6655
Bronaber Gwynd 57 SH7131
Bronant Dyfed 43 SN6467
Broncroft Shrops 59 SO5486
Brongest Dyfed 42 SN3245
Bronington Clwyd 71 SJ4839
Bronllys Powys 45 SO1434
Bronwydd Dyfed 31 SN4123
Bronydd Powys 45 SO2245
Bronygarth Shrops 58 SJ2637
Brook Dyfed 31 SN2609
Brook Hants 12 SU2714
Brook Hants 23 SU3429
Brook IOW 13 SZ3983
Brook Kent 29 TR0644
Brook Surrey 14 SU9237
Brook Surrey 14 TQ0546
Brook End Beds 51 TL0763
Brook End Beds 52 TL1547
Brook End Bucks 38 SP9244
Brook End Cambs 51 TL0773
Brook Hill Hants 12 SU2714
Brook House Clwyd 70 SJ0765
Brook Street Essex 27 TQ5793
Brook Street Kent 17 TQ9333
Brook Street Suffk 54 TL8248
Brook Street W Susx 15 TQ3026
Brooke Leics 63 SK8405
Brooke Norfk 67 TM2899
Brookfield Strath 115 NS4164
Brookhampton Hants 13 SU7106
Brookhampton Oxon 37 SU6098
Brookhampton Somset 21 ST6327
Brookhouse Lancs 87 SD5464
Brookhouse S York 75 SK5188
Brookhouse Green Ches 72 SJ8161
Brookhouses Derbys 74 SK0388
Brookland Kent 17 TQ9926
Brooklands Gt Man 79 SJ7890
Brookmans Park Herts 39 TL2404
Brooks Powys 58 SO1499
Brooks End Kent 29 TR2967
Brooks Green W Susx 14 TQ1224
Brooksby Leics 63 SK6715
Brookthorpe Gloucs 35 SO8312
Brookville Norfk 65 TL7396
Brookwood Surrey 25 SU9557
Broom Beds 39 TL1742
Broom Dur 96 NZ2441
Broom S York 75 SK4491
Broom Warwks 48 SP0853
Broom Green Norfk 66 TF9823
Broom Hill Dorset 12 SU0302
Broom Hill H & W 60 SO9175
Broom Hill Notts 62 SK5447
Broom Hill S York 83 SE4102
Broom Street Kent 28 TR0462
Broom's Green H & W 47 SO7132
Broome H & W 60 SO9078
Broome Norfk 67 TM3591
Broome Shrops 59 SO4080
Broome Park Nthumb 111 NU1012
Broomedge Ches 79 SJ7085
Broomer's Corner W Susx 14 TQ1220
Broomershill W Susx 14 TQ0619
Broomfield Essex 40 TL7010
Broomfield Kent 28 TQ8452
Broomfield Kent 29 TR1966
Broomfield Somset 20 ST2232
Broomfields Shrops 59 SJ4217
Broomfleet Humb 84 SE8727
Broomhall Surrey 25 SU9566
Broomhaugh Nthumb 103 NZ0261
Broomhill Nthumb 103 NU2401
Broomhill Green Ches 71 SJ6247
Broomley Nthumb 103 NZ0360
Broomsthorpe Norfk 66 TF8428
Brora Highld 147 NC9103
Broseley Shrops 60 SJ6701
Brotherhouse Bar Lincs 64 TF2614
Brotherlee Dur 95 NY9237
Brothertoft Lincs 77 TF2746
Brotherton N York 83 SE4825
Brotton Cleve 97 NZ6819
Broubster Highld 150 ND0359
Brough Cumb 95 NY7914
Brough Derbys 74 SK1882
Brough Highld 151 ND2273
Brough Humb 84 SE9326
Brough Notts 76 SK8458
Brough Shet 155 HU5665
Brough Lodge Shet 155 HU5892
Brough Sowerby Cumb 95 NY7912
Broughall Shrops 71 SJ5741
Broughton Border 108 NT1136
Broughton Bucks 38 SP8413
Broughton Bucks 38 SP8939
Broughton Cambs 52 TL2878
Broughton Clwyd 71 SJ3363
Broughton Gt Man 79 SD8201
Broughton Hants 23 SU3033
Broughton Humb 84 SE9608
Broughton Lancs 80 SD5234
Broughton N York 82 SD9451
Broughton N York 90 SE7673
Broughton Nhants 51 SP8375
Broughton Oxon 49 SP4138
Broughton S Glam 33 SS9270
Broughton Staffs 72 SJ7634
Broughton Astley Leics 50 SP5292
Broughton Beck Cumb 86 SD2882
Broughton Gifford Wilts 22 ST8763
Broughton Green H & W 47 SO9561
Broughton Hackett H & W 47 SO9254
Broughton Mains D & G 99 NX4545
Broughton Mills Cumb 86 SD2290
Broughton Moor Cumb 92 NY0533
Broughton Poggs Oxon 36 SP2303
Broughton Tower Cumb 86 SD2187
Broughton-in-Furness Cumb 86 SD2187
Broughty Ferry Tays 127 NO4630
Brow End Cumb 86 SD2674
Brow-of-the-Hill Norfk 65 TF6819
Brown Candover Hants 24 SU5739
Brown Edge Lancs 80 SD3614
Brown Edge Staffs 72 SJ9053
Brown Heath Ches 71 SJ4564
Brown Lees Staffs 72 SJ8756
Brown Street Suffk 54 TM0663
Brown's Green W Mids 61 SP0591
Brownber Cumb 87 NY7005
Brownheath Shrops 59 SJ4629
Brownhill Gramp 143 NJ8640
Brownhills Fife 127 NO5215
Brownhills W Mids 61 SK0405
Brownieside Nthumb 111 NU1623
Browninghill Green Hants 24 SU5859
Brownlow Heath Ches 72 SJ8360
Brownrigg Cumb 92 NY0420
Brownrigg Cumb 92 NY1652
Brownsham Devon 18 SS2826
Brownsover Warwks 50 SP5177
Brownston Devon 7 SX6952
Browston Green Norfk 67 TG4901
Broxa N York 91 SE9491
Broxbourne Herts 39 TL3606
Broxburn Loth 117 NT0872
Broxburn Loth 119 NT6977
Broxfield Nthumb 111 NU2016
Broxted Essex 40 TL5727
Broxton Ches 71 SJ4754
Broxwood H & W 46 SO3654
Broyle Side E Susx 16 TQ4513
Bruan Highld 151 ND3139
Bruar Tays 132 NN8265
Brucefield Highld 147 NH9386
Bruchag Strath 114 NS1157
Bruera Ches 71 SJ4360
Bruern Abbey Oxon 36 SP2620
Bruichladdich Strath 112 NR2661
Bruisyard Suffk 55 TM3266
Bruisyard Street Suffk 55 TM3365
Brumby Humb 84 SE8909
Brund Staffs 74 SK1061
Brundall Norfk 67 TG3308
Brundish Suffk 55 TM2769
Brundish Street Suffk 55 TM2671
Brunnian Cnwll 2 SW5036
Brunslow Shrops 59 SO3684
Bruntcliffe W York 82 SE2526
Brunthwaite W York 82 SE0546
Bruntingthorpe Leics 50 SP6089
Brunton Fife 126 NO3220
Brunton Nthumb 111 NU2024
Brunton Wilts 23 SU2456
Brushford Somset 20 SS9225
Brushford Barton Devon 8 SS6707
Bruton Somset 22 ST6835
Bryan's Green H & W 47 SO8868
Bryanston Dorset 11 ST8607
Bryant's Bottom Bucks 26 SU8599
Brydekirk D & G 101 NY1870
Brymbo Clwyd 71 SJ2953
Brympton Somset 10 ST5115
Bryn Ches 71 SJ6072
Bryn Gt Man 78 SD5600
Bryn Shrops 59 SO2985
Bryn W Glam 33 SS8192
Bryn Du Gwynd 68 SH3472
Bryn Gates Lancs 78 SD5901
Bryn Golau M Glam 33 ST0088
Bryn Saith Marchog Clwyd 70 SJ0750
Bryn-bwbach Gwynd 57 SH6236
Bryn-coch W Glam 32 SS7499
Bryn-Eden Gwynd 57 SH7129
Bryn-henllan Dyfed 30 SN0139
Bryn-mawr Gwynd 56 SH2433
Bryn-newydd Clwyd 70 SJ1842
Bryn-penarth Powys 58 SJ1004
Bryn-y-bal Clwyd 70 SJ2564
Bryn-y-maen Clwyd 69 SH8376
Bryn-yr-Eos Clwyd 70 SJ2840
Brynaman Dyfed 32 SN7114
Brynberian Dyfed 31 SN1035
Brynbryddan W Glam 32 SS7792
Bryncae M Glam 33 SS9982
Bryncethin M Glam 33 SS9183
Bryncir Gwynd 56 SH4844
Bryncroes Gwynd 56 SH2231
Bryncrug Gwynd 57 SH6103
Bryneglwys Clwyd 70 SJ1447
Brynfields Clwyd 71 SJ3044
Brynford Clwyd 70 SJ1774
Bryngwran Gwynd 68 SH3577
Bryngwyn Gwent 34 SO3909
Bryngwyn Powys 45 SO1849
Brynhoffnant Dyfed 42 SN3351
Bryning Lancs 80 SD4029
Brynithel Gwent 33 SO2101
Brynmawr Gwent 33 SO1911
Brynmenyn M Glam 33 SS9084
Brynmill W Glam 32 SS6392
Brynna M Glam 33 SS9883
Brynrefail Gwynd 68 SH4886
Brynrefail Gwynd 69 SH5562
Brynsadler M Glam 33 ST0280
Brynsiencyn Gwynd 68 SH4867
Brynteg Gwynd 68 SH4982
Bualintur Highld 128 NG4020
Buarth-draw Clwyd 70 SJ1779
Bubbenhall Warwks 61 SP3672
Bubwith Humb 84 SE7136
Buchanan Smithy Cent 115 NS4689
Buchanhaven Gramp 143 NK1247
Buchanty Tays 125 NN9328
Buchany Cent 124 NN7102
Buchlyvie Cent 115 NS5793
Buck's Cross Devon 18 SS3522
Buck's Mills Devon 18 SS3523
Buckabank Cumb 93 NY3749
Buckden Cambs 52 TL1967
Buckden N York 88 SD9477
Buckenham Norfk 67 TG3505
Buckerell Devon 9 ST1200
Buckfast Devon 7 SX7467
Buckfastleigh Devon 7 SX7366
Buckhaven Fife 118 NT3598
Buckholm Border 109 NT4738
Buckholt Gwent 34 SO5016
Buckhorn Weston Dorset 22 ST7524
Buckhurst Hill Essex 27 TQ4194
Buckie Gramp 142 NJ4265
Buckingham Bucks 49 SP6933
Buckland Bucks 38 SP8812
Buckland Devon 7 SX6743
Buckland Gloucs 48 SP0835
Buckland Hants 12 SZ3196
Buckland Herts 39 TL3533
Buckland Kent 29 TR3042
Buckland Oxon 36 SU3498
Buckland Surrey 26 TQ2150
Buckland Brewer Devon 18 SS4220
Buckland Common Bucks 38 SP9207
Buckland Dinham Somset 22 ST7551
Buckland Filleigh Devon 18 SS4609
Buckland in the Moor Devon 7 SX7273
Buckland Monachorum Devon 6 SX4968
Buckland Newton Dorset 11 ST6805
Buckland Ripers Dorset 11 SY6582
Buckland St Mary Somset 10 ST2613
Buckland-Tout-Saints Devon 7 SX7645
Bucklebury Berks 24 SU5570
Bucklerheads Tays 127 NO4636
Bucklers Hard Hants 13 SU4000
Bucklesham Suffk 55 TM2441
Buckley Clwyd 70 SJ2763
Buckley Green Warwks 48 SP1567
Buckley Mountain Clwyd 70 SJ2765
Bucklow Hill Ches 79 SJ7383
Buckminster Leics 63 SK8722
Bucknall Lincs 76 TF1668
Bucknall Staffs 72 SJ9047
Bucknell Oxon 49 SP5625
Bucknell Shrops 46 SO3574
Buckpool Gramp 142 NJ4165
Bucks Green W Susx 14 TQ0833
Bucks Hill Herts 26 TL0500
Bucks Horn Oak Hants 25 SU8041
Bucksburn Gramp 135 NJ8909
Buckshead Cnwll 3 SW8346
Buckton H & W 46 SO3873
Buckton Humb 91 TA1872
Buckton Nthumb 111 NU0838
Buckworth Cambs 52 TL1476
Budbrooke Warwks 48 SP2665
Budby Notts 75 SK6169
Budd's Titson Cnwll 18 SS2401
Buddileigh Staffs 72 SJ7449
Buddon Tays 127 NO5232
Bude Cnwll 18 SS2105
Budge's Shop Cnwll 5 SX3259
Budlake Devon 9 SS9800
Budle Nthumb 111 NU1535
Budleigh Salterton Devon 9 SY0682
Budlett's Common E Susx 16 TQ4723
Budock Water Cnwll 3 SW7831
Buerton Ches 72 SJ6843
Bugbrooke Nhants 49 SP6757
Bugford Devon 7 SX8350
Buglawton Ches 72 SJ8763
Bugle Cnwll 4 SX0158
Bugley Dorset 22 ST7824
Bugthorpe Humb 90 SE7757
Buildwas Shrops 59 SJ6204
Builth Road Powys 45 SO0353
Builth Wells Powys 45 SO0350
Bulbourne Herts 38 SP9313
Bulbridge Wilts 23 SU0830
Bulby Lincs 64 TF0526
Buldoo Highld 150 ND0067
Bulford Wilts 23 SU1643
Bulford Barracks Wilts 23 SU1843
Bulkeley Ches 71 SJ5354
Bulkington Warwks 61 SP3986
Bulkington Wilts 22 ST9458
Bulkworthy Devon 18 SS3914
Bull Bay Gwynd 68 SH4294
Bull's Green Herts 39 TL2717
Bull's Green Norfk 67 TM4194
Bullamore N York 89 SE3994
Bullbridge Derbys 74 SK3552
Bullbrook Berks 25 SU8869
Bullen's Green Herts 39 TL2105
Bulley Gloucs 35 SO7619
Bullgill Cumb 92 NY0938
Bullinghope H & W 46 SO5136
Bullington Hants 24 SU4541
Bullington Lincs 76 TF0877
Bullington End Bucks 38 SP8145
Bullockstone Kent 29 TR1665
Bulmer Essex 54 TL8440
Bulmer N York 90 SE6967
Bulmer Tye Essex 54 TL8438
Bulphan Essex 40 TQ6385
Bulstone Devon 9 SY1789
Bulstrode Herts 26 TL0302
Bulstrode Park Bucks 26 SU9888
Bulterley Heath Staffs 72 SJ7450
Bulverhythe E Susx 17 TQ7708
Bulwark Gramp 143 NJ9345
Bulwell Notts 62 SK5343
Bulwick Nhants 51 SP9694
Bumble's Green Essex 39 TL4005
Bunacaimb Highld 129 NM6588
Bunarkaig Highld 131 NN1887
Bunbury Ches 71 SJ5657
Bunbury Heath Ches 71 SJ5558
Bunchrew Highld 140 NH6246
Buncton W Susx 15 TQ1413
Bundalloch Highld 138 NG8927
Bunessan Strath 121 NM3821
Bungay Suffk 55 TM3389
Bunker's Hill Lincs 77 TF2653
Bunnahabhainn Strath 112 NR4173
Bunny Notts 62 SK5829
Buntait Highld 139 NH4030
Buntingford Herts 39 TL3629
Bunwell Norfk 66 TM1292
Bunwell Street Norfk 66 TM1193
Bupton Derbys 73 SK2237
Burbage Derbys 74 SK0472
Burbage Leics 50 SP4492
Burbage Wilts 23 SU2261
Burcher H & W 46 SO3360
Burchett's Green Berks 26 SU8481
Burchett's Green E Susx 16 TQ6631
Burcombe Wilts 23 SU0730
Burcot H & W 60 SO9871
Burcot Oxon 37 SU5695
Burcote Shrops 60 SO7495
Burcott Bucks 38 SP8415
Burcott Bucks 38 SP8823
Burdale N York 90 SE8762
Bures Suffk 54 TL9034
Burford H & W 46 SO5868
Burford Oxon 36 SP2512
Burg Strath 121 NM3845
Burgates Hants 14 SU7728
Burge End Herts 38 TL1432
Burgess Hill W Susx 15 TQ3218
Burgh Suffk 55 TM2351
Burgh by Sands Cumb 93 NY3259
Burgh Castle Norfk 67 TG4805
Burgh Heath Surrey 26 TQ2457
Burgh Hill E Susx 17 TQ7226
Burgh Le Marsh Lincs 77 TF5065
Burgh next Aylsham Norfk 67 TG2125
Burgh on Bain Lincs 76 TF2186
Burgh St Margaret Norfk 67 TG4413
Burgh St Peter Norfk 67 TM4693
Burghclere Hants 24 SU4761
Burghead Gramp 141 NJ1168
Burghfield Berks 24 SU6668
Burghfield Common Berks 24 SU6566
Burghill H & W 46 SO4844
Burghwallis S York 83 SE5311
Burham Kent 28 TQ7262
Buriton Hants 13 SU7419
Burland Ches 71 SJ6153
Burlawn Cnwll 4 SW9970
Burleigh Berks 25 SU9169
Burleigh Gloucs 35 SO8601
Burlescombe Devon 9 ST0716
Burleston Dorset 11 SY7794
Burlestone Devon 7 SX8248
Burley Hants 12 SU2102
Burley Leics 63 SK8810
Burley Shrops 59 SO4881
Burley Gate H & W 46 SO5947
Burley in Wharfedale W York 82 SE1646
Burley Lawn Hants 12 SU2103
Burley Street Hants 12 SU2004
Burley Wood Head W York 82 SE1544
Burleydam Ches 71 SJ6042
Burlingham Green Norfk 67 TG3610
Burlingjobb Powys 46 SO2558
Burlington Shrops 60 SJ7711
Burlton Shrops 59 SJ4526
Burmarsh Kent 17 TR1032
Burmington Warwks 48 SP2637
Burn N York 83 SE5928
Burn Cross S York 74 SK3496
Burn Naze Lancs 80 SD3443
Burn of Cambus Cent 124 NN7102
Burnage Gt Man 79 SJ8692
Burnaston Derbys 73 SK2832
Burnbanks Cumb 94 NY5016
Burnbrae Strath 116 NS8759
Burnby Humb 84 SE8346
Burndell W Susx 14 SU9802
Burnden Gt Man 79 SD7207
Burnedge Gt Man 79 SD9110
Burneside Cumb 87 SD5095
Burneston N York 89 SE3084
Burnett Avon 22 ST6665
Burnfoot Border 109 NT4113
Burnfoot Border 109 NT5116
Burnfoot D & G 100 NX9791
Burnfoot D & G 101 NY3388
Burnfoot D & G 101 NY3996
Burnfoot Tays 125 NN9904
Burnham Bucks 26 SU9282
Burnham Humb 84 TA0516
Burnham Deepdale Norfk 66 TF8044
Burnham Green Herts 39 TL2616
Burnham Market Norfk 66 TF8342
Burnham Norton Norfk 66 TF8343
Burnham Overy Norfk 66 TF8442
Burnham Overy Staithe Norfk 66 TF8444
Burnham Thorpe Norfk 66 TF8541
Burnham-on-Crouch Essex 40 TQ9496
Burnham-on-Sea Somset 20 ST3049
Burnhaven Gramp 143 NK1244
Burnhead D & G 100 NX8695
Burnhervie Gramp 142 NJ7319
Burnhill Green Staffs 60 SJ7800
Burnhope Dur 96 NZ1948
Burnhouse Strath 115 NS3850
Burniston N York 91 TA0193
Burnley Lancs 81 SD8432
Burnmouth Border 119 NT9560
Burnopfield Dur 96 NZ1757
Burnrigg Cumb 94 NY4856
Burnsall N York 88 SE0361
Burnside Fife 126 NO1608
Burnside Fife 117 NT0575
Burnside Gramp 147 NJ1769
Burnside Tays 134 NO4259
Burnside Tays 127 NO5050
Burnside of Duntrune Tays 127 NO4434
Burnt Heath Essex 41 TM0627
Burnt Hill Berks 24 SU5774
Burnt Houses Dur 96 NZ1223
Burnt Oak E Susx 16 TQ5126
Burnt Yates N York 89 SE2561
Burntcommon Surrey 26 TQ0354
Burntheath Derbys 73 SK2431
Burnthouse Cnwll 3 SW7636
Burntisland Fife 117 NT2385
Burntwood Staffs 61 SK0509
Burntwood Green Staffs 61 SK0608
Burnville Devon 5 SX4982
Burnworthy Somset 9 ST1915
Burpham Surrey 26 TQ0152
Burpham W Susx 14 TQ0308
Burradon Nthumb 111 NT9806
Burradon T & W 103 NZ2772
Burrafirth Shet 155 HP6113
Burras Cnwll 2 SW6734
Burraton Cnwll 5 SX4167
Burraton Devon 6 SX6153
Burravoe Shet 155 HU5180
Burrells Cumb 94 NY6718
Burrelton Tays 126 NO2037
Burridge Devon 19 SS5735
Burridge Devon 10 ST3106
Burridge Hants 13 SU5110
Burrill N York 89 SE2387
Burringham Humb 84 SE8309
Burrington Avon 21 ST4859
Burrington Devon 19 SS6416
Burrington H & W 46 SO4472
Burrough End Cambs 53 TL6255
Burrough Green Cambs 53 TL6355
Burrough on the Hill Leics 63 SK7510
Burrow Lancs 87 SD6174
Burrow Somset 20 SS9342
Burrow Bridge Somset 21 ST3530
Burrowhill Surrey 25 SU9762
Burrows Cross Surrey 14 TQ0846
Burry W Glam 32 SS4590
Burry Port Dyfed 32 SN4400
Burrygreen W Glam 32 SS4591
Burscough Lancs 78 SD4310
Burscough Bridge Lancs 80 SD4412
Bursea Humb 84 SE8033
Burshill Humb 85 TA0948
Bursledon Hants 13 SU4809
Burslem Staffs 72 SJ8649
Burstall Suffk 54 TM0944
Burstock Dorset 10 ST4202
Burston Norfk 54 TM1383
Burston Staffs 72 SJ9330
Burstow Surrey 15 TQ3141
Burstwick Humb 85 TA2227
Burtersett N York 88 SD8989
Burtholme Cumb 101 NY5463
Burthorpe Green Suffk 53 TL7764
Burthwaite Cumb 93 NY4149
Burthy Cnwll 3 SW9155
Burtle Hill Somset 21 ST3843
Burtoft Lincs 64 TF2635
Burton Ches 71 SJ3174
Burton Ches 71 SJ5063
Burton Dorset 11 SY6891
Burton Dorset 12 SZ1694
Burton Dyfed 30 SM9805
Burton Lincs 76 SK9574
Burton Nthumb 111 NU1833
Burton Somset 20 ST1944

Burton

Carnbo

Burton Somset 10 ST5313
Burton Wilts 35 ST8179
Burton Wilts 22 ST8232
Burton Agnes Humb 91 TA1062
Burton Bradstock Dorset 10 SY4889
Burton Coggles Lincs 63 SK9725
Burton Dassett Warwks 48 SP3951
Burton End Essex 39 TL5323
Burton End Suffk 53 TL6645
Burton Fleming Humb 91 TA0871
Burton Green Clwyd 71 SJ3458
Burton Green Warwks 61 SP2675
Burton Hastings Warwks 50 SP4189
Burton in Lonsdale N York 87 SD6572
Burton Joyce Notts 63 SK6443
Burton Latimer Nhants 51 SP9074
Burton Lazars Leics 63 SK7716
Burton Leonard N York 89 SE3263
Burton on the Wolds Leics 62 SK5821
Burton Overy Leics 50 SP6798
Burton Pedwardine Lincs 64 TF1142
Burton Pidsea Humb 85 TA2431
Burton Salmon N York 83 SE4927
Burton upon Stather Humb 84 SE8717
Burton upon Trent Staffs 73 SK2323
Burton's Green Essex 40 TL8226
Burton-in-Kendal Cumb 87 SD5376
Burtonwood Ches 78 SJ5692
Burwardsley Ches 71 SJ5156
Burwarton Shrops 59 SO6185
Burwash E Susx 16 TQ6724
Burwash Common E Susx 16 TQ6323
Burwash Weald E Susx 16 TQ6523
Burwell Cambs 53 TL5866
Burwell Lincs 77 TF3579
Burwen Gwynd 68 SH4293
Burwick Ork 155 ND4484
Bury Cambs 52 TL2883
Bury Gt Man 81 SD8011
Bury Somset 20 SS9427
Bury W Susx 14 TQ0113
Bury End Beds 38 TL1235
Bury End Bucks 26 SU9697
Bury Green Herts 39 TL4521
Bury St Edmunds Suffk 54 TL8564
Burythorpe N York 90 SE7964
Busby Strath 115 NS5756
Buscot Wilts 36 SU2298
Bush Cnwll 18 SS2307
Bush Gramp 135 NO7565
Bush Bank H & W 46 SO4551
Bush Green Norfk 55 TM2187
Bush Green Suffk 54 TL9157
Bush Hill Park Gt Lon 27 TQ3395
Bushbury W Mids 60 SJ9202
Bushby Leics 63 SK6503
Bushey Herts 26 TQ1395
Bushey Heath Herts 26 TQ1494
Bushley H & W 47 SO8734
Bushley Green H & W 47 SO8634
Bushmead Beds 52 TL1160
Bushton Wilts 36 SU0677
Busk Cumb 94 NY6042
Buslingthorpe Lincs 76 TF0785
Bussage Gloucs 35 SO8803
Bussex Somset 21 ST3535
Butcher Hill W York 81 SD9322
Butcher's Cross E Susx 16 TQ5525
Butcher's Pasture Essex 40 TL6024
Butcombe Avon 21 ST5161
Butleigh Somset 21 ST5233
Butleigh Wootton Somset 21 ST5035
Butler's Cross Bucks 38 SP8407
Butler's Hill Notts 75 SK5448
Butlers Green Staffs 72 SJ8150
Butlers Marston Warwks 48 SP3250
Butley Suffk 55 TM3650
Butley Corner Suffk 55 TM3849
Butt Green Ches 72 SJ6651
Butt Lane Staffs 72 SJ8254
Butt's Green Essex 40 TL7603
Buttercrambe N York 90 SE7358
Butterdean Border 119 NT7964
Butterknowle Dur 95 NZ1025
Butterleigh Devon 9 SS9708
Butterley Derbys 74 SK4051
Buttermere Cumb 93 NY1717
Buttermere Wilts 23 SU3461
Buttershaw W York 82 SE1329
Butterstone Tays 125 NO0645
Butterton Staffs 72 SJ8242
Butterton Staffs 73 SK0756
Butterwick Dur 96 NZ3830
Butterwick Lincs 64 TF3845
Butterwick N York 90 SE7277
Butterwick N York 91 SE9871
Buttington Powys 58 SJ2408
Buttonbridge Shrops 60 SO7379
Buttonoak Shrops 60 SO7578
Buttsash Hants 13 SU4206
Buttsbear Cross Cnwll 18 SS2604
Buxhall Suffk 54 TM0057
Buxhall Fen Street Suffk 54 TM0059
Buxted E Susx 16 TQ4923
Buxton Derbys 74 SK0572
Buxton Norfk 67 TG2322
Buxton Heath Norfk 66 TG1821
Bwlch Powys 33 SO1522
Bwlch-y-cibau Powys 58 SJ1717
Bwlch-y-ffridd Powys 58 SO0795
Bwlch-y-groes Dyfed 31 SN2436
Bwlch-y-sarnau Powys 45 SO0374
Bwlchgwyn Clwyd 70 SJ2653
Bwlchllan Dyfed 44 SN5758
Bwlchnewydd Dyfed 31 SN3624
Bwlchtocyn Gwynd 56 SH3125
Bwlchyddar Clwyd 58 SJ1722
Bwlchyfadfa Dyfed 42 SN4349
Bwlchymyrdd W Glam 32 SS5798
Byermoor T & W 96 NZ1857
Byers Garth Dur 96 NZ3140
Byers Green Dur 96 NZ2233
Byfield Nhants 49 SP5152
Byfleet Surrey 26 TQ0661
Byford H & W 46 SO3942
Byker T & W 103 NZ2764
Bylchau Clwyd 70 SH9762
Byley Ches 79 SJ7269
Bynea Dyfed 32 SS5499
Byrewalls Border 110 NT6642
Byrness Nthumb 102 NT7602
Bystock Devon 9 SY0283
Bythorn Cambs 51 TL0575
Byton H & W 46 SO3764
Bywell Nthumb 103 NZ0461
Byworth W Susx 14 SU9821

C

Cabourne Lincs 85 TA1401
Cabrach Gramp 141 NJ3826
Cabrach Strath 112 NR4964
Cabus Lancs 80 SD4948
Cabvie Lodge Highld 138 NH1567
Cackle Street E Susx 16 TQ4526
Cackle Street E Susx 16 TQ6919
Cackle Street E Susx 17 TQ8218
Cadbury Devon 9 SS9105
Cadbury Barton Devon 19 SS6917
Cadder Strath 116 NS6072
Caddington Beds 38 TL0619
Caddonfoot Border 109 NT4535
Cade Street E Susx 16 TQ6020
Cadeby Leics 62 SK4202
Cadeby S York 75 SE5100
Cadeleigh Devon 9 SS9108
Cadgwith Cnwll 3 SW7214
Cadham Fife 126 NO2801
Cadishead Gt Man 79 SJ7091
Cadle W Glam 32 SS6296
Cadley Lancs 80 SD5231
Cadley Wilts 23 SU2066
Cadley Wilts 23 SU2453
Cadmore End Bucks 37 SU7892
Cadnam Hants 12 SU3013
Cadney Humb 84 TA0103
Cadole Clwyd 70 SJ2062
Cadoxton S Glam 20 ST1269
Cadoxton Juxta-Neath W Glam 32 SS7598
Cadsden Bucks 38 SP8204
Cadwst Clwyd 58 SJ0235
Cae'r bryn Dyfed 32 SN5913
Cae'r-bont Powys 32 SN8011
Caeathro Gwynd 68 SH5061
Caehopkin Powys 33 SN8212
Caenby Lincs 76 SK9989
Caenby Corner Lincs 76 SK9689
Caeo Dyfed 44 SN6740
Caer Farchell Dyfed 30 SM7927
Caerau M Glam 33 SS8694
Caerau S Glam 33 ST1375
Caerdeon Gwynd 57 SH6518
Caergeiliog Gwynd 68 SH3178
Caergwrle Clwyd 71 SJ3057
Caerhun Gwynd 69 SH7770
Caerlanrig Border 109 NT3904
Caerleon Gwent 34 ST3490
Caernarfon Gwynd 68 SH4862
Caerphilly M Glam 33 ST1587
Caersws Powys 58 SO0392
Caerwedros Dyfed 42 SN3755
Caerwent Gwent 34 ST4790
Caerwys Clwyd 70 SJ1272
Caerynwch Gwynd 57 SH7617
Caggle Street Gwent 34 SO3717
Caim Gwynd 69 SH6280
Cairinis W Isls 154 NF8260
Cairinis W Isls 154 NB2133
Cairnbaan Strath 113 NR8390
Cairnbrogie Gramp 143 NJ8527
Cairnbulg Gramp 143 NK0365
Cairncross Border 119 NT8963
Cairncurran Strath 115 NS3170
Cairndow Strath 123 NN1810
Cairneyhill Fife 117 NT0486
Cairnfield House Gramp 142 NJ4162
Cairngarroch D & G 98 NX0549
Cairngrassie Gramp 135 NO9095
Cairnhall D & G 100 NX9086
Cairnie Gramp 142 NJ4844
Cairnorrie Gramp 143 NJ8641
Cairnryan D & G 98 NX0668
Cairnty Gramp 141 NJ3352
Caister-on-Sea Norfk 67 TG5112
Caistor Lincs 85 TA1101
Caistor St Edmund Norfk 67 TG2303
Cake Street Norfk 54 TM0690
Cakebole H & W 60 SO8772
Calais Street Suffk 54 TL9739
Calbourne IOW 13 SZ4286
Calceby Lincs 77 TF3875
Calcot Berks 24 SU6671
Calcot Clwyd 70 SJ1674
Calcot Gloucs 36 SP0810
Calcot Row Berks 24 SU6771
Calcots Gramp 141 NJ2563
Calcott Kent 29 TR1762
Calcott Shrops 59 SJ4413
Calcutt N York 83 SE3455
Calcutt Wilts 36 SU1193
Caldbeck Cumb 93 NY3240
Caldbergh N York 89 SE0985
Caldecote Cambs 52 TL1488
Caldecote Cambs 52 TL3456
Caldecote Herts 39 TL2338
Caldecote Nhants 49 SP6851
Caldecote Highfields Cambs 52 TL3559
Caldecott Leics 51 SP8693
Caldecott Nhants 51 SP9868
Caldecott Oxon 37 SU4996
Calder Bridge Cumb 86 NY0306
Calder Grove W York 82 SE3016
Calder Vale Lancs 80 SD5345
Calderbank Strath 116 NS7663
Calderbrook Gt Man 82 SD9418
Caldercote Bucks 38 SP8935
Caldercruix Strath 116 NS8167
Caldermill Strath 107 NS6641
Caldermore Gt Man 81 SD9316
Caldicot Gwent 34 ST4888
Caldwell N York 89 NZ1613
Caldy Mersyd 78 SJ2285
Caledfwlch Dyfed 44 SN6525
Calendra Cnwll 3 SW9240
Calenick Cnwll 3 SW8243
Calford Green Suffk 53 TL7045
Calfsound Ork 155 HY5738
Calgary Strath 121 NM3751
Califer Gramp 141 NJ0857
California Cent 116 NS9076
California Derbys 62 SK3335
California Norfk 67 TG5115
California Suffk 54 TM0641
California Cross Devon 7 SX7053
Calke Derbys 62 SK3721
Callakille Highld 137 NG6955
Callaly Nthumb 111 NU0509
Callander Cent 124 NN6207
Callanish W Isls 154 NB2133
Callaughton Shrops 59 SO6197
Callert Cottage Highld 130 NN1060
Callestick Cnwll 3 SW7750
Calligarry Highld 129 NG6203
Callington Cnwll 5 SX3669
Callingwood Staffs 73 SK1823
Callow H & W 46 SO4934
Callow End H & W 47 SO8350
Callow Hill H & W 60 SO7573
Callow Hill H & W 47 SP0164
Callow Hill Wilts 36 SU0384
Callows Grave H & W 46 SO5967
Calmore Hants 12 SU3414
Calmsden Gloucs 36 SP0508
Calne Wilts 35 ST9971
Calow Derbys 74 SK4071
Calshot Hants 13 SU4701
Calstock Cnwll 6 SX4368
Calstone Wellington Wilts 23 SU0268
Calthorpe Norfk 66 TG1831
Calthorpe Street Norfk 67 TG4025
Calthwaite Cumb 93 NY4640
Calton N York 88 SD9059
Calton Staffs 73 SK1049
Calton Green Staffs 73 SK1049
Calveley Ches 71 SJ5958
Calver Derbys 74 SK2374
Calver Hill H & W 46 SO3748
Calver Sough Derbys 74 SK2374
Calverhall Shrops 59 SJ6037
Calverleigh Devon 9 SS9214
Calverley W York 82 SE2036
Calvert Bucks 49 SP6824
Calverton Bucks 38 SP7939
Calverton Notts 75 SK6149
Calvine Tays 132 NN8065
Calvo Cumb 92 NY1453
Calzeat Border 108 NT1135
Cam Gloucs 35 ST7599
Camas Luinie Highld 138 NG9428
Camasachoirce Highld 130 NM7660
Camasine Highld 130 NM7561
Camastianavaig Highld 137 NG5039
Camasunary Highld 128 NG5118
Camault Muir Highld 139 NH5040
Camber E Susx 17 TQ9618
Camberley Surrey 25 SU8860
Camberwell Gt Lon 27 TQ3276
Camblesforth N York 83 SE6425
Cambo Nthumb 103 NZ0285
Cambois Nthumb 103 NZ3083
Camborne Cnwll 2 SW6440
Cambridge Cambs 53 TL4558
Cambridge Gloucs 35 SO7403
Cambrose Cnwll 2 SW6845
Cambus Cent 116 NS8594
Cambus O' May Gramp 134 NO4198
Cambusavie Platform Highld 147 NH7696
Cambusbarron Cent 116 NS7792
Cambuskenneth Cent 116 NS8094
Cambuslang Strath 116 NS6460
Cambuswallace Strath 108 NT0438
Camden Town Gt Lon 27 TQ2883
Cameley Avon 21 ST6157
Camelford Cnwll 4 SX1083
Camelon Cent 116 NS8680
Camer's Green H & W 47 SO7735
Camerory Highld 141 NJ0131
Camerton Avon 22 ST6857
Camerton Cumb 92 NY0330
Camghouran Tays 124 NN5556
Camieston Border 110 NT5730
Cammachmore Gramp 135 NO9195
Cammeringham Lincs 76 SK9482
Camore Highld 147 NH7889
Camp The Gloucs 35 SO9109
Campbeltown Strath 105 NR7120
Camperdown T & W 103 NZ2772
Cample D & G 100 NX8993
Campmuir Tays 126 NO2137
Camps Loth 117 NT0968
Camps End Cambs 53 TL6142
Campsall S York 83 SE5413
Campsie Strath 116 NS6079
Campsie Ash Suffk 55 TM3356
Campton Beds 38 TL1238
Camptown Border 110 NT6813
Camrose Dyfed 30 SM9220
Camserney Tays 125 NN8149
Camster Highld 151 ND2642
Camusnagaul Highld 145 NH0589
Camusnagaul Highld 130 NN0874
Camusteel Highld 137 NG7042
Camusterrach Highld 137 NG7141
Canada Hants 12 SU2818
Canal Foot Cumb 86 SD3177
Canaston Bridge Dyfed 30 SN0615
Candacraig Gramp 134 NO3499
Candle Street Suffk 54 TM0374
Candlesby Lincs 77 TF4567
Candover Green Shrops 59 SJ5005
Candyburn Strath 108 NT0741
Cane End Oxon 37 SU6779
Canewdon Essex 40 TQ9094
Canford Bottom Dorset 12 SU0305
Canford Cliffs Dorset 12 SZ0589
Canford Magna Dorset 12 SZ0398
Canhams Green Suffk 54 TM0565
Canisbay Highld 151 ND3472
Canklow S York 74 SK4291
Canley W Mids 61 SP3077
Cann Dorset 22 ST8721
Cannich Highld 139 NH3331
Canning Town Gt Lon 27 TQ4081
Cannington Somset 20 ST2539
Cannock Staffs 60 SJ9810
Cannock Wood Staffs 61 SK0412
Cannon Bridge H & W 46 SO4340
Canon Frome H & W 47 SO6443
Canon Pyon H & W 46 SO4548
Canonbie D & G 101 NY3976
Canons Ashby Nhants 49 SP5750
Canonstown Cnwll 2 SW5335
Canterbury Kent 29 TR1457
Cantley Norfk 67 TG3704
Cantley S York 83 SE6202
Cantlop Shrops 59 SJ5205
Canton S Glam 33 ST1676
Cantraywood Highld 140 NH7847
Cantsfield Lancs 87 SD6272
Canvey Island Essex 40 TQ7983
Canwick Lincs 76 SK9869
Canworthy Water Cnwll 5 SX2291
Caol Highld 130 NN1175
Caolas Scalpaigh W Isls 154 NG2198
Caoles Strath 120 NM0848
Caonich Highld 130 NN0692
Capel Kent 16 TQ6344
Capel Surrey 15 TQ1740
Capel Bangor Dyfed 43 SN6580
Capel Betws Lleucu Dyfed 44 SN6058
Capel Coch Gwynd 68 SH4682
Capel Curig Gwynd 69 SH7258
Capel Cynon Dyfed 42 SN3849
Capel Dewi Dyfed 31 SN4542
Capel Dewi Dyfed 32 SN4720
Capel Garmon Gwynd 69 SH8155
Capel Green Suffk 55 TM3649
Capel Gwyn Dyfed 32 SN4622
Capel Gwyn Gwynd 68 SH3475
Capel Gwynfe Dyfed 32 SN7222
Capel Hendre Dyfed 32 SN5911
Capel Isaac Dyfed 44 SN5926
Capel Iwan Dyfed 31 SN2936
Capel le Ferne Kent 29 TR2539
Capel Llanilltern M Glam 33 ST0979
Capel Mawr Gwynd 68 SH4171
Capel Seion Dyfed 43 SN6379
Capel St Andrew Suffk 55 TM3748
Capel St Mary Suffk 54 TM0838
Capel Trisant Dyfed 43 SN7175
Capel-Dewi Dyfed 43 SN6282
Capel-y-ffin Powys 46 SO2531
Capel-y-graig Gwynd 69 SH5469
Capelles Guern 152 GN0000
Capeluchaf Gwynd 68 SH4349
Capelulo Gwynd 69 SH7476
Capenhurst Ches 71 SJ3673
Capernwray Lancs 87 SD5371
Capheaton Nthumb 103 NZ0380
Caplaw Strath 115 NS4458
Capon's Green Suffk 55 TM2867
Cappercleuch Border 109 NT2423
Capstone Kent 28 TQ7865
Capton Devon 7 SX8353
Capton Somset 20 ST0839
Caputh Tays 125 NO0840
Car Colston Notts 63 SK7142
Caradon Town Cnwll 5 SX2971
Carbeth Inn Cent 115 NS5279
Carbis Cnwll 4 SX0059
Carbis Bay Cnwll 2 SW5238
Carbost Highld 136 NG3731
Carbost Highld 136 NG4248
Carbrook S York 74 SK3889
Carbrooke Norfk 66 TF9402
Carburton Notts 75 SK6172
Carclaze Cnwll 3 SX0254
Carclew Cnwll 3 SW7838
Carcroft S York 83 SE5409
Cardenden Fife 117 NT2195
Cardeston Shrops 59 SJ3912
Cardewlees Cumb 93 NY3551
Cardhu Gramp 141 NJ1943
Cardiff S Glam 33 ST1876
Cardigan Dyfed 42 SN1746
Cardinal's Green Cambs 53 TL6146
Cardington Beds 38 TL0847
Cardington Shrops 59 SO5095
Cardinham Cnwll 4 SX1268
Cardrain D & G 98 NX1231
Cardrona Border 109 NT3038
Cardross Strath 115 NS3477
Cardryne D & G 98 NX1132
Cardurnock Cumb 93 NY1758
Careby Lincs 64 TF0216
Careston Tays 134 NO5260
Carew Dyfed 30 SN0403
Carew Cheriton Dyfed 30 SN0402
Carew Newton Dyfed 30 SN0404
Carey H & W 46 SO5730
Carfin Strath 116 NS7759
Carfraemill Border 118 NT5053
Cargate Green Norfk 67 TG3912
Cargen D & G 100 NX9672
Cargenbridge D & G 100 NX9575
Cargill Tays 126 NO1536
Cargo Cumb 93 NY3659
Cargreen Cnwll 6 SX4362
Cargurrel Cnwll 3 SW8737
Carham Nthumb 110 NT7938
Carhampton Somset 20 ST0042
Carharrack Cnwll 3 SW7341
Carie Tays 124 NN6257
Carinish W Isls 154 NF8260
Carisbrooke IOW 13 SZ4888
Cark Cumb 87 SD3676
Carkeel Cnwll 5 SX4160
Carlabhagh W Isls 154 NB2043
Carland Cross Cnwll 3 SW8554
Carlbury Dur 96 NZ2115
Carlby Lincs 64 TF0413
Carlcroft Nthumb 110 NT8311
Carlecotes S York 82 SE1703
Carleen Cnwll 2 SW6130
Carlesmoor N York 89 SE2073
Carleton Cumb 93 NY4252
Carleton Cumb 94 NY5329
Carleton Lancs 80 SD3339
Carleton N York 82 SD9749
Carleton N York 89 SE3959
Carleton W York 83 SE4620
Carleton Forehoe Norfk 66 TG0905
Carleton Rode Norfk 66 TM1093
Carleton St Peter Norfk 67 TG3402
Carlidnack Cnwll 3 SW7729
Carlin How Cleve 97 NZ7019
Carlincraig Gramp 142 NJ6743
Carlingcott Avon 22 ST6958
Carlisle Cumb 93 NY3956
Carloggas Cnwll 4 SW8765
Carlops Border 117 NT1656
Carloway W Isls 154 NB2043
Carlton Beds 51 SP9555
Carlton Cambs 53 TL6452
Carlton Cleve 96 NZ3921
Carlton Cumb 86 NY0109
Carlton Leics 62 SK3904
Carlton N York 90 NZ5004
Carlton N York 88 SE0684
Carlton N York 90 SE6086
Carlton N York 83 SE6423
Carlton Notts 62 SK6041
Carlton S York 83 SE3610
Carlton Suffk 55 TM3764
Carlton W York 83 SE3327
Carlton Colville Suffk 55 TM5189
Carlton Curlieu Leics 50 SP6997
Carlton Green Cambs 53 TL6451
Carlton Husthwaite N York 90 SE4976
Carlton in Lindrick Notts 75 SK5883
Carlton Miniott N York 89 SE3981
Carlton Scroop Lincs 63 SK9445
Carlton-le-Moorland Lincs 76 SK9058
Carlton-on-Trent Notts 75 SK7963
Carluddon Cnwll 3 SX0255
Carluke Strath 116 NS8450
Carlyon Bay Cnwll 3 SX0552
Carmacoup Strath 107 NS7927
Carmarthen Dyfed 31 SN4120
Carmel Clwyd 70 SJ1676
Carmel Dyfed 32 SN5816
Carmel Gwynd 68 SH4954
Carmichael Strath 108 NS9238
Carminowe Cnwll 2 SW6623
Carmunnock Strath 115 NS5957
Carmyle Strath 116 NS6462
Carmyllie Tays 127 NO5442
Carn Brea Cnwll 2 SW6841
Carn-gorm Highld 138 NG9520
Carnaby Humb 91 TA1465
Carnbee Fife 127 NO5206
Carnbo Tays 125 NO0503

Cheney Longville
Clopton Corner

Cheney Longville *Shrops* 59 SO4284
Chenies *Bucks* 26 TQ0198
Chepstow *Gwent* 34 ST5393
Chequerbent *Gt Man* 79 SD6706
Chequers Corner *Norfk* 65 TF4908
Cherhill *Wilts* 36 SU0370
Cherington *Gloucs* 35 ST9098
Cherington *Warwks* 48 SP2936
Cheriton *Devon* 19 SS7346
Cheriton *Hants* 24 SU5828
Cheriton *Kent* 29 TR2037
Cheriton *W Glam* 32 SS4593
Cheriton Bishop *Devon* 8 SX7793
Cheriton Fitzpaine *Devon* 9 SS8606
Cheriton or Stackpole Elidor *Dyfed* 30 SR9897
Cherrington *Shrops* 72 SJ6619
Cherry Burton *Humb* 84 SE9841
Cherry Hinton *Cambs* 53 TL4856
Cherry Orchard *H & W* 47 SO8553
Cherry Willingham *Lincs* 76 TF0272
Chertsey *Surrey* 26 TQ0466
Cheselbourne *Dorset* 11 SY7699
Chesham *Bucks* 26 SP9601
Chesham *Gt Man* 81 SD8012
Chesham Bois *Bucks* 26 SU9699
Cheshunt *Herts* 27 TL3502
Chesley *Kent* 28 TQ8563
Cheslyn Hay *Staffs* 60 SJ9707
Chessetts Wood *Warwks* 61 SP1873
Chessington *Surrey* 26 TQ1863
Chester *Ches* 71 SJ4066
Chester Moor *Dur* 96 NZ2649
Chester-le-Street *Dur* 96 NZ2751
Chesterblade *Somset* 22 ST6641
Chesterfield *Derbys* 74 SK3871
Chesterfield *Staffs* 61 SK0905
Chesterhill *Loth* 118 NT3764
Chesters *Border* 110 NT6022
Chesters *Border* 110 NT6210
Chesterton *Cambs* 64 TL1295
Chesterton *Cambs* 53 TL4660
Chesterton *Gloucs* 35 SP0100
Chesterton *Oxon* 37 SP5621
Chesterton *Shrops* 60 SO7897
Chesterton *Staffs* 72 SJ8349
Chesterton Green *Warwks* 48 SP3558
Chesterwood *Nthumb* 102 NY8364
Chestfield *Kent* 29 TR1365
Chestnut Street *Kent* 28 TQ8763
Cheston *Devon* 7 SX6858
Cheswardine *Shrops* 72 SJ7130
Cheswell *Shrops* 72 SJ7116
Cheswick *Nthumb* 111 NU0346
Cheswick Green *W Mids* 61 SP1376
Chetnole *Dorset* 10 ST6008
Chettiscombe *Devon* 9 SS9614
Chettisham *Cambs* 53 TL5483
Chettle *Dorset* 11 ST9513
Chetton *Shrops* 60 SO6690
Chetwode *Bucks* 49 SP6429
Chetwynd *Shrops* 72 SJ7321
Chetwynd Aston *Shrops* 72 SJ7517
Cheveley *Cambs* 53 TL6861
Chevening *Kent* 27 TQ4857
Cheverton *IOW* 13 SZ4583
Chevington *Suffk* 53 TL7859
Chevington Drift *Nthumb* 103 NZ2598
Chevithorne *Devon* 9 SS9715
Chew Magna *Avon* 21 ST5763
Chew Moor *Gt Man* 79 SD6607
Chew Stoke *Avon* 21 ST5561
Chewton Keynsham *Avon* 21 ST6566
Chewton Mendip *Somset* 21 ST5953
Chichacott *Devon* 8 SX6096
Chicheley *Bucks* 38 SP9046
Chichester *W Susx* 14 SU8604
Chickerell *Dorset* 11 SY6480
Chickering *Suffk* 55 TM2176
Chicklade *Wilts* 22 ST9134
Chickward *H & W* 46 SO2853
Chidden *Hants* 13 SU6517
Chiddingfold *Surrey* 14 SU9635
Chiddingly *E Susx* 16 TQ5414
Chiddingstone *Kent* 16 TQ5045
Chiddingstone Causeway *Kent* 16 TQ5246
Chideock *Dorset* 10 SY4292
Chidham *W Susx* 14 SU7903
Chidswell *W York* 82 SE2623
Chieveley *Berks* 24 SU4774
Chignall Smealy *Essex* 40 TL6611
Chignall St James *Essex* 40 TL6610
Chigwell *Essex* 27 TQ4494
Chigwell Row *Essex* 27 TQ4693
Chilbolton *Hants* 23 SU3940
Chilcomb *Hants* 24 SU5028
Chilcombe *Dorset* 10 SY5291
Chilcompton *Somset* 21 ST6451
Chilcote *Leics* 61 SK2811
Child Okeford *Dorset* 11 ST8312
Child's Ercall *Shrops* 72 SJ6625
Childer Thornton *Ches* 71 SJ3677
Childrey *Oxon* 36 SU3687
Childswickham *H & W* 48 SP0738
Childwall *Mersyd* 78 SJ4189
Childwick Bury *Herts* 38 TL1410
Childwick Green *Herts* 38 TL1410
Chilfrome *Dorset* 10 SY5898
Chilgrove *W Susx* 14 SU8314
Chilham *Kent* 29 TR0653
Chilhampton *Wilts* 23 SU0933
Chilla *Devon* 18 SS4402
Chillaton *Devon* 5 SX4381
Chillenden *Kent* 29 TR2753
Chillerton *IOW* 13 SZ4883
Chillesford *Suffk* 55 TM3852
Chillingham *Nthumb* 111 NU0525
Chillington *Devon* 7 SX7942
Chillington *Somset* 10 ST3811
Chilmark *Wilts* 22 ST9732
Chilmington Green *Kent* 28 TQ9840
Chilson *Oxon* 36 SP3119
Chilsworthy *Cnwll* 5 SX4172
Chilsworthy *Devon* 18 SS3206
Chiltern Green *Beds* 38 TL1319
Chilthorne Domer *Somset* 21 ST5219
Chilton *Bucks* 37 SP6811
Chilton *Devon* 9 SS8604
Chilton *Dur* 96 NZ2829
Chilton *Kent* 29 TR2743
Chilton *Oxon* 37 SU4885
Chilton *Suffk* 54 TL8842
Chilton Candover *Hants* 24 SU5940
Chilton Cantelo *Somset* 21 ST5722
Chilton Foliat *Wilts* 36 SU3170
Chilton Polden *Somset* 21 ST3740
Chilton Street *Suffk* 53 TL7546
Chilton Trinity *Somset* 20 ST2939
Chilwell *Notts* 62 SK5135
Chilworth *Hants* 13 SU4018
Chilworth *Surrey* 14 TQ0347
Chimney *Oxon* 36 SP3501
Chineham *Hants* 24 SU6555
Chingford *Gt Lon* 27 TQ3894
Chinley *Derbys* 74 SK0482
Chinnor *Oxon* 37 SP7501
Chipchase Castle *Nthumb* 102 NY8775
Chipnall *Shrops* 72 SJ7231
Chippenham *Cambs* 53 TL6669
Chippenham *Wilts* 35 ST9173
Chipperfield *Herts* 26 TL0401
Chipping *Herts* 39 TL3531
Chipping *Lancs* 81 SD6243
Chipping Campden *Gloucs* 48 SP1539
Chipping Hill *Essex* 40 TL8215
Chipping Norton *Oxon* 48 SP3127
Chipping Ongar *Essex* 39 TL5503
Chipping Sodbury *Avon* 35 ST7282
Chipping Warden *Nhants* 49 SP4948
Chipstable *Somset* 20 ST0427
Chipstead *Kent* 27 TQ5056
Chipstead *Surrey* 27 TQ2756
Chirbury *Shrops* 58 SO2698
Chirk *Clwyd* 58 SJ2837
Chirnside *Border* 119 NT8756
Chirnsidebridge *Border* 119 NT8556
Chirton *Wilts* 23 SU0757
Chisbury *Wilts* 23 SU2766
Chiselborough *Somset* 10 ST4614
Chiseldon *Wilts* 36 SU1880
Chisholme *Border* 109 NT4112
Chislehampton *Oxon* 37 SU5999
Chislehurst *Gt Lon* 27 TQ4470
Chislet *Kent* 29 TR2264
Chisley *W York* 82 SE0028
Chiswellgreen *Herts* 38 TL1304
Chiswick *Gt Lon* 26 TQ2078
Chiswick End *Cambs* 52 TL3745
Chisworth *Derbys* 79 SJ9991
Chitcombe *E Susx* 17 TQ8120
Chithurst *W Susx* 14 SU8423
Chittering *Cambs* 53 TL4969
Chitterne *Wilts* 22 ST9843
Chittlehamholt *Devon* 19 SS6520
Chittlehampton *Devon* 19 SS6325
Chittlehampton *Devon* 19 SS6511
Chittoe *Wilts* 22 ST9566
Chivelstone *Devon* 7 SX7838
Chivenor *Devon* 19 SS5034
Chlenry *D & G* 98 NX1260
Chobham *Surrey* 25 SU9762
Cholderton *Wilts* 23 SU2242
Cholesbury *Bucks* 38 SP9307
Chollerford *Nthumb* 102 NY9170
Chollerton *Nthumb* 102 NY9372
Cholsey *Oxon* 37 SU5886
Cholstrey *H & W* 46 SO4659
Chop Gate *N York* 90 SE5599
Choppington *Nthumb* 103 NZ2484
Chopwell *T & W* 95 NZ1158
Chorley *Ches* 71 SJ5751
Chorley *Lancs* 81 SD5817
Chorley *Shrops* 60 SO6983
Chorley *Staffs* 61 SK0710
Chorleywood *Herts* 26 TQ0396
Chorleywood West *Herts* 26 TQ0296
Chorlton *Ches* 72 SJ7250
Chorlton Lane *Ches* 71 SJ4547
Chorlton-cum-Hardy *Gt Man* 79 SJ8193
Choulton *Shrops* 59 SO3788
Chowley *Ches* 71 SJ4756
Chrishall *Essex* 39 TL4439
Chrisswell *Strath* 114 NS2274
Christchurch *Cambs* 65 TL4996
Christchurch *Dorset* 12 SZ1592
Christchurch *Gloucs* 34 SO5613
Christchurch *Gwent* 34 ST3489
Christian Malford *Wilts* 35 ST9678
Christleton *Ches* 71 SJ4465
Christmas Common *Oxon* 37 SU7193
Christon *Avon* 21 ST3757
Christon Bank *Nthumb* 111 NU2123
Christow *Devon* 8 SX8385
Chuck Hatch *E Susx* 16 TQ4733
Chudleigh *Devon* 9 SX8679
Chudleigh Knighton *Devon* 8 SX8477
Chulmleigh *Devon* 19 SS6814
Chunal *Derbys* 74 SK0390
Church *Lancs* 81 SD7429
Church Ashton *Shrops* 72 SJ7317
Church Brampton *Nhants* 50 SP7165
Church Brough *Cumb* 95 NY7913
Church Broughton *Derbys* 73 SK2033
Church Crookham *Hants* 25 SU8051
Church Eaton *Staffs* 72 SJ8417
Church End *Beds* 38 SP9832
Church End *Beds* 38 SP9921
Church End *Beds* 38 TL0334
Church End *Beds* 51 TL0558
Church End *Beds* 51 TL1058
Church End *Beds* 39 TL1937
Church End *Cambs* 51 TL0873
Church End *Cambs* 52 TL2082
Church End *Cambs* 52 TL3278
Church End *Cambs* 53 TL4857
Church End *Essex* 40 TL6223
Church End *Essex* 40 TL7228
Church End *Essex* 40 TL7316
Church End *Gt Lon* 26 TQ2490
Church End *Hants* 24 SU6756
Church End *Herts* 38 TL1011
Church End *Herts* 39 TL2630
Church End *Herts* 39 TL4422
Church End *Lincs* 64 TF2234
Church End *Lincs* 77 TF4295
Church End *Warwks* 61 SP2490
Church End *Warwks* 61 SP2992
Church Enstone *Oxon* 48 SP3725
Church Fenton *N York* 83 SE5136
Church Green *Devon* 9 SY1796
Church Gresley *Derbys* 73 SK2918
Church Hanborough *Oxon* 36 SP4213
Church Hill *Ches* 72 SJ6465
Church Hill *Staffs* 60 SK0011
Church Houses *N York* 90 SE6697
Church Knowle *Dorset* 11 SY9481
Church Laneham *Notts* 75 SK8176
Church Langton *Leics* 50 SP7293
Church Lawford *Warwks* 50 SP4576
Church Lawton *Staffs* 72 SJ8255
Church Leigh *Staffs* 73 SK0235
Church Lench *H & W* 48 SP0251
Church Mayfield *Staffs* 73 SK1544
Church Minshull *Ches* 72 SJ6660
Church Norton *W Susx* 14 SZ8795
Church Preen *Shrops* 59 SO5498
Church Pulverbatch *Shrops* 59 SJ4303
Church Stoke *Powys* 58 SO2794
Church Stowe *Nhants* 49 SP6357
Church Street *Essex* 53 TL7943
Church Street *Kent* 28 TQ7174
Church Street *Suffk* 55 TM4883
Church Stretton *Shrops* 59 SO4593
Church Town *Humb* 84 SE7806
Church Village *M Glam* 33 ST0885
Church Warsop *Notts* 75 SK5668
Church Wilne *Derbys* 62 SK4431
Churcham *Gloucs* 35 SO7618
Churchbridge *Staffs* 60 SJ9808
Churchdown *Gloucs* 35 SO8819
Churchend *Essex* 41 TR0093
Churchfield *W Mids* 60 SP0192
Churchgate *Herts* 27 TL3402
Churchgate Street *Essex* 39 TL4811
Churchill *Avon* 21 ST4459
Churchill *Devon* 19 SS5940
Churchill *Devon* 10 ST2902
Churchill *H & W* 60 SO8879
Churchill *H & W* 47 SO9253
Churchill *Oxon* 48 SP2824
Churchinford *Devon* 9 ST2112
Churchover *Warwks* 50 SP5180
Churchstanton *Somset* 9 ST1914
Churchstow *Devon* 7 SX7145
Churchthorpe *Lincs* 77 TF3297
Churchtown *Derbys* 74 SK2662
Churchtown *Devon* 19 SS6744
Churchtown *Lancs* 80 SD3240
Churchtown *Lancs* 80 SD4843
Churchtown *Mersyd* 80 SD3618
Churnsike Lodge *Nthumb* 102 NY6677
Churston Ferrers *Devon* 7 SX9056
Churt *Surrey* 25 SU8538
Churton *Ches* 71 SJ4156
Churwell *W York* 82 SE2729
Chwilog *Gwynd* 56 SH4338
Chyandour *Cnwll* 2 SW4731
Chyanvounder *Cnwll* 2 SW6522
Chyeowling *Cnwll* 3 SW7941
Chyvarloe *Cnwll* 2 SW6523
Cil *Powys* 58 SJ1701
Cilcain *Clwyd* 70 SJ1765
Cilcennin *Dyfed* 44 SN5260
Cilcewydd *Powys* 58 SJ2204
Cilfrew *W Glam* 32 SN7700
Cilfynydd *M Glam* 33 ST0891
Cilgerran *Dyfed* 31 SN1942
Cilgwyn *Dyfed* 44 SN7429
Cilgwyn *Gwynd* 68 SH4953
Ciliau-Aeron *Dyfed* 44 SN5057
Cilmaengwyn *W Glam* 32 SN7405
Cilmery *Powys* 45 SO0051
Cilrhedyn *Dyfed* 31 SN2834
Cilsan *Dyfed* 32 SN5922
Ciltalgarth *Gwynd* 57 SH8940
Cilycwm *Dyfed* 44 SN7539
Cimla *W Glam* 32 SS7696
Cinder Hill *W Mids* 60 SO9294
Cinderford *Gloucs* 35 SO6514
Cippenham *Bucks* 26 SU9480
Cirencester *Gloucs* 35 SP0201
Citadilla *N York* 89 SE2299
City *Gt Lon* 27 TQ3281
City *S Glam* 33 SS9878
City Dulas *Gwynd* 68 SH4687
Clabhach *Strath* 120 NM1858
Clachaig *Strath* 114 NS1181
Clachan *Highld* 137 NG5436
Clachan *Strath* 122 NM7819
Clachan *Strath* 122 NM8543
Clachan *Strath* 113 NR7556
Clachan Mor *Strath* 120 NL9847
Clachan na Luib *W Isls* 154 NF8163
Clachan-a-Luib *W Isls* 154 NF8163
Clachan-Seil *Strath* 122 NM7718
Clachaneasy *D & G* 98 NX3574
Clachnaharry *Highld* 140 NH6446
Clachtoll *Highld* 148 NC0427
Clackavoid *Tays* 133 NO1463
Clackmannan *Cent* 116 NS9191
Clackmarass *Gramp* 141 NJ2458
Clacton-on-Sea *Essex* 41 TM1715
Cladich *Strath* 123 NN0921
Cladswell *H & W* 48 SP0558
Claggan *Highld* 122 NM7049
Claigan *Highld* 136 NG2354
Clandown *Avon* 22 ST6855
Clanfield *Hants* 13 SU6916
Clanfield *Oxon* 36 SP2801
Clannaborough *Devon* 8 SS7402
Clanville *Hants* 23 SU3148
Clanville *Somset* 21 ST6233
Claonaig *Strath* 113 NR8656
Clap Hill *Kent* 28 TR0537
Clapgate *Dorset* 11 SU0102
Clapgate *Herts* 39 TL4424
Clapham *Beds* 38 TL0352
Clapham *Devon* 9 SX8987
Clapham *Gt Lon* 27 TQ2975
Clapham *N York* 88 SD7469
Clapham *W Susx* 14 TQ0906
Clapham Folly *Beds* 38 TL0252
Clappersgate *Cumb* 87 NY3603
Clapton *Somset* 10 ST4106
Clapton *Somset* 21 ST6453
Clapton-in-Gordano *Avon* 34 ST4773
Clapton-on-the-Hill *Gloucs* 36 SP1617
Clapworthy *Devon* 19 SS6724
Clarach *Dyfed* 43 SN6084
Claravale *T & W* 103 NZ1364
Clarbeston *Dyfed* 30 SN0521
Clarbeston Road *Dyfed* 30 SN0121
Clarborough *Notts* 75 SK7383
Clare *Suffk* 53 TL7745
Clarebrand *D & G* 99 NX7665
Clarencefield *D & G* 100 NY0968
Clarewood *Nthumb* 103 NZ0169
Clarilaw *Border* 109 NT5218
Clark's Green *Surrey* 15 TQ1739
Clarken Green *Hants* 24 SU5651
Clarkston *Strath* 115 NS5757
Clashmore *Highld* 148 NC0331
Clashmore *Highld* 146 NH7489
Clashnessie *Highld* 148 NC0530
Clashnoir *Gramp* 141 NJ2222
Clathy *Tays* 125 NN9920
Clathymore *Tays* 125 NO0121
Clatt *Gramp* 142 NJ5326
Clatter *Powys* 58 SN9994
Clatterford End *Essex* 40 TL6113
Clatworthy *Somset* 20 ST0531
Claughton *Lancs* 80 SD5342
Claughton *Lancs* 87 SD5566
Claughton *Mersyd* 78 SJ3088
Clavelshay *Somset* 20 ST2531
Claverdon *Warwks* 48 SP1965
Claverham *Avon* 21 ST4566
Clavering *Essex* 39 TL4731
Claverley *Shrops* 60 SO7993
Claverton *Avon* 22 ST7864
Claverton Down *Avon* 22 ST7763
Clawdd-coch *S Glam* 33 ST0577
Clawdd-newydd *Clwyd* 70 SJ0852
Clawthorpe *Cumb* 87 SD5377
Clawton *Devon* 18 SX3599
Claxby *Lincs* 76 TF1194
Claxby *Lincs* 77 TF4571
Claxton *N York* 90 SE6959
Claxton *Norfk* 67 TG3303
Clay Common *Suffk* 55 TM4681
Clay Coton *Nhants* 50 SP5976
Clay Cross *Derbys* 74 SK3963
Clay End *Herts* 39 TL3024
Claybrooke Magna *Leics* 50 SP4988
Claydon *Oxon* 49 SP4549
Claydon *Suffk* 54 TM1349
Claygate *D & G* 101 NY3979
Claygate *Kent* 28 TQ7144
Claygate *Surrey* 26 TQ1563
Claygate Cross *Kent* 27 TQ6155
Clayhall *Gt Lon* 27 TQ4390
Clayhanger *Devon* 20 ST0222
Clayhanger *W Mids* 61 SK0404
Clayhidon *Devon* 9 ST1615
Clayhill *E Susx* 17 TQ8323
Clayhill *Hants* 12 SU3006
Clayhithe *Cambs* 53 TL5064
Clayock *Highld* 151 ND1659
Claypit Hill *Cambs* 52 TL3554
Claypits *Gloucs* 35 SO7606
Claypole *Lincs* 76 SK8449
Claythorpe *Lincs* 77 TF4178
Clayton *S York* 83 SE4507
Clayton *W Susx* 15 TQ2914
Clayton *W York* 82 SE1231
Clayton Green *Lancs* 81 SD5723
Clayton West *W York* 82 SE2510
Clayton-le-Moors *Lancs* 81 SD7530
Clayton-le-Woods *Lancs* 81 SD5622
Clayworth *Notts* 75 SK7387
Cleadale *Highld* 128 NM4789
Cleadon *T & W* 96 NZ3862
Clearbrook *Devon* 6 SX5265
Clearwell *Gloucs* 34 SO5608
Clearwell Meend *Gloucs* 34 SO5808
Cleasby *N York* 89 NZ2512
Cleat *Ork* 155 ND4584
Cleatlam *Dur* 95 NZ1118
Cleator *Cumb* 92 NY0113
Cleator Moor *Cumb* 92 NY0115
Cleckheaton *W York* 82 SE1825
Clee St Margaret *Shrops* 59 SO5684
Cleedownton *Shrops* 59 SO5880
Cleehill *Shrops* 46 SO5975
Cleekhimin *Strath* 116 NS7658
Cleestanton *Shrops* 46 SO5779
Cleethorpes *Humb* 85 TA3008
Cleeton St Mary *Shrops* 46 SO6178
Cleeve *Avon* 21 ST4666
Cleeve *Oxon* 37 SU6081
Cleeve Hill *Gloucs* 47 SO9827
Cleeve Prior *H & W* 48 SP0849
Cleghornie *Loth* 118 NT5983
Clehonger *H & W* 46 SO4637
Cleish *Tays* 117 NT0998
Cleland *Strath* 116 NS7958
Clement Street *Kent* 27 TQ5370
Clement's End *Beds* 38 TL0214
Clenamacrie *Strath* 122 NM9228
Clench Common *Wilts* 23 SU1765
Clenchwarton *Norfk* 65 TF5920
Clent *H & W* 60 SO9279
Clenterty *Gramp* 142 NJ7760
Cleobury Mortimer *Shrops* 60 SO6775
Cleobury North *Shrops* 59 SO6286
Cleongart *Strath* 105 NR6734
Clephanton *Highld* 140 NH8150
Clerkhill *D & G* 101 NY2697
Cleuch-head *D & G* 108 NS8200
Clevancy *Wilts* 36 SU0575
Clevedon *Avon* 34 ST4171
Cleveley *Oxon* 48 SP3923
Cleveleys *Lancs* 80 SD3143
Clevelode *H & W* 47 SO8347
Cleverton *Wilts* 35 ST9785
Clewer *Somset* 21 ST4351
Cley next the Sea *Norfk* 66 TG0444
Cliburn *Cumb* 94 NY5824
Cliddesden *Hants* 24 SU6349
Cliff *Warwks* 61 SP2197
Cliff End *E Susx* 17 TQ8813
Cliffe *Dur* 96 NZ2115
Cliffe *Kent* 28 TQ7376
Cliffe *Lancs* 81 SD7333
Cliffe *N York* 83 SE6631
Cliffe Woods *Kent* 28 TQ7373
Clifford *H & W* 46 SO2445
Clifford *W York* 83 SE4344
Clifford Chambers *Warwks* 48 SP1952
Clifford's Mesne *Gloucs* 47 SO7023
Cliffsend *Kent* 29 TR3464
Clifton *Avon* 34 ST5773
Clifton *Beds* 39 TL1639
Clifton *Cent* 123 NN3231
Clifton *Cumb* 94 NY5326
Clifton *Derbys* 73 SK1644
Clifton *Gt Man* 79 SD7703
Clifton *H & W* 47 SO8446
Clifton *Lancs* 80 SD4630
Clifton *N York* 83 SE5953
Clifton *Notts* 62 SK5434
Clifton *Nthumb* 103 NZ2082
Clifton *Oxon* 49 SP4931
Clifton *S York* 75 SK5296
Clifton *W York* 82 SE1622
Clifton *W York* 82 SE1948
Clifton Campville *Staffs* 61 SK2510
Clifton Dykes *Cumb* 44 NY5427
Clifton Hampden *Oxon* 37 SU5495
Clifton Reynes *Bucks* 38 SP9051
Clifton upon Dunsmore *Warwks* 50 SP5376
Clifton upon Teme *H & W* 47 SO7161
Cliftonville *Kent* 29 TR3771
Climping *W Susx* 14 SU9902
Clink *Somset* 22 ST7948
Clint *N York* 89 SE2659
Clint Green *Norfk* 66 TG0210
Clinterty *Gramp* 135 NJ8311
Clintmains *Border* 110 NT6132
Clipiau *Gwynd* 57 SH8410
Clippesby *Norfk* 67 TG4214
Clipsham *Leics* 63 SK9716
Clipston *Nhants* 50 SP7181
Clipston *Notts* 63 SK6334
Clipstone *Beds* 38 SP9426
Clipstone *Notts* 75 SK5963
Clitheroe *Lancs* 81 SD7441
Clive *Shrops* 59 SJ5124
Clixby *Lincs* 85 TA0904
Cloatley *Wilts* 35 ST9890
Clocaenog *Clwyd* 70 SJ0854
Clochan *Gramp* 142 NJ4060
Clochtow *Tays* 127 NO4852
Clock Face *Mersyd* 78 SJ5291
Cloddiau *Powys* 58 SJ2009
Clodock *H & W* 46 SO3227
Cloford *Somset* 22 ST7244
Clola *Gramp* 143 NK0043
Clophill *Beds* 38 TL0838
Clopton *Nhants* 51 TL0680
Clopton *Suffk* 55 TM2253
Clopton Corner *Suffk* 55 TM2254

Clopton Green
Corner Row

Clopton Green Suffk 53 TL7655
Clopton Green Suffk 54 TL9759
Clos du Valle Guern 152 GN0000
Closeburn D & G 100 NX8992
Closeburnmill D & G 100 NX9094
Closeclark IOM 153 SC2775
Closworth Somset 10 ST5610
Clothall Herts 39 TL2731
Clotton Ches 71 SJ5264
Cloudesley Bush Warwks 50 SP4686
Clough Gt Man 79 SD9408
Clough Foot W York 81 SD9123
Clough Head W York 82 SE0918
Cloughton N York 91 TA0194
Cloughton Newlands N York 91 TA0096
Clousta Shet 155 HU3057
Clova Tays 134 NO3273
Clovelly Devon 18 SS3124
Clovenfords Border 109 NT4536
Clovulin Highld 130 NN0063
Clow Bridge Lancs 81 SD8228
Clowne Derbys 75 SK4875
Clows Top H & W 60 SO7172
Cloy Clwyd 71 SJ3943
Cluanie Inn Highld 130 NH0711
Cluanie Lodge Highld 130 NH0910
Clubworthy Cnwll 5 SX2792
Clugston D & G 98 NX3557
Clun Shrops 59 SO3080
Clunas Highld 140 NH8846
Clunbury Shrops 59 SO3780
Clune Highld 140 NH7925
Clunes Highld 131 NN1988
Clungunford Shrops 46 SO3978
Clunie Gramp 142 NJ6350
Clunie Tays 126 NO1043
Clunton Shrops 59 SO3381
Clutton Avon 21 ST6259
Clutton Ches 71 SJ4654
Clutton Hill Avon 21 ST6359
Clwt-y-bont Gwynd 69 SH5762
Clydach Gwent 34 SO2213
Clydach W Glam 32 SN6800
Clydach Vale M Glam 33 SS9792
Clydebank Strath 115 NS4970
Clydey Dyfed 31 SN2535
Clyffe Pypard Wilts 36 SU0777
Clynder Strath 114 NS2484
Clynderwen Dyfed 31 SN1219
Clyne W Glam 32 SN8000
Clynnog-fawr Gwynd 68 SH4149
Clyro Powys 45 SO2143
Clyst Honiton Devon 9 SX9893
Clyst Hydon Devon 9 ST0301
Clyst St George Devon 9 SX9888
Clyst St Lawrence Devon 9 ST0200
Clyst St Mary Devon 9 SX9791
Cnoc W Isls 154 NB4931
Cnwch Coch Dyfed 43 SN6774
Coad's Green Cnwll 5 SX2976
Coal Aston Derbys 74 SK3679
Coal Pool W Mids 60 SP0199
Coal Street Suffk 55 TM2371
Coalbrookdale Shrops 60 SJ6604
Coalbrookvale Gwent 33 SO1909
Coalburn Strath 108 NS8134
Coalburns T & W 96 NZ1260
Coalcleugh Nthumb 95 NY8045
Coaley Gloucs 35 SO7701
Coalfell Cumb 94 NY5959
Coalhill Essex 40 TQ7597
Coalmoor Shrops 60 SJ6607
Coalpit Heath Avon 35 ST6780
Coalpit Hill Staffs 72 SJ8253
Coalport Shrops 60 SJ6902
Coalsnaughton Cent 116 NS9195
Coaltown of Balgonie Fife 117 NT2999
Coaltown of Wemyss Fife 118 NT3295
Coalville Leics 62 SK4214
Coanwood Nthumb 94 NY6859
Coat Somset 21 ST4520
Coatbridge Strath 116 NS7365
Coatdyke Strath 116 NS7465
Coate Wilts 23 SU0462
Coate Wilts 36 SU1882
Coates Cambs 64 TL3097
Coates Gloucs 35 SO9701
Coates Lincs 75 SK8181
Coates Lincs 76 SK9083
Coates W Susx 14 SU9917
Coatham Cleve 97 NZ5925
Coatham Mundeville Dur 96 NZ2820
Cobbaton Devon 19 SS6126
Coberley Gloucs 35 SO9616
Cobhall Common H & W 46 SO4535
Cobham Kent 28 TQ6768
Cobham Surrey 26 TQ1060
Coblers Green Essex 40 TL6819
Cobley Dorset 12 SU0220
Cobnash H & W 46 SO4560
Cobo Guern 152 GN0000
Cobridge Staffs 72 SJ8747
Coburby Gramp 143 NJ9164
Cock Alley Derbys 74 SK4170
Cock Bank Clwyd 71 SJ3545
Cock Bevington Warwks 48 SP0552
Cock Bridge Gramp 133 NJ2509
Cock Clarks Essex 40 TL8102
Cock End Suffk 53 TL7253
Cock Green Essex 40 TL6919
Cock Marling E Susx 17 TQ8718
Cock Street Kent 28 TQ7850
Cockayne N York 90 SE6198
Cockayne Hatley Beds 52 TL2649
Cockburnspath Border 119 NT7770
Cockenzie and Port Seton Loth 118 NT4075
Cocker Bar Lancs 80 SD5022
Cocker Brook Lancs 81 SD7425
Cockerdale W York 82 SE2329
Cockerham Lancs 80 SD4651
Cockermouth Cumb 92 NY1230
Cockernhoe Green Herts 38 TL1223
Cockett W Glam 32 SS6394
Cockfield Dur 96 NZ1224
Cockfield Suffk 54 TL9054
Cockfosters Gt Lon 27 TQ2796
Cocking W Susx 14 SU8717
Cocking Causeway W Susx 14 SU8819
Cockington Devon 7 SX8963
Cocklake Somset 21 ST4449
Cockle Park Nthumb 103 NZ2091
Cockley Beck Cumb 86 NY2501
Cockley Cley Norfk 66 TF7904
Cockpole Green Berks 37 SU7981
Cocks Cnwll 3 SW7652
Cockshutford Shrops 59 SO5885
Cockshutt Shrops 59 SJ4328
Cockthorpe Norfk 66 TF9842
Cockwells Cnwll 2 SW5234
Cockwood Devon 9 SX9780
Cockwood Somset 20 ST2242
Cockyard Derbys 74 SK0479
Cockyard H & W 46 SO4133
Coddenham Suffk 54 TM1354
Coddington Ches 71 SJ4555
Coddington H & W 47 SO7142
Coddington Notts 76 SK8354
Codford St Mary Wilts 22 ST9739
Codford St Peter Wilts 22 ST9639
Codicote Herts 39 TL2118
Codmore Hill W Susx 14 TQ0520
Codnor Derbys 74 SK4149
Codrington Avon 35 ST7278
Codsall Staffs 60 SJ8603
Codsall Wood Staffs 60 SJ8404
Coed Morgan Gwent 34 SO3511
Coed Talon Clwyd 70 SJ2659
Coed Ystumgwern Gwynd 57 SH5824
Coed-y-Bryn Dyfed 42 SN3545
Coed-y-caerau Gwent 34 ST3891
Coed-y-paen Gwent 34 ST3398
Coed-yr-ynys Powys 33 SO1520
Coedana Gwynd 68 SH4382
Coedely M Glam 33 ST0285
Coedkernew Gwent 34 ST2783
Coedpoeth Clwyd 70 SJ2851
Coedway Powys 59 SJ3315
Coelbren Powys 33 SN8511
Coffinswell Devon 7 SX8968
Coffle End Beds 51 TL0159
Cofton Hackett H & W 60 SP0075
Cogan S Glam 33 ST1771
Cogenhoe Nhants 51 SP8260
Cogges Oxon 36 SP3609
Coggeshall Essex 40 TL8522
Coggin's Mill E Susx 16 TQ5927
Coignafearn Highld 140 NH7018
Coilacriech Gramp 134 NO3296
Coilantogle Cent 124 NN5907
Coillore Highld 136 NG3537
Coiltry Highld 131 NH3506
Coity M Glam 33 SS9281
Col W Isls 154 NB4739
Colaboll Highld 146 NC5610
Colan Cnwll 4 SW8661
Colaton Raleigh Devon 9 SY0787
Colbost Highld 136 NG2148
Colburn N York 89 SE1999
Colbury Hants 12 SU3410
Colby Cumb 94 NY6620
Colby IOM 153 SC2370
Colby Norfk 67 TG2231
Colchester Essex 41 TL9925
Cold Ash Berks 24 SU5169
Cold Ashby Nhants 50 SP6576
Cold Ashton Avon 35 ST7572
Cold Aston Gloucs 36 SP1219
Cold Blow Dyfed 31 SN1212
Cold Brayfield Bucks 38 SP9252
Cold Cotes N York 88 SD7171
Cold Green H & W 47 SO6842
Cold Hanworth Lincs 76 TF0383
Cold Harbour Herts 38 TL1415
Cold Harbour Oxon 37 SU6379
Cold Harbour Wilts 22 ST8645
Cold Hatton Shrops 59 SJ6221
Cold Hatton Heath Shrops 59 SJ6321
Cold Hesledon Dur 96 NZ4146
Cold Hiendley W York 83 SE3714
Cold Higham Nhants 49 SP6653
Cold Kirby N York 90 SE5384
Cold Newton Leics 63 SK7106
Cold Northcott Cnwll 5 SX2086
Cold Norton Essex 40 TL8500
Cold Overton Leics 63 SK8010
Cold Weston Shrops 59 SO5583
Coldbackie Highld 149 NC6160
Coldbeck Cumb 88 NY7204
Coldean E Susx 15 TQ3308
Coldeast Devon 7 SX8174
Colden W York 82 SD9628
Colden Common Hants 13 SU4822
Coldfair Green Suffk 55 TM4360
Coldham Cambs 65 TF4303
Coldharbour Cnwll 3 SW7548
Coldharbour Devon 9 ST0612
Coldharbour Gloucs 34 SO5503
Coldharbour Surrey 15 TQ1443
Coldingham Border 119 NT9065
Coldmeece Staffs 72 SJ8532
Coldred Kent 29 TR2747
Coldridge Devon 8 SS6907
Coldstream Border 110 NT8439
Coldwaltham W Susx 14 TQ0216
Coldwell H & W 46 SO4235
Cole Somset 22 ST6733
Cole End Warwks 61 SP2089
Cole Green Herts 39 TL2811
Cole Green Herts 39 TL4330
Cole Henley Hants 24 SU4651
Cole's Cross Devon 7 SX7746
Colebatch Shrops 59 SO3187
Colebrook Devon 9 ST0006
Colebrook Devon 6 SX5457
Colebrooke Devon 8 SX7699
Coleby Humb 84 SE8919
Coleby Lincs 76 SK9760
Coleford Devon 8 SS7701
Coleford Gloucs 34 SO5710
Coleford Somset 22 ST6848
Coleford Water Somset 20 ST1133
Colegate End Norfk 55 TM1987
Colehill Dorset 12 SU0201
Coleman Green Herts 39 TL1812
Coleman's Hatch E Susx 16 TQ4433
Colemere Shrops 59 SJ4332
Colemore Hants 24 SU7030
Colemore Green Shrops 60 SO7197
Colenden Tays 126 NO1029
Coleorton Leics 62 SK4017
Colerne Wilts 35 ST8271
Coles Cross Dorset 10 ST3902
Coles Green Suffk 54 TM1041
Colesbourne Gloucs 35 SP0013
Colesden Beds 52 TL1255
Coleshill Bucks 26 SU9495
Coleshill Oxon 36 SU2393
Coleshill Warwks 61 SP2089
Colestocks Devon 9 ST0900
Coley Avon 21 ST5855
Colgate W Susx 15 TQ2332
Colgrain Strath 115 NS3280
Colinsburgh Fife 127 NO4703
Colinton Loth 117 NT2168
Colintraive Strath 114 NS0374
Colkirk Norfk 66 TF9126
Collace Tays 126 NO2032
Collafirth Shet 155 HU3482
Collaton Devon 7 SX7139
Collaton Devon 7 SX7952
Collaton St Mary Devon 7 SX8660
College Green Somset 21 ST5736
College of Roseisle Gramp 141 NJ1466
College Town Berks 25 SU8560
Collessie Fife 126 NO2813
Colleton Mills Devon 19 SS6615
Collier Row Gt Lon 27 TQ5091
Collier Street Kent 28 TQ7145
Collier's End Herts 39 TL3720
Collier's Green Kent 17 TQ7822
Colliers Green Kent 28 TQ7538
Colliery Row T & W 96 NZ3249
Collieston Gramp 143 NK0328
Collin D & G 100 NY0276
Collingbourne Ducis Wilts 23 SU2453
Collingbourne Kingston Wilts 23 SU2355
Collingham W York 83 SE3945
Collington H & W 47 SO6460
Collingtree Nhants 49 SP7555
Collins Green Ches 78 SJ5594
Collins Green H & W 47 SO7457
Colliston Tays 127 NO6045
Colliton Devon 9 ST0804
Collyweston Nhants 63 SK9902
Colmonell Strath 98 NX1485
Colmworth Beds 51 TL1058
Coln Rogers Gloucs 36 SP0809
Coln St Aldwyns Gloucs 36 SP1405
Coln St Dennis Gloucs 36 SP0810
Colnbrook Berks 26 TQ0277
Colne Cambs 52 TL3775
Colne Lancs 81 SD8939
Colne Bridge W York 82 SE1720
Colne Edge Lancs 81 SD8841
Colne Engaine Essex 40 TL8430
Colney Norfk 66 TG1807
Colney Heath Herts 39 TL2005
Colney Street Herts 26 TL1502
Colpy Gramp 142 NJ6432
Colquhar Border 109 NT3341
Colquite Cnwll 4 SX0570
Colscott Devon 18 SS3614
Colsterdale N York 89 SE1381
Colsterworth Lincs 63 SK9324
Colston Bassett Notts 63 SK7033
Colt Hill Hants 24 SU7551
Colt's Hill Kent 16 TQ6443
Coltfield Gramp 141 NJ1163
Coltishall Norfk 67 TG2719
Colton Cumb 86 SD3185
Colton N York 83 SE5444
Colton Norfk 66 TG1009
Colton Staffs 73 SK0420
Colton W York 83 SE3732
Columbjohn Devon 9 SX9699
Colva Powys 45 SO1952
Colvend D & G 92 NX8654
Colwall H & W 47 SO7542
Colwell Nthumb 102 NY9575
Colwich Staffs 73 SK0121
Colwick Notts 62 SK6140
Colwinston S Glam 33 SS9375
Colworth W Susx 14 SU9103
Colwyn Bay Clwyd 69 SH8578
Colyford Devon 10 SY2592
Colyton Devon 9 SY2494
Combe Berks 23 SU3760
Combe Devon 7 SX7238
Combe Devon 7 SX8448
Combe H & W 46 SO3463
Combe Oxon 36 SP4116
Combe Almer Dorset 11 SY9597
Combe Common Surrey 14 SU9436
Combe Fishacre Devon 7 SX8465
Combe Florey Somset 20 ST1531
Combe Hay Avon 22 ST7359
Combe Martin Devon 19 SS5846
Combe Moor H & W 46 SO3663
Combe Raleigh Devon 9 ST1502
Combe St Nicholas Somset 10 ST3011
Combeinteignhead Devon 7 SX9071
Comberbach Ches 79 SJ6477
Comberford Staffs 61 SK1907
Comberton Cambs 52 TL3856
Comberton H & W 46 SO4968
Combpyne Devon 10 SY2892
Combridge Staffs 73 SK0937
Combrook Warwks 48 SP3051
Combs Derbys 74 SK0478
Combs Suffk 54 TM0456
Combs Ford Suffk 54 TM0457
Combwich Somset 20 ST2542
Comers Gramp 135 NJ6707
Comhampton H & W 47 SO8367
Commercial Dyfed 31 SN1416
Commercial End Cambs 53 TL5563
Commins Coch Powys 57 SH8402
Common Edge Lancs 80 SD3232
Common End Cumb 92 NY0022
Common Moor Cnwll 5 SX2469
Common Platt Wilts 36 SU1186
Common Side Derbys 74 SK3375
Common The Wilts 23 SU2432
Commondale N York 90 NZ6610
Commonside Ches 71 SJ5473
Commonside Derbys 73 SK2441
Commonwood Clwyd 71 SJ3753
Commonwood Shrops 59 SJ4828
Compass Somset 20 ST2934
Compstall Gt Man 79 SJ9690
Compstonend D & G 99 NX6652
Compton Berks 37 SU5280
Compton Devon 7 SX8664
Compton Hants 23 SU3529
Compton Hants 13 SU4625
Compton Staffs 60 SO8284
Compton Surrey 25 SU9546
Compton W Susx 14 SU7714
Compton Wilts 23 SU1351
Compton Abbas Dorset 22 ST8618
Compton Abdale Gloucs 36 SP0516
Compton Bassett Wilts 36 SU0372
Compton Beauchamp Oxon 36 SU2786
Compton Bishop Somset 21 ST3955
Compton Chamberlayne Wilts 23 SU0229
Compton Dando Avon 21 ST6464
Compton Dundon Somset 21 ST4932
Compton Durville Somset 10 ST4117
Compton Greenfield Avon 34 ST5681
Compton Martin Avon 21 ST5457
Compton Pauncefoot Somset 21 ST6426
Compton Valence Dorset 10 SY5993
Compton Verney Warwks 48 SP3152
Comrie Fife 117 NT0289
Comrie Tays 124 NN7722
Conaglen House Highld 130 NN0268
Conchra Highld 138 NG8827
Concraigie Tays 125 NO0944
Conder Green Lancs 80 SD4556
Conderton H & W 47 SO9637
Condicote Gloucs 48 SP1528
Condorrat Strath 116 NS7373
Condover Shrops 59 SJ4905
Coney Hill Gloucs 35 SO8517
Coney Weston Suffk 54 TL9578
Coneyhurst Common W Susx 14 TQ1023
Coneysthorpe N York 90 SE7171
Conford Hants 14 SU8233
Congdon's Shop Cnwll 5 SX2878
Congerstone Leics 62 SK3605
Congham Norfk 65 TF7123
Conghurst Kent 17 TQ7628
Congl-y-wal Gwynd 57 SH7044
Congleton Ches 72 SJ8562
Congresbury Avon 21 ST4363
Congreve Staffs 60 SJ9013
Conheath D & G 100 NX9969
Conicavel Gramp 140 NH9853
Coningsby Lincs 76 TF2257
Conington Cambs 52 TL1885
Conington Cambs 52 TL3266
Conisbrough S York 75 SK5098
Conisholme Lincs 77 TF4095
Coniston Cumb 86 SD3097
Coniston Humb 86 TA1535
Coniston Humb 85 TA1434
Coniston Cold N York 81 SD9054
Conistone N York 88 SD9867
Connah's Quay Clwyd 71 SJ2969
Connel Strath 122 NM9134
Connel Park Strath 107 NS6012
Connor Downs Cnwll 2 SW5939
Conon Bridge Highld 139 NH5455
Cononley N York 82 SD9846
Consall Staffs 72 SJ9848
Consett Dur 95 NZ1051
Constable Burton N York 89 SE1690
Constable Lee Lancs 81 SD8123
Constantine Cnwll 3 SW7329
Constantine Bay Cnwll 4 SW8774
Contin Highld 139 NH4556
Conwy Gwynd 69 SH7877
Conyer Kent 28 TQ9664
Conyer's Green Suffk 54 TL8867
Cooden E Susx 17 TQ7107
Cook's Green Essex 41 TM1818
Cookbury Devon 18 SS4006
Cookbury Wick Devon 18 SS3905
Cookham Berks 26 SU8985
Cookham Dean Berks 26 SU8685
Cookham Rise Berks 26 SU8885
Cookhill Warwks 48 SP0558
Cookley H & W 60 SO8480
Cookley Suffk 55 TM3475
Cookley Green Oxon 37 SU6990
Cookney Gramp 135 NO8693
Cooks Green Suffk 54 TL9753
Cooksbridge E Susx 15 TQ4013
Cooksey Green H & W 47 SO9069
Cookshill Staffs 72 SJ9443
Cooksland Cnwll 4 SX0867
Cooksmill Green Essex 40 TL6306
Cookson Green Ches 71 SJ5774
Cookson's Green Dur 96 NZ2933
Coolham W Susx 14 TQ1122
Cooling Kent 28 TQ7575
Cooling Street Kent 28 TQ7474
Coombe Cnwll 2 SW6242
Coombe Cnwll 3 SW8340
Coombe Devon 8 SX8384
Coombe Devon 7 SX9373
Coombe Devon 9 SY1091
Coombe Gloucs 35 ST7694
Coombe Hants 13 SU6620
Coombe Wilts 23 SU1450
Coombe Bissett Wilts 23 SU1026
Coombe Cellars Devon 7 SX9072
Coombe Cross Hants 13 SU6620
Coombe End Somset 20 ST0329
Coombe Hill Gloucs 47 SO8826
Coombe Keynes Dorset 11 SY8484
Coombe Pafford Devon 7 SX9166
Coombe Street Somset 22 ST7631
Coombes W Susx 15 TQ1808
Coombeswood W Mids 60 SO9785
Cooper Street Kent 29 TR3060
Cooper Turning Gt Man 79 SD6308
Cooper's Corner Kent 16 TQ4849
Cooperhill Gramp 141 NH9953
Coopers Green E Susx 16 TQ4723
Coopers Green Herts 39 TL1909
Coopersale Common Essex 27 TL4702
Coopersale Street Essex 27 TL4701
Cootham W Susx 14 TQ0714
Cop Street Kent 27 TQ2959
Copdock Suffk 54 TM1242
Copford Green Essex 40 TL9222
Copgrove N York 89 SE3463
Copister Shet 155 HU4879
Cople Beds 38 TL1048
Copley Dur 95 NZ0825
Copley Gt Man 79 SJ9798
Copley W York 82 SE0822
Coplow Dale Derbys 74 SK1679
Copmanthorpe N York 83 SE5646
Copmere End Staffs 72 SJ8029
Copp Lancs 80 SD4239
Coppathorne Cnwll 18 SS2000
Coppenhall Staffs 72 SJ9019
Coppenhall Moss Ches 72 SJ7058
Copperhouse Cnwll 2 SW5637
Coppicegate Shrops 60 SO7379
Coppingford Cambs 52 TL1679
Coppins Corner Kent 28 TQ9448
Copplestone Devon 8 SS7702
Coppull Lancs 81 SD5614
Coppull Moor Lancs 81 SD5512
Copsale W Susx 15 TQ1724
Copster Green Lancs 81 SD6733
Copston Magna Warwks 50 SP4588
Copt Heath W Mids 61 SP1777
Copt Hewick N York 89 SE3471
Copthall Green Essex 27 TL4201
Copthorne Cnwll 5 SX2692
Copthorne W Susx 15 TQ3139
Copy's Green Norfk 66 TF9439
Copythorne Hants 12 SU3014
Coram Street Suffk 54 TM0042
Corbets Tey Gt Lon 27 TQ5685
Corbiere Jersey 152 JS0000
Corbridge Nthumb 103 NY9964
Corby Nhants 51 SP8988
Corby Glen Lincs 63 TF0024
Corby Hill Cumb 94 NY4857
Cordon Strath 105 NS0230
Cordwell Derbys 74 SK3176
Coreley Shrops 46 SO6173
Cores End Bucks 26 SU9087
Corfe Somset 20 ST2319
Corfe Castle Dorset 11 SY9681
Corfe Mullen Dorset 11 SY9896
Corfton Shrops 59 SO4985
Corgarff Gramp 133 NJ2708
Corhampton Hants 13 SU6120
Corks Pond Kent 28 TQ6540
Corley Warwks 61 SP3085
Corley Ash Warwks 61 SP2986
Corley Moor Warwks 61 SP2884
Cormuir Tays 134 NO3066
Cornard Tye Suffk 54 TL9041
Corndon Devon 8 SX6985
Corner Row Lancs 80 SD4134

Corney

Cross Green

Corney *Cumb* 86 SD1191
Cornforth *Dur* 96 NZ3134
Cornhill *Gramp* 142 NJ5858
Cornhill-on-Tweed *Nthumb* 110 NT8639
Cornholme *W York* 81 SD9126
Cornish Hall End *Essex* 53 TL6836
Cornoigmore *Strath* 120 NL9846
Cornriggs *Dur* 95 NY8441
Cornsay *Dur* 96 NZ1443
Cornsay Colliery *Dur* 96 NZ1643
Corntown *Highld* 139 NH5556
Corntown *M Glam* 33 SS9177
Cornwell *Oxon* 48 SP2727
Cornwood *Devon* 6 SX6059
Cornworthy *Devon* 7 SX8255
Corpach *Highld* 130 NN0976
Corpusty *Norfk* 66 TG1129
Corrachree *Gramp* 134 NJ4604
Corran *Cnwll* 3 SW9946
Corran *Highld* 130 NG8409
Corran *Highld* 130 NN0263
Corrany *IOM* 153 SC4589
Corrie *D & G* 101 NY2086
Corrie *Strath* 105 NS0242
Corriecravie *Strath* 105 NR9223
Corriegills *Strath* 105 NS0335
Corriegour Lodge Hotel *Highld* 131 NN2692
Corriemoille *Highld* 139 NH3663
Corrimony *Highld* 139 NH3730
Corringham *Essex* 40 TQ7083
Corringham *Lincs* 76 SK8691
Corris *Gwynd* 57 SH7508
Corris Uchaf *Gwynd* 57 SH7408
Corrow *Strath* 114 NN1800
Corry *Highld* 137 NG6424
Cors-y-Gedol *Gwynd* 57 SH6022
Corscombe *Devon* 8 SX6296
Corscombe *Dorset* 10 ST5105
Corse *Gloucs* 47 SO7826
Corse Lawn *Gloucs* 47 SO8330
Corsham *Wilts* 35 ST8770
Corsindae *Gramp* 135 NJ6808
Corsley *Wilts* 22 ST8246
Corsley Heath *Wilts* 22 ST8245
Corsock *D & G* 99 NX7675
Corston *Avon* 22 ST6965
Corston *Wilts* 35 ST9283
Corstorphine *Loth* 117 NT1972
Cortachy *Tays* 134 NO3959
Corton *Suffk* 67 TM5497
Corton *Wilts* 22 ST9340
Corton Denham *Somset* 21 ST6322
Coruanan Lodge *Highld* 130 NN0668
Corwen *Clwyd* 70 SJ0743
Coryates *Dorset* 10 SY6285
Coryton *Devon* 5 SX4583
Coryton *Essex* 40 TQ7382
Cosby *Leics* 50 SP5495
Coseley *W Mids* 60 SO9494
Cosford *Shrops* 60 SJ8005
Cosgrove *Nhants* 38 SP7942
Cosham *Hants* 13 SU6505
Cosheston *Dyfed* 30 SN0003
Coshieville *Tays* 124 NN7749
Cossall *Notts* 62 SK4842
Cossall Marsh *Notts* 62 SK4842
Cossington *Leics* 62 SK6013
Cossington *Somset* 21 ST3540
Costallack *Cnwll* 2 SW4525
Costessey *Norfk* 66 TG1711
Costock *Notts* 62 SK5726
Coston *Leics* 63 SK8422
Coston *Norfk* 66 TG0506
Cote *Oxon* 36 SP3502
Cote *Somset* 21 ST3444
Cotebrook *Ches* 71 SJ5765
Cotehill *Cumb* 93 NY4650
Cotes *Cumb* 87 SD4886
Cotes *Leics* 62 SK5520
Cotes *Staffs* 72 SJ8434
Cotes Heath *Staffs* 72 SJ8334
Cotesbach *Leics* 50 SP5382
Cotgrave *Notts* 63 SK6435
Cotham *Notts* 63 SK7947
Cothelstone *Somset* 20 ST1831
Cotherstone *Dur* 95 NZ0119
Cothill *Oxon* 37 SU4699
Cotleigh *Devon* 9 ST2002
Cotmanhay *Derbys* 62 SK4543
Coton *Cambs* 52 TL4058
Coton *Nhants* 50 SP6771
Coton *Shrops* 59 SJ5334
Coton *Staffs* 72 SJ8120
Coton *Staffs* 72 SJ9731
Coton *Staffs* 61 SK1804
Coton Clanford *Staffs* 72 SJ8723
Coton Hayes *Staffs* 72 SJ9832
Coton Hill *Shrops* 59 SJ4813
Coton in the Clay *Staffs* 73 SK1628
Coton in the Elms *Derbys* 73 SK2415
Coton Park *Derbys* 73 SK2617
Cott *Devon* 7 SX7861
Cottage End *Hants* 24 SU4143
Cottam *Humb* 91 SE9964
Cottam *Lancs* 80 SD5032
Cottam *Notts* 75 SK8179
Cottenham *Cambs* 53 TL4467
Cotterdale *N York* 88 SD8393
Cottered *Herts* 39 TL3129
Cotteridge *W Mids* 61 SP0480
Cotterstock *Nhants* 51 TL0490
Cottesbrooke *Nhants* 50 SP7173
Cottesmore *Leics* 63 SK9013
Cottingham *Humb* 84 TA0432
Cottingham *Nhants* 51 SP8490
Cottingley *W York* 82 SE1137
Cottisford *Oxon* 49 SP5831
Cottivett *Cnwll* 5 SX3662
Cotton *Suffk* 54 TM0666
Cotton End *Beds* 38 TL0845
Cotton Tree *Lancs* 81 SD9039
Cottown *Gramp* 142 NJ5026
Cottown *Gramp* 142 NJ7615
Cottown of Gight *Gramp* 143 NJ8140
Cottrell *S Glam* 33 ST0774
Cotts *Devon* 6 SX4365
Cotwall *Shrops* 59 SJ6017
Cotwalton *Staffs* 72 SJ9234
Couch's Mill *Cnwll* 4 SX1459
Coughton *H & W* 34 SO5921
Coughton *Warwks* 48 SP0860
Coulaghailtro *Strath* 113 NR7165
Coulags *Highld* 138 NG9645
Coulderton *Cumb* 86 NX9808
Coull *Gramp* 134 NJ5102
Coulport *Strath* 114 NS2187
Coulsdon *Gt Lon* 27 TQ2959
Coulston *Wilts* 22 ST9554
Coulter *Strath* 108 NT0234
Coultershaw Bridge *W Susx* 14 SU9719
Coultings *Somset* 20 ST2241
Coulton *N York* 90 SE6373
Coultra *Fife* 126 NO3523
Cound *Shrops* 59 SJ5505
Coundlane *Shrops* 59 SJ5705
Coundon *Dur* 96 NZ2329
Coundon Grange *Dur* 96 NZ2228
Countersett *N York* 88 SD9187
Countess *Wilts* 23 SU1542
Countess Cross *Essex* 40 TL8631
Countess Wear *Devon* 9 SX9489
Countesthorpe *Leics* 50 SP5895
Countisbury *Devon* 19 SS7449
Coup Green *Lancs* 81 SD5927
Coupar Angus *Tays* 126 NO2239
Coupland *Cumb* 94 NY7118
Coupland *Nthumb* 110 NT9330
Cour *Strath* 105 NR8248
Courance *D & G* 100 NY0590
Court Henry *Dyfed* 32 SN5522
Court-at-Street *Kent* 17 TR0935
Courteachan *Highld* 129 NM6897
Courteenhall *Nhants* 49 SP7653
Courtsend *Essex* 41 TR0293
Courtway *Somset* 20 ST2033
Cousland *Loth* 118 NT3768
Cousley Wood *E Susx* 16 TQ6533
Cove *Border* 119 NT7771
Cove *Devon* 20 SS9619
Cove *Gramp* 135 NJ9501
Cove *Hants* 25 SU8555
Cove *Highld* 144 NG8191
Cove *Strath* 114 NS2282
Cove Bottom *Suffk* 55 TM4979
Covehithe *Suffk* 55 TM5282
Coven *Staffs* 60 SJ9106
Coven Lawn *Staffs* 60 SJ9005
Coveney *Cambs* 53 TL4882
Covenham St Bartholomew *Lincs* 77 TF3394
Covenham St Mary *Lincs* 77 TF3394
Coventry *W Mids* 61 SP3378
Coverack *Cnwll* 3 SW7818
Coverack Bridges *Cnwll* 2 SW6630
Coverham *N York* 89 SE1086
Covington *Cambs* 51 TL0570
Covington *Strath* 108 NS9739
Cow Green *Suffk* 54 TM0565
Cow Honeybourne *H & W* 48 SP1143
Cowan Bridge *Lancs* 87 SD6376
Cowbeech *E Susx* 16 TQ6114
Cowbit *Lincs* 64 TF2518
Cowbridge *S Glam* 33 SS9974
Cowdale *Derbys* 74 SK0771
Cowden *Kent* 16 TQ4640
Cowden Pound *Kent* 16 TQ4642
Cowden Station *Kent* 16 TQ4741
Cowdenbeath *Fife* 117 NT1691
Cowers Lane *Derbys* 73 SK3046
Cowes *IOW* 13 SZ4996
Cowesby *N York* 89 SE4689
Cowesfield Green *Wilts* 23 SU2523
Cowfold *W Susx* 15 TQ2122
Cowgill *Cumb* 88 SD7586
Cowhill *Avon* 34 ST6091
Cowie *Cent* 116 NS8389
Cowley *Derbys* 74 SK3376
Cowley *Devon* 9 SX9095
Cowley *Gloucs* 35 SO9614
Cowley *Gt Lon* 26 TQ0582
Cowley *Oxon* 37 SP5304
Cowley *Oxon* 49 SP6628
Cowling *Lancs* 81 SD5917
Cowling *N York* 82 SD9643
Cowling *N York* 89 SE2387
Cowlinge *Suffk* 53 TL7154
Cowmes *W York* 82 SE1815
Cowpe *Lancs* 81 SD8320
Cowpen *Nthumb* 103 NZ2981
Cowpen Bewley *Cleve* 97 NZ4824
Cowplain *Hants* 13 SU6810
Cowshill *Dur* 95 NY8540
Cowslip Green *Avon* 21 ST4861
Cowthorpe *N York* 83 SE4252
Cox Common *Suffk* 55 TM4082
Coxall *Shrops* 46 SO3774
Coxbank *Ches* 72 SJ6541
Coxbench *Derbys* 62 SK3743
Coxbridge *Somset* 21 ST5436
Coxford *Cnwll* 4 SX1696
Coxford *Norfk* 66 TF8529
Coxgreen *Staffs* 60 SO8086
Coxheath *Kent* 28 TQ7451
Coxhoe *Dur* 96 NZ3136
Coxley *Somset* 21 ST5343
Coxley *W York* 82 SE2717
Coxley Wick *Somset* 21 ST5243
Coxpark *Cnwll* 5 SX4072
Coxtie Green *Essex* 27 TQ5696
Coxwold *N York* 90 SE5377
Coychurch *M Glam* 33 SS9379
Coylton *Strath* 107 NS4219
Coylumbridge *Highld* 132 NH9111
Coytrahen *M Glam* 33 SS8885
Crab Orchard *Dorset* 12 SU0806
Crabbs Cross *H & W* 48 SP0465
Crabtree *W Susx* 15 TQ2125
Crabtree Green *Clwyd* 71 SJ3344
Crackenthorpe *Cumb* 94 NY6622
Crackington Haven *Cnwll* 4 SX1496
Crackley *Staffs* 72 SJ8350
Crackley *Warwks* 61 SP2973
Crackleybank *Shrops* 60 SJ7611
Crackpot *N York* 88 SD9796
Cracoe *N York* 88 SD9760
Craddock *Devon* 9 ST0812
Cradle End *Herts* 39 TL4521
Cradley *H & W* 47 SO7347
Cradley *W Mids* 60 SO9485
Cradoc *Powys* 45 SO0130
Crafthole *Cnwll* 5 SX3654
Crafton *Bucks* 38 SP8819
Crag Foot *Lancs* 87 SD4873
Cragg Hill *W York* 82 SE2437
Cragg Vale *W York* 82 SE0023
Craggan *Highld* 141 NJ0226
Craghead *Dur* 96 NZ2150
Crai *Powys* 45 SN8924
Craibstone *Gramp* 142 NJ4959
Craichie *Tays* 127 NO5047
Craig *Tays* 127 NO6956
Craig Llangiwg *W Glam* 32 SN7204
Craig Penllyn *S Glam* 33 SS9777
Craig's End *Essex* 53 TL7137
Craig-y-Duke *W Glam* 32 SN7002
Craig-y-nos *Powys* 33 SN8415
Craigbank *Strath* 107 NS5911
Craigburn *Border* 117 NT2354
Craigcefnparc *W Glam* 32 SN6702
Craigcleuch *D & G* 101 NY3486
Craigdam *Gramp* 143 NJ8430
Craigdarroch *D & G* 107 NX7391
Craigdhu *Strath* 122 NM8205
Craigearn *Gramp* 142 NJ7214
Craigellachie *Gramp* 141 NJ2844
Craigend *Strath* 115 NS4670
Craigend *Tays* 126 NO1120
Craigendoran *Strath* 115 NS3181
Craighlaw *D & G* 98 NX3061
Craighouse *Strath* 113 NR5267
Craigie *Strath* 107 NS4232
Craigie *Tays* 126 NO1143
Craigiefold *Gramp* 143 NJ9165
Craigley *D & G* 99 NX7658
Craiglockhart *Fife* 117 NT2271
Craiglug *Gramp* 141 NJ3355
Craigmillar *Loth* 117 NT3071
Craignant *Shrops* 58 SJ2535
Craigneston *D & G* 107 NX7587
Craigneuk *Strath* 116 NS7765
Craigneuk *Strath* 116 NS7756
Craignure *Strath* 122 NM7236
Craigo *Tays* 135 NO6864
Craigrothie *Fife* 126 NO3810
Craigruie *Cent* 124 NN4920
Craigton *Gramp* 135 NJ8301
Craigton *Strath* 115 NS4954
Craigton *Tays* 127 NO5138
Craigton of Airlie *Tays* 126 NO3250
Crail *Fife* 127 NO6107
Crailing *Border* 110 NT6824
Crakehall *N York* 89 SE2489
Crakehill *N York* 89 SE4273
Crakemarsh *Staffs* 73 SK0936
Crambe *N York* 90 SE7364
Cramlington *Nthumb* 103 NZ2676
Cramond *Loth* 117 NT1976
Cramond Bridge *Loth* 117 NT1775
Cranage *Ches* 79 SJ7568
Cranberry *Staffs* 72 SJ8235
Cranborne *Dorset* 12 SU0513
Cranbrook *Kent* 28 TQ7736
Cranbrook Common *Kent* 28 TQ7838
Crane Moor *S York* 82 SE3001
Crane's Corner *Norfk* 66 TF9113
Cranfield *Beds* 38 SP9542
Cranford *Devon* 18 SS3421
Cranford *Gt Lon* 26 TQ1076
Cranford St Andrew *Nhants* 51 SP9277
Cranford St John *Nhants* 51 SP9276
Cranham *Gloucs* 35 SO8913
Cranham *Gt Lon* 27 TQ5787
Cranhill *Warwks* 48 SP1253
Crank *Mersyd* 78 SJ5099
Cranleigh *Surrey* 14 TQ0539
Cranmer Green *Suffk* 54 TM0171
Cranmore *IOW* 13 SZ3990
Cranmore *Somset* 22 ST6643
Cranoe *Leics* 50 SP7695
Cransford *Suffk* 55 TM3164
Cranshaws *Border* 118 NT6861
Cranstal *IOM* 153 NX4602
Cranswick *Humb* 84 TA0252
Crantock *Cnwll* 4 SW7960
Cranwell *Lincs* 76 TF0349
Cranwich *Norfk* 65 TL7794
Cranworth *Norfk* 66 TF9804
Craobh Haven *Strath* 122 NM7907
Crapstone *Devon* 6 SX5067
Crarae *Strath* 114 NR9897
Crask Inn *Highld* 149 NC5224
Crask of Aigas *Highld* 139 NH4642
Craster *Nthumb* 111 NU2519
Craswall *H & W* 46 SO2735
Crateford *Staffs* 60 SJ9009
Cratfield *Suffk* 55 TM3175
Crathes *Gramp* 135 NO7596
Crathie *Gramp* 133 NO2695
Crathie *Highld* 132 NN5793
Crathorne *N York* 89 NZ4407
Craven Arms *Shrops* 59 SO4382
Crawcrook *T & W* 103 NZ1363
Crawford *Lancs* 78 SD4902
Crawford *Strath* 108 NS9520
Crawfordjohn *Strath* 108 NS8823
Crawick *D & G* 107 NS7811
Crawley *Hants* 24 SU4235
Crawley *Oxon* 36 SP3412
Crawley *W Susx* 15 TQ2636
Crawley Down *W Susx* 15 TQ3437
Crawley Side *Dur* 95 NY9940
Crawshawbooth *Lancs* 81 SD8125
Crawton *Gramp* 135 NO8779
Crawton *N York* 90 SE6476
Craxe's Green *Essex* 40 TL9419
Cray *N York* 88 SD9479
Cray's Pond *Oxon* 37 SU6380
Crayford *Gt Lon* 27 TQ5175
Crayke *N York* 90 SE5670
Craymere Beck *Norfk* 66 TG0631
Crays Hill *Essex* 40 TQ7192
Craythorne *Staffs* 73 SK2426
Craze Lowman *Devon* 9 SS9814
Crazies Hill *Oxon* 37 SU7980
Creacombe *Devon* 18 SS3219
Creag Ghoraidh *W Isls* 154 NF7948
Creagan Inn *Strath* 122 NM9744
Creagorry *W Isls* 154 NF7948
Creaguaineach Lodge *Highld* 131 NN3068
Creamore Bank *Shrops* 59 SJ5130
Creaton *Nhants* 50 SP7071
Creca *D & G* 101 NY2270
Credenhill *H & W* 46 SO4543
Crediton *Devon* 8 SS8300
Creebank *D & G* 98 NX3477
Creebridge *D & G* 99 NX4165
Creech Heathfield *Somset* 20 ST2727
Creech St Michael *Somset* 20 ST2725
Creed *Cnwll* 3 SW9347
Creedy Park *Devon* 8 SS8301
Creekmouth *Gt Lon* 27 TQ4581
Creeting St Mary *Suffk* 54 TM0956
Creeton *Lincs* 64 TF0120
Creetown *D & G* 99 NX4759
Creggans Inn *Strath* 123 NN0902
Cregneash *IOM* 153 SC1867
Cregrina *Powys* 45 SO1252
Creich *Fife* 126 NO3221
Creigiau *M Glam* 33 ST0781
Crelly *Cnwll* 2 SW6732
Cremyll *Cnwll* 6 SX4553
Cressage *Shrops* 59 SJ5904
Cressbrook *Derbys* 74 SK1673
Cresselly *Dyfed* 30 SN0606
Cressex *Bucks* 26 SU8492
Cressing *Essex* 40 TL7920
Cresswell *Dyfed* 30 SN0506
Cresswell *Nthumb* 103 NZ2993
Cresswell *Staffs* 72 SJ9739
Creswell *Derbys* 75 SK5274
Creswell Green *Staffs* 61 SK0710
Cretingham *Suffk* 55 TM2260
Cretshengan *Strath* 113 NR7166
Crew Green *Powys* 59 SJ3215
Crewe *Ches* 71 SJ4253
Crewe *Ches* 72 SJ7056
Crewe Green *Ches* 72 SJ7255
Crewkerne *Somset* 10 ST4409
Crews Hill *H & W* 35 SO6722
Crews Hill Station *Herts* 27 TL3000
Crewton *Derbys* 62 SK3733
Crianlarich *Cent* 123 NN3825
Cribbs Causeway *Avon* 34 ST5780
Cribyn *Dyfed* 44 SN5250
Criccieth *Gwynd* 56 SH4938
Crich *Derbys* 74 SK3454
Crich Carr *Derbys* 74 SK3354
Crich Common *Derbys* 74 SK3553
Crichton *Loth* 118 NT3862
Crick *Gwent* 34 ST4890
Crick *Nhants* 50 SP5872
Crickadarn *Powys* 45 SO0942
Cricket St Thomas *Somset* 10 ST3708
Crickheath *Shrops* 59 SJ2922
Crickhowell *Powys* 33 SO2118
Cricklade *Wilts* 36 SU0993
Cricklewood *Gt Lon* 26 TQ2385
Cridling Stubbs *N York* 83 SE5221
Crieff *Tays* 125 NN8621
Criggan *Cnwll* 4 SX0160
Criggion *Powys* 59 SJ2915
Crigglestone *W York* 82 SE3116
Crimble *Gt Man* 81 SD8611
Crimond *Gramp* 143 NK0556
Crimonmogate *Gramp* 143 NK0358
Crimplesham *Norfk* 65 TF6503
Crimscote *Warwks* 48 SP2347
Crinan *Strath* 113 NR7894
Crindledyke *Strath* 116 NS8356
Cringleford *Norfk* 67 TG1905
Cringles *N York* 82 SE0448
Crinow *Dyfed* 31 SN1214
Cripp's Corner *E Susx* 17 TQ7721
Cripplesease *Cnwll* 2 SW5036
Cripplestyle *Dorset* 12 SU0812
Crizeley *H & W* 46 SO4532
Croachy *Highld* 140 NH6527
Croanford *Cnwll* 4 SX0371
Crochmare House *D & G* 100 NX8977
Crock Street *Somset* 10 ST3213
Crockenhill *Kent* 27 TQ5067
Crocker End *Oxon* 37 SU7086
Crocker's Ash *H & W* 34 SO5316
Crockerhill *W Susx* 14 SU9206
Crockernwell *Devon* 8 SX7592
Crockerton *Wilts* 22 ST8642
Crocketford *D & G* 100 NX8372
Crockey Hill *N York* 83 SE6246
Crockham Hill *Kent* 27 TQ4450
Crockhurst Street *Kent* 16 TQ6245
Crockleford Heath *Essex* 41 TM0426
Croes-goch *Dyfed* 30 SM8330
Croes-lan *Dyfed* 42 SN3844
Croes-y-mwyalch *Gwent* 34 ST3092
Croes-y-pant *Gwent* 34 SO3104
Croeserw *W Glam* 33 SS8795
Croesor *Gwynd* 57 SH6344
Croesyceiliog *Dyfed* 31 SN4016
Croesyceiliog *Gwent* 34 ST3096
Croft *Ches* 79 SJ6393
Croft *Devon* 5 SX5296
Croft *Leics* 50 SP5195
Croft *Lincs* 77 TF5061
Croft Michael *Cnwll* 2 SW6637
Croft-on-Tees *N York* 89 NZ2809
Croftamie *Cent* 115 NS4785
Crofton *Cumb* 93 NY3050
Crofton *Devon* 9 SX9680
Crofton *W York* 83 SE3817
Crofton *Wilts* 23 SU2562
Crofts *D & G* 99 NX7365
Crofts *Gramp* 141 NJ2850
Crofts Bank *Gt Man* 79 SJ7695
Crofts of Dipple *Gramp* 141 NJ3259
Crofts of Savoch *Gramp* 143 NK0460
Crofty *W Glam* 32 SS5294
Crogen *Gwynd* 58 SJ0036
Croggan *Strath* 122 NM7027
Croglin *Cumb* 94 NY5747
Crogo *D & G* 99 NX7576
Croik *Highld* 146 NH4591
Cromarty *Highld* 140 NH7867
Crombie *Fife* 117 NT0584
Cromdale *Highld* 141 NJ0728
Cromer *Herts* 39 TL2928
Cromer *Norfk* 67 TG2242
Cromford *Derbys* 73 SK2956
Cromhall *Avon* 35 ST6990
Cromhall Common *Avon* 35 ST6989
Cromor *W Isls* 154 NB4021
Crompton Fold *Gt Man* 79 SD9409
Cromwell *Notts* 75 SK7961
Cronberry *Strath* 107 NS6022
Crondall *Hants* 25 SU7948
Cronk-y-Voddy *IOM* 153 SC3085
Cronkbourne *IOM* 153 SC3677
Cronton *Mersyd* 78 SJ4988
Crook *Cumb* 87 SD4695
Crook *Dur* 96 NZ1635
Crook Inn *Border* 108 NT1026
Crook of Devon *Tays* 117 NO0400
Crookdake *Cumb* 93 NY1943
Crooke *Gt Man* 78 SD5507
Crooked End *Gloucs* 35 SO6217
Crooked Holme *Cumb* 101 NY5161
Crooked Soley *Wilts* 36 SU3172
Crookedholm *Strath* 107 NS4537
Crookes *S York* 74 SK3287
Crookhall *Dur* 95 NZ1150
Crookham *Berks* 24 SU5464
Crookham *Nthumb* 110 NT9138
Crookham Village *Hants* 25 SU7952
Crooklands *Cumb* 87 SD5383
Cropper *Derbys* 73 SK2335
Cropredy *Oxon* 49 SP4646
Cropston *Leics* 62 SK5510
Cropthorne *H & W* 47 SO9945
Cropton *N York* 90 SE7589
Cropwell Bishop *Notts* 63 SK6835
Cropwell Butler *Notts* 63 SK6837
Cros *W Isls* 154 NB5061
Crosbie *Strath* 114 NS2149
Crosbost *W Isls* 154 NB3924
Crosby *Cumb* 92 NY0738
Crosby *Humb* 84 SE8912
Crosby *IOM* 153 SC3279
Crosby *Mersyd* 78 SJ3198
Crosby Garret *Cumb* 88 NY7209
Crosby Ravensworth *Cumb* 94 NY6214
Crosby Villa *Cumb* 92 NY0939
Croscombe *Somset* 21 ST5944
Crosemere *Shrops* 59 SJ4329
Cross *Somset* 21 ST4154
Cross Ash *Gwent* 34 SO4019
Cross Bush *W Susx* 14 TQ0306
Cross Coombe *Cnwll* 3 SW7251
Cross End *Beds* 51 TL0658
Cross End *Essex* 54 TL8534
Cross Flatts *W York* 82 SE1040
Cross Gates *W York* 83 SE3534
Cross Green *Devon* 5 SX3888
Cross Green *Staffs* 60 SJ9105
Cross Green *Suffk* 54 TL8353

Ddol-Cownwy
Drumhead

Ddol-Cownwy Powys 58 SJ0117
Deal Kent 29 TR3752
Dean Cumb 92 NY0725
Dean Devon 19 SS6245
Dean Devon 19 SS7048
Dean Devon 7 SX7364
Dean Dorset 11 ST9715
Dean Hants 24 SU4431
Dean Hants 13 SU5619
Dean Lancs 81 SD8525
Dean Oxon 36 SP3422
Dean Somset 22 ST6743
Dean Bottom Kent 27 TQ5868
Dean Court Oxon 37 SP4705
Dean End Dorset 11 ST9717
Dean Head S York 74 SE2600
Dean Prior Devon 7 SX7363
Dean Row Ches 79 SJ8781
Dean Street Kent 28 TQ7453
Deanburnhaugh Border 109 NT3911
Deancombe Devon 7 SX7264
Deane Gt Man 79 SD6907
Deane Hants 24 SU5450
Deanhead W York 82 SE0415
Deanland Dorset 22 ST9918
Deanlane End W Susx 13 SU7412
Deanraw Nthumb 102 NY8162
Deans Loth 117 NT0369
Deanscales Cumb 92 NY0926
Deanshanger Nhants 49 SP7639
Deanshaugh Gramp 141 NJ3550
Deanston Cent 116 NN7101
Dearham Cumb 92 NY0736
Dearnley Gt Man 81 SD9215
Debach Suffk 55 TM2454
Debden Essex 53 TL5533
Debden Essex 27 TQ4496
Debden Green Essex 40 TL5831
Debenham Suffk 54 TM1763
Deblin's Green H & W 47 SO8148
Dechmont Loth 117 NT0370
Dechmont Road Loth 117 NT0269
Deddington Oxon 49 SP4631
Dedham Essex 41 TM0533
Dedham Heath Essex 41 TM0531
Dedworth Berks 26 SU9476
Deene Nhants 51 SP9492
Deenethorpe Nhants 51 SP9591
Deepcar S York 74 SK2897
Deepcut Surrey 25 SU9057
Deepdale Cumb 88 SD7184
Deepdale N York 88 SD8979
Deeping Gate Lincs 64 TF1509
Deeping St James Lincs 64 TF1609
Deeping St Nicholas Lincs 64 TF2115
Deerhurst Gloucs 47 SO8730
Deerhurst Walton Gloucs 47 SO8828
Deerton Street Kent 28 TQ9762
Defford H & W 47 SO9143
Defynnog Powys 45 SN9227
Deganwy Gwynd 69 SH7779
Degnish Strath 122 NM7812
Deighton N York 89 NZ3801
Deighton N York 83 SE6244
Deighton W York 82 SE1519
Deiniolen Gwynd 69 SH5763
Delabole Cnwll 4 SX0683
Delamere Ches 71 SJ5668
Delfrigs Gramp 143 NJ9620
Dell Quay W Susx 14 SU8302
Delley Devon 19 SS5424
Delliefure Highld 141 NJ0730
Delly End Oxon 36 SP3513
Delmonden Green Kent 17 TQ7330
Delnashaugh Inn Gramp 141 NJ1835
Delny Highld 146 NH7372
Delph Gt Man 82 SD9807
Delves Dur 95 NZ1149
Delvine Tays 126 NO1240
Dembleby Lincs 64 TF0437
Demelza Cnwll 4 SW9763
Denaby S York 75 SK4899
Denaby Main S York 75 SK4999
Denbies Surrey 26 TQ1450
Denbigh Clwyd 70 SJ0566
Denbrae Fife 126 NO3818
Denbury Devon 7 SX8268
Denby Derbys 62 SK3946
Denby Bottles Derbys 62 SK3846
Denby Dale W York 82 SE2208
Denchworth Oxon 36 SU3891
Dendron Cumb 86 SD2470
Denel End Beds 38 TL0335
Denfield Tays 125 NN9517
Denford Nhants 51 SP9976
Dengie Essex 41 TL9802
Denham Bucks 26 TQ0487
Denham Suffk 53 TL7561
Denham Suffk 55 TM1974
Denham End Suffk 53 TL7663
Denham Green Bucks 26 TQ0488
Denham Green Suffk 55 TM1974
Denhead Fife 127 NO4613
Denhead Gramp 143 NJ9952
Denhead of Gray Tays 126 NO3531
Denholm Border 110 NT5718
Denholme W York 82 SE0734
Denholme Clough W York 82 SE0732
Denio Gwynd 56 SH3635
Denmead Hants 13 SU6512
Denmore Gramp 135 NJ9411
Denne Park W Susx 15 TQ1628
Dennington Suffk 55 TM2867
Denny Cent 116 NS8082
Dennyloanhead Cent 116 NS8080
Denshaw Gt Man 82 SD9710
Denside Gramp 135 NO8095
Densole Kent 29 TR2141
Denston Suffk 53 TL7652
Denstone Staffs 73 SK0940
Denstroude Kent 29 TR1061
Dent Cumb 87 SD7086
Dent-de-Lion Kent 29 TR3269
Denton Cambs 52 TL1587
Denton Dur 96 NZ2118
Denton E Susx 16 TQ4502
Denton Gt Man 79 SJ9295
Denton Kent 28 TQ6673
Denton Kent 29 TR2147
Denton Lincs 63 SK8632
Denton N York 82 SE1448
Denton Nhants 51 SP8358
Denton Norfk 55 TM2788
Denton Oxon 37 SP5902
Denver Norfk 65 TF6001
Denwick Nthumb 111 NU2014
Deopham Norfk 66 TG0400
Deopham Green Norfk 66 TM0499
Depden Suffk 53 TL7857
Depden Green Suffk 53 TL7756
Deptford Gt Lon 27 TQ3777
Deptford Wilts 22 SU0138
Derby Derbys 62 SK3536
Derby Devon 19 SS5633
Derbyhaven IOM 153 SC2867
Derculich Tays 125 NN8852
Deri M Glam 33 SO1201
Derril Devon 18 SS3003
Derringstone Kent 29 TR2049
Derrington Staffs 72 SJ8922
Derriton Devon 18 SS3303
Derry Hill Wilts 35 ST9670
Derrythorpe Humb 84 SE8208
Dersingham Norfk 65 TF6830
Dervaig Strath 121 NM4352
Derwen Clwyd 70 SJ0750
Derwen Fawr Dyfed 44 SN5722
Derwenlas Powys 57 SN7298
Derwydd Dyfed 32 SN6117
Desborough Nhants 51 SP8083
Desford Leics 62 SK4703
Deskford Gramp 142 NJ5061
Detchant Nthumb 111 NU0836
Detling Kent 28 TQ7958
Deuxhill Shrops 60 SO6987
Devauden Gwent 34 ST4898
Devil's Bridge Dyfed 43 SN7376
Deviock Cnwll 5 SX3155
Devitts Green Warwks 61 SP2790
Devizes Wilts 22 SU0061
Devonport Devon 6 SX4554
Devonside Cent 116 NS9196
Devoran Cnwll 3 SW7939
Dewarton Loth 118 NT3763
Dewlish Dorset 11 SY7798
Dewsbury W York 82 SE2421
Dewsbury Moor W York 82 SE2321
Deytheur Powys 58 SJ2317
Dial Avon 21 ST5366
Dial Green W Susx 14 SU9227
Dial Post W Susx 15 TQ1519
Dibberford Dorset 10 ST4504
Dibden Hants 13 SU4008
Dibden Purlieu Hants 13 SU4106
Dickens Heath W Mids 61 SP1176
Dickleburgh Norfk 54 TM1682
Didbrook Gloucs 48 SP0531
Didcot Oxon 37 SU5290
Diddington Cambs 52 TL1965
Diddlebury Shrops 59 SO5085
Didley H & W 46 SO4532
Didling W Susx 14 SU8318
Didmarton Gloucs 35 ST8287
Didsbury Gt Man 79 SJ8491
Didworthy Devon 7 SX6862
Digby Lincs 76 TF0854
Digg Highld 136 NG4668
Diggle Gt Man 82 SE0007
Digmoor Lancs 78 SD4905
Digswell Herts 39 TL2415
Digswell Water Herts 39 TL2514
Dihewyd Dyfed 44 SN4855
Dilham Norfk 67 TG3325
Dilhorne Staffs 72 SJ9743
Dillington Cambs 52 TL1365
Dilston Nthumb 102 NY9763
Dilton Wilts 22 ST8548
Dilton Marsh Wilts 22 ST8449
Dilwyn H & W 46 SO4154
Dimple Derbys 74 SK2960
Dimple Gt Man 81 SD7015
Dinas Cnwll 4 SW9274
Dinas Dyfed 30 SN0138
Dinas Dyfed 31 SN2730
Dinas Gwynd 56 SH2735
Dinas M Glam 33 ST0091
Dinas Dinlle Gwynd 68 SH4356
Dinas Powys S Glam 33 ST1571
Dinas-Mawddwy Gwynd 57 SH8515
Dinder Somset 21 ST5744
Dinedor H & W 46 SO5336
Dingestow Gwent 34 SO4510
Dingle Mersyd 78 SJ3687
Dingleden Kent 17 TQ8131
Dingley Nhants 50 SP7787
Dingwall Highld 139 NH5458
Dinham Gwent 34 ST4792
Dinmael Clwyd 70 SJ0044
Dinnet Gramp 134 NO4598
Dinnington S York 75 SK5285
Dinnington Somset 10 ST4012
Dinnington T & W 103 NZ2073
Dinorwic Gwynd 69 SH5961
Dinton Bucks 37 SP7610
Dinton Wilts 22 SU0131
Dinwoodie D & G 100 NY1190
Dinworthy Devon 18 SS3015
Dipford Somset 20 ST2021
Dipley Hants 24 SU7457
Dippen Strath 105 NR7937
Dippenhall Surrey 25 SU8146
Dippermill Devon 18 SS4406
Dippertown Devon 5 SX4284
Dippin Strath 105 NS0422
Dipple Gramp 141 NJ3258
Dipple Strath 106 NS2002
Diptford Devon 7 SX7256
Dipton Dur 96 NZ1554
Diptonmill Nthumb 102 NY9361
Dirleton Loth 118 NT5184
Dirt Pot Nthumb 95 NY8545
Discoed Powys 46 SO2764
Diseworth Leics 62 SK4524
Dishforth N York 89 SE3873
Disley Ches 79 SJ9784
Diss Norfk 54 TM1180
Disserth Powys 45 SO0358
Distington Cumb 92 NY0023
Ditchampton Wilts 23 SU0831
Ditchburn Nthumb 111 NU1320
Ditcheat Somset 21 ST6236
Ditchingham Norfk 67 TM3391
Ditchley Oxon 36 SP3820
Ditchling E Susx 15 TQ3215
Ditherington Shrops 59 SJ5014
Ditteridge Wilts 35 ST8169
Dittisham Devon 7 SX8655
Ditton Ches 78 SJ4986
Ditton Kent 28 TQ7158
Ditton Green Cambs 53 TL6558
Ditton Priors Shrops 59 SO6089
Dixton Gloucs 47 SO9830
Dixton Gwent 34 SO5113
Dizzard Cnwll 4 SX1698
Dobcross Gt Man 82 SD9906
Dobroyd Castle W York 81 SD9323
Dobwalls Cnwll 5 SX2165
Doccombe Devon 8 SX7786
Dochgarroch Highld 140 NH6140
Dockenfield Surrey 25 SU8240
Docker Lancs 87 SD5774
Docking Norfk 65 TF7636
Docklow H & W 46 SO5657
Dockray Cumb 93 NY2649
Dockray Cumb 93 NY3921
Dod's Leigh Staffs 73 SK0134
Dodbrooke Devon 7 SX7444
Dodd's Green Ches 71 SJ6043
Doddinghurst Essex 27 TQ5999
Doddington Cambs 52 TL4090
Doddington Kent 28 TQ9357
Doddington Lincs 76 SK8970
Doddington Nthumb 111 NT9932
Doddington Shrops 46 SO6176
Doddiscombsleigh Devon 8 SX8586
Doddshill Norfk 65 TF6930
Doddy Cross Cnwll 5 SX3062
Dodford H & W 60 SO9373
Dodford Nhants 49 SP6160
Dodington Avon 35 ST7580
Dodington Somset 20 ST1740
Dodleston Ches 71 SJ3661
Dodscott Devon 19 SS5419
Dodside Strath 115 NS5053
Dodworth S York 82 SE3105
Dodworth Bottom S York 83 SE3204
Dodworth Green S York 82 SE3004
Doe Bank W Mids 61 SP1197
Doe Lea Derbys 75 SK4666
Dog Village Devon 9 SX9896
Dogdyke Lincs 76 TF2055
Dogley Lane W York 82 SE1813
Dogmersfield Hants 25 SU7852
Dogridge Wilts 36 SU0887
Dogsthorpe Cambs 64 TF1901
Dol-for Powys 57 SH8106
Dol-gran Dyfed 31 SN4334
Dolancothi Dyfed 44 SN6640
Dolanog Powys 58 SJ0612
Dolau Powys 45 SO1467
Dolbenmaen Gwynd 56 SH5043
Doley Shrops 72 SJ7429
Dolfor Powys 58 SO1087
Dolgarrog Gwynd 69 SH7767
Dolgellau Gwynd 57 SH7217
Dolgoch Gwynd 57 SH6504
Doll Highld 147 NC8803
Dollar Cent 117 NS9698
Dollarfield Cent 117 NS9697
Dolley Green Powys 46 SO2865
Dollwen Dyfed 43 SN6881
Dolphin Clwyd 70 SJ1973
Dolphinholme Lancs 80 SD5253
Dolphinton Strath 117 NT1046
Dolton Devon 19 SS5712
Dolwen Clwyd 69 SH8874
Dolwyddelan Gwynd 69 SH7352
Dolybont Dyfed 43 SN6288
Dolyhir Powys 46 SO2457
Domgay Powys 58 SJ2818
Donaldson's Lodge Nthumb 110 NT8741
Doncaster S York 83 SE5703
Doncaster Carr S York 83 SE5801
Donehill Devon 8 SX7277
Donhead St Andrew Wilts 22 ST9124
Donhead St Mary Wilts 22 ST9024
Donibristle Fife 117 NT1688
Doniford Somset 20 ST0842
Donington Lincs 64 TF2035
Donington on Bain Lincs 76 TF2382
Donington Southing Lincs 64 TF2034
Donisthorpe Leics 61 SK3113
Donkey Street Kent 17 TR1032
Donkey Town Surrey 25 SU9360
Donnington Berks 24 SU4668
Donnington Gloucs 48 SP1928
Donnington H & W 47 SO7034
Donnington Shrops 59 SJ5708
Donnington Shrops 60 SJ7114
Donnington W Susx 14 SU8501
Donnington Wood Shrops 60 SJ7012
Donyatt Somset 10 ST3314
Doomsday Green W Susx 15 TQ1929
Doonfoot Strath 106 NS3219
Doonholm Strath 106 NS3317
Dorback Lodge Highld 141 NJ0716
Dorchester Dorset 11 SY6990
Dorchester Oxon 37 SU5794
Dordon Warwks 61 SK2500
Dore S York 74 SK3181
Dores Highld 140 NH5934
Dorking Surrey 15 TQ1649
Dorking Tye Suffk 54 TL9236
Dormans Land Surrey 15 TQ4041
Dormans Park Surrey 15 TQ3940
Dormington H & W 46 SO5840
Dormston H & W 47 SO9857
Dorn Gloucs 48 SP2034
Dorney Berks 26 SU9378
Dornie Highld 138 NG8826
Dornoch Highld 147 NH7989
Dornock D & G 101 NY2366
Dorrery Highld 150 ND0754
Dorridge W Mids 61 SP1775
Dorrington Lincs 76 TF0852
Dorrington Shrops 59 SJ4702
Dorrington Shrops 72 SJ7340
Dorsington Warwks 48 SP1349
Dorstone H & W 46 SO3141
Dorton Bucks 37 SP6814
Dosthill Staffs 61 SP2199
Dottery Dorset 10 SY4595
Doublebois Cnwll 5 SX1964
Dougarie Strath 105 NR8837
Doughton Gloucs 35 ST8791
Douglas IOM 153 SC3775
Douglas Strath 108 NS8330
Douglas and Angus Tays 127 NO4233
Douglas Castle Strath 108 NS8431
Douglas Pier Strath 114 NS1999
Douglas Water Strath 108 NS8736
Douglas West Strath 108 NS8231
Douglastown Tays 126 NO4147
Doulting Somset 21 ST6443
Dounby Ork 155 HY2920
Doune Cent 116 NN7201
Doune Highld 146 NC4400
Dounepark Strath 106 NX1897
Dounie Highld 146 NH5690
Dousland Devon 6 SX5369
Dovaston Shrops 59 SJ3521
Dove Green Notts 75 SK4652
Dove Holes Derbys 74 SK0777
Dovenby Cumb 92 NY0933
Dover Gt Man 78 SD6000
Dover Kent 29 TR3241
Dovercourt Essex 41 TM2431
Doverdale H & W 47 SO8666
Doveridge Derbys 73 SK1133
Doversgreen Surrey 15 TQ2548
Dowally Tays 125 NO0048
Dowbridge Lancs 80 SD4331
Dowdeswell Gloucs 35 SP0019
Dowlais M Glam 33 SO0607
Dowland Devon 19 SS5610
Dowlish Ford Somset 10 ST3513
Dowlish Wake Somset 10 ST3712
Down Ampney Gloucs 36 SU0996
Down Hatherley Gloucs 35 SO8622
Down St Mary Devon 8 SS7404
Down Thomas Devon 6 SX5050
Downacarey Devon 5 SX3790
Downderry Cnwll 5 SX3154
Downe Gt Lon 27 TQ4361
Downend Avon 35 ST6577
Downend Berks 37 SU4775
Downend Gloucs 35 ST8398
Downend IOW 13 SZ5387
Downfield Tays 126 NO3932
Downgate Cnwll 5 SX2871
Downgate Cnwll 5 SX3672
Downham Cambs 53 TL5284
Downham Essex 40 TQ7296
Downham Gt Lon 27 TQ3871
Downham Lancs 81 SD7844
Downham Nthumb 110 NT8633
Downham Market Norfk 65 TF6103
Downhead Somset 21 ST5625
Downhead Somset 22 ST6945
Downhill Cnwll 4 SW8669
Downhill Tays 125 NO0930
Downholland Cross Lancs 78 SD3606
Downholme N York 89 SE1197
Downies Gramp 135 NO9294
Downing Clwyd 70 SJ1578
Downley Bucks 26 SU8495
Downside Somset 21 ST6244
Downside Somset 21 ST6450
Downside Surrey 26 TQ1057
Downton Hants 12 SZ2693
Downton Wilts 12 SU1821
Downton on the Rock H & W 46 SO4273
Dowsby Lincs 64 TF1129
Dowsdale Lincs 64 TF2810
Dowsland Green Essex 40 TL8724
Doxey Staffs 72 SJ8923
Doxford Nthumb 111 NU1823
Doynton Avon 35 ST7274
Draethen M Glam 34 ST2287
Draffan Strath 116 NS7945
Dragonby Humb 84 SE9014
Dragons Green W Susx 15 TQ1423
Drakeholes Notts 75 SK7090
Drakelow H & W 60 SO8180
Drakemyre Strath 115 NS2950
Drakes Broughton H & W 47 SO9248
Drakes Cross H & W 61 SP0876
Drakewalls Cnwll 6 SX4270
Draughton N York 82 SE0352
Draughton Nhants 50 SP7676
Drax N York 83 SE6726
Drax Hales N York 83 SE6725
Draycot Foliat Wilts 36 SU1777
Draycote Warwks 50 SP4470
Draycott Derbys 62 SK4433
Draycott Gloucs 48 SP1835
Draycott H & W 47 SO8548
Draycott Shrops 60 SO8093
Draycott Somset 21 ST4751
Draycott Somset 21 ST5521
Draycott in the Clay Staffs 73 SK1528
Draycott in the Moors Staffs 72 SJ9840
Drayford Devon 19 SS7813
Draynes Cnwll 5 SX2169
Drayton H & W 60 SO9075
Drayton Hants 13 SU6705
Drayton Leics 51 SP8392
Drayton Lincs 64 TF2439
Drayton Norfk 66 TG1813
Drayton Oxon 49 SP4241
Drayton Oxon 37 SU4894
Drayton Somset 21 ST4024
Drayton Bassett Staffs 61 SK1900
Drayton Beauchamp Bucks 38 SP9011
Drayton Parslow Bucks 38 SP8328
Drayton St Leonard Oxon 37 SU5996
Drebley N York 88 SE0559
Dreemskerry IOM 153 SC4791
Dreen Hill Dyfed 30 SM9214
Drefach Dyfed 31 SN3538
Drefach Dyfed 44 SN4945
Drefach Dyfed 32 SN5213
Drefelin Dyfed 31 SN3637
Dreghorn Strath 106 NS3538
Drellingore Kent 29 TR2441
Drem Loth 118 NT5079
Dresden Staffs 72 SJ9142
Drewsteignton Devon 8 SX7391
Driby Lincs 77 TF3874
Driffield Gloucs 36 SU0799
Driffield Humb 91 TA0257
Driffield Cross Roads Gloucs 36 SU0698
Drift Cnwll 2 SW4328
Drigg Cumb 86 SD0699
Drighlington W York 82 SE2228
Drimnin Highld 121 NM5554
Drimpton Dorset 10 ST4104
Drimsallie Highld 130 NM9578
Dringhoe Humb 85 TA1454
Dringhouses N York 83 SE5849
Drinkstone Suffk 54 TL9561
Drinkstone Green Suffk 54 TL9660
Drinsey Nook Notts 76 SK8773
Drive End Dorset 10 ST5808
Driver's End Herts 39 TL2220
Drointon Staffs 73 SK0226
Droitwich H & W 47 SO8963
Dron Tays 126 NO1416
Dronfield Derbys 74 SK3578
Dronfield Woodhouse Derbys 74 SK3378
Drongan Strath 107 NS4418
Dronley Tays 126 NO3435
Droop Dorset 11 ST7508
Dropping Well S York 74 SK3994
Droxford Hants 13 SU6018
Droylsden Gt Man 79 SJ9097
Druid Clwyd 70 SJ0443
Druids Heath W Mids 61 SK0502
Druidston Dyfed 30 SM8616
Druimachoish Highld 123 NN1246
Druimarbin Highld 130 NN0770
Druimdrishaig Strath 113 NR7370
Druimindarroch Highld 129 NM6884
Drum Strath 114 NR9276
Drum Tays 117 NO0400
Drumalbin Strath 108 NS9038
Drumbeg Highld 148 NC1232
Drumblade Gramp 142 NJ5840
Drumblair House Gramp 142 NJ6343
Drumbreddon D & G 98 NX0843
Drumbuie Highld 137 NG7730
Drumburgh Cumb 93 NY2659
Drumburn D & G 92 NX8854
Drumchapel Strath 115 NS5270
Drumchastle Tays 132 NN6858
Drumclog Strath 107 NS6438
Drumeldrie Fife 127 NO4403
Drumelzier Border 108 NT1334
Drumfearn Highld 129 NG6716
Drumfrennie Gramp 135 NO7298
Drumguish Highld 132 NH7900
Drumhead Gramp 134 NO6092

Drumin
East Pulham

Drumin Gramp 141 NJ1830
Drumjohn D & G 107 NX5297
Drumlamford Strath 98 NX2876
Drumlasie Gramp 135 NJ6405
Drumleaning Cumb 93 NY2751
Drumlemble Strath 104 NR6619
Drumlithie Gramp 135 NO7880
Drummoddie D & G 99 NX3845
Drummore D & G 98 NX1336
Drummore D & G 100 NX9074
Drummuir Gramp 141 NJ3843
Drumnadrochit Highld 139 NH5030
Drumnagorrach Gramp 142 NJ5252
Drumpark D & G 100 NX8779
Drumrunie Lodge Highld 145 NC1604
Drumshang Strath 106 NS2514
Drumuie Highld 136 NG4546
Drumvaich Cent 124 NN6704
Drumvillie Highld 140 NH9420
Drunzie Tays 126 NO1308
Druridge Nthumb 103 NZ2796
Drury Clwyd 71 SJ2964
Dry Doddington Lincs 63 SK8546
Dry Drayton Cambs 52 TL3861
Dry Sandford Oxon 37 SP4600
Dry Street Essex 40 TQ6986
Drybeck Cumb 94 NY6615
Drybridge Gramp 142 NJ4362
Drybridge Strath 106 NS3536
Drybrook Gloucs 35 SO6417
Dryburgh Border 110 NT5932
Dryhope Border 109 NT2624
Drym Cnwll 2 SW6133
Drymen Cent 115 NS4788
Drymuir Gramp 143 NJ9046
Drynoch Highld 136 NG4031
Dryslwyn Dyfed 32 SN5520
Dryton Shrops 59 SJ5905
Dubford Gramp 143 NJ7963
Dublin Suffk 54 TM1669
Duchally Highld 145 NC3817
Duck End Beds 38 TL0544
Duck End Cambs 52 TL2464
Duck End Essex 40 TL6526
Duck's Cross Beds 52 TL1156
Duckend Green Essex 40 TL7223
Duckington Ches 71 SJ4851
Ducklington Oxon 36 SP3507
Duddingston Loth 117 NT2872
Duddington Nhants 51 SK9800
Duddlestone Somset 20 ST2321
Duddleswell E Susx 16 TQ4628
Duddlewick Shrops 59 SO6583
Duddo Nthumb 110 NT9342
Duddon Ches 71 SJ5164
Duddon Bridge Cumb 86 SD1988
Dudleston Shrops 71 SJ3438
Dudleston Heath Shrops 59 SJ3736
Dudley T & W 103 NZ2573
Dudley W Mids 60 SO9490
Dudley Hill W York 82 SE1830
Dudley Port W Mids 60 SO9691
Dudnill Shrops 47 SO6474
Dudsbury Dorset 12 SZ0798
Dudswell Herts 38 SP9609
Duffield Derbys 62 SK3443
Duffryn M Glam 33 SS8495
Dufftown Gramp 141 NJ3240
Duffus Gramp 141 NJ1668
Dufton Cumb 94 NY6825
Duggleby N York 90 SE8767
Duirinish Highld 137 NG7831
Duisdalemore Highld 129 NG7013
Duisky Highld 130 NN0076
Duke Street Suffk 54 TM0742
Dukestown Gwent 33 SO1410
Dukinfield Gt Man 79 SJ9397
Dulas Gwynd 68 SH4789
Dulcote Somset 21 ST5644
Dulford Devon 9 ST0706
Dull Tays 125 NN8049
Dullatur Strath 116 NS7476
Dullingham Cambs 53 TL6357
Dullingham Ley Cambs 53 TL6456
Dulnain Bridge Highld 141 NH9925
Duloe Beds 52 TL1560
Duloe Cnwll 5 SX2358
Dulverton Somset 20 SS9127
Dulwich Gt Lon 27 TQ3373
Dumbarton Strath 115 NS3975
Dumbleton Gloucs 47 SP0135
Dumfries D & G 100 NX9776
Dumgoyne Cent 115 NS5283
Dummer Hants 24 SU5846
Dumpton Kent 29 TR3966
Dun Tays 135 NO6659
Dunalastair Tays 132 NN7158
Dunan Highld 137 NG5828
Dunan Strath 114 NS1571
Dunan Tays 124 NN4757
Dunaverty Strath 105 NR6807
Dunball Somset 21 ST3141
Dunbar Loth 118 NT6778
Dunbeath Highld 151 ND1629
Dunbeg Strath 122 NM8833
Dunblane Cent 116 NN7801
Dunbog Fife 126 NO2817
Dunbridge Hants 23 SU3226
Duncanston Highld 139 NH5856
Duncanstone Gramp 142 NJ5726
Dunchideock Devon 9 SX8787
Dunchurch Warwks 50 SP4871
Duncote Nhants 49 SP6750
Duncow D & G 100 NX9683
Duncrievie Tays 126 NO1309
Duncton W Susx 14 SU9617
Dundee Tays 126 NO4030
Dundon Somset 21 ST4832
Dundonald Strath 106 NS3634
Dundonnell Highld 145 NH0987
Dundraw Cumb 93 NY2149
Dundreggan Highld 131 NH3214
Dundrennan D & G 99 NX7447
Dundry Avon 21 ST5666
Dunecht Gramp 135 NJ7509
Dunfermline Fife 117 NT0987
Dunfield Gloucs 36 SU1497
Dunford Bridge S York 82 SE1502
Dungate Kent 28 TQ9159
Dungavel Strath 107 NS6537
Dunge Wilts 22 ST8954
Dunglass Loth 119 NT7671
Dungworth S York 74 SK2789
Dunham Notts 75 SK8074
Dunham Town Gt Man 79 SJ7387
Dunham Woodhouses Gt Man 79 SJ7287
Dunham-on-the-Hill Ches 71 SJ4772
Dunhampstead H & W 47 SO9160
Dunhampton H & W 47 SO8466
Dunholme Lincs 76 TF0279
Dunino Fife 127 NO5311
Dunipace Cent 116 NS8083
Dunk's Green Kent 27 TQ6152
Dunkeld Tays 125 NO0242
Dunkerton Avon 22 ST7159
Dunkeswell Devon 9 ST1407
Dunkeswick W York 82 SE3047
Dunkirk Avon 35 ST7885
Dunkirk Ches 71 SJ3872
Dunkirk Kent 29 TR0759
Dunkirk Staffs 72 SJ8152
Dunkirk Wilts 22 ST9962
Dunlappie Tays 134 NO5867
Dunley H & W 47 SO7869
Dunley Hants 24 SU4553
Dunlop Strath 115 NS4049
Dunmaglass Highld 140 NH5922
Dunmere Cnwll 4 SX0467
Dunmore Cent 116 NS8989
Dunmore Strath 113 NR7961
Dunn Street Kent 28 TQ7961
Dunnet Highld 151 ND2171
Dunnichen Tays 127 NO5048
Dunning Tays 125 NO0114
Dunnington Humb 85 TA1551
Dunnington N York 83 SE6652
Dunnington Warwks 48 SP0654
Dunnockshaw Lancs 81 SD8127
Dunoon Strath 114 NS1776
Dunphail Gramp 141 NJ0048
Dunragit D & G 98 NX1557
Duns Border 119 NT7853
Duns Tew Oxon 49 SP4528
Dunsa Derbys 74 SK2470
Dunsby Lincs 64 TF1026
Dunscar Gt Man 81 SD7113
Dunscore D & G 100 NX8684
Dunscroft S York 83 SE6409
Dunsdale Cleve 97 NZ6019
Dunsden Green Oxon 37 SU7377
Dunsdon Devon 18 SS3008
Dunsfold Surrey 14 TQ0035
Dunsford Devon 8 SX8189
Dunshelt Fife 126 NO2410
Dunshillock Gramp 143 NJ9848
Dunsill Notts 75 SK4661
Dunsley N York 90 NZ8511
Dunsley Staffs 60 SO8583
Dunsmore Bucks 38 SP8605
Dunsop Bridge Lancs 81 SD6649
Dunstable Beds 38 TL0122
Dunstall Staffs 73 SK1820
Dunstall Common H & W 47 SO8843
Dunstall Green Suffk 53 TL7460
Dunstan Nthumb 111 NU2419
Dunstan Steads Nthumb 111 NU2422
Dunster Somset 20 SS9943
Dunston Lincs 76 TF0662
Dunston Norfk 67 TG2202
Dunston Staffs 72 SJ9217
Dunston T & W 96 NZ2362
Dunston Heath Staffs 72 SJ9017
Dunstone Devon 6 SX5951
Dunstone Devon 7 SX7175
Dunsville S York 83 SE6407
Dunswell Humb 85 TA0735
Dunsyre Strath 117 NT0748
Dunterton Devon 5 SX3779
Dunthrop Oxon 48 SP3528
Duntisbourne Abbots Gloucs 35 SO9607
Duntisbourne Rouse Gloucs 35 SO9805
Duntish Dorset 11 ST6906
Duntocher Strath 115 NS4872
Dunton Beds 39 TL2344
Dunton Bucks 38 SP8224
Dunton Norfk 66 TF8830
Dunton Bassett Leics 50 SP5490
Dunton Green Kent 27 TQ5157
Dunton Wayletts Essex 40 TQ6590
Duntulm Highld 136 NG4174
Dunure Strath 106 NS2515
Dunvant W Glam 32 SS5993
Dunvegan Highld 136 NG2547
Dunwich Suffk 55 TM4770
Dunwood Staffs 72 SJ9455
Durdar Cumb 93 NY4051
Durgan Cnwll 3 SW7727
Durham Dur 96 NZ2742
Durisdeer D & G 108 NS8903
Durisdeermill D & G 108 NS8804
Durkar W York 82 SE3116
Durleigh Somset 20 ST2736
Durley Hants 13 SU5116
Durley Wilts 23 SU2364
Durley Street Hants 13 SU5217
Durlock Kent 29 TR2757
Durlock Kent 29 TR3164
Durlow Common H & W 47 SO6339
Durmgley Tays 127 NO4250
Durn Gt Man 82 SD9416
Durness Highld 149 NC4068
Duror Highld 122 NM9955
Durran Strath 122 NM9607
Durrington W Susx 14 TQ1105
Durrington Wilts 23 SU1544
Durris Gramp 135 NO7796
Dursley Gloucs 35 ST7598
Dursley Cross Gloucs 35 SO6920
Durston Somset 20 ST2928
Durweston Dorset 11 ST8508
Duston Nhants 49 SP7261
Duthil Highld 140 NH9324
Dutlas Powys 45 SO2177
Dutson Cnwll 5 SX3485
Dutton Ches 71 SJ5779
Duxford Cambs 53 TL4846
Duxford Oxon 36 SP3600
Dwygyfylchi Gwynd 69 SH7376
Dwyran Gwynd 68 SH4465
Dyce Gramp 135 NJ8812
Dye House Nthumb 95 NY9358
Dyer's End Essex 53 TL7238
Dyfatty Dyfed 32 SN4401
Dyffryn M Glam 33 SO0603
Dyffryn M Glam 33 SS8593
Dyffryn S Glam 33 ST0971
Dyffryn Ardudwy Gwynd 57 SH5823
Dyffryn Castell Dyfed 43 SN7782
Dyffryn Cellwen W Glam 33 SN8510
Dyke Devon 18 SS3123
Dyke Gramp 140 NH9858
Dyke Lincs 64 TF1022
Dykehead Cent 115 NS5997
Dykehead Strath 116 NS8759
Dykehead Tays 126 NO2453
Dykehead Tays 134 NO3859
Dykelands Gramp 135 NO7068
Dykends Tays 133 NO2557
Dykeside Gramp 142 NJ7243
Dylife Powys 43 SN8694
Dymchurch Kent 17 TR1029
Dymock Gloucs 47 SO7031
Dyrham Avon 35 ST7475
Dysart Fife 117 NT3093
Dyserth Clwyd 70 SJ0578

E

Eachway H & W 60 SO9876
Eachwick Nthumb 103 NZ1171
Eagland Hill Lancs 80 SD4345
Eagle Lincs 76 SK8766
Eagle Barnsdale Lincs 76 SK8865
Eagle Manor Lincs 76 SK8868
Eaglescliffe Cleve 96 NZ4215
Eaglesfield Cumb 92 NY0928
Eaglesfield D & G 101 NY2374
Eaglesham Strath 115 NS5751
Eagley Gt Man 81 SD7112
Eairy IOM 153 SC2977
Eakring Notts 75 SK6762
Ealand Humb 84 SE7811
Ealing Gt Lon 26 TQ1780
Eals Nthumb 94 NY6756
Eamont Bridge Cumb 94 NY5228
Earby Lancs 81 SD9046
Earcroft Lancs 81 SD6823
Eardington Shrops 60 SO7290
Eardisland H & W 46 SO4158
Eardisley H & W 46 SO3149
Eardiston H & W 47 SO6968
Eardiston Shrops 59 SJ3725
Earith Cambs 52 TL3875
Earl Shilton Leics 50 SP4697
Earl Soham Suffk 55 TM2363
Earl Sterndale Derbys 74 SK0966
Earl Stonham Suffk 54 TM1059
Earl's Croome H & W 47 SO8642
Earl's Down E Susx 16 TQ6419
Earl's Green Suffk 54 TM0366
Earle Nthumb 111 NT9826
Earlestown Mersyd 78 SJ5795
Earley Berks 24 SU7472
Earlham Norfk 67 TG1908
Earlish Highld 136 NG3861
Earls Barton Nhants 51 SP8563
Earls Colne Essex 40 TL8528
Earls Common H & W 47 SO9559
Earlsditton Shrops 47 SO6275
Earlsdon W Mids 61 SP3278
Earlsferry Fife 118 NO4800
Earlsfield Gt Lon 27 TQ2573
Earlsford Gramp 143 NJ8334
Earlsheaton W York 82 SE2621
Earlston Border 110 NT5738
Earlston Strath 106 NS4035
Earlswood Surrey 15 TQ2749
Earlswood Warwks 61 SP1174
Earlswood Common Gwent 34 ST4594
Earnley W Susx 14 SZ8196
Earnshaw Bridge Lancs 80 SD5222
Earsdon Nthumb 103 NZ1993
Earsdon T & W 103 NZ3272
Earsham Norfk 55 TM3288
Earswick N York 90 SE6157
Eartham W Susx 14 SU9309
Earthcott Avon 35 ST6585
Easby N York 90 NZ5708
Easdale Strath 122 NM7417
Easebourne W Susx 14 SU9023
Easenhall Warwks 50 SP4679
Eashing Surrey 25 SU9443
Easington Bucks 37 SP6810
Easington Cleve 97 NZ7417
Easington Dur 96 NZ4143
Easington Humb 85 TA3919
Easington Nthumb 111 NU1234
Easington Oxon 37 SU6697
Easington Colliery Dur 96 NZ4344
Easington Lane T & W 96 NZ3646
Easingwold N York 90 SE5269
Easole Street Kent 29 TR2652
Eassie and Nevay Tays 126 NO3344
East Aberthaw S Glam 20 ST0366
East Allington Devon 7 SX7748
East Anstey Devon 19 SS8626
East Anton Hants 23 SU3747
East Appleton N York 89 SE2395
East Ashey IOW 13 SZ5888
East Ashling W Susx 14 SU8107
East Aston Hants 24 SU4445
East Ayton N York 91 SE9985
East Balsdon Cnwll 5 SX2898
East Bank Gwent 33 SO2105
East Barkwith Lincs 76 TF1681
East Barming Kent 28 TQ7254
East Barnby N York 90 NZ8212
East Barnet Gt Lon 27 TQ2795
East Barns Loth 119 NT7176
East Barsham Norfk 66 TF9133
East Beckham Norfk 66 TG1639
East Bedfont Gt Lon 26 TQ0873
East Bergholt Suffk 54 TM0734
East Bierley W York 82 SE1929
East Bilney Norfk 66 TF9519
East Blatchington E Susx 16 TQ4800
East Bloxworth Dorset 11 SY8894
East Boldon T & W 96 NZ3661
East Boldre Hants 12 SU3700
East Bolton Nthumb 111 NU1216
East Bower Somset 21 ST3237
East Bradenham Norfk 66 TF9308
East Brent Somset 21 ST3451
East Bridgford Notts 63 SK6943
East Briscoe Dur 95 NY9719
East Buckland Devon 19 SS6831
East Budleigh Devon 9 SY0684
East Burnham Bucks 26 SU9584
East Burton Dorset 11 SY8287
East Butsfield Dur 95 NZ1145
East Butterwick Humb 84 SE8306
East Calder Loth 117 NT0867
East Carleton Norfk 66 TG1701
East Carlton Nhants 51 SP8389
East Carlton W York 82 SE2143
East Challow Oxon 36 SU3888
East Charleton Devon 7 SX7642
East Chelborough Dorset 10 ST5505
East Chevington Nthumb 103 NZ2699
East Chiltington E Susx 15 TQ3715
East Chinnock Somset 10 ST4913
East Chisenbury Wilts 23 SU1452
East Cholderton Hants 23 SU2945
East Clandon Surrey 26 TQ0651
East Claydon Bucks 49 SP7325
East Clevedon Avon 34 ST4171
East Coker Somset 10 ST5412
East Combe Somset 20 ST1631
East Compton Somset 21 ST6141
East Cornworthy Devon 7 SX8455
East Cote Cumb 92 NY1255
East Cottingwith Humb 84 SE7042
East Cowes IOW 13 SZ5095
East Cowick Humb 83 SE6620
East Cowton N York 89 NZ3003
East Cramlington Nthumb 103 NZ2776
East Cranmore Somset 22 ST6743
East Creech Dorset 11 SY9382
East Curthwaite Cumb 93 NY3348
East Dean E Susx 16 TV5598
East Dean H & W 35 SO6520
East Dean Hants 23 SU2726
East Dean W Susx 14 SU9012
East Dereham Norfk 66 TF9913
East Down Devon 19 SS6041
East Drayton Notts 75 SK7775
East Dulwich Gt Lon 27 TQ3375
East Dundry Avon 21 ST5766
East Ella Humb 84 TA0529
East End Avon 34 ST4770
East End Beds 38 SP9642
East End Beds 51 TL1055
East End Bucks 38 SP9344
East End Essex 39 TL4210
East End Hants 24 SU4161
East End Hants 12 SZ3696
East End Herts 39 TL4527
East End Humb 85 TA1931
East End Humb 85 TA2927
East End Kent 17 TQ8335
East End Kent 28 TQ9673
East End Oxon 36 SP3915
East End Somset 22 ST6746
East Everleigh Wilts 23 SU2053
East Farleigh Kent 28 TQ7353
East Farndon Nhants 50 SP7184
East Ferry Lincs 75 SK8199
East Firsby Lincs 76 TF0085
East Fortune Loth 118 NT5479
East Garforth W York 83 SE4133
East Garston Berks 36 SU3576
East Ginge Oxon 37 SU4486
East Goscote Leics 63 SK6413
East Grafton Wilts 23 SU2560
East Grange Gramp 141 NJ0961
East Green Suffk 55 TM4065
East Grimstead Wilts 23 SU2227
East Grinstead W Susx 15 TQ3938
East Guldeford E Susx 17 TQ9321
East Haddon Nhants 50 SP6668
East Hagbourne Oxon 37 SU5288
East Halton Humb 85 TA1319
East Ham Gt Lon 27 TQ4283
East Hanney Oxon 36 SU4193
East Hanningfield Essex 40 TL7701
East Hardwick W York 83 SE4618
East Harling Norfk 54 TL9986
East Harlsey N York 89 SE4299
East Harnham Wilts 23 SU1428
East Harptree Avon 21 ST5655
East Hartburn Cleve 96 NZ4217
East Hartford Nthumb 103 NZ2679
East Harting W Susx 14 SU7919
East Hatch Wilts 22 ST9228
East Hatley Cambs 52 TL2850
East Hauxwell N York 89 SE1693
East Haven Tays 127 NO5836
East Heath Berks 25 SU7967
East Heckington Lincs 64 TF1944
East Hedleyhope Dur 96 NZ1540
East Helmsdale Highld 147 ND0315
East Hendred Oxon 37 SU4588
East Heslerton N York 91 SE9276
East Hewish Avon 21 ST4064
East Hoathly E Susx 16 TQ5216
East Holme Dorset 11 SY8986
East Holywell T & W 103 NZ3073
East Horndon Essex 40 TQ6389
East Horrington Somset 21 ST5846
East Horsley Surrey 26 TQ0952
East Horton Nthumb 111 NU0330
East Howe Dorset 12 SZ0795
East Huntington N York 83 SE6155
East Huntspill Somset 21 ST3445
East Hyde Beds 38 TL1217
East Ilkerton Devon 19 SS7147
East Ilsley Berks 37 SU4980
East Keal Lincs 77 TF3863
East Kennett Wilts 23 SU1167
East Keswick W York 83 SE3644
East Kilbride Strath 116 NS6354
East Kimber Devon 5 SX4998
East Kirkby Lincs 77 TF3362
East Knighton Dorset 11 SY8185
East Knowstone Devon 19 SS8423
East Knoyle Wilts 22 ST8830
East Kyloe Nthumb 111 NU0639
East Lambrook Somset 10 ST4318
East Langdon Kent 29 TR3346
East Langton Leics 50 SP7292
East Laroch Highld 130 NN0858
East Lavant W Susx 14 SU8608
East Lavington W Susx 14 SU9416
East Layton N York 89 NZ1609
East Leake Notts 62 SK5526
East Learmouth Nthumb 110 NT8637
East Leigh Devon 8 SS6905
East Leigh Devon 7 SX6852
East Leigh Devon 7 SX7657
East Lexham Norfk 66 TF8517
East Linton Loth 118 NT5977
East Liss Hants 14 SU7827
East Lockinge Oxon 36 SU4287
East Lound Humb 75 SK7899
East Lulworth Dorset 11 SY8682
East Lutton N York 91 SE9469
East Lydeard Somset 20 ST1829
East Lydford Somset 21 ST5731
East Malling Kent 28 TQ7056
East Malling Heath Kent 28 TQ6955
East Marden W Susx 14 SU8014
East Markham Notts 75 SK7373
East Martin Hants 12 SU0719
East Marton N York 81 SD9050
East Meon Hants 13 SU6822
East Mere Devon 9 SS9916
East Mersea Essex 41 TM0414
East Molesey Surrey 26 TQ1467
East Morden Dorset 11 SY9194
East Morton D & G 108 NS8800
East Morton W York 82 SE0942
East Ness N York 90 SE6978
East Newton Humb 85 TA2638
East Norton Leics 50 SK7800
East Oakley Hants 24 SU5749
East Ogwell Devon 7 SX8370
East Orchard Dorset 11 ST8317
East Ord Nthumb 119 NT9751
East Panson Devon 5 SX3692
East Parley Dorset 12 SZ1097
East Peckham Kent 28 TQ6648
East Pennar Dyfed 30 SM9602
East Pennard Somset 21 ST5937
East Perry Cambs 52 TL1566
East Portlemouth Devon 7 SX7538
East Prawle Devon 7 SX7836
East Preston W Susx 14 TQ0602
East Pulham Dorset 11 ST7209

F

G

Gadgirth

Gonalston

Gadgirth Strath 106 NS4022
Gadlas Shrops 59 SJ3737
Gaer Powys 33 SO1721
Gaer-llwyd Gwent 34 ST4496
Gaerwen Gwynd 68 SH4871
Gagingwell Oxon 48 SP4025
Gailes Strath 106 NS3235
Gailey Staffs 60 SJ9110
Gainford Dur 96 NZ1716
Gainsborough Lincs 75 SK8189
Gainsford End Essex 53 TL7235
Gairloch Highld 144 NG8076
Gairlochy Highld 131 NN1784
Gairneybridge Tays 117 NT1397
Gaisby W York 82 SE1536
Gaisgill Cumb 87 NY6305
Gaitsgill Cumb 93 NY3846
Galashiels Border 109 NT4936
Galby Leics 50 SK6900
Galcantray Highld 140 NH8148
Galgate Lancs 80 SD4855
Galhampton Somset 21 ST6329
Gallanach Strath 120 NM2161
Gallanach Strath 122 NM8326
Gallantry Bank Ches 71 SJ5153
Gallatown Fife 117 NT2994
Galley Common Warwks 61 SP3091
Galleywood Essex 40 TL7003
Gallovie Highld 132 NN5589
Gallowfauld Tays 127 NO4342
Gallowhill Tays 126 NO1635
Gallows Green Essex 40 TL9226
Gallows Green H & W 47 SO9362
Gallowstree Common Oxon 37 SU6980
Gallt-y-foel Gwynd 69 SH5862
Galltair Highld 129 NG8120
Gally Hill Hants 25 SU8051
Gallypot Street E Susx 16 TQ4735
Galmisdale Highld 128 NM4784
Galmpton Devon 7 SX6940
Galmpton Devon 7 SX8856
Galphay N York 89 SE2572
Galston Strath 107 NS5036
Galton Dorset 11 SY7785
Gamballs Green Staffs 74 SK0367
Gambles Green Essex 40 TL7614
Gamblesby Cumb 94 NY6039
Gamelsby Cumb 93 NY2552
Gamesley Gt Man 79 SK0194
Gamlingay Cambs 52 TL2452
Gamlingay Cinques Cambs 52 TL2352
Gamlingay Great Heath Beds 52 TL2151
Gammersgill N York 88 SE0582
Gamrie Gramp 143 NJ7962
Gamston Notts 75 SK7176
Gamston Notts 62 SK5937
Ganarew H & W 34 SO5216
Ganavan Bay Strath 122 NM8632
Gang Cnwll 5 SX3068
Ganllwyd Gwynd 57 SH7324
Gannachy Tays 134 NO5970
Ganstead Humb 85 TA1434
Ganthorpe N York 90 SE6870
Ganton N York 91 SE9977
Ganwick Corner Herts 27 TQ2599
Gappah Devon 9 SX8677
Garbity Gramp 141 NJ3152
Garboldisham Norfk 54 TM0081
Garchory Gramp 134 NJ3010
Garden City Clwyd 71 SJ3269
Garden Village Derbys 74 SK2698
Gardeners Green Berks 25 SU8266
Gardenstown Gramp 143 NJ8064
Garderhouse Shet 155 HU3347
Gardham Humb 84 SE9542
Gare Hill Somset 22 ST7840
Garelochhead Strath 114 NS2491
Garford Oxon 36 SU4296
Garforth W York 83 SE4033
Garforth Bridge W York 83 SE3932
Gargrave N York 81 SD9354
Gargunnock Cent 116 NS7094
Garizim Gwynd 69 SH6975
Garlic Street Norfk 55 TM2183
Garlieston D & G 99 NX4746
Garlinge Kent 29 TR3369
Garlinge Green Kent 29 TR1152
Garlogie Gramp 135 NJ7805
Garmond Gramp 143 NJ8052
Garmondsway Dur 96 NZ3434
Garmouth Gramp 141 NJ3364
Garmston Shrops 59 SJ6006
Garn Gwynd 56 SH2834
Garn-Dolbenmaen Gwynd 56 SH4943
Garnant Dyfed 32 SN6713
Garnett Bridge Cumb 87 SD5299
Garnkirk Strath 116 NS6768
Garnswllt W Glam 32 SN6209
Garrabost W Isls 154 NB5133
Garrallan Strath 107 NS5418
Garras Cnwll 2 SW7023
Garreg Gwynd 57 SH6141
Garrigill Cumb 94 NY7441
Garriston N York 89 SE1592
Garroch D & G 99 NX5981
Garrochtrie D & G 98 NX1138
Garrochty Strath 114 NS0953
Garros Highld 136 NG4962
Garrowby Hall Humb 90 SE7957
Garsdale Cumb 88 SD7489
Garsdale Head Cumb 88 SD7891
Garsdon Wilts 35 ST9687
Garshall Green Staffs 72 SJ9633
Garsington Oxon 37 SP5802
Garstang Lancs 80 SD4945
Garston Herts 26 TL1100
Garston Mersyd 78 SJ4084
Gartachossan Strath 112 NR3461
Gartcosh Strath 116 NS6967
Garth Clwyd 70 SJ2542
Garth Gwent 34 ST3492
Garth M Glam 33 SS8690
Garth Powys 45 SN9549
Garth Powys 46 SO2772
Garth Penrhyncoch Dyfed 43 SN6484
Garth Row Cumb 87 SD5297
Garthamlock Strath 116 NS6566
Garthbrengy Powys 45 SO0433
Gartheli Dyfed 44 SN5856
Garthmyl Powys 58 SO1999
Garthorpe Humb 84 SE8418
Garthorpe Leics 63 SK8320
Garths Cumb 87 SD5489
Gartly Gramp 142 NJ5232
Gartmore Cent 115 NS5297
Gartness Cent 115 NS5086
Gartness Strath 116 NS7864
Gartocharn Strath 115 NS4286
Garton Humb 85 TA2635
Garton End Cambs 64 TF1900
Garton-on-the-Wolds Humb 91 SE9759
Gartsherrie Strath 116 NS7265
Gartymore Highld 147 ND0114
Garvald Loth 118 NT5870
Garvan Highld 130 NM9777
Garvard Strath 112 NR3791
Garve Highld 139 NH3961
Garvestone Norfk 66 TG0207
Garvock Strath 114 NS2570
Garway H & W 34 SO4522
Garway Common H & W 34 SO4622
Garway Hill H & W 46 SO4425
Garyvard W Isls 154 NB3619
Gasper Wilts 22 ST7633
Gastard Wilts 22 ST8868
Gasthorpe Norfk 54 TL9781
Gaston Green Essex 39 TL4917
Gatcombe IOW 13 SZ4985
Gate Burton Lincs 76 SK8382
Gate Helmsley N York 83 SE6955
Gatebeck Cumb 87 SD5485
Gateford Notts 75 SK5781
Gateforth N York 83 SE5628
Gatehead Strath 106 NS3936
Gatehouse Nthumb 102 NY7889
Gatehouse of Fleet D & G 99 NX5956
Gatelawbridge D & G 100 NX9096
Gateley Norfk 66 TF9624
Gatenby N York 89 SE3287
Gates Heath Ches 71 SJ4760
Gatesgarth Cumb 93 NY1915
Gateshaw Border 110 NT7722
Gateshead T & W 96 NZ2562
Gateside Fife 126 NO1809
Gateside Strath 115 NS3653
Gateside Strath 115 NS4858
Gateside Tays 127 NO4344
Gateslack D & G 108 NS8902
Gathurst Gt Man 78 SD5407
Gatley Gt Man 79 SJ8488
Gatton Surrey 27 TQ2752
Gattonside Border 109 NT5435
Gaufron Powys 45 SN9968
Gauldry Fife 126 NO3723
Gauldswell Tays 126 NO2151
Gaulkthorn Lancs 81 SD7526
Gaultree Norfk 65 TF4907
Gaunt's Common Dorset 12 SU0205
Gaunt's End Essex 39 TL5525
Gaunton's Bank Ches 71 SJ5647
Gautby Lincs 76 TF1772
Gavinton Border 119 NT7652
Gawber S York 83 SE3207
Gawcott Bucks 49 SP6831
Gawsworth Ches 79 SJ8969
Gawthorpe W York 82 SE2721
Gawthrop Cumb 87 SD6987
Gawthwaite Cumb 86 SD2784
Gay Bowers Essex 40 TL7904
Gay Street W Susx 14 TQ0820
Gaydon Warwks 48 SP3653
Gayhurst Bucks 38 SP8446
Gayle N York 88 SD8688
Gayles N York 89 NZ1207
Gayton Mersyd 78 SJ2780
Gayton Nhants 49 SP7054
Gayton Norfk 65 TF7219
Gayton Staffs 72 SJ9828
Gayton le Marsh Lincs 77 TF4284
Gayton Thorpe Norfk 65 TF7418
Gaywood Norfk 65 TF6320
Gazeley Suffk 53 TL7264
Gear Cnwll 3 SW7224
Gearraidh Bhaird W Isls 154 NB3619
Geary Highld 136 NG2661
Gedding Suffk 54 TL9457
Geddinge Kent 29 TR2346
Geddington Nhants 51 SP8983
Gedling Notts 62 SK6142
Gedney Lincs 65 TF4024
Gedney Broadgate Lincs 65 TF4022
Gedney Drove End Lincs 65 TF4629
Gedney Dyke Lincs 65 TF4126
Gedney Hill Lincs 64 TF3311
Gee Cross Gt Man 79 SJ9593
Geldeston Norfk 67 TM3991
Gelli Gwent 34 ST2792
Gelli M Glam 33 SS9794
Gelli Gynan Clwyd 70 SJ1854
Gellifor Clwyd 70 SJ1262
Gelligaer M Glam 33 ST1396
Gelligroes Gwent 33 ST1794
Gelligron W Glam 32 SN7104
Gellilydan Gwynd 57 SH6839
Gellinudd W Glam 32 SN7303
Gelly Dyfed 31 SN0819
Gellyburn Tays 125 NO0939
Gellywen Dyfed 31 SN2723
Gelston D & G 92 NX7758
Gelston Lincs 63 SK9145
Gembling Humb 91 TA1057
Gentleshaw Staffs 61 SK0511
George Green Bucks 26 SU9981
George Nympton Devon 19 SS7023
Georgefield D & G 101 NY2991
Georgeham Devon 18 SS4639
Georgia Cnwll 2 SW4836
Georth Ork 155 HY3625
Gerlan Gwynd 69 SH6366
Germansweek Devon 5 SX4394
Germoe Cnwll 2 SW5829
Gerrans Cnwll 3 SW8735
Gerrards Cross Bucks 26 TQ0088
Gerrick Cleve 90 NZ7012
Gestingthorpe Essex 54 TL8138
Geuffordd Powys 58 SJ2114
Gib Hill Ches 79 SJ6478
Gibraltar Lincs 77 TF5558
Gibsmere Notts 75 SK7148
Giddeahall Wilts 35 ST8674
Giddy Green Dorset 11 SY8386
Gidea Park Gt Lon 27 TQ5290
Gidleigh Devon 8 SX6788
Giffnock Strath 115 NS5658
Gifford Loth 118 NT5368
Giffordtown Fife 126 NO2811
Giggleswick N York 88 SD8063
Gilberdyke Humb 84 SE8329
Gilbert Street Hants 24 SU6432
Gilbert's Cross Staffs 60 SO8187
Gilbert's End H & W 47 SO8342
Gilchriston Loth 118 NT4865
Gilcrux Cumb 92 NY1138
Gildersome W York 82 SE2429
Gildingwells S York 75 SK5585
Gilesgate Moor Dur 96 NZ2942
Gileston S Glam 20 ST0166
Gilfach M Glam 33 ST1598
Gilfach Goch M Glam 33 SS9790
Gilfachrheda Dyfed 42 SN4158
Gilgarran Cumb 92 NY0323
Gill Cumb 93 NY4429
Gill's Green Kent 17 TQ7532
Gillamoor N York 90 SE6889
Gillan Cnwll 3 SW7825
Gillesbie D & G 100 NY1691
Gilling East N York 90 SE6176
Gilling West N York 89 NZ1805
Gillingham Dorset 22 ST8026
Gillingham Kent 28 TQ7768
Gillingham Norfk 67 TM4191
Gillock Highld 151 ND2159
Gillow Heath Staffs 72 SJ8858
Gills Highld 151 ND3272
Gilmanscleuch Border 109 NT3321
Gilmerton Loth 117 NT2868
Gilmerton Tays 125 NN8823
Gilmonby Dur 95 NY9912
Gilmorton Leics 50 SP5787
Gilsland Nthumb 102 NY6366
Gilson Warwks 61 SP1989
Gilstead W York 82 SE1239
Gilston Herts 39 TL4413
Gilston Loth 118 NT4456
Giltbrook Notts 62 SK4845
Gilwern Gwent 34 SO2414
Gimingham Norfk 67 TG2836
Ginclough Ches 79 SJ9576
Ginger Green E Susx 16 TQ6212
Gipping Suffk 54 TM0763
Gipsey Bridge Lincs 77 TF2849
Girdle Toll Strath 106 NS3440
Girlington W York 82 SE1334
Girlsta Shet 155 HU4250
Girsby Cleve 89 NZ3508
Girtford Beds 52 TL1649
Girthon D & G 99 NX6053
Girton Cambs 53 TL4262
Girton Notts 75 SK8265
Girvan Strath 106 NX1897
Gisburn Lancs 81 SD8248
Gisleham Suffk 55 TM5188
Gislingham Suffk 54 TM0771
Gissing Norfk 54 TM1485
Gittisham Devon 9 SY1398
Gladestry Powys 45 SO2355
Gladsmuir Loth 118 NT4573
Glais W Glam 32 SN7000
Glaisdale N York 90 NZ7705
Glamis Tays 126 NO3846
Glan-Duar Dyfed 44 SN5243
Glan-Dwyfach Gwynd 56 SH4843
Glan-Mule Powys 58 SO1690
Glan-rhyd W Glam 32 SN7809
Glan-y-don Clwyd 70 SJ1679
Glan-y-llyn M Glam 33 ST1183
Glan-y-nant Powys 58 SN9384
Glan-yr-afon Gwynd 69 SH6080
Glan-yr-afon Gwynd 70 SH9140
Glan-yr-afon Gwynd 70 SJ0142
Glan-yr-afon W Glam 32 SN6305
Glanaber Gwynd 69 SH6351
Glanafon Dyfed 30 SM9617
Glanaman Dyfed 32 SN6713
Glandford Norfk 66 TG0441
Glandwr Dyfed 31 SN1928
Glandyfi Dyfed 43 SN6996
Glangrwyne Powys 34 SO2416
Glanrhyd Dyfed 31 SN1442
Glanton Nthumb 111 NU0714
Glanton Pike Nthumb 111 NU0514
Glanvilles Wootton Dorset 11 ST6708
Glapthorn Nhants 51 TL0290
Glapwell Derbys 75 SK4766
Glasbury Powys 45 SO1739
Glascoed Clwyd 70 SH9973
Glascoed Gwent 34 SO3301
Glascote Staffs 61 SK2203
Glascwm Powys 45 SO1552
Glasfryn Clwyd 70 SH9250
Glasgow Strath 115 NS5865
Glasinfryn Gwynd 69 SH5868
Glasnacardoch Bay Highld 129 NM6795
Glasnakille Highld 128 NG5313
Glaspwll Powys 43 SN7397
Glass Houghton W York 83 SE4324
Glassenbury Kent 28 TQ7536
Glasserton D & G 99 NX4237
Glassford Strath 116 NS7247
Glasshouse Gloucs 35 SO7021
Glasshouse Hill Gloucs 35 SO7020
Glasshouses N York 89 SE1764
Glasson Cumb 101 NY2560
Glasson Lancs 80 SD4456
Glassonby Cumb 94 NY5738
Glasterlaw Tays 127 NO5951
Glaston Leics 51 SK8900
Glastonbury Somset 21 ST5038
Glatton Cambs 52 TL1586
Glazebrook Ches 79 SJ6992
Glazebury Ches 79 SJ6797
Glazeley Shrops 60 SO7088
Gleadsmoss Ches 79 SJ8168
Gleaston Cumb 86 SD2570
Glebe Highld 139 NH5118
Gledhow W York 82 SE3137
Gledpark D & G 99 NX6250
Gledrid Shrops 59 SJ3036
Glemsford Suffk 54 TL8348
Glen Auldyn IOM 153 SC4393
Glen Clunie Lodge Gramp 133 NO1383
Glen Maye IOM 153 SC2379
Glen Mona IOM 153 SC4588
Glen Nevis House Highld 130 NN1272
Glen Parva Leics 50 SP5798
Glen Trool Lodge D & G 99 NX4080
Glen Vine IOM 153 SC3378
Glenancross Highld 129 NM6691
Glenaros House Strath 121 NM5544
Glenbarr Strath 105 NR6736
Glenbarry Gramp 142 NJ5554
Glenbeg Highld 121 NM5862
Glenbeg Highld 141 NJ0028
Glenboig Strath 116 NS7268
Glenborrodale Highld 121 NM6061
Glenbranter Strath 114 NS1197
Glenbreck Border 108 NT0521
Glenbrittle House Highld 128 NG4121
Glenbuck Strath 107 NS7429
Glencally Tays 134 NO3562
Glencaple D & G 100 NX9968
Glencarron Lodge Highld 138 NH0650
Glencarse Tays 126 NO1921
Glenceitlein Highld 123 NN1548
Glencoe Highld 130 NN1058
Glencothe Border 108 NT0829
Glencraig Fife 117 NT1894
Glencrosh D & G 107 NX7689
Glendale Highld 136 NG1749
Glendaruel Strath 114 NR9983
Glendevon Tays 125 NN9904
Glendoe Lodge Highld 131 NH4009
Glendoick Tays 126 NO2022
Glenduckie Fife 126 NO2818
Gleneagles Tays 125 NN9208
Gleneagles Hotel Tays 125 NN9111
Glenegedale Strath 112 NR3351
Glenelg Highld 129 NG8119
Glenerney Gramp 141 NJ0146
Glenfarg Tays 126 NO1310
Glenfeshie Lodge Highld 132 NN8493
Glenfield Leics 62 SK5406
Glenfinnan Highld 130 NM9080
Glenfinntaig Lodge Highld 131 NN2286
Glenfoot Tays 126 NO1815
Glenfyne Lodge Strath 123 NN2215
Glengarnock Strath 115 NS3252
Glengolly Highld 151 ND1065
Glengorm Castle Strath 121 NM4457
Glengrasco Highld 136 NG4444
Glenholm Border 108 NT1033
Glenhoul D & G 107 NX6187
Glenisla Tays 133 NO2160
Glenkerry Border 109 NT2710
Glenkin Strath 114 NS1280
Glenkindie Gramp 142 NJ4314
Glenlivet Gramp 141 NJ1929
Glenlochar D & G 99 NX7364
Glenloig Strath 105 NR9435
Glenlomond Tays 126 NO1704
Glenluce D & G 98 NX1957
Glenmark Tays 134 NO4183
Glenmassen Strath 114 NS1088
Glenmavis Strath 116 NS7467
Glenmore Highld 136 NG4340
Glenmore Lodge Highld 133 NH9709
Glenquiech Tays 134 NO4261
Glenralloch Strath 113 NR8569
Glenridding Cumb 93 NY3817
Glenrothes Fife 117 NO2700
Glenshee Tays 125 NN9834
Glenshero Lodge Highld 132 NN5592
Glenstriven Strath 114 NS0878
Glentham Lincs 76 TF0090
Glentromie Lodge Highld 132 NN7897
Glentrool Village D & G 98 NX3578
Glentruim House Highld 132 NN6894
Glentworth Lincs 76 SK9488
Glenuig Highld 129 NM6677
Glenure Strath 123 NN0448
Glenurquhart Highld 140 NH7462
Glenvarragill Highld 136 NG4739
Glenwhilly D & G 98 NX1771
Glespin Strath 108 NS8127
Glewstone H & W 34 SO5521
Glinton Cambs 64 TF1505
Glooston Leics 50 SP7595
Glororum Nthumb 111 NU1633
Glossop Derbys 74 SK0393
Gloster Hill Nthumb 103 NU2504
Gloucester Gloucs 35 SO8318
Glusburn N York 82 SE0045
Glutt Lodge Highld 150 ND0036
Gluvian Cnwll 4 SW9164
Glympton Oxon 36 SP4221
Glyn Ceiriog Clwyd 70 SJ2038
Glyn-Neath W Glam 33 SN8806
Glynarthen Dyfed 42 SN3148
Glyncorrwg W Glam 33 SS8798
Glynde E Susx 16 TQ4509
Glyndebourne E Susx 16 TQ4510
Glyndyfrdwy Clwyd 70 SJ1442
Glyntaff M Glam 33 ST0889
Glyntawe Powys 33 SN8416
Glynteg Dyfed 31 SN3637
Gnosall Staffs 72 SJ8220
Gnosall Heath Staffs 72 SJ8220
Goadby Leics 50 SP7598
Goadby Marwood Leics 63 SK7726
Goat Lees Kent 28 TR0145
Goatacre Wilts 35 SU0276
Goatfield Strath 114 NN0100
Goatham Green E Susx 17 TQ8120
Goathill Dorset 11 ST6717
Goathland N York 90 NZ8301
Goathurst Somset 20 ST2534
Goathurst Common Kent 27 TQ4952
Gobowen Shrops 59 SJ3033
Godalming Surrey 25 SU9643
Godameavy Devon 6 SX5364
Goddard's Corner Suffk 55 TM2868
Goddard's Green Kent 17 TQ8134
Godford Cross Devon 9 ST1302
Godington Bucks 49 SP6427
Godley Gt Man 79 SJ9595
Godmanchester Cambs 52 TL2470
Godmanstone Dorset 11 SY6697
Godmersham Kent 28 TR0550
Godney Somset 21 ST4842
Godolphin Cross Cnwll 2 SW6031
Godre'r-graig W Glam 32 SN7506
Godshill Hants 12 SU1715
Godshill IOW 13 SZ5281
Godstone Staffs 73 SK0134
Godstone Surrey 27 TQ3551
Godsworthy Devon 5 SX5277
Godwinscroft Hants 12 SZ1996
Goetre Gwent 34 SO3206
Goff's Oak Herts 27 TL3202
Gofilon Gwent 34 SO2613
Gogar Loth 117 NT1672
Goginan Dyfed 43 SN6881
Golan Gwynd 57 SH5242
Golant Cnwll 3 SX1254
Golberdon Cnwll 5 SX3271
Golborne Gt Man 78 SJ6097
Golcar W York 82 SE0915
Gold Hill Cambs 65 TL5392
Gold Hill Dorset 11 ST8213
Goldcliff Gwent 34 ST3683
Golden Cross E Susx 16 TQ5312
Golden Green Kent 16 TQ6348
Golden Grove Dyfed 32 SN5919
Golden Hill Dyfed 30 SM9802
Golden Pot Hants 24 SU7143
Golden Valley Derbys 74 SK4251
Goldenhill Staffs 72 SJ8553
Golders Green Gt Lon 26 TQ2487
Goldfinch Bottom Berks 24 SU5063
Goldhanger Essex 40 TL9008
Golding Shrops 59 SJ5403
Goldington Beds 38 TL0750
Golds Green W Mids 60 SO9893
Goldsborough N York 90 NZ8314
Goldsborough N York 83 SE3856
Goldsithney Cnwll 2 SW5430
Goldstone Kent 29 TR2961
Goldstone Shrops 72 SJ7028
Goldsworth Surrey 25 SU9958
Goldthorpe S York 83 SE4604
Goldworthy Devon 18 SS3922
Golford Kent 28 TQ7936
Golford Green Kent 28 TQ7936
Gollanfield Highld 140 NH8053
Gollinglith Foot N York 89 SE1481
Golly Clwyd 71 SJ3358
Golsoncott Somset 20 ST0239
Golspie Highld 147 NC8300
Gomeldon Wilts 23 SU1835
Gomersal W York 82 SE2026
Gomshall Surrey 14 TQ0847
Gonalston Notts 63 SK6747

Gonerby Hill Foot

Griggs Green

Gonerby Hill Foot Lincs 63 SK9037
Gonfirth Shet 155 HU3661
Good Easter Essex 40 TL6212
Gooderstone Norfk 65 TF7602
Goodleigh Devon 19 SS6034
Goodmanham Humb 84 SE8843
Goodnestone Kent 28 TR0461
Goodnestone Kent 29 TR2554
Goodrich H & W 34 SO5719
Goodrington Devon 7 SX8958
Goodshaw Lancs 81 SD8125
Goodshaw Fold Lancs 81 SD8026
Goodstone Devon 7 SX7872
Goodwick Dyfed 30 SM9438
Goodworth Clatford Hants 23 SU3642
Goodyers End Warwks 61 SP3385
Goole Humb 84 SE7423
Goole Fields Humb 84 SE7520
Goom's Hill H & W 47 SP0154
Goonbell Cnwll 3 SW7249
Goonhavern Cnwll 3 SW7853
Goonvrea Cnwll 2 SW7149
Goose Green Avon 35 ST6774
Goose Green Essex 41 TM1327
Goose Green Essex 41 TM1325
Goose Green Gt Man 78 SD5603
Goose Green Kent 27 TQ6451
Goose Green Kent 28 TQ8437
Goose Green W Susx 14 TQ1118
Goose Pool H & W 46 SO4636
Goosecruives Gramp 135 NO7583
Gooseford Devon 8 SX6792
Gooseham Cnwll 18 SS2316
Goosehill Green H & W 47 SO9361
Goosemoor Somset 20 SS9635
Goosey Oxon 36 SU3591
Goosnargh Lancs 81 SD5536
Goostrey Ches 79 SJ7770
Gorddinog Gwynd 69 SH6773
Gordon Border 110 NT6443
Gordon Arms Hotel Border 109 NT3025
Gordonstown Gramp 142 NJ5656
Gordonstown Gramp 142 NJ7138
Gore Powys 46 SO2558
Gore Pit Essex 40 TL8719
Gore Street Kent 29 TR2765
Gorebridge Loth 118 NT3461
Gorefield Cambs 65 TF4112
Gores Wilts 23 SU1158
Gorey Jersey 152 JS0000
Goring Oxon 37 SU6080
Goring Heath Oxon 37 SU6579
Goring-by-Sea W Susx 14 TQ1102
Gorleston on Sea Norfk 67 TG5204
Gorrachie Gramp 142 NJ7358
Gorran Cnwll 3 SW9942
Gorran Haven Cnwll 3 SX0141
Gorran High Lanes Cnwll 3 SW9843
Gorrig Dyfed 31 SN4142
Gors Dyfed 43 SN6277
Gorse Hill Wilts 36 SU1586
Gorsedd Clwyd 70 SJ1576
Gorseinon W Glam 32 SS5998
Gorseybank Derbys 73 SK2953
Gorsgoch Dyfed 44 SN4850
Gorslas Dyfed 32 SN5713
Gorsley Gloucs 47 SO6925
Gorsley Common Gloucs 47 SO6825
Gorst Hill H & W 60 SO7373
Gorstage Ches 71 SJ6172
Gorstan Highld 139 NH3862
Gorstello Ches 71 SJ3562
Gorsty Common H & W 46 SO4437
Gorsty Hill Staffs 73 SK1028
Gorten Strath 122 NM7432
Gorthleck Highld 139 NH5420
Gorton Gt Man 79 SJ8896
Gosbeck Suffk 54 TM1555
Gosberton Lincs 64 TF2331
Gosberton Clough Lincs 64 TF1929
Gosfield Essex 40 TL7829
Gosford Devon 9 SY1097
Gosforth Cumb 86 NY0603
Gosforth T & W 103 NZ2368
Gosland Green Ches 71 SJ5758
Gosling Street Somset 21 ST5433
Gosmore Herts 39 TL1827
Gospel End Staffs 60 SO8993
Gospel Green W Susx 14 SU9431
Gosport Hants 13 SZ6099
Gossard Green Beds 38 SP9643
Gossington Gloucs 35 SO7302
Goswick Nthumb 111 NU0644
Gotham Notts 62 SK5330
Gotherington Gloucs 47 SO9529
Gotton Somset 20 ST2428
Goudhurst Kent 28 TQ7237
Goulceby Lincs 77 TF2579
Gourdas Gramp 142 NJ7741
Gourdie Tays 126 NO3532
Gourdon Gramp 135 NO8270
Gourock Strath 114 NS2477
Govan Strath 115 NS5465
Goveton Devon 7 SX7546
Gowdall Humb 83 SE6222
Gower Highld 139 NH5058
Gowerton W Glam 32 SS5896
Gowkhall Fife 117 NT0589
Gowthorpe Humb 84 SE7654
Goxhill Humb 85 TA1021
Goxhill Humb 85 TA1844
Grabhair W Isls 154 NB3915
Graby Lincs 64 TF0929
Grade Cnwll 2 SW7114
Gradeley Green Ches 71 SJ5851
Graffham W Susx 14 SU9217
Grafham Cambs 52 TL1669
Grafham Surrey 14 TQ0241
Grafton H & W 46 SO4936
Grafton H & W 46 SO5761
Grafton H & W 47 SO9837
Grafton N York 89 SE4163
Grafton Oxon 36 SP2600
Grafton Shrops 59 SJ4319
Grafton Flyford H & W 47 SO9655
Grafton Regis Nhants 49 SP7546
Grafton Underwood Nhants 51 SP9280
Grafty Green Kent 28 TQ8748
Graianrhyd Clwyd 70 SJ2156
Graig Clwyd 70 SJ0872
Graig Gwynd 69 SH8071
Graig-fechan Clwyd 70 SJ1454
Grain Kent 28 TQ8876
Grains Bar Gt Man 79 SD9608
Grainsby Lincs 77 TF2799
Grainthorpe Lincs 77 TF3896
Graiselound Humb 75 SK7698
Grampound Cnwll 3 SW9348
Grampound Road Cnwll 3 SW9150
Gramsdal W Isls 154 NF8155
Gramsdale W Isls 154 NF8155
Granborough Bucks 49 SP7625
Granby Notts 63 SK7536
Grand Chemins Jersey 152 JS0000
Grandborough Warwks 50 SP4966
Grandes Rocques Guern 152 GN0000
Grandtully Tays 125 NN9153
Grange Cumb 93 NY2517
Grange Kent 28 TQ7968
Grange Mersyd 78 SJ2286
Grange Tays 126 NO2625
Grange Crossroads Gramp 142 NJ4754
Grange Gate Dorset 11 SY9182
Grange Hall Gramp 141 NJ0660
Grange Hill Gt Lon 27 TQ4492
Grange Lindores Fife 126 NO2516
Grange Moor W York 82 SE2215
Grange Villa Dur 96 NZ2352
Grange-over-Sands Cumb 87 SD4077
Grangehall Strath 108 NS9642
Grangemill Derbys 74 SK2457
Grangemouth Cent 116 NS9281
Grangepans Cent 117 NT0181
Grangetown Cleve 97 NZ5420
Gransmoor Humb 91 TA1259
Gransmore Green Essex 40 TL6922
Granston Dyfed 30 SM8934
Grantchester Cambs 53 TL4355
Grantham Lincs 63 SK9135
Granton Fife 117 NT2376
Grantown-on-Spey Highld 141 NJ0328
Grantsfield H & W 46 SO5260
Grantshouse Border 119 NT8065
Grappenhall Ches 79 SJ6486
Grasby Lincs 85 TA0804
Grasmere Cumb 86 NY3307
Grass Green Essex 53 TL7338
Grasscroft Gt Man 82 SD9704
Grassendale Mersyd 78 SJ3985
Grassgarth Cumb 93 NY3444
Grassington N York 88 SE0063
Grassmoor Derbys 74 SK4067
Grassthorpe Notts 75 SK7967
Grateley Hants 23 SU2741
Gratwich Staffs 73 SK0231
Graveley Cambs 52 TL2563
Graveley Herts 39 TL2327
Gravelly Hill W Mids 61 SP1090
Gravelsbank Shrops 59 SJ3300
Graveney Kent 28 TR0562
Gravesend Kent 28 TQ6574
Gravir W Isls 154 NB3915
Grayingham Lincs 76 SK9396
Grayrigg Cumb 87 SD5796
Grays Essex 27 TQ6177
Grayshott Hants 14 SU8735
Grayson Green Cumb 92 NX9925
Grayswood Surrey 14 SU9134
Graythorpe Cleve 97 NZ5227
Grazeley Berks 24 SU6966
Greasbrough S York 74 SK4195
Greasby Mersyd 78 SJ2587
Greasley Notts 62 SK4846
Great Abington Cambs 53 TL5348
Great Addington Nhants 51 SP9675
Great Alne Warwks 48 SP1259
Great Altcar Lancs 78 SD3305
Great Amwell Herts 39 TL3712
Great Asby Cumb 94 NY6713
Great Ashfield Suffk 54 TL9967
Great Ayton N York 90 NZ5610
Great Baddow Essex 40 TL7304
Great Badminton Avon 35 ST8082
Great Bardfield Essex 40 TL6730
Great Barford Beds 52 TL1351
Great Barr W Mids 61 SP0495
Great Barrington Gloucs 36 SP2113
Great Barrow Ches 71 SJ4768
Great Barton Suffk 54 TL8967
Great Barugh N York 90 SE7479
Great Bavington Nthumb 102 NY9880
Great Bealings Suffk 55 TM2348
Great Bedwyn Wilts 23 SU2764
Great Bentley Essex 41 TM1021
Great Billing Nhants 51 SP8162
Great Bircham Norfk 65 TF7732
Great Blakenham Suffk 54 TM1150
Great Blencow Cumb 93 NY4532
Great Bolas Shrops 72 SJ6421
Great Bookham Surrey 26 TQ1354
Great Bosullow Cnwll 2 SW4133
Great Bourton Oxon 49 SP4545
Great Bowden Leics 50 SP7488
Great Bradley Suffk 53 TL6753
Great Braxted Essex 40 TL8614
Great Bricett Suffk 54 TM0350
Great Brickhill Bucks 38 SP9030
Great Bridge W Mids 60 SO9892
Great Bridgeford Staffs 72 SJ8827
Great Brington Nhants 50 SP6665
Great Bromley Essex 41 TM0826
Great Broughton Cumb 92 NY0731
Great Broughton N York 90 NZ5405
Great Budworth Ches 79 SJ6677
Great Burdon Dur 96 NZ3116
Great Burstead Essex 40 TQ6892
Great Busby N York 90 NZ5205
Great Canfield Essex 40 TL5918
Great Carlton Lincs 77 TF4085
Great Casterton Leics 63 TF0008
Great Chart Kent 28 TQ9841
Great Chatfield Wilts 22 ST8563
Great Chatwell Staffs 60 SJ7914
Great Chell Staffs 72 SJ8652
Great Chesterford Essex 39 TL5042
Great Cheverell Wilts 22 ST9854
Great Chishill Cambs 39 TL4238
Great Clacton Essex 41 TM1716
Great Cliffe W York 82 SE3015
Great Clifton Cumb 92 NY0429
Great Coates Humb 85 TA2309
Great Comberton H & W 47 SO9542
Great Comp Kent 27 TQ6356
Great Corby Cumb 93 NY4754
Great Cornard Suffk 54 TL8840
Great Cowden Humb 85 TA2342
Great Coxwell Oxon 36 SU2693
Great Cransley Nhants 51 SP8376
Great Cressingham Norfk 66 TF8501
Great Crosthwaite Cumb 93 NY2524
Great Cubley Derbys 73 SK1638
Great Dalby Leics 63 SK7414
Great Doddington Nhants 51 SP8864
Great Doward H & W 34 SO5416
Great Dunham Norfk 66 TF8714
Great Dunmow Essex 40 TL6222
Great Durnford Wilts 23 SU1338
Great Easton Essex 40 TL6025
Great Easton Leics 51 SP8492
Great Eccleston Lancs 80 SD4240
Great Edstone N York 90 SE7083
Great Ellingham Norfk 66 TM0196
Great Elm Somset 22 ST7449
Great Englebourne Devon 7 SX7756
Great Everdon Nhants 49 SP5957
Great Eversden Cambs 52 TL3653
Great Finborough Suffk 54 TM0158
Great Fransham Norfk 66 TF8913
Great Gaddesden Herts 38 TL0211
Great Gidding Cambs 52 TL1183
Great Givendale Humb 84 SE8153
Great Glemham Suffk 55 TM3361
Great Glen Leics 50 SP6597
Great Gonerby Lincs 63 SK8938
Great Gransden Cambs 52 TL2655
Great Green Cambs 39 TL2844
Great Green Norfk 55 TM2889
Great Green Suffk 54 TL9155
Great Green Suffk 54 TL9365
Great Habton N York 90 SE7576
Great Hale Lincs 64 TF1442
Great Hallingbury Essex 39 TL5119
Great Hanwood Shrops 59 SJ4409
Great Harrowden Nhants 51 SP8770
Great Harwood Lancs 81 SD7332
Great Haseley Oxon 37 SP6401
Great Hatfield Humb 85 TA1842
Great Haywood Staffs 73 SJ9922
Great Heck N York 83 SE5920
Great Henny Essex 54 TL8637
Great Hinton Wilts 22 ST9059
Great Hockham Norfk 66 TL9592
Great Holland Essex 41 TM2019
Great Horkesley Essex 41 TL9731
Great Hormead Herts 39 TL4029
Great Horton W York 82 SE1431
Great Horwood Bucks 49 SP7731
Great Houghton Nhants 50 SP7958
Great Houghton S York 83 SE4206
Great Hucklow Derbys 74 SK1777
Great Kelk Humb 91 TA1058
Great Kimble Bucks 38 SP8205
Great Kingshill Bucks 26 SU8797
Great Langdale Cumb 86 NY2906
Great Langton N York 89 SE2996
Great Leighs Essex 40 TL7217
Great Limber Lincs 85 TA1308
Great Linford Bucks 38 SP8542
Great Livermere Suffk 54 TL8871
Great Longstone Derbys 74 SK2071
Great Lumley T & W 96 NZ2949
Great Lyth Shrops 59 SJ4507
Great Malvern H & W 47 SO7746
Great Maplestead Essex 54 TL8034
Great Marton Lancs 80 SD3235
Great Massingham Norfk 66 TF7922
Great Melton Norfk 66 TG1206
Great Meols Mersyd 78 SJ2390
Great Milton Oxon 37 SP6202
Great Missenden Bucks 26 SP8901
Great Mitton Lancs 81 SD7138
Great Mongeham Kent 29 TR3551
Great Moulton Norfk 54 TM1690
Great Munden Herts 39 TL3524
Great Musgrave Cumb 94 NY7613
Great Ness Shrops 59 SJ3919
Great Nurcott Somset 20 SS9036
Great Oak Gwent 34 SO3810
Great Oakley Essex 41 TM1927
Great Oakley Nhants 51 SP8785
Great Offley Herts 38 TL1427
Great Ormside Cumb 94 NY7017
Great Orton Cumb 93 NY3254
Great Ouseburn N York 89 SE4461
Great Oxendon Nhants 50 SP7383
Great Oxney Green Essex 40 TL6606
Great Pattenden Kent 28 TQ7344
Great Paxton Cambs 52 TL2063
Great Plumpton Lancs 80 SD3833
Great Plumstead Norfk 67 TG3010
Great Ponton Lincs 63 SK9230
Great Potheridge Devon 19 SS5114
Great Preston W York 83 SE4029
Great Purston Nhants 49 SP5139
Great Raveley Cambs 52 TL2581
Great Rissington Gloucs 36 SP1917
Great Rollright Oxon 48 SP3231
Great Rudbaxton Dyfed 30 SM9620
Great Ryburgh Norfk 66 TF9527
Great Ryle Nthumb 111 NU0212
Great Ryton Shrops 59 SJ4803
Great Saling Essex 40 TL6925
Great Salkeld Cumb 94 NY5536
Great Sampford Essex 53 TL6435
Great Sankey Ches 78 SJ5688
Great Saredon Staffs 60 SJ9508
Great Saughall Ches 71 SJ3669
Great Saxham Suffk 53 TL7862
Great Shefford Berks 36 SU3875
Great Shelford Cambs 53 TL4651
Great Smeaton N York 89 NZ3404
Great Snoring Norfk 66 TF9434
Great Somerford Wilts 35 ST9682
Great Soudley Shrops 72 SJ7229
Great Stainton Dur 96 NZ3322
Great Stambridge Essex 40 TQ8991
Great Staughton Cambs 52 TL1264
Great Steeping Lincs 77 TF4364
Great Stonar Kent 29 TR3359
Great Strickland Cumb 94 NY5522
Great Stukeley Cambs 52 TL2274
Great Sturton Lincs 76 TF2176
Great Sutton Ches 71 SJ3775
Great Sutton Shrops 59 SO5183
Great Swinburne Nthumb 102 NY9375
Great Tew Oxon 48 SP4028
Great Tey Essex 40 TL8925
Great Torrington Devon 18 SS4919
Great Tosson Nthumb 103 NU0200
Great Totham Essex 40 TL8611
Great Totham Essex 40 TL8713
Great Tows Lincs 76 TF2290
Great Urswick Cumb 86 SD2674
Great Wakering Essex 40 TQ9487
Great Waldingfield Suffk 54 TL9144
Great Walsingham Norfk 66 TF9437
Great Waltham Essex 40 TL6913
Great Warley Essex 27 TQ5890
Great Washbourne Gloucs 47 SO9834
Great Weeke Devon 8 SX7187
Great Weldon Nhants 51 SP9289
Great Welnetham Suffk 54 TL8759
Great Wenham Suffk 54 TM0738
Great Whittington Nthumb 103 NZ0070
Great Wigborough Essex 41 TL9615
Great Wilbraham Cambs 53 TL5557
Great Wishford Wilts 23 SU0735
Great Witchingham Norfk 66 TG1020
Great Witcombe Gloucs 35 SO9114
Great Witley H & W 47 SO7566
Great Wolford Warwks 48 SP2534
Great Wratting Essex 53 TL6848
Great Wymondley Herts 39 TL2128
Great Wyrley Staffs 60 SJ9907
Great Wytheford Shrops 59 SJ5719
Great Yarmouth Norfk 67 TG5207
Great Yeldham Essex 53 TL7638
Greatfield Wilts 36 SU0785
Greatford Lincs 64 TF0811
Greatgate Staffs 73 SK0539
Greatham Cleve 97 NZ4927
Greatham Hants 14 SU7730
Greatham W Susx 14 TQ0415
Greatstone-on-Sea Kent 17 TR0822
Greatworth Nhants 49 SP5542
Grebby Lincs 77 TF4368
Greeba IOM 153 SC3081
Green Clwyd 70 SJ0668
Green Bank Cumb 87 SD3780
Green Cross Surrey 14 SU8637
Green Down Somset 21 ST5753
Green End Beds 38 TL0147
Green End Beds 51 TL0864
Green End Beds 51 TL1063
Green End Beds 52 TL1252
Green End Cambs 52 TL2274
Green End Cambs 52 TL3856
Green End Cambs 53 TL4668
Green End Cambs 53 TL4861
Green End Cambs 52 TL1683
Green End Herts 39 TL2630
Green End Herts 39 TL3222
Green End Herts 39 TL3333
Green End Warwks 61 SP2686
Green Hammerton N York 83 SE4556
Green Head Cumb 93 NY3649
Green Heath Staffs 60 SJ9913
Green Hill Wilts 36 SU0686
Green Hills Cambs 53 TL6072
Green Lane Devon 8 SX7877
Green Lane H & W 48 SP0664
Green Moor S York 74 SK2899
Green Oak Humb 84 SE8127
Green Ore Somset 21 ST5750
Green Quarter Cumb 87 NY4603
Green Street E Susx 17 TQ7611
Green Street Gloucs 35 SO8915
Green Street H & W 47 SO8749
Green Street Herts 39 TL4521
Green Street Herts 26 TQ1998
Green Street Green Gt Lon 27 TQ4563
Green Street Green Kent 27 TQ5870
Green Tye Herts 39 TL4418
Greenburn Loth 116 NS9360
Greencroft Hall Dur 96 NZ1549
Greenend Oxon 36 SP3221
Greenfield Beds 38 TL0534
Greenfield Clwyd 70 SJ1977
Greenfield Gt Man 82 SD9904
Greenfield Highld 131 NH2000
Greenfield Oxon 37 SU7191
Greenfield Strath 114 NS2490
Greenford Gt Lon 26 TQ1482
Greengairs Strath 116 NS7870
Greengates W York 82 SE1937
Greengill Cumb 92 NY1037
Greenhalgh Lancs 80 SD4035
Greenham Berks 24 SU4865
Greenham Somset 20 ST0820
Greenhaugh Nthumb 102 NY7987
Greenhead Nthumb 102 NY6565
Greenheys Gt Man 79 SD7104
Greenhill Cent 116 NS8279
Greenhill D & G 100 NY1079
Greenhill H & W 47 SO7248
Greenhill Kent 29 TR1666
Greenhill Strath 108 NS9332
Greenhillocks Derbys 74 SK4049
Greenhithe Kent 27 TQ5875
Greenholm Strath 107 NS5437
Greenholme Cumb 87 NY5905
Greenhouse Border 109 NT5523
Greenhow Hill N York 89 SE1164
Greenland Highld 151 ND2367
Greenland S York 74 SK3988
Greenlands Bucks 37 SU7785
Greenlaw Border 110 NT7146
Greenlea D & G 100 NY0375
Greenloaning Tays 125 NN8307
Greenmoor Hill Oxon 37 SU6481
Greenmount Gt Man 81 SD7714
Greenock Strath 115 NS2876
Greenodd Cumb 86 SD3182
Greens Norton Nhants 49 SP6649
Greensgate Norfk 66 TG1015
Greenshields Strath 108 NT0243
Greenside T & W 96 NZ1362
Greenside W York 82 SE1716
Greenstead Essex 41 TM0125
Greenstead Green Essex 40 TL8227
Greensted Essex 39 TL5403
Greenstreet Green Suffk 54 TM0349
Greenway Gloucs 47 SO7033
Greenway H & W 60 SO7470
Greenway S Glam 33 ST0573
Greenway Somset 21 ST3124
Greenwich Gt Lon 27 TQ3877
Greet Gloucs 48 SP0230
Greete Shrops 46 SO5770
Greetham Leics 63 SK9214
Greetham Lincs 77 TF3070
Greetland W York 82 SE0821
Gregson Lane Lancs 81 SD5926
Greinton Somset 21 ST4136
Grenaby IOM 153 SC2672
Grendon Nhants 51 SP8760
Grendon Warwks 61 SP2799
Grendon Green H & W 46 SO5957
Grendon Underwood Bucks 37 SP6820
Grenofen Devon 6 SX4971
Grenoside S York 74 SK3393
Greosabhagh W Isls 154 NG1593
Gresford Clwyd 71 SJ3454
Gresham Norfk 66 TG1638
Greshornish House Hotel Highld 136 NG3454
Gressenhall Norfk 66 TF9615
Gressenhall Green Norfk 66 TF9616
Gressingham Lancs 87 SD5769
Gresty Green Ches 72 SJ7053
Greta Bridge Dur 95 NZ0813
Gretna D & G 101 NY3167
Gretna Green D & G 101 NY3168
Gretton Gloucs 47 SP0030
Gretton Nhants 51 SP8994
Gretton Shrops 59 SO5195
Grewelthorpe N York 89 SE2376
Grey Friars Suffk 55 TM4770
Grey Green Humb 84 SE7807
Grey's Green Oxon 37 SU7182
Greygarth N York 89 SE1872
Greylake Somset 21 ST3833
Greyrigg D & G 100 NY0888
Greysouthen Cumb 92 NY0729
Greystoke Cumb 93 NY4430
Greystone Tays 127 NO5343
Greywell Hants 24 SU7151
Gribb Dorset 10 ST3703
Gribthorpe Humb 84 SE7635
Griff Warwks 61 SP3689
Griffithstown Gwent 34 ST2998
Griffydam Leics 62 SK4118
Griggs Green Hants 14 SU8231

Grimeford Village

Hardwicke

Grimeford Village *Lancs*	**81**	SD6112
Grimesthorpe *S York*	**74**	SK3689
Grimethorpe *S York*	**83**	SE4109
Grimley *H & W*	**47**	SO8360
Grimmet *Strath*	**106**	NS3210
Grimoldby *Lincs*	**77**	TF3988
Grimpo *Shrops*	**59**	SJ3526
Grimsargh *Lancs*	**81**	SD5834
Grimsby *Humb*	**85**	TA2710
Grimscote *Nhants*	**49**	SP6553
Grimscott *Cnwll*	**18**	SS2606
Grimshader *W Isls*	**154**	NB4025
Grimshaw *Lancs*	**81**	SD7024
Grimshaw Green *Lancs*	**80**	SD4912
Grimsthorpe *Lincs*	**64**	TF0422
Grimston *Humb*	**85**	TA2735
Grimston *Leics*	**63**	SK6821
Grimston *Norfk*	**65**	TF7222
Grimston Hill *Notts*	**75**	SK6865
Grimstone *Dorset*	**10**	SY6394
Grimstone End *Suffk*	**54**	TL9368
Grinacombe Moor *Devon*	**5**	SX4191
Grindale *Humb*	**91**	TA1271
Grindle *Shrops*	**60**	SJ7503
Grindleford *Derbys*	**74**	SK2477
Grindleton *Lancs*	**81**	SD7545
Grindley Brook *Shrops*	**71**	SJ5242
Grindlow *Derbys*	**74**	SK1877
Grindon *Cleve*	**96**	NZ3925
Grindon *Nthumb*	**110**	NT9144
Grindon *Staffs*	**73**	SK0854
Grindon Hill *Nthumb*	**102**	NY8268
Grindonrigg *Nthumb*	**110**	NT9243
Gringley on the Hill *Notts*	**75**	SK7390
Grinsdale *Cumb*	**93**	NY3758
Grinshill *Shrops*	**59**	SJ5223
Grinton *N York*	**88**	SE0498
Griomaisiader *W Isls*	**154**	NB4025
Grishipoll *Strath*	**120**	NM1859
Grisling Common *E Susx*	**16**	TQ4322
Gristhorpe *N York*	**91**	TA0981
Griston *Norfk*	**66**	TL9499
Gritley *Ork*	**155**	HY5504
Grittenham *Wilts*	**36**	SU0382
Grittleton *Wilts*	**35**	ST8580
Grizebeck *Cumb*	**86**	SD2384
Grizedale *Cumb*	**86**	SD3394
Groby *Leics*	**62**	SK5207
Groes *Clwyd*	**70**	SJ0064
Groes-faen *M Glam*	**33**	ST0680
Groes-Wen *M Glam*	**33**	ST1286
Groesffordd *Gwynd*	**56**	SH2739
Groesffordd Marli *Clwyd*	**70**	SJ0073
Groesllwyd *Powys*	**58**	SJ2111
Groeslon *Gwynd*	**68**	SH4755
Groeslon *Gwynd*	**68**	SH5260
Grogarry *W Isls*	**154**	NF7739
Grogport *Strath*	**105**	NR8144
Groigearraidh *W Isls*	**154**	NF7739
Gromford *Suffk*	**55**	TM3858
Gronant *Clwyd*	**70**	SJ0983
Groombridge *E Susx*	**16**	TQ5337
Grosebay *W Isls*	**154**	NG1593
Grosmont *Gwent*	**46**	SO4024
Grosmont *N York*	**90**	NZ8305
Groton *Suffk*	**54**	TL9641
Grotton *Gt Man*	**79**	SD9604
Grouville *Jersey*	**152**	JS0000
Grove *Bucks*	**38**	SP9122
Grove *Dorset*	**11**	SY6972
Grove *Dyfed*	**30**	SM9900
Grove *Kent*	**29**	TR2362
Grove *Notts*	**75**	SK7479
Grove *Oxon*	**36**	SU4090
Grove Green *Kent*	**28**	TQ7856
Grove Park *Gt Lon*	**27**	TQ4072
Grove Vale *W Mids*	**61**	SP0394
Grovenhurst *Kent*	**28**	TQ7140
Grovesend *Avon*	**35**	ST6589
Grovesend *W Glam*	**32**	SN5900
Grubb Street *Kent*	**27**	TQ5869
Gruinard *Highld*	**144**	NG9489
Gruinart *Strath*	**112**	NR2966
Grula *Highld*	**136**	NG3826
Gruline *Strath*	**121**	NM5440
Grumbla *Cnwll*	**2**	SW4029
Grundisburgh *Suffk*	**55**	TM2251
Gruting *Shet*	**155**	HU2749
Gualachulain *Highld*	**123**	NN1145
Guanockgate *Lincs*	**64**	TF3710
Guardbridge *Fife*	**127**	NO4518
Guarlford *H & W*	**47**	SO8145
Guay *Tays*	**125**	NN9948
Guestling Green *E Susx*	**17**	TQ8513
Guestling Thorn *E Susx*	**17**	TQ8516
Guestwick *Norfk*	**66**	TG0626
Guide *Lancs*	**81**	SD7025
Guide Bridge *Gt Man*	**79**	SJ9297
Guide Post *Nthumb*	**103**	NZ2585
Guilden Down *Shrops*	**59**	SO3082
Guilden Morden *Cambs*	**39**	TL2744
Guilden Sutton *Ches*	**71**	SJ4468
Guildford *Surrey*	**25**	SU9949
Guildstead *Kent*	**28**	TQ8262
Guildtown *Tays*	**126**	NO1331
Guilsborough *Nhants*	**50**	SP6772
Guilsfield *Powys*	**58**	SJ2211
Guilton *Kent*	**29**	TR2858
Guiltreehill *Strath*	**106**	NS3610
Guineaford *Devon*	**19**	SS5537
Guisborough *Cleve*	**97**	NZ6015
Guiseley *W York*	**82**	SE1942
Guist *Norfk*	**66**	TG0025
Guiting Power *Gloucs*	**48**	SP0924
Gullane *Loth*	**118**	NT4882
Gulling Green *Suffk*	**54**	TL8256
Gulval *Cnwll*	**2**	SW4831
Gulworthy *Devon*	**6**	SX4572
Gumfreston *Dyfed*	**31**	SN1001
Gumley *Leics*	**50**	SP6889
Gummow's Shop *Cnwll*	**4**	SW8657
Gun Green *Kent*	**17**	TQ7731
Gun Hill *E Susx*	**16**	TQ5614
Gun Hill *Warwks*	**61**	SP2889
Gunby *Humb*	**84**	SE7035
Gunby *Lincs*	**63**	SK9121
Gunby *Lincs*	**77**	TF4666
Gundleton *Hants*	**24**	SU6133
Gunn *Devon*	**19**	SS6333
Gunnerside *N York*	**88**	SD9598
Gunnerton *Nthumb*	**102**	NY9074
Gunness *Humb*	**84**	SE8411
Gunnislake *Cnwll*	**6**	SX4371
Gunnista *Shet*	**155**	HU5043
Gunthorpe *Cambs*	**64**	TF1802
Gunthorpe *Norfk*	**66**	TG0134
Gunthorpe *Notts*	**63**	SK6844
Gunton *Suffk*	**67**	TM5395
Gunville *IOW*	**13**	SZ4788
Gunwalloe *Cnwll*	**2**	SW6522
Gupworthy *Somset*	**20**	SS9734
Gurnard *IOW*	**13**	SZ4795
Gurnett *Ches*	**79**	SJ9271
Gurney Slade *Somset*	**21**	ST6249
Gurnos *W Glam*	**32**	SN7709
Gushmere *Kent*	**28**	TR0457
Gussage All Saints *Dorset*	**11**	SU0010
Gussage St Andrew *Dorset*	**11**	ST9714
Gussage St Michael *Dorset*	**11**	ST9811
Guston *Kent*	**29**	TR3244
Gutcher *Shet*	**155**	HU5499
Guthrie *Tays*	**127**	NO5650
Guy's Marsh *Dorset*	**22**	ST8420
Guyhirn *Cambs*	**65**	TF4003
Guyhirn Gull *Cambs*	**65**	TF3904
Guyzance *Nthumb*	**103**	NU2103
Gwaenysgor *Clwyd*	**70**	SJ0781
Gwalchmai *Gwynd*	**68**	SH3876
Gwastadnant *Gwynd*	**69**	SH6157
Gwaun-Cae-Gurwen *W Glam*	**32**	SN6911
Gwbert on Sea *Dyfed*	**42**	SN1650
Gwealavellan *Cnwll*	**2**	SW6041
Gwealeath *Cnwll*	**2**	SW6922
Gweek *Cnwll*	**2**	SW7026
Gwehelog *Gwent*	**34**	SO3804
Gwenddwr *Powys*	**45**	SO0643
Gwendreath *Cnwll*	**3**	SW7217
Gwennap *Cnwll*	**3**	SW7340
Gwenter *Cnwll*	**3**	SW7417
Gwernaffield *Clwyd*	**70**	SJ2065
Gwernesney *Gwent*	**34**	SO4101
Gwernogle *Dyfed*	**44**	SN5333
Gwernymynydd *Clwyd*	**70**	SJ2162
Gwersyllt *Clwyd*	**71**	SJ3153
Gwespyr *Clwyd*	**70**	SJ1183
Gwindra *Cnwll*	**3**	SW9552
Gwinear *Cnwll*	**2**	SW5937
Gwithian *Cnwll*	**2**	SW5841
Gwredog *Gwynd*	**68**	SH4085
Gwrhay *Gwent*	**33**	ST1899
Gwyddelwern *Clwyd*	**70**	SJ0746
Gwyddgrug *Dyfed*	**44**	SN4635
Gwynfryn *Clwyd*	**70**	SJ2552
Gwystre *Powys*	**45**	SO0665
Gwytherin *Clwyd*	**69**	SH8761
Gyfelia *Clwyd*	**71**	SJ3245
Gyrn-goch *Gwynd*	**68**	SH4048

H

Habberley *H & W*	**60**	SO8177
Habberley *Shrops*	**59**	SJ3903
Habergham *Lancs*	**81**	SD8033
Habertoft *Lincs*	**77**	TF5069
Habin *W Susx*	**14**	SU8022
Habrough *Humb*	**85**	TA1413
Hacconby *Lincs*	**64**	TF1025
Haceby *Lincs*	**64**	TF0236
Hacheston *Suffk*	**55**	TM3059
Hack Green *Ches*	**72**	SJ6448
Hackbridge *Gt Lon*	**27**	TQ2865
Hackenthorpe *S York*	**74**	SK4183
Hackford *Norfk*	**66**	TG0502
Hackforth *N York*	**89**	SE2492
Hackland *Ork*	**155**	HY3920
Hackleton *Nhants*	**51**	SP8055
Hacklinge *Kent*	**29**	TR3454
Hackman's Gate *H & W*	**60**	SO8978
Hackness *N York*	**91**	SE9790
Hackness *Somset*	**21**	ST3345
Hackney *Gt Lon*	**27**	TQ3484
Hackthorn *Lincs*	**76**	SK9982
Hackthorpe *Cumb*	**94**	NY5423
Hacton *Gt Lon*	**27**	TQ5585
Hadden *Border*	**110**	NT7836
Haddenham *Bucks*	**37**	SP7308
Haddenham *Cambs*	**53**	TL4675
Haddington *Lincs*	**76**	SK9162
Haddington *Loth*	**118**	NT5173
Haddiscoe *Norfk*	**67**	TM4497
Haddo *Gramp*	**143**	NJ8337
Haddon *Cambs*	**64**	TL1392
Hade Edge *W York*	**82**	SE1404
Hadfield *Derbys*	**74**	SK0296
Hadham Cross *Herts*	**39**	TL4218
Hadham Ford *Herts*	**39**	TL4321
Hadleigh *Essex*	**40**	TQ8187
Hadleigh *Suffk*	**54**	TM0242
Hadleigh Heath *Suffk*	**54**	TL9941
Hadley *H & W*	**47**	SO8564
Hadley *Shrops*	**60**	SJ6711
Hadley End *Staffs*	**73**	SK1320
Hadley Wood *Gt Lon*	**27**	TQ2698
Hadlow *Kent*	**27**	TQ6350
Hadlow Down *E Susx*	**16**	TQ5324
Hadnall *Shrops*	**59**	SJ5220
Hadstock *Essex*	**53**	TL5644
Hadzor *H & W*	**47**	SO9162
Haffenden Quarter *Kent*	**28**	TQ8840
Hafod-y-bwch *Clwyd*	**71**	SJ3147
Hafod-y-coed *Gwent*	**34**	SO2200
Hafodunos *Clwyd*	**69**	SH8666
Hafodyrynys *Gwent*	**34**	ST2298
Haggate *Lancs*	**81**	SD8735
Haggbeck *Cumb*	**101**	NY4773
Haggerston *Nthumb*	**111**	NU0443
Haggington Hill *Devon*	**19**	SS5547
Haggs *Cent*	**116**	NS7879
Hagley *H & W*	**46**	SO5641
Hagley *H & W*	**60**	SO9180
Hagmore Green *Suffk*	**54**	TL9539
Hagnaby *Lincs*	**77**	TF3462
Hagnaby *Lincs*	**77**	TF4879
Hagworthingham *Lincs*	**77**	TF3469
Haigh *Gt Man*	**78**	SD6009
Haighton Green *Lancs*	**81**	SD5634
Hail Weston *Cambs*	**52**	TL1662
Haile *Cumb*	**86**	NY0308
Hailes *Gloucs*	**48**	SP0430
Hailey *Herts*	**39**	TL3710
Hailey *Oxon*	**37**	SU6485
Hailey *Oxon*	**36**	SP3512
Hailsham *E Susx*	**16**	TQ5909
Hainault *Gt Lon*	**27**	TQ4591
Haine *Kent*	**29**	TR3566
Hainford *Norfk*	**67**	TG2218
Hainton *Lincs*	**76**	TF1884
Hainworth *W York*	**82**	SE0638
Haisthorpe *Humb*	**91**	TA1264
Hakin *Dyfed*	**30**	SM8905
Halam *Notts*	**75**	SK6754
Halbeath *Fife*	**117**	NT1288
Halberton *Devon*	**9**	ST0112
Halcro *Highld*	**151**	ND2360
Hale *Ches*	**78**	SJ4782
Hale *Cumb*	**87**	SD5078
Hale *Gt Man*	**79**	SJ7786
Hale *Hants*	**12**	SU1818
Hale *Somset*	**22**	ST7427
Hale *Surrey*	**25**	SU8448
Hale Bank *Ches*	**78**	SJ4784
Hale Green *E Susx*	**16**	TQ5514
Hale Nook *Lancs*	**80**	SD3944
Hale Street *Kent*	**28**	TQ6749
Halebarns *Gt Man*	**79**	SJ7985
Hales *Norfk*	**67**	TM3797
Hales *Staffs*	**72**	SJ7134
Hales Green *Derbys*	**73**	SK1841
Hales Place *Kent*	**29**	TR1459
Halesgate *Lincs*	**64**	TF3226
Halesowen *W Mids*	**60**	SO9683
Halesworth *Suffk*	**55**	TM3877
Halewood *Mersyd*	**78**	SJ4585
Halford *Devon*	**7**	SX8174
Halford *Shrops*	**59**	SO4383
Halford *Warwks*	**48**	SP2645
Halfpenny *Cumb*	**87**	SD5387
Halfpenny Green *Staffs*	**60**	SO8291
Halfpenny Houses *N York*	**89**	SE2284
Halfway *Berks*	**24**	SU4068
Halfway *Dyfed*	**44**	SN6430
Halfway *Powys*	**44**	SN8232
Halfway *S York*	**75**	SK4381
Halfway Bridge *W Susx*	**14**	SU9321
Halfway House *Shrops*	**59**	SJ3411
Halfway Houses *Kent*	**28**	TQ9372
Halifax *W York*	**82**	SE0925
Halistra *Highld*	**136**	NG2459
Halkirk *Highld*	**151**	ND1359
Halkyn *Clwyd*	**70**	SJ2171
Hall *Strath*	**115**	NS4154
Hall Cliffe *W York*	**82**	SE2918
Hall Cross *Lancs*	**80**	SD4230
Hall Dunnerdale *Cumb*	**86**	SD2195
Hall End *Beds*	**38**	TL0045
Hall End *Beds*	**38**	TL0737
Hall End *W Mids*	**60**	SP0092
Hall Green *W Mids*	**61**	SP1181
Hall's Green *Essex*	**39**	TL4108
Hall's Green *Herts*	**39**	TL2728
Hallam Fields *Derbys*	**62**	SK4739
Halland *E Susx*	**16**	TQ4916
Hallaton *Leics*	**50**	SP7896
Hallatrow *Avon*	**21**	ST6357
Hallbankgate *Cumb*	**94**	NY5859
Hallbeck *Cumb*	**87**	SD6288
Hallen *Avon*	**34**	ST5580
Hallfield Gate *Derbys*	**74**	SK3958
Hallgarth *Dur*	**96**	NZ3243
Hallin *Highld*	**136**	NG2558
Halling *Kent*	**28**	TQ7063
Hallington *Lincs*	**77**	TF3085
Hallington *Nthumb*	**102**	NY9875
Halliwell *Gt Man*	**79**	SD6910
Halloughton *Notts*	**75**	SK6951
Hallow *H & W*	**47**	SO8258
Hallow Heath *H & W*	**47**	SO8259
Hallrule *Border*	**110**	NT5914
Hallsands *Devon*	**7**	SX8138
Hallthwaites *Cumb*	**86**	SD1885
Halltoft End *Lincs*	**64**	TF3645
Hallworthy *Cnwll*	**4**	SX1787
Hallyne *Border*	**109**	NT1940
Halmer End *Staffs*	**72**	SJ7948
Halmond's Frome *H & W*	**47**	SO6747
Halnaker *W Susx*	**14**	SU9007
Halsall *Lancs*	**78**	SD3710
Halse *Nhants*	**49**	SP5640
Halse *Somset*	**20**	ST1428
Halsetown *Cnwll*	**2**	SW5038
Halsham *Humb*	**85**	TA2727
Halsinger *Devon*	**19**	SS5138
Halstead *Essex*	**40**	TL8130
Halstead *Kent*	**27**	TQ4861
Halstead *Leics*	**63**	SK7505
Halstock *Dorset*	**10**	ST5308
Halsway *Somset*	**20**	ST1337
Haltcliff Bridge *Cumb*	**93**	NY3636
Haltham *Lincs*	**77**	TF2463
Halton *Bucks*	**38**	SP8710
Halton *Ches*	**78**	SJ5481
Halton *Clwyd*	**71**	SJ3039
Halton *Lancs*	**87**	SD5064
Halton *Nthumb*	**103**	NY9967
Halton *W York*	**83**	SE3533
Halton East *N York*	**82**	SE0454
Halton Fenside *Lincs*	**77**	TF4263
Halton Gill *N York*	**88**	SD8776
Halton Green *Lancs*	**87**	SD5165
Halton Holegate *Lincs*	**77**	TF4165
Halton Lea Gate *Nthumb*	**94**	NY6458
Halton Quay *Cnwll*	**5**	SX4165
Halton Shields *Nthumb*	**103**	NZ0168
Halton West *N York*	**81**	SD8454
Haltwhistle *Nthumb*	**102**	NY7064
Halvergate *Norfk*	**67**	TG4106
Halwell *Devon*	**7**	SX7753
Halwill *Devon*	**18**	SX4299
Halwill Junction *Devon*	**18**	SS4400
Ham *Devon*	**9**	ST2301
Ham *Gloucs*	**35**	SO9721
Ham *Gloucs*	**35**	ST6898
Ham *Gt Lon*	**26**	TQ1772
Ham *Kent*	**29**	TR3254
Ham *Somset*	**20**	ST2825
Ham *Somset*	**22**	ST6748
Ham *Wilts*	**23**	SU3262
Ham Common *Dorset*	**22**	ST8125
Ham Green *Avon*	**34**	ST5375
Ham Green *H & W*	**47**	SO7544
Ham Green *H & W*	**47**	SP0163
Ham Green *Kent*	**28**	TQ8468
Ham Green *Kent*	**17**	TQ8926
Ham Hill *Kent*	**28**	TQ6960
Ham Street *Somset*	**21**	ST5534
Hamble *Hants*	**13**	SU4806
Hambleden *Bucks*	**37**	SU7886
Hambledon *Hants*	**13**	SU6414
Hambledon *Surrey*	**25**	SU9638
Hambleton *Lancs*	**80**	SD3742
Hambleton *N York*	**83**	SE5530
Hambleton Moss Side *Lancs*	**80**	SD3842
Hambridge *Somset*	**21**	ST3921
Hambridge *Somset*	**21**	ST5936
Hambrook *Avon*	**35**	ST6478
Hambrook *W Susx*	**14**	SU7806
Hamels *Herts*	**39**	TL3724
Hameringham *Lincs*	**77**	TF3167
Hamerton *Cambs*	**52**	TL1379
Hamilton *Strath*	**116**	NS7255
Hamlet *Dorset*	**10**	ST5908
Hamlins *E Susx*	**16**	TQ5908
Hammerpot *W Susx*	**14**	TQ0605
Hammersmith *Gt Lon*	**26**	TQ2378
Hammerwich *Staffs*	**61**	SK0707
Hammerwood *E Susx*	**16**	TQ4339
Hammond Street *Herts*	**39**	TL3304
Hammoon *Dorset*	**11**	ST8114
Hamnavoe *Shet*	**155**	HU3735
Hamnavoe *Shet*	**155**	HU4971
Hampden Park *E Susx*	**16**	TQ6002
Hampden Row *Bucks*	**26**	SP8501
Hamperden End *Essex*	**40**	TL5730
Hampnett *Gloucs*	**36**	SP0915
Hampole *S York*	**83**	SE5010
Hampreston *Dorset*	**12**	SZ0598
Hampsfield *Cumb*	**87**	SD4080
Hampson Green *Lancs*	**80**	SD4954
Hampstead *Gt Lon*	**27**	TQ2685
Hampstead Norrey's *Berks*	**37**	SU5276
Hampsthwaite *N York*	**89**	SE2559
Hampt *Cnwll*	**5**	SX3874
Hampton *Devon*	**10**	SY2696
Hampton *Gt Lon*	**26**	TQ1369
Hampton *H & W*	**48**	SP0243
Hampton *Kent*	**29**	TR1568
Hampton *Shrops*	**60**	SO7486
Hampton *Wilts*	**36**	SU1892
Hampton Bishop *H & W*	**46**	SO5637
Hampton Green *Ches*	**71**	SJ5149
Hampton Heath *Ches*	**71**	SJ5049
Hampton in Arden *W Mids*	**61**	SP2080
Hampton Loade *Shrops*	**60**	SO7486
Hampton Lovett *H & W*	**47**	SO8865
Hampton Lucy *Warwks*	**48**	SP2557
Hampton on the Hill *Warwks*	**48**	SP2564
Hampton Poyle *Oxon*	**37**	SP5015
Hampton Wick *Gt Lon*	**26**	TQ1769
Hamptworth *Wilts*	**12**	SU2419
Hamrow *Norfk*	**66**	TF9124
Hamsey *E Susx*	**15**	TQ4012
Hamsey Green *Gt Lon*	**27**	TQ3559
Hamstall Ridware *Staffs*	**73**	SK1019
Hamstead *IOW*	**13**	SZ4091
Hamstead *W Mids*	**61**	SP0592
Hamstead Marshall *Berks*	**24**	SU4165
Hamsterley *Dur*	**95**	NZ1156
Hamsterley *Dur*	**96**	NZ1231
Hamstreet *Kent*	**17**	TR0033
Hamwood *Avon*	**21**	ST3756
Hamworthy *Dorset*	**11**	SY9991
Hanbury *H & W*	**47**	SO9664
Hanbury *Staffs*	**73**	SK1727
Hanby *Lincs*	**64**	TF0231
Hanchet End *Suffk*	**53**	TL6446
Hanchurch *Staffs*	**72**	SJ8441
Hand and Pen *Devon*	**9**	SY0495
Hand Green *Ches*	**71**	SJ5460
Handale *Cleve*	**97**	NZ7215
Handbridge *Ches*	**71**	SJ4065
Handcross *W Susx*	**15**	TQ2629
Handforth *Ches*	**79**	SJ8583
Handley *Ches*	**71**	SJ4657
Handley *Derbys*	**74**	SK3761
Handley Green *Essex*	**40**	TL6501
Handsacre *Staffs*	**73**	SK0915
Handsworth *S York*	**74**	SK4186
Handsworth *W Mids*	**61**	SP0489
Handy Cross *Bucks*	**26**	SU8590
Hanford *Dorset*	**11**	ST8411
Hanford *Staffs*	**72**	SJ8741
Hanging Langford *Wilts*	**23**	SU0337
Hangleton *E Susx*	**15**	TQ2607
Hangleton *W Susx*	**14**	TQ0803
Hanham *Avon*	**35**	ST6472
Hankelow *Ches*	**72**	SJ6645
Hankerton *Wilts*	**35**	ST9790
Hankham *E Susx*	**16**	TQ6105
Hanley *Staffs*	**72**	SJ8847
Hanley Castle *H & W*	**47**	SO8442
Hanley Child *H & W*	**47**	SO6565
Hanley Swan *H & W*	**47**	SO8142
Hanley William *H & W*	**47**	SO6766
Hanlith *N York*	**88**	SD8961
Hanmer *Clwyd*	**71**	SJ4539
Hannaford *Devon*	**19**	SS6029
Hannah *Lincs*	**77**	TF4979
Hannington *Hants*	**24**	SU5355
Hannington *Nhants*	**51**	SP8170
Hannington *Wilts*	**36**	SU1793
Hannington Wick *Wilts*	**36**	SU1795
Hanscombe End *Beds*	**38**	TL1133
Hanslope *Bucks*	**38**	SP8046
Hanthorpe *Lincs*	**64**	TF0823
Hanwell *Gt Lon*	**26**	TQ1579
Hanwell *Oxon*	**49**	SP4343
Hanworth *Gt Lon*	**26**	TQ1271
Hanworth *Norfk*	**67**	TG1935
Happendon *Strath*	**108**	NS8533
Happisburgh *Norfk*	**67**	TG3831
Happisburgh Common *Norfk*	**67**	TG3728
Hapsford *Ches*	**71**	SJ4774
Hapton *Lancs*	**81**	SD7931
Hapton *Norfk*	**66**	TM1796
Harberton *Devon*	**7**	SX7758
Harbertonford *Devon*	**7**	SX7856
Harbledown *Kent*	**29**	TR1357
Harborne *W Mids*	**60**	SP0284
Harborough Magna *Warwks*	**50**	SP4778
Harborough Parva *Warwks*	**50**	SP4878
Harbottle *Nthumb*	**102**	NT9304
Harbourneford *Devon*	**7**	SX7162
Harbours Hill *H & W*	**47**	SO9565
Harbridge *Hants*	**12**	SU1410
Harbridge Green *Hants*	**12**	SU1410
Harbury *Warwks*	**48**	SP3759
Harby *Leics*	**63**	SK7431
Harby *Notts*	**76**	SK8770
Harcombe *Devon*	**9**	SX8881
Harcombe *Devon*	**9**	SY1590
Harcombe Bottom *Devon*	**10**	SY3395
Harden *W Mids*	**60**	SK0100
Harden *W York*	**82**	SE0838
Hardenhuish *Wilts*	**35**	ST9174
Hardgate *D & G*	**100**	NX8167
Hardgate *Gramp*	**135**	NJ7901
Hardgate *N York*	**89**	SE2662
Hardgate *Strath*	**115**	NS5072
Hardham *W Susx*	**14**	TQ0317
Hardhorn *Lancs*	**80**	SD3537
Hardingham *Norfk*	**66**	TG0403
Hardingstone *Nhants*	**49**	SP7657
Hardington *Somset*	**22**	ST7452
Hardington Mandeville *Somset*	**10**	ST5111
Hardington Marsh *Somset*	**10**	ST5009
Hardington Moor *Somset*	**10**	ST5112
Hardisworthy *Devon*	**18**	SS2320
Hardley *Hants*	**13**	SU4205
Hardley Street *Norfk*	**67**	TG3701
Hardmead *Bucks*	**38**	SP9347
Hardraw *N York*	**88**	SD8691
Hardsough *Lancs*	**81**	SD7920
Hardstoft *Derbys*	**75**	SK4363
Hardway *Hants*	**13**	SU6001
Hardway *Somset*	**22**	ST7234
Hardwick *Bucks*	**38**	SP8019
Hardwick *Cambs*	**52**	TL3758
Hardwick *Lincs*	**76**	SK8675
Hardwick *Nhants*	**51**	SP8469
Hardwick *Norfk*	**55**	TM2289
Hardwick *Oxon*	**36**	SP3806
Hardwick *Oxon*	**49**	SP5729
Hardwick *S York*	**75**	SK4885
Hardwick *W Mids*	**61**	SP0798
Hardwick Green *H & W*	**47**	SO8133
Hardwicke *Gloucs*	**35**	SO7912
Hardwicke *Gloucs*	**47**	SO9027

Hardy's Green

Henbury

Hardy's Green *Essex* 40 TL9320
Hare Croft *W York* 82 SE0835
Hare Green *Essex* 41 TM1025
Hare Hatch *Berks* 37 SU8077
Hare Street *Essex* 39 TL4209
Hare Street *Essex* 27 TL5300
Hare Street *Herts* 39 TL3929
Harebeating *E Susx* 16 TQ5910
Hareby *Lincs* 77 TF3365
Harefield *Gt Lon* 26 TQ0590
Harehill *Derbys* 73 SK1735
Harehills *W York* 82 SE3135
Harehope *Nthumb* 111 NU0920
Harelaw *Border* 109 NT5323
Harelaw *Dur* 96 NZ1652
Hareplain *Kent* 28 TQ8339
Harescough *Cumb* 94 NY6042
Harescombe *Gloucs* 35 SO8310
Haresfield *Gloucs* 35 SO8010
Harestock *Hants* 24 SU4631
Harewood *W York* 83 SE3245
Harewood End *H & W* 46 SO5227
Harford *Devon* 6 SX6359
Hargate *Norfk* 66 TM1191
Hargrave *Ches* 71 SJ4862
Hargrave *Nhants* 51 TL0370
Hargrave *Suffk* 53 TL7760
Hargrave Green *Suffk* 53 TL7759
Harker *Cumb* 101 NY3960
Harkstead *Suffk* 54 TM1834
Harlaston *Staffs* 61 SK2110
Harlaxton *Lincs* 63 SK8832
Harle Syke *Lancs* 81 SD8635
Harlech *Gwynd* 57 SH5831
Harlescott *Shrops* 59 SJ4916
Harlesden *Gt Lon* 26 TQ2183
Harlesthorpe *Derbys* 75 SK4976
Harleston *Devon* 7 SX7945
Harleston *Norfk* 55 TM2483
Harleston *Suffk* 54 TM0160
Harlestone *Nhants* 49 SP7064
Harley *S York* 74 SK3698
Harley *Shrops* 59 SJ5901
Harlington *Beds* 38 TL0330
Harlington *Gt Lon* 26 TQ0877
Harlington *S York* 83 SE4802
Harlosh *Highld* 136 NG2841
Harlow *Essex* 39 TL4410
Harlow Hill *Nthumb* 103 NZ0768
Harlthorpe *Humb* 84 SE7337
Harlton *Cambs* 52 TL3852
Harlyn Bay *Cnwll* 4 SW8775
Harman's Cross *Dorset* 11 SY9880
Harmby *N York* 89 SE1289
Harmer Green *Herts* 39 TL2515
Harmer Hill *Shrops* 59 SJ4822
Harmondsworth *Gt Lon* 26 TQ0577
Harmston *Lincs* 76 SK9662
Harnage *Shrops* 59 SJ5604
Harnham *Nthumb* 103 NZ0781
Harnhill *Gloucs* 36 SP0600
Harold Hill *Gt Lon* 27 TQ5392
Harold Wood *Gt Lon* 27 TQ5590
Haroldston West *Dyfed* 30 SM8615
Haroldswick *Shet* 155 HP6312
Harome *N York* 90 SE6481
Harpenden *Herts* 38 TL1314
Harpford *Devon* 9 SY0990
Harpham *Humb* 91 TA0861
Harpley *H & W* 47 SO6861
Harpley *Norfk* 65 TF7825
Harpole *Nhants* 49 SP6961
Harpsdale *Highld* 151 ND1355
Harpsden *Oxon* 37 SU7680
Harpswell *Lincs* 76 SK9389
Harpur Hill *Derbys* 74 SK0671
Harpurhey *Gt Man* 79 SD8501
Harraby *Cumb* 93 NY4154
Harracott *Devon* 19 SS5527
Harrapool *Highld* 129 NG6523
Harrietfield *Tays* 125 NN9829
Harrietsham *Kent* 28 TQ8652
Harringay *Gt Lon* 27 TQ3188
Harrington *Lincs* 77 TF3671
Harrington *Nhants* 50 SP7780
Harringworth *Nhants* 51 SP9197
Harriseahead *Staffs* 72 SJ8655
Harriston *Cumb* 92 NY1541
Harrogate *N York* 82 SE3054
Harrold *Beds* 51 SP9457
Harrop Dale *Gt Man* 82 SE0008
Harrow *Gt Lon* 26 TQ1588
Harrow Green *Suffk* 54 TL8654
Harrow on the Hill *Gt Lon* 26 TQ1587
Harrow Weald *Gt Lon* 26 TQ1591
Harrowbarrow *Cnwll* 5 SX4070
Harrowden *Beds* 38 TL0647
Harrowgate Village *Dur* 96 NZ2917
Harston *Cambs* 53 TL4250
Harston *Leics* 63 SK8331
Harswell *Humb* 84 SE8240
Hart *Cleve* 97 NZ4734
Hart Station *Cleve* 97 NZ4836
Hartburn *Nthumb* 103 NZ0885
Hartest *Suffk* 54 TL8352
Hartfield *E Susx* 16 TQ4735
Hartford *Cambs* 52 TL2572
Hartford *Ches* 71 SJ6372
Hartford *Somset* 20 SS9529
Hartford End *Essex* 40 TL6817
Hartfordbridge *Hants* 25 SU7757
Hartforth *N York* 89 NZ1606
Harthill *Ches* 71 SJ4955
Harthill *Loth* 116 NS9064
Harthill *S York* 75 SK4980
Hartington *Derbys* 74 SK1260
Hartington *Nthumb* 103 NZ0288
Hartland *Devon* 18 SS2524
Hartland Quay *Devon* 18 SS2224
Hartlebury *H & W* 60 SO8471
Hartlepool *Cleve* 97 NZ5032
Hartley *Cumb* 88 NY7808
Hartley *Kent* 27 TQ6066
Hartley *Kent* 17 TQ7634
Hartley *Nthumb* 103 NZ3475
Hartley Green *Kent* 27 TQ6067
Hartley Green *Staffs* 72 SJ9829
Hartley Wespall *Hants* 24 SU6958
Hartley Wintney *Hants* 24 SU7656
Hartlip *Kent* 28 TQ8464
Hartoft End *N York* 90 SE7493
Harton *N York* 90 SE7061
Harton *Shrops* 59 SO4888
Harton *T & W* 103 NZ3765
Hartpury *Gloucs* 47 SO7924
Hartshead *W York* 82 SE1822
Hartshead Moor Side *W York* 82 SE1625
Hartshill *Staffs* 72 SJ8546
Hartshill *Warwks* 61 SP3194
Hartshorne *Derbys* 62 SK3221
Hartside *Nthumb* 111 NT9716
Hartsop *Cumb* 93 NY4013
Hartswell *Somset* 20 ST0827
Hartwell *Nhants* 38 SP7850
Hartwith *N York* 89 SE2161
Hartwood *Strath* 116 NS8459
Hartwoodmyres *Border* 109 NT4324
Harvel *Kent* 28 TQ6563
Harvington *H & W* 60 SO8775
Harvington *H & W* 48 SP0549
Harwell *Notts* 75 SK6891
Harwell *Oxon* 37 SU4989
Harwich *Essex* 41 TM2531
Harwood *Gt Man* 79 SD7410
Harwood *Nthumb* 95 NY8233
Harwood *Nthumb* 103 NZ0189
Harwood Dale *N York* 91 SE9695
Harwood Lee *Gt Man* 81 SD7411
Harworth *Notts* 75 SK6191
Hasbury *W Mids* 60 SO9582
Hascombe *Surrey* 25 TQ0039
Haselbech *Nhants* 50 SP7177
Haselbury Plucknett *Somset* 10 ST4710
Haseley *Warwks* 48 SP2367
Haseley Green *Warwks* 48 SP2369
Haseley Knob *Warwks* 61 SP2371
Haselor *Warwks* 48 SP1257
Hasfield *Gloucs* 47 SO8227
Hasguard *Dyfed* 30 SM8509
Haskayne *Lancs* 78 SD3508
Hasketon *Suffk* 55 TM2450
Hasland *Derbys* 74 SK3969
Hasland Green *Derbys* 74 SK3968
Haslemere *Surrey* 14 SU9032
Haslingden *Lancs* 81 SD7823
Haslingden Grane *Lancs* 81 SD7522
Haslingfield *Cambs* 52 TL4052
Haslington *Ches* 72 SJ7355
Hassall *Ches* 72 SJ7657
Hassall Green *Ches* 72 SJ7858
Hassell Street *Kent* 29 TR0946
Hassingham *Norfk* 67 TG3605
Hassness *Cumb* 93 NY1816
Hassocks *W Susx* 15 TQ3015
Hassop *Derbys* 74 SK2272
Haste Hill *Surrey* 14 SU9032
Haster *Highld* 151 ND3251
Hasthorpe *Lincs* 77 TF4869
Hastingleigh *Kent* 29 TR0945
Hastings *E Susx* 17 TQ8209
Hastings *Somset* 10 ST3116
Hastingwood *Essex* 39 TL4807
Hastoe *Herts* 38 SP9209
Haswell *Dur* 96 NZ3743
Haswell Plough *Dur* 96 NZ3742
Hatch *Beds* 52 TL1547
Hatch Beauchamp *Somset* 20 ST3020
Hatch End *Beds* 51 TL0760
Hatch End *Gt Lon* 26 TQ1390
Hatchet Gate *Hants* 12 SU3701
Hatching Green *Herts* 38 TL1312
Hatchmere *Ches* 71 SJ5571
Hatcliffe *Humb* 76 TA2100
Hatfield *H & W* 46 SO5959
Hatfield *Herts* 39 TL2308
Hatfield *S York* 83 SE6609
Hatfield Broad Oak *Essex* 39 TL5416
Hatfield Heath *Essex* 39 TL5215
Hatfield Peverel *Essex* 40 TL7911
Hatfield Woodhouse *S York* 83 SE6708
Hatford *Oxon* 36 SU3395
Hatherden *Hants* 23 SU3450
Hatherleigh *Devon* 8 SS5404
Hathern *Leics* 62 SK5022
Hatherop *Gloucs* 36 SP1505
Hathersage *Derbys* 74 SK2381
Hathersage Booths *Derbys* 74 SK2480
Hatherton *Ches* 72 SJ6847
Hatherton *Staffs* 60 SJ9510
Hatley St George *Cambs* 52 TL2751
Hatt *Cnwll* 5 SX4062
Hattingley *Hants* 24 SU6437
Hatton *Ches* 78 SJ5982
Hatton *Derbys* 73 SK2130
Hatton *Gramp* 143 NK0537
Hatton *Gt Lon* 26 TQ0975
Hatton *Lincs* 76 TF1776
Hatton *Shrops* 59 SO4790
Hatton *Tays* 127 NO4642
Hatton *Warwks* 48 SP2367
Hatton Heath *Ches* 71 SJ4561
Hatton of Fintray *Gramp* 143 NJ8316
Haugh *Lincs* 77 TF4175
Haugh *Strath* 107 NS4925
Haugh *W York* 81 SD9311
Haugh Head *Nthumb* 111 NU0026
Haugh of Glass *Gramp* 142 NJ4238
Haugh of Urr *D & G* 100 NX8066
Haugham *Lincs* 77 TF3381
Haughhead Inn *Strath* 116 NS6079
Haughley *Suffk* 54 TM0262
Haughley Green *Suffk* 54 TM0264
Haughton *Notts* 75 SK6872
Haughton *Powys* 59 SJ3018
Haughton *Shrops* 59 SJ3726
Haughton *Shrops* 59 SJ5516
Haughton *Shrops* 60 SJ7408
Haughton *Shrops* 60 SO6896
Haughton *Staffs* 72 SJ8620
Haughton Green *Gt Man* 79 SJ9393
Haughton le Skerne *Dur* 96 NZ3116
Haughton Moss *Ches* 71 SJ5756
Haultwick *Herts* 39 TL3323
Haunton *Staffs* 61 SK2310
Hautes Croix *Jersey* 152 JS0000
Hauxley *Nthumb* 103 NU2703
Hauxton *Cambs* 53 TL4452
Havannah *Ches* 72 SJ8664
Havant *Hants* 13 SU7106
Haven *H & W* 46 SO4054
Haven Bank *Lincs* 76 TF2352
Haven Side *Humb* 85 TA1827
Havenstreet *IOW* 13 SZ5690
Havercroft *W York* 83 SE3913
Haverfordwest *Dyfed* 30 SM9515
Haverhill *Suffk* 53 TL6745
Haverigg *Cumb* 86 SD1578
Havering-atte-Bower *Essex* 27 TQ5193
Haversham *Bucks* 38 SP8242
Haverthwaite *Cumb* 87 SD3483
Haverton Hill *Cleve* 97 NZ4822
Havyat *Avon* 21 ST4761
Havyatt *Somset* 21 ST5338
Hawarden *Clwyd* 71 SJ3165
Hawbridge *H & W* 47 SO9049
Hawbush Green *Essex* 40 TL7820
Hawcoat *Cumb* 86 SD2071
Hawe's Green *Norfk* 67 TM2399
Hawen *Dyfed* 42 SN3446
Hawes *N York* 88 SD8789
Hawford *H & W* 47 SO8460
Hawick *Border* 109 NT5014
Hawk Green *Gt Man* 79 SJ9687
Hawkchurch *Devon* 10 ST3400
Hawkedon *Suffk* 53 TL7953
Hawkenbury *Kent* 28 TQ8045
Hawkeridge *Wilts* 22 ST8653
Hawkerland *Devon* 9 SY0588
Hawkes End *W Mids* 61 SP2982
Hawkesbury *Avon* 35 ST7686
Hawkesbury *Warwks* 61 SP3784
Hawkesbury Upton *Avon* 35 ST7786
Hawkhill *Nthumb* 111 NU2212
Hawkhurst *Kent* 17 TQ7530
Hawkhurst Common *E Susx* 16 TQ5217
Hawkinge *Kent* 29 TR2139
Hawkley *Hants* 24 SU7429
Hawkridge *Devon* 19 SS8630
Hawksdale *Cumb* 93 NY3648
Hawkshaw *Gt Man* 81 SD7615
Hawkshead *Cumb* 87 SD3598
Hawkshead Hill *Cumb* 86 SD3398
Hawksland *Strath* 108 NS8439
Hawkspur Green *Essex* 40 TL6532
Hawkstone *Shrops* 59 SJ5830
Hawkswick *N York* 88 SD9570
Hawksworth *Notts* 63 SK7543
Hawksworth *W York* 82 SE1641
Hawkwell *Essex* 40 TQ8591
Hawley *Hants* 25 SU8657
Hawley *Kent* 27 TQ5471
Hawling *Gloucs* 36 SP0622
Hawnby *N York* 90 SE5489
Haworth *W York* 82 SE0337
Hawstead *Suffk* 54 TL8559
Hawstead Green *Suffk* 54 TL8658
Hawthorn *Dur* 96 NZ4145
Hawthorn *Hants* 24 SU6733
Hawthorn *M Glam* 33 ST0987
Hawthorn Hill *Berks* 25 SU8773
Hawthorn Hill *Lincs* 76 TF2155
Hawthorpe *Lincs* 64 TF0427
Hawton *Notts* 75 SK7851
Haxby *N York* 90 SE6058
Haxby Gates *N York* 83 SE6056
Haxey *Humb* 75 SK7799
Haxey Turbary *Humb* 84 SE7501
Haxted *Surrey* 16 TQ4245
Haxton *Wilts* 23 SU1449
Hay *Cnwll* 3 SW8651
Hay *Cnwll* 3 SW9243
Hay *Cnwll* 3 SW9552
Hay *Cnwll* 4 SW9770
Hay Green *Norfk* 65 TF5418
Hay Street *Herts* 39 TL3926
Hay-on-Wye *Powys* 45 SO2342
Haydock *Mersyd* 78 SJ5697
Haydon *Avon* 22 ST6853
Haydon *Dorset* 11 ST6715
Haydon *Somset* 20 ST2523
Haydon Bridge *Nthumb* 102 NY8464
Haydon Wick *Wilts* 36 SU1387
Haye *Cnwll* 5 SX3570
Hayes *Gt Lon* 26 TQ0980
Hayes *Gt Lon* 27 TQ4066
Hayes End *Gt Lon* 26 TQ0882
Hayfield *Derbys* 74 SK0386
Hayfield *Strath* 123 NN0723
Haygate *Shrops* 59 SJ6410
Hayhillock *Tays* 127 NO5242
Hayle *Cnwll* 2 SW5537
Hayley Green *W Mids* 60 SO9582
Haymoor Green *Ches* 72 SJ6850
Hayne *Devon* 9 SS9515
Hayne *Devon* 8 SX7685
Haynes *Beds* 38 TL0740
Haynes West End *Beds* 38 TL0640
Hayscastle *Dyfed* 30 SM8925
Hayscastle Cross *Dyfed* 30 SM9125
Haysden *Kent* 16 TQ5745
Hayton *Cumb* 92 NY1041
Hayton *Cumb* 94 NY5157
Hayton *Humb* 84 SE8245
Hayton *Notts* 75 SK7284
Hayton's Bent *Shrops* 59 SO5280
Haytor Vale *Devon* 8 SX7777
Haytown *Devon* 18 SS3814
Haywards Heath *W Susx* 15 TQ3324
Haywood *H & W* 46 SO4834
Haywood *S York* 83 SE5812
Haywood Oaks *Notts* 75 SK6055
Hazards Green *E Susx* 16 TQ6812
Hazel Grove *Gt Man* 79 SJ9287
Hazel Street *Kent* 28 TQ6939
Hazel Stub *Suffk* 53 TL6544
Hazelbank *Strath* 116 NS8345
Hazelbury Bryan *Dorset* 11 ST7408
Hazeleigh *Essex* 40 TL8203
Hazeley *Hants* 24 SU7458
Hazelford *Notts* 75 SK7249
Hazelhurst *Gt Man* 79 SD9600
Hazelslade *Staffs* 60 SK0212
Hazelton Walls *Fife* 126 NO3322
Hazelwood *Derbys* 62 SK3245
Hazlemere *Bucks* 26 SU8895
Hazlerigg *T & W* 103 NZ2372
Hazles *Staffs* 73 SK0047
Hazleton *Gloucs* 36 SP0718
Heacham *Norfk* 65 TF6737
Headbourne Worthy *Hants* 24 SU4832
Headbrook *H & W* 46 SO2854
Headcorn *Kent* 28 TQ8344
Headingley *W York* 82 SE2836
Headington *Oxon* 37 SP5207
Headlam *Dur* 96 NZ1818
Headless Cross *H & W* 48 SP0365
Headlesscross *Strath* 116 NS9158
Headley *Hants* 24 SU5162
Headley *Hants* 14 SU8236
Headley *Surrey* 26 TQ2054
Headley Down *Hants* 14 SU8336
Headley Heath *H & W* 61 SP0676
Headon *Notts* 75 SK7476
Heads *Strath* 116 NS7247
Heads Nook *Cumb* 94 NY5054
Heage *Derbys* 74 SK3750
Healaugh *N York* 88 SE0199
Healaugh *N York* 83 SE5047
Heald Green *Gt Man* 79 SJ8485
Heale *Devon* 19 SS6446
Heale *Somset* 20 ST2420
Heale *Somset* 21 ST3825
Healey *Lancs* 81 SD8816
Healey *N York* 89 SE1780
Healey *Nthumb* 95 NZ0158
Healey *W York* 82 SE2719
Healeyfield *Dur* 95 NZ0648
Healing *Humb* 85 TA2110
Heamoor *Cnwll* 2 SW4631
Heanor *Derbys* 62 SK4346
Heanton Punchardon *Devon* 19 SS5035
Heapey *Lancs* 81 SD5920
Heapham *Lincs* 76 SK8788
Hearn *Hants* 14 SU8337
Hearts Delight *Kent* 28 TQ8862
Heasley Mill *Devon* 19 SS7332
Heast *Highld* 129 NG6417
Heath *Derbys* 75 SK4567
Heath *W York* 83 SE3520
Heath and Reach *Beds* 38 SP9228
Heath Common *W Susx* 14 TQ0915
Heath End *Bucks* 26 SU8898
Heath End *Hants* 24 SU4161
Heath End *Hants* 24 SU5862
Heath End *Leics* 62 SK3621
Heath End *Surrey* 25 SU8549
Heath End *Warwks* 48 SP2360
Heath Green *H & W* 61 SP0771
Heath Hall *D & G* 100 NX9979
Heath Hayes *Staffs* 60 SK0110
Heath Hill *Shrops* 60 SJ7613
Heath House *Somset* 21 ST4146
Heath Town *W Mids* 60 SO9399
Heathbrook *Shrops* 59 SJ6228
Heathcote *Derbys* 74 SK1460
Heathcote *Shrops* 72 SJ6528
Heathencote *Nhants* 49 SP7147
Heather *Leics* 62 SK3910
Heathfield *Devon* 8 SX8376
Heathfield *E Susx* 16 TQ5821
Heathfield *N York* 89 SE1367
Heathfield *Somset* 20 ST1626
Heathstock *Devon* 9 ST2402
Heathton *Shrops* 60 SO8192
Heatley *Gt Man* 79 SJ7088
Heatley *Staffs* 73 SK0626
Heaton *Gt Man* 79 SD6909
Heaton *Lancs* 87 SD4460
Heaton *Staffs* 72 SJ9562
Heaton *T & W* 103 NZ2666
Heaton *W York* 82 SE1335
Heaton Chapel *Gt Man* 79 SJ8891
Heaton Mersey *Gt Man* 79 SJ8690
Heaton Norris *Gt Man* 79 SJ8890
Heaton's Bridge *Lancs* 80 SD4011
Heaverham *Kent* 27 TQ5758
Heaviley *Gt Man* 79 SJ9088
Heavitree *Devon* 9 SX9492
Hebburn *T & W* 103 NZ3164
Hebden *N York* 88 SE0263
Hebden Bridge *W York* 82 SD9927
Hebden Green *Ches* 71 SJ6365
Hebing End *Herts* 39 TL3122
Hebron *Dyfed* 31 SN1827
Hebron *Gwynd* 68 SH4584
Hebron *Nthumb* 103 NZ1989
Heckfield *Hants* 24 SU7260
Heckfield Green *Suffk* 54 TM1875
Heckfordbridge *Essex* 40 TL9421
Heckington *Lincs* 64 TF1444
Heckmondwike *W York* 82 SE1824
Heddington *Wilts* 22 ST9966
Heddon-on-the-Wall *Nthumb* 103 NZ1366
Hedenham *Norfk* 67 TM3193
Hedge End *Hants* 13 SU4912
Hedgerley *Bucks* 26 SU9687
Hedgerley Green *Bucks* 26 SU9787
Hedging *Somset* 20 ST3029
Hedley on the Hill *Nthumb* 95 NZ0759
Hednesford *Staffs* 60 SJ9912
Hedon *Humb* 85 TA1928
Hedsor *Bucks* 26 SU9086
Hegdon Hill *H & W* 46 SO5853
Heglibister *Shet* 155 HU3851
Heighington *Dur* 96 NZ2422
Heighington *Lincs* 76 TF0269
Heightington *H & W* 60 SO7671
Heiton *Border* 110 NT7130
Hele *Cnwll* 5 SX2198
Hele *Devon* 19 SS5347
Hele *Devon* 9 SS9902
Hele *Devon* 7 SX7470
Hele *Somset* 20 ST1824
Hele Lane *Devon* 19 SS7910
Helensburgh *Strath* 115 NS2982
Helenton *Strath* 106 NS3830
Helford *Cnwll* 3 SW7526
Helford Passage *Cnwll* 3 SW7626
Helhoughton *Norfk* 66 TF8626
Helions Bumpstead *Essex* 53 TL6541
Hell Corner *Berks* 23 SU3864
Hellaby *S York* 75 SK5092
Helland *Cnwll* 4 SX0771
Hellandbridge *Cnwll* 4 SX0671
Hellescott *Cnwll* 5 SX2888
Hellesdon *Norfk* 67 TG2010
Hellesvear *Cnwll* 2 SW5040
Hellidon *Nhants* 49 SP5158
Hellifield *N York* 81 SD8556
Hellingly *E Susx* 16 TQ5812
Hellington *Norfk* 67 TG3103
Helm *Nthumb* 103 NZ1896
Helmdon *Nhants* 49 SP5943
Helme *W York* 82 SE0912
Helmingham *Suffk* 54 TM1857
Helmington Row *Dur* 96 NZ1835
Helmsdale *Highld* 147 ND0315
Helmshore *Lancs* 81 SD7821
Helmsley *N York* 90 SE6183
Helmswell Cliff *Lincs* 76 SK9489
Helperby *N York* 89 SE4469
Helperthorpe *N York* 91 SE9570
Helpringham *Lincs* 64 TF1440
Helpston *Cambs* 64 TF1205
Helsby *Ches* 71 SJ4975
Helsey *Lincs* 77 TF5172
Helston *Cnwll* 2 SW6527
Helstone *Cnwll* 4 SX0881
Helton *Cumb* 94 NY5021
Helwith *N York* 88 NZ0702
Helwith Bridge *N York* 88 SD8069
Hemblington *Norfk* 67 TG3411
Hemel Hempstead *Herts* 38 TL0507
Hemerdon *Devon* 6 SX5657
Hemingbrough *N York* 83 SE6730
Hemingby *Lincs* 76 TF2374
Hemingfield *S York* 83 SE3801
Hemingford Abbots *Cambs* 52 TL2871
Hemingford Grey *Cambs* 52 TL2970
Hemingstone *Suffk* 54 TM1454
Hemington *Nhants* 51 TL0985
Hemington *Somset* 22 ST7253
Hemley *Suffk* 55 TM2842
Hemlington *Cleve* 90 NZ5014
Hemp Green *Suffk* 55 TM3769
Hempholme *Humb* 85 TA0850
Hempnall *Norfk* 67 TM2494
Hempnall Green *Norfk* 67 TM2493
Hempriggs *Gramp* 141 NJ1063
Hempstead *Essex* 53 TL6338
Hempstead *Gloucs* 35 SO8116
Hempstead *Kent* 28 TQ7964
Hempstead *Norfk* 66 TG1037
Hempstead *Norfk* 67 TG4028
Hempton *Norfk* 66 TF9129
Hempton *Oxon* 49 SP4431
Hemsby *Norfk* 67 TG4917
Hemswell *Lincs* 76 SK9290
Hemsworth *W York* 83 SE4213
Hemyock *Devon* 9 ST1313
Henbury *Avon* 34 ST5678
Henbury *Ches* 79 SJ8773

Hendersyde Park
Hobbles Green

Hendersyde Park Border	110	NT7435
Hendham Devon	7	SX7450
Hendomen Powys	58	SO2197
Hendon Gt Lon	26	TQ2389
Hendra Cnwll	3	SW7237
Hendra Cnwll	4	SX0275
Hendre Gwent	34	SO4614
Hendre M Glam	33	SS9381
Hendy Dyfed	32	SN5803
Heneglwys Gwynd	68	SH4276
Henfield W Susx	15	TQ2115
Henford Devon	5	SX3794
Henghurst Kent	28	TQ9536
Hengoed M Glam	33	ST1594
Hengoed Powys	45	SO2253
Hengoed Shrops	58	SJ2833
Hengrave Suffk	54	TL8268
Henham Essex	39	TL5428
Henhurst Kent	28	TQ6669
Heniarth Powys	58	SJ1208
Henlade Somset	20	ST2623
Henley Dorset	11	ST6904
Henley Gloucs	35	SO9016
Henley Shrops	59	SO4588
Henley Shrops	46	SO5476
Henley Somset	21	ST4232
Henley Suffk	54	TM1551
Henley W Susx	14	SU8925
Henley Green W Mids	61	SP3681
Henley Park Surrey	25	SU9352
Henley Street Kent	28	TQ6667
Henley's Down E Susx	17	TQ7312
Henley-in-Arden Warwks	48	SP1566
Henley-on-Thames Oxon	37	SU7682
Henllan Clwyd	70	SJ0268
Henllan Dyfed	31	SN3540
Henllan Amgoed Dyfed	31	SN1819
Henllys Gwent	34	ST2691
Henlow Beds	39	TL1738
Hennock Devon	8	SX8381
Henny Street Essex	54	TL8738
Henry's Moat (Castell Hendre) Dyfed	30	SN0427
Henryd Gwynd	69	SH7774
Hensall N York	83	SE5923
Henshaw Nthumb	102	NY7664
Hensingham Cumb	92	NX9816
Henstead Suffk	55	TM4885
Hensting Hants	13	SU4922
Henstridge Somset	22	ST7219
Henstridge Ash Somset	22	ST7220
Henstridge Marsh Somset	22	ST7320
Henton Oxon	37	SP7602
Henton Somset	21	ST4945
Henwick H & W	47	SO8355
Henwood Cnwll	5	SX2673
Heol Senni Powys	45	SN9223
Heol-las W Glam	32	SS6998
Heol-y-Cyw M Glam	33	SS9484
Hepburn Nthumb	111	NU0624
Hepple Nthumb	103	NT9901
Hepscott Nthumb	103	NZ2284
Heptonstall W York	82	SD9828
Hepworth Suffk	54	TL9874
Hepworth W York	82	SE1606
Herbrandston Dyfed	30	SM8707
Hereford H & W	46	SO5139
Hereson Kent	29	TR3865
Heribusta Highld	136	NG3970
Heriot Loth	118	NT3953
Hermiston Loth	117	NT1870
Hermit Hill S York	74	SE3200
Hermitage Berks	24	SU5072
Hermitage Border	101	NY5095
Hermitage Dorset	11	ST6506
Hermitage Hants	13	SU7505
Hermon Dyfed	31	SN2031
Hermon Gwynd	68	SH3968
Herne Kent	29	TR1865
Herne Bay Kent	29	TR1768
Herne Common Kent	29	TR1765
Herne Hill Gt Lon	27	TQ3274
Herne Pound Kent	28	TQ6654
Herner Devon	19	SS5826
Hernhill Kent	29	TR0660
Herodsfoot Cnwll	5	SX2160
Heronden Kent	29	TR2954
Herongate Essex	40	TQ6291
Heronsford Strath	98	NX1283
Heronsgate Herts	26	TQ0294
Herriard Hants	24	SU6646
Herring's Green Beds	38	TL0844
Herringfleet Suffk	67	TM4797
Herringswell Suffk	53	TL7270
Herringthorpe S York	75	SK4492
Herrington T & W	96	NZ3453
Hersden Kent	29	TR2062
Hersham Cnwll	18	SS2507
Hersham Surrey	26	TQ1164
Herstmonceux E Susx	16	TQ6312
Herston Dorset	11	SZ0178
Herston Ork	155	ND4191
Hertford Herts	39	TL3212
Hertford Heath Herts	39	TL3510
Hertingfordbury Herts	39	TL3012
Hesketh Bank Lancs	80	SD4423
Hesketh Lane Lancs	81	SD6141
Heskin Green Lancs	80	SD5315
Hesleden Dur	96	NZ4438
Hesleden N York	88	SD8874
Hesleyside Nthumb	102	NY8183
Heslington N York	83	SE6250
Hessay N York	83	SE5253
Hessenford Cnwll	5	SX3057
Hessett Suffk	54	TL9361
Hessle Humb	84	TA0326
Hessle W York	83	SE4317
Hest Bank Lancs	87	SD4666
Hestley Green Suffk	54	TM1567
Heston Gt Lon	26	TQ1277
Hestwall Ork	155	HY2618
Heswall Mersyd	78	SJ2681
Hethe Oxon	49	SP5929
Hethersett Norfk	66	TG1404
Hethersgill Cumb	101	NY4767
Hetherside Cumb	101	NY4366
Hetherson Green Ches	71	SJ5250
Hethpool Nthumb	110	NT8928
Hett Dur	96	NZ2836
Hetton N York	88	SD9658
Hetton Steads Nthumb	111	NU0335
Hetton-le-Hole T & W	96	NZ3547
Heugh Nthumb	103	NZ0873
Heugh Head Border	119	NT8762
Heughhead Gramp	134	NJ3811
Heveningham Suffk	55	TM3372
Hever Kent	16	TQ4745
Heversham Cumb	87	SD4983
Hevingham Norfk	67	TG1921
Hewas Water Cnwll	3	SW9649
Hewelsfield Gloucs	34	SO5602
Hewenden W York	82	SE0736
Hewish Avon	21	ST4064
Hewish Somset	10	ST4208
Hewood Dorset	10	ST3502
Hexham Nthumb	102	NY9364
Hextable Kent	27	TQ5170
Hexthorpe S York	83	SE5602
Hexton Herts	38	TL1030
Hexworthy Cnwll	5	SX3581
Hexworthy Devon	7	SX6572
Hey Lancs	81	SD8843
Hey Houses Lancs	80	SD3429
Heybridge Essex	40	TL8508
Heybridge Essex	40	TQ6398
Heybridge Basin Essex	40	TL8707
Heybrook Bay Devon	6	SX4949
Heydon Cambs	39	TL4339
Heydon Norfk	66	TG1127
Heydour Lincs	63	TF0039
Heyhead Gt Man	79	SJ8285
Heylipoll Strath	120	NL9743
Heylor Shet	155	HU2980
Heyrod Gt Man	79	SJ9799
Heysham Lancs	87	SD4160
Heyshaw N York	89	SE1761
Heyshott W Susx	14	SU8917
Heyside Gt Man	79	SD9307
Heytesbury Wilts	22	ST9242
Heythrop Oxon	48	SP3527
Heywood Gt Man	79	SD8510
Heywood Wilts	22	ST8753
Hibaldstow Humb	84	SE9702
Hickleton S York	83	SE4805
Hickling Norfk	67	TG4124
Hickling Notts	63	SK6928
Hickling Green Norfk	67	TG4123
Hickling Heath Norfk	67	TG4022
Hickmans Green Kent	29	TR0658
Hicks Forstal Kent	29	TR1863
Hickstead W Susx	15	TQ2620
Hidcote Bartrim Gloucs	48	SP1742
Hidcote Boyce Gloucs	48	SP1742
High Ackworth W York	83	SE4417
High Angerton Nthumb	103	NZ0985
High Ardwell D & G	98	NX0745
High Auldgirth D & G	100	NX9187
High Bankhill Cumb	94	NY5542
High Beach Essex	27	TQ4198
High Bentham N York	87	SD6669
High Bewaldeth Cumb	93	NY2234
High Bickington Devon	19	SS6020
High Bickwith N York	88	SD8076
High Biggins Cumb	87	SD6078
High Blantyre Strath	116	NS6756
High Bonnybridge Cent	116	NS8379
High Borrans Cumb	87	NY4300
High Bradley N York	82	SE0049
High Bray Devon	19	SS6934
High Brooms Kent	16	TQ5941
High Bullen Devon	19	SS5320
High Buston Nthumb	111	NU2308
High Callerton Nthumb	103	NZ1670
High Casterton Cumb	87	SD6278
High Catton Humb	84	SE7153
High Close N York	96	NZ1715
High Cogges Oxon	36	SP3709
High Common Norfk	66	TF9905
High Coniscliffe Dur	96	NZ2215
High Crosby Cumb	93	NY4559
High Cross Cnwll	3	SW7429
High Cross Hants	13	SU7126
High Cross Herts	39	TL3618
High Cross Strath	115	NS4046
High Cross W Susx	15	TQ2417
High Cross Warwks	48	SP2067
High Cross Bank Derbys	73	SK2817
High Disley Ches	79	SJ9784
High Drummore D & G	98	NX1235
High Dubmire T & W	96	NZ3249
High Easter Essex	40	TL6214
High Eggborough N York	83	SE5721
High Ellington N York	89	SE2083
High Ercall Shrops	59	SJ5917
High Etherley Dur	96	NZ1728
High Ferry Lincs	77	TF3549
High Flats W York	82	SE2107
High Garrett Essex	40	TL7727
High Grange Dur	96	NZ1731
High Grantley N York	89	SE2369
High Green Cumb	87	NY4103
High Green H & W	47	SO8745
High Green Norfk	66	TG1305
High Green Norfk	54	TM1689
High Green Norfk	67	TM2898
High Green S York	74	SK3397
High Green Shrops	60	SO7083
High Green Suffk	54	TL8560
High Green W York	82	SE2014
High Halden Kent	28	TQ8937
High Halstow Kent	28	TQ7875
High Ham Somset	21	ST4231
High Harrington Cumb	92	NY0025
High Harrogate N York	82	SE3155
High Haswell Dur	96	NZ3643
High Hatton Shrops	59	SJ6124
High Hawsker N York	91	NZ9207
High Hesket Cumb	93	NY4744
High Hoyland S York	82	SE2710
High Hunsley Humb	84	SE9535
High Hurstwood E Susx	16	TQ4926
High Hutton N York	90	SE7568
High Ireby Cumb	93	NY2237
High Kilburn N York	90	SE5179
High Killerby N York	91	TA0683
High Knipe Cumb	94	NY5219
High Lands Dur	96	NZ1226
High Lane Ches	79	SJ8868
High Lane Gt Man	79	SJ9585
High Lane H & W	47	SO6760
High Lanes Cnwll	2	SW5637
High Laver Essex	39	TL5208
High Legh Ches	79	SJ7084
High Leven Cleve	89	NZ4512
High Littleton Avon	21	ST6458
High Lorton Cumb	92	NY1625
High Marnham Notts	75	SK8070
High Melton S York	83	SE5001
High Mickley Nthumb	103	NZ0761
High Moorsley T & W	96	NZ3345
High Newport T & W	96	NZ3754
High Newton Cumb	87	SD4082
High Nibthwaite Cumb	86	SD2989
High Offley Staffs	72	SJ7826
High Ongar Essex	40	TL5603
High Onn Staffs	72	SJ8216
High Park Corner Essex	41	TM0320
High Pennyvenie Strath	107	NS4907
High Post Wilts	23	SU1536
High Roding Essex	40	TL6017
High Row Cumb	93	NY3535
High Row Cumb	93	NY3821
High Salter Lancs	87	SD6062
High Salvington W Susx	14	TQ1206
High Scales Cumb	93	NY1845
High Seaton Cumb	92	NY0231
High Shaw N York	88	SD8691
High Side Cumb	93	NY2330
High Spen T & W	96	NZ1359
High Stoop Dur	95	NZ1040
High Street Cambs	52	TL3762
High Street Cnwll	3	SW9653
High Street Kent	17	TQ7430
High Street Kent	29	TR0862
High Street Suffk	55	TM4171
High Street Suffk	55	TM4355
High Throston Cleve	97	NZ4833
High Town Staffs	60	SJ9911
High Toynton Lincs	77	TF2869
High Trewhitt Nthumb	111	NU0105
High Urpeth Dur	96	NZ2354
High Valleyfield Fife	117	NT0086
High Warden Nthumb	102	NY9067
High Westwood Dur	95	NZ1155
High Woolaston Gloucs	34	ST5899
High Worsall Cleve	89	NZ3809
High Wray Cumb	87	SD3799
High Wych Herts	39	TL4614
High Wycombe Bucks	26	SU8693
Higham Derbys	74	SK3859
Higham Kent	16	TQ6048
Higham Kent	28	TQ7171
Higham Lancs	81	SD8136
Higham S York	82	SE3107
Higham Suffk	53	TL7465
Higham Suffk	54	TM0335
Higham Dykes Nthumb	103	NZ1375
Higham Ferrers Nhants	51	SP9668
Higham Gobion Beds	38	TL1032
Higham Hill Gt Lon	27	TQ3590
Higham on the Hill Leics	61	SP3895
Highampton Devon	18	SS4804
Highams Park Gt Lon	27	TQ3891
Highbridge Hants	13	SU4621
Highbridge Somset	21	ST3247
Highbrook W Susx	15	TQ3630
Highburton W York	82	SE1813
Highbury Gt Lon	27	TQ3185
Highbury Somset	22	ST6949
Highclere Hants	24	SU4359
Highcliffe Dorset	12	SZ2193
Highcliffiane Derbys	73	SK2947
Higher Alham Somset	22	ST6741
Higher Ansty Dorset	11	ST7604
Higher Ballam Lancs	80	SD3630
Higher Bartle Lancs	80	SD5033
Higher Berry End Beds	38	SP9834
Higher Bockhampton Dorset	11	SY7292
Higher Brixham Devon	7	SX9155
Higher Burrowton Devon	9	SY0097
Higher Burwardsley Ches	71	SJ5156
Higher Chillington Somset	10	ST3810
Higher Combe Somset	20	SS9030
Higher Coombe Dorset	10	SY5391
Higher Gabwell Devon	7	SX9169
Higher Halstock Leigh Dorset	10	ST5107
Higher Harpers Lancs	81	SD8237
Higher Heysham Lancs	87	SD4160
Higher Hurdsfield Ches	79	SJ9374
Higher Irlam Gt Man	79	SJ7295
Higher Kingcombe Dorset	10	ST5400
Higher Kinnerton Clwyd	71	SJ3261
Higher Melcombe Dorset	11	ST7402
Higher Muddiford Devon	19	SS5638
Higher Nyland Dorset	22	ST7322
Higher Ogden Gt Man	82	SD9512
Higher Pentire Cnwll	2	SW6525
Higher Penwortham Lancs	80	SD5128
Higher Studfold N York	88	SD8170
Higher Town Cnwll	3	SW8044
Higher Town Cnwll	4	SX0061
Higher Town IOS	2	SV9215
Higher Tregantle Cnwll	5	SX4052
Higher Walton Ches	78	SJ5985
Higher Walton Lancs	81	SD5727
Higher Wambrook Somset	10	ST2908
Higher Waterston Dorset	11	SY7295
Higher Whatcombe Dorset	11	ST8301
Higher Wheelton Lancs	81	SD6022
Higher Whiteleigh Cnwll	5	SX2494
Higher Whitley Ches	78	SJ6180
Higher Wraxhall Dorset	10	ST5601
Higher Wych Ches	71	SJ4943
Higherford Lancs	81	SD8640
Highfield Devon	8	SX7097
Highfield Humb	84	SE7236
Highfield Strath	115	NS3150
Highfield T & W	96	NZ1458
Highfields S York	83	SE5406
Highgate E Susx	16	TQ4234
Highgate Gt Lon	27	TQ2887
Highgate Head Derbys	74	SK0486
Highgreen Manor Nthumb	102	NY8091
Highlane S York	74	SK4081
Highlaws Cumb	92	NY1449
Highleadon Gloucs	47	SO7623
Highleigh W Susx	14	SZ8498
Highley Shrops	60	SO7483
Highmoor Cumb	93	NY2647
Highmoor Oxon	37	SU7084
Highmoor Cross Oxon	37	SU7084
Highmoor Hill Gwent	34	ST4689
Highnam Gloucs	35	SO7817
Highnam Green Gloucs	35	SO7920
Highridge Avon	21	ST5567
Highstead Kent	29	TR2166
Highsted Kent	28	TQ9061
Highstreet Green Essex	53	TL7634
Highstreet Green Surrey	14	SU9835
Hightae D & G	100	NY0978
Highter's Heath W Mids	61	SP0879
Hightown Ches	72	SJ8762
Hightown Hants	12	SU1704
Hightown Mersyd	78	SD3003
Hightown Green Suffk	54	TL9756
Highway H & W	46	SO4549
Highway Wilts	36	SU0474
Highweek Devon	7	SX8472
Highwood Staffs	73	SK0931
Highwood Hill Gt Lon	26	TQ2193
Highworth Wilts	36	SU2092
Hilden Park Kent	16	TQ5747
Hildenborough Kent	16	TQ5648
Hildersham Cambs	53	TL5448
Hilderstone Staffs	72	SJ9534
Hilderthorpe Humb	91	TA1766
Hilfield Dorset	10	ST6305
Hilgay Norfk	65	TL6298
Hill Avon	35	ST6495
Hill Warwks	50	SP4566
Hill Brow Hants	14	SU7926
Hill Chorlton Staffs	72	SJ7939
Hill Common Norfk	67	TG4122
Hill Common Somset	20	ST1426
Hill Deverill Wilts	22	ST8640
Hill Dyke Lincs	77	TF3447
Hill End Dur	95	NZ0136
Hill End Fife	117	NT0395
Hill End Gloucs	47	SO9037
Hill Green Kent	28	TQ8362
Hill Head Hants	13	SU5402
Hill of Beath Fife	117	NT1590
Hill of Fearn Highld	147	NH8377
Hill Ridware Staffs	73	SK0817
Hill Side H & W	47	SO7561
Hill Side W York	82	SE1717
Hill Top Dur	95	NY9924
Hill Top Hants	13	SU4003
Hill Top S York	74	SK3992
Hill Top W Mids	60	SO9993
Hill Top W York	82	SE0712
Hill Top W York	83	SE3315
Hillam N York	83	SE5028
Hillbeck Cumb	95	NY7915
Hillborough Kent	29	TR2168
Hillbutts Dorset	11	ST9901
Hillcott Wilts	23	SU1158
Hillend Fife	117	NT1483
Hillend Loth	117	NT2566
Hillend Strath	116	NS8267
Hillend W Glam	31	SS4190
Hillersland Gloucs	34	SO5614
Hillerton Devon	8	SX7298
Hillesden Bucks	49	SP6828
Hillesley Gloucs	35	ST7689
Hillfarrance Somset	20	ST1624
Hillfoot Strath	115	NS5472
Hillgrove W Susx	14	SU9428
Hillhampton H & W	46	SO5847
Hillhead Devon	7	SX9054
Hillhead Strath	108	NS9840
Hillhead of Cocklaw Gramp	143	NK0844
Hillhead of Durno Gramp	142	NJ7128
Hilliard's Cross Staffs	61	SK1511
Hilliclay Highld	151	ND1764
Hillingdon Gt Lon	26	TQ0782
Hillington Norfk	65	TF7225
Hillington Strath	115	NS5164
Hillis Corner IOW	13	SZ4793
Hillmorton Warwks	50	SP5373
Hillock Vale Lancs	81	SD7629
Hillowtan D & G	100	NX7763
Hillpool H & W	60	SO8976
Hillpound Hants	13	SU5715
Hills Town Derbys	75	SK4869
Hillside Devon	7	SX7060
Hillside Gramp	135	NO9197
Hillside T & W	135	NO6960
Hillstreet Hants	12	SU3416
Hillswick Shet	155	HU2877
Hilltown Devon	8	SX5380
Hillwell Shet	155	HU3714
Hilmarton Wilts	35	SU0175
Hilperton Wilts	22	ST8759
Hilperton Marsh Wilts	22	ST8659
Hilsea Hants	13	SU6503
Hilston Humb	85	TA2833
Hilston Park Gwent	34	SO4418
Hiltingbury Hants	13	SU4221
Hilton Border	119	NT8750
Hilton Cambs	52	TL2966
Hilton Cleve	89	NZ4611
Hilton Cumb	94	NY7320
Hilton Derbys	73	SK2430
Hilton Dorset	11	ST7802
Hilton Dur	96	NZ1622
Hilton Shrops	60	SO7795
Hilton of Cadboll Highld	147	NH8776
Himbleton H & W	47	SO9458
Himley Staffs	60	SO8891
Hincaster Cumb	87	SD5084
Hinchley Wood Surrey	26	TQ1565
Hinckley Leics	50	SP4294
Hinderclay Suffk	54	TM0276
Hinderwell N York	97	NZ7916
Hindford Shrops	59	SJ3333
Hindhead Surrey	14	SU8835
Hindle Fold Lancs	81	SD7332
Hindley Gt Man	78	SD6104
Hindley Nthumb	95	NZ0459
Hindley Green Gt Man	79	SD6403
Hindlip H & W	47	SO8858
Hindolveston Norfk	66	TG0329
Hindon Wilts	22	ST9132
Hindringham Norfk	66	TF9836
Hingham Norfk	66	TG0202
Hinksford Staffs	60	SO8689
Hinnington Shrops	60	SJ7404
Hinstock Shrops	72	SJ6925
Hintlesham Suffk	54	TM0843
Hinton Avon	35	ST7376
Hinton Gloucs	35	SO6803
Hinton H & W	46	SO3338
Hinton Hants	12	SZ2195
Hinton Shrops	59	SJ4008
Hinton Shrops	59	SO6582
Hinton Admiral Hants	12	SZ2096
Hinton Ampner Hants	13	SU6027
Hinton Blewett Somset	21	ST5956
Hinton Charterhouse Avon	22	ST7758
Hinton Green H & W	48	SP0240
Hinton Marsh Hants	24	SU5828
Hinton Martell Dorset	11	SU0106
Hinton on the Green H & W	48	SP0240
Hinton Parva Wilts	36	SU2383
Hinton St George Somset	10	ST4212
Hinton St Mary Dorset	11	ST7816
Hinton Waldrist Oxon	36	SU3799
Hinton-in-the-Hedges Nhants	49	SP5636
Hints Shrops	46	SO6174
Hints Staffs	61	SK1502
Hinwick Beds	51	SP9361
Hinxhill Kent	28	TR0442
Hinxton Cambs	53	TL4945
Hinxworth Herts	39	TL2340
Hipperholme W York	82	SE1225
Hipsburn Nthumb	111	NU2311
Hipswell N York	89	SE1898
Hirn Gramp	135	NJ7200
Hirnant Powys	58	SJ0422
Hirst Nthumb	103	NZ2787
Hirst Courtney N York	83	SE6124
Hirwaen Clwyd	70	SJ1361
Hirwaun M Glam	33	SN9505
Hiscott Devon	19	SS5426
Histon Cambs	53	TL4463
Hitcham Suffk	54	TL9851
Hitcham Causeway Suffk	54	TL9852
Hitcham Street Suffk	54	TL9851
Hitchin Herts	39	TL1829
Hither Green Gt Lon	27	TQ3874
Hittisleigh Devon	8	SX7395
Hittisleigh Cross Devon	8	SX7395
Hive Humb	84	SE8230
Hixon Staffs	73	SK0025
Hoaden Kent	29	TR2759
Hoar Cross Staffs	73	SK1323
Hoarwithy H & W	46	SO5429
Hoath Kent	29	TR2064
Hoathly Kent	28	TQ6536
Hobarris Shrops	46	SO3178
Hobbles Green Suffk	53	TL7053

Huncote
Inverarity

Huncote Leics 50 SP5197
Hundalee Border 110 NT6418
Hundall Derbys 74 SK3876
Hunderthwaite Dur 95 NY9821
Hundle Houses Lincs 77 TF2453
Hundleby Lincs 77 TF3966
Hundleton Dyfed 30 SM9600
Hundon Suffk 53 TL7348
Hundred Acres Hants 13 SU5911
Hundred End Lancs 80 SD4122
Hundred House Powys 45 SO1154
Hundred The H & W 46 SO5264
Hungarton Leics 63 SK6907
Hungate End Bucks 38 SP7946
Hunger Hill Lancs 80 SD5411
Hungerford Berks 23 SU3368
Hungerford Hants 12 SU1612
Hungerford Somset 20 ST0440
Hungerford Newtown Berks 36 SU3571
Hungerstone H & W 46 SO4435
Hungerton Lincs 63 SK8729
Hungryhatton Shrops 72 SJ6626
Hunmanby N York 91 TA0977
Hunningham Warwks 48 SP3767
Hunnington H & W 60 SO9681
Hunny Hill IOW 13 SZ4990
Hunsdon Herts 39 TL4114
Hunsingore N York 83 SE4253
Hunslet W York 82 SE3130
Hunsonby Cumb 94 NY5835
Hunstanton Norfk 65 TF6740
Hunstanworth Dur 95 NY9448
Hunston Suffk 54 TL9768
Hunston W Susx 14 SU8601
Hunston Green Suffk 54 TL9866
Hunstrete Avon 21 ST6462
Hunsworth W York 82 SE1827
Hunt End H & W 48 SP0364
Hunt's Corner Norfk 54 TM0588
Hunt's Cross Mersyd 78 SJ4385
Hunter's Inn Devon 19 SS6548
Hunters Quay Strath 114 NS1879
Hunterston Ches 72 SJ6946
Huntham Somset 21 ST3426
Hunthill Lodge Tays 134 NO4771
Huntingdon Cambs 52 TL2471
Huntingdon H & W 46 SO2553
Huntingfield Suffk 55 TM3374
Huntingford Dorset 22 ST8030
Huntington H & W 46 SO4841
Huntington Loth 118 NT4874
Huntington N York 83 SE6156
Huntington Staffs 60 SJ9712
Huntley Gloucs 35 SO7219
Huntly Gramp 142 NJ5339
Hunton Hants 24 SU4840
Hunton Kent 28 TQ7149
Hunton N York 89 SE1892
Hunton Bridge Herts 26 TL0800
Hunts Green Bucks 38 SP8903
Hunts Green Warwks 61 SP1897
Huntscott Somset 20 SS9144
Huntsham Devon 20 ST0020
Huntshaw Devon 19 SS5023
Huntshaw Cross Devon 19 SS5222
Huntspill Somset 21 ST3145
Huntstile Somset 20 ST2633
Huntworth Somset 21 ST3134
Hunwick Dur 96 NZ1832
Hunworth Norfk 66 TG0635
Hurcott Somset 10 ST3916
Hurdcott Wilts 23 SU1733
Hurdsfield Ches 79 SJ9274
Hurley Berks 37 SU8283
Hurley Warwks 61 SP2495
Hurley Bottom Berks 37 SU8283
Hurley Common Warwks 61 SP2496
Hurlford Strath 107 NS4536
Hurlston Green Lancs 80 SD3911
Hurn Dorset 12 SZ1296
Hurn's End Lincs 77 TF4249
Hursley Hants 13 SU4225
Hurst Berks 25 SU7973
Hurst Dorset 11 SY7990
Hurst N York 88 NZ0402
Hurst Somset 10 ST4518
Hurst Green E Susx 17 TQ7327
Hurst Green Essex 41 TM0916
Hurst Green Lancs 81 SD6838
Hurst Green Surrey 27 TQ3951
Hurst Hill W Mids 60 SO9393
Hurst Wickham W Susx 15 TQ2816
Hurstbourne Priors Hants 24 SU4346
Hurstbourne Tarrant Hants 23 SU3853
Hurstley H & W 46 SO3548
Hurstpierpoint W Susx 15 TQ2716
Hurstway Common H & W 46 SO2949
Hurstwood Lancs 81 SD8831
Hurtiso Ork 155 HY5001
Hurtmore Surrey 25 SU9445
Hurworth Burn Dur 96 NZ4033
Hurworth-on-Tees Dur 89 NZ3009
Hury Dur 95 NY9519
Husbands Bosworth Leics 50 SP6484
Husborne Crawley Beds 38 SP9635
Husthwaite N York 90 SE5175
Hut Green N York 83 SE5623
Hutcherleigh Devon 7 SX7850
Huthwaite N York 90 NZ4801
Huthwaite Notts 75 SK4659
Huttoft Lincs 77 TF5176
Hutton Avon 21 ST3558
Hutton Border 119 NT9053
Hutton Cumb 93 NY4326
Hutton Essex 40 TQ6395
Hutton Humb 84 TA0253
Hutton Lancs 80 SD4926
Hutton Bonville N York 89 NZ3300
Hutton Buscel N York 91 SE9784
Hutton Conyers N York 89 SE3273
Hutton Cranswick Humb 84 TA0252
Hutton End Cumb 93 NY4538
Hutton Hall Cleve 90 NZ6014
Hutton Hang N York 89 SE1788
Hutton Henry Dur 96 NZ4236
Hutton Lowcross Cleve 90 NZ5914
Hutton Magna Dur 89 NZ1212
Hutton Mulgrave N York 90 NZ8309
Hutton Roof Cumb 93 NY3734
Hutton Roof Cumb 87 SD5677
Hutton Rudby N York 89 NZ4606
Hutton Sessay N York 89 SE4776
Hutton Wandesley N York 83 SE5050
Hutton-le-Hole N York 90 SE7090
Huxham Devon 9 SX9497
Huxham Green Somset 21 ST5936
Huxley Ches 71 SJ5061
Huyton Mersyd 78 SJ4490
Hycemoor Cumb 86 SD0989
Hyde Gloucs 35 SO8801
Hyde Gt Man 79 SJ9494
Hyde Hants 12 SU1612
Hyde End Berks 24 SU7266
Hyde Heath Bucks 26 SP9300
Hyde Lea Staffs 72 SJ9120
Hyde Park Corner Somset 20 ST2832
Hydestile Surrey 25 SU9640
Hykeham Moor Lincs 76 SK9366
Hylands Essex 40 TL6704
Hyndford Bridge Strath 108 NS9141
Hynish Strath 120 NL9839
Hyssington Powys 59 SO3194
Hystfield Gloucs 35 ST6695
Hythe Hants 13 SU4207
Hythe Kent 29 TR1634
Hythe Somset 21 ST4452
Hythe End Berks 26 TQ0172
Hyton Cumb 86 SD0987

I

Ibberton Dorset 11 ST7807
Ible Derbys 74 SK2457
Ibsley Hants 12 SU1509
Ibstock Leics 62 SK4009
Ibstone Bucks 37 SU7593
Ibthorpe Hants 23 SU3753
Iburndale N York 90 NZ8707
Ibworth Hants 24 SU5654
Icelton Avon 21 ST3765
Ickburgh Norfk 66 TL8195
Ickenham Gt Lon 26 TQ0786
Ickford Bucks 37 SP6407
Ickham Kent 29 TR2258
Ickleford Herts 39 TL1831
Icklesham E Susx 17 TQ8716
Ickleton Cambs 39 TL4943
Icklingham Suffk 53 TL7772
Ickornshaw N York 82 SD9642
Ickwell Green Beds 52 TL1545
Icomb Gloucs 36 SP2122
Idbury Oxon 36 SP2319
Iddesleigh Devon 19 SS5708
Ide Devon 9 SX8990
Ide Hill Kent 27 TQ4851
Ideford Devon 9 SX8977
Iden E Susx 17 TQ9123
Iden Green Kent 28 TQ7437
Iden Green Kent 17 TQ8031
Idle W York 82 SE1737
Idless Cnwll 3 SW8147
Idlicote Warwks 48 SP2844
Idmiston Wilts 23 SU1937
Idridgehay Derbys 73 SK2849
Idrigill Highld 136 NG3863
Idstone Oxon 36 SU2584
Iffley Oxon 37 SP5203
Ifield W Susx 15 TQ2537
Ifold W Susx 14 TQ0231
Iford Dorset 12 SZ1393
Iford E Susx 15 TQ4007
Ifton Gwent 34 ST4688
Ifton Heath Shrops 59 SJ3237
Ightam Kent 27 TQ5956
Ightfield Shrops 71 SJ5938
Iken Suffk 55 TM4155
Ilam Staffs 73 SK1350
Ilchester Somset 21 ST5222
Ilderton Nthumb 111 NU0121
Ilford Gt Lon 27 TQ4486
Ilford Somset 10 ST3617
Ilfracombe Devon 19 SS5247
Ilkeston Derbys 62 SK4641
Ilketshall St Andrew Suffk 55 TM3887
Ilketshall St Margaret Suffk 55 TM3485
Ilkley W York 82 SE1147
Illand Cnwll 5 SX2878
Illey W Mids 60 SO9881
Illidge Green Ches 72 SJ7963
Illingworth W York 82 SE0728
Illogan Cnwll 2 SW6743
Illston on the Hill Leics 50 SP7099
Ilmer Bucks 37 SP7605
Ilmington Warwks 48 SP2143
Ilminster Somset 10 ST3614
Ilsingston Dorset 11 SY7592
Ilsington Devon 7 SX7875
Ilston W Glam 32 SS5590
Ilton N York 89 SE1978
Ilton Somset 10 ST3517
Imachar Strath 105 NR8640
Immingham Humb 85 TA1814
Immingham Dock Humb 85 TA1916
Impington Cambs 53 TL4463
Ince Ches 71 SJ4576
Ince Blundell Mersyd 78 SD3203
Ince-in-Makerfield Gt Man 78 SD5904
Inchbae Lodge Hotel Highld 146 NH4069
Inchbare Tays 134 NO6065
Inchberry Gramp 141 NJ3055
Inchinnan Strath 115 NS4769
Inchlaggan Highld 131 NH1701
Inchmichael Tays 126 NO2425
Inchnacardoch Hotel Highld 131 NH3810
Inchnadamph Highld 145 NC2521
Inchture Tays 126 NO2728
Inchvuilt Highld 139 NH2438
Inchyra Tays 126 NO1820
Indian Queens Cnwll 4 SW9159
Ingate Place Suffk 55 TM4288
Ingatestone Essex 40 TQ6499
Ingbirchworth S York 82 SE2205
Ingerthorpe N York 89 SE2866
Ingestre Staffs 72 SJ9724
Ingham Lincs 76 SK9483
Ingham Norfk 67 TG3926
Ingham Suffk 54 TL8570
Ingham Corner Norfk 67 TG3927
Ingleborough Norfk 65 TF4715
Ingleby Derbys 62 SK3426
Ingleby Arncliffe N York 89 NZ4400
Ingleby Barwick Cleve 89 NZ4414
Ingleby Cross N York 89 NZ4500
Ingleby Greenhow N York 90 NZ5706
Ingleigh Green Devon 8 SS6007
Inglesbatch Avon 22 ST7061
Inglesham Wilts 36 SU2098
Ingleston D & G 99 NX6048
Ingleston D & G 100 NX9865
Ingleton Dur 96 NZ1720
Ingleton N York 87 SD6972
Inglewhite Lancs 80 SD5439
Ingmire Hall Cumb 87 SD6391
Ingoe Nthumb 103 NZ0374
Ingoldisthorpe Norfk 65 TF6832
Ingoldmells Lincs 77 TF5668
Ingoldsby Lincs 64 TF0129
Ingram Nthumb 111 NU0115
Ingrave Essex 40 TQ6291
Ingrow W York 82 SE0539
Ings Cumb 87 SD4498
Ingst Avon 34 ST5887
Ingthorpe Leics 63 SK9908
Ingworth Norfk 67 TG1929
Inkberrow H & W 47 SP0157
Inkerman Dur 95 NZ1139
Inkhorn Gramp 143 NJ9239
Inkpen Berks 23 SU3664
Inkstack Highld 151 ND2570
Inmarsh Wilts 22 ST9460
Innellan Strath 114 NS1570
Innerleithen Border 109 NT3336
Innerleven Fife 118 NO3700
Innermessan D & G 98 NX0862
Innerwick Loth 119 NT7273
Innesmill Gramp 141 NJ2863
Insch Gramp 142 NJ6228
Insh Highld 132 NH8101
Inskip Lancs 80 SD4637
Inskip Moss Side Lancs 80 SD4539
Instow Devon 18 SS4730
Insworke Cnwll 6 SX4252
Intake S York 74 SK3884
Inver Gramp 133 NO2293
Inver Highld 147 NH8682
Inver Tays 125 NO0142
Inver-boyndie Gramp 142 NJ6664
Inverailort Highld 129 NM7681
Inveralligin Highld 138 NG8457
Inverallochy Gramp 143 NK0365
Inveran Highld 146 NH5797
Inveraray Strath 123 NN0908
Inverarish Highld 137 NG5535
Inverarity Tays 127 NO4544
Inverarnan Cent 123 NN3118
Inveravon Cent 117 NS9579
Inverawe Strath 122 NN0231
Inverbervie Gramp 135 NO8272
Inverbroom Highld 145 NH1883
Invercreran House Hotel Strath 122 NN0146
Inverdruie Highld 132 NH8911
Inveresk Loth 118 NT3471
Inveresragan Strath 122 NM9835
Inverey Gramp 133 NO0889
Inverfarigaig Highld 139 NH5123
Inverfolia Strath 122 NM9544
Invergarry Highld 131 NH3001
Invergeldie Tays 124 NN7327
Invergloy Highld 131 NN2288
Invergordon Highld 140 NH7068
Invergowrie Tays 126 NO3430
Inverguseran Highld 129 NG7407
Inverhadden Tays 124 NN6757
Inverherive Hotel Cent 123 NN3626
Inverie Highld 129 NG7600
Inverinan Strath 122 NM9917
Inverinate Highld 138 NG9221
Inverkeilor Tays 127 NO6649
Inverkeithing Fife 117 NT1383
Inverkeithny Gramp 142 NJ6247
Inverkip Strath 114 NS2072
Inverkirkaig Highld 145 NC0719
Inverlael Highld 145 NH1885
Inverlair Highld 131 NN3479
Inverliever Lodge Strath 122 NM8905
Inverlochy Strath 123 NN1927
Invermarkie Gramp 142 NJ4239
Invermoriston Highld 139 NH4216
Inverneg Strath 115 NS3497
Inverness Highld 140 NH6645
Invernoaden Strath 114 NS1297
Inveroran Hotel Strath 123 NN2741
Inverquharity Tays 134 NO4057
Inverquhomery Gramp 143 NK0146
Inverroy Highld 131 NN2581
Inversanda Highld 130 NM9459
Invershiel Highld 138 NG9319
Invershin Highld 146 NH5796
Invershore Highld 151 ND2435
Inversnaid Hotel Cent 123 NN3308
Inverugie Gramp 143 NK0948
Inveruglas Strath 123 NN3109
Inveruglass Highld 132 NH8000
Inverurie Gramp 142 NJ7721
Inwardleigh Devon 8 SX5699
Inworth Essex 40 TL8717
Iping W Susx 14 SU8522
Ipplepen Devon 7 SX8366
Ipsden Oxon 37 SU6285
Ipstones Staffs 73 SK0149
Ipswich Suffk 54 TM1644
Irby Mersyd 78 SJ2584
Irby in the Marsh Lincs 77 TF4663
Irby upon Humber Humb 85 TA1904
Irchester Nhants 51 SP9265
Ireby Cumb 93 NY2338
Ireby Lancs 87 SD6575
Ireland Beds 38 TL1341
Ireleth Cumb 86 SD2277
Ireshopeburn Dur 95 NY8638
Ireton Wood Derbys 73 SK2847
Irlam Gt Man 79 SJ7294
Irnham Lincs 64 TF0226
Iron Acton Avon 35 ST6783
Iron Bridge Cambs 65 TL4898
Iron Cross Warwks 48 SP0552
Ironbridge Shrops 60 SJ6703
Ironmacannie D & G 99 NX6675
Irons Bottom Surrey 15 TQ2446
Ironville Derbys 75 SK4351
Irstead Norfk 67 TG3620
Irthington Cumb 101 NY4961
Irthlingborough Nhants 51 SP9470
Irton N York 91 TA0184
Irvine Strath 106 NS3238
Isauld Highld 150 NC9865
Isbister Shet 155 HU3790
Isfield E Susx 16 TQ4417
Isham Nhants 51 SP8873
Isington Hants 25 SU7842
Islandpool H & W 60 SO8780
Isle Abbotts Somset 21 ST3520
Isle Brewers Somset 21 ST3621
Isle of Dogs Gt Lon 27 TQ3779
Isle of Whithorn D & G 99 NX4736
Isleham Cambs 53 TL6474
Isleornsay Highld 129 NG7012
Islesteps D & G 100 NX9672
Islet Village Guern 152 GN0000
Isley Walton Leics 62 SK4224
Islibhig W Isls 154 NB0029
Islington Gt Lon 27 TQ3184
Islip Nhants 51 SP9879
Islip Oxon 37 SP5211
Ibberton Dorset 11 ST7807
Ible Derbys 74 SK2457
Ibsley Hants 12 SU1509
Ibstock Leics 62 SK4009
Ibstone Bucks 37 SU7593
Ibthorpe Hants 23 SU3753
Iburndale N York 90 NZ8707
Ibworth Hants 24 SU5654
Icelton Avon 21 ST3765
Ickburgh Norfk 66 TL8195
Ickenham Gt Lon 26 TQ0786
Ickford Bucks 37 SP6407
Ickham Kent 29 TR2258
Ickleford Herts 39 TL1831
Icklesham E Susx 17 TQ8716
Ickleton Cambs 39 TL4943
Icklingham Suffk 53 TL7772
Ickornshaw N York 82 SD9642
Ickwell Green Beds 52 TL1545
Icomb Gloucs 36 SP2122
Idbury Oxon 36 SP2319
Iddesleigh Devon 19 SS5708
Ide Devon 9 SX8990
Ide Hill Kent 27 TQ4851
Ideford Devon 9 SX8977
Iden E Susx 17 TQ9123
Iden Green Kent 28 TQ7437
Iden Green Kent 17 TQ8031
Idle W York 82 SE1737
Idless Cnwll 3 SW8147
Idlicote Warwks 48 SP2844
Idmiston Wilts 23 SU1937
Idridgehay Derbys 73 SK2849
Idrigill Highld 136 NG3863
Idstone Oxon 36 SU2584
Iffley Oxon 37 SP5203
Ifield W Susx 15 TQ2537
Ifold W Susx 14 TQ0231
Iford Dorset 12 SZ1393
Iford E Susx 15 TQ4007
Ifton Gwent 34 ST4688
Ifton Heath Shrops 59 SJ3237
Ightam Kent 27 TQ5956
Ightfield Shrops 71 SJ5938
Iken Suffk 55 TM4155
Ilam Staffs 73 SK1350
Ilchester Somset 21 ST5222
Ilderton Nthumb 111 NU0121
Ilford Gt Lon 27 TQ4486
Ilford Somset 10 ST3617
Ilfracombe Devon 19 SS5247
Ilkeston Derbys 62 SK4641
Ilketshall St Andrew Suffk 55 TM3887
Ilketshall St Margaret Suffk 55 TM3485
Ilkley W York 82 SE1147
Illand Cnwll 5 SX2878
Illey W Mids 60 SO9881
Illidge Green Ches 72 SJ7963
Illingworth W York 82 SE0728
Illogan Cnwll 2 SW6743
Illston on the Hill Leics 50 SP7099
Ilmer Bucks 37 SP7605
Ilmington Warwks 48 SP2143
Ilminster Somset 10 ST3614
Ilsingston Dorset 11 SY7592
Ilsington Devon 7 SX7875
Ilston W Glam 32 SS5590
Ilton N York 89 SE1978
Ilton Somset 10 ST3517
Imachar Strath 105 NR8640
Immingham Humb 85 TA1814
Immingham Dock Humb 85 TA1916
Impington Cambs 53 TL4463
Ince Ches 71 SJ4576
Ince Blundell Mersyd 78 SD3203
Ince-in-Makerfield Gt Man 78 SD5904
Inchbae Lodge Hotel Highld 146 NH4069
Inchbare Tays 134 NO6065
Inchberry Gramp 141 NJ3055
Inchinnan Strath 115 NS4769
Inchlaggan Highld 131 NH1701
Inchmichael Tays 126 NO2425
Inchnacardoch Hotel Highld 131 NH3810
Inchnadamph Highld 145 NC2521
Inchture Tays 126 NO2728
Inchvuilt Highld 139 NH2438
Inchyra Tays 126 NO1820
Indian Queens Cnwll 4 SW9159
Ingate Place Suffk 55 TM4288
Ingatestone Essex 40 TQ6499
Ingbirchworth S York 82 SE2205
Ingerthorpe N York 89 SE2866
Ingestre Staffs 72 SJ9724
Ingham Lincs 76 SK9483
Ingham Norfk 67 TG3926
Ingham Suffk 54 TL8570
Ingham Corner Norfk 67 TG3927
Ingleborough Norfk 65 TF4715
Ingleby Derbys 62 SK3426
Ingleby Arncliffe N York 89 NZ4400
Ingleby Barwick Cleve 89 NZ4414
Ingleby Cross N York 89 NZ4500
Ingleby Greenhow N York 90 NZ5706
Ingleigh Green Devon 8 SS6007
Inglesbatch Avon 22 ST7061
Inglesham Wilts 36 SU2098
Ingleston D & G 99 NX6048
Ingleston D & G 100 NX9865
Ingleton Dur 96 NZ1720
Ingleton N York 87 SD6972
Inglewhite Lancs 80 SD5439
Ingmire Hall Cumb 87 SD6391
Ingoe Nthumb 103 NZ0374
Ingoldisthorpe Norfk 65 TF6832
Ingoldmells Lincs 77 TF5668
Ingoldsby Lincs 64 TF0129
Ingram Nthumb 111 NU0115
Ingrave Essex 40 TQ6291
Ingrow W York 82 SE0539
Ings Cumb 87 SD4498
Ingst Avon 34 ST5887
Ingthorpe Leics 63 SK9908
Ingworth Norfk 67 TG1929
Inkberrow H & W 47 SP0157
Inkerman Dur 95 NZ1139
Inkhorn Gramp 143 NJ9239
Inkpen Berks 23 SU3664
Inkstack Highld 151 ND2570
Inmarsh Wilts 22 ST9460
Innellan Strath 114 NS1570
Innerleithen Border 109 NT3336
Innerleven Fife 118 NO3700
Innermessan D & G 98 NX0862
Innerwick Loth 119 NT7273
Innesmill Gramp 141 NJ2863
Insch Gramp 142 NJ6228
Insh Highld 132 NH8101
Inskip Lancs 80 SD4637
Inskip Moss Side Lancs 80 SD4539
Instow Devon 18 SS4730
Insworke Cnwll 6 SX4252
Intake S York 74 SK3884
Inver Gramp 133 NO2293
Inver Highld 147 NH8682
Inver Tays 125 NO0142
Inver-boyndie Gramp 142 NJ6664
Inverailort Highld 129 NM7681
Inveralligin Highld 138 NG8457
Inverallochy Gramp 143 NK0365
Inveran Highld 146 NH5797
Inveraray Strath 123 NN0908
Inverarish Highld 137 NG5535
Inverarity Tays 127 NO4544

Inverarnan

Kilstay

Inverarnan *Cent* **123** NN3118
Inveravon *Cent* **117** NS9579
Inverawe *Strath* **122** NN0231
Inverbervie *Gramp* **135** NO8272
Inverbroom *Highld* **145** NH1883
Invercreran House Hotel *Strath* **122** NN0146
Inverdruie *Highld* **132** NH8911
Inveresk *Loth* **118** NT3471
Inveresragan *Strath* **122** NM9835
Inverey *Gramp* **133** NO0889
Inverfarigaig *Highld* **139** NH5123
Inverfolia *Strath* **122** NM9544
Invergarry *Highld* **131** NH3001
Invergeldie *Tays* **124** NN7327
Invergloy *Highld* **131** NN2288
Invergordon *Highld* **140** NH7068
Invergowrie *Tays* **126** NO3430
Inverguseran *Highld* **129** NG7407
Inverhadden *Tays* **124** NN6757
Inverherive Hotel *Cent* **123** NN3626
Inverie *Highld* **129** NG7600
Inverinan *Strath* **122** NM9917
Inverinate *Highld* **138** NG9221
Inverkeilor *Tays* **127** NO6649
Inverkeithing *Fife* **117** NT1383
Inverkeithny *Gramp* **142** NJ6247
Inverkip *Strath* **114** NS2072
Inverkirkaig *Highld* **145** NC0719
Inverlael *Highld* **145** NH1885
Inverlair *Highld* **131** NN3479
Inverliever Lodge *Strath* **122** NM8905
Inverlochy *Strath* **123** NN1927
Invermarkie *Gramp* **142** NJ4239
Invermoriston *Highld* **139** NH4216
Inverneg *Strath* **115** NS3497
Inverness *Highld* **140** NH6645
Invernoaden *Strath* **114** NS1297
Inveroran Hotel *Strath* **123** NN2741
Inverquharity *Tays* **134** NO4057
Inverquhomery *Gramp* **143** NK0146
Inverroy *Highld* **131** NN2581
Inversanda *Highld* **130** NM9459
Invershiel *Highld* **138** NG9319
Invershin *Highld* **146** NH5796
Invershore *Highld* **151** ND2435
Inversnaid Hotel *Cent* **123** NN3308
Inverugie *Gramp* **143** NK0948
Inveruglas *Strath* **123** NN3109
Inveruglass *Highld* **132** NH8000
Inverurie *Gramp* **142** NJ7721
Inwardleigh *Devon* **8** SX5699
Inworth *Essex* **40** TL8717
Iping *W Susx* **14** SU8522
Ipplepen *Devon* **7** SX8366
Ipsden *Oxon* **37** SU6285
Ipstones *Staffs* **73** SK0149
Ipswich *Suffk* **54** TM1644
Irby *Mersyd* **78** SJ2584
Irby in the Marsh *Lincs* **77** TF4663
Irby upon Humber *Humb* **85** TA1904
Irchester *Nhants* **51** SP9265
Ireby *Cumb* **93** NY2338
Ireby *Lancs* **87** SD6575
Ireland *Beds* **38** TL1341
Ireleth *Cumb* **86** SD2277
Ireshopeburn *Dur* **95** NY8638
Ireton Wood *Derbys* **73** SK2847
Irlam *Gt Man* **79** SJ7294
Irnham *Lincs* **64** TF0226
Iron Acton *Avon* **35** ST6783
Iron Bridge *Cambs* **65** TL4898
Iron Cross *Warwks* **48** SP0552
Ironbridge *Shrops* **60** SJ6703
Ironmacannie *D & G* **99** NX6675
Irons Bottom *Surrey* **15** TQ2446
Ironville *Derbys* **75** SK4351
Irstead *Norfk* **67** TG3620
Irthington *Cumb* **101** NY4961
Irthlingborough *Nhants* **51** SP9470
Irton *N York* **91** TA0184
Irvine *Strath* **106** NS3238
Isauld *Highld* **150** NC9865
Isbister *Shet* **155** HU3790
Isfield *E Susx* **16** TQ4417
Isham *Nhants* **51** SP8873
Isington *Hants* **25** SU7842
Islandpool *H & W* **60** SO8780
Isle Abbotts *Somset* **21** ST3520
Isle Brewers *Somset* **21** ST3621
Isle of Dogs *Gt Lon* **27** TQ3779
Isle of Whithorn *D & G* **99** NX4736
Isleham *Cambs* **53** TL6474
Isleornsay *Highld* **129** NG7012
Islesteps *D & G* **100** NX9672
Islet Village *Guern* **152** GN0000
Isley Walton *Leics* **62** SK4224
Islibhig *W Isls* **154** NB0029
Islington *Gt Lon* **27** TQ3184
Islip *Nhants* **51** SP9879
Islip *Oxon* **37** SP5214
Islivig *W Isls* **154** NB0029
Isombridge *Shrops* **59** SJ6113
Istead Rise *Kent* **27** TQ6370
Itchen Abbas *Hants* **24** SU5333
Itchen Stoke *Hants* **24** SU5532
Itchingfield *W Susx* **15** TQ1328
Itchington *Avon* **35** ST6587
Itteringham *Norfk* **66** TG1430
Itton *Devon* **8** SX6899
Itton *Gwent* **34** ST4995
Ivegill *Cumb* **93** NY4143
Ivelet *N York* **88** SD9398
Iver *Bucks* **26** TQ0381
Iver Heath *Bucks* **26** TQ0283
Iveston *Dur* **96** NZ1350
Ivinghoe *Bucks* **38** SP9416
Ivinghoe Aston *Bucks* **38** SP9517
Ivington *H & W* **46** SO4756
Ivington Green *H & W* **46** SO4656
Ivy Cross *Dorset* **22** ST8623
Ivy Hatch *Kent* **27** TQ5854
Ivy Todd *Norfk* **66** TF8909
Ivybridge *Devon* **6** SX6356
Ivychurch *Kent* **17** TR0327
Iwade *Kent* **28** TQ9067
Iwerne Courtney
or Shroton *Dorset* **11** ST8512
Iwerne Minster *Dorset* **11** ST8614
Ixworth *Suffk* **54** TL9370
Ixworth Thorpe *Suffk* **54** TL9173

J

Jack Green *Lancs* **81** SD5925
Jack Hill *N York* **82** SE1951
Jack's Bush *Hants* **23** SU2636
Jack-in-the-Green *Devon* **9** SY0195
Jacksdale *Notts* **75** SK4451
Jackson Bridge *W York* **82** SE1607
Jackton *Strath* **115** NS5952
Jacobs Well *Surrey* **25** TQ0053
Jacobstow *Cnwll* **5** SX1995
Jacobstowe *Devon* **8** SS5801
Jameston *Dyfed* **30** SS0598
Jamestown *Highld* **139** NH4756
Jamestown *Strath* **115** NS3981
Janets-town *Highld* **151** ND3551
Janetstown *Highld* **151** ND1932
Jardine Hall *D & G* **100** NY1088
Jarrow *T & W* **103** NZ3364
Jarvis Brook *E Susx* **16** TQ5329
Jasper's Green *Essex* **40** TL7226
Jawcraig *Cent* **116** NS8475
Jaywick *Essex* **41** TM1413
Jealott's Hill *Berks* **25** SU8673
Jeator Houses *N York* **89** SE4394
Jedburgh *Border* **110** NT6420
Jeffreston *Dyfed* **31** SN0906
Jemimaville *Highld* **140** NH7165
Jerbourg *Guern* **152** GN0000
Jerusalem *Lincs* **76** SK9170
Jesmond *T & W* **103** NZ2566
Jevington *E Susx* **16** TQ5601
Jingle Street *Gwent* **34** SO4710
Jockey End *Herts* **38** TL0413
Jodrell Bank *Ches* **79** SJ7970
John O'Groats *Highld* **151** ND3872
John's Cross *E Susx* **17** TQ7421
Johnby *Cumb* **93** NY4332
Johnshaven *Gramp* **135** NO7967
Johnson's Street *Norfk* **67** TG3717
Johnston *Dyfed* **30** SM9310
Johnston *Dyfed* **31** SN3919
Johnstone *D & G* **109** NT2400
Johnstone *Strath* **115** NS4263
Johnstonebridge *D & G* **100** NY1092
Johnstown *Clwyd* **71** SJ3046
Joppa *Dyfed* **43** SN5666
Joppa *Loth* **118** NT3173
Joppa *Strath* **106** NS4119
Jordans *Bucks* **26** SU9791
Jordanston *Dyfed* **30** SM9132
Jordanthorpe *S York* **74** SK3580
Joyden's Wood *Kent* **27** TQ5072
Jubilee Corner *Kent* **28** TQ8447
Jump *S York* **83** SE3801
Jumper's Town *E Susx* **16** TQ4632
Juniper Green *Loth* **117** NT1968
Jurby *IOM* **153** SC3598
Jurston *Devon* **8** SX6984

K

Kaber *Cumb* **88** NY7911
Kames *Strath* **114** NR9771
Kames *Strath* **107** NS6926
Kea *Cnwll* **3** SW8142
Keadby *Humb* **84** SE8311
Keal Cotes *Lincs* **77** TF3660
Kearby Town End *N York* **83** SE3447
Kearsley *Gt Man* **79** SD7504
Kearsley *Nthumb* **103** NZ0275
Kearsney *Kent* **29** TR2844
Kearstwick *Cumb* **87** SD6079
Kearton *N York* **88** SD9998
Keasden *N York* **88** SD7266
Keason *Cnwll* **5** SX3168
Keaton *Devon* **7** SX6454
Keckwick *Ches* **78** SJ5783
Keddington *Lincs* **77** TF3488
Keddington Corner *Lincs* **77** TF3589
Kedington *Suffk* **53** TL7046
Kedleston *Derbys* **73** SK3040
Keelby *Lincs* **85** TA1610
Keele *Staffs* **72** SJ8045
Keele University *Staffs* **72** SJ8144
Keeley Green *Beds* **38** TL0046
Keelham *W York* **82** SE0732
Keeston *Dyfed* **30** SM9019
Keevil *Wilts* **22** ST9258
Kegworth *Leics* **62** SK4826
Kehelland *Cnwll* **2** SW6241
Keig *Gramp* **142** NJ6119
Keighley *W York* **82** SE0541
Keillour *Tays* **125** NN9725
Keiloch *Gramp* **133** NO1891
Keils *Strath* **113** NR5268
Keinton Mandeville *Somset* **21** ST5430
Keir Mill *D & G* **100** NX8593
Keirsleywell Row *Nthumb* **94** NY7751
Keisby *Lincs* **64** TF0328
Keisley *Cumb* **94** NY7124
Keiss *Highld* **151** ND3461
Keith *Gramp* **142** NJ4250
Keithick *Tays* **126** NO2038
Keithock *Tays* **134** NO6063
Keithtown *Gramp* **139** NH5256
Kelbrook *Lancs* **81** SD9044
Kelburn *Strath* **114** NS2156
Kelby *Lincs* **63** TF0041
Keld *Cumb* **94** NY5514
Keld *N York* **88** NY8900
Keld Head *N York* **90** SE7884
Keldholme *N York* **90** SE7086
Kelfield *Humb* **84** SE8201
Kelfield *N York* **83** SE5938
Kelham *Notts* **75** SK7755
Kelhead *D & G* **100** NY1469
Kellacott *Devon* **5** SX4088
Kellamergh *Lancs* **80** SD4029
Kellas *Gramp* **141** NJ1654
Kellas *Tays* **127** NO4535
Kellaton *Devon* **7** SX8039
Kelleth *Cumb* **87** NY6605
Kelling *Norfk* **66** TG0942
Kellington *N York* **83** SE5524
Kelloe *Dur* **96** NZ3436
Kelloholm *D & G* **107** NS7411
Kells *Cumb* **92** NX9616
Kelly *Devon* **5** SX3981
Kelly Bray *Cnwll* **5** SX3671
Kelmarsh *Nhants* **50** SP7379
Kelmscot *Oxon* **36** SU2499
Kelsale *Suffk* **55** TM3865
Kelsall *Ches* **71** SJ5268
Kelshall *Herts* **39** TL3336
Kelsick *Cumb* **93** NY1950
Kelso *Border* **110** NT7234
Kelstedge *Derbys* **74** SK3363
Kelstern *Lincs* **77** TF2489
Kelsterton *Clwyd* **70** SJ2770
Kelston *Avon* **22** ST7067
Keltneyburn *Tays* **124** NN7749
Kelty *Fife* **117** NT1494
Kelvedon *Essex* **40** TL8619
Kelvedon Hatch *Essex* **27** TQ5698
Kelynack *Cnwll* **2** SW3729
Kemacott *Devon* **19** SS6647
Kemback *Fife* **126** NO4115
Kemberton *Shrops* **60** SJ7204
Kemble *Gloucs* **35** ST9897
Kemble Wick *Gloucs* **35** ST9895
Kemerton *H & W* **47** SO9536
Kemeys Commander *Gwent* **34** SO3404
Kemnay *Gramp* **142** NJ7316
Kemp Town *E Susx* **15** TQ3303
Kempe's Corner *Kent* **28** TR0346
Kempley *Gloucs* **47** SO6629
Kempley Green *Gloucs* **47** SO6728
Kemps Green *Warwks* **61** SP1470
Kempsey *H & W* **47** SO8549
Kempsford *Gloucs* **36** SU1696
Kempshott *Hants* **24** SU6050
Kempston *Beds* **38** TL0347
Kempston Hardwick *Beds* **38** TL0344
Kempton *Shrops* **59** SO3682
Kemsing *Kent* **27** TQ5558
Kemsley *Kent* **28** TQ9166
Kemsley Street *Kent* **28** TQ8062
Kenardington *Kent* **17** TQ9732
Kenchester *H & W* **46** SO4342
Kencot *Oxon* **36** SP2504
Kendal *Cumb* **87** SD5192
Kenderchurch *H & W* **46** SO4028
Kendleshire *Avon* **35** ST6679
Kenfig Hill *M Glam* **33** SS8382
Kenidjack *Cnwll* **2** SW3632
Kenilworth *Warwks* **61** SP2871
Kenley *Gt Lon* **27** TQ3260
Kenley *Shrops* **59** SJ5500
Kenmore *Highld* **137** NG7557
Kenmore *Tays* **124** NN7745
Kenn *Avon* **21** ST4268
Kenn *Devon* **9** SX9285
Kennacraig *Strath* **113** NR8262
Kennards House *Cnwll* **5** SX2883
Kenneggy *Cnwll* **2** SW5628
Kennerleigh *Devon* **8** SS8107
Kennessee Green *Mersyd* **78** SD3801
Kennet *Cent* **116** NS9291
Kennethmont *Gramp* **142** NJ5428
Kennett *Cambs* **53** TL7068
Kennford *Devon* **9** SX9186
Kenninghall *Norfk* **54** TM0386
Kennington *Kent* **28** TR0245
Kennington *Oxon* **37** SP5201
Kennoway *Fife* **126** NO3502
Kenny *Somset* **10** ST3117
Kennyhill *Suffk* **53** TL6679
Kennythorpe *N York* **90** SE7865
Kenovay *Strath* **120** NL9946
Kensaleyre *Highld* **136** NG4151
Kensham Green *Kent* **17** TQ8229
Kensington *Gt Lon* **27** TQ2579
Kensworth *Beds* **38** TL0319
Kensworth Common *Beds* **38** TL0317
Kent End *Wilts* **36** SU0594
Kent Green *Ches* **72** SJ8458
Kent Street *E Susx* **17** TQ7816
Kent Street *Kent* **28** TQ6654
Kent's Green *Gloucs* **47** SO7423
Kent's Oak *Hants* **23** SU3224
Kentallen *Highld* **122** NN0057
Kentchurch *H & W* **46** SO4125
Kentford *Suffk* **53** TL7066
Kentisbeare *Devon* **9** ST0608
Kentisbury *Devon* **19** SS6243
Kentisbury Ford *Devon* **19** SS6242
Kentish Town *Gt Lon* **27** TQ2884
Kentmere *Cumb* **87** NY4504
Kenton *Devon* **9** SX9583
Kenton *Gt Lon* **26** TQ1788
Kenton *Suffk* **55** TM1965
Kenton *T & W* **103** NZ2267
Kenton Bank Foot *Nthumb* **103** NZ2069
Kentra *Highld* **129** NM6569
Kents Bank *Cumb* **87** SD3975
Kenwick *Shrops* **59** SJ4230
Kenwyn *Cnwll* **3** SW8145
Kenyon *Ches* **79** SJ6395
Keoldale *Highld* **149** NC3866
Keppoch *Highld* **138** NG8924
Kepwick *N York* **89** SE4690
Keresley *W Mids* **61** SP3282
Keresley Green *Warwks* **61** SP3283
Kergilliak *Cnwll* **3** SW7833
Kernborough *Devon* **7** SX7941
Kerne Bridge *H & W* **34** SO5818
Kerridge *Ches* **79** SJ9376
Kerridge-end *Ches* **79** SJ9475
Kerris *Cnwll* **2** SW4427
Kerry *Powys* **58** SO1490
Kerrycroy *Strath* **114** NS1061
Kersall *Notts* **75** SK7162
Kersbrook *Devon* **9** SY0683
Kerscott *Devon* **19** SS6329
Kersey *Suffk* **54** TM0044
Kersey Tye *Suffk* **54** TL9843
Kersey Upland *Suffk* **54** TL9942
Kershader *W Isls* **154** NB3320
Kershopefoot *D & G* **101** NY4782
Kersoe *H & W* **47** SO9940
Kerswell *Devon* **9** ST0806
Kerswell Green *H & W* **47** SO8646
Kerthen Wood *Cnwll* **2** SW5833
Kesgrave *Suffk* **55** TM2245
Kessingland *Suffk* **55** TM5286
Kessingland Beach *Suffk* **55** TM5385
Kestle *Cnwll* **3** SW9845
Kestle Mill *Cnwll* **4** SW8459
Keston *Gt Lon* **27** TQ4164
Keswick *Cumb* **93** NY2623
Keswick *Norfk* **67** TG2004
Ketsby *Lincs* **77** TF3676
Kettering *Nhants* **51** SP8678
Ketteringham *Norfk* **66** TG1603
Kettins *Tays* **126** NO2338
Kettle Green *Herts* **39** TL4118
Kettlebaston *Suffk* **54** TL9650
Kettlebridge *Fife* **126** NO3007
Kettlebrook *Staffs* **61** SK2103
Kettleburgh *Suffk* **55** TM2660
Kettleholm *D & G* **100** NY1577
Kettleshulme *Ches* **79** SJ9879
Kettlesing *N York* **82** SE2256
Kettlesing Bottom *N York* **89** SE2357
Kettlestoft *Ork* **155** HY6538
Kettlestone *Norfk* **66** TF9631
Kettlethorpe *Lincs* **76** SK8475
Kettlewell *N York* **88** SD9672
Ketton *Leics* **63** SK9704
Kew *Gt Lon* **26** TQ1876
Kewstoke *Avon* **21** ST3363
Kexbrough *S York* **82** SE3009
Kexby *Lincs* **76** SK8785
Kexby *N York* **84** SE7050
Key Green *Ches* **72** SJ8963
Key Green *N York* **90** NZ8004
Key Street *Kent* **28** TQ8764
Key's Toft *Lincs* **77** TF4858
Keyham *Leics* **63** SK6706
Keyhaven *Hants* **12** SZ3091
Keyingham *Humb* **85** TA2425
Keymer *W Susx* **15** TQ3115
Keynsham *Avon* **21** ST6568
Keysoe *Beds* **51** TL0762
Keysoe Row *Beds* **51** TL0861
Keyston *Cambs* **51** TL0475
Keyworth *Notts* **62** SK6130
Kibbear *Somset* **20** ST2222
Kibblesworth *T & W* **96** NZ2456
Kibworth Beauchamp *Leics* **50** SP6893
Kibworth Harcourt *Leics* **50** SP6894
Kidbrooke *Gt Lon* **27** TQ4176
Kidburngill *Cumb* **92** NY0621
Kidd's Moor *Norfk* **66** TG1103
Kiddemore Green *Staffs* **60** SJ8509
Kidderminster *H & W* **60** SO8376
Kiddington *Oxon* **49** SP4123
Kidlington *Oxon* **37** SP4913
Kidmore End *Oxon* **37** SU6979
Kidsdale *D & G* **99** NX4336
Kidsgrove *Staffs* **72** SJ8454
Kidstones *N York* **88** SD9581
Kidwelly *Dyfed* **31** SN4006
Kiel Crofts *Strath* **122** NM9039
Kielder *Nthumb* **102** NY6293
Kiells *Strath* **112** NR4168
Kilbarchan *Strath* **115** NS4063
Kilbeg *Highld* **129** NG6506
Kilberry *Strath* **113** NR7164
Kilbirnie *Strath* **115** NS3154
Kilbride *Strath* **122** NM8525
Kilbride *Strath* **113** NR7279
Kilbride *Strath* **114** NS0367
Kilburn *Derbys* **62** SK3845
Kilburn *Gt Lon* **26** TQ2483
Kilburn *N York* **90** SE5179
Kilby *Leics* **50** SP6295
Kilchamaig *Strath* **113** NR8060
Kilchattan *Strath* **112** NR3795
Kilchattan *Strath* **114** NS1054
Kilcheran *Strath* **122** NM8239
Kilchoan *Highld* **121** NM4863
Kilchrenan *Strath* **122** NN0322
Kilconquhar *Fife* **127** NO4802
Kilcot *Gloucs* **47** SO6925
Kilcoy *Highld* **139** NH5751
Kilcreggan *Strath* **114** NS2480
Kildale *N York* **90** NZ6009
Kildalloig *Strath* **105** NR7518
Kildary *Highld* **147** NH7674
Kildavaig *Strath* **114** NR9866
Kildavanan *Strath* **114** NS0266
Kildonan *Highld* **147** NC9120
Kildonan *Strath* **105** NS0321
Kildonan Lodge *Highld* **147** NC9022
Kildonnan *Highld* **128** NM4885
Kildrochet House *D & G* **98** NX0856
Kildrummy *Gramp* **142** NJ4617
Kildwick *N York* **82** SE0046
Kilfinan *Strath* **114** NR9378
Kilfinnan *Highld* **131** NN2795
Kilford *Clwyd* **70** SJ0766
Kilgetty *Dyfed* **31** SN1207
Kilgrammie *Strath* **106** NS2502
Kilgwrrwg Common *Gwent* **34** ST4797
Kilham *Humb* **91** TA0664
Kilham *Nthumb* **110** NT8832
Kilkenneth *Strath* **120** NL9444
Kilkenzie *Strath* **105** NR6724
Kilkhampton *Cnwll* **18** SS2511
Killamarsh *Derbys* **75** SK4581
Killay *W Glam* **32** SS6092
Killearn *Cent* **115** NS5286
Killerby *Dur* **96** NZ1919
Killerton *Devon* **9** SS9700
Killichonan *Tays* **132** NN5458
Killiechronan *Strath* **121** NM5441
Killiecrankie *Tays* **132** NN9162
Killilan *Highld* **138** NG9430
Killin *Cent* **124** NN5733
Killinghall *N York* **89** SE2858
Killington *Cumb* **87** SD6188
Killington *Devon* **19** SS6646
Killingworth *T & W* **103** NZ2770
Killiow *Cnwll* **3** SW8042
Killivose *Cnwll* **3** SW8049
Killochyett *Border* **118** NT4545
Kilmacolm *Strath* **115** NS3567
Kilmahog *Cent* **124** NN6108
Kilmahumaig *Strath* **113** NR7893
Kilmaluag *Highld* **136** NG4374
Kilmany *Fife* **126** NO3821
Kilmarie *Highld* **129** NG5517
Kilmarnock *Strath* **107** NS4237
Kilmartin *Strath* **113** NR8398
Kilmaurs *Strath* **106** NS4141
Kilmelford *Strath* **122** NM8512
Kilmeny *Strath* **112** NR3965
Kilmersdon *Somset* **22** ST6952
Kilmeston *Hants* **13** SU5825
Kilmichael *Strath* **113** NR8593
Kilmichael *Strath* **105** NR6922
Kilmichael of Inverlussa *Strath* **113** NR7786
Kilmington *Devon* **10** SY2797
Kilmington *Wilts* **22** ST7736
Kilmington Common *Wilts* **22** ST7735
Kilmington Street *Wilts* **22** ST7835
Kilmorack *Highld* **139** NH4944
Kilmore *Highld* **129** NG6507
Kilmore *Highld* **122** NM5270
Kilmore *Strath* **122** NM8825
Kilmory *Strath* **113** NR7074
Kilmory *Strath* **105** NR9621
Kilmuir *Highld* **136** NG2547
Kilmuir *Highld* **136** NG3770
Kilmuir *Highld* **140** NH6749
Kilmuir *Highld* **147** NH7573
Kilmun *Strath* **114** NS1781
Kiln Green *Berks* **37** SU8178
Kiln Pit Hill *Nthumb* **95** NZ0355
Kilnave *Strath* **112** NR2871
Kilncadzow *Strath* **116** NS8848
Kilndown *Kent* **16** TQ7035
Kilnhill *Cumb* **93** NY2132
Kilnhouses *Ches* **71** SJ6366
Kilnhurst *S York* **75** SK4597
Kilninver *Strath* **122** NM8221
Kilnsea *Humb* **85** TA4115
Kilnsey *N York* **88** SD9767
Kilnwick *Humb* **84** SE9949
Kilnwick Percy *Humb* **84** SE8249
Kiloran *Strath* **112** NR3996
Kilpatrick *Strath* **105** NR9026
Kilpeck *H & W* **46** SO4430
Kilpin *Humb* **84** SE7726
Kilpin Pike *Humb* **84** SE7626
Kilrenny *Fife* **127** NO5704
Kilrie *Ches* **79** SJ7478
Kilsby *Nhants* **50** SP5671
Kilspindie *Tays* **126** NO2125
Kilstay *D & G* **98** NX1238

Kilsyth
Kyrle

Kilsyth Strath 116 NS7178
Kiltarlity Highld 139 NH5041
Kilton Cleve 97 NZ7018
Kilton Thorpe Cleve 97 NZ6917
Kilvaxter Highld 136 NG3869
Kilve Somset 20 ST1442
Kilvington Notts 63 SK8042
Kilwinning Strath 106 NS3043
Kimberley Norfk 66 TG0603
Kimberley Notts 62 SK4944
Kimberworth S York 74 SK4093
Kimble Wick Bucks 38 SP8007
Kimblesworth Dur 96 NZ2547
Kimbolton Cambs 51 TL1067
Kimbolton H & W 46 SO5261
Kimcote Leics 50 SP5886
Kimmeridge Dorset 11 SY9179
Kimmerston Nthumb 111 NT9535
Kimpton Hants 23 SU2746
Kimpton Herts 39 TL1718
Kimworthy Devon 18 SS3112
Kinbrace Highld 150 NC8631
Kinbuck Cent 125 NN7905
Kincaple Fife 127 NO4618
Kincardine Fife 116 NS9387
Kincardine Highld 146 NH6089
Kincardine O'Neil Tays 134 NO5999
Kinclaven Tays 126 NO1538
Kincorth Gramp 135 NJ9403
Kincorth House Gramp 141 NJ0161
Kincraig Highld 132 NH8305
Kincraigie Tays 125 NN9849
Kindallachan Tays 125 NN9949
Kinerarach Strath 113 NR6553
Kineton Gloucs 48 SP0926
Kineton Warwks 48 SP3350
Kinfauns Tays 126 NO1622
Kinfig M Glam 32 SS8081
Kinfold Strath 106 NS3634
King Sterndale Derbys 74 SK0972
King's Acre H & W 46 SO4841
King's Bromley Staffs 73 SK1216
King's Cliffe Nhants 51 TL0097
King's Coughton Warwks 48 SP0859
King's Heath W Mids 61 SP0781
King's Hill Warwks 61 SP3274
King's Lynn Norfk 65 TF6120
King's Mills Guern 152 GN0000
King's Moss Lancs 78 SD5000
King's Newton Derbys 62 SK3825
King's Norton Leics 50 SK6800
King's Norton W Mids 61 SP0579
King's Nympton Devon 19 SS6819
King's Pyon H & W 46 SO4450
King's Somborne Hants 23 SU3531
King's Stag Dorset 11 ST7210
King's Stanley Gloucs 35 SO8103
King's Sutton Oxon 49 SP4936
King's Walden Herts 39 TL1623
Kingarth Strath 114 NS0956
Kingcausie Gramp 135 NO8699
Kingcoed Gwent 34 SO4305
Kingerby Lincs 76 TF0592
Kingford Devon 18 SS2806
Kingham Oxon 48 SP2624
Kingholm Quay D & G 100 NX9773
Kinghorn Fife 117 NT2686
Kinglassie Fife 117 NT2298
Kingoldrum Tays 126 NO3355
Kingoodie Tays 126 NO3329
Kings Bridge W Glam 32 SS5997
Kings Caple H & W 46 SO5528
Kings Green Gloucs 47 SO7734
Kings Hill W Mids 60 SO9896
Kings House Hotel Highld 123 NN2654
Kings Langley Herts 26 TL0702
Kings Meaburn Cumb 94 NY6221
Kings Muir Border 109 NT2539
Kings Newnham Warwks 50 SP4577
Kings Ripton Cambs 52 TL2676
Kings Weston Avon 34 ST5477
Kings Worthy Hants 24 SU4932
Kingsand Cnwll 6 SX4350
Kingsash Bucks 38 SP8805
Kingsbarns Fife 127 NO5912
Kingsbridge Devon 7 SX7344
Kingsbridge Somset 20 SS9837
Kingsburgh Highld 136 NG3955
Kingsbury Gt Lon 26 TQ1988
Kingsbury Warwks 61 SP2196
Kingsbury Episcopi Somset 21 ST4321
Kingsclere Hants 24 SU5258
Kingscote Gloucs 35 ST8196
Kingscott Devon 19 SS5318
Kingscross Strath 105 NS0428
Kingsdon Somset 21 ST5126
Kingsdown Kent 29 TR3748
Kingsdown Wilts 22 ST8167
Kingsdown Wilts 36 SU1688
Kingseat Fife 117 NT1290
Kingsey Bucks 37 SP7406
Kingsfold W Susx 15 TQ1636
Kingsford Gramp 135 NJ8506
Kingsford H & W 60 SO8181
Kingsford Strath 115 NS4447
Kingsgate Kent 29 TR3970
Kingshall Street Suffk 54 TL9161
Kingsheanton Devon 19 SS5537
Kingshouse Hotel Cent 124 NN5620
Kingshurst W Mids 61 SP1688
Kingside Hill Cumb 92 NY1551
Kingskerswell Devon 7 SX8767
Kingskettle Fife 126 NO3008
Kingsland Dorset 10 SY4597
Kingsland Gwynd 68 SH2581
Kingsland H & W 46 SO4461
Kingsley Ches 71 SJ5574
Kingsley Hants 25 SU7838
Kingsley Staffs 73 SK0146
Kingsley Green W Susx 14 SU8930
Kingsley Park Nhants 49 SP7762
Kingslow Shrops 60 SO7998
Kingsmead Hants 13 SU5813
Kingsmuir Fife 127 NO5308
Kingsmuir Tays 127 NO4849
Kingsnorth Kent 28 TR0039
Kingstanding W Mids 61 SP0794
Kingsteignton Devon 7 SX8773
Kingsthorne H & W 46 SO4931
Kingsthorpe Nhants 49 SP7563
Kingston Cambs 52 TL3455
Kingston Cnwll 5 SX3675
Kingston Devon 6 SX6347
Kingston Devon 9 SY0687
Kingston Dorset 11 ST7509
Kingston Dorset 11 SY9579
Kingston Hants 12 SU1401
Kingston IOW 13 SZ4781
Kingston Kent 29 TR1950
Kingston Loth 118 NT5482
Kingston W Susx 14 TQ0802
Kingston Bagpuize Oxon 36 SU4098
Kingston Blount Oxon 37 SU7399
Kingston by Sea W Susx 15 TQ2305
Kingston Deverill Wilts 22 ST8437
Kingston Lisle Oxon 36 SU3287
Kingston near Lewes E Susx 15 TQ3908
Kingston on Soar Notts 62 SK5027
Kingston on Spey Gramp 141 NJ3365
Kingston Russell Dorset 10 SY5791
Kingston Seymour Avon 21 ST4066
Kingston St Mary Somset 20 ST2229
Kingston Stert Oxon 37 SP7200
Kingston upon Thames Gt Lon 26 TQ1869
Kingstone H & W 46 SO4235
Kingstone Oxon 36 SU2685
Kingstone Somset 10 ST3713
Kingstone Staffs 73 SK0629
Kingstown Cumb 93 NY3959
Kingswear Devon 7 SX8851
Kingswells Gramp 135 NJ8606
Kingswinford W Mids 60 SO8888
Kingswood Avon 35 ST6473
Kingswood Bucks 37 SP6919
Kingswood Gloucs 35 ST7491
Kingswood Kent 28 TQ8350
Kingswood Powys 58 SJ2302
Kingswood Somset 20 ST1037
Kingswood Surrey 26 TQ2455
Kingswood Warwks 61 SP1871
Kingswood Brook Warwks 61 SP1970
Kingswood Common H & W 46 SO2954
Kingswood Common Staffs 60 SJ8302
Kingthorpe Lincs 76 TF1275
Kington Avon 35 ST6290
Kington H & W 46 SO2956
Kington H & W 47 SO9956
Kington Langley Wilts 35 ST9276
Kington Magna Dorset 22 ST7622
Kington St Michael Wilts 35 ST9077
Kingussie Highld 132 NH7500
Kingweston Somset 21 ST5230
Kinharrachie Gramp 143 NJ9231
Kinharvie D & G 100 NX9266
Kinkell Bridge Tays 125 NN9316
Kinknockie Gramp 143 NK0041
Kinleith Loth 117 NT1866
Kinlet Shrops 60 SO7180
Kinloch Highld 149 NC3434
Kinloch Highld 149 NC5552
Kinloch Highld 128 NM4099
Kinloch Tays 126 NO1444
Kinloch Tays 126 NO2644
Kinloch Hourn Highld 130 NG9506
Kinloch Rannoch Tays 132 NN6658
Kinlochard Cent 124 NN4502
Kinlochbervie Highld 148 NC2256
Kinlocheil Highld 130 NM9779
Kinlochewe Highld 138 NH0261
Kinlochlaggan Highld 131 NN5289
Kinlochleven Highld 131 NN1861
Kinlochmoidart Highld 129 NM7072
Kinlochnanuagh Highld 129 NM7384
Kinloss Gramp 141 NJ0661
Kinmel Bay Clwyd 70 SH9880
Kinmount House D & G 100 NY1368
Kinmuck Gramp 143 NJ8119
Kinmundy Gramp 143 NJ8817
Kinnabus Strath 104 NR2942
Kinnadie Gramp 143 NJ9743
Kinnaird Tays 133 NN9559
Kinnaird Tays 126 NO2428
Kinnaird Castle Tays 134 NO6357
Kinneddar Gramp 141 NJ2269
Kinneff Gramp 135 NO8477
Kinnelhead D & G 108 NT0201
Kinnell Tays 127 NO6150
Kinnerley Shrops 59 SJ3320
Kinnersley H & W 46 SO3449
Kinnersley H & W 47 SO8743
Kinnerton Powys 46 SO2463
Kinnerton Shrops 59 SO3796
Kinnerton Green Clwyd 71 SJ3361
Kinnesswood Tays 126 NO1702
Kinninvie Dur 95 NZ0521
Kinnordy Tays 126 NO3655
Kinoulton Notts 63 SK6730
Kinross Tays 126 NO1102
Kinrossie Tays 126 NO1832
Kinsbourne Green Herts 38 TL1016
Kinsey Heath Ches 72 SJ6642
Kinsham H & W 46 SO3665
Kinsham H & W 47 SO9335
Kinsley W York 83 SE4114
Kinson Dorset 12 SZ0796
Kintbury Berks 23 SU3866
Kintessack Gramp 141 NJ0060
Kintillo Tays 126 NO1317
Kinton H & W 46 SO4174
Kinton Shrops 59 SJ3719
Kintore Gramp 143 NJ7916
Kintour Strath 112 NR4551
Kintra Strath 120 NM3125
Kintraw Strath 122 NM8204
Kinveachy Highld 140 NH9018
Kinver Staffs 60 SO8483
Kiplin N York 89 SE2897
Kippax W York 83 SE4130
Kippen Cent 116 NS6494
Kippford or Scaur D & G 92 NX8354
Kipping's Cross Kent 16 TQ6440
Kirbister Ork 155 HY3607
Kirby Bedon Norfk 67 TG2705
Kirby Bellars Leics 63 SK7117
Kirby Cane Norfk 67 TM3794
Kirby Corner W Mids 61 SP2976
Kirby Cross Essex 41 TM2120
Kirby Fields Leics 62 SK5203
Kirby Grindalythe N York 91 SE9067
Kirby Hill N York 89 NZ1406
Kirby Hill N York 89 SE3968
Kirby Knowle N York 89 SE4687
Kirby le Soken Essex 41 TM2121
Kirby Misperton N York 90 SE7779
Kirby Muxloe Leics 62 SK5104
Kirby Row Norfk 67 TM3792
Kirby Sigston N York 89 SE4194
Kirby Underdale Humb 90 SE8058
Kirby Wiske N York 89 SE3784
Kirconnel D & G 100 NX9868
Kirdford W Susx 14 TQ0126
Kirk Highld 151 ND2859
Kirk Bramwith S York 83 SE6211
Kirk Deighton N York 83 SE3950
Kirk Ella Humb 84 TA0129
Kirk Hallam Derbys 62 SK4540
Kirk Hammerton N York 83 SE4655
Kirk Ireton Derbys 73 SK2650
Kirk Langley Derbys 73 SK2838
Kirk Merrington Dur 96 NZ2631
Kirk Michael IOM 153 SC3190
Kirk of Shotts Strath 116 NS8462
Kirk Sandall S York 83 SE6108
Kirk Smeaton N York 83 SE5216
Kirk Yetholm Border 110 NT8228
Kirkabister Shet 155 HU4938
Kirkandrews D & G 99 NX6048
Kirkandrews upon Eden Cumb 93 NY3558
Kirkbampton Cumb 93 NY3056
Kirkbean D & G 92 NX9759
Kirkbride Cumb 93 NY2256
Kirkbridge N York 89 SE2590
Kirkbuddo Tays 127 NO5043
Kirkburn Border 109 NT2938
Kirkburn Humb 84 SE9855
Kirkburton W York 82 SE1912
Kirkby Lincs 76 TF0592
Kirkby Mersyd 78 SJ4099
Kirkby N York 90 NZ5305
Kirkby Fleetham N York 89 SE2894
Kirkby Green Lincs 76 TF0857
Kirkby Hall N York 89 SE2795
Kirkby in Ashfield Notts 75 SK4856
Kirkby la Thorpe Lincs 76 TF0946
Kirkby Lonsdale Cumb 87 SD6178
Kirkby Malham N York 88 SD8960
Kirkby Mallory Leics 50 SK4500
Kirkby Malzeard N York 89 SE2374
Kirkby Mills N York 90 SE7085
Kirkby on Bain Lincs 77 TF2462
Kirkby Overblow N York 83 SE3249
Kirkby Stephen Cumb 88 NY7708
Kirkby Thore Cumb 94 NY6325
Kirkby Underwood Lincs 64 TF0727
Kirkby Wharf N York 83 SE5041
Kirkby Woodhouse Notts 75 SK4954
Kirkby-in-Furness Cumb 86 SD2282
Kirkbymoorside N York 90 SE6986
Kirkcaldy Fife 117 NT2892
Kirkcambeck Cumb 101 NY5368
Kirkchrist D & G 99 NX6751
Kirkcolm D & G 98 NX0268
Kirkconnel D & G 107 NS7311
Kirkconnell D & G 99 NX6760
Kirkcowan D & G 98 NX3260
Kirkcudbright D & G 99 NX6850
Kirkdale Mersyd 78 SJ3493
Kirkfieldbank Strath 108 NS8643
Kirkgunzeon D & G 100 NX8666
Kirkham Lancs 80 SD4232
Kirkham N York 90 SE7365
Kirkhamgate W York 82 SE2922
Kirkharle Nthumb 103 NZ0182
Kirkhaugh Nthumb 94 NY6949
Kirkheaton Nthumb 103 NZ0177
Kirkheaton W York 82 SE1818
Kirkhill Highld 139 NH5545
Kirkhope Strath 108 NS9606
Kirkhouse Cumb 94 NY5759
Kirkhouse Green S York 83 SE6213
Kirkibost Highld 129 NG5518
Kirkinch Tays 126 NO3044
Kirkinner D & G 99 NX4251
Kirkintilloch Strath 116 NS6573
Kirkland Cumb 92 NY0718
Kirkland Cumb 93 NY2648
Kirkland Cumb 94 NY6432
Kirkland D & G 107 NS7213
Kirkland D & G 99 NX4356
Kirkland D & G 100 NX8190
Kirkland D & G 100 NY0389
Kirkland Guards Cumb 93 NY1840
Kirkleatham Cleve 97 NZ5921
Kirklevington Cleve 89 NZ4309
Kirkley Suffk 67 TM5391
Kirklington N York 89 SE3181
Kirklington Notts 75 SK6757
Kirklinton Cumb 101 NY4367
Kirkliston Loth 117 NT1274
Kirkmabreck D & G 99 NX4856
Kirkmaiden D & G 98 NX1236
Kirkmichael Strath 106 NS3408
Kirkmichael Tays 133 NO0759
Kirkmuirhill Strath 107 NS7842
Kirknewton Loth 117 NT1166
Kirknewton Nthumb 110 NT9130
Kirkney Gramp 142 NJ5132
Kirkoswald Cumb 94 NY5541
Kirkoswald Strath 106 NS2407
Kirkpatrick D & G 100 NX9090
Kirkpatrick Durham D & G 100 NX7870
Kirkpatrick-Fleming D & G 101 NY2770
Kirksanton Cumb 86 SD1380
Kirkstall W York 82 SE2635
Kirkstead Lincs 76 TF1762
Kirkstile D & G 101 NY3690
Kirkstile Gramp 142 NJ5235
Kirkstone Pass Inn Cumb 87 NY4007
Kirkstyle Highld 151 ND3472
Kirkthorpe W York 83 SE3621
Kirkton D & G 100 NX9781
Kirkton Fife 126 NO3625
Kirkton Gramp 142 NJ6425
Kirkton Gramp 143 NJ8243
Kirkton Highld 137 NG8227
Kirkton Highld 138 NG9141
Kirkton Tays 125 NN9618
Kirkton Manor Border 109 NT2238
Kirkton of Airlie Tays 126 NO3151
Kirkton of Auchterhouse Tays 126 NO3438
Kirkton of Barevan Highld 140 NH8347
Kirkton of Collace Tays 126 NO1931
Kirkton of Glenbuchat Gramp 141 NJ3715
Kirkton of
Logie Buchan Gramp 143 NJ9829
Kirkton of Menmuir Tays 134 NO5364
Kirkton of Monikie Tays 127 NO5138
Kirkton of Rayne Gramp 142 NJ6930
Kirkton of Skene Gramp 135 NJ8007
Kirkton of Strathmartine Tays 126 NO3735
Kirkton of Tealing Tays 126 NO4038
Kirktown Gramp 143 NJ9965
Kirktown Gramp 143 NK0852
Kirktown of Bourtie Gramp 143 NJ8025
Kirktown of Fetteresso Gramp 135 NO8486
Kirktown of Mortlach Gramp 141 NJ3138
Kirktown of Slains Gramp 143 NK0329
Kirkwall Ork 155 HY4411
Kirkwhelpington Nthumb 103 NY9984
Kirmington Humb 85 TA1011
Kirmond le Mire Lincs 76 TF1892
Kirn Strath 114 NS1878
Kirriemuir Tays 126 NO3853
Kirstead Green Norfk 67 TM2997
Kirtlebridge D & G 101 NY2372
Kirtling Cambs 53 TL6857
Kirtling Green Suffk 53 TL6855
Kirtlington Oxon 37 SP4919
Kirtomy Highld 150 NC7463
Kirton Gramp 134 NJ6113
Kirton Lincs 64 TF3038
Kirton Notts 75 SK6969
Kirton Suffk 55 TM2740
Kirton End Lincs 64 TF2940
Kirton Holme Lincs 64 TF2642
Kirton in Lindsey Lincs 76 SK9398
Kirtonhill Strath 115 NS3875
Kirwaugh D & G 99 NX4054
Kishorn Highld 138 NG8440
Kislingbury Nhants 49 SP6959
Kite Green Warwks 48 SP1666
Kitebrook Warwks 48 SP2431
Kites Hardwick Warwks 50 SP4768
Kitleigh Cnwll 18 SX2499
Kitt Green Gt Man 78 SD5405
Kittisford Somset 20 ST0822
Kittle W Glam 32 SS5789
Kitts Green W Mids 61 SP1587
Kittybrewster Gramp 135 NJ9207
Kitwood Hants 24 SU6633
Kivernoll H & W 46 SO4632
Kiveton Park S York 75 SK4982
Knaith Lincs 75 SK8284
Knaith Park Lincs 76 SK8485
Knap Corner Dorset 22 ST8023
Knaphill Surrey 25 SU9658
Knaplock Somset 19 SS8633
Knapp Somset 20 ST3025
Knapp Hill Hants 13 SU4023
Knapthorpe Notts 75 SK7458
Knapton N York 83 SE5652
Knapton N York 90 SE8876
Knapton Norfk 67 TG3034
Knapton Green H & W 46 SO4452
Knapwell Cambs 52 TL3362
Knaresborough N York 89 SE3557
Knarsdale Nthumb 94 NY6754
Knaven Gramp 143 NJ8943
Knayton N York 89 SE4387
Knebworth Herts 39 TL2520
Knedlington Humb 84 SE7327
Kneesall Notts 75 SK7064
Kneesworth Cambs 39 TL3444
Kneeton Notts 63 SK7146
Knelston W Glam 32 SS4688
Knenhall Staffs 72 SJ9237
Knettishall Suffk 54 TL9780
Knightacott Devon 19 SS6539
Knightcote Warwks 48 SP4054
Knightley Staffs 72 SJ8125
Knightley Dale Staffs 72 SJ8123
Knighton Devon 6 SX5349
Knighton Dorset 10 ST6111
Knighton Dorset 12 SZ0497
Knighton Leics 62 SK6001
Knighton Powys 46 SO2872
Knighton Somset 20 ST1944
Knighton Staffs 72 SJ7240
Knighton Staffs 72 SJ7527
Knighton Wilts 36 SU2971
Knighton on Teme H & W 47 SO6369
Knightsbridge Gloucs 47 SO8926
Knightsmill Cnwll 4 SX0780
Knightwick H & W 47 SO7356
Knill H & W 46 SO2960
Knipton Leics 63 SK8231
Knitsley Dur 95 NZ1048
Kniveton Derbys 73 SK2050
Knock Cumb 94 NY6727
Knock Gramp 142 NJ5452
Knock Highld 129 NG6709
Knock W Isls 154 NB4931
Knock Castle Strath 114 NS1963
Knockally Highld 151 ND1429
Knockan Highld 145 NC2110
Knockando Gramp 141 NJ1941
Knockbain Highld 139 NH5543
Knockbain Highld 140 NH6256
Knockdee Highld 151 ND1760
Knockdown Wilts 35 ST8388
Knockeen Strath 106 NX3195
Knockenkelly Strath 105 NS0427
Knockentiber Strath 106 NS4039
Knockespock House Gramp 142 NJ5423
Knockhall Kent 27 TQ5974
Knockholt Kent 27 TQ4658
Knockholt Pound Kent 27 TQ4859
Knockin Shrops 59 SJ3322
Knockinlaw Strath 107 NS4239
Knockmill Kent 27 TQ5761
Knocknain D & G 98 NW9764
Knocksheen D & G 99 NX5882
Knockvennie Smithy D & G 99 NX7571
Knodishall Suffk 55 TM4262
Knole Somset 21 ST4825
Knole Park Avon 34 ST5983
Knolls Green Ches 79 SJ8079
Knolton Clwyd 71 SJ3739
Knook Wilts 22 ST9341
Knossington Leics 63 SK8008
Knott End-on-Sea Lancs 80 SD3548
Knotting Beds 51 TL0063
Knotting Green Beds 51 TL0062
Knottingley W York 83 SE5023
Knotty Green Bucks 26 SU9392
Knowbury Shrops 46 SO5775
Knowe D & G 98 NX3171
Knowehead D & G 107 NX6090
Knoweside Strath 106 NS2512
Knowl Green Essex 53 TL7841
Knowl Hill Berks 37 SU8279
Knowle Avon 34 ST6070
Knowle Devon 18 SS4938
Knowle Devon 8 SS7801
Knowle Devon 9 ST0007
Knowle Devon 9 SY0582
Knowle Shrops 46 SO5973
Knowle Somset 20 SS9643
Knowle W Mids 61 SP1876
Knowle Cross Devon 9 SY0397
Knowle Green Lancs 81 SD6338
Knowle Hill Surrey 25 SU9966
Knowle St Giles Somset 10 ST3411
Knowlefield Cumb 93 NY4057
Knowlton Dorset 12 SU0209
Knowlton Kent 29 TR2853
Knowsley Mersyd 78 SJ4395
Knowstone Devon 19 SS8323
Knox N York 89 SE2957
Knox Bridge Kent 28 TQ7840
Knucklas Powys 46 SO2574
Knuston Nhants 51 SP9266
Knutsford Ches 79 SJ7578
Knutton Staffs 72 SJ8347
Knypersley Staffs 72 SJ8856
Krumlin W York 82 SE0518
Kuggar Cnwll 3 SW7216
Kyle of Lochalsh Highld 137 NG7627
Kyleakin Highld 137 NG7526
Kylerhea Highld 129 NG7820
Kyles Scalpay W Isls 154 NG2198
Kylesku Highld 148 NC2233
Kylesmorar Highld 129 NM8093
Kylestrome Highld 148 NC2234
Kyloe Nthumb 111 NU0540
Kynaston H & W 47 SO6435
Kynaston Shrops 59 SJ3520
Kynnersley Shrops 72 SJ6716
Kyre Green H & W 46 SO6162
Kyre Park H & W 47 SO6263
Kyrewood H & W 46 SO5967
Kyrle Somset 20 ST0522

L'Ancresse
Letchmore Heath

L

L'Ancresse Guern 152 GN0000
L'Eree Guern 152 GN0000
L'Etacq Jersey 152 JS0000
La Beilleuse Guern 152 SY5206
La Fontenelle Guern 152 GN0000
La Fosse Guern 152 GN0000
La Greve Guern 152 GN0000
La Greve de Lecq Jersey 152 JS0000
La Hougue Bie Jersey 152 JS0000
La Houguette Guern 152 GN0000
La Passee Guern 152 GN0000
La Pulente Jersey 152 JS0000
La Rocque Jersey 152 JS0000
La Rousaillerie Guern 152 GN0000
La Villette Guern 152 GN0000
Labbacott Devon 18 SS4021
Lacadal W Isls 154 NB4234
Lacasaigh W Isls 154 NB3321
Laceby Humb 85 TA2106
Lacey Green Bucks 37 SP8200
Lach Dennis Ches 79 SJ7071
Lackenby Cleve 97 NZ5619
Lackford Suffk 53 TL7970
Lackford Green Suffk 53 TL7970
Lacock Wilts 22 ST9168
Ladbroke Warwks 49 SP4158
Ladderedge Staffs 72 SJ9654
Laddingford Kent 28 TQ6948
Lade Bank Lincs 77 TF3954
Ladock Cnwll 3 SW8950
Lady Hall Cumb 86 SD1986
Lady Village Ork 155 HY6841
Lady's Green Suffk 53 TL7559
Ladybank Fife 126 NO3009
Ladycross Cnwll 5 SX3188
Ladygill Strath 108 NS9428
Ladykirk Border 110 NT8847
Ladykirk Ho Border 110 NT8845
Ladyridge H & W 46 SO5931
Ladywood H & W 47 SO8661
Ladywood W Mids 61 SP0586
Lag D & G 100 NX8786
Laga Highld 121 NM6361
Lagavulin Strath 104 NR4045
Lagg Strath 105 NR9521
Laggan Highld 131 NN2997
Laggan Highld 132 NN6194
Laggan Strath 98 NX0982
Laid Highld 149 NC4159
Laide Highld 144 NG9091
Laig Highld 128 NM4687
Laigh Church Strath 115 NS4647
Laigh Fenwick Strath 107 NS4542
Laigh Glenmuir Strath 107 NS6120
Laighstonehall Strath 116 NS7054
Laindon Essex 40 TQ6889
Lairg Highld 146 NC5806
Laisterdyke W York 82 SE1932
Laithes Cumb 93 NY4633
Lake Devon 19 SS5531
Lake Devon 5 SX5289
Lake Dorset 11 SY9990
Lake IOW 13 SZ5883
Lake Wilts 23 SU1339
Lake Side Cumb 87 SD3787
Lakenheath Suffk 53 TL7182
Laker's Green Surrey 14 TQ0335
Lakesend Norfk 65 TL5196
Lakley Lanes Bucks 38 SP8250
Laleham Surrey 26 TQ0568
Laleston M Glam 33 SS8779
Lamancha Border 117 NT2052
Lamanva Cnwll 3 SW7631
Lamarsh Essex 54 TL8835
Lamas Norfk 67 TG2423
Lamb Roe Lancs 81 SD7337
Lambden Border 110 NT7443
Lamberhurst Kent 28 TQ6736
Lamberhurst Down Kent 16 TQ6735
Lamberton Border 119 NT9658
Lambeth Gt Lon 27 TQ3178
Lambfair Green Suffk 53 TL7153
Lambley Notts 63 SK6345
Lambley Nthumb 94 NY6658
Lambourn Berks 36 SU3278
Lambourne End Essex 27 TQ4794
Lambs Green W Susx 15 TQ2136
Lambston Dyfed 30 SM9016
Lamerton Devon 5 SX4577
Lamesley T & W 96 NZ2557
Lamington Strath 108 NS9731
Lamlash Strath 105 NS0231
Lamonby Cumb 93 NY4036
Lamorick Cnwll 4 SX0364
Lamorna Cnwll 2 SW4424
Lamorran Cnwll 3 SW8741
Lampen Cnwll 4 SX1867
Lampeter Dyfed 44 SN5747
Lampeter Velfrey Dyfed 31 SN1514
Lamphey Dyfed 30 SN0100
Lamplugh Cumb 92 NY0820
Lamport Nhants 50 SP7574
Lamyatt Somset 21 ST6536
Lana Devon 18 SS3007
Lana Devon 5 SX3496
Lanark Strath 108 NS8843
Lanarth Cnwll 3 SW7621
Lancaster Lancs 87 SD4761
Lancaut Gloucs 34 ST5396
Lanchester Dur 96 NZ1647
Lancing W Susx 15 TQ1804
Land-hallow Highld 151 ND1833
Landbeach Cambs 53 TL4765
Landcross Devon 18 SS4523
Landerberry Gramp 135 NJ7404
Landewednack Cnwll 2 SW7012
Landford Wilts 12 SU2519
Landimore W Glam 32 SS4692
Landkey Devon 19 SS6031
Landkey Town Devon 19 SS5931
Landore W Glam 32 SS6695
Landrake Cnwll 5 SX3760
Lands End Cnwll 2 SW3425
Landscove Devon 7 SX7766
Landshipping Dyfed 30 SN0211
Landue Cnwll 5 SX3579
Landulph Cnwll 6 SX4361
Landwade Suffk 53 TL6268
Landywood Staffs 60 SJ9805
Lane Cnwll 4 SW8260
Lane Bottom Lancs 81 SD8735
Lane End Bucks 37 SU8091
Lane End Ches 79 SJ6890
Lane End Cnwll 4 SX0369
Lane End Hants 13 SU5525
Lane End Kent 27 TQ5671
Lane End Lancs 81 SD8747
Lane End Wilts 22 ST8145
Lane End Waberthwaite Cumb 86 SD1093
Lane Ends Derbys 73 SK2334
Lane Ends Dur 96 NZ1833
Lane Ends Lancs 81 SD7930
Lane Ends N York 82 SD9743
Lane Green Staffs 60 SJ8703
Lane Head Dur 89 NZ1211
Lane Head Gt Man 79 SJ6296
Lane Head W Mids 35 SO9700
Lane Heads Lancs 80 SD4339
Lane Side Lancs 81 SD7922
Laneast Cnwll 5 SX2283
Laneham Notts 75 SK8076
Lanehead Dur 95 NY8441
Lanehead Nthumb 102 NY7985
Laneshaw Bridge Lancs 81 SD9240
Langaford Devon 18 SX4199
Langaller Somset 20 ST2626
Langar Notts 63 SK7234
Langbank Strath 115 NS3873
Langbar N York 82 SE0951
Langbaurgh N York 90 NZ5511
Langcliffe N York 88 SD8264
Langdale End N York 91 SE9391
Langdon Cnwll 5 SX3089
Langdon Beck Dur 95 NY8531
Langdown Hants 13 SU4206
Langdyke Fife 126 NO3304
Langenhoe Essex 41 TM0018
Langford Avon 21 ST4560
Langford Beds 39 TL1841
Langford Devon 9 ST0203
Langford Essex 40 TL8309
Langford Notts 75 SK8258
Langford Oxon 36 SP2402
Langford Budville Somset 20 ST1122
Langford End Beds 52 TL1753
Langham Dorset 22 ST7725
Langham Essex 41 TM0333
Langham Leics 63 SK8411
Langham Norfk 66 TG0141
Langham Suffk 54 TL9769
Langham Moor Essex 41 TM0131
Langham Wick Essex 41 TM0231
Langho Lancs 81 SD7034
Langholm D & G 101 NY3684
Langland W Glam 32 SS6087
Langley Berks 26 TQ0178
Langley Ches 79 SJ9471
Langley Derbys 62 SK4445
Langley Essex 39 TL4334
Langley Gloucs 47 SP0028
Langley Gt Man 79 SD8506
Langley Hants 13 SU4401
Langley Herts 39 TL2122
Langley Kent 28 TQ8052
Langley Nthumb 102 NY8261
Langley Oxon 36 SP2915
Langley Somset 20 ST0828
Langley W Susx 14 SU8029
Langley Warwks 48 SP1962
Langley Burrell Wilts 35 ST9375
Langley Castle Nthumb 102 NY8362
Langley Common Derbys 73 SK2937
Langley Green Derbys 73 SK2738
Langley Green Essex 40 TL8722
Langley Green Warwks 48 SP1962
Langley Marsh Somset 20 ST0729
Langley Mill Derbys 62 SK4446
Langley Moor Dur 96 NZ2540
Langley Park Dur 96 NZ2145
Langley Street Norfk 67 TG3601
Langleybury Herts 26 TL0700
Langney E Susx 16 TQ6302
Langold Notts 75 SK5886
Langore Cnwll 5 SX2986
Langport Somset 21 ST4226
Langrick Lincs 77 TF2648
Langridge Avon 35 ST7469
Langridge Ford Devon 19 SS5722
Langrigg Cumb 92 NY1645
Langrish Hants 13 SU7023
Langsett S York 74 SE2100
Langshaw Border 109 NT5139
Langside Tays 125 NN7913
Langstone Gwent 34 ST3789
Langstone Hants 13 SU7204
Langthorne N York 89 SE2491
Langthorpe N York 89 SE3867
Langthwaite N York 88 NZ0001
Langtoft Humb 91 TA0066
Langtoft Lincs 64 TF1212
Langton Dur 96 NZ1619
Langton Lincs 76 TF2368
Langton Lincs 77 TF3970
Langton N York 90 SE7966
Langton by Wragby Lincs 76 TF1476
Langton Green Kent 16 TQ5439
Langton Green Suffk 54 TM1474
Langton Herring Dorset 10 SY6182
Langton Matravers Dorset 11 SZ0078
Langtree Devon 18 SS4515
Langtree Week Devon 18 SS4715
Langwathby Cumb 94 NY5733
Langwell House Highld 147 ND1122
Langworth Lincs 76 TF0676
Langworthy Devon 5 SX4894
Lanieth Cnwll 3 SW9752
Lanivet Cnwll 4 SX0464
Lank Cnwll 4 SX0875
Lanlivery Cnwll 4 SX0759
Lanner Cnwll 2 SW7139
Lanoy Cnwll 5 SX2977
Lanreath Cnwll 4 SX1857
Lansallos Cnwll 4 SX1751
Lanteglos Cnwll 4 SX0882
Lanteglos Highway Cnwll 3 SX1453
Lanton Border 110 NT6221
Lanton Nthumb 110 NT9231
Lapford Devon 19 SS7308
Laphroaig Strath 104 NR3845
Lapley Staffs 60 SJ8712
Lapworth Warwks 61 SP1671
Larachbeg Highld 122 NM6948
Larbert Cent 116 NS8582
Larbreck Lancs 80 SD4040
Largie Gramp 142 NJ6131
Largiemore Strath 114 NR9486
Largoward Fife 127 NO4607
Largs Strath 114 NS2059
Largybeg Strath 105 NS0423
Largymore Strath 105 NS0424
Larkbeare Devon 9 SY0797
Larkfield Kent 28 TQ7058
Larkfield Strath 114 NS2475
Larkhall Strath 116 NS7651
Larkhill Wilts 23 SU1244
Larling Norfk 54 TL9889
Lartington Dur 95 NZ0117
Lasborough Gloucs 35 ST8294
Lasham Hants 24 SU6742
Lashbrook Devon 18 SS4305
Lashenden Kent 28 TQ8440
Lask Edge Staffs 72 SJ9156
Lassodie Fife 117 NT1292
Lasswade Loth 117 NT3065
Lastingham N York 90 SE7290
Latcham Somset 21 ST4447
Latchford Herts 39 TL3920
Latchford Oxon 37 SP6501
Latchingdon Essex 40 TL8800
Latchley Cnwll 5 SX4173
Latebrook Staffs 72 SJ8453
Lately Common Gt Man 79 SJ6797
Lathbury Bucks 38 SP8744
Latheron Highld 151 ND2033
Latheronwheel Highld 151 ND1832
Lathones Fife 127 NO4708
Latimer Bucks 26 TQ0099
Latteridge Avon 35 ST6684
Lattiford Somset 22 ST6926
Latton Wilts 36 SU0995
Lauder Border 118 NT5347
Laugharne Dyfed 31 SN3010
Laughterton Lincs 76 SK8375
Laughton E Susx 16 TQ4913
Laughton Leics 50 SP6688
Laughton Lincs 76 SK8497
Laughton Lincs 64 TF0731
Laughton-en-le-Morthen S York 75 SK5187
Launcells Cnwll 18 SS2405
Launcells Cross Cnwll 18 SS2605
Launceston Cnwll 5 SX3384
Launton Oxon 37 SP6022
Laurencekirk Gramp 135 NO7171
Laurieston Cent 116 NS9179
Laurieston D & G 99 NX6864
Lavendon Bucks 51 SP9153
Lavenham Suffk 54 TL9149
Lavernock S Glam 20 ST1868
Laversdale Cumb 101 NY4762
Laverstock Wilts 23 SU1630
Laverstoke Hants 24 SU4948
Laverton Gloucs 48 SP0735
Laverton N York 89 SE2273
Laverton Somset 22 ST7753
Lavister Clwyd 71 SJ3758
Law Strath 116 NS8252
Law Hill Strath 116 NS8251
Lawers Tays 124 NN6739
Lawford Essex 41 TM0831
Lawford Somset 20 ST1336
Lawgrove Tays 125 NO0926
Lawhitton Cnwll 5 SX3582
Lawkland N York 88 SD7766
Lawkland Green N York 88 SD7765
Lawley Shrops 60 SJ6608
Lawnhead Staffs 72 SJ8325
Lawrence End Herts 38 TL1419
Lawrenny Dyfed 30 SN0106
Lawshall Suffk 54 TL8654
Lawshall Green Suffk 54 TL8853
Lawton H & W 46 SO4459
Laxay W Isls 154 NB3321
Laxdale W Isls 154 NB4234
Laxey IOM 153 SC4384
Laxfield Suffk 55 TM2972
Laxford Bridge Highld 148 NC2346
Laxo Shet 155 HU4463
Laxton Humb 84 SE7925
Laxton Nhants 51 SP9596
Laxton Notts 75 SK7267
Laycock W York 82 SE0341
Layer Breton Essex 40 TL9417
Layer Marney Essex 40 TL9217
Layer-de-la-Haye Essex 41 TL9620
Layham Suffk 54 TM0240
Layland's Green Berks 23 SU3866
Laymore Dorset 10 ST3804
Layter's Green Bucks 26 SU9890
Laytham Humb 84 SE7439
Laythes Cumb 93 NY2455
Lazenby Cleve 97 NZ5719
Lazonby Cumb 94 NY5439
Le Bigard Guern 152 GN0000
Le Bourg Guern 152 GN0000
Le Bourg Jersey 152 JS0000
Le Gron Guern 152 GN0000
Le Haguais Jersey 152 JS0000
Le Hocq Jersey 152 JS0000
Le Villocq Guern 152 GN0000
Lea Derbys 74 SK3257
Lea H & W 35 SO6521
Lea Lincs 75 SK8286
Lea Shrops 59 SJ4108
Lea Shrops 59 SO3589
Lea Wilts 35 ST9586
Lea Bridge Derbys 74 SK3156
Lea Heath Staffs 73 SK0225
Lea Marston Warwks 61 SP2093
Lea Town Lancs 80 SD4730
Lea Yeat Cumb 88 SD7686
Leachkin Highld 140 NH6344
Leadburn Loth 117 NT2355
Leaden Roding Essex 40 TL5913
Leadenham Lincs 76 SK9452
Leadgate Dur 96 NZ1251
Leadgate Nthumb 95 NZ1159
Leadhills Strath 108 NS8815
Leadingcross Green Kent 28 TQ8951
Leadmill Derbys 74 SK2380
Leafield Oxon 36 SP3115
Leagrave Beds 38 TL0523
Leahead Ches 72 SJ6864
Lealholm Side N York 90 NZ7607
Leake N York 89 SE4390
Leake Common Side Lincs 77 TF3952
Lealholm N York 90 NZ7607
Lealt Highld 137 NG5060
Leam Derbys 74 SK2379
Leamington Hastings Warwks 50 SP4467
Leamington Spa Warwks 48 SP3265
Leamonsley Staffs 61 SK1009
Leamside Dur 96 NZ3146
Leap Cross E Susx 16 TQ5810
Leasgill Cumb 87 SD4983
Leasingham Lincs 76 TF0548
Leasingthorne Dur 96 NZ2530
Leatherhead Surrey 26 TQ1656
Leathley N York 82 SE2347
Leaton Shrops 59 SJ4618
Leaton Shrops 59 SJ6111
Leaveland Kent 28 TR0053
Leavenheath Suffk 54 TL9537
Leavening N York 90 SE7863
Leaves Green Gt Lon 27 TQ4161
Lebberston N York 91 TA0782
Lechlade Gloucs 36 SU2199
Leck Lancs 87 SD6476
Leck Gruinart Strath 112 NR2768
Leckbuie Tays 124 NN7040
Leckford Hants 23 SU3737
Leckhampstead Berks 36 SU4375
Leckhampstead Bucks 49 SP7237
Leckhampstead Thicket Berks 36 SU4276
Leckhampton Gloucs 35 SO9419
Leckmelm Highld 145 NH1689
Leckwith S Glam 33 ST1574
Leconfield Humb 84 TA0143
Ledaig Strath 122 NM9037
Ledburn Bucks 38 SP9021
Ledbury H & W 47 SO7137
Leddington Gloucs 47 SO6834
Ledgemoor H & W 46 SO4150
Ledicot H & W 46 SO4162
Ledmore Junction Highld 145 NC2412
Ledsham Ches 71 SJ3574
Ledsham W York 83 SE4529
Ledston W York 83 SE4328
Ledston Luck W York 83 SE4330
Ledstone Devon 7 SX7446
Ledwell Oxon 49 SP4128
Lee Devon 18 SS4846
Lee Gt Lon 27 TQ3875
Lee Hants 12 SU3617
Lee Shrops 59 SJ4032
Lee Brockhurst Shrops 59 SJ5427
Lee Chapel Essex 40 TQ6987
Lee Clump Bucks 38 SP9004
Lee Common Bucks 38 SP9103
Lee Green Ches 72 SJ6661
Lee Mill Devon 6 SX5955
Lee Moor Devon 6 SX5762
Lee Street Surrey 15 TQ2743
Lee-on-the-Solent Hants 13 SU5600
Leebotwood Shrops 59 SO4798
Leece Cumb 86 SD2469
Leedon Beds 38 SP9325
Leeds Kent 28 TQ8253
Leeds W York 82 SE2932
Leeds Beck Lincs 76 TF2065
Leedstown Cnwll 2 SW6034
Leek Staffs 72 SJ9856
Leek Wootton Warwks 48 SP2868
Leeming N York 89 SE2989
Leeming W York 82 SE0434
Leeming Bar N York 89 SE2889
Lees Derbys 73 SK2637
Lees Gt Man 79 SD9504
Lees W York 82 SE0437
Lees Green Derbys 73 SK2637
Lees Hill Cumb 101 NY5568
Leesthorpe Leics 63 SK7813
Leeswood Clwyd 70 SJ2660
Leetown Tays 126 NO2121
Leftwich Ches 79 SJ6672
Legbourne Lincs 77 TF3784
Legburthwaite Cumb 93 NY3219
Legerwood Border 110 NT5843
Legsby Lincs 76 TF1385
Leicester Leics 62 SK5804
Leicester Forest East Leics 62 SK5202
Leigh Devon 19 SS7212
Leigh Dorset 10 ST6108
Leigh Gloucs 47 SO8626
Leigh Gt Man 79 SJ6599
Leigh H & W 47 SO7853
Leigh Kent 16 TQ5446
Leigh Shrops 59 SJ3303
Leigh Surrey 15 TQ2246
Leigh Wilts 36 SU0692
Leigh Beck Essex 40 TQ8183
Leigh Delamere Wilts 35 ST8879
Leigh Green Kent 17 TQ9033
Leigh Knoweglass Strath 116 NS6350
Leigh Park Dorset 12 SZ0299
Leigh Sinton H & W 47 SO7750
Leigh upon Mendip Somset 22 ST6947
Leigh Woods Avon 34 ST5672
Leigh-on-Sea Essex 40 TQ8286
Leighland Chapel Somset 20 ST0336
Leighterton Gloucs 35 ST8290
Leighton N York 89 SE1679
Leighton Powys 58 SJ2306
Leighton Shrops 59 SJ6105
Leighton Somset 22 ST7043
Leighton Bromswold Cambs 52 TL1175
Leighton Buzzard Beds 38 SP9225
Leinthall Earls H & W 46 SO4467
Leinthall Starkes H & W 46 SO4369
Leintwardine H & W 46 SO4074
Leire Leics 50 SP5290
Leiston Suffk 55 TM4462
Leitfie Tays 126 NO2545
Leith Loth 117 NT2776
Leitholm Border 110 NT7944
Lelant Cnwll 2 SW5437
Lelley Humb 85 TA2032
Lem Hill H & W 60 SO7275
Lemmington Hall Nthumb 111 NU1211
Lempitlaw Border 110 NT7832
Lemreway W Isls 154 NB3711
Lemsford Herts 39 TL2212
Lenchwick H & W 48 SP0347
Lendalfoot Strath 106 NX1390
Lendrick Cent 124 NN5506
Lendrum Terrace Gramp 143 NK1141
Lenham Kent 28 TQ8952
Lenham Heath Kent 28 TQ9149
Lenie Highld 139 NH5126
Lennel Border 110 NT8540
Lennox Plunton D & G 99 NX6051
Lennoxlove Loth 118 NT5172
Lennoxtown Strath 116 NS6277
Lent Bucks 26 SU9381
Lenton Lincs 64 TF0230
Lenton Notts 62 SK5539
Lenwade Norfk 66 TG0918
Lenzie Strath 116 NS6572
Leochel-Cushnie Gramp 134 NJ5210
Leominster H & W 46 SO4959
Leonard Stanley Gloucs 35 SO8003
Leoville Jersey 152 JS0000
Lepe Hants 13 SZ4498
Lephin Highld 136 NG1749
Leppington N York 90 SE7661
Lepton W York 82 SE2015
Lerryn Cnwll 4 SX1457
Lerwick Shet 155 HU4741
Les Arquets Guern 152 GN0000
Les Hubits Guern 152 GN0000
Les Lohiers Guern 152 GN0000
Les Murchez Guern 152 GN0000
Les Nicolles Guern 152 GN0000
Les Quartiers Guern 152 GN0000
Les Quennevais Jersey 152 JS0000
Les Sages Guern 152 GN0000
Les Villets Guern 152 GN0000
Lesbury Nthumb 111 NU2311
Leslie Fife 126 NO2501
Leslie Gramp 142 NJ5924
Lesmahagow Strath 108 NS8139
Lesnewth Cnwll 4 SX1390
Lessingham Norfk 67 TG3928
Lessonhall Cumb 93 NY2250
Lestowder Cnwll 3 SW7924
Leswalt D & G 98 NX0163
Letchmore Heath Herts 26 TQ1597

Letchworth
Littlewindsor

Letchworth Herts	39	TL2232
Letcombe Bassett Oxon	36	SU3784
Letcombe Regis Oxon	36	SU3886
Letham Border	110	NT6709
Letham Fife	126	NO3014
Letham Tays	127	NO5348
Letham Grange Tays	127	NO6345
Lethendy Tays	126	NO1341
Lethenty Gramp	142	NJ5820
Lethenty Gramp	143	NJ8140
Letheringham Suffk	55	TM2757
Letheringsett Norfk	66	TG0638
Lett's Green Kent	27	TQ4559
Lettaford Devon	8	SX7084
Letterfearn Highld	138	NG8823
Letterfinlay Lodge Hotel Highld	131	NN2491
Lettermorar Highld	129	NM7389
Letters Highld	145	NH1687
Lettershaw Strath	108	NS8920
Letterston Dyfed	30	SM9429
Lettoch Highld	141	NJ0219
Lettoch Highld	141	NJ1032
Letton H & W	46	SO3346
Letton H & W	46	SO3770
Letty Green Herts	39	TL2810
Letwell S York	75	SK5686
Leuchars Fife	127	NO4521
Leumrabhagh W Isls	154	NB3711
Leurbost W Isls	154	NB3725
Levalsa Moor Cnwll	3	SX0049
Levedale Staffs	72	SJ8916
Level's Green Essex	39	TL4724
Leven Fife	118	NO3800
Leven Humb	85	TA1045
Levencorroch Strath	105	NS0021
Levens Cumb	87	SD4886
Levens Green Herts	39	TL3522
Levenshulme Gt Man	79	SJ8794
Levenwick Shet	155	HU4021
Leverburgh W Isls	154	NG0286
Leverington Cambs	65	TF4411
Leverstock Green Herts	38	TL0806
Leverton Lincs	77	TF4047
Levington Suffk	55	TM2339
Levisham N York	90	SE8390
Lew Oxon	36	SP3206
Lewannick Cnwll	5	SX2780
Lewdown Devon	5	SX4586
Lewes E Susx	15	TQ4110
Leweston Dorset	10	ST6312
Leweston Dyfed	30	SM9322
Lewis Wych H & W	46	SO3357
Lewisham Gt Lon	27	TQ3774
Lewiston Highld	139	NH5129
Lewknor Oxon	37	SU7197
Leworthy Devon	18	SS3201
Leworthy Devon	19	SS6738
Lewson Street Kent	28	TQ9661
Lewth Lancs	80	SD4836
Lewtrenchard Devon	5	SX4586
Lexden Essex	41	TL9625
Lexworthy Somset	20	ST2535
Ley Cnwll	4	SX1766
Ley Hill Bucks	26	SP9902
Leybourne Kent	28	TQ6858
Leyburn N York	89	SE1190
Leycett Staffs	72	SJ7946
Leygreen Herts	39	TL1624
Leyland Lancs	80	SD5422
Leyland Green Mersyd	78	SD5500
Leylodge Gramp	135	NJ7613
Leys Gramp	143	NK0052
Leys Tays	126	NO2537
Leys of Cossans Tays	126	NO3849
Leysdown-on-Sea Kent	28	TR0370
Leysmill Tays	127	NO6047
Leysters H & W	46	SO5664
Leyton Gt Lon	27	TQ3786
Leytonstone Gt Lon	27	TQ3987
Lezant Cnwll	5	SX3479
Lezayre IOM	153	SC4294
Lezerea Cnwll	2	SW6833
Lhanbryde Gramp	141	NJ2761
Libanus Powys	45	SN9925
Libberton Strath	108	NS9943
Liberton Loth	117	NT2769
Lichfield Staffs	61	SK1109
Lickey H & W	60	SO9975
Lickey End H & W	60	SO9772
Lickey Rock H & W	60	SO9774
Lickfold W Susx	14	SU9226
Liddaton Green Devon	5	SX4582
Liddesdale Highld	130	NM7759
Liddington Wilts	36	SU2081
Lidgate Derbys	74	SK3077
Lidgate Suffk	53	TL7258
Lidget S York	75	SE6500
Lidgett Notts	75	SK6365
Lidham Hill E Susx	17	TQ8316
Lidlington Beds	38	SP9939
Lidsing Kent	28	TQ7862
Liff Tays	126	NO3332
Lifford W Mids	61	SP0580
Lifton Devon	5	SX3885
Liftondown Devon	5	SX3685
Lighthazles W York	82	SE0220
Lighthorne Warwks	48	SP3355
Lightwater Surrey	25	SU9362
Lightwood Staffs	72	SJ9241
Lightwood Green Ches	71	SJ6342
Lightwood Green Clwyd	71	SJ3840
Lilbourne Nhants	50	SP5676
Lilburn Tower Nthumb	111	NU0224
Lilleshall Shrops	72	SJ7315
Lilley Berks	37	SU4479
Lilley Herts	38	TL1126
Lilliesleaf Border	109	NT5325
Lillingstone Dayrell Bucks	49	SP7039
Lillingstone Lovell Bucks	49	SP7140
Lillington Dorset	10	ST6212
Lilliput Dorset	12	SZ0489
Lilstock Somset	20	ST1645
Lilyhurst Shrops	60	SJ7413
Limbrick Lancs	81	SD6016
Limbury Beds	38	TL0724
Lime Street H & W	47	SO8130
Limebrook H & W	46	SO3766
Limefield Gt Man	81	SD8012
Limekilnburn Strath	116	NS7050
Limekilns Fife	117	NT0883
Limerigg Cent	116	NS8571
Limerstone IOW	13	SZ4482
Limestone Brae Nthumb	95	NY7949
Limington Somset	21	ST5422
Limmerhaugh Strath	107	NS6127
Limpenhoe Norfk	67	TG3903
Limpley Stoke Wilts	22	ST7860
Limpsfield Surrey	27	TQ4053
Limpsfield Chart Surrey	27	TQ4251
Linby Notts	75	SK5351
Linchmere W Susx	14	SU8630
Lincluden D & G	100	NX9677
Lincoln Lincs	76	SK9771
Lincomb H & W	47	SO8268
Lincombe Devon	7	SX7440
Lindal in Furness Cumb	86	SD2475
Lindale Cumb	87	SD4180
Lindfield W Susx	15	TQ3425
Lindford Hants	14	SU8036
Lindley W York	82	SE1217
Lindley Green N York	82	SE2248
Lindores Fife	126	NO2616
Lindow End Ches	79	SJ8178
Lindridge H & W	47	SO6769
Lindsell Essex	40	TL6427
Lindsey Suffk	54	TL9745
Lindsey Tye Suffk	54	TL9845
Liney Somset	21	ST3535
Linford Essex	40	TQ6779
Linford Hants	12	SU1806
Lingbob W York	82	SE0935
Lingdale Cleve	97	NZ6716
Lingen H & W	46	SO3667
Lingfield Surrey	15	TQ3843
Lingley Green Ches	78	SJ5588
Lingwood Norfk	67	TG3508
Linicro Highld	136	NG3966
Linkend H & W	47	SO8231
Linkenholt Hants	23	SU3657
Linkhill Kent	17	TQ8127
Linkinhorne Cnwll	5	SX3173
Linktown Fife	117	NT2790
Linkwood Gramp	141	NJ2361
Linley Shrops	59	SO3592
Linley Green H & W	47	SO6953
Linleygreen Shrops	60	SO6898
Linlithgow Loth	117	NS9977
Linshiels Nthumb	110	NT8906
Linsidemore Highld	146	NH5499
Linslade Beds	38	SP9125
Linstead Parva Suffk	55	TM3377
Linstock Cumb	93	NY4258
Linthurst H & W	60	SO9972
Linthwaite W York	82	SE1014
Lintlaw Border	119	NT8258
Lintmill Gramp	142	NJ5165
Linton Border	110	NT7726
Linton Cambs	53	TL5646
Linton Derbys	73	SK2716
Linton H & W	47	SO6625
Linton Kent	28	TQ7550
Linton N York	88	SD9962
Linton W York	83	SE3946
Linton Heath Derbys	73	SK2816
Linton Hill Gloucs	47	SO6624
Linton-on-Ouse N York	90	SE4860
Linwood Hants	12	SU1809
Linwood Lincs	76	TF1186
Linwood Strath	115	NS4464
Lional W Isls	154	NB5263
Lions Green E Susx	16	TQ5518
Liphook Hants	14	SU8431
Lipley Shrops	72	SJ7330
Liscard Mersyd	78	SJ2991
Liscombe Somset	19	SS8732
Liskeard Cnwll	5	SX2564
Liss Hants	14	SU7727
Liss Forest Hants	14	SU7828
Lissett Humb	91	TA1458
Lissington Lincs	76	TF1083
Liston Essex	54	TL8544
Lisvane S Glam	33	ST1883
Liswerry Gwent	34	ST3487
Litcham Norfk	66	TF8817
Litchard M Glam	33	SS9081
Litchborough Nhants	49	SP6354
Litchfield Hants	24	SU4653
Litherland Mersyd	78	SJ3397
Litlington Cambs	39	TL3142
Litlington E Susx	16	TQ5201
Little Abington Cambs	53	TL5349
Little Addington Nhants	51	SP9673
Little Airies D & G	99	NX4248
Little Almshoe Herts	39	TL2026
Little Alne Warwks	48	SP1461
Little Altcar Mersyd	78	SD3006
Little Amwell Herts	39	TL3511
Little Asby Cumb	87	NY6909
Little Aston Staffs	61	SK0900
Little Atherfield IOW	13	SZ4679
Little Ayton N York	90	NZ5610
Little Baddow Essex	40	TL7707
Little Badminton Avon	35	ST8084
Little Bampton Cumb	93	NY2755
Little Bardfield Essex	40	TL6531
Little Barford Beds	52	TL1756
Little Barningham Norfk	66	TG1333
Little Barrington Gloucs	36	SP2012
Little Barrow Ches	71	SJ4769
Little Barugh N York	90	SE7679
Little Bavington Nthumb	102	NY9878
Little Bayton Warwks	61	SP3585
Little Bealings Suffk	55	TM2247
Little Bedwyn Wilts	23	SU2866
Little Bentley Essex	41	TM1125
Little Berkhamsted Herts	39	TL2907
Little Billing Nhants	51	SP8061
Little Billington Beds	38	SP9322
Little Birch H & W	46	SO5130
Little Bispham Lancs	80	SD3141
Little Blakenham Suffk	54	TM1048
Little Blencow Cumb	93	NY4532
Little Bloxwich W Mids	60	SK0003
Little Bognor W Susx	14	TQ0020
Little Bolehill Derbys	73	SK2954
Little Bookham Surrey	26	TQ1254
Little Bourton Oxon	49	SP4544
Little Bowden Leics	50	SP7487
Little Bradley Suffk	53	TL6852
Little Brampton H & W	46	SO3061
Little Brampton Shrops	59	SO3681
Little Braxted Essex	40	TL8314
Little Brechin Tays	134	NO5862
Little Brickhill Bucks	38	SP9132
Little Bridgeford Staffs	72	SJ8727
Little Brington Nhants	49	SP6663
Little Bromley Essex	41	TM0928
Little Broughton Cumb	92	NY0731
Little Budworth Ches	71	SJ5965
Little Burstead Essex	40	TQ6692
Little Bytham Lincs	64	TF0118
Little Canfield Essex	40	TL5821
Little Carlton Lincs	77	TF3985
Little Carlton Notts	75	SK7757
Little Casterton Leics	64	TF0109
Little Catwick Humb	85	TA1244
Little Catworth Cambs	51	TL1072
Little Cawthorpe Lincs	77	TF3583
Little Chalfont Bucks	26	SU9997
Little Charlinch Somset	20	ST2437
Little Chart Kent	28	TQ9446
Little Chatfield Wilts	22	ST8563
Little Chesterford Essex	39	TL5141
Little Cheveney Kent	28	TQ7243
Little Cheverell Wilts	22	ST9953
Little Chishill Cambs	39	TL4137
Little Clacton Essex	41	TM1618
Little Clanfield Oxon	36	SP2701
Little Clifton Cumb	92	NY0528
Little Coates Humb	85	TA2408
Little Comberton H & W	47	SO9643
Little Common E Susx	17	TQ7107
Little Comp Kent	27	TQ6356
Little Compton Warwks	48	SP2630
Little Corby Cumb	93	NY4757
Little Cornard Suffk	54	TL9039
Little Cowarne H & W	46	SO6051
Little Coxwell Oxon	36	SU2893
Little Crakehall N York	89	SE2390
Little Cransley Nhants	51	SP8376
Little Cressingham Norfk	66	TF8700
Little Crosby Mersyd	78	SD3201
Little Crosthwaite Cumb	93	NY2327
Little Cubley Derbys	73	SK1537
Little Dalby Leics	63	SK7714
Little Dens Gramp	143	NK0643
Little Dewchurch H & W	46	SO5231
Little Ditton Cambs	53	TL6658
Little Doward H & W	34	SO5416
Little Driffield Humb	91	TA0058
Little Dunham Norfk	66	TF8612
Little Dunkeld Tays	125	NO0342
Little Dunmow Essex	40	TL6521
Little Durnford Wilts	23	SU1234
Little Eaton Derbys	62	SK3641
Little Ellingham Norfk	66	TM0099
Little Elm Somset	22	ST7146
Little Everdon Nhants	49	SP5957
Little Eversden Cambs	52	TL3753
Little Faringdon S York	36	SP2201
Little Fencote N York	89	SE2893
Little Fenton N York	83	SE5235
Little Fransham Norfk	66	TF9011
Little Gaddesden Herts	38	SP9913
Little Garway H & W	46	SO4424
Little Gidding Cambs	52	TL1282
Little Glemham Suffk	55	TM3458
Little Gorsley H & W	47	SO6924
Little Gransden Cambs	52	TL2755
Little Green Notts	63	SK7243
Little Green Somset	22	ST7248
Little Grimsby Lincs	77	TF3291
Little Gringley Notts	75	SK7380
Little Habton N York	90	SE7477
Little Hadham Herts	39	TL4322
Little Hale Lincs	64	TF1441
Little Hallam Derbys	62	SK4640
Little Hallingbury Essex	39	TL5017
Little Hanford Dorset	11	ST8411
Little Harrowden Nhants	51	SP8771
Little Hartlip Kent	28	TQ8464
Little Haseley Oxon	37	SP6400
Little Hatfield Humb	85	TA1743
Little Hautbois Norfk	67	TG2521
Little Haven Dyfed	30	SM8512
Little Hay Staffs	61	SK1102
Little Hayfield Derbys	74	SK0388
Little Haywood Staffs	73	SK0021
Little Heath Berks	24	SU6573
Little Heath Staffs	72	SJ8917
Little Heath W Mids	61	SP3482
Little Hereford H & W	46	SO5568
Little Hermitage Kent	28	TQ7170
Little Horkesley Essex	40	TL9532
Little Hormead Herts	39	TL4028
Little Horsted E Susx	16	TQ4718
Little Horton W York	82	SE1531
Little Horton Wilts	23	SU0462
Little Horwood Bucks	38	SP7930
Little Houghton Nhants	51	SP8059
Little Houghton S York	83	SE4205
Little Hucklow Derbys	74	SK1678
Little Hulton Gt Man	79	SD7203
Little Hungerford Berks	24	SU5173
Little Hutton N York	89	SE4576
Little Ingestre Staffs	72	SJ9824
Little Irchester Nhants	51	SP9066
Little Kelk Humb	91	TA0959
Little Keyford Somset	22	ST7746
Little Kimble Bucks	38	SP8207
Little Kineton Warwks	48	SP3350
Little Kingshill Bucks	26	SU8999
Little Knox D & G	100	NX8060
Little Langdale Cumb	86	NY3103
Little Langford Wilts	23	SU0436
Little Lashbrook Devon	18	SS4007
Little Laver Essex	39	TL5409
Little Leigh Ches	71	SJ6175
Little Leighs Essex	40	TL7117
Little Lever Gt Man	79	SD7507
Little Linford Bucks	38	SP8444
Little Linton Cambs	53	TL5547
Little Load Somset	21	ST4724
Little London Cambs	65	TL4196
Little London E Susx	16	TQ5620
Little London Essex	39	TL4729
Little London Essex	53	TL6835
Little London Gloucs	35	SO7018
Little London Hants	23	SU3749
Little London Hants	24	SU6259
Little London Lincs	64	TF2321
Little London Lincs	77	TF3374
Little London Lincs	65	TF4323
Little London Norfk	65	TF5621
Little London Oxon	37	SP6412
Little London Powys	58	SO0488
Little London W York	82	SE2039
Little Longstone Derbys	74	SK1871
Little Madeley Staffs	72	SJ7745
Little Malvern H & W	47	SO7640
Little Mancot Clwyd	71	SJ3266
Little Maplestead Essex	54	TL8234
Little Marcle H & W	47	SO6736
Little Marland Devon	18	SS5012
Little Marlow Bucks	26	SU8787
Little Massingham Norfk	65	TF7824
Little Melton Norfk	66	TG1607
Little Mill Gwent	34	SO3203
Little Milton Oxon	37	SP6100
Little Missenden Bucks	26	SU9299
Little Mongham Kent	29	TR3351
Little Moor Somset	21	ST3232
Little Musgrave Cumb	94	NY7612
Little Ness Shrops	59	SJ4019
Little Neston Ches	71	SJ2976
Little Newcastle Dyfed	30	SM9829
Little Newsham Dur	96	NZ1217
Little Norton Somset	10	ST4715
Little Norton Staffs	60	SK0207
Little Oakley Essex	41	TM2129
Little Oakley Nhants	51	SP8985
Little Odell Beds	51	SP9557
Little Offley Herts	38	TL1328
Little Onn Staffs	72	SJ8315
Little Ormside Cumb	94	NY7016
Little Orton Cumb	93	NY3555
Little Ouseburn N York	89	SE4460
Little Oxendon Nhants	50	SP7283
Little Packington Warwks	61	SP2184
Little Pannell Wilts	22	SU0053
Little Pattenden Kent	28	TQ7445
Little Paxton Cambs	52	TL1862
Little Petherick Cnwll	4	SW9172
Little Plumpton Lancs	80	SD3832
Little Plumstead Norfk	67	TG3112
Little Ponton Lincs	63	SK9232
Little Posbrook Hants	13	SU5304
Little Potheridge Devon	19	SS5214
Little Preston Nhants	49	SP5854
Little Preston W York	83	SE3930
Little Raveley Cambs	52	TL2579
Little Reedness Humb	84	SE8022
Little Ribston N York	83	SE3853
Little Rissington Gloucs	36	SP1819
Little Rollright Oxon	48	SP2930
Little Rowsley Derbys	74	SK2566
Little Ryburgh Norfk	66	TF9628
Little Ryle Nthumb	111	NU0111
Little Ryton Shrops	59	SJ4803
Little Salkeld Cumb	94	NY5636
Little Sampford Essex	40	TL6533
Little Sandhurst Berks	25	SU8262
Little Saredon Staffs	60	SJ9407
Little Saughall Ches	71	SJ3768
Little Saxham Suffk	54	TL8063
Little Scatwell Highld	139	NH3856
Little Sessay N York	89	SE4674
Little Shelford Cambs	53	TL4551
Little Silver Devon	9	SS8601
Little Silver Devon	9	SS9109
Little Singleton Lancs	80	SD3739
Little Skipwith N York	83	SE6538
Little Smeaton N York	83	SE5216
Little Snoring Norfk	66	TF9532
Little Sodbury Avon	35	ST7582
Little Sodbury End Avon	35	ST7483
Little Somborne Hants	23	SU3832
Little Somerford Wilts	35	ST9684
Little Soudley Shrops	72	SJ7128
Little Stainforth N York	88	SD8166
Little Stainton Dur	96	NZ3420
Little Stanney Ches	71	SJ4174
Little Staughton Beds	51	TL1062
Little Steeping Lincs	77	TF4362
Little Stonham Suffk	54	TM1160
Little Stretton Leics	50	SK6600
Little Stretton Shrops	59	SO4491
Little Strickland Cumb	94	NY5619
Little Stukeley Cambs	52	TL2175
Little Sugnall Staffs	72	SJ8031
Little Sutton Ches	71	SJ3776
Little Sutton Shrops	59	SO5182
Little Swinburne Nthumb	102	NY9477
Little Sypland D & G	99	NX7253
Little Tew Oxon	48	SP3828
Little Tey Essex	40	TL8923
Little Thetford Cambs	53	TL5376
Little Thirkleby N York	89	SE4778
Little Thornage Norfk	66	TG0538
Little Thornton Lancs	80	SD3541
Little Thorpe Dur	96	NZ4242
Little Thurlow Suffk	53	TL6751
Little Thurlow Green Suffk	53	TL6851
Little Thurrock Essex	27	TQ6277
Little Torrington Devon	18	SS4916
Little Totham Essex	40	TL8811
Little Town Ches	79	SJ6494
Little Town Cumb	93	NY2319
Little Town Lancs	81	SD6635
Little Twycross Leics	62	SK3405
Little Urswick Cumb	86	SD2673
Little Wakering Essex	40	TQ9388
Little Walden Essex	39	TL5441
Little Waldingfield Suffk	54	TL9245
Little Walsingham Norfk	66	TF9337
Little Waltham Essex	40	TL7012
Little Warley Essex	40	TQ6090
Little Washbourne Gloucs	47	SO9833
Little Weighton Humb	84	SE9833
Little Weldon Nhants	51	SP9289
Little Welnetham Suffk	54	TL8859
Little Welton Lincs	77	TF3087
Little Wenham Suffk	54	TM0839
Little Wenlock Shrops	59	SJ6406
Little Weston Somset	21	ST6225
Little Whitefield IOW	13	SZ5889
Little Whittington Nthumb	102	NY9869
Little Wilbraham Cambs	53	TL5458
Little Witcombe Gloucs	35	SO9115
Little Witley H & W	47	SO7863
Little Wittenham Oxon	37	SU5693
Little Wolford Warwks	48	SP2635
Little Woodcote Surrey	27	TQ2861
Little Wratting Suffk	53	TL6847
Little Wymington Beds	51	SP9565
Little Wymondley Herts	39	TL2127
Little Wyrley Staffs	60	SK0105
Little Wytheford Shrops	59	SJ5619
Little Yeldham Essex	53	TL7839
Littlebeck N York	90	NZ8804
Littleborough Devon	19	SS8210
Littleborough Gt Man	81	SD9316
Littleborough Notts	75	SK8282
Littlebourne Kent	29	TR2057
Littlebredy Dorset	10	SY5889
Littlebury Essex	39	TL5139
Littlebury Green Essex	39	TL4838
Littlecott Wilts	23	SU1352
Littledean Gloucs	35	SO6713
Littledown Hants	23	SU3457
Littleham Devon	18	SS4323
Littleham Devon	9	SY0381
Littlehampton W Susx	14	TQ0201
Littleharle Tower Nthumb	103	NZ0183
Littlehempston Devon	7	SX8162
Littlehoughton Nthumb	111	NU2216
Littlemill Gramp	134	NO3295
Littlemill Highld	140	NH9150
Littlemoor Derbys	74	SK3663
Littlemore Oxon	37	SP5302
Littleover Derbys	62	SK3334
Littleport Cambs	53	TL5686
Littleport Bridge Cambs	53	TL5787
Littler Ches	71	SJ6366
Littlestone-on-Sea Kent	17	TR0824
Littlethorpe Leics	50	SP5496
Littlethorpe N York	89	SE3269
Littleton Avon	21	ST5563
Littleton Ches	71	SJ4466
Littleton D & G	99	NX6355
Littleton Dorset	11	ST8904
Littleton Hants	24	SU4532
Littleton Somset	21	ST4930
Littleton Surrey	25	SU9847
Littleton Surrey	26	TQ0668
Littleton Tays	126	NO3350
Littleton Drew Wilts	35	ST8380
Littleton-on-Severn Avon	34	ST5989
Littletown Dur	96	NZ3343
Littletown IOW	13	SZ5390
Littlewick Green Berks	37	SU8379
Littlewindsor Dorset	10	ST4304

Littlewood

Long Meadowend

Littlewood Staffs 60 SJ9807
Littleworth Bucks 38 SP8823
Littleworth H & W 47 SO8850
Littleworth H & W 47 SO9962
Littleworth Oxon 36 SU3197
Littleworth Staffs 72 SJ9323
Littleworth Staffs 60 SK0111
Littleworth W Susx 15 TQ1920
Littleworth Common Bucks 26 SU9386
Littleworth End Cambs 52 TL2266
Littley Green Essex 40 TL6917
Litton Derbys 74 SK1675
Litton N York 88 SD9074
Litton Somset 21 ST5954
Litton Cheney Dorset 10 SY5490
Liurbost W Isls 154 NB3725
Liverpool Mersyd 78 SJ3490
Liversedge W York 82 SE1923
Liverton Cleve 97 NZ7115
Liverton Devon 7 SX8075
Liverton Mines Cleve 97 NZ7117
Liverton Street Kent 28 TQ8750
Livingston Loth 117 NT0668
Livingston Village Loth 117 NT0366
Lixton Devon 7 SX6950
Lixwm Clwyd 70 SJ1671
Lizard Cnwll 2 SW7012
Llaingoch Gwynd 68 SH2382
Llaithddu Powys 58 SO0680
Llan Powys 57 SH8800
Llan-y-pwll Clwyd 71 SJ3752
Llanaber Gwynd 57 SH6018
Llanaelhaearn Gwynd 56 SH3844
Llanafan Dyfed 43 SN6872
Llanafan-fechan Powys 45 SN9750
Llanallgo Gwynd 68 SH5085
Llanarmon Gwynd 56 SH4239
Llanarmon Dyffryn Ceiriog Clwyd 58 SJ1532
Llanarmon-yn-Ial Clwyd 70 SJ1956
Llanarth Dyfed 42 SN4257
Llanarth Gwent 34 SO3710
Llanarthne Dyfed 32 SN5320
Llanasa Clwyd 70 SJ1081
Llanbabo Gwynd 68 SH3787
Llanbadarn Fawr Dyfed 43 SN6081
Llanbadarn Fynydd Powys 45 SO0977
Llanbadarn-y-garreg Powys 45 SO1148
Llanbadoc Gwent 34 ST3799
Llanbadrig Gwynd 68 SH3794
Llanbeder Gwent 34 ST3890
Llanbedr Gwynd 57 SH5826
Llanbedr Powys 45 SO1446
Llanbedr Powys 34 SO2320
Llanbedr-Dyffryn-Clwyd Clwyd 70 SJ1459
Llanbedr-y-cennin Gwynd 69 SH7669
Llanbedrgoch Gwynd 68 SH5180
Llanbedrog Gwynd 56 SH3231
Llanberis Gwynd 69 SH5760
Llanbethery S Glam 20 ST0369
Llanbister Powys 45 SO1173
Llanblethian S Glam 33 SS9873
Llanboidy Dyfed 31 SN2123
Llanbradach M Glam 33 ST1490
Llanbrynmair Powys 57 SH8902
Llancadle S Glam 20 ST0368
Llancarfan S Glam 33 ST0470
Llancayo Gwent 34 SO3603
Llancillo H & W 46 SO3625
Llancloudy H & W 34 SO4921
Llancynfelyn Dyfed 43 SN6492
Llandaff S Glam 33 ST1577
Llandanwg Gwynd 57 SH5728
Llandawke Dyfed 31 SN2811
Llanddaniel Fab Gwynd 68 SH4970
Llanddarog Dyfed 32 SN5016
Llanddeiniol Dyfed 43 SN5571
Llanddeiniolen Gwynd 69 SH5465
Llandderfel Gwynd 58 SH9837
Llanddeusant Dyfed 44 SN7724
Llanddeusant Gwynd 68 SH3485
Llanddew Powys 45 SO0530
Llanddewi W Glam 32 SS4588
Llanddewi Brefi Dyfed 44 SN6655
Llanddewi Rhydderch Gwent 34 SO3512
Llanddewi Velfrey Dyfed 31 SN1415
Llanddewi Ystradenni Powys 45 SO1068
Llanddewi'r Cwm Powys 45 SO0348
Llanddoget Gwynd 69 SH8063
Llanddona Gwynd 69 SH5779
Llanddowror Dyfed 31 SN2514
Llanddulas Clwyd 70 SH9178
Llanddwywe Gwynd 57 SH5822
Llanddyfnan Gwynd 68 SH5078
Llandecwyn Gwynd 57 SH6337
Llandefaelog Powys 45 SO0332
Llandefaelogtrer-graig Powys 45 SO1229
Llandefalle Powys 45 SO1035
Llandegai Gwynd 69 SH5971
Llandegfan Gwynd 69 SH5674
Llandegla Clwyd 70 SJ2051
Llandegley Powys 45 SO1463
Llandegveth Gwent 34 ST3395
Llandegwning Gwynd 56 SH2629
Llandeilo Dyfed 32 SN6222
Llandeilo Graban Powys 45 SO0944
Llandeilo'r Fan Powys 45 SN8934
Llandeloy Dyfed 30 SM8626
Llandenny Gwent 34 SO4104
Llandevaud Gwent 34 ST4090
Llandevenny Gwent 34 ST4186
Llandinabo H & W 46 SO5128
Llandinam Powys 58 SO0288
Llandissilio Dyfed 31 SN1221
Llandogo Gwent 34 SO5203
Llandough S Glam 33 SS9972
Llandough S Glam 33 ST1673
Llandovery Dyfed 44 SN7634
Llandow S Glam 33 SS9473
Llandre Dyfed 43 SN6286
Llandre Dyfed 44 SN6741
Llandre Isaf Dyfed 31 SN1328
Llandrillo Clwyd 58 SJ0337
Llandrillo-yn-Rhos Clwyd 69 SH8380
Llandrindod Wells Powys 45 SO0561
Llandrinio Powys 58 SJ2817
Llandudno Gwynd 69 SH7882
Llandudno Junction Gwynd 69 SH7977
Llandudwen Gwynd 56 SH2736
Llandulas Powys 45 SN8841
Llandwrog Gwynd 68 SH4555
Llandybie Dyfed 32 SN6115
Llandyfaelog Dyfed 31 SN4111
Llandyfan Dyfed 32 SN6417
Llandyfriog Dyfed 31 SN3341
Llandyfrydog Gwynd 68 SH4485
Llandygwydd Dyfed 31 SN2443
Llandynan Clwyd 70 SJ1845
Llandyrnog Clwyd 70 SJ1065
Llandyssil Powys 58 SO1995
Llandysul Dyfed 31 SN4140
Llanedeyrn S Glam 33 ST2181
Llanedi Dyfed 32 SN5806
Llaneglwys Powys 45 SO0538
Llanegryn Gwynd 57 SH6005
Llanegwad Dyfed 32 SN5221
Llaneilian Gwynd 68 SH4692
Llanelian-yn-Rhos Clwyd 69 SH8676
Llanelidan Clwyd 70 SJ1150
Llanelieu Powys 45 SO1834
Llanellen Gwent 34 SO3010
Llanelli Dyfed 32 SN5000
Llanelltyd Gwynd 57 SH7119
Llanelly Gwent 34 SO2314
Llanelwedd Powys 45 SO0451
Llanenddwyn Gwynd 57 SH5823
Llanengan Gwynd 56 SH2926
Llanerch Gwynd 57 SH8816
Llanerch Powys 59 SO3093
Llanerchymedd Gwynd 68 SH4184
Llanerfyl Powys 58 SJ0309
Llanfachraeth Gwynd 68 SH3182
Llanfachreth Gwynd 57 SH7522
Llanfaelog Gwynd 68 SH3373
Llanfaelrhys Gwynd 56 SH2026
Llanfaenor Gwent 34 SO4317
Llanfaes Gwynd 69 SH6077
Llanfaes Powys 45 SO0328
Llanfaethlu Gwynd 68 SH3186
Llanfair Gwynd 57 SH5728
Llanfair Caereinion Powys 58 SJ1006
Llanfair Clydogau Dyfed 44 SN6251
Llanfair Dyffryn Clwyd Clwyd 70 SJ1355
Llanfair Kilgeddin Gwent 34 SO3506
Llanfair P G Gwynd 68 SH5271
Llanfair Talhaiarn Clwyd 70 SH9270
Llanfair Waterdine Shrops 45 SO2376
Llanfair-is-gaer Gwynd 68 SH5065
Llanfair-Nant-Gwyn Dyfed 31 SN1637
Llanfair-y-Cwmmwd Gwynd 68 SH4466
Llanfair-yn-Neubwll Gwynd 68 SH3076
Llanfairfechan Gwynd 69 SH6874
Llanfairynghornwy Gwynd 68 SH3290
Llanfallteg Dyfed 31 SN1520
Llanfallteg West Dyfed 31 SN1419
Llanfarian Dyfed 43 SN5877
Llanfechain Powys 58 SJ1920
Llanfechelli Gwynd 68 SH3791
Llanferres Clwyd 70 SJ1860
Llanfflewyn Gwynd 68 SH3588
Llanfigael Gwynd 68 SH3282
Llanfihangel Glyn Myfyr Clwyd 70 SH9849
Llanfihangel Nant Bran Powys 45 SN9434
Llanfihangel Rhydithon Powys 45 SO1566
Llanfihangel Rogiet Gwent 34 ST4587
Llanfihangel Tal-y-llyn Powys 45 SO1128
Llanfihangel yn Nhowyn Gwynd 68 SH3277
Llanfihangel-ar-Arth Dyfed 31 SN4540
Llanfihangel-nant-Melan Powys 45 SO1758
Llanfihangel-uwch-Gwili Dyfed 32 SN4922
Llanfihangel-y-Creuddyn Dyfed 43 SN6675
Llanfihangel-y-pennant Gwynd 57 SH5244
Llanfihangel-y-pennant Gwynd 57 SH6708
Llanfihangel-y-traethau Gwynd 57 SH5934
Llanfihangel-yng-Ngwynfa Powys 58 SJ0816
Llanfilo Powys 45 SO1132
Llanfoist Gwent 34 SO2813
Llanfor Gwynd 58 SH9336
Llanfrechfa Gwent 34 ST3293
Llanfrothen Gwynd 57 SH6241
Llanfrynach Powys 45 SO0725
Llanfwrog Clwyd 70 SJ1157
Llanfwrog Gwynd 68 SH3084
Llanfyllin Powys 58 SJ1419
Llanfynydd Clwyd 70 SJ2856
Llanfynydd Dyfed 44 SN5527
Llanfyrnach Dyfed 31 SN2231
Llangadfan Powys 58 SJ0110
Llangadog Dyfed 31 SN4207
Llangadog Dyfed 44 SN7028
Llangadwaladr Clwyd 58 SJ1830
Llangadwaladr Gwynd 68 SH3869
Llangaffo Gwynd 68 SH4468
Llangain Dyfed 31 SN3815
Llangammarch Wells Powys 45 SN9346
Llangan S Glam 33 SS9577
Llangarron H & W 34 SO5220
Llangasty-Talyllin Powys 45 SO1326
Llangathen Dyfed 32 SN5822
Llangattock Powys 33 SO2117
Llangattock Lingoed Gwent 34 SO3620
Llangattock-Vibon-Avel Gwent 34 SO4515
Llangedwyn Clwyd 58 SJ1824
Llangefni Gwynd 68 SH4675
Llangeinor M Glam 33 SS9187
Llangeinwen Gwynd 68 SH4465
Llangeitho Dyfed 44 SN6259
Llangeler Dyfed 31 SN3739
Llangelynin Gwynd 57 SH5707
Llangendeirne Dyfed 32 SN4513
Llangennech Dyfed 32 SN5601
Llangennith W Glam 31 SS4291
Llangenny Powys 34 SO2417
Llangernyw Clwyd 69 SH8767
Llangian Gwynd 56 SH2928
Llangiwg W Glam 32 SN7205
Llangloffan Dyfed 30 SM9032
Llanglydwen Dyfed 31 SN1826
Llangoed Gwynd 69 SH6079
Llangoedmor Dyfed 42 SN2046
Llangollen Clwyd 70 SJ2141
Llangolman Dyfed 31 SN1127
Llangors Powys 45 SO1327
Llangovan Gwent 34 SO4505
Llangower Gwynd 58 SH9032
Llangranog Dyfed 42 SN3154
Llangristiolus Gwynd 68 SH4373
Llangrove H & W 34 SO5219
Llangua Gwent 46 SO3925
Llangunllo Powys 45 SO2171
Llangunnor Dyfed 31 SN4320
Llangurig Powys 43 SN9079
Llangwm Clwyd 70 SH9644
Llangwm Dyfed 30 SM9909
Llangwm Gwent 34 ST4299
Llangwm-isaf Gwent 34 SO4300
Llangwnnadl Gwynd 56 SH2033
Llangwyfan Clwyd 70 SJ1166
Llangwyllog Gwynd 68 SH4379
Llangwyryfon Dyfed 43 SN5970
Llangybi Dyfed 44 SN6053
Llangybi Gwent 34 ST3796
Llangybi Gwynd 56 SH4341
Llangyfelach W Glam 32 SS6498
Llangynhafal Clwyd 70 SJ1263
Llangynidr Powys 33 SO1519
Llangynin Dyfed 31 SN2517
Llangynllo Dyfed 42 SN3544
Llangynog Dyfed 31 SN3314
Llangynog Powys 58 SJ0526
Llangynog Powys 45 SO0145
Llangynwyd M Glam 33 SS8588
Llanhamlach Powys 45 SO0926
Llanharan M Glam 33 ST0083
Llanharry M Glam 33 ST0080
Llanhennock Gwent 34 ST3592
Llanhilleth Gwent 33 SO2100
Llanidan Gwynd 68 SH4966
Llanidloes Powys 58 SN9584
Llaniestyn Gwynd 56 SH2733
Llanigon Powys 45 SO2139
Llanilar Dyfed 43 SN6275
Llanilid M Glam 33 SS9781
Llanina Dyfed 42 SN4059
Llanio Dyfed 44 SN6457
Llanishen Gwent 34 SO4703
Llanishen S Glam 33 ST1781
Llanllechid Gwynd 69 SH6268
Llanlleonfel Powys 45 SN9350
Llanllowell Gwent 34 ST3998
Llanllugan Powys 58 SJ0502
Llanllwch Dyfed 31 SN3818
Llanllwchaiarn Powys 58 SO1292
Llanllwni Dyfed 44 SN4741
Llanllyfni Gwynd 68 SH4751
Llanmadoc W Glam 32 SS4493
Llanmaes S Glam 20 SS9769
Llanmartin Gwent 34 ST3989
Llanmerewig Powys 58 SO1593
Llanmihangel S Glam 33 SS9871
Llanmiloe Dyfed 31 SN2408
Llanmorlais W Glam 32 SS5294
Llannefydd Clwyd 70 SH9870
Llannon Dyfed 32 SN5308
Llannor Gwynd 56 SH3537
Llanon Dyfed 42 SN5166
Llanover Gwent 34 SO3109
Llanpumsaint Dyfed 31 SN4229
Llanrhaeadr-ym-Mochnant Clwyd 58 SJ1226
Llanrhidian W Glam 32 SS4992
Llanrhos Gwynd 69 SH7980
Llanrhychwyn Gwynd 69 SH7761
Llanrhyddlad Gwynd 68 SH3389
Llanrhystud Dyfed 43 SN5369
Llanrian Dyfed 30 SM8231
Llanrothal H & W 34 SO4718
Llanrug Gwynd 69 SH5363
Llanrumney S Glam 34 ST2280
Llanrwst Gwynd 69 SH8061
Llansadurnen Dyfed 31 SN2810
Llansadwrn Dyfed 44 SN6931
Llansadwrn Gwynd 69 SH5575
Llansaint Dyfed 31 SN3808
Llansamlet W Glam 32 SS6897
Llansanffraid Glan Conwy Gwynd 69 SH8076
Llansannan Clwyd 70 SH9365
Llansannor S Glam 33 SS9977
Llansantffraed Powys 45 SO1223
Llansantffraed-Cwmdeuddwr Powys 45 SN9667
Llansantffraed-in-Elvel Powys 45 SO0954
Llansantffraid Dyfed 42 SN5167
Llansantffraid-ym-Mechain Powys 58 SJ2220
Llansawel Dyfed 44 SN6136
Llansilin Clwyd 58 SJ2128
Llansoy Gwent 34 SO4402
Llanspyddid Powys 45 SO0128
Llanstadwell Dyfed 30 SM9404
Llansteffan Dyfed 31 SN3510
Llanstephan Powys 45 SO1141
Llantarnam Gwent 34 ST3093
Llanteg Dyfed 31 SN1810
Llanthewy Skirrid Gwent 34 SO3416
Llanthony Gwent 46 SO2827
Llantilio Pertholey Gwent 34 SO3116
Llantilio-Crossenny Gwent 34 SO3914
Llantrisant Gwent 34 ST3996
Llantrisant Gwynd 68 SH3584
Llantrisant M Glam 33 ST0483
Llantrithyd S Glam 33 ST0472
Llantwit Fardre M Glam 33 ST0886
Llantwit Major S Glam 20 SS9668
Llantysilio Clwyd 70 SJ1943
Llanuwchllyn Gwynd 57 SH8730
Llanvaches Gwent 34 ST4391
Llanvair Discoed Gwent 34 ST4492
Llanvapley Gwent 34 SO3614
Llanvetherine Gwent 34 SO3617
Llanveynoe H & W 46 SO3031
Llanvihangel Crucorney Gwent 34 SO3220
Llanvihangel Gobion Gwent 34 SO3409
Llanvihangel-Ystern-Llewern Gwent 34 SO4313
Llanwarne H & W 46 SO5027
Llanwddyn Powys 58 SJ0219
Llanwenarth Gwent 34 SO2714
Llanwenog Dyfed 44 SN4945
Llanwern Gwent 34 ST3688
Llanwinio Dyfed 31 SN2626
Llanwnda Dyfed 30 SM9339
Llanwnda Gwynd 68 SH4758
Llanwnnen Dyfed 44 SN5347
Llanwnog Powys 58 SO0293
Llanwonno M Glam 33 ST0395
Llanwrda Dyfed 44 SN7131
Llanwrin Powys 57 SH7803
Llanwrthwl Powys 45 SN9763
Llanwrtyd Powys 45 SN8647
Llanwrtyd Wells Powys 45 SN8846
Llanwyddelan Powys 58 SJ0801
Llanyblodwel Shrops 58 SJ2323
Llanybri Dyfed 31 SN3312
Llanybydder Dyfed 44 SN5244
Llanycefn Dyfed 31 SN0923
Llanychaer Bridge Dyfed 30 SM9835
Llanycrwys Dyfed 44 SN6445
Llanymawddwy Gwynd 58 SH9019
Llanymynech Shrops 58 SJ2621
Llanynghenedl Gwynd 68 SH3181
Llanynis Powys 45 SN9950
Llanynys Clwyd 70 SJ1062
Llanyre Powys 45 SO0462
Llanystumdwy Gwynd 56 SH4738
Llanywern Powys 45 SO1028
Llawhaden Dyfed 31 SN0717
Llawnt Shrops 58 SJ2430
Llawryglyn Powys 58 SN9291
Llay Clwyd 71 SJ3355
Llechcynfarwy Gwynd 68 SH3880
Llechfaen Powys 45 SO0828
Llechryd Dyfed 31 SN2143
Llechylched Gwynd 68 SH3476
Lledrod Dyfed 43 SN6470
Llidiadnenog Dyfed 44 SN5437
Llidiardau Gwynd 57 SH8738
Llidiart-y-parc Clwyd 70 SJ1143
Llithfaen Gwynd 56 SH3542
Lloc Clwyd 70 SJ1376
Llong Clwyd 70 SJ2662
Llowes Powys 45 SO1941
Llwydcoed M Glam 33 SN9904
Llwydiarth Powys 58 SJ0315
Llwyn Clwyd 70 SJ0864
Llwyn-drain Dyfed 31 SN2634
Llwyn-du Gwent 34 SO2816
Llwyn-on M Glam 33 SO0111
Llwyn-y-brain Dyfed 31 SN1914
Llwyn-y-Groes Dyfed 44 SN5956
Llwyncelyn Dyfed 42 SN4459
Llwyndafydd Dyfed 42 SN3755
Llwynderw Powys 58 SJ2104
Llwyndyrys Gwynd 56 SH3740
Llwyngwril Gwynd 57 SH5909
Llwynhendy Dyfed 32 SS5399
Llwynmawr Clwyd 58 SJ2237
Llwynypia M Glam 33 SS9993
Llyn-y-pandy Clwyd 70 SJ2065
Llynclys Shrops 58 SJ2824
Llynfaes Gwynd 68 SH4178
Llys-y-fran Dyfed 30 SN0424
Llysfaen Clwyd 69 SH8977
Llyswen Dyfed 44 SN4661
Llyswen Powys 45 SO1337
Llysworney S Glam 33 SS9673
Llywel Powys 45 SN8630
Load Brook S York 74 SK2788
Loan Cent 117 NS9675
Loanend Nthumb 119 NT9450
Loanhead Loth 117 NT2865
Loaningfoot D & G 92 NX9655
Loans Strath 106 NS3431
Lobb Devon 18 SS4737
Lobhillcross Devon 5 SX4686
Loch Baghasdail W Isls 154 NF7919
Loch Euphoirt W Isls 154 NF8563
Loch Katrine Pier Cent 124 NN4907
Loch Loyal Lodge Highld 149 NC6146
Loch Maree Hotel Highld 144 NG9170
Loch nam Madadh W Isls 154 NF9169
Lochailort Highld 129 NM7682
Lochaline Highld 121 NM6744
Lochans D & G 98 NX0656
Locharbriggs D & G 100 NX9980
Lochavich Strath 122 NM9415
Lochawe Strath 123 NN1227
Lochboisdale W Isls 154 NF7919
Lochbuie Strath 121 NM6025
Lochcarron Highld 138 NG8939
Lochdon Strath 122 NM7233
Lochdonhead Strath 122 NM7233
Lochead Strath 113 NR7778
Lochearnhead Cent 124 NN5823
Lochee Tays 126 NO3731
Locheilside Station Highld 130 NM9978
Lochend Highld 140 NH5937
Locheport W Isls 154 NF8563
Lochfoot D & G 100 NX8973
Lochgair Strath 114 NR9290
Lochgelly Fife 117 NT1893
Lochgilphead Strath 113 NR8688
Lochgoilhead Strath 114 NN2001
Lochieheads Fife 126 NO2513
Lochill Gramp 141 NJ2964
Lochindorb Lodge Highld 140 NH9635
Lochinver Highld 145 NC0922
Lochluichart Highld 139 NH3363
Lochmaben D & G 100 NY0882
Lochmaddy W Isls 154 NF9169
Lochore Fife 117 NT1796
Lochranza Strath 105 NR9350
Lochside Gramp 135 NO7364
Lochside Highld 140 NH8152
Lochton Strath 98 NX2579
Lochty Fife 127 NO5208
Lochty Tays 134 NO5362
Lochuisge Highld 122 NM7955
Lochwinnoch Strath 115 NS3559
Lochwood D & G 100 NY0896
Lockengate Cnwll 4 SX0361
Lockerbie D & G 100 NY1381
Lockeridge Wilts 23 SU1467
Lockerley Hants 23 SU3025
Locking Avon 21 ST3659
Lockington Humb 84 SE9947
Lockington Leics 62 SK4627
Lockleywood Shrops 72 SJ6928
Locks Heath Hants 13 SU5107
Locksbottom Gt Lon 27 TQ4265
Locksgreen IOW 13 SZ4490
Lockton N York 90 SE8489
Loddington Leics 63 SK7902
Loddington Nhants 51 SP8178
Loddiswell Devon 7 SX7248
Loddon Norfk 67 TM3698
Lode Cambs 53 TL5362
Lode Heath W Mids 61 SP1580
Loders Dorset 10 SY4994
Lodge Green W Mids 61 SP2583
Lodsworth W Susx 14 SU9223
Lofhouse Gate W York 83 SE3324
Lofthouse N York 89 SE1073
Lofthouse W York 83 SE3325
Loftus Cleve 97 NZ7218
Logan Strath 107 NS5820
Loganbeck Cumb 86 SD1890
Loganlea Loth 117 NS9762
Loggerheads Staffs 72 SJ7336
Logie Fife 126 NO4020
Logie Gramp 141 NJ0150
Logie Tays 135 NO6963
Logie Coldstone Gramp 134 NJ4304
Logie Pert Tays 135 NO6664
Logierait Tays 125 NN9752
Logierieve Gramp 143 NJ9127
Login Dyfed 31 SN1623
Lolworth Cambs 52 TL3664
Lon-las W Glam 32 SS7097
Lonbain Highld 137 NG6852
Londesborough Humb 84 SE8645
London Gt Lon 27 TQ2879
London Apprentice Cnwll 3 SX0049
London Beach Kent 28 TQ8836
London Colney Herts 39 TL1803
Londonderry N York 89 SE3087
Londonthorpe Lincs 63 SK9537
Londubh Highld 144 NG8680
Long Ashton Avon 34 ST5570
Long Bank H & W 60 SO7674
Long Bennington Lincs 63 SK8344
Long Bredy Dorset 10 SY5690
Long Buckby Nhants 50 SP6367
Long Cause Devon 7 SX7961
Long Clawson Leics 63 SK7227
Long Common Hants 13 SU5014
Long Compton Staffs 72 SJ8522
Long Compton Warwks 48 SP2832
Long Crendon Bucks 37 SP6908
Long Crichel Dorset 11 ST9710
Long Ditton Surrey 26 TQ1766
Long Drax N York 83 SE6828
Long Duckmanton Derbys 75 SK4471
Long Eaton Derbys 62 SK4833
Long Green Ches 71 SJ4770
Long Green H & W 47 SO8433
Long Hanborough Oxon 36 SP4114
Long Hedges Lincs 77 TF3547
Long Itchington Warwks 50 SP4165
Long Lane Shrops 59 SJ6315
Long Lawford Warwks 50 SP4776
Long Load Somset 21 ST4623
Long Marston Herts 38 SP8915
Long Marston N York 83 SE5051
Long Marston Warwks 48 SP1548
Long Marton Cumb 94 NY6624
Long Meadowend Shrops 59 SO4181

Long Melford

Lydiard Tregoze

Long Melford *Suffk* 54 TL8645
Long Newnton *Gloucs* 35 ST9192
Long Newton *Loth* 118 NT5164
Long Preston *N York* 88 SD8358
Long Riston *Humb* 85 TA1242
Long Sight *Gt Man* 79 SD9206
Long Stratton *Norfk* 67 TM1992
Long Street *Bucks* 38 SP7947
Long Sutton *Hants* 24 SU7347
Long Sutton *Lincs* 65 TF4322
Long Sutton *Somset* 21 ST4725
Long Thurlow *Suffk* 54 TM0068
Long Waste *Shrops* 59 SJ6115
Long Whatton *Leics* 62 SK4723
Long Wittenham *Oxon* 37 SU5493
Longbenton *T & W* 103 NZ2668
Longborough *Gloucs* 48 SP1729
Longbridge *W Mids* 60 SP0177
Longbridge *Warwks* 48 SP2762
Longbridge Deverill *Wilts* 22 ST8640
Longburgh *Cumb* 93 NY3058
Longburton *Dorset* 11 ST6412
Longcliffe *Derbys* 73 SK2255
Longcombe *Devon* 7 SX8359
Longcot *Oxon* 36 SU2790
Longcroft *Cumb* 93 NY2158
Longcross *Surrey* 25 SU9865
Longden *Shrops* 59 SJ4406
Longden Common *Shrops* 59 SJ4305
Longdon *H & W* 47 SO8336
Longdon *Staffs* 61 SK0714
Longdon Green *Staffs* 61 SK0813
Longdon Heath *H & W* 47 SO8338
Longdon upon Tern *Shrops* 59 SJ6115
Longdown *Devon* 9 SX8691
Longdowns *Cnwll* 3 SW7434
Longfield *Kent* 27 TQ6069
Longford *Derbys* 73 SK2137
Longford *Gloucs* 35 SO8320
Longford *Gt Lon* 26 TQ0576
Longford *Kent* 27 TQ5156
Longford *Shrops* 72 SJ6434
Longford *Shrops* 72 SJ7218
Longford *W Mids* 61 SP3583
Longforgan *Tays* 126 NO2929
Longformacus *Border* 119 NT6957
Longframlington *Nthumb* 103 NU1300
Longham *Dorset* 12 SZ0698
Longham *Norfk* 66 TF9416
Longhaven *Gramp* 143 NJ9538
Longhaven *Gramp* 143 NK1039
Longhirst *Nthumb* 103 NZ2289
Longhope *Gloucs* 35 SO6918
Longhope *Ork* 155 ND3190
Longhorsley *Nthumb* 103 NZ1494
Longhoughton *Nthumb* 111 NU2415
Longlands *Cumb* 93 NY2636
Longlane *Derbys* 73 SK2437
Longlevens *Gloucs* 35 SO8519
Longley *W York* 82 SE0522
Longley *W York* 82 SE1406
Longley Green *H & W* 47 SO7350
Longleys *Tays* 126 NO2643
Longmanhill *Gramp* 142 NJ7362
Longmoor Camp *Hants* 14 SU7931
Longmorn *Gramp* 141 NJ2358
Longmoss *Ches* 79 SJ8974
Longnewton *Border* 110 NT5827
Longnewton *Cleve* 96 NZ3816
Longney *Gloucs* 35 SO7612
Longniddry *Loth* 118 NT4476
Longnor *Shrops* 59 SJ4800
Longnor *Staffs* 74 SK0864
Longparish *Hants* 24 SU4345
Longpark *Cumb* 101 NY4362
Longridge *Lancs* 81 SD6037
Longridge *Loth* 116 NS9462
Longridge *Staffs* 72 SJ9015
Longriggend *Strath* 116 NS8270
Longrock *Cnwll* 2 SW5031
Longsdon *Staffs* 72 SJ9654
Longshaw Common *Gt Man* 78 SD5302
Longside *Gramp* 143 NK0347
Longslow *Shrops* 72 SJ6535
Longstanton *Cambs* 52 TL3966
Longstock *Hants* 23 SU3537
Longstone *Dyfed* 31 SN1409
Longstowe *Cambs* 52 TL3054
Longstreet *Wilts* 23 SU1451
Longthorpe *Cambs* 64 TL1698
Longthwaite *Cumb* 93 NY4323
Longton *Lancs* 80 SD4825
Longton *Staffs* 72 SJ9143
Longtown *Cumb* 101 NY3768
Longtown *H & W* 46 SO3229
Longueville *Jersey* 152 JS0000
Longville in the Dale *Shrops* 59 SO5393
Longwick *Bucks* 38 SP7905
Longwitton *Nthumb* 103 NZ0788
Longwood *D & G* 99 NX7060
Longwood *Shrops* 59 SJ6007
Longwood House *Hants* 13 SU5324
Longworth *Oxon* 36 SU3899
Longyester *Loth* 118 NT5465
Lonmay *Gramp* 143 NK0159
Lonmore *Highld* 136 NG2646
Looe *Cnwll* 5 SX2553
Loose *Kent* 28 TQ7552
Loosebeare *Devon* 8 SS7105
Loosegate *Lincs* 64 TF3125
Loosley Row *Bucks* 37 SP8100
Lootcherbrae *Gramp* 142 NJ6053
Lopcombe Corner *Wilts* 23 SU2535
Lopen *Somset* 10 ST4214
Loppington *Shrops* 59 SJ4629
Lorbottle *Nthumb* 111 NU0306
Lordington *W Susx* 14 SU7809
Lords Wood *Kent* 28 TQ7762
Lordsbridge *Norfk* 65 TF5712
Lornty *Tays* 126 NO1746
Loscoe *Derbys* 62 SK4247
Loscombe *Dorset* 10 SY4997
Lossiemouth *Gramp* 141 NJ2370
Lostford *Shrops* 59 SJ6231
Lostock Gralam *Ches* 79 SJ6974
Lostock Green *Ches* 79 SJ6973
Lostock Hall Fold *Gt Man* 79 SD6509
Lostock Junction *Gt Man* 79 SD6708
Lostwithiel *Cnwll* 4 SX1059
Lothbeg *Highld* 147 NC9410
Lothersdale *N York* 82 SD9545
Lothmore *Highld* 147 NC9611
Loudwater *Bucks* 26 SU9090
Loughborough *Leics* 62 SK5319
Loughor *W Glam* 32 SS5698
Loughton *Bucks* 38 SP8337
Loughton *Essex* 27 TQ4296
Loughton *Shrops* 59 SO6182
Lound *Lincs* 64 TF0618
Lound *Notts* 75 SK6986
Lound *Suffk* 67 TM5099
Lounston *Devon* 7 SX7875
Lount *Leics* 62 SK3819
Louth *Lincs* 77 TF3287
Love Clough *Lancs* 81 SD8127
Lovedean *Hants* 13 SU6812
Lover *Wilts* 12 SU2120
Loversall *S York* 75 SK5798
Loves Green *Essex* 40 TL6404
Lovesome Hill *N York* 89 SE3699
Loveston *Dyfed* 31 SN0808
Lovington *Somset* 21 ST5930
Low Ackworth *W York* 83 SE4517
Low Angerton *Nthumb* 103 NZ0984
Low Barbeth *D & G* 98 NX0166
Low Barlings *Lincs* 76 TF0873
Low Bell End *N York* 90 SE7197
Low Bentham *N York* 87 SD6469
Low Biggins *Cumb* 87 SD6077
Low Borrowbridge *Cumb* 87 NY6101
Low Bradfield *S York* 74 SK2691
Low Bradley *N York* 82 SE0048
Low Braithwaite *Cumb* 93 NY4242
Low Burnham *Humb* 84 SE7802
Low Buston *Nthumb* 111 NU2207
Low Catton *Humb* 84 SE7053
Low Coniscliffe *Dur* 89 NZ2513
Low Crosby *Cumb* 93 NY4459
Low Dinsdale *Dur* 89 NZ3411
Low Eggborough *N York* 83 SE5623
Low Ellington *N York* 89 SE1983
Low Fell *T & W* 96 NZ2559
Low Gartachorrans *Cent* 115 NS4685
Low Gate *Nthumb* 102 NY9063
Low Gettbridge *Cumb* 94 NY5259
Low Grantley *N York* 89 SE2370
Low Green *N York* 89 SE2059
Low Habberley *H & W* 60 SO8077
Low Ham *Somset* 21 ST4329
Low Harrogate *N York* 82 SE2955
Low Hawsker *N York* 91 NZ9207
Low Hesket *Cumb* 93 NY4646
Low Hill *H & W* 60 SO8473
Low Hutton *N York* 90 SE7667
Low Knipe *Cumb* 94 NY5119
Low Laithe *N York* 89 SE1963
Low Langton *Lincs* 76 TF1576
Low Leighton *Derbys* 79 SK0085
Low Lorton *Cumb* 92 NY1525
Low Marnham *Notts* 75 SK8069
Low Middleton *Nthumb* 111 NU1035
Low Mill *N York* 90 SE6795
Low Moor *Lancs* 81 SD7341
Low Moor *W York* 82 SE1628
Low Moorsley *T & W* 96 NZ3446
Low Mowthorpe *N York* 91 SE8966
Low Newton *Cumb* 87 SD4082
Low Rogerscales *Cumb* 92 NY1426
Low Row *Cumb* 93 NY1944
Low Row *Cumb* 93 NY3536
Low Row *Cumb* 102 NY5863
Low Row *N York* 88 SD9797
Low Salchrie *D & G* 98 NX0365
Low Santon *Humb* 84 SE9412
Low Street *Essex* 28 TQ6677
Low Street *Norfk* 67 TG3423
Low Tharston *Norfk* 66 TM1895
Low Torry *Fife* 117 NT0186
Low Toynton *Lincs* 77 TF2770
Low Valley *S York* 83 SE4003
Low Walworth *Dur* 96 NZ2417
Low Wood *Cumb* 87 SD3483
Low Worsall *N York* 89 NZ3909
Low Wray *Cumb* 87 NY3701
Lowbands *H & W* 47 SO7731
Lowca *Cumb* 92 NX9821
Lowdham *Notts* 63 SK6646
Lowe *Shrops* 59 SJ4930
Lowe Hill *Staffs* 73 SJ9955
Lower Aisholt *Somset* 20 ST2035
Lower Ansty *Dorset* 11 ST7603
Lower Apperley *Gloucs* 47 SO8527
Lower Arncott *Oxon* 37 SP6018
Lower Ashton *Devon* 8 SX8484
Lower Assendon *Oxon* 37 SU7484
Lower Ballam *Lancs* 80 SD3631
Lower Barewood *H & W* 46 SO3956
Lower Bartle *Lancs* 80 SD4933
Lower Beeding *W Susx* 15 TQ2127
Lower Benefield *Nhants* 51 SP9988
Lower Bentley *H & W* 47 SO9865
Lower Beobridge *Shrops* 60 SO7891
Lower Birchwood *Derbys* 75 SK4354
Lower Boddington *Nhants* 49 SP4852
Lower Boscaswell *Cnwll* 2 SW3734
Lower Bourne *Surrey* 25 SU8444
Lower Brailes *Warwks* 48 SP3139
Lower Breakish *Highld* 129 NG6723
Lower Bredbury *Gt Man* 79 SJ9191
Lower Broadheath *H & W* 47 SO8157
Lower Buckenhill *H & W* 46 SO6033
Lower Bullingham *H & W* 46 SO5138
Lower Burgate *Hants* 12 SU1515
Lower Burrowton *Devon* 9 SY0097
Lower Burton *H & W* 46 SO4256
Lower Caldecote *Beds* 52 TL1746
Lower Cam *Gloucs* 35 SO7400
Lower Canada *Avon* 21 ST3558
Lower Catesby *Nhants* 49 SP5159
Lower Chapel *Powys* 45 SO0235
Lower Chicksgrove *Wilts* 22 ST9729
Lower Chute *Wilts* 23 SU3153
Lower Clapton *Gt Lon* 27 TQ3485
Lower Clent *H & W* 60 SO9279
Lower Clopton *Warwks* 48 SP1745
Lower Creedy *Devon* 8 SS8402
Lower Crossings *Derbys* 74 SK0480
Lower Cumberworth *W York* 82 SE2209
Lower Cwmtwrch *Powys* 32 SN7610
Lower Darwen *Lancs* 81 SD6825
Lower Dean *Beds* 51 TL0569
Lower Denby *W York* 82 SE2307
Lower Diabaig *Highld* 137 NG7960
Lower Dicker *E Susx* 16 TQ5511
Lower Dinchope *Shrops* 59 SO4584
Lower Down *Shrops* 59 SO3484
Lower Dunsforth *N York* 89 SE4464
Lower Egleton *H & W* 47 SO6245
Lower Elkstone *Staffs* 74 SK0658
Lower Ellastone *Staffs* 73 SK1142
Lower End *Bucks* 37 SP6809
Lower End *Bucks* 38 SP9238
Lower End *Nhants* 51 SP8861
Lower Everleigh *Wilts* 23 SU1854
Lower Exbury *Hants* 13 SZ4299
Lower Eythorne *Kent* 29 TR2849
Lower Failand *Avon* 34 ST5173
Lower Farringdon *Hants* 24 SU7035
Lower Feltham *Gt Lon* 26 TQ0971
Lower Fittleworth *W Susx* 14 TQ0118
Lower Foxdale *IOM* 153 SC2779
Lower Frankton *Shrops* 59 SJ3732
Lower Freystrop *Dyfed* 30 SM9512
Lower Froyle *Hants* 24 SU7544
Lower Gabwell *Devon* 7 SX9169
Lower Gledfield *Highld* 146 NH5890
Lower Godney *Somset* 21 ST4742
Lower Gornal *W Mids* 60 SO9191
Lower Gravenhurst *Beds* 38 TL1035
Lower Green *Essex* 39 TL4334
Lower Green *Gt Man* 79 SJ7098
Lower Green *Herts* 39 TL1832
Lower Green *Herts* 39 TL4233
Lower Green *Kent* 16 TQ5640
Lower Green *Kent* 16 TQ6341
Lower Green *Nhants* 50 SP8159
Lower Green *Norfk* 66 TF9837
Lower Green *Staffs* 60 SJ9007
Lower Green *Suffk* 53 TL7465
Lower Hacheston *Suffk* 55 TM3156
Lower Halliford *Surrey* 26 TQ0866
Lower Halstock Leigh *Dorset* 10 ST5207
Lower Halstow *Kent* 28 TQ8567
Lower Hamworthy *Dorset* 11 SY9990
Lower Hardres *Kent* 29 TR1553
Lower Harpton *H & W* 46 SO2760
Lower Hartshay *Derbys* 74 SK3851
Lower Hartwell *Bucks* 38 SP7912
Lower Hatton *Staffs* 72 SJ8236
Lower Hawthwaite *Cumb* 86 SD2189
Lower Hergest *H & W* 46 SO2755
Lower Heyford *Oxon* 49 SP4824
Lower Heysham *Lancs* 87 SD4160
Lower Higham *Kent* 28 TQ7172
Lower Holbrook *Suffk* 54 TM1834
Lower Hordley *Shrops* 59 SJ3929
Lower Horncroft *W Susx* 14 TQ0017
Lower Howsell *H & W* 47 SO7848
Lower Irlam *Gt Man* 79 SJ7193
Lower Kilburn *Derbys* 62 SK3744
Lower Kilcott *Avon* 35 ST7889
Lower Killeyan *Strath* 104 NR2742
Lower Kingcombe *Dorset* 10 SY5599
Lower Kingswood *Surrey* 26 TQ2453
Lower Kinnerton *Ches* 71 SJ3462
Lower Langford *Avon* 21 ST4560
Lower Largo *Fife* 126 NO4102
Lower Leigh *Staffs* 73 SK0135
Lower Lemington *Gloucs* 48 SP2134
Lower Llanfadog *Powys* 45 SN9567
Lower Lovacott *Devon* 19 SS5227
Lower Loxhore *Devon* 19 SS6137
Lower Lydbrook *Gloucs* 34 SO5916
Lower Lye *H & W* 46 SO4066
Lower Machen *Gwent* 34 ST2288
Lower Maes-coed *H & W* 46 SO3430
Lower Mannington *Dorset* 12 SU0604
Lower Marston *Somset* 22 ST7644
Lower Meend *Gloucs* 34 SO5504
Lower Middleton Cheney *Nhants* 49 SP5041
Lower Milton *Somset* 21 ST5347
Lower Moor *W Mids* 47 SO9747
Lower Morton *Avon* 35 ST6491
Lower Nazeing *Essex* 39 TL3906
Lower Norton *Warwks* 48 SP2363
Lower Nyland *Dorset* 22 ST7521
Lower Penarth *S Glam* 20 ST1869
Lower Penn *Staffs* 60 SO8796
Lower Pennington *Hants* 12 SZ3193
Lower Penwortham *Lancs* 80 SD5327
Lower Peover *Ches* 79 SJ7474
Lower Place *Gt Man* 81 SD9011
Lower Pollicott *Bucks* 37 SP7013
Lower Pond Street *Essex* 39 TL4537
Lower Quinton *Warwks* 48 SP1847
Lower Rainham *Kent* 28 TQ8167
Lower Raydon *Suffk* 54 TM0338
Lower Roadwater *Somset* 20 ST0339
Lower Salter *Lancs* 87 SD6063
Lower Seagry *Wilts* 35 ST9580
Lower Sheering *Essex* 39 TL4914
Lower Shelton *Beds* 38 SP9942
Lower Shiplake *Oxon* 37 SU7679
Lower Shuckburgh *Warwks* 49 SP4862
Lower Slaughter *Gloucs* 36 SP1622
Lower Soothill *W York* 82 SE2523
Lower Soudley *Gloucs* 35 SO6609
Lower Standen *Kent* 29 TR2340
Lower Stanton St Quintin *Wilts* 35 ST9180
Lower Stoke *Kent* 28 TQ8375
Lower Stone *Gloucs* 35 ST6794
Lower Stonnall *Staffs* 61 SK0803
Lower Stow Bedon *Norfk* 66 TL9694
Lower Street *Dorset* 11 SY8399
Lower Street *E Susx* 16 TQ7012
Lower Street *Norfk* 67 TG2635
Lower Street *Suffk* 53 TL7852
Lower Street *Suffk* 54 TM1052
Lower Stretton *Ches* 79 SJ6281
Lower Stroud *Dorset* 10 SY4598
Lower Sundon *Beds* 38 TL0526
Lower Swanwick *Hants* 13 SU4909
Lower Swell *Gloucs* 48 SP1725
Lower Tadmarton *Oxon* 48 SP4036
Lower Tale *Devon* 9 ST0601
Lower Tean *Staffs* 73 SK0138
Lower Thurlton *Norfk* 67 TM4299
Lower Town *Cnwll* 2 SW6528
Lower Town *Devon* 7 SX7172
Lower Town *Dyfed* 30 SM9637
Lower Town *H & W* 47 SO6342
Lower Trebullett *Cnwll* 5 SX3277
Lower Tregantle *Cnwll* 5 SX3953
Lower Treluswell *Cnwll* 3 SW7735
Lower Tysoe *Warwks* 48 SP3445
Lower Ufford *Suffk* 55 TM2952
Lower Upcott *Devon* 9 SX8880
Lower Upham *Hants* 13 SU5219
Lower Upnor *Kent* 28 TQ7571
Lower Vexford *Somset* 20 ST1135
Lower Walton *Ches* 78 SJ6086
Lower Waterston *Dorset* 11 SY7395
Lower Weare *Somset* 21 ST4053
Lower Welson *H & W* 46 SO2950
Lower Westmancote *H & W* 47 SO9337
Lower Whatcombe *Dorset* 11 ST8401
Lower Whatley *Somset* 22 ST7447
Lower Whitley *Ches* 71 SJ6179
Lower Wick *Gloucs* 35 ST7096
Lower Wick *H & W* 47 SO8352
Lower Wield *Hants* 24 SU6340
Lower Wigginton *Herts* 38 SP9409
Lower Willingdon *E Susx* 16 TQ5803
Lower Winchendon *Bucks* 37 SP7312
Lower Woodend *Bucks* 37 SU8187
Lower Woodford *Wilts* 23 SU1235
Lower Wraxhall *Dorset* 10 ST5700
Lower Wyche *H & W* 47 SO7743
Lower Wyke *W York* 82 SE1525
Lowerhouse *Lancs* 81 SD8032
Lowesby *Leics* 63 SK7207
Lowestoft *Suffk* 67 TM5493
Loweswater *Cumb* 92 NY1421
Lowfield Heath *W Susx* 15 TQ2739
Lowgill *Cumb* 87 SD6297
Lowgill *Lancs* 87 SD6564
Lowick *Cumb* 86 SD2885
Lowick *Nhants* 51 SP9881
Lowick *Nthumb* 111 NU0139
Lowick Bridge *Cumb* 86 SD2986
Lowick Green *Cumb* 86 SD2985
Lowlands *Dur* 96 NZ1325
Lowlands *Gwent* 34 ST2996
Lowsonford *Warwks* 48 SP1868
Lowther *Cumb* 94 NY5323
Lowther Castle *Cumb* 94 NY5223
Lowthorpe *Humb* 91 TA0860
Lowton *Devon* 8 SS6604
Lowton *Gt Man* 78 SJ6197
Lowton *Somset* 20 ST1918
Lowton Common *Gt Man* 79 SJ6397
Lowton St Mary's *Gt Man* 79 SJ6397
Loxbeare *Devon* 9 SS9116
Loxhill *Surrey* 25 TQ0038
Loxhore *Devon* 19 SS6138
Loxhore Cott *Devon* 19 SS6138
Loxley *Warwks* 48 SP2553
Loxley Green *Staffs* 73 SK0630
Loxter *H & W* 47 SO7140
Loxton *Avon* 21 ST3755
Loxwood *W Susx* 14 TQ0331
Lubenham *Leics* 50 SP7087
Lucas Green *Surrey* 25 SU9460
Lucasgate *Lincs* 77 TF4147
Luccombe *Somset* 20 SS9243
Luccombe Village *IOW* 13 SZ5879
Lucker *Nthumb* 111 NU1530
Luckett *Cnwll* 5 SX3873
Lucking Street *Essex* 54 TL8134
Luckington *Wilts* 35 ST8383
Lucknam *Wilts* 35 ST8272
Luckwell Bridge *Somset* 20 SS9038
Lucott *Somset* 19 SS8645
Lucton *H & W* 46 SO4364
Lucy Cross *N York* 89 NZ2112
Ludborough *Lincs* 77 TF2995
Ludbrook *Devon* 7 SX6654
Ludchurch *Dyfed* 31 SN1411
Luddenden *W York* 82 SE0426
Luddenden Foot *W York* 82 SE0325
Luddenham Court *Kent* 28 TQ9963
Luddesdown *Kent* 28 TQ6666
Luddington *Humb* 84 SE8316
Luddington *Warwks* 48 SP1652
Luddington in the Brook *Nhants* 51 TL1083
Ludford *Lincs* 76 TF1989
Ludford *Shrops* 46 SO5174
Ludgershall *Bucks* 37 SP6517
Ludgershall *Wilts* 23 SU2650
Ludgvan *Cnwll* 2 SW5033
Ludham *Norfk* 67 TG3818
Ludlow *Shrops* 46 SO5175
Ludney *Somset* 10 ST3812
Ludwell *Wilts* 22 ST9122
Ludworth *Dur* 96 NZ3641
Luffenhall *Herts* 39 TL2928
Luffincott *Devon* 5 SX3394
Luffness *Loth* 118 NT4780
Lugar *Strath* 107 NS5921
Lugg Green *H & W* 46 SO4462
Luggate Burn *Loth* 118 NT5974
Luggiebank *Strath* 116 NS7672
Lugsdale *Ches* 78 SJ5285
Lugton *Strath* 115 NS4152
Lugwardine *H & W* 46 SO5540
Luib *Highld* 137 NG5627
Lulham *H & W* 46 SO4141
Lullington *Derbys* 61 SK2412
Lullington *E Susx* 16 TQ5202
Lullington *Somset* 22 ST7851
Lulsgate Bottom *Avon* 21 ST5165
Lulsley *H & W* 47 SO7455
Lulworth Camp *Dorset* 11 SY8381
Lumb *Lancs* 81 SD8324
Lumb *W York* 82 SE0221
Lumbutts *W York* 82 SD9523
Lumby *N York* 83 SE4830
Lumloch *Strath* 116 NS6370
Lumphanan *Gramp* 134 NJ5804
Lumphinnans *Fife* 117 NT1792
Lumsden *Gramp* 142 NJ4722
Lunan *Tays* 127 NO6851
Lunanhead *Tays* 127 NO4752
Luncarty *Tays* 125 NO0929
Lund *Humb* 84 SE9647
Lund *N York* 83 SE6532
Lundford Magna *Lincs* 76 TF1989
Lundie *Cent* 124 NN7304
Lundie *Tays* 126 NO2836
Lundin Links *Fife* 126 NO4002
Lundy Green *Norfk* 67 TM2392
Lunna *Shet* 155 HU4869
Lunsford *Kent* 28 TQ6959
Lunsford's Cross *E Susx* 17 TQ7210
Lunt *Mersyd* 78 SD3402
Luntley *H & W* 46 SO3955
Luppitt *Devon* 9 ST1606
Lupridge *Devon* 7 SX7153
Lupset *W York* 82 SE3119
Lupton *Cumb* 87 SD5581
Lurgashall *W Susx* 14 SU9326
Lurley *Devon* 9 SS9215
Lusby *Lincs* 77 TF3467
Luscombe *Devon* 7 SX7957
Luson *Devon* 6 SX6050
Luss *Strath* 115 NS3692
Lusta *Highld* 136 NG2656
Lustleigh *Devon* 8 SX7881
Luston *H & W* 46 SO4863
Luthermuir *Gramp* 135 NO6568
Luthrie *Fife* 126 NO3319
Lutley *W Mids* 60 SO9382
Luton *Beds* 38 TL0921
Luton *Devon* 9 ST0802
Luton *Devon* 9 SX9076
Luton *Kent* 28 TQ7766
Lutterworth *Leics* 50 SP5484
Lutton *Devon* 6 SX5959
Lutton *Devon* 7 SX6961
Lutton *Dorset* 11 SY8980
Lutton *Lincs* 65 TF4325
Lutton *Nhants* 52 TL1187
Luxborough *Somset* 20 SS9738
Luxulyan *Cnwll* 4 SX0558
Luzley *Gt Man* 79 SD9600
Lybster *Highld* 151 ND2435
Lydbury North *Shrops* 59 SO3486
Lydcott *Devon* 19 SS6936
Lydd *Kent* 17 TR0420
Lydden *Kent* 29 TR2645
Lydden *Kent* 29 TR3567
Lyddington *Leics* 51 SP8797
Lyde Green *Hants* 24 SU7057
Lydeard St Lawrence *Somset* 20 ST1332
Lydford *Devon* 5 SX5185
Lydford on Fosse *Somset* 21 ST5630
Lydgate *Gt Man* 82 SD9516
Lydgate *W York* 81 SD9225
Lydham *Shrops* 59 SO3391
Lydiard Green *Wilts* 36 SU0885
Lydiard Millicent *Wilts* 36 SU0986
Lydiard Tregoze *Wilts* 36 SU1085

Lydiate

Meidrim

Lydiate *Mersyd* 78 SD3604
Lydiate Ash *H & W* 60 SO9775
Lydlinch *Dorset* 11 ST7413
Lydney *Gloucs* 35 SO6303
Lydstep *Dyfed* 31 SS0898
Lye *W Mids* 60 SO9284
Lye Cross *Avon* 21 ST4962
Lye Green *Bucks* 38 SP9703
Lye Green *E Susx* 16 TQ5134
Lye Green *Warwks* 48 SP1965
Lye Head *H & W* 60 SO7573
Lye's Green *Wilts* 22 ST8146
Lyford *Oxon* 36 SU3994
Lymbridge Green *Kent* 29 TR1244
Lyme *Border* 109 NT2041
Lyme Regis *Dorset* 10 SY3492
Lyminge *Kent* 29 TR1641
Lymington *Hants* 12 SZ3295
Lyminster *W Susx* 14 TQ0204
Lymm *Ches* 79 SJ6887
Lympne *Kent* 17 TR1135
Lympsham *Somset* 21 ST3354
Lympstone *Devon* 9 SX9984
Lynbridge *Devon* 19 SS7248
Lynch *Somset* 20 SS9047
Lynch Green *Norfk* 66 TG1505
Lynchat *Highld* 132 NH7801
Lyndhurst *Hants* 12 SU3008
Lyndon *Leics* 63 SK9004
Lyndon Green *W Mids* 61 SP1485
Lyne *Surrey* 26 TQ0166
Lyne Down *H & W* 47 SO6431
Lyne of Skene *Gramp* 135 NJ7610
Lyneal *Shrops* 59 SJ4433
Lyneham *Devon* 8 SX8579
Lyneham *Oxon* 36 SP2720
Lyneham *Wilts* 35 SU0278
Lyneholmford *Cumb* 101 NY5172
Lynemouth *Nthumb* 103 NZ2991
Lyness *Ork* 155 ND3094
Lyng *Norfk* 66 TG0617
Lyng *Somset* 21 ST3329
Lynhales *H & W* 46 SO3255
Lynmouth *Devon* 19 SS7249
Lynn *Shrops* 72 SJ7815
Lynn *Staffs* 61 SK0704
Lynn of Shenval *Gramp* 141 NJ2129
Lynsted *Kent* 28 TQ9460
Lynstone *Cnwll* 18 SS2005
Lynton *Devon* 19 SS7249
Lyon's Gate *Dorset* 11 ST6505
Lyonshall *H & W* 46 SO3355
Lytchett Matravers *Dorset* 11 SY9495
Lytchett Minster *Dorset* 11 SY9693
Lyth *Highld* 151 ND2762
Lytham *Lancs* 80 SD3627
Lytham St Anne's *Lancs* 80 SD3427
Lythbank *Shrops* 59 SJ4607
Lythe *N York* 90 NZ8413
Lythmore *Highld* 150 ND0566

M

Mabe Burnthouse *Cnwll* 3 SW7634
Mabie *D & G* 100 NX9570
Mablethorpe *Lincs* 77 TF5085
Macclesfield *Ches* 79 SJ9173
Macclesfield Forest *Ches* 79 SJ9772
Macduff *Gramp* 142 NJ7064
Macharioch *Strath* 105 NR7309
Machen *M Glam* 33 ST2189
Machire *Strath* 112 NR2164
Machrie *Strath* 105 NR8934
Machrihanish *Strath* 104 NR6320
Machrins *Strath* 112 NR3693
Machynlleth *Powys* 57 SH7400
Machynys *Dyfed* 32 SS5198
Mackworth *Derbys* 62 SK3137
Macmerry *Loth* 118 NT4372
Maddaford *Devon* 8 SX5494
Madderty *Tays* 125 NN9522
Maddington *Wilts* 23 SU0744
Maddiston *Cent* 116 NS9476
Madehurst *W Susx* 14 SU9810
Madeley *Shrops* 60 SJ6904
Madeley *Staffs* 72 SJ7744
Madeley Heath *Staffs* 72 SJ7845
Madford *Devon* 9 ST1411
Madingley *Cambs* 52 TL3960
Madley *H & W* 46 SO4238
Madresfield *H & W* 47 SO8047
Madron *Cnwll* 2 SW4531
Maen-y-groes *Dyfed* 42 SN3858
Maenaddwyn *Gwynd* 68 SH4684
Maenan *Gwynd* 69 SH7965
Maenclochog *Dyfed* 31 SN0827
Maendy *S Glam* 33 ST0076
Maenporth *Cnwll* 3 SW7829
Maentwrog *Gwynd* 57 SH6640
Maer *Cnwll* 18 SS2008
Maer *Staffs* 72 SJ7938
Maerdy *Dyfed* 44 SN6527
Maerdy *M Glam* 33 SS9798
Maes-glas *Gwent* 34 ST2985
Maesbrook *Shrops* 59 SJ3021
Maesbury *Shrops* 59 SJ3026
Maesbury Marsh *Shrops* 59 SJ3125
Maesgwynne *Dyfed* 31 SN2024
Maeshafn *Clwyd* 70 SJ2061
Maesllyn *Dyfed* 42 SN3644
Maesmynis *Powys* 45 SO0146
Maesmynis *Powys* 45 SO0349
Maesteg *M Glam* 33 SS8590
Maesybont *Dyfed* 32 SN5616
Maesycwmmer *M Glam* 33 ST1594
Magdalen Laver *Essex* 39 TL5108
Maggieknockater *Gramp* 141 NJ3145
Maggots End *Essex* 39 TL4827
Magham Down *E Susx* 16 TQ6011
Maghull *Mersyd* 78 SD3703
Magor *Gwent* 34 ST4286
Maiden Bradley *Wilts* 22 ST8038
Maiden Head *Avon* 21 ST5666
Maiden Law *Dur* 96 NZ1749
Maiden Newton *Dorset* 10 SY5997
Maiden Wells *Dyfed* 30 SR9799
Maidencombe *Devon* 7 SX9268
Maidenhayne *Devon* 10 SY2795
Maidenhead *Berks* 26 SU8980
Maidens *Strath* 106 NS2107
Maidens Green *Berks* 25 SU8972
Maidenwell *Lincs* 77 TF3179
Maidford *Nhants* 49 SP6052
Maids Moreton *Bucks* 49 SP7035
Maidstone *Kent* 28 TQ7555
Maidwell *Nhants* 50 SP7476
Mainclee *Gwent* 34 ST3288
Mains of Bainakettle *Gramp* 134 NO6274
Mains of Balhall *Tays* 134 NO5163
Mains of Dalvey *Highld* 141 NJ1132
Mains of Haulkerton *Gramp* 135 NO7172
Mainsforth *Dur* 96 NZ3131
Mainsriddle *D & G* 92 NX9456
Mainstone *Shrops* 58 SO2787
Maisemore *Gloucs* 35 SO8121
Major's Green *H & W* 61 SP1077
Makeney *Derbys* 62 SK3544
Malborough *Devon* 7 SX7139
Malcoff *Derbys* 74 SK0782
Malden *Surrey* 26 TQ2166
Malden Rushett *Gt Lon* 26 TQ1761
Maldon *Essex* 40 TL8506
Malham *N York* 88 SD9063
Mallaig *Highld* 129 NM6796
Mallaigvaig *Highld* 129 NM6897
Malleny Mills *Loth* 117 NT1665
Mallows Green *Essex* 39 TL4726
Malltraeth *Gwynd* 68 SH4068
Mallwyd *Gwynd* 57 SH8612
Malmesbury *Wilts* 35 ST9387
Malmsmead *Somset* 19 SS7947
Malpas *Ches* 71 SJ4847
Malpas *Cnwll* 3 SW8442
Malpas *Gwent* 34 ST3090
Maltby *Cleve* 89 NZ4613
Maltby *Lincs* 77 TF3183
Maltby *S York* 75 SK5392
Maltby le Marsh *Lincs* 77 TF4681
Malting Green *Essex* 41 TL9720
Maltman's Hill *Kent* 28 TQ9043
Malton *N York* 90 SE7871
Malvern Link *H & W* 47 SO7947
Malvern Wells *H & W* 47 SO7742
Malzie *D & G* 99 NX3754
Mamble *H & W* 60 SO6871
Mamhilad *Gwent* 34 SO3003
Manaccan *Cnwll* 3 SW7624
Manafon *Powys* 58 SJ1102
Manais *W Isls* 154 NG1089
Manaton *Devon* 8 SX7581
Manby *Lincs* 77 TF3986
Mancetter *Warwks* 61 SP3296
Manchester *Gt Man* 79 SJ8497
Mancot *Clwyd* 71 SJ3167
Mandally *Highld* 131 NH2900
Manea *Cambs* 53 TL4789
Maney *W Mids* 61 SP1195
Manfield *N York* 89 NZ2113
Mangerton *Dorset* 10 SY4995
Mangotsfield *Avon* 35 ST6676
Mangrove Green *Herts* 38 TL1224
Manhay *Cnwll* 2 SW6930
Manish *W Isls* 154 NG1089
Mankinholes *W York* 82 SD9523
Manley *Ches* 71 SJ5071
Manmoel *Gwent* 33 SO1803
Mannel *Strath* 120 NL9840
Manning's Heath *W Susx* 15 TQ2028
Manningford Bohune *Wilts* 23 SU1357
Manningford Bruce *Wilts* 23 SU1358
Manningham *W York* 82 SE1435
Mannington *Dorset* 12 SU0605
Manningtree *Essex* 41 TM1031
Mannofield *Gramp* 135 NJ9104
Manor Park *Gt Lon* 27 TQ4285
Manorbier *Dyfed* 30 SS0697
Manorbier Newton *Dyfed* 30 SN0400
Manordeilo *Dyfed* 44 SN6726
Manorhill *Border* 110 NT6632
Manorowen *Dyfed* 30 SM9336
Mansell Gamage *H & W* 46 SO3944
Mansell Lacy *H & W* 46 SO4245
Mansergh *Cumb* 87 SD6082
Mansfield *Notts* 75 SK5361
Mansfield *Strath* 107 NS6214
Mansfield Woodhouse *Notts* 75 SK5363
Mansriggs *Cumb* 86 SD2980
Manston *Dorset* 11 ST8115
Manston *Kent* 29 TR3466
Manston *W York* 83 SE3634
Manswood *Dorset* 11 ST9708
Manthorpe *Lincs* 63 SK9137
Manthorpe *Lincs* 64 TF0715
Manton *Humb* 84 SE9302
Manton *Leics* 63 SK8704
Manton *Notts* 75 SK6078
Manton *Wilts* 23 SU1768
Manuden *Essex* 39 TL4926
Manwood Green *Essex* 39 TL5412
Maperton *Somset* 22 ST6726
Maple Cross *Herts* 26 TQ0393
Maplebeck *Notts* 75 SK7060
Mapledurham *Oxon* 37 SU6776
Mapledurwell *Hants* 24 SU6851
Maplehurst *W Susx* 15 TQ1824
Maplescombe *Kent* 27 TQ5664
Mapleton *Derbys* 73 SK1647
Mapleton *Kent* 16 TQ4649
Mapperley *Derbys* 62 SK4342
Mapperley Park *Notts* 62 SK5842
Mapperton *Dorset* 10 SY5099
Mappleborough Green *Warwks* 48 SP0866
Mappleton *Humb* 85 TA2243
Mapplewell *S York* 83 SE3210
Mappowder *Dorset* 11 ST7306
Marazanvose *Cnwll* 3 SW7950
Marazion *Cnwll* 2 SW5130
Marbury *Ches* 71 SJ5645
March *Cambs* 65 TL4196
March *Strath* 108 NS9914
Marcham *Oxon* 37 SU4596
Marchamley *Shrops* 59 SJ5929
Marchamley Wood *Shrops* 59 SJ5831
Marchington *Staffs* 73 SK1330
Marchington Woodlands *Staffs* 73 SK1128
Marchros *Gwynd* 56 SH3125
Marchwiel *Clwyd* 71 SJ3547
Marchwood *Hants* 12 SU3810
Marcross *S Glam* 20 SS9269
Marden *H & W* 46 SO5146
Marden *Kent* 28 TQ7444
Marden *Wilts* 23 SU0857
Marden Ash *Essex* 27 TL5502
Marden Beech *Kent* 28 TQ7442
Marden Thorn *Kent* 28 TQ7642
Mardens Hill *E Susx* 16 TQ5032
Mardlebury *Herts* 39 TL2618
Mardy *Gwent* 34 SO3015
Marefield *Leics* 63 SK7407
Mareham le Fen *Lincs* 77 TF2761
Mareham on the Hill *Lincs* 77 TF2867
Marehay *Derbys* 62 SK3947
Marehill *W Susx* 14 TQ0618
Maresfield *E Susx* 16 TQ4624
Marfleet *Humb* 85 TA1429
Marford *Clwyd* 71 SJ3556
Margam *W Glam* 32 SS7887
Margaret Marsh *Dorset* 22 ST8218
Margaretting *Essex* 40 TL6701
Margaretting Tye *Essex* 40 TL6800
Margate *Kent* 29 TR3571
Margnaheglish *Strath* 105 NS0332
Margrie *D & G* 99 NX5950
Margrove Park *Cleve* 97 NZ6515
Marham *Norfk* 65 TF7009
Marhamchurch *Cnwll* 18 SS2203
Marholm *Cambs* 64 TF1401
Marian-glas *Gwynd* 68 SH5084
Mariansleigh *Devon* 19 SS7422
Marine Town *Kent* 28 TQ9274
Marionburgh *Gramp* 135 NJ7006
Marishader *Highld* 136 NG4963
Maristow *Devon* 6 SX4764
Marjoriebanks *D & G* 100 NY0883
Mark *D & G* 98 NX1157
Mark *Somset* 21 ST3847
Mark Causeway *Somset* 21 ST3547
Mark Cross *E Susx* 16 TQ5010
Mark Cross *E Susx* 16 TQ5831
Mark's Corner *IOW* 13 SZ4692
Markbeech *Kent* 16 TQ4742
Markby *Lincs* 77 TF4878
Markeaton *Derbys* 62 SK3237
Market Bosworth *Leics* 62 SK4002
Market Deeping *Lincs* 64 TF1310
Market Drayton *Shrops* 72 SJ6734
Market Harborough *Leics* 50 SP7387
Market Lavington *Wilts* 22 SU0154
Market Overton *Leics* 63 SK8816
Market Rasen *Lincs* 76 TF1089
Market Stainton *Lincs* 76 TF2279
Market Street *Norfk* 67 TG2921
Market Weighton *Humb* 84 SE8741
Market Weston *Suffk* 54 TL9877
Markfield *Leics* 62 SK4809
Markham *Gwent* 33 SO1601
Markham Moor *Notts* 75 SK7173
Markinch *Fife* 126 NO2901
Markington *N York* 89 SE2865
Marks Tey *Essex* 40 TL9023
Marksbury *Avon* 22 ST6662
Markshall *Essex* 40 TL8425
Markwell *Cnwll* 5 SX3758
Markyate *Herts* 38 TL0616
Marl Bank *H & W* 47 SO7840
Marlborough *Wilts* 23 SU1868
Marlbrook *H & W* 46 SO5154
Marlbrook *H & W* 60 SO9774
Marlcliff *Warwks* 48 SP0950
Marldon *Devon* 7 SX8663
Marle Green *E Susx* 16 TQ5816
Marlesford *Suffk* 55 TM3258
Marley *Kent* 29 TR1850
Marley *Kent* 29 TR3353
Marley Green *Ches* 71 SJ5845
Marley Hill *T & W* 96 NZ2058
Marlingford *Norfk* 66 TG1309
Marloes *Dyfed* 30 SM7908
Marlow *Bucks* 26 SU8486
Marlow *H & W* 46 SO4076
Marlpit Hill *Kent* 16 TQ4347
Marlpits *E Susx* 16 TQ4528
Marlpits *E Susx* 16 TQ7013
Marlpool *Derbys* 62 SK4345
Marnhull *Dorset* 22 ST7818
Marple *Gt Man* 79 SJ9588
Marple Bridge *Gt Man* 79 SJ9688
Marr *S York* 83 SE5105
Marrick *N York* 88 SE0798
Marros *Dyfed* 31 SN2008
Marsden *T & W* 103 NZ3964
Marsden *W York* 82 SE0411
Marsden Height *Lancs* 81 SD8636
Marsett *N York* 88 SD9085
Marsh *Bucks* 38 SP8109
Marsh *M Glam* 10 ST2510
Marsh *W York* 82 SE0235
Marsh Baldon *Oxon* 37 SU5699
Marsh Gibbon *Bucks* 37 SP6422
Marsh Green *Devon* 9 SY0493
Marsh Green *Kent* 16 TQ4344
Marsh Green *Shrops* 59 SJ6014
Marsh Green *Staffs* 72 SJ8858
Marsh Lane *Derbys* 74 SK4079
Marsh Lane *Gloucs* 34 SO5807
Marsh Street *Somset* 20 SS9944
Marsh The *Powys* 59 SO3197
Marshall's Heath *Herts* 39 TL1614
Marshalswick *Herts* 39 TL1608
Marsham *Norfk* 67 TG1923
Marshborough *Kent* 29 TR3057
Marshbrook *Shrops* 59 SO4489
Marshchapel *Lincs* 77 TF3599
Marshfield *Avon* 35 ST7873
Marshfield *Gwent* 34 ST2582
Marshgate *Cnwll* 4 SX1592
Marshland Green *Gt Man* 79 SJ6899
Marshland St James *Norfk* 65 TF5209
Marshside *Mersyd* 80 SD3619
Marshwood *Dorset* 10 SY3899
Marske *N York* 89 NZ1000
Marske-by-the-Sea *Cleve* 97 NZ6322
Marston *Ches* 79 SJ6775
Marston *H & W* 46 SO3557
Marston *Lincs* 63 SK8943
Marston *Oxon* 37 SP5208
Marston *Staffs* 60 SJ8313
Marston *Staffs* 72 SJ9227
Marston *Warwks* 61 SP2094
Marston *Wilts* 22 ST9656
Marston Green *W Mids* 61 SP1785
Marston Jabbet *Warwks* 61 SP3788
Marston Magna *Somset* 21 ST5922
Marston Meysey *Wilts* 36 SU1297
Marston Montgomery *Derbys* 73 SK1337
Marston Moretaine *Beds* 38 SP9941
Marston on Dove *Derbys* 73 SK2329
Marston St Lawrence *Nhants* 49 SP5341
Marston Stannet *H & W* 46 SO5655
Marston Trussell *Nhants* 50 SP6985
Marstow *H & W* 34 SO5518
Marsworth *Bucks* 38 SP9114
Marten *Wilts* 23 SU2860
Marthall *Ches* 79 SJ7975
Martham *Norfk* 67 TG4518
Martin *Hants* 12 SU0619
Martin *Kent* 29 TR3447
Martin *Lincs* 76 TF1259
Martin *Lincs* 77 TF2466
Martin Dales *Lincs* 76 TF1762
Martin Drove End *Hants* 12 SU0520
Martin Hussingtree *H & W* 47 SO8860
Martindale *Cumb* 93 NY4319
Martinhoe *Devon* 19 SS6648
Martinscroft *Ches* 79 SJ6589
Martinstown *Dorset* 11 SY6489
Martlesham *Suffk* 55 TM2547
Martletwy *Dyfed* 30 SN0310
Martley *H & W* 47 SO7560
Martock *Somset* 21 ST4619
Marton *Ches* 71 SJ6267
Marton *Ches* 79 SJ8568
Marton *Cleve* 97 NZ5115
Marton *Humb* 85 TA1739
Marton *Humb* 91 TA2069
Marton *Lincs* 76 SK8381
Marton *N York* 89 SE4162
Marton *N York* 90 SE7383
Marton *Shrops* 58 SJ2802
Marton *Warwks* 48 SP4068
Marton-le-Moor *N York* 89 SE3770
Martyr Worthy *Hants* 24 SU5132
Martyr's Green *Surrey* 26 TQ0857
Marwick *Ork* 155 HY2324
Marwood *Devon* 19 SS5437
Mary Tavy *Devon* 5 SX5079
Marybank *Highld* 139 NH4853
Maryburgh *Highld* 139 NH5456
Maryculter *Gramp* 135 NO8599
Marygold *Border* 119 NT8159
Maryhill *Gramp* 143 NJ8245
Maryhill *Strath* 115 NS5669
Marykirk *Gramp* 135 NO6865
Maryland *Gwent* 34 SO5105
Marylebone *Gt Lon* 27 TQ2782
Marylebone *Gt Man* 78 SD5807
Marypark *Gramp* 141 NJ1938
Maryport *Cumb* 92 NY0336
Maryport *D & G* 98 NX1434
Marystow *Devon* 5 SX4382
Maryton *Tays* 127 NO6856
Marywell *Gramp* 135 NO9399
Marywell *Tays* 134 NO5895
Marywell *Tays* 127 NO6544
Masham *N York* 89 SE2280
Mashbury *Essex* 40 TL6511
Mason *T & W* 103 NZ2073
Masongill *N York* 87 SD6675
Mastin Moor *Derbys* 75 SK4575
Matching *Essex* 39 TL5212
Matching Green *Essex* 39 TL5311
Matching Tye *Essex* 39 TL5111
Matfen *Nthumb* 103 NZ0371
Matfield *Kent* 28 TQ6541
Mathern *Gwent* 34 ST5290
Mathon *H & W* 47 SO7346
Mathry *Dyfed* 30 SM8832
Matlaske *Norfk* 66 TG1534
Matlock *Derbys* 74 SK3059
Matlock Bank *Derbys* 74 SK3060
Matlock Bath *Derbys* 74 SK2958
Matlock Dale *Derbys* 74 SK2959
Matson *Gloucs* 35 SO8515
Matterdale End *Cumb* 93 NY3923
Mattersey *Notts* 75 SK6889
Mattersey Thorpe *Notts* 75 SK6889
Mattingley *Hants* 24 SU7357
Mattishall *Norfk* 66 TG0511
Mattishall Burgh *Norfk* 66 TG0512
Mauchline *Strath* 107 NS4927
Maud *Gramp* 143 NJ9148
Maufant *Jersey* 152 JS0000
Maugersbury *Gloucs* 48 SP2025
Maughold *IOM* 153 SC4991
Mauld *Highld* 139 NH4038
Maulden *Beds* 38 TL0538
Maulds Meaburn *Cumb* 94 NY6216
Maunby *N York* 89 SE3586
Maund Bryan *H & W* 46 SO5650
Maundown *Somset* 20 ST0628
Mautby *Norfk* 67 TG4812
Mavesyn Ridware *Staffs* 73 SK0816
Mavis Enderby *Lincs* 77 TF3666
Maw Green *Ches* 72 SJ7057
Maw Green *W Mids* 60 SP0196
Mawbray *Cumb* 92 NY0846
Mawdesley *Lancs* 80 SD4914
Mawdlam *M Glam* 32 SS8081
Mawgan *Cnwll* 2 SW7025
Mawgan Cross *Cnwll* 2 SW7024
Mawgan Porth *Cnwll* 4 SW8567
Mawla *Cnwll* 2 SW7045
Mawnan *Cnwll* 3 SW7827
Mawnan Smith *Cnwll* 3 SW7728
Mawthorpe *Lincs* 77 TF4672
Maxey *Cambs* 64 TF1208
Maxstoke *Warwks* 61 SP2386
Maxted Street *Kent* 29 TR1244
Maxton *Border* 110 NT6130
Maxton *Kent* 29 TR3041
Maxwell Town *D & G* 100 NX9676
Maxworthy *Cnwll* 5 SX2593
May Bank *Staffs* 72 SJ8547
May's Green *Oxon* 37 SU7480
May's Green *Surrey* 26 TQ0957
Mayals *W Glam* 32 SS6089
Maybole *Strath* 106 NS2909
Maybury *Surrey* 26 TQ0159
Mayes Green *Surrey* 14 TQ1239
Mayfield *E Susx* 16 TQ5826
Mayfield *Loth* 118 NT3565
Mayfield *Staffs* 73 SK1545
Mayford *Surrey* 25 SU9956
Mayland *Essex* 40 TL9201
Maynard's Green *E Susx* 16 TQ5818
Maypole *Gwent* 34 SO4716
Maypole *Kent* 29 TR2064
Maypole *W Mids* 61 SP0778
Maypole Green *Norfk* 67 TM4195
Maypole Green *Suffk* 54 TL9159
Maypole Green *Suffk* 55 TM2767
Mead *Devon* 18 SS2217
Meadgate *Avon* 22 ST6758
Meadle *Bucks* 38 SP8005
Meadowfield *Dur* 96 NZ2439
Meadowhall *S York* 74 SK3991
Meadowtown *Shrops* 59 SJ3001
Meadwell *Devon* 5 SX4081
Meal Bank *Cumb* 87 SD5495
Mealrigg *Cumb* 92 NY1345
Mealsgate *Cumb* 93 NY2042
Meamskirk *Strath* 115 NS5455
Meanwood *W York* 82 SE2837
Mearbeck *N York* 88 SD8160
Meare *Somset* 21 ST4541
Meare Green *Somset* 21 ST3326
Meare Green *Somset* 20 ST2922
Mears Ashby *Nhants* 51 SP8366
Measham *Leics* 62 SK3311
Meathop *Cumb* 87 SD4380
Meaux *Humb* 85 TA0839
Meavy *Devon* 6 SX5467
Medbourne *Leics* 51 SP8093
Meddon *Devon* 18 SS2717
Meden Vale *Notts* 75 SK5870
Medlam *Lincs* 77 TF3156
Medlar *Lancs* 80 SD4135
Medmenham *Berks* 37 SU8084
Medomsley *Dur* 95 NZ1154
Medstead *Hants* 24 SU6537
Meer Common *H & W* 46 SO3652
Meerbrook *Staffs* 72 SJ9860
Meesden *Herts* 39 TL4332
Meeson *Shrops* 72 SJ6421
Meeth *Devon* 19 SS5408
Meeting Green *Suffk* 53 TL7455
Meeting House Hill *Norfk* 67 TG3028
Meidrim *Dyfed* 31 SN2920

Moel Tryfan
Necton

Moel Tryfan Gwynd	68	SH5156
Moelfre Clwyd	58	SJ1828
Moelfre Gwynd	68	SH5186
Moffat D & G	108	NT0805
Mogerhanger Beds	52	TL1449
Moira Leics	62	SK3115
Mol-chlach Highld	128	NG4513
Molash Kent	28	TR0251
Mold Clwyd	70	SJ2363
Moldgreen W York	82	SE1516
Molehill Green Essex	40	TL5624
Molehill Green Essex	40	TL7120
Molescroft Humb	84	TA0140
Molesden Nthumb	103	NZ1484
Molesworth Cambs	51	TL0775
Molland Devon	19	SS8028
Mollington Ches	71	SJ3870
Mollington Oxon	49	SP4447
Mollinsburn Strath	116	NS7171
Monachty Dyfed	44	SN5061
Monday Boys Kent	28	TQ9045
Mondynes Gramp	135	NO7779
Monewden Suffk	55	TM2358
Moneydie Tays	125	NO0629
Moneygrow Green Berks	26	SU8977
Moniaive D & G	107	NX7890
Monifieth Tays	127	NO4932
Monikie Tays	127	NO4938
Monimail Fife	126	NO2914
Monington Dyfed	42	SN1344
Monk Bretton S York	83	SE3607
Monk Fryston N York	83	SE5029
Monk Sherborne Hants	24	SU6056
Monk Soham Suffk	55	TM2165
Monk Soham Green Suffk	55	TM2066
Monk Street Essex	40	TL6128
Monk's Gate W Susx	15	TQ2027
Monken Hadley Gt Lon	26	TQ2497
Monkhide H & W	46	SO6144
Monkhill Cumb	93	NY3458
Monkhopton Shrops	59	SO6293
Monkland H & W	46	SO4557
Monkleigh Devon	18	SS4520
Monknash S Glam	33	SS9170
Monkokehampton Devon	8	SS5805
Monks Eleigh Suffk	54	TL9647
Monks Heath Ches	79	SJ8474
Monks Horton Kent	28	TQ8356
Monks Kirby Warwks	50	SP4683
Monks Risborough Bucks	38	SP8104
Monkseaton T & W	103	NZ3472
Monksilver Somset	20	ST0737
Monkspath W Mids	61	SP1376
Monksthorpe Lincs	77	TF4465
Monkswood Gwent	34	SO3402
Monkton E Susx	9	ST1803
Monkton Kent	29	TR2964
Monkton S Glam	33	SS9270
Monkton Strath	106	NS3527
Monkton T & W	103	NZ3363
Monkton Combe Avon	22	ST7762
Monkton Deverill Wilts	22	ST8537
Monkton Farleigh Wilts	22	ST8065
Monkton Heathfield Somset	20	ST2526
Monkton Up Wimborne Dorset	11	SU0113
Monkton Wyld Dorset	10	SY3396
Monkwearmouth T & W	96	NZ3958
Monkwood Hants	24	SU6630
Monmore Green W Mids	60	SO9297
Monmouth Gwent	34	SO5012
Monnington on Wye H & W	46	SO3743
Monreith D & G	98	NX3541
Mont Saint Guern	152	GN0000
Montacute Somset	10	ST4916
Montcliffe Gt Man	81	SD6611
Montford Shrops	59	SJ4114
Montford Bridge Shrops	59	SJ4215
Montgarrie Gramp	142	NJ5717
Montgarswood Strath	107	NS5227
Montgomery Powys	58	SO2296
Montgreenan Strath	106	NS3343
Monton Gt Man	79	SJ7699
Montrose Tays	135	NO7157
Monxton Hants	23	SU3144
Monyash Derbys	74	SK1566
Monymusk Gramp	142	NJ6815
Monzie Tays	125	NN8725
Moodiesburn Strath	116	NS6970
Moonzie Fife	126	NO3317
Moor Allerton W York	82	SE3038
Moor Crichel Dorset	11	ST9908
Moor End Beds	38	SP9719
Moor End Devon	19	SS6609
Moor End Humb	84	SE8137
Moor End Lancs	80	SD3744
Moor End N York	83	SE6038
Moor End W York	82	SE0528
Moor Green Herts	39	TL3226
Moor Head W York	82	SE1337
Moor Head W York	82	SE2329
Moor Monkton N York	83	SE5156
Moor Row Cumb	92	NY0014
Moor Row Cumb	93	NY2149
Moor Row Dur	96	NZ1515
Moor Side Lancs	80	SD4935
Moor Side Lancs	80	SD4334
Moor Side Lincs	77	TF2557
Moor Street Kent	28	TQ8265
Moor Street W Mids	60	SO9982
Moorbath Dorset	10	SY4395
Moorby Lincs	77	TF2964
Moorcot H & W	46	SO3555
Moordown Dorset	12	SZ0994
Moore Ches	78	SJ5784
Moorend Gloucs	35	SO7303
Moorends S York	83	SE6915
Moorgreen Hants	13	SU4815
Moorgreen Notts	62	SK4847
Moorhall Derbys	74	SK3074
Moorhampton H & W	46	SO3746
Moorhouse Cumb	93	NY2551
Moorhouse Cumb	93	NY3356
Moorhouse Notts	75	SK7566
Moorhouse W York	83	SE4810
Moorhouse Bank Surrey	27	TQ4353
Moorland Somset	21	ST3332
Moorlinch Somset	21	ST3936
Moorsholm Cleve	90	NZ6814
Moorside Cumb	86	NY0701
Moorside Dorset	22	ST7919
Moorside Gt Man	79	SD9407
Moorside W York	82	SE2436
Moorstock Kent	29	TR1038
Moorswater Cnwll	5	SX2364
Moorthorpe W York	83	SE4611
Moortown Devon	6	SX5274
Moortown Hants	12	SU1503
Moortown IOW	13	SZ4283
Moortown Lincs	76	TF0798
Moortown Shrops	59	SJ6118
Moortown W York	82	SE2939
Morangie Highld	147	NH7683
Morar Highld	129	NM6793
Morborne Cambs	64	TL1391
Morchard Bishop Devon	8	SS7707
Morcombelake Dorset	10	SY4094
Morcott Leics	51	SK9200
Morda Shrops	58	SJ2827
Morden Dorset	11	SY9195
Morden Gt Lon	27	TQ2666
Mordiford H & W	46	SO5737
Mordon Dur	96	NZ3226
More Shrops	59	SO3491
Morebath Devon	20	SS9525
Morebattle Border	110	NT7724
Morecambe Lancs	87	SD4364
Moredon Wilts	36	SU1487
Morefield Highld	145	NH1195
Morehall Kent	29	TR2136
Moreleigh Devon	7	SX7652
Morenish Tays	124	NN6035
Moresby Cumb	92	NX9921
Moresby Parks Cumb	92	NX9919
Morestead Hants	13	SU5025
Moreton Dorset	11	SY8089
Moreton Essex	39	TL5307
Moreton H & W	46	SO5064
Moreton Mersyd	78	SJ2689
Moreton Oxon	37	SP6904
Moreton Staffs	72	SJ7817
Moreton Staffs	73	SK1429
Moreton Corbet Shrops	59	SJ5623
Moreton Jeffries H & W	46	SO6048
Moreton Mill Shrops	59	SJ5723
Moreton Morrell Warwks	48	SP3155
Moreton on Lugg H & W	46	SO5045
Moreton Paddox Warwks	48	SP3154
Moreton Pinkney Nhants	49	SP5749
Moreton Say Shrops	59	SJ6334
Moreton Valence Gloucs	35	SO7809
Moreton-in-Marsh Gloucs	48	SP2032
Moretonhampstead Devon	8	SX7586
Morfa Dyfed	42	SN3053
Morfa Bychan Gwynd	57	SH5437
Morfa Dinlle Gwynd	68	SH4358
Morfa Glas W Glam	33	SN8606
Morfa Nefyn Gwynd	56	SH2840
Morgan's Vale Wilts	12	SU1920
Morganstown S Glam	33	ST1281
Morham Loth	118	NT5571
Moriah Dyfed	43	SN6279
Morland Cumb	94	NY6022
Morley Ches	79	SJ8282
Morley Derbys	62	SK3940
Morley Dur	96	NZ1227
Morley W York	82	SE2627
Morley Green Ches	79	SJ8281
Morley St Botolph Norfk	66	TM0799
Mornick Cnwll	5	SX3272
Morningside Loth	117	NT2470
Morningside Strath	116	NS8355
Morningthorpe Norfk	67	TM2192
Morpeth Nthumb	103	NZ1986
Morphie Gramp	135	NO7164
Morrey Staffs	73	SK1218
Morridge Side Staffs	73	SK0254
Morridge Top Staffs	74	SK0365
Morriston W Glam	32	SS6697
Morston Norfk	66	TG0043
Mortehoe Devon	18	SS4545
Morthen S York	75	SK4788
Mortimer Berks	24	SU6564
Mortimer Common Berks	24	SU6565
Mortimer West End Hants	24	SU6363
Mortimer's Cross H & W	46	SO4263
Mortlake Gt Lon	26	TQ2075
Morton Cumb	93	NY3854
Morton Cumb	93	NY4539
Morton Derbys	74	SK4060
Morton IOW	13	SZ6085
Morton Lincs	75	SK8091
Morton Lincs	64	TF0923
Morton Norfk	66	TG1216
Morton Notts	75	SK7251
Morton Shrops	59	SJ2924
Morton Hall Lincs	76	SK8863
Morton Tinmouth Dur	96	NZ1821
Morton-on-Swale N York	89	SE3291
Morvah Cnwll	2	SW4035
Morval Cnwll	5	SX2556
Morvich Highld	138	NG9621
Morville Shrops	60	SO6794
Morville Heath Shrops	60	SO6893
Morwenstow Cnwll	18	SS2015
Mosborough S York	74	SK4281
Moscow Strath	107	NS4840
Mose Shrops	60	SO7590
Mosedale Cumb	93	NY3532
Moseley H & W	47	SO8159
Moseley W Mids	60	SO9498
Moseley W Mids	61	SP0783
Moses Gate Gt Man	79	SD7306
Moss Clwyd	71	SJ3053
Moss S York	83	SE5914
Moss Strath	120	NL9544
Moss Bank Mersyd	78	SJ5197
Moss Edge Lancs	80	SD4243
Moss End Ches	79	SJ6778
Moss Side Cumb	93	NY1952
Moss Side Lancs	80	SD3730
Moss Side Mersyd	78	SD3802
Moss-side Highld	140	NH8555
Mossat Gramp	142	NJ4719
Mossbank Shet	155	HU4575
Mossbay Cumb	92	NX9927
Mossblown Strath	106	NS4024
Mossbrow Gt Man	79	SJ7089
Mossburnford Border	110	NT6616
Mossdale D & G	99	NX6670
Mossdale Strath	107	NS4904
Mossend Strath	116	NS7460
Mosser Mains Cumb	92	NY1125
Mossgiel Strath	107	NS4828
Mossknowe D & G	101	NY2769
Mossley Ches	72	SJ8861
Mossley Gt Man	82	SD9701
Mosspaul Hotel Border	109	NY3999
Mosstodloch Gramp	141	NJ3259
Mossy Lea Lancs	80	SD5312
Mossyard D & G	99	NX5451
Mosterton Dorset	10	ST4505
Moston Gt Man	79	SD8701
Moston Shrops	59	SJ5626
Moston Green Ches	72	SJ7261
Mostyn Clwyd	70	SJ1580
Motcombe Dorset	22	ST8525
Mothecombe Devon	6	SX6047
Motherby Cumb	93	NY4228
Motherwell Strath	116	NS7457
Motspur Park Gt Lon	26	TQ2267
Mottingham Gt Lon	27	TQ4272
Mottisfont Hants	23	SU3226
Mottistone IOW	13	SZ4083
Mottram in Longdendale Gt Man	79	SJ9995
Mottram St Andrew Ches	79	SJ8778
Mouilpied Guern	152	GN0000
Mouldsworth Ches	71	SJ5071
Moulin Tays	132	NN9459
Moulsecoomb E Susx	15	TQ3307
Moulsford Oxon	37	SU5883
Moulsoe Bucks	38	SP9141
Moultavie Highld	146	NH6371
Moulton Ches	79	SJ6569
Moulton Lincs	64	TF3023
Moulton N York	89	NZ2303
Moulton Nhants	50	SP7866
Moulton S Glam	33	ST0770
Moulton Suffk	53	TL6964
Moulton Chapel Lincs	64	TF2918
Moulton Seas End Lincs	64	TF3227
Moulton St Mary Norfk	67	TG3907
Mount Cnwll	3	SW7856
Mount Cnwll	4	SX1468
Mount W York	82	SE0917
Mount Ambrose Cnwll	2	SW7043
Mount Bures Essex	40	TL9032
Mount Hawke Cnwll	2	SW7147
Mount Hermon Cnwll	2	SW6915
Mount Lothian Loth	117	NT2757
Mount Pleasant Ches	72	SJ8456
Mount Pleasant Derbys	74	SK3448
Mount Pleasant Dur	96	NZ2634
Mount Pleasant E Susx	16	TQ4216
Mount Pleasant H & W	47	SP0064
Mount Pleasant Norfk	66	TL9994
Mount Pleasant Suffk	53	TL7347
Mount Sorrel Wilts	23	SU0324
Mount Tabor W York	82	SE0527
Mountain W York	82	SE0930
Mountain Ash M Glam	33	ST0499
Mountain Cross Border	117	NT1547
Mountain Street Kent	29	TR0652
Mountfield E Susx	17	TQ7320
Mountgerald House Highld	139	NH5661
Mountjoy Cnwll	4	SW8760
Mountnessing Essex	40	TQ6297
Mounton Gwent	34	ST5193
Mountsorrel Leics	62	SK5814
Mountstuart Strath	114	NS1159
Mousehill Surrey	25	SU9441
Mousehole Cnwll	2	SW4626
Mouswald D & G	100	NY0672
Mow Cop Ches	72	SJ8557
Mowhaugh Border	110	NT8120
Mowmacre Hill Leics	62	SK5807
Mowsley Leics	50	SP6489
Mowtie Gramp	135	NO8388
Moy Highld	140	NH7634
Moy Highld	131	NN4282
Moye Highld	138	NG8818
Moyles Court Hants	12	SU1608
Moylgrove Dyfed	42	SN1144
Muasdale Strath	105	NR6840
Much Birch H & W	46	SO5030
Much Cowarne H & W	46	SO6147
Much Dewchurch H & W	46	SO4831
Much Hadham Herts	39	TL4219
Much Hoole Lancs	80	SD4723
Much Hoole Town Lancs	80	SD4722
Much Marcle H & W	47	SO6532
Much Wenlock Shrops	59	SO6299
Muchalls Gramp	135	NO9092
Muchelney Somset	21	ST4224
Muchelney Ham Somset	21	ST4423
Muchlarnick Cnwll	5	SX2156
Mucking Essex	40	TQ6881
Muckingford Essex	40	TQ6779
Muckleford Dorset	10	SY6393
Mucklestone Staffs	72	SJ7237
Muckley Shrops	59	SO6495
Muckton Lincs	77	TF3781
Mucomir Highld	131	NN1884
Mud Row Kent	28	TR0072
Muddiford Devon	19	SS5638
Muddles Green E Susx	16	TQ5413
Mudeford Dorset	12	SZ1892
Mudford Somset	21	ST5719
Mudford Sock Somset	21	ST5519
Mudgley Somset	21	ST4545
Mugdock Cent	115	NS5577
Mugeary Highld	136	NG4439
Mugginton Derbys	73	SK2842
Muggintonlane End Derbys	73	SK2844
Muggleswick Dur	95	NZ0449
Muir of Fowlis Gramp	134	NJ5612
Muir of Miltonduff Gramp	141	NJ1859
Muir of Ord Highld	139	NH5250
Muir of Thorn Tays	125	NO0637
Muirden Gramp	142	NJ7054
Muirdrum Tays	127	NO5637
Muiresk Gramp	142	NJ6948
Muirhead Fife	126	NO2805
Muirhead Strath	116	NS6869
Muirhead Tays	126	NO3434
Muirhouses Cent	117	NT0180
Muirkirk Strath	107	NS6927
Muirmill Cent	116	NS7283
Muirshearlich Highld	131	NN1380
Muirtack Gramp	143	NJ9937
Muirton Tays	125	NN9211
Muirton Mains Highld	139	NH4553
Muirton of Ardblair Tays	126	NO1643
Muker N York	88	SD9097
Mulbarton Norfk	67	TG1901
Mulben Gramp	141	NJ3550
Mulfra Cnwll	2	SW4534
Mulindry Strath	112	NR3659
Mullacott Cross Devon	19	SS5144
Mullion Cnwll	2	SW6719
Mullion Cove Cnwll	2	SW6617
Mumby Lincs	77	TF5174
Muncher's Green Herts	39	TL3126
Munderfield Row H & W	47	SO6451
Munderfield Stocks H & W	47	SO6550
Mundesley Norfk	67	TG3136
Mundford Norfk	66	TL8093
Mundham Norfk	67	TM3397
Mundon Hill Essex	40	TL8602
Mungrisdale Cumb	93	NY3630
Munlochy Highld	140	NH6453
Munnoch Strath	114	NS2548
Munsley H & W	47	SO6640
Munslow Shrops	59	SO5287
Murchington Devon	8	SX6888
Murcot H & W	48	SP0640
Murcott Oxon	37	SP5815
Murcott Wilts	35	ST9591
Murkle Highld	151	ND1668
Murlaggan Highld	130	NN0192
Murrell Green Hants	24	SU7455
Murroes Tays	127	NO4635
Murrow Cambs	64	TF3707
Mursley Bucks	38	SP8128
Murston Kent	28	TQ9264
Murthill Tays	134	NO4657
Murthly Tays	126	NO1038
Murton Cumb	94	NY7221
Murton Dur	96	NZ3847
Murton N York	83	SE6452
Murton Nthumb	111	NT9748
Murton T & W	103	NZ3270
Musbury Devon	10	SY2794
Muscoates N York	90	SE6879
Musselburgh Loth	118	NT3472
Muston Leics	63	SK8237
Muston N York	91	TA0979
Mustow Green H & W	60	SO8774
Muswell Hill Gt Lon	27	TQ2889
Mutehill D & G	99	NX6848
Mutford Suffk	55	TM4888
Muthill Tays	125	NN8717
Mutterton Devon	9	ST0205
Muxton Shrops	60	SJ7114
Mybster Highld	151	ND1652
Myddfai Dyfed	44	SN7730
Myddle Shrops	59	SJ4623
Mydroilyn Dyfed	42	SN4555
Mylor Cnwll	3	SW8135
Mylor Bridge Cnwll	3	SW8036
Mynachlog ddu Dyfed	31	SN1430
Myndd-llan Clwyd	70	SJ1572
Myndtown Shrops	59	SO3989
Mynydd Buch Dyfed	43	SN7276
Mynydd Isa Clwyd	70	SJ2563
Mynydd Llandygai Gwynd	69	SH6065
Mynydd-bach Gwent	34	ST4894
Mynydd-bach W Glam	32	SS6597
Mynyddgarreg Dyfed	31	SN4208
Mynytho Gwynd	56	SH3031
Myrebird Gramp	135	NO7398
Myredykes Border	102	NY5998
Mytchett Surrey	25	SU8855
Mytholm W York	82	SD9827
Mytholmroyd W York	82	SE0126
Mythop Lancs	80	SD3634
Myton-on-Swale N York	89	SE4366

N

Na Buirgh W Isls	154	NG0394
Naast Highld	144	NG8283
Nab's Head Lancs	81	SD6229
Naburn N York	83	SE5945
Nackholt Kent	28	TR0543
Nackington Kent	29	TR1554
Nacton Suffk	55	TM2240
Nafferton Humb	91	TA0559
Nag's Head Gloucs	35	ST8898
Nailbridge Gloucs	35	SO6415
Nailsbourne Somset	20	ST2128
Nailsea Avon	34	ST4770
Nailstone Leics	62	SK4106
Nailsworth Gloucs	35	ST8499
Nairn Highld	140	NH8856
Nalderswood Surrey	15	TQ2445
Nancegollan Cnwll	2	SW6332
Nancledra Cnwll	2	SW4936
Nanhoron Gwynd	56	SH2731
Nannerch Clwyd	70	SJ1669
Nanpantan Leics	62	SK5017
Nanpean Cnwll	3	SW9556
Nanquidno Cnwll	2	SW3629
Nanstallon Cnwll	4	SX0367
Nant Gwynant Gwynd	69	SH6350
Nant Peris Gwynd	69	SH6058
Nant-ddu Powys	33	SO0014
Nant-glas Powys	45	SN9965
Nant-y-Bwch Gwent	33	SO1210
Nant-y-caws Dyfed	32	SN4518
Nant-y-derry Gwent	34	SO3306
Nant-y-gollen Shrops	58	SJ2428
Nant-y-moel M Glam	33	SS9392
Nant-y-pandy Gwynd	69	SH6973
Nanternis Dyfed	42	SN3756
Nantgaredig Dyfed	32	SN4921
Nantgarw M Glam	33	ST1285
Nantglyn Clwyd	70	SJ0061
Nantgwyn Powys	45	SN9776
Nantlle Gwynd	68	SH5153
Nantmawr Shrops	58	SJ2524
Nantmel Powys	45	SO0366
Nantmor Gwynd	57	SH6046
Nantwich Ches	72	SJ6552
Nantyffyllon M Glam	33	SS8492
Naphill Bucks	26	SU8496
Napleton H & W	47	SO8648
Nappa N York	81	SD8553
Napton on the Hill Warwks	49	SP4661
Narberth Dyfed	31	SN1015
Narborough Leics	50	SP5497
Narborough Norfk	65	TF7412
Narkurs Cnwll	5	SX3255
Nasareth Gwynd	68	SH4749
Naseby Nhants	50	SP6978
Nash Bucks	38	SP7833
Nash Gt Lon	27	TQ4063
Nash Gwent	34	ST3483
Nash H & W	46	SO3062
Nash Shrops	46	SO6071
Nash End H & W	60	SO7781
Nash Lee Bucks	38	SP8408
Nash Street Kent	27	TQ6469
Nash's Green Hants	24	SU6745
Nassington Nhants	51	TL0696
Nastend Gloucs	35	SO7906
Nasty Herts	39	TL3524
Nateby Cumb	88	NY7706
Nateby Lancs	80	SD4644
Natland Cumb	87	SD5289
Naughton Suffk	54	TM0249
Naunton Gloucs	48	SP1123
Naunton H & W	47	SO8645
Naunton H & W	47	SO8739
Naunton Beauchamp H & W	47	SO9652
Navenby Lincs	76	SK9858
Navestock Essex	27	TQ5397
Navestock Side Essex	27	TQ5697
Navidale House Hotel Highld	147	ND0316
Navity Highld	140	NH7864
Nawton N York	90	SE6584
Nayland Suffk	54	TL9734
Nazeing Essex	39	TL4106
Nazeing Gate Essex	39	TL4105
Neacroft Hants	12	SZ1896
Neal's Green Warwks	61	SP3384
Neap Shet	155	HU5058
Near Cotton Staffs	73	SK0646
Near Sawry Cumb	87	SD3795
Neasden Gt Lon	26	TQ2185
Neasham Dur	89	NZ3210
Neath W Glam	32	SS7597
Neatham Hants	24	SU7440
Neatishead Norfk	67	TG3420
Nebo Dyfed	43	SN5465
Nebo Gwynd	68	SH4850
Nebo Gwynd	69	SH8355
Nebo Gwynd	68	SH4690
Necton Norfk	66	TF8709

Newtown

Oakham

Newtown *Ches* 71 SJ5375
Newtown *Ches* 71 SJ6247
Newtown *Ches* 72 SJ9060
Newtown *Cnwll* 2 SW5729
Newtown *Cnwll* 3 SW7423
Newtown *Cnwll* 3 SX1052
Newtown *Cnwll* 5 SX2978
Newtown *Cumb* 92 NY1048
Newtown *Cumb* 101 NY5062
Newtown *Cumb* 94 NY5224
Newtown *D & G* 107 NS7710
Newtown *Derbys* 79 SJ9984
Newtown *Devon* 9 SY0699
Newtown *Devon* 19 SS7625
Newtown *Dorset* 10 ST4802
Newtown *Dorset* 12 SZ0393
Newtown *Gloucs* 35 SO6702
Newtown *Gt Man* 78 SD5604
Newtown *Gwent* 33 SO1709
Newtown *H & W* 46 SO4757
Newtown *H & W* 46 SO5333
Newtown *H & W* 46 SO6145
Newtown *H & W* 47 SO7037
Newtown *H & W* 47 SO8755
Newtown *H & W* 60 SO9478
Newtown *Hants* 12 SU2710
Newtown *Hants* 24 SU4763
Newtown *Hants* 13 SU6013
Newtown *Highld* 131 NH3504
Newtown *IOW* 13 SZ4290
Newtown *Lancs* 80 SD5118
Newtown *M Glam* 33 ST0598
Newtown *Nthumb* 111 NT9631
Newtown *Nthumb* 103 NU0300
Newtown *Nthumb* 103 NU0425
Newtown *Powys* 58 SO1091
Newtown *Shrops* 59 SJ4222
Newtown *Shrops* 59 SJ4731
Newtown *Staffs* 60 SJ9904
Newtown *Wilts* 22 ST9129
Newtown *Wilts* 23 SU2963
Newtown Linford *Leics* 62 SK5209
Newtown of Beltrees *Strath* 115 NS3758
Newtown St Boswells *Border* 110 NT5732
Newtown Unthank *Leics* 62 SK4904
Newtyle *Tays* 126 NO2941
Newyears Green *Gt Lon* 26 TQ0788
Newyork *Strath* 122 NM9611
Nextend *H & W* 46 SO3357
Neyland *Dyfed* 30 SM9605
Niarbyl *IOM* 153 SC2177
Nibley *Avon* 35 ST6982
Nibley *Gloucs* 35 SO6606
Nibley Green *Gloucs* 35 ST7396
Nicholashayne *Devon* 9 ST1016
Nicholaston *W Glam* 32 SS5288
Nickies Hill *Cumb* 101 NY5367
Nidd *N York* 89 SE3060
Nigg *Gramp* 135 NJ9402
Nigg *Highld* 147 NH8071
Nightcott *Devon* 19 SS8925
Nimlet *Avon* 35 ST7470
Nine Elms *Wilts* 36 SU1085
Nine Wells *Dyfed* 30 SM7924
Ninebanks *Nthumb* 94 NY7853
Nineveh *H & W* 47 SO6265
Ninfield *E Susx* 16 TQ7012
Ningwood *IOW* 13 SZ3989
Nisbet *Border* 110 NT6725
Nisbet Hill *Border* 119 NT7950
Niton *IOW* 13 SZ5076
Nitshill *Strath* 115 NS5260
No Man's Heath *Ches* 71 SJ5148
No Man's Heath *Warwks* 61 SK2808
No Man's Land *Cnwll* 4 SW9470
No Man's Land *Cnwll* 5 SX2756
Noah's Ark *Kent* 27 TQ5557
Noak Bridge *Essex* 40 TQ6990
Noak Hill *Essex* 27 TQ5494
Noblethorpe *W York* 82 SE2805
Nobold *Shrops* 59 SJ4710
Nobottle *Nhants* 49 SP6763
Nocton *Lincs* 76 TF0564
Nogdam End *Norfk* 67 TG3900
Noke *Oxon* 37 SP5413
Nolton *Dyfed* 30 SM8618
Nolton Haven *Dyfed* 30 SM8618
Nomansland *Devon* 19 SS8313
Nomansland *Wilts* 12 SU2517
Noneley *Shrops* 59 SJ4828
Nonington *Kent* 29 TR2552
Nook *Cumb* 101 NY4679
Nook *Cumb* 87 SD5481
Norbiton *Gt Lon* 26 TQ1969
Norbreck *Lancs* 80 SD3140
Norbridge *H & W* 47 SO7144
Norbury *Ches* 71 SJ5547
Norbury *Derbys* 73 SK1241
Norbury *Gt Lon* 27 TQ3069
Norbury *Shrops* 59 SO3692
Norbury *Staffs* 72 SJ7823
Norbury Common *Ches* 71 SJ5548
Norbury Junction *Staffs* 72 SJ7923
Norchard *H & W* 47 SO8568
Norcott Brook *Ches* 78 SJ6080
Norcross *Lancs* 80 SD3341
Nordelph *Norfk* 65 TF5501
Norden *Gt Man* 81 SD8614
Nordley *Shrops* 60 SO6996
Norham *Nthumb* 110 NT9047
Norland Town *W York* 82 SE0622
Norley *Ches* 71 SJ5772
Norleywood *Hants* 12 SZ3597
Norlington *E Susx* 16 TQ4413
Norman Cross *Cambs* 52 TL1690
Norman's Bay *E Susx* 16 TQ6805
Norman's Green *Devon* 9 ST0503
Normanby *Cleve* 97 NZ5418
Normanby *Humb* 84 SE8816
Normanby *Lincs* 76 SK9988
Normanby *N York* 90 SE7381
Normanby le Wold *Lincs* 76 TF1295
Normandy *Surrey* 25 SU9351
Normanton *Derbys* 62 SK3433
Normanton *Leics* 63 SK8140
Normanton *Leics* 63 SK9305
Normanton *Lincs* 63 SK9446
Normanton *Notts* 75 SK7054
Normanton *W York* 83 SE3822
Normanton *Wilts* 23 SU1340
Normanton le Heath *Leics* 62 SK3712
Normanton on Soar *Notts* 62 SK5122
Normanton on the Wolds *Notts* 62 SK6232
Normanton on Trent *Notts* 75 SK7868
Normoss *Lancs* 80 SD3437
Norney *Surrey* 25 SU9444
Norrington Common *Wilts* 22 ST8864
Norris Green *Cnwll* 5 SX4169
Norristhorpe *W York* 82 SE2123
North Anston *S York* 75 SK5184
North Aston *Oxon* 49 SP4828
North Baddesley *Hants* 13 SU3920
North Ballachulish *Highld* 130 NN0560
North Barrow *Somset* 21 ST6129
North Barsham *Norfk* 66 TF9135
North Benfleet *Essex* 40 TQ7588
North Bersted *W Susx* 14 SU9201
North Berwick *Loth* 118 NT5485
North Biddick *T & W* 96 NZ3153
North Bitchburn *Dur* 96 NZ1732
North Boarhunt *Hants* 13 SU6010
North Bockhampton *Hants* 12 SZ1797
North Bovey *Devon* 8 SX7484
North Bradley *Wilts* 22 ST8555
North Brentor *Devon* 5 SX4881
North Brewham *Somset* 22 ST7236
North Bridge *Surrey* 14 SU9636
North Brook End *Cambs* 39 TL2944
North Buckland *Devon* 18 SS4840
North Burlingham *Norfk* 67 TG3609
North Cadbury *Somset* 21 ST6327
North Carlton *Lincs* 76 SK9477
North Carlton *Notts* 75 SK5984
North Cave *Humb* 84 SE8932
North Cerney *Gloucs* 35 SP0107
North Charford *Hants* 12 SU1919
North Charlton *Nthumb* 111 NU1622
North Cheam *Gt Lon* 26 TQ2365
North Cheriton *Somset* 22 ST6925
North Chideock *Dorset* 10 SY4294
North Cliffe *Humb* 84 SE8736
North Clifton *Notts* 75 SK8272
North Close *Dur* 96 NZ2532
North Cockerington *Lincs* 77 TF3790
North Collingham *Notts* 76 SK8362
North Common *E Susx* 15 TQ3921
North Connel *Strath* 122 NM9034
North Cornelly *M Glam* 33 SS8181
North Corner *Cnwll* 3 SW7818
North Corry *Highld* 122 NM8353
North Cotes *Lincs* 77 TA3400
North Country *Cnwll* 2 SW6943
North Cove *Suffk* 55 TM4689
North Cowton *N York* 89 NZ2803
North Crawley *Bucks* 38 SP9244
North Cray *Gt Lon* 27 TQ4872
North Creake *Norfk* 66 TF8538
North Curry *Somset* 21 ST3125
North Dalton *Humb* 84 SE9351
North Deighton *N York* 83 SE3951
North Duffield *N York* 83 SE6837
North Duntulm *Highld* 136 NG4274
North Elham *Kent* 29 TR1844
North Elkington *Lincs* 77 TF2890
North Elmham *Norfk* 66 TF9820
North Elmsall *W York* 83 SE4712
North End *Avon* 21 ST4266
North End *Cumb* 93 NY3259
North End *Dorset* 22 ST8427
North End *Essex* 40 TL6618
North End *Hants* 12 SU1016
North End *Hants* 24 SU5828
North End *Hants* 13 SU6502
North End *Humb* 85 TA1022
North End *Humb* 85 TA1941
North End *Humb* 85 TA2831
North End *Humb* 85 TA3101
North End *Leics* 62 SK5715
North End *Lincs* 76 TF0499
North End *Lincs* 64 TF2341
North End *Lincs* 77 TF4289
North End *Mersyd* 78 SD3004
North End *Nhants* 51 SP9668
North End *Norfk* 66 TL9992
North End *Nthumb* 103 NU1301
North End *W Susx* 14 SU9703
North End *W Susx* 14 TQ1109
North Erradale *Highld* 144 NG7480
North Evington *Leics* 62 SK6204
North Fambridge *Essex* 40 TQ8597
North Ferriby *Humb* 84 SE9826
North Frodingham *Humb* 85 TA1053
North Gorley *Hants* 12 SU1611
North Green *Norfk* 55 TM2288
North Green *Suffk* 55 TM3162
North Green *Suffk* 55 TM3966
North Grimston *N York* 90 SE8467
North Halling *Kent* 28 TQ7065
North Hayling *Hants* 13 SU7303
North Hazelrigg *Nthumb* 111 NU0533
North Heasley *Devon* 19 SS7333
North Heath *W Susx* 14 TQ0621
North Hele *Somset* 20 ST0323
North Hill *Cnwll* 5 SX2776
North Hillingdon *Gt Lon* 26 TQ0784
North Hinksey *Oxon* 37 SP4905
North Huish *Devon* 7 SX7156
North Hykeham *Lincs* 76 SK9465
North Kelsey *Humb* 84 TA0401
North Kessock *Highld* 140 NH6548
North Killingholme *Humb* 85 TA1417
North Kilvington *N York* 89 SE4285
North Kilworth *Leics* 50 SP6183
North Kingston *Hants* 12 SU1603
North Kyme *Lincs* 76 TF1552
North Landing *Humb* 91 TA2471
North Lee *Bucks* 38 SP8308
North Lees *N York* 89 SE2973
North Leigh *Kent* 29 TR1347
North Leigh *Oxon* 36 SP3813
North Leverton with
Habblesthorpe *Notts* 75 SK7882
North Littleton *H & W* 48 SP0847
North Lopham *Norfk* 54 TM0382
North Luffenham *Leics* 63 SK9303
North Marden *W Susx* 14 SU8016
North Marston *Bucks* 37 SP7722
North Middleton *Loth* 118 NT3559
North Middleton *Nthumb* 111 NT9924
North Milmain *D & G* 98 NX0852
North Molton *Devon* 19 SS7329
North Moreton *Oxon* 37 SU5689
North Mundham *W Susx* 14 SU8702
North Muskham *Notts* 75 SK7958
North Newbald *Humb* 84 SE9136
North Newington *Oxon* 49 SP4240
North Newnton *Wilts* 23 SU1257
North Newton *Somset* 20 ST3031
North Nibley *Gloucs* 35 ST7495
North Oakley *Hants* 24 SU5354
North Ockendon *Gt Lon* 27 TQ5985
North Ormesby *Cleve* 97 NZ5119
North Ormsby *Lincs* 77 TF2893
North Otterington *N York* 89 SE3689
North Owersby *Lincs* 76 TF0594
North Perrott *Somset* 10 ST4709
North Petherton *Somset* 20 ST2833
North Petherwin *Cnwll* 5 SX2789
North Pickenham *Norfk* 66 TF8606
North Piddle *H & W* 47 SO9654
North Pool *Devon* 7 SX7741
North Poorton *Dorset* 10 SY5298
North Poulner *Hants* 12 SU1606
North Quarme *Somset* 20 SS9236
North Queensferry *Fife* 117 NT1380
North Radworthy *Devon* 19 SS7534
North Rauceby *Lincs* 76 TF0246
North Reston *Lincs* 77 TF3883
North Rigton *N York* 82 SE2749
North Ripley *Hants* 12 SZ1699
North Rode *Ches* 72 SJ8866
North Row *Cumb* 93 NY2232
North Runcton *Norfk* 65 TF6416
North Scale *Cumb* 86 SD1869
North Scarle *Lincs* 76 SK8466
North Seaton *Nthumb* 103 NZ2986
North Seaton Colliery *Nthumb* 103 NZ2985
North Shian *Strath* 122 NM9143
North Shields *T & W* 103 NZ3568
North Shoebury *Essex* 40 TQ9286
North Shore *Lancs* 80 SD3037
North Side *Cambs* 64 TL2799
North Side *Cumb* 92 NX9929
North Skelton *Cleve* 97 NZ6718
North Somercotes *Lincs* 77 TF4296
North Stainley *N York* 89 SE2876
North Stainmore *Cumb* 95 NY8314
North Stifford *Essex* 40 TQ6080
North Stoke *Avon* 35 ST7069
North Stoke *Oxon* 37 SU6186
North Stoke *W Susx* 14 TQ0110
North Street *Berks* 24 SU6371
North Street *Cambs* 53 TL5868
North Street *Hants* 12 SU1518
North Street *Hants* 24 SU6433
North Street *Kent* 28 TQ8174
North Street *Kent* 28 TR0157
North Sunderland *Nthumb* 111 NU2131
North Tamerton *Cnwll* 5 SX3197
North Tawton *Devon* 8 SS6601
North Third *Cent* 116 NS7589
North Thoresby *Lincs* 77 TF2998
North Tidworth *Wilts* 23 SU2349
North Town *Berks* 26 SU8882
North Town *Devon* 19 SS5109
North Town *Somset* 21 ST5642
North Tuddenham *Norfk* 66 TG0314
North Walbottle *T & W* 103 NZ1767
North Walsham *Norfk* 67 TG2830
North Waltham *Hants* 24 SU5646
North Warnborough *Hants* 24 SU7351
North Weald Basset *Essex* 39 TL4904
North Wheatley *Notts* 75 SK7585
North Whilborough *Devon* 7 SX8766
North Wick *Avon* 21 ST5865
North Widcombe *Somset* 21 ST5758
North Willingham *Lincs* 76 TF1688
North Wingfield *Derbys* 74 SK4065
North Witham *Lincs* 63 SK9221
North Wootton *Dorset* 11 ST6514
North Wootton *Norfk* 65 TF6424
North Wootton *Somset* 21 ST5641
North Wraxall *Wilts* 35 ST8175
North Wroughton *Wilts* 36 SU1481
Northacre *Norfk* 66 TL9598
Northall *Bucks* 38 SP9520
Northall Green *Norfk* 66 TF9914
Northallerton *N York* 89 SE3694
Northam *Devon* 18 SS4529
Northam *Hants* 13 SU4312
Northampton *H & W* 47 SO8365
Northampton *Nhants* 49 SP7560
Northaw *Herts* 27 TL2702
Northay *Somset* 10 ST2811
Northborough *Cambs* 64 TF1507
Northbourne *Kent* 29 TR3352
Northbridge Street *E Susx* 17 TQ7324
Northbrook *Hants* 24 SU5139
Northbrook *Oxon* 37 SP4922
Northchapel *W Susx* 14 SU9529
Northchurch *Herts* 38 SP9708
Northcott *Devon* 9 ST0912
Northcott *Devon* 9 ST1209
Northcott *Devon* 5 SX3392
Northcourt *Oxon* 37 SU4998
Northdown *Kent* 29 TR3770
Northedge *Derbys* 74 SK3665
Northend *Bucks* 37 SU7392
Northend *Warwks* 48 SP3952
Northend Woods *Bucks* 26 SU9089
Northenden *Gt Man* 79 SJ8289
Northfield *Gramp* 135 NJ9008
Northfield *Humb* 84 TA0326
Northfield *W Mids* 60 SP0279
Northfields *Lincs* 64 TF0208
Northfleet *Kent* 27 TQ6374
Northiam *E Susx* 17 TQ8324
Northill *Beds* 52 TL1446
Northington *Gloucs* 35 SO7008
Northington *Hants* 24 SU5637
Northlands *Lincs* 77 TF3453
Northleach *Gloucs* 36 SP1114
Northleigh *Devon* 19 SS6034
Northleigh *Devon* 9 SY1995
Northlew *Devon* 19 SX5099
Northload Bridge *Somset* 21 ST4939
Northmoor *Somset* 20 SS9028
Northmoor *Oxon* 36 SP4202
Northmuir *Tays* 126 NO3854
Northney *Hants* 13 SU7303
Northolt *Gt Lon* 26 TQ1384
Northop *Clwyd* 70 SJ2468
Northop Hall *Clwyd* 70 SJ2667
Northorpe *Lincs* 76 SK8997
Northorpe *Lincs* 64 TF0917
Northorpe *Lincs* 64 TF2036
Northorpe *W York* 82 SE2221
Northover *Somset* 21 ST4838
Northover *Somset* 21 ST5223
Northowram *W York* 82 SE1126
Northport *Dorset* 11 SY9288
Northrepps *Norfk* 67 TG2439
Northton *W Isls* 154 NF9989
Northway *Somset* 20 ST1329
Northway *W Glam* 32 SS5889
Northwich *Ches* 79 SJ6673
Northwick *Avon* 34 ST5686
Northwick *H & W* 47 SO8458
Northwick *Somset* 21 ST3548
Northwold *Norfk* 65 TL7597
Northwood *Derbys* 74 SK2664
Northwood *Gt Lon* 26 TQ0990
Northwood *IOW* 13 SZ4992
Northwood *Shrops* 59 SJ4633
Northwood *Staffs* 72 SJ8949
Northwood End *Beds* 38 TL0941
Northwood Green *Gloucs* 35 SO7216
Norton *Avon* 21 ST3463
Norton *Ches* 78 SJ5581
Norton *Cleve* 96 NZ4421
Norton *Cnwll* 4 SX0869
Norton *E Susx* 16 TQ4701
Norton *Gloucs* 47 SO8524
Norton *Gwent* 34 SO4420
Norton *H & W* 47 SO8751
Norton *H & W* 48 SP0447
Norton *Herts* 39 TL2334
Norton *IOW* 12 SZ3488
Norton *N York* 90 SE7971
Norton *Nhants* 49 SP5963
Norton *Notts* 75 SK5771
Norton *Powys* 46 SO3067
Norton *S York* 83 SE5415
Norton *S York* 74 SK3681
Norton *Shrops* 59 SJ5609
Norton *Shrops* 60 SJ7200
Norton *Shrops* 59 SO4681
Norton *Shrops* 59 SO6382
Norton *Suffk* 54 TL9565
Norton *W Glam* 32 SS6188
Norton *W Susx* 14 SU9206
Norton *Wilts* 35 ST8884
Norton Bavant *Wilts* 22 ST9043
Norton Bridge *Staffs* 72 SJ8630
Norton Canes *Staffs* 60 SK0107
Norton Canon *H & W* 46 SO3847
Norton Corner *Norfk* 66 TG0928
Norton Disney *Lincs* 76 SK8859
Norton Ferris *Wilts* 22 ST7936
Norton Fitzwarren *Somset* 20 ST1925
Norton Green *IOW* 12 SZ3488
Norton Green *Staffs* 60 SK0107
Norton Hawkfield *Avon* 21 ST5964
Norton Heath *Essex* 40 TL6004
Norton in Hales *Shrops* 72 SJ7038
Norton in the Moors *Staffs* 72 SJ8951
Norton Lindsey *Warwks* 48 SP2263
Norton Little Green *Suffk* 54 TL9766
Norton Malreward *Avon* 21 ST6064
Norton Mandeville *Essex* 40 TL5804
Norton St Philip *Somset* 22 ST7755
Norton sub Hamdon *Somset* 10 ST4615
Norton Subcourse *Norfk* 67 TM4198
Norton Wood *H & W* 46 SO3648
Norton-Juxta-Twycross *Leics* 61 SK3207
Norton-le-Clay *N York* 89 SE4071
Norwell *Notts* 75 SK7761
Norwell Woodhouse *Notts* 75 SK7362
Norwich *Norfk* 67 TG2308
Norwick *Shet* 155 HP6414
Norwood *Cent* 116 NS8793
Norwood *Kent* 17 TR0530
Norwood *S York* 75 SK4681
Norwood End *Essex* 40 TL5608
Norwood Green *Gt Lon* 26 TQ1378
Norwood Green *W York* 82 SE1326
Norwood Hill *Surrey* 15 TQ2343
Norwoodside *Cambs* 65 TL4197
Noseley *Leics* 50 SP7398
Noss Mayo *Devon* 6 SX5547
Nosterfield *N York* 89 SE2780
Nosterfield End *Cambs* 53 TL6344
Nostie *Highld* 138 NG8527
Notgrove *Gloucs* 36 SP1020
Nottage *M Glam* 33 SS8177
Notter *Cnwll* 5 SX3960
Nottingham *Notts* 62 SK5739
Nottington *Dorset* 11 SY6682
Notton *W York* 83 SE3413
Notton *Wilts* 35 ST9169
Nottswood Hill *Gloucs* 35 SO7018
Nounsley *Essex* 40 TL7910
Noutard's Green *H & W* 47 SO8066
Nox *Shrops* 59 SJ4110
Nuffield *Oxon* 37 SU6687
Nun Monkton *N York* 90 SE5057
Nunburnholme *Humb* 84 SE8447
Nuncargate *Notts* 75 SK5054
Nunclose *Cumb* 94 NY4945
Nuneaton *Warwks* 61 SP3691
Nuneham Courtenay *Oxon* 37 SU5599
Nunhead *Gt Lon* 27 TQ3475
Nunkeeling *Humb* 85 TA1449
Nunney *Somset* 22 ST7345
Nunney Catch *Somset* 22 ST7344
Nunnington *H & W* 46 SO5543
Nunnington *N York* 90 SE6679
Nunnykirk *Nthumb* 103 NZ0793
Nuns Moor *T & W* 103 NZ2266
Nunsthorpe *Humb* 85 TA2607
Nunthorpe *Cleve* 97 NZ5314
Nunthorpe *N York* 83 SE6050
Nunthorpe Village *Cleve* 90 NZ5413
Nunton *Wilts* 23 SU1526
Nunwick *N York* 89 SE3274
Nunwick *Nthumb* 102 NY8774
Nup End *Bucks* 38 SP8619
Nupdown *Avon* 35 ST6395
Nupend *Gloucs* 35 SO7806
Nuptow *Berks* 25 SU8873
Nursling *Hants* 12 SU3716
Nursted *Hants* 13 SU7521
Nursteed *Wilts* 23 SU0260
Nurton *Staffs* 60 SO8399
Nutbourne *W Susx* 14 SU7705
Nutbourne *W Susx* 14 TQ0718
Nutfield *Surrey* 27 TQ3050
Nuthall *Notts* 62 SK5243
Nuthampstead *Herts* 39 TL4034
Nuthurst *W Susx* 15 TQ1925
Nutley *E Susx* 16 TQ4427
Nutley *Hants* 24 SU6044
Nuttal Lane *Gt Man* 81 SD7915
Nutwell *S York* 83 SE6304
Nybster *Highld* 151 ND3663
Nyetimber *W Susx* 14 SZ8998
Nyewood *W Susx* 14 SU8021
Nymet Rowland *Devon* 19 SS7108
Nymet Tracey *Devon* 8 SS7200
Nympsfield *Gloucs* 35 SO8000
Nynehead *Somset* 20 ST1422
Nythe *Somset* 21 ST4234
Nyton *W Susx* 14 SU9305

O

Oad Street *Kent* 28 TQ8762
Oadby *Leics* 50 SK6200
Oak Cross *Devon* 8 SX5399
Oak Tree *Dur* 89 NZ3613
Oakall Green *H & W* 47 SO8161
Oakamoor *Staffs* 73 SK0444
Oakbank *Loth* 117 NT0766
Oakdale *Gwent* 33 ST1898
Oake *Somset* 20 ST1525
Oaken *Staffs* 60 SJ8602
Oakenclough *Lancs* 80 SD5447
Oakengates *Shrops* 60 SJ7010
Oakenholt *Clwyd* 70 SJ2571
Oakenshaw *Dur* 96 NZ1937
Oakenshaw *W York* 82 SE1727
Oaker Side *Derbys* 74 SK2760
Oakerthorpe *Derbys* 74 SK3854
Oakford *Devon* 20 SS9121
Oakford *Dyfed* 42 SN4558
Oakfordbridge *Devon* 20 SS9122
Oakgrove *Ches* 79 SJ9169
Oakham *Leics* 63 SK8608

P

Pant Mawr

Pica

Pant Mawr Powys 43 SN8482
Pant-glas Gwynd 68 SH4747
Pant-Gwyn Dyfed 44 SN5925
Pant-lasau W Glam 32 SN6600
Pant-pastynog Clwyd 70 SJ0461
Pant-y-dwr Powys 45 SN9874
Pant-y-ffridd Powys 58 SJ1502
Pant-y-gog M Glam 33 SS9090
Pant-y-mwyn Clwyd 70 SJ1964
Pantasaph Clwyd 70 SJ1675
Panteg Dyfed 30 SM9234
Pantersbridge Cnwll 4 SX1667
Pantglas Powys 43 SN7797
Panton Lincs 76 TF1778
Pantperthog Gwynd 57 SH7404
Pantyffynnon Dyfed 32 SN6210
Pantygasseg Gwent 34 ST2599
Pantymenyn Dyfed 31 SN1426
Panxworth Norfk 67 TG3513
Papcastle Cumb 92 NY1031
Papigoe Highld 151 ND3851
Pappie Loth 118 NT5972
Papplewick Notts 75 SK5451
Papworth Everard Cambs 52 TL2862
Papworth St Agnes Cambs 52 TL2664
Par Cnwll 3 SX0753
Paramour Street Kent 29 TR2961
Parbold Lancs 80 SD4911
Parbrook Somset 21 ST5736
Parbrook W Susx 14 TQ0825
Parc Gwynd 57 SH8834
Parc Seymour Gwent 34 ST4091
Parcllyn Dyfed 42 SN2451
Pardshaw Cumb 92 NY0924
Parham Suffk 55 TM3060
Park D & G 100 NX9091
Park Gramp 135 NO7898
Park Nthumb 102 NY6861
Park Bottom Cnwll 2 SW6642
Park Bridge Gt Man 79 SD9402
Park Corner Berks 26 SU8582
Park Corner E Susx 16 TQ5336
Park Corner Oxon 37 SU6988
Park End Beds 38 SP9952
Park End Nthumb 102 NY8675
Park End Staffs 72 SJ7851
Park Gate H & W 60 SO9371
Park Gate Hants 13 SU5108
Park Gate W York 82 SE1841
Park Green Essex 39 TL4628
Park Green Suffk 54 TM1364
Park Head Cumb 94 NY5841
Park Head Derbys 74 SK3654
Park Hill Gloucs 34 ST5799
Park Royal Gt Lon 26 TQ1982
Park Street W Susx 14 TQ1131
Parkend Gloucs 34 SO6108
Parkers Green Kent 16 TQ6148
Parkeston Essex 41 TM2332
Parkeston Quay Essex 41 TM2332
Parkfield Bucks 37 SP8002
Parkfield Cnwll 5 SX3167
Parkgate Ches 70 SJ2878
Parkgate Ches 79 SJ7873
Parkgate Cumb 93 NY2146
Parkgate D & G 100 NY0288
Parkgate E Susx 17 TQ7214
Parkgate Essex 40 TL6829
Parkgate Kent 27 TQ5064
Parkgate Kent 17 TQ8534
Parkgate Surrey 15 TQ2043
Parkhall Strath 115 NS4871
Parkham Devon 18 SS3921
Parkham Ash Devon 18 SS3620
Parkhill Notts 75 SK6952
Parkhill House Gramp 143 NJ8914
Parkhouse Gwent 34 SO5003
Parkmill W Glam 32 SS5489
Parkside Clwyd 71 SJ3855
Parkside Dur 96 NZ4248
Parkside Strath 116 NS8058
Parkstone Dorset 12 SZ0391
Parley Green Dorset 12 SZ1097
Parlington W York 83 SE4235
Parmoor Bucks 37 SU7989
Parndon Essex 39 TL4308
Parr Bridge Gt Man 79 SD7001
Parracombe Devon 19 SS6745
Parrah Green Ches 72 SJ7145
Parrog Dyfed 30 SN0539
Parson Drove Cambs 64 TF3708
Parson's Cross S York 74 SK3492
Parson's Heath Essex 41 TM0226
Parson's Hill Derbys 73 SK2926
Parsonby Cumb 92 NY1438
Partick Strath 115 NS5467
Partington Gt Man 79 SJ7191
Partney Lincs 77 TF4068
Parton Cumb 93 NY2750
Parton Cumb 92 NX9820
Parton D & G 99 NX6970
Partridge Green W Susx 15 TQ1919
Partrishow Powys 34 SO2722
Parwich Derbys 73 SK1854
Paslow Wood Common Essex 27 TL5802
Passenham Nhants 38 SP7839
Passfield Hants 14 SU8234
Passingford Bridge Essex 27 TQ5097
Paston Cambs 64 TF1802
Paston Norfk 67 TG3234
Pasturefields Staffs 73 SJ9924
Patchacott Devon 5 SX4798
Patcham E Susx 15 TQ3008
Patchetts Green Herts 26 TQ1497
Patching W Susx 14 TQ0806
Patchole Devon 19 SS6142
Patchway Avon 34 ST6082
Pateley Bridge N York 89 SE1565
Paternoster Heath Essex 40 TL9115
Pateshall H & W 46 SO5262
Path of Condie Tays 125 NO0711
Pathe Somset 21 ST3730
Pathhead Fife 117 NT2992
Pathhead Loth 118 NT3964
Pathhead Strath 107 NS6114
Pathlow Warwks 48 SP1758
Patmore Heath Herts 39 TL4425
Patna Strath 106 NS4110
Patney Wilts 23 SU0758
Patrick IOM 153 SC2482
Patrick Brompton N York 89 SE2190
Patricroft Gt Man 79 SJ7597
Patrington Humb 85 TA3122
Patrixbourne Kent 29 TR1855
Patterdale Cumb 93 NY3915
Pattingham Staffs 60 SO8299
Pattishall Nhants 49 SP6754
Pattiswick Green Essex 40 TL8124
Patton Shrops 59 SO5895
Paul Cnwll 2 SW4627
Paul's Dene Wilts 23 SU1432
Paulerspury Bucks 49 SP7145
Paull Humb 85 TA1626
Paulton Avon 21 ST6556
Paunton H & W 47 SO6650
Pauperhaugh Nthumb 103 NZ1099
Pave Lane Shrops 72 SJ7616
Pavenham Beds 51 SP9955
Pawlett Somset 20 ST2942
Pawston Nthumb 110 NT8532
Paxford Gloucs 48 SP1837
Paxton Border 119 NT9353
Payden Street Kent 28 TQ9254
Payhembury Devon 9 ST0901
Paythorne Lancs 81 SD8251
Paytoe H & W 46 SO4171
Peacehaven E Susx 15 TQ4101
Peak Dale Derbys 74 SK0976
Peak Forest Derbys 74 SK1179
Peak Hill Lincs 64 TF2615
Peakirk Cambs 64 TF1606
Peanmeanach Highld 129 NM7180
Pearson's Green Kent 28 TQ6943
Peartree Green H & W 46 SO5932
Pease Pottage W Susx 15 TQ2633
Peasedown St John Avon 22 ST7057
Peasehill Derbys 74 SK4049
Peaseland Green Norfk 66 TG0516
Peasemore Berks 37 SU4577
Peasenhall Suffk 55 TM3569
Peaslake Surrey 14 TQ0844
Peasley Cross Mersyd 78 SJ5294
Peasmarsh E Susx 17 TQ8822
Peasmarsh Somset 10 ST3312
Peasmarsh Surrey 25 SU9946
Peat Inn Fife 127 NO4509
Peathill Gramp 143 NJ9366
Peatling Magna Leics 50 SP5992
Peatling Parva Leics 50 SP5889
Peaton Shrops 59 SO5385
Pebmarsh Essex 40 TL8533
Pebworth H & W 48 SP1347
Pecket Well W York 82 SD9929
Peckforton Ches 71 SJ5356
Peckham Gt Lon 27 TQ3476
Peckleton Leics 62 SK4701
Pedair-ffordd Powys 58 SJ1124
Pedlinge Kent 17 TR1335
Pedmore W Mids 60 SO9182
Pedwell Somset 21 ST4236
Peebles Border 109 NT2540
Peel IOM 153 SC2483
Peel Lancs 80 SD3531
Peel Common Hants 13 SU5703
Peene Kent 29 TR1837
Peening Quarter Kent 17 TQ8828
Pegsdon Beds 38 TL1130
Pegswood Nthumb 103 NZ2287
Pegwell Kent 29 TR3664
Peinchorran Highld 137 NG5233
Peinlich Highld 136 NG4158
Pelaw T & W 96 NZ3061
Pelcomb Dyfed 30 SM9218
Pelcomb Bridge Dyfed 30 SM9317
Pelcomb Cross Dyfed 30 SM9218
Peldon Essex 41 TL9816
Pell Green E Susx 16 TQ6432
Pelsall W Mids 60 SK0203
Pelsall Wood W Mids 60 SK0204
Pelton Dur 96 NZ2553
Pelton Fell Dur 96 NZ2551
Pelutho Cumb 92 NY1249
Pelynt Cnwll 5 SX2055
Pemberton Dyfed 32 SN5300
Pemberton Gt Man 78 SD5503
Pembles Cross Kent 28 TQ8947
Pembrey Dyfed 31 SN4301
Pembridge H & W 46 SO3958
Pembroke Dyfed 30 SM9801
Pembroke Dock Dyfed 30 SM9603
Pembury Kent 16 TQ6240
Pen Rhiwfawr W Glam 32 SN7410
Pen-bont Rhydybeddau Dyfed 43 SN6783
Pen-ffordd Dyfed 31 SN0722
Pen-groes-oped Gwent 34 SO3106
Pen-llyn Gwynd 68 SH3582
Pen-lon Gwynd 68 SH4365
Pen-rhiw Dyfed 31 SN2440
Pen-twyn Gwent 33 SO2000
Pen-twyn Gwent 34 SO2603
Pen-twyn Gwent 34 SO5209
Pen-y-bont Clwyd 58 SJ2123
Pen-y-Bont-Fawr Powys 58 SJ0824
Pen-y-bryn Dyfed 31 SN1742
Pen-y-bryn M Glam 33 SS8384
Pen-y-cae Powys 33 SN8413
Pen-y-cae-mawr Gwent 34 ST4195
Pen-y-cefn Clwyd 70 SJ1175
Pen-y-clawdd Gwent 34 SO4507
Pen-y-coedcae M Glam 33 ST0587
Pen-y-cwn Dyfed 30 SM8523
Pen-y-darren M Glam 33 SO0506
Pen-y-fai M Glam 33 SS8981
Pen-y-felin Clwyd 70 SJ1569
Pen-y-garn Dyfed 43 SN6285
Pen-y-genffordd Powys 45 SO1729
Pen-y-graig Gwynd 56 SH2033
Pen-y-Gwryd Hotel Gwynd 69 SH6655
Pen-y-lan S Glam 33 SS9976
Pen-y-pass Gwynd 69 SH6455
Pen-y-stryt Clwyd 70 SJ1952
Pen-yr-Heol Gwent 34 SO4311
Pen-yr-Heolgerrig M Glam 33 SO0306
Penair Cnwll 3 SW8445
Penallt Gwent 34 SO5210
Penally Dyfed 31 SS1199
Penalt H & W 46 SO5629
Penare Cnwll 3 SW9940
Penarth S Glam 33 ST1871
Penblewin Dyfed 31 SN1216
Penbryn Dyfed 42 SN2951
Pencader Dyfed 31 SN4436
Pencaenewydd Gwynd 56 SH4040
Pencaitland Loth 118 NT4468
Pencalenick Cnwll 3 SW8545
Pencarnisiog Gwynd 68 SH3573
Pencarreg Dyfed 44 SN5445
Pencarrow Cnwll 4 SX1082
Pencelli Powys 45 SO0925
Penclawdd W Glam 32 SS5495
Pencoed M Glam 33 SS9581
Pencombe H & W 46 SO5952
Pencoyd H & W 46 SO5126
Pencraig H & W 34 SO5620
Pencraig Powys 58 SJ0426
Pendeen Cnwll 2 SW3834
Penderyn M Glam 33 SN9408
Pendine Dyfed 31 SN2208
Pendlebury Gt Man 79 SD7802
Pendleton Lancs 81 SD7539
Pendock H & W 47 SO7832
Pendoggett Cnwll 4 SX0279
Pendomer Somset 10 ST5210
Pendoylan S Glam 33 ST0576
Pendre M Glam 33 SS9181
Penegoes Powys 57 SH7600
Penelewey Cnwll 3 SW8140
Pengam Gwent 33 ST1597
Pengam S Glam 33 ST2177
Penge Gt Lon 27 TQ3570
Pengelly Cnwll 3 SW8551
Pengelly Cnwll 4 SX0783
Pengorffwysfa Gwynd 68 SH4692
Pengover Green Cnwll 5 SX2765
Pengrugla Cnwll 3 SW9947
Pengwern Clwyd 70 SJ0276
Penhale Cnwll 2 SW6918
Penhale Cnwll 4 SW9057
Penhale Cnwll 4 SX0860
Penhale Cnwll 5 SX4153
Penhallow Cnwll 3 SW7651
Penhalurick Cnwll 2 SW7038
Penhalvean Cnwll 2 SW7038
Penhill Wilts 36 SU1588
Penhow Gwent 34 ST4290
Penhurst E Susx 16 TQ6916
Peniarth Gwynd 57 SH6105
Penicuik Loth 117 NT2359
Peniel Clwyd 70 SJ0362
Peniel Dyfed 31 SN4324
Penifiler Highld 136 NG4841
Peninver Strath 105 NR7524
Penisar Waun Gwynd 69 SH5563
Penistone S York 82 SE2403
Penjerrick Cnwll 3 SW7730
Penkelly Cnwll 4 SX1854
Penketh Ches 78 SJ5587
Penkill Strath 106 NX2398
Penkridge Staffs 60 SJ9213
Penlean Cnwll 5 SX2098
Penley Clwyd 71 SJ4040
Penllergaer W Glam 32 SS6198
Penllyn S Glam 33 SS9775
Penmachno Gwynd 69 SH7950
Penmaen Gwent 33 ST1897
Penmaen W Glam 32 SS5288
Penmaenan Gwynd 69 SH7175
Penmaenmawr Gwynd 69 SH7276
Penmaenpool Gwynd 57 SH6918
Penmark S Glam 20 ST0568
Penmon Gwynd 69 SH6280
Penmorfa Gwynd 57 SH5540
Penmynydd Gwynd 68 SH5074
Penn Bucks 26 SU9193
Penn W Mids 60 SO8895
Penn Street Bucks 26 SU9295
Pennal Gwynd 57 SH6900
Pennan Gramp 143 NJ8465
Pennant Clwyd 58 SJ0234
Pennant Powys 43 SN8897
Pennant-Melangell Powys 58 SJ0226
Pennard W Glam 32 SS5688
Pennerley Shrops 59 SO3599
Pennicott Devon 9 SS8701
Pennington Cumb 86 SD2677
Pennington Hants 12 SZ3195
Pennington Green Gt Man 79 SD6206
Pennorth Powys 45 SO1125
Pennsylvania Avon 35 ST7473
Penny Bridge Cumb 86 SD3083
Penny Bridge Dyfed 30 SN0001
Penny Green Notts 75 SK5475
Penny Hill Lincs 64 TF3526
Pennycross Strath 121 NM5025
Pennygate Norfk 67 TG3423
Pennyghael Strath 121 NM5125
Pennyglen Strath 106 NS2710
Pennymoor Devon 19 SS8611
Penparc Dyfed 42 SN2047
Penparcau Dyfed 43 SN5980
Penpedairheol Gwent 34 SO3303
Penpedairheol M Glam 33 ST1497
Penperlleni Gwent 34 SO3204
Penpethy Cnwll 4 SX0886
Penpillick Cnwll 3 SX0856
Penpol Cnwll 3 SW8139
Penpoll Cnwll 3 SX1454
Penponds Cnwll 2 SW6339
Penpont D & G 100 NX8494
Penpont Powys 45 SN9728
Penquit Devon 7 SX6454
Penrest Cnwll 5 SX3377
Penrherber Dyfed 31 SN2938
Penrhiw-pal Dyfed 42 SN3445
Penrhiwceiber M Glam 33 ST0597
Penrhiwllan Dyfed 31 SN3641
Penrhos Gwent 34 SO4111
Penrhos Gwynd 68 SH2781
Penrhos Gwynd 56 SH3433
Penrhos Powys 32 SN8011
Penrhos garnedd Gwynd 69 SH5670
Penrhyn Bay Gwynd 69 SH8281
Penrhyn-side Gwynd 69 SH8181
Penrhyncoch Dyfed 43 SN6384
Penrhyndeudraeth Gwynd 57 SH6139
Penrice W Glam 32 SS4987
Penrioch Strath 105 NR8744
Penrith Cumb 94 NY5130
Penrose Cnwll 4 SW8770
Penrose Cnwll 5 SX2589
Penruddock Cumb 93 NY4227
Penryn Cnwll 3 SW7834
Pensarn Clwyd 70 SH9578
Pensarn Dyfed 31 SN4119
Pensax H & W 47 SO7269
Pensby Mersyd 78 SJ2782
Penselwood Somset 22 ST7531
Pensford Avon 21 ST6263
Pensham H & W 47 SO9444
Penshaw T & W 96 NZ3354
Penshurst Kent 16 TQ5243
Penshurst Station Kent 16 TQ5246
Pensilva Cnwll 5 SX2970
Pensnett W Mids 60 SO9189
Penson Cnwll 4 SX0874
Penstone Devon 8 SS7700
Penstrowed Powys 58 SO0691
Pentewan Cnwll 3 SX0147
Pentir Gwynd 69 SH5766
Pentire Cnwll 4 SW7961
Pentlepoir Dyfed 31 SN1105
Pentlow Essex 54 TL8146
Pentlow Street Essex 54 TL8245
Pentney Norfk 65 TF7214
Penton Grafton Hants 23 SU3247
Penton Mewsey Hants 23 SU3247
Pentraeth Gwynd 68 SH5278
Pentre Clwyd 70 SJ0862
Pentre Clwyd 70 SJ2840
Pentre Clwyd 71 SJ3267
Pentre Gwent 34 SO3106
Pentre M Glam 33 SS9696
Pentre Powys 58 SO0685
Pentre Powys 58 SO1589
Pentre Shrops 59 SJ3617
Pentre Bach Clwyd 70 SJ2175
Pentre bach Dyfed 44 SN5547
Pentre Berw Gwynd 68 SH4772
Pentre Ffwrndan Clwyd 70 SJ2572
Pentre Gwynfryn Gwynd 57 SH5927
Pentre Halkyn Clwyd 70 SJ2072
Pentre Hodrey Shrops 46 SO3277
Pentre Isaf Clwyd 70 SH9871
Pentre Llanrhaeadr Clwyd 70 SJ0863
Pentre Llifior Powys 58 SO1598
Pentre Meyrick S Glam 33 SS9675
Pentre Saron Clwyd 70 SJ0260
Pentre ty gwyn Dyfed 44 SN8135
Pentre'r Felin Gwynd 69 SH8069
Pentre'r-felin Dyfed 44 SN6148
Pentre'r-felin Powys 45 SN9230
Pentre'rbryn Dyfed 42 SN3954
Pentre-ba^ch Powys 45 SN9132
Pentre-bont Gwynd 69 SH7351
Pentre-cagel Dyfed 31 SN3340
Pentre-celyn Clwyd 70 SJ1453
Pentre-celyn Powys 57 SH8905
Pentre-chwyth W Glam 32 SS6794
Pentre-clawdd Shrops 59 SJ2931
Pentre-cwrt Dyfed 31 SN3838
Pentre-dwr W Glam 32 SS6995
Pentre-Gwenlais Dyfed 32 SN6016
Pentre-llwyn-llwyd Powys 45 SN9654
Pentre-llyn Dyfed 43 SN6175
Pentre-llyn-cymmer Clwyd 70 SH9752
Pentre-Maw Powys 57 SH8803
Pentre-piod Gwent 34 SO2601
Pentre-poeth Gwent 34 ST2686
Pentre-tafarn-y-fedw Gwynd 69 SH8162
Pentrebach M Glam 33 SO0604
Pentrebeirdd Powys 58 SJ1813
Pentredwr Clwyd 70 SJ1946
Pentrefelin Gwynd 68 SH4392
Pentrefelin Gwynd 57 SH5239
Pentrefoelas Clwyd 69 SH8751
Pentregalar Dyfed 31 SN1831
Pentregat Dyfed 42 SN3551
Pentrich Derbys 74 SK3852
Pentridge Hill Dorset 12 SU0317
Pentyrch M Glam 33 ST1081
Penwithick Cnwll 3 SX0256
Penwood Hants 24 SU4461
Penwyllt Powys 33 SN8515
Penybanc Dyfed 44 SN6123
Penybont Powys 45 SO1164
Penycae Clwyd 70 SJ2745
Penycaerau Gwynd 56 SH1927
Penyffordd Clwyd 71 SJ3061
Penygarnedd Powys 58 SJ1023
Penygraig M Glam 33 ST0090
Penygroes Dyfed 32 SN5813
Penygroes Gwynd 68 SH4752
Penysarn Gwynd 68 SH4590
Penywaun M Glam 33 SN9804
Penywern W Glam 32 SN7609
Penzance Cnwll 2 SW4730
Peopleton H & W 47 SO9350
Peover Heath Ches 79 SJ7973
Peper Harow Surrey 25 SU9344
Peplow Shrops 59 SJ6224
Pepper's Green Essex 40 TL6110
Peppershill Oxon 37 SP6709
Pepperstock Beds 38 TL0817
Perceton Strath 106 NS3540
Percie Gramp 134 NO5992
Percyhorner Gramp 143 NJ9665
Perelle Guern 152 GN0000
Periton Somset 20 SS9545
Perivale Gt Lon 26 TQ1682
Perkins Village Devon 9 SY0291
Perkinsville Dur 96 NZ2553
Perlethorpe Notts 75 SK6470
Perran Wharf Cnwll 3 SW7738
Perranarworthal Cnwll 3 SW7738
Perranporth Cnwll 3 SW7554
Perranuthnoe Cnwll 2 SW5329
Perranwell Cnwll 3 SW7739
Perranwell Cnwll 3 SW7752
Perranzabuloe Cnwll 3 SW7752
Perrott's Brook Gloucs 35 SP0106
Perry W Mids 61 SP0792
Perry Barr W Mids 61 SP0791
Perry Green Essex 40 TL8022
Perry Green Herts 39 TL4317
Perry Green Wilts 35 ST9689
Perry Street Somset 10 ST3305
Pershall Staffs 72 SJ8129
Pershore H & W 47 SO9446
Pertenhall Beds 51 TL0865
Perth Tays 126 NO1123
Perthy Shrops 59 SJ3633
Perton H & W 46 SO5940
Perton Staffs 60 SO8699
Pertwood Wilts 22 ST8936
Pet Street Kent 29 TR0846
Peter Tavy Devon 5 SX5177
Peter's Green Herts 38 TL1419
Peterborough Cambs 64 TL1998
Peterchurch H & W 46 SO3438
Peterculter Gramp 135 NJ8300
Peterhead Gramp 143 NK1246
Peterlee Dur 96 NZ4241
Peters Marland Devon 18 SS4713
Petersfield Hants 13 SU7423
Petersham Gt Lon 26 TQ1873
Peterston-Super-Ely S Glam 33 ST0876
Peterstone Wentlooge Gwent 34 ST2679
Peterstow H & W 46 SO5624
Petham Kent 29 TR1251
Petherwin Gate Cnwll 5 SX2889
Petrockstow Devon 19 SS5109
Petsoe End Bucks 38 SP8949
Pett E Susx 17 TQ8714
Pett Bottom Kent 29 TR1552
Pettaugh Suffk 54 TM1659
Petterden Tays 127 NO4240
Pettinain Strath 108 NS9543
Pettistree Suffk 55 TM3055
Petton Devon 20 ST0124
Petton Shrops 59 SJ4326
Petts Wood Gt Lon 27 TQ4567
Petty France Avon 35 ST7885
Pettycur Fife 117 NT2686
Pettymuk Gramp 143 NJ9023
Petworth W Susx 14 SU9721
Pevensey E Susx 16 TQ6405
Pevensey Bay E Susx 16 TQ6504
Pewsey Wilts 23 SU1660
Pheasant's Hill Bucks 37 SU7887
Phepson H & W 47 SO9459
Philadelphia T & W 96 NZ3352
Philham Devon 18 SS2522
Philiphaugh Border 109 NT4327
Phillack Cnwll 2 SW5638
Philleigh Cnwll 3 SW8639
Philpot End Essex 40 TL6118
Philpstoun Loth 117 NT0577
Phocle Green H & W 47 SO6326
Phoenix Green Hants 24 SU7555
Phoines Highld 132 NN7093
Pibsbury Somset 21 ST4426
Pica Cumb 92 NY0222

Piccadilly
Powburn

Piccadilly *Warwks* 61 SP2398
Piccotts End *Herts* 38 TL0409
Pickering *N York* 90 SE7984
Picket Piece *Hants* 23 SU3947
Picket Post *Hants* 12 SU1906
Pickford *W Mids* 61 SP2881
Pickford Green *W Mids* 61 SP2781
Pickhill *N York* 89 SE3483
Picklescott *Shrops* 59 SO4399
Pickmere *Ches* 79 SJ6977
Pickney *Somset* 20 ST1929
Pickstock *Shrops* 72 SJ7223
Pickup Bank *Lancs* 81 SD7122
Pickwell *Devon* 18 SS4540
Pickwell *Leics* 63 SK7811
Pickwick *Wilts* 35 ST8670
Pickworth *Leics* 63 SK9913
Pickworth *Lincs* 64 TF0433
Pict's Cross *H & W* 46 SO5526
Pictillum *Gramp* 142 NJ7317
Picton *Ches* 71 SJ4371
Picton *Clwyd* 70 SJ1182
Picton *N York* 89 NZ4107
Picton Ferry *Dyfed* 31 SN2717
Piddinghoe *E Susx* 16 TQ4303
Piddington *Bucks* 37 SU8094
Piddington *Nhants* 51 SP8054
Piddington *Oxon* 37 SP6317
Piddlehinton *Dorset* 11 SY7197
Piddletrenthide *Dorset* 11 SY7099
Pidley *Cambs* 52 TL3377
Pie Corner *H & W* 47 SO6461
Piercebridge *Dur* 96 NZ2115
Pierowall *Ork* 155 HY4348
Piff's Elm *Gloucs* 47 SO9026
Pig Oak *Dorset* 12 SU0202
Pig Street *H & W* 46 SO3647
Pigdon *Nthumb* 103 NZ1588
Pigeon Green *Warwks* 48 SP2260
Pikehall *Derbys* 74 SK1959
Pilford *Dorset* 12 SU0301
Pilgrims Hatch *Essex* 27 TQ5895
Pilham *Lincs* 76 SK8693
Pill *Avon* 34 ST5275
Pillaton *Cnwll* 5 SX3664
Pillatonmill *Cnwll* 5 SX3663
Pillerton Hersey *Warwks* 48 SP2948
Pillerton Priors *Warwks* 48 SP2947
Pilleth *Powys* 46 SO2667
Pilley *Hants* 12 SZ3298
Pilley *S York* 74 SE3300
Pilley Bailey *Hants* 12 SZ3398
Pillgwenlly *Gwent* 34 ST3186
Pillhead *Devon* 18 SS4726
Pilling *Lancs* 80 SD4048
Pilling Lane *Lancs* 80 SD3749
Pilning *Avon* 34 ST5684
Pilot Inn *Kent* 17 TR0818
Pilsbury *Derbys* 74 SK1163
Pilsdon *Dorset* 10 SY4199
Pilsgate *Cambs* 64 TF0605
Pilsley *Derbys* 74 SK2371
Pilsley *Derbys* 74 SK4262
Pilson Green *Norfk* 67 TG3713
Piltdown *E Susx* 16 TQ4422
Pilton *Devon* 19 SS5534
Pilton *Leics* 63 SK9102
Pilton *Nhants* 51 TL0284
Pilton *Somset* 21 ST5941
Pilton Green *W Glam* 32 SS4487
Pimlico *Lancs* 81 SD7443
Pimlico *Nhants* 49 SP6140
Pimperne *Dorset* 11 ST9009
Pin Green *Herts* 39 TL2525
Pinchbeck *Lincs* 64 TF2425
Pinchbeck Bars *Lincs* 64 TF1925
Pinchbeck West *Lincs* 64 TF2024
Pincheon Green *S York* 83 SE6517
Pinchinthorpe *Cleve* 90 NZ5714
Pincock *Lancs* 80 SD5417
Pindon End *Bucks* 38 SP7847
Pinfold *Lancs* 80 SD3811
Pinford End *Suffk* 54 TL8459
Pinged *Dyfed* 31 SN4203
Pingewood *Berks* 24 SU6969
Pinhoe *Devon* 9 SX9694
Pinkett's Booth *W Mids* 61 SP2781
Pinkney *Wilts* 35 ST8686
Pinley *W Mids* 61 SP3577
Pinley Green *Warwks* 48 SP2066
Pinmill *Suffk* 55 TM2037
Pinminnoch *Strath* 106 NX1993
Pinmore *Strath* 106 NX2091
Pinn *Devon* 9 SY1086
Pinner *Gt Lon* 26 TQ1289
Pinner Green *Gt Lon* 26 TQ1289
Pinsley Green *Ches* 71 SJ5846
Pinvin *H & W* 47 SO9549
Pinwherry *Strath* 98 NX2086
Pinxton *Derbys* 75 SK4554
Pipe and Lyde *H & W* 46 SO5043
Pipe Gate *Shrops* 72 SJ7340
Pipehill *Staffs* 61 SK0907
Piperhill *Highld* 140 NH8650
Pipers Pool *Cnwll* 5 SX2584
Pipewell *Nhants* 51 SP8485
Pippacott *Devon* 19 SS5237
Pippin Street *Lancs* 81 SD5924
Pipton *Powys* 45 SO1637
Pirbright *Surrey* 25 SU9455
Pirbright Camp *Surrey* 25 SU9356
Pirnie *Border* 110 NT6528
Pirnmill *Strath* 105 NR8744
Pirton *H & W* 47 SO8847
Pirton *Herts* 38 TL1431
Pishill *Oxon* 37 SU7389
Pistyll *Gwynd* 56 SH3241
Pitagowan *Tays* 132 NN8165
Pitblae *Gramp* 143 NJ9864
Pitcairngreen *Tays* 125 NO0627
Pitcalnie *Highld* 147 NH8072
Pitcaple *Gramp* 142 NJ7225
Pitcarity *Tays* 134 NO3365
Pitch Green *Bucks* 37 SP7703
Pitch Place *Surrey* 25 SU8839
Pitch Place *Surrey* 25 SU9852
Pitchcombe *Gloucs* 35 SO8508
Pitchcott *Bucks* 37 SP7720
Pitcher Row *Lincs* 64 TF2933
Pitchford *Shrops* 59 SJ5303
Pitchroy *Gramp* 141 NJ1738
Pitcombe *Somset* 22 ST6732
Pitcot *M Glam* 33 SS8974
Pitcox *Loth* 118 NT6475
Pitfichie *Gramp* 142 NJ6716
Pitglassie *Gramp* 142 NJ6943
Pitgrudy *Highld* 147 NH7991
Pitkennedy *Tays* 127 NO5454
Pitlessie *Fife* 126 NO3309
Pitlochry *Tays* 132 NN9458
Pitmachie *Gramp* 142 NJ6728
Pitmain *Highld* 132 NH7400
Pitmedden *Gramp* 143 NJ8827
Pitmuies *Tays* 127 NO5649
Pitmunie *Gramp* 142 NJ6614
Pitney *Somset* 21 ST4528
Pitroddie *Tays* 126 NO2125
Pitscottie *Fife* 126 NO4112
Pitsea *Essex* 40 TQ7488
Pitses *Gt Man* 79 SD9403
Pitsford *Nhants* 50 SP7567
Pitstone *Bucks* 38 SP9415
Pitt *Devon* 9 ST0316
Pitt *Hants* 24 SU4528
Pitt Court *Gloucs* 35 ST7496
Pitt's Wood *Kent* 16 TQ6149
Pittarrow *Gramp* 135 NO7274
Pittenweem *Fife* 127 NO5502
Pitteuchar *Fife* 117 NT2899
Pittington *Dur* 96 NZ3244
Pittodrie House Hotel *Gramp* 142 NJ6924
Pitton *Wilts* 23 SU2131
Pittulie *Gramp* 143 NJ9567
Pity Me *Dur* 96 NZ2645
Pityme *Cnwll* 4 SW9576
Pivington *Kent* 28 TQ9146
Pixey Green *Suffk* 55 TM2475
Pixham *Surrey* 26 TQ1750
Plain Street *Cnwll* 4 SW9778
Plains *Strath* 116 NS7966
Plaish *Shrops* 59 SO5296
Plaistow *Derbys* 74 SK3456
Plaistow *Gt Lon* 27 TQ4082
Plaistow *H & W* 47 SO6939
Plaistow *W Susx* 14 TQ0030
Plaitford *Hants* 12 SU2719
Plank Lane *Gt Man* 79 SJ6399
Plas Cymyran *Gwynd* 68 SH2975
Plastow Green *Hants* 24 SU5361
Platt *Kent* 27 TQ6257
Platt Bridge *Gt Man* 78 SD6002
Platt Lane *Shrops* 59 SJ5136
Platts Heath *Kent* 28 TQ8750
Plawsworth *Dur* 96 NZ2647
Plaxtol *Kent* 27 TQ6053
Play Hatch *Oxon* 37 SU7376
Playden *E Susx* 17 TQ9221
Playford *Suffk* 55 TM2147
Playing Place *Cnwll* 3 SW8141
Playley Green *Gloucs* 47 SO7631
Plealey *Shrops* 59 SJ4206
Plean *Cent* 116 NS8386
Pleasance *Fife* 126 NO2312
Pleasington *Lancs* 81 SD6426
Pleasley *Derbys* 75 SK5064
Pleasleyhill *Notts* 75 SK5064
Pleck *Dorset* 11 ST7010
Pledgdon Green *Essex* 40 TL5626
Pledwick *W York* 83 SE3316
Pleinheaume *Guern* 152 GN0000
Plemont *Jersey* 152 JS0000
Plemstall *Ches* 71 SJ4570
Plenmeller *Nthumb* 102 NY7163
Pleshey *Essex* 40 TL6614
Plockton *Highld* 137 NG8033
Ploughfield *H & W* 46 SO3841
Plowden *Shrops* 59 SO3887
Ploxgreen *Shrops* 59 SJ3604
Pluckley *Kent* 28 TQ9245
Pluckley Station *Kent* 28 TQ9243
Pluckley Thorne *Kent* 28 TQ9244
Plucks Gutter *Kent* 29 TR2663
Plumbland *Cumb* 92 NY1539
Plumgarths *Cumb* 87 SD4994
Plumley *Ches* 79 SJ7274
Plumpton *Cumb* 94 NY4937
Plumpton *E Susx* 15 TQ3613
Plumpton *Nhants* 49 SP5948
Plumpton End *Nhants* 49 SP7245
Plumpton Green *E Susx* 15 TQ3616
Plumpton Head *Cumb* 94 NY5035
Plumstead *Gt Lon* 27 TQ4478
Plumstead *Norfk* 66 TG1334
Plumstead Green *Norfk* 66 TG1235
Plumtree *Notts* 62 SK6132
Plumtree Green *Kent* 28 TQ8245
Plungar *Leics* 63 SK7634
Plurenden *Kent* 28 TQ9337
Plush *Dorset* 11 ST7102
Plusha *Cnwll* 5 SX2580
Plushabridge *Cnwll* 5 SX3072
Plwmp *Dyfed* 42 SN3652
Plymouth *Devon* 6 SX4754
Plympton *Devon* 6 SX5456
Plymstock *Devon* 6 SX5152
Plymtree *Devon* 9 ST0502
Pockley *N York* 90 SE6385
Pocklington *Humb* 84 SE8048
Pode Hole *Lincs* 64 TF2121
Podimore *Somset* 21 ST5424
Podington *Beds* 51 SP9462
Podmore *Staffs* 72 SJ7835
Point Clear *Essex* 41 TM1015
Pointon *Lincs* 64 TF1131
Pokesdown *Dorset* 12 SZ1292
Polapit Tamar *Cnwll* 5 SX3389
Polbain *Highld* 144 NB9910
Polbathic *Cnwll* 5 SX3456
Polbeth *Loth* 117 NT0264
Polbrock *Cnwll* 4 SX0169
Pole Elm *H & W* 47 SO8450
Pole Moor *W York* 82 SE0615
Polebrook *Nhants* 51 TL0686
Polegate *E Susx* 16 TQ5804
Polelane Ends *Ches* 79 SJ6479
Polesworth *Warwks* 61 SK2602
Polgigga *Cnwll* 2 SW3723
Polglass *Highld* 144 NC0307
Polgooth *Cnwll* 3 SW9950
Polgown *D & G* 107 NS7103
Poling *W Susx* 14 TQ0404
Poling Corner *W Susx* 14 TQ0405
Polkerris *Cnwll* 3 SX0952
Pollard Street *Norfk* 67 TG3332
Pollington *Humb* 83 SE6119
Polloch *Highld* 129 NM7668
Pollokshaws *Strath* 115 NS5661
Pollokshields *Strath* 115 NS5763
Polmassick *Cnwll* 3 SW9745
Polmear *Cnwll* 3 SX0853
Polmont *Cent* 116 NS9378
Polnish *Highld* 129 NM7582
Polperro *Cnwll* 5 SX2051
Polruan *Cnwll* 3 SX1250
Polsham *Somset* 21 ST5142
Polstead *Suffk* 54 TL9938
Polstead Heath *Suffk* 54 TL9940
Poltalloch *Strath* 113 NR8196
Poltescoe *Cnwll* 3 SW7215
Poltimore *Devon* 9 SX9696
Polton *Loth* 117 NT2864
Polwarth *Border* 119 NT7450
Polyphant *Cnwll* 5 SX2682
Polzeath *Cnwll* 4 SW9378
Pomathorn *Loth* 117 NT2459
Ponde *Powys* 45 SO1037
Ponders End *Gt Lon* 27 TQ3596
Pondersbridge *Cambs* 64 TL2692
Ponsanooth *Cnwll* 3 SW7537
Ponsonby *Cumb* 86 NY0505
Ponsongath *Cnwll* 3 SW7518
Ponsworthy *Devon* 7 SX7073
Pont Cyfyng *Gwynd* 69 SH7357
Pont Morlais *Dyfed* 32 SN5307
Pont Pen-y-benglog *Gwynd* 69 SH6560
Pont Rhyd-sarn *Gwynd* 57 SH8528
Pont Rhyd-y-cyff *M Glam* 33 SS8788
Pont Robert *Powys* 58 SJ1012
Pont Walby *M Glam* 33 SN8906
Pont-ar-gothi *Dyfed* 32 SN5021
Pont-ar-Hydfer *Powys* 45 SN8627
Pont-ar-llechau *Dyfed* 44 SN7224
Pont-Ebbw *Gwent* 34 ST2985
Pont-faen *Powys* 45 SN9934
Pont-gareg *Dyfed* 31 SN1441
Pont-Nedd-Fechan *Powys* 33 SN9007
Pont-rhyd-y-fen *W Glam* 32 SS7994
Pont-rug *Gwynd* 68 SH5162
Pont-y-blew *Clwyd* 71 SJ3138
Pont-y-pant *Gwynd* 69 SH7554
Pont-yr-hafod *Dyfed* 30 SM9026
Pont-yr-Rhyl *M Glam* 33 SS9089
Pontac *Jersey* 152 JS0000
Pontamman *Dyfed* 32 SN6312
Pontantwn *Dyfed* 32 SN4412
Pontardawe *W Glam* 32 SN7204
Pontarddulais *W Glam* 32 SN5903
Pontarsais *Dyfed* 31 SN4428
Pontblyddyn *Clwyd* 70 SJ2760
Pontdolgoch *Powys* 58 SO0193
Pontefract *W York* 83 SE4521
Ponteland *Nthumb* 103 NZ1672
Ponterwyd *Dyfed* 43 SN7481
Pontesbury *Shrops* 59 SJ3906
Pontesbury Hill *Shrops* 59 SJ3905
Pontesford *Shrops* 59 SJ4106
Pontfadog *Clwyd* 70 SJ2338
Pontfaen *Dyfed* 30 SN0234
Pontgarreg *Dyfed* 42 SN3353
Ponthenry *Dyfed* 32 SN4709
Ponthir *Gwent* 34 ST3292
Ponthirwaun *Dyfed* 42 SN2645
Pontllanfraith *Gwent* 33 ST1895
Pontlliw *W Glam* 32 SS6199
Pontlottyn *M Glam* 33 SO1106
Pontlyfni *Gwynd* 68 SH4352
Pontnewydd *Gwent* 34 ST2896
Pontnewynydd *Gwent* 34 SO2701
Pontop *Dur* 96 NZ1453
Pontrhydfendigaid *Dyfed* 43 SN7366
Pontrhydygroes *Dyfed* 43 SN7472
Pontrhydyrun *Gwent* 34 ST2997
Pontrilas *H & W* 46 SO3927
Ponts Green *E Susx* 16 TQ6715
Pontshaen *Dyfed* 42 SN4446
Pontshill *H & W* 35 SO6421
Pontsticill *M Glam* 33 SO0511
Pontwelly *Dyfed* 31 SN4140
Pontyates *Dyfed* 32 SN4708
Pontyberem *Dyfed* 32 SN5010
Pontybodkin *Clwyd* 70 SJ2759
Pontyclun *M Glam* 33 ST0381
Pontycymer *M Glam* 33 SS9091
Pontyglasier *Dyfed* 31 SN1436
Pontygwaith *M Glam* 33 ST0094
Pontygynon *Dyfed* 31 SN1237
Pontymoel *Gwent* 34 SO2900
Pontypool *Gwent* 34 SO2800
Pontypool Road *Gwent* 34 ST3099
Pontypridd *M Glam* 33 ST0789
Pontywaun *Gwent* 34 ST2292
Pooksgreen *Hants* 12 SU3710
Pool *Cnwll* 2 SW6641
Pool *IOS* 2 SV8714
Pool *W York* 82 SE2445
Pool Head *H & W* 46 SO5550
Pool of Muckhart *Cent* 117 NO0000
Pool Quay *Powys* 58 SJ2511
Pool Street *Essex* 53 TL7636
Poole *Dorset* 11 SZ0090
Poole Keynes *Wilts* 35 ST9995
Poolewe *Highld* 144 NG8580
Pooley Bridge *Cumb* 93 NY4724
Pooley Street *Norfk* 54 TM0581
Poolfold *Staffs* 72 SJ8959
Poolhill *Gloucs* 47 SO7229
Pooting's *Kent* 16 TQ4549
Popham *Hants* 24 SU5543
Poplar *Gt Lon* 27 TQ3780
Poplar Street *Suffk* 55 TM4465
Porchbrook *H & W* 60 SO7270
Porchfield *IOW* 13 SZ4491
Poringland *Norfk* 67 TG2701
Porkellis *Cnwll* 2 SW6933
Porlock *Somset* 19 SS8846
Porlock Weir *Somset* 19 SS8647
Port Appin *Strath* 122 NM9045
Port Askaig *Strath* 112 NR4369
Port Bannatyne *Strath* 114 NS0767
Port Carlisle *Cumb* 101 NY2461
Port Charlotte *Strath* 112 NR2558
Port Clarence *Cleve* 97 NZ4921
Port Dolgarrog *Gwynd* 69 SH7766
Port Driseach *Strath* 114 NR9973
Port Einon *W Glam* 32 SS4685
Port Ellen *Strath* 104 NR3645
Port Elphinstone *Gramp* 142 NJ7720
Port Erin *IOM* 153 SC1969
Port Gaverne *Cnwll* 4 SX0080
Port Glasgow *Strath* 115 NS3274
Port Henderson *Highld* 137 NG7573
Port Isaac *Cnwll* 4 SW9980
Port Logan *D & G* 98 NX0940
Port Mor *Highld* 128 NM4279
Port Mulgrave *N York* 97 NZ7917
Port Na Craig *Tays* 125 NN9357
Port nan Giuran *W Isls* 154 NB5537
Port nan Long *W Isls* 154 NF8978
Port Nis *W Isls* 154 NB5363
Port of Menteith *Cent* 115 NN5801
Port of Ness *W Isls* 154 NB5363
Port Quin *Cnwll* 4 SW9780
Port Ramsay *Strath* 122 NM8845
Port Soderick *IOM* 153 SC3472
Port St Mary *IOM* 153 SC2067
Port Sunlight *Mersyd* 78 SJ3384
Port Talbot *W Glam* 32 SS7689
Port Tennant *W Glam* 32 SS6893
Port Wemyss *Strath* 112 NR1651
Port William *D & G* 98 NX3343
Port-an-Eorna *Highld* 137 NG7732
Portachoillan *Strath* 113 NR7557
Portavadie *Strath* 114 NR9369
Portbury *Avon* 34 ST5075
Portchester *Hants* 13 SU6105
Porteath *Cnwll* 4 SW9679
Portencalzie *D & G* 98 NX0171
Portencross *Strath* 114 NS1748
Portesham *Dorset* 10 SY6085
Portessie *Gramp* 142 NJ4366
Portfield Gate *Dyfed* 30 SM9215
Portgate *Devon* 5 SX4285
Portgordon *Gramp* 142 NJ3964
Portgower *Highld* 147 ND0013
Porth *Cnwll* 4 SW8362
Porth *M Glam* 33 ST0291
Porth Dinllaen *Gwynd* 56 SH2740
Porth Navas *Cnwll* 3 SW7527
Porth-y-Waen *Shrops* 58 SJ2623
Porthallow *Cnwll* 3 SW7923
Porthallow *Cnwll* 5 SX2251
Porthcawl *M Glam* 33 SS8177
Porthcothan *Cnwll* 4 SW8672
Porthcurno *Cnwll* 2 SW3822
Porthgain *Dyfed* 30 SM8132
Porthgwarra *Cnwll* 2 SW3721
Porthill *Staffs* 72 SJ8448
Porthkea *Cnwll* 3 SW8242
Porthkerry *S Glam* 20 ST0866
Porthleven *Cnwll* 2 SW6225
Porthmadog *Gwynd* 57 SH5638
Porthmeor *Cnwll* 2 SW4337
Portholland *Cnwll* 3 SW9541
Porthoustock *Cnwll* 3 SW8021
Porthpean *Cnwll* 3 SX0250
Porthtowan *Cnwll* 2 SW6947
Porthwgan *Clwyd* 71 SJ3846
Porthyrhyd *Dyfed* 32 SN5215
Portincaple *Strath* 114 NS2393
Portinfer *Jersey* 152 JS0000
Portington *Humb* 84 SE7831
Portinnisherrich *Strath* 122 NM9711
Portinscale *Cumb* 93 NY2523
Portishead *Avon* 34 ST4675
Portknockie *Gramp* 142 NJ4868
Portlethen *Gramp* 135 NO9196
Portling *D & G* 92 NX8753
Portloe *Cnwll* 3 SW9339
Portlooe *Cnwll* 5 SX2452
Portmahomack *Highld* 147 NH9184
Portmellon *Cnwll* 3 SX0144
Portmore *Hants* 12 SZ3397
Portnacroish *Strath* 122 NM9247
Portnaguran *W Isls* 154 NB5537
Portnahaven *Strath* 112 NR1652
Portnalong *Highld* 136 NG3434
Portobello *Loth* 117 NT3073
Portobello *T & W* 96 NZ2856
Portobello *W Mids* 60 SO9598
Porton *Wilts* 23 SU1836
Portontown *Devon* 5 SX4176
Portpatrick *D & G* 98 NW9954
Portreath *Cnwll* 2 SW6545
Portree *Highld* 136 NG4843
Portscatho *Cnwll* 3 SW8735
Portsea *Hants* 13 SU6300
Portskerra *Highld* 150 NC8765
Portskewett *Gwent* 34 ST4988
Portslade *E Susx* 15 TQ2506
Portslade-by-Sea *E Susx* 15 TQ2605
Portslogan *D & G* 98 NW9858
Portsmouth *Hants* 13 SU6400
Portsmouth *W York* 81 SD9026
Portsonachan Hotel *Strath* 123 NN0420
Portsoy *Gramp* 142 NJ5866
Portswood *Hants* 13 SU4214
Portuairk *Highld* 128 NM4368
Portway *H & W* 46 SO4844
Portway *H & W* 46 SO4935
Portway *H & W* 61 SP0872
Portway *W Mids* 60 SO9787
Portwrinkle *Cnwll* 5 SX3553
Portyerrock *D & G* 99 NX4738
Posbury *Devon* 8 SX8197
Posenhall *Shrops* 59 SJ6501
Poslingford *Suffk* 53 TL7648
Posso *Border* 109 NT2033
Post Green *Dorset* 11 SY9593
Postbridge *Devon* 8 SX6579
Postcombe *Oxon* 37 SP7000
Postling *Kent* 29 TR1439
Postwick *Norfk* 67 TG2907
Potarch *Gramp* 134 NO6097
Pothole *Cnwll* 3 SW9750
Potsgrove *Beds* 38 SP9530
Pott Row *Norfk* 65 TF7022
Pott Shrigley *Ches* 79 SJ9479
Pott's Green *Essex* 40 TL9122
Potten End *Herts* 38 TL0109
Potten Street *Kent* 29 TR2567
Potter Brompton *N York* 91 SE9777
Potter Heigham *Norfk* 67 TG4119
Potter Row *Bucks* 26 SP9002
Potter Somersal *Derbys* 73 SK1335
Potter's Cross *Staffs* 60 SO8484
Potter's Forstal *Kent* 28 TQ8946
Potter's Green *E Susx* 16 TQ5023
Potter's Green *Herts* 39 TL3520
Pottergate Street *Norfk* 66 TM1591
Potterhanworth *Lincs* 76 TF0566
Potterhanworth Booths *Lincs* 76 TF0767
Potterne *Wilts* 22 ST9958
Potterne Wick *Wilts* 22 ST9957
Potters Bar *Herts* 26 TL2401
Potters Brook *Lancs* 80 SD4852
Potters Crouch *Herts* 38 TL1105
Potters Green *W Mids* 61 SP3782
Potters Marston *Leics* 50 SP4996
Pottersheath *Herts* 39 TL2318
Potterspury *Nhants* 49 SP7543
Potterton *Gramp* 143 NJ9415
Potterton *W York* 83 SE4038
Potthorpe *Norfk* 66 TF9422
Pottle Street *Wilts* 22 ST8140
Potto *N York* 89 NZ4703
Potton *Beds* 52 TL2249
Poughill *Cnwll* 18 SS2207
Poughill *Devon* 19 SS8508
Poulner *Hants* 12 SU1606
Poulshot *Wilts* 22 ST9659
Poulston *Devon* 7 SX7754
Poulton *Gloucs* 36 SP0901
Poulton *Mersyd* 78 SJ3091
Poulton Priory *Gloucs* 36 SP0900
Poulton-le-Fylde *Lancs* 80 SD3439
Pound Bank *H & W* 60 SO7374
Pound Green *E Susx* 16 TQ5123
Pound Green *H & W* 60 SO7579
Pound Green *Suffk* 53 TL7153
Pound Hill *W Susx* 15 TQ2937
Pound Street *Hants* 24 SU4561
Poundffald *W Glam* 32 SS5694
Poundgates *E Susx* 16 TQ4928
Poundon *Bucks* 49 SP6425
Poundsbridge *Kent* 16 TQ5341
Poundsgate *Devon* 7 SX7072
Poundstock *Cnwll* 18 SX2099
Pounsley *E Susx* 16 TQ5221
Pouton *D & G* 99 NX4645
Povey Cross *Surrey* 15 TQ2642
Pow Green *H & W* 47 SO7144
Powburn *Nthumb* 111 NU0616

Powderham

Reedness

Powderham Devon 9 SX9684
Powerstock Dorset 10 SY5196
Powfoot D & G 100 NY1465
Powhill Cumb 93 NY2355
Powick H & W 47 SO8351
Powmill Tays 117 NT0297
Poxwell Dorset 11 SY7384
Poyle Surrey 26 TQ0376
Poynings W Susx 15 TQ2611
Poynter's Lane End Cnwll 2 SW6743
Poyntington Dorset 21 ST6520
Poynton Ches 79 SJ9283
Poynton Shrops 59 SJ5617
Poynton Green Shrops 59 SJ5618
Poys Street Suffk 55 TM3570
Poyston Cross Dyfed 30 SM9819
Poystreet Green Suffk 54 TL9758
Praa Sands Cnwll 2 SW5828
Pratt's Bottom Gt Lon 27 TQ4762
Praze-an-Beeble Cnwll 2 SW6335
Predannack Wollas Cnwll 2 SW6616
Prees Shrops 59 SJ5533
Prees Green Shrops 59 SJ5531
Prees Heath Shrops 71 SJ5538
Prees Higher Heath Shrops 59 SJ5635
Prees Lower Heath Shrops 59 SJ5732
Preesall Lancs 80 SD3647
Preesgweene Shrops 59 SJ2936
Pren-gwyn Dyfed 42 SN4244
Prendwick Nthumb 111 NU0012
Prenteg Gwynd 57 SH5841
Prenton Mersyd 78 SJ3086
Prescot Mersyd 78 SJ4692
Prescott Devon 9 ST0814
Prescott Shrops 59 SJ4220
Prescott Shrops 60 SO6681
Presnerb Tays 133 NO1866
Pressen Nthumb 110 NT8335
Prestatyn Clwyd 70 SJ0682
Prestbury Ches 79 SJ8976
Prestbury Gloucs 47 SO9723
Presteigne Powys 46 SO3164
Prestleigh Somset 21 ST6340
Prestolee Gt Man 79 SD7505
Preston Border 119 NT7957
Preston Devon 7 SX7451
Preston Devon 7 SX8574
Preston Devon 7 SX8962
Preston Dorset 11 SY7083
Preston E Susx 15 TQ3106
Preston Gloucs 47 SO6834
Preston Gloucs 36 SP0400
Preston Herts 39 TL1824
Preston Humb 85 TA1830
Preston Kent 28 TR0260
Preston Kent 29 TR2460
Preston Lancs 80 SD5329
Preston Leics 63 SK8602
Preston Loth 118 NT5977
Preston Nthumb 111 NU1825
Preston Shrops 59 SJ5211
Preston Somset 20 ST0935
Preston Suffk 54 TL9450
Preston Wilts 36 SU2774
Preston Bagot Warwks 48 SP1765
Preston Bissett Bucks 49 SP6529
Preston Bowyer Somset 20 ST1326
Preston Brockhurst Shrops 59 SJ5324
Preston Brook Ches 78 SJ5680
Preston Candover Hants 24 SU6041
Preston Capes Nhants 49 SP5754
Preston Crowmarsh Oxon 37 SU6190
Preston Deanery Nhants 50 SP7855
Preston Green Warwks 48 SP1665
Preston Gubbals Shrops 59 SJ4919
Preston Montford Shrops 59 SJ4314
Preston on Stour Warwks 48 SP2049
Preston on Tees Cleve 96 NZ4315
Preston on the Hill Ches 78 SJ5780
Preston on Wye H & W 46 SO3842
Preston Patrick Cumb 87 SD5483
Preston Plucknett Somset 10 ST5316
Preston Street Kent 29 TR2561
Preston upon the Weald Moors Shrops 72 SJ6815
Preston Wynne H & W 46 SO5546
Preston-under-Scar N York 88 SE0691
Prestonpans Loth 118 NT3874
Prestwich Gt Man 79 SD8104
Prestwick Nthumb 103 NZ1872
Prestwick Strath 106 NS3525
Prestwood Bucks 26 SP8700
Prestwood Staffs 60 SO8786
Price Town M Glam 33 SS9391
Prickwillow Cambs 53 TL5982
Priddy Somset 21 ST5250
Priest Hutton Lancs 87 SD5273
Priestacott Devon 18 SS4206
Priestcliffe Derbys 74 SK1471
Priestcliffe Ditch Derbys 74 SK1371
Priestend Bucks 37 SP6905
Priestland Strath 107 NS5737
Priestley Green W York 82 SE1326
Priestweston Shrops 59 SO2997
Priestwood Green Kent 28 TQ6564
Primethorpe Leics 50 SP5293
Primrose Green Norfk 66 TG0716
Primrose Hill Cambs 52 TL3889
Primrose Hill Derbys 75 SK4358
Primrose Hill Lancs 78 SD3809
Primrose Hill W Mids 60 SO9487
Primrosehill Border 119 NT7857
Primsidemill Border 110 NT8126
Princes Gate Dyfed 31 SN1312
Princes Risborough Bucks 38 SP8003
Princethorpe Warwks 61 SP4070
Princetown Devon 6 SX5873
Prinsted W Susx 14 SU7605
Prion Clwyd 70 SJ0562
Prior Rigg Cumb 101 NY4568
Priors Halton Shrops 46 SO4975
Priors Hardwick Warwks 49 SP4756
Priors Marston Warwks 49 SP4957
Priors Norton Gloucs 47 SO8624
Priory Wood H & W 46 SO2645
Prisk S Glam 33 ST0176
Priston Avon 22 ST6960
Pristow Green Norfk 54 TM1388
Prittlewell Essex 40 TQ8687
Privett Hants 13 SU6727
Prixford Devon 19 SS5536
Probus Cnwll 3 SW8947
Prospect Cumb 92 NY1140
Prospidnick Cnwll 2 SW6431
Protstonhill Gramp 143 NJ8163
Providence Avon 34 ST5370
Prudhoe Nthumb 103 NZ0962
Prussia Cove Cnwll 2 SW5528
Publow Avon 21 ST6264
Puckeridge Herts 39 TL3823
Puckington Somset 10 ST3718
Pucklechurch Avon 35 ST6976
Puckrup Gloucs 47 SO8836
Puddinglake Ches 79 SJ7269
Puddington Ches 71 SJ3273
Puddington Devon 19 SS8310
Puddledock Norfk 66 TM0592
Puddlehill Herts 38 TL0023
Puddletown Dorset 11 SY7594
Pudsey W York 82 SE2232
Pulborough W Susx 14 TQ0418
Puleston Shrops 72 SJ7322
Pulford Ches 71 SJ3758
Pulham Dorset 11 ST7008
Pulham Market Norfk 55 TM1986
Pulham St Mary Norfk 55 TM2085
Pullens Green Avon 34 ST6192
Pulley Shrops 59 SJ4709
Pulloxhill Beds 38 TL0634
Pumpherston Loth 117 NT0669
Pumsaint Dyfed 44 SN6540
Puncheston Dyfed 30 SN0129
Puncknowle Dorset 10 SY5388
Punnett's Town E Susx 16 TQ6220
Purbrook Hants 13 SU6707
Purbrook Park Hants 13 SU6707
Purfleet Essex 27 TQ5578
Puriton Somset 21 ST3241
Purleigh Essex 40 TL8402
Purley Berks 37 SU6675
Purley Gt Lon 27 TQ3161
Purlogue Shrops 46 SO2877
Purlpit Wilts 22 ST8766
Purls Bridge Cambs 53 TL4786
Purse Caundle Dorset 11 ST6917
Purshall Green H & W 60 SO8971
Purslow Shrops 59 SO3680
Purston Jaglin W York 83 SE4319
Purtington Somset 10 ST3908
Purton Gloucs 35 SO6904
Purton Gloucs 35 SO6705
Purton Wilts 36 SU0987
Purton Stoke Wilts 36 SU0990
Pury End Nhants 49 SP7145
Pusey Oxon 36 SU3596
Putley H & W 47 SO6337
Putley Green H & W 47 SO6437
Putloe Gloucs 35 SO7709
Putney Gt Lon 26 TQ2374
Putron Village Guern 152 GN0000
Putsborough Devon 18 SS4440
Puttenham Herts 38 SP8814
Puttenham Surrey 25 SU9247
Puttock End Essex 54 TL8040
Puttock's End Essex 40 TL5719
Putton Dorset 11 SY6480
Puxley Nhants 49 SP7542
Puxton Avon 21 ST4063
Pwll Dyfed 32 SN4801
Pwll Trap Dyfed 31 SN2616
Pwll-du Gwent 34 SO2411
Pwll-glas Clwyd 70 SJ1154
Pwll-y-glaw W Glam 32 SS7993
Pwllcrochan Dyfed 30 SM9202
Pwllgloyw Powys 45 SO0333
Pwllheli Gwynd 56 SH3735
Pwllmeyric Gwent 34 ST5292
Pydew Gwynd 69 SH8079
Pye Bridge Derbys 75 SK4452
Pye Corner Gwent 34 ST3485
Pye Corner Herts 39 TL4412
Pye Green Staffs 60 SJ9813
Pyecombe W Susx 15 TQ2813
Pyle M Glam 33 SS8282
Pyleigh Somset 20 ST1330
Pylle Somset 21 ST6038
Pymore Cambs 53 TL4986
Pymore Dorset 10 SY4694
Pyrford Surrey 26 TQ0358
Pyrton Oxon 37 SU6896
Pytchley Nhants 51 SP8574
Pyworthy Devon 18 SS3102

Q

Quabbs Shrops 58 SO2180
Quadring Lincs 64 TF2233
Quadring Eaudike Lincs 64 TF2433
Quainton Bucks 37 SP7420
Quaker's Yard M Glam 33 ST0995
Quaking Houses Dur 96 NZ1850
Quarley Hants 23 SU2743
Quarndon Derbys 62 SK3340
Quarr Hill IOW 13 SZ5792
Quarrier's Homes Strath 115 NS3666
Quarrington Lincs 64 TF0544
Quarrington Hill Dur 96 NZ3337
Quarry Bank Ches 71 SJ5465
Quarry Bank W Mids 60 SO9386
Quarrywood Gramp 141 NJ1763
Quarter Strath 116 NS7251
Quarter Strath 114 NS1961
Quatford Shrops 60 SO7391
Quatt Shrops 60 SO7588
Quebec Dur 96 NZ1743
Quedgeley Gloucs 35 SO8014
Queen Adelaide Cambs 53 TL5681
Queen Camel Somset 21 ST5924
Queen Charlton Avon 21 ST6367
Queen Dart Devon 19 SS8316
Queen Oak Dorset 22 ST7831
Queen Street Kent 28 TQ6845
Queen Street Wilts 35 SU0287
Queen's Bower IOW 13 SZ5684
Queen's Head Shrops 59 SJ3327
Queen's Park Beds 38 TL0349
Queen's Park Nhants 49 SP7562
Queenborough Kent 28 TQ9172
Queenhill H & W 47 SO8537
Queensbury W York 82 SE1030
Queensferry Clwyd 71 SJ3168
Queenslie Strath 116 NS6565
Queenzieburn Strath 116 NS6977
Quendon Essex 39 TL5130
Queniborough Leics 63 SK6412
Quenington Gloucs 36 SP1404
Quernmore Lancs 87 SD5160
Quernmore Park Hall Lancs 87 SD5162
Queslett W Mids 61 SP0695
Quethiock Cnwll 5 SX3164
Quick's Green Berks 37 SU5876
Quidenham Norfk 54 TM0287
Quidhampton Hants 24 SU5150
Quidhampton Wilts 23 SU1030
Quina Brook Shrops 59 SJ5232
Quinberry End Nhants 49 SP6250
Quinton Nhants 49 SP7754
Quinton W Mids 60 SO9984
Quinton Green Nhants 50 SP7853
Quintrell Downs Cnwll 4 SW8460
Quither Devon 5 SX4481
Quixhall Staffs 73 SK1041
Quixwood Border 119 NT7863
Quoditch Devon 5 SX4097
Quorndon Leics 62 SK5616
Quothquan Strath 108 NS9939
Quoyburray Ork 155 HY5005
Quoyloo Ork 155 HY2420

R

Rabbit's Cross Kent 28 TQ7847
Rableyheath Herts 39 TL2319
Raby Cumb 93 NY1951
Raby Mersyd 71 SJ3179
Rachan Mill Border 108 NT1134
Rachub Gwynd 69 SH6267
Rackenford Devon 19 SS8518
Rackham W Susx 14 TQ0413
Rackheath Norfk 67 TG2814
Rackwick Ork 155 ND2099
Radbourne Derbys 73 SK2836
Radcliffe Gt Man 79 SD7806
Radcliffe Nthumb 103 NU2602
Radcliffe on Trent Notts 63 SK6439
Radclive Bucks 49 SP6734
Radcot Oxon 36 SU2899
Raddington Somset 20 ST0225
Radernie Fife 127 NO4609
Radford Semele Warwks 48 SP3464
Radlet Somset 20 ST2038
Radlett Herts 26 TL1600
Radley Devon 19 SS7323
Radley Oxon 37 SU5398
Radley Green Essex 40 TL6205
Radmore Green Ches 71 SJ5955
Radnage Bucks 37 SU7897
Radstock Avon 22 ST6854
Radstone Nhants 49 SP5840
Radway Warwks 48 SP3648
Radway Green Ches 72 SJ7754
Radwell Beds 51 TL0057
Radwell Herts 39 TL2335
Radwinter Essex 53 TL6037
Radwinter End Essex 53 TL6139
Radyr S Glam 33 ST1280
RAF College (Cranwell) Lincs 76 TF0049
Rafford Gramp 141 NJ0556
Raftra Cnwll 2 SW3723
Ragdale Leics 63 SK6619
Ragdon Shrops 59 SO4591
Raginnis Cnwll 2 SW4625
Raglan Gwent 34 SO4107
Ragnall Notts 75 SK8073
Raigbeg Highld 140 NH8128
Rainbow Hill H & W 47 SO8555
Rainford Mersyd 78 SD4700
Rainham Gt Lon 27 TQ5282
Rainham Kent 28 TQ8165
Rainhill Mersyd 78 SJ4991
Rainhill Stoops Mersyd 78 SJ5090
Rainow Ches 79 SJ9475
Rainsough Gt Man 79 SD8002
Rainton N York 89 SE3675
Rainworth Notts 75 SK5858
Raisbeck Cumb 87 NY6407
Raise Cumb 94 NY7046
Raisthorpe N York 90 SE8561
Rait Tays 126 NO2226
Raithby Lincs 77 TF3084
Raithby Lincs 77 TF3766
Raithwaite N York 90 NZ8611
Rake W Susx 14 SU8027
Rakewood Gt Man 82 SD9414
Ralia Highld 132 NN7097
Ram Dyfed 44 SN5846
Ram Hill Avon 35 ST6779
Ram Lane Kent 28 TQ9646
Ramasaig Highld 136 NG1644
Rame Cnwll 3 SW7233
Rame Cnwll 6 SX4249
Rampisham Dorset 10 ST5602
Rampside Cumb 86 SD2366
Rampton Cambs 53 TL4267
Rampton Notts 75 SK8078
Ramridge End Beds 38 TL1023
Ramsbottom Gt Man 81 SD7916
Ramsbury Wilts 36 SU2771
Ramscraigs Highld 151 ND1427
Ramsdean Hants 13 SU7022
Ramsdell Hants 24 SU5857
Ramsden H & W 47 SO9246
Ramsden Oxon 36 SP3515
Ramsden Bellhouse Essex 40 TQ7194
Ramsden Heath Essex 40 TQ7095
Ramsey Cambs 52 TL2885
Ramsey Essex 41 TM2130
Ramsey IOM 153 SC4594
Ramsey Forty Foot Cambs 52 TL3087
Ramsey Heights Cambs 52 TL2484
Ramsey Island Essex 40 TL9405
Ramsey Mereside Cambs 52 TL2889
Ramsey St Mary's Cambs 52 TL2587
Ramsgate Kent 29 TR3865
Ramsgill N York 89 SE1170
Ramshaw Dur 95 NY9547
Ramsholt Suffk 55 TM3141
Ramshope Nthumb 102 NT7304
Ramshorn Staffs 73 SK0845
Ramsley Devon 8 SX6593
Ramsnest Common Surrey 14 SU9432
Ranby Lincs 76 TF2278
Ranby Notts 75 SK6580
Rand Lincs 76 TF1078
Randwick Gloucs 35 SO8306
Ranfurly Strath 115 NS3865
Rangemore Staffs 73 SK1822
Rangeworthy Avon 35 ST6986
Rank's Green Essex 40 TL7418
Rankinston Strath 107 NS4513
Ranksborough Leics 63 SK8311
Rann Lancs 81 SD7124
Rannoch Station Tays 124 NN4257
Ranochan Highld 129 NM8282
Ranscombe Somset 20 SS9443
Ranskill Notts 75 SK6587
Ranton Staffs 72 SJ8524
Ranton Green Staffs 72 SJ8423
Ranworth Norfk 67 TG3514
Raploch Cent 116 NS7894
Rapness Ork 155 HY5141
Rapps Somset 10 ST3316
Rascarrel D & G 92 NX7948
Rashfield Strath 114 NS1483
Rashwood H & W 47 SO9165
Raskelf N York 90 SE4971
Rassau Gwent 33 SO1511
Rastrick W York 82 SE1421
Ratagan Highld 138 NG9119
Ratby Leics 62 SK5105
Ratcliffe Culey Leics 61 SP3299
Ratcliffe on Soar Notts 62 SK4928
Ratcliffe on the Wreake Leics 63 SK6314
Ratfyn Wilts 23 SU1642
Rathen Gramp 143 NJ9960
Rathillet Fife 126 NO3620
Rathmell N York 88 SD8059
Ratho Loth 117 NT1370
Rathven Gramp 142 NJ4465
Ratlake Hants 13 SU4123
Ratley Warwks 48 SP3847
Ratling Kent 29 TR2453
Ratlinghope Shrops 59 SO4096
Rattan Row Norfk 65 TF5114
Rattar Highld 151 ND2673
Ratten Row Cumb 93 NY3240
Ratten Row Cumb 93 NY3949
Ratten Row Lancs 80 SD4241
Rattery Devon 7 SX7461
Rattlesden Suffk 54 TL9758
Ratton Village E Susx 16 TQ5901
Rattray Tays 126 NO1845
Raughton Cumb 93 NY3947
Raughton Head Cumb 93 NY3745
Raunds Nhants 51 SP9972
Raven Meols Mersyd 78 SD2905
Ravenfield S York 75 SK4895
Ravenglass Cumb 86 SD0896
Ravenhills Green H & W 47 SO7454
Raveningham Norfk 67 TM3996
Ravenscar N York 91 NZ9801
Ravenscliffe Staffs 72 SJ8452
Ravensdale IOM 153 SC3592
Ravensden Beds 51 TL0754
Ravenshead Notts 75 SK5654
Ravensmoor Ches 71 SJ6150
Ravensthorpe Nhants 50 SP6670
Ravensthorpe W York 82 SE2220
Ravenstone Bucks 38 SP8451
Ravenstone Leics 62 SK4013
Ravenstonedale Cumb 88 NY7203
Ravenstruther Strath 116 NS9245
Ravensworth N York 89 NZ1308
Raw N York 91 NZ9305
Rawcliffe Humb 83 SE6822
Rawcliffe N York 83 SE5854
Rawcliffe Bridge Humb 83 SE6921
Rawdon W York 82 SE2139
Rawling Street Kent 28 TQ9059
Rawmarsh S York 75 SK4396
Rawnsley Staffs 60 SK0212
Rawreth Essex 40 TQ7893
Rawridge Devon 9 ST2006
Rawtenstall Lancs 81 SD8123
Raydon Suffk 54 TM0438
Raylees Nthumb 102 NY9291
Rayleigh Essex 40 TQ8090
Raymond Hill Devon 10 SY3296
Rayne Essex 40 TL7222
Raynes Park Gt Lon 26 TQ2368
Rea Gloucs 35 SO8016
Reach Cambs 53 TL5666
Read Lancs 81 SD7634
Reading Berks 24 SU7173
Reading Street Kent 17 TQ9230
Reading Street Kent 29 TR3869
Reagill Cumb 94 NY6017
Rearquhar Highld 146 NH7492
Rearsby Leics 63 SK6514
Rease Heath Shrops 72 SJ6454
Reay Highld 150 NC9664
Reculver Kent 29 TR2269
Red Ball Devon 9 ST0917
Red Bull Ches 72 SJ8254
Red Cross Cambs 53 TL4754
Red Cross Cnwll 18 SS2605
Red Dial Cumb 93 NY2546
Red Hill Dorset 12 SZ0995
Red Hill Warwks 48 SP1356
Red Lodge Suffk 53 TL6970
Red Lumb Gt Man 81 SD8415
Red Rock Gt Man 78 SD5809
Red Roses Dyfed 31 SN2011
Red Row T & W 103 NZ2599
Red Street Staffs 72 SJ8251
Red Wharf Bay Gwynd 68 SH5281
Redberth Dyfed 31 SN0804
Redbourn Herts 38 TL1012
Redbourne Lincs 76 SK9799
Redbrook Clwyd 71 SJ5041
Redbrook Gloucs 34 SO5309
Redbrook Street Kent 28 TQ9336
Redburn Highld 140 NH9447
Redburn Nthumb 102 NY7764
Redcar Cleve 97 NZ6024
Redcastle D & G 100 NX8165
Redcastle Highld 139 NH5849
Redding Cent 116 NS9278
Reddingmuirhead Cent 116 NS9177
Reddish Gt Man 79 SJ8993
Redditch H & W 48 SP0467
Rede Suffk 54 TL8055
Redenhall Norfk 55 TM2684
Redenham Hants 23 SU3049
Redesmouth Nthumb 102 NY8682
Redford Gramp 135 NO7570
Redford Tays 127 NO5644
Redford W Susx 14 SU8626
Redfordgreen Border 109 NT3616
Redgate M Glam 33 ST0188
Redgorton Tays 125 NO0828
Redgrave Suffk 54 TM0477
Redhill Avon 21 ST4962
Redhill Gramp 135 NJ7704
Redhill Herts 39 TL3033
Redhill Surrey 27 TQ2750
Redisham Suffk 55 TM4084
Redland Avon 34 ST5775
Redland Ork 155 HY3724
Redlingfield Suffk 54 TM1870
Redlingfield Green Suffk 54 TM1871
Redlynch Somset 22 ST7033
Redlynch Wilts 12 SU2021
Redmain Cumb 92 NY1333
Redmarley H & W 47 SO7666
Redmarley D'Abitot Gloucs 47 SO7531
Redmarshall Cleve 96 NZ3821
Redmile Leics 63 SK7935
Redmire N York 88 SE0491
Redmyre Gramp 135 NO7575
Rednal Shrops 59 SJ3628
Rednal W Mids 60 SP0076
Redpath Border 110 NT5835
Redruth Cnwll 2 SW6942
Redstocks Wilts 22 ST9362
Redstone Tays 126 NO1834
Redstone Cross Dyfed 31 SN1015
Redvales Gt Man 79 SD8008
Redwick Avon 34 ST5486
Redwick Gwent 34 ST4184
Redworth Dur 96 NZ2423
Reed Herts 39 TL3636
Reedham Norfk 67 TG4201
Reedness Humb 84 SE7923

Rowden
Sandhurst

Rowden Devon 8 SX6499
Rowen Gwynd 69 SH7671
Rowfield Derbys 73 SK1948
Rowfoot Nthumb 102 NY6860
Rowford Somset 20 ST2327
Rowhedge Essex 41 TM0221
Rowhook W Susx 14 TQ1234
Rowington Warwks 48 SP2069
Rowland Derbys 74 SK2172
Rowland's Castle Hants 13 SU7310
Rowland's Gill T & W 96 NZ1658
Rowledge Surrey 25 SU8243
Rowley Dur 95 NZ0848
Rowley Humb 84 SE9732
Rowley Shrops 59 SJ3006
Rowley Green W Mids 61 SP3483
Rowley Hill W York 82 SE1914
Rowley Regis W Mids 60 SO9787
Rowlstone H & W 46 SO3727
Rowly Surrey 14 TQ0440
Rowner Hants 13 SU5801
Rowney Green H & W 61 SP0471
Rownhams Hants 12 SU3817
Rowrah Cumb 92 NY0518
Rows of Trees Ches 79 SJ8379
Rowsham Bucks 38 SP8417
Rowsley Derbys 74 SK2565
Rowstock Oxon 37 SU4789
Rowston Lincs 76 TF0856
Rowthorne Derbys 75 SK4764
Rowton Ches 71 SJ4464
Rowton Shrops 59 SJ3612
Rowton Shrops 59 SJ6119
Rowton Shrops 59 SO4180
Rowtown Surrey 26 TQ0363
Roxburgh Border 110 NT6930
Roxby Humb 84 SE9116
Roxby N York 97 NZ7616
Roxton Beds 52 TL1554
Roxwell Essex 40 TL6408
Roy Bridge Highld 131 NN2681
Royal Oak Dur 96 NZ2023
Royal Oak Lancs 78 SD4103
Royal's Green Ches 71 SJ6242
Roydhouse W York 82 SE2112
Roydon Essex 39 TL4010
Roydon Norfk 65 TF7023
Roydon Norfk 54 TM1080
Roydon Hamlet Essex 39 TL4107
Royston Herts 39 TL3540
Royston S York 83 SE3611
Royton Gt Man 79 SD9107
Rozel Jersey 152 JS0000
Ruabon Clwyd 71 SJ3043
Ruaig Strath 120 NM0747
Ruan High Lanes Cnwll 3 SW9039
Ruan Lanihorne Cnwll 3 SW8942
Ruan Major Cnwll 2 SW7016
Ruan Minor Cnwll 2 SW7115
Ruardean Gloucs 35 SO6217
Ruardean Hill Gloucs 35 SO6317
Ruardean Woodside Gloucs 35 SO6216
Rubery H & W 60 SO9977
Ruckcroft Cumb 94 NY5344
Ruckhall Common H & W 46 SO4539
Ruckinge Kent 17 TR0233
Ruckland Lincs 77 TF3378
Ruckley Shrops 59 SJ5300
Rudby N York 89 NZ4706
Rudchester Nthumb 103 NZ1167
Ruddington Notts 62 SK5732
Ruddle Gloucs 35 SO6811
Ruddlemoor Cnwll 3 SX0054
Rudford Gloucs 35 SO7721
Rudge Somset 22 ST8251
Rudgeway Avon 35 ST6386
Rudgwick W Susx 14 TQ0834
Rudhall H & W 47 SO6225
Rudheath Ches 79 SJ6772
Rudley Green Essex 40 TL8303
Rudloe Wilts 35 ST8470
Rudry M Glam 33 ST2086
Rudston Humb 91 TA0967
Rudyard Staffs 72 SJ9557
Ruecastle Border 110 NT6120
Rufford Lancs 80 SD4615
Rufforth N York 83 SE5251
Rug Clwyd 70 SJ0543
Rugby Warwks 50 SP5075
Rugeley Staffs 73 SK0418
Ruggaton Devon 19 SS5545
Ruishton Somset 20 ST2625
Ruislip Gt Lon 26 TQ0987
Ruletown Head Border 110 NT6113
Rumbach Gramp 141 NJ3852
Rumbling Bridge Tays 117 NT0199
Rumburgh Suffk 55 TM3481
Rumby Hill Dur 96 NZ1634
Rumford Cent 116 NS9377
Rumford Cnwll 4 SW8970
Rumney S Glam 33 ST2178
Rumwell Somset 20 ST1923
Runcorn Ches 78 SJ5182
Runcton W Susx 14 SU8802
Runcton Holme Norfk 65 TF6109
Runfold Surrey 25 SU8647
Runhall Norfk 66 TG0507
Runham Norfk 67 TG4610
Runham Norfk 67 TG5108
Runnington Somset 20 ST1221
Runsell Green Essex 40 TL7905
Runshaw Moor Lancs 80 SD5319
Runswick N York 97 NZ8016
Runtaleave Tays 133 NO2867
Runwell Essex 40 TQ7594
Ruscombe Berks 37 SU7976
Rush Green Ches 79 SJ6987
Rush Green Essex 41 TM1515
Rush Green Gt Lon 27 TQ5187
Rush Green Herts 39 TL2123
Rush Green Herts 39 TL3325
Rushall H & W 47 SO6435
Rushall Norfk 55 TM1982
Rushall W Mids 60 SK0200
Rushall Wilts 23 SU1255
Rushbrooke Suffk 54 TL8961
Rushbury Shrops 59 SO5191
Rushden Herts 39 TL3031
Rushden Nhants 51 SP9566
Rushenden Kent 28 TQ9071
Rusher's Cross E Susx 16 TQ6028
Rushett Common Surrey 14 TQ0242
Rushford Devon 5 SX4576
Rushford Norfk 54 TL9281
Rushlake Green E Susx 16 TQ6218
Rushmere Suffk 55 TM4986
Rushmere St Andrew Suffk 55 TM1946
Rushmoor Surrey 25 SU8740
Rushock H & W 46 SO3058
Rushock H & W 60 SO8871
Rusholme Gt Man 79 SJ8594
Rushton Ches 71 SJ5863
Rushton Nhants 51 SP8482
Rushton Shrops 59 SJ6008
Rushton Spencer Staffs 72 SJ9362
Rushwick H & W 47 SO8254
Rushyford Dur 96 NZ2728
Ruskie Cent 116 NN6200
Ruskington Lincs 76 TF0851
Rusland Cumb 87 SD3488
Rusper W Susx 15 TQ2037
Ruspidge Gloucs 35 SO6611
Russ Hill Surrey 15 TQ2240
Russel's Green Suffk 55 TM2572
Russell Green Essex 40 TL7413
Russell's Green E Susx 16 TQ7011
Russell's Water Oxon 37 SU7089
Rusthall Kent 16 TQ5639
Rustington W Susx 14 TQ0402
Ruston N York 91 SE9583
Ruston Parva Humb 91 TA0661
Ruswarp N York 90 NZ8809
Ruthall Shrops 59 SO5990
Rutherford Border 110 NT6430
Rutherglen Strath 116 NS6161
Ruthernbridge Cnwll 4 SX0166
Ruthin Clwyd 70 SJ1258
Ruthrieston Gramp 135 NJ9204
Ruthven Gramp 142 NJ5046
Ruthven Highld 140 NH8132
Ruthven Highld 132 NN7699
Ruthven Tays 126 NO2848
Ruthven House Tays 126 NO3047
Ruthvoes Cnwll 4 SW9260
Ruthwaite Cumb 93 NY2336
Ruthwell D & G 100 NY0967
Ruxley Corner Gt Lon 27 TQ4770
Ruxton Green H & W 34 SO5419
Ruyton-XI-Towns Shrops 59 SJ3922
Ryal Nthumb 103 NZ0174
Ryall Dorset 10 SY4095
Ryall H & W 47 SO8640
Ryarsh Kent 28 TQ6660
Rycote Oxon 37 SP6705
Rydal Cumb 87 NY3606
Ryde IOW 13 SZ5992
Rye E Susx 17 TQ9220
Rye Cross H & W 47 SO7735
Rye Foreign E Susx 17 TQ8922
Rye Harbour E Susx 17 TQ9319
Rye Street H & W 47 SO7835
Ryebank Shrops 59 SJ5131
Ryeford H & W 35 SO6322
Ryehill Humb 85 TA2225
Ryeish Green Nhants 24 SU7267
Ryhall Leics 64 TF0310
Ryhill W York 83 SE3814
Ryhope T & W 96 NZ4152
Rylah Derbys 75 SK4667
Ryland Lincs 76 TF0179
Rylands Notts 62 SK5335
Rylstone N York 88 SD9658
Ryme Intrinseca Dorset 10 ST5810
Ryther N York 83 SE5539
Ryton N York 90 SE7975
Ryton Shrops 60 SJ7602
Ryton T & W 103 NZ1564
Ryton Warwks 61 SP4086
Ryton Woodside T & W 96 NZ1462
Ryton-on-Dunsmore Warwks 61 SP3874

S

Sabden Lancs 81 SD7837
Sabine's Green Essex 27 TQ5496
Sacombe Herts 39 TL3319
Sacombe Green Herts 39 TL3419
Sacriston T & W 96 NZ2447
Sadberge Dur 96 NZ3416
Saddell Strath 105 NR7832
Saddington Leics 50 SP6691
Saddle Bow Norfk 65 TF6015
Saddlescombe W Susx 15 TQ2711
Sadgill Cumb 87 NY4805
Saffron Walden Essex 39 TL5438
Sageston Dyfed 30 SN0503
Saham Hills Norfk 66 TF9003
Saham Toney Norfk 66 TF8901
Saighton Ches 71 SJ4462
St Abbs Border 119 NT9167
St Agnes Cnwll 2 SW7150
St Agnes Loth 118 NT6763
St Albans Herts 38 TL1407
St Allen Cnwll 3 SW8250
St Andrew Guern 152 GN0000
St Andrew's Major S Glam 33 ST1371
St Andrews Fife 127 NO5116
St Andrews Well Dorset 10 SY4793
St Ann's D & G 100 NY0793
St Ann's Chapel Cnwll 5 SX4170
St Ann's Chapel Devon 7 SX6647
St Anne's Lancs 80 SD3228
St Anthony Cnwll 3 SW7825
St Anthony's Hill E Susx 16 TQ6201
St Arvans Gwent 34 ST5296
St Asaph Clwyd 70 SJ0374
St Athan S Glam 20 ST0167
St Aubin Jersey 152 JS0000
St Austell Cnwll 3 SX0152
St Bees Cumb 86 NX9711
St Blazey Cnwll 3 SX0654
St Blazey Gate Cnwll 3 SX0653
St Boswells Border 110 NT5930
St Brelade Jersey 152 JS0000
St Brelades Bay Jersey 152 JS0000
St Breock Cnwll 4 SW9771
St Breward Cnwll 4 SX0977
St Briavels Gloucs 34 SO5604
St Bride's Major M Glam 33 SS8974
St Brides Dyfed 30 SM8010
St Brides Netherwent Gwent 34 ST4289
St Brides super-Ely S Glam 33 ST0977
St Brides Wentlooge Gwent 34 ST2982
St Budeaux Devon 6 SX4558
St Buryan Cnwll 2 SW4025
St Catherine Avon 35 ST7769
St Catherines Strath 123 NN1207
St Chloe Gloucs 35 SO8401
St Clears Dyfed 31 SN2816
St Cleer Cnwll 5 SX2468
St Clement Cnwll 3 SW8543
St Clement Jersey 152 JS0000
St Clether Cnwll 5 SX2084
St Colmac Strath 114 NS0467
St Columb Major Cnwll 4 SW9163
St Columb Minor Cnwll 4 SW8362
St Columb Road Cnwll 4 SW9159
St Combs Gramp 143 NK0563
St Cross South Elmham Suffk 55 TM2984
St Cyrus Gramp 135 NO7464
St David's Tays 125 NN9420
St Davids Dyfed 30 SM7525
St Day Cnwll 3 SW7242
St Decumans Somset 20 ST0642
St Dennis Cnwll 4 SW9557
St Devereux H & W 46 SO4431
St Dogmaels Dyfed 42 SN1645
St Dogwells Dyfed 30 SM9727
St Dominick Cnwll 5 SX4067
St Donats S Glam 20 SS9368
St Edith's Marsh Wilts 22 ST9764
St Endellion Cnwll 4 SW9978
St Enoder Cnwll 3 SW8956
St Erme Cnwll 3 SW8449
St Erney Cnwll 5 SX3759
St Erth Cnwll 2 SW5535
St Erth Praze Cnwll 2 SW5735
St Ervan Cnwll 4 SW8970
St Ewe Cnwll 3 SW9746
St Fagans S Glam 33 ST1277
St Fergus Gramp 143 NK0952
St Fillans Tays 124 NN6924
St Florence Dyfed 31 SN0801
St Gennys Cnwll 4 SX1497
St George Clwyd 70 SH9775
St George's S Glam 33 ST1076
St George's Hill Surrey 26 TQ0862
St Georges Avon 21 ST3762
St Germans Cnwll 5 SX3657
St Giles in the Wood Devon 19 SS5319
St Giles-on-the-Heath Cnwll 5 SX3690
St Harmon Powys 45 SN9872
St Helen Auckland Dur 96 NZ1826
St Helena Norfk 66 TG1816
St Helens Cumb 92 NY0232
St Helens E Susx 17 TQ8212
St Helens IOW 13 SZ6289
St Helens Mersyd 78 SJ5195
St Helier Gt Lon 27 TQ2567
St Helier Jersey 152 JS0000
St Hilary Cnwll 2 SW5431
St Hilary S Glam 33 ST0173
St Hill Devon 9 ST0908
St Hill W Susx 15 TQ3835
St Illtyd Gwent 34 SO2202
St Ippollitts Herts 39 TL1927
St Ishmaels Dyfed 30 SM8307
St Issey Cnwll 4 SW9271
St Ive Cnwll 5 SX3167
St Ives Cambs 52 TL3171
St Ives Cnwll 2 SW5140
St Ives Dorset 12 SU1204
St James's End Nhants 49 SP7460
St James Norfk 67 TG2720
St James South Elmham Suffk 55 TM3281
St John Cnwll 5 SX4053
St John Jersey 152 JS0000
St John's IOM 153 SC2781
St John's Chapel Devon 19 SS5329
St John's Chapel Dur 95 NY8837
St John's Fen End Norfk 65 TF5312
St John's Highway Norfk 65 TF5214
St John's Kirk Strath 108 NS9836
St John's Town of Dalry D & G 99 NX6281
St John's Wood Gt Lon 27 TQ2683
St Johns Dur 95 NZ0633
St Johns H & W 47 SO8454
St Johns Kent 27 TQ5356
St Johns Surrey 25 SU9857
St Jude's IOM 153 SC3996
St Just Cnwll 2 SW3731
St Just Lane Cnwll 3 SW8535
St Just-in-Roseland Cnwll 3 SW8435
St Katherines Gramp 142 NJ7834
St Keverne Cnwll 3 SW7921
St Kew Cnwll 4 SX0276
St Kew Highway Cnwll 4 SX0375
St Keyne Cnwll 5 SX2461
St Laurence Kent 29 TR3665
St Lawrence Cnwll 4 SX0466
St Lawrence Essex 41 TL9604
St Lawrence IOW 13 SZ5376
St Lawrence Jersey 152 JS0000
St Leonard's Street Kent 28 TQ6756
St Leonards Bucks 38 SP9007
St Leonards Dorset 12 SU1103
St Leonards E Susx 17 TQ8009
St Levan Cnwll 2 SW3822
St Lythans S Glam 33 ST1072
St Mabyn Cnwll 4 SX0473
St Madoes Tays 126 NO1921
St Margaret South Elmham Suffk 55 TM3183
St Margaret's at Cliffe Kent 29 TR3544
St Margarets H & W 46 SO3533
St Margarets Herts 39 TL3811
St Margarets Hope Ork 155 ND4493
St Marks IOM 153 SC2974
St Martin Cnwll 5 SX2555
St Martin Guern 152 GN0000
St Martin Jersey 152 JS0000
St Martin's Tays 126 NO1530
St Martin's Green Cnwll 3 SW7323
St Martin's Moor Shrops 59 SJ3135
St Martins Shrops 59 SJ3236
St Mary Jersey 152 JS0000
St Mary Bourne Hants 24 SU4250
St Mary Church S Glam 33 ST0071
St Mary Cray Gt Lon 27 TQ4768
St Mary Hill S Glam 33 SS9678
St Mary in the Marsh Kent 17 TR0627
St Mary's Ork 155 HY4701
St Mary's Bay Kent 17 TR0827
St Mary's Grove Avon 21 ST4669
St Mary's Hoo Kent 28 TQ8076
St Marychurch Devon 7 SX9166
St Maughans Gwent 34 SO4617
St Maughans Green Gwent 34 SO4717
St Mawes Cnwll 3 SW8433
St Mawgan Cnwll 4 SW8765
St Mellion Cnwll 5 SX3965
St Mellons S Glam 34 ST2281
St Merryn Cnwll 4 SW8874
St Mewan Cnwll 3 SW9951
St Michael Caerhays Cnwll 3 SW9642
St Michael Church Somset 20 ST3030
St Michael Penkevil Cnwll 3 SW8541
St Michael South Elmham Suffk 55 TM3483
St Michael's on Wyre Lancs 80 SD4641
St Michaels H & W 46 SO5865
St Michaels Kent 17 TQ8835
St Minver Cnwll 4 SW9677
St Monans Fife 127 NO5201
St Neot Cnwll 4 SX1868
St Neots Cambs 52 TL1860
St Newlyn East Cnwll 3 SW8256
St Nicholas Dyfed 30 SM9035
St Nicholas S Glam 33 ST0974
St Nicholas at Wade Kent 29 TR2666
St Ninians Cent 116 NS7991
St Olaves Norfk 67 TM4599
St Osyth Essex 41 TM1215
St Ouen Jersey 152 JS0000
St Owens Cross H & W 46 SO5324
St Paul's Walden Herts 39 TL1922
St Pauls Cray Gt Lon 27 TQ4768
St Peter Jersey 152 JS0000
St Peter Port Guern 152 GN0000
St Peter's Guern 152 GN0000
St Peter's Kent 29 TR3868
St Peter's Hill Cambs 52 TL2372
St Petrox Dyfed 30 SR9797
St Pinnock Cnwll 5 SX2063
St Quivox Strath 106 NS3723
St Ruan Cnwll 2 SW7115
St Sampson Guern 152 GN0000
St Saviour Guern 152 GN0000
St Saviour Jersey 152 JS0000
St Stephen Cnwll 3 SW9453
St Stephen's Coombe Cnwll 3 SW9451
St Stephens Cnwll 5 SX3285
St Stephens Cnwll 5 SX4158
St Teath Cnwll 4 SX0680
St Tudy Cnwll 4 SX0676
St Twynnells Dyfed 30 SR9597
St Veep Cnwll 3 SX1455
St Vigeans Tays 127 NO6443
St Wenn Cnwll 4 SW9664
St Weonards H & W 46 SO4924
Saintbury Gloucs 48 SP1139
Salachail Strath 123 NN0551
Salcombe Devon 7 SX7439
Salcombe Regis Devon 9 SY1588
Salcott Essex 40 TL9413
Sale Gt Man 79 SJ7991
Sale Green H & W 47 SO9358
Saleby Lincs 77 TF4578
Salehurst E Susx 17 TQ7524
Salem Dyfed 44 SN6226
Salem Dyfed 43 SN6684
Salem Gwynd 69 SH5456
Salen Highld 121 NM6864
Salen Strath 121 NM5743
Salesbury Lancs 81 SD6832
Salford Beds 38 SP9339
Salford Gt Man 79 SJ8197
Salford Oxon 48 SP2828
Salford Priors Warwks 48 SP0751
Salfords Surrey 15 TQ2846
Salhouse Norfk 67 TG3114
Saline Fife 117 NT0292
Salisbury Wilts 23 SU1429
Salkeld Dykes Cumb 94 NY5437
Salle Norfk 66 TG1024
Salmonby Lincs 77 TF3273
Salperton Gloucs 36 SP0720
Salph End Beds 38 TL0852
Salsburgh Strath 116 NS8262
Salt Staffs 72 SJ9527
Salt Cotes Cumb 93 NY1853
Salta Cumb 92 NY0845
Saltaire W York 82 SE1438
Saltash Cnwll 6 SX4258
Saltburn Highld 146 NH7270
Saltburn-by-the-Sea Cleve 97 NZ6621
Saltby Leics 63 SK8526
Saltcoats Cumb 86 SD0797
Saltcoats Strath 106 NS2441
Saltcotes Lancs 80 SD3728
Saltdean E Susx 15 TQ3802
Salterbeck Cumb 92 NX9926
Salterforth Lancs 81 SD8845
Salterswall Ches 71 SJ6266
Salterton Wilts 23 SU1236
Saltfleet Lincs 77 TF4593
Saltfleetby All Saints Lincs 77 TF4590
Saltfleetby St Clements Lincs 77 TF4691
Saltfleetby St Peter Lincs 77 TF4489
Saltford Avon 22 ST6867
Salthouse Norfk 66 TG0743
Saltley W Mids 61 SP1088
Saltmarsh Gwent 34 ST3482
Saltmarshe Humb 84 SE7824
Saltney Ches 71 SJ3865
Salton N York 90 SE7179
Saltrens Devon 18 SS4522
Saltwick Nthumb 103 NZ1780
Saltwood Kent 29 TR1535
Salvington W Susx 14 TQ1205
Salwarpe H & W 47 SO8762
Salwayash Dorset 10 SY4596
Sambourne Warwks 48 SP0662
Sambrook Shrops 72 SJ7124
Samlesbury Lancs 81 SD5930
Samlesbury Bottoms Lancs 81 SD6228
Sampford Arundel Somset 20 ST1118
Sampford Brett Somset 20 ST0741
Sampford Courtenay Devon 8 SS6301
Sampford Moor Somset 20 ST1118
Sampford Peverell Devon 9 ST0314
Sampford Spiney Devon 6 SX5372
Samson's Corner Essex 41 TM0818
Samsonlane Ork 155 HY6526
Samuelston Loth 118 NT4870
Sanaigmore Strath 112 NR2370
Sancreed Cnwll 2 SW4129
Sancton Humb 84 SE8939
Sand Somset 21 ST4346
Sand Cross E Susx 16 TQ5820
Sand Hills W York 83 SE3739
Sand Hole Humb 84 SE8137
Sand Hutton N York 90 SE6958
Sand Side Cumb 86 SD2282
Sandaig Highld 129 NG7102
Sandal Magna W York 83 SE3417
Sandale Cumb 93 NY2440
Sandavore Highld 128 NM4785
Sandbach Ches 72 SJ7560
Sandbank Strath 114 NS1680
Sandbanks Dorset 12 SZ0487
Sandend Gramp 142 NJ5566
Sanderstead Gt Lon 27 TQ3461
Sandford Avon 21 ST4259
Sandford Cumb 94 NY7316
Sandford Devon 8 SS8202
Sandford Dorset 11 SY9289
Sandford Hants 12 SU1601
Sandford IOW 13 SZ5381
Sandford Shrops 59 SJ3423
Sandford Shrops 59 SJ5833
Sandford Strath 107 NS7143
Sandford Orcas Dorset 21 ST6220
Sandford St Martin Oxon 49 SP4226
Sandford-on-Thames Oxon 37 SP5301
Sandgate Kent 29 TR2035
Sandhaven Gramp 143 NJ9667
Sandhead D & G 98 NX0949
Sandhill S York 75 SK4496
Sandhills Dorset 10 ST5800
Sandhills Dorset 11 ST6810
Sandhills Oxon 37 SP5507
Sandhills Surrey 14 SU9337
Sandhills W Mids 61 SK0604
Sandhoe Nthumb 102 NY9666
Sandhole Strath 114 NS0098
Sandholme Humb 84 SE8230
Sandholme Lincs 64 TF3337
Sandhurst Berks 25 SU8361
Sandhurst Gloucs 47 SO8223

Stanley
Stratton Strawless

Stanley W York 83 SE3422
Stanley Common Derbys 62 SK4042
Stanley Crook Dur 96 NZ1637
Stanley Ferry W York 83 SE3522
Stanley Gate Lancs 78 SD4405
Stanley Moor Staffs 72 SJ9251
Stanley Pontlarge Gloucs 47 SP0030
Stanmer E Susx 15 TQ3309
Stanmore Berks 37 SU4778
Stanmore Gt Lon 26 TQ1692
Stanmore Hants 24 SU4628
Stannersburn Nthumb 102 NY7286
Stanningley W York 82 SE2234
Stannington Nthumb 103 NZ2179
Stannington S York 74 SK2987
Stannington Station Nthumb 103 NZ2181
Stansbatch H & W 46 SO3461
Stansfield Suffk 53 TL7852
Stanshope Staffs 73 SK1253
Stanstead Suffk 54 TL8449
Stanstead Abbots Herts 39 TL3811
Stanstead Street Suffk 54 TL8448
Stansted Kent 27 TQ6062
Stansted Mountfitchet Essex 39 TL5125
Stanton Derbys 73 SK2718
Stanton Devon 7 SX7050
Stanton Gloucs 48 SP0634
Stanton Gwent 34 SO3021
Stanton Nthumb 103 NZ1390
Stanton Staffs 73 SK1245
Stanton Suffk 54 TL9673
Stanton Butts Cambs 52 TL2372
Stanton by Bridge Derbys 62 SK3726
Stanton by Dale Derbys 62 SK4637
Stanton Drew Avon 21 ST5963
Stanton Fitzwarren Wilts 36 SU1790
Stanton Harcourt Oxon 36 SP4105
Stanton Hill Notts 75 SK4760
Stanton in Peak Derbys 74 SK2364
Stanton Lacy Shrops 46 SO4978
Stanton Long Shrops 59 SO5791
Stanton on the Wolds Notts 63 SK6330
Stanton Prior Avon 22 ST6762
Stanton St Bernard Wilts 23 SU0961
Stanton St John Oxon 37 SP5709
Stanton St Quintin Wilts 35 ST9079
Stanton Street Suffk 54 TL9566
Stanton under Bardon Leics 62 SK4610
Stanton upon Hine Heath Shrops 59 SJ5624
Stanton Wick Avon 21 ST6162
Stantway Gloucs 35 SO7313
Stanwardine in the Field Shrops 59 SJ4124
Stanwardine in the Wood Shrops 59 SJ4227
Stanway Essex 40 TL9424
Stanway Gloucs 48 SP0632
Stanway Green Essex 40 TL9523
Stanway Green Suffk 55 TM2470
Stanwell Surrey 26 TQ0574
Stanwell Moor Surrey 26 TQ0474
Stanwick Nhants 51 SP9771
Stanwix Cumb 93 NY4057
Staoinebrig W Isls 154 NF7532
Stape N York 90 SE7994
Stapehill Dorset 12 SU0500
Stapeley Ches 72 SJ6749
Stapenhill Staffs 73 SK2521
Staple Kent 29 TR2756
Staple Somset 20 ST1141
Staple Cross Devon 20 ST0320
Staple Cross E Susx 17 TQ7822
Staple Fitzpaine Somset 10 ST2618
Staple Hill H & W 60 SO9773
Staplefield W Susx 15 TQ2728
Stapleford Cambs 53 TL4751
Stapleford Herts 39 TL3117
Stapleford Leics 63 SK8018
Stapleford Lincs 76 SK8857
Stapleford Notts 62 SK4837
Stapleford Wilts 23 SU0737
Stapleford Abbotts Essex 27 TQ5194
Stapleford Tawney Essex 27 TQ5099
Staplegrove Somset 20 ST2126
Staplehay Somset 20 ST2121
Staplehurst Kent 28 TQ7843
Staplers IOW 13 SZ5189
Staplestreet Kent 29 TR0660
Staplet Cumb 101 NY5071
Stapleton H & W 46 SO3265
Stapleton Leics 50 SP4398
Stapleton N York 89 NZ2612
Stapleton Shrops 59 SJ4704
Stapleton Somset 21 ST4621
Stapley Somset 9 ST1913
Staploe Beds 52 TL1560
Staplow H & W 47 SO6941
Star Dyfed 31 SN2434
Star Fife 126 NO3103
Star Somset 21 ST4358
Starbeck N York 83 SE3255
Starbotton N York 88 SD9574
Starcross Devon 9 SX9781
Stareton Warwks 61 SP3371
Starkholmes Derbys 74 SK3058
Starklin H & W 60 SO8574
Starling Gt Man 79 SD7710
Starlings Green Essex 39 TL4631
Starr's Green E Susx 17 TQ7615
Starston Norfk 55 TM2384
Start Devon 7 SX8044
Startforth Dur 95 NZ0415
Startley Wilts 35 ST9482
Statenborough Kent 29 TR3155
Statham Ches 79 SJ6787
Stathe Somset 21 ST3728
Stathern Leics 63 SK7731
Station Town Dur 96 NZ4036
Staughton Green Cambs 52 TL1365
Staughton Highway Cambs 52 TL1364
Staunton Gloucs 34 SO5512
Staunton Gloucs 47 SO7829
Staunton Green H & W 46 SO3661
Staunton in the Vale Notts 63 SK8043
Staunton on Arrow H & W 46 SO3660
Staunton on Wye H & W 46 SO3644
Staveley Cumb 87 SD3786
Staveley Cumb 87 SD4698
Staveley Derbys 75 SK4374
Staveley N York 89 SE3662
Staverton Devon 7 SX7964
Staverton Gloucs 47 SO8923
Staverton Nhants 49 SP5361
Staverton Wilts 22 ST8560
Staverton Bridge Gloucs 35 SO8722
Stawell Somset 21 ST3738
Stawley Somset 20 ST0622
Staxigoe Highld 151 ND3852
Staxton N York 91 TA0179
Staylittle Dyfed 43 SN6489
Staylittle Powys 43 SN8891
Staynall Lancs 80 SD3643
Staythorpe Notts 75 SK7554
Stead W York 82 SE1446
Stean N York 89 SE0973
Steane Nhants 49 SP5538
Stearsby N York 90 SE6171
Steart Somset 20 ST2745
Stebbing Essex 40 TL6624
Stebbing Green Essex 40 TL6823
Stebbing Park Essex 40 TL6524
Stechford W Mids 61 SP1287
Stede Quarter Kent 28 TQ8738
Stedham W Susx 14 SU8622
Steel Nthumb 95 NY9458
Steel Cross E Susx 16 TQ5331
Steel Heath Shrops 59 SJ5436
Steele Road Border 101 NY5293
Steen's Bridge H & W 46 SO5357
Steep Hants 13 SU7425
Steep Lane W York 82 SE0223
Steephill IOW 13 SZ5477
Steeple Dorset 11 SY9080
Steeple Essex 40 TL9303
Steeple Ashton Wilts 22 ST9056
Steeple Aston Oxon 49 SP4725
Steeple Barton Oxon 49 SP4424
Steeple Bumpstead Essex 53 TL6841
Steeple Claydon Bucks 49 SP7026
Steeple Gidding Cambs 52 TL1381
Steeple Langford Wilts 23 SU0337
Steeple Morden Cambs 39 TL2842
Steeton W York 82 SE0344
Stein Highld 136 NG2656
Stella T & W 103 NZ1763
Stelling Minnis Kent 29 TR1447
Stembridge Somset 21 ST4220
Stenalees Cnwll 3 SX0156
Stenhouse D & G 100 NX8093
Stenhousemuir Cent 116 NS8783
Stenigot Lincs 77 TF2480
Stenscholl Highld 136 NG4767
Stenton Loth 118 NT6274
Steornabhagh W Isls 154 NB4232
Stepaside Dyfed 31 SN1407
Stepney Gt Lon 27 TQ3681
Stepping Hill Gt Man 79 SJ9187
Steppingley Beds 38 TL0035
Stepps Strath 116 NS6568
Sternfield Suffk 55 TM3861
Sterridge Devon 19 SS5545
Stert Wilts 23 SU0259
Stetchworth Cambs 53 TL6459
Steven's Crouch E Susx 17 TQ7115
Stevenage Herts 39 TL2325
Stevenston Strath 106 NS2742
Steventon Hants 24 SU5447
Steventon Oxon 37 SU4691
Steventon End Essex 53 TL5942
Stevington Beds 51 SP9853
Stewartby Beds 38 TL0142
Stewarton Strath 115 NS4245
Stewkley Bucks 38 SP8526
Stewley Somset 10 ST3118
Stewton Lincs 77 TF3587
Steyne Cross IOW 13 SZ6487
Steyning W Susx 15 TQ1711
Steynton Dyfed 30 SM9107
Stibb Cnwll 18 SS2210
Stibb Cross Devon 18 SS4314
Stibb Green Wilts 23 SU2262
Stibbard Norfk 66 TF9828
Stibbington Cambs 51 TL0898
Stichill Border 110 NT7138
Sticker Cnwll 3 SW9750
Stickford Lincs 77 TF3560
Sticklepath Devon 8 SX6494
Sticklepath Somset 20 ST0436
Stickling Green Essex 39 TL4732
Stickney Lincs 77 TF3457
Stidd Lancs 81 SD6536
Stiff Green Kent 28 TQ8761
Stiffkey Norfk 66 TF9742
Stifford's Bridge H & W 47 SO7347
Stile Bridge Kent 28 TQ7547
Stileway Somset 21 ST4641
Stilligarry W Isls 154 NF7638
Stillingfleet N York 83 SE5940
Stillington Cleve 96 NZ3723
Stillington N York 90 SE5867
Stilton Cambs 52 TL1689
Stinchcombe Gloucs 35 ST7298
Stinsford Dorset 11 SY7091
Stiperstones Shrops 59 SJ3600
Stirchley Shrops 60 SJ6907
Stirchley W Mids 61 SP0581
Stirling Cent 116 NS7993
Stirling Gramp 143 NK1242
Stirtloe Cambs 52 TL1966
Stirton N York 82 SD9752
Stisted Essex 40 TL8024
Stitchcombe Wilts 36 SU2369
Stithians Cnwll 3 SW7336
Stivichall W Mids 61 SP3376
Stixwould Lincs 76 TF1765
Stoak Ches 71 SJ4273
Stobo Border 109 NT1837
Stoborough Dorset 11 SY9286
Stoborough Green Dorset 11 SY9285
Stobs Castle Border 109 NT5008
Stobswood Nthumb 103 NZ2195
Stock Avon 21 ST4561
Stock Essex 40 TQ6998
Stock Green H & W 47 SO9859
Stock Wood H & W 47 SP0058
Stockbridge Hants 23 SU3535
Stockbriggs Strath 107 NS7936
Stockbury Kent 28 TQ8461
Stockcross Berks 24 SU4368
Stockdale Cnwll 3 SW7837
Stockdalewath Cumb 93 NY3845
Stocker's Hill Kent 28 TQ9650
Stockerston Leics 51 SP8397
Stocking H & W 47 SO6230
Stocking Green Bucks 38 SP8047
Stocking Pelham Herts 39 TL4529
Stockingford Warwks 61 SP3391
Stockland Devon 9 ST2404
Stockland Bristol Somset 20 ST2443
Stockland Green Kent 16 TQ5642
Stockleigh English Devon 8 SS8506
Stockleigh Pomeroy Devon 9 SS8703
Stockley Wilts 22 ST9967
Stockley Hill H & W 46 SO3738
Stocklinch Somset 10 ST3817
Stockmoor H & W 46 SO3954
Stockport Gt Man 79 SJ8990
Stocksbridge S York 74 SK2698
Stocksfield Nthumb 103 NZ0561
Stockstreet Essex 40 TL8222
Stockton H & W 46 SO5261
Stockton Norfk 67 TM3894
Stockton Shrops 58 SJ2601
Stockton Shrops 72 SJ7716
Stockton Shrops 60 SO7299
Stockton Warwks 49 SP4363
Stockton Wilts 22 ST9838
Stockton Brook Staffs 72 SJ9151
Stockton Heath Ches 78 SJ6185
Stockton on Teme H & W 47 SO7167
Stockton on the Forest N York 83 SE6556
Stockton-on-Tees Cleve 96 NZ4419
Stockwell Gloucs 35 SO9414
Stockwell End W Mids 60 SJ8900
Stockwell Heath Staffs 73 SK0521
Stockwood Avon 21 ST6368
Stockwood Dorset 10 ST5906
Stodday Lancs 87 SD4658
Stodmarsh Kent 29 TR2260
Stody Norfk 66 TG0535
Stoer Highld 148 NC0328
Stoford Somset 10 ST5613
Stoford Wilts 23 SU0835
Stogumber Somset 20 ST0937
Stogursey Somset 20 ST2042
Stoke Devon 18 SS2324
Stoke Hants 24 SU4051
Stoke Hants 13 SU7202
Stoke Kent 28 TQ8274
Stoke W Mids 61 SP3778
Stoke Abbott Dorset 10 ST4500
Stoke Albany Nhants 51 SP8088
Stoke Ash Suffk 54 TM1170
Stoke Bardolph Notts 63 SK6441
Stoke Bliss H & W 47 SO6563
Stoke Bruerne Nhants 49 SP7449
Stoke by Clare Suffk 53 TL7443
Stoke Canon Devon 9 SX9398
Stoke Charity Hants 24 SU4839
Stoke Climsland Cnwll 5 SX3674
Stoke Cross H & W 47 SO6250
Stoke D'Abernon Surrey 26 TQ1258
Stoke Doyle Nhants 51 TL0286
Stoke Dry Leics 51 SP8596
Stoke Edith H & W 46 SO6040
Stoke End Warwks 61 SP1797
Stoke Farthing Wilts 23 SU0525
Stoke Ferry Norfk 65 TF7000
Stoke Fleming Devon 7 SX8648
Stoke Gabriel Devon 7 SX8557
Stoke Gifford Avon 35 ST6279
Stoke Golding Leics 61 SP3997
Stoke Goldington Bucks 38 SP8348
Stoke Green Bucks 26 SU9882
Stoke Hammond Bucks 38 SP8829
Stoke Heath H & W 47 SO9468
Stoke Heath Shrops 72 SJ6529
Stoke Heath W Mids 61 SP3681
Stoke Holy Cross Norfk 67 TG2301
Stoke Lacy H & W 47 SO6249
Stoke Lyne Oxon 49 SP5628
Stoke Mandeville Bucks 38 SP8310
Stoke Newington Gt Lon 27 TQ3386
Stoke Orchard Gloucs 47 SO9128
Stoke Poges Bucks 26 SU9783
Stoke Pound H & W 47 SO9667
Stoke Prior H & W 46 SO5256
Stoke Prior H & W 47 SO9467
Stoke Rivers Devon 19 SS6335
Stoke Rochford Lincs 63 SK9127
Stoke Row Oxon 37 SU6884
Stoke St Gregory Somset 21 ST3427
Stoke St Mary Somset 20 ST2622
Stoke St Michael Somset 22 ST6646
Stoke St Milborough Shrops 59 SO5682
Stoke sub Hamdon Somset 10 ST4717
Stoke Talmage Oxon 37 SU6799
Stoke Trister Somset 22 ST7428
Stoke upon Tern Shrops 59 SJ6328
Stoke Wake Dorset 11 ST7606
Stoke Wharf H & W 47 SO9567
Stoke-by-Nayland Suffk 54 TL9836
Stoke-on-Trent (Hanley) Staffs 72 SJ8847
Stoke-upon-Trent Staffs 72 SJ8745
Stokeford Dorset 11 SY8687
Stokeham Notts 75 SK7876
Stokeinteignhead Devon 7 SX9170
Stokenchurch Bucks 37 SU7696
Stokenham Devon 7 SX8042
Stokesay Shrops 59 SO4381
Stokesby Norfk 67 TG4310
Stokesley N York 90 NZ5208
Stolford Somset 20 ST0332
Stolford Somset 20 ST2345
Ston Easton Somset 21 ST6253
Stondon Massey Essex 27 TL5800
Stone Bucks 37 SP7812
Stone Gloucs 35 ST6895
Stone H & W 60 SO8675
Stone Kent 27 TQ5774
Stone Kent 17 TQ9427
Stone S York 75 SK5589
Stone Somset 21 ST5834
Stone Staffs 72 SJ9034
Stone Allerton Somset 21 ST3951
Stone Bridge Corner Cambs 64 TF2700
Stone Chair W York 82 SE1227
Stone Cross E Susx 16 TQ5128
Stone Cross E Susx 16 TQ6104
Stone Cross E Susx 16 TQ6431
Stone Cross Kent 16 TQ5239
Stone Cross Kent 28 TR0236
Stone Cross Kent 29 TR3257
Stone Hill S York 83 SE6809
Stone House Cumb 88 SD7685
Stone Rows Leics 61 SK3214
Stone Street Kent 27 TQ5754
Stone Street Suffk 54 TL9639
Stone Street Suffk 54 TM0143
Stone Street Suffk 55 TM3882
Stone-edge-Batch Avon 34 ST4671
Stonea Cambs 65 TL4593
Stonebridge Avon 21 ST3859
Stonebridge Norfk 54 TL9290
Stonebridge W Mids 61 SP2182
Stonebroom Derbys 74 SK4059
Stonebury Herts 39 TL3828
Stonechrubie Highld 145 NC2419
Stonecross Green Suffk 54 TL8257
Stonecrouch Kent 16 TQ7033
Stoneferry Humb 85 TA1031
Stonefield Castle Hotel Strath 113 NR8671
Stonegarthside Cumb 101 NY4780
Stonegate E Susx 16 TQ6628
Stonegate N York 90 NZ7708
Stonegrave N York 90 SE6577
Stonehall H & W 47 SO8848
Stonehaugh Nthumb 102 NY7976
Stonehaven Gramp 135 NO8786
Stonehill Green Gt Lon 27 TQ5070
Stonehouse Ches 71 SJ5070
Stonehouse D & G 100 NX8268
Stonehouse Devon 6 SX4654
Stonehouse Gloucs 35 SO8005
Stonehouse Nthumb 94 NY6958
Stonehouse Strath 116 NS7546
Stoneleigh Warwks 61 SP3372
Stoneley Green Ches 71 SJ6151
Stonely Cambs 52 TL1167
Stoner Hill Hants 13 SU7225
Stones Green Essex 41 TM1626
Stonesby Leics 63 SK8224
Stonesfield Oxon 36 SP3917
Stonethwaite Cumb 93 NY2613
Stonetree Green Kent 29 TR0637
Stonewells Gramp 141 NJ2865
Stonewood Kent 27 TQ5972
Stoney Cross Hants 12 SU2611
Stoney Middleton Derbys 74 SK2375
Stoney Stanton Leics 50 SP4994
Stoney Stoke Somset 22 ST7032
Stoney Stratton Somset 21 ST6539
Stoney Stretton Shrops 59 SJ3809
Stoneybridge H & W 60 SO9476
Stoneybridge W Isls 154 NF7532
Stoneyburn Loth 117 NS9862
Stoneygate Leics 62 SK6002
Stoneyhills Essex 40 TQ9597
Stoneykirk D & G 98 NX0853
Stoneywood Cent 116 NS7982
Stoneywood Gramp 135 NJ8811
Stonham Aspal Suffk 54 TM1359
Stonnall Staffs 61 SK0603
Stonor Oxon 37 SU7388
Stonton Wyville Leics 50 SP7395
Stony Cross H & W 46 SO5466
Stony Cross H & W 47 SO7247
Stony Houghton Derbys 75 SK4966
Stony Stratford Bucks 38 SP7840
Stonyford Hants 12 SU3215
Stonywell Staffs 61 SK0712
Stoodleigh Devon 19 SS6532
Stoodleigh Devon 20 SS9218
Stopham W Susx 14 TQ0219
Stopsley Beds 38 TL1023
Stoptide Cnwll 4 SW9475
Storeton Mersyd 78 SJ3084
Storeyard Green H & W 47 SO7144
Stormy Corner Lancs 78 SD4707
Stornoway W Isls 154 NB4232
Storridge H & W 47 SO7548
Storrington W Susx 14 TQ0814
Storth Cumb 87 SD4779
Storwood Humb 84 SE7144
Stotfield Gramp 141 NJ2270
Stotfold Beds 39 TL2136
Stottesdon Shrops 60 SO6782
Stoughton Leics 63 SK6402
Stoughton Surrey 25 SU9851
Stoughton W Susx 14 SU8011
Stoul Highld 129 NM7594
Stoulton H & W 47 SO9049
Stour Provost Dorset 22 ST7921
Stour Row Dorset 22 ST8221
Stourbridge W Mids 60 SO8983
Stourpaine Dorset 11 ST8609
Stourport-on-Severn H & W 60 SO8171
Stourton Staffs 60 SO8684
Stourton W York 83 SE3230
Stourton Warwks 48 SP2936
Stourton Wilts 22 ST7734
Stourton Caundle Dorset 11 ST7115
Stout Somset 21 ST4331
Stove Shet 155 HU4224
Stoven Suffk 55 TM4481
Stow Border 118 NT4544
Stow Lincs 76 SK8882
Stow Bardolph Norfk 65 TF6206
Stow Bedon Norfk 66 TL9596
Stow cum Quy Cambs 53 TL5260
Stow Longa Cambs 51 TL1070
Stow Maries Essex 40 TQ8399
Stow-on-the-Wold Gloucs 48 SP1925
Stowbridge Norfk 65 TF6007
Stowe Gloucs 34 SO5606
Stowe Shrops 46 SO3173
Stowe by Chartley Staffs 73 SK0026
Stowehill Nhants 49 SP6458
Stowell Somset 22 ST6822
Stowey Somset 21 ST5959
Stowford Devon 5 SX4398
Stowford Devon 19 SS6541
Stowford Devon 5 SX4387
Stowford Devon 9 SY1189
Stowlangtoft Suffk 54 TL9568
Stowmarket Suffk 54 TM0458
Stowting Kent 29 TR1242
Stowting Common Kent 29 TR1243
Stowupland Suffk 54 TM0760
Straanruie Highld 141 NH9916
Strachan Gramp 135 NO6792
Strachur Strath 114 NN0901
Stradbroke Suffk 55 TM2373
Stradbrook Wilts 22 ST9152
Stradishall Suffk 53 TL7452
Stradsett Norfk 65 TF6605
Stragglethorpe Lincs 76 SK9152
Stragglethorpe Notts 63 SK6537
Straight Soley Wilts 36 SU3172
Straiton Loth 117 NT2766
Straiton Strath 106 NS3804
Straloch Gramp 143 NJ8620
Straloch Tays 133 NO0463
Stramshall Staffs 73 SK0735
Strang IOM 153 SC3578
Strangford H & W 46 SO5827
Stranraer D & G 98 NX0560
Strata Florida Dyfed 43 SN7465
Stratfield Mortimer Berks 24 SU6664
Stratfield Saye Hants 24 SU6861
Stratfield Turgis Hants 24 SU6959
Stratford Beds 52 TL1748
Stratford Gt Lon 27 TQ3884
Stratford St Andrew Suffk 55 TM3560
Stratford St Mary Suffk 54 TM0434
Stratford sub Castle Wilts 23 SU1332
Stratford Tony Wilts 23 SU0926
Stratford-upon-Avon Warwks 48 SP2055
Strath Highld 144 NG7978
Strathan Highld 145 NC0821
Strathan Highld 149 NC5764
Strathan Highld 130 NM9791
Strathaven Strath 116 NS7044
Strathblane Cent 115 NS5679
Strathcarron Sta Highld 138 NG9442
Strathcoil Strath 122 NM6830
Strathdon Gramp 134 NJ3512
Strathkanaird Highld 145 NC1501
Strathkinness Fife 127 NO4516
Strathmashie House Tays 132 NN5891
Strathmiglo Fife 126 NO2109
Strathpeffer Highld 139 NH4858
Strathtay Tays 125 NN9153
Strathwhillan Strath 105 NS0235
Strathy Highld 150 NC8464
Strathy Inn Highld 150 NC8365
Strathyre Cent 124 NN5617
Stratton Cnwll 18 SS2306
Stratton Dorset 11 SY6593
Stratton Gloucs 35 SP0103
Stratton Audley Oxon 49 SP6025
Stratton St Margaret Wilts 36 SU1786
Stratton St Michael Norfk 67 TM2093
Stratton Strawless Norfk 67 TG2220

T

Tarvie
Tillybirloch

Tarvie Tays 133 NO0164
Tarvin Ches 71 SJ4966
Tarvin Sands Ches 71 SJ4967
Tasburgh Norfk 67 TM1996
Tasley Shrops 60 SO6894
Taston Oxon 36 SP3521
Tatenhill Staffs 73 SK2021
Tathall End Bucks 38 SP8246
Tatham Lancs 87 SD6069
Tathwell Lincs 77 TF3182
Tatsfield Surrey 27 TQ4156
Tattenhall Ches 71 SJ4858
Tatterford Norfk 66 TF8628
Tattersett Norfk 66 TF8429
Tattershall Lincs 76 TF2157
Tattershall Bridge Lincs 76 TF1956
Tattershall Thorpe Lincs 76 TF2159
Tattingstone Suffk 54 TM1337
Tattingstone White Horse Suffk 54 TM1338
Tatworth Somset 10 ST3205
Tauchers Gramp 141 NJ3749
Taunton Somset 20 ST2224
Taverham Norfk 66 TG1613
Taverners Green Essex 40 TL5618
Tavernspite Dyfed 31 SN1812
Tavistock Devon 6 SX4874
Taw green Devon 8 SX6597
Tawstock Devon 19 SS5529
Taxal Derbys 79 SK0079
Taychreggan Hotel Strath 123 NN0421
Tayinloan Strath 105 NR6946
Taynton Gloucs 35 SO7222
Taynton Oxon 36 SP2313
Taynuilt Strath 122 NN0031
Tayport Fife 127 NO4628
Tayvallich Strath 113 NR7487
Tealby Lincs 76 TF1590
Teangue Highld 129 NG6609
Teanord Highld 140 NH5964
Tebay Cumb 87 NY6104
Tebworth Beds 38 SP9926
Tedburn St Mary Devon 8 SX8194
Teddington Gloucs 47 SO9633
Teddington Gt Lon 26 TQ1670
Tedstone Delamere H & W 47 SO6958
Tedstone Wafer H & W 47 SO6759
Teesport Cleve 97 NZ5423
Teesside Park Cleve 97 NZ4618
Teeton Nhants 50 SP6970
Teffont Evias Wilts 22 ST9931
Teffont Magna Wilts 22 ST9932
Tegryn Dyfed 31 SN2233
Teigh Leics 63 SK8615
Teigncombe Devon 8 SX6787
Teigngrace Devon 7 SX8574
Teignmouth Devon 7 SX9473
Teindside Border 109 NT4408
Telford Shrops 60 SJ6908
Tellisford Somset 22 ST8055
Telscombe E Susx 15 TQ4003
Telscombe Cliffs E Susx 15 TQ4001
Tempar Tays 124 NN6857
Templand D & G 100 NY0886
Temple Cnwll 4 SX1473
Temple Loth 117 NT3158
Temple Strath 115 NS5469
Temple Balsall W Mids 61 SP2076
Temple Bar Dyfed 44 SN5354
Temple Cloud Avon 21 ST6257
Temple End Suffk 53 TL6650
Temple Ewell Kent 29 TR2844
Temple Grafton Warwks 48 SP1255
Temple Guiting Gloucs 48 SP0928
Temple Hirst N York 83 SE6024
Temple Normanton Derbys 74 SK4167
Temple Pier Highld 139 NH5330
Temple Sowerby Cumb 94 NY6127
Templecombe Somset 22 ST7022
Templeton Devon 19 SS8813
Templeton Dyfed 31 SN1111
Templetown Dur 95 NZ1050
Tempsford Beds 52 TL1653
Ten Mile Bank Norfk 65 TL5996
Tenbury Wells H & W 46 SO5968
Tenby Dyfed 31 SN1300
Tendring Essex 41 TM1424
Tendring Green Essex 41 TM1325
Tendring Heath Essex 41 TM1326
Tenpenny Heath Essex 41 TM0820
Tenterden Kent 17 TQ8833
Terling Essex 40 TL7715
Tern Shrops 59 SJ6216
Ternhill Shrops 59 SJ6332
Terregles D & G 100 NX9377
Terrington N York 90 SE6770
Terrington St Clement Norfk 65 TF5520
Terrington St John Norfk 65 TF5314
Terry's Green Warwks 61 SP1073
Teston Kent 28 TQ7053
Testwood Hants 12 SU3514
Tetbury Gloucs 35 ST8993
Tetbury Upton Gloucs 35 ST8895
Tetchill Shrops 59 SJ3932
Tetcott Devon 5 SX3396
Tetford Lincs 77 TF3374
Tetney Lincs 77 TA3100
Tetney Lock Lincs 85 TA3402
Tetsworth Oxon 37 SP6801
Tettenhall W Mids 60 SJ8800
Tettenhall Wood W Mids 60 SO8899
Tetworth Cambs 52 TL2253
Teversal Notts 75 SK4861
Teversham Cambs 53 TL4958
Teviothead Border 109 NT4005
Tewel Gramp 135 NO8085
Tewin Herts 39 TL2714
Tewkesbury Gloucs 47 SO8932
Teynham Kent 28 TQ9662
Thackley W York 82 SE1738
Thackthwaite Cumb 92 NY1423
Thackthwaite Cumb 93 NY4225
Thakeham W Susx 14 TQ1017
Thame Oxon 37 SP7005
Thames Ditton Surrey 26 TQ1567
Thamesmead Gt Lon 27 TQ4780
Thanington Kent 29 TR1356
Thankerton Strath 108 NS9738
Tharston Norfk 66 TM1894
Thatcham Berks 24 SU5167
Thatto Heath Mersyd 78 SJ5093
Thaxted Essex 40 TL6131
The Bank Ches 72 SJ8457
The Bank Shrops 59 SO6199
The Beeches Gloucs 36 SP0302
The Biggins Cambs 53 TL4788
The Blythe Staffs 73 SK0428
The Bourne H & W 47 SO9856
The Braes Highld 137 NG5234
The Bratch Staffs 60 SO8693
The Broad H & W 46 SO4961
The Brunt Loth 118 NT6873
The Bungalow IOM 153 SC3986
The Bush Kent 28 TQ6649
The Butts Gloucs 35 SO8916
The Chequer Clwyd 71 SJ4840
The City Beds 52 TL1159
The City Bucks 37 SU7896
The Common Oxon 48 SP2927
The Common Wilts 35 SU0285
The Corner Kent 28 TQ7041
The Corner Shrops 59 SO4387
The Cronk IOM 153 SC3395
The Den Strath 115 NS3251
The Flatt Cumb 101 NY5678
The Forge H & W 46 SO3459
The Forstal E Susx 16 TQ5435
The Forstal Kent 28 TQ8946
The Forstal Kent 28 TR0438
The Fouralls Shrops 72 SJ6831
The Green Cumb 86 SD1884
The Green Essex 40 TL7719
The Grove H & W 47 SO8741
The Haven W Susx 14 TQ0830
The Haw Gloucs 47 SO8427
The Hill Cumb 86 SD1783
The Hirsel Border 110 NT8240
The Holt Berks 37 SU8078
The Horns Kent 17 TQ7429
The Leacon Kent 17 TQ9833
The Lee Bucks 38 SP9004
The Lhen IOM 153 NX3801
The Lochs Gramp 141 NJ3062
The Middles Dur 96 NZ2051
The Moor Kent 17 TQ7529
The Mumbles W Glam 32 SS6187
The Mythe Gloucs 47 SO8934
The Narth Gwent 34 SO5206
The Neuk Gramp 135 NO7397
The Quarry Gloucs 35 ST7499
The Quarter Kent 28 TQ8844
The Reddings Gloucs 35 SO9121
The Rookery Staffs 72 SJ8555
The Ross Tays 124 NN7621
The Sands Surrey 25 SU8846
The Shoe Wilts 35 ST8074
The Smithies Shrops 60 SO6897
The Spike Cambs 53 TL4848
The Spring Warwks 61 SP2873
The Square Gwent 34 ST2796
The Stair Kent 16 TQ6047
The Stocks Kent 17 TQ9127
The Straits Hants 25 SU7839
The Strand Wilts 22 ST9259
The Thrift Herts 39 TL3139
The Towans Cnwll 2 SW5538
The Vauld H & W 46 SO5349
The Wyke Shrops 60 SJ7206
Theakston N York 89 SE3085
Thealby Humb 84 SE8917
Theale Berks 24 SU6471
Theale Somset 21 ST4646
Thearne Humb 85 TA0736
Theberton Suffk 55 TM4365
Thedden Grange Hants 24 SU6839
Theddingworth Leics 50 SP6685
Theddlethorpe All Saints Lincs 77 TF4688
Theddlethorpe St Helen Lincs 77 TF4788
Thelbridge Cross Devon 19 SS7911
Thelnetham Suffk 54 TM0178
Thelveton Norfk 54 TM1681
Thelwall Ches 79 SJ6587
Themelthorpe Norfk 66 TG0524
Thenford Nhants 49 SP5241
Theobald's Green Wilts 23 SU0268
Therfield Herts 39 TL3337
Thetford Norfk 54 TL8783
Thethwaite Cumb 93 NY3744
Theydon Bois Essex 27 TQ4499
Thicket Prior Humb 83 SE6943
Thickwood Wilts 35 ST8272
Thimbleby Lincs 77 TF2470
Thimbleby N York 89 SE4495
Thingwall Mersyd 78 SJ2784
Thirkleby N York 89 SE4778
Thirlby N York 90 SE4883
Thirlestane Border 118 NT5647
Thirlspot Cumb 93 NY3118
Thirn N York 89 SE2185
Thirsk N York 89 SE4281
Thirtleby Humb 85 TA1634
Thistleton Lancs 80 SD4037
Thistleton Leics 63 SK9118
Thistley Green Suffk 53 TL6676
Thixendale N York 90 SE8460
Thockrington Nthumb 102 NY9578
Tholomas Drove Cambs 65 TF4006
Tholthorpe N York 89 SE4766
Thomas Chapel Dyfed 31 SN1008
Thomas Close Cumb 93 NY4340
Thomas Town Warwks 48 SP0763
Thomastown Gramp 142 NJ5736
Thompson Norfk 66 TL9296
Thong Kent 28 TQ6770
Thoralby N York 88 SE0086
Thoresby Notts 75 SK6371
Thoresthorpe Lincs 77 TF4577
Thoresway Lincs 76 TF1696
Thorganby Lincs 76 TF2097
Thorganby N York 83 SE6841
Thorgill N York 90 SE7096
Thorington Suffk 55 TM4174
Thorington Street Suffk 54 TM0035
Thorlby N York 82 SD9653
Thorley Herts 39 TL4718
Thorley IOW 12 SZ3689
Thorley Houses Herts 39 TL4620
Thorley Street IOW 12 SZ3788
Thormanby N York 90 SE4974
Thorn's Flush Surrey 14 TQ0440
Thornaby-on-Tees Cleve 97 NZ4518
Thornage Norfk 66 TG0536
Thornborough Bucks 49 SP7433
Thornborough N York 89 SE2979
Thornbury Avon 35 ST6390
Thornbury Devon 18 SS4008
Thornbury H & W 47 SO6259
Thornbury W York 82 SE1933
Thornby Cumb 93 NY2851
Thornby Nhants 50 SP6775
Thorncliff Staffs 73 SK0158
Thorncombe Dorset 10 ST3703
Thorncombe Street Surrey 25 SU9941
Thorncott Green Beds 52 TL1547
Thorncross IOW 13 SZ4381
Thorndon Suffk 54 TM1469
Thorndon Cross Devon 8 SX5394
Thorne S York 83 SE6812
Thorne Somset 10 ST5217
Thorne St Margaret Somset 20 ST1020
Thornecroft Devon 7 SX7767
Thornehillhead Devon 18 SS4116
Thorner W York 83 SE3740
Thornes Staffs 61 SK0703
Thornes W York 83 SE3219
Thorney Bucks 26 TQ0379
Thorney Cambs 64 TF2804
Thorney Notts 76 SK8572
Thorney Somset 21 ST4223
Thorney Hill Hants 12 SZ2099
Thorney Toll Cambs 64 TF3404
Thornfalcon Somset 20 ST2823
Thornford Dorset 10 ST6012
Thorngrafton Nthumb 102 NY7865
Thorngrove Somset 21 ST3632
Thorngumbald Humb 85 TA2026
Thornham Norfk 65 TF7343
Thornham Magna Suffk 54 TM1070
Thornham Parva Suffk 54 TM1072
Thornhaugh Cambs 64 TF0600
Thornhill Cent 116 NN6600
Thornhill D & G 100 NX8795
Thornhill Derbys 74 SK1983
Thornhill Hants 13 SU4612
Thornhill M Glam 33 ST1584
Thornhill W York 82 SE2518
Thornhill Lees W York 82 SE2419
Thornhills W York 82 SE1523
Thornholme Humb 91 TA1164
Thornicombe Dorset 11 ST8703
Thornington Nthumb 110 NT8833
Thornley Dur 95 NZ1137
Thornley Dur 96 NZ3639
Thornley Gate Cumb 95 NY8356
Thornliebank Strath 115 NS5559
Thorns Suffk 53 TL7455
Thorns Green Gt Man 79 SJ7884
Thornsett Derbys 79 SK0086
Thornthwaite Cumb 93 NY2225
Thornthwaite N York 89 SE1758
Thornton Bucks 49 SP7435
Thornton Cleve 89 NZ4713
Thornton Dyfed 30 SM9007
Thornton Fife 117 NT2897
Thornton Humb 84 SE7645
Thornton Lancs 80 SD3342
Thornton Leics 62 SK4607
Thornton Lincs 77 TF2467
Thornton Mersyd 78 SD3301
Thornton Nthumb 111 NT9547
Thornton Tays 126 NO3946
Thornton W York 82 SE0932
Thornton Curtis Humb 85 TA0817
Thornton Dale N York 90 SE8383
Thornton Green Ches 71 SJ4473
Thornton Heath Gt Lon 27 TQ3168
Thornton Hough Mersyd 78 SJ3080
Thornton in Lonsdale N York 87 SD6873
Thornton le Moor Lincs 76 TF0496
Thornton Rust N York 88 SD9689
Thornton Steward N York 89 SE1787
Thornton Watlass N York 89 SE2385
Thornton-in-Craven N York 81 SD9048
Thornton-le-Beans N York 89 SE3990
Thornton-le-Clay N York 90 SE6865
Thornton-le-Moor N York 89 SE3988
Thornton-le-Moors Ches 71 SJ4474
Thornton-le-Street N York 89 SE4186
Thorntonhall Strath 115 NS5955
Thorntonloch Loth 119 NT7574
Thornwood Common Essex 39 TL4604
Thornydykes Border 110 NT6148
Thornythwaite Cumb 93 NY3922
Thoroton Notts 63 SK7642
Thorp Arch W York 83 SE4345
Thorpe Derbys 73 SK1550
Thorpe Humb 84 SE9946
Thorpe Lincs 77 TF4981
Thorpe N York 88 SE0161
Thorpe Norfk 67 TM4398
Thorpe Notts 75 SK7649
Thorpe Surrey 26 TQ0168
Thorpe Abbotts Norfk 55 TM1979
Thorpe Acre Leics 62 SK5119
Thorpe Arnold Leics 63 SK7720
Thorpe Audlin W York 83 SE4715
Thorpe Bassett N York 90 SE8673
Thorpe Bay Essex 40 TQ9185
Thorpe by Water Leics 51 SP8996
Thorpe Common S York 74 SK3895
Thorpe Constantine Staffs 61 SK2508
Thorpe End Norfk 67 TG2810
Thorpe Green Essex 41 TM1623
Thorpe Green Lancs 81 SD5923
Thorpe Green Suffk 54 TL9354
Thorpe Hesley S York 74 SK3796
Thorpe in Balne S York 83 SE5910
Thorpe in the Fallows Lincs 76 SK9180
Thorpe Langton Leics 50 SP7492
Thorpe Larches Dur 96 NZ3826
Thorpe le Street Humb 84 SE8343
Thorpe Lea Surrey 26 TQ0170
Thorpe Malsor Nhants 51 SP8378
Thorpe Mandeville Nhants 49 SP5244
Thorpe Market Norfk 67 TG2436
Thorpe Morieux Suffk 54 TL9453
Thorpe on the Hill Lincs 76 SK9065
Thorpe on the Hill W York 83 SE3126
Thorpe Salvin S York 75 SK5281
Thorpe Satchville Leics 63 SK7311
Thorpe St Andrew Norfk 67 TG2508
Thorpe St Peter Lincs 77 TF4860
Thorpe Thewles Cleve 96 NZ3923
Thorpe Tilney Lincs 76 TF1257
Thorpe Underwood N York 89 SE4659
Thorpe Underwood Nhants 50 SP7981
Thorpe Waterville Nhants 51 TL0281
Thorpe Willoughby N York 83 SE5731
Thorpe-le-Soken Essex 41 TM1722
Thorpeness Suffk 55 TM4759
Thorpland Norfk 65 TF6108
Thorrington Essex 41 TM0919
Thorverton Devon 9 SS9202
Thrales End Beds 38 TL1116
Thrandeston Suffk 54 TM1176
Thrapston Nhants 51 SP9978
Threapland Cumb 92 NY1539
Threapland N York 88 SD9860
Threapwood Ches 71 SJ4344
Threapwood Staffs 73 SK0342
Threapwood Head Staffs 73 SK0342
Threave Strath 106 NS3306
Three Ashes H & W 34 SO5122
Three Bridges W Susx 15 TQ2837
Three Burrows Cnwll 3 SW7446
Three Chimneys Kent 28 TQ8238
Three Cocks Powys 45 SO1737
Three Crosses W Glam 32 SS5794
Three Cups Corner E Susx 16 TQ6320
Three Gates H & W 47 SO6862
Three Hammers Cnwll 5 SX2287
Three Holes Norfk 65 TF5000
Three Lane Ends Gt Man 79 SD8309
Three Leg Cross E Susx 16 TQ6831
Three Legged Cross Dorset 12 SU0805
Three Mile Cross Berks 24 SU7167
Three Mile Stone Cnwll 3 SW7745
Three Miletown Loth 117 NT0675
Three Oaks E Susx 17 TQ8314
Threehammer Common Norfk 67 TG3419
Threekingham Lincs 64 TF0836
Threepwood Border 109 NT5143
Threlkeld Cumb 93 NY3125
Threshfield N York 88 SD9863
Thrigby Norfk 67 TG4612
Thringarth Dur 95 NY9322
Thringstone Leics 62 SK4217
Thrintoft N York 89 SE3192
Thriplow Cambs 53 TL4346
Throapham S York 75 SK5387
Throckenhalt Lincs 64 TF3509
Throcking Herts 39 TL3330
Throckley T & W 103 NZ1566
Throckmorton H & W 47 SO9850
Throop Dorset 11 SY8292
Throop Dorset 12 SZ1195
Throphill Nthumb 103 NZ1285
Thropton Nthumb 103 NU0202
Throsk Cent 116 NS8591
Througham Gloucs 35 SO9108
Throughgate D & G 100 NX8784
Throwleigh Devon 8 SX6690
Throwley Kent 28 TQ9955
Throwley Forstal Kent 28 TQ9854
Thrumpton Notts 62 SK5031
Thrumpton Notts 75 SK7080
Thrumster Highld 151 ND3345
Thrunscoe Humb 85 TA3107
Thrup Oxon 36 SU2999
Thrupp Gloucs 35 SO8603
Thrupp Oxon 37 SP4716
Thrushelton Devon 5 SX4487
Thrushesbush Essex 39 TL4909
Thrussington Leics 63 SK6515
Thruxton H & W 46 SO4334
Thruxton Hants 23 SU2945
Thrybergh S York 75 SK4695
Thulston Derbys 62 SK4031
Thundersley Essex 40 TQ7988
Thurcaston Leics 62 SK5610
Thurcroft S York 75 SK4988
Thurdon Cnwll 18 SS2810
Thurgarton Norfk 66 TG1834
Thurgarton Notts 75 SK6949
Thurgoland S York 82 SE2901
Thurlaston Leics 50 SP5099
Thurlaston Warwks 50 SP4670
Thurlbear Somset 20 ST2621
Thurlby Lincs 76 SK9061
Thurlby Lincs 64 TF0916
Thurlby Lincs 77 TF4776
Thurleigh Beds 51 TL0558
Thurlestone Devon 7 SX6742
Thurlow Suffk 53 TL6750
Thurloxton Somset 20 ST2730
Thurlstone S York 82 SE2303
Thurlton Norfk 67 TM4198
Thurlwood Ches 72 SJ8057
Thurmaston Leics 62 SK6109
Thurnby Leics 63 SK6403
Thurne Norfk 67 TG4015
Thurnham Kent 28 TQ8057
Thurning Nhants 51 TL0882
Thurning Norfk 66 TG0729
Thurnscoe S York 83 SE4505
Thursby Cumb 93 NY3250
Thursden Lancs 81 SD9034
Thursford Norfk 66 TF9833
Thursley Surrey 25 SU9039
Thurso Highld 151 ND1168
Thurstaston Mersyd 78 SJ2484
Thurston Suffk 54 TL9265
Thurston Clough Gt Man 82 SD9707
Thurston Planch Suffk 54 TL9364
Thurstonfield Cumb 93 NY3156
Thurstonland W York 82 SE1610
Thurton Norfk 67 TG3200
Thurvaston Derbys 73 SK2437
Thuxton Norfk 66 TG0307
Thwaite N York 88 SD8998
Thwaite Suffk 54 TM1168
Thwaite Head Cumb 87 SD3490
Thwaite St Mary Norfk 67 TM3395
Thwaites W York 82 SE0741
Thwaites Brow W York 82 SE0740
Thwing Humb 91 TA0470
Tibbermore Tays 125 NO0423
Tibbers D & G 100 NX8696
Tibberton Gloucs 35 SO7521
Tibberton H & W 47 SO9057
Tibberton Shrops 72 SJ6820
Tibbie Shiels Inn Border 109 NT2420
Tibenham Norfk 54 TM1389
Tibshelf Derbys 75 SK4461
Tibthorpe Humb 84 SE9555
Ticehurst E Susx 16 TQ6830
Tichborne Hants 24 SU5730
Tickencote Leics 63 SK9809
Tickenham Avon 34 ST4571
Tickford End Bucks 38 SP8843
Tickhill S York 75 SK5993
Ticklerton Shrops 59 SO4890
Ticknall Derbys 62 SK3523
Tickton Humb 84 TA0541
Tidbury Green W Mids 61 SP1075
Tidcombe Wilts 23 SU2858
Tiddington Oxon 37 SP6404
Tiddington Warwks 48 SP2255
Tidebrook E Susx 16 TQ6130
Tideford Cnwll 5 SX3559
Tideford Cross Cnwll 5 SX3461
Tidenham Gloucs 34 ST5595
Tideswell Derbys 74 SK1575
Tidmarsh Berks 24 SU6374
Tidmington Warwks 48 SP2538
Tidpit Hants 12 SU0718
Tiers Cross Dyfed 30 SM9010
Tiffield Nhants 49 SP7051
Tigerton Tays 134 NO5364
Tigh a Ghearraidh W Isls 154 NF7172
Tigharry W Isls 154 NF7172
Tighnabruaich Strath 114 NR9873
Tigley Devon 7 SX7660
Tilbrook Cambs 51 TL0869
Tilbury Essex 27 TQ6476
Tilbury Green Essex 53 TL7441
Tile Cross W Mids 61 SP1687
Tile Hill W Mids 61 SP2777
Tilehouse Green W Mids 61 SP1776
Tilehurst Berks 24 SU6673
Tilford Surrey 25 SU8743
Tilgate W Susx 15 TQ2734
Tilgate Forest Row W Susx 15 TQ2632
Tilham Street Somset 21 ST5535
Tillers Green Gloucs 47 SO6932
Tillicoultry Cent 116 NS9197
Tillietudlem Strath 116 NS8045
Tillingham Essex 41 TL9904
Tillington H & W 46 SO4644
Tillington W Susx 14 SU9621
Tillington Common H & W 46 SO4545
Tilly Essex 40 TL5926
Tillybirloch Gramp 135 NJ6807

Tillycairn

Treuddyn

Tillycairn *Gramp*	**134**	NO4697
Tillyfourie *Gramp*	**135**	NJ6412
Tillygreig *Gramp*	**143**	NJ8822
Tillyrie *Tays*	**126**	NO1006
Tilmanstone *Kent*	**29**	TR3051
Tiln *Notts*	**75**	SK7084
Tilney All Saints *Norfk*	**65**	TF5618
Tilney High End *Norfk*	**65**	TF5617
Tilney St Lawrence *Norfk*	**65**	TF5414
Tilshead *Wilts*	**23**	SU0347
Tilstock *Shrops*	**59**	SJ5437
Tilston *Ches*	**71**	SJ4650
Tilstone Bank *Ches*	**71**	SJ5659
Tilstone Fearnall *Ches*	**71**	SJ5660
Tilsworth *Beds*	**38**	SP9824
Tilton on the Hill *Leics*	**63**	SK7405
Tiltups End *Gloucs*	**35**	ST8497
Timberland *Lincs*	**76**	TF1258
Timbersbrook *Ches*	**72**	SJ8962
Timberscombe *Somset*	**20**	SS9542
Timble *N York*	**82**	SE1853
Timewell *Devon*	**20**	SS9625
Timpanheck *D & G*	**101**	NY3274
Timperley *Gt Man*	**79**	SJ7888
Timsbury *Avon*	**22**	ST6758
Timsbury *Hants*	**23**	SU3424
Timsgarry *W Isls*	**154**	NB0534
Timsgearraidh *W Isls*	**154**	NB0534
Timworth *Suffk*	**54**	TL8669
Timworth Green *Suffk*	**54**	TL8669
Tincleton *Dorset*	**11**	SY7692
Tindale *Cumb*	**94**	NY6159
Tindale Crescent *Dur*	**96**	NZ1927
Tingewick *Bucks*	**49**	SP6532
Tingley *W York*	**82**	SE2826
Tingrith *Beds*	**38**	TL0032
Tinhay *Devon*	**5**	SX3985
Tinker's Hill *Hants*	**24**	SU4047
Tinkersley *Derbys*	**74**	SK2664
Tinsley *S York*	**74**	SK4090
Tinsley Green *W Susx*	**15**	TQ2839
Tintagel *Cnwll*	**4**	SX0588
Tintern Parva *Gwent*	**34**	SO5200
Tintinhull *Somset*	**21**	ST4919
Tintwistle *Derbys*	**79**	SK0197
Tinwald *D & G*	**100**	NY0081
Tinwell *Leics*	**63**	TF0006
Tipp's End *Norfk*	**65**	TL5095
Tippacott *Devon*	**19**	SS7647
Tiptoe *Hants*	**12**	SZ2597
Tipton *W Mids*	**60**	SO9492
Tipton Green *W Mids*	**60**	SO9592
Tipton St John *Devon*	**9**	SY0991
Tiptree *Essex*	**40**	TL8916
Tiptree Heath *Essex*	**40**	TL8815
Tir-y-fron *Clwyd*	**70**	SJ2859
Tirabad *Powys*	**45**	SN8741
Tiretigan *Strath*	**113**	NR7162
Tirley *Gloucs*	**47**	SO8328
Tirphil *M Glam*	**33**	SO1303
Tirril *Cumb*	**94**	NY5026
Tisbury *Wilts*	**22**	ST9429
Tisman's Common *W Susx*	**14**	TQ0632
Tissington *Derbys*	**73**	SK1752
Titchberry *Devon*	**18**	SS2427
Titchfield *Hants*	**13**	SU5405
Titchfield Common *Hants*	**13**	SU5206
Titchmarsh *Nhants*	**51**	TL0279
Titchwell *Norfk*	**65**	TF7643
Tithby *Notts*	**63**	SK6937
Titley *H & W*	**46**	SO3360
Titmore Green *Herts*	**39**	TL2126
Titsey *Surrey*	**27**	TQ4054
Tittensor *Staffs*	**72**	SJ8738
Tittleshall *Norfk*	**66**	TF8921
Titton *H & W*	**60**	SO8370
Tiverton *Ches*	**71**	SJ5560
Tiverton *Devon*	**9**	SS9512
Tivetshall St Margaret *Norfk*	**54**	TM1787
Tivetshall St Mary *Norfk*	**54**	TM1686
Tivington *Somset*	**20**	SS9345
Tivy Dale *S York*	**82**	SE2707
Tixall *Staffs*	**72**	SJ9722
Tixover *Leics*	**51**	SK9700
Toab *Shet*	**155**	HU3811
Toadhole *Derbys*	**74**	SK3856
Toadmoor *Derbys*	**74**	SK3451
Tobermory *Strath*	**121**	NM5055
Toberonochy *Strath*	**122**	NM7408
Tobha Mor *W Isls*	**154**	NF7536
Tocher *Gramp*	**142**	NJ6932
Tochieneal *Gramp*	**142**	NJ5165
Tockenham *Wilts*	**36**	SU0379
Tockenham Wick *Wilts*	**36**	SU0381
Tocketts *Cleve*	**97**	NZ6217
Tockington *Avon*	**34**	ST6086
Tockwith *N York*	**83**	SE4652
Todber *Dorset*	**22**	ST7919
Todburn *Nthumb*	**103**	NZ1295
Toddington *Beds*	**38**	TL0128
Toddington *Gloucs*	**48**	SP0333
Todds Green *Herts*	**39**	TL2226
Todenham *Gloucs*	**48**	SP2335
Todhills *Cumb*	**101**	NY3762
Todhills *Dur*	**96**	NZ2133
Todhills *Tays*	**127**	NO4239
Todmorden *W York*	**81**	SD9324
Todwick *S York*	**75**	SK4984
Toft *Cambs*	**52**	TL3656
Toft *Ches*	**79**	SJ7576
Toft *Lincs*	**64**	TF0717
Toft *Shet*	**155**	HU4376
Toft *Warwks*	**50**	SP4770
Toft Hill *Dur*	**96**	NZ1528
Toft Hill *Lincs*	**77**	TF2462
Toft Monks *Norfk*	**67**	TM4294
Toft next Newton *Lincs*	**76**	TF0388
Toftrees *Norfk*	**66**	TF8927
Tofts *Highld*	**151**	ND3668
Toftwood *Norfk*	**66**	TF9811
Togston *Nthumb*	**103**	NU2402
Tokavaig *Highld*	**129**	NG6011
Tokers Green *Oxon*	**37**	SU7077
Tolastadh *W Isls*	**154**	NB5347
Toldavas *Cnwll*	**2**	SW4226
Toldish *Cnwll*	**4**	SW9259
Toll Bar *S York*	**83**	SE5507
Tolland *Somset*	**20**	ST1032
Tollard Farnham *Dorset*	**11**	ST9515
Tollard Royal *Wilts*	**11**	ST9417
Tollbar End *W Mids*	**61**	SP3675
Toller Fratrum *Dorset*	**10**	SY5797
Toller Porcorum *Dorset*	**10**	SY5698
Toller Whelme *Dorset*	**10**	ST5101
Tollerton *N York*	**90**	SE5164
Tollerton *Notts*	**62**	SK6134
Tollesbury *Essex*	**40**	TL9510
Tolleshunt D'Arcy *Essex*	**40**	TL9211
Tolleshunt Knights *Essex*	**40**	TL9114
Tolleshunt Major *Essex*	**40**	TL9011
Tolpuddle *Dorset*	**11**	SY7994
Tolsta *W Isls*	**154**	NB5347
Tolvan *Cnwll*	**2**	SW7028
Tolver *Cnwll*	**2**	SW4832
Tolworth *Gt Lon*	**26**	TQ1966
Tomaknock *Tays*	**125**	NN8721
Tomatin *Highld*	**140**	NH8028
Tomchrasky *Highld*	**131**	NH2512
Tomdoun *Highld*	**131**	NH1500
Tomich *Highld*	**146**	NC6005
Tomich *Highld*	**139**	NH3027
Tomich *Highld*	**139**	NH5348
Tomich *Highld*	**146**	NH6971
Tomintoul *Gramp*	**141**	NJ1619
Tomlow *Warwks*	**49**	SP4563
Tomnacross *Highld*	**139**	NH5141
Tomnavoulin *Gramp*	**141**	NJ2126
Tompkin *Staffs*	**72**	SJ9451
Ton *Gwent*	**34**	SO3301
Ton *Gwent*	**34**	ST3695
Ton-teg *M Glam*	**33**	ST0986
Tonbridge *Kent*	**16**	TQ5846
Tondu *M Glam*	**33**	SS8984
Tonedale *Somset*	**20**	ST1321
Tong *Kent*	**28**	TQ9556
Tong *Shrops*	**60**	SJ7907
Tong *W York*	**82**	SE2230
Tong Green *Kent*	**28**	TQ9853
Tong Norton *Shrops*	**60**	SJ7908
Tong Street *W York*	**82**	SE1930
Tonge *Leics*	**62**	SK4223
Tongham *Surrey*	**25**	SU8848
Tongland *D & G*	**99**	NX6954
Tongue *Highld*	**149**	NC5956
Tongue End *Lincs*	**64**	TF1518
Tongwynlais *S Glam*	**33**	ST1382
Tonna *W Glam*	**32**	SS7798
Tonwell *Herts*	**39**	TL3316
Tonypandy *M Glam*	**33**	SS9991
Tonyrefail *M Glam*	**33**	ST0188
Toot Baldon *Oxon*	**37**	SP5600
Toot Hill *Essex*	**27**	TL5102
Toot Hill *Hants*	**12**	SU3818
Toothill *Wilts*	**36**	SU1183
Tooting *Gt Lon*	**27**	TQ2771
Tooting Bec *Gt Lon*	**27**	TQ2872
Top End *Beds*	**51**	TL0362
Top of Hebers *Gt Man*	**79**	SD8607
Top-y-rhos *Clwyd*	**70**	SJ2558
Topcliffe *N York*	**89**	SE3976
Topcroft *Norfk*	**67**	TM2693
Topcroft Street *Norfk*	**67**	TM2691
Topham *S York*	**83**	SE6217
Toppesfield *Essex*	**53**	TL7437
Toppings *Gt Man*	**81**	SD7213
Toprow *Norfk*	**66**	TM1698
Topsham *Devon*	**9**	SX9688
Torbeg *Strath*	**105**	NR8929
Torboll *Highld*	**147**	NH7599
Torbreck *Highld*	**140**	NH6441
Torbryan *Devon*	**7**	SX8266
Torcastle *Highld*	**131**	NN1378
Torcross *Devon*	**7**	SX8241
Tore *Highld*	**140**	NH6052
Torfrey *Cnwll*	**3**	SX1154
Torinturk *Strath*	**113**	NR8164
Torksey *Lincs*	**76**	SK8378
Tormarton *Avon*	**35**	ST7678
Tormitchell *Strath*	**106**	NX2394
Tormore *Strath*	**105**	NR8932
Tornagrain *Highld*	**140**	NH7650
Tornaveen *Gramp*	**134**	NJ6106
Torness *Highld*	**139**	NH5826
Tornewton *Devon*	**7**	SX8167
Toronto *Dur*	**96**	NZ1930
Torosay Castle *Strath*	**122**	NM7335
Torpenhow *Cumb*	**93**	NY2039
Torphichen *Loth*	**117**	NS9672
Torphins *Gramp*	**134**	NJ6202
Torpoint *Cnwll*	**6**	SX4355
Torquay *Devon*	**7**	SX9164
Torquhan *Border*	**118**	NT4448
Torr *Devon*	**6**	SX5851
Torran *Highld*	**137**	NG5949
Torrance *Strath*	**116**	NS6173
Torranyard *Strath*	**115**	NS3544
Torre *Somset*	**20**	ST0439
Torridon *Highld*	**138**	NG9055
Torridon House *Highld*	**138**	NG8657
Torrin *Highld*	**129**	NG5721
Torrisdale *Highld*	**149**	NC6761
Torrisdale Square *Strath*	**105**	NR7936
Torrish *Highld*	**147**	NC9718
Torrisholme *Lancs*	**87**	SD4563
Torrobull *Highld*	**146**	NC5904
Torry *Gramp*	**135**	NJ9405
Torryburn *Fife*	**117**	NT0286
Tortan *H & W*	**60**	SO8472
Torteval *Guern*	**152**	GN0000
Torthorwald *D & G*	**100**	NY0378
Tortington *W Susx*	**14**	TQ0004
Tortworth *Avon*	**35**	ST7093
Torvaig *Highld*	**136**	NG4944
Torver *Cumb*	**86**	SD2894
Torwood *Cent*	**116**	NS8385
Torwoodlee *Border*	**109**	NT4738
Torworth *Notts*	**75**	SK6586
Toscaig *Highld*	**137**	NG7138
Toseland *Cambs*	**52**	TL2462
Tosside *Lancs*	**81**	SD7656
Tostock *Suffk*	**54**	TL9563
Totaig *Highld*	**136**	NG2050
Tote *Highld*	**136**	NG4149
Tote *Highld*	**137**	NG5160
Tote Hill *W Susx*	**14**	SU8624
Tothill *Lincs*	**77**	TF4181
Totland *IOW*	**12**	SZ3287
Totley *S York*	**74**	SK3079
Totley Brook *S York*	**74**	SK3180
Totnes *Devon*	**7**	SX8060
Toton *Notts*	**62**	SK5034
Totronald *Strath*	**120**	NM1656
Totscore *Highld*	**136**	NG3866
Tottenham *Gt Lon*	**27**	TQ3390
Tottenhill *Norfk*	**65**	TF6411
Totteridge *Gt Lon*	**26**	TQ2494
Totternhoe *Beds*	**38**	SP9821
Tottington *Gt Man*	**81**	SD7712
Tottleworth *Lancs*	**81**	SD7331
Totton *Hants*	**12**	SU3613
Touchen End *Berks*	**26**	SU8776
Toulston *N York*	**83**	SE4543
Toulton *Somset*	**20**	ST1931
Toulvaddie *Highld*	**147**	NH8880
Tovil *Kent*	**28**	TQ7554
Tow Law *Dur*	**95**	NZ1138
Towan *Cnwll*	**4**	SW8774
Towan *Cnwll*	**3**	SX0148
Toward *Strath*	**114**	NS1368
Toward Quay *Strath*	**114**	NS1167
Towcester *Nhants*	**49**	SP6948
Towednack *Cnwll*	**2**	SW4838
Towersey *Oxon*	**37**	SP7305
Towie *Gramp*	**134**	NJ4312
Town End *Cambs*	**65**	TL4195
Town End *Cumb*	**87**	NY3406
Town End *Cumb*	**94**	NY6325
Town End *Cumb*	**87**	SD3687
Town End *Cumb*	**87**	SD4483
Town Green *Lancs*	**78**	SD4005
Town Green *Norfk*	**67**	TG3612
Town Head *Cumb*	**87**	NY4103
Town Head *N York*	**88**	SD8258
Town Head *N York*	**82**	SE1748
Town Kelloe *Dur*	**96**	NZ3536
Town Lane *Gt Man*	**79**	SJ6999
Town Littleworth *E Susx*	**15**	TQ4117
Town Moor *T & W*	**103**	NZ2465
Town of Lowdon *Mersyd*	**78**	SJ6196
Town Row *E Susx*	**16**	TQ5630
Town Street *Suffk*	**53**	TL7785
Town Yetholm *Border*	**110**	NT8128
Townend *Strath*	**115**	NS3976
Towngate *Cumb*	**94**	NY5246
Towngate *Lincs*	**64**	TF1310
Townhead *Cumb*	**92**	NY0735
Townhead *Cumb*	**94**	NY6334
Townhead *D & G*	**100**	NY0088
Townhead *S York*	**82**	SE1602
Townhead of Greenlaw *D & G*	**99**	NX7464
Townhill *Loth*	**117**	NT1089
Townlake *Devon*	**5**	SX4074
Towns End *Hants*	**24**	SU5659
Townsend *Somset*	**10**	ST3614
Townshend *Cnwll*	**2**	SW5932
Townwell *Avon*	**35**	ST7090
Towthorpe *Humb*	**91**	SE8962
Towthorpe *N York*	**90**	SE6258
Towton *N York*	**83**	SE4839
Towyn *Clwyd*	**70**	SH9779
Toxteth *Mersyd*	**78**	SJ3588
Toy's Hill *Kent*	**27**	TQ4651
Toynton All Saints *Lincs*	**77**	TF3963
Toynton Fen Side *Lincs*	**77**	TF3961
Toynton St Peter *Lincs*	**77**	TF4063
Trabboch *Strath*	**107**	NS4421
Trabbochburn *Strath*	**107**	NS4621
Traboe *Cnwll*	**3**	SW7421
Tracebridge *Somset*	**20**	ST0621
Tradespark *Highld*	**140**	NH8656
Traethsaith *Dyfed*	**42**	SN2851
Trafford Park *Gt Man*	**79**	SJ7896
Trallong *Powys*	**45**	SN9629
Tranent *Loth*	**118**	NT4072
Tranmere *Mersyd*	**78**	SJ3187
Trannack *Cnwll*	**2**	SW5633
Trantelbeg *Highld*	**150**	NC8952
Trantlemore *Highld*	**150**	NC8953
Tranwell *Nthumb*	**103**	NZ1883
Trap *Dyfed*	**32**	SN6518
Trap's Green *Warwks*	**48**	SP1069
Trapshill *Berks*	**23**	SU3763
Traquair *Border*	**109**	NT3334
Trash Green *Berks*	**24**	SU6569
Traveller's Rest *Devon*	**19**	SS6127
Trawden *Lancs*	**81**	SD9138
Trawscoed *Dyfed*	**43**	SN6672
Trawsfynydd *Gwynd*	**57**	SH7035
Tre Aubrey *S Glam*	**33**	ST0372
Tre'R-Ddol *Dyfed*	**43**	SN6692
Tre-gagle *Gwent*	**34**	SO5207
Tre-Gibbon *M Glam*	**33**	SN9905
Tre-groes *Dyfed*	**42**	SN4044
Tre-Mostyn *Clwyd*	**70**	SJ1479
Tre-Vaughan *Dyfed*	**31**	SN3921
Tre-wyn *Gwent*	**34**	SO3222
Trealaw *M Glam*	**33**	ST0092
Treales *Lancs*	**80**	SD4332
Treamble *Cnwll*	**3**	SW7856
Trearddur Bay *Gwynd*	**68**	SH2579
Treaslane *Highld*	**136**	NG3953
Treator *Cnwll*	**4**	SW9075
Trebanog *M Glam*	**33**	ST0190
Trebanos *W Glam*	**32**	SN7103
Trebartha *Cnwll*	**5**	SX2677
Trebarvah *Cnwll*	**2**	SW7130
Trebarwith *Cnwll*	**4**	SX0586
Trebeath *Cnwll*	**5**	SX2587
Trebehor *Cnwll*	**2**	SW3724
Trebelzue *Cnwll*	**4**	SW8464
Trebetherick *Cnwll*	**4**	SW9378
Treborough *Somset*	**20**	ST0136
Trebudannon *Cnwll*	**4**	SW8961
Trebullett *Cnwll*	**5**	SX3278
Treburgett *Cnwll*	**4**	SX0579
Treburick *Cnwll*	**4**	SW8971
Treburley *Cnwll*	**5**	SX3577
Treburrick *Cnwll*	**4**	SW8670
Trebyan *Cnwll*	**4**	SX0763
Trecastle *Powys*	**45**	SN8829
Trecogo *Cnwll*	**5**	SX3080
Trecott *Devon*	**8**	SS6300
Trecwn *Dyfed*	**30**	SM9632
Trecynon *M Glam*	**33**	SN9903
Tredaule *Cnwll*	**5**	SX2381
Tredavoe *Cnwll*	**2**	SW4528
Tredegar *Gwent*	**33**	SO1408
Tredethy *Cnwll*	**4**	SX0672
Tredington *Gloucs*	**47**	SO9029
Tredington *Warwks*	**48**	SP2543
Tredinnick *Cnwll*	**4**	SW9270
Tredinnick *Cnwll*	**4**	SX0459
Tredinnick *Cnwll*	**4**	SX1666
Tredinnick *Cnwll*	**5**	SX2357
Tredinnick *Cnwll*	**5**	SX2957
Tredomen *Powys*	**45**	SO1231
Tredrissi *Dyfed*	**31**	SN0742
Tredrizzick *Cnwll*	**4**	SW9577
Tredunhock *Gwent*	**34**	ST3794
Tredustan *Powys*	**45**	SO1332
Treen *Cnwll*	**2**	SW4337
Treen *Cnwll*	**2**	SW3923
Treesmill *Cnwll*	**3**	SX0855
Treeton *S York*	**75**	SK4387
Trefacca *Powys*	**45**	SO1431
Trefasser *Dyfed*	**30**	SM8938
Trefdraeth *Gwynd*	**68**	SH4170
Trefeglwys *Powys*	**58**	SN9690
Trefenter *Dyfed*	**43**	SN6068
Treffgarne *Dyfed*	**30**	SM9523
Treffgarne Owen *Dyfed*	**30**	SM8625
Trefforest *M Glam*	**33**	ST0888
Treffynnon *Dyfed*	**30**	SM8528
Trefil *Gwent*	**33**	SO1212
Trefilan *Dyfed*	**44**	SN5456
Treflach Wood *Shrops*	**58**	SJ2625
Trefnannau *Powys*	**58**	SJ2316
Trefnant *Clwyd*	**70**	SJ0570
Trefonen *Shrops*	**58**	SJ2526
Trefor *Gwynd*	**68**	SH3780
Treforda *Cnwll*	**4**	SX0988
Trefrew *Cnwll*	**4**	SX1084
Trefriw *Gwynd*	**69**	SH7863
Tregadillett *Cnwll*	**5**	SX2983
Tregaian *Gwynd*	**68**	SH4580
Tregare *Gwent*	**34**	SO4110
Tregarne *Cnwll*	**3**	SW7823
Tregaron *Dyfed*	**44**	SN6759
Tregarth *Gwynd*	**69**	SH6067
Tregaswith *Cnwll*	**4**	SW8962
Tregatta *Cnwll*	**4**	SX0587
Tregawne *Cnwll*	**4**	SX0066
Tregear *Cnwll*	**3**	SW8650
Tregeare *Cnwll*	**5**	SX2486
Tregeiriog *Clwyd*	**58**	SJ1733
Tregele *Gwynd*	**68**	SH3592
Tregellist *Cnwll*	**4**	SX0177
Tregenna *Cnwll*	**3**	SW8743
Tregenna *Cnwll*	**4**	SX0973
Tregeseal *Cnwll*	**2**	SW3731
Tregew *Cnwll*	**3**	SW8034
Tregidden *Cnwll*	**3**	SW7523
Tregiddle *Cnwll*	**2**	SW6723
Tregidgeo *Cnwll*	**3**	SW9647
Tregiskey *Cnwll*	**3**	SX0146
Treglemais *Dyfed*	**30**	SM8229
Tregole *Cnwll*	**5**	SX1998
Tregolls *Cnwll*	**3**	SW7335
Tregonce *Cnwll*	**4**	SW9373
Tregonetha *Cnwll*	**4**	SW9563
Tregony *Cnwll*	**3**	SW9244
Tregoodwell *Cnwll*	**4**	SX1183
Tregoose *Cnwll*	**2**	SW6823
Tregoss *Cnwll*	**4**	SW9660
Tregowris *Cnwll*	**3**	SW7722
Tregoyd *Powys*	**45**	SO1937
Tregrehan Mills *Cnwll*	**3**	SX0453
Tregullon *Cnwll*	**4**	SX0664
Tregunna *Cnwll*	**4**	SW9673
Tregunnon *Cnwll*	**5**	SX2283
Tregurrian *Cnwll*	**4**	SW8565
Tregustick *Cnwll*	**4**	SW9866
Tregynon *Powys*	**58**	SO0998
Trehafod *M Glam*	**33**	ST0490
Trehan *Cnwll*	**5**	SX4058
Treharris *M Glam*	**33**	ST0996
Treharrock *Cnwll*	**4**	SX0178
Trehemborne *Cnwll*	**4**	SW8773
Treherbert *Dyfed*	**44**	SN5847
Treherbert *M Glam*	**33**	SS9498
Treheveras *Cnwll*	**3**	SW8046
Trehunist *Cnwll*	**5**	SX3263
Trekelland *Cnwll*	**5**	SX3480
Trekenner *Cnwll*	**5**	SX3478
Treknow *Cnwll*	**4**	SX0586
Trelan *Cnwll*	**3**	SW7418
Trelash *Cnwll*	**4**	SX1890
Trelassick *Cnwll*	**3**	SW8752
Trelawne *Cnwll*	**5**	SX2154
Trelawnyd *Clwyd*	**70**	SJ0979
Treleague *Cnwll*	**3**	SW7821
Treleaver *Cnwll*	**3**	SW7716
Trelech *Dyfed*	**31**	SN2830
Trelech a'r Betws *Dyfed*	**31**	SN3026
Treleddyd-fawr *Dyfed*	**30**	SM7528
Trelew *Cnwll*	**3**	SW8135
Trelewis *M Glam*	**33**	ST1096
Treligga *Cnwll*	**4**	SX0484
Trelights *Cnwll*	**4**	SW9979
Trelill *Cnwll*	**4**	SX0478
Trelinnoe *Cnwll*	**5**	SX3181
Trelion *Cnwll*	**3**	SW9252
Trelissick *Cnwll*	**3**	SW8339
Trelleck *Gwent*	**34**	SO5005
Trelleck Grange *Gwent*	**34**	SO4901
Trelogan *Clwyd*	**70**	SJ1180
Trelonk *Cnwll*	**3**	SW8941
Trelow *Cnwll*	**4**	SW9269
Trelowarren *Cnwll*	**2**	SW7124
Trelowia *Cnwll*	**5**	SX2956
Treluggan *Cnwll*	**3**	SW8838
Trelystan *Powys*	**58**	SJ2503
Tremadog *Gwynd*	**57**	SH5640
Tremail *Cnwll*	**4**	SX1686
Tremaine *Cnwll*	**5**	SX2389
Tremar *Cnwll*	**5**	SX2568
Trematon *Cnwll*	**5**	SX3959
Trembraze *Cnwll*	**5**	SX2565
Tremeirchion *Clwyd*	**70**	SJ0873
Tremethick Cross *Cnwll*	**2**	SW4430
Tremollett *Cnwll*	**5**	SX2975
Tremore *Cnwll*	**4**	SX0164
Trenance *Cnwll*	**3**	SW8022
Trenance *Cnwll*	**4**	SW8568
Trenance *Cnwll*	**4**	SW9270
Trenarren *Cnwll*	**3**	SX0348
Trenault *Cnwll*	**5**	SX2683
Trench *Shrops*	**60**	SJ6912
Trench Green *Oxon*	**37**	SU6877
Trencreek *Cnwll*	**4**	SW8260
Trencreek *Cnwll*	**4**	SX1896
Trendeal *Cnwll*	**3**	SW8952
Trendrine *Cnwll*	**2**	SW4739
Treneague *Cnwll*	**4**	SW9871
Trenear *Cnwll*	**2**	SW6731
Treneglos *Cnwll*	**5**	SX2088
Trenerth *Cnwll*	**2**	SW6035
Trenewan *Cnwll*	**4**	SX1753
Trenewth *Cnwll*	**4**	SX0778
Trengothal *Cnwll*	**2**	SW3724
Trengune *Cnwll*	**4**	SX1893
Treninnick *Cnwll*	**4**	SW8160
Trenowah *Cnwll*	**4**	SW7959
Trenoweth *Cnwll*	**3**	SW7533
Trent *Dorset*	**10**	ST5918
Trent Port *Lincs*	**76**	SK8381
Trent Vale *Staffs*	**72**	SJ8643
Trentham *Staffs*	**72**	SJ8740
Trentishoe *Devon*	**19**	SS6448
Trentlock *Derbys*	**62**	SK4831
Treoes *S Glam*	**33**	SS9478
Treorchy *M Glam*	**33**	SS9597
Trequite *Cnwll*	**4**	SX0377
Trerhyngyll *S Glam*	**33**	ST0077
Trerulefoot *Cnwll*	**5**	SX3358
Tresahor *Cnwll*	**3**	SW7431
Tresawle *Cnwll*	**3**	SW8846
Trescott *Staffs*	**60**	SO8597
Trescowe *Cnwll*	**2**	SW5731
Tresean *Cnwll*	**4**	SW7858
Tresham *Gloucs*	**35**	ST7991
Tresillian *Cnwll*	**3**	SW8646
Tresinney *Cnwll*	**4**	SX1081
Treskinnick Cross *Cnwll*	**5**	SX2098
Treslea *Cnwll*	**4**	SX1368
Tresmeer *Cnwll*	**5**	SX2387
Tresparrett *Cnwll*	**4**	SX1491
Tressait *Tays*	**132**	NN8160
Tresta *Shet*	**155**	HU3650
Tresta *Shet*	**155**	HU6090
Treswell *Notts*	**75**	SK7879
Treswithian *Cnwll*	**2**	SW6241
Trethawle *Cnwll*	**5**	SX2662
Trethevey *Cnwll*	**4**	SX0789
Trethewey *Cnwll*	**2**	SW3823
Trethomas *M Glam*	**33**	ST1888
Trethosa *Cnwll*	**3**	SW9454
Trethurgy *Cnwll*	**3**	SX0355
Tretio *Dyfed*	**30**	SM7829
Tretire *H & W*	**46**	SO5123
Tretower *Powys*	**33**	SO1821
Treuddyn *Clwyd*	**70**	SJ2557

Trevadlock

Upper Moor

Trevadlock Cnwll 5 SX2679
Trevague Cnwll 5 SX2379
Trevalga Cnwll 4 SX0890
Trevalyn Clwyd 71 SJ3856
Trevanger Cnwll 4 SW9677
Trevanson Cnwll 4 SW9773
Trevarrack Cnwll 2 SW4731
Trevarren Cnwll 4 SW9160
Trevarrian Cnwll 4 SW8566
Trevarrick Cnwll 3 SW9843
Trevarth Cnwll 3 SW7240
Trevaughan Dyfed 31 SN2015
Treveal Cnwll 2 SW4740
Treveal Cnwll 4 SW7858
Treveale Cnwll 3 SW8751
Treveighan Cnwll 4 SX0779
Trevellas Downs Cnwll 3 SW7452
Trevelmond Cnwll 5 SX2063
Trevempor Cnwll 4 SW8159
Treveneague Cnwll 2 SW5432
Treveor Cnwll 3 SW9841
Treverbyn Cnwll 3 SW8849
Treverbyn Cnwll 4 SX0157
Treverva Cnwll 3 SW7531
Trevescan Cnwll 2 SW3524
Trevethin Gwent 34 SO2801
Trevia Cnwll 4 SX0983
Trevigro Cnwll 5 SX3369
Trevilla Cnwll 3 SW8239
Trevilledor Cnwll 4 SW8867
Trevilson Cnwll 3 SW8455
Trevine Dyfed 30 SM8432
Treviscoe Cnwll 3 SW9455
Treviskey Cnwll 3 SW9340
Trevissick Cnwll 3 SX0248
Trevithal Cnwll 2 SW4626
Trevithick Cnwll 4 SW8862
Trevithick Cnwll 3 SW9645
Trevivian Cnwll 4 SX1785
Trevoll Cnwll 4 SW8358
Trevone Cnwll 4 SW8975
Trevor Clwyd 70 SJ2742
Trevor Gwynd 56 SH3746
Trevorgans Cnwll 2 SW4025
Trevorrick Cnwll 4 SW8672
Trevorrick Cnwll 4 SW9273
Trevose Cnwll 4 SW8675
Trew Cnwll 2 SW6129
Trewalder Cnwll 4 SX0782
Trewalkin Powys 45 SO1531
Trewarlett Cnwll 5 SX3380
Trewarmett Cnwll 4 SX0686
Trewarthenick Cnwll 3 SW9044
Trewassa Cnwll 4 SX1486
Trewaves Cnwll 2 SW5926
Treween Cnwll 5 SX2182
Trewellard Cnwll 2 SW3733
Trewen Cnwll 5 SX2583
Trewen Cnwll 4 SX0577
Trewennack Cnwll 2 SW6728
Trewent Dyfed 30 SS0197
Trewern Powys 58 SJ2811
Trewetha Cnwll 4 SX0080
Trewethern Cnwll 4 SX0076
Trewidland Cnwll 5 SX2559
Trewillis Cnwll 3 SW7717
Trewince Cnwll 3 SW8633
Trewint Cnwll 4 SX1072
Trewint Cnwll 5 SX2180
Trewint Cnwll 5 SX2963
Trewirgie Cnwll 3 SW8845
Trewithian Cnwll 3 SW8737
Trewoodloe Cnwll 5 SX3271
Trewoofe Cnwll 2 SW4425
Trewoon Cnwll 2 SW6819
Trewoon Cnwll 3 SW9952
Treworgan Cnwll 3 SW8349
Treworlas Cnwll 3 SW8938
Treworld Cnwll 4 SX1190
Treworthal Cnwll 3 SW8839
Treyarnon Cnwll 4 SW8673
Treyford W Susx 14 SU8218
Triangle W York 82 SE0422
Trickett's Cross Dorset 12 SU0800
Triermain Cumb 102 NY5966
Triffleton Dyfed 30 SM9724
Trillacott Cnwll 5 SX2689
Trimdon Dur 96 NZ3634
Trimdon Colliery Dur 96 NZ3735
Trimdon Grange Dur 96 NZ3635
Trimingham Norfk 67 TG2838
Trimley Suffk 55 TM2737
Trimley Heath Suffk 55 TM2738
Trimley Lower Street Suffk 55 TM2636
Trimpley H & W 60 SO7978
Trims Green Herts 39 TL4717
Trimsaran Dyfed 32 SN4504
Trimstone Devon 19 SS5043
Trinafour Tays 132 NN7264
Trinant Gwent 33 ST2099
Tring Herts 38 SP9211
Tring Wharf Herts 38 SP9212
Tringford Herts 38 SP9113
Trinity Jersey 152 JS0000
Trinity Tays 134 NO6061
Trinity Gask Tays 125 NN9718
Triscombe Somset 20 SS9237
Triscombe Somset 20 ST1535
Trislaig Highld 130 NN0874
Trispen Cnwll 3 SW8450
Tritlington Nthumb 103 NZ2092
Troan Cnwll 4 SW8957
Trochry Tays 125 NN9740
Troedrhiwfuwch M Glam 33 SO1204
Troedyraur Dyfed 42 SN3245
Troedyrhiw M Glam 33 SO0702
Trofarth Clwyd 69 SH8571
Trois Bois Jersey 152 JS0000
Troon Cnwll 2 SW6638
Troon Strath 106 NS3230
Troston Suffk 54 TL8972
Troswell Cnwll 5 SX2592
Trotshill H & W 47 SO8855
Trottiscliffe Kent 27 TQ6460
Trotton W Susx 14 SU8322
Trough Gate Lancs 81 SD8821
Troughend Nthumb 102 NY8692
Troutbeck Cumb 93 NY3927
Troutbeck Cumb 87 NY4002
Troutbeck Bridge Cumb 87 NY4000
Troway Derbys 74 SK3879
Trowbridge Wilts 22 ST8558
Trowell Notts 62 SK4839
Trowle Common Wilts 22 ST8458
Trowse Newton Norfk 67 TG2406
Troy W York 82 SE2439
Trudoxhill Somset 22 ST7443
Trull Somset 20 ST2122
Trumfleet S York 83 SE6011
Trumpan Highld 136 NG2261
Trumpet H & W 47 SO6539
Trumpington Cambs 53 TL4454
Trumpsgreen Surrey 25 SU9967
Trunch Norfk 67 TG2834
Trunnah Lancs 80 SD3442
Truro Cnwll 3 SW8244
Truscott Cnwll 5 SX2985
Trusham Devon 8 SX8582
Trusley Derbys 73 SK2535
Trysull Staffs 60 SO8594
Tubney Oxon 36 SU4399
Tuckenhay Devon 7 SX8156
Tuckhill Shrops 60 SO7888
Tuckingmill Cnwll 2 SW6540
Tuckingmill Wilts 22 ST9329
Tuckton Dorset 12 SZ1492
Tucoyse Cnwll 3 SW9645
Tuddenham Suffk 53 TL7371
Tuddenham Suffk 55 TM1948
Tudeley Kent 16 TQ6245
Tudhoe Dur 96 NZ2535
Tudorville H & W 46 SO5922
Tudweiloig Gwynd 56 SH2436
Tuesley Surrey 25 SU9642
Tuffley Gloucs 35 SO8314
Tufton Dyfed 30 SN0428
Tufton Hants 24 SU4546
Tugby Leics 63 SK7601
Tugford Shrops 59 SO5587
Tughall Nthumb 111 NU2126
Tullibody Cent 116 NS8595
Tullich Highld 140 NH6328
Tullich Highld 147 NH8576
Tullich Strath 123 NN0815
Tulliemet Tays 125 NO0052
Tulloch Cent 124 NN5120
Tulloch Gramp 143 NJ8031
Tulloch Station Highld 131 NN3580
Tullochgorm Strath 114 NR9695
Tullybeagles Lodge Tays 125 NO0136
Tullynessle Gramp 142 NJ5519
Tulse Hill Gt Lon 27 TQ3172
Tumble Dyfed 32 SN5411
Tumbler's Green Essex 40 TL8025
Tumby Lincs 76 TF2359
Tumby Woodside Lincs 77 TF2757
Tummel Bridge Tays 132 NN7659
Tunbridge Wells Kent 16 TQ5839
Tundergarth D & G 101 NY1780
Tungate Norfk 67 TG2629
Tunstall Humb 85 TA3031
Tunstall Kent 28 TQ8961
Tunstall Lancs 87 SD6073
Tunstall N York 89 SE2196
Tunstall Norfk 67 TG4107
Tunstall Staffs 72 SJ7727
Tunstall Staffs 72 SJ8651
Tunstall Suffk 55 TM3655
Tunstall T & W 96 NZ3953
Tunstead Derbys 74 SK1074
Tunstead Norfk 67 TG3022
Tunstead Milton Derbys 79 SK0180
Tunworth Hants 24 SU6748
Tupsley H & W 46 SO5340
Tur Langton Leics 50 SP7194
Turgis Green Hants 24 SU6959
Turkdean Gloucs 36 SP1017
Turleigh Wilts 22 ST8060
Turleygreen Shrops 60 SO7685
Turn Lancs 81 SD8118
Turnastone H & W 46 SO3536
Turnberry Strath 106 NS2005
Turnchapel Devon 6 SX4953
Turnditch Derbys 73 SK2946
Turner Green Lancs 81 SD6030
Turner's Green E Susx 16 TQ6319
Turner's Green Warwks 48 SP1969
Turner's Hill W Susx 15 TQ3435
Turners Puddle Dorset 11 SY8393
Turnford Herts 39 TL3604
Turnhouse Loth 117 NT1674
Turnworth Dorset 11 ST8207
Turriff Gramp 142 NJ7250
Turton Bottoms Gt Man 81 SD7315
Turvey Beds 38 SP9452
Turville Bucks 37 SU7691
Turville Heath Bucks 37 SU7490
Turweston Bucks 49 SP6037
Tushielaw Inn Border 109 NT3017
Tushingham cum Grindley Ches 71 SJ5246
Tutbury Staffs 73 SK2128
Tutnall H & W 60 SO9970
Tutshill Gloucs 34 ST5494
Tuttington Norfk 67 TG2227
Tutwell Cnwll 5 SX3875
Tuxford Notts 75 SK7471
Twatt Ork 155 HY2724
Twatt Shet 155 HU3253
Twechar Strath 116 NS6975
Tweedmouth Nthumb 119 NT9952
Tweedsmuir Border 108 NT1024
Twelve Oaks E Susx 16 TQ6820
Twelveheads Cnwll 3 SW7542
Twemlow Green Ches 79 SJ7868
Twenty Lincs 64 TF1520
Twerton Avon 22 ST7264
Twickenham Gt Lon 26 TQ1673
Twigworth Gloucs 35 SO8422
Twineham W Susx 15 TQ2519
Twineham Green W Susx 15 TQ2520
Twinhoe Avon 22 ST7559
Twinstead Essex 54 TL8636
Twiss Green Ches 79 SJ6595
Twitchen Devon 19 SS7930
Twitchen Shrops 46 SO3779
Twitham Kent 29 TR2656
Two Bridges Devon 6 SX6174
Two Dales Derbys 74 SK2763
Two Gates Staffs 61 SK2101
Two Mile Oak Cross Devon 7 SX8468
Two Pots Devon 19 SS5344
Two Waters Herts 38 TL0505
Twycross Leics 62 SK3304
Twyford Berks 37 SU7976
Twyford Bucks 49 SP6626
Twyford Hants 13 SU4824
Twyford Leics 63 SK7210
Twyford Lincs 63 SK9323
Twyford Norfk 66 TG0123
Twyford Common H & W 46 SO5135
Twyn-carno M Glam 33 SO1108
Twyn-y-Sheriff Gwent 34 SO4005
Twyn-yr-Odyn S Glam 33 ST1173
Twynholm D & G 99 NX6654
Twyning Gloucs 47 SO8936
Twyning Green Gloucs 47 SO9036
Twynllanan Dyfed 44 SN7524
Twywell Nhants 51 SP9578
Ty'n-dwr Clwyd 70 SJ2341
Ty'n-y-bryn M Glam 33 ST0087
Ty'n-y-coedcae M Glam 33 ST1988
Ty'n-y-groes Gwynd 69 SH7771
Ty-croes Dyfed 32 SN6010
Ty-nant Clwyd 70 SH9944
Ty-nant Gwynd 58 SH9026
Tyberton H & W 46 SO3839
Tyburn W Mids 61 SP1391
Tycrwyn Powys 58 SJ1018
Tydd Gote Lincs 65 TF4518
Tydd St Giles Cambs 65 TF4216
Tydd St Mary Lincs 65 TF4418
Tye Hants 13 SU7302
Tye Green Essex 39 TL5424
Tye Green Essex 53 TL5935
Tye Green Essex 40 TL7821
Tyersal W York 82 SE1932
Tyldesley Gt Man 79 SD6802
Tyler Hill Kent 29 TR1461
Tyler's Green Essex 39 TL5005
Tylers Green Bucks 26 SU9093
Tylers Green Surrey 27 TQ3552
Tylorstown M Glam 33 ST0095
Tylwch Powys 58 SN9780
Tyn-y-nant M Glam 33 ST0685
Tyndrum Cent 123 NN3230
Tyneham Dorset 11 SY8880
Tynemouth T & W 103 NZ3669
Tynewydd M Glam 33 SS9398
Tyninghame Loth 118 NT6179
Tynron D & G 100 NX8093
Tynygongl Gwynd 68 SH5082
Tynygraig Dyfed 43 SN6969
Tyringham Bucks 38 SP8547
Tyseley W Mids 61 SP1184
Tythegston M Glam 33 SS8578
Tytherington Avon 35 ST6688
Tytherington Ches 79 SJ9175
Tytherington Somset 22 ST7644
Tytherington Wilts 22 ST9141
Tytherleigh Devon 10 ST3103
Tywardreath Cnwll 3 SX0854
Tywardreath Highway Cnwll 3 SX0755
Tywyn Gwynd 57 SH5800
Tywyn Gwynd 69 SH7878

U

Ubbeston Green Suffk 55 TM3271
Ubley Avon 21 ST5258
Uckerby N York 89 NZ2402
Uckfield E Susx 16 TQ4721
Uckinghall H & W 47 SO8637
Uckington Gloucs 47 SO9124
Uckington Shrops 59 SJ5709
Uddingston Strath 116 NS6960
Uddington Strath 108 NS8633
Udimore E Susx 17 TQ8719
Udny Green Gramp 143 NJ8726
Udny Station Gramp 143 NJ9024
Uffcott Wilts 36 SU1277
Uffculme Devon 9 ST0612
Uffington Oxon 36 SU3089
Uffington Shrops 59 SJ5313
Ufford Cambs 64 TF0903
Ufford Suffk 55 TM2952
Ufton Warwks 48 SP3762
Ufton Nervet Berks 24 SU6367
Ugadale Strath 105 NR7828
Ugborough Devon 7 SX6755
Uggeshall Suffk 55 TM4480
Ugglebarnby N York 90 NZ8707
Ughill Derbys 74 SK2590
Ugley Essex 39 TL5228
Ugley Green Essex 39 TL5227
Ugthorpe N York 90 NZ7911
Uig Highld 136 NG1952
Uig Highld 136 NG3963
Uig Strath 120 NM1654
Uig W Isls 154 NB0533
Uigshader Highld 136 NG4346
Uisken Strath 121 NM3919
Ulbster Highld 151 ND3241
Ulcat Row Cumb 93 NY4022
Ulceby Humb 85 TA1014
Ulceby Lincs 77 TF4272
Ulceby Cross Lincs 77 TF4173
Ulceby Skitter Humb 85 TA1215
Ulcombe Kent 28 TQ8448
Uldale Cumb 93 NY2437
Uley Gloucs 35 ST7898
Ulgham Nthumb 103 NZ2392
Ullapool Highld 145 NH1294
Ullenhall Warwks 48 SP1267
Ullenwood Gloucs 35 SO9416
Ulleskelf N York 83 SE5239
Ullesthorpe Leics 50 SP5087
Ulley S York 75 SK4687
Ullingswick H & W 46 SO5949
Ullinish Lodge Hotel Highld 136 NG3237
Ullock Cumb 92 NY0724
Ulpha Cumb 86 SD1993
Ulpha Cumb 87 SD4581
Ulrome Humb 85 TA1656
Ulsta Shet 155 HU4680
Ulting Wick Essex 40 TL8009
Ulverley Green W Mids 61 SP1382
Ulverston Cumb 86 SD2878
Ulwell Dorset 12 SZ0280
Umachan Highld 137 NG6050
Umberleigh Devon 19 SS6023
Unapool Highld 148 NC2333
Under Burnmouth D & G 101 NY4783
Under River Kent 27 TQ5552
Underbarrow Cumb 87 SD4692
Undercliffe W York 82 SE1834
Underdale Shrops 59 SJ5013
Underley Hall Cumb 87 SD6179
Underling Green Kent 28 TQ7546
Underwood Notts 75 SK4750
Undley Suffk 53 TL6981
Undy Gwent 34 ST4386
Union Mills IOM 153 SC3577
Union Street E Susx 16 TQ7031
Unstone Derbys 74 SK3777
Unstone Green Derbys 74 SK3776
Unsworth Gt Man 79 SD8207
Unthank Cumb 93 NY3948
Unthank Cumb 93 NY4536
Unthank Cumb 94 NY6040
Unthank Derbys 74 SK3075
Unthank Nthumb 111 NT9848
Unthank End Cumb 93 NY4535
Up Cerne Dorset 11 ST6502
Up Exe Devon 9 SS9402
Up Holland Lancs 78 SD5205
Up Marden W Susx 14 SU7913
Up Mudford Somset 10 ST5718
Up Nately Hants 24 SU6951
Up Somborne Hants 23 SU3932
Up Sydling Dorset 10 ST6201
Upavon Wilts 23 SU1354
Upchurch Kent 28 TQ8467
Upcott Devon 19 SS5838
Upcott Devon 19 SS7529
Upcott H & W 46 SO3250
Upcott Somset 20 SS9025
Updown Hill Surrey 25 SU9363
Upend Cambs 53 TL7058
Upgate Norfk 66 TG1318
Upgate Street Norfk 66 TM0992
Upgate Street Norfk 67 TM2891
Uphall Dorset 10 ST5502
Uphall Loth 117 NT0671
Upham Devon 19 SS8808
Upham Hants 13 SU5320
Uphampton H & W 46 SO3963
Uphampton H & W 47 SO8364
Uphill Avon 21 ST3158
Uplawmoor Strath 115 NS4355
Upleadon Gloucs 47 SO7527
Upleatham Cleve 97 NZ6319
Uplees Kent 28 TR0064
Uploders Dorset 10 SY5093
Uplowman Devon 9 ST0115
Uplyme Devon 10 SY3293
Upminster Gt Lon 27 TQ5686
Upottery Devon 9 ST2007
Uppaton Devon 5 SX4380
Upper Affcot Shrops 59 SO4486
Upper Ardchronie Highld 146 NH6188
Upper Arley H & W 60 SO7680
Upper Arncott Oxon 37 SP6117
Upper Astrop Nhants 49 SP5137
Upper Basildon Berks 37 SU5976
Upper Batley W York 82 SE2325
Upper Beeding W Susx 15 TQ1910
Upper Benefield Nhants 51 SP9789
Upper Bentley H & W 47 SO9966
Upper Bighouse Highld 150 NC8856
Upper Birchwood Derbys 75 SK4355
Upper Boat M Glam 33 ST1086
Upper Boddington Nhants 49 SP4852
Upper Borth Dyfed 43 SN6088
Upper Brailes Warwks 48 SP3039
Upper Breakish Highld 129 NG6823
Upper Breinton H & W 46 SO4640
Upper Broadheath H & W 47 SO8056
Upper Broughton Notts 63 SK6826
Upper Bucklebury Berks 24 SU5468
Upper Burgate Hants 12 SU1516
Upper Bush Kent 28 TQ6966
Upper Caldecote Beds 52 TL1645
Upper Canada Avon 21 ST3658
Upper Canterton Hants 12 SU2612
Upper Catesby Nhants 49 SP5259
Upper Catshill H & W 60 SO9674
Upper Chapel Powys 45 SO0040
Upper Cheddon Somset 20 ST2328
Upper Chicksgrove Wilts 22 ST9529
Upper Chute Wilts 23 SU2953
Upper Clapton Gt Lon 27 TQ3487
Upper Clatford Hants 23 SU3543
Upper Clynnog Gwynd 56 SH4646
Upper Coberley Gloucs 35 SO9816
Upper Cokeham W Susx 15 TQ1605
Upper Cotton Staffs 73 SK0547
Upper Cound Shrops 59 SJ5505
Upper Cudworth S York 83 SE3909
Upper Cumberworth W York 82 SE2008
Upper Cwmtwrch Powys 32 SN7511
Upper Dallachy Gramp 141 NJ3662
Upper Deal Kent 29 TR3651
Upper Dean Beds 51 TL0467
Upper Denby W York 82 SE2207
Upper Denton Cumb 102 NY6165
Upper Dicker E Susx 16 TQ5509
Upper Dinchope Shrops 59 SO4583
Upper Dounreay Highld 150 ND0065
Upper Dovercourt Essex 41 TM2330
Upper Drumbane Cent 124 NN6606
Upper Dunsforth N York 89 SE4463
Upper Eashing Surrey 25 SU9543
Upper Egleton H & W 47 SO6344
Upper Elkstone Staffs 74 SK0558
Upper Ellastone Staffs 73 SK1043
Upper End Derbys 74 SK0875
Upper Enham Hants 23 SU3650
Upper Ethrie Highld 140 NH7662
Upper Farmcote Shrops 60 SO7791
Upper Farringdon Hants 24 SU7135
Upper Framilode Gloucs 35 SO7510
Upper Froyle Hants 24 SU7543
Upper Godney Somset 21 ST4842
Upper Gravenhurst Beds 38 TL1136
Upper Green Berks 23 SU3763
Upper Green Essex 53 TL5935
Upper Green Gwent 34 SO3818
Upper Green Suffk 53 TL7464
Upper Grove Common H & W 46 SO5526
Upper Hackney Derbys 74 SK2861
Upper Hale Surrey 25 SU8349
Upper Halliford Surrey 26 TQ0968
Upper Halling Kent 28 TQ6964
Upper Hambleton Leics 63 SK9007
Upper Harbledown Kent 29 TR1158
Upper Hardres Court Kent 29 TR1550
Upper Hardwick H & W 46 SO4057
Upper Hartfield E Susx 16 TQ4634
Upper Hartshay Derbys 74 SK3850
Upper Hatherley Gloucs 35 SO9220
Upper Hatton Staffs 72 SJ8237
Upper Haugh S York 74 SK4297
Upper Hayton Shrops 59 SO5181
Upper Heaton W York 82 SE1719
Upper Helmsley N York 83 SE6956
Upper Hergest H & W 46 SO2654
Upper Heyford Nhants 49 SP6659
Upper Heyford Oxon 49 SP4925
Upper Hiendley W York 83 SE3913
Upper Hill H & W 46 SO4753
Upper Hockenden Kent 27 TQ5069
Upper Hopton W York 82 SE1918
Upper Howsell H & W 47 SO7848
Upper Hulme Staffs 73 SK0160
Upper Ifold Surrey 14 TQ0033
Upper Inglesham Wilts 36 SU2096
Upper Kilcott Avon 35 ST7988
Upper Killay W Glam 32 SS5892
Upper Kinchrackine Strath 123 NN1627
Upper Lambourn Berks 36 SU3080
Upper Landywood Staffs 60 SJ9805
Upper Langford Avon 21 ST4659
Upper Langwith Derbys 75 SK5169
Upper Largo Fife 127 NO4203
Upper Leigh Staffs 73 SK0136
Upper Ley Gloucs 35 SO7217
Upper Littleton Avon 21 ST5564
Upper Longdon Staffs 61 SK0614
Upper Ludstone Shrops 60 SO8095
Upper Lybster Highld 151 ND2537
Upper Lydbrook Gloucs 34 SO6015
Upper Lyde H & W 46 SO4944
Upper Lye H & W 46 SO3965
Upper Maes-coed H & W 46 SO3334
Upper Midhope Derbys 74 SK2199
Upper Milton H & W 60 SO8172
Upper Minety Wilts 35 SU0091
Upper Moor H & W 47 SO9747

Upper Moor Side
Water

Upper Moor Side *W York* **82** SE2430
Upper Mulben *Gramp* **141** NJ3551
Upper Netchwood *Shrops* **59** SO6092
Upper Nobut *Staffs* **73** SK0335
Upper Norwood *W Susx* **14** SU9317
Upper Padley *Derbys* **74** SK2478
Upper Pennington *Hants* **12** SZ3095
Upper Pickwick *Wilts* **35** ST8571
Upper Pollicott *Bucks* **37** SP7013
Upper Pond Street *Essex* **39** TL4636
Upper Poppleton *N York* **83** SE5553
Upper Quinton *Warwks* **48** SP1846
Upper Ratley *Hants* **23** SU3223
Upper Rochford *H & W* **47** SO6367
Upper Ruscoe *D & G* **99** NX5661
Upper Sapey *H & W* **47** SO6863
Upper Seagry *Wilts* **35** ST9480
Upper Shelton *Beds* **38** SP9843
Upper Sheringham *Norfk* **66** TG1441
Upper Shuckburgh *Warwks* **49** SP5061
Upper Skelmorlie *Strath* **114** NS2067
Upper Slaughter *Gloucs* **48** SP1523
Upper Soudley *Gloucs* **35** SO6510
Upper Spond *H & W* **46** SO3152
Upper Standen *Kent* **29** TR2139
Upper Staploe *Beds* **52** TL1459
Upper Stepford *D & G* **100** NX8681
Upper Stoke *Norfk* **67** TG2502
Upper Stondon *Beds* **38** TL1435
Upper Stowe *Nhants* **49** SP6456
Upper Street *Hants* **12** SU1518
Upper Street *Norfk* **67** TG3217
Upper Street *Norfk* **67** TG3616
Upper Street *Norfk* **54** TM1779
Upper Street *Suffk* **53** TL7851
Upper Street *Suffk* **54** TM1050
Upper Street *Suffk* **54** TM1434
Upper Strensham *H & W* **47** SO8939
Upper Sundon *Beds* **38** TL0428
Upper Swell *Gloucs* **48** SP1726
Upper Tankersley *S York* **74** SK3499
Upper Tasburgh *Norfk* **67** TM2095
Upper Tean *Staffs* **73** SK0139
Upper Threapwood *Ches* **71** SJ4345
Upper Town *Avon* **21** ST5265
Upper Town *Derbys* **73** SK2351
Upper Town *Derbys* **74** SK2361
Upper Town *Dur* **95** NZ0737
Upper Town *H & W* **46** SO5848
Upper Town *Suffk* **54** TL9267
Upper Tysoe *Warwks* **48** SP3343
Upper Ufford *Suffk* **55** TM2952
Upper Upham *Wilts* **36** SU2277
Upper Upnor *Kent* **28** TQ7570
Upper Victoria *Tays* **127** NO5336
Upper Vobster *Somset* **22** ST7049
Upper Wardington *Oxon* **49** SP4945
Upper Weald *Bucks* **38** SP8037
Upper Weedon *Nhants* **49** SP6258
Upper Wellingham *E Susx* **16** TQ4313
Upper Weston *Avon* **22** ST7267
Upper Weybread *Suffk* **55** TM2379
Upper Wick *H & W* **47** SO8252
Upper Wield *Hants* **24** SU6238
Upper Winchendon *Bucks* **37** SP7414
Upper Woodford *Wilts* **23** SU1237
Upper Wootton *Hants* **24** SU5754
Upper Wraxall *Wilts* **35** ST8074
Upper Wyche *H & W* **47** SO7643
Upperby *Cumb* **93** NY4153
Upperglen *Highld* **136** NG3151
Uppermill *Gt Man* **82** SD9905
Upperthong *W York* **82** SE1208
Upperthorpe *Derbys* **75** SK4580
Upperthorpe *Humb* **84** SE7500
Upperton *W Susx* **14** SU9522
Uppertown *Derbys* **74** SK3264
Uppertown *Highld* **151** ND3576
Upperup *Gloucs* **36** SU0496
Upperwood *Derbys* **73** SK2956
Uppincott *Devon* **9** SS9006
Uppingham *Leics* **51** SP8699
Uppington *Dorset* **12** SU0206
Uppington *Shrops* **59** SJ5909
Upsall *N York* **89** SE4586
Upsettlington *Border* **110** NT8846
Upshire *Essex* **27** TL4101
Upstreet *Kent* **29** TR2263
Upthorpe *Suffk* **54** TL9772
Upton *Berks* **26** SU9779
Upton *Bucks* **37** SP7711
Upton *Cambs* **64** TF1000
Upton *Cambs* **52** TL1778
Upton *Ches* **71** SJ4069
Upton *Ches* **78** SJ5087
Upton *Cnwll* **18** SS2004
Upton *Cnwll* **5** SX2772
Upton *Cumb* **93** NY3139
Upton *Devon* **9** ST0902
Upton *Devon* **7** SX7043
Upton *Dorset* **11** SY7483
Upton *Dorset* **11** SY9893
Upton *Dyfed* **30** SN0204
Upton *Hants* **23** SU3555
Upton *Hants* **12** SU3716
Upton *Humb* **85** TA1454
Upton *Leics* **61** SP3699
Upton *Lincs* **76** SK8686
Upton *Mersyd* **78** SJ2788
Upton *Nhants* **49** SP7159
Upton *Norfk* **67** TG3912
Upton *Notts* **75** SK7354
Upton *Notts* **75** SK7476
Upton *Oxon* **36** SP2312
Upton *Oxon* **37** SU5187
Upton *Somset* **20** SS9928
Upton *Somset* **21** ST4526
Upton *W York* **83** SE4713
Upton *Warwks* **48** SP1257
Upton *Wilts* **22** ST8731
Upton Cheyney *Avon* **35** ST6970
Upton Cressett *Shrops* **59** SO6592
Upton Crews *H & W* **47** SO6527
Upton Cross *Cnwll* **5** SX2872
Upton End *Beds* **38** TL1234
Upton Grey *Hants* **24** SU6948
Upton Heath *Ches* **71** SJ4169
Upton Hellions *Devon* **8** SS8403
Upton Lovell *Wilts* **22** ST9440
Upton Magna *Shrops* **59** SJ5512
Upton Noble *Somset* **22** ST7139
Upton Pyne *Devon* **9** SX9198
Upton Scudamore *Wilts* **22** ST8647
Upton Snodsbury *H & W* **47** SO9454
Upton St Leonards *Gloucs* **35** SO8615
Upton Towans *Cnwll* **2** SW5740
Upton upon Severn *H & W* **47** SO8540
Upton Warren *H & W* **47** SO9267
Upwaltham *W Susx* **14** SU9413
Upware *Cambs* **53** TL5470
Upwell *Norfk* **65** TF4902
Upwey *Dorset* **11** SY6685
Upwick Green *Herts* **39** TL4524
Upwood *Cambs* **52** TL2582
Urchfont *Wilts* **23** SU0357
Urdimarsh *H & W* **46** SO5248
Ure Bank *N York* **89** SE3172
Urlay Nook *Cleve* **89** NZ4014
Urmston *Gt Man* **79** SJ7694
Urquhart *Gramp* **141** NJ2862
Urra *N York* **90** NZ5601
Urray *Highld* **139** NH5052
Usan *Tays* **127** NO7254
Ushaw Moor *Dur* **96** NZ2242
Usk *Gwent* **34** SO3700
Usselby *Lincs* **76** TF0993
Usworth *T & W* **96** NZ3057
Utley *W York* **82** SE0542
Uton *Devon* **8** SX8298
Utterby *Lincs* **77** TF3093
Uttoxeter *Staffs* **73** SK0933
Uwchmynydd *Gwynd* **56** SH1525
Uxbridge *Gt Lon* **26** TQ0584
Uyeasound *Shet* **155** HP5901
Uzmaston *Dyfed* **30** SM9714

V

Vale *Guern* **152** GN0000
Valley *Gwynd* **68** SH2979
Valley End *Surrey* **25** SU9564
Valley Truckle *Cnwll* **4** SX0982
Valtos *Highld* **137** NG5163
Valtos *W Isls* **154** NB0936
Van *M Glam* **33** ST1686
Vange *Essex* **40** TQ7186
Varteg *Gwent* **34** SO2606
Vatsetter *Shet* **155** HU5389
Vatten *Highld* **136** NG2843
Vaynor *M Glam* **33** SO0410
Velindre *Powys* **45** SO1836
Vellow *Somset* **20** ST0938
Velly *Devon* **18** SS2924
Venn *Cnwll* **18** SS2608
Venn *Devon* **7** SX8549
Venn Ottery *Devon* **9** SY0891
Venngreen *Devon* **18** SS3711
Vennington *Shrops* **59** SJ3309
Venny Tedburn *Devon* **8** SX8297
Venterdon *Cnwll* **5** SX3675
Ventnor *IOW* **13** SZ5677
Venton *Devon* **6** SX5956
Vernham Dean *Hants* **23** SU3356
Vernham Street *Hants* **23** SU3457
Vernolds Common *Shrops* **59** SO4780
Verwood *Dorset* **12** SU0809
Veryan *Cnwll* **3** SW9139
Veryan Green *Cnwll* **3** SW9140
Vickerstown *Cumb* **86** SD1868
Victoria *Cnwll* **4** SW9861
Victoria *Gwent* **33** SO1707
Victoria *S York* **82** SE1705
Vidlin *Shet* **155** HU4765
Viewfield *Gramp* **141** NJ2864
Viewpark *Strath* **116** NS7061
Vigo *Kent* **27** TQ6361
Ville la Bas *Jersey* **152** JS0000
Villiaze *Guern* **152** GN0000
Vine's Cross *E Susx* **16** TQ5917
Vinehall Street *E Susx* **17** TQ7520
Virginia Water *Surrey* **25** TQ0067
Virginstow *Devon* **5** SX3792
Virley *Essex* **40** TL9414
Vobster *Somset* **22** ST7048
Voe *Shet* **155** HU4062
Vowchurch *H & W* **46** SO3636
Vulcan Village *Ches* **78** SJ5894

W

Wackerfield *Dur* **96** NZ1522
Wacton *Norfk* **66** TM1791
Wadborough *H & W* **47** SO9047
Waddesdon *Bucks* **37** SP7416
Waddeton *Devon* **7** SX8756
Waddicar *Mersyd* **78** SJ3999
Waddingham *Lincs* **76** SK9896
Waddington *Lancs* **81** SD7343
Waddington *Lincs* **76** SK9764
Waddon *Devon* **9** SX8879
Waddon *Dorset* **10** SY6285
Wadebridge *Cnwll* **4** SW9972
Wadeford *Somset* **10** ST3110
Wadenhoe *Nhants* **51** TL0183
Wadesmill *Herts* **39** TL3617
Wadhurst *E Susx* **16** TQ6431
Wadshelf *Derbys* **74** SK3170
Wadswick *Wilts* **22** ST8467
Wadworth *S York* **75** SK5696
Waen *Clwyd* **70** SH9962
Waen *Clwyd* **70** SJ1065
Waen *Powys* **58** SJ2319
Waen Fach *Powys* **58** SJ2017
Waen-pentir *Gwynd* **69** SH5766
Waen-wen *Gwynd* **69** SH5768
Wagbeach *Shrops* **59** SJ3602
Wainfelin *Gwent* **34** SO2701
Wainfleet All Saints *Lincs* **77** TF4959
Wainfleet Bank *Lincs* **77** TF4759
Wainford *Norfk* **55** TM3490
Wainhouse Corner *Cnwll* **4** SX1895
Wains Hill *Avon* **34** ST3970
Wainscott *Kent* **28** TQ7470
Wainstalls *W York* **82** SE0428
Waitby *Cumb* **88** NY7508
Waithe *Lincs* **77** TA2800
Wake Green *W Mids* **61** SP0982
Wakefield *W York* **83** SE3320
Wakerley *Nhants* **51** SP9599
Wakes Colne *Essex* **40** TL8928
Wal-wen *Clwyd* **70** SJ2076
Walberswick *Suffk* **55** TM4974
Walberton *W Susx* **14** SU9705
Walbottle *T & W* **103** NZ1666
Walbutt *D & G* **99** NX7468
Walby *Cumb* **101** NY4460
Walcombe *Somset* **21** ST5546
Walcot *Humb* **84** SE8720
Walcot *Lincs* **64** TF0635
Walcot *Lincs* **76** TF1356
Walcot *Shrops* **59** SJ5912
Walcot *Shrops* **59** SO3485
Walcot *Warwks* **48** SP1358
Walcot *Wilts* **36** SU1684
Walcot Green *Norfk* **54** TM1280
Walcote *Leics* **50** SP5683
Walcott *Norfk* **67** TG3532
Walden *N York* **88** SE0082
Walden Head *N York* **88** SD9880
Walden Stubbs *N York* **83** SE5516
Walderslade *Kent* **28** TQ7663
Walderton *W Susx* **14** SU7910
Walditch *Dorset* **10** SY4892
Waldley *Derbys* **73** SK1236
Waldridge *Dur* **96** NZ2549
Waldringfield *Suffk* **55** TM2845
Waldron *E Susx* **16** TQ5419
Wales *S York* **75** SK4882
Wales *Somset* **21** ST5824
Walesby *Lincs* **76** TF1392
Walesby *Notts* **75** SK6870
Walford *H & W* **46** SO3872
Walford *H & W* **34** SO5820
Walford *Shrops* **59** SJ4320
Walford *Staffs* **72** SJ8133
Walford Heath *Shrops* **59** SJ4419
Walgherton *Ches* **72** SJ6948
Walgrave *Nhants* **51** SP8071
Walhampton *Hants* **12** SZ3396
Walk Mill *Lancs* **81** SD8729
Walkden *Gt Man* **79** SD7302
Walker *T & W* **103** NZ2864
Walker Fold *Lancs* **81** SD6741
Walker's Green *H & W* **46** SO5247
Walker's Heath *W Mids* **61** SP0578
Walkerburn *Border* **109** NT3637
Walkeringham *Notts* **75** SK7792
Walkerith *Notts* **75** SK7892
Walkern *Herts* **39** TL2826
Walkerton *Fife* **126** NO2301
Walkhampton *Devon* **6** SX5369
Walkington *Humb* **84** SE9936
Walkley *S York* **74** SK3388
Walkwood *H & W* **48** SP0364
Wall *Cnwll* **2** SW6036
Wall *Nthumb* **102** NY9168
Wall *Staffs* **61** SK1006
Wall End *Cumb* **86** SD2383
Wall End *H & W* **46** SO4457
Wall Heath *W Mids* **60** SO8889
Wall Houses *Nthumb* **103** NZ0368
Wall under Haywood *Shrops* **59** SO5092
Wallacetown *Strath* **106** NS2703
Wallacetown *Strath* **106** NS3422
Wallands Park *E Susx* **15** TQ4010
Wallasey *Mersyd* **78** SJ2992
Wallend *Kent* **28** TQ8775
Waller's Green *H & W* **47** SO6739
Wallhead *Cumb* **101** NY4660
Wallingford *Oxon* **37** SU6089
Wallington *Gt Lon* **27** TQ2864
Wallington *Hants* **13** SU5806
Wallington *Herts* **39** TL2933
Wallington Heath *W Mids* **60** SJ9903
Wallis *Dyfed* **30** SN0125
Wallisdown *Dorset* **12** SZ0694
Walliswood *W Susx* **14** TQ1138
Walls *Shet* **155** HU2449
Wallsend *T & W* **103** NZ2966
Wallthwaite *Cumb* **93** NY3526
Wallyford *Loth* **118** NT3671
Walmer *Kent* **29** TR3750
Walmer Bridge *Lancs* **80** SD4724
Walmersley *Gt Man* **81** SD8013
Walmestone *Kent* **29** TR2559
Walmley *W Mids* **61** SP1393
Walmley Ash *W Mids* **61** SP1492
Walmsgate *Lincs* **77** TF3677
Walpole *Somset* **20** ST3042
Walpole *Suffk* **55** TM3674
Walpole Cross Keys *Norfk* **65** TF5119
Walpole Highway *Norfk* **65** TF5114
Walpole St Andrew *Norfk* **65** TF5017
Walpole St Peter *Norfk* **65** TF5016
Walrow *Somset* **21** ST3447
Walsall *W Mids* **60** SP0198
Walsall Wood *W Mids* **61** SK0403
Walsden *W York* **81** SD9321
Walsgrave on Sowe *W Mids* **61** SP3881
Walshall Green *Herts* **39** TL4430
Walsham le Willows *Suffk* **54** TM0071
Walshaw *Gt Man* **81** SD7711
Walshaw *W York* **82** SD9731
Walshford *N York* **83** SE4153
Walsoken *Norfk* **65** TF4710
Walston *Strath* **117** NT0545
Walsworth *Herts* **39** TL1930
Walter Ash *Bucks* **37** SU8398
Walters Green *Kent* **16** TQ5140
Walterston *S Glam* **33** ST0671
Walterstone *H & W* **46** SO3425
Waltham *Humb* **85** TA2603
Waltham *Kent* **29** TR1048
Waltham Abbey *Essex* **27** TL3800
Waltham Chase *Hants* **13** SU5614
Waltham Cross *Herts* **27** TL3600
Waltham on the Wolds *Leics* **63** SK8024
Waltham St Lawrence *Berks* **37** SU8276
Waltham's Cross *Essex* **40** TL6930
Walthamstow *Gt Lon* **27** TQ3689
Walton *Bucks* **38** SP8936
Walton *Cambs* **64** TF1702
Walton *Cumb* **101** NY5264
Walton *Derbys* **74** SK3568
Walton *Leics* **50** SP5987
Walton *Powys* **46** SO2559
Walton *Shrops* **59** SJ5818
Walton *Shrops* **46** SO4679
Walton *Somset* **21** ST4636
Walton *Staffs* **72** SJ8528
Walton *Staffs* **72** SJ8932
Walton *Suffk* **55** TM2935
Walton *W Susx* **14** SU8104
Walton *W York* **83** SE3516
Walton *W York* **83** SE4447
Walton *Warwks* **48** SP2853
Walton Cardiff *Gloucs* **47** SO9032
Walton East *Dyfed* **30** SN0223
Walton Elm *Dorset* **11** ST7717
Walton Grounds *Nhants* **49** SP5135
Walton Lower Street *Suffk* **55** TM2834
Walton on the Hill *Surrey* **26** TQ2255
Walton on the Naze *Essex* **41** TM2522
Walton on the Wolds *Leics* **62** SK5919
Walton Park *Avon* **34** ST4172
Walton West *Dyfed* **30** SM8612
Walton-in-Gordano *Avon* **34** ST4273
Walton-le-Dale *Lancs* **81** SD5628
Walton-on-Thames *Surrey* **26** TQ1066
Walton-on-the-Hill *Staffs* **72** SJ9520
Walton-on-Trent *Derbys* **73** SK2118
Walwen *Clwyd* **70** SJ1179
Walwen *Clwyd* **70** SJ1771
Walwick *Nthumb* **102** NY9070
Walworth *Dur* **96** NZ2318
Walworth *Gt Lon* **27** TQ3277
Walworth Gate *Dur* **96** NZ2320
Walwyn's Castle *Dyfed* **30** SM8711
Wambrook *Somset* **10** ST2907
Wampool *Cumb* **93** NY2454
Wanborough *Surrey* **25** SU9348
Wanborough *Wilts* **36** SU2082
Wandel *Strath* **108** NS9427
Wandon End *Herts* **38** TL1322
Wandsworth *Gt Lon* **27** TQ2574
Wangford *Suffk* **55** TM4679
Wanlip *Leics* **62** SK5910
Wanlockhead *D & G* **108** NS8712
Wannock *E Susx* **16** TQ5703
Wansford *Cambs* **64** TL0799
Wansford *Humb* **84** TA0656
Wanshurst Green *Kent* **28** TQ7645
Wanstead *Gt Lon* **27** TQ4088
Wanstrow *Somset* **22** ST7141
Wanswell *Gloucs* **35** SO6801
Wantage *Oxon* **36** SU3988
Wants Green *H & W* **47** SO7557
Wapley *Avon* **35** ST7179
Wappenbury *Warwks* **48** SP3769
Wappenham *Nhants* **49** SP6245
Warbister *Ork* **155** HY3932
Warbleton *E Susx* **16** TQ6018
Warborough *Oxon* **37** SU5993
Warboys *Cambs* **52** TL3080
Warbreck *Lancs* **80** SD3238
Warbstow *Cnwll* **5** SX2090
Warburton *Gt Man* **79** SJ7089
Warcop *Cumb* **94** NY7415
Ward End *W Mids* **61** SP1188
Ward Green *Suffk* **54** TM0464
Warden *Kent* **28** TR0271
Warden *Nthumb* **102** NY9166
Warden Law *T & W* **96** NZ3649
Warden Street *Beds* **38** TL1244
Wardhedges *Beds* **38** TL0635
Wardington *Oxon* **49** SP4846
Wardle *Ches* **71** SJ6156
Wardle *Gt Man* **81** SD9116
Wardley *Gt Man* **79** SD7602
Wardley *Leics* **51** SK8300
Wardlow *Derbys* **74** SK1874
Wardsend *Ches* **79** SJ9382
Wardy Hill *Cambs* **53** TL4782
Ware *Herts* **39** TL3514
Ware Street *Kent* **28** TQ7956
Wareham *Dorset* **11** SY9287
Warehorne *Kent* **17** TQ9832
Waren Mill *Nthumb* **111** NU1434
Warenford *Nthumb* **111** NU1328
Warenton *Nthumb* **111** NU1030
Wareside *Herts* **39** TL3915
Waresley *Cambs* **52** TL2554
Waresley *H & W* **60** SO8470
Warfield *Berks* **25** SU8872
Warfleet *Devon* **7** SX8750
Wargate *Lincs* **64** TF2330
Wargrave *Berks* **37** SU7978
Warham *H & W* **46** SO4838
Warham All Saints *Norfk* **66** TF9541
Warham St Mary *Norfk* **66** TF9441
Wark *Nthumb* **110** NT8238
Wark *Nthumb* **102** NY8577
Warkleigh *Devon* **19** SS6422
Warkton *Nhants* **51** SP8979
Warkworth *Nhants* **49** SP4840
Warkworth *Nthumb* **111** NU2406
Warlaby *N York* **89** SE3491
Warland *W York* **82** SD9420
Warleggan *Cnwll* **4** SX1569
Warleigh *Avon* **22** ST7964
Warley Town *W York* **82** SE0524
Warlingham *Surrey* **27** TQ3658
Warmanbie *D & G* **101** NY1969
Warmbrook *Derbys* **73** SK2853
Warmfield *W York* **83** SE3720
Warmingham *Ches* **72** SJ7061
Warmington *Nhants* **51** TL0790
Warmington *Warwks* **49** SP4147
Warminster *Wilts* **22** ST8745
Warmley *Avon* **35** ST6673
Warmsworth *S York* **75** SE5400
Warmwell *Dorset* **11** SY7585
Warndon *H & W* **47** SO8856
Warnford *Hants* **13** SU6223
Warnham *W Susx* **15** TQ1533
Warnham Court *W Susx* **15** TQ1533
Warningcamp *W Susx* **14** TQ0307
Warninglid *W Susx* **15** TQ2426
Warren *Ches* **79** SJ8870
Warren *Dyfed* **30** SR9397
Warren Row *Berks* **37** SU8180
Warren Street *Kent* **28** TQ9252
Warren's Green *Herts* **39** TL2628
Warrenby *Cleve* **97** NZ5825
Warrenhill *Strath* **108** NS9438
Warrington *Bucks* **51** SP8953
Warrington *Ches* **78** SJ6088
Warriston *Loth* **117** NT2575
Warsash *Hants* **13** SU4906
Warslow *Staffs* **74** SK0858
Warsop *Notts* **75** SK5667
Warsop Vale *Notts* **75** SK5467
Warter *Humb* **84** SE8750
Warter Priory *Humb* **84** SE8449
Warthermaske *N York* **89** SE2078
Warthill *N York* **83** SE6755
Wartling *E Susx* **16** TQ6509
Wartnaby *Leics* **63** SK7123
Warton *Lancs* **80** SD4128
Warton *Lancs* **87** SD4972
Warton *Nthumb* **103** NU0002
Warton *Warwks* **61** SK2803
Warwick *Cumb* **93** NY4656
Warwick *Warwks* **48** SP2865
Warwick Bridge *Cumb* **93** NY4756
Warwicksland *Cumb* **101** NY4577
Wasdale Head *Cumb* **86** NY1808
Wash *Derbys* **74** SK0682
Wash *Devon* **7** SX7665
Washaway *Cnwll* **4** SX0369
Washbourne *Devon* **7** SX7954
Washbrook *Somset* **21** ST4250
Washbrook *Suffk* **54** TM1142
Washfield *Devon* **9** SS9315
Washfold *N York* **88** NZ0502
Washford *Somset* **20** ST0541
Washford Pyne *Devon* **19** SS8111
Washingborough *Lincs* **76** TF0170
Washington *T & W* **96** NZ3155
Washington *W Susx* **14** TQ1112
Washwood Heath *W Mids* **61** SP1088
Wasing *Berks* **24** SU5764
Waskerley *Dur* **95** NZ0445
Wasperton *Warwks* **48** SP2658
Wasps Nest *Lincs* **76** TF0764
Wass *N York* **90** SE5579
Watchet *Somset* **20** ST0743
Watchfield *Oxon* **36** SU2490
Watchfield *Somset* **21** ST3446
Watchgate *Cumb* **87** SD5398
Watchill *Cumb* **93** NY1842
Watcombe *Devon* **7** SX9267
Watendlath *Cumb* **93** NY2716
Water *Devon* **8** SX7580

West Witton

Widworthy

West Witton N York	88	SE0588
West Woodburn Nthumb	102	NY8987
West Woodhay Berks	23	SU3963
West Woodlands Somset	22	ST7743
West Woodside Cumb	93	NY3049
West Worldham Hants	24	SU7436
West Worthing W Susx	15	TQ1302
West Wratting Essex	53	TL6052
West Wycombe Bucks	37	SU8294
West Wylam Nthumb	103	NZ1063
West Yatton Wilts	35	ST8575
West Yoke Kent	27	TQ6065
West Youlstone Cnwll	18	SS2615
Westbere Kent	29	TR1961
Westborough Lincs	63	SK8544
Westbourne W Susx	13	SU7507
Westbrook Berks	24	SU4272
Westbrook Kent	29	TR3470
Westbrook Wilts	22	ST9565
Westbury Bucks	49	SP6235
Westbury Shrops	59	SJ3509
Westbury Wilts	22	ST8751
Westbury Leigh Wilts	22	ST8649
Westbury on Severn Gloucs	35	SO7114
Westbury-on-Trym Avon	34	ST5777
Westbury-sub-Mendip Somset	21	ST5049
Westby Lancs	80	SD3831
Westcliff-on-Sea Essex	40	TQ8685
Westcombe Somset	22	ST6739
Westcote Gloucs	36	SP2120
Westcott Bucks	37	SP7116
Westcott Devon	9	ST0204
Westcott Somset	19	SS8720
Westcott Surrey	15	TQ1448
Westcott Barton Oxon	49	SP4325
Westcourt Wilts	23	SU2261
Westdean E Susx	16	TV5299
Westdown Camp Wilts	23	SU0447
Westdowns Cnwll	4	SX0582
Wested Kent	27	TQ5166
Westend Gloucs	35	SO7807
Westend Town Nthumb	102	NY7865
Westenhanger Kent	29	TR1237
Wester Drumashie Highld	140	NH6032
Wester Essenside Border	109	NT4320
Wester Ochiltree Loth	117	NT0374
Wester Pitkierie Fife	127	NO5505
Westerdale Highld	151	ND1251
Westerdale N York	90	NZ6605
Westerfield Suffk	54	TM1747
Westergate W Susx	14	SU9305
Westerham Kent	27	TQ4454
Westerhope T & W	103	NZ1966
Westerland Devon	7	SX8662
Westerleigh Avon	35	ST6979
Westerton Tays	127	NO6754
Westerton W Susx	14	SU8807
Westfield Avon	22	ST6753
Westfield Cumb	92	NX9926
Westfield E Susx	17	TQ8115
Westfield Loth	116	NS9472
Westfield Norfk	66	TF9909
Westfield Strath	116	NS7273
Westfield Sole Kent	28	TQ7761
Westfields Dorset	11	ST7206
Westfields H & W	46	SO4941
Westfields of Rattray Tays	126	NO1746
Westford Somset	20	ST1220
Westgate Dur	95	NY9038
Westgate Humb	84	SE7707
Westgate Norfk	66	TF9740
Westgate Hill W York	82	SE2029
Westgate on Sea Kent	29	TR3270
Westgate Street Norfk	67	TG1921
Westhall Suffk	55	TM4280
Westham Dorset	11	SY6679
Westham E Susx	16	TQ6404
Westham Somset	21	ST4046
Westhampnett W Susx	14	SU8806
Westhay Somset	21	ST4342
Westhead Lancs	78	SD4407
Westhide H & W	46	SO5843
Westhill Gramp	135	NJ8307
Westholme Somset	21	ST5741
Westhope H & W	46	SO4651
Westhope Shrops	59	SO4786
Westhorp Nhants	49	SP5152
Westhorpe Lincs	64	TF2231
Westhorpe Suffk	54	TM0468
Westhoughton Gt Man	79	SD6506
Westhouse N York	87	SD6773
Westhouses Derbys	74	SK4157
Westhumble Surrey	26	TQ1651
Westlake Devon	6	SX6253
Westland Green Herts	39	TL4222
Westleigh Devon	18	SS4728
Westleigh Devon	9	ST0617
Westleton Suffk	55	TM4369
Westley Shrops	59	SJ3607
Westley Suffk	54	TL8264
Westley Waterless Cambs	53	TL6156
Westlington Bucks	37	SP7610
Westlinton Cumb	101	NY3964
Westmarsh Kent	29	TR2761
Westmeston E Susx	15	TQ3313
Westmill Herts	39	TL3627
Westminster Gt Lon	27	TQ2979
Westmuir Tays	126	NO3652
Westnewton Cumb	92	NY1344
Westoe T & W	103	NZ3765
Weston Avon	22	ST7366
Weston Berks	36	SU3973
Weston Ches	78	SJ5080
Weston Ches	72	SJ7352
Weston Devon	9	ST1400
Weston Devon	9	SY1688
Weston Dorset	11	SY6871
Weston H & W	46	SO3656
Weston Hants	13	SU7221
Weston Herts	39	TL2530
Weston Lincs	64	TF2924
Weston Nhants	49	SP5846
Weston Notts	75	SK7767
Weston Shrops	59	SO6093
Weston Shrops	59	SJ2927
Weston Shrops	59	SJ5629
Weston Shrops	46	SO3273
Weston Staffs	72	SJ9726
Weston W York	82	SE1747
Weston Beggard H & W	46	SO5841
Weston by Welland Nhants	50	SP7791
Weston Colley Hants	24	SU5039
Weston Colville Cambs	53	TL6153
Weston Corbett Hants	24	SU6846
Weston Coyney Staffs	72	SJ9343
Weston Favell Nhants	50	SP7962
Weston Green Cambs	53	TL6252
Weston Heath Shrops	60	SJ7713
Weston Hills Lincs	64	TF2720
Weston in Arden Warwks	61	SP3886
Weston Jones Staffs	72	SJ7624
Weston Longville Norfk	66	TG1115
Weston Lullingfields Shrops	59	SJ4224
Weston Patrick Hants	24	SU6946
Weston Rhyn Shrops	58	SJ2835
Weston Subedge Gloucs	48	SP1241
Weston Turville Bucks	38	SP8510
Weston under Penyard H & W	35	SO6322
Weston under Wetherley Warwks	48	SP3669
Weston Underwood Bucks	38	SP8650
Weston Underwood Derbys	73	SK2942
Weston-in-Gordano Avon	34	ST4474
Weston-on-the-Green Oxon	37	SP5318
Weston-Super-Mare Avon	21	ST3260
Weston-under-Lizard Staffs	60	SJ8010
Weston-upon-Trent Derbys	62	SK4027
Westonbirt Gloucs	35	ST8589
Westoning Beds	38	TL0332
Westoning Woodend Beds	38	TL0232
Westonzoyland Somset	21	ST3534
Westow N York	90	SE7565
Westpeek Devon	5	SX3493
Westport Somset	21	ST3820
Westquarter Cent	116	NS9178
Westra S Glam	33	ST1470
Westridge Green Berks	37	SU5679
Westrigg Loth	116	NS9067
Westrop Wilts	36	SU2093
Westruther Border	110	NT6349
Westry Cambs	65	TL4098
Westthorpe Derbys	75	SK4579
Westward Cumb	93	NY2744
Westward Ho! Devon	18	SS4329
Westwell Kent	28	TQ9947
Westwell Oxon	36	SP2209
Westwell Leacon Kent	28	TQ9647
Westwick Cambs	53	TL4265
Westwick Dur	95	NZ0715
Westwick Norfk	67	TG2726
Westwood Devon	9	SY0199
Westwood Kent	27	TQ6070
Westwood Kent	29	TR3667
Westwood Notts	75	SK4551
Westwood Wilts	22	ST8059
Westwood Heath W Mids	61	SP2776
Westwoodside Humb	75	SE7400
Wetham Green Kent	28	TQ8468
Wetheral Cumb	93	NY4654
Wetherby W York	83	SE4048
Wetherden Suffk	54	TM0062
Wetheringsett Suffk	54	TM1266
Wethersfield Essex	40	TL7131
Wetherup Street Suffk	54	TM1464
Wetley Rocks Staffs	72	SJ9649
Wettenhall Ches	71	SJ6261
Wetton Staffs	73	SK1055
Wetwang Humb	91	SE9359
Wetwood Staffs	72	SJ7733
Wexcombe Wilts	23	SU2758
Wexham Bucks	26	SU9882
Wexham Street Bucks	26	SU9883
Weybourne Norfk	66	TG1142
Weybread Suffk	55	TM2480
Weybread Street Suffk	55	TM2479
Weybridge Surrey	26	TQ0764
Weycroft Devon	10	SY3099
Weydale Highld	151	ND1564
Weyhill Hants	23	SU3146
Weymouth Dorset	11	SY6779
Whaddon Bucks	38	SP8034
Whaddon Cambs	52	TL3546
Whaddon Gloucs	35	SO8313
Whaddon Wilts	22	ST8861
Whaddon Wilts	23	SU1926
Whale Cumb	94	NY5221
Whaley Derbys	75	SK5171
Whaley Bridge Derbys	79	SK0180
Whaley Thorns Derbys	75	SK5271
Whaligoe Highld	151	ND3140
Whalley Lancs	81	SD7336
Whalley Banks Lancs	81	SD7335
Whalton Nthumb	96	NZ1318
Whamley Nthumb	102	NY8766
Whaplode Lincs	64	TF3224
Whaplode Drove Lincs	64	TF3213
Wharf Warwks	49	SP4352
Wharfe N York	88	SD7869
Wharles Lancs	80	SD4435
Wharley End Beds	38	SP9442
Wharncliffe Side S York	74	SK2994
Wharram-le-Street N York	90	SE8665
Wharton Ches	72	SJ6666
Wharton H & W	46	SO5055
Whashton Green N York	89	NZ1405
Whasset Cumb	87	SD5080
Whaston N York	89	NZ1506
Whatcote Warwks	48	SP2944
Whateley Warwks	61	SP2299
Whatfield Suffk	54	TM0246
Whatley Somset	10	ST3607
Whatley Somset	22	ST7347
Whatley's End Avon	35	ST6581
Whatlington E Susx	17	TQ7618
Whatsole Street Kent	29	TR1144
Whatstandwell Derbys	74	SK3354
Whatton Notts	63	SK7439
Whauphill D & G	99	NX4049
Whaw N York	88	NY9804
Wheal Rose Cnwll	2	SW7144
Wheatacre Norfk	67	TM4694
Wheatfield Oxon	37	SU6899
Wheathampstead Herts	39	TL1714
Wheathill Shrops	59	SO6282
Wheathill Somset	21	ST5830
Wheatley Hants	25	SU7840
Wheatley Oxon	37	SP5905
Wheatley W York	82	SE0726
Wheatley Hill Dur	96	NZ3738
Wheatley Hills S York	83	SE5904
Wheatley Lane Lancs	81	SD8337
Wheaton Aston Staffs	60	SJ8512
Wheatsheaf Clwyd	71	SJ3253
Wheddon Cross Somset	20	SS9238
Wheel Inn Cnwll	2	SW6921
Wheelbarrow Town Kent	29	TR1445
Wheeler's Green Oxon	24	SU7672
Wheeler's Street Kent	28	TQ8444
Wheelerend Common Bucks	37	SU8093
Wheelerstreet Surrey	25	SU9440
Wheelock Ches	72	SJ7559
Wheelock Heath Ches	72	SJ7557
Wheelton Lancs	81	SD6021
Wheldale W York	83	SE4526
Wheldrake N York	83	SE6844
Whelford Gloucs	36	SU1699
Whelpley Hill Bucks	38	SP9904
Whelpo Cumb	93	NY3139
Whelston Clwyd	70	SJ2076
Whempstead Herts	39	TL3221
Whenby N York	90	SE6369
Whepstead Suffk	54	TL8358
Wherstead Suffk	54	TM1540
Wherwell Hants	23	SU3841
Wheston Derbys	74	SK1376
Whetsted Kent	28	TQ6646
Whetstone Gt Lon	27	TQ2693
Whetstone Leics	50	SP5597
Wheyrigg Cumb	93	NY1948
Whicham Cumb	86	SD1382
Whichford Warwks	48	SP3134
Whickham T & W	96	NZ2061
Whiddon Devon	18	SX4799
Whiddon Down Devon	8	SX6992
Whight's Corner Suffk	54	TM1242
Whigstreet Tays	127	NO4844
Whilton Nhants	49	SP6364
Whimble Devon	18	SS3503
Whimple Devon	9	SY0497
Whimpwell Green Norfk	67	TG3829
Whin Lane End Lancs	80	SD3941
Whinburgh Norfk	66	TG0009
Whinnie Liggate D & G	99	NX7252
Whinnow Cumb	93	NY3051
Whinny Hill Cleve	96	NZ3818
Whinnyfold Gramp	143	NK0733
Whippingham IOW	13	SZ5193
Whipsnade Beds	38	TL0117
Whipton Devon	9	SX9493
Whisby Lincs	76	SK9067
Whissendine Leics	63	SK8214
Whissonsett Norfk	66	TF9123
Whistlefield Strath	114	NS2393
Whistlefield Inn Strath	114	NS1492
Whistley Green Berks	25	SU7974
Whiston Mersyd	78	SJ4791
Whiston Nhants	51	SP8460
Whiston S York	75	SK4489
Whiston Staffs	60	SJ8914
Whiston Staffs	73	SK0347
Whiston Cross Shrops	60	SJ7903
Whiston Eaves Staffs	73	SK0446
Whiston Lane End Mersyd	78	SJ4690
Whitacre Fields Warwks	61	SP2592
Whitbeck Cumb	86	SD1184
Whitbourne H & W	47	SO7257
Whitburn Loth	116	NS9464
Whitburn T & W	96	NZ4062
Whitby Ches	71	SJ3975
Whitby N York	91	NZ8910
Whitbyheath Ches	71	SJ3974
Whitchester Border	119	NT7159
Whitchurch Avon	21	ST6167
Whitchurch Bucks	38	SP8020
Whitchurch Devon	6	SX4972
Whitchurch Dyfed	30	SM8025
Whitchurch H & W	34	SO5517
Whitchurch Hants	24	SU4648
Whitchurch Oxon	37	SU6377
Whitchurch S Glam	33	ST1579
Whitchurch Shrops	71	SJ5341
Whitchurch Canonicorum Dorset	10	SY3995
Whitchurch Hill Oxon	37	SU6378
Whitcombe Dorset	11	SY7188
Whitcot Shrops	59	SO3791
Whitcott Keysett Shrops	58	SO2782
White Ball Somset	20	ST1019
White Chapel H & W	48	SP0740
White Chapel Lancs	81	SD5541
White Colne Essex	40	TL8729
White Coppice Lancs	81	SD6118
White Cross Cnwll	2	SW6821
White End H & W	47	SO7834
White Kirkley Dur	95	NZ0235
White Lackington Dorset	11	SY7198
White Ladies Aston H & W	47	SO9252
White Mill Dyfed	32	SN4621
White Notley Essex	40	TL7818
White Ox Mead Avon	22	ST7258
White Pit Lincs	77	TF3777
White Roding Essex	40	TL5613
White Stake Lancs	80	SD5125
White Stone H & W	46	SO5642
White Waltham Berks	26	SU8577
White-le-Head Dur	96	NZ1654
Whiteacre Kent	29	TR1148
Whiteacre Heath Warwks	61	SP2292
Whiteash Green Essex	40	TL7930
Whitebirk Lancs	81	SD7028
Whitebridge Highld	139	NH4815
Whitebrook Gwent	34	SO5306
Whitecairns Gramp	143	NJ9218
Whitechapel Gt Lon	27	TQ3381
Whitechurch Dyfed	31	SN1536
Whitecliffe Gloucs	34	SO5609
Whitecraig Loth	118	NT3470
Whitecroft Gloucs	35	SO6206
Whitecrook D & G	98	NX1656
Whitecross Cnwll	2	SW5234
Whitecross Cnwll	4	SW9672
Whiteface Highld	146	NH7088
Whitefarland Strath	105	NR8642
Whitefaulds Strath	106	NS2909
Whitefield Devon	19	SS7035
Whitefield Gt Man	79	SD8006
Whitefield Somset	20	ST0729
Whitefield Lane End Mersyd	78	SJ4589
Whiteford Gramp	142	NJ7126
Whitegate Ches	71	SJ6269
Whitehall Hants	24	SU7452
Whitehall Ork	155	HY6528
Whitehall W Susx	15	TQ1321
Whitehaven Cumb	92	NX9718
Whitehill Hants	14	SU7934
Whitehill Kent	28	TR0059
Whitehills Gramp	142	NJ6565
Whitehouse Gramp	142	NJ6114
Whitehouse Strath	113	NR8161
Whitehouse Common W Mids	61	SP1397
Whitekirk Loth	118	NT5981
Whitelackington Somset	10	ST3815
Whiteley Hants	13	SU5209
Whiteley Bank IOW	13	SZ5581
Whiteley Green Ches	79	SJ9278
Whiteley Village Surrey	26	TQ0962
Whitemans Green W Susx	15	TQ3025
Whitemire Gramp	140	NH9854
Whitemoor Cnwll	4	SW9757
Whitemoor Derbys	62	SK3647
Whitemoor Notts	62	SK5441
Whitemoor Staffs	72	SJ8861
Whitenap Hants	12	SU3620
Whiteness Shet	155	HU3844
Whiteoak Green Oxon	36	SP3414
Whiteparish Wilts	23	SU2423
Whiterashes Gramp	143	NJ8523
Whiterow Gramp	141	NJ0257
Whiterow Highld	151	ND3648
Whiteshill Gloucs	35	SO8406
Whitesmith E Susx	16	TQ5213
Whitestaunton Somset	10	ST2810
Whitestone Devon	9	SX8694
Whitestone Cross Devon	9	SX8993
Whitestreet Green Suffk	54	TL9739
Whitewall Corner N York	90	SE7969
Whiteway Dorset	22	ST7264
Whiteway Gloucs	35	SO9110
Whitewell Lancs	81	SD6646
Whiteworks Devon	6	SX6171
Whitfield Avon	35	ST6791
Whitfield Kent	29	TR3045
Whitfield Nhants	49	SP6039
Whitfield Nthumb	94	NY7857
Whitfield Hall Nthumb	94	NY7756
Whitford Clwyd	70	SJ1478
Whitford Devon	10	SY2595
Whitgift Humb	84	SE8122
Whitgreave Staffs	72	SJ9028
Whithorn D & G	99	NX4440
Whiting Bay Strath	105	NS0425
Whitington Norfk	65	TL7199
Whitkirk W York	83	SE3633
Whitland Dyfed	31	SN1916
Whitlaw Border	109	NT5012
Whitletts Strath	106	NS3623
Whitley Berks	24	SU7270
Whitley N York	83	SE5620
Whitley S York	74	SK3494
Whitley Wilts	22	ST8866
Whitley Bay T & W	103	NZ3571
Whitley Chapel Nthumb	95	NY9257
Whitley Heath Staffs	72	SJ8126
Whitley Lower W York	82	SE2217
Whitley Row Kent	27	TQ4952
Whitlock's End W Mids	61	SP1076
Whitlow S York	74	SK3182
Whitminster Gloucs	35	SO7708
Whitmore Dorset	12	SU0609
Whitmore Staffs	72	SJ8140
Whitnage Devon	9	ST0215
Whitnash Warwks	48	SP3263
Whitney-on-Wye H & W	46	SO2747
Whitrigg Cumb	93	NY2038
Whitrigg Cumb	93	NY2257
Whitrigglees Cumb	93	NY2457
Whitsbury Hants	12	SU1219
Whitsford Devon	19	SS6633
Whitsome Border	119	NT8650
Whitson Gwent	34	ST3883
Whitstable Kent	29	TR1066
Whitstone Cnwll	5	SX2698
Whittingehame Loth	118	NT6073
Whittingham Nthumb	111	NU0611
Whittingslow Shrops	59	SO4388
Whittington Derbys	74	SK3875
Whittington Gloucs	35	SP0120
Whittington H & W	47	SO8753
Whittington Lancs	87	SD6075
Whittington Shrops	59	SJ3231
Whittington Staffs	61	SK1508
Whittington Staffs	60	SO8682
Whittington Warwks	61	SP2999
Whittington Moor Derbys	74	SK3773
Whittle-le-Woods Lancs	81	SD5821
Whittlebury Nhants	49	SP6943
Whittlesey Cambs	64	TL2697
Whittlesford Cambs	53	TL4748
Whittlestone Head Lancs	81	SD7119
Whitton Cleve	96	NZ3822
Whitton Humb	84	SE9024
Whitton Nthumb	103	NU0501
Whitton Powys	46	SO2767
Whitton Shrops	46	SO5772
Whitton Suffk	54	TM1447
Whittonditch Wilts	36	SU2872
Whittonstall Nthumb	95	NZ0757
Whitway Hants	24	SU4559
Whitwell Derbys	75	SK5276
Whitwell Herts	39	TL1820
Whitwell IOW	13	SZ5277
Whitwell Leics	63	SK9208
Whitwell N York	89	SE2899
Whitwell Street Norfk	66	TG1022
Whitwell-on-the-Hill N York	90	SE7265
Whitwick Leics	62	SK4315
Whitwood W York	83	SE4024
Whitworth Lancs	81	SD8818
Whixall Shrops	59	SJ5134
Whixley N York	89	SE4458
Whorlton Dur	95	NZ1014
Whorlton N York	90	NZ4802
Whyle H & W	46	SO5561
Whyteleafe Surrey	27	TQ3358
Wibdon Gloucs	34	ST5797
Wibsey W York	82	SE1430
Wibtoft Warwks	50	SP4887
Wichenford H & W	47	SO7860
Wichling Kent	28	TQ9256
Wick Avon	35	ST7072
Wick Devon	9	ST1704
Wick Dorset	12	SZ1591
Wick H & W	47	SO9645
Wick Highld	151	ND3650
Wick M Glam	33	SS9271
Wick Somset	20	ST2144
Wick Somset	21	ST4026
Wick W Susx	14	TQ0203
Wick Wilts	12	SU1621
Wick End Beds	38	SP9850
Wick St Lawrence Avon	21	ST3665
Wicken Cambs	53	TL5770
Wicken Nhants	49	SP7439
Wicken Bonhunt Essex	39	TL4933
Wickenby Lincs	76	TF0982
Wicker Street Green Suffk	54	TL9742
Wickersley S York	75	SK4791
Wickford Essex	40	TQ7493
Wickham Berks	36	SU3971
Wickham Hants	13	SU5711
Wickham Bishops Essex	40	TL8412
Wickham Green Berks	24	SU4072
Wickham Green Suffk	54	TM0969
Wickham Heath Berks	24	SU4169
Wickham Market Suffk	55	TM3055
Wickham Skeith Suffk	54	TM0969
Wickham St Paul Essex	54	TL8336
Wickham Street Suffk	53	TL7654
Wickham Street Suffk	54	TM0869
Wickhambreaux Kent	29	TR2158
Wickhambrook Suffk	53	TL7554
Wickhamford H & W	48	SP0641
Wickhampton Norfk	67	TG4205
Wicklewood Norfk	66	TG0702
Wickmere Norfk	66	TG1733
Wickstreet E Susx	16	TQ5308
Wickwar Avon	35	ST7288
Widdington Essex	39	TL5331
Widdop Lancs	81	SD9233
Widdrington Nthumb	103	NZ2595
Widdrington Station T & W	103	NZ2494
Wide Open T & W	103	NZ2472
Widecombe in the Moor Devon	8	SX7176
Widegates Cnwll	5	SX2858
Widemouth Bay Cnwll	18	SS2002
Widford Essex	40	TL6904
Widford Herts	39	TL4216
Widford Oxon	36	SP2712
Widham Wilts	36	SU0988
Widmer End Bucks	26	SU8896
Widmerpool Notts	63	SK6327
Widmore Gt Lon	27	TQ4268
Widnes Ches	78	SJ5184
Widworthy Devon	9	SY2199

Wigan
Woodminton

Wigan Gt Man 78 SD5805
Wigborough Somset 10 ST4415
Wiggaton Devon 9 SY1093
Wiggenhall St Germans Norfk 65 TF5914
Wiggenhall St Mary Magdalen Norfk 65 TF5911
Wiggenhall St Mary the Virgin Norfk 65 TF5813
Wiggens Green Essex 53 TL6642
Wiggenstall Staffs 74 SK0960
Wiggington Shrops 59 SJ3335
Wigginton Herts 38 SP9310
Wigginton N York 90 SE6058
Wigginton Oxon 48 SP3833
Wigginton Staffs 61 SK2006
Wigglesworth N York 81 SD8156
Wiggold Gloucs 36 SP0404
Wiggonby Cumb 93 NY2952
Wiggonholt W Susx 14 TQ0616
Wighill N York 83 SE4746
Wighton Norfk 66 TF9439
Wigley Derbys 74 SK3171
Wigley Hants 12 SU3217
Wigmore H & W 46 SO4169
Wigmore Kent 28 TQ7964
Wigsley Notts 76 SK8570
Wigsthorpe Nhants 51 TL0482
Wigston Leics 50 SP6198
Wigston Fields Leics 50 SK6000
Wigston Parva Leics 50 SP4689
Wigthorpe Notts 75 SK5983
Wigtoft Lincs 64 TF2636
Wigton Cumb 93 NY2548
Wigtown D & G 99 NX4355
Wigtwizzle S York 74 SK2495
Wike W York 83 SE3342
Wilbarston Nhants 51 SP8188
Wilberfoss Humb 84 SE7350
Wilburton Cambs 53 TL4775
Wilby Nhants 51 SP8666
Wilby Norfk 54 TM0389
Wilby Suffk 55 TM2472
Wilcot Wilts 23 SU1360
Wilcrick Gwent 34 ST4088
Wilday Green Derbys 74 SK3274
Wildboarclough Ches 79 SJ9868
Wilden Beds 51 TL0955
Wilden H & W 60 SO8272
Wildhern Hants 23 SU3550
Wildhill Herts 39 TL2606
Wildmanbridge Strath 116 NS8253
Wildmoor H & W 60 SO9575
Wildsworth Lincs 75 SK8097
Wilford Notts 62 SK5637
Wilkesley Ches 71 SJ6241
Wilkhaven Highld 147 NH9486
Wilkieston Fife 117 NT1268
Wilkin's Green Herts 39 TL1907
Wilksby Lincs 77 TF2862
Willand Devon 9 ST0310
Willards Hill E Susx 17 TQ7124
Willaston Ches 71 SJ3377
Willaston Ches 72 SJ6852
Willcott Shrops 59 SJ3718
Willen Bucks 38 SP8741
Willenhall W Mids 60 SO9798
Willenhall W Mids 61 SP3676
Willerby Humb 84 TA0230
Willerby N York 91 TA0079
Willersey Gloucs 48 SP1039
Willersley H & W 46 SO3147
Willesborough Kent 28 TR0441
Willesborough Lees Kent 28 TR0342
Willesden Gt Lon 26 TQ2284
Willesleigh Devon 19 SS6033
Willesley Wilts 35 ST8588
Willett Somset 20 ST1033
Willey Shrops 60 SO6799
Willey Warwks 50 SP4984
Willey Green Surrey 25 SU9351
Williamscot Oxon 49 SP4845
Williamstown M Glam 33 ST0090
Willian Herts 39 TL2230
Willicote Warwks 48 SP1849
Willingale Essex 40 TL5907
Willingdon E Susx 16 TQ5902
Willingham Cambs 52 TL4070
Willingham Lincs 76 SK8784
Willingham Green Cambs 53 TL6254
Willington Beds 52 TL1150
Willington Derbys 73 SK2928
Willington Dur 96 NZ1935
Willington Kent 28 TQ7853
Willington Warwks 48 SP2639
Willington Corner Ches 71 SJ5266
Willington Quay T & W 103 NZ3267
Willitoft Humb 84 SE7434
Williton Somset 20 ST0840
Willoughby Lincs 64 TF0537
Willoughby Lincs 77 TF4771
Willoughby Warwks 50 SP5167
Willoughby Hills Lincs 64 TF3545
Willoughby Waterleys Leics 50 SP5792
Willoughby-on-the-Wolds Notts 63 SK6325
Willoughton Lincs 76 SK9293
Willow Green Ches 71 SJ6076
Willows Green Essex 40 TL7219
Willsbridge Avon 35 ST6670
Willsworthy Devon 8 SX5381
Willtown Somset 21 ST3924
Wilmcote Warwks 48 SP1658
Wilmington Avon 22 ST6962
Wilmington Devon 9 SY2199
Wilmington E Susx 16 TQ5404
Wilmington Kent 27 TQ5372
Wilmslow Ches 79 SJ8481
Wilnecote Staffs 61 SK2200
Wilpshire Lancs 81 SD6832
Wilsden W York 82 SE0936
Wilsford Lincs 63 TF0042
Wilsford Wilts 23 SU1057
Wilsford Wilts 23 SU1339
Wilsham Devon 19 SS7548
Wilshaw W York 82 SE1109
Wilsill N York 89 SE1864
Wilsley Green Kent 28 TQ7736
Wilsley Pound Kent 28 TQ7837
Wilson H & W 46 SO5523
Wilson Leics 62 SK4024
Wilsontown Strath 116 NS9455
Wilstead Beds 38 TL0643
Wilsthorpe Lincs 64 TF0913
Wilstone Herts 38 SP9014
Wilstone Green Herts 38 SP9013
Wilton Cleve 97 NZ5819
Wilton Cumb 86 NY0311
Wilton H & W 46 SO5824
Wilton N York 90 SE8582
Wilton Wilts 23 SU0931
Wilton Wilts 23 SU2661
Wilton Dean Border 109 NT4914
Wimbish Essex 53 TL5936
Wimbish Green Essex 53 TL6035
Wimblebury Staffs 60 SK0111
Wimbledon Gt Lon 26 TQ2370
Wimblington Cambs 65 TL4192
Wimborne Minster Dorset 11 SZ0199
Wimborne St Giles Dorset 12 SU0311
Wimbotsham Norfk 65 TF6205
Wimpstone Warwks 48 SP2148
Wincanton Somset 22 ST7128
Winceby Lincs 77 TF3268
Wincham Ches 79 SJ6775
Winchburgh Loth 117 NT0975
Winchcombe Gloucs 48 SP0228
Winchelsea E Susx 17 TQ9017
Winchelsea Beach E Susx 17 TQ9116
Winchester Hants 24 SU4829
Winchet Hill Kent 28 TQ7340
Winchfield Hants 24 SU7654
Winchmore Hill Bucks 26 SU9395
Winchmore Hill Gt Lon 27 TQ3194
Wincle Ches 72 SJ9566
Wincobank S York 74 SK3891
Winder Cumb 92 NY0417
Windermere Cumb 87 SD4098
Winderton Warwks 48 SP3240
Windhill Highld 139 NH5348
Windlehurst Gt Man 79 SJ9586
Windlesham Surrey 25 SU9364
Windmill Cnwll 4 SW8974
Windmill Derbys 74 SK1677
Windmill Hill E Susx 16 TQ6412
Windmill Hill Somset 10 ST3116
Windrush Gloucs 36 SP1913
Windsole Gramp 142 NJ5560
Windsor Berks 26 SU9576
Windsor Green Suffk 54 TL8954
Windsoredge Gloucs 35 SO8400
Windy Arbour Warwks 61 SP2971
Windy Hill Clwyd 71 SJ3054
Windygates Fife 118 NO3400
Windyharbour Ches 79 SJ8270
Wineham W Susx 15 TQ2320
Winestead Humb 85 TA2924
Winewall Lancs 81 SD9140
Winfarthing Norfk 54 TM1085
Winford Avon 21 ST5464
Winford IOW 13 SZ5584
Winforton H & W 46 SO2946
Winfrith Newburgh Dorset 11 SY8084
Wing Bucks 38 SP8822
Wing Leics 63 SK8903
Wingate Dur 96 NZ4036
Wingates Gt Man 79 SD6507
Wingates Nthumb 103 NZ0995
Wingerworth Derbys 74 SK3867
Wingfield Beds 38 TL0026
Wingfield Suffk 55 TM2277
Wingfield Wilts 22 ST8256
Wingfield Green Suffk 55 TM2177
Wingham Kent 29 TR2457
Wingmore Kent 29 TR1946
Wingrave Bucks 38 SP8719
Winkburn Notts 75 SK7058
Winkfield Berks 25 SU9072
Winkfield Row Berks 25 SU8971
Winkfield Street Berks 25 SU8972
Winkhill Staffs 73 SK0651
Winkhurst Green Kent 16 TQ4949
Winkleigh Devon 19 SS6308
Winksley N York 89 SE2571
Winkton Dorset 12 SZ1696
Winlaton T & W 96 NZ1762
Winlaton Mill T & W 96 NZ1860
Winless Highld 151 ND3054
Winllan Powys 58 SJ2221
Winmarleigh Lancs 80 SD4647
Winnall H & W 47 SO8167
Winnall Hants 24 SU4829
Winnersh Berks 25 SU7870
Winnington Ches 79 SJ6474
Winscales Cumb 92 NY0226
Winscombe Avon 21 ST4257
Winsford Ches 72 SJ6566
Winsford Somset 20 SS9034
Winsham Devon 19 SS5038
Winsham Somset 10 ST3706
Winshill Staffs 73 SK2623
Winshwen W Glam 32 SS6896
Winskill Cumb 94 NY5834
Winslade Hants 24 SU6548
Winsley Wilts 22 ST7960
Winslow Bucks 49 SP7727
Winslow Oxon 36 SU2685
Winson Gloucs 36 SP0808
Winsor Hants 12 SU3114
Winster Cumb 87 SD4193
Winster Derbys 74 SK2460
Winston Dur 96 NZ1416
Winston Suffk 54 TM1861
Winston Green Suffk 54 TM1761
Winstone Gloucs 35 SO9509
Winswell Devon 18 SS4913
Winterborne Came Dorset 11 SY7088
Winterborne Clenston Dorset 11 ST8303
Winterborne Herringston Dorset 11 SY6888
Winterborne Houghton Dorset 11 ST8204
Winterborne Kingston Dorset 11 SY8697
Winterborne Monkton Dorset 11 SY6787
Winterborne Stickland Dorset 11 ST8304
Winterborne Tomson Dorset 11 SY8897
Winterborne Whitechurch Dorset 11 ST8300
Winterborne Zelston Dorset 11 SY8997
Winterbourne Avon 35 ST6480
Winterbourne Berks 24 SU4572
Winterbourne Abbas Dorset 10 SY6190
Winterbourne Bassett Wilts 36 SU0974
Winterbourne Dauntsey Wilts 23 SU1734
Winterbourne Earls Wilts 23 SU1734
Winterbourne Gunner Wilts 23 SU1735
Winterbourne Monkton Wilts 36 SU0971
Winterbourne Steepleton Dorset 10 SY6289
Winterbourne Stoke Wilts 23 SU0741
Winterbrook Oxon 37 SU6088
Winterburn N York 88 SD9358
Winteringham Humb 84 SE9221
Winterley Ches 72 SJ7457
Wintersett W York 83 SE3815
Winterslow Wilts 23 SU2332
Winterton Humb 84 SE9218
Winterton-on-Sea Norfk 67 TG4919
Winthorpe Lincs 77 TF5665
Winthorpe Notts 75 SK8156
Winton Cumb 88 NY7810
Winton Dorset 12 SZ0893
Winton E Susx 16 TQ5103
Winton N York 89 SE4196
Wintringham N York 90 SE8873
Winwick Cambs 51 TL1080
Winwick Ches 78 SJ6092
Winwick Nhants 50 SP6273
Wirksworth Derbys 73 SK2854
Wirswall Ches 71 SJ5444
Wisbech Cambs 65 TF4609
Wisbech St Mary Cambs 65 TF4208
Wisborough Green W Susx 14 TQ0525
Wiseman's Bridge Dyfed 31 SN1406
Wiseton Notts 75 SK7189
Wishanger Gloucs 35 SO9109
Wishaw Strath 116 NS7955
Wishaw Warwks 61 SP1794
Wisley Surrey 26 TQ0659
Wispington Lincs 76 TF2071
Wissenden Kent 28 TQ9041
Wissett Suffk 55 TM3679
Wissington Suffk 40 TL9533
Wistanstow Shrops 59 SO4385
Wistanswick Shrops 72 SJ6629
Wistaston Ches 72 SJ6853
Wistaston Green Ches 72 SJ6854
Wisterfield Ches 79 SJ8371
Wiston Dyfed 30 SN0218
Wiston Strath 108 NS9532
Wiston W Susx 15 TQ1512
Wistow Cambs 52 TL2780
Wistow Leics 50 SP6495
Wistow N York 83 SE5935
Wiswell Lancs 81 SD7437
Witby Mills Avon 22 ST6657
Witcham Cambs 53 TL4680
Witchampton Dorset 11 ST9806
Witchford Cambs 53 TL5078
Witcombe Somset 21 ST4721
Witham Essex 40 TL8214
Witham Friary Somset 22 ST7441
Witham on the Hill Lincs 64 TF0516
Withcall Lincs 77 TF2883
Withdean E Susx 15 TQ3007
Witherenden Hill E Susx 16 TQ6426
Witheridge Devon 19 SS8014
Witherley Leics 61 SP3297
Withern Lincs 77 TF4282
Withernsea Humb 85 TA3427
Withernwick Humb 85 TA1940
Withersdale Street Suffk 55 TM2680
Withersfield Essex 53 TL6548
Witherslack Cumb 87 SD4384
Witherslack Hall Cumb 87 SD4385
Withiel Cnwll 4 SW9965
Withiel Florey Somset 20 SS9833
Withielgoose Cnwll 4 SX0065
Withington Ches 79 SJ8169
Withington Gloucs 35 SP0215
Withington Gt Man 79 SJ8492
Withington H & W 46 SO5643
Withington Shrops 59 SJ5713
Withington Staffs 73 SK0335
Withington Green Ches 79 SJ8071
Withington Marsh H & W 46 SO5544
Withleigh Devon 9 SS9012
Withnell Lancs 81 SD6322
Withybed Green H & W 60 SP0172
Withybrook Warwks 50 SP4383
Withycombe Somset 20 ST0141
Withyditch Avon 22 ST6959
Withyham E Susx 16 TQ4935
Withypool Devon 19 SS8435
Withywood Avon 21 ST5667
Witley Surrey 25 SU9439
Witnesham Suffk 54 TM1751
Witney Oxon 36 SP3510
Wittering Cambs 64 TF0502
Wittersham Kent 17 TQ9027
Witton Norfk 67 TG3109
Witton Norfk 67 TG3331
Witton W Mids 61 SP0790
Witton Gilbert Dur 96 NZ2345
Witton Green Norfk 67 TG4102
Witton le Wear Dur 96 NZ1431
Witton Park Dur 96 NZ1730
Wiveliscombe Somset 20 ST0827
Wivelrod Hants 24 SU6738
Wivelsfield E Susx 15 TQ3420
Wivelsfield Green E Susx 15 TQ3519
Wivelsfield Station W Susx 15 TQ3219
Wivenhoe Essex 41 TM0321
Wivenhoe Cross Essex 41 TM0423
Wiveton Norfk 66 TG0442
Wix Essex 41 TM1628
Wix Green Essex 41 TM1728
Wixford Warwks 48 SP0854
Wixhill Shrops 59 SJ5528
Wixoe Essex 53 TL7143
Woburn Beds 38 SP9433
Woburn Sands Bucks 38 SP9235
Wokefield Park Berks 24 SU6765
Woking Surrey 25 TQ0058
Wokingham Berks 25 SU8168
Wolborough Devon 7 SX8570
Wold Newton Humb 91 TA0473
Wold Newton Humb 77 TF2496
Woldingham Surrey 27 TQ3755
Wolf Hills Nthumb 94 NY7258
Wolf's Castle Dyfed 30 SM9526
Wolfclyde Strath 108 NT0236
Wolferlow H & W 47 SO6661
Wolferton Norfk 65 TF6528
Wolfhampcote Warwks 50 SP5265
Wolfhill Tays 126 NO1533
Wolfsdale Dyfed 30 SM9321
Wollaston Nhants 51 SP9062
Wollaston Shrops 59 SJ3212
Wollaton Notts 62 SK5239
Wolleigh Devon 8 SX8080
Wollerton Shrops 59 SJ6130
Wollescote W Mids 60 SO9283
Wolseley Bridge Staffs 73 SK0220
Wolsingham Dur 95 NZ0737
Wolstanton Staffs 72 SJ8548
Wolstenholme Gt Man 81 SD8414
Wolston Warwks 50 SP4175
Wolsty Cumb 92 NY1050
Wolvercote Oxon 37 SP4910
Wolverhampton W Mids 60 SO9198
Wolverley H & W 60 SO8379
Wolverley Shrops 59 SJ4731
Wolverton Bucks 38 SP8141
Wolverton Hants 24 SU5558
Wolverton Kent 29 TR2642
Wolverton Warwks 48 SP2062
Wolverton Wilts 22 ST7831
Wolverton Common Hants 24 SU5659
Wolvesnewton Gwent 34 ST4599
Wolvey Warwks 50 SP4387
Wolvey Heath Warwks 50 SP4388
Wolviston Cleve 97 NZ4525
Wombleton N York 90 SE6683
Wombourne Staffs 60 SO8793
Wombwell S York 83 SE4002
Womenswold Kent 29 TR2250
Womersley N York 83 SE5319
Wonastow Gwent 34 SO4810
Wonersh Surrey 14 TQ0145
Wonford Devon 9 SX9491
Wonson Devon 8 SX6789
Wonston Hants 24 SU4739
Wooburn Bucks 26 SU9087
Wooburn Green Bucks 26 SU9188
Wooburn Moor Bucks 26 SU9189
Wood Bevington Warwks 48 SP0554
Wood Burcot Nhants 49 SP6946
Wood Dalling Norfk 66 TG0827
Wood Eaton Staffs 72 SJ8417
Wood End Beds 38 TL0046
Wood End Beds 51 TL0866
Wood End Cambs 52 TL3675
Wood End Gt Lon 26 TQ1081
Wood End Herts 39 TL3225
Wood End W Mids 60 SJ9400
Wood End Warwks 61 SP1171
Wood End Warwks 61 SP2498
Wood End Warwks 61 SP2987
Wood Enderby Lincs 77 TF2764
Wood Green Gt Lon 27 TQ3090
Wood Hayes W Mids 60 SJ9402
Wood Lane Shrops 59 SJ4132
Wood Lane Staffs 72 SJ8149
Wood Norton Norfk 66 TG0127
Wood Row W York 83 SE3827
Wood Street Norfk 67 TG3722
Wood Street Surrey 25 SU9550
Wood Top Lancs 81 SD5643
Wood Walton Cambs 52 TL2180
Wood's Corner E Susx 16 TQ6619
Wood's Green E Susx 16 TQ6333
Woodale N York 88 SE0279
Woodall S York 75 SK4880
Woodbastwick Norfk 67 TG3315
Woodbeck Notts 75 SK7777
Woodborough Notts 63 SK6347
Woodborough Wilts 23 SU1159
Woodbridge Devon 9 SY1895
Woodbridge Dorset 22 ST8518
Woodbridge Suffk 55 TM2649
Woodbury Devon 9 SY0087
Woodbury Salterton Devon 9 SY0189
Woodchester Gloucs 35 SO8302
Woodchurch Kent 17 TQ9434
Woodchurch Mersyd 78 SJ2786
Woodcombe Somset 20 SS9546
Woodcote Gt Lon 27 TQ2962
Woodcote Oxon 37 SU6482
Woodcote Shrops 72 SJ7615
Woodcote Green H & W 60 SO9172
Woodcott Hants 24 SU4354
Woodcroft Gloucs 34 ST5495
Woodcutts Dorset 11 ST9717
Woodditton Cambs 53 TL6559
Woodeaton Oxon 37 SP5312
Wooden Dyfed 31 SN1105
Woodend Highld 130 NM7861
Woodend Loth 116 NS9269
Woodend Nhants 49 SP6149
Woodend Staffs 73 SK1726
Woodend W Susx 14 SU8108
Woodend Green Essex 39 TL5528
Woodfalls Wilts 12 SU1920
Woodford Devon 7 SX7950
Woodford Gloucs 35 ST6995
Woodford Gt Lon 27 TQ4191
Woodford Gt Man 79 SJ8882
Woodford Nhants 51 SP9676
Woodford Bridge Gt Lon 27 TQ4291
Woodford Halse Nhants 49 SP5452
Woodford Wells Gt Lon 27 TQ4093
Woodgate Devon 9 ST1015
Woodgate H & W 47 SO9666
Woodgate Norfk 66 TF8915
Woodgate Norfk 66 TG0215
Woodgate W Mids 60 SO9982
Woodgate W Susx 14 SU9304
Woodgreen Hants 12 SU1717
Woodgreen Oxon 36 SP3610
Woodhall N York 88 SD9790
Woodhall Hill W York 82 SE2035
Woodhall Spa Lincs 76 TF1963
Woodham Bucks 37 SP7018
Woodham Dur 96 NZ2826
Woodham Lincs 76 TF2267
Woodham Ferrers Essex 40 TQ7999
Woodham Mortimer Essex 40 TL8104
Woodham Walter Essex 40 TL8007
Woodhaven Fife 126 NO4126
Woodhead Gramp 142 NJ7838
Woodhill Somset 21 ST3527
Woodhorn Nthumb 103 NZ2988
Woodhorn Demesne Nthumb 103 NZ3088
Woodhouse Leics 62 SK5314
Woodhouse S York 74 SK4284
Woodhouse W York 82 SE2935
Woodhouse W York 83 SE3821
Woodhouse Eaves Leics 62 SK5214
Woodhouse Green Staffs 72 SJ9162
Woodhouse Mill S York 75 SK4385
Woodhouselee Loth 117 NT2364
Woodhouselee D & G 101 NY3975
Woodhouses Cumb 93 NY3252
Woodhouses Gt Man 79 SD9100
Woodhouses Staffs 61 SK0709
Woodhouses Staffs 73 SK1518
Woodhuish Devon 7 SX9152
Woodhurst Cambs 52 TL3176
Woodingdean E Susx 15 TQ3505
Woodkirk W York 82 SE2725
Woodland Devon 7 SX7968
Woodland Devon 6 SX6256
Woodland Dur 95 NZ0726
Woodland Gramp 143 NJ8723
Woodland Kent 29 TR1441
Woodland Strath 106 NX1795
Woodland Head Devon 8 SX7796
Woodland Street Somset 21 ST5337
Woodland View S York 74 SK3188
Woodlands Dorset 12 SU0509
Woodlands Gramp 135 NO7895
Woodlands Hants 12 SU3211
Woodlands Kent 27 TQ5660
Woodlands N York 83 SE3254
Woodlands S York 83 SE5308
Woodlands Somset 20 ST1640
Woodlands Park Berks 26 SU8678
Woodlands St Mary Berks 36 SU3375
Woodleigh Devon 7 SX7349
Woodlesford W York 83 SE3629
Woodley Berks 25 SU7773
Woodley Gt Man 79 SJ9392
Woodley Green Berks 26 SU8480
Woodmancote Gloucs 47 SO9727
Woodmancote Gloucs 35 SP0008
Woodmancote Gloucs 35 ST7597
Woodmancote H & W 47 SO9142
Woodmancote W Susx 14 SU7707
Woodmancote W Susx 15 TQ2314
Woodmancott Hants 24 SU5642
Woodmansey Humb 84 TA0538
Woodmansgreen W Susx 14 SU8627
Woodmansterne Surrey 27 TQ2759
Woodmanton Devon 9 SY0186
Woodmarsh Wilts 22 ST8555
Woodmill Staffs 73 SK1320
Woodminton Wilts 22 SU0022

Woodnesborough
Zouch

Woodnesborough Kent 29 TR3157
Woodnewton Nhants 51 TL0394
Woodnook Notts 75 SK4752
Woodplumpton Lancs 80 SD4934
Woodrising Norfk 66 TF9803
Woodrow H & W 60 SO8974
Woodseaves Shrops 72 SJ6831
Woodseaves Staffs 72 SJ7925
Woodsend Wilts 36 SU2176
Woodsetts S York 75 SK5483
Woodsford Dorset 11 SY7590
Woodside Berks 25 SU9371
Woodside Cumb 92 NY0434
Woodside Essex 39 TL4704
Woodside Fife 127 NO4207
Woodside Gt Lon 27 TQ3467
Woodside Hants 12 SZ3294
Woodside Herts 39 TL2406
Woodside Tays 126 NO2037
Woodside Green Kent 28 TQ9053
Woodstock Dyfed 30 SN0325
Woodstock Oxon 37 SP4416
Woodston Cambs 64 TL1897
Woodthorpe Derbys 75 SK4574
Woodthorpe Leics 62 SK5417
Woodthorpe Lincs 77 TF4380
Woodton Norfk 67 TM2994
Woodtown Devon 18 SS4123
Woodvale Mersyd 78 SD3010
Woodville Derbys 62 SK3118
Woodwall Green Staffs 72 SJ7831
Woody Bay Devon 19 SS6748
Woodyates Dorset 12 SU0219
Woofferton Shrops 46 SO5268
Wookey Somset 21 ST5145
Wookey Hole Somset 21 ST5347
Wool Dorset 11 SY8486
Woolacombe Devon 18 SS4643
Woolage Green Kent 29 TR2349
Woolage Village Kent 29 TR2350
Woolaston Gloucs 34 ST5899
Woolaston Common Gloucs 34 SO5801
Woolavington Somset 21 ST3441
Woolbeding W Susx 14 SU8722
Woolbrook Devon 9 SY1289
Woolcotts Somset 20 SS9631
Wooldale W York 82 SE1508
Wooler Nthumb 111 NT9927
Wooley Bridge Derbys 79 SK0194
Woolfardisworthy Devon 18 SS3321
Woolfardisworthy Devon 19 SS8208
Woolfold Gt Man 81 SD7811
Woolfords Strath 117 NT0056
Woolhampton Berks 24 SU5766
Woolhanger Devon 19 SS6945
Woolhope H & W 46 SO6135
Woolland Dorset 11 ST7707
Woollard Avon 21 ST6364
Woollensbrook Herts 39 TL3609
Woolley Avon 22 ST7468
Woolley Cambs 52 TL1574
Woolley Cnwll 18 SS2516
Woolley Derbys 74 SK3760
Woolley W York 83 SE3212
Woolmer Green Herts 39 TL2518
Woolmere Green H & W 47 SO9663
Woolmerston Somset 20 ST2833
Woolminstone Somset 10 ST4108
Woolpack Kent 28 TQ8537
Woolpit Suffk 54 TL9762
Woolpit Green Suffk 54 TL9761
Woolscott Warwks 50 SP5068
Woolsgrove Devon 8 SS7902
Woolsington T & W 103 NZ1870
Woolstaston Shrops 59 SO4598
Woolsthorpe Lincs 63 SK8333
Woolsthorpe Lincs 63 SK9224
Woolston Ches 79 SJ6489
Woolston Devon 7 SX7141
Woolston Devon 7 SX7150
Woolston Hants 13 SU4310
Woolston Shrops 59 SJ3224
Woolston Shrops 59 SO4287
Woolston Somset 20 ST0939
Woolston Somset 21 ST6527
Woolston Green Devon 7 SX7766
Woolstone Bucks 38 SP8738
Woolstone Gloucs 47 SO9630
Woolstone Oxon 36 SU2987
Woolton Mersyd 78 SJ4286
Woolton Hill Hants 24 SU4361
Woolverstone Suffk 54 TM1738
Woolverton Somset 22 ST7953
Woolwich Gt Lon 27 TQ4478
Woonton H & W 46 SO3552
Woonton H & W 46 SO5562
Wooperton Nthumb 111 NU0420
Woore Shrops 72 SJ7342
Wootten Breadmead Beds 38 TL0243
Wootten Green Suffk 55 TM2372
Wootton Beds 38 TL0044
Wootton H & W 46 SO3252
Wootton Hants 12 SZ2498
Wootton Humb 85 TA0815
Wootton IOW 13 SZ5392
Wootton Kent 29 TR2246
Wootton Nhants 49 SP7656
Wootton Oxon 37 SP4419
Wootton Oxon 37 SP4701
Wootton Shrops 59 SJ3327
Wootton Staffs 72 SJ8227
Wootton Staffs 73 SK1044
Wootton Bassett Wilts 36 SU0682
Wootton Bridge IOW 13 SZ5492
Wootton Common IOW 13 SZ5391
Wootton Courtenay Somset 20 SS9343
Wootton Fitzpaine Dorset 10 SY3695
Wootton Rivers Wilts 23 SU1962
Wootton St Lawrence Hants 24 SU5953
Wootton Wawen Warwks 48 SP1563
Worbarrow Dorset 11 SY8779
Worcester H & W 47 SO8554
Worcester Park Gt Lon 26 TQ2165
Wordsley W Mids 60 SO8987
Worfield Shrops 60 SO7595
Worgret Dorset 11 SY9087
Workhouse End Beds 38 TL1052
Workington Cumb 92 NY0028
Worksop Notts 75 SK5879
Worlaby Humb 84 TA0113
Worlaby Lincs 77 TF3476
World's End Berks 37 SU4877
Worlds End Bucks 38 SP8509
Worlds End Hants 13 SU6311
Worlds End W Susx 15 TQ3220
Worle Avon 21 ST3562
Worleston Ches 72 SJ6556
Worlingham Suffk 55 TM4489
Worlington Devon 19 SS7713
Worlington Suffk 53 TL6973
Worlingworth Suffk 55 TM2368
Wormald Green N York 89 SE3065
Wormbridge H & W 46 SO4230
Wormegay Norfk 65 TF6611
Wormelow Tump H & W 46 SO4930
Wormhill Derbys 74 SK1274
Wormhill H & W 46 SO4239
Wormingford Essex 40 TL9332
Worminghall Bucks 37 SP6308
Wormington Gloucs 48 SP0336
Worminster Somset 21 ST5743
Wormiston Border 117 NT2345
Wormit Tays 126 NO4026
Wormleighton Warwks 49 SP4553
Wormley Herts 39 TL3605
Wormley Surrey 25 SU9438
Wormley Hill S York 83 SE6616
Wormleybury Herts 39 TL3506
Wormshill Kent 28 TQ8857
Wormsley H & W 46 SO4247
Worplesdon Surrey 25 SU9753
Worrall S York 74 SK3092
Worrall Hill Gloucs 34 SO6014
Worsbrough S York 83 SE3602
Worsbrough Bridge S York 83 SE3503
Worsbrough Dale S York 83 SE3604
Worsley Gt Man 79 SD7500
Worsley Mesnes Gt Man 78 SD5703
Worstead Norfk 67 TG3025
Worsthorne Lancs 81 SD8732
Worston Devon 6 SX5953
Worston Lancs 81 SD7742
Worth Kent 29 TR3355
Worth Somset 21 ST5144
Worth W Susx 15 TQ3036
Worth Abbey Surrey 15 TQ3134
Worth Matravers Dorset 11 SY9777
Wortham Suffk 54 TM0877
Worthen Shrops 59 SJ3204
Worthenbury Clwyd 71 SJ4146
Worthing Norfk 66 TF9919
Worthing W Susx 15 TQ1403
Worthington Leics 62 SK4020
Worthybrook Gwent 34 SO4711
Worting Hants 24 SU5952
Wortley S York 74 SK3099
Wortley W York 82 SE2732
Worton N York 88 SD9589
Worton Wilts 22 ST9757
Wortwell Norfk 55 TM2784
Wotherton Shrops 58 SJ2800
Wothorpe Cambs 64 TF0205
Wotter Devon 6 SX5661
Wotton Surrey 14 TQ1247
Wotton Underwood Bucks 37 SP6815
Wotton-under-Edge Gloucs 35 ST7593
Woughton on the Green Bucks 38 SP8737
Wouldham Kent 28 TQ7164
Woundale Shrops 60 SO7793
Wrabness Essex 41 TM1731
Wrafton Devon 18 SS4935
Wragby Lincs 76 TF1378
Wragby W York 83 SE4116
Wramplingham Norfk 66 TG1106
Wrangaton Devon 7 SX6758
Wrangbrook W York 83 SE4913
Wrangle Lincs 77 TF4250
Wrangle Common Lincs 77 TF4253
Wrangle Lowgate Lincs 77 TF4451
Wrangway Somset 20 ST1218
Wrantage Somset 20 ST3022
Wrawby Humb 84 TA0108
Wraxall Avon 34 ST4971
Wraxall Somset 21 ST6036
Wray Lancs 87 SD6067
Wray Castle Cumb 87 NY3700
Wraysbury Berks 25 TQ0074
Wrayton Lancs 87 SD6172
Wrea Green Lancs 80 SD3931
Wreaks End Cumb 86 SD2286
Wreay Cumb 93 NY4348
Wreay Cumb 93 NY4423
Wrecclesham Surrey 25 SU8244
Wrekenton T & W 96 NZ2759
Wrelton N York 90 SE7686
Wrenbury Ches 71 SJ5947
Wrench Green N York 91 SE9689
Wreningham Norfk 66 TM1698
Wrentham Suffk 55 TM4982
Wrenthorpe W York 82 SE3122
Wrentnall Shrops 59 SJ4203
Wressle Humb 84 SE7131
Wressle Humb 84 SE9709
Wrestlingworth Beds 52 TL2547
Wretton Norfk 65 TF6900
Wrexham Clwyd 71 SJ3350
Wribbenhall H & W 60 SO7975
Wrickton Shrops 59 SO6486
Wright's Green Essex 39 TL5017
Wrightington Bar Lancs 80 SD5313
Wrinehill Staffs 72 SJ7547
Wrington Avon 21 ST4762
Wringworthy Cnwll 5 SX2658
Writhlington Somset 22 ST6954
Writtle Essex 40 TL6706
Wrockwardine Shrops 59 SJ6212
Wroot Humb 84 SE7103
Wrose W York 82 SE1636
Wrotham Kent 27 TQ6158
Wrotham Heath Kent 27 TQ6357
Wrottesley Staffs 60 SJ8200
Wroughton Wilts 36 SU1480
Wroxall IOW 13 SZ5579
Wroxall Warwks 61 SP2271
Wroxeter Shrops 59 SJ5608
Wroxham Norfk 67 TG3017
Wroxton Oxon 49 SP4141
Wyaston Derbys 73 SK1842
Wyatt's Green Essex 40 TQ5999
Wyberton Lincs 64 TF3240
Wyboston Beds 52 TL1656
Wybunbury Ches 72 SJ6949
Wych Dorset 10 SY4791
Wych Cross E Susx 15 TQ4131
Wychbold H & W 47 SO9266
Wychnor Staffs 73 SK1715
Wyck Hants 24 SU7539
Wyck Rissington Gloucs 36 SP1821
Wycliffe Dur 95 NZ1114
Wycoller Lancs 81 SD9339
Wycomb Leics 63 SK7724
Wycombe Marsh Bucks 26 SU8892
Wyddial Herts 39 TL3731
Wye Kent 28 TR0546
Wyesham Gwent 34 SO5211
Wyfordby Leics 63 SK7918
Wyke Devon 9 SX8799
Wyke Devon 10 SY2996
Wyke Dorset 22 ST7926
Wyke Shrops 59 SJ6402
Wyke Surrey 25 SU9251
Wyke W York 82 SE1526
Wyke Champflower Somset 22 ST6634
Wyke Regis Dorset 11 SY6677
Wykeham N York 90 SE8175
Wykeham N York 91 SE9683
Wyken Shrops 60 SO7695
Wyken W Mids 61 SP3780
Wykey Shrops 59 SJ3824
Wykin Leics 61 SP4095
Wylam Nthumb 103 NZ1164
Wylde Green W Mids 61 SP1294
Wylye Wilts 22 SU0037
Wymeswold Leics 62 SK6023
Wymington Beds 51 SP9564
Wymondham Leics 63 SK8418
Wymondham Norfk 66 TG1001
Wyndham M Glam 33 SS9392
Wynds Point H & W 47 SO7640
Wynford Eagle Dorset 10 SY5896
Wynyard Park Cleve 96 NZ4326
Wyre Piddle H & W 47 SO9647
Wysall Notts 62 SK6027
Wyson H & W 46 SO5267
Wythall H & W 61 SP0774
Wytham Oxon 37 SP4708
Wythburn Cumb 93 NY3214
Wythenshawe Gt Man 79 SJ8386
Wythop Mill Cumb 93 NY1729
Wyton Cambs 52 TL2772
Wyton Humb 85 TA1733
Wyverstone Suffk 54 TM0468
Wyverstone Street Suffk 54 TM0367
Wyville Lincs 63 SK8729

Y

Y Felinheli Gwynd 68 SH5267
Y Ferwig Dyfed 42 SN1849
Y Ffor Gwynd 56 SH3939
Y Gyffylliog Clwyd 70 SJ0557
Y Maerdy Clwyd 70 SJ0144
Y Nant Clwyd 70 SJ2850
Y Rhiw Gwynd 56 SH2227
Yaddlethorpe Humb 84 SE8806
Yafford IOW 13 SZ4481
Yafforth N York 89 SE3494
Yalberton Devon 7 SX8658
Yalding Kent 28 TQ6950
Yanwath Cumb 94 NY5127
Yanworth Gloucs 36 SP0713
Yapham Humb 84 SE7851
Yapton W Susx 14 SU9703
Yarborough Avon 21 ST3857
Yarbridge IOW 13 SZ6086
Yarburgh Lincs 77 TF3592
Yarcombe Devon 9 ST2408
Yard Devon 19 SS7721
Yardley W Mids 61 SP1386
Yardley Gobion Nhants 49 SP7644
Yardley Hastings Nhants 51 SP8657
Yardley Wood W Mids 61 SP1079
Yardro Powys 45 SO2258
Yarford Somset 20 ST2029
Yarkhill H & W 46 SO6042
Yarley Somset 21 ST5044
Yarlington Somset 21 ST6529
Yarlsber N York 87 SD7072
Yarm Cleve 89 NZ4112
Yarmouth IOW 12 SZ3589
Yarnacott Devon 19 SS6230
Yarnbrook Wilts 22 ST8654
Yarner Devon 8 SX7778
Yarnfield Staffs 72 SJ8632
Yarnscombe Devon 19 SS5623
Yarnton Oxon 37 SP4711
Yarpole H & W 46 SO4764
Yarrow Border 109 NT3528
Yarrow Somset 21 ST3746
Yarrow Feus Border 109 NT3325
Yarrowford Border 109 NT4030
Yarsop H & W 46 SO4047
Yarwell Nhants 51 TL0697
Yate Avon 35 ST7081
Yateley Hants 25 SU8161
Yatesbury Wilts 36 SU0671
Yattendon Berks 24 SU5574
Yatton Avon 21 ST4365
Yatton H & W 46 SO4366
Yatton H & W 47 SO6330
Yatton Keynell Wilts 35 ST8676
Yaverland IOW 13 SZ6185
Yawl Devon 10 SY3194
Yawthorpe Lincs 76 SK8992
Yaxham Norfk 66 TG0010
Yaxley Cambs 64 TL1891
Yaxley Suffk 54 TM1273
Yazor H & W 46 SO4046
Yeading Gt Lon 26 TQ1182
Yeadon W York 82 SE2041
Yealand Conyers Lancs 87 SD5074
Yealand Redmayne Lancs 87 SD4975
Yealand Storrs Lancs 87 SD5075
Yealmbridge Devon 6 SX5852
Yealmpton Devon 6 SX5851
Yearby Cleve 97 NZ5921
Yearngill Cumb 92 NY1443
Yearsley N York 90 SE5874
Yeaton Shrops 59 SJ4319
Yeaveley Derbys 73 SK1840
Yeavering Nthumb 110 NT9330
Yedingham N York 91 SE8979
Yelford Oxon 36 SP3604
Yelland Devon 18 SS4931
Yelling Cambs 52 TL2662
Yelvertoft Nhants 50 SP5975
Yelverton Devon 6 SX5267
Yelverton Norfk 67 TG2902
Yenston Somset 22 ST7121
Yeo Mill Somset 19 SS8426
Yeo Vale Devon 18 SS4223
Yeoford Devon 8 SX7899
Yeolmbridge Cnwll 5 SX3187
Yeovil Somset 10 ST5515
Yeovil Marsh Somset 10 ST5418
Yeovilton Somset 21 ST5423
Yerbeston Dyfed 30 SN0609
Yesnaby Ork 155 HY2215
Yetlington Nthumb 111 NU0209
Yetminster Dorset 10 ST5910
Yetson Devon 7 SX8056
Yettington Devon 9 SY0585
Yetts o'Muckhart Cent 117 NO0001
Yew Green Warwks 48 SP2367
Yews Green W York 82 SE0931
Yielden Beds 51 TL0167
Yieldingtree H & W 60 SO8977
Yieldshields Strath 116 NS8750
Yiewsley Gt Lon 26 TQ0680
Ynysboeth M Glam 33 ST0695
Ynysddu Gwent 33 ST1792
Ynysforgan W Glam 32 SS6799
Ynyshir M Glam 33 ST0292
Ynyslas Dyfed 43 SN6193
Ynysmaerdy M Glam 33 ST0383
Ynysmeudwy W Glam 32 SN7305
Ynystawe W Glam 32 SN6800
Ynyswen M Glam 33 SS9597
Ynyswen Powys 33 SN8313
Ynysybwl M Glam 33 ST0594
Ynysymaengwyn Gwynd 57 SH5902
Yockenthwaite N York 88 SD9078
Yockleton Shrops 59 SJ3910
Yokefleet Humb 84 SE8124
Yoker Strath 115 NS5069
Yonder Bognie Gramp 142 NJ6046
York Lancs 81 SD7133
York N York 83 SE6051
York Town Hants 25 SU8660
Yorkletts Kent 29 TR0963
Yorkley Gloucs 35 SO6307
Yorton Heath Shrops 59 SJ5022
Youlgreave Derbys 74 SK2064
Youlthorpe Humb 84 SE7655
Youlton N York 90 SE4963
Young's End Essex 40 TL7319
Youngsbury Herts 39 TL3618
Yoxall Staffs 73 SK1418
Yoxford Suffk 55 TM3969
Yoxford Little Street Suffk 55 TM3869
Ysbyty Cynfyn Dyfed 43 SN7578
Ysbyty Ifan Gwynd 69 SH8448
Ysbyty Ystwyth Dyfed 43 SN7371
Ysceifiog Clwyd 70 SJ1571
Ysgubor-y-Coed Dyfed 43 SN6895
Ystalyfera W Glam 32 SN7608
Ystrad M Glam 33 SS9895
Ystrad Aeron Dyfed 44 SN5256
Ystrad Meurig Dyfed 43 SN7067
Ystrad Mynach M Glam 33 ST1494
Ystrad-ffyn Dyfed 44 SN7846
Ystradfellte Powys 33 SN9313
Ystradgynlais Powys 32 SN7910
Ystradowen S Glam 33 ST0077
Ystumtuen Dyfed 43 SN7378
Ythanbank Gramp 143 NJ9033
Ythanwells Gramp 142 NJ6338
Ythsie Gramp 143 NJ8830

Z

Zeal Monachorum Devon 8 SS7204
Zeals Wilts 22 ST7831
Zelah Cnwll 3 SW8151
Zennor Cnwll 2 SW4538
Zoar Cnwll 3 SW7619
Zouch Notts 62 SK5023